The Concise Encyclopedia of Sociology

The Concise Encyclopedia of Sociology

Edited by George Ritzer and J. Michael Ryan

A John Wiley & Sons, Ltd., Publication

This edition first published 2011

Blackwell Publishing was acquired by John Wiley & Sons in February 2007. Blackwell's publishing program has been merged with Wiley's global Scientific, Technical, and Medical business to form Wiley-Blackwell.

Registered Office
John Wiley & Sons Ltd, The Atrium, Southern Gate, Chichester, West Sussex, PO19 8SQ, United Kingdom

Editorial Offices
350 Main Street, Malden, MA 02148-5020, USA

9600 Garsington Road, Oxford, OX4 2DQ, UK

The Atrium, Southern Gate, Chichester, West Sussex, PO19 8SQ, UK

For details of our global editorial offices, for customer services, and for information about how to apply for permission to reuse the copyright material in this book please see our website at www.wiley.com/wiley-blackwell.

Library of Congress Cataloging-in-Publication Data

The concise encyclopedia of sociology / edited by George Ritzer and J. Michael Ryan.
p. cm.
Includes bibliographical references and index.
ISBN 978-1-4051-8353-6 (hardcover : alk. paper) – ISBN 978-1-4051-8352-9 (pbk. : alk. paper)
1. Sociology–Encyclopedias. I. Ritzer, George. II. Ryan, J. Michael.
HM425.C66 2011
301.03–dc22

2010036832

A catalogue record for this book is available from the British Library.

This book is published in the following electronic formats: ePDFs 9781444392630;
Wiley Online Library 9781444392654; ePub 9781444392647

Set in 9.5/11pt Ehrhardt by SPi Publisher Services, Pondicherry, India
Printed in Singapore by Ho Printing Singapore Pte Ltd

2 2011

Contents

Contributors

Gabriele Abels, *University of Tübingen*
Barry D. Adam, *University of Windsor*
Michele Adams, *Tulane University*
Patricia Adler, *University of Colorado*
Peter Adler, *University of Denver*
Michael Agar, *University of Maryland*
Kristine J. Ajrouch, *Eastern Michigan University*
Syed Farid Alatas, *National University of Singapore*
Richard Alba, *University at Albany*
Dawn Aliberti, *Case Western Reserve University*
Graham Allan, *Keele University*
Christopher W. Allinson, *The University of Leeds*
Jutta Allmendinger, *Social Science Research Center Berlin*
Mats Alvesson, *Lunds Universitet*
Hans van Amersfoort, *University of Amsterdam*
Peter B. Andersen, *University of Copenhagen*
Eric Anderson, *University of Bath*
Christopher Andrews, *University of Maryland*
Robert J. Antonio, *University of Kansas*
Lemonik Arthur, *Rhode Island College*
Mikaila Mariel Lemonik Arthur, *Rhode Island College*
Elyshia Aseltine, *University of Austin at Texas*
Zeynep Atalay, *University of Maryland*
Lonnie, Athens, *Seton Hall University*
Muhammad Najib Azca, *Universitas Gadjah Mada*
Abdallah M. Badahdah, *University of North Dakota*
Hans A. Baer, *The University of Melbourne*
Stephen J. Bahr, *Brigham Young University*
Alan Bairner, *Loughborough University*
J. I. (Hans) Bakker, *University of Guelph*
Jack Barbalet, *University of Western Sydney*
Kendra Barber, *University of Maryland*
Eileen Barker, *London School of Economics and Political Science*
Nina Baur, *Technial University, Berlin*
Rob Beamish, *Queen's University*
Thomas D. Beamish, *University of California, Davis*
Frank D. Bean, *University of California, Irvine*
Dawn Beichner, *Illinois state University*
David Bell, *University of Leeds*
T. J. Berard, *Kent State University*
Mabel Berezin, *Cornell University*
Joseph Berger
Pierre van den Berghe, *University of Washington*
Yasemin Besen-Cassino, *Montclair State University*
Peter Beyer, *University of Ottawa*
William Bezdek, *Oakland University*
Alex Bierman, *California State University, Northridge*
Nicole Woolsey Biggart, *University of California, Davis*
David B. Bills, *University of Iowa*
Sam Binkley, *Emerson College*
Jon Binnie, *Manchester Metropolitan University*
Manuela Boatca, *Catholic University of Eichstätt-Ingolstadt*
Connie de Boer, *University of Amsterdam*
John Bongaarts, *Population Council*
Kimberly Bonner, *University of Maryland*
Alfons Bora, *Bielefeld University*
Christine A. Bose, *University at Albany, SUNY*
Geoffrey Bowker, *Santa Clara University*
Gaspar Brandle, *Universidad de Murcia*
David G. Bromley, *Virginia Commonwealth University*
Susan K. Brown
Clifton D. Bryant, *Virginia Tech*
Ian Buchanan, *Cardiff University*
Claudia Buchmann, *The Ohio State University*
Steven M. Buechler, *Minnesota State University, Mankato*
Dirk Bunzel, *University of Oulu*
Melissa L. Burgess,
Marcos Burgos, *The Graduate Center, The City University of New York*
Joseph Burke, *Independent Researcher*
Peter J. Burke, *University of California, Riverside*
Tom R. Burns, *Stanford University*
Roger Burrows, *University of York*
Ryan Calder, *University of California, Berkeley*
Thomas Calhoun, *Jackson State University*
Peter L. Callero, *Western Oregon University*
John L. Campbell, *Dartmouth College*
James R. Carey, *University of California Davis*
Dianne Cyr Carmody, *Old Dominion University*
Moira Carmody, *University of Western Sydney*
Laura M. Carpenter, *Vanderbilt University*
Deborah Carr, *Rutgers University*
Michael C Carroll
Allison Carter, *Rowan University*
Chris Carter, *University of St Andrews*
Michael J. Carter, *University of California, Riverside*

John M. Chamberlain,
J. K. Chambers, *University of Toronto*
Gordon C. Chang, *University of California, San Diego*
Jean Francois Chanlat, *Université Paris-Dauphine*
Kathy Charmaz, *Sonoma State University*
Christopher Chase-Dunn, *University of California, Riverside*
David Cheal, *University of Winnipeg*
Roland Chilton, *University of Massachusetts, Amherst*
James L. Chriss, *Cleveland State University*
Doris, Chu, *Arakansas State University, Jonesboro*
Peter, Chua, *San Jose State University*
Jeffrey M. Clair
D. Anthony Tyeeme Clark, *University of Illinois, Urbana-Champaign*
Jesse K. Clark, *University of Georgia*
Adele E. Clarke, *University of California School of Nursing*
Stewart Clegg, *University of Technology, Sydney*
Jay Coakley, *University of Colorado, Colorado Springs*
Rodney Coates, *Miami University*
Allan Cochrane, *The Open University*
William C. Cockerham, *University of Alabama, Birmingham*
Walker Connor, *Trinity College*
Peter Conrad, *Brandeis University*
Daniel Thomas Cook, *Rutgers University*
Karen S. Cook, *Stanford University*
Mamadi Corra, *East Carolina University*
Karen Corteen, *University of Chester*
Zoë Blumberg Corwin, *University of Southern California*
Lloyd, Cox, *Macquarie University*
Ann Cronin, *University of Surrey*
Graham Crow, *University of Southhampton*
Kyle Crowder, *University of North Carolina, Chapel Hill*
Gregory J. Crowley, *Coro Center for Civic Leadership*
Geoff Cumming, *La Trobe University*
Kimberly Cunningham, *City University of New York Graduate Center*
John Curra, *Eastern Kentucky University*
Steven Dandaneau, *University of Tennessee, Knoxville*
Tim Dant, *Lancaster University*
Julia O'Connell Davidson, *The University of Nottingham*
Hartley Dean, *London School of Ecomomics and Political Science*
James Joseph Dean, *Sonoma State University*
Paul Dean, *University of Maryland*
Mary Jo Deegan, *University of Nebraska-Lincoln*
Mathieu Deflem, *University of South Carolina*
Regina Deil-Amen, *University of Arizona*
Gerard Delanty, *University of Sussex*
David H. Demo, *University of North Carolina, Greensboro*
Kimy N. Dennis, *North Carolina State University*
Rutledge M. Dennis, *George Mason University*
Esther Dermott, *University of Bristol*
Steve Derne, *SUNY Geneseo*
Marjorie L. Devault, *Syracuse University*
Joel A. Devine, *Tulane University*
Mario Diani, *Università degli studi di Trento*
James Dickinson, *Rider University*
Andreas Diekmann, *Swiss Federal Institute of Techology, Zurich*
Michele, Dillon, *University of New Hampshire*
Robert Dingwall, *Director of Dingwall Enterprises: Consulting, Research, Writing*
Karel Dobbelaere, *Katholieke Universiteit Leuven*
Nigel Dodd, *The London School of Economics*
Lena Dominelli, *Durham University*
Gwendolyn Dordick, *The City College of New York, CUNY*
David Downes
Rachel Dowty, *Louisiana State University*
Jaap Dronkers, *European University Institute*
John Drysdale, *American University*
Harriet Orcutt Duleep, *College of William and Mary*
Diana Dumais, *University of New Hampshire*
Riley Dunlap, *Oklahoma State University*
Jennifer Dunn, *Southern Illinois University, Carbondale*
Jennifer Earl, *University of California, Santa Barbara*
Martha Easton, *Elmira College*
Bob, Edwards, *East Carolina University*
Rosalind, Edwards, *London South Bank University*
Brad van Eeden-Moorefield,
Noah Efron, *Bar-Ilan University*
Anne Eisenberg, *State University of New York at Geneseo*
S. N. Eisendstat, *The Van Leer Jerusalem Institute*
Richard Ekins
Tony Elger, *University of Warwick*
David L. Elliott, *University of Missouri, Columbia*
Irma T. Elo, *University of Pennsylvania*
Chamsy El-Ojeili, *Victoria University of Wellington*
Debbie Epstein, *Cardiff University*
Eugene P. Ericksen, *Temple University*
Julia A. Ericksen, *Temple University*
Lena Eriksson, *The University of York*
David T. Evans, *University of Glasgow*
Dianne Fabii, *Rutgers University*
William W. Falk, *University of Maryland*
Xitao Fan, *University of Virginia*
Thomas J. Fararo, *University of Pittsburgh*
George Farkas, *Cornell University*
Margaret E. Farrar, *Augustana College*

Anne Fearfull, *University of St Andrews*
Gordon Fellman, Brandeis University
Sarah Fenstermaker, *University of California, Santa Barbara*
April Few-Demo, *Virginia Polytechnic Institute and State University*
Mark G. Field, *Harvard University*
Glenn Firebaugh, *Pennsylvania State University*
Juanita M. Firestone, *University of Texas, San Antonio*
David M. Flores, *University of Nevada, Reno*
John Foran, *University of California, Santa Barbara*
Marion Fourcade-Gourinchas, *University of California, Berkeley*
Gelya Frank
Boris, Frankel, *The University of Melbourne*
Adrian Franklin, *University of Tasmania*
Judith J. Friedman, *Rutgers, The State University of New Jersey*
Irene Hanson Frieze, *University of Pittsburgh*
Catarina Fritz, *Minnesota State University, Mankato*
Hongyun Fu, *Tulane University*
Stephan Fuchs, *University of Virginia*
Steve Fuller, *University of Warwick*
Caroline Fusco, *University of Toronto*
Karl Gabriel, *Westfälische Wilhelms-Universität Münster*
Gloria Gadsden, *East Stroudsburg University*
Larry Gaines, *California State University, San Bernardino*
Andrew Gamble, *University of Cambridge*
Markus Gangl, *University of Wisconsin-Madison*
Robert Garner, *University of Leicester*
Nicolas Garnham, *University of Westminster*
Rosemary Gartner, *University of Toronto*
Gil Geis, *University of Califonria, Irvine*
Gary Genosko, *Lakehead University*
Linda K. George, *Duke University Center for the Study of Aging and Human Development*
Simone Ghezzi, *Università di Milano-Bicocca*
Wayne Gillespie, *East Tennessee State University*
Stephanie Gilmore, *Dickinson College*
Giuseppe Giordan, *University of Padova*
Evi Girling, *Keele University*
Henry A. Giroux, *McMaster University*
Richard Giulianotti
Norval D. Glenn, *The University of Texas at Austin*
Julian, Go *Boston University*
Ernest Goetz, *Texas A&M University*
Ralph Gomes, *Howard University*
Erich Goode, *New York University*
Lyn Gorman, *Charles Sturt University*
Kevin Fox Gotham, *Tulane University*
Royston Greenwood, *University of Alberta*
Julie Gregory, *Queen's University*
Arthur L. Greil, *Alfred University*
Sean Patrick Griffin, *Penn State Abington*
Axel Groenemeyer, *University of Dortmund*
David, Grusky *Stanford University*
Stephen Obeng Gyimah, *Queen's University*
Joanna Hadjicostandi, *The University of Texas of the Permian Basin*
Catherine Hakim, *London School of Economics*
John R. Hall, *University of California, Davis*
Lesley A. Hall, *Wellcome Library*
Matthew Hall, *Pennsylvania State University*
Peter M. Hall, *University of Missouri*
Thomas D. Hall, *DePauw University*
Karen Bettez Halnon, *Penn State Abington*
Laura Hamilton, *Indiana University*
Martyn Hammersley, *The Open University*
David J. Harding, *University of Michigan*
Simon Hardy, *University of Worcester*
Austin Harrington, *University of Leeds*
Dave Harris, *University of College Plymouth St Mark and St John*
Anthony Ryan Hatch, *Georgia Stage University*
Keith Hayward, *University of Kent*
Brian Heaphy, *The University of Manchester*
Sue Heath, *University of Southampton*
John Heeren, *California State University, San Bernardino*
Karen A. Hegtvedt, *Emory University*
Laura Auf der Heide, *Cornell University*
Scott, Heil *City University of New York, Graduate Center*
Gert Hekma, *University of Amsterdam*
Thomas Henricks, *Elon University*
Stuart Henry, *San Diego State University*
Robin K. Henson, *University of North Texas*
Sabine Hering, *University of Siegen*
Donald J. Hernandez, *State University of New York at Albany*
Purseay P. M. A. R. Heugens, *Rotterdam School of Management, Erasmus University*
Annette Hill, *University of Westminster*
Michael R. Hill, *University of Nebraska, Lincoln*
Matt Hills, *Cardiff University*
Daniel Hillyard, *Southern Illinois University, Carbondale*
Wendy Hilton-Morrow, *Augustana College*
Michelle J. Hindin, *Johns Hopkins University*
Susan W. Hinze, *Case Western Reserve University*
Randy Hodson, *Ohio State University*
Douglas B. Holt, *Said Business School University of Oxford*
Burkart Holzner, *University of Pittsburgh*
Allan V. Horwitz, *Rutgers University*
Janet Hoskins, *University of Southern California*
James House, *University of Michigan*

Jeffrey Houser
Andrea N. Hunt, *NC State University*
Stephen Hunt, *University of West of England*
Ray Hutchison, *University of Wisconsin, Green Bay*
Mark Hutter, *Rowan University*
Michael Indergaard, *St John's University*
Ronald Inglehart, *University of Michigan*
Keiko Inoue
Paul Ingram, *Columbia University*
Stevi Jackson, *University of York*
Martin M. Jacobsen, *West Texas A&M University*
Rita Jalali, *International Consultant*
Lynn Jamieson, *The University of Edinburgh*
James M. Jasper, *CUNY Graduate Center*
Alayna Jehle, *R & D Strategic Solutions*
Richard Jenkins, *University of Sheffield*
Chris Jenks, *Brunel University*
Elyse Jennings, *University of Michigan*
Laura Jennings, *University of South Carolina Upstate*
Paul Jones, *University of Liverpool*
Joan R. Kahn, *University of Maryland*
Vasiliki Kantzara, *Panteion University of Social and Political Science*
Susanne Karstedt, *University of Leeds*
Walda Katz-Fishman, *Howard University*
Tally Katz-Gerro, *University of Haifa*
Erin Kaufmann
Douglas Kellner, *Columbia University*
Russell Kelly, *University of Trier, Germany*
Markus Kemmelmeier, *University of Nevada, Reno*
Anne Kerr, *University of Leeds*
Ann H. Kim, *York University*
Michael S. Kimmel, *SUNY at Stony Brook*
Dave King, *University of Liverpool*
William J. Kinney, *University of St. Thomas*
Susan Kippax, *University of New South Wales*
Roger E. Kirk, *Baylor Univesity*
Sharon Kirmeyer, *Centers for Disease Control and Prevention*
Sunita Kishor, *ICF Macro*
Peter Kivisto, *Augustana College*
Christian Klesse, *Manchester Metropolitan University*
Andrew Kliman, *Pace University*
Wolfgang Knoebl, *Goettingen University*
Nikos Kokosalakis, *Panteion University*
Mark Konty, *Eastern Kentucky University*
Marek Korczynski, *Loughborough University*
Joseph Kotarba, *University of Houston*
Robert Kozinets, *Schulich School of Business*
Robert van Krieken, *University of Sydney*
Mary M. Kritz, *Cornell University*
Amy Kroska, *University of Oklahoma*
Catherine Krull, *Queen's University*
Abdi M. Kusow, *Oakland University*
Craig D. Lair, *Gettysburg College*
Siegfried Lamnek,
Rainhart Lang, *Technical University of Chemnitz*
Beryl Langer, *La Trobe University*
Lauren Langman, *Loyola University Chicago*
Patti Lather, *Ohio State University*
Abraham D. Lavender, *Florida International University*
Ian Law, *University of Leeds*
Jacob Lederman, *The City University of New York*
Susan Hagood Lee, *Boston University*
Dirk vom Lehn, *King's College London*
Terri LeMoyne, *University of Tennessee, Chattanooga*
Patrica Lengermann
Athena Leoussi, *University of Reading*
Ron J. Lesthaeghe, *University of Michigan*
Jack Levin, *Northeastern University*
Don Levy, *Southeast Missouri State University*
Tyson E. Lewis
Victor Lidz, *Drexel University College of Medicine*
John Lie, *University of California, Berkeley*
Jan Lin, *Occidental College*
Amy Lind, *University of Cincinnati*
Michael Lipscomb, *Winthrop University*
Sonia Livingstone, *London School of Economics*
Omar Lizardo, *University of Notre Dame*
Omar Lizardo
Elizabeth Long, *Rice University*
Charles F. Longino Jr
Michael Lovaglia
David W. Lovell, *University of New South Wales at the Australian Defence Force Academy*
Ray Loveridge, *Saïd Business School, University of Oxford*
John Loy, *University of Rhode Island*
Steve Loyal, *University of College Dublin*
Chao-Chin Lu, *Brigham Young University*
Jeffrey W. Lucas, *University of Maryland*
Glenn Lucke, *University of Virginia*
Wolfgang Ludwig-Mayerhofer, *University of Siegen*
Richard Machalek, *University of Wyoming*
Vicky M. MacLean, *Middle Tennessee State Universisty*
Michael Macy, *Cornell University*
Jennifer Smith Maguire, *University of Leicester*
Joseph, Maguire *Loughborough University*
Matthew C. Mahutga, *University of California, Riverside*
Regan, Main
Dominic Malcolm, *Loughborough University*
Evans Mandes, *George Mason University*
Peter Manning, *Northeastern University*
Barry Markovsky, *University of South Carolina*
Randal Marlin, *Carleton University*
Heather Marsh, *University of Maryland*
Randy Martin, *New York University*

Mark Mather, *Population Reference Bureau*
Ross Matsueda, *University of Washington*
Steffen Mau, *University of Bremen*
Allan Mazur, *Syracuse University*
Doug McAdam, *Stanford University*
E. Doyle McCarthy, *Fordham University*
Charles McCormick, *University of Albany*
Peter McDonald, *The Australian National University*
PJ McGann, *University of Michigan*
Patrick J. W. McGinty, *Western Illinois University*
Brian McNair, *University of Strathclyde, Glasgow*
Clark McPhail, *University of Illinois, Urbana-Champaign*
Michelle Meagher, *University of Alberta*
Barbara F. Meeker, *University of Maryland*
Dominique Meekers, *Tulane Univesity*
Robert F. Meier, *University of Nebraska at Omaha*
Roslyn Arlin Mickelson, *University of North Carolina, Charlotte*
Dan E. Miller, *University of Dayton*
Toby Miller, *University of California, Riverside*
Monica K. Miller
Andrew Milner, *Monash University*
Joya Misra, *University of Massachusetts*
Tariq Modood, *University of Bristol*
Linda D. Molm, *The University of Arizona*
Jesús Romero Moñivas, *San Pablo-CEU*
Christopher D. Moore, *Lakeland College*
Laura M. Moore, *Hood College*
Yuri Jack Gomez Morales, *Universidad Nacional de Colombia*
David H. Morgan, *Keele University*
Thomas J. Morrione, *Colby College*
Marietta Morrissey, *University of Toledo*
Ross Mouer, *Monash University*
Siamak Movahedi, *University of Massachusetts, Boston*
Anna S. Mueller, *University of Texas*
Carol Mueller, *Arizona State University*
Chandra Mukerji, *University of California, San Diego*
Albert M. Muniz, *DePaul University*
Paul T. Munroe, *Towson University*
Peter Murphy, *Monash University*
Stephen L. Muzzatti, *Ryerson University*
Joane Nagel, *University of Kansas*
Nancy A. Naples, *University of Connecticut*
Victor Nee, *Cornell University*
Sarah Nettleton, *University of York*
Leonard Nevarez, *Vassar College*
Brett Nicholls, *University of Otago*
Gillian Niebrugge, *American University*
Donald A. Nielsen, *College of Charleston*
François Nielsen, *University of North Carolina*
Natalia, Nikolova, *University of Technology, Sydney*
Takako Nomi, *University of Chicago*
Samuel Nunn, *Indiana University-Purdue University, Indianapolis*
Richard E. Ocejo, *John Jay College of Criminal Justice - CUNY*
Jarron M. Saint Onge, *University of Houston*
Anthony J. Onwuegbuzie, *Sam Houston State University*
Terri L. Orbuch, *Oakland University*
James D. Orcutt, *Florida State University*
W. Edward Orser, *UMBC An honors University in Maryland*
Anthony M. Orum, *University of Illinois at Chicago*
Timothy J. Owens, *Purdue University*
Enzo, Pace, *University of Padova*
Esperanza Palma, *University of Autonoma Metropolitan Azacapotzalco*
Sangeeta Parashar, *Montclair State University*
Patricia Parker, *North Carolina State*
Vincent N. Parrillo, *William Paterson University*
Ray Paternoster, *University of Maryland*
Vrushali Patil, *Florida International University*
Michael Quinn Patton, *Utilization-Focused Evaluation*
George Pavlich, *University of Alberta*
Jennifer Pearson, *Wichita State University*
Cynthia Fabrizio Pelak, *The University of Memphis*
Anssi Peräkylä, *University of Helsinki*
Robin D. Perrin, *Pepperdine University*
Nick Perry, *University of Auckland*
Frances G. Pestello, *University of Dayton*
Thomas Pettigrew, *Universtiy of California, Santa Cruz*
Mary Pickering, *San Jose State University*
Michael Pickering, *Loughborough*
Jan Nederveen Pieterse, *University of California, Santa Barbara*
Tyrone S. Pitsis, *University of Technology, Sydney*
Rebecca F. Plante, *Ithaca College*
Jennifer Platt, *University of Sussex*
Ken Plummer, *University of Essex*
Massimiliano A. Polichetti, *Civil Servant under the Italian Ministry for Culture*
Francesca Polletta, *University of California, Irvine*
Karen Polonko, *Old Dominion University*
Suet-ling Pong, *Pennsylvania State University*
Henry N. Pontell, *University of California, Irvine*
Silvia Posocco, *Birkbeck College, University of London*
Brian Powell, *Indiana University, Bloomington*
Jason L. Powell, *Liverpool University*
Joel Powell, *Minnesota State University, Moorhead*
Beverly M. Pratt, *University of Maryland*
Harland Prechel, *Texas A&M University*
Peter Preisendörfer, *University of Mainz*

Stella Quah, *National University of Singapore*
Matt Qvortrup, *Robert Gordon University*
Sara Raley, *McDaniel College*
Francesco Ramella, *Urbino University "Carlo Bo"*
Sheetal Ranjan, *William Paterson University*
Mark K. Rank, *Washington University in St Louis*
Lisa Rashotte, *University of North Carolina, Charlotte*
William K. Rawlins, *Ohio University*
Anne Warfield Rawls, *Bentley College*
Larry Ray, *University of Kent*
Michael Reay
Andreas Reckwitz, *University of Konstanz*
Jo Reger, *Oakland University*
D. A. Reisman, *Nanyang Business School*
Larissa Remennick, *Bar-lian University*
PJ Rey, *University of Maryland*
Cecilia L. Ridgeway, *Stanford University*
Cathering Riegle-Crum
Arnout van de Rijt, *State University of New York, Stony Brook*
George Ritzer, *Universtiy of Maryland, College Park*
Polly Rizova, *Willamette University*
Tracy Roberts, *University of Maryland*
Roland Robertson, *University of Aberdeen*
Paul Rock, *London School of Economics*
Richard G. Rogers, *University of Colorado*
Deana A. Rohlinger, *Florida State University*
Chris Rojek, *Brunel University*
Paul Roman, *University of Georgia*
Christopher Rootes, *University of Kent*
Jennifer Rothchild, *University of Minnesota, Morris*
Nicole Rousseau, *Kent State University*
David Rowe, *University of Western Sydney*
Karen Rowlingson, *University of Birmingham*
Janet M. Ruane, *Montclair State University*
Martin Ruef, *Princeton University*
Joseph D. Rumbo, *James Madison University*
Philip Rumney, *University of West of England*
Leila J. Rupp, *University of California, Santa Barbara*
Barbara Ryan, *Widener University*
J. Michael Ryan, *University of Maryland, College Park*
Michael T. Ryan, *Dodge City Community College*
Nicholas Sammond, *University of Toronto*
Jimy M. Sanders, *University of South Carolina*
Stephen K. Sanderson, *University of California, Riverside*
Diana Santillan, *The George Washington University*
Roberta Sassatelli, *University of Milan*
Sharon L. Sassler, *Cornell University*
R. Keith Sawyer, *Washington University*
Lawrence A. Scaff, *Wayne State University*
Thomas L. Scheff, *University of California, Santa Barbara*
Teresa L. Scheid, *University of North Carolina, Charlotte*
Scott Schieman, *University of Toronto*
Hubert Schijf
Kathryn S. Schiller, *University at Albany, State University of New York*
Lucia Schmidt, *Universität Bielefeld*
Mark A. Schneider, *Southern Illinois University, Carbondale*
Kurt Schock, *Rutgers University*
Claudia W. Scholz
Juliet Schor, *Boston College*
Jonathan E. Schroeder, *University of Exeter*
Hans-Joachim Schubert, *Niederrhein University of Applied Science*
Russell K. Schutt, *University of Massachusetts, Boston*
Gerhard Schutte, *University of Wisconsin, Parkside*
Thomas A. Schwandt, *University of Illinois, Urbana-Champaign*
Jennifer Schwartz, *Washington State University*
Joseph Scimecca, *George Mason University*
Melissa Scopilliti
Jerome Scott, *Community educator & organizer, Atlanta, GA (retired)*
Sheila Scraton, *Leeds Metropolitan University*
Dusko, Sekulic, *Faculty of Law*
Eve Shapiro, *University of Connecticut, Storrs*
Yossi Shavit, *Tel Aviv University*
Benjamin Shepard, *New York City College of Technology of the City University of New York*
Diane S. Shinberg, *University of Memphis*
Yuichi Shionoya, *Hitotsubashi University*
Cynthia Siemsen, *California State University, Chico*
Alexandra E. Sigillo, *University of Nevada, Reno*
Daniel Silver, *University of Toronto*
Brent Simpson, *University of South Carolina*
Barbara Sims, *Penn State University, Harrisburg*
John Sinclair, *The University of Melbourne*
Leslie Sklair, *London School of Economics*
James Slevin, *University of Roskilde*
Michelle Smirnova, *University of Maryland*
David Norman Smith, *University of Kansas*
Gregory W. H. Smith, *University of Salford*
Irving Smith, *United States Military Academy*
Melanie Smith, *University of Greenwich*
Philip Smith, *Yale University*
David A. Snow, *University of California*
Patricia Snyder, *University of Florida*
Jessica Sperling, *The Graduate Center, The City University of New York*
Lyn Spillman, *University of Notre Dame*
Steven Stack, *Wayne State University*
Mark Stafford, *Texas State University*
James Ronald Stanfield, *Colorado State University*

Clifford L. Staples, *The University of North Dakota*
Silvia Staub-Bernasconi, *Zentrum für postgraduale Studien Sozialer Arbeit, Zurich*
Robert A. Stebbins, *University of Calgary*
George Steinmetz, *University of Michigan*
Judith Stepan-Norris, *University of California, Irvine*
Jeff Stepnisky, *MacEwan University*
Fred Stevens, *Maastricht University*
Gillian Stevens, *University of Illinois*
Nick Stevenson, *University of Nottingham*
Todd Stillman, *Independent Researcher*
John Stone, *Boston University*
Rob Stones, *University of Essex*
John Storey, *University of Sunderland*
Robin Stryker, *University of Minnesota*
Lyndsey Stults, *Trinity College*
Ivan Y. Sun, *University of Delaware*
Hung-En Sung, *John Jay College of Criminal Justice, CUNY*
William H. Swatos, Jr, *Association for the Sociology of Religion*
Mark Tausig, *University of Akron*
Verta Taylor, *University of California, Santa Barbara*
Victor E. Taylor, *York College of PA*
Yvette Taylor, *Newcastle University*
Tenisha Tevis, *University of the Pacific*
Richard Tewksbury, *University of Louisville*
Elizabeth Thorn, *University of Maryland*
Karen Throsby, *The University of Warwick*
Shane Thye, *Universtiy of South Carolina*
William G. Tierney, *University of Southern California*
David B. Tindall, *University of British Columbia*
Charles R. Tittle, *North Carolina State University*
Robert Tonkinson, *University of Western Australia*
Alberto Toscano, *Goldsmiths University of London*
Ruth Triplett, *Old Dominion University*
Trutz von Trotha, *University of Siegen*
Lisa Troyer, *University of Connecticut*
Charalambos Tsekeris, *Panteion University*
Frank van Tubergen, *Utrecht University*
Andrew Tudor, *University of York*
Kenneth D. Tunnell, *Eastern Kentucky University*
Bryan S. Turner, *City University of New York*
Charles Turner, *University of Warwick*
Stephen Turner, *University of South Florida*
Rodanthi Tzanelli, *University of Leeds*
Jeffrey T. Ulmer, *Penn State University*
Wout Ultee, *Radboud University, Nijmegan*
Carey L. Usher, *Mary Baldwin College*
Stephen Valocchi, *Trinity College*
Tancy Vandecar-Burdin, *Old Dominion University*
Mark VanLandingham, *Tulane University*
Ian Varcoe, *University of Leeds*
Tiina Vares, *University of Canterbury*
Matthias Zick Varul, *University of Exeter*
Lois A. Vitt, *Institute for Socio-Financial Studies*
Faye Linda Wachs, *California State Polytechnic, Pomana*
David Wagner, *University at Albany, SUNY*
Matthew Waites, *University of Glasgow*
Anne Waldschmidt, *University of Cologne*
Henry A. Walker, *University of Arizona*
Philip Walsh, *York University*
Susan Walzer, *Skidmore College*
Yong Wang, *Montclair State University*
Jason Wasserman
Leslie Wasson, *Chapman University*
John R. Weeks, *San Diego State University*
Darin Weinberg, *University of Cambridge*
Raymond M. Weinstein, *University of South Carolina, Aiken*
Eben A. Weitzman, *University of Massachusetts, Boston*
Barry Wellman, *University of Toronto*
Christian Welzel, *Jacobs University*
Christine A. Wernet, *University of South Carolina, Aiken*
Jonathan H. Westover, *Utah Valley University*
Michael J. White, *Brown University*
John T. Whitehead, *East Tennessee State University*
Owen Whooley, *New York University*
Vanessa R. Wight, *Columbia University*
Melissa M. Wilcox, *Whitman College*
Joyce E. Williams, *Texas Woman's University*
Matthew Williams, *Boston College*
Janet M. Wilmoth, *Syracuse University*
Nico Wilterdink, *Universiteit van Amsterdam*
Howard Winant, *University of California, Santa Barbara*
Emma Wincup, *University of Leeds*
Kristina B. Wolff, *University of Maine, Farmington*
Helen Wood, *Demontford Leicester*
Stephen Wood, *University of Sheffield*
John Wooldredge, *University of Cincinnati*
Susan L. Wortmann, *University of Nebraska, Lincoln*
Delores F. Wunder, *Southern Illinois University, Carbondale*
Gad Yair, *The Hebrew Universty*
Michael Yaksich, *Honda R & D Americas, Inc.*
David Yamane, *Wake Forest University*
Kosaku Yoshino, *Sophia University*
Reef Youngreen of Massachusetts, Boston
Milan Zafirovski, *University of North Texas*
Jonke van der Zee
Jane Zeni, *University of Missouri, St Louis*
Jens O. Zinn of Kent
Kathrin Zippel, *Northeastern University*
Robert Zussman, *University of Massachusetts, Amherst*

Introduction

The origins of sociology are usually traced back to 1839 and the coining of the term by Auguste Comte, one of the important thinkers in the history of the discipline. However, others trace intellectual concern for sociological issues much further back, and it could be argued that scholars (and non-scholars) have been thinking sociologically since the early history of humankind. However, it was not until about a half-century after Comte's creation of the concept that sociology began to develop as a formal and clearly distinct discipline, primarily, at least at first, in Europe and the United States. It was another French thinker, Émile Durkheim, who in the late 1800s was responsible for distinguishing clearly the subject matter of sociology from neighboring fields such as psychology and biology. Sociology became institutionalized in France (thanks, importantly, to Durkheim's efforts), as well as in Germany, Great Britain, and the United States. While sociology in the United States did not take the early lead in the development of key ideas and theories, it did move strongly in the direction of institutionalization (as did sociology in other nations, especially Great Britain). Sociology has grown enormously in the one hundred-plus years since the work of Durkheim and the early institutionalization of the field and is today a truly globe-straddling discipline. The sociological literature is now huge and highly diverse, and is growing exponentially. Journals, and therefore journal articles, devoted to sociology and its many subfields have proliferated rapidly, as has the number of books devoted to sociological topics. This is part of a broader issue identified by another early leader in sociology, Georg Simmel, who was concerned with the increasing gap between our cultural products and our ability to comprehend them. Sociology is one of those cultural products and this concise encyclopedia is devoted to the goal of allowing interested readers to gain a better understanding of it.

Framing *The Concise Encyclopedia of Sociology*

The magnitude and the diversity of the sociological literature represent a challenge to a wide range of people-scholars and students in sociology and closely related disciplines (some of which were at one time part of sociology) such as criminology, social work, and urban studies; in all of the other social sciences; and in many other disciplines. More generally, many others, including secondary school students and interested laypeople, often need to gain a sense not only of the discipline in general, but also of a wide range of specific topics and issues in the domain of sociology. Journalists and documentary filmmakers are others who frequently seek out ideas and insights from sociology. This concise encyclopedia gathers together in one place state-of-the-art information on, and analyses of, much of what constitutes contemporary sociology.

The Concise Encyclopedia of Sociology is drawn largely from entries that can be found in the full version of the *Blackwell Encyclopedia of Sociology* (2007). That project constitutes what is arguably the largest and greatest single reference work in sociology and one that by being continually updated online, promises to stay that way. Despite its unrivalled position as the single best sociological resource available, however, the full-length *Encyclopedia of Sociology* can be inaccessible to the average student, scholar, or layperson interested in sociology. Hence, the idea was born to create a more concise, manageable, and affordable version of the full-length project so that the great wealth of expertise and knowledge that it represents can be utilized by more people. The two leading figures on that project – the editor-in-chief and the senior managing editor – thus created this project.

Despite being a concise version, an effort was made to cast a very wide net in terms of areas to be included. It turned out that a majority of the entries for a given area also fit into one or more – in some cases 4 or 5 – other areas. In order to clarify and simplify matters for readers, 22 general categories were created that now form the organizational base of the Lexicon to be found soon after this introduction. The Lexicon represents the best way to get a quick overview of both sociology today and the contents of the concise encyclopedia (more on the Lexicon below).

An effort was made to ensure that the authors of the entries would be from many different parts of the world. The following are among the many countries from which authors have been drawn: Australia, Austria, Belgium, Canada, China, Denmark, Finland, France, Germany, Greece, Hungary, Ireland, Israel, Italy, Japan, The Netherlands, New Zealand, Norway, Portugal, Singapore, South Korea, Spain, Sweden, Switzerland, the United Kingdom, the United States, and Zambia.

As a result of the international diversity of authors, the entries themselves are extraordinarily diverse. The entries include topics and people that are not typically included in a work like this emanating from the West and the North. This is truly a work that represents global sociology. While a major effort was made to be sure that there was representation from all parts of the world, there are certain to be omissions and oversights. Another kind of diversity is reflected in the fact that legendary figures in the field of sociology (S. N. Eisenstadt, Kenneth Plummer, Thomas J. Scheff), contemporary leaders (Linda D. Molm, Karen S. Cook, Roland Robertson, Chandra Mukerji, Doug Kellner), young scholars (Karen Bettez Halnon, Lloyd Cox), and even some graduate students (Paul Dean, Joseph Burke) are represented as authors in these pages. This diversity of authorship helped guarantee that the entries in this volume would range all the way from the expected "old chestnuts" to those on hot, new, cutting-edge topics.

Another useful reference source found in this encyclopedia is the timeline of sociology. While this cannot cover everything that everyone would consider of particular significance, it is a listing of over 600 of the most influential events, figures, and publications to have made an impact on the field. As with the entries themselves, the timeline covers a lot of ground both temporally (stretching back over 2,500 years) and geographically (ranging from the Philippines to Argentina to Poland and many places in between).

Although many of the entries in these pages were drawn from the full-length version of this project, and this had already undergone a rigorous editorial process, all entries once again underwent another careful round of editing, and often several rewrites. Further, nearly 20 percent of these entries are original to this project. Thus, all entries in this project have been reviewed and re-reviewed by the editors for both accuracy and interest.

As pointed out above, the overall design of this ambitious project can be gleaned from the Lexicon. First, a glance at the 22 broad headings gives the reader a sense of the great sweep of sociology that includes such diverse subfields as crime and deviance, demography/population, education, family, gender, health and medicine, media, politics, popular culture, race/ethnicity, religion, science, sexuality, social psychology, social stratification, sport, and urbanization. Second, a more detailed examination of the topics listed under each of the broad headings in the Lexicon yields a further sense not only of that sweep, but also of the enormous depth of work in sociology. Thus, the coverage of the field in this volume is both wide and deep, especially for a project of this nature. To take just one example, the crime and deviance category includes not only a general entry on crime, but also entries on such specific topics as capital punishment, child abuse, cybercrime, hate crimes, male rape, political crime, victimization, and many more. To take another example, entries on the economy range all the way from major events (Industrial Revolution and the rise of post-industrial society), theories (rational choice), and people (Karl Marx) to a wide array of other topics including money, occupations, poverty, wealth, shopping, and the ethnic/informal economy. Similar and often even greater depth is reflected in the lists of terms under most of the other headings in the Lexicon.

Sociology is a highly dynamic discipline that is constantly undergoing changes of various types and magnitudes. This greatly complicates getting a sense of the expanse of sociology. This is traceable to changes both within the field and in the larger social world that it studies.

In terms of changes in sociology, the concise encyclopedia includes many traditional concepts, such as primary groups, dyad and triad, norms, values, culture, and so on, but supplements these with a broad assortment of more recently coined and/or popularized concepts, such as distanciation and disembedding, glocalization, simulation, implosion, postpositivism, and imagined communities.

More generally, changes in the relative importance of various subareas in the discipline lead to increases (and decreases) in attention to them. Among the areas that seem to be attracting greater interest are globalization (see below) as well as the sociology of consumption and sport. A significant number of entries in the concise encyclopedia can be included under one (or more) of these headings.

The entries included in the concise encyclopedia also reflect recent changes in the larger social world. For example, the study of cybercrime is a relatively recent addition to the area of crime because the cyberspace in which it occurs is itself relatively new. Furthermore, new ways of engaging in criminal behavior on the Internet are constantly being invented. For example, a relatively new crime has emerged that involves the sending of emails to large numbers of people around the world claiming that help is needed in transferring money from one country to another. In return, the email recipient is offered a significant share of the money. Those who respond with a willingness to help are eventually lured into transferring considerable sums to the sender of the emails in order, they are told, to help with the transfer by, for example, bribing officials. People have lost tens and even hundreds of thousands of dollars in such scams. While the perpetrators are hard to find, victims are not and are subject to prosecution for illegal activities on their part (e.g., deceiving others in order to get needed funds).

A more general recent social change that is profoundly affecting sociology is globalization. This is clearly an emerging and multifaceted process that is dramatically altering the landscape of the world. Sociology (and many other disciplines including political science, international relations, and economics) has been compelled to deal with the process and its various aspects in many different ways. Thus, we have seen the emergence of various theories and methods devoted to dealing with this topic. Furthermore, the many different aspects and dimensions of the process of globalization have attracted the notice of sociologists (and other scholars). Much consideration has been paid to the economic dimensions of globalization, but there are myriad other aspects – social, cultural, political, and the like – that are also drawing increasing attention from sociologists. Thus, in addition to a general entry on globalization, this concise encyclopedia includes a number of more specific entries on such issues as world cities, the global justice movement, and the globalization of sport, sexuality, and so on. Further, such topics and issues will emerge as globalization as a process continues to evolve and develop. Sociology will respond by devoting attention to them.

By its very nature, sociology is also highly topical and its focus is often drawn to the most recent and publicly visible developments, events, and people. There are, of course, far too many of these to cover completely in this single volume, and in any case the topics covered are constantly changing with current events. However, in order to give a sense of this topicality, some of the most important such issues are covered here. For example, changes in science are dealt with under entries on the human genome, new reproductive technologies, genetic engineering, and the measurement of risk. Topical issues in health and medicine include AIDS, aging, mental health, and well-being, stress and health, and health care delivery systems. A flavor of the many new topics in culture of interest to sociologists is offered here in entries on popular culture icons and forms, postmodern culture, surveillance, brand culture, and online social networking.

The dynamic character of sociology makes it extremely interesting, but also very difficult to grasp in some general sense. Thus, it is useful to offer a definition of sociology, although the fact is that the complexity and diversity of the discipline have led to many different definitions and wide disagreement over precisely how to define it. While we recognize that it is one among many definitions, the following is a variant on one that we feel can be usefully employed and is consistent with the thrust of most definitions in the discipline: Sociology is the study of individuals, groups, organizations, cultures, societies, and transnational relationships and of the various interrelationships among and between them.

Unpacking this definition gives us yet another way of gaining an impression of the field of sociology. On the one hand, it is clear that sociology spans the workings of a number of levels of analysis all the way from individuals to groups, organizations, cultures, societies, and transnational processes. On the other, sociology is deeply concerned with the interrelationship among and between all of those levels of analysis. Thus, at the extremes, one might be concerned with the relationship between individuals and the transnational relationships involved in globalization. While globalization is certainly affecting individuals (for example, outsourcing is leading to the loss of jobs in some areas of the world and to the creation of others elsewhere around the globe), it is also the case that globalization is the outcome of the actions of various people (business leaders, politicians, workers). Sociology is attuned to such extreme micro (individual) and macro (global) relationships as well as everything in between. A slightly different way of saying this is that sociology is concerned, at its extremes, with the relationship between individual agents and the structures (e.g., of global transnational relationships) within which they exist and which they construct and are constantly reconstructing.

Using *The Concise Encyclopedia of Sociology*

One way of gaining an impression of the expanse of sociology is, of course, to read every entry in this concise encyclopedia. Since few (save the co-editors) are likely to undertake such an enormous task, a first approach would be to scan the entire Lexicon and then select headings and terms of special interest. The reader could then begin building from there to encompass areas and topics of less direct and immediate interest.

However, readers without time to work their way through the entire encyclopedia would be well advised to focus on several rather general Lexicon entries: Key Concepts, Key Figures, Theory, and Methods. Let us look at each of these in a bit more detail.

In a sense the vast majority of entries in this concise encyclopedia are key concepts in sociology, but a large number of the most important and widely used concepts in the discipline have been singled out for inclusion under the heading of Key Concepts. An understanding of this range of ideas, as well as of the content of each, will go a long way toward giving the reader an appreciation of the field. For example, one can begin at the level of the individual with the ideas of mind and self, and then move through such concepts as agency, interaction, everyday life, groups (primary and secondary), organizations, institutions, society, and globalization. This would give the reader a sound grasp of the scope of sociology, at least in terms of the extent of its concerns, all the way from individuals and their thoughts and actions to global relationships and processes. Readers could then work their way through the key concepts in a wide range of other ways and directions, but in the end they would emerge with a pretty good conception of the discipline.

A second way to proceed is through the topics under the heading of Key Figures. This is, in some ways, a more accessible way of gaining a broad understanding of the discipline because it ties key ideas to specific people and their biographical and social contexts. One could begin with Auguste Comte and the invention of the concept of sociology. One could then move back in time from Comte to even earlier figures such as Ibn Khaldun and then push forward to later key figures such as W. E. B. Du Bois, Talcott Parsons, and Robert Merton (US), Michel Foucault and Pierre Bourdieu (France), Karl Mannheim and Norbert Elias (Great Britain, although both were born in Germany), and so on. While we have restricted coverage in this concise encyclopedia to deceased key figures, it is also possible to gain a sense of the contributions of living key sociologists, either through entries written by them for these volumes (e.g., Kenneth Plummer, Thomas Scheff) or through innumerable topical entries that inevitably deal with their ideas. For example, the entry on structuration theory deals with one of the major contributions of Anthony Giddens, glocalization is closely associated with the work of Roland Robertson, while ethnomethodology was "invented" by Harold Garfinkel.

All of those mentioned in the previous paragraph are theorists, but there are many other key figures in or associated with the discipline as well. One can read entries on these people and gain an understanding of specific areas in sociology, including demography (Kingsley Davis), race relations (W. E. B. Du Bois), feminism (Betty Friedan), sexuality (Alfred Kinsey), gender (Simone de Beauvoir), media (Marshall McLuhan), urbanization (Jane Jacobs), and many more.

A distinctive quality of sociology is that it has sets of elaborated theories and methods. Even though there is no overall agreement on which theory or method to use, they provide the keys to understanding the discipline as a whole. We have already encountered a number of theorists, but the encyclopedia is also loaded with broad discussions of both general theories and specific theoretical ideas. Among the more classical theories that are covered are structural functionalism, system theory, structuralism, Marxism and neo-Marxism, critical theory, conflict theory, feminism, phenomenology, symbolic interactionism, labeling theory, role theory, dramaturgy, ethnomethodology, existential sociology, semiotics, psychoanalysis, behaviorism, social exchange theory, and rational choice theories. In addition, much attention is given to newer theories such as recent feminist theories, actor-network theory, chaos theory, queer theory, expectation states theory, as well as a variety of the "posts" – postpositivism, poststructuralism, post-Fordism, and a range of postmodern perspectives.

The methods entries have similarly diverse coverage, which can be divided roughly into qualitative and quantitative methods. All are of varying degrees of utility in studying virtually any topic of concern in sociology. Among the notable qualitative methods covered are ethnography, feminist methodology, interviewing, verstehen, and participant and non-participant observation. More quantitative methods covered include a variety of demographic techniques, experiments, social network analysis, and survey research. Also covered under the heading of methods is a wide range of statistical techniques. Finally, a series of broad methodological issues is dealt with, such as validity, reliability, objectivity, and many others.

Of course, since sociology is constantly expanding, so too are its key concepts, figures, theories, and methods. For example, globalization is, as we have seen, a relatively new issue and sociological concept. It is leading to a reconceptualization of the work of classical theorists (such as Marx and Weber) and of the relevance of their ideas (imperialism, rationalization) to globalization, the generation of a wide range of new concepts (e.g., glocalization, empire, McDonaldization, time–space distanciation) needed to get a handle on it, and theories (transnationalism, network society) and methods (quantitative cross-national studies as well as methods that rely on data not derived from the nation-state) appropriate to the study of global issues and processes. We can expect that in the coming years other new topics will come to the fore, with corresponding implications for how we think about the work of classical theorists as well as leading to the generation of new or revised concepts, theories, and methods.

It is safe to say that the *Blackwell Encyclopedia of Sociology* represents the largest and most complete, diverse, global, and up-to-date repository of sociological knowledge in the history of the discipline. It stands as a resource for professional sociologists, scholars in other fields, students, and interested laypeople. We are confident that this concise version has managed to maintain the essence and high academic quality that made the full-length version the success that it has been and will prove just as invaluable a resource to senior scholars, young professionals, graduate students, undergraduate students, and laypeople alike.

George Ritzer and J. Michael Ryan
Co-editors *The Concise Encyclopedia of Sociology*
University of Maryland, College Park
August 2010

Acknowledgments

We must begin by thanking all those who worked on the larger version of the *Blackwell Encyclopedia of Sociology*. It is through the dedication, commitment, skill, and hard work of all those involved in that project that this project was born.

We are particularly indebted to those authors who took the time to complete the often arduous task of trimming their longer entries for use in this concise version. It was no easy task to trim entries of such importance to a concise yet thorough form, but all of our authors did so impressively.

In addition, we are indebted to the host of new authors who served as replacements for authors who were unable to contribute to this project. They have indeed helped to give this concise version a fresh new flavour. In particular we would like to thank Rob Beamish who really helped to pull us through some tight spots. His commitment to this project was much appreciated.

There were a number of undergraduates whose assistance was also invaluable in completing this project. The biggest thanks goes to Marla Bonner, whose hard work and dedication were absolutely essential in keeping this project on target and schedule. She handled many of the day-to-day details with such skill and aplomb that it enabled us to focus our time on reading and editing. She was the real backbone to the project. In addition, we would like to thank Noam Weiss and Beatriz Arcoverde who also served as valuable assistants.

An especially heartfelt thanks goes to the outstanding team at Blackwell for their endless support on this and other projects. Justin Vaughan, our publisher, has been wonderfully encouraging, supportive, and understanding throughout the many years that we have worked with him. He has our gratitude as both publisher and friend. Ben Thatcher has also been an absolutely invaluable contributor to this project. His professional skills were matched only by his sense of humor in serving as the glue that kept this project together.

Timeline

J. Michael Ryan

This timeline provides a listing of over 635 of the most influential events, figures, and publications to have made an impact on the field of sociology.

551–479 BCE	Confucius theorizes life and society. His work is primarily known through the *Analects of Confucius*, compiled by his disciples posthumously
469–399 BCE	Socrates lays the foundation of western philosophy
384–322 BCE	Aristotle makes further contributions to western science and philosophy
360 BCE	Plato debates the nature of ethics and politics in *Republic*
1377	Ibn-Khaldun writes *Muqaddimah*, which many consider one of the first important works in sociology
1516	Thomas More's *Utopia*, in which the term "utopia" is coined
1651	Thomas Hobbes's *Leviathan* discusses the requirement of surrender of sovereignty to the state needed to prevent a "war of all against all"
1692–3	Edmund Halley publishes the first life table
1712–78	Rousseau, Jean-Jacques
1713	James Waldegrave introduces an early form of game theory
1723–90	Smith, Adam
1724–1804	Kant, Immanuel
1739	David Hume publishes *Treatise on Human Nature* advocating the study of humanity through direct observation rather than abstract philosophy
1748	Baron de Montesquieu argues that society is the source of all laws in *The Spirit of the Laws*
1759–97	Wollstonecraft, Mary
1760–1825	Saint-Simon, Claude-Henri
1762	Jean-Jacques Rousseau publishes *The Social Contract*, which prioritizes contracts between people and the social will over government control
1764	Reverend Thomas Bayes's *Essay Towards Solving a Problem in the Doctrine of Chances*, published posthumously, contains a statement of his Bayes theorem, the foundation of Bayesian statistics
1766–1834	Malthus, Thomas Robert
1770–1831	Hegel, G. W. F.
1772–1823	Ricardo, David
1776	Monarchical rule over America ends
1776	Adam Smith discusses the invisible hand of capitalism in *An Inquiry into the Nature and Causes of the Wealth of Nations*
1781	Kant argues against the radical empiricism of Hume in *Critique of Pure Reason*
1783–1830	Simon Bolivar
1788	Kant argues for the essence of free will in *Critique of Practical Reason*
1789	Jeremy Bentham develops the greatest happiness principle in *Introduction to the Principles of Morals and Legislation*, introducing a theory of social morals
1789	Condorcet coins the term "social science"
1789	French Revolution begins
1790	First US Census taken
1792	Wollstonecraft's *A Vindication of the Rights of Woman*, an early feminist classic

1798	Malthus theorizes demographics with his *Essay on the Principle of Population*
1798–1857	Comte, Auguste
1801	First British Census taken
1802–76	Martineau, Harriet
1804–72	Feuerbach, Ludwig
1805–59	Tocqueville, Alexis de
1805	The method of least squares presented by Adrien Marie Legendre in *New Methods for Determining the Orbits of Comets*
1806–73	Mill, John Stuart
1807	Hegel's *Phenomenology of Mind*, a key source on Hegel's idealism
1809–82	Darwin, Charles
1817	Ricardo's *The Principles of Political Economy and Taxation*, a classic in political economy laying out the advantages of free trade
1818–83	Marx, Karl
1820–95	Engels, Friedrich
1820–1903	Spencer, Herbert
1833–1911	Dilthey, William
1834	Statistical Society of London (later Royal Statistical Society) founded
1835–82	Jevons, William
1835–1909	Lombroso, Cesare
1837	Hegel's *Philosophy of History*, a dialectical analysis of the goal of human history
1837	Martineau's *Society in America*, an early sociological classic based on the author's travels through America
1839	Comte coins the term "sociology"
1839	American Statistical Association founded
1840	Tocqueville offers early insight into the United States in *Democracy in America*
1840–1902	Krafft-Ebing, Richard von
1840–1910	Sumner, William Graham
1842	Comte's *Course in Positive Philosophy* lays out a positivistic approach
1842–1910	James, William
1843	Mill in *A System of Logic* says that science needs both inductive and deductive reasoning
1843–1904	Tarde, Gabriel
1844	Marx's early humanistic thinking is laid out in *Economic and Philosophic Manuscripts* of 1844 (not published until 1932)
1844–1900	Nietzsche, Friedrich
1846	Marx authors *The German Ideology*, proposing a methodology of historical materialism
1848	Marx and Engels inspire the masses and call for revolution with the *Communist Manifesto*
1848	Mill debates the principles of socialism in his *Principles of Political Economy*
1848–1923	Pareto, Vilfredo
1850	Spencer introduces his ideas of social structure and change in *Social Statics*
1851	Feuerbach's *Lectures on the Essence of Religion*
1851	The Crystal Palace opens during first World's Fair in London
1854–1926	Small, Albion W.
1855–1936	Tönnies, Ferdinand
1856–1939	Freud, Sigmund
1857	In Britain, the Society of the Study of Social Problems is created
1857–1913	Saussure, Ferdinand de
1857–1929	Veblen, Thorstein
1857–61	Marx lays the groundwork for his later work on political economy and capitalism in *Grundrisse: Foundations of the Critique of Political Economy*
1857–84	The National Association for the Promotion of Social Science operates in Britain
1858–1917	Durkheim, Émile
1858–1918	Simmel, Georg

1858–1922	Sarasvati, Pandita Ramabai
1858–1941	Mosca, Gaetano
1858–1942	Boas, Franz
1859	Charles Darwin writes about evolution through natural selection in *The Origin of Species*
1859–1939	Ellis, Havelock
1859–1952	Dewey, John
1859–1938	Husserl, Edmund
1860–1935	Addams, Jane
1860–1935	Gilman, Charlotte Perkins
1861–96	Rizal, José
1863–1931	Mead, George Herbert
1863–1941	Sombart, Werner
1863–1947	Thomas, William I.
1864–1920	Weber, Max
1864–1929	Cooley, Charles Horton
1864–1929	Hobhouse, L. T.
1864–1944	Park, Robert E.
1867	Marx publishes one of the greatest insights into capitalism with *Capital*, vol. 1: *A Critique of Political Economy*
1868–1935	Hirschfeld, Magnus
1868–1963	Du Bois, W. E. B.
1869–1940	Goldman, Emma
1870–1954	Weber, Marianne
1871–1919	Luxemburg, Rosa
1871	The Trade Union Act makes unions legal in Britain
1873	Spencer's *Study of Sociology* becomes the first book used as a text to teach sociology in the United States, although no formal sociology class yet exists
1875–1962	Yanagita, Kunio
1876–96	Spencer writes his three-volume work on *Principles of Sociology*
1876–1924	Gökalp, Ziya
1876–1936	Michels, Robert
1877–1945	Halbwachs, Maurice
1877	Galton introduces the statistical phenomenon of regression and uses this term, although he originally termed it "reversion"
1881–1955	Radcliffe-Brown, Alfred R.
1882–1958	Znaniecki, Florian
1882–1970	MacIver, Robert
1883–1950	Schumpeter, Joseph A.
1883–1972	Takata, Yasuma
1884	Engels argues that women are subordinated by society, not biology, in *The Origins of the Family, Private Property, and the State*
1884–1942	Malinowski, Bronislaw K.
1885–1971	Lukács, Georg
1886	Krafft-Ebing publishes *Psychopathia Sexualis*, one of the first systematic studies of sexuality
1886	Sarasvati authors *The High-Caste Hindu Woman*, raising public consciousness about the plight of Hindu women and marking the beginning of family and kinship studies in India
1886–1964	Polanyi, Karl
1886–1966	Burgess, Ernest W.
1887	Tönnies's *Gemeinschaft und Gesellschaft* introduces his concepts of the same name
1887	Rizal publishes his first novel, *Noli Me Tangere* [*Touch Me Not*], describing the problems of Filipino society and blaming Spanish colonial rule
1887–1949	Sarkar, Benoy Kumar

1889	Charles Booth publishes his pioneering study of London poverty as *Life and Labour of the People of London*
1889–1968	Sorokin, Pitirim A.
1889–1976	Heidegger, Martin
1890	William James's *Principles of Psychology* is an early scientific work in psychology noted for its emphasis on the self
1890	Tarde distinguishes between the imitative and inventive in *Laws of Imitation*
1890	The first course in sociology is taught at the University of Kansas in Lawrence
1890	Sir James Frazer authors *The Golden Bough*, a comparative study of mythology and religion
1890–1947	Lewin, Kurt
1891	The first department of sociology and history is founded at the University of Kansas in Lawrence
1891	Walter Francis Wilcox's *The Divorce Problem: A Study in Statistics*
1891–1937	Gramsci, Antonio
1892	Small founds first major Department of Sociology at the University of Chicago
1892–1940	Benjamin, Walter
1893	Durkheim discusses the transition from mechanical to organic solidarity in *The Division of Labor in Society*
1893	New Zealand becomes the first country in the world to grant women the right to vote
1893	The first journal of sociology, *Revue Internationale de Sociologie*, is edited by René Worms in Paris
1893	The first sociological society, the Institut International de Sociologie, is founded in France
1893	Pearson introduces the term "standard deviation"
1893–1947	Mannheim, Karl
1893–1950	Sutherland, Edwin H.
1893–1956	Johnson, Charles Spurgeon
1893–1981	Marshall, Thomas Humphrey
1894	Kidd publishes *Social Evolution*, setting forth his ideas about the constant strife between individual and public interest
1894–1956	Kinsey, Alfred
1894–1962	Frazier, E. Franklin
1894–1966	Suzuki, Eitaro
1895	Durkheim presents a methodological foundation for sociology in *Rules of the Sociological Method*
1895	The first large-scale census of the German Empire is taken
1895	The first Department of Sociology in Europe is founded by Durkheim at the University of Bordeaux
1895	The Fabians found the London School of Economics (LSE)
1895	The *American Journal of Sociology* (*AJS*) is begun by Albion Small
1895	Nietzsche attacks sociology in *Twilight of the Idols*
1895–1973	Horkheimer, Max
1895–1988	Mendieta y Núñez, Lucio
1895–1990	Mumford, Lewis
1896–1988	Kurauchi, Kazuta
1897	Durkheim uses *Suicide* to demonstrate how even the most seemingly individual of acts still has a basis in the social
1897	*Rivista Italiana di Sociologia* appears in Italy
1897–1957	Reich, Wilhelm
1897–1962	Bataille, Georges
1897–1990	Elias, Norbert
1898	Durkheim founds the journal *L'Année Sociologique* (later *Annales de Sociologie*)
1898–1979	Marcuse, Herbert
1899	Veblen develops his idea of conspicuous consumption in *The Theory of the Leisure Class*

1899	Du Bois's *The Philadelphia Negro: A Social Study* is one of the first urban ethnographies
1899–1959	Schütz, Alfred
1899–1960	Becker, Howard
1899–1977	Thomas, Dorothy Swain
1900	Freud introduces his early principles of psychoanalysis in *Interpretation of Dreams*
1900	Husserl lays the groundwork of phenomenology in *Logical Investigations*
1900	Simmel discusses the tragedy of culture in *The Philosophy of Money*
1900	Pearson introduces the chi-squared test and the name for it in an article in the London, Edinburgh, and Dublin *Philosophical Magazine and Journal of Science*
1900–80	Fromm, Erich
1900–87	Blumer, Herbert
1901–74	Cox, Oliver Cromwell
1901–76	Lazarsfeld, Paul
1901–78	Mead, Margaret
1901–81	Lacan, Jacques
1901–91	Lefebvre, Henri
1902	Cooley's *Human Nature and Social Order* is an early classic that influenced symbolic interactionism, noted for its emphasis on the "looking-glass self"
1902	Ebenezer Howard inspires urban reform with his *Garden Cities of To-morrow*
1902	Durkheim becomes the first Professor of Sociology in Europe with his appointment to a position at the Sorbonne
1902	The United States Census Bureau is founded
1902–79	Parsons, Talcott
1902–85	Braudel, Fernand
1902–92	Imanishi, Kinji
1903	Du Bois introduces the concepts of the veil and double consciousness in *The Souls of Black Folk*
1903	The LSE houses the first British Department of Sociology
1903	Durkheim and his nephew Marcel Mauss's *Primitive Classification* shows the basis of classification in the social world rather than the mind
1903	Formation of the Sociological Society in London; operates on a UK-wide basis
1903–69	Adorno, Theodor W.
1903–96	Bernard, Jessie
1904	Robert Park's *The Crowd and the Public* is an early contribution to the study of collective behavior
1904	Spearman develops rank correlation
1904–80	Bateson, Gregory
1904–90	Skinner, Burrhus Frederic
1905	American Sociological Society (ASS: later ASA) founded at a meeting held at Johns Hopkins University in Baltimore, Maryland
1905	Weber ties the rise of the capitalist spirit to Calvinism in *The Protestant Ethic and the Spirit of Capitalism*
1905–6	Lester Ward serves as the first President of the ASS
1905–80	Sartre, Jean-Paul
1905–83	Aron, Raymond
1905–99	Komarovsky, Mirra
1906	First ASS meeting is held in Providence, Rhode Island
1906	Sombart's *Why Is There No Socialism in the United States?*
1906	Hobhouse publishes *Morals in Evolution: A Study in Comparative Ethics*
1906–75	Arendt, Hannah
1907	Hobhouse becomes the first Professor of Sociology at a British university, the LSE (although Edvard Westermarck had held the position part-time a few weeks before Hobhouse)
1907	James's Pragmatism helps set the stage for the rise of symbolic interactionism

1907	Eugenics Society founded in the UK
1908	Simmel publishes *Soziologie*, a wide-ranging set of essays on various social phenomena
1908	*Sociological Review* founded
1908	William Sealy Gosset, who went by the pseudonym "student," introduces the statistic z for testing hypotheses on the mean of the normal distribution in his paper "The probable error of a mean" (*Biometrika*)
1908–86	Beauvoir, Simone de
1908–97	Davis, Kingsley
1908–2006	Galbraith, John Kenneth
1908–2009	Lévi-Strauss, Claude
1909	German Sociological Association founded with Tönnies serving as the first President
1909	Freud delivers first lectures on psychoanalysis in the United States at Clark University
1909–2002	Riesman, David
1910	Addams's *Twenty Years at Hull House* contains recollections and reflections of the social reformer and feminist
1910–89	Homans, George
1910–2003	Merton, Robert K.
1911	Frederick W. Taylor authors *The Principles of Scientific Management*, laying out his ideas of the same name
1911–63	Kuhn, Manford
1911–79	Germani, Gino
1911–80	McLuhan, Marshall
1912	Durkheim equates religion with the social in *The Elementary Forms of the Religious Life*
1912–96	Lemert, Edwin M.
1913	James Broadus Watson introduces the term "behaviorism"
1913	The first assembly line introduced in a Ford factory
1913–2003	Coser, Lewis
1914–18	World War I
1914–96	Maruyama, Masao
1914–2000	Whyte, William Foote
1915	Pareto's *General Treatise on Sociology* is a major contribution to sociology by a thinker most associated with economics
1915	Sir Patrick Geddes authors *Cities in Evolution*, an essay on the growth of cities
1915–80	Barthes, Roland
1916	Saussure distinguishes between the signifier and the signified in *Course in General Linguistics*
1916–62	Mills, C. Wright
1916–96	Strauss, Anselm
1916–2006	Jacobs, Jane
1917	Russian Revolution begins
1917	Sociology taught for the first time in India at Calcutta University
1917–99	Whyte, William H.
1918	Znaniecki and Thomas use multiple methods in *The Polish Peasant in Europe and America*
1918	Weber's lecture on "Science as vocation"
1918	The first Chair in Sociology in Germany is established at the University of Frankfurt
1918	The phrase "analysis of variance" appears in Sir Ronald Aylmer Fisher's "The causes of human variability" (*Eugenics Review*)
1918–22	Oswald Spengler's *Decline of the West* argues that the development of civilizations follows a recognizable series of repetitive rises and falls
1918–90	Althusser, Louis
1918–2002	Blau, Peter
1918–2006	Tsurumi, Kazuko
1919	Sorokin's doctoral dissertation, *System of Sociology*, is published secretly after the Russian Revolution

1919	Hirschfeld opens the Institute for Sexual Research in Berlin
1919	The New School for Social Research is founded
1919	Takata Yasuma writes *Shakaigaku Genri* [*Treatise on Sociology*], in which he attempts a general sociological theory based on methodological individualism
1919	First Sociology Department in India formed at Bombay University
1920	Znaniecki becomes the first Chair in Sociology in Poland at the University of Poznan
1920–76	Braverman, Harry
1920–80	Gouldner, Alvin
1920–92	Bottomore, Thomas Burton
1921	Park and Burgess author *Introduction to the Science of Sociology*, the first major sociology textbook
1921–88	Williams, Raymond
1921–2002	Rawls, John
1921–2004	Duncan, Otis Dudley
1921–2006	Friedan, Betty
1922	Weber's *Economy and Society* is published in three volumes posthumously, introducing his comparative historical methodology
1922	Malinowski publishes *Argonauts of the Western Pacific*, in which he classifies ethnographic research into three parts based on complexity
1922	Social Science Research Council established in the United States
1922–82	Goffman, Erving
1922–92	Rosenberg, Morris
1922–96	Kuhn, Thomas
1922–97	Castoriadis, Cornelius
1922–	Casanova, Pablo González
1923	Lukács's *History and Class Consciousness* anticipates a more humanist interpretation of Marx; it is a key source on the concept of "reification"
1923	The Institute of Social Research, also known as the Frankfurt School, is founded
1923	Weber's *General Economic History* (published posthumously)
1923–2003	Kitsuse, John I.
1923–2010	Eisenstadt, Shmuel N.
1924	Hisatoshi Tanabe founds Tokyo Shakaigaku Kenkyukai (Tokyo Society of Sociological Study)
1924	Sutherland presents the first systematic textbook study of crime in *Criminology*
1924	Hobhouse publishes *Social Development: Its Nature and Conditions*
1924–33	Elton Mayo conducts the Hawthorne Experiments on worker productivity and concludes that the very act of studying something can change it, a principle that has come to be known as the "Hawthorne effect"
1924–98	Lyotard, Jean-François
1925	Mauss develops his theory of gift exchange in *The Gift*
1925	Halbwachs helps establish social memory studies with *The Social Frameworks of Memory*
1925	Park and Burgess invigorate urban sociology with *The City*
1925	Fisher's Statistical Methods for Research Workers becomes a landmark text in the field of statistics
1925–61	Fanon, Franz
1925–82	Emerson, Richard M.
1925–86	Certeau, Michel de
1925–94	Liebow, Elliot
1925–95	Deleuze, Gilles
1925–95	Gellner, Ernst
1926–84	Foucault, Michel
1926–95	Coleman, James
1926–2002	Illich, Ivan

1927	Heidegger's *Being and Time* is an existentialist analysis of individuals' relationship to modern society
1927	Znaniecki founds the Polish Sociological Institute
1927–40	Benjamin collects notes that later become *The Arcades Project*, an early classic on, among many other things, consumption sites
1927–98	Luhmann, Niklas
1928	William I. Thomas and Dorothy S. Thomas introduce the Thomas theorem – what humans perceive as real will be real in its consequences – in *The Child in America*
1928–2003	Hess, Beth
1928–2007	Syed Hussein Alatas
1929	Mannheim's *Ideology and Utopia* elaborates his sociology of knowledge
1929	The Great Depression begins in the United States and spreads to the rest of the world
1929	Robert S. Lynd and Helen M. Lynd conduct the Middletown studies
1929	k-statistics are introduced by Sir Ronald Aylmer Fisher
1929–68	King, Jr, Martin Luther
1929–2007	Baudrillard, Jean
1929–2008	Tilly, Charles
1929–2009	Ralf Dahrendorf
1930	J. L. Moreno invents sociometry, the cornerstone of network analysis
1930	Yanagita introduces his theory of shükenron (concentric area theory) in his book *Kagyükö* [*On Snails*]
1930–2002	Bourdieu, Pierre
1930–2004	Derrida, Jacques
1930–	Wallerstein, Immanuel
1931	The Sociology Department at Harvard is established by Sorokin
1931	Population Association of America (PAA) founded
1931	The term "factor analysis" introduced by Louis L. Thurstone in "Multiple factor analysis" (*Psychological Review*)
1931–94	Debord, Guy
1931–2007	Rorty, Richard
1932	Schütz's *The Phenomenology of the Social World* introduces phenomenology into mainstream social theory
1933–77	Shariati, Ali
1933–84	Milgram, Stanley
1934	Mead develops ideas central to symbolic interactionism in *Mind, Self, and Society*
1934	The term "confidence interval" coined by Jerzy Neyman in "On the two different aspects of the representative method" (*Journal of the Royal Statistical Society*)
1934	The F distribution tabulated by G. W. Snedecor in *Calculation and Interpretation of Analysis of Variance and Covariance*
1934–92	Lorde, Audre
1935	Mannheim suggests a planned society in *Man and Society in an Age of Reconstruction*
1935	*American Sociological Review* (*ASR*) begins with Frank Hankins as editor
1935	The term "null hypothesis" is used by Fisher in *The Design of Experiments*
1935–75	Sacks, Harvey
1935–91	Bonfil Batalla, Guillermo
1935–2002	Sainsaulieu, Renaud
1935–2003	Faletto, Enzo
1935–2003	Said, Edward W.
1936	John Maynard Keynes introduces his economic theory in *General Theory of Employment, Interest, and Money*
1936–79	Poulantzas, Nicos
1937	Parsons helps bring European theory to the United States in *The Structure of Social Action*
1937	Mass Observation research unit set up by Tom Harrison, Charles Madge, and Humphrey Jennings

1938	Skinner's *The Behavior of Organisms* is a major contribution to psychological behaviorism
1938	*Journal of Marriage and the Family* founded
1938–2002	Nozick, Robert
1939	Elias develops his figurational sociology in *The Civilizing Process*
1939–45	World War II
1939–2004	Lechner, Norbert
1940–91	Fajnzylber, Fernando
1941	Kinji Imanishi publishes *Seibutsu no Sekai* [*The World of Living Things*], which is a philosophical statement of his views on the origins and interactions of organisms with their environment and development of the biosphere
1941	William Lloyd Warner authors *The Social Life of a Modern Community*, the first volume in the Yankee City series
1942	Schumpeter's *Capitalism, Socialism, and Democracy*, best known for the idea of "creative destruction" in capitalism
1942	William Henry Beveridge publishes *Social Insurance and Allied Services*, known as the Beveridge Report, establishing the foundations for the welfare state
1942–2004	Anzaldúa, Gloria
1943	Sartre further develops existentialism in *Being and Nothingness*
1943	William Foote Whyte's *Street Corner Society* is a classic ethnography on street corner life in Boston
1943	The statistical P-value is discussed in *Statistical Adjustment of Data* by W. E. Deming
1944	Polanyi's *The Great Transformation* discusses issues of socialism, free trade, and the Industrial Revolution
1945	Kingsley Davis and Wilbert Moore lay the groundwork for stratification in "Some principles of stratification" (*ASR*)
1945	United Nations founded
1946	Parsons establishes the Department of Social Relations at Harvard
1947	Kinsey Institute founded at Indiana University at Bloomington
1947	Horkheimer and Adorno criticize the Enlightenment in *The Dialectic of Enlightenment*
1948	Alfred Kinsey, Wardell Pomeroy, and Clyde Martin revolutionize the way many think about sexuality with *The Sexual Behavior of the Human Male*
1948	E. Franklin Frazier is elected the first black President of the ASS
1948	Oliver Cromwell Cox authors his famous analysis in *Caste, Class, and Race*
1948–2002	Rosenfeld, Rachel
1949	Lévi-Strauss helps develop structuralist thinking with his *The Elementary Structures of Kinship*
1949	Merton's *Social Theory and Social Structure* appears, the first edition of a classic collection of essays
1949	Simone de Beauvoir challenges the traditional concept of "woman" in *The Second Sex*
1949	International Sociological Association founded with Louis Wirth serving as the first President
1949	Stoufer et al., *The American Soldier: Adjustment During Army Life*, vol. 1, is a major empirical study of the American military
1950	David Reisman, Nathan Glazer, and Reuel Denney develop inner- and other-directedness in *The Lonely Crowd*
1951	C. Wright Mills offers an analysis of working life in the United States in *White Collar*
1951	Parsons furthers his structural functional theory in *The Social System*
1951	Parsons develops action theory in *Toward a General Theory of Action*
1951	Society for the Study of Social Problems (SSSP) founded in the United States
1951	SSSP begins publishing the journal *Social Problems*
1951	British Sociological Association is founded
1951	Asch experiments are published demonstrating the power of group conformity
1951	Arendt's *The Origins of Totalitarianism* is a classic work in political theory, especially totalitarianism
1951	Indian Sociological Society founded at Bombay

1952	International Social Science Council established
1952	*Current Sociology*, an official journal of the International Sociological Association, is launched
1952	American Psychiatric Association publishes first edition of the *Diagnostic and Statistical Manual* (*DSM*)
1952	Dorothy Swain Thomas is elected the first female President of the ASS
1952	Sociological Bulletin first published at Bombay University
1953	Skinner's *Science and Human Behavior* is a further contribution to psychological behaviorism
1953	Ludwig Wittgenstein's ideas of language games are presented in his work *Philosophical Investigations*
1954	Abraham Maslow makes famous his hierarchy of needs in *Motivation and Personality*
1954	Manford Kuhn and Thomas McPartland lay the groundwork for structural symbolic interactionism in "An empirical investigation of self-attitudes" (*ASR*)
1954	The United States Supreme Court decision in *Brown v. Board of Education of Topeka, Kansas*, ends officially sanctioned segregation in that country
1955	L. J. Moreno's *Sociometry* is a major contribution to social psychology
1955	Gino Germani's *Estructura Social de la Argentina* [*The Social Structure of Argentina*] uses empirical data from the Argentinian national census of 1947 to analyze contemporary Argentina
1956	Mills argues that there has been a convergence of economic, political, and military power and that members of this elite largely share a common social background in *The Power Elite*
1956	Dahrendorf's *Class and Class Conflict in Industrial Society* becomes a central work in conflict theory
1956	Coser integrates a Simmelian approach with structural functionalism in the *Functions of Social Conflict*
1957	Barthes helps develop semiology in *Mythologies*
1957	Chomsky revolutionizes the field of linguistics and helps spark the cognitive revolution with *Syntactic Structures*
1957	Richard Hoggart's *The Uses of Literacy* is an early contribution and exemplification of the Birmingham School
1957	Maruyama Masao writes *Denken in Japan* [*Japanese Thought*], which still serves as a reference point for ongoing debates on the intellectual development of modern Japan
1957	Michael Young and Peter Willmott author *Family and Kinship in East London*, exploring changes in kinship networks and contacts of families in East London as they are affected by urban change
1958	Galbraith challenges the idea of consumer sovereignty in *The Affluent Society*
1958	Homans's article "Social behavior as exchange" (*AJS*) develops his notion of exchange theory
1958	Raymond Williams presents his first major analysis of culture in *Culture and Society*
1959	Cuban Revolution is launched by Fidel Castro awakening the call for social and political reforms across Latin America and the rest of the world
1959	Karl Popper's *The Logic of Scientific Discovery* argues that scientific results can never be proven, merely falsified
1959	Mills critiques structural functionalism in *The Sociological Imagination*, also introducing his concept of the same name
1959	Goffman's early statement on dramaturgy is developed in *The Presentation of Self in Everyday Life*
1959	Thibaut and Kelley's *The Social Psychology of Groups* is an early psychological contribution to exchange theory
1959	ASS changes its name to the American Sociological Association (ASA)
1960	*Journal of Health and Social Behavior* (*JHSB*) founded
1960	Morris Janowitz's *The Professional Soldier: A Social and Political Portrait*

1960	Alvin Gouldner's "The norm of reciprocity: a preliminary statement" (*ASR*)
1960	Margaret Stacey authors her first major work, *Tradition and Change: A Study of Banbury*
1961	Homans further develops his exchange theory in *Social Behavior: Its Elementary Forms*
1961	Fanon's *The Wretched of the Earth* is a powerful influence on revolutionary movements
1961	Goffman introduces the idea of a total institution in *Asylums: Essays on the Social Situation of Mental Patients and Other Inmates*
1961	Jane Jacobs analyzes urban culture in *The Death and Life of Great American Cities*
1961	*International Journal of Comparative Sociology* founded
1962	Richard Emerson introduces his first major statement on exchange theory in "Power-dependence relations" (*ASR*)
1962	Thomas Kuhn in *The Structure of Scientific Revolutions* offers a revolutionary rather than evolutionary theory of scientific change
1962	Habermas's *The Structural Transformation of the Public Sphere* is an important early contribution to current debate on civil society
1962	Herbert Gans's *Urban Villagers* is a classic in urban sociology
1963	Goffman publishes *Stigma*, one of the first major works in labeling theory
1963	Betty Friedan's *The Feminine Mystique* marks the beginning of the second wave of feminism for many
1963	Australian Sociological Association founded (originally known as the Sociological Association of Australia and New Zealand)
1963	Stanley Milgram's experiments are outlined in his article "Behavioral study of obedience" (*Journal of Abnormal and Social Psychology*)
1963	*Demography* journal founded by Donald Bogue
1963	S. N. Eisenstadt presents analytic tools helpful for cultural comparison in *The Political Systems of Empires*
1963	European Fertility Project begun by Ansley Coale
1963	First issue of *Sociology of Education* published
1963	Nathan Glazer and Daniel P. Moynihan's *Beyond the Melting Pot* is known for its focus on assimilation
1963	Martin Luther King, Jr delivers his "I have a dream" speech in Washington, DC
1963	Becker's *Outsiders: Studies in the Sociology of Deviance* is a key document in the sociology of deviance, especially labeling theory
1964	Blau's major integrative statement in exchange theory is laid out in *Exchange and Power in Social Life*
1964	McLuhan discusses the global village in *Understanding Media: The Extensions of Man*
1964	Marcuse publishes *One-Dimensional Man: Studies in the Ideology of Advances in Industrial Society*, outlining what he sees as society's destructive impact on individuals
1964	Center for Contemporary Cultural Studies founded under the leadership of Richard Hoggart at the University of Birmingham, UK
1964	Aaron V. Cicourel's *Method and Measurement in Sociology*
1965	Social Science Research Council established in the UK (name changed to Economic and Social Research Council in 1983)
1965	Foucault argues that the madman has taken the place of the leper in *Madness and Civilization*
1965	*Australian and New Zealand Journal of Sociology* founded (later changed to *Journal of Sociology* in 1998)
1966	William Masters and Virginia Johnson's further research into human sexuality in *Human Sexual Response*
1966	Berger and Luckmann further develop social constructionism in *The Social Construction of Reality: A Treatise in the Sociology of Knowledge*
1966	Scheff's *Being Mentally Ill: A Sociological Theory* becomes a major work in studies of mental illness, social constructionism, and labeling theory interactions
1967	Derrida's *On Grammatology* becomes a central text in the emerging area of poststructuralism

1967	Debord criticizes both the media and consumption in *Society of the Spectacle*
1967	Garfinkel's *Studies in Ethnomethodology* develops the field of the same name
1967	*Sociology*, the official journal of the British Sociological Association, is founded
1967	Barney Glaser and Anselm Strauss's *The Discovery of Grounded Theory: Strategies for Qualitative Research* introduces their theory of the same name
1967	Liebow's *Tally's Corner: A Study of Negro Streetcorner Men* is an important ethnographic study carried out in Washington, DC
1967	Gans's *The Levittowners* is another classic ethnography, this time in a paradigmatic suburban development
1967	Otis Dudley Duncan authors *The American Occupational Structure*, detailing how parents transmit their societal status to their children
1968	Student revolts begin in Paris and spread throughout Europe
1968	Paul Ehrlich's *The Population Bomb* issues an early, perhaps overheated, warning about the population explosion
1968	John Goldthorpe, David Lockwood, Frank Bechhofer, and Jennifer Platt, in *The Affluent Worker: Industrial Attitudes and Behavior*, argue that the growing affluence of sections of the working class in Britain does not entail the end of class division, but that class remains a central feature of British life even in a prosperous, consumer society
1968	*Chinese Sociology and Anthropology* founded
1969	Blumer gives one of the first systematic statements of symbolic interactionism in *Symbolic Interactionism: Perspectives and Methods*
1969	Althusser lays the groundwork of structural Marxism in *For Marx*
1969	Native Americans take over Alcatraz Island in California, launching their civil rights movement
1969	The gay rights movement is launched during the Stonewall Riots in New York City
1969	Faletto and Cardoso author *Dependencia y Desarrollo en América Latina* [*Dependency and Development in Latin America*], which attempts to systematize an interpretive model of economic development in Latin America
1970	Students protesting the American invasion of Cambodia are shot by National Guardsmen at Kent State University in Kent, Ohio, setting off a wave of student strikes across the United States
1970	Gouldner critiques trends in sociology, especially structural functionalism, in *The Coming Crisis of Western Sociology*
1970	Baudrillard's *Consumer Society: Myths and Structures* becomes a classic text in the study of consumption
1970	Thomas S. Szasz launches a critique of psychiatry in *The Manufacture of Madness: A Comparative Study of the Inquisition and the Mental Health Movement*
1970	The first Women's Studies Program in the United States opens at San Diego State College
1970	Fajnzylber publishes his first important work, *Sistema Industrial y Exportación de Manufacturas: Análisis de la Experiencia Brasileña* [*The Industrial System and Manufactured Goods: An Analysis of the Brazilian Experience*]
1971	Habermas presents a prehistory of modern positivism with the intention of analyzing knowledge-constitutive interests in control, understanding, and emancipation in *Knowledge and Human Interests*
1971	Antonio Gramsci's *Prison Notebooks* are published, making his ideas, including hegemony, better known
1971	Phillip Zimbardo conducts his famous prison experiments at Stanford
1971	Sociologists for Women in Society (SWS) founded
1972	The First General Social Survey (GSS) is taken
1972	The destruction of the Pruitt-Igoe housing complex in St Louis marks the end of the modernist reign for some postmodernists
1972	*Journal on Armed Forces and Society* founded
1972	Philippine *Sociological Review* founded
1973	Baudrillard challenges Marx in *The Mirror of Production*

1973	Clifford Geertz introduces his notion of "thick descriptions" in *The Interpretation of Cultures*
1973	David Rosenhan questions taken-for-granted notions of sanity and insanity in "On being sane in insane places" (*Science*)
1973	The United States Supreme Court decision in *Roe v. Wade* gives women the right to choose in issues of abortion
1973	Mark Granovetter's "The strength of weak ties" (*AJS*) introduces his concept of the same name
1973	Bell's *The Coming of Post-Industrial Society* documents and anticipates dramatic social change
1974	Immanuel Wallerstein develops world-systems theory in the first of his three-volume work, *The Modern World-System*
1974	First issue of *Theory and Society* published
1974	Goffman's *Frame Analysis: An Essay on the Organization of Experience* introduces the influential idea of frames
1974	Glen Elder, Jr's *Children of the Great Depression* sets the stage for the development of the life course perspective
1974	The National Commission for the Protection of Human Subjects of Biomedical and Behavioral Research is established
1974	Henri Lefebvre brings spatial concerns to the forefront of social analysis in *The Production of Space*
1975	George Ritzer's *Sociology: A Multiple Paradigm Science* outlines the paradigmatic status of sociology and constitutes a contribution to metatheory
1975	Randall Collins develops a micro perspective on conflict theory in *Conflict Sociology: Toward an Explanatory Science*
1975	E. O. Wilson's *Sociobiology: A New Synthesis* is a key statement in the development of sociobiology
1975	Foucault outlines the history and theory of the carceral system in *Discipline and Punish: The Birth of the Prison*
1975	Foucault employs his idea of an archeology of knowledge in *The Birth of the Clinic: An Archeology of Medical Perception*
1975	Castoriadis's *The Imaginary Institution of Society* presents an interdisciplinary critique of contemporary capitalist societies, in part by formulating an alternative to both foundationalist social science and poststructural relativism
1975	Peter Singer's *Animal Liberation* becomes an important text in the animal rights movement
1975	Canadian *Journal of Sociology* founded
1976	Baudrillard argues that we can no longer engage in symbolic exchange in his *Symbolic Exchange and Death*
1976	Elijah Anderson's *A Place on the Corner* becomes a cornerstone of classical ethnography
1977	Bourdieu introduces habitus, field, and his constructivist structuralism in *Outline of a Theory of Practice*
1977	Albert Bandura's *Social Learning Theory* introduces the perspective of the same name
1977	James House's "The three faces of social psychology" (*Sociometry*) provides perspective for the field
1977	Joseph Berger, M. Hamit Fisek, Robert Norman, and Morris Zelditch's *Status Characteristics and Social Interaction: An Expectation States Approach* introduces the theory of the same name
1977	Richard Sennett's *The Fall of Public Man* demonstrates the impoverishment of the social world
1977	R. W. Connell's *Ruling Class, Ruling Culture: Studies of Conflict, Power, and Hegemony in Australian Life* deals with Australian class relations and culture
1977	Norbert Lechner urges Latin Americans to use political reflection as a guide to theoretical analysis in *La Crisis del Estado en América Latina*

1978	The publication of Edward Said's *Orientalism* is a foundational historical moment in the rise of postcolonial studies
1978	Derrida's *Writing and Difference* is another key contribution to poststructuralism
1978	Nancy Chodorow expands on Freud in *The Reproduction of Mothering: Psychoanalysis and the Sociology of Gender*
1978	The Society for Applied Sociology founded
1979	Roy Bhaskar authors *The Possibility of Naturalism: A Philosophical Critique of the Contemporary Human Sciences*, a cornerstone of critical realism
1979	Arlie Hochschild introduces the idea of emotional labor in "Emotion work, feeling rules, and social structure"
1979	Lyotard's *The Postmodern Condition* declares war on the modern grand narrative and totalizations
1979	Bruno Latour and Steve Woolgar's *Laboratory Life: The Social Construction of Scientific Facts* introduces actor-network theory (ANT)
1979	Rorty argues for a pragmatic philosophy in *Philosophy and the Mirror of Nature*
1979	Theda Skocpol's *States and Social Revolutions* makes the case for the importance of the state in social revolutions
1979	Morris Rosenberg broadens understandings of the self-concept in *Conceiving the Self*
1979	Chinese Sociological Association is founded
1980	Foucault publishes the first of his three-volume *The History of Sexuality*, which becomes a classic in poststructuralist and queer theories
1980	Stuart Hall's "Encoding/decoding" appears in *Culture, Media, Language* and argues that audiences interpret the same television material in different ways
1980	Adrienne Rich introduces the lesbian continuum in "Compulsory heterosexuality and the lesbian existence"
1980	Sheldon Stryker develops structural identity theory in *Symbolic Interactionism: A Social Structural Version*
1980	Ali Shariati publishes *On the Sociology of Islam*
1980	The Institute of Sociology of the Chinese Academy of Social Sciences founded
1981	Gary Becker authors *A Treatise on the Family*, a key text in the sociology of the family
1981	Alain Touraine outlines the techniques of "sociological intervention" in *The Voice and the Eye*
1981	Leonard Pearlin's "The stress process" (*JHSB*) outlines the concept of the same name
1981	Willer and Anderson's *Networks, Exchange and Coercion*
1981	First AIDS case reported in the United States
1982	First issue of *Theory, Culture, and Society* is published
1982	Luhmann's early work on systems theory is presented in *The Differentiation of Society*
1982	Margaret Archer's "Morphogenesis versus structuration: on combining structure and action" (*BJS*) makes the case for systems theory vs. structuration theory
1982–3	Jeffrey Alexander updates functionalism in his four-volume *Theoretical Logic in Sociology*
1983	Karen Cook, Richard Emerson, Mary Gillmore, and Toshio Yamagishi further develop exchange theory in "The distribution of power in exchange networks: theory and experimental results" (*AJS*)
1983	Baudrillard's *Simulations* introduces his famous concept of the same name
1983	Nancy Hartsock authors "The feminist standpoint: developing the Ground for a specifically feminist historical materialism," a key contribution to standpoint theory
1983	Hochschild analyzes the emotional labor of airline attendants and bill collectors in *The Managed Heart: Commercialization of Human Feeling*
1983	First issue of *Sociological Theory* published

1983	Barry Wellman's contribution to network analysis in "Network analysis: some basic principles" (*Sociological Theory*)
1983	Melvin Kohn and Carmi Schooler's *Work and Personality: An Inquiry into the Impact of Social Stratification* is a key work on the relationship between class and work
1983	Paul DiMaggio and Walter Powell's "The iron cage revisited: institutional isomorphism and collective rationality in organizational fields" will achieve the most cumulative citations in ASR history
1984	Anthony Giddens's most developed statement on structuration theory appears in *The Constitution of Society: Outline of the Theory of Structuration*
1984	Habermas develops his ideas of communicative rationality in *The Theory of Communicative Action*, vol. 1: *Reason and the Rationalization of Society*
1984	Certeau's *The Practice of Everyday Life* accords great power to the agent
1984	Bourdieu's *Homo Academicus* is a study of academia from the author's distinctive theoretical perspective
1984	Bourdieu's *Distinction: A Social Critique of the Judgment of Taste*
1984	Luhmann develops his systems theory in *Social Systems*
1985	Gayatri Spivak's "Can the subaltern speak? Speculations on widow sacrifice" (*Wedge 7/8*) becomes a classic in postcolonial studies
1985	Deleuze and Guattari's *Anti-Oedipus: Capitalism and Schizophrenia* makes an important contribution to poststructural/postmodern theory
1985	Jeffrey Alexander and Paul Colomy's "Toward neo-functionalism" (*Sociological Theory*) develops the short-lived theory of the same name
1985	Ernesto Laclau and Chantal Mouffe's *Hegemony and Socialist Strategy: Towards a Radical Democratic Politics* marks an important shift in neo-Marxian theory
1985	European *Sociological Review* founded
1986	Ulrich Beck develops the notion of risk in *Risk Society: Towards a New Modernity*
1986	Lacan revises Freudian psychoanalysis in the context of Saussurean linguistics in *Écrits*
1986	Paul Virilio's *Speed and Politics* introduces the idea of speed through his notion of dromology
1986	International Sociology founded
1987	Dorothy Smith presents a phenomenological feminist critique in *The Everyday World as Problematic: A Feminist Sociology*
1987	Gilles Lipovetsky develops a post-postmodernism in *The Empire of Fashion: Dressing Modern Democracy*
1987	Candace West and Don Zimmerman differentiate sex, sex category, and gender in "Doing gender" (*Gender and Society*)
1988	Noam Chomsky and Edward Herman argue that the mass media are a political tool of political propaganda in *Manufacturing Consent: The Political Economy of the Mass Media*
1988	Barry Markovsky, David Willer, and Travis Patton author "Power relations in exchange networks" (*ASR*)
1988	Linda Molm emphasizes rewards in exchange theory in "The structure and use of power: a comparison of reward and punishment power" (*Social Psychology Quarterly*)
1988	*Journal of Historical Sociology* founded
1989	Žižek develops his ideas of ideology critique and cultural analysis in *The Sublime Object of Ideology*
1989	Bauman's *Modernity and the Holocaust* argues that the Holocaust was an instantiation of modernity and argues for a sociology of morality
1989	David Harvey further develops social geography and the idea of time–space compression in *The Condition of Postmodernity: An Enquiry into the Origins of Cultural Change*
1989	Edward Soja brings spatial concerns to the forefront once again in *Postmodern Geographies: The Reassertion of Space in Critical Social Theory*

1989	Trinh Minh-ha's *Woman, Native, Other: Writing Postcoloniality and Feminism*
1989	Michael Moore's first major documentary, *Roger & Me*, exposes the effects of plant closures on social life in Flint, Michigan
1989	Berlin Wall falls
1990	James S. Coleman develops rational choice theory in *Foundations of Social Theory*
1990	Judith Butler's *Gender Trouble* challenges traditional ideas of sex, gender, and sexuality
1990	Giddens introduces his idea of the juggernaut in *The Consequences of Modernity*
1990	Donna Haraway contributes to postmodern feminism with "A manifesto for cyborgs: science, technology, and socialist feminism"
1990	Patricia Hill Collins develops intersectionality in *Black Feminist Thought: Knowledge, Consciousness, and Empowerment*
1990	Tamito Yoshida publishes *Jyoho to Jiko Soshiki-sei no Riron* [*Theory of Information and Self-Organizing Systems*], outlining his general systems theory
1990	*Sociétés Contemporaines* founded
1990–2	The National Comorbidity Survey administers structured psychiatric exams to respondents to assess levels of disorder
1991	Jameson's *Postmodernism, or the Cultural Logic of Late Capitalism* integrates neo-Marxian and postmodern ideas
1991	Kenneth Gergen brings postmodernity to bear on the self in *The Saturated Self: Dilemmas of Identity in Contemporary Life*
1991	Giddens's *Modernity and Self-Identity: Self and Society in the Late Modern Age* is a discussion of important microsociological issues
1991	Sharon Zukin links power to geography in *Landscapes of Power: From Detroit to Disney World*
1991	The term "new urbanism" is introduced at a meeting of urban reformers in California
1991	Steven Best and Douglas Kellner's *Postmodern Theory: Critical Interrogations* is a useful overview of postmodern theory
1991	Saskia Sassen introduces the term "global city" in her book *The Global City: New York, London, Tokyo*
1991	*Berliner Journal für Soziologie* founded in Berlin
1992	Francis Fukuyama argues in *The End of History and the Last Man* that the progression of human history as a struggle between ideologies is largely at an end, with liberal democracy coming out the winner
1992	Marc Auge's *Non-Places: An Introduction to an Anthropology of Supermodernity* introduces the ideas of non-place and supermodernity
1992	Roland Robertson develops the idea of glocalization in *Globalization: Social Theory and Global Culture*
1992	First European Conference of Sociology is held in Vienna
1992	Bourdieu and Wacquant's *An Invitation to Reflexive Sociology* presents an overview of Bourdieu's ideas
1992	Bauman's *Intimations of Postmodernity* contains contributions to postmodern theory by a modernist
1992	European Sociological Association founded
1992	Mitchell Duneier's *Slim's Table: Race, Respectability, and Masculinity* becomes a classic in ethnographic studies
1992	*International Journal of Japanese Sociology* founded
1993	Bruno Latour establishes actor-network theory (ANT) in *We Have Never Been Modern*
1993	Ritzer's *The McDonaldization of Society: An Investigation into the Changing Character of Contemporary Social Life* brings Weber's thesis of rationalization to bear on contemporary society and consumption
1994	Homi Bhabha contributes to studies of both culture and postcolonialism with *The Location of Culture*

1994	Cornell West's *Race Matters* is an important contribution to multidisciplinary thinking on race
1994	Cairo hosts UN International Conference on Population and Development, which leads to major reforms in population planning
1994	Giddens's *Beyond Left and Right: The Future of Radical Politics* marks a shift in his work to more practical issues
1995	Benjamin Barber's *Jihad vs. McWorld* contrasts a homogenizing and heterogenizing approach to global politics
1995	Michel Maffesoli develops neotribalism in *The Time of Tribes*
1995	Soziale Systeme founded
1996	Castells argues the importance of information in *The Rise of the Network Society*
1996	Appadurai's *Modernity at Large: Cultural Dimensions of Globalization* introduces the idea of "scapes"
1996	Samuel Huntington argues the importance of cultural civilizations in *The Clash of Civilizations and the Remaking of World Order*
1996	Asia Pacific Sociological Association founded
1997	Chomsky authors *Media Control: The Spectacular Achievements of Propaganda*, summarizing his views on the media as well as terrorism
1997	Peter Burke outlines his model of a cybernetic identity theory in "An identity model of network exchange" (*ASR*)
1997	Hochschild's *The Time Bind: When Work Becomes Home and Home Becomes Work* discusses the time bind placed on contemporary families, the importance of the "second shift," and even the "third shift"
1997	Kathryn Edin and Laura Lein demonstrate the inefficiencies of the welfare system in the United States in *Making Ends Meet: How Single Mothers Survive Welfare and Low-Wage Work*
1998	*Interventions: International Journal of Postcolonial Studies* founded
1998	Arts and Humanities Research Board established in the UK (changed to Arts and Humanities Research Council in 2005)
1999	Barry Glassner publishes a critical insight into the role of fear in US culture in *The Culture of Fear: Why Americans are Afraid of the Wrong Things*
2000	Michael Hardt and Antonio Negri's *Empire* argues that imperialism is being replaced by an empire without a national base
2000	Robert Putnam's *Bowling Alone: The Collapse and Revival of American Community*
2000	Bauman's *Liquid Modernity* provides new imagery in a theory of the contemporary world
2001	Edward Lawler advocates the role of emotion in "An affect theory of social exchange" (*AJS*)
2001	September 11, 2001: terrorists hijack airplanes and destroy the World Trade Center in New York City and parts of the Pentagon in Washington, DC
2001	Barbara Ehrenreich brings light to the difficulties of living on the minimum wage in *Nickled and Dimed: On Not Getting By in America*
2001	The Netherlands becomes the first country in the world to recognize same-sex marriage
2002	Leslie Sklair argues for alternatives to global capitalism in *Globalization: Capitalism and Its Alternatives*
2002	African Sociological Association formed
2003	Chandra Mohanty's *Feminism Without Borders: Decolonizing Theory, Practicing Solidarity*
2003	John Urry brings chaos theory to bear on globalization in *Global Complexity*
2003	Annette Lareau argues that class-based childrearing practices perpetuate social inequality in *Unequal Childhoods: Race, Class, and Family Life*
2004	Michael Burawoy, President of the ASA, launches a major debate on public sociology with his presidential address

2004	Hardt and Negri release *Multitude: War and Democracy in the Age of Empire* as a follow-up to their 2000 work on empire
2005	ASA holds Centennial meeting in San Francisco, California
2005	Hurricane Katrina sparks new conversations on urban reform, racism, and class relations

Lexicon

Crime and Deviance

Addiction and Dependency
Aggression
Alcoholism and Alcohol Abuse
Capital Punishment
Child Abuse
Crime
Crime, Broken Windows Theory of
Crime, Corporate
Crime, Organized
Crime, Political
Crime, Radical/Marxist Theories of
Crime, Social Control Theory of
Crime, Social Learning Theory of
Crime, White-Collar
Criminal Justice System
Criminology
Criminology: Research Methods
Cybercrime
Death Penalty as a Social Problem
Deinstitutionalization
Deterrence Theory
Deviance
Deviance, Academic
Deviance, Constructionist Perspectives
Deviance, Crime and
Deviance, Criminalization of
Deviance, Explanatory Theories of
Deviance, Medicalization of
Deviance, Normative Definitions of
Deviance, Positivist Theories of
Deviance, Reactivist Definitions of
Deviance, Theories of
Deviant Beliefs/Cognitive Deviance
Deviant Careers
Domestic Violence
Drug Use
Drugs, Drug Abuse, and Drug Policy
Hate Crimes
Homophobia
Identity, Deviant
Labeling
Labeling Theory
Madness
Mental Disorder
Moral Panics
Positive Deviance
Race and Crime
Race and the Criminal Justice System
Rape/Sexual Assault as Crime
Sexual Deviance
Social Control
Sociocultural Relativism
Subcultures, Deviant
Suicide
Victimization
Violence
Violent Crime
Zimbardo Prison Experiment

Culture, Popular Culture, Media, and Sport

Acculturation
Agency (and Intention)
Body and Cultural Sociology
Censorship
Certeau, Michel de
Civilizations
Civilizing Process
Collective Action
Consumption and the Internet
Counterculture
Critical Theory/Frankfurt School
Cultural Capital
Cultural Critique
Cultural Feminism
Cultural Imperialism
Cultural Relativism
Cultural Studies
Cultural Studies, British
Culture
Culture Industries
Culture Jamming
Culture, Nature and
Culture of Poverty
Cyberculture
Deconstruction
Discourse
Distinction
Economy, Culture and
Emotion: Cultural Aspects

Demography and Ecology

Economy and Consumption

Consumption and the Body
Consumption, Cathedrals and Landscapes of
Consumption, Green/Sustainable
Consumption and the Internet
Crime, Corporate
Culture Jamming
Culture of Poverty
Dependency and World-Systems Theories
Development: Political Economy
Distinction
Division of Labor
Divisions of Household Labor
Dual Labor Markets
Economic Determinism
Economic Development
Economic Sociology: Classical Political Economic Perspectives
Economic Sociology: Neoclassical Economic Perspective
Economy, Culture and
Ethnic/Informal Economy
Exchange-Value
Exploitation
Feminization of Poverty
Fordism/Post-Fordism
Gender, Work, and Family
Global Economy
Globalization, Consumption and
Hawthorne Effect
Income Inequality and Income Mobility
Industrial Revolution
Industrialization
Inequality, Wealth
Institutionalism
International Gender Division of Labor
Japanese-Style Management
Labor/Labor Power
Labor Markets
Leisure
Leisure Class
Lifestyle
McDonaldization
Markets
Marx, Karl
Marxism and Sociology
Migration and the Labor Force
Modernization
Money
Moral Economy
Polanyi, Karl
Political Economy
Population and Development
Post-Industrial Society
Poverty
Privatization
Property, Private
Public and Private
Rationalization
Reflexive Modernization
Schumpeter, Joseph A.
Sexualities and Consumption
Smith, Adam
Sport and Capitalism
State and Economy
Taxes: Progressive, Proportional, and Regressive
Taylorism
Transition Economies
Transnationals
Unemployment as a Social Problem
Unions
Urban Poverty
Use-Value
Value
Wealth
Weber, Max
Welfare State
Work, Sociology of

Education

Affirmative Action
Bell Curve
Community College
Critical Pedagogy
Demographic Techniques: Time Use
Deviance, Academic
Education
Educational Inequality
Feminist Pedagogy
Gender, Education and
Hidden Curriculum
Literacy/Illiteracy
Meritocracy
School Segregation, Desegregation
Self-Fulfilling Prophecy
Sex Education
Status Attainment
Tracking

Family and Friendship

Carework
Childhood
Cohabitation
Demographic Techniques: Time Use
Divisions of Household Labor
Divorce

Domestic Violence
Family Demography
Family Diversity
Family, History of
Family Poverty
Family Structure
Family Theory
Fatherhood
Gender, Work, and Family
Households
Intimacy
Kinship
Lesbian and Gay Families
Lone-Parent Families
Love and Commitment
Marriage
Matriarchy
Motherhood
Same-Sex Marriage/Civil Unions
Youth/Adolescence

Gender and Sexuality

AIDS, Sociology of
Beauvoir, Simone de
Bifurcated Consciousness, Line of Fault
Bisexuality
Black Feminist Thought
Body and Sexuality
Carework
Childhood Sexuality
Coming Out/Closets
Compulsory Heterosexuality
Consciousness Raising
Cultural Feminism
Cybersexualities and Virtual Sexuality
Demographic Techniques: Time Use
Doing Gender
Drag Queens and Drag Kings
Emotion Work
Essentialism and Constructionism
Everyday Life
Fatherhood
Female Genital Cutting
Female Masculinity
Femininities/Masculinities
Feminism
Feminism, First, Second, and Third Waves
Feminist Methodology
Feminist Pedagogy
Feminist Standpoint Theory
Feminization of Poverty
Gender Bias
Gender, the Body and
Gender, Development and
Gender, Education and
Gender Ideology and Gender Role Ideology
Gender Oppression
Gender, Work, and Family
Globalization, Sexuality and
Hegemonic Masculinity
Heterosexuality
Homophobia
Homophobia and Heterosexism
Homosexuality
Inequality/Stratification, Gender
International Gender Division of Labor
Intersectionality
Intersexuality
Kinsey, Alfred
Lesbian Feminism
Lesbian and Gay Families
Lesbianism
Liberal Feminism
Male Rape
Martineau, Harriet
Matrix of Domination
New Reproductive Technologies
Patriarchy
Population and Gender
Pornography and Erotica
Postmodern Feminism
Postmodern Sexualities
Privilege
Prostitution
Queer Theory
Radical Feminism
Rape Culture
Repressive Hypothesis
Safer Sex
Same-Sex Marriage/Civil Unions
Sex Education
Sex and Gender
Sex Panics
Sex Tourism
Sexism
Sexual Citizenship
Sexual Deviance
Sexual Harassment
Sexual Health
Sexual Politics
Sexual Practices
Sexualities and Consumption
Sexualities and Culture Wars
Sexuality
Sexuality, Masculinity and
Sexuality, Religion and
Sexuality Research: Ethics
Sexuality Research: History

Sexuality Research: Methods
Sexuality and Sport
Socialist Feminism
Socialization, Gender
Strategic Essentialism
Stratification, Gender and
Third World and Postcolonial Feminisms/Subaltern
Transgender, Transvestism, and Transsexualism
Womanism
Women, Sexuality and
Women's Health
Women's Movements

Health and Medicine, Gerontology and Aging

Age, Period, and Cohort Effects
Aging, Demography of
Aging, Mental Health, and Well-Being
Aging, Sociology of
AIDS, Sociology of
Body and Society
Complementary and Alternative Medicine
Death and Dying
Deviance, Medicalization of
Epidemiology
Euthanasia
Health Care Delivery Systems
Health and Culture
Health and Medicine
HIV/AIDS and Population
Life Course
Managed Care
Medical Sociology
Medical Sociology and Genetics
Medicine, Sociology of
Sexual Health
Social Capital
Social Epidemiology
Socialist Medicine
Socialized Medicine
Socioeconomic Status, Health, and Mortality
Sociology in Medicine
Women's Health

Key Concepts

Accommodation
Accounts
Acculturation
Agency (and Intention)
Alienation
Anarchism
Anomie
Assimilation
Attitudes and Behavior
Authoritarian Personality
Authoritarianism
Authority and Legitimacy
Base and Superstructure
Behaviorism
Bifurcated Consciousness, Line of Fault
Body and Society
Bourgeoisie and Proletariat
Bureaucratic Personality
Capitalism
Caste: Inequalities Past and Present
Chaos
Charisma
Charisma, Routinization of
Citizenship
Civil Religion
Civil Society
Civilizations
Civilizing Process
Class
Class Conflict
Class Consciousness
Collective Action
Collective Consciousness
Commodities, Commodity Fetishism, and Commodification
Communism
Community
Complexity and Emergence
Conspicuous Consumption
Consumption
Counterculture
Crime
Criminology
Crowd Behavior
Cultural Capital
Cultural Imperialism
Cultural Relativism
Culture
Culture: Conceptual Clarifications
Culture Industries
Culture of Poverty
Deconstruction
Definition of the Situation
Deinstitutionalization
Democracy
Demography
Deviance
Dialectic
Dialectical Materialism

Outsider-Within
Patriarchy
Phenomenology
Place
Play
Politics
Positivism
Post-Industrial Society
Postmodern Social Theory
Postpositivism
Poststructuralism
Power
Power Elite
Practice Theory
Pragmatism
Praxis
Prejudice
Primary Groups
Primitive Religion
Property, Private
Public Sphere
Quantitative Methods
Race
Rational Legal Authority
Rationalization
Reference Groups
Reflexive Modernization
Reflexivity
Reification
Religion, Sociology of
Revolutions
Rite of Passage
Ritual
Role
Role-Taking
Sacred/Profane
Science
Secondary Data Analysis
Secondary Groups
Secularization
Segregation
Self
Self-Concept
Self-Fulfilling Prophecy
Semiotics
Sexism
Significant Others
Signs
Simulation
Social Capital
Social Change
Social Control
Social Fact
Social Influence
Social Movements
Social Network Theory
Social Order
Social Psychology
Social Structure
Social System
Socialism
Socialization
Socialization, Adult
Socialization, Primary
Society
Sociolinguistics
Sociological Imagination
Sociology
Solidarity
Solidarity, Mechanical and Organic
Space
Species-Being
State
Status
Stereotyping and Stereotypes
Stigma
Stranger, The
Strategic Essentialism
Structuralism
Structure and Agency
Subculture
Subjectivity
Suicide
Symbolic Classification
Symbolic Exchange
Symbolic Interaction
Theory
Time-Space
Tolerance
Tradition
Trust
Urban
Use-Value
Value
Values
Verstehen

Key Figures

Addams, Jane
Beauvoir, Simone de
Benjamin, Walter
Blau, Peter
Blumer, Herbert George
Bourdieu, Pierre
Braverman, Harry
Certeau, Michel de
Comte, Auguste
Cooley, Charles Horton

Davis, Kingsley
Derrida, Jacques
Du Bois, W. E. B.
Durkheim, Émile
Elias, Norbert
Engels, Friedrich
Feuerbach, Ludwig
Foucault, Michel
Freud, Sigmund
Goffman, Erving
Gramsci, Antonio
Hegel, G. W. F.
Homans, George
Khaldun, Ibn
Kinsey, Alfred
McLuhan, Marshall
Malthus, Thomas Robert
Mannheim, Karl
Marcuse, Herbert
Martineau, Harriet
Marx, Karl
Mead, George Herbert
Merton, Robert K.
Milgram, Stanley (Experiments)
Mills, C. Wright
Nietzsche, Friedrich
Park, Robert E. and Burgess, Ernest W.
Parsons, Talcott
Polanyi, Karl
Saussure, Ferdinand de
Schumpeter, Joseph A.
Schütz, Alfred
Simmel, Georg
Smith, Adam
Thomas, William I.
Tocqueville, Alexis de
Tönnies, Ferdinand
Weber, Max

Management and Organizations

Bureaucratic Personality
Capitalism, Social Institutions of
Charisma, Routinization of
Consumption, Cathedrals and Landscapes of
Crime, Corporate
Ideal Type
Institutional Theory, New
Japanese-Style Management
Labor Markets
Labor Process
Leadership
McDonaldization
Management
Management, Theories of
Military Sociology
Organization Theory
Organizations
Organizations as Social Structures
Outsourcing
Rational Legal Authority
Transnationals

Methods

ANOVA (Analysis of Variance)
Bell Curve
Biography
Chance and Probability
Computer-Aided/Mediated Analysis
Confidence Intervals
Content Analysis
Convenience Sample
Conversation Analysis
Correlation
Criminology: Research Methods
Demographic Data: Censuses, Registers, Surveys
Demographic Techniques: Population Projections and Estimates
Demographic Techniques: Population Pyramids and Age/Sex Structure
Demographic Techniques: Time Use
Descriptive Statistics
Emic/Etic
Empiricism
Epistemology
Ethics, Fieldwork
Ethics, Research
Ethnography
Experiment
Experimental Design
Experimental Methods
Factor Analysis
Feminist Methodology
General Linear Model
Gini Coefficient
Grounded Theory
Hawthorne Effect
Hermeneutics
Historical and Comparative Methods
Hypotheses
Institutional Review Boards and Sociological Research
Intersubjectivity
Interviewing, Structured, Unstructured, and Postmodern

Measures of Centrality
Methods
Methods, Mixed
Multivariate Analysis
Objectivity
Observation, Participant and Non-Participant
Outliers
Paradigms
Postpositivism
Qualitative Methods
Quantitative Methods
Random Sample
Reflexivity
Regression and Regression Analysis
Reliability
Sampling, Qualitative (Purposive)
Secondary Data Analysis
Sexuality Research: Ethics
Sexuality Research: Methods
Social Epistemology
Social Network Analysis
Standardization
Statistical Significance Testing
Statistics
Subjectivity
Survey Research
Theory and Methods
Theory Construction
Validity, Qualitative
Validity, Quantitative
Variables
Variables, Control
Variables, Dependent
Variables, Independent
Variance
Verstehen

Politics and Law

Anarchism
Authoritarianism
Authority and Legitimacy
Citizenship
Civil Society
Communism
Conservatism
Crime, Political
Criminal Justice System
Democracy
Development: Political Economy
Empire
Fascism
Global Politics
Gramsci, Antonio
Identity Politics/Relational Politics
Imagined Communities
Imperialism
Law, Sociology of
Liberalism
Marginalization, Outsiders
Nation-State
Nationalism
Neoliberalism
NGO/INGO
Political Economy
Political Sociology
Politics
Politics and Media
Populism
Power Elite
Privatization
Public Sphere
Race and the Criminal Justice System
Rational Legal Authority
Recognition
Revolutions
Sexual Citizenship
Sexual Politics
Social Problems, Politics of
Socialism
State
State and Economy
Tocqueville, Alexis de
Violence
War
Welfare State
World Conflict

Race and Ethnicity

Accommodation
Acculturation
Affirmative Action
Assimilation
Authoritarian Personality
Black Feminist Thought
Caste: Inequalities Past and Present
Civil Rights Movement
Colonialism (Neocolonialism)
Conflict (Racial/Ethnic)
Decolonization
Diaspora
Discrimination
Diversity
Double Consciousness
Du Bois, W. E. B.
Ethnic Enclaves
Ethnic Groups

Ethnic/Informal Economy
Ethnicity
Ethnocentricism
Immigration
Indigenous Movements
Indigenous Peoples
Intersectionality
Multiculturalism
Nation-State
Nationalism
Orientalism
Outsider-Within
Passing
Prejudice
Race
Race and Crime
Race and the Criminal Justice System
Racism, Structural and Institutional
Refugees
School Segregation, Desegregation
Segregation
Solidarity
Stratification, Race/Ethnicity and
Third World and Postcolonial Feminisms/ Subaltern
Tolerance
Transnationalism
Whiteness
Womanism

Religion

Asceticism
Belief
Buddhism
Charisma
Church
Civil Religion
Fundamentalism
Globalization, Religion and
Islam
Judaism
Myth
New Religious Movements
Orthodoxy
Primitive Religion
Religion, Sociology of
Ritual
Sacred
Sacred/Profane
Scientology
Secularization
Sexuality, Religion and
Theology

Science

Actor-Network Theory
Chance and Probability
Ecology
Eugenics
Experiment
Fact, Theory, and Hypothesis: Including the History of the Scientific Fact
Genetic Engineering as a Social Problem
Human Genome and the Science of Life
Induction and Observation in Science
Kuhn, Thomas and Scientific Paradigms
Matthew Effect
Merton, Robert K.
Paradigms
Science
Science, Social Construction of
Scientific Knowledge, Sociology of
Scientific Revolution
Technology, Science, and Culture

Social Change, Social Movements, and Globalization

Accommodation
Animal Rights Movements
Anti-War and Peace Movements
Capitalism
Chicago School
Civil Rights Movement
Civil Society
Collective Action
Collective Identity
Colonialism (Neocolonialism)
Consumer Culture, Children's
Counterculture
Crowd Behavior
Cultural Imperialism
Decolonization
Dependency and World-Systems Theories
Development: Political Economy
Economic Development
Elias, Norbert
Empire
Endogenous Development
Environmental Movements
Feminization of Poverty
Gay and Lesbian Movement
Gender, Development and
Global Economy
Global Justice as a Social Movement
Global Politics

Global/World Cities
Globalization
Globalization, Consumption and
Globalization, Culture and
Globalization and Global Justice
Globalization, Religion and
Globalization, Sexuality and
Globalization, Sport and
Glocalization
Grobalization
Human Rights
Hybridity
Imagined Communities
Immigration
Immigration Policy
Imperialism
Income Inequality, Global
Indigenous Movements
Industrial Revolution
Industrialization
McDonaldization
Media and Globalization
Migration: International
Migration and the Labor Force
Modernization
Nation-State
Nationalism
Neoliberalism
New Social Movement Theory
NGO/INGO
Orientalism
Population and Development
Privatization
Reflexive Modernization
Refugees
Resource Mobilization Theory
Revolutions
Scientific Revolution
Second Demographic Transition
Secularization
Sex Tourism
Social Change
Social Movements
Social Movements, Networks and
Social Movements, Non-Violent
Social Movements, Participatory Democracy in
Social Movements, Repression of
Student Movements
Terrorism
Transition Economies
Transnationals
Urbanization
Women's Movements
World Conflict

Social Problems

Abortion as a Social Problem
Alcoholism and Alcohol Abuse
Capital Punishment
Caste: Inequalities Past and Present
Class Conflict
Crime
Crime, Organized
Crime, Political
Crime, White-Collar
Criminal Justice System
Death Penalty as a Social Problem
Deterrence Theory
Deviance, Academic
Deviant Careers
Disability as a Social Problem
Discrimination
Divorce
Domestic Violence
Drug Use
Drugs, Drug Abuse, and Drug Policy
Ecological Problems
Eugenics
Gambling as a Social Problem
Genetic Engineering as a Social Problem
Genocide
Globalization and Global Justice
Homelessness
Homophobia
Homophobia and Heterosexism
Human Rights
Immigration Policy
Infertility
Marginalization, Outsiders
Migration: Undocumented/Illegal
Queer Theory
Race and the Criminal Justice System
Refugees
Sexual Harassment
Social Problems, Concept and Perspectives
Social Problems, Politics of
Social Services
Social Work: History and Institutions
Social Work: Theory and Methods
Surveillance
Tolerance
Unemployment as a Social Problem
Victimization
Violence
Welfare Dependency and Welfare Underuse

Social Psychology, Interaction, Groups, and Socialization

Accounts
Affect Control Theory
Aggression
Asch Experiments
Attitudes and Behavior
Attribution Theory
Authority and Conformity
Behaviorism
Blau, Peter
Blumer, Herbert George
Cognitive Dissonance Theory (Festinger)
Collective Action
Cooley, Charles Horton
Crime, Social Learning Theories of
Definition of the Situation
Doing Gender
Double Consciousness
Dyad/Triad
Emotion: Cultural Aspects
Emotion: Social Psychological Aspects
Emotion Work
Ethnomethodology
Exchange Network Theory
Existential Sociology
Experimental Methods
Facework
Generalized Other
Goffman, Erving
Group Processes
Groups
Homans, George
Identity Control Theory
Identity, Deviant
Identity Politics/Relational Politics
Identity: Social Psychological Aspects
Identity Theory
Impression Formation
Individualism
In-Groups and Out-Groups
Interaction
Interpersonal Relationships
Intersubjectivity
Intimacy
Language
Looking-Glass Self
Mass Media and Socialization
Master Status
Mead, George Herbert
Mediated Interaction
Mesostructure
Microsociology
Milgram, Stanley (Experiments)
Mind
Networks
Norms
Phenomenology
Play
Power
Power, Theories of
Power-Dependence Theory
Pragmatism
Prejudice
Primary Groups
Psychological Social Psychology
Public Opinion
Rational Choice Theories
Reference Groups
Rite of Passage
Role
Role-Taking
Role Theory
Secondary Groups
Self
Self-Concept
Self-Esteem, Theories of
Self-Fulfilling Prophecy
Significant Others
Simmel, Georg
Social Cognition
Social Comparison Theory
Social Distance
Social Exchange Theory
Social Identity Theory
Social Influence
Social Justice, Theories of
Social Learning Theory
Social Order
Social Psychology
Social Worlds
Socialization
Socialization, Adult
Socialization, Agents of
Socialization, Gender
Socialization, Primary
Sociometry
Status
Status Construction Theory
Stereotyping and Stereotypes
Stigma
Symbolic Interaction
Thomas, William I.
Trust
Values
Weak Ties (Strength of)
Zimbardo Prison Experiment

Social Stratification

Bourgeoisie and Proletariat
Caste: Inequalities Past and Present
Class
Class Conflict
Class Consciousness
Culture of Poverty
Discrimination
Dual Labor Markets
Educational Inequality
Elites
Family Poverty
Feminization of Poverty
Gay and Lesbian Movement
Gender Oppression
Gini Coefficient
Income Inequality, Global
Income Inequality and Income Mobility
Inequality, Wealth
Inequality/Stratification, Gender
Leisure Class
Lifestyle
Marx, Karl
Meritocracy
Mobility, Horizontal and Vertical
Poverty
Power Elite
Privilege
School Segregation, Desegregation
Socioeconomic Status, Health, and Mortality
Status Attainment
Strategic Essentialism
Stratification: Functional and Conflict Theories
Stratification, Gender and
Stratification and Inequality, Theories of
Stratification, Race/Ethnicity and
Third World and Postcolonial Feminisms/Subaltern
Urban Poverty
Wealth

Theory

Accounts
Actor-Network Theory
Affect Control Theory
Anomie
Attribution Theory
Authoritarian Personality
Base and Superstructure
Behaviorism
Benjamin, Walter
Bifurcated Consciousness, Line of Fault
Biosociological Theories
Black Feminist Thought
Blau, Peter
Blumer, Herbert George
Body and Cultural Sociology
Bourdieu, Pierre
Braverman, Harry
Certeau, Michel de
Chaos
Charisma
Charisma, Routinization of
Class Consciousness
Cognitive Dissonance Theory (Festinger)
Collective Conscience
Commodities, Commodity Fetishism, and Commodification
Complexity and Emergence
Compositional Theory of Urbanism
Comte, Auguste
Conflict Theory
Conversation Analysis
Cooley, Charles Horton
Crime, Broken Windows Theory of
Crime, Radical/Marxist Theories of
Crime, Social Control Theory of
Crime, Social Learning Theories of
Critical Theory/Frankfurt School
Cultural Critique
Cultural Feminism
Cultural Studies
Cultural Studies, British
Culture Industries
Culture, Nature and
Deconstruction
Demographic Transition Theory
Dependency and World-Systems Theories
Derrida, Jacques
Deterrence Theory
Deviance, Constructionist Perspectives
Deviance, Explanatory Theories of
Deviance, Positivist Theories of
Deviance, Theories of
Dialectic
Dialectical Materialism
Distanciation and Disembedding
Distinction
Division of Labor
Dramaturgy
Du Bois, W. E. B.
Durkheim, Émile
Dyad/Triad
Economic Determinism
Economic Sociology: Classical Political Economic Perspectives

Rationalization
Reflexive Modernization
Reification
Resource Mobilization Theory
Ritual
Role Theory
Saussure, Ferdinand de
Schütz, Alfred
Self-Esteem, Theories of
Semiotics
Signs
Simmel, Georg
Simulation
Situationists
Smith, Adam
Social Exchange Theory
Social Fact
Social Influence
Social Justice, Theories of
Social Learning Theory
Social Network Theory
Social Structure
Social System
Social Theory and Sport
Socialist Feminism
Society
Sociolinguistics
Sociological Imagination
Solidarity, Mechanical and Organic
Space
Species-Being
Status Construction Theory
Stranger, The
Strategic Essentialism
Stratification: Functional and Conflict Theories
Stratification and Inequality, Theories of
Structural Functional Theory
Structuralism
Structuration Theory
Structure and Agency
Surveillance
Symbolic Exchange
Symbolic Interaction
System Theories
Terrorism
Theoretical Research Programs
Theory
Theory Construction
Theory and Methods
Third World and Postcolonial Feminisms/Subaltern
Thomas, William I.
Time-Space
Tocqueville, Alexis de
Tönnies, Ferdinand
Trust
Urbanism, Subcultural Theory of
Use-Value
Value
Verstehen
Weak Ties (Strength of)
Weber, Max
Work, Sociology of

Urbanization

Arcades
Blockbusting
Built Environment
Chicago School
City
Community
Compositional Theory of Urbanism
Ethnic Enclaves
Gentrification
Global/World Cities
Homelessness
Metropolis
New Urbanism
Rural Sociology
Suburbs
Urban
Urban Ecology
Urban Policy
Urban Political Economy
Urban Poverty
Urban Renewal and Redevelopment
Urban Revolution
Urban Space
Urban Tourism
Urbanism, Subcultural Theory of
Urbanization

A

abortion as a social problem

Abortion has been legal in the USA and in almost all western European countries since the early 1970s, and in Belgium and Ireland since the early 1990s. Although abortion was legal in the Soviet Union for several years prior to its collapse, abortion politics have subsequently come to the fore in some Eastern European countries (e.g., Poland) as a result of government attempts at scaling-back abortion. Legal access to abortion continues to be highly restricted in Mexico and in several Central and South American countries. Abortion is most intensely debated in the USA, where legal and congressional initiatives to amend the US Supreme Court's recognition (*Roe v. Wade*, 1973) of a woman's legal right to an abortion continue unabated. Abortion activism is pursued by several religious and secular organizations, and abortion politics dominate presidential and congressional elections and debates over judicial appointments. Grassroots efforts to restrict abortion have met with some success; post-*Roe* Supreme Court decisions have imposed various restrictions, most notably the imposition of spousal and parental notification requirements. Currently, the issue of late-term abortion is intensely debated (though most abortions are performed in the first trimester of pregnancy).

Notwithstanding the intensity of pro-choice and pro-life activism, American public opinion on abortion has remained steadfastly consistent. Since 1975, approximately one-fifth of Americans agree that abortion should be illegal in all circumstances, another one-fifth believe that abortion should be legal in all circumstances, and a broad majority (approx. 60 percent) are of the opinion that abortion should be legal but restricted. Americans are most likely to endorse abortion as an option in cases of rape, and when pregnancy poses a physical threat to the mother or fetus; fewer endorse economic need as a reason justifying abortion.

According to the Alan Guttmacher Institute (http://www.alanguttmacher.org), abortion is one of the most common surgical procedures performed in the USA: 1.29 million abortions were performed in 2002, with almost half of all unintended pregnancies ending in abortion. The abortion rate has declined from its peak of 29 (per 1,000 women ages 15 to 44) in the early 1980s, to 20 currently. There has been an especially noticeable decrease among 15- to 19-year-old girls (from 43.5 in the mid-to-late 1980s to 24.0 currently). By contrast, the overall abortion rate in England and Wales is considerably lower, at 17.0 (for women aged 15–44).

Many Americans argue that the number of abortions alone constitutes a social problem; others suggest that the aging and declining prevalence of abortion providers is a social problem in ferment. The majority of obstetricians who perform abortion are age 50 or over, and the proportion of US counties without abortion providers increased from 77 percent in the late 1970s to 86 percent in the late 1990s (Finer & Henshaw 2003: 6). A majority of women who face the dilemma of an unintended pregnancy report using contraception during the month they became pregnant (53 percent), though not always correctly (Finer et al. 2005). Other abortion-inducing circumstances include inadequate finances, relationship problems, concerns over readiness for motherhood, and psychological and physical health problems. Nonetheless, 60 percent of those who get an abortion are already mothers, and 12 percent have previously had an abortion. Across all age groups, the incidence of abortion is greater among women who are single, poor, and non-white (Hispanic, black, or other ethnic minority). Rural women are less likely to have access to abortion providers, and to use abortion in the case of an unwanted pregnancy.

Given the socio-demographic trends in abortion usage, pro-choice supporters argue that it is not abortion per se that is a social problem but the social and economic circumstances of many women's lives. In particular, they argue that women's lack of resources, including the absence of health insurance, the lack of access to and effective use of contraception, and the absence of school sexual education programs, contributes to unintended pregnancies. Abortion supporters also point out that restrictions on abortion (e.g., spousal and parental notification), do not recognize the high incidence of spousal and family violence and the well-grounded fears that many women and teenagers may have in disclosing their pregnancies.

SEE ALSO: Family, Sociology of; Social Problems, Politics of

REFERENCES

Finer, L. B. & Henshaw, S. K. (2003) Abortion incidence and services in the United States in 2000. *Perspectives on Sexual and Reproductive Health* 35: 6–15.

Finer, L. B., Frohwirth, L., Dauphinee, L., Singh, S., & Moore, A. (2005) Reasons US women have abortions: quantitative and qualitative perspectives. *Perspectives on Sexual and Reproductive Health* 37: 110–18.

MICHELE DILLON AND DIANA DUMAIS

accommodation

Accommodation was one of the four features of Robert Park and Ernest Burgess's model of social interaction. Though the concept illustrated racial and ethnic social changes taking place in the USA and the rest of the world during the last half of the nineteenth century and the first two or three decades of the twentieth, and for this reason lacks a certain relevance today, there are still aspects of the term, as defined by Park and Burgess, which might provide insights into specific patterns of racial and ethnic interaction and aid in our understanding of the dynamics of social change. Utilizing Simmel's model of dominance and its pivotal role in superordinate and subordinate relations, Park and Burgess describe accommodation as a procedure which limits conflicts and cements relations, in that groups and individuals recognize dominant individuals and groups as well as their positions within these super- and subordinate relations. On the surface, and in theory, this logic appears to be one of "live and let live," and appears to be grounded in an idea similar to that of social and cultural pluralism. However, the reality is quite different. However, whether referring to majority and minority populations, in population percentages, or populations differing in ethnicity, religion, or culture, accommodation refers to those arrangements, implied or explicit, which regulate the types of exchanges and relations between groups. These arrangements, spoken or unspoken, written or unwritten, determine which rights, privileges, and obligations shall accrue to some groups and be denied to others. Indeed, the history of multicultural and multiethnic nations has been a history of "forced" accommodation, and the USA, Canada, and the nations of Latin America have all forced major segments of their societies to accommodate to majority, sometimes minority, values and standards. Hence, in the USA the accommodation was linguistic, religious, and cultural; in Canada, linguistic and cultural, and in Latin America, indigenous populations were largely oppressed and suppressed by Europeans and mixed populations which largely excluded indigenous populations from the body politic. In the USA, Canada, and throughout Latin America accommodation meant giving in to the dominant groups by following the procedures and guidelines constructed by them.

SEE ALSO: Acculturation; Assimilation; Park, Robert E. and Burgess, Ernest W.

SUGGESTED READING

Dennis, R. M. (ed.) (2008) *Biculturalism, Self Identity and Societal Transformation*. Emerald Publishing, Bingley.

RUTLEDGE M. DENNIS

accounts

An account, as the term is most commonly used in sociology, refers to statements that explain disruptions in the social and moral order. In this sense, accounts are linguistic devices by which actors attempt to reposition themselves as socially acceptable and morally reputable in the face of imputations of deviance or failure. Although the concept of accounts has roots in C. Wright Mills's 1940 article on "Situated actions and the vocabularies of motives," in Gresham Sykes and David Matza's 1957 article on "Techniques of neutralization," and more generally in the work of Erving Goffman, the term itself was introduced in its distinctive sociological sense by Marvin Scott and Sanford Lyman in their 1968 article, entitled simply "Accounts."

Accounts may be classified by what they accomplish, by their functions and consequences, both for individual actors and for the social and moral order. First, accounts may restore breaches in the social order. Second, accounts, even taken narrowly as explanations of disruptions of an ongoing moral order, are deeply implicated in processes of social control.

Third, and more generally, accounts are a form of making meaning. Whether, as some suggest, this meaning making emerges from a deep-felt human urge or, as is more demonstrable, from specific social situations that challenge existing understandings, accounts provide interpretations of behavior and its motives. Understood narrowly, accounts are efforts to give socially acceptable meanings to particular and otherwise discredited behaviors. Understood more broadly, as plotted narratives, accounts are efforts to connect a series of events and behaviors into a coherent story, with a beginning, a middle, and an end, causally related and with a more or less explicit moral content. Fourth, and more specifically, accounts create identities. Because accounts involve the imputation of motives, and the selective avowal and disavowal of behaviors as motivated, they also involve claims as to what is and is not a part of the self. When offered with deep-felt belief on the part of the speaker, as is often the case in response to illness, divorce, or other disruptions of a previous routine, accounts contribute to the formation of both personal (internally held) and social (publicly enacted) identities. When offered cynically, as self-conscious efforts to manipulate impressions, whether for the enhancement of status or to avoid sanctions, accounts may not contribute to the formation of personal identities but nonetheless still contribute to the formation of social identities.

SEE ALSO: Accounts, Deviant; Identity Theory; Mills, C. Wright; Social Order

SUGGESTED READINGS

Orbuch, T. L. (1997) People's accounts count: the sociology of accounts. *Annual Review of Sociology* 23: 455–78.

Scott, M. B. & Lyman, S. (1968) Accounts. *American Sociological Review* 33: 46–62.

ROBERT ZUSSMAN

acculturation

Acculturation can be defined as the process of bringing previously separated and disconnected cultures into contact with one another. Acculturation is not the absorption of different cultures as a result of a mere physical contact or superficial exposure. The processes of cultural transmission and cultural borrowing are the result of conscious decision-making on the part of an individual or a group that is approaching a culturally distinct group. If no force or coercion is involved, the individual or group must decide whether and to what extent the new culture will be accepted or rejected. E. Franklin Frazier (1957) made the distinction between "material acculturation" and "ideational acculturation." Material acculturation involves the conveying of language and other cultural tools whereas ideational acculturation involves the conveying of morals and norms. Individuals and groups can consciously decide to accept the language and cultural tools of a new culture without accepting and internalizing the morals and norms of the new culture.

The process of acculturation is complex and is not a simple matter of the cultural majority forcing its culture upon the cultural minority. Some individuals and groups respond favorably and with relative ease to the possibility of acculturation whereas others respond unfavorably and with unease. How the individual or group perceives the process of acculturation and how the larger society perceives this process are both significant. If the larger society views the possibility of an incoming group's acculturation as favorable and with ease, there will be less hostility and discomfort throughout the process. If the acculturation of an incoming group is viewed unfavorably and with unease by the larger society, there will be greater hostility, discomfort, and the process will require more effort on the part of this incoming group.

SEE ALSO: Accommodation; Assimilation; Culture

REFERENCE

Frazier, E. F. (1957) *Race and Cultural Contact in the Modern World*. Beacon Press, Boston, MA.

SUGGESTED READING

Myrdal, G. (1944) *An American Dilemma*. Harper & Row, New York.

KIMYA N. DENNIS

actor-network theory

Actor-network theory originated in the 1980s as a movement within the sociology of science, centered at the Paris School of Mines. Key developers were Bruno Latour, Michel Callon, Antoine Hennion, and John Law. It was sharply critical of earlier historical and sociological analyses of science, which had drawn a clear divide between the "inside" of a science (to be analyzed in terms of its adherence or not to a unitary scientific method) and its "outside" (the field of its application).

Actor-network theorists made three key moves. First, they argued for a semiotic network reading of scientific practice. Human and non-human actors (actants) were assumed to be subject to the same analytic categories, just as a ring or a prince could hold the same structural position in a fairy tale. They could be enrolled in a network or not, could hold or not hold certain moral positions, and so forth. This profound ontological position has been the least understood but the most generative aspect of the theory. Second, they argued that in producing their theories, scientists weave together human and non-human actors into relatively stable network nodes, or "black boxes." Thus a given astronomer can tie together her telescope, some distant stars, and a funding agency into an impregnable fortress, and to challenge her results you would need to find your own telescope, stars, and funding sources. Practically, this entailed an agnostic position on the "truth" of science. Indeed, they argued for a principle of symmetry according to which the same set of explanatory factors should be used to account for failed and successful scientific theories. There is no ultimate arbiter of right and wrong. Third, they maintained that in the process of constructing these relatively stable network configurations, scientists produced contingent nature – society divides. Nature and society were not pre-given entities that could be used to explain anything else; they were the outcomes of the *work* of doing technoscience. Latour called this the "Janus face" of science. As it was being produced it was seen as contingent; once produced it was seen as always and already true.

Together, these three moves made the central analytical unit the work of the intermediary. There is no society out there to which scientists respond as they build their theories, nor is there a nature which constrains them to a single telling of their stories. Rather, the technoscientist stands between nature and society, politics and technology. She can act as a spokesperson for her array of actants (things in the world, people in her lab), and if successful can black-box these to create the effect of truth.

The theory has given rise to a number of concepts which have proven useful in a wide range of technoscientific analyses. It has remained highly influential as a methodological tool for analyzing truth-making in all its forms. The call to "follow the actors" – to see what they do rather than report on what they say they do – has been liberating for those engaged in studying scientists, who frequently hold their own truth and practice as if above the social and political fray. Their attention to the work of representation on paper led to the ideas of "immutable mobiles" and "centers of calculation," which trace the power of technoscience to its ability to function as a centralizing networked bureaucracy. Indeed, the anthropological eye of actor-networked theorists – looking at work practices and not buying into actors' categories – has led to a rich meeting between the sociology of work, the Chicago School of sociology, and actor-network theory. Latour's later work on the distribution of political and social values between the technical world and the social institution has opened up a powerful discourse about the political and moral force of technology.

The actor-network theory itself has changed significantly in recent years, including Latour's (1999) tongue-in-cheek denial of each of its central terms and the hyphen connecting them. This has been in response to a number of critiques that the theory privileged the powerful, Machiavellian technoscientist as world-builder, without giving much opportunity for representing the invisible technicians within the networks and alternative voices from without (Star 1995).

SEE ALSO: Science and Culture; Science, Social Construction of; Technology, Science, and Culture

REFERENCES

Latour, B. (1999) On recalling ANT. In: Law, J. & Hassard, J. (eds.), *Actor Network Theory and After*. Blackwell, Oxford, pp. 15–25.

Star, S. L. (ed.) (1995) *Ecologies of Knowledge: Work and Politics in Science and Technology*. SUNY Press, New York.

SUGGESTED READING

Latour, B. (1987) *Science in Action: How to Follow Scientists and Engineers through Society*. Open University Press, Milton Keynes.

GEOFFREY BOWKER

Addams, Jane (1860–1935)

Feminist pragmatist, social settlement leader, and Nobel Laureate, Jane Addams was a charismatic world leader with an innovative intellectual legacy in sociology and one of the most important sociologists in the world. From 1890 to 1935, she led dozens of women in sociology, although after 1920 most of these women were forced out of sociology and into other fields such as social work, applied psychology, and pedagogy.

Jane Addams was born on September 6, 1860, in Cedarville, Illinois. In 1887, accompanied by her college friend Ellen Gates Starr, Addams visited the social settlement Toynbee Hall in London's East End. It provided a model in 1889 for the friends to co-found their social settlement, Hull-House, in Chicago.

Hull-House became the institutional anchor for women's gender-segregated work in sociology and liaisoned with the most important male sociological center during this era, the University of Chicago. Addams led an international social movement which brought together all classes; social groups; ages, especially the young and the elderly; and the oppressed to form a democratic community able to articulate and enact their ideals and needs. She described her work in *Twenty Years at Hull-House* (1910) and *The Second Twenty Years at Hull-House* (1930). Her combined thought and practice is called "feminist pragmatism": an American theory uniting liberal values and a belief in a rational public with a cooperative, nurturing, and liberating model of the self, the other, and the community. Education and democracy are mechanisms to organize and improve society, learn about community, participate in group decisions, and become a "citizen." Democracy emerges from different groups with distinct perspectives, histories, communities, and structures of the self. She discussed these concepts in *Democracy and Social Ethics* (1902); *Newer Ideals of Peace* (1907); *The Spirit of Youth and the City Streets* (1909).

Addams' intellectual legacy as a feminist pragmatist articulated radical changes in American life and politics, altering the possibilities for human growth and action, especially for the poor and oppressed.

SEE ALSO: Chicago School; Feminist Pedagogy

SUGGESTED READING

Deegan, M. J. (1988) *Jane Addams and the Men of the Chicago School, 1892–1920*. Transaction Books, New Brunswick, NJ.

MARY JO DEEGAN

addiction and dependency

Terms such as addiction and dependency are frequently used to describe patterns of illicit drug use. However, there are no universal definitions of these terms and they are frequently used inconsistently and interchangeably. As a result, it is difficult to estimate the number of drug users who can be described as addicted or dependent. Addiction tends to refer to dependence on a particular drug or drugs, which has developed to the extent that it has a severe and harmful impact on an individual drug user. The term implies that the drug user is unable to give up drug use without incurring adverse effects.

Dependency can refer to physical and/or emotional dependency and drug users may experience one or both forms. Drug users can become physically dependent on drugs, thus continuing with their drug use in order to avoid the physical discomfort of withdrawal. They can also become emotionally dependent on drugs; for example, relying upon drug use to seek pleasure or to avoid pain. Drugscope (a UK-based independent center of expertise on drugs) suggests that the term dependency is preferable to addiction because the latter is linked to negative images of drug use.

Sociologists have been influential in highlighting the importance of societal reaction to drug use. Drawing upon the insights of symbolic interactionism, Howard Becker's classic study *Outsiders: Studies in the Sociology of Deviance* (1963) drew attention to the processes by which individuals became drug users within a deviant subculture. Employing the notion of a career, he highlighted how the labeling of individuals as deviants by the public and agents of social control (including criminal justice agencies and medical professionals) helped to increase levels of drug use. He argued that by attaching a stigmatizing label to a drug user, the individual responds to this new identity. Other influential research, such as Jock Young's *The Drugtakers* (1971), has highlighted the role of the media in amplifying drug use.

Sociological analysis of drug use has played a significant role in challenging the medicalization of so-called deviant behavior. Sociologists have challenged the practice of referring to drug use as a disease with the implication that it can be cured solely through medical treatment. In particular, feminist sociologists have been highly critical of this approach, which fails to recognize the links between women's subordinate position in society and their use of illicit drugs.

SEE ALSO: Deviance, Medicalization of; Deviant Careers; Drug Use; Labeling Theory

REFERENCES

Becker, H. (2003) *Outsiders: Studies in the Sociology of Deviance*. Free Press, New York.

Young, J. (1971) *The Drugtakers: The Social Meaning of Drug Use*. MacGibbon and Kee, London.

SUGGESTED READING

Ettore, E. (2007) *Revisioning Women and Drug Use: Gender, Power and the Body*. Palgrave Macmillan, Basingstoke.

EMMA WINCUP

adoption

Adoption is a legal act through which a child is placed under the permanent care and guardianship of one or more individuals who are not his or her biological parents. The parental rights and responsibilities of the child's birth parents are dissolved and transferred to the adoptive parents. Current estimates suggest that about 4 percent of Americans are adopted.

The pre-existing connection between adopter and adoptee may be that of relatives or non-relatives. Relative adopters are more likely to be black, poor, and have low levels of education. Non-relative adopters are more likely to be white and have higher levels of income and education – often adopting due to infertility. Adoptions are governed by state laws which often privilege heterosexual, married couples of child-bearing age.

In the USA, the small number of parents who willingly place their children for adoption are generally white, relatively advantaged, and have high educational aspirations. An increasing number of adoptions are also coming through the foster care system, in which birth parents are typically black or Hispanic and come from very poor backgrounds. International adoptions have also risen in recent years.

Assumptions about the primacy of biological ties between parent and child are prevalent; however, studies indicate that adoptive families are more similar than different from biological families. In fact, adoptive family contexts generally erode any detrimental effects of conditions prior to adoption. Most adoptees and their families do well on critical measures of life success and are personally satisfied with the outcomes of adoption.

SEE ALSO: Fatherhood; Marriage; Motherhood

SUGGESTED READINGS

Feigelman, W. (1997) Adopted adults: comparisons with persons raised in conventional families. *Adoption Quarterly* 2: 79–88.

Fisher, A. P. (2003) Still "not quite as good as having your own"? Toward a sociology of adoption. *Annual Review of Sociology* 29: 335–61.

Hamilton, L., Cheng, S., and Powell, B. (2007) Adoptive parents, adaptive parents: evaluating the importance of biological ties for parental investment. *American Sociological Review* 72: 95–116.

LAURA HAMILTON

Affect control theory

Affect control theory (ACT) is grounded in symbolic interactionist insights about the importance of using language and symbols to define situations. The theory begins with the assertion that people reduce uncertainty by developing "working understandings" of their social worlds. They label parts of social situations, using language available to them. After creating this definition, they are motivated to maintain it. ACT assumes that our labeling of situations evokes affective meanings. These affective meanings, rather than specific labels, are what we try to maintain during interaction. The theory is formalized in three parts: the measurement of affect, event reaction equations, and mathematical statement of the control process.

SCOPE

Scope statements specify the conditions under which a theory applies. There are specific conditions that limit ACT's applicability: a social behavior must be directed toward an object (e.g., another person); there must be at least one observer who is a member of a language culture already identified by ACT researchers (e.g., the USA, Canada, or Japan); and the theory only applies to labeled aspects of social experiences (e.g., identities and behaviors).

SENTIMENTS

ACT assumes that people affectively respond to every social event (the *affective reaction principle*). The theory describes these affective responses along three dimensions of meaning: evaluation (goodness or badness), potency (powerfulness or weakness), and activity (liveliness or quietness). These are cross-cultural, universal dimensions describe substantial variation in affective meaning and can be measured mathematically. The affective meanings associated with labeled concepts (identities, behaviors, emotions, and so forth) are called *sentiments*. Although stable within a culture, sentiments vary cross-culturally. ACT researchers have used evaluation, potency and activity ratings to index meanings in different cultures, including the USA, Canada, Japan, Germany, China, and Northern Ireland.

IMPRESSIONS

Social interaction changes our perceptions of labeled actors and behaviors. In response to observing a Mother Dragging her Daughter through the park, our feelings about that mother, that daughter, and perhaps even what it means to drag someone may change. In ACT, we call these situated meanings *impressions*. To predict impressions, events are simplified into Actor Behaves toward Object sentences. Event reactions are quantified using impression formation equations created by regressing pre-event sentiments onto post-event impressions. Once generated, ACT can predict how people will feel after an interaction using only their initial definition of the situation.

CONTROL AND RECONSTRUCTION

ACT proposes that actors work to experience impressions that are consistent with their sentiments (the *affect control principle*). Discrepancies between sentiments and impressions reveal how well interactions we experience are confirming cultural prescriptions. Affect control theory defines *deflection* as the discrepancy (measured mathematically) between sentiments and impressions. Using mathematical equations that predict deflection researchers (using a computer program called *INTERACT*) can predict future behaviors that minimize deflection. However, when deflection is inexorably large, the observer may need to reconstruct the event using different labels (e.g., using Scrooge instead of Businessman) in order to reduce deflection.

TRAITS, EMOTIONS, AND OTHER THEORETICAL ELABORATIONS

If we take these same equations and hold the actor's *identity* constant, we can solve for a trait that can be added to the actor's identity to make "sense" of experiences (e.g., adding the trait Bad to Mother to produce the identity Bad Mother). ACT also uses these equations to make predictions about the emotions that actors and objects are likely to feel in social interaction. Researchers have elaborated the basic Actor–Behavior–Object grammar of ACT to include settings and nonverbal behaviors.

SEE ALSO: Emotion: Social Psychological Aspects; Identity Theory; Identity Control Theory; Social Identity Theory; Symbolic Interaction

SUGGESTED READINGS

MacKinnon, N. J. (1994) *Symbolic Interactionism as Affect Control*. SUNY Press, New York.

Osgood, C. E., May, W. H., & Miron, M. S. (1975) *Cross-Cultural Universals of Affective Meaning*. University of Illinois Press, Urbana, IL.

Heise, D. R. (1979) *Understanding Events: Affect and the Construction of Social Action*. Cambridge: Cambridge University Press.

Heise, D. R. (2007) *Expressive Order: Confirming Sentiments in Social Actions*. Springer, New York.

JESSE K. CLARK

affirmative action

The term affirmative action encompasses a broad range of voluntary and mandated policies and procedures intended to provide equal access to educational and employment opportunities for members of historically excluded groups. Foremost among the bases for historical exclusion have been race, ethnicity, and sex, although consideration is sometimes extended to other groups (e.g., Vietnam veterans, the disabled). Both the concept of affirmative action and its application have undergone a series of transformations and interpretations. These shifts have contributed to considerable ambivalence in levels of public support for and opposition to affirmative action policies.

There is no single model of affirmative action. Affirmative action efforts may be either public or private. Definitions of protected groups range from very restricted to very broad. Enforcement mechanisms may be quite rigorous or virtually non-existent.

Affirmative action is in many ways an outgrowth of the Civil Rights Movements. In particular, Title VII of the 1964 Civil Rights Act prohibited discrimination in any areas of employment that was based on race, color, creed, or sex. The year after the passage of the Civil Rights Act, President Lyndon Johnson signed Executive Order 11246, which prohibited discrimination against minorities by federal contractors. While American presidents had routinely been issuing similar Executive Orders for some time, EO 11246 was different in two important ways. First, it included sex rather than merely race as a protected category. Second, it established an enforcement mechanism, the Office of Federal Contract Compliance (OFCC). While not a powerful entity, the OFCC was an important step in institutionalizing affirmative action. Affirmative action received a further boost with the passage of the 1972 Equal Employment Opportunity Act (EEOA). The EEOA required federal agencies to adopt affirmative action. By 2000, this legislation covered about 3.5 million federal employees (Harper & Reskin 2005).

Whether applied to employment or to education, affirmative action has been a politically sensitive issue. Much of the contention has been grounded in differing understandings and interpretations of affirmative action. While most participants in the affirmative action debate agree on the social benefits of racially and culturally diverse workforces and student bodies, they differ sharply on how to achieve this. Opponents of affirmative action often emphasize the apparent contradictions between group-based remedies and the American commitment to individualism and meritocracy. Many maintain that affirmative action unfairly stigmatizes members of protected categories, who can never be certain that their success was due to their individual merit. Advocates discuss the benefits of more exclusive hiring and admissions criteria and the need in a fair society to provide reparations for indisputable histories of disadvantage.

SEE ALSO: Discrimination; School Segregation, Desegregation

REFERENCE

Harper, S. & Reskin, B. (2005) Affirmative action at school and on the job. *Annual Review of Sociology* 31: 357–79.

SUGGESTED READING

Oppenheimer, D. B. (1989) Distinguishing five models of affirmative action. *Berkeley Women's Law Journal* 4: 42–61.

DAVID B. BILLS AND ERIN KAUFMAN

age, period, and cohort effects

Age, period, and cohort are variables often used in social research that are so closely interrelated that the effects of one cannot be studied without consideration of the effects of the others. Each variable is a perfect linear function of the other two, which means that when any two are statistically held constant, the third has no variance. It follows that the effects of all three cannot be simultaneously estimated with any conventional statistical analysis – a phenomenon known as the age–period–cohort conundrum.

The age–period–cohort conundrum is important because all three variables are important for the explanation of a wide range of social and psychological phenomena. Age, the amount of time passed since an entity came into existence (by birth, in the case of human individuals), almost always needs to be an independent or control variable when human individuals are the units of analysis. Almost as important are cohort, the time when an entity came into existence, and period, the time when measurement was taken. All three are closely and causally related to a wide range of influences on human characteristics and behaviors.

To illustrate the APC conundrum, consider a hypothetical case in which a cross-sectional study of adults shows that at one point in time there was a positive linear relationship of age to support for a certain social policy. From these data alone one cannot tell whether the relationship reflects age or cohort effects, or both, because age and cohort are perfectly correlated in cross-sectional data. Now, consider panel data showing that specific individuals on average became more supportive of the policy as they grew older. From these data alone, one cannot tell whether the change resulted from period or age related influences, or both, because in panel data age and period are perfectly correlated. These two sets of data together suggest positive age effects, but they do not prove such effects because there is a logically possible alternative explanation. They could have resulted from positive period effects offset at each age level by opposite-signed cohort effects. This explanation seems rather improbable, because according to theory and some empirical evidence, most period and cohort effects on attitudes result ultimately from the same influences and thus should usually be reinforcing rather than offsetting. However, "usually" is not "always," and thus a confident conclusion about age effects is not warranted without consideration of other relevant information.

This hypothetical example illustrates the importance for attempts to disentangle age, period, and cohort effects (cohort analyses) of theory and what Converse (1976) has called "side information" – information other than the APC data at hand. Good cohort analysis is not "plug and play" but rather requires human judgment at each stage of the process.

SEE ALSO: Demography

REFERENCE

Converse, P. E. (1976) *The Dynamics of Party Support: Cohort Analyzing Party Identification*. Sage, Beverly Hills, CA.

SUGGESTED READING

Glenn, N. D. (2005) *Cohort Analysis*, rev. edn. Sage, Thousand Oaks, CA.

NORVAL D. GLENN

agency (and intention)

Agency is the faculty for action. This faculty may be uniquely human. Action differs from the (mere) behavior of non-human organisms, which is driven by innate or conditioned reflexes and instincts. Non-human organisms have no or little control over how they behave. They do not have a sense of self or, if they do, it is not reflexive. Their behavior is caused by forces they cannot comprehend or influence. Human actors are different because they are conscious and aware of the world, themselves, and other actors. To some extent, what they do, and who they are, is up to them. They are open to the world, and not stuck in the immediately pressing here and now of a local niche. Human identity is not fixed from the start, and so human beings have to make themselves into who they will become. This makes predictions of actions difficult, if not impossible. Action is contingent; behavior is necessary. An actor can act, but also not, and can also act in different ways. While actors may have reasons for their actions, such reasons do not determine actions in the same rigid way that natural forces cause behavior.

The faculty for agency is located in the human mind. The mind is the seat of reflexivity, deliberation, and intentionality. Before we act, we rehearse possibilities and alternatives. The mind also houses the sense of who we are as individual persons. Humans have minds and selves, and these together are the sources for action. Action is motivated, but not caused, by intentions. These intentions give actions their meaning. To understand agency, action, and actors, sociology needs to understand and interpret the meanings and intentions that actions have for their actors. This is difficult, since intentions and meanings presumably are mental states inside the head, and so cannot be directly observed, unlike overt behavior. While each of us can introspect our own intentions, what happens in other minds may ultimately be inaccessible. In fact, for Freud, we do not even know, and chronically deceive ourselves, about what happens in our own minds.

Much depends on how our agentic core is developed. One possibility is rational choice and exchange theory. This holds person, intention, and action constant. In this tradition of scholarship, there is no genuine problem or difficulty with agency because it is settled by *fiat*. By axiom or definition, all actors are deemed rational.

On the other hand, in the symbolic interactionism tradition, agency is more contingent and open-ended. This is not for the external observer to decide, but emerges from the practice of social life itself. The faculty for agency is not ready made, but emerges through a process of social formation and re-formation. To understand agency, one needs to take the "actor's point of view" and see the actors' worlds from their own perspectives. Since all action is symbolically structured, most importantly through language and culture, the key to agency and action is interpretation, not explanation.

According to ethnomethodologists, members of ordinary everyday society do not so much act as enact the social practices of common sense. There are very narrow limits on what actors can be consciously aware of and define or redefine. Members are not the authors of these practices but one outcome of them. Members are the means by which society reproduces itself. Social practices cannot be defined and redefined at will.

Yet another possibility is a constructivist, rather than realist, notion of agency. Constructivism sees agency not as a faculty that is, in fact, had by actors but as a property that may, or may not, be ascribed to them. Agency then becomes an attribution, akin to the granting of a privilege that can also be withdrawn and withheld. This constructivist turn in the study of agency makes variation in attributions the key. Agency now becomes a second-order construct, not a first-order essence or natural kind. Allowing for variation might make it possible to render agency more amenable to empirical research, whereas up to now it has been bogged down in conceptual and semantic analysis.

SEE ALSO: Constructionism; Ethnomethodology; Micro–Macro Links; Rational Choice Theories; Structure and Agency; Symbolic Interaction

SUGGESTED READING

Emirbayer, M. & Mische, A. (1998) What is agency? *American Journal of Sociology* 104: 962–1023.

STEPHAN FUCHS

aggression

Aggression is any behavior that is directed toward injuring, harming, or inflicting pain on another living being or group of beings. Generally, the victim(s) of aggression must wish to avoid such behavior in order for it to be considered true aggression. *Hostile aggression* is an aggressive act that results from anger, and is intended to inflict pain or injury. *Instrumental aggression* is regarded as a means to an end other than pain or injury. The concept of aggression is broad, and includes many categories of behavior (street crime, child abuse, war, etc.). Theories on aggression are commonly categorized according to the three variables that are present whenever any aggressive act is committed. First, *aggressors* are examined in terms of the causes of their actions. Research/theories have devoted particular attention to biological, psychopathological, social learning, and rational choice explanations for aggression, in addition to a variety of other influences (such as drugs, alcohol, arousal, etc.). The phenomenon of aggression is complex, and many factors may affect those who engage in it. Second, *situational* factors may have an important impact on aggression. Issues such as frustration–aggression, environmental stressors, and sociocultural influences (such as the popular culture) have received significant examination in this regard. *Targets* or *victims* constitute the third component of aggressive behavior. Demographic factors (such as race, gender), and the retaliatory capacity of victims are of importance here. Effects of aggression on victims, such as *learned helplessness* and *blaming the victim*, are also of significant concern.

SEE ALSO: Learned Helplessness, Social Learning Theory

SUGGESTED READINGS

Bandura, A. (1973) *Aggression: A Social Learning Analysis*. Prentice-Hall, Englewood Cliffs, NJ.

Miller, N. E. (1941) The frustration–aggression hypothesis. *Psychological Review* 48: 337–42.

WILLIAM J. KINNEY

aging, demography of

The demography of aging began to emerge as a distinct subfield within demography during the second half of the twentieth century, when low fertility and mortality rates were creating dramatic shifts in the age structure of developed countries. Early in this field's development, demography of aging researchers were focused on defining old age and aging, documenting changes in the age structure, identifying mortality trends, describing the health status of older adults, explaining the geographical distribution and mobility of older adults, understanding the life course and cohort flow, and exploring living arrangements, family support, and retirement trends. More recently demographers have become increasingly concerned with population aging as it relates to social transfer programs, social institutions such as the economy and the family, and the overall quality of life for different age groups (e.g., children, working-aged adults, older adults). Formal demographers, who are focused on understanding demographic trends related to fertility, mortality, and migration, and social demographers, who examine the social causes and consequences of demographic trends, use quantitative methods to understand population aging. Formal demographers tend to document worldwide trends in population aging and national changes in mortality, morbidity, disability, and geographical distribution. Social demographers examine a range of issues related to population aging including the potential demand placed on health care systems, the impact of changing family structure on care provision, the economic implications of an aging population, and the motivations for residential mobility. In doing so, researchers in the demography of aging provide a justification for studying older adults, identify the social causes of aging, and consider the various consequences of shifting population age structure.

SEE ALSO: Aging, Sociology of; Demographic Techniques: Population Pyramids and Age/Sex Structure

SUGGESTED READINGS

Preston, S. & Martin, L. (eds.) (1994) *Demography of Aging*. National Academy Press, Washington, DC.

Wilmoth, J. & Longino, Jr., C. (2007) Demographic perspectives on aging. In: Wilmoth, J. and Ferraro, K. (eds.), *Gerontology: Perspectives and Issues*, 3rd edn. Springer, New York, pp. 35–56.

JANET M. WILMOTH AND CHARLES F. LONGINO, JR.

aging, mental health, and well-being

Social factors are strongly implicated in mental health and well-being throughout life, including old age. Sociologists argue that mental health and subjective well-being are powerful indicators of how well societies serve their members both individually and collectively. That is, effective societies not only meet the basic needs of their members, but also provide the conditions and opportunities that sustain emotional health and perceptions that life is good.

The vast majority of Americans are relatively free of psychiatric or emotional symptoms and are generally satisfied with their lives. This pattern is at least as strong for older adults as for young and middle-aged adults. Comparison of research based on older samples with those from age-heterogeneous samples reveals only a few rather subtle, but important, differences. The most distinctive aspect of depression and distress in later life is the prominent role of physical illness and disability in increasing risk of depression. Many studies suggest that physical illness and/or disability is the strongest single predictor of depression and distress; in contrast, physical health is of negligible importance during young adulthood and middle age. In contrast, demographic variables are weaker predictors of depression and distress in late life than earlier in adulthood. Racial or ethnic differences are minimally important during later life and even gender differences in depression, which are very large in young adulthood, narrow substantially by late life.

SEE ALSO: Aging, Sociology of

SUGGESTED READING

George, L. K. (2004) Social and economic factors related to psychiatric disorders in late life. In Blazer, D. G., Steffens, D. C., & Busse, E. W. (eds.), *Textbook of Geriatric Psychiatry*, 3rd edn. American Psychiatric Publishing, Washington, DC, pp. 139–61.

LINDA K. GEORGE

aging, sociology of

The sociology of aging is both broad and deep. The breadth of the field can be highlighted in several ways. First, the sociology of aging encompasses investigations of aging as a process, of older adults as a group, and of old age as a distinctive stage of the life course. Second, aging research is performed at multiple levels of analysis, from macro-level studies of age structure within and across societies, to meso-level studies of labor-force participation and family structure, to micro-level investigations of health and well-being. Third, aging research uses the full repertoire of methods that characterize the discipline, including life tables and other demographic methods, survey research, ethnographic methods, and observational studies. The depth of the field results from the accumulation of scientific studies that now span more than three-quarters of a century.

A large proportion of sociological research on aging rests on the challenges posed by an aging society, although that impetus is not always explicit. Studies of public and private transfers of money, time, and in-kind services rest in large part on their salience for sustaining an aging population. Studies of health, disability, and quality of life are important not only because they address threats to well-being, but also because they shed light on the factors that keep older adults from excessive reliance on public programs. Even studies of the caregivers of impaired older adults rest not only on concern about the health risks of chronic stress, but also on the desire to enable families to bear as much of the cost of care as possible, thus relieving public programs. Thus, age structure and its social implications is a significant and far-reaching arm of aging research.

Multiple forces, both social and non-social, determine the process and experience of aging. Historically, there was a tendency to attribute the aging process and the experience of late life to inherent biological and developmental processes. Most of us are relatively ignorant of the extent to which the process and experience of aging vary across historical time, finding it difficult, for example, to imagine a time when there was no retirement or when the odds of dying were essentially the same during childhood, adulthood, and old age. And yet, retirement as a predictable life course transition and odds favoring survival to old age both emerged in the twentieth century.

The vast majority of aging research falls under the general topic of aging and well-being, with well-being broadly defined to include any social asset (e.g., economic resources, life satisfaction). Social scientific interest in aging was spurred by concerns about the well-being of older adults in both absolute and relative (to other age groups) terms. This is probably not surprising. The history of sociology in general has been driven by concerns about social disadvantage – its prevalence, antecedents, and consequences. The types of well-being examined in relation to aging are numerous. A partial list of the forms of well-being frequently studied in late life include longevity, physical health, disability, mental health, subjective well-being, economic status, and identity or sense of self.

Since the late 1980s, the life course perspective has assumed increasing influence in sociological research, especially research on aging. The life course perspective focuses on the complex links between social/historical change and personal biography. In addition, the life course perspective is ideally suited to linking macro- and meso-level social conditions to individual behaviors and well-being, to tracing the effects of both structural opportunities and constraints of human agency (i.e., personal choices) over the long haul, and documenting the many ways that the past is indeed prologue to the future. Thus, life course research is an important and exciting part of the sociology of aging.

SEE ALSO: Age, Period, and Cohort Effects; Aging, Demography of; Aging, Mental Health, and Well-Being; Demographic Transition Theory; Life Course

SUGGESTED READINGS

Binstock, R. H. & George, L. K. (eds.), *Handbook of Aging and the Social Sciences*, 3rd edn. Academic Press, San Diego, CA, pp. 208–28.

George, L. K. (2003) What life course perspectives offer the study of aging and health. In: Settersten, R. A. (ed.), *Invitation to the Life Course*. Baywood Publishing, Amityville, NY, pp. 161–90.

LINDA K. GEORGE

AIDS, sociology of

AIDS (acquired immune deficiency syndrome) is caused by a retrovirus, the human immunodeficiency virus (HIV), identified in 1984. It is currently estimated that over 35 million people are living with HIV, the vast majority living in low- to middle-income countries. HIV/AIDS is not evenly distributed and prevalence rates range from 1 percent to 25 percent in the adult population. While some countries, such as those in northern Europe, have "concentrated" epidemics mainly confined to gay men, others such as those in southern Africa, are experiencing "generalized" epidemics where the entire sexually active population is affected. Others such as Russia are experiencing an accelerating epidemic, initially confined to transmission among injecting drug users but now becoming generalized. The USA and countries in South America and in the Asia-Pacific region are experiencing multiple epidemics – among people who inject drugs, among gay men, and increasingly among the poor. While the global incidence rate and incidence itself appears to have peaked in the late 1990s, the estimated annual number of new infections over the last few years appears to have stabilized at the alarmingly high rate of 2 to 4 million per year and there continue to be more new HIV infections each year than there are AIDS-related deaths. The world is facing a global pandemic: a pandemic marked by inequalities of gender, race, class, and sexual orientation.

Although there is no cure for HIV, effective treatment, in the form of anti-retroviral therapies, has slowed the progression from HIV to AIDS to death in almost all who have treatment access. While in the income-rich world there has been an 80 percent fall in AIDS-related deaths, in low-income countries only a very small proportion of those in need of treatment are currently receiving effective therapy. Prospects for treatment access continue to be thwarted by poverty and global inequalities, as well as pharmaceutical patent rights. The number of new cases still outpaces the expansion of treatment access and the demand for treatment will continue to grow as people continue to become infected.

As a blood borne virus, HIV is most commonly transmitted by sexual intercourse (vaginal and anal) with an HIV infected person. It is also transmitted by the sharing of HIV-contaminated needles and syringes, from an HIV-positive mother to child during birth and breast feeding, and via the use of contaminated blood products. There is at present no effective prophylactic vaccine. Consistent condom use for sex and the use of clean needles and syringes for drug injection are the most efficacious prevention strategies currently available. Abstinence from both sex and drug use has not been shown to be an effective strategy and there continues to be debate about the effectiveness of sexual monogamy. Male circumcision has been shown to reduce the likelihood of sexual transmission from women to men, but male circumcision alone is unlikely to curb the epidemic. Clinical trials continue the search for other efficacious prevention tools, for example, microbicides.

More than efficacious prevention technologies – even when combined – are needed. Changes in social relations are also necessary. Gender inequality is one of the key social drivers of HIV-transmission and the gendered patterns of social and economic dependency which result in women having little access to education and other resources need to be changed. Human rights are central to an effective response. All people have the right to HIV-prevention information and HIV-prevention technologies, and people living with HIV have the right to effective treatment as well as the right to equality before the law, privacy, liberty of movement, work, equal access to education, housing, health care, social security, assistance, and welfare. Stigma and discrimination undermine an effective response.

Social transformation is necessary. Evidence indicates that HIV transmission rates fall in countries where governments acknowledge that HIV is a virus that affects everyone, fund prevention and health promotion including education programs, promote condom use and needle and syringe programs, support social movements by funding at-risk communities to combat HIV-transmission, and provide treatment, care and support to all those living with HIV/AIDS. In the absence of these factors and in the presence of moral agendas that thwart the promotion of effective technologies, such as condoms, prevention efforts falter.

HIV/AIDS is an issue of global governance. The policies and practices of AIDS prevention, treatment and support not only affect health care systems, they also affect the nature of social relations and the values and ideologies that underpin them. The challenge is to address the social, cultural and economic dimensions of health, to address issues of power, and to fight discrimination.

SEE ALSO: Drug Use; Gender, Development and; Globalization, Sexuality and; HIV/AIDS and Population; Human Rights

SUGGESTED READINGS

Barnett, A. & Whiteside, A. (2006) *AIDS in the Twenty-First Century: Disease and Globalization*, 2nd edn. Palgrave, New York.

Epstein, Helen (2007) *The Invisible Cure: Africa, the West, and the Fight against AIDS*. Farrar, Straus and Giroux, New York.

SUSAN KIPPAX

alcoholism and alcohol abuse

Normative structures surrounding alcohol use vary greatly over history and geography. In many settings drinking only accompanies rituals of celebration and social solidarity. There is however a long history of solitary and group drunkenness with adverse consequences. Dangers of alcohol consumption are recognized in its prohibition throughout Islam. In general, however, history shows eons of socially integrated alcohol use. Concepts of societal-level alcohol-related problems first emerged some 500 years ago. These social problems grew with industrialization, urbanization, immigration, and population increase.

Medical definitions of alcohol problems are sociologically constructed, focused on failures in role performance and/or destructive behaviors. These behaviors can range from breaking small groups' rules to committing murder in an intoxicated rage. Alcoholism has an additional sociological element in its definition, namely the loss of self-control wherein drinking is repeated despite substantial costs to the drinker.

Alcohol problems have emerged globally in concert with "modernization" and social change. Cultures where alcohol has been consumed non-problematically for centuries have seen the emergence of alcohol problems. Patterns of consumption (time, place, amount) change, traditional forms of social control over intoxication fall away, and industrialization creates roles that are intolerant of routine drinking.

Men drink more than women in all societies. Industrialization, women's employment, and gender equality for women are associated with drinking patterns similar to men's. Because of alcohol's potency, drinking among youth generates substantial social control efforts in industrialized societies, with these controls actually encouraging the dangerous behavior called "binge drinking." By contrast, in China mandating a minimum age for drinking has only recently been considered.

Many sociologists are skeptical about the disease model of alcoholism since personal will and social support are core to the achievement of abstinence. Applications of sociology are however central in achieving social control over alcohol problems since complete prohibition has proven to be ineffective.

SEE ALSO: Drugs, Drug Abuse, and Drug Policy; Social Control; Social Problems, Politics of

SUGGESTED READING

Gusfield, J. R. (1996) *Contested Meanings: The Construction of Alcohol Problems.* University of Wisconsin Press, Madison, WI.

PAUL ROMAN

alienation

Alienation is the social and psychological separation between oneself and one's life experiences. Alienation is a concept originally applied to work and work settings but today is also used to characterize separation from the political sphere. To be alienated is to live in a society but not to feel that one is a part of its ongoing activities.

Theories of alienation start with the writings of Marx, who identified the capacity for self-directed *creative activity* as the core distinction between humans and animals. If people cannot express their *species being* (their creativity), they are reduced to the status of animals or machines. Marx argued that, under capitalism, workers lose control over their work and, as a consequence, are alienated in at least four ways. First, they are alienated from the *products* of their labor. They no longer determine what is to be made nor what use will be made of it. Work is reduced to being a means to an end – a means to acquire money to buy the material necessities of life. Second, workers are alienated from the *process* of work. Someone else controls the pace, pattern, tools, and techniques of their work. Third, because workers are separated from their activity, they become alienated from *themselves*. Non-alienated work, in contrast, entails the same enthusiastic absorption and self-realization as hobbies and leisure pursuits. Fourth, alienated labor is an isolated endeavor, not part of a collectively planned effort to meet a group need. Consequently, workers are alienated from *others* as well as from themselves. Marx argued that these four aspects of alienation reach their peak under industrial capitalism and that alienated work, which is inherently dissatisfying, would naturally produce in workers a desire to change the existing system. Alienation, in Marx's view, thus plays a crucial role in leading to social revolution to change society toward a non-alienated future.

Today, the core of alienation research has moved away from the social philosophical approach of Marx, based on projecting a future that *could be*, and toward a more empirical study of the causes and consequences of alienation within the world of work as it *actually exists*. The contemporary approach substitutes measures of job satisfaction for Marx's more expansive conception of alienation. Related concepts include job commitment, effort bargaining, and, conversely, resistance. In the political sphere voting behavior and a sense of political efficacy have emerged as central empirical indicators of underlying alienation from society's power structures. Theories of alienation, as exercises in social philosophy, help to keep alive questions about the future of society by envisioning possible alternatives that do not yet exist. Such exercises are necessary if the social sciences are to retain a transformative potential beyond the tyranny of *what is* and toward *what could be*.

SEE ALSO: Anomie; Capitalism; Labor Process; Marx, Karl

SUGGESTED READINGS

Hodson, R. (2001) *Dignity at Work*. Cambridge University Press, New York.

Marx, K. (1971) [1844] The economic and philosophic manuscripts of 1844. In: Jordon, Z. A. (ed.), *Karl Marx*. Michael Joseph, London.

RANDY HODSON

American Sociological Association

The American Sociological Association (ASA), founded in 1905, is the largest and most influential organization of professional sociologists in the USA. In 1959, the organization's original name was formally changed from the American Sociological Society (ASS) to its current moniker, the American Sociological Association. In 2009, the ASA reported some 14,000 dues-paying members and operating investments valued at approximately $4.6 million. A comprehensive, independent history of the organization has yet to be written.

The first ASS presidents comprised the major white male intellectual architects of what became the American sociological tradition. The pioneering work of the ASS is chronicled in the *Papers and Proceedings of the American Sociological Association* (1906–28) and the *American Journal of Sociology* (*AJS*). The *AJS*, founded in 1895 by Albion W. Small at the University of Chicago, served as the voice of the ASS until 1935 when the ASS membership established a separate journal, the *American Sociological Review* (*ASR*). Today, the ASA publishes several journals, including *Footnotes*, the organization's professional newsletter. Since 1963, the day-to-day bureaucratic operations of the association are administered by an Executive Officer and an ever-growing paid staff, now housed in Washington, DC. In consequence, the annually-elected ASA presidents have become less responsible for ordinary bureaucratic tasks and the ASA executive office has itself become a consequential force in shaping and promoting the public image of disciplinary sociology in the United States.

Whereas the ASA is national in scope, several regional, state and special interest organizations provide more focused, more accessible and often more convivial professional sociological outlets. Many sociologists participate in both the ASA and one (sometimes more) of the smaller sociological organizations or regional societies. Some smaller organizations work alongside or within the ASA while others thrive as fully separate and sometimes competitive entities.

SEE ALSO: Sociology

SUGGESTED READING

Rosich, K. J. (2005) *A History of the American Sociological Association, 1981–2004*. American Sociological Association, Washington, DC.

MICHAEL R. HILL

Americanization

The term "Americanization," which broadly deals with American influence on something, has multiple specific meanings. Within the USA, Americanization has been most prominently understood in relation to immigrant acculturation, or immigrants' adoption of US cultural norms and values. This Americanization concept was at its most popular in the early twentieth century. A large influx of immigrants had arrived to the USA between the 1870s and the 1920s, and the rapid growth of the foreign-born population caused concern that these newcomers would maintain their heritage culture rather than adopting US ways. World War I increased nationalist fervor and thus led to a heightened sense of nativism; immigrant cultures and languages were seen as not only deficient but also threatening, and "Americanization" of immigrants was therefore understood as imperative. However, this Americanization sentiment lessened following the 1924 immigration restrictions. It further decreased in popularity with the post-World War II-era's codification of human rights and with the increasing permissibility of cultural distinction following the civil rights era. Today, speaking of "Americanizing" immigrants is often seen as unacceptable and culturally biased.

Outside of the USA, Americanization has been most commonly used to signify the spreading of US cultural, political, and economic norms and practices to other nations. This understanding of Americanization is thus related to globalization and westernization. Though exact contents and processes of this "Americanization" are broad and oft-debated, US political influences have included the spreading of democracy, particularly during the cold war era; economic influences have included deregulation and free market principles; and cultural influences have included concepts of individualism and specific US cultural products, such as music, television, and film. While US practices and culture have sometimes been adopted voluntarily by other nations, Americanization has also been seen as hegemonic and forcibly imposed due to the USA's economic and political power. Americanization has thus been seen, at varying times and by varying actors, as both a positive and negative phenomenon.

SEE ALSO: Assimilation; Cultural Imperialism; McDonaldization

SUGGESTED READING

Ritzer, G. & Ryan, M. (2004) Americanisation, McDonaldisation, and globalisation. In: Campbell, N., Davies, J., & McKay, G. (eds.), *Issues in Americanization and Culture*. Edinburgh University Press, Edinburgh, pp. 41–60.

JESSICA SPERLING

anarchism

Anarchism signifies the condition of being without rule. Anarchism, then, has often been equated with chaos. This interpretation was lent weight by the period of anarchist "propaganda by deed" towards the end of the nineteenth century. For most anarchists, though, their political allegiances involve opposition to the intrusiveness, destructiveness, and artificiality of state authority, the rejection of all forms of domination and hierarchy, and the desire to construct a social order based on free association. Anarchism is, however, a heterogeneous political field, containing a host of variations – for instance, organization versus spontaneity, peaceful transition versus violence, individualist versus collectivist means and ends, romanticism versus science, and existential versus structural critique of domination.

Although anarchism has been traced back, say, to millenarian sects of the Middle Ages, anarchism is properly a nineteenth-century ideology and movement, and anarchists are perhaps best remembered through Marx's encounters with Max Stirner, Pierre-Joseph Proudhon, and Mikhail Bakunin. Nevertheless, anarchism and communism were not clearly distinguished as varieties of socialism until the period after the Second International. From this time onwards, Marxists equated anarchism with extreme individualism, with opposition to any form of organization or authority, and with mistakenly taking the state (instead of capital) as primary in understanding exploitation and domination.

In the twentieth century, anarchism provided the underpinnings of larger movements and rebellions – for instance, revolutionary syndicalism (the trade unions as revolutionary weapons and models of a future social order) in strongholds such as France, Spain, and Italy; and the collectivization of land and factories during the Spanish Civil War. MIT linguist and political activist Noam Chomsky is probably the best-known contemporary representative of this strand of anarchist thought.

Between 1914 and 1938, anarchism as an ideology and a movement went into serious decline. However, it was widely viewed as at least implicit in the counter-cultural opposition of the 1960s and 1970s. More recently, "primitivist" anarchists connected modernity's obsessions with science and progress with the domination of human beings and nature and with the loss of authenticity and spontaneity. For some, poststructuralism has strong anarchist resonances – underscoring difference against totalizing and scientistic Marxian theory and politics, decentralist, and attentive to the micro-operations of power. Finally, the anti-globalization movement is sometimes said to represent a "new anarchism," opposing neoliberal capitalism and statism, decentralist and localist in its aims, and characterized by openness and by "horizontal" organizational tendencies.

SEE ALSO: Capitalism; Communism; Socialism

SUGGESTED READINGS

Carter, A. (1971) *The Political Theory of Anarchism*. Routledge & Kegan Paul, London.
Woodcock, G. (ed.) (1977) *The Anarchist Reader*. Harvester Press, Brighton.

CHAMSY EL-OJEILI

animal rights movement

The animal rights movement, which emerged in the 1970s, seeks to end the use of animals as sources of food and experimental subjects. It has challenged traditional animal welfare which seeks to eliminate the unnecessary suffering of animals. Strategically, the animal rights movement is characterized by its willingness to engage in grassroots campaigning and activism which, at its extremes, has included, sometimes violent, forms of direct action.

General arguments employed to explain the emergence of the animal rights movement include those based on post-material values, occupation and gender, the latter being seen as particularly appropriate not least given that a preponderance of animal rights activists are women.

Other explanations provide room for the independent explanatory validity of people's genuine concern for animals and what is done to them. This includes the influence of a radical philosophy for animals, and particularly work by Singer (1975) and Regan (1984), greater knowledge of their capabilities, and increasing coverage of animal issues in the media.

SEE ALSO: New Social Movement Theory; Social Movements

REFERENCES

Regan, T. (1984) *The Case for Animal Rights*. Routledge, London.

Singer, P. (1975) *Animal Liberation*. Jonathan Cape, London.

ROBERT GARNER

anomie

Anomie refers to the lack or ineffectiveness of normative regulation in society. The concept was first introduced in sociology by Émile Durkheim (1893) who argued, against Marx, that the division of labor brings about problematic consequences only under exceptional circumstances, either because of a lack of regulation or because the level of regulation does not match the degree of development of the division of labor. In his famous study on suicide, Durkheim (1897) relied on the anomie perspective to introduce the anomic type of suicide. Anomic suicide takes place when normative regulations are absent, such as in the world of trade and industry (chronic anomie), or when abrupt transitions in society, such as fiscal crises, lead to a loss in the effectiveness of norms to regulate behavior (acute anomie).

Durkheim's anomie concept was expanded by Robert K. Merton (1968), who argued that a state of anomie occurs as a result of the unusually strong emphasis in US society on the dominant cultural goals (individual success) without a corresponding emphasis on the legitimate means (education, work) to reach those goals. Anomie refers to the resulting demoralization or deinstitutionalization of legitimate norms.

Following Merton's work, anomie became among the most applied concepts in American sociology during the 1950s and 1960s. Theoretically, anomie was perceived among non-Marxists as a useful alternative to alienation. In matters of empirical research, an important development was Leo Srole's concept of anomia, which refers to the social-psychological mental states of individuals who are confronted with social conditions of anomie. Caught in the polarization between micro and macro perspectives, the theoretical relation between anomia and anomie has not yet been adequately addressed.

During the 1970s and early 1980s, the concept of anomie was much less discussed. Since the late 1980s, however, there has been a revival of the anomie concept in at least two areas of inquiry. First, Merton's perspective of anomie and social structure is now widely recognized as one of the most influential contributions in criminological sociology. The theoretical approach has now been broadened as comprising an anomie theory (of social organization) as well as a strain theory (of deviance). In contemporary criminological sociology, strain theory is much more influential than anomie theory.

Second, Durkheim's anomie concept is applied in research on societies undergoing rapid social and economic change, such as many of the eastern European countries since the collapse of communism. It remains to be seen if and how this renewed concept of anomie will integrate with the related literature on globalization and inequality that is traditionally rather hostile toward Durkheimian and functional-structuralist theories. Perhaps a new integrated perspective can emerge that will transcend the prior dichotomies between anomie and rival concepts such as alienation.

SEE ALSO: Alienation; Durkheim, Émile; Merton, Robert K.; Norms; Structural Functional Theory

REFERENCES

Durkheim, É. (1933) [1893] *The Division of Labor in Society*, trans. G. Simpson. Free Press, Glencoe, IL.

Durkheim, É. (1952) [1897] *Suicide: A Study in Sociology*, trans. J. A. Spaulding & G. Simpson. Routledge & Kegan Paul, London.

Merton, R. K. (1968) *Social Theory and Social Structure*, enlarged edn. Free Press, New York.

Srole, L. (1956) Social integration and certain corollaries: an exploratory study. *American Sociological Review* 21: 709–16.

SUGGESTED READING

Featherstone, R. & Deflem, M. (2003) Anomie and strain: context and consequences of Merton's two theories. *Sociological Inquiry* 73: 471–89.

MATHIEU DEFLEM

ANOVA (analysis of variance)

Analysis of Variance (ANOVA) is a statistical technique for detecting differences among the means of groups within a sample. It is one of several techniques of the "general linear model."

In the basic case, a sample is divided into groups based on values of one discrete independent variable with a small number of categories. Within each group, the means for a second variable, the dependent variable, are calculated. The difference in the means for the different groups is compared to the variation of the individual cases within each group around that group's mean. The larger the difference in the means (relative to the variation around each mean), the more likely it is that the means are significantly different, and the less likely that one would make a type I (alpha) error by saying that the groups have different means in the population from which the sample is drawn.

Key to ANOVA, the F statistic comprises the ratio of the mean squared error between groups and the mean squared error within groups. The larger the difference between means of each group, the larger the F ratio is (holding constant the variation around the individual means). The larger the variation around each individual mean, the smaller is the F ratio (holding constant the difference between the means for each group). To make reliable inferences about the population based on the sample, ANOVA assumes: the sample was drawn randomly from the population, and the distribution of the dependent variable around the mean(s) is normal, not skewed in either direction.

F ratios are distributed in a family of curves based on the degrees of freedom for the between group means (number of groups of the independent variable minus one) and the degrees of freedom within groups (number of individual cases minus the number of values of the independent variable).

SEE ALSO: General Linear Model; Statistical Significance Testing

SUGGESTED READING

Agresti, A. & Finlay, B. (1997). *Statistical Methods for the Social Sciences*, 3rd edn. Prentice Hall, Upper Saddle River, NJ.

PAUL T. MUNROE

anti-war and peace movements

While many people in the USA are only aware of anti-war and peace movements from the 1960s and 1970s period of social unrest, these movements have been in existence since long before. Peace and anti-war movements are social movements that concentrate on a variety of issues related to violence, armed conflict, war, domination and oppression. The goals of the movements vary according to the dominant issue of the moment as well as the time and place in which they exist. For example, while there is an active international anti-nuclear arms movement, these efforts rarely receive mainstream attention in the USA.

Common themes of anti-war and peace groups range from ending a specific conflict to the abolition of war, the elimination of weapons as well as the creation of non-violent mechanisms to solve conflicts; such as through the creation of government sponsored committees or departments dedicated to peace rather than defense. Tactics utilized by these groups vary and often mirror the ideology of the group. Non-violent approaches include large boycotts, protests, hunger strikes, sit-ins, speeches, letter-writing campaigns, lobbying politicians, voting, education, and outreach. Others have used violence such as self-immolation, the destruction of property and even assassination as a mechanism to end war.

People and groups resist war and armed conflict for a wide variety of reasons such as economic exploitation, violation of human rights, destruction of property, environmental harm, the immorality of killing, the ideological justifications for war as well as the financial costs. Individuals may work individually or organize their own local groups, join larger national groups and work within educational and religious institutions to advance their cause. As our consciousness expands globally, strategies for change have become more transnational with groups around the world organizing to protest and disrupt meetings of world leaders to draw attention to situations they believe are unjust. The emergence of the Internet and other advances in technology has provided a new means of coalition building, which has been expanded as it is easier to reach people around the globe. For example, when the USA was preparing to invade Iraq in 2003, the peace movement was able to organize simultaneous protests of millions of people around the world.

While anti-war and peace movements are often successful in influencing public debate and beliefs about armed conflict and current military actions, rarely have they been able to stop wars. For example, the anti-war movement of the 1960s and 1970s galvanized the nation and created enough pressure on government officials to change their actions concerning the war. Part of this success was the number of people within government and politics who were openly against the war and worked to end it as soon as possible. Successful change arises out of a combination of people working within and outside of social and political institutions. One key element helping end the Vietnam War was the media coverage of the protests and of the war itself. More recent conflicts and peace movement activities have not had the same level of support thus making the efforts of the anti-war movement more challenging due to the invisibility of their efforts or of war itself, in the mainstream media.

SEE ALSO: Social Movements; War

SUGGESTED READINGS
Marullo, S. & Meyer, D. (2004). Antiwar and peace movements. In: Snow, D., Soule, S., & Kriesi, H. (eds.), *The Blackwell Companion to Social Movements*. Blackwell, Oxford.
Waller, M. R. & Rycenga, J. (2001). *Frontline Feminisms: Women, War, and Resistance*. Routledge, New York.
Wittner, L. (1984) *Rebels against War: The American Peace Movement, 1933–1983*. Temple University Press, Philadelphia.

KRISTINA B. WOLFF

arcades

Originating in Paris in the 1820s, arcades were decorative passages or walkways through blocks of buildings. Glass-roofed and supported by ornate ironwork columns, arcades formed interior streets; sites of conspicuous consumption for the wealthy, and places of spectacle for the poor. Hemmed in by concession stands and eclectic emporia, arcade shop fronts offered the observer a visual experience of illuminated shop-signs, *objets d'art*, and a cornucopia of commodities from around the world. Sociologically speaking, the importance of the Parisian arcades lies in their role as progenitor of modern consumerism and more tangentially as a prototype of the contemporary shopping mall.

The unearthing of the arcade as a site of sociological and philosophical importance is closely associated with the German literary theorist, Walter Benjamin. Benjamin was fascinated by the arcades, "mythical" qualities, viewing them as both "threatening" and "alluring" – places in which the emotions were stimulated and where the spheres of public and private life were blurred and challenged. In *The Arcades Project* (*Das Passagen-Werk*), Benjamin viewed the arcades as a metaphor for the composition and dynamic form of modern industrial capitalism. He described arcade shop fronts as "dream houses," where everything desirable becomes a commodity (frequently on the first floor of the arcades, sexual pleasures could be bought and drinking and gambling were common). For Benjamin, the continual flow of goods, the "sensual immediacy" of the displays, and the visual appeal of transitory fashions were all fragments of the "commodity fetish." Yet while newness itself becomes a fetish, the modern commodity has a built-in obsolescence – the novel inevitably becomes the outmoded. This tension is apparent in the fate of the arcades themselves. Following Haussman's "creative destruction" of Second Empire Paris in the 1860s, most of the arcades were destroyed to make way for the wide boulevards that characterize Paris today. Likewise, by the time of Benjamin's research, the arcades had largely been superseded by the modern department store with its more rationalized forms of mass urban consumption. However, surviving examples of original arcades can still be found in Paris today.

SEE ALSO: Benjamin, Walter; Cathedrals and Landscapes of Consumption

SUGGESTED READINGS
Buck-Morss, S. (1989) *The Dialectics of Seeing: Walter Benjamin and the Arcades Project*. Cambridge: MIT Press, Cambridge, MA.
Geist, J. F. (1983) *Arcades*. MIT Press, Cambridge, MA.

KEITH HAYWARD

asceticism

The concept of asceticism shows the unity of efforts through which an individual desires to progress in his moral, religious and spiritual life. The original meaning of the term refers to any exercise, physical, intellectual or moral, practiced with method and rigor, in hopes of self-improvement and progress. Notwithstanding the great flexibility that characterizes the application of asceticism, the concept always alludes to a search towards perfection based on the submission of the body to the spirit, recalling the symbolic distinction between exterior and interior life.

Following the evolution of the concept of asceticism within different historical and social contexts, it is possible to see its strategic importance within the social sciences, especially in regard to understanding the western world. Aside from the combination of physical and intellectual exercises, which have always had their own social relevance, asceticism refers to the complex relationship between nature and culture, as well as to the classic religious relationship between faith and reason; such aspects are the fruit of a continual and dynamic negotiation that develops within concrete social and cultural contexts.

Far from disappearing, asceticism is present even in the contemporary world, and not only in the context of oriental religious and experiences, such as some practices of Hinduism and Buddhism. While in a strictly religious sphere, new forms of asceticism could be tantric practices or yoga. Deborah Lupton (1996) relates asceticism to the issue of food and the awareness of the body and Enzo Pace (1983) puts it in the context of political activism.

SEE ALSO: Body and Society; Buddhism; Hinduism; Sexuality, Religion and

REFERENCES

Lupton, D. (1996) *Food, the Body and the Self.* Sage, London.

Pace, E. (1983) *Asceti e mistici in una società secolarizzata.* Marsilio, Venice.

GIUSEPPE GIORDAN

asch experiments

Solomon Asch (1907–96) conducted pioneering social psychological experiments on group conformity, and processes of person perception. His conformity experiments are of particular importance. In these experiments, college students were told they were participating in a study on visual perception (by matching the length of one line to three others). In truth, the experiment was intended to measure the extent of conformity to group norms and perceptions, even when those norms/perceptions conflicted with their own interpretation of reality. After a series of confederates intentionally gave incorrect answers in the experiment, approximately one-third of the participants conformed to these incorrect answers in a majority of trials. Approximately one-fourth refused to conform in any of the trials. And, while the majority of individual responses given in the experiment reflected independence from the group, a clear majority (approximately three-fourths) of the participants displayed a capacity to engage in this extreme form of conformity at least once during the course of the experiment. Asch's conformity experiments had a huge impact on the early development of social psychology, and served as inspiration for numerous future studies, including Milgram's research on obedience and Zimbardo's mock prison study at Stanford University.

Asch also conducted experiments on person perception that had an equally profound impact on the early theoretical development of social psychology. These experiments on *central* and *peripheral* personality traits led to a deeper understanding of how impressions of others are formed and structured.

SEE ALSO: Authority and Conformity; Milgram, Stanley (Experiments); Zimbardo Prison Experiment

SUGGESTED READINGS

Asch, S. E. (1952) *Social Psychology.* Prentice Hall, New York.

Asch, S. E. (1955) Opinions and social pressure. *Scientific American* (November): 31–55.

Asch, S. E. (1956) Studies of independence and conformity: a minority of one against a unanimous majority. *Psychological Monographs* 70 (whole no. 416).

WILLIAM J. KINNEY

assimilation

Assimilation is reemerging as a core concept for comprehending the long-run consequences of immigration, both for the immigrants and their descendants and for the society that receives them.

This new phase could be described as a second life for a troubled concept. In its first life, assimilation was enthroned as the reigning idea in the study of ethnicity and race. In the USA, where the theoretical development of assimilation mainly took place, this period began with the studies of the Chicago School in the early twentieth century and ended not long after the canonical statement of assimilation theory, Milton Gordon's *Assimilation in American Life*, appeared in the mid-1960s. In this first phase, assimilation did double duty – on the one hand, as popular ideology for interpreting the American experience and, correlatively, an ideal expressing the direction in which ethnic and racial divisions were evolving in the USA; and, on the other, as the foundational concept for the social scientific understanding of processes of change undergone by immigrants and, even more, the ensuing generations.

One profound alteration to the social scientific apparatus for studying immigrant-group incorporation is that it is no longer exclusively based on assimilation. Very abstractly, three patterns describe today how immigrants and their descendants become "incorporated into," that is, a recognized part of, an immigration society: the pattern of assimilation involves a progressive, typically multigenerational, process of socioeconomic, cultural, and social integration into the "mainstream," that part of the society where racial and ethnic origins have at most minor effects on the life chances of individuals; a second pattern entails racial exclusion, absorption into a racial minority status, which implies persistent and substantial disadvantages vis-à-vis the members of the mainstream; a third pattern is that of a pluralism in which individuals and groups are able to draw social and economic advantages by keeping some aspects of their lives within the confines of an ethnic matrix (e.g., ethnic economic niches, ethnic communities).

SEE ALSO: Acculturation; Immigration; Whiteness

SUGGESTED READINGS

Alba, R. & Nee, V. (2003) *Remaking the American Mainstream: Assimilation and Contemporary Immigration*. Harvard University Press, Cambridge, MA.

Gordon, M. (1964) *Assimilation in American Life*. Oxford University Press, New York.

RICHARD ALBA AND VICTOR NEE

attitudes and behavior

The role of attitudes in guiding behavior is an enduring social psychological concern. Two explanatory paradigms have emerged. One approach is grounded in positivism and deductive theorizing. The other is inductive and phenomenological, emphasizing process and construction.

Gordon Allport in the mid-1930s (1935: "Attitudes"), articulated the positivist approach, when he defined attitudes as mental states which direct one's response, placing attitudes in a causal, directive role. This laid the groundwork for a deductive, scientific approach to the relationship between attitudes and behavior. Attitudes were intrapersonal, psychological tendencies expressed through favorable or unfavorable evaluation of objects.

This approach has dominated contemporary research. Martin Fishbein and Icek Ajzen in the Theory of Reasoned Action have become the most widely known exemplars of this approach. Their four-stage, recursive model posits that attitudes explain behavioral intentions, if it is not coerced and nothing else intervenes. The core assumption is consistency. Attitudes are conceptualized as generic, transsituational, psychological expressions that guide behavior across circumstances.

Attiudes, because they are mental constructs present a measurement problem. Attitude scaling techniques were developed to address this problem. Techniques developed by Likert, Thurstone, Guttman, and Osgood have become the backbone of attitudinal data collection strategies. The common core of all attitude measurement is asking questions out of context to reveal these internal sentiments.

Some researchers, such as Fishbein, discourage the measurement of behavior, opting instead for the measurement of behavioral intention. This allows surveys to be the primary measurement tool for both attitudes and behavioral intentions. Through questions, respondents are asked to reveal what they intend to do or what they have done. Although a causal relationship is hypothesized, designs allow for the simultaneous measurement of attitudes and behavior.

The phenomenological approach also emerged early, most notably in the works of Thomas and Znaniecki (1918: *The Polish Peasant in Europe and America*) and Faris (1928: "Attitudes and behavior"). In this approach attitudes and behaviors are interpersonal, not intrapersonal, phenomena. Social context is central to understanding the ways in which attitudes and behavior come together. This approach assumes that attitudes and behavior and thus their relationship are complex and situational.

Blumer challenged the very idea of a bivariate, objective, intrapersonal conceptualization of these concepts. For him the key to understanding the relationship between mental conceptualizations and actions was the actor's definition of the situation. Actors continually interpret and reinterpret the situations in which they find themselves, in order to create and coordinate their actions with others.

This line of thinking was extended by Deutscher and his collaborators (1973; 1993). By reviewing and critiquing the extant attitude-behavior work, they conclude that a situational approach, in which social actors construct behavior and give it meaning in social situations, is what is needed. They emphasize that "it's what's in between attitude and behavior" that counts. Situations are open, indefinite, and subject to continuous interpretation, reinterpretation and modification by the social actors embedded in them. People imbue situations with meaning, then act on the basis of that meaning. Behavior is constructed in concert with others, not solely by individuals.

Attitudes are important for understanding both behavior and its change. Relevant studies appear in almost every field of sociology, including law, criminology, family, and substance use. Given the affective and motivational nature of attitude conceptualization, work in the sociology of emotions, motive, and language have relevance for understanding the complexity of this relationship and resolving some of these intellectual disputes in understanding the relationship between thoughts and actions.

SEE ALSO: Definition of the Situation; Psychological Social Psychology; Social Cognition; Social Psychology

REFERENCES

Deutscher, I. (1973) *What We Say/What We Do: Sentiments and Acts*. Scott Foresman, Glenview, IL.

Deutscher, I., Pestello, F. P., & Pestello, H. F. G. (1993) *Sentiments and Acts*. Aldine de Gruyter, New York.

SUGGESTED READINGS

Blumer, H. (1955) Attitudes and the social act. *Social Problems* 3: 59–65.

Likert, R. (1932) The method of constructing an attitude scale. *Archives of Psychology* 140: 44–53.

FRANCES G. PESTELLO

attribution theory

There is no one theory of attribution; rather, several perspectives are collectively referred to as attribution theory. Attribution theory attempts to elucidate how people explain human behaviors by inferring the causes of those behaviors. Frtiz Heider (1958) provided the building blocks for developing attribution research. He proposed that in their search for causal structures of events, people attribute causality either to elements within the environment or to elements within the person. He noted that people tend to overestimate the role of internal causes, such attitudes, when explaining others' behavior. Further, he assumed that people tend to make an internal attribution of causes if they view an action as intentionally caused.

Correspondence inference theory identifies the conditions under which an observed behavior can be said to correspond to a particular disposition or quality within the actor. The process of correspondence inference works backward and is divided into two stages: the attribution of intention and the attribution of dispositions. Another important contribution to attribution research is Kelley's (1967) theory of covariation analysis which is concerned with the accuracy of attributing causes to effects. His theory in the essay "Attribution theory in social psychology" hinges on the principle of covariation between possible causes and effects. Three types of information are utilized to make causal attribution: consensus, distinctiveness, and consistency. Consensus refers to whether all people act the same way toward the same stimulus or only the observed person. Distinctiveness concerns whether the observed person behaves in the same way to different stimuli. Consistency refers to whether the observed person behaves in the same way toward the same stimulus over time and in different situations. The attribution to personal or environmental factors depends on the combination of these qualities.

Bernard Weiner's (1986) theory of achievement and emotion focuses on the emotional and behavioral consequences of the attribution process. This theory proposes three dimensions of perceived causality: the locus of the cause (within the person versus outside the person), the stability of the cause (stable versus unstable), and the controllability over the cause (controllable versus uncontrollable). The resultant emotions depend on the type of attribution that observers make. Weiner differentiated between two groups of affects. First, "outcome-dependent" affects which are experienced as a result of the attainment or non-attainment of a given outcome, and not by the cause of that outcome. The second group is called "attribution-linked" affects which are experienced as a result of appraisal and assignment of a cause.

In the process of making attributions, people make mistakes by either overestimating or underestimating the impact of situational or personal factors when explaining their behaviors or the behaviors of others. These errors are termed biases in attribution. Correspondence bias, also called fundamental attribution error, is one of them which refers to observers' tendency to exaggerate or overestimate the influence of dispositional factors when explaining people's behavior.

SEE ALSO: Accounts; Labeling Theory; Stigma; Stratification

REFERENCE

Heider, F. (1958) *The Psychology of Interpersonal Relations*. Wiley, New York.

Weiner, B. (1986) *An Attributional Theory of Motivation and Emotion*. Springer Verlag, New York.

SUGGESTED READINGS

Kelley, H. H. & Michela, J. L. (1980) Attribution theory and research. *Annual Review of Psychology* 31: 457–501.

Weiner, B. (2008) Reflections on the history of attribution theory and research: people, personalities, publications, problems. *Social Psychology* 39: 151–6.

ABDALLAH M. BADAHDAH

authoritarian personality

The authoritarian personality is a psychological syndrome of traits that correlates highly with outgroup prejudice. Three personality traits in particular characterize the syndrome: deference to authorities, aggression toward outgroups, and rigid adherence to cultural conventions. Thus, authoritarians hold a rigidly hierarchical view of the world.

Nazi Germany inspired the first conceptualizations. The Frankfurt School, combining Marxism, psychoanalysis, and sociology, introduced the syndrome to explain Hitler's popularity among working-class Germans. Social psychologists soon demonstrated the syndrome in the USA. In 1950, the major publication by Adorno et al., *The Authoritarian Personality,* appeared. The product of two German refugees and two US social psychologists from Berkeley, this publication firmly established the concept in social science. Its easily administered F (for fascism) Scale led to an explosion of more than 2,000 published research papers. Critics disparaged the work on political, methodological, and theoretical grounds.

Methodological critics unearthed a host of problems. The most important objection concerned the 1950 study's neglect of the social context. Authoritarianism rises in times of societal threat, and recedes in times of calm. Crises invoke authoritarian leadership and encourage equalitarians to accept such leadership. Moreover, the syndrome's link to behavior is strongly related to the situational context in which authoritarians find themselves.

Nonetheless, research throughout the world with various measures shows that authoritarians reveal similar susceptibilities. In particular, high scorers favor extreme right-wing politics and exhibit prejudice against outgroups. This remarkable global consistency of results suggests that the authoritarian personality is a general personality syndrome with early origins in childhood that center on universal issues of authority and security. A plethora of theories attempt to define the personality type and its origins. The original Berkeley theory stressed the effects of a stern father in early life. Later formulations emphasize the syndrome's focus on strength and weakness, its intense orientation to the ingroup, and the importance of modeling of authoritarian behavior by parents.

SEE ALSO: Authoritarianism; Authority and Conformity; Authority and Legitimacy; Critical Theory/Frankfurt School

REFERENCE

Adorno, T. W., Frenkel-Brunswik, E., Levinson, D. J., & Sanford, R. N. (1950) *The Authoritarian Personality*. Harper & Row, New York.

THOMAS F. PETTIGREW

authoritarianism

The concept of authoritarianism has been used mainly to refer to a type of authority whose power is exercised within diffuse legal, institutional, or de facto boundaries that easily leads to arbitrary acts against groups and individuals. Those who are in power are not accountable to constituencies and public policy does not derive from social consent.

Within sociology and political science, particularly within comparative politics, authoritarianism has been understood as a modern type of political regime. This notion has had an important conceptual development since the 1970s, which clarified some ambiguities within political analyses that tended to mix up this type of regime with fascism and other forms of totalitarianism. The concept of authoritarianism has included a range of regimes, from personal dictatorships such as Franco's in Spain in the 1930s, hegemonic party regimes like the Mexican regime founded after the 1910 revolution, and the military governments of South America established during the 1960s and 1970s. The context in which this type of regime was founded was generally a protracted situation of instability such as a revolution (Mexico), a civil war (Spain), a democratic crisis (Chile), and deterioration of the economy and political polarization (Argentina). Most countries where an authoritarian regime was founded had neither a liberal democratic rule nor an opportunity to develop a state of law, and the construction of the nation was mediated not primarily by the concept of the citizen but rather by the notion of "the people."

Authoritarianisms are political systems with limited, not responsible, political pluralism; without elaborate ideology, but with distinctive mentalities; without extensive or intensive political mobilization, except at some points in their development; and in which a leader or occasionally a small group exercises power within formally ill-defined, but actually quite predictable, limits.

SEE ALSO: Authority and Legitimacy; Fascism; Modernization; Populism

SUGGESTED READINGS

Collier, D. (ed.) (1979) *The New Authoritarianism in Latin America*. Princeton University Press, Princeton, NJ.

Linz, J. (1964) A theory of authoritarian regime: the case of Spain. In: Allardt, E. & Littunen,Y. (eds.) (1964) *Cleavages, Ideologies, and Party Systems: Transactions of the Westermarck Society*, Helsinki, vol. 10, pp. 291–341.

ESPERANZA PALMA

authority and conformity

A common phenomenon in social groups (some would say a requirement) is the existence of authority: the right or power to give orders and enforce standards. Authority is only meaningful if people comply with those rules and orders. Conformity, compliance with orders and standards, is the corollary to authority.

Macro-level perspectives tend to focus on *authority*. Because authority is a characteristic of a position in society it can be thought of as a structural component, although cultural transmission passes on the meanings that go with a position of authority. Max Weber's discussion of the types of legitimate authority is a classic example. Recent studies in this area examine the economic authority of multinational corporations, the political authority of state actors, the effects of religious authority on mass movements, as well as the conflicts created when these forms of authority meet head-on in the process of globalization.

Micro-level perspectives tend to focus on *conformity*, seeking to explain why people comply with the orders of authority or the standards of the group. Experiments by Asch, Milgram, and Zimbardo demonstrated the ease with which a person could be induced into making choices that person knew to be false or unethical. The "Utrecht studies" replicated these classic findings and helped identify the conditions that produce resistance to conformity. Studies in social influence take a more generalized approach to conformity by applying general theories of behavior like social identity theory. Conformity to group standards is viewed in this perspective as one outcome of group membership. Identity theories provide an individual-level theoretical mechanism for conforming behavior, namely the motivation to have one's environmental inputs align with one's definitions of self. People conform because to do otherwise is to invite a heightened level of psychological discomfort as a person becomes aware that they are not acting on their self-meanings.

SEE ALSO: Authority and Legitimacy; Milgram, Stanley (Experiments); Rational Legal Authority; Social Identity Theory; Zimbardo Prison Experiment

SUGGESTED READINGS

Blass, T. (ed.) (2000) *Obedience to Authority: Current Perspectives on the Milgram Pardigm*. Lawrence Erlbaum Associates, Mahwah, NJ.

Meeus, W. H. J. & Raaijmakers, Q. A. W. (1995) Obedience in modern society: the Utrecht studies. *Journal of Social Issues* 51: 155–75.

MARK KONTY

authority and legitimacy

Authority is often defined as legitimate power, and contrasted to pure power. In the case of legitimate authority, compliance is voluntary and based on a belief in the right of the authority to demand compliance.

Max Weber provided a famous classification of forms of legitimate authority in terms of the defining type of legitimating belief. Weber identifies four distinct "bases" of legitimacy, three of which are directly associated with forms of authority. The fourth – value-rational faith – legitimates authority indirectly by providing a standard of justice to which particular earthly authorities might claim to correspond. The forms of authority are charismatic, traditional, and rational-legal. Each of these forms can serve on its own as the core of a system of domination. Traditional authority is based on unwritten rules; rational-legal authority on written rules. Unwritten rules may be justified by the belief that they have held true since time immemorial, while written rules are more typically justified by the belief that they have been properly enacted in accordance with other laws. Charismatic authority is command which is not based on rules. What the charismatic leader says overrides and replaces any written rule.

Charismatic authority originates in the extraordinary qualities of the person holding this authority, not in another source, such as the will of the people.

SEE ALSO: Democracy; Legitimacy; Power Elite; Representation; Weber, Max

SUGGESTED READINGS

Lukes, S. (1991) Perspectives on authority. In: *Moral Conflict and Politics*. Clarendon Press, Oxford, pp. 141–54.

Peters, R. S. (1958) Authority. *Proceedings of the Aristotelian Society* 32: 207–24.

Weber, M. (1978) [1968] *Economy and Society: An Outline of Interpretive Sociology*, 3 vols., ed. G. Roth & C. Wittich. University of California Press, Berkeley, CA.

STEPHEN TURNER

B

bankruptcy

Financial and bankruptcy law refers to the laws applied to savings, investments, and loss, among other economic areas. Financial law deals with the broad range of saving and investment products as well as the services related to these products. These include personal finance, corporate finance, credit trade, budgeting, and stocks. Bankruptcy law, on the other hand, regulates the declaration of an individual or company's inability to pay creditors. It is also related to financial stress, asset sales, and macro-economic fluctuations.

Financial law plays a very important role in the world economy and typically covers the following areas: banking – including banks, trust companies, saving banks, savings, loans, and credit unions; brokerage services including broker disputes; commodities; consumer lenders; insurance; investments; mortgages; mutual funds; and stocks and bonds.

Bankruptcy law involves the development of plans that allow debtors to resolve debts through the division of their assets among creditors. This may also allow a debtor to stay in business and use revenues to resolve his debts. Bankruptcy law also allows some debtors to be discharged of all financial obligations after their assets are distributed even though debts have not been paid in full.

Bankruptcy laws diverge enormously across different countries. In the USA the focus has been on salvaging the business as a whole, while British law is designed more to support creditors. Developing countries ("third world") and economies in transition ("second world") vary economically – but also legally. Thus, each one typically adopted its own version of the bankruptcy laws. No one is certain about which model is best. The reason is that no one knows the answers to some basic questions: are the rights of the creditors superior to the rights of the owners? Is it better to rehabilitate than to liquidate?

For example, the effects of strict, liquidation-prone laws are not wholly bad or wholly beneficial. Consumers borrow less and interest rates fall – but entrepreneurs are deterred and firms become more risk-averse. Until such time as these questions are settled and as long as the corporate debt crisis deepens, we are likely to witness a flowering of disparate versions of bankruptcy laws all over the world as we watch the numbers of bankruptcies increase.

SEE ALSO: Consumption; Wealth

SUGGESTED READING

Manning, R. D. (2000) *Credit Card Nation: The Consequences of America's Addiction to Credit*. Basic Books, New York.

JUANITA M. FIRESTONE AND CLAUDIA W. SCHOLZ

base and superstructure

In the Preface to the first published installment of his critique of political economy, Marx presented the classic statement of the base and superstructure metaphor. In a sketch of his work's "guiding thread," Marx (1907: lv) noted that humankind enters determinate, necessary social relations of production appropriate to a determinate developmental stage of the material forces of production. These relations, comprised of real individuals, their activity, and the material conditions in which they live, constitute the "economic structure" – the real basis of the legal and political superstructure and determinate forms of social consciousness. Consciousness does not determine social being; being determines consciousness.

The material infrastructure, Marx maintained, was the real locus of fundamental transformation – not new ideas or changes in the superstructure. The social relations of production – property relations – initially facilitate but later fetter the development of the material forces of production, leading to social change. As "the economic foundation" transforms, "the whole immense superstructure sooner or later revolutionizes itself" (Marx 1907: lv). This formulation suggests that the "economic foundation" – the economy – directly determines the superstructure.

The Preface's compressed style facilitates narrow readings and misinterpretations but there was a reason for Marx's cryptic prose. The short, tight Preface reinforced revolutionaries' enthusiasm for change even though the ensuing dry economic analysis of this incomplete segment of Marx's critique revealed little about capitalism's fundamental contradictions. The specific fissure points of a social formation's weaknesses could lead to radical social transformation, the Preface indicated, and that promising sketch could entice one to read this installment of the critique and the next (whenever it might appear).

After Marx's death, Engels rejected mechanistic interpretations of Marx's Preface, arguing the base was determinate "only in the last instance." But Engels' scientific socialism and the Marx/Darwin parallels he had emphasized, reinforced an unreflexive determinism. Nevertheless, a close reading of Marx's Preface demonstrates that economic or technological determinist interpretations were misguided understandings of the base/superstructure metaphor.

The material forces of production consist of raw materials, machinery, technology, production facilities, and labor power. The conscious, revolutionary subject – the proletariat – is one of the productive forces. Similarly, the social relations of production include workers' aggregation in increasingly larger factories which could influence class consciousness and fuel revolutionary enthusiasm. Read this way, Marx's position is not objectively (or structurally) deterministic.

Because it is in "the legal, political, religious, artistic or philosophical, in short, ideological forms" that humankind became "conscious of this conflict," Marx (1907: lv–lvi) wanted to emphasize that the social relations of production must be changed for real social transformation to follow:

> A social formation does not collapse before all the forces of production, of which it is capable, are developed and new, superior relations of production do not take their place before the material conditions of existence have matured in the womb of the old society itself. Therefore humankind always sets for itself only the tasks that it can solve, since closer examination shows that the task itself only arises where the material conditions for its solution are already at hand or at least in the process of being grasped. (Marx 1907: lvi)

Change entails conscious human action. Louis Althusser argued that capitalist reproduction dominates the base/superstructure relation. He claimed that ideology is pervasive and operates through ideological state apparatuses (ISAs). Ideology provides an "imaginary relation" to the relations of production that helps reproduce those relations rather than exposing their contradictions. The ISAs repress real understanding and reproduce the relations of production, leaving the base determinate in the last instance. By downplaying conscious, historical subjects and emphasizing a system of structures, Althusser removes the revolutionary subject from the metaphor and misrepresents Marx in a different way than the economic determinists.

SEE ALSO: Capitalism; Capitalism, Social Institutions of; Marx, Karl; Materialism

REFERENCE

Marx, K. (1907) [1859] *Zur Kritik der politischen Ökonomie* (*Towards the Critique of Political Economy*). Dietz, Stuttgart.

SUGGESTED READINGS

Althusser, L. (1972 [1969]) *Lenin and Philosophy, and Other Essays*, trans. B. Brewster. NLB, London.

Marx, K. (1970) [1859] *A Contribution to the Critique of Political Economy*, trans. S. Ryazanskaya. Progress Publishers, Moscow.

ROB BEAMISH

Baudrillard, Jean (1929–2007)

A highly original and influential French theorist, Baudrillard is difficult to situate in relation to traditional sociology and social theory. Initially associated with postmodern and poststructuralist theory, his work combines philosophy, social theory, and an idiosyncratic cultural metaphysics that reflects on key events of phenomena of the epoch. A sharp critic of contemporary society, culture, and thought, Baudrillard is often seen as a major guru of French postmodern theory, although he can also be read as a thinker who combines theory and social and cultural criticism in original and provocative ways, and as a writer who has developed his own style and forms of writing. He was an extremely prolific author who published over 50 books and commented on some of the most salient cultural and sociological phenomena of the contemporary era, including the erasure of the distinctions of gender, race, and class that structured modern societies in a new postmodern consumer, media, and high-tech society; the mutating roles of art and aesthetics; fundamental changes in politics, culture, and human beings; and the impact of new media, information, and cybernetic technologies on the creation of a qualitatively different social order, providing fundamental mutations of human and social life.

During the late 1960s, Baudrillard began publishing a series of books that would eventually make him world famous. Influenced by Lefebvre, Barthes, and a number of other French thinkers,

Baudrillard undertook serious work in the field of social theory, semiology, and psychoanalysis in the 1960s and published his first book, *The System of Objects*, in 1968 (1996), followed by a book on *The Consumer Society* in 1970 (1998), and *For a Critique of the Political Economy of the Sign* in 1972 (1981). Combining semiological studies, Marxian political economy, and sociology of the consumer society, Baudrillard began his lifelong task of exploring the system of objects and signs which forms our everyday life.

The early Baudrillard described the meanings invested in the objects of everyday life (e.g., the power accrued through identification with one's automobile when driving) and the structural system through which objects were organized into a new, modern society (e.g., the prestige or sign-value of a new sports car). Baudrillard claims that commodities are bought and displayed as much for their sign-value as their use-value, and that the phenomenon of sign-value has become an essential constituent of the commodity and consumption in the consumer society.

The discourse of "the end" signifies his announcing a postmodern break or rupture in history. We are now, Baudrillard claims, in a new era of simulation in which social reproduction (information processing, communication, knowledge industries, and so on) replaces production as the organizing form of society. For Baudrillard, modern societies are organized around the production and consumption of commodities, while postmodern societies are organized around *simulation* and the play of images and signs, denoting a situation in which codes, models, and signs are the organizing forms of a new social order where simulation rules.

Baudrillard's postmodern world is also one of radical *implosion*, in which social classes, genders, political differences, and once autonomous realms of society and culture collapse into each other, erasing previously defined boundaries and differences. If modern societies, for classical social theory, were characterized by differentiation, for Baudrillard postmodern societies are characterized by dedifferentiation, or implosion.

In addition, his postmodern universe is one of *hyperreality* in which entertainment, information, and communication technologies provide experiences more intense and involving than the scenes of banal everyday life, as well as the codes and models that structure everyday life. The realm of the hyperreal (i.e., media simulations of reality, Disneyland and amusement parks, malls and consumer fantasylands, TV sports, and other excursions into ideal worlds) is more real than real, whereby the models, images, and codes of the hyperreal come to control thought and behavior.

Baudrillard is an example of the "global popular," a thinker who has followers and readers throughout the world. Baudrillard's influence has been largely at the margins of a diverse number of disciplines ranging from social theory to philosophy to art history, thus it is difficult to gauge his impact on the mainstream of any specific academic discipline. He now appears in retrospect as a completely idiosyncratic thinker who went his own way and developed his own mode of writing and thought that will continue to provoke contemporary and future students of critical theory.

SEE ALSO: Hyperreality; Implosion; Postmodern Culture; Postmodern Social Theory; Semiotics; Simulation

SUGGESTED READINGS

Baudrillard, J. (1983a) *Simulations*. Semiotext(e), New York.

Baudrillard, J. (1993) [1976] *Symbolic Exchange and Death*. Sage, London.

Baudrillard, J. (2002) *The Spirit of Terrorism: And Requiem for the Twin Towers*. Verso, London.

Kellner, D. (1989) *Jean Baudrillard: From Marxism to Postmodernism and Beyond*. Polity Press and Stanford University Press, Cambridge and Palo Alto, CA.

Kellner, D. (ed.) (1994) *Jean Baudrillard: A Critical Reader*. Blackwell, Oxford.

DOUGLAS KELLNER

Beauvoir, Simone de (1908–86)

The French existentialist philosopher, writer, and social essayist Simone de Beauvoir is most widely known for her pioneering work *Le Deuxieme Sexe* (1949) or *The Second Sex*. Her exposé of woman as "Other" and her calling attention to the feminine condition of oppression as historically linked to motherhood are considered her major contributions to modern feminist thought. While not generally acknowledged as a sociologist, Beauvoir nevertheless contributed to sociology in *The Second Sex, The Coming of Age* (*La Vieillesse* 1970), a study of old age, and to a lesser extent, her writings on the media and death and dying. Simone de Beauvoir is also internationally read and widely known for her novels, autobiographies, and travelogues. Beauvoir's theorizing corrects androcentric biases found in earlier gender-neutral theoretical frameworks, particularly in her use of social categories to inform individually oriented philosophical theories of self-determination and freedom. She systematically examined the historically situated or lived experiences of women relative to men. Deeply influenced by the existential philosophy of her lifelong companion Jean-Paul Sartre, Simone de Beauvoir extended Sartrean existential philosophy to encompass social and cultural determinants of the human condition. She used existential philosophy, as a guide for understanding herself as a woman and as a framework for understanding the condition of women, more generally. True to her existentialist philosophy, Beauvoir's writings avoid any attempt to discover a single universal "truth" as prescriptive for intellectual or personal freedom for all women. Her efforts to understand women's historical oppression, contemporary situation, and future prospects drew from fiction and literary criticism, as well as from biology, historical anthropology, political economy, and psychoanalysis. However, Beauvoir found extant writings either erroneous or incomplete and developed her own distinctively sociological argument emphasizing the crucial feminist insight that, "One is not born, but rather becomes, a woman." Consistent with existentialist philosophy, Beauvoir saw the human condition as defined foremost by the freedom to choose, as humans are born with no fixed essence or nature. Despite this freedom, however, it is *external social forces* that undeniably shape transcendent possibilities for self creation. Thus for a woman to be defined as Other is to be defined as second to man, less than man, and for man's pleasure. Beauvoir's theorizing took a distinctively sociological dimension in *The Second Sex*, contributing to the social basis for the study of gender. Similarly, the scope of her research methodology contributed to revisionist history, as she theorized from sources and documentation from women themselves, including letters, diaries, autobiographies, case histories, political and social essays, and novels.

SEE ALSO: Feminism; Sex and Gender

REFERENCE

De Beauvoir, S. (1949) *The Second Sex*, trans. and ed. H. M. Parshley. Alfred A. Knopf, New York, 1953.

SUGGESTED READINGS

Bair, D. (1990) *Simone de Beauvoir: A Biography*. Touchstone, New York.

Deegan, M. J. (1991) Simone de Beauvoir. In: Deegan, M. J. (ed), *Women in Sociology: A Bio-bibliographical Sourcebook*. Greenwood Press, New York.

Walsh, M. (2000) Beauvoir, feminisms and ambiguities. *Hecate* (May): 26.

VICKY M. MACLEAN AND PATRICIA PARKER

behaviorism

Behaviorism was a dominant school of American psychological thought from the 1930s through the 1960s. Its principal founder, John B. Watson, clearly defined behaviorism as follows: "Psychology, as the behaviorist views it, is a purely objective branch of natural science. Its theoretical goal is the prediction and control of behavior. The behaviorist recognizes no dividing line between man and brute" (Watson 1914: 158). B. F. Skinner, who developed the dominant theory of behaviorism for 30 years, was squarely on the nurture side of the nature–nurture controversy and on the deterministic side of the free will–determinism issue. He disavowed favorite psychological constructs such as consciousness, freedom, indwelling agents, dignity, and creativity. In each case Skinner argued that these examples either represent constructs from one's own biological/environmental histories or are behaviors in which the antecedents (controlling agents) are not clearly understood.

Although Skinner's radical behaviorism is no longer a major player in psychological theory, the applications that his research fostered are very much a part of the contemporary scene. These applications span many areas in contemporary psychology, including clinical psychology and therapy. He gave us a strong hint of his application of learning called operant conditioning in his one and only novel, *Walden Two*, a book first published in 1948 and still in print. The novel represented Skinner's attempt to engineer a utopian society based upon Skinnerian operant principles. Sometimes called social engineering, Skinner's novel was his solution to the horrors of World War II. He hoped to engineer out of the human repertoire all negative emotions, leaving only the positive ones. This is an example of behavioral modification, and many of its elements (positive reinforcement, successive approximations, gradual change in behavior through desensitization) have been incorporated successfully in therapy today.

The principal set of events that led to the demise of behaviorism as a compelling theory was the growth of connectionism and the cognitive revolution of the 1970s, which was theoretically friendlier to the biological causes of behavior. More specifically, the Chomsky (1971)–Skinner (1957) debates of the 1960s concerning the origins and development of native languages sealed the fate of radical behaviorism, since Skinner was never able to deal with the irrepressible novelty of human speech. Young children usually speak grammatically and in novel form with each new utterance, a fact that is anathema to any learning paradigm of language acquisition.

The legacy of behaviorism for modern psychology was its insistence upon measurable behavior, thus transforming psychology from its introspective and subjective past into the world of scientific inquiry. This process allowed psychology to embrace new disciplines such as statistics and measurement theory in attempts to add legitimacy to its new endeavors at the expense of more humanistic approaches to psychology.

SEE ALSO: Social Learning Theory; Theory

REFERENCES

Chomsky, N. (1971) The case against B. F. Skinner. *New York Review of Books* (December 30): 18–24.

Skinner, B. F. (1948) *Walden Two.* Macmillan, New York.

Skinner, B. F. (1957) *Verbal Behavior.* Appleton-Century-Crofts, New York.

Watson, J. (1914) *Behavior: An Introduction to Comparative Psychology.* Holt, Rinehart, Winston, New York.

EVANS MANDES

belief

Belief is a key psychological and biographical phenomenon within sociological frames of religion. Thomas O'Dea (1966) pivots Max Weber's "process of rationalization" as essential to understanding belief and belief patterns surrounding religious experiences. With the historic dismissal of certain fantastical and mystical traditions as "irrational," rational theologies were developed to maintain the power of religious institutions. Rationalized theologies – developed via rationalization processes, i.e., "from *mythos* to *logos*" (p. 46) – are not necessarily philosophically or mathematically logical. However, these rationalization processes are legitimated via leadership role-play, i.e., clergy, clerics, priests, rabbis, and so on.

While O'Dea focuses on the structure – power – dimensions of belief, Peter Berger (1969) focuses on the social psychological dimensions. Within modern – as opposed to traditional – societies, religion transforms into a "free subjective choice," therefore losing "its intersubjectively obligatory character" (pp. 166–7). As this occurs, religious experiences no longer remain "external to the individual consciousness." Rather they are also experienced "*within* consciousness" (p. 167). Berger refers to this as the "consciousness of believers," i.e., belief.

Uniting both structural and social psychological perspectives, Weber (1993) defines belief as a committed seriousness to the "cognitive validity" of and "practical commitment" to a set of ideas, even at the expense of personal interests (p. xliii). As implied, this cognitive validity and practical commitment emerge through rationalization.

SEE ALSO: Church; Primitive Religion; Religion, Sociology of

REFERENCES

Berger, P. L. (1969) *The Sacred Canopy: Elements of a Sociological Theory of Religion.* Doubleday, New York.

O'Dea, T. F. (1966) *The Sociology of Religion.* Prentice Hall, Upper Saddle River, NJ.

Weber, M. (1993) *The Sociology of Religion.* Beacon Press, Boston, MA.

BEVERLY M. PRATT

bell curve

The bell curve provides a foundation for the majority of statistical procedures in sociology. Conceptually it is a histogram, but with such fine distinctions between outcomes that it is a line in the shape of a bell. Beneath this curve are all possible outcomes, with the outcomes on the x-axis and the y-axis describing the proportion or probability for each outcome. The "tails" of the curve extend indefinitely. The shape is symmetrical and unimodal, so that the distribution's mean, median, and mode are identical and in the center of the distribution. In the distribution one standard deviation from the mean is 34.13 percent of the area under the curve, two standard deviations is 47.72 percent of the area under the curve, and three standard deviations is 49.87 percent of the area under the curve. Since the distribution is symmetrical, the distance from the mean will be the same regardless of whether the standard deviations are above or below the mean.

The bell curve can be used for hypothesis testing. The central limit theorem states that, *even when individual scores are not normally distributed*, in random samples of a sufficient size, the distribution of sample means will be approximately normally distributed around the population mean. Thus, sociologists can examine the probability of producing a specific sample mean, based on a hypothesized population mean. If a sample mean is unlikely to occur based on the hypothesized population mean, the sociologist can reject the hypothesized population mean. Similarly, relationships between variables can be tested by studying how likely it would be to find a specific relationship in a sample if there was no relationship in the population.

SEE ALSO: Quantitative Methods

SUGGESTED READINGS
Agresti, A. & Finlay, B. (1997) *Statistical Methods for the Social Sciences*. Prentice Hall, Upper Saddle River, NJ.
Healey, J. F. (2005) *Statistics: A Tool for Social Research*. Thomson Wadsworth, Belmont, CA.

ALEX BIERMAN

Benjamin, Walter (1892–1940)

Walter Benjamin was a German literary critic and philosopher whose work draws on historical materialism and Jewish mysticism.

"The work of art in the age of mechanical reproduction" is perhaps Benjamin's most famous essay, and has become a central text for art history and cultural studies. Benjamin argues that our ability to reproduce art inaugurates a new age in which authenticity is made increasingly meaningless. Film in particular irrevocably transforms people's experiences of art, rendering contemplation and judgment impossible in the face of a stream of moving images. The consequences of the aestheticization of politics, Benjamin fears, are fascism and war.

The second aspect of Benjamin's work relevant for sociologists is the figure of the flâneur. Described in his essay "Paris, capital of the nineteenth century," the flâneur represents a particularly modern sensibility: a detached observer of urban life who is connected to yet not synonymous with the bourgeoisie.

While Benjamin only completed one book-length work in his life (*The Origin of German_Tragic Drama*), he spent 13 years collecting information for an exhaustive study of the Parisian arcades. The arcades, for Benjamin, embodied both the infrastructure and the ruins of capitalism. This unfinished masterwork, *Das Passagenarbeit*, is perhaps the best example of Benjamin's methodology.

In 1933 Benjamin became affiliated with the Institute for Social Research. When the Institute moved from Paris to New York, Benjamin made an attempt to emigrate to the USA via Spain. Upon trying to cross the Franco-Spanish border on September 25, 1940, a local official refused his group entry and threatened to turn them over to the authorities. Rather than face the Gestapo, Benjamin took his own life that night. The next day, the rest of his party was permitted to cross the border. Benjamin is buried in Port Bou, Spain.

SEE ALSO: Arcades; Consumption, Mass Consumption, and Consumer Culture; Critical Theory/Frankfurt School

SUGGESTED READINGS
Benjamin, W. (1968) *Illuminations: Essays and Reflections*, ed. H. Arendt, trans. H. Zohn. Schocken Books, New York.
Benjamin, W. (2002) *The Arcades Project*, ed. H. Eiland, trans. K. McLaughlin & R. Tiedemann. Belknap Press, Cambridge, MA.

MARGARET E. FARRAR

bifurcated consciousness, line of fault

Dorothy Smith's influential feminist essay, "A sociology for women," begins by calling attention to a "line of fault": "a point of rupture in my/our experience as woman/women within the social forms of consciousness – the culture or ideology of our society – in relation to the world known otherwise, the world directly felt, sensed, responded to, prior to its social expression" (1987: 49). She was pointing to the shift away from embodied experience into a governing, conceptual mode of consciousness associated with the "ruling relations" of industrial capitalism (1999). She saw in most women's lives in that period a distinctive subjectivity, a "bifurcated consciousness" organized by women's household labor and the tasks assigned to them, historically, in the occupational division of labor. As mothers, wives, community volunteers, nurses, secretaries, and so on, Smith argued, women engage with people's bodily existence, performing essential but invisible work within organizations. In such positions, women hold in their consciousness both embodied and institutional ways of seeing and thinking. When attention is directed to this disjuncture, a "line of fault" opens the organization of social life to analytic scrutiny.

Smith first wrote of women's bifurcated consciousness in the early 1970s (1974). Her injunction to "begin with women's experience" parallels in some ways the writings of other socialist feminists of the time, such as Sheila Rowbotham, Sandra Harding, and Donna Haraway, as well as Patricia Hill Collins's account of a "black feminist thought" tied to a position as "outsider within." Smith's distinctive approach also drew from the materialist method of Marx, the social psychology of George Herbert Mead, and the phenomenology of Alfred Schutz. In later writings, she and her students developed "institutional ethnography" (Smith 2005; 2006), an "alternative sociology" designed to explore the disjunctures of life within textually mediated societies.

SEE ALSO: Black Feminist Thought; Consciousness Raising; Double Consciousness;

Feminist Methodology; Feminist Standpoint Theory; Matrix of Domination

REFERENCES

Smith, D. E. (1974) Women's perspective as a radical critique of sociology. *Sociological Inquiry* 44: 7–13.

Smith, D. E. (1987) *The Everyday World as Problematic: A Feminist Sociology*. Northeastern University Press, Boston.

Smith, D. E. (1999) *Writing the Social: Critique, Theory, and Investigations*. University of Toronto Press, Toronto.

Smith, D. E. (2005) *Institutional Ethnography: A Sociology for People*. AltaMira, Lanham, MD.

Smith, D. E. (ed.) (2006) *Institutional Ethnography as Practice*. Rowman & Littlefield, Lanham, MD.

MARJORIE L. DE VAULT

biodemography

Although still a modest subfield within demography, biodemography is arguably the fastest growing part of demography and one of the most innovative and stimulating. The two main branches today involve: (1) biological-demographic research directly related to human health, with emphasis on health surveys, a field of research that might be called biomedical demography (or "epidemography" because it is a cross between demography and epidemiology), and (2) research at the intersection of demography and biology, an endeavor that will be referred to as biological demography. The first branch is characterized by demographers engaging in collaborative research with epidemiologists. This is very important, for both fields and for deeper understanding of human health. Researchers in the second branch face an even bigger challenge. Both of the two main branches of biodemography have many smaller branches. As in any innovative, rapidly growing interdisciplinary field, these smaller branches form tangles and thickets. Consequently, it is difficult to present a coherent structure for the evolving research in biodemography. One way to proceed is to make use of the hierarchical ordering of knowledge within biology. This provides a basis for ordering the research subdivisions that range from the molecular and cellular to the ecological and evolutionary. This ordering of biodemography by levels is useful because, as physiologist George Bartholomew noted over four decades ago, the significance of every level of biological organization can be found above and explanations of the mechanism in the level below. For example, the results of studies on different APOE gene alleles shed important light on molecular mechanisms for different risks of ischemic heart disease, Alzheimer's disease, and other chronic conditions, thus providing information on a person's individual risk of these chronic diseases and, in turn, informing the design of population surveys and model construction for epidemiological forecasting.

SEE ALSO: Biosociological Theories; Demography

SUGGESTED READING

Carey J. R. (2008) Biodemography: research prospects and directions. *Demographic Research* 19: 1749–58.

JAMES R. CAREY

biography

Biography has long been a part of the social sciences, having been introduced in different disciplines as "case histories" (psychiatry), "life histories" (anthropology), "personal documents" (sociology, psychology), and, more recently, "life stories" (linguistics, oral history), each focused on understanding individuals as the unit of analysis. Recent years have seen more interdisciplinary dialogue seeking to redefine the importance of individual lives to broader social and cultural phenomena. Anthropology, which made the recording of individual lives in an interview setting a cornerstone of ethnographic methodology, is but one of many disciplinary sources for narrative and biographical approaches in the social sciences today. But it remains a pivotal and innovative site for working through issues of representation through the modernist period and the period of postmodernist critique.

When the subject of a biography is alive, then there is clearly a process of exchange in which certain documents and confidences are offered in response to certain questions, and the accounts of the biographical subject and the writer come to construct each other. These new "collaborative biographies" mark a shift away from viewing the observer/observed relationship as "a scaffolding separate from content, to the view that the relationship is inseparable from content" (Freeman 1989: 432).

The intersection of history with personal experience and the individual life with the collective heritage makes biography a particularly significant locus for the analysis of historical memory. The microcosm of one person's biography does not disqualify each unique narrative from any hope of generalization, but can be seen precisely as part of its value. Each narrative enlarges our sense of human possibilities, and enriches our understandings of what it has meant to live in a particular society and culture.

In summary, three key "moments" can be observed in the use of biography in the social sciences.

First, a period when life histories were "collected" as data which would then be subjected to criteria of cultural typicality or, in other disciplines than anthropology, analyzed through schemata designed to destabilize conventional biographical assumptions while establishing diverse disciplinary imperatives. Second, a period when concerns of representing the humanity of the oppressed or the exotic took center stage, in what has retrospectively come to be seen as a kind of "tactical humanism." Third, what could be called the narrative turn, in which the primary concern has been how lived worlds have been constructed by language and made to mask certain unspoken relations of power, often articulated as part of a Foucauldian linkage of knowledge and power.

SEE ALSO: Ethnography; Methods; Phenomenology; Psychoanalysis

REFERENCE

Freeman, J. (1990) *Hearts of Sorrow: Vietnamese–American Lives*. Stanford University Press, Stanford, CA.

SUGGESTED READING

Bertaux, D. (1981) *Biography and Society: The Life History Approach in the Social Sciences*. Sage, London.

JANET HOSKINS AND GELYA FRANK

biosociological theories

Biosociological theories integrate biology into sociological explanations of human behavior. They do so by incorporating theoretical ideas and empirical discoveries from various branches of behavioral biology including evolutionary biology (especially *sociobiology* and *behavioral ecology*), ecology, ethology, neurobiology, endocrinology, primatology, and population genetics. Biosociological theories inform and guide the work of many contemporary *evolutionary sociologists*. Most biosociological theories can be grouped loosely into three categories: those that focus on: (1) the biological basis of evolved human nature, (2) the relationship between human nature and the evolutionary history of human societies, and (3) how an evolved "small-group ape" experiences and copes with life at the scale of industrial and post-industrial societal formations.

Recently, biosociological theorists have expressed increasing dissatisfaction with the *tabula rasa* ("blank slate") view of human nature. Like an increasing number of *evolutionary psychologists*, biosociological theorists have begun to subscribe to a new understanding of the human brain as densely populated by a rich array of *cognitive algorithms*, or innate mental mechanisms, that help generate complex patterns of social behavior. These cognitive algorithms are regarded as evolved adaptations to the selection pressures that were present in the ancestral environments in which humans evolved.

Biosociological theorists like Jonathan Turner and Alexandra Maryanski (2008) have reconstructed the *phylogeny* (evolutionary history) of human societies to explain how early *hominids* (primates ancestral to humans) evolved from living in fluid, transient groups with weak social ties to much more stable, durable groups with strong social ties. Their analysis attributes this transition to ecological changes that displaced early hominids from the security of arboreal environments into much more hazardous savannah environments. These new, open-plains environments subjected ancestral hominids to intensified selection pressures that eventually yielded much more highly organized and cohesive societies. The ability of early humans to overcome an ape heritage consisting of weak social ties and transient social relationships was made possible, in large part, by the evolutionary enhancement of human emotional capabilities.

Other biosociological theorists like Douglas Massey (2005) contend that humans are, by nature, a small-group ape that is best adapted to social life at the scale of small, hunter-gatherer bands. However, the past 10,000 years of evolution has produced societies with very large and densely concentrated populations and unprecedented degrees of organizational complexity. Thus, Massey describes contemporary humans as "strangers in a strange land," occupants of societies that are alien to the evolved psychological attributes of a small-group ape. Some biosociological theorists like Massey observe that humans living in large-scale, urban-industrial societies routinely organize themselves into social networks resembling those that typify smaller, pre-industrial societies. For example, the long-documented tendency of big-city residents to organize themselves into small-scale "urban villages," often constructed along ethnic-group lines, is construed as evidence of the persistence of a human preference for living in social networks at the scale of the hunter-gatherer band. Yet, while approximating a "tribal scale" social existence, such social networks do not always succeed in buffering humans from evolutionarily novel threats posed by contemporary societies. Various features of urban environments are seen as subjecting humans to unprecedented stresses, the effects of which can pose serious health threats to an organism arguably better adapted to ancestral patterns of societal organization.

SEE ALSO: Biosociology; Crime, Biosocial Theories of; Evolution; Society and Biology

REFERENCES

Massey, D. S. (2005) *Strangers in a Strange Land: Humans in an Urbanizing World.* W. W. Norton, New York.

Turner, J. H. & Maryanski, A. (2008) *On the Origin of Societies by Natural Selection.* Paradigm Publishers, Boulder, CO.

RICHARD MACHALEK

biosociology

In their broadest senses *sociobiology* and *biosociology* refer to the modern study of biology as it relates – within a Darwinian framework – to social behavior. Sociobiology is the better known term, made famous when the *New York Times* gave prominence to controversy surrounding a 1975 book, *Sociobiology: The New Synthesis*, by Harvard entomologist E. O. Wilson. Here biosociology is the preferred term because, etymologically, it refers to a subdiscipline within sociology, and it avoids some negative connotations of sociobiology.

Sociobiology introduced two theoretical problems that annoyed traditional sociologists. First is its focus on *ultimate* causes of human nature, ignoring those *proximate* mechanisms through which behavior operates. A well-known example is the selectionist theory of sex differences in mating strategy. Males produce offspring with an ejaculation; females must invest a prolonged period of pregnancy and nursing. Therefore males maximize genetic fitness (i.e., the representation of their genes in succeeding generations) by indiscriminately spreading their seed among many females, whereas females are selective, devoting their limited pregnancies to the finest sires and, if feasible, withholding sexual favors until they receive from the male a commitment for child support. The theory speaks of evolution long ago, ignoring those proximate influences – our psychology and culture – that are the explanatory currency of the social sciences. Thus it cannot explain or even query why one culture is polygamous, another monogamous; why marriages in some societies are arranged by parents and in others by romantic attraction; why divorce and birth rates are sometimes high, sometimes low.

Also, some of sociobiology's claims defy common observation. Most sociologists do not maximize their genetic fitness, instead limiting their children to two or less, and some "waste" resources by adopting unrelated infants.

The development of "evolutionary psychology" eliminated some of these annoyances. Its most important innovation has been to re-introduce proximate causation in the form of a thinking brain with specialized modules for parenting, emotional communication, kinship, mate choice, sex, aggression, child care, and so on.

Evolutionary psychologists emphasize that it is our minds that have evolved, not our disembodied behaviors. This is an ingenious corrective to sociobiology's exclusive focus on ultimate causes. With our mind as a proximate mechanism, it is easy to incorporate learning, socialization, and cultural differences. But evolutionary psychology introduces problems of its own. Its modular mind is a postulation that lacks empirical verification.

Also, evolutionary psychology usually ignores our nonhuman primate cousins. Consider, for example, the theory of male and female mating strategies, which should apply to apes as well as humans. But the hypothesized sex difference is not apparent in most apes, casting doubt on the theory's underlying reasoning.

Biosociology largely abjures speculations about ultimate causes, evolved in the unknowable past. Instead the focus is on proximate causes, e.g., the neurohormonal mechanisms underlying human behavior. Biosociology emphasizes that human behavior follows a primate pattern and therefore values comparative studies of other primate species, whereas analogs with insects, birds, and fish are regarded as too distant to be useful. Biosociology's research methods are diverse but usually have a tight link to theory. Biosocial hypotheses should be falsifiable by practical empirical means.

Few sociologists have requisite training in biology, so most relevant research is conducted in neighboring disciplines including psychology, primatology, anthropology, genetics, and experimental economics. Primatology has had the greatest impact, leaving no doubt that human behavior in face-to-face groups fits the general pattern of higher primates – with the supremely important addition of language-based cultures. The human body surface (facial appearance and expressions, physique, and postures) is now known to be an important component of social interaction and a powerful influence on life course. Beneath the body surface, the neurohormonal system affects, and is affected by, social interaction. Testosterone and cortisol have become important variables in studies of dominance and antisocial behavior. Neuroimaging pinpoints areas of the brain that are activated during certain tasks, showing, for example, that putting one's negative feelings of sadness or anger into words, as occurs in talk therapy, lessens the response of the amygdala, damping down the emotional distress. Behavioral genetics demonstrates that some personality traits, long thought to be determined by early childhood socialization, are strongly inherited and highly correlated in identical twins raised apart. Population geneticists, tracing specific variants of the Y chromosome in men, and mitochondrial DNA in women, infer the migratory paths of major ancestral groups of *Homo sapiens* during the past 50,000 years. This sampling of findings barely suggests the potential of biology to revise our understanding of human interaction.

SEE ALSO: Biosociological Theories; Evolutionary Sociology; Society and Biology

SUGGESTED READINGS

Barkow, J., Cosmides, L. & Tooby, J. (1992) *The Adapted Mind.* Oxford University Press, New York.

Goodall, J. (1986) *The Chimpanzees of Gombe.* Harvard University Press, Cambridge, MA.

Mazur, A. (2005) *Biosociology of Dominance and Deference.* Rowman & Littlefield, Boulder, CO.

Walsh, A. (1995) *Biosociology: An Emerging Paradigm.* Praeger, Westport, CT.

ALLAN MAZUR

bisexuality

There are at least four different meanings associated with the term bisexuality. Firstly, in early sexology bisexuality was conceived of as a primordial state of hermaphroditism prior to sexual differentiation. Secondly, bisexuality has been invoked to describe the co-presence of "feminine" and "masculine" psychological traits in a human being. Thirdly, bisexuality has provided the concept to account for people's propensity to be sexually attracted to both men and women. This is currently the most common understanding of bisexuality. Fourthly, bisexuality is frequently seen as a pervasive "middle ground" (of merged gender, sex or sexuality). This representation of bisexuality includes the notion that "we're all bisexual, really," which may imply either an essential androgyny or a universal "latent bisexuality" in the sense of an abstracted potential to love people of both genders (or irrespective of gender) (see Hemmings 2002).

Bisexuality plays a rather paradoxical role in the history of sexuality. Although it has been integral, if not central, to most modern theories of sexuality, it has rarely been acknowledged or taken seriously in or for itself. Steven Angelides (2000) shows that notions of bisexuality have been foundational elements of an emerging *economy of (hetero) sexuality* in various scientific discourses throughout the nineteenth and twentieth centuries, ranging from (evolutionary) biology and medical sexology to Freudian psychoanalysis.

Only the emergence of self-conscious and assertive bisexual social movement networks in many countries since the late 1970s has resulted in the consolidation of a bisexual identity. Bisexuals have been active in a range of social movements around gender and sexuality, in particular the feminist, lesbian and gay, S/M, polyamory, and queer movements. The marginalization of bisexuality in many environments (including gay male and lesbian feminist social and political spaces) has led many bisexuals to campaign around this aspect of their identity. Bisexual activists developed the concept biphobia to account for the specific forms of discrimination faced by bisexuals in various social contexts. Among others, biphobia entails a range of stereotypes such as the beliefs that bisexuals would be shallow, narcissistic, untrustworthy, morally bankrupt, promiscuous, incapable of monogamy, HIV carriers, fence sitters, etc. Biphobic representation intersects with other discriminatory discourses, in particular the ones around sexism, racism, and classism. It overlaps, but at the same time remains distinct from homophobia and lesbophobia.

SEE ALSO: Heterosexuality; Homosexuality; Sexuality; Coming-Out/Closets; Gay and Lesbian Movement; Gay/Homosexuality; Homophobia and Heterosexism; Identity and Sexuality; Lesbianism; Queer Theory

REFERENCES

Angelides, S. (2000) *A History of Bisexuality.* University of Chicago Press, Chicago, IL.

Hemmings, C. (2002) *Bisexual Spaces: A Geography of Sexuality and Gender.* Routledge, London.

SUGGESTED READINGS

Atkins, D. (ed.) (2002) *Bisexual Women in the Twenty-First Century.* Harrington Park Press, New York.

Klesse, C. (2007) *The Spectre of Promiscuity: Gay and Bisexual Non-Monogamies and Polyamories*, Ashgate, Aldershot.

Rodríguez Rust, P. (ed.) (2000) *Bisexuality in the United States: A Social Science Reader.* Columbia University Press, New York.

Storr, M. (1999) *Bisexuality: A Critical Reader.* Routledge, London.

CHRISTIAN KLESSE

black feminist thought

Black feminist thought is a collection of ideas, writings, and art that articulates a standpoint of and for black women of the African diaspora. It describes black women as a unique group that exists in a "place" in US social relations where intersectional processes of race, ethnicity, gender, class, and sexual orientation shape black women's individual and collective consciousness and actions. As a standpoint theory, black feminist thought conceptualizes identities as fluid and interdependent socially constructed "locations" within a historical context. It is grounded in black women's historical experience with enslavement, anti-lynching movements, Civil Rights and Black Power movements, sexual politics, capitalism, and patriarchy.

Distinctive tenets of black feminist thought include: (1) the legitimization of partial, subjugated knowledges as a unique, diverse standpoint; (2) black women's multiple oppressions resulting in ideologies and challenges that are unique; (3) black feminist consciousness as a self-reflexive process toward black women's liberation through activism; and (4) the replacement of deleterious images of black womanhood. Black feminist thought has been expressed historically through collective social and political activism (National Black Feminist Organization; Combahee River Collective). Black feminists assert that all black women have the common experience of negotiating oppression(s) despite occupying different social locations and possessing variable privileges.

Black feminists broke from mainstream feminists in the 1970s. At this time, black feminist thought began to reflect a provocative, sophisticated critique of the mainstream white women's movement and theorizations. Black feminist writings do not advocate a wholly separatist movement from mainstream feminism but do call for the inclusion of all women's experiences in scientific inquiry. Attention to the interlocking nature of race, ethnicity, gender, class, and sexual orientation over the course of time and geography is a recurrent theme in writings. The 1980s saw black feminists building a "praxis" bridge between the ivory tower and the community. Black feminist literature illuminated the historical contributions of black women in American civil rights and women's movements. In the 1990s and early twenty-first century, black women scholars also began to spotlight black women's experiences of intimate violence and resistance.

Black feminist thought is conducive to qualitative, quantitative, or mixed-method designs. Black feminists incorporate traditional data and non-traditional and non-literal data (e.g., diaries, creative arts) to document the personal experiences of participants. Methodological critiques have included the difficulty of operationalizing black feminist concepts and the lack of predictive power in regard to behavioral outcomes. Future research directions should include attempts to demonstrate black feminist thought's utility in empirical research.

SEE ALSO: Feminism; Feminist Standpoint Theory; Outsider-Within; Womanism

SUGGESTED READINGS

Collins, P. H. (1991) *Black Feminist Thought: Knowledge, Consciousness, and the Politics of Empowerment.* Routledge, New York.

Few, A., Stephens, D., & Rouse-Arnette, M. (2003) Sister-to-sister talk: transcending boundaries in qualitative research with black women. *Family Relations* 52: 205–15.

James, J. & Sharply-Whiting, T. D. (eds.) (2000) *The Black Feminist Reader*. Blackwell, Cambridge, MA.

APRIL L. FEW

Blau, Peter (1918–2002)

Peter Blau is one of the most influential figures in post-war American sociology. His long career and range of substantive interests span the range from small-groups and social exchange theory to organizational theory, the analysis of status attainment, and finally general sociological theory. In spite of its apparent "heterogeneity," it can be argued that a single strand runs through Blau's diverse body of work. For Blau, the study of the structural limits posed by large-scale distributions of actors, positions, and resources on the opportunities and choices of individuals constituted the central subject matter of sociology. Nevertheless Blau made seminal contributions to many sociological fields. His life's work can be divided into four major components: status attainment, his work on organizations, his exchange theory, and his macrostructural theory.

STATUS ATTAINMENT AND MOBILITY

Blau and Duncan's classic monograph *The American Occupational Structure* (1967) introduced to a sociological audience multiple regression and path analysis, which is today the bread and butter of quantitative sociology.

ORGANIZATIONAL THEORY

Blau's first major contributions to sociology were in the field of organizations. His first important publication – an elaboration of his dissertation research – was *Dynamics of Bureaucracy* (1955), which at the time formed part of a rising post-Weberian wave of organizational studies. This research consisted in exploring how far the received image of the Weberian bureaucracy as an efficient, mechanical system of roles, positions, and duties held up under close scrutiny in the empirical study of social interaction within organizations. Blau (1955) contributed to this strand of research by highlighting the ways in which the real life of the organization was structured along informal channels of interaction and socio-emotional exchange, and how the incipient status systems formed through these back-channels were as important to the continued functioning of these organizations as the formal status structure. Thus, Blau was primarily concerned with the interplay between formal structure, informal practices, and bureaucratic pressures and how these processes affect organizational change.

EXCHANGE THEORY AND SMALL GROUP BEHAVIOR

From his original study of social activity in bureaucracies, Blau developed a "microstructural" theory of exchange and social integration in small groups. His work on this type of non-economic exchange and its interaction with the status and power structure of the group (flows of advice, esteem, and reputation) would later become important in the influential formalization of exchange theory in the hands of Richard Emerson. To this day Blau is seen in social psychology (along with George Homans) as one of the intellectual progenitors of modern exchange theory in structural social psychology.

MACROSTRUCTURAL THEORY

For Blau (1977), social structure consisted of the networks of social relations that organize patterns of interaction across different social positions. For Blau, the basic components of social structure were not natural persons, but instead social positions. Thus, the "parts" of social structure are classes of people like men and women, rich and poor, etc. The relations between these components are none other than the actual network connections that may (or may not) obtain between members of different positions.

SEE ALSO: Exchange Network Theory; Merton, Robert K.; Organizations as Social Structures; Social Exchange Theory; Social Structure

REFERENCE

Blau, P. (1977) A macrosociological theory of social structure. *American Journal of Sociology* 83 (1): 26–54.

SUGGESTED READINGS

Blau, P. M. (1970) A formal theory of differentiation in organizations. *American Sociological Review* 35: 201–18.

Blau, P. M. (1974) Presidential address: parameters of social structure. *American Sociological Review* 39: 615–35.

OMAR LIZARDO

blockbusting

Blockbusting was prohibited by the Civil Rights (Fair Housing) Act of 1968, which declared it an illegal practice "for profit, to induce or attempt to induce" housing sales "by representations regarding the entry or prospective entry into the neighborhood of a person or persons of a particular race, color, religion, etc." (Section 804[e]). Blockbusting practices occurred sporadically throughout the twentieth century (sometimes under other names, like "panic peddling"), but reached their peak in the 1950s and 1960s when they served to accelerate massive racial change in residential areas in a large number of American cities.

Blockbusters functioned in settings where rigid patterns of residential segregation prevailed, resulting from private discrimination and institutionalized though real estate, banking, and governmental practices. They preyed upon the racial prejudices and fears of white residents by selling or renting to African Americans – or even by spreading rumors of black settlement – to panic property owners unwilling to accept residential integration. Such actions severely depressed housing values, enabling the operators to purchase houses well below prior market values. "White flight" often ensued, further depressing prices. In turn, blockbusters sold the properties to African American home-seekers, previously denied such residential options within the rigid confines of housing segregation, at mark-ups considerably in excess of normal business margins. The profit from such transactions was sometimes referred to as "the color tax" or "black tax," the price African Americans had to pay to gain new housing opportunity. Since prospective African American home buyers often lacked access to conventional financing, blockbusters also often profited from loan arrangements, which protected their investment, but left purchasers exposed to considerable risk.

Following adoption of the Fair Housing Act, flagrant instances of blockbusting have declined. The anti-blockbusting provisions of the law were upheld by a series of federal court decisions, and stronger enforcement mechanisms were added in subsequent federal legislation.

SEE ALSO: Racism, Structural and Institutional; Urban Policy; Urban Political Economy

SUGGESTED READING

Helper, R. (1969) *Racial Policies and Practices of Real Estate Brokers.* University of Minnesota Press, Minneapolis, MN.

W. EDWARD ORSER

Blumer, Herbert George (1900–87)

Herbert George Blumer emerged from a rural Missouri background and matured into an internationally acclaimed scholar (University of Missouri, BA 1921, MA 1922; University of Chicago, PhD, 1928) whose work defined a pioneering and enduringly relevant theoretical and methodological position in sociology and social psychology. He taught at Chicago from 1928 until 1951, leaving there to become the first chair of the Department of Sociology at the University of California at Berkeley, a post that he held until he retired in 1967. He earned the American Sociological Association's "Career of Distinguished Scholarship Award" in 1983. Among his many non-academic activities, he served with the Department of State's Office of War Information (1943–5) and chaired the Board of Arbitration for the U.S. Steel Corporation and the United Steel Workers of America.

Blumer's preeminent contribution to the social sciences is his formulation of a sociological perspective known as "symbolic interactionism." Based upon the philosophy and social psychology of George Herbert Mead and John Dewey, it is grounded in pragmatists' assumptions about human action and the reflexive socially grounded nature of the self.

Blumer's perspective and its associated empirically oriented methodological position characterize social action and social structures of any size or complexity as ongoing processes of individual and collective action predicated on the human capacity for self-indication and the construction of meaning. He rejects psychological behaviorism and deductively formulated, positivistic, and structural-functional sociology because they belittle the role of individuals in creating, sustaining, and changing the social world through self-indication, interpretation, and action. Instead, he affirms the significance of socially emergent individual and collective definition accompanying and directing attempts to handle life, which he depicts as an ongoing stream of situations. His non-reified conceptions of social structures as processes of action and interaction and of society as a "network of interaction" inform his analyses of macro- as well as micro-social phenomena.

Blumer (1969) set out his theory in *Symbolic Interactionism: Perspective and Method* as it pertains to human group life, action and interaction, objects, actors, and interconnections among individual and group lines of action. His perspective's three fundamental premises are: (1) people act individually and collectively on the basis of the meanings of "objects" in their world, (2) the meanings of these material (an automobile), abstract (justice), or social (a friend) objects are constructed in interactions that people have with one another, and (3) during interaction people use interpretive processes to alter these meanings.

Blumer, like G. H. Mead and John Dewey, characterizes acts as being built up from processes of self-indication and interpretation, which mediate between stimulus and response. Accordingly, he argues that we create symbols, or stimuli to which we attach meanings, and then act in regard to these meanings. Indication and the creation of objects are significant processes in so far as they inform the construction of action. Without self-indication and symbolic interaction, in fact, the social world would not exist.

Building upon this fundamental understanding, Blumer crafted what frequently became discipline-defining analyses of a wide range of subjects, including: research methods, collective behavior, industrialization, social movements, fashion, race relations, industrial and labor relations, social problems, morale, public opinion, social attitudes, social change, public sector social science research, and social psychology. Consistent with his perspective as a symbolic interactionist, and pertinent to his investigation of each of these areas and to social phenomena in general, he assigns social interaction and processes of individual and collective definition key roles in creating, maintaining, and changing social reality. This core element of his view remains a central feature of the perspective today.

SEE ALSO: Mead, George Herbert; Methods; Social Psychology; Symbolic Interaction

REFERENCE

Blumer, H. (1969) *Symbolic Interactionism: Perspective and Method.* Prentice Hall, Englewood Cliffs, NJ.

SUGGESTED READINGS

Blumer, H. (1939) Collective behavior. In Park, R. E. (ed.), *An Outline of the Principles of Sociology*. Barnes and Nobel, New York, pp. 219–80.

Blumer, H. (1990) *Industrialization as an Agent of Social Change*, ed. D. R. Maines & T. J. Morrione. Aldine de Gruyter, Hawthorne, NY.

Blumer, H. (2004) George Herbert Mead and human conduct, ed. T. J. Morrione. AltaMira Press, Walnut Creek, CA.

THOMAS J. MORRIONE

body and cultural sociology

Diverse theoretical traditions have been influential in the development of the contemporary sociology of the body, such as philosophical anthropology, Marxist humanism, and phenomenology. However, Michel Foucault (1926–84) has been a dominant influence in late twentieth-century historical and sociological approaches. Systematic sociological interest in the body began in the 1980s with *The Body and Society* (Turner 1984) and *Five Bodies* (O'Neill 1985). The journal *Body and Society* was launched in 1995 to cater for this expanding academic market.

Taking a wider perspective, there has been a persistent but erratic and uncertain interest from symbolic interactionism in body, identity, self, and interaction. Erving Goffman in *The Presentation of Self in Everyday Life* (1959) demonstrated the importance of the body for identity in disruptions to interaction. While the body began to appear in the study of micro-interactions, it also had major implications for the historical sociology of the norms of civilized behavior undertaken by Norbert Elias in *The Civilizing Process* (1978). Domestic utensils, such as the fork or spittoon, were important features of the regulation of manners through the training of the body.

Academic interest in the body was a response to significant changes in post-war society, namely, the rise of consumerism and the growth of leisure industries. In the late twentieth century, there was increasing social and economic emphasis on leisure and consumption rather than production. The growth of a new hedonistic culture was identified by Daniel Bell in *The Cultural Contradictions of Capitalism* (1976). Bell described new contradictions in a society that still required a disciplined labor force, but also encouraged and promoted hedonism through advertising, credit, and consumerism. Leisure industries, mass consumption, and extended credit have developed in tandem with the emphasis on youthfulness, activism, and the body beautiful. The body became a major conduit for the commodification of the everyday world and a symbol of the youth cultures of post-war society. In addition, aging, disease, and death no longer appear to be immutable facts about the human condition but contingent possibilities that are constantly transformed by medical science. Cosmetic surgery has become a growth industry in western societies through which the body can be constructed.

The post-war baby boomers became the social carriers of a popular culture that focused on the athletic, groomed, and sexual body as an icon of liberalism and the do-it-yourself culture that followed the events of 1968. There are two salient social phenomena that illustrate these developments in consumerism – the global growth of mass sport, especially international football, and popular dance. Popular dance forms have become a global "dancescape" in which the body is sexually charged as part of the gay scene. Finally, the playful body or the postmodern body is one that can be endlessly recreated and reshaped.

Research on the body is confronted by two distinctive options. There is either the cultural decoding of the body as a system of meaning that has a definite structure existing separately from the intentions and conceptions of individuals, or there is the phenomenological study of embodiment that attempts to understand human practices that are organized around the life course (of birth, maturation, reproduction, and death). The work of Pierre Bourdieu offers a possible solution to this persistent tension between meaning and experience or between representation and practice. Bourdieu's development of the notions of habitus and practice in *Outline of a Theory of Practice* (1977) provides research strategies for looking simultaneously at how status difference is inscribed on the body and how we experience the world through our bodies, which are ranked in terms of their cultural capital. This reconciliation of these traditions can be assisted by distinguishing between the idea of the body as representation and embodiment as practice and experience.

Since the 1980s, a variety of perspectives on the body have emerged. It is unlikely and possibly undesirable that any single theoretical synthesis will finally develop. The creative tension between seeing the body as cultural representation and experience will continue to produce innovative and creative research. There are, of course, new issues on the horizon which sociologists will need to examine: the posthuman body, cybernetics, genetic modification, and the genetic mapping of the body are obvious issues. The wealth and quality of this research suggest that the sociology of the body is not a passing fashion but an aspect of mainstream sociology.

SEE ALSO: Body and Sexuality; Body and Society; Consumption and the Body; Elias, Norbert; Emotion Work; Foucault, Michel; Gender, Consumption and; Sport and the Body

REFERENCES
O'Neill, John (1985) *Five Bodies: The Human Shape of Modern Society*. Cornell University Press, Ithaca, NY.
Turner, Bryan S. (1984) *The Body and Society: Explorations in Social Theory*. Blackwell, Oxford.

SUGGESTED READING
Foucault, Michel (1977) *The History of Sexuality*. Tavistock, London.

BRYAN S. TURNER

body and sexuality

The sex, gender and sexuality of the human body have both intertwined and disjointed histories within society, deeming some classifications as normal/healthy and others as pathological/sickly. Eighteenth-century science especially exacerbated the oppositional nature between categories of sex, gendered experiences and sexuality, constructing them as universally biologically determined.

The discovery of the hormone in 1905 provided the first biological justification for a difference between female and male bodies. Although the previous common belief was that there were two types of hormones – one for each sex – studies conducted in the 1920s found female hormones in male animals serving to refute this theory. After a number of theories were tested – among which were that female sex hormones either had no effect or that they caused disease and/or homosexuality – eventually it was understood that male and female sex hormones work cooperatively and even synergistically in both male and female bodies. While both sexes came to be defined by biological differences, the woman's body, defined primarily by her reproductive capabilities, took on an especially gendered understanding and became further medicalized according to a heteronormative model. The development of the contraceptive pill in the 1950s transformed female sex hormones into big business; simultaneously constructing heterosexual vaginal intercourse as the sexual norm resulting in pregnancy.

Simone de Beauvoir was the first to recognize and challenge the notion of the male sex as "normal" – casting the woman as the "other" in addition to distinguishing between sex and gender. Similar to the medical understanding of the female body as primarily defined by its reproductive capacity, female sexuality was understood as singularly oriented towards procreation – in contrast with a more lustful conception of male sexuality.

From the beginning to the middle of the nineteenth century, the Early Victorian ideal of true love dominated the discourse, idealizing true womanhood, true manhood and true "love" which was free of sensuality and defined by its purity. It was not until the latter half of the nineteenth century that "heterosexuality" and "homosexuality" came to be named and documented. Such a change in discourse has been argued to have resulted from the growth of the consumer economy which replaced the Victorian work ethic with a new pleasure ethic. In conjunction with this shift and rise of erotica, the male-dominated medical field defined male–female relationships as healthy and natural. This conception served to shift the rhetoric from the previous label of the sex-enjoying woman as a "nymphomaniac" to the sex-rejecting woman as suffering from "anesthesia." As such, the true love model was replaced with the normal love model, one which was replete with sexuality, subsequently assigning people a "sexual orientation."

Dr. Krafft-Ebing's influential *Psychopathia Sexualis* (1892) argued that people had a "sexual instinct" that was oriented towards members of the opposite sex with an inherent "purpose" for procreation. This publication served to naturalize heterosexuality subsequently establishing the "oppositeness" of sexes which was the source of the universal, normal, erotic attraction between males and females. Further the post-World War II "cult of domesticity" served to re-associate the woman with the home and men with work outside the home, thereby reifying this oppositeness of sexes – and their mutual dependence upon one another in order to maintain a family and/or household. These trends simultaneously pathologized same-sex attraction and nonconformist gender identities/behaviors.

Alfred Kinsey et al. (1948) challenged this hetero-homo dichotomy (and associated positive/negative values), in providing evidence that homosexual experiences are much more common than previously thought. He challenged the "natural" divide between heterosexuality and homosexuality and instead emphasized how "Only the human mind invents categories and tries to force facts into separate pigeon holes. The living world is a continuum." Gore Vidal further argued that "there is no such thing as a homosexual or heterosexual person. There are only homo- or heterosexual acts." These new perspectives challenged this dichotomy and the privileging of "heterosexuality" as normal or healthy behavior, relegating all other acts to the pathological bin.

SEE ALSO: Body and Cultural Sociology; Body and Society; Compulsory Heterosexulity; Gender, the Body and; Sexuality; Sexuality Research: History

REFERENCES

Kinsey, A., Pomeroy, W. B. & Martin, C. E. (1948) *Sexual Behavior in the Human Male*. W. B. Saunders, Philadelphia.

SUGGESTED READINGS

Beauvoir, S. de (1973) *The Second Sex*. Vintage Books, New York.

Foucault, M. (1978) *The History of Sexuality, Vol. 1: An Introduction*. Vintage Books, New York.

MICHELLE SMIRNOVA

body and society

Since the late 1980s there has been growing interest in the sociology of the body. The sociology of the body has been divided analytically into two distinctive, often contradictory, approaches. These two traditions represent alternative answers to the question: is the human body socially constructed? In social constructionist approaches, the body is treated as a system of cultural representations. In the phenomenological tradition, the "lived body" is studied in the everyday world of social interaction.

The body is often studied as a cultural representation of social life. In this sociological and anthropological tradition, research considers the ways in which the body enters into political discourse as a representation of power, and how power is exercised over the body. This approach to the body, which has been dominated by the legacy of Michel Foucault, is concerned with questions of representation and control in which diet is for example a regulation or government of the body. The Foucauldian perspective is not concerned to understand our experiences of embodiment; it does not aim to grasp the lived experience of the body from a phenomenology of the body.

The principal starting point for an analysis of the lived body has been the research of the French philosopher Maurice Merleau-Ponty. In the *Phenomenology of Perception* (1982) he examined how perception of reality occurs from the specific location of our body, and hence he showed how cognition is always an embodied perception of the world. Phenomenology is a critique of the dualism of the mind and body, in which body is seen to be passive and inert. Research inspired by the phenomenological tradition has been important in showing the intimate connections between body, experience, and identity. For example, traumatic experiences of disease have a major impact on self-perception and identity, and hence loss of a body part can have devastating consequences for self-identity. This division between the body as representation and as experience has dominated the sociological debate about the body, and there have been many attempts to reconcile this difference.

While there is therefore a sociological and anthropological tradition which examines the body as a symbolic system, we can also examine how human beings are embodied and how they learn a variety of cultural practices that are necessary for walking, sitting, dancing, and so forth. The study of embodiment has been the particular concern of anthropologists who have been influenced by the concept of "body techniques" (Mauss 1973). These anthropological assumptions have in turn been developed by Pierre Bourdieu through the concepts of hexis and habitus in which our dispositions and tastes are organized. For example, within the habitus of social classes, Bourdieu showed in *Distinction* (1984) that the body is invested with symbolic capital in which the body is a living expression of the hierarchies of social power. The body is permanently cultivated and represented by the aesthetic preferences of different social classes. The different sports that are supported by different social classes illustrate this form of distinction. Weightlifting is part of the habitus of the working class; mountaineering, of upper social strata.

If the body is understood exclusively as a system of cultural representation, it becomes very difficult to develop an adequate sociology of the body as lived experience. Sociologists have therefore become interested in bodily performances, which cannot be grasped simply as static cultural representations.

The contemporary anthropology and sociology of the body has also been continuously influenced by feminist social theory. Simone de Beauvoir's *The Second Sex* (1972) was a major contribution to the study of the patriarchal regulation of the female body. Feminist theories of the body have employed social constructionism to show how the differences between male and female bodies, that we take for granted as if they were facts of nature, are socially produced. More recently, there has been increasing interest in the question of men's bodies, health, and masculinity.

The underlying theory of gender inequalities was the idea of patriarchy and much empirical research in sociology has subsequently explored how the social and political subordination of women is expressed somatically in psychological depression and physical illness. Creative scholarship went into historical research on body image, diet, obesity, and eating disorders.

SEE ALSO: Body and Cultural Sociology; Body and Sexuality; Bourdieu, Pierre; Disability as a Social Problem; Foucault, Michel; Sex and Gender

REFERENCE

Mauss, M. (1973) Techniques of the Body. *Economy and Society* 2: 70–88.

SUGGESTED READINGS

Featherstone, M., Hepworth, M., & Turner, B. S. (eds.) (1991) *The Body: Social Processes and Cultural Theory*. Sage, London.

Foucault, M. (1973) *The Birth of the Clinic: The Archaeology of Medical Perception*. Tavistock, London.

Turner, B. S. (1984) *The Body and Society: Explorations in Social Theory*. Blackwell, Oxford.

BRYAN S. TURNER

Bourdieu, Pierre (1930–2002)

Born in August 1930, Pierre Bourdieu followed an adventurous life trajectory from rural southern-western France (at the foot of the Pyrénées mountains) to a fruitful educational career and his enrolment at the prestigious École Normale Supérieure as a philosophy major. Against the spirit of his time, overwhelmingly characterized by Sartrean existentialism, early Bourdieu focused on the study of logic and the history of science under Alexandre Koyré, Jules Vuillemin, Eric Weil, Martial Guéroult, Gaston Bachelard, and Georges Canguilhem.

His military service in Algeria and his systematic engagement in anthropological work on Kabylia, mainly focusing on the structural effects of power and stratification within the context of colonialism and native cultural practices, strongly prompted him to turn to the disciplines of ethnology, sociology, and statistics. This was, however, a reflexive turn because, at about the same time, Bourdieu directed the newfound instruments and tools of social science back onto his own childhood village in a parallel effort to better understand *both* the collapse of the European peasant society (during the postwar decades) *and* the specificity/peculiarity of the sociological gaze itself.

Bourdieu's long-term empirical field studies served as a useful springboard for his groundbreaking *Outline of a Theory of Practice* (1977), where he sophisticatedly explains his signature concern for a relational method of sociological work based on *reflexivity* – that is, a continuous turn of one's sociological tools upon one's scientific practice, so as to critically reflect on the wider social conditions and concrete operations of construction of the object. This particular epistemological need to master (in a fashioned way) the various distortions that the analytic posture (the *scholastic point of view*) implicitly introduces in the mutual relation between the subject and the object (the observer and the observed) constitutes the cornerstone of Bourdieu's lifework.

The circular dialectic between actual social life and the relevant sociological accounts, as well as between symbolic structures and the actions of social agents, was strategically designed to resolve the old and persistent dilemmas of sociology: naturalism versus anti-naturalism, objectivism versus subjectivism, quantity versus quality, structure versus agency, culture versus practice, determination versus freedom.

Most importantly, Bourdieu insisted on the existence of *both* invisible objective structures *and* agents' subjective interpretations of their lived experiences and situations. The former involves the dynamic and anti-reificatory/anti-essentialist conception of *social fields* – that is, the designation of relatively autonomous spaces of hidden forces and patterned struggles over specific forms of authority (such as *cultural capital*, a generalized theorization of capital as congealed and convertible "social energy"). The latter involves the Aristotelian-Thomist conception of *habitus* to further elaborate an anti-mechanistic, anti-rationalist, and dispositional philosophy of action as springing from socially shaped (power loaded) *and* individually embodied (mental) schemata of perception and appreciation.

Late Bourdieu entered the public sphere to critically engage major political issues and used his carefully developed concepts and research to illuminate social problems, over against a growing political apathy, the naturalization of *doxa* (the attitude of everyday life) and the increasing mediatization of public intellectuals.

Contrary to the dominant trends of postmodernism, Bourdieu believed not only in social science as a unifying knowledge project, but also in sociology's unexhausted capacity to "inform a 'rational utopianism' needed to salvage institutions of social justice from the new barbarism of the unfettered market and withdrawing state" (Wacquant 2002: 556).

SEE ALSO: Cultural Capital; Epistemology; Habitus/Field; Knowledge, Sociology of; Micro-Macro Links; Objectivity; Power; Reflexivity; Structure and Agency

REFERENCES

Bourdieu, P. (1977) *Outline of a Theory of Practice*. Cambridge University Press, Cambridge.

Wacquant, L. (2002) The sociological life of Pierre Bourdieu. *International Sociology* 17, 4, 549–56.

SUGGESTED READING

Bourdieu, P. (1984) *Distinction: A Social Critique of the Judgment of Taste*. Harvard University Press, Cambridge, MA.

CHARALAMBOS TSEKERIS

bourgeoisie and proletariat

The *Communist Manifesto*'s powerful imagery has permanently identified Marx with "bourgeoisie," "proletariat," and "class struggle" even though, he maintained, Adam Smith, David Ricardo, James Mill, and J. B. Say, among others, were first to identify the struggles of "the three great classes" – landed property and the capitalist and working classes – as central to political economy.

"Bourgeois" began as a twelfth-century, French, juridical term designating citizens or freemen in a city or burgh. During the late seventeenth century, "bourgeoisie" identified members of the emerging third estate and by 1789 connoted an entrepreneurial class (Thierry 1856). Merging bourgeoisie, the capitalist class, and a particular epoch of industrialization and exploitation into one image, Marx and Engels politicized the term. "Proletarians" originally identified the poorest Roman citizens who had no resources other than their children (*proles*). In 1762, Rousseau (1966: 157) revived *prolétaries* to describe members of "the lowest social class" – an image that resonated through 1789. By 1830, proletariat was increasingly associated with the industrial, working class and incorporated into German and English vernacular and political writing. In December 1842, Engels (Marx and Engels 1985: 442) noted that industry created wealth along with "absolutely poor people, who live from hand to mouth" – "proletarians." Marx (Marx and Engels 1982: 181–2) used Engels and Moses Hess's *Deutsche-Französiche Jahrbücher* contributions and his critique of Hegel's *Philosophy of Right* to identify the proletariat as a particular "estate [*Stand*] of society." Through "the formation [*Bildung*] of a class with *radical chains*, a class of bourgeois society which is no class of bourgeois society," it was "the *positive* possibility for German emancipation." The *Manifesto* identified the proletarianization – immiseration and mechanized exploitation – of workers as critical ingredients for social revolution.

SEE ALSO: Capitalism; Class Conflict; Marx, Karl

REFERENCES

Marx, K. and Engels, F. (1982) *Marx–Engels Gesamtausgabe* (*Marx–Engels Complete Works*) part 1, vol. 2. Dietz, Berlin.

Marx, K. and Engels, F. (1985) *Marx–Engels Gesamtausgabe* (*Marx–Engels Complete Works*) part 1, vol. 3. Dietz, Berlin.

Rousseau, J. J. (1966) [1762] *Du contrat social*. Garnier-Flammarion, Paris.

Thierry, A. (1856) *Essai sur l'histoire de la formation et des progrès du tiers état*. Furne, Paris.

ROB BEAMISH

brand culture

Brand research emerged from the allied fields of management, marketing, and strategy, which generally emphasize pragmatic models of brand "effects" driven by quantitative analysis. Recently, sociologists, anthropologists, and geographers have looked at brands from critical perspectives, acknowledging the importance of brands in society, and providing a necessary counterpoint to managerial and psychological views of branding. Brands are not only mediators of cultural meaning – brands themselves have become ideological referents that shape cultural rituals, economic activities, and social norms. Furthermore, brands may pre-empt cultural spheres of religion, politics, and myth, as they promote an ideology linked to political and theological models that equate consumption with happiness

Brand culture refers to the cultural influences and implications of brands in two ways. First, we live in a branded world: brands infuse culture with meaning, and branding profoundly influences contemporary society. Second, brand culture constitutes a third dimension for brand research – brand culture provides the necessary cultural, historical and political grounding to understand brands in context. In other words, neither managers nor consumers completely control branding processes – cultural codes constrain how brands work to produce meaning and value. The brand culture perspective sheds light on the gap often seen between managerial intention and market response.

If brands exist as cultural, ideological, and sociological objects, then understanding brands requires tools developed to understand culture, ideology, and society, in conjunction with more typical branding concepts, such as *brand equity*, *strategy*, and *value*. The brand culture concept acknowledges brands' representational and rhetorical power both as valuable cultural artifacts and as engaging and deceptive bearers of meaning, reflecting broad societal, cultural, and ideological codes.

SEE ALSO: Brands and Branding; Commodities, Commodity Fetishism, and Commodification; Consumer Society; Consumption; Shopping

SUGGESTED READINGS

Bently, L., Davis, J., & Ginsburg, J. (eds.) (2008) *Trade Marks and Brands: An Interdisciplinary Critique*. Cambridge University Press, Cambridge.

Holt, D. B. (2004) *How Brands Become Icons: The Principles of Cultural Branding*. Harvard Business School Press, Boston.

Schroeder, J. E. (2005) The artist and the brand. *European Journal of Marketing* 39: 1291–305.

Schroeder, J. E. & Salzer-Mörling, M. (eds.) (2006) *Brand Culture*. Routledge, London.

JONATHAN E. SCHROEDER

brands and branding

Brands are the names, signs, and symbols designed to identify the offerings of one producer from those of the competition. As such, brands can be distinguished from the more generic constructs of goods and services. Brands and branding have played a crucial role in the development of market economies by allowing producers a way to differentiate similar offerings. Brands have also profoundly changed the ways in which consumers make consumption decisions, relate to the market, define themselves, and interact with other consumers. They can be considered one of the chief sources of meaning in modern consumer culture.

Branding is a young discipline which evolved considerably in the twentieth century. In recent decades the practice of branding has been applied extensively (and well beyond packaged goods), being used on museums, political parties, universities, and religions. Recent decades have also witnessed a dramatic evolution in the ways in which brands are researched and understood. Marketing has its roots in economics and psychology. As a consequence of this lineage, brands were long studied from perspectives which stressed individual, passive, and rational consumers. Recently, the fields of marketing and consumer behavior have embraced sociological and anthropological perspectives. These perspectives treat brands as culturally embedded, social creations and view consumers (and their various social aggregations) as active interpreters and co-creators of brands.

Large brands, particularly global, multinational brands have become the target of a great deal of criticism and opposition, often seen as being emblematic of and responsible for the contemporary consumer society and its impact on global and local cultures, media, the environment, and human rights. There has been a growing anti-branding movement that is reflected in the guerilla anti-marketing actions of groups like AdBusters, the Billboard Liberation Front, and the Church of Stop Shopping.

SEE ALSO: Consumer Society; Consumption

SUGGESTED READINGS

Holt, D. B. (2002) Why do brands cause trouble? A dialectical theory of consumer culture and branding. *Journal of Consumer Research* 29 (June): 70–90.

Klein, N. (1999) *No Logo: Taking Aim at the Brand Bullies*. Picador, New York.

Muñiz, A. M. Jr. & O'Guinn, T. C. (2001) Brand community. *Journal of Consumer Research* 27 (March): 412–32.

ALBERT M. MUÑIZ, JR.

Braverman, Harry (1922–1976)

Harry Braverman, journalist, publisher, and a director of Monthly Review Press (1967–76), is best known for his book *Labor and Monopoly Capital*, published in 1974. This helped to continue the Marxist tradition within class theory when current analysis was centering on the rise of the middle class and the increasingly diamond-shaped nature of the class structure.

In Braverman's version of Marxist theory, the capitalist labor process, geared as it was to profitable production through generating more value from workers than is returned in the form of wages, had brought the worker and the labor process under the direct control of the capitalist and this has meant the deskilling of jobs and individuals. The industrialization of the twentieth century had through the scientific study of work and the assembly line created jobs with minimal training times and very short job cycles (often well under a minute).

A central message of Braverman for the late twentieth century was that the advent of new technologies (computerized or otherwise), the increasing employment in service jobs, and modern participative management approaches would continue the deskilling trend, and not reverse it as many anticipated.

The major criticism that has been made of the deskilling thesis is that control of labor need not become an end in itself for management and the achievement of its prime objective – profitability – may not always be furthered by deskilling work. For example, the number of workers may be reduced by increasing the discretion of a smaller core workforce; or more fluid forms of work organization may aid the profitable adjustment to fluctuating product market conditions and new technological opportunities.

Nevertheless, a key legacy of Braverman was to ensure that scientific management and its effects on workers were not increasingly treated as simply a benchmark of the first era of mass production. Much work in the twenty-first century remains low skilled: there have been clear cases where technology has reduced the skill level required in particular jobs and the discretion given to individuals, and many of the jobs created with the great growth in the service sector are low skilled, e.g., those in fast-food chains or call centers.

SEE ALSO: Division of Labor; Fordism/Post-Fordism; Labor Process; Taylorism; Work, Sociology of

SUGGESTED READING

Braverman, H. (1984) *Labor and Monopoly Capital: The Degradation of Work in the Twentieth Century*. Monthly Review Press, New York.

STEPHEN WOOD

British Sociological Association

The British Sociological Association (BSA) is the national learned society for sociology. It was founded in 1951, when sociology was starting to develop in British universities, and expanded rapidly as sociology expanded. It now has a wide range of functions (not, as in some associations, including the certification of sociologists' qualifications). It both organizes activities for sociologists, and represents them in the wider society.

Membership is open to all sociologists, and to other interested individuals; most members are university staff and students or researchers outside universities. Subscription rates are related to income, reflecting egalitarian principles also shown in its broader concern for gender equality. Funding also comes from the profits from publications and conferences.

There is an annual BSA conference, with distinguished plenary speakers and other papers in many parallel sessions, attended by several hundred participants. The association also runs over 40 study groups on specialist fields, such as sociology of education; the Medical Sociology group is particularly strong. The first BSA journal, *Sociology*, started in 1967; this was followed by *Work, Employment, and Society* in 1987, the electronic journal *Sociological Research OnLine* in 1996, and *Cultural Sociology* in 2007. A members' newsletter appears three times a year. Summer schools for graduate students, and other training activities, are regularly organized. Codes of practice, on subjects such as the ethics of research practice, guidelines on non-sexist language, and postgraduate research supervision, have also been promulgated. Other activities have arisen from the felt need to respond to external situations, often in cooperation with other learned societies on national issues of policy for social science.

For fuller details, see the BSA website, www.britsoc.co.uk.

SEE ALSO: American Sociological Association; Professions, Organized

SUGGESTED READING

Platt, J. (2000) *The British Sociological Association: A Sociological History*. Taylor and Francis, London.

JENNIFER PLATT

Buddhism

Buddhism is a neologism, created in Europe in the middle of the nineteenth century CE, from the Sanskrit word "Buddha," literally the awakened one. It is derived from an epithet attributed to Siddharta Gautama. Gautama was born in Northern India and most scholars estimate he lived between 563 and 483 BCE. The term Buddha defines all those beings who succeed through their own spiritual merits in being released from worldly pain to gain eternal bliss and omniscience.

In presenting himself as a model, the Buddha provides the disciple with all the indications needed to emulate him completely. This is something which occurs more through the seduction of conviction than through a process of persuasion based solely on his inscrutable superiority. The community of the emulator-disciples is called sangha, and together with the Buddha and his dharma forms the so-called triple gem (triratna), the foremost elements of this tradition.

Anyone who undertakes to travel the path leading to nirvana realizes from the first steps that no one else can travel this demanding path in his or her stead. All of the Buddha's teachings hinge on this premise and the emphasis returns time and time again to the central position of individual responsibility; for the Buddha is first and foremost the master (guru) who expounds the theoretical and practical means that can be used to achieve liberation.

SEE ALSO: Religion, Sociology of

SUGGESTED READINGS

Phra Prayuth, P. (1995) *Buddhadharma: Natural Laws and Values for Life*. SUNY Press, Albany, NY.

Polichetti, M. A. (1993) The spread of Tibetan buddhism in the west. *Tibet Journal* 18 (3): 65–7.

Tenzin, G. (14th Dalai Lama) (1995) *The World of Tibetan Buddhism: An Overview of Its Philosophy and Practice*. Wisdom Publications, Boston, MA.

MASSIMILIANO A. POLICHETTI

built environment

The *built environment* consists of all elements of the human-made physical environment. Commonly treated as wholly discrete from and in juxtaposition against the "natural environment," Dunlap and Catton's (1983) distinction between the "built," the "modified," and the "natural" environments critically captures the intermediate and continuous possibilities between and among these divisions.

Use of the term commonly diverges across disciplines, applications, and intended scale. Within engineering the built environment typically references infrastructural elements, technology, and systems (e.g., roads, bridges, depots; activities, technologies, practices, and structures implicated in the generation, transmission, and delivery of energy, sewerage/sanitation, communication, information). The building trades and applied architects and designers more narrowly address site planning, design, and materials. Alternatively, planners, urban designers, developers, and social scientists frequently use the term in a more inclusive, aggregated, and theoretical manner.

In recent years, two broad themes have gained prominence vis-à-vis the discourse of the built environment: an environmental imperative concerning development and sustainability that addresses its consequences for the natural environment; and its role in shaping human behavior.

SEE ALSO: Urban Space

REFERENCE

Dunlap, R. E. & Catton, W. R. (1983) What environmental sociologists have in common (whether concerned with "built" or "natural environments"). *Sociological Inquiry* 53 (2/3): 113–35.

SUGGESTED READING

Crysler, C. G. (2003) *Writing Spaces: Discourses of Architecture, Urbanism, and the Built Environment, 1960–2000*. Routledge, New York.

JOEL A. DEVINE

bureaucracy

Bureaucracy offers a way of organizing the administration of human affairs. It refers to a structure of offices or a process of formulating and implementing policy. Bureaucracies typically make binding decisions and thus embody a form of power.

The first major theorist of bureaucracy was Georg Friedrich Hegel, though bureaucracy only became a major subject of investigation in the work of Max Weber. Weber formulated the classic model of bureaucracy, characterized by hierarchy of command, specialized tasks, rules for decision-making, specialized training, and professional impartiality. For Weber, bureaucracy promoted administrative efficiency, but it could also pursue its own interests and clash with political mandates. He was in fact a sharp critic of bureaucracy, and unlike Hegel, he suggested that it presented a number of problems for modern society and the nation-state.

At the root of these problems is the instrumental rationality that bureaucracy embodies, making it an especially formidable type of control. The technical advantage of bureaucracy is its efficiency or the logical adaptation of means to ends, but at the expense of an unconstrained discussion of the ends themselves. Some writers have expressed concerns that the proliferation of bureaucratic rule represents a step toward total domination and the mechanization of life. Others have worried that bureaucratization seems inevitable and defies resistance because it is promoted by converging economic, political, and technical factors. In actuality bureaucracies do not conform to a single logic or a monolithic type, but assume different forms conditioned by social, cultural, and political considerations. They evolve informal patterns of communication and innovation. Technological changes in post-industrial society, such as rapid electronic communications, can even seem to promise a way of circumventing hierarchical bureaucratic processes. In light of such contrasting observations, the question of bureaucracy's compatibility with democratic governance is certain to endure as a concern in modern society.

SEE ALSO: Bureaucratic Personality; Rational Legal Authority; Weber, Max

SUGGESTED READING

Blau, P. & Meyer, M. (1987) *Bureaucracy in Modern Society*, 3rd edn. McGraw-Hill, New York.

Weber, M. (1968) [1922] *Economy and Society*. Bedminster, New York.

LAWRENCE A. SCAFF

bureaucratic personality

In his seminal work on the dysfunctions of bureaucracy, Robert Merton suggested that the values and attitudes necessary for the bureaucratic official to make a useful contribution are embraced to such a degree that the needs of the organization become secondary to the workings of the bureaucracy itself. Attention switches from the goals of the organization to the details of the control system. Rules become ends in themselves rather than means to ends, and are applied in a ritualistic manner regardless of circumstances. Rigid compliance with formal procedures, and a punctilious insistence on observing regulations, may cause the bureaucrat to lose sight of what really needs to be done. Behavior becomes so rule oriented that it is impossible to satisfy clients, giving rise to pejorative connotations of impersonality and petty officialdom. Merton saw the bureaucrat as having internalized an externally rationalized order that yields a relatively stable pattern of stimulus-response connections. This pattern is widely regarded as constituting personality.

Merton observed that the sentiments associated with the bureaucratic personality emanate from several sources. One is the bureaucrat's career structure. Rewards resulting from conformity, such as regular salary increases and pension benefits, cause the individual to overreact to formal requirements. Moreover, fixed progression keeps competition between colleagues to a minimum, and encourages an esprit de corps that often takes on a higher priority than work objectives. Another is the tendency for bureaucratic procedures to become "sanctified," the official performing them in an impersonal manner according to the demands of the training manual rather than the requirements of individual cases. Additionally, administrators are so mindful of their organizational status that they often fail to discard it when dealing with clients, thus giving the impression of a domineering attitude.

SEE ALSO: Bureaucracy; Merton, Robert K.; Rational Choice Theories; Weber, Max

SUGGESTED READINGS

Allinson, C. W. (1984) *Bureaucratic Personality and Organization Structure*. Gower, Aldershot.

Merton, R. K. (1940) Bureaucratic structure and personality. *Social Forces* 18: 560–8.

CHRISTOPHER W. ALLINSON

C

capital punishment

In both the USA and the world there are few punishments that are as old or as controversial as the punishment of death. In the international community the death penalty is as old as the code of King Hammaurabi of Babylon which called for capital punishment for some 25 different crimes. In the USA use of capital punishment dates to at least 1608 when Captain George Kendall of the Jamestown colony in Virginia was executed for allegedly being a Spanish spy. Today the death penalty still exists, though it is not as pervasive or as frequently used as in the past. As of 2009 there were 91 countries in the world that have abolished the death penalty as a possible punishment for any crime, 11 that have abolished it for "ordinary crimes" but retain it for others such as treason, and 33 more countries that have not officially abolished it but can be considered to have abolished the death penalty in practice in that they have not executed anyone since the 1990s. In total, there are 135 countries around the world that have abolished the death penalty for ordinary crimes either in law or in practice. There are 62 countries that have retained the death penalty for ordinary crimes: among these are China, Japan, Libya, Egypt, Iran, Afghanistan, Pakistan, and the USA. Most of these international executions have occurred in China.

Although the USA is officially a "death penalty country," there is a great deal of diversity in its use with a handful of states using the death penalty relatively frequently, some using it infrequently and some that are abolitionist with no death penalty. As of January of 2009 there were 36 states that had the death penalty as a possible punishment (2 of these states, however, have not executed anyone since 1976), and 14 states (plus the District of Columbia) that have no death penalty. Within death penalty states there is great variation in its use. The rate of execution is as high as 0.235 per 10,000 population in Oklahoma to 0.002 in Colorado, a ratio of approximately 117 to 1. Clearly, then there is a great deal of heterogeneity across death penalty states in how aggressively it is imposed.

On January 17, 1977, the first execution in the USA in almost ten years took place when Gary Mark Gilmore was executed by firing squad in the state of Utah. Gilmore was what has become known as a "voluntary" execution because he surrendered his legal right to appeal his death sentence, and his death begins the modern era of the death penalty in the United States. Since the resumption of executions in 1977 until February of 2009, there have been 1,149 executions in the USA. Two states, Texas and Virginia, account for nearly one-half (46 percent) of the total number, consistent with the past 83 percent of all executions in the USA having occurred in Southern states. The peak year for executions was 1999 when there were 98. Since then there has been a steady decline in the number of executions each year, and in 2008 there were only 37 executions. There are a number of reasons for the steady decline in the number of executions, one of the most important being the fact that there have been numerous "death row exonerations" – instances where persons placed on death row awaiting execution were found upon further investigation (DNA evidence, for example) to have been innocent. Since 1977 there have been 130 death row exonerations, or 1 exoneration for every 9 executions. In the past, the most frequent method of executing someone in the USA was through electrocution. Since 1977, however, all death penalty states have moved toward the use of lethal injection as the preferred method of putting prisoners to death. Of the 1,149 executions since 1977, 85 percent were done by lethal injection.

In trying to figure out the future of the death penalty, it is unlikely to be completely abolished either in the world or in the USA in the near future. The majority of the death penalty countries in the world are countries with large Islamic populations where capital punishment is both practiced and widely accepted culturally. The death penalty is also not likely to be abolished in the USA. The majority of executions both today and in the past have been conducted in Southern states and also for cultural and religious (Christian Evangelical) reasons capital punishment enjoys popular support there.

SEE ALSO: Criminal Justice System; Death and Dying; Death Penalty as a Social Problem

SUGGESTED READINGS
Bedau, H. and Cassell, P. (2004) *Debating the Death Penalty*. Oxford University Press, New York.
Paternoster, R., Brame, R., & Bacon, S. (2008) *The Death Penalty: America's Experience with Capital Punishment*. Oxford University Press, New York.

PURSEY P. M. A. R. HEUGENS

Capitalism

Capital, as a noun referring to the funds individuals or corporations use as the basis for financial operations, is first employed in 1709 within "An Act for Enlarging the Capital Stock of the Bank of England." Capitalism, representing a system where capital is advanced to increase wealth, did not come into use until William Thackeray's 1854 novel, *The Newcomes*.

Capitalism may refer to an economic, political and/or social system (e.g. feudalism, capitalism, communism), a broad historical period, or specific forms within that period (e.g. mercantile, industrial, finance, monopoly, or late capitalism). It is often politically encumbered through association with Marx's and other socialist or communist critiques of capitalism (although Marx never used "capitalism" in *The Manifesto* or *Capital* – first employing it in his late-1870s correspondence). Werner Sombart tried to depoliticize the term, maintaining it was an analytical concept applicable to a specific socio-economic system.

As such, capitalism is a system that provides for needs and wants, animated by a particular ethos, coordinated and organized by established practices, regulations, and laws, privileging particular types of knowledge (e.g. scientific, technical, and instrumentally rational). Capitalism's ethos involves an historically unique approach to acquisition, positive attitudes towards unfettered competition, and the predominance of goal-rational action (Weber 1927: 352–68). Capitalist production is not directly aimed at human need; it centers on abstract value and potentially unlimited accumulation. Each economic unit competes to extend its economic power as far and advantageously as possible within the existing legal system.

Although forms of capitalism existed in the ancient world, thirteenth-century Italy, and the Low Countries, Weber (1927: 275-8) identified five criteria characterizing capitalism, as a "pure type," in the modern era.

First, capitalism exists when "the provision of everyday wants" is met through capitalist enterprise. The whole economic system would collapse if those enterprises ceased their productive activities.

Second, capitalism depends on rational calculation and precise accounting. It is the first economic/social system aimed at the pursuit of unlimited wealth and everything is viewed in terms of accumulation: people are producers or consumers; nature is a repository of resources; enhancing managerial techniques, technical capacities, and performance outcomes is constantly required; progress involves the creation of new wants, better technology, reduced costs, and increased speeds of capital circulation. Firms calculate the components and costs of production – e.g. raw material, machinery, wages, transport, advertising – and the potential consumer demand to ensure, as much as possible, profit maximization. Enterprises determine when and how far they can extend their economic reach while complying with existing law. Goal-rational action pervades capitalism as people, objects, and events are evaluated in means/ends terms.

Third, capitalism presupposes an enduring, predictable legal system. Entrepreneurs, enterprises, or managers must be certain of property and ownership rights, their easy purchase and sale, and enforceable contracts. Agents of capital must have the legal freedom to undertake the production of any product or service where profit appears attainable and be able to pursue that objective through a variety of organizational forms.

Fourth, capitalism presupposes the presence of individuals "who are not only legally in the position, but are also economically compelled, to sell their labor on the market without restriction" (Weber 1927: 277). Capitalism could not exist and develop without "such a propertyless stratum . . . a class compelled to sell its labor services to live." Living "under the compulsion of the whip of hunger," Weber maintained, enabled employers to "unambiguously [determine workers' wages] by agreement in advance."

Finally, capitalism requires the complete commercialization of economic life where the primary goal is gaining and expanding economic advantage while building commercial wealth. Of critical importance is the sale and purchase of shares in an enterprise or particular property. Through share ownership, individuals or corporations gain access to capital resources well beyond a single individual's wealth, enabling firms to dominate increasingly larger markets and ultimately globalize their activities. The stock market provides the opportunity for wealth through shrewd investment and moves capital to areas of anticipated need and growth; the fluctuation of share values also measures enterprises' efficiency and profitability over the short and long term.

Capitalism entails a number of dynamic tensions concerning power, control and freedom. Although capitalism has flourished in periods of war, it requires sufficiently long periods of social and political stability for investors, speculators, and producers to make long-term plans with some confidence. Capitalism requires the personal, internal control of individuals' actions, along with institutional regulation – Michel Foucault's notion of disciplining docile bodies – with ultimate power residing in the legal system. Thus, despite certain rhetoric to the contrary, capitalism requires a strong, stable state although state powers must be limited. There is a constant tension and shifting of the private sector/public sector balance of power.

State power must be restricted so that individuals or firms may engage in saving, risk-taking, and profit-making activities without the fear of arbitrary state intervention or the confiscation of property. At the same time, particularly after the 1929 depression, private enterprise has depended on the state and public sector for key infrastructural resources, policies, laws and security. The state, even the neoliberal one, plays a major role in managing the financial environment within which corporations act: for example, governments establish the money supply, determine interest rates, influence access to credit, implement budgets (including deficits and deficit financing), set rates for progressive income and corporate taxes, influence currency value, regulate securities exchanges, establish tariff rates and trade policies, legislate on collective bargaining rights, minimum wage, unemployment insurance, fund and oversee education, and are increasingly involved in health care. The state is a major economic actor.

Sociology's emergence and early development within industrial capitalism is not mere coincidence. Capitalism's social impact and its analytical ethos provided the substance and form for sociology to develop as an empirically based, theoretically informed, critical discipline.

SEE ALSO: Capitalism, Social Institutions of; Communism; Economy (Sociological Approach); Globalization; Socialism

REFERENCE

Weber, M. (1927) [1923] *General Economic History*, trans. F. Knight. Free Press, Glencoe, IL.

SUGGESTED READING

Blaug, M. (1997) *Economic Theory in Retrospect*, 5th edn. Cambridge University Press, New York.

ROB BEAMISH

capitalism, social institutions of

The concept of capitalism refers to the idea that certain societies allow economic actors to rationally organize the social and financial capital at their disposal in pursuit of perpetually renewed private profits. The organizational forms actors have chosen to organize economic transactions vary, but an oft-used classification distinguishes between formal organizations, markets for the exchange of capital, goods, and services, and organization-market "hybrids" like interorganizational networks and alliances. As these organizational forms represent the core engines of production and exchange in capitalist societies, they are typically referred to as the economic institutions of capitalism.

But although economic institutions are necessary ingredients of capitalist societies, they are not sufficient conditions to support the maintenance of a capitalist system of production. The success of economic institutions is contingent on the presence of a set of public or private arrangements for the regulation and enforcement of exchange transactions between two or more autonomous capitalist actors: the social institutions of capitalism. The conditions these social institutions ought to promote are fourfold. First, social peace, the condition in which potential conflict is diminished and in which cooperation is supported. Second, individual freedom, encompassing guarantees to at least some actors that they will have the leeway to engage in exchange agreements and co-dictate the terms of those. Third, transferable property rights, which are attached to physical commodities or services, such that they may be exchanged in the marketplace without much friction in the form of transaction costs. Fourth, enforceable contracts, instruments facilitating the making and keeping of mutual promises about future exchanges.

Whether the social institutions of capitalism referenced above should be classified as public or private depends on their position vis-à-vis the relationships they govern, as well as on the nature of the sanctions they rely on to regulate capitalist exchange. Private institutions arise within long-lasting exchange relationships between two or more capitalist actors, and serve to make those relationships self-enforcing and self-policing. Nevertheless, not all background conditions necessary for capitalist production can always be provided by such intrinsically more efficient private institutions. Social peace and individual freedom have a strong public goods character. Everyone benefits when these conditions are in place, but no single actor can produce them by individual means or even has the incentive to contribute to their advancement. Under such conditions, the rational pursuit of private objectives by self-interested individuals may produce collectively disastrous outcomes. The classical way out of the dilemma of the provision of public goods is the (partial) abdication of individual authority to public institutions. Individuals may jointly agree on certain collective limitations to their natural rights and freedoms, in return for long-run stability (social peace) and greater security that they actually get to enjoy the rights they do retain (e.g., certain forms of individual freedom). In all modern capitalist societies, these collective limitations have taken the form of the state.

The state is a versatile creature in that it can not only provide for social peace and individual freedom, but also for transferable property rights and enforceable contracts. But states are public institutions, and as such often criticized for being slow, inefficient, and breeding the bureaucratic personality. Fortunately, whereas state bureaucracy and public sector governmentality probably represent the only feasible solutions to the problem of providing social peace and individual freedom, private institutional alternatives are available for the provision of transferable property rights and enforceable contracts. These institutions include: kinship ties, clans, trust, and reputation. By stipulating and policing pro-social norms, such private institutions circumvent any resort to public institutions and may even fill the voids in case the latter are absent or deficient in a given setting.

SEE ALSO: Capitalism; Communism; Property, Private; Social Capital

SUGGESTED READING

Heugens, P. P. M. A. R., van Oosterhout, J., & Vromen, J. J. (2004) *The Social Institutions of Capitalism: Evolution and Design of Social Contracts*. Edward Elgar, Cheltenham.

PURSEY P. M. A. R. HEUGENS

carework

Carework refers to the work of caring for others, including unpaid care for family members and friends, as well as paid care for others. Caring work includes taking care of children, the elderly, the sick, and the disabled, as well as domestic work such as cleaning and cooking. As reproductive labor, carework is necessary to society. By deploying the term "carework," scholars and advocates emphasize the importance of recognizing that care is not simply a natural response to those in need, but hard physical, mental, and emotional work, which is often unequally distributed. Because care tends to be economically devalued, many scholars who study carework emphasize the skill required for care, and the importance of valuing care.

The scholarship on carework addresses several key issues. Understanding the balance in care provision among families, states, and markets is a central concern. There are important differences between countries where much carework is provided or subsidized by the state, those where almost all carework is provided through families, and those where much carework is provided through the market. Scholarship also highlights the tensions between paid versus unpaid care, as well as between care quality and costs for care. Care – whether provided within the family or in institutions – improves significantly with lower careworker–recipient ratios; yet such care is costly.

Finally, as all of these points suggest, inequalities provide a key approach for analyzing carework. Carework clearly reinforces gender inequality, but also inequalities of race, ethnicity, class, sexuality, ability, and nation. Care is a profound and central experience in many people's lives; it is critical to analyze the experience of care with more subtlety, recognizing that care may be empowering as well as oppressive – and may be both at the same time.

SEE ALSO: Division of Household Labor; Gender, Work, and Family; Inequality/Stratification, Gender

SUGGESTED READING

Folbre, N. (2001) *The Invisible Heart: Economics and Family Values*. New Press, New York.

JOYA MISRA

caste: inequalities past and present

To categorize different forms of stratification systems sociologists most frequently examine the way resources such as wealth, power, and prestige are acquired in society. In some societies, such valued resources are acquired on the basis of achievement or merit. In others, these resources are accorded to individuals on the basis of ascribed, not achieved, characteristics. The idea of ascribed and achieved status is used to contrast caste systems with class systems. In class systems one's opportunities in life, at least in theory, are determined by one's actions, allowing a degree of individual mobility that is not possible in caste systems. In caste systems a person's social position is determined by birth, and social intercourse outside one's caste is prohibited. Caste systems are to be found among the Hindus in India. Examples of caste-like systems can also be found in other non-Hindu societies such as Japan, during the Tokugawa period, and South Africa, during the era of apartheid.

The term "caste" itself is often used to denote large-scale kinship groups that are hierarchically organized within a rigid system of stratification. Early Hindu literary classics describe a society divided into four *varnas*: *Brahman* (poet-priest), *Kshatriya* (warrior-chief), *Vaishya* (trader), and *Shudra* (menial, servant). The *varnas* formed ranked categories characterized by differential access to spiritual and material privileges. They excluded the Untouchables, who were despised because they engaged in occupations that were considered unclean and polluting.

This hierarchical system persisted throughout the Hindu subcontinent for millennia. The basis of caste ranking was the sacred concept of purity and pollution. Brahmans were considered ritually pure because they were engaged in priestly duties. Untouchables were regarded as impure since they were employed in manual labor and with ritually polluting objects. Usually those who had high ritual status also had economic and political power. Relations between castes were generally regulated by beliefs about pollution. Thus, there were restrictions on interdining and intermarriage between castes was not allowed. Violations of these rules entailed purification rites and sometimes expulsion from the caste. Traditional Hindu religious beliefs about *samsara* (reincarnation) and *karma* (quality of actions) provided the justification for the operation of this hierarchical society. A person's actions in previous lives determined his or her social ranking in this life.

British colonialism had a significant impact on the Indian social structure – from western ideas, the legal system, to English educational institutions. After the country became independent in 1947, the movement from a traditional to a modern economy, together with India's democratic electoral system, further eroded the institution of caste. The Indian leaders enacted legislative and legal measures to create a more egalitarian society. A new constitution was adopted, which abolished untouchability and prohibited discrimination in public places. In addition, special benefits were provided for those who had suffered most from the caste system.

What progress has the country made toward improving the lives of the Untouchables, who now form 16 percent of the population? Has the traditional caste system disintegrated? In urban areas, divisions based on income, education, and occupations have become more important than caste cleavages for social and economic purposes. In rural areas, the dominant castes are no longer from the higher castes but belong to the middle and lower peasant castes. Yet for most Indians who live in rural areas (nearly 72 percent) caste factors remain an integral part of their daily lives.

With the support of government scholarships and job reservations, a small proportion of the Untouchable community has managed to gain entry into the middle class – as schoolteachers, clerks, bank tellers, typists, and government officials. Reservation of seats in the legislature has made the political arena somewhat more accessible. The majority of Dalits, however, remain landless agricultural laborers, powerless, desperately poor, and illiterate, and continue to face discrimination. As in the past, rural and urban areas in India will continue to witness inter-caste conflicts. Yet, more significantly, like ethnic conflicts elsewhere between groups, these conflicts have more to do with control over political and economic resources and less over caste beliefs and values.

SEE ALSO: Affirmative Action; Conflict (Racial/Ethnic); Racial Hierarchy; Stratification, Race/Ethnicity and

SUGGESTED READINGS

Dumont, L. (1970) *Homo Hierarchicus*. University of Chicago Press, Chicago, IL.

Jaffrelot, C. (2003) *India's Silent Revolution: The Rise of the Lower Castes in North India*. Hurst, London.

Jalali, R. (1993) Preferential policies and the movement of the disadvantaged: the case of the scheduled castes in India. *Ethnic and Racial Studies* 16 (1): 95–120.

RITA JALALI

censorship

Censorship has generally been of interest to social theorists when considered as a matter of state control over "free speech" and/or mass-mediated content. This governmental censorship has tended to focus on notions of protecting "vulnerable" (young/lower-class/female) audiences from representations of sex, violence, and criminality which, it is assumed, may deprave, corrupt, or desensitize them.

Media-sociological work on censorship argues that it has worked to support the ideological power of hegemonic blocs, tending to repress expression which does not fall into normative cultural categories, as well as especially restricting popular rather than "literary" culture. "Educated," middle-class audiences for elite culture are not as likely to be represented as "vulnerable" as audiences for popular film and television. In the USA, the cinema Production Code of 1930 infamously detailed exactly what could not be shown in classical Hollywood films: sexual relations between heterosexual characters were elided; morally bad characters were depicted as never triumphing thanks to their crimes; and homosexual relationships could not be shown nor even strongly implied.

As well as restricting popular culture through codes of conduct for producers or industry self-regulation, censorship can also be said to act productively. Though it has historically produced gaps and absences in pop culture, it has also shaped texts and genres, especially by favoring moral messages such as "crime will be punished."

Censorship debates have been recurrently linked to moral panics surrounding new media technologies. One of these was the UK's "video nasties" panic in the 1980s (Critcher 2003), when the new media technology of video recording was felt to have undermined media regulation by making "adult" horror texts depicting violence and gore available to "children." More recently, the Internet has occasioned similar outcries, with the availability of online pornography supposedly threatening state and industry regulation of such imagery.

SEE ALSO: Moral Panics

REFERENCE

Critcher, C. (2003) *Moral Panics and the Media*. Open University Press, Buckingham.

MATT HILLS

Certeau, Michel de (1925–86)

Born in 1925 in Chambéry, France, Michel de Certeau obtained degrees in classics and philosophy at the universities of Grenoble, Lyon, and Paris. Joining the Society of Jesus in 1950, he was ordained in 1956. He completed a doctorate on the mystical writings of Jean-Joseph Surin at the Sorbonne in 1960 and taught in Paris and San Diego. He died of stomach cancer in 1986.

Certeau's career can be divided into three stages. The first was largely concerned with traditional religious history; then, after "the Events of May" (1968), his work took a very different turn, becoming both contemporary and sociocultural; then, after a highly productive decade writing about contemporary issues, Certeau's thoughts returned to the history of religion and he produced what would be his last book, a two-volume history of seventeenth-century mysticism in Europe.

The first stage of Certeau's career culminated in a profound retheorization of history, the fruit of which is to be seen in *L'écriture de l'histoire* (*The Writing of History*), first published in 1975. Greatly influenced by Lacanian psychoanalysis, Certeau argued that history is a machine for calming the anxiety most westerners feel in the face of death. It works by raising the specter of death within a memorial framework that gives the appearance that we will live forever after all.

The second stage of Certeau's career began abruptly in May 1968 when the streets of Paris erupted in a paroxysm of student and blue-collar protest. The essays written on the run in these heady days (*The Capture of Speech*) are of lasting interest to social theorists for the way they begin to theorize everyday forms of resistance. Certeau was given an opportunity to expand on these preliminary investigations in the early 1970s when he was given a large research grant to study French culture on a broad scale. The legacy of this work is the two volumes of *The Practice of Everyday Life* (a third was planned, but never completed). In terms of their uptake in sociology, Certeau's most important and influential concepts come from this period: strategy and tactics, place and space.

Both strategy and tactics are determined as *calculations*. The essential difference between strategy and tactics is the way they relate to the variables that everyday life inevitably throws at us all. Strategy works to limit the sheer number of variables that can affect it by creating some kind of protected zone, a place in which the environment can be rendered predictable if not properly tame. Tactics, by contrast, is the approach one takes to everyday life when one is unable to take measures against its variables. Tactics refers to the set of practices that strategy has not been able to domesticate. They are not in themselves subversive, but they function symbolically as daily proof of the partiality of strategic control.

Certeau began to work in earnest on his mysticism project, which culminates the third and final stage of his career, when he returned to France after nearly a decade in California. This project revisits the topic with which Certeau's career began, but as with his critique of historiography, its aim was not merely to add yet another catalogue of curiosities to an already well-stocked cabinet. Rather, he wanted to understand the logic of mysticism, to try to understand it for itself as its own peculiar kind of discourse.

IAN BUCHANAN

SEE ALSO: Everyday Life; Place; Space

SUGGESTED READING
Buchanan, I. (2000) *Michel de Certeau: Cultural Theorist*. Sage, London.
Certeau, M. de (1984) *The Practice of Everyday Life*, trans. S. Rendall. University of California Press, Berkeley, CA.

chance and probability

Chance is an informal concept, sometimes meaning probability, sometimes meaning randomness. Probability is a formal mathematical concept expressed in its most simple form as dependent probability, which is a number between zero and one that represents the likelihood that, for example, a person with one property will have another property. Thus the probability of a live birth being female is a dependent probability in which the two properties are live birth and female. Probabilities may also be assigned to beliefs. It is commonly asserted that social processes are probabilistic and that causal relations in social sciences are probabilistic. This means that the causal relationships or processes are not deterministic. However, it is only very infrequently that dependent probabilities can be assigned to nondeterministic processes or causal relations. Thus actual numerical probabilities generally play no formal role in sociological theories.

The primary role of probability ideas is in relation to statistics, and generally probability usages in social statistics rely, confusingly, on notions of error. The term error in the social sciences is not used only for errors of observation but more broadly, for the distribution of observation that results from actual nondeterministic, entangled, causal processes. Thus "error" would appear whether or not there was error of observation at all. The standard method of modeling causal relations in the social sciences uses linear equations which do not contain probabilities and treat indeterminacy as error. A close relationship with relatively little variation around the line defined by the equation produces a high correlation while a relationship in which there is more variation produces a low correlation. Models can be built containing large sets of such relationships and interpreted in terms of causation.

SEE ALSO: Fact, Theory, and Hypothesis: Including the History of the Scientific Fact; Statistics

SUGGESTED READING
Freedman, D. A. (2005) *Statistical Models: Theory and Practice*. Cambridge University Press, New York.

STEPHEN TURNER

chaos

Chaos theory emerged in the physical sciences as an explanatory framework for processes that appeared disorderly, such as turbulence or weather patterns, but which had complex mathematical models behind their seeming randomness. However, theories which are predictive chemistry or physics fall short of explanation for the diverse phenomena and larger standard error margins of human behavior. The apparent promise of chaos or complexity theories for sociology is their tolerance for ambiguity, uncertainty or unpredictability, and their assertion that apparent disorder in human behavior may in fact be orderly at a higher level than we are measuring.

Few sociological studies have been published that successfully apply chaos or complexity mathematics to empirical social research results. Journal articles use concepts and models of chaos or complexity as metaphors, and they may fail to distinguish between the two theories.

Promising sociological research directions may be found in the incorporation of fuzzy set theory to social science research methods. "Fuzzification," according to its originator Lotfi Zadeh (1965), is a methodology used to generalize a specific theory from a crisp (discrete) to a continuous (fuzzy) form. Members of a fuzzy set may or may not have full membership in the discrete sense, but are assigned a value indicating their degree of possible membership.

SEE ALSO: Mathematical Sociology; Scientific Knowledge, Sociology of

REFERENCE
Kiel, L. D. & Elliott, E. W. (eds.) (1997) *Chaos Theory in the Social Sciences: Foundations and Applications*. University of Michigan Press, Ann Arbor, MI.

SUGGESTED READING
Zadeh, L. (1965) Fuzzy sets. *Information and Control* 8: 338–53.

LESLIE WASSON

charisma

The term "charisma" is one of the most enduring conceptions in the annals of sociology. Its origin, meaning "gift," as derived from the Greek, is close to Max Weber's understanding of the term which has subsequently passed into common vocabularies.

In a sociological sense, charisma refers to the qualities of those who possess, or are believed to possess, powers of leadership either as a virtue of exceptional personality or derived from some unusual inspiration such as a magical, divine or diabolical source, powers not possessed by the ordinary person (Weber 1947).

Charisma is a source of instability and innovation and therefore constitutes a dynamic element in social change. The concept of a cultural breakthrough was essential to Weber's understanding of the process of social transformation. At each "turning point" in a society's development, he argued, there are two possible directions in which it could advance. If it were to proceed in one direction, the society would undergo profound transformation in the established order, but if it were to take the other, the existing order would be reinforced. The breakthrough juncture in social change is associated with the idea of charisma and prophets representing the prototypes of leaders with such qualities. Charismatic leadership is, in Weber's account, the source which precipitates it. Thus pure charisma is alien to the established institutions of society and prevailing economic arrangements in particular.

Charismatic authority is considered legitimate because it is based on the magnetic, compelling personal style of leadership. By contrast, bureaucratic authority is considered legitimate because it is founded on abstract rules. Traditional authority is rendered legitimate since it rests on precedence. Charismatic leadership and legal-rational systems of domination stand at opposite poles. Of all these forms of authority, charismatic leadership is the least stable. Such leaders are unpredictable, their lifestyles chaotic, their moods labile, and their commands often unfathomable. Moreover, the authority of charismatic leaders depends entirely on the support of their followers. If the followers lose faith, the leader is left with no power of command. For this reason the charismatic leader's position is precarious.

For Weber, charismatic leadership tends to become routinized. The first phase of a religious movement passes fairly quickly. Charismatic phenomena are unstable and temporary and can prolong their existence only by becoming routinized – that is, by transformation into institutionalized structures.

SEE ALSO: Charisma, Routinization of; New Religious Movements; Religion, Sociology of; Weber, Max

REFERENCE

Weber, M. (1947) *Theory of Social Action*, trans. A. M. Henderson & T. Parsons, ed. T. Parsons. Oxford University Press, New York, pp. 358–9.

SUGGESTED READING

Weber, M. (1978) *Economy and Society: An Outline of Interpretive Sociology*, ed. G. Roth & C. Wittich. University of California Press, Berkeley, CA.

STEPHEN HUNT

charisma, routinization of

The routinization of charisma relates to Max Weber's (1968: 212–54) typology of pure types of legitimate, social power (*reinen Typen legitimer Herrschaft*) (Weber 1956: 122–5; 1968: 212–7). Charisma stems from "an exceptional [*außeralltäglich*] (originally attributed to prophets, people with healing or legal knowledge, great hunters or war heroes: as magically instilled), valued quality" endowing a person with "supernatural, superhuman, or at least specifically exceptional – not those normally found – powers and qualities that are divine gifts [*gottgesandt*] or exemplary [*vorbildlich*] and thus valued in a *leader* [*Führer*]" (Weber 1956: 140; 1968: 241). Attributed to various persons, charisma exists among those "conventionally assessed" as "the 'greatest' heroes, prophets, and saviours" (Weber 1956: 140; 1968: 241).

Charismatic power creates "an emotion-based communalization [*Vergemeinschaftung*];" there are no officials, staff, formal rules or abstract legal principles – "*duty* to the leader" binds people, creating legitimate order (Weber 1956: 141; 1968: 243). Opposing the existing order, charismatic leaders can foment revolutionary change.

Rooted in individuals' perceived powers and qualities, charismatic power is unstable. Stability requires a routine – routinized – solution to succession which is achieved through traditionalization, rationalization, or a combination. For example, succession may require finding another charismatic leader; the original leader or community may designate a successor possessing specific qualities; an hereditary link between leader and an heir may be claimed and ultimately routinized; succession might entail a traditionalized confirmation by ordeal. Routinization reduces disciples' emotion-based duty obligations, establishing a more regularized life.

SEE ALSO: Authority and Legitimacy; Charisma; Rational Legal Authority; Weber, Max

REFERENCES

Weber, M. (1956) *Wirtschaft und Gesellschaft: Grundriss der Verstehenden Soziologie* (*Economy and Society: An Outline of Interpretive Sociology*), 2 vols., ed. J. Winckelmann. J. C. B. Mohr, Tübingen.
Weber, M. (1968) *Economy and Society: An Outline of Interpretive Sociology*, 3 vols., ed. G. Roth & C.

Wittich, trans. E. Fischoff, H. Gerth, et al. Bedminster Press, New York.

ROB BEAMISH

Chicago School

The Chicago School of Urban Sociology refers to work of faculty and graduate students at the University of Chicago during the period 1915 to 1935. This small group of scholars (the full-time faculty in the department of sociology never numbered more than 6 persons) developed a new sociological theory and research methodology in a conscious effort to create a science of society using the city of Chicago as a social laboratory. The Chicago School is represented by three generations of faculty. The first included Albion Small (founder of the department), W. I. Thomas, Charles R. Henderson, Graham Taylor, and George E. Vincent. The second generation included Small, Thomas, Ernest Burgess, Ellsworth Faris, and Robert Park. It was this group that trained the graduate students responsible for the classic studies of the Chicago School. The third generation included Park, Burgess, Louis Wirth, and William Ogburn. This group of faculty would remain intact until the time Park retired from the university in 1934. The Chicago School continues to define the contours of urban sociology, most clearly in the contributions of urban ecology and applied research.

The sociology faculty pioneered empirical research using qualitative and quantitative methods to develop a "science of sociology." Park formulated a new theoretical model based upon his observation that the city was more than a geographic phenomenon; the basic concepts of human ecology were borrowed from the natural sciences. Competition and segregation led to formation of *natural areas*, each with a separate and distinct *moral order*. The city was "a mosaic of little worlds that touch but do not interpenetrate." Burgess's model for the growth of the city showed a central business district surrounded by the zone in transition, the zone of workingmen's homes, the residential zone, and the commuter zone (see Figure 1). Roderick McKenzie expanded the basic model of human ecology in his later study of the metropolitan community.

The research and publication program of the Chicago School was carried out under the auspices of a Local Community Research Committee, an interdisciplinary group comprised of faculty and graduate students from sociology, political science (Charles Merriam), and anthropology (Robert Redfield). Support came from the Laura Spellman Rockefeller Memorial (more than $600,000 from 1924 to 1934). Graduate students under the guidance of Park and Burgess mapped local community areas and studied the spatial organization of juvenile delinquency, family disorganization, and cultural life in the city. The research program produced a diverse array of studies broadly organized around the themes of urban institutions (the hotel, taxi, dance hall), social disorganization (juvenile delinquency, the homeless man), and natural areas themselves. Among the notable Chicago School studies are Frederick Thrasher, *The Gang* (1926); Louis Wirth, *The Ghetto* (1928); and Harvey W. Zorbaugh, *The Gold Coast and the Slum* (1929).

The Chicago School dominated urban sociology and sociology more generally in the first half of the twentieth century. By 1950 some 200 students had completed graduate study at Chicago, and more than half of the presidents of the American Sociological Association were faculty or students at Chicago. The *American Journal of Sociology*, started by Small in 1895, served as the official journal of the American Sociological Association from 1906 to 1935.

There were early critiques of the Chicago School, including Missa Alihan's 1938 critique of the determinism inherent in Park's human ecology (Park wrote that "on the whole" the criticisms were correct). Burgess's concentric zones were soon replaced by a variety of models showing multiple nuclei and eventually the decentralized, polycentered city. Recent attention has focused on the role of women in the development of the Chicago School. Burgess would later note that systematic urban research at Chicago started with the Hull-House studies begun by Edith Abbot and Sophonsia Breckenridge in 1908. The influence of the early work of the Chicago School may be seen in some later studies, notably St. Clair Drake and Horace Cayton's *Black Metropolis* (1945), community studies directed by Morris Janowitz in the 1970s, and William Julius Wilson's work on poverty neighborhoods in 1980–95.

In addition to urban sociology, there are claims to various other Chicago Schools in ethnic studies, crime and delinquency, symbolic interaction, and other fields. Park felt that Thomas's work formed the foundation for the department, but wrote that he was not aware that he was creating a "school" or a "doctrine." The Chicago School label developed in large measure from critiques by scholars from other universities. Urban geographers have claimed that while Chicago was the model for urban theory of the twentieth century, Los Angeles is the model for urban theory of the future. It should be noted that the Los Angeles School (a title coined by the authors themselves, in contrast to the Chicago

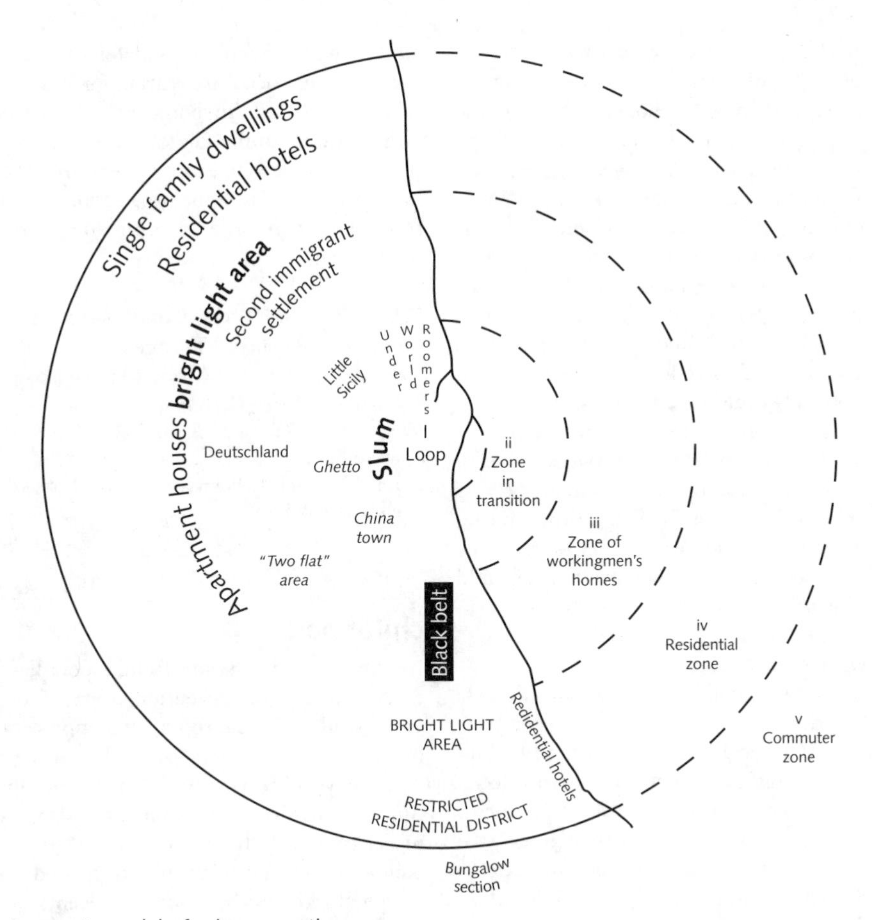

Figure 1 Burgess's model of urban growth

School) is more appropriately urban studies, rather than urban sociology.

SEE ALSO: Addams, Jane; American Sociological Association; Compositional Theory of Urbanism; Park, Robert E. and Burgess, Ernest W.; Urban Ecology

SUGGESTED READINGS

Abbott, A. (1999) *Department and Discipline: Chicago Sociology at One Hundred*. University of Chicago Press, Chicago.

Deegan, M. J. (1986) *Jane Addams and the Men of the Chicago School, 1892–1918*. Transaction Books, New Brunswick, NJ.

Matthews, F. H. (1977) *Quest for an American Sociology: Robert E. Park and the Chicago School*. McGill-Queen's University Press, Montreal.

RAY HUTCHISON

child abuse

Child abuse includes all forms of physical, emotional and sexual ill-treatment, neglect, and exploitation. Globally, hundreds of millions of children are victims of violence; the vast majority of perpetrators are parents-family caretakers. In the USA, over 3 million children are reported to official agencies for severe maltreatment each year. These official figures are just the tip of the iceberg, as more than a third of adults in the USA report having experienced abuse and/or neglect as a child.

TYPES

Child physical abuse involves a parent or caretaker intentionally inflicting physical pain on the child. Physical violence against children ranges from extremes such as punching, beating, kicking (16 percent), to the less severe such as spanking (90 percent). Note that engaging in the less severe or "culturally acceptable" levels of harsh parenting and/or corporal punishment significantly increases the likelihood that parents will proceed to more severely abuse the child. Child sexual abuse involves a caretaker using a child for sexual gratification. Such violence ranges from extremes of actual penetration, molestation with genital contact (17 percent girls, 4 percent boys), to the less severe noncontact abuse (proposition, exhibition). Child emotional abuse involves a parent-caregiver inflicting psychological pain on the child, including yelling, ridiculing, degrading or humiliating, isolating, ignoring, rejecting, terrorizing, or corrupting a child. Severe emotional violence against children (10–15 percent) is often distinguished from less severe (65–85 percent) by whether it forms a pattern and the degree of potential or actual harm. Child neglect involves a parent-caretaker's failure to provide for the child's basic needs. This includes physical, medical, educational, supervision and/or emotional neglect, although most focus on severe physical neglect like abandonment or malnourishment (14 percent girls, 21 percent boys). Finally, prenatal neglect (refusal to obtain care) or abuse (smoking, drinking, taking illegal drugs during pregnancy) constitutes another category of maltreatment and is associated with a higher risk of child abuse after birth.

CONSEQUENCES

The consequences of child abuse are considerable for the child, the adult they become, and for society. In fact, even the less severe forms of child abuse, like spanking, have many negative effects. Some consequences differ by type of maltreatment. For example, child neglect is most strongly associated with lower cognitive development and educational achievement for the child; while child physical abuse is more strongly related to higher levels of child aggression and subsequent violence. However, all forms of child maltreatment are associated with adverse effects including increased risk of mental health problems such as depression; substance abuse of legal and illegal drugs as a teenager; risky sexual behavior as a teenager; delinquency and arrests; and poorer physical health when older.

THE CYCLE OF CHILD ABUSE

Aside from the obvious trauma, reasons for the profound effects of child abuse include changes in the child's brain and CNS that result from child maltreatment; modeling effects; presence of toxic belief systems; and the defense mechanisms that children develop to cope with fear and despair. These include denial, depression, substance abuse, risky sex – all of the factors that in turn increase the chances that these maltreated children will grow up to abuse and/or neglect their own children.

PREVENTION

The problem of child abuse and neglect crosses all class, cultural, religious, racial, ethnic, gender, economic, and geographic boundaries. The sheer pervasiveness, brutality, and forms of child abuse point to the need to search for the underlying structural causes. Anchored in the UN Convention on the Rights of the Child, the weight of evidence points to the need to extend to children the rights of human beings and equal protection under the law from violence in order to begin an end to the abuse of children.

SEE ALSO: Childhood; Childhood Sexuality; Domestic Violence; Violence

SUGGESTED READINGS

The Adverse Childhood Experiences Study, www.cdc.gov/nccdphp/ACE/.

Family Research Laboratory, Murray Straus, www.unh.edu/frl/cbb.htm.

KAREN POLONKO

childhood

In the past few decades, childhood has received extensive academic attention from sociology. Previous studies on the topic have approached childhood primarily from a psychological perspective. They have especially focused on childhood as a time for cognitive development and psychological maturity. In the discipline of sociology, the area of childhood has not been fully neglected, but rather marginalized until relatively recently. Children have typically been portrayed as adults in training, so their individual needs, motives and desires have been ignored. In fact, children's needs and desires have been associated with crime and deviance. Sociology of childhood has emerged as an important area of study in the past few decades. Instead of looking at childhood as a universal experience of cognitive development, sociology of childhood focuses on the role of societies and different cultures in defining and shaping childhood experiences. This approach also focuses on the role of socialization.

The first interest in sociology has come from feminist scholars and scholars of gender studies. Especially studies of subordinate groups such as women and minorities started including another subordinate, marginalized group: children. Secondly, traditional gender roles have associated women closely with children.

The most substantial body of work in childhood has been in the area of *socialization*. Socialization refers to the process during which children learn and internalize the rules of society. The process of socialization has been studied from the perspective of two different paradigms.

The first paradigm, *the deterministic model,* assumes children are passive creatures. The initial assumption in this paradigm is that children are new, inexperienced members of society, who need to be taught the rules of that particular society. In this paradigm the children do not contribute to their education and socialization, but are rather passive recipients.

The second paradigm, *the functionalist model,* focuses more on creating order in society. The main assumption in this view is that children are disruptive and chaotic by nature. Their disruptive nature poses a threat to society's order and stability. That is why they need to learn the rules of society. Socialization, according to functionalists, provides the education process for children to learn and obey the rules of society. This process is crucial to ensure the order and stability of society. While the functionalist model was popular particularly in the 1950s, this view has lost its popularity.

The third paradigm, the reproductive model, moved the debate on childhood away from the role of socialization in maintaining order to sustaining inequalities. Some sociologists argue that socialization of children becomes a mechanism to reinforce and sustain existing social inequalities. Especially through parental resources and education, many theorists argue children are socialized intro privileged social roles.

Today, there are three trends in the contemporary sociological literature on childhood. First, a burgeoning literature on childhood focuses on children as actors. While previous literature has studied childhood from the perspectives of parents, educators and adults, the views and perspectives of children were rarely acknowledged. A recent wave of research acknowledges children as actors with distinct motivations and aspirations instead of simply seeing them as passive recipients. In this sociological view children are not portrayed as smaller, unformed adults, lower in the developmental chain, but rather as distinct actors.

Another new approach in contemporary sociological literature focuses on social inequality among children. Instead of categorizing all children together, this view opts for exploring the inner differences within and between them. Some theorists point to the role of race, class and gender in understanding inequality among children in the USA. Many theorists also offer cross-national comparisons in children's relative deprivation and poverty.

Finally, contemporary sociology explores the boundaries of childhood. Some sociologists point to the blurred line between childhood and adulthood. Especially due to work and consumption, childhood is shortened. New research argues, however, that while the period of childhood might be shortened, transition to adulthood is taking longer than ever before.

SEE ALSO: Child Abuse; Childhood Sexuality; Consumer Culture, Children's; Socialization; Youth/Adolescence

SUGGESTED READINGS

Corsaro, W. A. (2005) *The Sociology of Childhood.* Pine Forge Press: Thousand Oaks, CA.

Liebel, M. (2004) *A Will of Their Own: A Cross-Cultural Perspective on Working Children.* Zed Books: New York.

Zelizer, V. A. (1985) *Pricing the Priceless Child: The Changing Social Value of Children.* Basic Books: New York.

YASEMIN BESEN-CASSINO

childhood sexuality

Bringing the two sensitive areas of childhood and sexuality together ends a dominant and ideological taboo, especially when the issue of childhood sexuality highlights the rights of all children to make informed choices about their own bodies, sexual desires, practices, and identity and when it challenges heterosexual norms. There is a limited understanding of childhood sexuality due to methodological, practical and ethical dilemmas. Publications on this sensitive and controversial issue are predominantly concerned with child sexual abuse. Childhood sexuality is conceptualized in two essential ways. One view is that children are naturally sexually innocent beings in danger from abuse from adults on whom they are also dependent for protection. The second view is that children are naturally sexual beings who need adult guidance to protect and guide them through their sexual development. In the USA and the UK explanations of childhood sexuality predominantly focus on childhood development models which presume that biological developments are signifiers of a child's capacity to make sense of, and to make appropriate decisions regarding, sex and sexuality via adult guidance. Contemporary approaches within social science have problematized these conceptualizations and developmental models of childhood sexuality.

More radical approaches contextualize childhood sexualities in relation to external individual and structural influences. Concerns with childhood sexuality in the USA and the UK concentrate on two key areas. One, adolescent (hetero)sexual activity, can be seen in discussions and interventions regarding teenage pregnancies. In other words what children are doing with/to each other sexually.

Two, pedophilia and child pornography, hence what adults are doing to children sexually. Socially, politically, and legislatively, protectionist and welfarist discourses prevail concerning the protection of pre (hetero)sexual children and "childhood innocence" together with the natural trajectory of heterosexuality. Resistance to dominant conceptualizations and constructions of childhood (hetero)sexuality such as oppositional desires, practices, and identities, including among children themselves ought to be acknowledged.

SEE ALSO: Child Abuse; Childhood; Compulsory Heterosexuality; Sexuality

SUGGESTED READINGS

Plummer, K. (1991) Understanding childhood sexualities. In: Sandfort, T., Brongersma, E., & van Naerssen, A. (eds.), *Male Intergenerational Intimacy: Historical, Socio-Psychological, and Legal Perspectives*. Harrington Park Press, New York.

Sandfort, T. & Rademakers, J. (eds.) (2000) *Childhoood Sexuality: Normal Sexual Behavior and Development*. Haworth Press, New York.

KAREN CORTEEN

church

The sociological phenomenon of "church" – from the Greek word "ecclesia" – has been theoretically discussed from Emile Durkheim to Thomas O'Dea to Peter Berger. Durkheim's seminal text – *The Elementary Forms of Religious Life* – defines church as "a society whose members are united because they imagine the sacred world and its relations with the profane world in the same way and because they translate this common representation into identical practices" (1995: 41); this definition, thereby, coincides with religion. In other words, church is a defined group of individuals who profess similar religious worldviews, encompassed as either a small group of individuals – i.e., a neighborhood place of worship – or as an entire people group throughout the world – i.e., Buddhists, Catholics, Muslims, Orthodox Jews, etc.

Building upon the scholarly work of both theorists and theologians, Thomas O'Dea signifies church as separate from "sects" and "mysticisms." Specifically, church contains the following attributes: membership designated at birth; formal administration of "grace" – i.e., salvation; demographic representation of social locations; disposition to convert others; and ability to "adjust to and compromise with the existing society and its values and institutions" (1966: 68). Sects are differentiated from churches based on their separatism and "withdrawal from or defiance of" (p. 68) institutional norms from the greater society. Additionally, mysticisms are differentiated from churches due to emphasis on individualized religious responses within smaller groups of people. Churches, sects, and mysticisms, however, historically appear in response to each other, O'Dea argues, from at least Christianity's conception.

Regarding the "institution of church," Berger suggests that the Christian church, specifically, "represents a very unusual case of the institutional specialization of religion, that is, of an institution specifically concerned with religion in counterposition with all other institutions of society" (1969: 123). The Christian religion legitimates the sacred/profane duality, emphasizing the existence of church as a sociological phenomena.

SEE ALSO: Belief; Buddhism; Christianity; Durkheim, Émile; Islam; Judaism; Religion

REFERENCES

Berger, P. L. (1969) *The Sacred Canopy: Elements of a Sociological Theory of Religion*. Doubleday, New York.

Durkheim, E. (1995) *The Elementary Forms of Religious Life*. Free Press, New York.

O'Dea, T. F. (1966) *The Sociology of Religion*. Prentice Hall, Upper Saddle River, NJ.

BEVERLY M. PRATT

citizenship

Citizenship refers to membership in a political community organized as a territorial or national state. The nature and content of citizenship varies with the form of state. Citizenship in the classic Greek *polis*, for instance, provided membership to a political elite, whereas modern liberal democratic citizenship provides opportunity to vote in a political election cycle. Sociological theories, however, recognize that citizenship has more than a mere political dimension.

Types of citizenship can be characterized in terms of two distinct axes or dimensions, one being *access* to citizenship status and the other being the *quality* of the rights and duties that attach to citizenship. Rules of access to citizenship separate citizens from noncitizens. Two alternative legal possibilities include *jus sanguinis* or citizenship by descent and *jus soli* or citizenship by birthplace. Which of these operates can have large consequences for persons who have moved across national boundaries either through the internationalization of economic activity and labor markets or the transformation of political units, both of which have relocated significant numbers of people transnationally over the last century.

Under conditions of *jus sanguinis* it is not sufficient to be born in a country to have access to its citizenship. To be a German or a Japanese citizen, for instance, it is not sufficient to be born in Germany or Japan. In these cases, citizenship is based on descent or appropriate ethnic-cultural qualities, and birth in its territory has no bearing on access to citizenship, even for second- and third-generation settlers. The range of possibilities under *jus soli* arrangements, on the other hand, is broader. American and Australian citizenship, for instance, can be acquired by virtue of being born in those countries. French citizenship, on the other hand, is attributed to a person born in France if at least one parent was also born in France (or a French colony or territory prior to independence). The legal requirements of acquisition of citizenship by naturalization are also quite variable between nation-states.

The second axis of citizenship, which is that of quality, refers to what is provided by formal membership of a political community once it is attained. The quality of citizenship comprises the rights and duties that are available to persons as citizens. The rights and duties of citizenship include not only those of political participation but also those that relate to legal and social capacities. Marshall (1950), for instance, distinguishes civil, political, and social citizenship.

The civil component of citizenship, according to Marshall, consists of those rights and duties that derive from legal institutions and especially courts of law. Civil rights include equal treatment before the law, rights of contract and property, and freedom from constraint by the state. Political rights are typically understood as rights of participation in the nation's political processes and especially the right to vote and stand for election. The social rights of citizenship are described by Marshall as rights to a basic level of material well-being through state provision independently of a person's market capacities. Accounts of the quality of citizenship have also been supplemented by reflection on recent social movements, which leads to consideration of rights associated with gender, ethnic, and green citizenship.

Citizenship is generally treated in terms of the rights that are available to citizens and denied to non-citizens, but there are also duties of citizenship, and the relationship between rights and duties in citizenship has drawn interest from sociological writers. Citizenship duties or obligations arguably have a role in the maintenance of social order and integration, but for most writers this aspect of citizenship remains secondary to the importance of citizenship in providing otherwise unobtainable capacities to persons through the rights of citizenship.

One development that has affected issues of citizenship is the changing composition of national communities, through migration, from culturally homogeneous populations to mosaics of national, ethnic, religious, and racial diversity. These changes pose problems of integration and social segmentation. Today, the question of access to rights by outsiders is associated with the broader questions of the increasing internationalization of national economies and displacement of persons through war and national decomposition and the consequent movement of large numbers of people across national boundaries. This raises questions concerning the impact of international organizations on national citizenship rights. Indeed, in Western Europe today there are in effect different levels of citizenship participation insofar as non-national residents may have civil and social rights and even certain political rights by virtue of the laws of their host countries that operate in terms of EU-sponsored human rights protocols and other transnational directives.

SEE ALSO: Democracy; Migration and the Labor Force; Sexual Citizenship

REFERENCES

Barbalet, J. M. (1989) *Citizenship: Rights, Struggle and Class Inequality*. University of Minnesota Press, Minneapolis, MN.

Janoski, T. (1998) *Citizenship and Civil Society: A Framework of Rights and Obligations in Liberal, Traditional and Social Democratic Regimes*. Cambridge University Press, New York.

SUGGESTED READING

Marshall, T. H. (1950) *Citizenship and Social Class*. Cambridge University Press, Cambridge.

JACK BARBALET

city

Cities were a feature of all the great ancient civilizations. Relatively small by modern standards, they, nevertheless, facilitated a far more diverse range of activities than was possible in other forms of human settlement. The city and the urban way of life that accompanies it, however, inasmuch as they have interested sociologists, are of more recent origin and are closely linked to the rise of industrialism.

In the nineteenth century, the city and urbanism began to exert a powerful fascination upon social theorists and sociologists. Karl Marx and Friedrich Engels saw the rise of the city as an integral part of human development and they recognized, as did Max Weber, that differing cultural and historical conditions lead to different types of cities. In addition, however, they argued that the human condition that is experienced in cities is the product of economic structure. Engels went so far as to examine the human condition of the working class in nineteenth-century Manchester in what has come to be seen as a pioneering exercise in social inquiry.

Ferdinand Tönnies drew an unfavorable contrast between the social bonds that are experienced in rural societies (*Gemeinschaft*) with the much weaker ties that are common to towns and cities (*Gesellschaft*). This pessimistic view of life in the city was shared by Georg Simmel who regarded the unique characteristic of the modern city as the intensification of nervous stimuli contrasting with the slower, more habitual and even quality of rural existence. Émile Durkheim, on the other hand, whilst acknowledging that city life brings with it impersonality, alienation, and the potential for conflict, also believed that the organic solidarity that emerges in the city can be the basis of a deeper form of social cohesion than that of mechanical solidarity found in pre-urban societies.

The industrial age made urban centers increasingly attractive to immigrants, both internal, from the rural hinterland, and external, from other parts of the world. As a consequence, all modern industrial societies became heavily urbanized and since the second half of the twentieth century, globalization has also become a growing influence on the social transformation of developing countries.

In this period, cities have become the centers of economic, industrial, and political power. For some social commentators, cities are dynamic, full of creative energy and offering a previously unknown range of diverse opportunities. For others, they are infernal places, characterized by violence, crime, corruption, and ill-health. More realistically, they are a blend of the attributes that are indicated at both ends of this spectrum. What is undeniable, however, is that they are unequal and divided social spaces that have continued throughout the twentieth and into the twenty-first centuries to be the objects of sociological analysis and research.

The study of cities has involved focusing on the built environment, on the social life of urban people and on the relationship between the two. A hugely significant work in this respect was *The Death and Life of Great American Cities* written in 1961 by Jane Jacobs. However, the origins of urban sociology can be traced to the work of the Chicago School in the 1920s and 1930s. Robert E. Park was the founder of an ecological approach which likened cities to biological organisms. Many subsequent studies of cities have been influenced by this approach even though its emphasis on the natural development of the city ignores the importance of economic and political decisions about planning.

Louis Wirth was responsible for introducing the idea of urbanism as a way of life. Extending the concerns of earlier social thinkers, he argued that in cities people may live in close proximity but they do not truly know each other. Weak social bonds, a more frenetic pace of life and the centrality of competition rather than cooperation characterize their lives. Despite Wirth's undoubted influence, it has been suggested that both he and Park were overly affected by their experiences of North American cities. Indeed even in the USA at the time they were writing, although arguably less so today, it was possible to find close-knit communities resembling villages which helped to preserve ethnic difference even in huge ethnically diverse cities such as Chicago itself and New York.

There is no doubt, however, that the idea of life in the city as being a distinctive form of human existence has continued to figure in sociological debate. Indeed this belief has intensified with the emergence of what is generally known as the post-industrial city. Since it was previously thought that the modern city and industrialism are inextricably linked, the idea of a city with very little industrial activity has proved difficult to understand.

More recent major contributors to the sociological understanding of the city include Henri Lefebvre, David Harvey, and Manuel Castells. Like Simmel, Lefebvre was interested in the relationship between the social space of the city and the mental life of its citizens. In addition, he sought to demonstrate the extent to which urbanization in and of itself has come to replace industrialization as the key determinant of capitalist accumulation. For Harvey and Castells, however, the city remains a product of industrial capitalism rather than its major driving force. More specifically, according to Harvey, industrial capitalism continually restructures space and, for that reason, urbanism has been an important product – arguably the most visible product – of industrialization. For Castells, the spatial form of the city is bound up with the overall mechanism of its development. That is to say, he does not regard the city solely as a distinct location but also as an integral part of the entire process of collective consumption. In such ways has the sociological debate moved from seeing cities as natural spatial processes to socially and physically constructed features of the social and economic systems of power.

Theoretical considerations have arguably underpinned most emerging concerns within the overall study of the city. These include suburbanization, inner city decay, urban conflict, urban renewal (including gentrification and civic boosterism) and spatially identifiable inequalities. Sharon Zukin, for example, has powerfully demonstrated the ways in which access to "public" spaces in modern cities is increasingly controlled. Studies have also taken into account the relationship between globalization and the city, including the emergence of what are described as global cities, the rapid growth of cities in the developing world and the city as the agent of consumer capitalism.

SEE ALSO: Built Environment; Chicago School; Global/World Cities; Simmel, Georg; Urbanization

SUGGESTED READINGS

Castells, M. (1977) *The Urban Question: A Marxist Approach*. Edward Arnold, London.

Harvey, D. (1973) *Social Justice and the City*. Edward Arnold, London.

Jacobs, J. (1992) *The Death and Life of Great American Cities*. Vintage Books, New York.

Lefebvre, H. (2003) *The Urban Revolution*. University of Minnesota Press, Minneapolis, MN.

Short, J. F. Jr. (ed.) (1971) *The Social Fabric of the Metropolis. Contributions of the Chicago School of Urban Sociology*. University of Chicago Press, Chicago, IL.

ALAN BAIRNER

civil religion

Civil religion refers to the cultural beliefs, practices, and symbols that relate a nation to the ultimate conditions of its existence. Bellah (1967) argues that civil religion is an understanding of the American experience in the light of ultimate and universal reality, and can be found in presidential inaugural addresses, sacred texts (the Declaration of Independence) and places (Gettysburg), and community rituals (Memorial Day parades). Like Rousseau and Durkheim, Bellah sees legitimation as a problem faced by every nation, and civil religion as one solution under the right social conditions. Civil religion comes into existence only in the modern period when church and state are legally separated as well as structurally differentiated.

Bellah's essay stimulated debates and research. Wimberly (1976) found evidence for the existence of civil religion as a dimension of society in the USA distinct from politics and organized religion. Some research also tested the concept of civil religion cross-nationally, finding unique constellations of legitimating myths and symbols in Israel, Japan, Mexico, and Sri Lanka. Before a consensus could emerge on civil religion, however, the concept lost favor among sociologists (Mathisen 1989).

The emergence of religious nationalism worldwide highlighted the divisive potential of politicized religion over against the integrative effect of civil religion. Examining the situation in the USA after the rise of the New Christian Right in the 1980s, Wuthnow (1988) found not a single civil religion, but two – one conservative, one liberal – in dispute and therefore incapable of creating a unifying collective consciousness. By the 1990s, other concepts emerged, most notably "public religion" and concern with the role of religion in "civil society."

SEE ALSO: Civil Society; Religion, Sociology of; Semiotics

REFERENCES

Bellah, Robert N. (1967) Civil religion in America. *Daedalus* 96: 1–21.

Mathisen, J. A. (1989) Twenty years after Bellah: whatever happened to American civil religion? *Sociological Analysis* 50: 129–47.

Wimberly, R. C. (1976) Testing the civil religion hypothesis. *Sociological Analysis* 37: 341–52.

Wuthnow, R. (1988) *The Restructuring of American Religion*. Princeton University Press, Princeton, NJ.

DAVID YAMANE

Civil Rights Movement

The struggle for civil rights for African Americans is one which has spanned centuries. After emancipation from slavery and the Fourteenth Amendment which granted them citizenship, African Americans were still denied basic civil rights guaranteed by the US constitution. In the South, Jim Crow was a system of segregation that was institutionalized after the 1896 *Plessey v. Ferguson* decision which stated that "separate but equal" public facilities were constitutional. In practice however, public spaces for African Americans were almost always inferior to those of whites.

Prior to the modern Civil Rights Movement African American hopes for racial equality rested in integrated education. A series of lawsuits filed by the National Association for the Advancement of Colored People (NAACP) sought to overturn *Plessey*. The 1954 *Brown v. Board of Education* decision desegregated schools in the South and proved that Jim Crow could be challenged and defeated. This was a monumental legislative achievement but more was needed to dismantle racial segregation in all aspects of public life.

In 1955 the Montgomery Bus Boycott was started when Rosa Parks was arrested for refusing to give up her seat to a white passenger. This act of defiance had occurred before but because of Mrs Parks' standing in the community she was considered the perfect symbol on which to launch a boycott to protest segregated seating. Reverend Dr. Martin Luther King, Jr., and other local black leaders established the Montgomery Improvement Association which organized the boycott that lasted for a year and successfully integrated buses in Montgomery, Alabama. The success of the Montgomery Bus Boycott ignited the modern Civil Rights Movement. The Southern Christian Leadership Conference (SCLC) was established shortly after to organize non-violent desegregation efforts elsewhere. In what Dr. King called the *zeitgeist* or "the spirit of the times," non-violent protests quickly spread to other Southern cities.

In the early 1960s students began to wage their own protests against segregation. Sit-ins, such as those started by college students in Greensboro, North Carolina, sparked non-violent direct action protest. Other forms of non-violent direct-action protests such as wade-ins, pray-ins, and read-ins followed. These students formed the Student Non-Violent Coordinating Committee (SNCC) as a separate organization in the movement devoted to the younger generations of activists. Following the sit-ins, the Congress of Racial Equality (CORE), founded in 1942, sent black and white youth on Freedom Rides throughout the South to test the Supreme Court ruling against segregation in interstate travel terminals. These youth were met with incredible violence that the media displayed to the world. In 1963 hundreds of thousands of people marched on Washington to call the government's attention to the neglect of the rights of African Americans. This display of mass support pushed President Kennedy toward the Civil Rights Act of 1964 which outlawed racial discrimination in public schools, government, and employment.

While civil rights organizations denounced racism in society, within their organizations they maintained gender and sexual identity inequities. Male ministers were often the visible and hierarchical leadership of the movement while women such as Ella Baker and Fannie Lou Hamer, who were equally talented grassroots leaders, were expected to stay behind the scenes. Furthermore, differences in gender and sexual orientation were muted in place of achieving a shared experience of living in a racist society. Gay activists such as Bayard Rustin and James Baldwin faced homophobia within the movement and were admonished to keep quiet about the oppression of homosexuals so that their sexual orientation could not be used against the movement.

As a social movement, the Civil Rights Movement created disruption and generated the power needed by African Americans to overturn institutionalized segregation. As a rational and well-planned movement, the Civil Rights Movement provided a precedent for movements that followed led by students, women, Latinos, American Indians, gays and lesbians, anti-war activists, farm workers, environmentalists, and others. The Civil Rights Movement also illustrated the importance of faith as an impetus for social justice movements. Black churches as religious institutions provided organizational centers, resource mobilization, and movement leadership which contributed to the success of the movement.

On a global scale, the Civil Rights Movement exposed the world to the shortcomings of democracy in the USA. While the Civil Rights Movement illegalized *de jure* racism, it did not eliminate *de facto* racism. The institutional barriers removed by the Civil Rights Movement allowed for the growth of the black middle class, and helped to racially integrate many public institutions, yet the dilemma of racial inequality has persisted.

SEE ALSO: Indigenous Movements; Race; Stratification, Race/Ethnicity and; Social Movements, Nonviolent

SUGGESTED READINGS

Morris, A. D. (1984) *The Origins of the Civil Rights Movement: Black Communities Organizing for Change*. Free Press, New York.

Robnett, B. (1997) *How Long? How Long? African-American Women in the Struggle for Civil Rights*. Oxford University Press, New York.

KENDRA BARBER

civil society

Civil society is often understood as a defense against excessive state power and atomized individualism, which otherwise threatens to create conditions for authoritarianism. The term can be traced to Roman civil law (*ius civile*) but its contemporary use to describe contractual relations, the rise of public opinion, representative government, civic freedoms, plurality, and "civility" first appeared in seventeenth- and eighteenth-century political philosophy notably in Hobbes's theory of a "social contract" between civil and political branches of the state and then Locke's theory of natural rights that inhere in civil society.

Civil society is a relatively autonomous sphere separate from and constraining the state. Though initially based on socially exclusive networks (aristocratic men in coffeehouse society) civil society theories envisaged a space for debate and private association at a time when such liberal principles were not widely shared. Ferguson (1966 [1767]) saw the development of civil society as bound to the progress of humanity from simple, clan-based militaristic societies to complex commercial ones. Civil society establishes a new order requiring dispersal of power and office, the rule of law, and liberal (i.e., tolerant) sentiments, in which people's lives and property are secure. However, civil society does not refer to just *any* kind of informal or private social relations, which exist in all societies, but to morally guided relations that make possible trust in anonymous social exchanges. Tocqueville, Durkheim, and then contemporary writers such as Putnam (1993) developed these ideas and stressed the importance of active and informal networks for stable democracy. Conversely, societies with weak civil society, low trust, and high levels of corruption for example will be vulnerable to authoritarianism.

Gramsci reintroduced the concept into Marxism in the 1920s when – attempting to combat economic reductionism – he defined civil society as a sphere of cultural struggle against bourgeois hegemony. This formulation was influential among Eurocommunist parties in the 1970 and 1980s, although ironically a significant revival of the concept came with the anti-communist movements of 1989, in which civil society defined social spaces for public discussion, local initiatives, and voluntary citizens' associations against the state. In the event many commentators view post-communist civil societies with disappointment, in the face of cultures of distrust, informal dealings, and the strengthening of particularistic visions and elements.

Alongside and possibly supplanting national state–civil society relations, some suggest that there is a global civil society made up of international non-governmental organizations, transnational social movements, and digitally mediated social networks. Although this idea has been influential, there is a conflict between the goal of creating transnational cosmopolitan values and the unregulated growth of world markets brought by global neoliberalism that has resulted in heightened levels of social inequality, which neither states nor international organizations have the capacity to address. Global political and corporate institutions are not (yet?) embedded within constraining networks of a global civil society and there is a risk here of an excessively elastic and insufficiently complex concept.

SEE ALSO: Democracy; Gramsci, Antonio; Marx, Karl; Public Sphere

REFERENCES

Ferguson, A. (1966) [1767] *An Essay on the History of Civil Society*. Edinburgh University Press, Edinburgh.

Putnam, R. D. (1993) *Making Democracy Work: Civic Traditions in Modern Italy*. Princeton University Press, Princeton, NJ.

LARRY RAY

civilizations

The central analytical core of the concept of civilization as presented here is the combination of ontological or cosmological visions, of visions of transmundane and mundane reality, with the definition, construction, and regulation of the major arenas of social life and interaction.

The central core of civilizations is the symbolic and institutional interrelation between the formulation, promulgation, articulation, and continuous reinterpretation of the basic ontological visions prevalent in a society, its basic ideological premises and core symbols on the one hand, and on the other the definition, structuration, and regulation of the major arenas of institutional life, of the political arena, of authority and its accountability, of the economy, of family life, social stratification, and of the construction of collective identities.

The impact of such ontological visions and premises on institutional formation is effected through various processes of social interaction and control that develop in a society. Such processes of control – and the opposition to them – are not limited to the exercise of power in the "narrow" political sense; as even sophisticated Marxists have stressed, they involve not only class relations or "modes of production." Rather, they are activated by major elites and influentials in a society.

The structure of such elite groups is closely related, on the one hand, to the basic cultural orientations prevalent in a society. On the other hand, and in connection with the types of cultural orientations and their transformations into basic premises of the social order, these elite groups tend to exercise different modes of control over the allocation of basic resources in the society.

In most human societies the distinct ideological and institutional civilizational dimensions were embedded in the major political, kinship, and ecological settings. The full development of these distinct civilizational dimensions – and of some awareness of their distinctiveness – occurred only in some very specific historical settings, namely, the so-called axial civilizations – even if some very important steps in that direction can be identified in some archaic civilizations such as the ancient Egyptian, Assyrian, or Mesoamerican ones, and especially in what may be called proto-axial ones, such as in the Iranian-Zoroastrian one, i.e. those civilizations that crystallized during the half-millennium from 500 BCE to the first century of the Christian era, within which new types of ontological visions, conceptions of a basic tension between the transcendental and mundane orders, emerged and were institutionalized in many parts of the world: above all, ancient Israel, followed by Second-Commonwealth Judaism and Christianity; ancient Greece; possibly Zoroastrianism in Iran; early imperial China; Hinduism and Buddhism; and, beyond the axial age proper, Islam. In all these cases the emergence of the axial civilizations that civilizations crystallized as distinct entities and an explicit consciousness thereof developed.

In these civilizations there developed a strong tendency to define certain collectivities and institutional – cultural or religious – arenas as distinct from "ethnic" or "political" ones – as most appropriate for the implementation of their respective transcendental visions.

Within all these civilizations there developed continual processes of change and of heterodox tendencies to far-reaching transformations. In close connection with these processes, heterodoxies there developed the strong sectarian heterodox visions that had been a permanent component in the dynamics of these civilizations, but with some partial exceptions, especially among some Islamic sects, they did not give rise to radical transformation of the political arena, its premises, and symbols. The most dramatic transformation from within one of the axial civilizations has probably been the emergence of modernity as a distinct new civilization, which first crystallized in Western Europe and then expanded to most other parts of the world, giving continual rise to the development of multiple, continually changing modernities.

This change took place in the realm of European-Christian civilization through the transformation of the sectarian visions through the Reformation and later the great revolutions, in which there developed a very strong emphasis on the bringing together of the City of God and the City of Man.

SEE ALSO: Culture; Empire; Political Sociology

SUGGESTED READINGS

Arnason, J. (2003) *Civilizations in Dispute*. Brill, Leiden.

Tiryakian, E. & Arjomand, S. A. (eds.) (2004) *Rethinking Civilizational Analysis*. Sage, London.

Castoriadis, C. (1987) *The Imaginary Constitution of Society*. Polity Press, Cambridge.

Eisenstadt, S. N., Arnason, J. P., & Wittrock, B. (eds.) 2005. *Axial Civilizations and World History*, Koninklijke Brill NV, Leiden.

Eisenstadt, S. N. (ed.) (2002) *Multiple Modernities*. Transaction, New Brunswick.

S. N. EISENSTADT

civilizing process

The concept of "the civilizing process" rests on a conception of "civilization" as a verb, aiming at understanding those social and political conditions, practices, and strategies which have produced changing conceptions of civility. There is a concern to link analysis of social, cultural, political and economic structures, processes, and lines of development to analysis of changing forms of subjective and intersubjective forms and relationships.

The concept is used in the greatest depth by the German sociologist Norbert Elias and his followers, but it also usefully captures a cluster of developments examined by a variety of other social theorists who have also observed and analyzed the emergence of a specifically modern disciplined character, mode of conduct, or habitus. Elias's approach shows: (1) that what is experienced as "civilization" is founded on a psychic structure or habitus which had changed over time, and (2) that it can only be understood in connection with changes in broader social relationships.

The concept is an important element of research and theory in social and historical studies of the self, identity, emotions and the body, the sociology of sport, social histories of crime and punishment, studies of genocide and the conduct of war, the sociology of organizations, and discussions of international relations and globalization. A central methodological problem concerns whether there has been too much emphasis placed on it as an unplanned process, and not enough attention paid to it as a civilizing mission or offensive. Anthropologists have also drawn attention to the continuities in human behavior across all cultural and historical contexts.

The themes which will dominate future discussion of the civilizing process include extending the analysis of civilizing processes beyond advanced industrial societies, the regulation of crime and corruption, the application of the concept to international relations, and the analysis of globalization.

SEE ALSO: Elias, Norbert

SUGGESTED READING

Elias, N. (2000) *The Civilizing Process: Sociogenetic and Psychogenetic Investigations*, rev. edn. Blackwell, Oxford.

ROBERT VAN KRIEKEN

class

Class refers to a stratification system that divides a society into a hierarchy of social positions. It is also a particular social position within a class stratification system: lower class, working class, middle class, upper class, or other such class designation. It is a method of social ranking that involves money, power, culture, taste, identity, access, and exclusion. Conceptualizations of class belong not only to sociology, but also to the popular press, the marketplace, the political process, and to those who perceive themselves as being located within a particular class position. People who do perceive class distinctions are "class conscious" and may feel the impact of class in powerful ways. Others barely notice it or refuse to concede its existence despite living with its effects. To some people, class connotes differing economic circumstances, lifestyles, and tastes; to others it is about social status, esteem, and respect.

New students of sociology will quickly encounter the concept of class. They will become familiar with the writings of Karl Marx and Max Weber and other prominent social theorists, who have contrasted, debated, explained, and elaborated the works of these foundational figures over the past century. They will be introduced to the research methods and applications that have alternately advanced and constrained class studies, especially in the USA. They will also find that the topic of class is both ideologically and emotionally charged, and that its usage in academic as well as interpersonal settings can be fraught with controversy and strong sentiment.

Marx made the concept of class central to his theory of social conflict. A class structure requires a power relationship: in Marxist terms, those who own productive property and those who do not, those who dominate and those who are subordinate. He divided industrial society into owners of capital (capitalists) and workers (the proletariat). In developed capitalist economies, the capitalist class owns most of society's assets and wields most of its economic and political power although the working class constitutes the majority of the population. In between capitalists and workers is a class that consists of professionals, shopkeepers, craftsmen, and other independent proprietors. Like capitalists, they own their own means of production and hire workers to assist them. They contribute much of the labor in creating or selling their products and services, and therefore can be their own "workers." Members of this class sometimes identify their interests with capitalists, and sometimes their interests lie with those of the working class.

Weber, like Marx, believed that economic stratification produces social classes, but he argued that other forms of social stratification occur independently of economics. Weber's was a three-dimensional model of stratification consisting of: (1) *social classes* that have an economic base; (2) *parties* which are oriented toward the acquisition of social power; and (3) *status* groups delineated in terms of social estimations of honor or esteem. Whereas Marx dealt mainly with the conflict of capitalists and workers, Weber added other groups with opposing interests: workers and managers, finance capitalists and borrowers, and sellers and purchasers of products and services.

In Weberian terms, classes are aggregates of individuals who share similar "life chances" with respect to education, work, healthcare, and in their ability to build personal wealth. Dominant classes achieve a monopoly on more lucrative markets; less dominant classes get only partial market participation. Classes reflect a particular community of interests, and class members share more than economic position or situation. They share cultural tastes and outlooks – lifestyles, educational credentials, occupational positions – that can cloak the economic basis for the particular class interest underneath.

Research traditions within sociology use both *objective* and *subjective* social class measures. Objective social class is defined in terms of objective criteria such as income, occupation and education as decided upon by the investigator. Subjective social class, by contrast, is measured in terms of how people identify themselves as class members within a hierarchy of social classes defined within the research. The class structures of several American communities (and cities) were identified in classic studies from the late 1930s through the late 1960s. In 1941, W. Lloyd Warner and his associates, studying a New England community, conceptualized classes as groups of people, judged as superior or inferior in prestige and acceptability to those "below or above them." Coleman and Neugarten, for their 1950s study of Kansas City, converted class to status groupings to test symbols of social status such as neighborhood, social clubs, educational attainment, and occupations. True to Weber's conceptions, the results showed that social status awareness was concentrated on status symbols and the relative status rank of individuals. The top and bottom status groups were seen as relatively small and defined as the "rich" and "poor," leaving one large middle class, a perception of class that persists in the USA today.

Community research helped to soften the Marxist class model and to demonstrate that a continuum exists among classes ranked primarily by occupational prestige, lifestyle, and status attainment. Attention was shifted away from economic interests towards subjective differences among individuals. Americans are popularly thought to be unburdened by the class distinctions that exist in older societies, although recent research suggests that the USA is not a classless society. Class differences and the movement of families up, and especially down, the economic ladder present a contradictory but compelling picture of stagnating mobility and emerging elites. Despite controversy and disagreement among researchers, it appears that interest in the concept of class is on the rise.

SEE ALSO: Class Conflict; Class Consciousness; Leisure Class; Marx, Karl; Weber, Max

SUGGESTED READINGS

Coleman, R. P. and Neugarten, B. L. (1971) *Social Status in the City*. Jossey-Bass, San Francisco, CA.

Warner, W. L., Meeker, M. L., & Eells, K. (1949.) *Social Class in America*. Science Research Associates, Chicago, IL.

Weber, M. (1982) The distribution of power: class, status, party. In: *Classes, Power, and Conflict*. University of California Press, Berkeley, CA.

Wright, E. O. (2005) Foundations of a neo-Marxist class analysis. In: E. O. Wright (ed.), *Approaches to Class Analysis*. Cambridge University Press, Cambridge.

LOIS A. VITT

class conflict

Marx famously stated "the history of all societies up to the present is the history of the class struggle." In his interpretation, the term class is used to refer to the main strata in all stratified society as constituted by a social group whose members share the same relationship to the forces of production. This was evident, according to Marx, in western societies which developed through the epochs of primitive communism, ancient society, feudal society, and industrial capitalism. Primitive communism, based on a communal mode of production and distribution, typified by a subsistence economy, represents the only example of a classless society. From then on, all societies are divided into essentially two major classes that are in an antagonistic relationship: masters and slaves in ancient society, lords and serfs under feudalism, and bourgeoisie and proletariat under the capitalist order. During each historical epoch the labor power required for production was supplied by the majority subject class. While, for Marx, class conflict arises in the exploitative situation evoked by the relationship to the forces of production, it is also evident through the development of such forces by an emerging class. The superiority of the capitalist forces of production, by way of illustration, led to a rapid transformation of the social structure, but only after the revolutionary triumph of the emergent class over the feudal order.

In terms of class conflict, or potential class conflict, Marx distinguished between a "class in itself" and a "class for itself." The former comprises a social grouping whose constituents share the same relationship to the forces of production. However, for Marx, a social grouping only fully becomes a class when it forms a "class for itself." At this stage, its members have achieved class consciousness and solidarity – a full awareness of their true situation of exploitation and oppression. Members of a class subsequently develop a common identity, recognize their shared interest, and unite, so creating class cohesion and ultimately taking recourse to revolutionary violence.

Much of Marx's work was concerned with class conflict in capitalist industrial society. Class antagonisms could not be resolved within its structure. Thus, the contradictions inherent in capitalism and its accompanying socio-political structures would bring class conflict to its ultimate realization. As capitalism develops, the workforce is concentrated in large factories where production becomes a social enterprise and thus illuminates the exploitation of the proletariat and its shared grievances. The increasing use of machinery would result in a homogeneous class since such technology brings a leveling process of deskilling, enhancing a sense of common experience, and engendering an increasing sense of alienation.

Marx believed that the class struggle that would overthrow the capitalist order would ensure that private property would be replaced by communally owned property, though industrial manufacture would remain as the basic modus operandi of production in the new society, communally owned but at a higher level of technological development. Since history is about class struggle, history would eventually come to an end. The socialist society that would replace capitalism would contain no dialectical contradictions, while, in effect, the working class would abolish itself.

SEE ALSO: Bourgeoisie and Proletariat; Class; Class Consciousness; Conflict Theory; False Consciousness; Marx, Karl

SUGGESTED READINGS

Darendorf, R. (1959) *Class and Class Conflict in Industrial Society*. Routledge & Kegan Paul, London.

Marx, K. & Engels, F. (1977) [1848] The communist manifesto. In: McLellan, D. (ed.), *Karl Marx: Selected Writings*. Oxford University Press, Oxford, pp. 221–46.

STEPHEN HUNT

class consciousness

For Marx, the transition from the objective conditions of a class "in itself" to one "in and for itself" results from workers experiencing and interpreting contradictions between "the existing individualist relations of production and the emerging collective forces of production" (Mann 1973: 12).

While the variation in Marxian discussions of the objective conditions is relatively consistent and circumscribed – a class's objective position within the social relations of production; amassing of workers in increasingly larger factories and in specific urban locations; material conditions of work; forms and processes of exploitation; absolute and relative deprivation – the development of class consciousness is more varied. Lenin, at one extreme, maintained workers could only achieve "trade union consciousness," requiring a vanguard party to reach revolutionary consciousness. Gramsci, at the other, argued organic intellectuals, developing within the working class, would challenge the existing hegemony. For class consciousness to become revolutionary, workers must identify as members of a single class, oppose other classes, believing their total situation (indeed, society as a whole) must and can be transformed into a better, envisioned, social totality.

E. P. Thompson (1968: 9–11) best captures the class/class consciousness dialectic: "class happens when some men, as a result of common experiences (inherited or shared), feel and articulate the identity of their interests as between themselves, and as against other men whose interests are different from (and usually opposed to) theirs." While class experience stems from one's location in the social relations of production, class consciousness is how those experiences are "expressed in cultural terms." Class is not a thing; it is how people "live their history."

SEE ALSO: Bourgeoisie and Proletariat; Class; Class Conflict; False Consciousness; Marx, Karl

REFERENCES

Mann, M. (1973) *Consciousness and Action among the Western Working Class*. Macmillan, London.

Thompson, E. P. (1968) *The Making of the English Working Class*. Penguin, Harmondsworth.

ROB BEAMISH

cognitive dissonance theory (Festinger)

Cognitive dissonance theory posits that individuals seek to maintain consistency among multiple cognitions (e.g., thoughts, behaviors, attitudes, values, beliefs). Inconsistent cognitions produce unpleasant arousal that leads individuals to reduce dissonance by: (1) changing one's cognition so that all cognitions are in agreement, (2) adopting cognitions that strengthen the "desirable" cognition, or (3) reducing the importance assigned to the inconsistency.

Heider's (1946: *The Psychology of Interpersonal Relations*) balance theory stated that people strive for balanced relationships between individuals and objects within their environment. Because unstable cognitions are difficult to maintain, people make adjustments in order to regain consistency. Festinger (1957) theorized that the driving force behind the need for balance was the aversive arousal caused by inconsistent cognitions.

Aronson (1969) introduced a "self-concept" theory, which presumed that individuals are motivated by a threat to the self-concept caused by inconsistent cognitions.

Bem (1965) offered a non-motivational explanation for attitudinal change. His "self-perception" theory stated that people's attitudes are established by reflecting on their behavior and then forming attitudes consistent with that behavior. Thus, a change in behavior leads to a change in attitude.

Zanna & Cooper (1974: "Dissonance and the pill: an attribution approach to studying the arousal properties of dissonance") concluded that arousal caused by internal imbalance motivates attitude change, while arousal caused by external factors does not influence attitude change.

Steele & Liu (1983: "Dissonance processes as self-affirmation") suggested that attitude change resulting from dissonance is caused by a need for a positive self-image rather than a need for cognitive consistency.

Cooper & Fazio (1984: "A new look at dissonance theory") suggested that dissonance occurs when individuals violate a societal norm.

Dissonance studies have used several paradigms to arouse dissonance such as "forced compliance" and "hypocrisy" models. In addition to dissonance arousal and relief, researchers have also applied cognitive dissonance theory to many real-world areas including culture, social support, and health and prevention.

SEE ALSO: Attitudes and Behavior; Psychology

REFERENCES

Aronson, E. (1969) The theory of cognitive dissonance: a current perspective. In: Berkowitz, L. (ed.), *Advances in Experimental Social Psychology*, vol. 4. Academic Press, New York, pp. 2–34.

Bem, D. (1965) An experimental analysis of self-persuasion. *Journal of Experimental Social Psychology* 1: 199–218.

ALEXANDRA E. SIGILLO, MONICA K. MILLER, AND ALAYNA JEHLE

cohabitation

The past few decades have brought dramatic changes in the residential arrangements of romantically involved unmarried adults. Indeed, as sexual activity has become uncoupled from marriage, growing numbers of young couples have begun sharing a home and a bed without the legal sanction of marriage. Cohabitation, as this type of living arrangement is commonly known, has become a normative part of the adult life course.

Determining the prevalence of cohabitation is a challenging task. Given the nature of today's dating and mating patterns, measuring trends in cohabitation is a highly subjective undertaking. Legal marriages are officially recorded via state licenses; no such formality is imposed on cohabiting couples. The process of entering into cohabiting unions can be rather indeterminate. Some couples may first spend a night or two together, but then find themselves staying overnight several times a week before ultimately acknowledging that they "live together." During this process, individuals may retain their separate addresses, even if they rarely sleep there, yet remain unwilling to tell family and friends that they cohabit. Other romantic couples proceed quickly and quite consciously into coresidential relationships, but without specific plans to marry. For others, cohabitation is a stepping stone to marriage – a way to test for compatibility or cement their relationship.

Most cohabiting unions are of relatively short duration, lasting on average only a year or two. A small fraction continue to cohabit indefinitely or represent an alternative to marriage. In the USA roughly half of all cohabiting unions end within the first year. In contrast, only about 1 in 10 lasts 5 or more years. Despite common beliefs that living together is a good way to assess compatibility for marriage, couples that lived together prior to marriage have elevated rates of marital dissolution. Cohabitation therefore does not appear to reduce subsequent divorce by winnowing out the least stable couples from marriage. However, the association between cohabitation and relationship disruption has not been firmly established.

Those who choose to live together tend to be different from adults who marry without first cohabiting, in that they tend to have lower levels of education, more unstable employment histories, and less traditional orientations towards the family. Another way in which cohabiting couples differ from those who are married is in their divergent backgrounds. For example, cohabiting couples are more likely to consist of partners from different racial backgrounds than are married couples, suggesting that living together is more acceptable than is marriage for interracial partnerships. Cohabitation is also less selective than is marriage with respect to education.

SEE ALSO: Divorce; Family Structure; Lesbian and Gay Families; Love and Commitment; Marriage

SUGGESTED READINGS

Blackwell, D. L. & Lichter, D. (2000) Mate selection among married and cohabiting couples. *Journal of Family Issues* 21: 275–302.

Sassler, S. (2004) The process of entering into cohabiting unions. *Journal of Marriage and Family* 66: 491–505.

SHARON L. SASSLER

collective action

The term "collective action" is hopelessly broad. Taken at face value, it could plausibly refer to *all* forms of human behavior involving two or more people. For our purposes, however, collective action refers to *emergent and at least minimally coordinated action by two or more people that is motivated by a desire to change some aspect of social life or to resist changes proposed by others*. While many aspects of collective action have been the subject of theory and research, we organize the entry around the two questions that have received the most scholarly attention.

The first concerns the origins of collective action. *Strain* theories presume that collective action is a response to some form of disruption in the normal functioning of society. In contrast, *resource mobilization* theorists argue that there is always sufficient "strain" in society to provide the motivation for collective action; what varies are the organizational capacity and resources required to do so. The distinctive contribution of *political process* theory has been to reassert the fundamental political character and origins of collective action. The main emphasis has been on the role of catalytic events that weaken established regimes, thereby creating new "opportunities" for successful action by challenging groups.

The second question focuses on differential participation in collective action. Why does one person come to take part while another does not? The oldest accounts of activism are *psychological*. The emphasis is on character traits or states of mind that presumably dispose an individual to participate. Running very much counter to these psychological theories is an important *rationalist* tradition in the study of collective action. More specifically, we can expect individuals to participate when: (1) they receive selective incentives for doing so and (2) effective systems of monitoring and sanctioning work are operating to deny benefits to those who fail to take part. A third perspective holds that strong *attitudinal support* for the aims of a movement compels individual activism.

All of the previous accounts of participation can be thought of as "dispositional." The final theory rests on a very different assumption. People participate not simply because prior dispositions impel them to, but because their *network location* in the world puts them at "risk" for participation. The causal emphasis is on existing ties to others in the movement that serve to *pull* them into collective action even as various dispositions are *pushing* them in that direction.

SEE ALSO: Civil Rights Movement; Resource Mobilization Theory; Revolutions; Social Change; Social Movements; Social Movements, Networks and

SUGGESTED READINGS

Diani, M. & McAdam, D. (eds.) (2003) *Social Movements and Networks.* Oxford University Press, Oxford.

McAdam, D. (1999) [1982] *Political Process and the Development of Black Insurgency, 1930–1970.* University of Chicago Press, Chicago, IL.

McCarthy, J. D. & Zald, M. N. (1977) Resource mobilization and social movements: a partial theory. *American Journal of Sociology* 82: 1212–41.

Olson, M., Jr. (1965) *The Logic of Collective Action.* Harvard University Press, Cambridge, MA.

Tilly, C. (1978) *From Mobilization to Revolution.* Addison-Wesley, Reading, MA.

DOUG MCADAM

collective consciousness

Two components of French sociologist Émile Durkheim's project are to establish sociology as a discipline in its own right, distinct from psychology, and to understand and demonstrate the dependence of human beings upon their societies. These come together in Durkheim's *L'ame collective* [the collective mind]. This concept, commonly referred to by sociologists as the "collective consciousness" or "conscience collective," exemplifies the crucial role that the social plays in human behavior.

In *The Division of Labor in Society*, Durkheim (1893) defines the collective consciousness as "the totality of beliefs and sentiments common to average members of the same society . . . it is an entirely different thing from particular consciences, although it can only be realized through them" (1933/1893: 38, 39). To understand how the collective consciousness functions, one must first understand Durkheim's distinction between what he deems mechanical and organic societies.

In *The Division of Labor in Society*, Durkheim illustrates the different mechanisms of social order through two societal types. The first type, the *mechanical* society, is a traditional, simpler society composed of economically self-sustaining members who, living in close proximity, are more alike than different. They are unified by language, religious beliefs, values, rituals; and activities common to, and respected by all. Together, these representations comprise the collective consciousness, a real, external, and coercive societal entity that pre-exists, outlives, is found in, and acts upon all people in the same manner. In a mechanical society, the function of the collective consciousness is to enforce social similarity and to discourage individual variation, which, in such a society, could undermine collective unity.

As populations grow, dynamic density increases and people interact more and more intensely.

Significantly, it is marked by an increase in occupational specialization: the division of labor. The changed and differentiated division of labor has a paradoxical effect: it creates interdependent individuality. That is, individuals increasingly perform heterogenous tasks, thus increasing their interdependence on each other and society, but they also perform increasingly specialized tasks, thus increasing their individuality. Their individual consciousnesses are increasingly developed and distinctive from the conscience collective. Durkheim deems such a societal arrangment *organic*. To Giddens (1972), Durkheim's collective consciousness in organic solidarity, now generated by the interdependence brought on by the specialized division of labor, is embodied in the state. Whereas the collective consciousness in mechanical society enforced what was necessary for society, in organic solidarity the state, informed by workers' guilds, consciously deliberates and collectively enacts what is best for society.

SEE ALSO: Anomie; Division of Labor; Émile Durkheim; Social Control; Solidarity, Mechanical and Organic

REFERENCES

Durkheim, É. (1933) [1893] *The Division of Labor in Society*. Free Press, New York.
Giddens, A. (1972) *Emile Durkheim Selected Writings*. Cambridge University Press, Cambridge.

SUSAN WORTMANN

collective identity

Within social movement theory, collective identity refers to the shared definition of a group that derives from its members' common interests, experiences, and solidarities. It is the social movement's answer to who we are, locating the movement within a field of political actors. Collective identity is neither fixed nor innate, but, rather, emerges through struggle as different political actors, including the movement, interact and react to each other. The salience of any given collective identity affects the mobilization, trajectory, and even impacts of social movements. Consequently, collective identity has become a central concept in the study of social movements.

The concept of collective identity emerged in the 1980s in Europe within new social movement (NSM) theory. Most locate its origin in the work of Alberto Melucci (1995). Researchers, dissatisfied by what they believed to be the overly structural depiction of social movements offered by the dominant resource mobilization and political process theories, adopted concepts from new social movement theory, like collective identity, to bring the cultural back into the study of social movements. Researchers acknowledge the relevance of collective identity not only for "new" social movements, but also for a variety of movements, both "old" and "new."

Collective identity is not predetermined. Political actors do not share a de facto identity as a result of their common structural position. Rather, identity emerges through various processes in which movement actors instill it with significance, relevance, and form. The three major processes through which movements construct an identity are: (1) the establishment of boundaries, (2) negotiation, and (3) the development of consciousness. In boundary making, social movements create new group values and structures that delineate who they are in relation to other political actors. In negotiation, movements engage with other political actors, continually enacting their shared identity and working to influence symbolic meanings. Finally, the development of consciousness imbues the collective identity with a larger purpose by embedding it within an ideological framework that assigns blame for the injustice against which the movement is mobilized. Further, collective identity becomes manifest in the day-to-day activities of the social movement. Movements not only have a collective identity, they also act in accordance with that identity. The line between "being" and "doing" is blurred.

SEE ALSO: Identity Politics/Relational Politics; Identity Theory; New Social Movement Theory; Social Movements; Social Movements, Networks and

REFERENCE

Melucci, A. (1995) The process of collective identity. In: Johnson, H. & Klandermas, B. (eds.), *Social Movements and Culture*. University of Minnesota Press, Minneapolis, MN, pp. 41–63.

SUGGESTED READING

Polletta, F. & Jasper, J. (2001) Collective identity and social movements. *Annual Review of Sociology* 27: 283–305.

OWEN WHOOLEY

colonialism (neocolonialism)

Colonialism refers to the direct political control of a society and its people by a foreign ruling state. Essentially it is a political phenomenon. The ruling state monopolizes political power and keeps the subordinated society and its people in a legally inferior position. But colonialism has had significant cultural, social, and economic correlates and ramifications. Neocolonialism is the continued exercise of political or economic influence over a society in the absence of formal political control.

Traditionally, the concept of colonialism has been associated with "colonization," which refers to the transplantation or settlement of peoples from one territory to another. The word colonization is derived from the Latin *colonia*, meaning the settlement of people from home. But popular and scholarly uses of the term later shifted the meaning. Colonialism came to refer to political control with or without settlement. The concept also took on a more explicit ethnic, racial, and geographical component. It increasingly came to refer to the establishment of political control by European or western powers over Asia, Latin America, and Africa. It also signified political control by one "race" over another "race," where the latter is deemed inferior to the former.

Analytically, colonialism is related to but also distinguishable from imperialism. While imperialism also refers to control by one society over another, it does not have to take the form of direct political control. It can also occur through informal political means (such as temporary military occupation), the exercise of economic power (control over finance or imposition of embargoes), or cultural influence (the spread of Hollywood movies around the world). Colonialism, by contrast, is a more specific variant of imperialism, referring to a situation whereby control is exerted directly and for a sustained duration of time. The ruling power officially declares political control over another territory and its people and institutionalizes the control through declarations of law. The colonized country is then a part of the mother country but subordinate to it. In this sense, colonialism can be seen as one particular form of imperialism among others.

The term neocolonialism refers to relations of unequal power between countries despite the formal independence of those countries. The term suggests that, even after colonized societies attain independence, they are kept in a position of political and economic inferiority that reproduces the position they had had when they were formal colonies. In this view, formerly colonized nations remain subject to unequal exchange with western countries, become dependent upon them for capital and technology necessary for their own industrialization, and serve as places for labor exploitation and continued resource extraction by foreign firms. Politically, formerly colonized nations remain subject to various mechanisms of outside control by western powers, either through debt bondage and international institutions like the World Bank or through political pressure or direct military intervention.

SEE ALSO: Decolonization; Dependency and World-Systems Theories; Orientalism; Third World and Postcolonial Feminisms/Subaltern

SUGGESTED READINGS

Brewer, A. (1990) *Marxist Theories of Imperialism: A Critical Survey*. Routledge, London.

Memmi, A. (1967) *The Colonizer and the Colonized*. Beacon Press, Boston, MA.

JULIAN GO

coming out/closets

The term coming out and the metaphor of the closet are closely connected. Both concepts have played a significant role in sexual politics since the 1950s. The idea of coming out was popularized in the radical politics of gay liberation movements throughout the 1960s and 1970s. On its most basic level, coming-out refers to a person's public disclosure of his or her gay male, lesbian, bisexual, or any other non-heterosexual identity. Gay liberationists considered coming out to be a political act, since heterosexist oppression aims at the erasure of same-sex desire. Gay liberationists mapped the interplay of various modes of oppression through the concept of the closet: criminalization, pathologization, police violence, bullying and queer-bashing, and the circulation of distorted images in media, education, and political discourse. The closet stands for the imposition of a psychic and socio-cultural reality reigned by secrecy, shame, lack of recognition, and isolation. In a book that became very influential during the 1990s, Sedgwick (1990) suggested that the closet should be understood more broadly. Putting forward the notion of the epistemology of the closet, Sedgwick argued that *all* forms of desire are organized around the alternatives of disclosure or secrecy and *all* social institutions are interested in regulating what can or should be known. Her work explored how cultural anxieties around the heterosexual/homosexual binary shaped the conceptualization of truth, secrecy, and personhood in western culture far beyond the policing of homosexuality.

As a political strategy, coming out involved various levels of reference, including self-acceptance, the sharing of one's identification with others (friends, family, colleagues, and so on) and coming out to society (for example through the participation at Gay Pride events). The gay liberationist slogan "Out of the closets and into the streets" shows that the ultimate aim was full participation in society. The street is not only a site of heightened visibility. It describes an integral element of the wider public sphere. In the liberationist approach, coming out was embedded in a collective strategy of community building. It allowed for the organization of political and self-help groups, the creation of gay neighborhoods in larger cities and laid the base for the emergence of a pink economy. This in turn provided the resources for survival in a hostile society and the continuation of an ongoing struggle for transformation. The consolidation of identity politics in subsequent generations of activism reinforced (often essentialist) notions of globally universal gay and lesbian identities. The emergence of gay and lesbian public spheres provides the backdrop to Herdt's (1992) analysis of coming out as a rite-of-passage. His study of a youth coming-out group in Chicago defines coming out as a ritualistic process of re-socialization, in which young men and women shun values derived from an older *homosexual* epistemological framework (governed by secrecy, shame, pathology, and stereotype) through a shift towards a *gay* (liberationist) paradigm (based on self-assertion and the recognition of gayness as a valid cultural force). Research since the 1990s emphasized that coming out is an ongoing multi-layered (and not necessarily linear) process throughout which people manage knowledge regarding their identities or sexual practices across fragmented cultural terrains. Moreover, the metaphor of coming out has been adapted in various fields of sexual and gender politics. There have been discussions about coming out, for example, in queer, bisexual, SM, polyamory, and transgender movements. Coming out entails different challenges in each context. Moreover, since the constituencies of these groups are not mutually exclusive, many people negotiate multiply stigmatized identifications in their coming-out processes.

US research indicates that at the turn of the millennium not all gay men and lesbians consider coming out to be a major issue in their lives any more. This "routinization" and "normalization" of *some* non-heterosexual cultural forms has given rise to the speculation about "the end of the closet". Yet as we have seen, there are multiple closets. Moreover, heterosexism has always been uneven across different spheres of society. Social location in terms of class, gender, race/ethnicity, and religious affiliation plays a significant role in mediating the nature and severity of the repercussions, which may follow the revelation of stigmatized erotic, sexual, or gender identifications. Black and ethnic minority activists have criticized the generalized demand to come out. They argued that many black non-heterosexuals need and value family and community support against racism. Coming out may endanger this support, so that coming out may feel too risky for many black non-heterosexuals in the face of enduring racism within heterosexual and non-heterosexual communities. For others, coming out may be irrelevant, if gay, lesbian or bisexual identities do not resonate with their salient cultural identifications. Same-sex desire carries different meanings in different cultural contexts.

SEE ALSO: Compulsory Heterosexuality; Gay and Lesbian Movement; Homophobia and Heterosexism; Homosexuality; Identity Politics/ Relational Politics; Transgender, Transvestism, and Transsexualism; Sexual Politics

REFERENCES

Herdt, G. (1992) (ed.) *Gay Culture in America*. Beacon Press, Boston, MA.

Sedgwick, E. K. (1990) *The Epistemology of the Closet*. University of California Press, Berkeley, CA.

SUGGESTED READING

Weeks, J. (1990) *Coming Out*, 2nd edn. Quartet Books, New York.

CHRISTIAN KLESSE

commodities, commodity fetishism, and commodification

Commodities are things that are useful, or that satisfy fundamental human needs – such as food or shelter – or more ephemeral needs, such as the desire to appear attractive or successful. As it is understood today, however, a commodity is a product that is bought and sold. This narrowing of the term came about with the rise of capitalism as the central organizing principle of Euro-American economic and social life.

The pioneering critique of capitalism by the philosopher Karl Marx in the mid nineteenth century brought the commodity to the fore as a unit of analysis in the study of capitalist social relations. In that work, Marx suggested that commodities' seeming simple utility masked the social and material relations that brought them into existence – especially the human labor necessary to produce them. Although a commodity was useful to the person who bought it because it satisfied some need, it was also useful to the person who sold it because its sale yielded value in excess of the cost of the labor and materials necessary to produce it.

Marx's theory responded to those of economists such as Adam Smith and David Ricardo, for whom the price of food, clothing, or fuel, for example, was seen as set by forces of supply and demand, and into which the very social struggle over the price of labor did not figure. Struggling to earn a living, individual laborers were blinded to these social relations, which they had in common with other workers, seeing commodities as simple objects of utility and not as repositories of those relations.

Marx referred to this designation of commodities as mere objects of utility as *commodity fetishism*, sarcastically suggesting that the classical economists' description of commodities as containing their own value, although seemingly scientific, was actually fantastical and wrong-headed. Marx drew upon emerging anthropological theory, which described religious practices in European colonies in Africa and East Asia as "fetishistic" because adherents to those religions ostensibly believed that their gods or ancestors dwelt in idols. Economists who treated commodities as having value in and of themselves were to Marx no better than primitive shamans or hucksters peddling a false religion.

By the end of the nineteenth century, rapid industrial development led social critics such as Max Weber and Thorstein Veblen to describe the commodity to a largely middle-class audience as a means of understanding the anxiety deriving from significant changes in social life, and for suggesting reforms designed to stave off workers' revolts in Europe and North America. During the twentieth century, women were increasingly positioned as the managers of household consumption, and men and children as the victims or beneficiaries of their purchases. Commodities were seen as bearing more than *practical* use value; they also carried *social* values, encouraging their users to be passive, consuming members of society rather than active and productive citizens. This transition has come to be called the "*commodification* of everyday life," or the rise of "consumer culture," and suggests a loss of personal and civic autonomy. This more reformist analysis of commodification has targeted an audience of consumers in order to alienate them from commodity relations, in the hopes of bolstering political and civic spheres activity, rather than creating the intellectual support for revolution.

Analyses by Frankfurt School theorists such as Max Horkheimer and Theodor Adorno sought to demonstrate how this commodification of daily life in a democratic capitalist society naturalized consumption as civic activity. These approaches suggested the possibility of the gradual overthrow of commodity relations as the central organizing principle of social life. Arguing against this, poststructuralists such as Jean Baudrillard maintained that the commodity relation was so fundamental to capitalist consciousness that its alienation offered no prospect of redemption, except by undermining the notion of value itself. The seeming fatalism of this approach has in turn been critiqued by the cultural-studies school, in works by Stuart Hall, Susan Willis, Sut Jhally, and others, which may broadly be understood as supporting a practical critique of consumption in social life, and which have also argued for the study of (and resistance to) the globalization of social and cultural relations under capitalism.

SEE ALSO: Consumer Society; Consumption, Mass Consumption, and Consumer Culture; Critical Theory/Frankfurt School

SUGGESTED READINGS

Appadurai, A. (ed.) (1986) *The Social Life of Things: Commodities in Cultural Perspective*. Cambridge University Press, Cambridge.

Apter, E. & Pietz, W. (eds.) (1993) *Fetishism as Cultural Discourse*. Cornell University Press, Ithaca, NJ.

Horkheimer, M. & Adorno, T. (1975) *Dialectic of Enlightenment*. HarperCollins, San Francisco, CA.

Tucker, R. C. (ed.) (1978) *The Marx–Engels Reader*, 2nd edn. W. W. Norton, New York.

NICHOLAS SAMMOND

communism

"Communism" is both a principle of social organization advocated since at least the time of ancient Greece, and a modern political movement – associated with the works of Karl Marx (1818–83) and his disciples – that held state power in a number of countries during the twentieth century. The core proposition of communism is that private ownership of property must cease, because it is the fundamental cause of social evils, including egoism, excess, and conflict. The relationship between communism's harmonious vision and its brutal implementation, however, is complex.

First systematically presented in Plato's *Republic*, communist schemes thereafter appeared episodically, in works such as Thomas More's *Utopia* (1516) and Morelly's *Code of Nature* (1755). They were shadowed by thoughtful critics. Aristotle, for example, declared: "that which is common to the greatest number has the least care bestowed upon it." Even among thinkers concerned by the gulf between rich and poor communism is seen as creating its own social problems, including jealousy and hatred between equals. Many stress the practical difficulties of sustaining communist outcomes.

Communism's moral vision has appeared in many different types of productive system, occasionally inspiring short-lived social experiments. The French Revolution of 1789–99 gave a fillip to many ideas, including communism, though there was a growing recognition that industry – with its potential to create vast amounts of wealth – signaled the dawn of a new age. Gracchus Babeuf's abortive "Conspiracy of the Equals" (1796) was an important historical link between communism and the socialism that emerged in the 1820s and 1830s.

The key difference between "communism" and "socialism" is that the abolition of private ownership to produce equal distribution was the central prescription of the former, while conscious and rational organization of economic activity to produce abundance is basic to the latter. There are clear affinities between the egalitarian and communitarian themes within pre-socialist communism, and the socialist critique of unrestrained individualism produced by the market. But socialism and communism interacted in unexpected ways: Marx's 1848 *Communist Manifesto* was more radical and worker-oriented than the appeals of his socialist competitors.

Marx harnessed communism to the emerging industrial working class in a historical story of class struggle reaching its ultimate stage in the clash between proletarians and capitalists. Communism would create a genuinely human society, the details of which were sketchy, but the precondition of which was material abundance. Humans would move from the current realm of necessity to the realm of freedom, in which the principle of distribution would be: "From each according to his ability, to each according to his needs!"

Marx's disciple, V. I. Lenin (1870–1924) also used the title "communist" to outmaneuver his socialist competitors. Lenin's communism – with its unmistakable Russian stamp – stressed leadership of the working class by a communist elite, a commitment to revolution, and the creation of a "dictatorship of the proletariat." Beginning in 1917 this communism was eventually established in at least fourteen countries, encompassing perhaps one-third of the world's population at its height. Most of these states collapsed near the end of the twentieth century.

Modern communism amounted to one-party states with central control over at least the major means of production, distribution, and exchange. Such control proved effectual for industrialization, despite its human costs. Soviet communism nevertheless played a crucial role in the defeat of Hitler and the subsequent, rapid creation of a Soviet "superpower."

If communism is not a serious model for an alternative social and political system, it remains a moral beacon for those frustrated by rampant individualism and disgusted by the increasing commodification of life in market societies.

SEE ALSO: Marx, Karl; Socialism

SUGGESTED READING

Marx, K. & Engels, F. (1969) *Manifesto of the Communist Party*. In: Marx, K. & Engels, F. *Selected Works*, vol. 1. Progress Publishers, Moscow, pp. 98–137.

DAVID W. LOVELL

community

"Community" is concerned with people having something in common, although there is much debate about precisely what that thing is. The most conventional approach relates to people sharing a geographical area (typically a neighborhood), an idea captured in references to *local* communities. Place is central to such an understanding because of the assumption that people are necessarily brought together by the fact of living in close proximity. This view is contested by those who argue that shared place does not always promote social connections between people. It is an established axiom of urban sociology that modern city spaces can be characterized as anonymous and impersonal, devoid of the collective connectedness associated with the idea of "community." Indeed, the theme of urbanization and increased geographical mobility leading to a loss of traditional patterns of community has been a very powerful one in sociological thought from the very beginning of the discipline. Against this background, the search for the basis of community has led other writers to highlight the importance of people being brought together by common interests or by common identities, neither of which requires co-presence. Occupational communities such as the academic community provide one example of groups of people whose common interests derived from work-based attachments may hold them together despite their being geographically dispersed, while religious communities illustrate the parallel point that a community of identity does not necessitate members being together in the same place. In this vein, Benedict Anderson has described nations as "imagined communities" whose members cannot possibly all have close, face-to-face connections.

Whether the basis of a community is common residence, common interest, common identity, or some combination of these factors, it is necessarily the case that the relationships that are involved will be exclusive to some degree. Put another way, communities operate by distinguishing those who belong ("insiders") from those who do not ("outsiders"). Community is an important dimension of social divisions as well as togetherness because inclusion in community relationships promises benefits (such as access to material resources, social support, or raised social status) that set members apart from others. A strong sense of this difference from non-members, of "us" and "them," is a characteristic of some of the most tightly bonded communities. Conversely, communities to which access is more open are correspondingly looser entities whose members do not have such a marked group identity, loyalty, and solidarity. People's sense of belonging to communities thus varies considerably in its intensity. The same point about variation applies to the degree of commitment that communities require of their members. The contrast between communities that bind members together tightly through similarity and those that have more points of connection with outside groups is captured in the distinction between the two types of social capital, respectively "bonding" and "bridging," that Robert Putnam develops in *Bowling Alone* (2000).

Arguably the most enduring challenge facing community researchers relates to the definition and operationalization of the concept of "community." The corruption of Ferdinand Tönnies's distinction between *Gemeinschaft* and *Gesellschaft* (translated as "community" and "association") into the idea that a continuum could be identified between strong rural communities and urban social patterns that lacked depth and durability has rightly been criticized for its geographical determinism: people's "community" relationships are not the simple product of their spatial location. It is quite another thing to acknowledge that local context matters to how people live their everyday lives, and ethnography is a favored tool among researchers who seek to capture the nuances of particular community settings. Immersion in a community allows ethnographers to capture the distinctiveness of its culture and to appreciate how belonging to that community is understood by its members. Other approaches focus less on the symbolic meaning of community and more on the mechanics of its operation. Social network analysis has proved particularly illuminating regarding the nature, purpose, and extent of people's connections to others, and it is more open than ethnography is to quantification. Barry Wellman (Wellman & Berkowitz 1998) has used this approach to argue convincingly that technological developments in communications (including the development of Internet communities) have freed individuals from dependence on others in their vicinity. Nevertheless, network analysis also reveals that many people's community ties continue to have a strong local component, especially if family and kin members are included in that calculation. Overall, research findings point to the continuing importance of communities of all types, both place-based and others. These findings cast doubt on those general theories of social change that anticipate the demise of community.

SEE ALSO: Civil Society; Imagined Communities; Networks; New Urbanism; Place; Tönnies, Ferdinand

REFERENCE

Wellman, B. & Berkowitz, S. (eds.) (1988) *Social Structures: A Network Approach*. Cambridge University Press, Cambridge.

SUGGESTED READINGS

Anderson, B. (1991) *Imagined Communities: Reflections on the Origin and Spread of Nationalism*. Verso, London.

Putnam, R. (2000) *Bowling Alone: The Collapse and Revival of American Community*. Simon & Schuster, New York.

Tönnies, F. (1955) *Community and Association*. Routledge & Kegan Paul, London.

GRAHAM CROW

community college

Although American community colleges (formerly known as junior colleges) have existed since the late nineteenth century, little sociological attention has been paid to these institutions until recently. The conceptual frameworks that do exist highlight the juxtaposition of the community college's function of expanding access to higher education while also limiting opportunity for many students.

Previously enrolling only about 10 percent of all undergraduates, the community college experienced unprecedented growth in the three decades following World War II. Between 1944 and 1947 community college enrollment doubled and community colleges grew exponentially in the 1960s and 1970s. Since the 1980s the number of community colleges has stabilized at over 1,100, or over one-fourth of all higher education institutions in the USA. This level of enrollment accounts for 45 percent of first-time college students and 37 percent of all undergraduates in US colleges and universities.

As a great invention of US higher education in the twentieth century, the community college has made college accessible to those people who may otherwise not be able to attend any college, especially to the working-class and minority populations who were traditionally under-represented in four-year colleges. Because of its open-door admissions policy, low tuition cost, diversity of course offerings, and flexible course schedule, community college is actually accessible to every applicant who may even not finish high school and is touted by its proponents as "democracy's college" or "people's college."

SEE ALSO: Education; Educational Inequality

SUGGESTED READING

Levinson, D. L. (2005) *Community Colleges: A Reference Handbook*. ABC-CLIO, Santa Barbara, CA.

REGINA DEIL-AMEN, TENISHA TEVIS, AND JINCHUN YU

complementary and alternative medicine

Various terms have been bandied around over the past several decades for a wide array of heterodox medical systems, ranging from professionalized to folk medical systems. Within the US context, the term that has become commonplace in various circles is *complementary and alternative medicine*, whereas, for example, in Australia it is simply *complementary medicine*. What has come to be termed complementary and alternative medicine (CAM) is actually an amorphous category that encompasses many medical systems and therapies in various national contexts, but particularly anglophone countries such as the United States, Canada, United Kingdom, Australia, and New Zealand. Whereas alternative practitioners and laypeople have tended to speak of holistic health, CAM and integrative medicine are in large part biomedical constructions. Most typologies of CAM tend to privilege western and Asian therapies over indigenous, folk, and religious therapies. Since the 1990s numerous biomedical practitioners have written overviews of CAM and have called for an evidence-based approach. In 1999 the National Institutes of Health's Office of Alternative Medicine (established in 1992 as a result of a Congressional mandate) was renamed the National Center for Complementary and Alternative Medicine. Furthermore, health insurance companies, health maintenance organizations, and hospitals have become increasingly interested in CAM therapies as a way of satisfying patients' demands and curtailing costs. While CAM or integrative medicine often adheres to a notion of holism by invoking the mantra of mind-body-spirit connections, in reality it gives little attention to the political-economic and social structural determinants of illness. Integrative medicine, which purports to blend the best of biomedicine and CAM, appears to function as a style of health care in which biomedicine treats alternative therapists as subordinates and alternative therapies as adjunct.

SEE ALSO: Health Care Delivery Systems; Medicine, Sociology of

SUGGESTED READING

Baer, H. (2004) *Towards an Integrative Medicine: From Holistic Health to Complementary and Alternative Medicine*. Altamira Press, Walnut Creek, CA.

HANS A. BAER

complexity and emergence

Complex phenomena reside between simplicity and randomness. When the laws governing a system are relatively simple, the system's behavior is easy to understand, explain, and predict. At the other extreme, some systems seem to behave randomly. Small variations in the state of the system at one time could result in very large changes to later states of the system. Such systems are often said to be *chaotic*. Complex systems are somewhere in between these two extremes: complexity is not easy to explain, but it is not so chaotic that understanding is completely impossible.

An interest in complexity is often accompanied by an interest in *emergence* – the processes whereby the global behavior of a system results from the actions and interactions of agents. There is no central controller or plan. Higher-level order emerges from the interaction of the individual components. Such systems are self-organizing, with control distributed throughout the system. Emergent systems are often complex in that they manifest order at the global system level that is difficult to explain by analyzing the individual components of the system in isolation.

Beginning in the mid-1990s, several scientific developments converged to create a qualitatively more advanced approach to complex systems, and complexity theory began to influence a wide range of disciplines, from biology to economics. The study of complex systems can provide new perspectives on important unresolved issues facing the social sciences – the relations between individuals and groups, the emergence of unintended effects from collective action, and the relation between the disciplines of economics and sociology.

SEE ALSO: Chaos

SUGGESTED READING

Sawyer, R. K. (2006) *Social Emergence: Societies as Complex Systems*. Cambridge University Press, New York.

R. KEITH SAWYER

compositional theory of urbanism

At the heart of urban sociology is the question: what are the consequences of urban life? Compositional theory represents one of the first serious statements that countered the popular turn-of-the-century premise that cities were alienating. Compositional theories of urbanism assert that urban–rural differences in social problems are due mainly to social characteristics (i.e., class, race/ethnicity, age) of city dwellers, not the urban environment.

Even in large, dense, heterogeneous areas, people find their own social worlds. City dwellers create and sustain personal networks that lend emotional and social support and provide stakes in conformity. These intimate social circles may be based on kinship, ethnicity, neighborhood, occupation, or lifestyle, but basic group dynamics and the quality and extent of social relationships are unaffected by the urban environment. Early qualitative evidence, such as Gans's (1962) *The Urban Villagers*, demonstrated the endurance and vitality of social ties in urban settings. Keller (1968) in *The Urban Neighborhood* specifies how the strength of neighborhood ties varies by neighborhood composition, for example by social class or family structure.

Compositional theorists attribute aggregate-level behavioral differences primarily to the different kinds of people in urban compared to suburban and rural areas rather than to effects of urbanism itself. People's characteristics – social class, age/lifecycle, family status, race/ethnicity – shape their behaviors and define their ways of life. What accounts for the greater unconventionality in cities is the concentration of individuals with certain traits, such as being younger, less often married, and more heterogeneous in terms of race/ethnicity, religion, and social class. Much of the relationship between urbanity (e.g., population density) and pathology (e.g., delinquency, welfare, mental illness) disappears once demographic factors are taken into account. Attention should be directed toward the social, economic, and political forces that shape expectations, opportunities, and roles available to various demographic groups.

SEE ALSO: City; Urbanism/Urban Culture

REFERENCES

Gans, H. J. (1962) *The Urban Villagers*. Free Press, New York.
Keller, S. (1968) *The Urban Neighborhood*. Random House, New York.

JENNIFER SCHWARTZ

compulsory heterosexuality

Popularized by Rich (1981), compulsory heterosexuality is the cultural assumption that both males and females are biologically predisposed to heterosexuality. The assumption that biology excludes a naturalized explanation of homosexuality limits humans to only heterosexual attraction. Therefore, the operation of compulsory heterosexuality usually involves the hegemonic manner in which heterosexuality is reified and naturalized, while homosexuality is considered the product of either psychological dysfunction or personal deviant choice. From this understanding homosexuality is deviant because it is thought to go against supposed natural inclinations. Hegemonic understandings of heterosexuality have often been supported by the misconception that other animals are also exclusively heterosexual, even though Bagemihl (1999) has shown homosexuality, as temporary sexual behavior and as a form of long-term relationship coupling, exists widely throughout the animal kingdom.

One result of the naturalization of heterosexuality and stigmatization of homosexuality, bisexuality, and transgenderism manifests itself in cultural and institutional inequality for non-heterosexuals. The institutionalization of heterosexuality can be found at all levels of western societies, in which power and privilege are usually dispersed unevenly to the benefit of heterosexuals. Restricting civil marriage to heterosexuals, for example, provides that group of people with significant insurance, taxation, and many other economic and social privileges that are denied to gay and lesbian couples.

Rich goes on to argue that validation of heterosexuals at the expense of non-heterosexuals influences the reproduction of male privilege in a patriarchal society by both political means and social violence. She contends that in a society in which men control most aspects of women's institutional lives, including their right to birth control, abortion, and occupational equality, women are essentially bound to a binary system of oppression. Should they choose not to participate in heterosexual family structure, they are stigmatized and further denied social and institutional support. Rich asserts that the naturalization of heterosexuality is so hegemonic that even feminists have failed to account for the overwhelming effects it has on oppressing women.

In recent years, much of the discussion of compulsory heterosexuality has shifted to the examination of heterosexism, which assumes that heterosexuality is and ought to remain culturally and institutionally privileged. Although heterosexism is thought to operate with less overt homophobia than compulsory heterosexuality as well as with more covert mechanisms, some have suggested that prejudice toward those other than heterosexuals increasingly reflects ambivalence: a combination of both positive and negative attitudes and behaviors. Ambivalence, of course, normally does little to change the status quo, thereby slowing the progress that gays and lesbians make toward full civil and cultural equality.

SEE ALSO: Heterosexuality; Homophobia and Heterosexism; Homosexuality

REFERENCES

Bagemihl, B. (1999) *Biological Exuberance: Animal Homosexuality and Natural Diversity*. St. Martin's Press, New York.

Rich, A. C. (1981) *Compulsory Heterosexuality and Lesbian Existence*. Only Women Press, London.

ERIC ANDERSON

computer-aided/mediated analysis

Software for qualitative data analysis (QDA) allows the analyst to systematically index and organize the data and then to retrieve the data reliably and flexibly in many different ways. For example, it can facilitate finding all the data *the analyst has previously identified* as indicating a particular theme or conceptual category, and it can facilitate parsing these data into subgroups based on demographic or other categorical or quantitative variables. It can also find all the cases where a theme was not present, or where combinations of themes are present, and so on.

There is no one best software program for analyzing qualitative data. Furthermore, there is no one best program for a particular type of research or analytic method. Researchers will sometimes ask "what's the best program for a study of health services?" or "what's the best program for doing grounded theory?" or "what's the best program for analyzing focus groups?" None of these questions has a good answer. Instead, choice needs to be approached based on the structure of the data, the specific things the analyst will want to do as part of the analysis, and the needs of the researcher around issues like ease of use, cost, time available, collaboration, and so on.

Qualitative data analysis software is not an analysis methodology and it will not automatically analyze data. It provides tools which, in the hands of a competent researcher, can make possible analyses of great depth and rigor. It can facilitate the analyses of data sets of sizes that would not be feasible by hand. However, a cautionary note is in order here: there has been an increasing number of projects in recent years in which researchers, believing that software will make it all possible, collect data sets of sizes that make meaningful analyses back-breaking, even with software. QDA software, appropriately matched to a project's needs and thoughtfully applied, can greatly enhance the qualitative research enterprise.

SEE ALSO: Information Technology; Technology, Science, and Culture; Validity, Quantitative

SUGGESTED READING

Weitzman, E. A. (2003) Software and qualitative research. In: Denzin, N. & Lincoln, Y. (eds.), *Collecting and Interpreting Qualitative Materials*, 2nd edn. Sage, Thousand Oaks, CA, pp. 310–39.

EBEN A. WEITZMAN

Comte, Auguste (1798–1857)

As Saint-Simon's secretary from 1817 to 1824, Comte drew heavily from his mentor's ideas but Comte was a strong, independent thinker who passionately pursued his own grand agenda. His 1822 *Plan de travaux scientifiques nécessaires pour réorganiser la société* outlined how the moral, intellectual, and social landscape of Europe should be changed.

Comte believed that human societies and the knowledge forms that structured them progressed through three stages – the theological, metaphysical, and positivist. The development of knowledge proceeded along the hierarchy of complexity – from astronomy and physics, the least complex, to chemistry and physiology, ultimately reaching social physics (Comte's initial term for social science).

Comte's six-volume *Cours de philosophie positive* (1830–42) was to establish positivism – systematic, observationally based knowledge – in all realms of study. In volume four of the *Cours*, written in 1839, Comte combined the Latin *socius* (companion, associate) with the Greek *lógos* (logic, thought) to identify "sociology" as the highest, most encompassing and complex form of knowledge. Sociology was the queen of the sciences. Some think Adolphe Quetelet's 1835 *Physique sociale* spurred the change in terminology but the deeper reason was an increasing appreciation for history in Comte's thought. The Latin/Greek neologism indicated that sociology focused on the logic of, and thought about, human association in more than mathematical terms.

Since social physics consisted of social statics and social dynamics, Comte sought change through scientifically informed, ordered progress. These conceptions complemented Comte's use of organic analogies as he discussed society's anatomy and physiology. The law of the three stages, the triumph of positive science, the conceptions of order, progress, social statics and dynamics, and social anatomy and physiology made Comte an early, passionate advocate for the unity of the sciences – the use of the scientific method in the study of both natural and social phenomena.

SEE ALSO: Durkheim, Émile; Positivism; Sociology

SUGGESTED READING

Comte, A. (1974) *The Essential Comte*, trans. M. Clarke. Croom Helm, London.

ROB BEAMISH

confidence intervals

A confidence interval (CI) is an *interval estimate* of a population parameter. It is a range of values, calculated from data, that is likely to include the true value of the parameter. When a newspaper reports "support for the government is 43 percent, in a poll with an error margin of 3 percent", the 43 percent is a *point estimate* of true support. The CI is 43 ± 3 percent, or (40 to 46 percent), and 3 percent is the *margin of error*. The endpoints of the CI are the *lower* and *upper limits* or *bounds*.

The *level of confidence*, C, is a percentage, commonly 95 percent although other levels are used. Figure 1 shows a simulation of 20 random samples. The CIs will, in the long run, capture the population mean μ on C percent of occasions. We can say "we are 95 percent confident our particular interval includes μ?" but not "the probability is 0.95 our interval includes μ" because that suggests μ varies, whereas μ is fixed but unknown. Any value in our CI is *plausible* for the parameter, whereas values outside the interval are relatively implausible.

The graphic representing a CI in Figure 1 is ambiguous. It is, unfortunately, also used for standard error (SE) bars – an interval $\pm$ SE about a mean, and typically about half the width of the 95 percent CI. Therefore every figure showing bars must state clearly what they represent.

Advantages of CIs include: (1) they give point and interval estimates in meaningful units; (2) there is a link with null hypothesis significance testing because any value outside a 95 percent CI would, given the data, be rejected as a null hypothesis at the 0.05 significance level, and any value inside the CI would not be rejected; (3) CI width gives

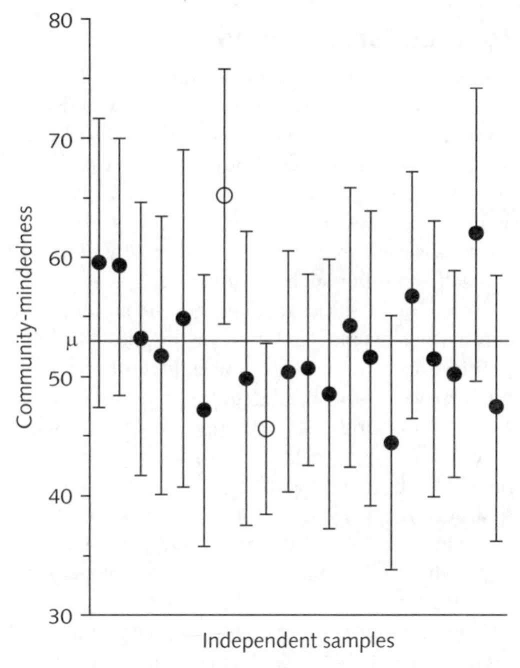

Figure 1 Means and 95 percent confidence intervals (CIs) for 20 independent samples, showing sample-to-sample variation

Each sample has size $n = 30$, and comes from a normally-distributed population with mean $\mu = 53$. The intervals vary in width because each is based on the standard deviation of that sample. In the long run, 95 percent of CIs are expected to include μ. Here, two CIs (open circles) do not include μ. Note that this is more often captured by the central region of a CI than by regions near the upper or lower limits of an interval. In practice, μ is not known and only one sample is taken.

information about precision, which may be more useful than a calculation of statistical power; and (4) they help combine evidence over experiments, and thus encourage meta-analysis.

SEE ALSO: Effect Sizes; Experimental Design; Independent Variables; Random Sampling; Statistical Significance Testing

SUGGESTED READINGS

Altman, D. G., Machin, D., Bryant, T. N., & Gardner, M. J. (2000) *Statistics With Confidence: Confidence Intervals and Statistical Guidelines*, 2nd edn. British Medical Journal Books, London.

Cumming, G., & Finch, S. (2005) Inference by eye: confidence intervals, and how to read pictures of data. *American Psychologist* 60: 170–80.

GEOFF CUMMING

conflict, racial and ethnic

Conflict is a basic process in social life. In certain situations it can lead to the destruction of some groups, in others it may act as a cohesive force. Racial and ethnic groups may be the source and the result of the two faces of social conflict, acting as a boundary marker between groups that see themselves as distinctive in their interests and values from other such groups.

Much of classical sociological theory analyzed conflict against the backdrop of the industrial and political revolutions of the late eighteenth and early nineteenth centuries in Europe and focused on class, status and party groups as the principal bases of group struggle. Divisions arising out of racial or ethnic membership tended to be assigned to a peripheral position in the analysis despite the overwhelming significance of war, colonialism, nationalism and genocide that formed an equally central part of the historical record.

Contemporary research on ethnicity and racial divisions has focused on trying to understand the processes of ethnogenesis, the construction and perpetuation of ethnic and racial boundaries, and the impact of forces like globalization and transnationalism on racial and ethnic conflict. While traditional patterns of international migration continue to play an important role in the generation of racial and ethnic diversity, they have been modified and changed by political and economic factors in complex and unpredictable ways. In the USA large numbers of Mexican migrants, both legal and unauthorized, have continued the growth of the Latino population into the largest single minority group. In Europe, the relations between immigrants and ethnic minorities – not least the increasing number of Muslim migrants from Turkey and North Africa – will be a major element in determining the conflict and stability of the emerging political structure, no matter whether the European Union becomes a superstate or remains a looser federation.

Several different theoretical perspectives can be found supporting contemporary studies of ethnic and racial conflict. Some, like rational choice theory, are methodologically individualistic and apply a cost–benefit formula to account for ethnic preferences and to explain the dynamics of racial and ethnic group formation. These have been criticized on the grounds that they fail to appreciate the collective dynamics of much ethnic behavior and underestimate the irrational side of racial violence. Other common perspectives see ethnicity and racial divisions as a type of social stratification: theories employing neo-Marxist categories stress the economic components underlying much ethnic conflict; while those following in the tradition of scholars like Weber and Furnivall provide a more pluralistic interpretation of the differences in ethnic and racial power. In general, these differences originate from the forces of conquest and migration, and are then perpetuated by the processes of group monopolization once an ethnic or racial boundary has been created. In this way, a hierarchical ordering of racial and ethnic groups is created which will eventually generate conflict as circumstances start to change and disadvantaged groups challenge the status quo. Other theories point to social-psychological factors, like prejudice and ethnocentrism, or even sociobiological imperatives, like kin selection, as important explanations for the persistence of ethnic divisions and the ubiquity of racial conflict.

SEE ALSO: Genocide; Race; Race, Definitions of

SUGGESTED READINGS

Stone, J. & Dennis, R. (eds.) (2003) *Race and Ethnicity: Comparative and Theoretical Approaches*. Blackwell, Malden, MA.

Stone, J. & Rizova, P. (2007) Rethinking racial conflict in an era of global terror. *Ethnic & Racial Studies* 30 (4): 534–45.

JOHN STONE AND POLLY RIZOVA

conflict theory

The term "conflict theory" came into wide use in sociology during the 1960s, when it was seen as an alternative to and rival of functionalism. Initially, the term seemed merely to identify a more politically neutral Marxian perspective, but for some it meant something much broader. The strongest contemporary advocate of conflict theory is Randall Collins. For him, conflict theory includes not only Marx and the Marxists, but also Weber and a number of other social theorists extending back to earlier times. He sees as early forerunners of modern conflict theory such thinkers as Machiavelli and Pareto. Collins (1974; 1975) has done more than any sociologist to develop a synthesized conflict theory that owes more to Weber than to any other sociologist. Sociologists have often regarded Lewis Coser's *The Functions of Social Conflict* (1956) as a version of conflict theory, but it is more a functionalist analysis of the role of conflict in social life than a use of conflict propositions to explain various social phenomena.

Conflict theory presupposes the following: (1) conflict or struggle between individuals and groups who have opposing interests or who are competing for scarce resources is the essence of social life; (2) competition and conflict occur over many types of resources in many settings, but power and economic resources are the principal sources of conflict and competition; (3) conflict and struggle typically result in some individuals and groups dominating and controlling others, and patterns of domination and subordination tend to be self-perpetuating; (4) dominant social groups have a disproportionate influence on the allocation of resources and on the structure of society.

Marxian conflict theory is the more prominent of two major lines of work. For Marxists, social class is the source of conflict in all societies above the level of primitive egalitarian communities. Class conflict – between masters and slaves or landlords and peasants, for example – pervades history and is the engine of historical change. Marxists have focused most of their attention, though, on the class structure of modern capitalist society. The most prominent feature of capitalist society is the class struggle between capitalists and workers. Marx assumed, and nearly all later Marxists have assumed as well, that to understand the structure, functioning, and evolution of capitalist society you had to start from the fact that capitalists have as their main objective maximizing profits and accumulating capital. They do this by exploiting the working class, i.e., by paying them wages that are less than the full value of the goods they produce. Workers are motivated to resist capitalist exploitation as much as they can, and thus there is an inherent antagonism between capitalists and workers. This class struggle is the foundation of capitalism and the root cause of all other forms of struggle or conflict within capitalism.

In the 1970s some sociologists began to rethink the traditional interpretation of Weber handed down by Talcott Parsons, viewing Weber as offering a kind of conflict theory that was similar to Marxian theory in certain ways, but different in crucial respects. Collins (1975; 1986) developed this idea most thoroughly. He argued that Weber was a complex and multidimensional thinker who later in life evolved into a conflict theorist. Like Marx, Weber emphasized the role of conflict, struggle, and discord in social life, viewing them as pervasive features of society and the keys to understanding it.

Conflict theory is alive and well in modern sociology and many sociologists work within that framework, broadly conceived. It has contributed much to sociological understanding and is being extended in new ways through linkage with perspectives normally thought far removed from it, such as sociobiology (Sanderson 2001) and Durkheimian social theory (Collins 2004).

SEE ALSO: Class Conflict; Critical Theory/ Frankfurt School; Dependency and World-Systems Theories; Marx, Karl; Stratification: Functional and Conflict Theories; Weber, Max

REFERENCES

Collins, R. (1974) Reassessments of sociological history: the empirical validity of the conflict tradition. *Theory and Society* 1: 147–78.

Collins, R. (1975) *Conflict Sociology: Toward an Explanatory Science*. Academic Press, New York.

Collins, R. (1986) *Max Weber: A Skeleton Key*. Sage, Beverly Hills, CA.

Collins, R. (2004) *Interaction Ritual Chains*. Princeton University Press, Princeton, NJ.

Sanderson, S. (2001) *The Evolution of Human Sociality*. Rowman & Littlefield, Boulder, CO.

STEPHEN K. SANDERSON

consciousness raising

Consciousness raising (CR) was a cornerstone of radical feminist organizing in the late 1960s and early 1970s. Many of the women involved in the anti-war, new left, and civil rights movements were disillusioned as they found themselves relegated to the role of providing services to men. As a result of this awareness, they began small consciousness raising groups to work for women's liberation.

CR groups constituted one segment of the contemporary women's movement classified as the small group, younger branch, or radical feminist sector (Firestone 1970: *The Dialectic of Sex*).

Meeting in small groups and talking about their lives, they recognized that other women were experiencing the same frustrations and blockages in their professional and personal lives as they were. They began a discourse that would later spill over to the larger more generalized women's movement and society itself. However, their high energy and "true believer" spirit led to strident encounters both within groups and with outside forces.

Since the 1980s, consciousness raising no longer plays the same role in the women's movement as diversity and international and transnational feminism call for a widening circle of feminist awareness and increased concern for the differences among women.

SEE ALSO: Radical Feminism

SUGGESTED READING

Ryan, B. (1992) *Feminism and the Women's Movement: Dynamics of Change in Social Movement Ideology and Activism*. Routledge, New York.

BARBARA RYAN

conservatism

Conservatism has been one of the principal ideologies of the modern era. It first developed in reaction to the French Revolution and became a key part of the Counter-Enlightenment which challenged many of the ideas of liberalism, in particular its abstract individualism, its universalism and its demands for equality. Conservatives stressed the importance of history and tradition, the particular and the local. First used as a party label in England in the 1830s, Conservatism gradually spread elsewhere, but Conservatives tended to regard it not as an overarching doctrine or transnational movement, but as composed of several distinct national traditions. Conservative thinkers have been highly diverse, ranging from Edmund Burke to Joseph de Maistre, and from Michael Oakeshott to Leo Strauss. Because Conservatives are so averse to rationalism and to universalism, Conservatism has not usually been presented as a universal doctrine in the grand manner of liberalism or socialism, organised around a distinct set of values and principles. It takes the form of a number of separate national traditions, each with its own peculiarities because of its unique national history and the statecraft that is deemed appropriate to conserve it.

Conservatism is a fundamentally defensive doctrine, concerned with the presentation of existing institutions and interests, and with resisting the pressures for reform and change when these are seen to threaten them. Arising from this is a profound skepticism about human reason, human goodness, human knowledge, and human capacity. Conservatives are generally pessimistic about the state of the world and human society, and believe that most schemes of improvement are at best well-meaning and at worse malicious attempts to change society which will end up making it worse. The Conservative instinct is always to hang on to what is familiar and known, rather than to risk what is unknown and untried.

SEE ALSO: Individualism; Liberalism; Nationalism; Tradition

SUGGESTED READING

O'Sullivan, N. (1986) *Conservatism*. Dent, London.

ANDREW GAMBLE

conspicuous consumption

The term conspicuous consumption entered the sociological lexicon via Thorstein Veblen's biting analysis of the spending patterns of the rich and *nouveau riches* in the late nineteenth century. *The Theory of the Leisure Class* (1994 [1899]) is an account of how these groups spent enormous energy and money constructing an ostentatious style of life. They built and decorated ornate homes, adorned their persons with clothing and jewelry, designed elaborate carriages, and employed large numbers of servants dressed in expensive uniforms. Throughout, the principles of waste, luxury, and ornamentation ruled the choices they made. The motive that animated their efforts was the desire for social esteem, which itself was dependent on the possession of wealth. But having money was not enough. It must be put "in evidence," or become conspicuous.

The theory of conspicuous consumption is the centerpiece of Veblen's larger analysis of class society and its relation to styles of life and work. Veblen believed that the desire to attain status, or social esteem, eventually became the dominant motive in individuals' decisions about work and consumption, even eclipsing biological or physical pressures to consume. In a status system based on wealth, the credibility and verifiability of individuals' claims to status become a significant issue. Particularly before the era of paper money, wealth was not easily transportable, and ensuring its safety also militated against public display of money itself. Therefore, proxy measures of wealth-holding developed, chief among them the ability to forgo productive labor, and the ability to consume luxuriously, or what Veblen termed *conspicuous leisure* and *conspicuous consumption*. For both leisure and consumption, public visibility is central. The need to put spending "in evidence" is because public display solves the informational problems associated with wealth-based status competitions. Thus, the role of public visibility, or what Veblen calls conspicuousness, becomes central to the operation of the system.

One feature of Veblen's theory of conspicuous consumption is that agents are deeply intentional in their spending decisions, making choices for the purpose of maximizing their social status. Consumption is neither personally expressive, nor impulsive. Consumption is valued for what others make of it, rather than for intrinsic product benefits or functions.

The theory of conspicuous consumption also predicts that people will tend to spend more heavily on socially visible goods, in contrast to products that are used in private. Appearance goods such as dress, footwear, and jewelry have traditionally been central to status competitions. So too have vehicles, from carriages to SUVs and BMWs. The third item in the trio of status display is the home, where ornamentation, size, and materials all figure centrally in the social value of a dwelling.

SEE ALSO: Bourdieu, Pierre; Brands and Branding; Consumption; Cultural Capital;

REFERENCE

Veblen, T. (1994) [1899] *The Theory of the Leisure Class*. Penguin, New York.

SUGGESTED READINGS

Campbell, C. (1994) Conspicuous confusion? A critique of Veblen's theory of conspicuous consumption. *Sociological Theory* 12 (2): 34–47.

Schor, J. B. (1998) *The Overspent American: Upscaling, Downshifting, and the New Consumer*. Basic Books, New York.

JULIET B. SCHOR

consumer culture, children's

Children's consumer culture refers to the institutional, material and symbolic arrangements which organize a young person's involvement in, and movement through, the early life course in terms of commercial interests and values. Children are both subject to and arise as subjects in consumer contexts. The meanings which adhere to commercial goods are at once imposed upon children, childhood, and their social worlds and are taken up by children as resources with which they create selves, identities, and relationships.

Beginning in the early 1900s in the USA, an emergent set of institutions, practices, and forms of knowledge began gradually coalescing around the social figure of the "child consumer." Initially, in the 1910 to 1930 period, most efforts to sell children's goods focused on appealing to adults', particularly mothers', perspectives. In the ensuing decades, merchandisers, advertisers, designers, and market researchers came to recognize "the child" as a consumer – i.e., as an economic agent with wants of her or his own as well as with a growing social right to be desirous of what the commerical world offered. The rise of the child as an agentive, knowing consumer has served as a counterweight to moral concerns expressed about commercial exploitation by framing children's consumption as essentially a matter of choice rather than of persuasion or trickery.

The reach of children's consumer culture extends beyond the child consumer proper and beyond the purchase of products and into changing definitions of the early life course. Increasingly specialized commercial goods, media, and spaces made for children's use have contributed to creating nuanced distinctions between different age grades of children and between genders, resulting in compartmentalized micro-markets and micro-cultures – e.g., the contemporary "tween." Children themselves make use of the meanings and goods available to them to forge relationships among and make distinctions between peers and between "children" and "adults."

SEE ALSO: Childhood; Consumer Society

SUGGESTED READINGS

Cook, D. T. (2004) *The Commodification of Childhood*. Duke University Press, Durham, NC.

Pugh, A. (2009) *Longing and Belonging*. University of California Press, Berkeley, CA.

Schor, J. (2004) *Born to Buy*. Scribner's, New York.

DANIEL THOMAS COOK

consumer society

The notion of "consumer society" emerged after World War II. It was used to suggest that the society which we live in is a late variant of capitalism characterized by the primacy of consumption over production. It also suggests that our societies produce one type of human being as its norm, the "consumer." While the link between consumption and identity is crucial in contemporary societies, even in so-called "tribal" societies people use objects as an important source of identity and a means of social relations, to distinguish themselves or mark alliances; even in these societies one can find forms of conspicuous consumption which mostly serve to reinforce social hierarchies. Still our societies seem to be different in that material culture has grown enormously, it has become ever more differentiated, and is increasingly produced and consumed via market-mediated social relationships. In subsistence economies, production and consumption were not specialized and separated spheres of action, held together by an equally specialized sphere of exchange: the fundamental cultural dichotomy on which social order rested was that of sacred/profane rather than of production/consumption. Because of the disentanglement of production and consumption we find ourselves confronted with objects whose meaning is beyond our everyday life and yet we are mobilized as "consumers" to use these objects in meaningful ways.

Analytically we may speak of "consumer society" whenever consumption has become more visible as a relatively specialized sphere of action – with its places, institutions, professions, and narratives. Consumer culture thus produces consumers, but does so in a variety of ways. Both market actors (advertising executives, marketing experts, shop-assistants) as well as political actors contribute to this. Historically we may speak of "consumer society" as a historical type of society in which the satisfaction of daily need is accomplished through the acquisition and use of "commodities": goods which are produced for exchange and are on sale on the market (Sassatelli 2007). From a long-term perspective, global commodity flows and knowledge flows, and in particular colonial goods and materialistic values, have played an important role in the development of consumer culture in the west. More recently, figures such as cultural intermediaries have acquired power and have become agents of change, promoting new styles of consumption which potentially cut across traditional social divisions and mix hedonism and asceticism.

Contemporary western consumer cultures are characterized by mass design and the aestheticization of ordinary objects. They are also characterized by marked standardization of the consumer experience, through strategies of "thematization" not only in theme-parks, but also in a general thematic organization of restaurants, shops, and spaces within shopping centers (Gottdiener 1997). There is an increased global visibility of consumer culture and of the political investment of the consumer: witness to this is the crucial intercultural function of global brands which provide a contested terrain for social mobilization and protest as well as dispersed, ordinary and perhaps banal forms of cosmopolitism; the cultural and political dynamism generated by consumption in societies in transition from communist to capitalist systems; or the cultural contestation which has followed the political replacement of the notion of citizen with that of consumer to promote the privatization of services. Contemporary studies of consumption across the globe take into consideration globalization dynamics which are often understood under the rubric of McDonaldization and Americanization (Ritzer and Ryan 2004). Still, the diverse local and national cultures play an important role in metabolizing mass-marketed consumer goods, global commodities and global or US chains as much as various national and local culture construct particular visions of the USA, US consumer lifestyles and business procedures.

SEE ALSO: Consumer Culture, Children's; Consumption; Consumption, Cathedrals and Landscapes of; Globalization, Consumption and

REFERENCES

Featherstone, M. (1991) *Consumer Culture and Postmodernism*. Sage, London.

Gottdiener, M. (1997) *The Theming of America: Dreams, Visions and Commercial Spaces*. Westview Press, Boulder, CO.

Ritzer, G. & Ryan, M. (2004) Americanisation, McDonaldisation, and globalisation. In: Campbell, N, Davies, J. & McKay, G. (eds.), *Issues in Americanisation and Culture*. Edinburgh University Press, Edinburgh, pp. 41–60.

Sassatelli, R. (2007) *Consumer Culture: History, Theory, Politics*. Sage, London.

SUGGESTED READING

Baudrillard, J. (1998) *The Consumer Society: Myths and Structures*. Sage, Lonodn.

ROBERTA SASSATELLI

consumption

Consumption has been defined by economists in utilitarian terms as individuals taking care of their needs and maximizing their utilities in market exchanges with the act of consumption taking place for the most part in private life. Even Marx saw it this way; while the shares of consumption for individuals were determined by property and production relations, the moment of consumption was a matter for individuals in their private lives. Thorstein Veblen and Marcel Mauss were the first social theorists to conceptualize a social logic of emulation and competition for prestige and power in consumer practices. Competition for prestige was not invented in modern societies; it could be found in the gift giving rituals that Mauss analyzed in tribal cultures. It could also be found in the idle pursuits of nobles in agrarian societies when useful work was considered ignoble according to Veblen.

In the nineteenth century, capitalist development and the industrial revolution were primarily focused on the capital goods sector and industrial infrastructure. Members of the working class worked for low wages for long hours, as much as 16 hours per day 6 days per week which did not leave much time or money for consumer activities. Henry Ford understood that mass production presupposed mass consumption. Frederick Taylor's theory of scientific management unleashed incredible productivity and reduced the costs of every commodity produced on assembly lines. Ford instituted the first 8-hour work day and paid a premium wage of $5 a day during World War I. Consumer goods had a shorter "life expectancy" than producer goods; further, planned obsolescence made commodities that would disintegrate within a predictable span of time and/or use, e.g. so many miles for a car tire. The fashion cycle also accelerated the depreciation of commodities even before they were physically used up. Buying on installment plans or on store credit made it possible to stretch out payments for the more expensive items. Initially the advertising form informed potential buyers of the qualities and availability of new commodities without manipulating their needs or desires. The consumer society collapsed after the stock market crash of 1929; corporations returned to lower wages and longer hours. Yet the American labor movement in collaboration with corporations in the core of the economy reestablished the conditions for this Fordist strategy after 1938, and the consumer society emerged from the ashes of World War II in the USA.

Consumption has two levels: individual consumption with its logic of emulation and competition for prestige and power and collective consumption that corresponds to social needs. Lefebvre notes that while modern capitalism is efficient at taking care of individual needs for material products and goods, there are social needs that are poorly recognized and met: health care, education, child care, care for the elderly, public spaces for recreation and leisure, love, and community. Social goods are different from individual goods, they are not necessarily used up in the same way as a beer is used up in individual acts of consumption. Millions of citizens have made use of Central Park in New York City, but they have yet to use it up.

Baudrillard's analysis of consumption begins with a critical analysis of the commodity form as the cellular form of modern society. Marx distinguished the use value of the commodity from its exchange value. Commodity logic reduced everything and everyone to exchange value. Commodity exchange integrated the members of different classes, but in a process that produced and reproduced the domination of capital. On the other hand, Marx saw the use value of commodities as corresponding to needs that were not equivalent and "natural." Baudrillard argues that needs are in no way natural, and that in our consumer society needs are produced just like commodities and are just as abstract and equivalent as exchange values. The code of consumption through the mediation of the advertising form attaches sign exchange value to all commodities. Consumption in its deepest meaning involves the consumption of these differential values which reproduces the code and the mode of production. While workers in modernity are often conscious of being exploited at work, Baudrillard sees this as a more profound form of alienation since consumers take pleasure or at least satisfaction from their consumer activities.

Michel de Certeau has looked at how consumers use commodities and the meanings attached to them through the media and the advertising form. Do consumers submit to the "terrorism of the code" as Baudrillard seems to assume? De Certeau's research and the work of the Birmingham school of cultural studies suggest otherwise. Gottdiener finds a struggle over meaning between producers and users of consumer goods. Youth in the 1960s appropriated working class clothing like blue jeans and modified them in various ways as a sign of protest and a sign of their proletarianization in the consumer society. Producers responded and reestablished the sign exchange value of their goods with various modifications: stitching, rips, pre-faded forms, etc.

SEE ALSO: Baudrillard, Jean; Certeau, Michel de; Conspicuous Consumption; Exchange-Value

SUGGESTED READINGS

Baudrillard, J. (1998) *The Consumer Society*. Sage, London.

Debord, G. (1970) *Society of the Spectacle*. Black and Red, Detroit.

de Certeau, M. (1984) *The Practice of Everyday Life*. University of California Press, Berkeley and Los Angeles, CA.

Gottdiener, M. (2001) *The Theming of America*. Westview, Boulder, CO.

Lefebvre, H. (2002) *Critique of Everyday Life*, vol. 2, 1st edn. Verso, London.
Mauss, M. (1967) *The Gift*. W. W. Norton & Co., New York.
Veblen, T. (1953) *Theory of the Leisure Class*. Mentor, New York.

MICHAEL T. RYAN

consumption, cathedrals and landscapes of

Although George Ritzer (2005) is the theorist most responsible for popularizing the phrase "cathedrals of consumption," it has been used at least since Kowinski, who stated that "malls are sometimes called cathedrals of consumption, meaning that they are the monuments of a new faith, the consumer religion, which has largely replaced the old" (1985: 218). These geographies are self-contained consumption settings that utilize postmodern techniques such as implosion, the compression of time and space, and simulation to create spectacular locales designed to attract consumers. They can be considered cathedrals because, much like their religious counterparts, they "are seen as fulfilling people's need to connect with each other and with nature, as well as their need to participate in festivals. [They] provide the kind of centeredness traditionally provided by religious temples, and they are constructed to have similar balance, symmetry, and order" (Ritzer 2005: 8).

Ritzer (2005) has built upon his notion of cathedrals of consumption to describe what he terms "landscapes of consumption," or "geographic areas that encompass two, or more, cathedrals of consumption" (p. 149). This definition can be extended to define landscapes of consumption as *locales that encompass two or more cathedrals of consumption that allow, encourage, and even compel people to consume*. The prototypical example of this would be the Las Vegas strip – an area where multiple cathedrals of consumption exist side-by-side in the same geographic setting and entice consumers not only through their individual appeal but also through the techniques made possible by their synergistic proximity.

Sharon Zukin (1991) has also contributed much to the idea of landscape. She uses the term landscape to describe a configuration of material geographic surroundings and their related social and symbolic practices. She argues that landscape is the major cultural product of our time and that landscape and power are deeply and intricately connected. Through this, large-scale, bureaucratic, economic structures attempt to impose a new order upon an existing geographic location. Although there is sometimes resistance to these attempts, ultimately capital wins out and landscapes are imposed. Zukin also argues that landscapes, contrary to the assertions of many postmodern social theorists, tend towards "repetition and singularity" and not towards ephemeral aestheticism.

Elsewhere, Ritzer, Ryan, and Stepnisky (2005) have extended the idea of landscapes of consumption with their case study of Easton Town Center in Columbus, Ohio. They argue that Easton serves as a prototype of a consumer setting that is becoming increasingly prevalent – one that seeks to simulate the look and feel of a nostalgic small town America. By encompassing two or more landscapes of consumption within one setting, Easton is able to expand the spectacle of landscape to a community level (Ryan 2005).

SEE ALSO: Consumption; Consumption, Mass Consumption and Consumer Culture; Shopping Malls

REFERENCES

Kowinski, W. S. (1985) *The Malling of America: An Inside Look at the Great Consumer Paradise*. William Morrow, New York.
Ritzer, G. (2005) *Enchanting a Disenchanted World: Revolutionizing the Means of Consumption*, 2nd edn. Pine Forge Press, Thousand Oaks, CA.
Ritzer, G., Ryan, J. M., & Stepnisky, J. (2005) Innovation in consumer settings: landscapes and beyond. In: Ratneshwar, S. and Mick, C. (eds.), *Inside Consumption: Frontiers of Research on Consumer Motives, Goals, and Desires*, Routledge, London, pp. 292–308.
Ryan, J. M. (2005) Easton: a 21st century (r)evolution in consumption, community, urbanism, and space. MA thesis. College Park, MD, University of Maryland.
Zukin, S. (1991) *Landscapes of Power: From Detroit to Disney World*. University of California Press, Berkeley, CA.

SUGGESTED READING

Ritzer, G. & Ryan, J. M. (2004) The globalization of nothing. In: Dasgupta, S. (ed.), *The Changing Face of Globalization*. Sage, Thousand Oaks, CA, pp. 298–317.

J. MICHAEL RYAN

consumption, green/sustainable

Sustainable/green consumption encompasses those disciplines, discourses, policy initiatives and practices that involve the design, implementation, and promotion of consumption practices and production technologies that seek to remedy any negative effects of human economic activity. This implies that current patterns of resource extraction, production, and consumption levels are unsustainable, and if left unchecked, will lead to environmental and social crises. Proponents of sustainable/green consumption attempt to raise consumer awareness of the obscured costs of pursuing a consumer lifestyle by demystifying the upstream (extraction and production) and downstream (disposal) consequences of consumption. They also assert that each individual consumer can help to reduce the adverse global effects of overconsumption by changing how they produce, obtain, use, and view resources.

While the meaning of the concept sustainable/green consumption is generally agreed upon, there is less agreement as to what its goals should be and how public policy should be used to achieve them. While some merely aspire to maintain existing economic systems, more hard line advocates aim to reign in harmful consumption practices and promote practices that can best sustain ecosystems. Still others seek to develop and implement consumption practices and production technologies to redress accrued environmental degradation and restore the Earth's ecosystems.

For policy-driven ecological economists and environmental scientists, sustainable/green consumption has become aligned with "sustainable development." These researchers aim to discover how developing nations can modernize their economies in ways that minimize environmental harm. For developed nations, sustainable development relies on regulatory incentives and "social marketing" campaigns to develop more sustainable production and distribution technologies and stimulate consumer awareness and implementation of environmentally friendly consumption practices. However, because individual consumer rights are so integral to modern democratic socioeconomic systems, the proper role of policymakers in regulating sustainable consumption has been widely disputed on the basis of overestimating the potential to change consumers' behaviors through regulation.

The "ecological modernization" approach also holds that economic growth and resolutions to ecological problems need not be mutually exclusive (Spaargaren and van Vliet 2000). However, it differs from sustainable development by reconceptualizing the consumer as an active – albeit highly rational – chooser. Ecological modernization seeks to reconcile the gap between policy and practice through a range of consciousness-raising strategies to influence consumer choices and promote sustainable/green consumption as a rational and ethical solution to the damage wrought by wasteful consumption.

The issue of how to promote environmentally beneficial consumption practices has thus become pivotal. Although some have framed sustainable/green consumption as an individualistic "cultural politics" rather than as a movement connected to larger social and environmental justice issues, others contend that this underestimates the breadth and depth of consumer objections to altering their lifestyles.

However, despite the obstacles posed by the individualistic orientation of consumers and consumerism, there is mounting evidence of greater participation in sustainable/green consumption; much of which has emerged from the margins of consumer societies. However, there is a need for more – and more systematic – studies of alternative consumer movements and the factors that give rise to them. Similarly, across the social and natural sciences, there is a lack of applied study into the implementation, effectiveness, and modification of policies designed to encourage sustainable/green consumption practices. For sustainable/green consumption to be better understood, these practices and policies must be examined in greater detail from a wide range of disciplines and methods.

SEE ALSO: Consumption; Environmental Movements; Environmental Sociology; Globalization, Consumption and

REFERENCE

Spaargaren, G. and van Vliet, B. (2000) Lifestyles, consumption and the environment: the ecological modernisation of domestic consumption. *Environmental Politics* 10 (1): 50–76.

SUGGESTED READING

Organisation for Economic Co-operation and Development (1997) *Sustainable Consumption and Production*. OECD Publications, Paris.

JOSEPH D. RUMBO

consumption and the body

The relationship between the body and material culture in the post-industrial world is defined through consumption. How one experiences the body, manages corporeal identity, and participates in social rituals as an embodied subject is, to a great extent, commodified. Changes in perspectives on the body are intertwined with the advent of consumer culture and the concomitant development of mass media and advertising. The appropriation of meanings for advertising promotes what is termed the "floating signifier" effect (Baudrillard 1975) or the shift in the use value attached to objects such that any meaning or quality can be associated with any object. The body acts as both a carrier of these multiple and shifting meanings and a means for expression as the body becomes what Featherstone (1991) refers to as the "visible carrier of the self."

Bourdieu (1984) notes that the body is not simply a surface to be read, but is a three-dimensional expression of social relations that take the form of corporeal or mental schema, referred to as habitus. Through the process of routine symbolic consumption, identity is constructed and embodied. The literal embodiment of class manifests in size, shape, weight, posture, demeanor, tastes, preference, and movement through social space. Other authors have applied similar principles to studying other facets of identity such as gender and/or race. Scholars note that the politics of cultural legitimation and the cultural capital conferred by one's taste reveal relations of power and privilege. Consumers who occupy different social locations may appropriate the symbols of other groups and thereby use such signifiers as a route to mobility. Some theorists argue that global consumer culture and the circulation of "lifestyle" commodities undermine the stability of embodied signifiers.

Scholarship on bodies and identity is diverse and varied. Two important trends appear as to how the body is viewed in consumer culture: (1) the dominated body and (2) the expressive body. In the first case, many theories have focused on the tyranny of the marketplace and its objectification and alienation of bodies. In the second case, opportunities for bodies to use consumer culture for expressive purposes provide a context for resistance and social change.

First, the body is viewed as subject to domination through commodification. Drawing on Marxist perspectives, the fetishization of bodies ultimately leads to the reproduction of socially unequal bodies. The bodies of the privileged are legitimated and idealized through participation in rituals of consumption. The individual is then subject to the tyranny of the market regardless of relative position. He or she is not tyrannized by an outsider, but becomes engaged in endless rituals of self-surveillance guided by idealized marketplace images conveyed through the mass media. Critiques of the dominated body approach focus on the cultural manufacture of meanings and identities. Baudrillard (1975) notes that individual desires are disguised expressions of social differences in a system of cultural meanings that is produced through commodities. For Baudrillard, the commodified body still acts as a marker of social distinction, but not a permanent one. This leads to the second way in which bodies are understood as sites of contestable meaning. The expressive body has the ability to participate in what Giddens (1991) terms "reflexive self-fashioning." Through participation in consumer culture, awareness that identity can be self-consciously constructed is generated.

SEE ALSO: Body and Cultural Sociology; Conspicuous Consumption; Globalization, Consumption and

REFERENCES

Baudrillard, J. (1975) *The Mirror of Production.* Teleos Press, St. Louis.

Bourdieu, P. (1984) *Distinction: A Social Critique of the Judgment of Taste.* Harvard University Press, Cambridge, MA.

Featherstone, M. (1991) The body in consumer culture. In: Featherstone, M., Hepworth, M., & Giddens, A. (1991) *Modernity and Self-Identity: Self and Society in the Late Modern Age.* Polity Press, Cambridge.

FAYE LINDA WACHS

consumption and the Internet

The study of consumption within the social sciences has been recently extended to include consumption of and on the Internet. Mass adoption of the Internet in the early to mid-1990s throughout western countries and beyond raises new questions about consumer culture, as the Internet facilitates the shift from mass to specialized, flexible, and dispersed forms of consumption. Taking "the Internet" as a "black box," a technology diffusing through the marketplace and into workplaces, homes, schools, and communities, some research asks how the Internet itself is being consumed: can the spread of the Internet be understood like the diffusion of any other consumer good and is there a widening or lessening "digital divide" akin to other social inequalities? Other research inquires into the many and diverse goods and services made available through the Internet: does e-commerce from business to consumers work in similar ways to high street shopping? Or, more broadly, what are the emerging cultural and social practices by which online content/services are consumed by users?

As "Internet studies" (itself a contested label) attracts the attention of multiple disciplines, consumption studies must negotiate its contribution in this research agenda, including negotiating the "optimistic"/"pessimistic" opposition that shaped the early phase of "Internet studies." Some ask whether the Internet affords new and emancipatory possibilities that can liberate people from well-established and hierarchical practices of material and symbolic consumption "offline." Research reveals some democratizing effects as a function of the Internet's heterarchical, even anarchic network structure, including positive implications for construction of identities in a domain where anonymity, expressiveness, experimentation, and tolerance shape the field of consumption. As consumers become "prosumers" – a hybrid of producers and consumers – what is the creative or democratic potential of online consumption practices?

More pessimistically, researchers show that the Internet affords new forms of commercial exploitation and social control, again extending and developing practices of production, distribution, and consumption offline to the online domain. This includes risks associated with the commercial or state invasion of privacy, the exploitation of personal data, opportunities to monitor, target or exploit consumers, and the reproduction of social inequality and exclusion online as offline.

The field has moved on from the assumption of a separate domain called "cyberspace" or a clear virtual/real distinction, leaving behind simple assertions of technological determinism (asking about the impacts or effects of the Internet on consumption) in favor of either a social determinism (stressing the importance of the offline context in shaping online consumption practices) or a "soft technological determinism" (seeking to understand in a more subtle and careful manner just whether and how consumption online differs from consumption offline, supplementing and diversifying the possibilities and practices of consumption in general).

Consumption online is integrated into daily life. While the material and symbolic conditions of consumption on the Internet may differ, they are not of a different order from offline consumption. Online, the (re)emergence of familiar cultural norms and social conventions is apparent, though for a minority of engaged consumers, radical or alternative forms of consumption, communication, community building and new digital literacies are also evident. Online too, the signs are growing that the emancipatory potential of the Internet is subject to increasing attempts to privatize, commercialize, control, and profit from the activities of consumers online, some defended under a "neoliberal" freeing of the market, on- as offline, others contested as incursions into public freedoms, privacy, and rights.

SEE ALSO: Consumption, Mass Consumption, and Consumer Culture; Cyberculture; Internet

SUGGESTED READINGS

Lievrouw, L. & Livingstone, S. (eds.) (2006). *Handbook of New Media: Social Shaping and Social Consequences*, updated student edn. Sage, London.

Miller, D. & Slater, D. (2000) *The Internet: An Ethnographic Approach*. Berg, London.

Wellman, B. & Haythornthwaite, C. (eds.) (2002) *The Internet in Everyday Life*. Blackwell, Malden, MA.

SONIA LIVINGSTONE

content analysis

Content analysis is a method of research that examines cultural artifacts by observing and analyzing these objects in systematic ways. Researchers seek to understand messages within texts while also searching for the meanings being produced and interpreted by the audience and producer of the text. Anything that is in or can be converted to printed form can be examined using content analysis.

This unobtrusive method lends well to both quantitative and qualitative techniques. A quantitative approach studies text by using narrowly defined parameters, concentrating on a particular set of images, words or phrases to be counted within specific documents. Qualitative approaches work with a less closely defined set of parameters. Researchers typically perform one or two stages of analysis before eliminating materials from their analysis. Both approaches examine the data in a series of analytic phases and establish a clear set of systematic rules, including defining the unit of analysis used to study the text, before the examination begins.

The process of creating the criteria for analysis, examining the documents, locating, marking, and tallying the unit of analysis is called *coding*. Researchers study both *manifest content*, which are words and phrases that are obvious in their meaning, and *latent content*, which are words and phrases that are more subjective in their interpretation. Manifest content is considered the more objective and reliable largely due to ease of identification.

The benefits of this type of analysis are that it is unobtrusive, transparent and the material examined provides an accurate representation of society since it is created without the intent of being a subject of study. Content analysis is a complement to other forms of analyses on texts and messages, which include frame analysis, textual analysis, and discourse analysis.

SEE ALSO: Discourse; Methods

SUGGESTED READINGS

Krippendorff, K. (2003) *Content Analysis: An Introduction to Its Methodology*. Sage, Newbury Park, CA.

Neuendorf, K. (2001) *The Content Analysis Handbook*. Sage, Newbury Park, CA.

KRISTINA B. WOLFF

convenience sample

A convenience sample refers to a subset of a research population that is utilized because of ease of access. Sampling is a practical solution to the fact that research populations are often too large or expensive to be studied in their entirety. (A research population is the largest collection of elements, people, artifacts, or other units of interest to the researcher.) Consequently, researchers will work with samples – subsets of research populations. The convenience sample is also known as an "accidental" sample since elements are selected by virtue of being in the right place at the right time. Reporters often utilize a convenience sample when they interview individuals who are close at hand. Educators who administer surveys to their students are also employing a convenience sample.

A convenience sample is a type of *nonprobability* sampling. Nonprobability samples are *not* based on a random selection process. A random selection process utilizes a sampling frame (a list of all elements in the population of interest) and chance to determine which elements from the population are selected for the sample. The selection of names from a hat illustrates a random selection process. A random selection process gives every element in the larger population an equal chance of being selected for the sample and thus gives us our best chance of obtaining a *representative* sample. When we use a nonprobability sample we cannot make any claim that our sample does a good job at representing the larger population from which it is selected. Nonprobability samples are not appropriate for generalizing sample findings back to populations and thus are weak with regard to *external validity* – the ability to use sample findings to make accurate statements about entire populations.

SEE ALSO: Quantitative Methods; Random Sample; Sampling, Qualitative (Purposive)

SUGGESTED READING

Ruane, J. (2005) *Essentials of Research Methods: A Guide to Social Science Research*. Blackwell Publishing, Malden, MA.

JANET M. RUANE

conversation analysis

Conversation analysis (CA) is a method for investigating the structure and process of social interaction between humans. It focuses primarily on talk, but integrates also the nonverbal aspects of interaction in its research design. As their data, CA studies use video or audio recordings made from naturally occurring interaction. As their results, CA studies yield descriptions of recurrent structures and practices of social interaction. Some of these, such as turn taking or sequence structure, are involved in all interaction, whereas others are more specific and have to do with particular actions, such as asking questions or delivering and receiving news, assessments, or complaints. CA studies can focus either on ordinary conversations taking place between acquaintances or family members, or on institutional encounters where the participants accomplish their institutional tasks through their interaction. CA elucidates basic aspects of human sociality that reside in talk, and it examines the ways in which specific social institutions are invoked in, and operate through, talk.

CA was started by Harvey Sacks and his coworkers – most importantly Emanuel Schegloff and Gail Jefferson – at the University of California in the 1960s. The initial formation of Sacks's ideas is documented in his lectures from 1964 to 1972 (Sacks 1992a; 1992b). CA was developed in an intellectual environment shaped by Goffman's work on the moral underpinnings of social interaction and Garfinkel's ethnomethodology focusing on the interpretive procedures underlying social action. Sacks started to study the real-time sequential ordering of actions: the rules, patterns, and structures in the relations between actions. Thereby, he made a radical shift in the perspective of social scientific inquiry into social interaction: instead of treating social interaction as a screen upon which other processes (moral, inferential, or others) were projected, Sacks started to study the very structures of the interaction itself.

There are perhaps three basic features shared by CA studies: (1) they focus on *action*, (2) the *structures* of which they seek to explicate, and thereby (3) they investigate the achievement of *intersubjective understanding*. As general research topics, these three would be shared by many "schools" of social science. The uniqueness of CA, however, is in the way in which it shows how "action," "structure," and "intersubjectivity" are practically achieved and managed in talk and interaction.

SEE ALSO: Discourse; Ethnomethodology; Goffman, Erving; Sociolinguistics; Symbolic Interaction

REFERENCES

Sacks, H. (1992a) *Lectures on Conversation*, vol. 1. Blackwell, Oxford.
Sacks, H. (1992b) *Lectures on Conversation*, vol. 2. Blackwell, Oxford.

ANSSI PERÄKYLÄ

Cooley, Charles Horton (1864–1929)

Charles Horton Cooley was a prominent member of the founding generation of American sociologists. Named a full professor of sociology at the University of Michigan in 1907, he was then elected president of the American Sociological Association in 1918. It was his aim and achievement to apply the ideas of pragmatism to the development of a sociological theory of social action, social order, and social change, which he ultimately accomplished with his trilogy: *Human Nature and the Social Order* ([1902] 1964), *Social Organization* ([1909] 1963), and *Social Process* ([1918] 1966).

In *Human Nature and the Social Order* Cooley examines the "distributive aspect" of the relationship between self and society, namely the development of the self through symbolically mediated interaction. A "looking-glass self," according to Cooley has three "principal elements": first the imagination of our appearance to the other person; second the imagination of his judgment of that appearance; and third some sort of self-feeling, such as "pride or mortification" (Cooley [1902] 1964: 184).

In *Social Organization* Cooley defines the "collective aspects" of social action (primary group, public opinion, democracy, social classes and institutions). Organizations are, over time and space, expanded structures of action such as "enduring sentiments, beliefs, customs" and large institutions such as "the government, the church and laws," but also micro-societal "apperceptive systems." "Organized attitudes" are resources for individuals and, simultaneously, they also limit their activities. "The individual," according to Cooley, "is always cause as well as effect of the institution" (Cooley [1909] 1963: 313–19).

In *Social Process* Cooley set up his conception of social change as a creative search and experiment process. Individual actions have their origin in "habits" of the social world. But those generalized meanings never provide complete answers to specific situations; they must therefore continuously be reconstructed in tentative trial phases. Most significant in the sequence of action (habit, conflict, experiment and new habit), is the experimental stage of "imaginative reconstruction." The "test of intelligence is the power to act successfully in new situations" (Cooley [1918] 1966: 351–8).

SEE ALSO: Chicago School; Looking-Glass Self; Mead, George Herbert; Pragmatism; Primary Groups; Symbolic Interaction

REFERENCES

Cooley, C. H. (1964) [1902] *Human Nature and the Social Order*. Schocken, New York.
Cooley, C. H. (1963) [1909] *Social Organization: A Study of the Larger Mind*. Schocken, New York.
Cooley, C. H. (1966) [1918] *Social Process*. Southern Illinois Press, Carbondale and Edwardsville, IL.

HANS-JOACHIM SCHUBERT

corporate social responsibility

The fundamental idea of corporate social responsibility (CSR) "is that business and society are interwoven rather than distinct entities" and that business must therefore meet particular societal expectations regarding their social, environmental, and economic activities (Wood 1991: 695). The concept refers to the discourses, practices, policy initiatives, and disciplines that shape these societal expectations, as well as internal value systems, voluntary practices of corporations, and legal requirements pertaining to those activities.

While modern conceptions of the term have appeared since the mid-to-late twentieth century, the general idea is not new. Original legal formulations placed restrictions on corporate activities and allowed corporate charters to be revoked when they "failed to act in the public good" (Banerjee 2008: 53). However, by the end of the 1800s, major restrictions on corporations were removed and their primary legal obligation became maximizing financial returns for shareholders.

The demand for modern conceptions of CSR has been driven by social movement groups, ethical consumers, and socially responsible investors (and corporations themselves). However, there has been little agreement among groups about the content areas (e.g. environment, labor practices, community relations, and human rights), standards, and governance of social responsibility. While the business community has generally sought voluntary (i.e. self-regulated) mechanisms, most social movement groups have advocated at least some level of legally-binding structures. Nonetheless, nearly all corporate practices of CSR to date (especially in the USA) have materialized through voluntary social reporting and codes of conduct.

While proponents see voluntary efforts as important steps in orienting corporations to the public good, critical perspectives emphasize voluntary CSR initiatives as an organized strategy by corporations to preempt stricter laws and regulations. Critical perspectives argue that if corporations' only legal responsibility is to make profits, it is impossible for them to adopt socially responsible practices.

SEE ALSO: Capitalism; Capitalism, Social Institutions of; Crime, Corporate; Environment, Sociology of the; Social Movements

SUGGESTED READINGS

Banerjee, S. (2008) Corporate social responsibility: the good, the bad, and the ugly. *Critical Sociology* 34 (1): 51–79.

Wood, D. (1991) Corporate social performance revisited. *Academy of Management Review* 16 (4): 691–718.

PAUL DEAN

correlation

Correlation refers to the relationship between two or more variables. Many different forms of correlation exist, but they all reflect a quantitative, statistical means for describing relationships. A correlation statistic is inherently *bivariate* (i.e., two variables) in nature.

Correlation speaks to whether or not variables are systematically related in some predictable fashion. For example, assuming no irrigational intervention, annual rainfall is likely related to growth in agricultural crops, such that crops receiving more rain likely will be more productive. Of course, this relationship probably varies somewhat depending on the type of crop, amount of sunlight, and many other variables.

Scatterplots can be used to graphically display the relationship, where each axis represents one of the variables and the the paired data for each observation are plotted. Perfect linear relationships result in the formation of a line by the plotted observations. As the relationship weakens, the plotted points will diverge from a straight line to form a more circular pattern.

The most common manifestation of bivariate correlation is the Pearson product-moment correlation coefficient, which was named after Karl Pearson (1857–1936), who popularized the statistic originally introduced by Francis Galton (1822–1911). The statistic is more commonly known as Pearson r or just r. A large section of statistical work can be traced to the simple correlation coefficient.

Pearson r ranges from $+1$ to -1, inclusive. A coefficient of 0 would represent no relationship. Coefficients of $+1$ would represent a perfect, positive (i.e., direct) relationship and those of -1 would represent a perfect, negative (i.e., indirect, inverse) relationship. Thus, the absolute value of the coefficient speaks to the strength of the relationship and the sign indicates directionality, either positive or negative. Importantly, r can be squared to yield an effect size statistic indicating the amount of shared variance between two variables.

SEE ALSO: Descriptive Statistics; General Linear Model; Statistical Significance Testing

SUGGESTED READINGS

Henson, R. K. (2000) Demystifying parametric analyses: illustrating canonical correlation as the multivariate general linear model. *Multiple Linear Regression Viewpoints* 26 (1): 11–19.

Hinkle, D. E., Wiersma, W., & Jurs, S. G. (2003) *Applied Statistics for the Behavioral Sciences*, 5th edn. Houghton Mifflin, Boston, MA.

ROBIN K. HENSON

counterculture

Similar in meaning to the more inclusive term "subculture," counterculture designates a group whose norms, values, symbolic references, and styles of life deviate from those of the dominant culture. Indeed, sociological commentary on the counterculture of the 1960s is so deeply informed by the rubric of subculture as to render the terms inseparable in many respects. Yet while subculture is the generic term typically applied to a range of such groups, from post war British youth cultures to inner-city African American youth cultures, counterculture is typically invoked with specific reference to the youth movements that swept American and Western European societies in the late to mid-1970s. First introduced by Roszak (1968), the term came to refer to a diffuse movement of students, youth, and other marginalia whose mobilizing strategies rejected that of traditional social movements, and appealed to diffuse concepts of anti-technological sentiment to achieve spontaneous and widespread reforms. It had an alternative strategy of political agitation to that of other subcultures.

The appeal was more to a presumed mentalist, spiritual, and lifestyle development which, members of the counterculture argued, would serve as a basis for overturning hierarchical structures implicit within advanced technological societies.

The counterculture of the 1960s is typically traced to early reactions to the conformity and mediocrity associated with the years of the postwar economic expansion. Beatniks and others drew on African American expressive traditions to fashion a vanguard sensibility in music, drugs, philosophy, literature, and poetry. Amid accelerating popular opposition to the war in Vietnam and an emerging student left, together with the growth of hippie enclaves and the increasing thematization of drug experiences in music, film, and media, a distinctly oppositional culture formed around what was termed a new "consciousness." Rejecting not only the values of the mainstream middle class from which it emerged, but also the class-based political traditions of an older generation of leftist opposition, the counterculture advocated an immediate and practical approach to social reform, beginning with the individual reform of personal relationships and daily habits, and the adoption of utopian egalitarianism in one's everyday style of life.

SEE ALSO: Cultural Studies; Subculture

REFERENCE

Roszak, T. (1968) *The Making of a Counter Culture: Reflections on the Technocratic Society and* Its *Youthful Opposition*. University of California Press, Berkeley, CA.

SUGGESTED READING

Brooks, D. (2000) *Bobo's in Paradise: The New Upper Class and How They Got There*. Simon & Schuster, New York.

SAM BINKLEY

creative destruction

The concept of "creative destruction" was made famous by the economist Joseph A. Schumpeter. For Schumpeter, creative destruction "is the essential fact about capitalism" (Schumpeter 1975 [1942]: 82) and is meant to highlight the dynamic nature of capitalist systems. It refers to how capitalism continuously revolutionizes itself as new products and business processes are created that render obsolete and destroy those that are existing. The classic example of this is how the creation of the automobile led to the destruction of the horse and buggy industry: after the former was created the latter could not compete as an effective means of transport and it was destroyed as a result.

There are two aspects of creative destruction that should be kept in mind.

The first is that the source of creative destruction comes "*from within*" the economic system itself and not from sources outside of it (p. 83, emphasis in original). In other words, change is endogenous to capitalism as entrepreneurs and innovators create the goods, technologies, and organizations that replace and destroy what already exists.

The second aspect is that the type of change involved in the process of creative destruction is *qualitative* in nature and highlights how firms seek a competitive advantage through the creation of qualitatively different products or processes. In fact, creative destruction rests upon the revolutionary nature of such qualitatively different goods, businesses, technologies, etc., being introduced into the economy This is what Schumpeter means when he says that the history of capitalism is a "history of revolutions" where the creation of the new upsets, overturns, and destroys the old.

SEE ALSO: Economic Development; Social Change.

REFERENCE

Schumpeter, J. 1975 [1942]. *Capitalism, Socialism, and Democracy*. Harper and Brothers, New York.

CRAIG D. LAIR

crime

Criminologists differ on how they define crime. One definition is a legal definition: crime is a violation of criminal law. Criminologist Edwin Sutherland calls this the conventional definition of crime because it is commonly used. He adds that it is typical to distinguish a crime from a tort. A crime is a violation against the state whereas a tort is a violation against an individual. An example of this occurred in the twentieth-century O. J. Simpson case. In criminal court Simpson was acquitted of murder but was found liable for wrongful death in civil court.

Within the legal definition of crime, crime is distinguished from delinquency by the age of the offender. In most states an offender must be 18 to be arrested and prosecuted as a criminal. Under 18 the youth is processed as a delinquent in a separate juvenile or family court and legally there is no criminal conviction.

Sociologist Émile Durkheim argues that crime is normal; even a society of saints has persons with faults that society judges and punishes. In other words, each society has a collective conscience that punishes faults so as to reinforce the common values that most members should strive to emulate. In fact, Durkheim notes, the absence of crime might be a problem. It might mean that a society is overly repressive and does not allow enough innovation. So no society should congratulate itself for completely eliminating crime.

On the other hand, criminologists Michael Gottfredson and Travis Hirschi define crimes as "acts of force or fraud undertaken in pursuit of self-interest" (1990: 15). So contrary to Sutherland, they see crime as ordinary and mundane, stemming from human nature which focuses on pursuing pleasure and avoiding pain. They see commonalities in crime, deviance, sin, and accident rather than conceptualizing them as distinct phenomena. They argue that sin and crime are often the same actions; the difference is that religion sanctions sin while the government punishes crime.

Herman and Julia Schwendinger define crime as acts against human rights. Using their definition, some could argue that various national leaders are criminals if they are violating human rights, even though as president or leader of their countries they are arguably acting lawfully.

Restorative justice, a recent perspective but one with ancient history, focuses on harms instead of "crimes." Contrary to the legal definition of crime, restorative justice proponents disagree that the "state" is the aggrieved party. They argue that the definition of crime is a harm, injury, or wrong done to another individual. The response of society should be first to acknowledge the hurt and injury that has occurred. Then there should be attention to the needs of the victim and then the offender. Thus a crime is seen not simply as an occasion for the state to inflict punishment, but as an opportunity for the community to intervene and help both the victim and the offender.

Perspectives such as that of the Schwendingers and the restorative justice perspective, see the usual emphasis on crime as too narrow. Such criminologists think that the criminal justice system puts too much emphasis on street crime and not enough on crimes of the powerful. These criminologists contend that corporations can and do perpetrate "crimes" or injuries. Jeffrey Reiman argues that while the FBI focuses on homicide, many more Americans are dying from occupational hazards at work or from hospital malpractice. But because our country protects both corporations and doctors, there is considerably less enforcement of statutes pertaining to workplace crime. The result is that "the rich get richer and the poor get prison."

John Hagan emphasizes that crime and our conceptions of crime are changeable. For example, in the 1920s the USA defined the manufacture, distribution, and sale of alcohol as criminal. Today alcohol production and consumption is a vital part of our economy. Instead of pursuing bootleggers, contemporary police are pursuing drug dealers.

Two common ways of measuring crime are arrest statistics reported in the FBI Uniform Crime Report (UCR) and victimization studies such as the National Crime Victimization Survey (NCVS). The FBI Crime Index is composed of violent and property offenses. Murder, rape, robbery, and aggravated assault make up the Violent Crime Index. Larceny-theft, burglary, and arson compose the Property Crime Index.

In 2007, in the USA, there were over 11.2 million offenses reported to the police for an Index Crime rate of 3,370.4 *offenses* per 100,000 residents. This rate was down 2 percent from 2006 and down 32 percent from 1993. Some attribute this decline to less reporting of crime to the police, more effective use of policing, increased incarceration, changes in demand for illegal drugs, especially crack cocaine, decreased availability of guns, improvement in the economy, and changes in youth attitudes. Criminologist John Conklin has done a thorough analysis of the dramatic crime decline in the 1990s. He concludes that the increased use of imprisonment was the major factor in the crime decline, followed by changes in the crack market and a switch to marijuana.

The NCVS reads descriptions of personal and property crimes to survey respondents who answer whether they have been a victim of such incidents in the past 6 months. Victimization studies have helped criminologists study crime because they allow for the analysis of crimes that do not get reported to the police, what some call the dark figure of crime. In 2006 US residents aged 12 or older experienced approximately 25 million violent and property victimizations. The rate of violent victimization decreased 44 percent from 1993 to 2006. Concerning property crime, from 1993 to 2006, the household burglary rate fell 40 percent; the rate of theft declined 40 percent; and the auto theft rate decreased 49 percent.

In summary, police, prosecutors, correctional officials, and criminologists act on the assumption that the conventional definition of crime is both generally accepted and valid. But there are other definitions of crime, especially the definitions proposed by critical criminologists and restorative justice theoreticians, that raise important questions about our understanding of crime and our reaction to it.

SEE ALSO: Crime, Corporate; Crime, Political; Crime, Radical/Marxist Theories of; Criminal Justice System; Criminology; Deviance, Crime and; Victimization

REFERENCE

Gottfredson, M. R. & Hirschi, T. (1990) *A General Theory of Crime*. Stanford University Press, Stanford, CA.

SUGGESTED READINGS

Braithwaite, J. (2002) *Restorative Justice and Responsive Regulation*. Oxford University Press, Oxford.

Conklin, J. (2003) *Why the Crime Rates Fell*. Allyn & Bacon, Boston, MA.

JOHN T. WHITEHEAD

crime, broken windows theory of

The term "broken windows" is used to signify the characteristics of neighborhood deterioration. They argue that if a broken window in a building or in a car is left untended, other signs of disorder will increase. Wilson and Kelling (1982) suggest that an unrepaired broken window is a signal that no one cares for the neighborhood. They argued that if the window is left broken, it can lead to more serious crime problems.

Philip Zimbardo (1969), a psychologist, tested the broken window theory with some experiments. He arranged that a car without a license plate be parked in a Bronx neighborhood and a comparable car be parked in Palo Alto, California. The car in the Bronx was destroyed within ten minutes; while the car in Palo Alto was left untouched for more than a week. After Zimbardo smashed the car in Palo Alto, passersby started to vandalize the car. In each case once each car started to be destroyed and looked abandoned, with more destruction, vandalism, and stealing soon following.

Signs of neighborhood deterioration or disorder, such as broken windows, can lead to the breakdown of social controls. In stable neighborhoods, residents tend to watch out and care more for their property, children, and public safety. Residents in these neighborhoods are more attached to their neighborhood and more likely to consider their neighborhood as their home. Thus, any broken windows or other signs of disorder in these stable neighborhoods will soon be addressed and fixed. In these stable neighborhoods, more informal social controls are exercised by residents, the result being that crime is less likely to invade such areas. On the other hand, when a neighborhood can no longer regulate signs of public disorder, such as broken windows, more deterioration and even serious crime can result (Wilson and Kelling 1982).

SEE ALSO: Crime; Crime, Social Control Theory of

REFERENCES

Zimbardo, P. G. (1969) *The Cognitive Control of Motivation*. Scott, Foresman, Glenview, IL.

Wilson, J. Q. & Kelling, G. (1982) Broken windows: the police and neighborhood safety. *Atlantic Monthly* (March): 29–38.

DORIS CHU

crime, corporate

Corporate crime involves organizational lawbreaking and includes offenses such as antitrust violations, the filing of false earnings statements, and misleading advertising. Corporate wrongdoing made headlines in the USA in the early 2000s with scandals involving Enron, Adelphia, WorldCom, Arthur Andersen, and a host of other commercial giants.

The legal concept of corporate criminal liability rests upon the idea that a business entity is something beyond an aggregation of its human members. Corporate decisions are said to represent an amalgam of inputs that often lead to action that no individual in the group would have carried out alone.

The major stamp of approval on the idea of criminal culpability of corporations in the USA was accorded in 1908 by the Supreme Court in *New York Central v. United States,* a case concerned with illegal rebates offered to preferred companies by the railroad. The company insisted that to penalize it was to harm innocent stockholders, but the judges ruled that if the authorities could not punish the corporate entity there would be no effective means to cope with illegal business practices.

A particularly provocative sociological dialog on corporate crime is found in an exchange between Donald Cressey and a pair of Australian scholars, John Braithwaite and Brent Fisse. Cressey maintained that it is impossible to formulate a social psychological theory of corporate crime. Braithwaite and Fisse insisted that sound theories can be based on analyses of corporate behaviors, such as those reflected in policies adopted by boards of directors.

SEE ALSO: Crime; Crime, White-Collar

SUGGESTED READINGS

Braithwaite, J. & Fisse, B. (1990) On the plausibility of corporate crime control. *Advances in Criminological Theory* 2: 15–37.

Cressey, D. (1988) Poverty of theory in corporate crime research. *Advances in Criminological Theory* 1: 31–56.

GILBERT GEIS

crime, organized

Though the study of organized crime is primarily a sociological pursuit, the phenomenon is a subject of study in numerous other disciplines, including anthropology, economics, history, and political science. Despite, if not because of, this broad and varied inquiry into the topic, there is little consensus on what constitutes "organized crime."

Perhaps the broadest interpretation of organized crime is offered by sociologist Joseph Albini in his book, *The American Mafia: Genesis of a Legend* (1971). His analysis identifies four types of organized crime: political-social (e.g., Ku Klux Klan), mercenary (predatory/theft-oriented), in-group (gangs), and syndicated (offers goods and services, and infiltrates legitimate businesses). Most scholars have opted to focus on the latter.

Four characteristics are most frequently cited in the academic literature when defining syndicated organized crime: a continuing enterprise, using rational means, profiting through illegal activities, utilizing the corruption of officials. Some authors have argued that groups must also use or threaten violence, and be involved in multiple criminal enterprises, to merit inclusion in the organized crime discussion.

SEE ALSO: Crime, Corporate; Crime, White-Collar

SUGGESTED READING

Hagan, F. (1983) The organized crime continuum: a further specification of a new conceptual model. *Criminal Justice Review* 8: 52–7.

SEAN PATRICK GRIFFIN

crime, political

Political crime is an illegal offense *against* the state (oppositional crime) with the intention of affecting its policies or an illegal offense *by* the state and its agents. Individually based political crimes benefit individuals as do occupational political crimes committed within legitimate occupations and intended to benefit office holders. Organizational political crimes benefit the state and its policies.

Some scholars, claiming that all crime is politically constructed, suggest using *social harm* as a broader definition of crime. Those most egregious behaviors arguably have been carried out by state agents who generally are free from legal prosecution. Under a broader definition, the state's unethical behaviors would be subject to the criminal label. More recent literature suggests using human rights violations as a definition.

In recent years the terms *state crime*, which better articulates the state's role and *state-corporate crime*, which focuses on the political activities of the state in conjunction with industry, have proven useful for detailing harmful actions within public and private bureaucracies.

There is no widely accepted theoretical explanation for political crime or method for studying it. Various sociological theories have been used; research methods mainly have been case studies. Although egregious, political crime has received scant coverage in text books and today often is omitted from survey classes.

SEE ALSO: Crime; Political Sociology

SUGGESTED READINGS

Ermann, M. D. & Lundman, R. J. (2001) *Corporate and Governmental Deviance*. Oxford University, New York.
Tunnell, K. D. (1993) *Political Crime in Contemporary America*. Garland, New York.

KENNETH D. TUNNELL

crime, radical/Marxist theories of

Marxist criminological theory asserts that crime is the result of structural inequalities that are inherently associated with capitalist economic systems. Although Marx himself wrote very little about crime, theorists have relied on his economic theory to provide a foundation for a *critical* theory of criminal behavior.

Marxist criminologists argue that a society where some people, because of their place in the capitalist system, are able to accrue a great deal of wealth and material goods, and some are not, is setting itself up for criminal behavior. Such behavior results from a lack of attention by those in power to the growing tensions among the working classes, who see a great divide between what the culture teaches them they can, and should, achieve, and the actual opportunities that could assist them in such achievement.

On another level, Marxist criminologists argue that the criminal justice system, the system through which people who break the law are processed, should become more equitable. There should be an expectation that all individuals who come in contact with the system will be treated justly and equitably, with the rich receiving the same treatment as the poor. A system where "the rich get richer and the poor get prison" (Reiman 2001) should be abolished once and for all. Corporate fraud, or suite crime, that bilks retirement funds from longtime and loyal employees should be punishable by hard prison time no less than crimes of the street. When differences exist between the haves and the have-nots when it comes to the meting out of justice, it becomes clear that the system is, in fact, unjust.

SEE ALSO: Capitalism; Crime; Crime, White-Collar; Marx, Karl

REFERENCE

Reiman, J. (2001) *The Rich Get Richer and the Poor Get Prison*. Allyn & Bacon, Boston, MA.

SUGGESTED READING

Sims, B. (1997) Crime, punishment, and the American dream: toward a Marxist integration. *Journal of Research in Crime and Delinquency* 34 (1): 5–24.

BARBARA SIMS

crime, social control theory of

The social control theory of crime is fundamentally a theory of conformity. Instead of theorizing about the motivations for criminal behavior, control theorists ask, "Why do people conform?" Their answers to this question stress the importance of strong group relationships, active institutional participation, and conventional moral values in constraining and regulating individual behavior. When these controlling influences are weak or rendered ineffective, people are freer to deviate from legal and moral norms. Thus, in explaining conformity, control theorists highlight the conditions under which crime and delinquency become possible, if not likely, outcomes.

The most influential formulation of control theory was presented by Travis Hirschi in his 1969 book, *Causes of Delinquency*. Hirschi identified four conceptually distinct elements of the social bond that, when strong and viable, maintain conformity to conventional rules of conduct: (1) emotional *attachment* to family and other conventional groups; (2) *commitment* to conventional lines of action, such as educational or occupational careers; (3) *involvement* in conventional activities with little free time to spare; and (4) *belief* in core moral values of society. To the extent that these elements are weak or ineffectual, individuals are freer to deviate than are individuals who are more strongly bonded to society.

In contrast to Hirschi's *relational* focus on the strength of the social bond, many earlier versions of control theory employed a *dualistic* conception of internal or personal controls versus external or social controls. Examples include Reiss's (1951) analysis of delinquency as the "failure of personal and social controls" and Reckless's (1961) containment theory, which placed special emphasis on the importance of a "good self-concept" as an inner "buffer" against environmental pressures toward delinquency. In his more recent work with Gottfredson, Hirschi (1990) has also moved toward a psychologically oriented explanation by arguing that *low self-control* is the basic source of criminal behavior.

SEE ALSO: Crime; Deviance, Explanatory Theories of; Social Control

REFERENCES

Gottfredson, M. R., & Hirschi, T. (1990) *A General Theory of Crime*. Stanford University Press, Stanford, CA.
Hirschi, T. (1969) *Causes of Delinquency*. University of California Press, Berkeley, CA.
Reckless, W. C. (1961) A new theory of delinquency and crime. *Federal Probation* 25: 42–6.
Reiss, A. J., Jr. (1951) Delinquency as the failure of personal and social controls. *American Sociological Review* 16, 196–207.

JAMES D. ORCUTT

crime, social learning theory of

The social learning theory of crime basically argues that some people learn to commit crimes through the same process through which others learn to conform. The theory assumes that people are "blank slates" at birth, having neither a motivation to commit crime nor to conform. The theory then asks two questions. First, at the micro-level, it asks why an individual commits crimes. The answer to this question stresses the process of learning which involves the interaction between thought or cognition, behavior and environment. Second, at the macro-level, social learning theory asks why some groups have higher crime rates than others. The answer to this question involves the concepts of culture conflict, differential social organization and social structure.

Social learning theory is rooted in the work of the Chicago School theorists of the early twentieth century. Along with social control theory, social learning theory is now considered one of, if not the, dominant theory of crime and deviance today. Its dominance is largely due to the work of two theorists, Edwin Sutherland and Ronald Akers. In 1939, Sutherland published the first version of his theory of social learning in his textbook *Principles of Criminology* with the final version published first in 1947. With this theory, he presented criminology with a purely sociological theory of crime that addressed his concerns about the biological and psychological theories of crime that were dominant at the time. Akers later revised Differential Association, rewriting it in the language of modern learning theory and expanding on it to make it more comprehensive. Besides his theoretical contributions, Akers has also been a leader in empirically testing social learning theory across a variety of groups and crimes.

SEE ALSO: Crime, Radical/Marxist Theories of; Crime, Social Control Theory of; Criminology

SUGGESTED READINGS:

Akers, R. (1998) *Social Learning and Social Structure: A General Theory of Crime and Deviance*. Northeastern University Press, Boston, MA.

Sutherland, E. (1947) *Principles of Criminology*, 4th edn. J. B. Lippincott, Philadelphia.

RUTH TRIPLETT

crime, white-collar

The term white-collar crime was coined by Edwin H. Sutherland in his 1939 presidential address to the American Sociological Society. Sutherland's focus was on crimes and regulatory offenses in business, politics, and the professions that were committed by persons in the upper classes. To be classified as a white-collar crime the behavior had to be carried out in the course of the offender's occupational pursuits.

A major aim of Sutherland was to overthrow common explanations of crime, such as feeblemindedness and psychiatric disorders, traits that were not characteristic of the majority of upperworld offenders.

A subsequent influential definition of white-collar crime was advanced by a Yale Law School research team that emphasized the legal nature of the offense rather than the social and occupational position of the offender. The Yale focus paved the way for studies of persons who violated specific statutes.

Sutherland maintained that many white-collar offenders escape conviction only because they come from the same social class as judges, have gone to the same elite schools, and live in the same neighborhoods. In addition, prosecutors often are reluctant to pursue an offender charged with the violation of a complex statute and defended by the stars of the legal profession.

The study of white-collar crime has always been something of an outlier in the sociological domain, in part because it tends to be resistant to quantification. Besides, an understanding of the dynamics of white-collar crime often requires knowledge of economics, jurisprudence, and regulatory practice, among other matters. Nor are white-collar offenders, unlike juvenile delinquents, likely to become accessible for fieldwork research.

SEE ALSO: Crime; Crime, Political

SUGGESTED READINGS

Geis, G. (2007). *White-Collar and Corporate Crime*. Prentice Hall, Upper Saddle River, NJ.

Sutherland, E. H. (1983) [1949]. *White Collar Crime*. Yale University Press, New Haven, CT.

GILBERT GEIS

criminal justice system

The Criminal justice system in any nation is a set of legal and social institutions designed to apprehend, prosecute and punish criminals; maintain social order by controlling crime and ensuring public safety. The three main branches of a criminal justice system are: (1) law enforcement; (2) courts; and (3) corrections. Each of these branches is linked to each of the others in the process of ensuring safety and delivering justice to the public. (1) The law enforcement comprises the police system and is primarily responsible for prevention, detection, and investigation of crime. They are the first responders to a crime scene and investigate the details. Based on their investigations or suspicions they arrest individuals and present them to the prosecutor who makes the decision about whether to press charges against the offender. The police officers also help in collecting evidence and testify for prosecution. (2) After the arrest, the courts make decisions about bail, court proceedings, preliminary hearings, arraignments, pre-trial motions, and plea bargains. If an offender remains in the system, the courts continue with the process of delivering justice by determining the guilt of the offender and ascertaining the punishment. In the USA there are various levels of courts starting with the "lower courts" all the way through to the highest federal appellate court which is the "US Supreme Court." (3) The correctional branch of the criminal justice system is responsible for managing the defendants at both the pre-trial stage and post-trial stage where they have been determined guilty and convicted. The correctional system includes the jails and the prisons; it also includes community probation, intermediate sanctions and parole. Jails and prisons are used for incarceration of individuals whereas probation, intermediate sanctions and parole are used when the individual is granted conditional release during or after serving their sentence.

SEE ALSO: Crime; Criminology; Deviance, Crime and

SUGGESTED READING

Schmalleger, F. (2007) *Criminal Justice Today: An Introductory Text for the 21st Century*, 9th edn. Prentice Hall, Upper Saddle River, NJ.

SHEETAL RANJAN

criminology

Edwin Sutherland defined criminology as the study of law making, law breaking and the response to law breaking. The American Society of Criminology calls it the study related to the measurement, etiology, consequences, prevention, control, and treatment of crime and delinquency. It is noteworthy that the term criminology is often used with "Criminal Justice." "Criminology" is concerned with law breaking where the greater emphasis is on the nature, extent and causes of crime. "Criminal Justice" is concerned with the response to law breaking and therefore the emphasis is on policing, courts and corrections. These two areas often overlap as one cannot be studied in isolation from the other. In recent years, criminology as a field of study has developed greatly with numerous universities having separate departments of criminology distinct from sociology, anthropology, political science etc.

The timeline detailing the development of criminological thought starts from Classical Criminology (from the 1700s) to Positivist Criminology (from the1800s) moving to the period of Formative Sociology (from the 1900s) and Sociological developments thereafter. There is some overlap in these timelines and some of these theories continue to gain and recede in popularity during different times.

Classical criminology emerged in response to the cruel and arbitrary social controls during the European Holy Inquisition. The philosophy developed by Cesare Beccaria and Jeremy Bentham related to human nature and how/ why it can be controlled by the state. It was argued that criminal behaviors can be deterred by punishment that was certain, severe and swift. These were the founding principles on which eighteenth-century reforms were based.

The Positivists rejected the idea that "crime can be committed by anyone" and instead suggested that criminals were "atavistic" or less developed individuals and therefore biologically pre disposed to crime due to physical or mental shortcomings. Cesare Lombroso with his theory of "born criminal" is regarded as the founder of this movement. The development of Positivist thought marked the shift from "punishment" to theorizing that the offender does not control his behavior and that scientific method can be applied to the study of criminals.

The period from 1900 to the 1950s can be considered the formative years for the development of sociological perspectives related to criminology. This period is marked by the developments in the Chicago School of the social disorganization perspectives and ecological theories of crime (social structure theories). It is also marked by the concept of Differential Association (social process theories) as proposed by Edwin Sutherland and the Strain theory proposed by Robert Merton.

Coming from the Chicago School, Edwin Sutherland proposed the Differential Association theory suggesting a social learning approach to understand why people commit crime. He proposed that criminal behavior is learned by interaction with others. This learning occurs within intimate personal groups and includes techniques for committing the crime and the motives and rationalizations for committing it as well.

Durkheim first introduced the concept of "Anomie" or (deregulation) in his book *Suicide* published in 1897. Merton developed this concept further in his "Strain" theory. Merton argues that crime occurs when there is a gap between cultural aspirations for economic success and structural impossibilities in achieving these goals. This gap between means and ends results in anomie or "cultural-chaos."

Recent developments in criminological thought are related to the development of the conflict perspectives and other multi-factor theories. The conflict perspective can be traced to Marxist ideology that inequality between social classes results in conditions that make the rich richer and poor poorer. The root cause of crime according to the conflict perspective is the constant struggle for power, control and material wealth. Because those in power make the laws, the laws tend to favor the wealthy and therefore the poor tend to commit crime.

This perspective includes multiple areas of conflict such as racism, sexism, globalism etc that can also be considered to contribute to crime.

Among the multi-factor theories are the life course and latent trait theories. These two theories differ primarily in the discussion related to the onset and persistence of crime. Life course theories reflect the view that criminality is a multi-dynamic process influenced by a variety of characteristics, traits and experiences. They believe that behavior changes for the better or worse are possible at any time in the life course. On the contrary the latent trait theories reflect the view that criminal behavior is controlled by a master trait present in a person at birth or soon after. This trait does not change throughout the life course of a person.

SEE ALSO: Anomie; Crime; Crime, Radical/Marxist Theories of; Crime, Social Learning Theories of; Criminal Justice System; Criminology: Research Methods; Deviance, Criminalization of; Merton, Robert K.; Race and the Criminal Justice System

SUGGESTED READINGS

Beccaria, C. (1963) [1764] *On Crimes and Punishments*, trans. H. Paolucci. Bobbs-Merrill, Indianapolis, IN.

Becker, H. S. (1963) *Outsiders: Studies in the Sociology of Deviance*. Free Press, New York.

Lombroso-Ferrero, G. (1972) [1911] *The Criminal Man*. Patterson Smith, Patterson, NJ.

Merton, R. K. (1938) Socia structure and anomie. *American Sociological Review* 3: 672–82.

Sutherland, E. H., Cressey, D. R., & Luckenbill, D. F. (1992) *Principles of Criminology*, 11th edn. General Hall, Dix Hills, NY.

SHEETAL RANJAN

criminology: research methods

Research methods are procedures for obtaining information on individual or aggregate phenomena in order to: (1) create a general explanation or *theory* to explain a phenomenon; (2) test the applicability of an existing theory; or (3) test the effectiveness of a policy or program. Criminologists examine juvenile delinquency, adult criminality, and victimization. Criminal justice researchers focus primarily on issues related to police, courts, and prisons. The methods employed for these topics are borrowed from the behavioral and social sciences.

Data is information gathered during a study, either qualitative or quantitative in form. Qualitative data involves verbal statements describing particular processes whereas quantitative data involves numerical information. Qualitative research is common for theory development and quantitative research for theory/hypothesis testing.

Ethnography is qualitative research involving detailed descriptions of the phenomena of interest. An example of ethnography is a study of prison inmate social systems and adaptation to incarceration. Observations are made about types of prison inmates and how they interact in order to formulate a theory of why some inmates adapt to incarceration more easily than others.

Quantitative research involves attaching numerical values to information. Some information is numeric by nature (e.g., years of age), whereas other information is assigned numerical values (e.g., a person's sex, where "male" is coded as "0" and "female" as "1"). Numeric data are gathered when a researcher intends to apply statistics in order to produce new information that cannot be obtained verbally.

The research design of a quantitative study is experimental, quasi-experimental, or non-experimental, reflecting differences in the ability to establish the causal order of events. Steps involved in quantitative research often include the following:

1. Begin with a theoretical model, or a general perspective of an individual or social process. For example, a "conflict" perspective argues that many social problems in a capitalist society (discrimination, poverty, environmental pollution, crime) are consequences of economic/power conflicts between groups.
2. Apply the model to a particular problem (e.g., crime).
3. Relevant theoretical concepts are transformed into operational definitions that can be observed (e.g., "economic power" may be measured as earned income). These definitions are placed into a hypothesis, or a statement about the predicted relationship between variables (e.g., persons with lower incomes are more likely to be arrested). The specific nature of any hypothesis means that the more general theory can never be tested directly.
4. Plan the data collection, involving determination of (a) target population to which the results will be generalized, (b) units of analysis (individuals, organizations, cities, etc.), (c) time dimension of the data (1 versus 2 + points in time), (d) research design based on the hypothesis and level of rigor desired (e.g., matched pairs, factorial, pretest-posttest), (e) probability sample representing the target population (drawn with simple random sampling, systematic random sampling, sampling

proportionate to size, etc.), (f) data collection instrument for compiling the information (e.g., survey questionnaire), and (g) procedures for gathering information (telephone, mail, face-to-face, reviewing archived data, etc.).

5 Collect the data by obtaining completed instruments for all sampled cases.
6 Check data for accuracy (typically accomplished with computers).
7 Examine data using statistics to test the hypotheses and describe the empirical relationships. Investigators must apply these statistics correctly in order to derive accurate conclusions.

SEE ALSO: Criminal Justice System; Criminology; Ethnography

SUGGESTED READINGS

Campbell, D. & Stanley, J. (1963) *Experimental and Quasi-Experimental Designs for Research.* Rand McNally, Chicago, IL.

Moser, C. A. & Kalton, G. (1972) *Survey Methods in Social Investigation*, 2nd edn. Basic Books, New York.

JOHN WOOLDREDGE

critical pedagogy

Critical pedagogy challenges both students and teachers to channel their experiences of oppression into educating and empowering marginalized peoples. Critical pedagogues approach education as a process of social, cultural, political, and individual transformation, where social equity can be nourished or social inequity perpetuated. According to critical pedagogues, notions defining rational classification of people into categories that diminish their social affect and importance keep them oppressed. Oppressed peoples thus require not only awareness of inequities they suffer but also an understanding of ways that oppressive social mechanisms and beliefs endure, and of resistance strategies. Reflection on one's own experiences of oppression and the feelings of frustration, shame, guilt, and rage that accompany those experiences help shape practices of critical pedagogy. Critical pedagogues redirect these feelings that can incite violent acts, submission, and/or ongoing repression into dynamic dialogue that defines literacy in terms of participatory citizenship.

Methods of critical pedagogy are as diverse as the people who practice them. However, some common elements and general themes include reworking roles of student and teacher, questioning economic categories of worth and success, and ongoing engagement with the social, cultural, and political interactions that perpetuate disenfranchised and marginalized identities. In a traditional educational environment, students listen to a lecturing teacher, who controls the flow of questions and answers. Part of the traditional student and teacher relationship is that students consume decontextualized knowledge produced by the teacher (and those who dictate what the teacher teaches). This arrangement, according to critical approaches to pedagogy, disenfranchises people by removing their control over experiential reflection, and neglecting to address emotionally charged daily experiences through which cultural symbols gain greater meaning.

Critical pedagogy incites critique of social values based on economic measures of worth and identity. When economic value defines products and peoples who can or cannot afford them, participation in community governance pits those who have against those who have not, and freedoms may only be afforded by people with enough money to buy them. Critical pedagogues teach people how to effectively participate in community governance (voting, legislating, finding alternative resources), thereby empowering people who are in no position to challenge oppressive economic systems and values based on economic leverage.

SEE ALSO: Feminist Pedagogy; Pedagogy

SUGGESTED READING

McLaren, P. (2002) *Life in Schools: An Introduction to Critical Pedagogy in the Foundations of Education.* Allyn and Bacon Publishers, Boston, MA.

RACHEL A. DOWTY

critical race theory

Critical race theory refers to a historical and contemporary body of scholarship that aims to interrogate the discourses, ideologies, and social structures that produce and maintain conditions of racial injustice. Critical race theory analyzes how race and racism are foundational elements in historical and contemporary social structures and social experiences. In defining critical race theory, it is important to first make a distinction between the historical tradition of theorizing about race and racism in western societies and a specific body of American legal scholarship that emerged in the 1970s and 1980s in response to the successes and failures of the US Civil Rights Movement struggles for the freedom and liberation of people of color of the 1950s and 1960s. Strongly influenced by prior freedom movements against colonialism, segregation, and racial violence, contemporary critical race theorists practice an "intellectual activism" that aims not only to theorize, but also to resist these conditions of racial oppression. Using this broader framework, critical race theory can be viewed as a diagnostic body of "intellectual activism" scholarship that seeks to identify the pressure points for anti-racist struggle. Given the breadth and scope of critical race theories, this essay will highlight several core themes that tie together this eclectic body of social and political thought.

The first core theme deals with how critical race theories frame its two focal objects of study: race and racism. Critical race theory understands the concept of race as a social construction that is produced as a result of the cultural and political meanings ascribed to it through social interactions and relationships across multiple levels of social organization. Since the 1600s, race has been a constitutive feature of global social, political, economic, and cultural organization. Critical race theories have demonstrated how race concepts and their accompanying racisms were foundational to the administration of colonial social systems, the rise and expansion of global capitalism, and the emergence of the human biological sciences and medicine of the eighteenth, nineteenth, and twentieth centuries. Historically speaking, however, there are not, and have never been, monolithic conceptions of race and/or racism. Critical race theorists have rejected the notion that racism is synonymous with maligned individual prejudice and have embraced a more structural and institutional understanding of racism. In highlighting the institutional basis of racism, critical race theorists challenge the idea that people of color are solely responsible for their own oppression. Drawing on these formulations, contemporary critical race theories understand racism as a vast and complicated system of institutionalized practices that structure the allocation of social, economic, and political power in unjust and racially coded ways.

A second core theme is that critical race theory has traditionally used and continues to represent an interdisciplinary and theoretically eclectic approach to the study of race and racism. The interdisciplinary and, indeed, extra-disciplinary nature of critical race theory enables the analysis of a wide range of social, economic, and political phenomena that shape race and racism as social structures. Critical race theory draws upon an interdisciplinary body of scholarship that has intellectual roots and practitioners in sociology, critical legal studies, political theory and philosophy, neo-Marxist British cultural studies, African American literary criticism, history, and pragmatist philosophy.

Some critical race theorists, particularly black feminist theorists, have embraced an intersectional theoretical approach to analyzing the ways in which systems of gender, sexuality, and nationalism are implicated in the production and maintenance of racism. Drawing on psychoanalytic and literary theories, critical race theorists have analyzed the relationships between forms of cultural racism and colonial domination. Critical race theorists have also documented and critiqued the role of nation states in the formation of racial categories in the enactment of different forms of political oppressions. Critical racial theories have long recognized and opposed the centrality of western science to the construction of racial meanings and racist practices. Critical race theorists have exposed and criticized the ways that the myths of American democracy, meritocracy, and progress and the ideology of individualism function to justify changing forms of racial domination.

Finally, many critical race theories often go beyond diagnosis and critique to offer arguments and proposals for specific social policies that, if implemented, might work to undo the systemic disadvantages that impair the life chances and conditions of people of color in the USA. These theories continue to challenge entrenched racial inequalities in health, education, criminal injustice, political representation, and economic opportunity and seek to foster a more just and equal society.

SEE ALSO: Black Feminist Thought; Intersectionality; Race

SUGGESTED READINGS

Collins, P. H. (2005) *Black Sexual Politics: African Americans, Gender, and the New Racism*. Routledge, New York.

Winant, H. (2001). *The World Is a Ghetto: Race and Democracy Since World War II*. Basic Books, New York.

ANTHONY RYAN HATCH

critical theory/Frankfurt School

Critical theory and the Frankfurt School are virtually interchangeable identifiers that give apparent unity to the complex social and political concerns, epistemological questions, and critical analyses produced by the variety of thinkers affiliated with the *Institut für Sozialforschung* (Institute for Social Research). The *Institut*'s key figures included Theodor Adorno, Erich Fromm, Max Horkheimer, Leo Lowenthal, Herbert Marcuse, and Frederick Pollock. Others, such as Henryk Grossmann, Otto

Kircheimer, Franz Neuman, and Karl Wittfogel had longstanding membership while individuals like Walter Benjamin, Bertolt Brecht, Hanns Eisler, and Karl Korsch were also affiliated with *Institut* projects and publications.

Founded in Frankfurt, Germany in 1923, the *Institut* emerged from organized discussions involving young intellectuals (many of Jewish descent), associated with the German Communist Party, eager to explore Marxist theory and practice while resisting Marxism's "Bolshevization." Although never a unified theory or school, key themes provided some cohesion: feelings of marginalization (as Jews in Germany, communists, intellectuals aligning with the working class, radical democrats in the Weimar Republic, for example) stimulated interest in issues of authoritarianism, propaganda, mass culture, domination, alienation, "authenticity," genuine creativity (avant-garde art and music), and human fulfillment. Drawing from a neo-Hegelian conception of totality and Freudian psychology, critical theorists proposed a determinate, comprehensive reason (*Vernunft*) to critique the domination of instrumental rationality in the modern world.

During its initial period, inspired by Korch's radical conception of socialization and Georg Lukács's focus on culture and class consciousness, *Institut* members wanted to develop a self-confident, active proletariat, engaged with intellectuals, which would transcend philosophy by actualizing it. Under Carl Grünberg's leadership, the *Institut* pursed projects that revitalized Grünberg's *Archiv für die Geschichte des Sozialismus und der Arbeiterbewegung* (Archive for the History of Socialism and the Workers' Movement). Grünberg's affiliation to Frankfurt University allowed, for the first time, students in Germany to formally study Marx's work and pursue his critique of political economy while completing university degrees. The *Institut* was also a silent but vital collaborator in the first Marx–Engels Institute-led, publication of the *Marx–Engels Gesamtausgabe* – making Marx's critically important, early philosophical works available to socialist theorists and reinforcing key themes in Marcuse's and Fromm's work.

In 1930, under Horkheimer, the "managerial scholar," the *Institut* began to shift from labor history and political economy to broader questions of social theory, epistemology and philosophy, replacing Grünberg's *Archiv* with the *Zeitschrift für Sozialforschung* (*Journal for Social Research*) as its major intellectual outlet. Horkheimer's inaugural lecture emphasized the need to grasp the connections among the economic conditions of life, individual psychic development and changes in the cultural sphere. He sought a multidisciplinary program involving philosophy, sociology, economics, history and psychology to critically interrogate the domination of instrumental reason in the modern world. Marcuse and Adorno's memberships in 1932 and 1938 strengthened and focused Horkheimer's growing anti-positivist, neo-Hegelian intellectual agenda.

When Hitler took power in 1933, the *Institut* relocated to the USA. Horkheimer's 1937 essay "Traditional and critical theory" confirmed the *Institut*'s ongoing agenda, introducing the term that camouflaged its Marxism, making the *Institut* more acceptable to American social scientists. But the term "critical theory" increasingly identified the *Institut*'s emerging, specific (and no longer Marxist) philosophy of "determinate negation." Adorno and Horkheimer sketched out aspects in *Dialektik der Aufklärung: Philosophische Fragmente* (*Dialectic of Enlightenment/the Enlightenment: Philosophical Fragments*) in 1944, continuing the critique of positivism and instrumental reason and reinforcing the need for a totalizing, determinate and comprehensive reason. The monograph also included a trenchant indictment of "the administered society" and America's "cultural industries," drawing parallels to fascist Germany. Adorno's *Negative Dialectics* (1966) and his *Aesthetic Theory* (1970) were the closest the Frankfurt School came to a systematic presentation of its philosophy.

By 1950, the *Institut* was re-established in Frankfurt where it was warmly received as a citadel of critical thought, inspiring university students across Europe to critically engage with the past and present. Remaining in America, Marcuse's *Eros and Civilization* (1955) and *One Dimensional Man* (1964) popularized key aspects of critical theory, providing an intellectual focal point for the student movement. Scholars like Jürgen Habermas, Alfred Schmidt, Albrecht Wellmer, Thomas McCarthy, Douglas Kellner, Steve Best, and Axel Honneth are among current critical theorists who continue to revise and develop the Frankfurt School's critique of modernity and instrumental reason.

SEE ALSO: Alienation; Consumption; Cultural Critique; Freud, Sigmund; Marcuse, Herbert; Marx, Karl

SUGGESTED READINGS

Jay, M. (1973) *The Dialectical Imagination*. Little, Brown, Boston, MA.

Kellner, D. (1989) *Critical Theory, Marxism, and Modernity*. Johns Hopkins University Press, Baltimore, MD.

Wiggerhaus, R. (1995) *The Frankfurt School*, trans. M. Robertson. MIT Press, Cambridge, MA.

ROB BEAMISH

crowd behavior

Crowd behavior is a misleading concept suggesting unanimous and continuous action by actors with similar motives. Three decades of observations of hundreds of demonstrations, celebrations and sporting events have debunked those stereotypes. Late-twentieth-century students of collective phenomena discarded "the crowd" as a useful descriptive or explanatory concept. They embraced "the gathering" as a concept that refers only to two or more persons in a common location in space and time without reference to the solitary or collective actions in which they might engage. The majority of gatherings are temporary; they have a life course beginning with an assembling process that brings persons from initially disparate locations to a subsequent common location; they end with a dispersing process that vacates that location. The most characteristic feature of temporary gatherings is the alternating and varied individual and collective actions that compose them.

ASSEMBLING

Studies of assembling processes consistently indicate factors responsible for who assembles and who does not. Various designations and prescriptions constitute assembling instructions and ordinarily emanate from some family member, friend, colleague, or acquaintance in the same social networks as the recipients. Research shows that whether recipients assemble or not is primarily a function of their availability at the time in question and their access to the alternate location. Research also shows that most individuals don't assemble alone; instead, most people assemble for most gatherings with one or more companions, with whom they remain until they disperse together.

ACTIONS IN GATHERINGS

Individuals engage in many solitary actions but also in a variety of collective actions with or in relation to their companions or other individuals and small groups. Collective actions develop in at least three ways. The most common are interdependently generated collective actions exemplified by the conversations that occur among companions or with strangers in close proximity. Third-party generated collective actions are common in political or religious gatherings when a speaker solicits singing, chanting, praying, or other actions and at least some (but seldom all) gathering members comply. Independently generated collective actions are illustrated by gathering members engaging in unsolicited clapping and cheering immediately following some speaker's or performer's audible or visible actions.

DISPERSING

Most temporary gatherings routinely disperse without incident or injury because individuals and their companions exit in staggered and orderly fashion. Explosions, fires, or floods requiring immediate and often simultaneous dispersal of gatherings illustrate emergency dispersals. Individuals may fear the risk of injury or fatality to themselves or their companions but incapacitating fear (panic) is rare. Research shows that reason trumps fear and altruism trumps selfishness. Individuals are far more likely to attend to and extricate their companions than to abandon them. Coerced dispersals occur when state agents of social control judge that gatherings threaten routine social order or the political status quo.

SEE ALSO: Collective Action; Group Processes

SUGGESTED READINGS

McPhail, C. (2006) The crowd and collective action: bringing symbolic interaction back in. *Symbolic Interaction* 29: 433–64.

Schweingruber, D. S. and McPhail, C. (1999) A method for systematically observing and recording collective action. *Sociological Methods and Research* 27: 451–98.

CLARK MCPHAIL

cultural capital

Cultural capital is a concept that was first developed by French sociologist Pierre Bourdieu and has become an important component in analyses of culture, social class, and inequality. Cultural capital is one of many forms of capital – economic, social, symbolic – that individuals draw from to achieve upward mobility, gain distinction, and enhance their lives. Being "rich" or "high" in cultural capital means to possess knowledge and understanding of certain cultural products and practices. In this sense, "accumulating," i.e. knowing and learning about, such cultural things as language, food, music, art, literature, and clothing is similar to accumulating economic capital (money, property) in that individuals can use them to achieve higher status within a given field.

Cultural capital exists in three forms. The first is the "embodied state." The accumulation of cultural capital begins at birth in the space of the family. Individuals essentially "inherit" certain practices such as habits, manners, speech patterns, and lifestyle from their families. They "embody" these cultural practices that remain with them for long periods of time.

The second form in which cultural capital exists is the "objectified state." This includes material objects – e.g. paintings, writings, buildings – that have economic (material) as well as symbolic (nonmaterial) value. For example, a bottle of wine has material value (price) and an individual need only possess a degree of economic capital (money) to obtain it. But wine also has certain symbolic properties that give it high nonmaterial value (vintage, region, grape varietal, actual taste, etc.). In order to fully use this object for personal advantage or gain (i.e. to enhance one's social status vis-à-vis communities of wine aficionados), one must not only possess the means to obtain its material contents (economic capital), but also possess the means to understand its symbolic contents (cultural capital). In other words, material objects have embodied cultural capital that grants them status beyond their material worth.

The third form is the "institutionalized state." After the family, cultural capital is distributed in many ways and in a great number of spaces, or formal institutions. The most common social structure in which cultural capital is embedded is education. The transmission of cultural capital through the university (the degree) legitimates its bearer, as opposed to the self-learned person, whose cultural capital can always be questioned. The university becomes a universally recognized guarantor of an individual's cultural capital.

As these different states imply, cultural capital is very much related to other forms of capital. In general, possessing high economic capital correlates strongly with possessing high cultural capital, but this is not always the case. For example, academics are generally high in cultural capital but relatively low in economic capital, whereas professional athletes are generally high in economic capital and low in cultural capital (Thornton 1996). Most importantly, it is the relationships between the forms of capital that leads to the "reproduction" of the social world. Universities, for example, can be prohibitive to certain social groups in terms of the amount of capital that they require for admission: economic (tuition), cultural (language skills, study habits), and social (networks, communities). High levels of each form of capital enhance one's ability to attend elite schools, which leads to the further accumulation and legitimization of cultural capital. And one can transfer such knowledge towards the accumulation of economic capital.

Cultural capital adds an important dimension to our understanding of social class and inequality. It demonstrates how people can possess power and achieve high status and be denied access to power and status in significant ways other than material wealth. Cultural capital also provides an insightful bridge for the gap between the fundamental sociological concepts of structure and agency. While individuals behave as agents with embodied cultural practices, they only accumulate such knowledge through action within social structures (e.g. the family, education).

SEE ALSO: Bourdieu, Pierre; Social Capital; Structure and Agency; Habitus/Field

REFERENCE

Thornton, S. (1996) *Club Cultures: Music, Media, and Subcultural Capital.* Wesleyan Press, London.

SUGGESTED READINGS

Bourdieu, P. (1984) *Distinction: A Social Critique of the Judgment of Taste.* Harvard University Press, Cambridge, MA.

Bourdieu, P. (1986) The forms of capital. In Richardson, J. (ed.), *Handbook of Theory and Research for the Sociology of Education.* Greenwood, New York, pp. 241–58.

RICHARD E. OCEJO

cultural citizenship

The idea of cultural citizenship has emerged through three main phases of debate. Firstly there was an attempt to extend the categories of citizenship to include questions of culture. Here there was a retracing of the debates on citizenship that was largely concerned with questions of rights and duties in the context of national societies to include issues related to culture. This work owed a great deal to attempts to link sociology and cultural studies found in the work of Raymond Williams, Stuart Hall, and others. According to Bryan Turner (2001) this debate was explicitly concerned with the participation of citizens within an explicitly national culture.

During phase one of the cultural citizenship debate issues related to the commodification of culture, access to the relevant cultural capital and the decline in cultural authority of the traditional arts dominated. Cultural citizenship was crucially a normative category that aimed to develop the conditions for a popular participatory democracy and a culturally inclusive society. However, the contours of this debate began to change through a greater recognition of the cultural pluralization of western democracies that had accompanied increasingly global societies. That cultures were no longer rooted to the spot in an age of virtuality, mass tourism, hybridity, migration and immigration, and other cultural mobilities became increasingly apparent. Notably Pakulski (1997) argued that from children to the disabled and from ethnic communities to diverse sexualities there were new demands being made for representation without normalizing distortion. If the previous set of debates was concerned with questions of participation and the distribution of cultural resources the second phase of the debate was more explicitly focused on issues related to cultural recognition. Finally, there are now signs that the debate on cultizenship could be entering into a third phase beyond questions related to identity to include the recent neoliberal assault on cultural practices more generally.

SEE ALSO: Citizenship; Cultural Studies; Multiculturalism

REFERENCES

Pakulski, J. (1997) Cultural citizenship. *Citizenship Studies* 1 (1): 73–86.

Turner, B. S. (2001) Outline of a general theory of cultural citizenship. In: Stevenson, N. (ed.), *Culture and Citizenship*. Sage, London, pp. 11–32.

SUGGESTED READINGS

Miller, T. (2007) *Cultural Citizenship*. Temple University Press, Philadelphia.

Stevenson, N. (2003) *Cultural Citizenship: Cosmopolitan Questions*, Open University Press, Milton Keynes.

NICK STEVENSON

cultural critique

Cultural critique is a broad field of study that employs many different theoretical traditions to analyze and critique cultural formations. Because culture is always historically and contextually determined, each era has had to develop its own methods of cultural analysis in order to respond to new technological innovations, new modes of social organization, new economic formations, and novel forms of oppression, exploitation, and subjugation.

The modern European tradition of cultural critique can be traced back to Immanuel Kant's (1724–1804) seminal essay entitled "What is Enlightenment?" Here, Kant opposed theocratic and authoritarian forms of culture with a liberal, progressive, and humanist culture of science, reason, and critique. By organizing society under the guiding principles of critical reason, Kant believed that pre-Enlightenment superstition and ignorance would be replaced by both individual liberty and universal peace.

Friedrich Nietzsche (1844–1900) historicized Kant's version of critique through a technique called genealogy. Nietzsche argued that Kant's necessary universals are born from historical struggles between competing interests. Nietzsche rested his faith not in universal categories of reason but rather in the aristocratic will to power to combat the "herd mentality" of German mass culture.

Like Nietzsche, Karl Marx (1818–83) also rejected universal and necessary truths outside of history. Using historical materialism as his major critical tool, Marx argued that the dominant culture legitimated current exploitative economic relations. In short, the class that controls the economic base also controls the production of cultural and political ideas. Whereas Nietzsche traced central forms of mass culture back to the hidden source of power animating them, Marx traced cultural manifestations back to their economic determinates. Here culture is derived from antagonistic social relations conditioned by capitalism, which distorts both the content and the form of ideas. Thus for Marx, cultural critique is essentially ideological critique exposing the interests of the ruling class within its seemingly natural and universal norms.

With the Frankfurt School of social theory, cultural critique attempted to synthesize the most politically progressive and theoretically innovative strands of the former cultural theories. Max Horkheimer (1895–1971), Theodor Adorno (1903–69), and Herbert Marcuse (1898–1979) are three of the central members of the Frankfurt School who utilized a transdisciplinary method that incorporated elements of critical reason, genealogy, historical materialism, sociology, and psychoanalysis to analyze culture. While heavily rooted in Marxism, the members of the Frankfurt School increasingly distanced themselves from Marx's conception of the centrality of economic relations, focusing instead on cultural and political methods of social control produced through new media technologies and a burgeoning culture industry.

While the Frankfurt School articulated cultural conditions in a stage of monopoly capitalism and fascist tendencies, British cultural studies emerged in the 1960s when, first, there was widespread global resistance to consumer capitalism and an upsurge of revolutionary movements. British cultural studies originally was developed by Richard Hoggart, Raymond Williams, and E. P. Thompson to preserve working-class culture against colonization by the culture industry. Both British cultural studies and the Frankfurt School recognized the central role of new consumer and media culture in the erosion of working-class resistance to capitalist hegemony. British cultural studies turned toward the oppositional potentials within youth subcultures.

Currently, cultural critique is attempting to respond to a new era of global capitalism, hybridized cultural forms, and increasing control of information by a handful of media conglomerates. As a response to these economic, social, and political trends, cultural critique has expanded its theoretical repertoire to include multicultural, postcolonial, and feminist critiques of culture. Thus, cultural criticism is reevaluating its own internal complicity with racism, sexism, colonialism, and homophobia and in the process gaining a new level of self-reflexivity that enables it to become an increasingly powerful tool for social emancipation.

SEE ALSO: Counterculture; Cultural Studies; Cultural Studies, British; Culture Industries; Mass Culture and Mass Society

SUGGESTED READINGS

Durham, M. G. & Kellner, D. (2001) *Media and Cultural Studies*. Blackwell, Malden, MA.

Kellner, D. (1989) *Critical Theory, Marxism, and Modernity*. Johns Hopkins University Press, Baltimore, MD.

DOUGLAS KELLNER AND TYSON E. LEWIS

cultural feminism

Foundationally, cultural feminism is a social movement that reclaims and redefines female identity and it seeks to understand women's social locations by concentrating on men's and women's gender differences. It is believed that women can be liberated from their subordination in society through individual change, the redefinition of femininity and masculinity and the creation of "women-centered" culture. Embedded within these efforts is a belief in essentialist gender differences.

Cultural feminists state that women are inherently nurturing, kind, gentle, non-violent and egalitarian. *First wave* feminists stressed the superiority of women's values, believing these would conquer masculine traits of selfishness, lack of self-control and violence. They worked for creating social change via the suffrage movement, women's right to free expression, a celebration and recognition of women's culture and by helping poor and working-class women. *Second wave* cultural feminists emerged out of the radical feminist movement in the early 1970s. They also sought to create change via highlighting women's uniqueness and feminine qualities, creating women-only spaces free from male dominance. Women are viewed as a "sisterhood," each sharing commonalities based on gender.

Women's subordination is attributed to men's nature; men are viewed as the "enemy" due to their biological maleness. Cultural feminists see women's qualities as powerful assets for women and argue women are treated secondary to men because western thought and society does not value women's virtues. Cultural feminism challenges male values of hierarchy, domination and independence and work to change society through emphasizing women's natural ability to solve conflict through cooperation, nonviolence and pacifism.

This form of feminism created a surge in scholarship, art, and literature focusing on issues specifically related to and about women. Some of the women-centered spaces and events include the establishment of domestic violence shelters, rape crisis centers, women's centers, music festivals, businesses and organizations and helped support the emergence of women and gender studies classes and programs in higher education. In sociology, for example, it provides a foundation for feminist methods, feminist sociology and the sociology of sex and gender.

As gender became a central form of analysis, "new" forms of scholarship emerged particularly within the areas of psychology, literature and rhetoric; embedded within this scholarship is the inherent belief that women have certain innate qualities that should be recognized and honored by society rather than remaining invisible or denigrated. Within this new scholarship was the development of feminist epistemology and standpoint theory; both recognize women's unique perspectives based on their experiences as women. *Standpoint theory* posits that women's understanding of the world is different from men's, even if it is shaped by men's definitions. This difference is based on women's experiences and knowledge or "ways of knowing," both formal and informal.

Cultural feminism is one of the most successful and influential branches of feminism, but it does not exist without criticism. One of the most common critiques is that of its reliance on applying biological definitions of "woman"; partially because this reifies the societal beliefs it seeks to redefine. By not challenging patriarchal systems that create and perpetuate the ideology that women are inferior to men, cultural feminism fails to address larger systemic issues and relies on meeting needs within the established social structures rather than challenging these structures. Additionally, by grouping all women as similar, the complexities of race, class, ethnicity and sexuality remain placed in subordinate positions or are completely ignored, thus confining the analysis.

SEE ALSO: Feminist Standpoint Theory; Lesbian Feminism; Radical Feminism

SUGGESTED READINGS

Alcoff, L. (1988) Cultural feminism versus post-structuralism: the identity crisis in feminist theory. *Signs: A Journal of Women in Culture and Society* 13: 405–36.

Donovan, J. (1985) *Feminist Theory: The Intellectual Traditions of American Feminism*. F. Ungar Publishing, New York.

KRISTINA B. WOLFF

cultural imperialism

Cultural imperialism is the process and practice of promoting one culture over another and often occurs through programs designed to assist other nations, particularly developing nations. Historically this occurred during *colonization* where one nation overpowers another weaker country for economic or political gain. Culture can be imposed in a wide variety of ways such as through restructuring education, religious, and political institutions.

Cultural imperialism is different from *cultural diffusion* primarily due to the mechanisms involved in changing culture and the roles power plays in the process. *Cultural diffusion* occurs "naturally" when people and groups from other cultures interact with each other. It does not result in the purposeful reduction or elimination of various cultural aspects.

Contemporary practices that result in cultural imperialism often take the form of development or assistance programs for struggling nations or communities. For example it is not uncommon for organizations such as the World Bank or United Nations to place conditions on loans or grants they provide to nations. Often monies are designated for specific projects that benefit outside corporations or countries such as building roads rather than creating schools or clinics. Aid that is designed for health care and education, often accompanies the requirement to teach English or practice western medicine which can negatively impact the existing culture.

One way people rectify the tension between needing support from outside agencies and maintaining their traditional cultural practices is through language or music. Historically, some colonial powers have outlawed traditional dress, language or religions as a means to maintain power. Often this results in the loss of culture as well as forcing groups into exile. As with the Native North Americans who were forced to change their language, customs, and dress, other nations such as China, Germany, and the Soviet Union have forced populations to abandon their traditional cultural practices.

For many, contemporary globalization, or *globalism*, is the new vehicle by which cultural imperialism can occur. People supporting the expansion of "free markets" contend that cultures are naturally fluid and therefore cultural imperialism is a "natural" result of trade. If western practices and ideas are adopted then it is believed that the cultural practices associated with them are better. Research focusing on the economic aspects argues that the spread of US corporations, such as the establishment of McDonald's, Starbucks, and Wal-Mart around the world, represent positive change that brings jobs and inexpensive goods.

Challenges to this belief include a questioning of what is being transferred or imposed upon other nations, who or what benefits from cultural shifts and what cultural aspects become lost. The rapid expansion of globalization reflects a specific type of American popular culture that is manipulated and controlled by corporations. These businesses tend to push out locally owned establishments which also results in a loss and shift of culture. Other areas of resistance include fighting for access to land and water, protection of local farming practices, and other cultural traditions.

SEE ALSO: Colonialism (Neocolonialism); Culture Studies; Globalization; Imperialism

SUGGESTED READINGS

Alexander, M. J. & Mohanty, C. (1997) *Feminist Genealogies, Colonial Legacies, Democratic Futures*. Routledge, New York.

Ritzer, G. & Ryan, M. (2002) The globalization of nothing. *Social Thought and Research* 25 (1–2): 51.

Rothkopf, D. (1997) In praise of cultural imperialism? *Foreign Policy* 107: 38.

KRISTINA B. WOLFF

cultural lag

The thesis of "cultural lag" formulated by the North American sociologist William F. Ogburn can be considered among the earliest sociological attempts to explain social change from social-cultural premises and not psycho-biological ones. Indeed, social change is one of the most important theoretical problems in sociology. Almost all the sociologists that belonged to so-called classical sociology sought to understand the process of social change.

The thesis of cultural lag is well-known among scholars of technology because Ogburn has been considered a technological determinist for his explanation of social change with respect to material culture (or technology). Ogburn developed the theory of cultural lag mainly in *Social Change with Respect to Cultural and Original Nature*, published in 1922 (cf. Ogburn 1966). Throughout the book, Ogburn builds the explanatory key to social change, not appealing to the traditional explanation in terms of evolution of inherited mental ability or, as he also calls it, "original nature". Previously, sociologists emphasized biological factors as variables of social change. However, with the elimination of the biological factor, Ogburn appeals to purely cultural factors to explain social change, and here is where he introduces his theory of cultural lag formulated in the following way:

> A cultural lag occurs when one of two parts of culture which are correlated changes before or in greater degree than the other part does, thereby causing less adjustment between the two parts that existed previously. (1966: 96)

According to Ogburn, material culture is the field that changes first and the rest of socio-cultural environments – organizational, axiological, juridical, ideological, etc. – have to adapt to it in order to avoid the temporary maladjustment or the lack of harmony between technology and cultural ambience. However, he recognizes that material culture does not always change as it has before, although in modern societies this is, in fact, the main form of social change – usually the social dimension adjusts to changes in the technological dimension. This means that the several parts of a given culture react with regard to changes at different rates and in different ways. According to Ogburn, this process of adaptation or adjustment of the cultural non-material fields to technology can take a great deal of time, and through that transition what he calls cultural lag takes place; that is to say, a "cultural delay" or "maladjustment" between the new technology and the diverse aspects of the social field. In other words, culture tends to lag behind the advances of technology. Thus, for Ogburn, the explanation of social change in modern societies consists fundamentally in four factors related to the material culture: inventions, accumulation of inventions, their diffusion and the adaptation to them.

This approach implies a "middle" technological determinism (neither "hard nor "soft"), because Ogburn puts the emphasis on a temporary maladjustment. That is to say, technology does not cause a mechanical and instantaneous change, but rather the theory of cultural lag only shows that the technical invention *chronologically comes before* the subsequent changes in the social field. These social changes then have to adjust to the technological invention. In this sense, there is a "middle" technological determinism because the adjustment has its own rhythm marked by society and not by the technological innovation.

SEE ALSO: Material Culture; Technology, Science, and Culture

REFERENCE

Ogburn, W. F. (1966) *Social Change with Respect to Cultural and Original Nature.* Dell Publishing, New York.

SUGGESTED READING

Romero Moñivas, J. (2007) La Tesis del Cultural lag. In: Reyes, R. (ed.), *Diccionario crítico de ciencias sociales.* Plaza & Valdés, Editorial Complutense, Madrid.

JESÚS ROMERO MOÑIVAS

cultural relativism

The concept of cultural relativism refers to the idea that one needs to understand all cultures within the context of their own terms (i.e., values, norms, standards, customs, knowledges, lifeways, worldviews, etc.) rather than judge them from the perspective of one's own culture. This ideal of cross-cultural understanding requires an epistemological "suspension" of one's own cultural biases in order to comprehend an unfamiliar cultural world.

At the turn of the twentieth century, Franz Boas applied the concept of cultural relativism to the theories and methods of anthropology, shifting cross-cultural research from the "armchair" to "the field," and encouraging his students to engage with the people they studied through the cultural immersion and participant-observation that now characterizes ethnographic fieldwork. Along with the concept of "historical particularism" (the idea that each culture has its own particular history and dialectics), the principles espoused by Boas and his students (such as Ruth Benedict and Margaret Mead) questioned the conventional view that placed cultures in an evolutionary hierarchy ranging from "primitive" to "civilized." Rather than view certain cultures as "backward," "stuck in the past," "strange," "barbaric," "savage," or "living history," Boas-inspired anthropologists argue that the study of cultural diversity, through the lens of cultural relativism, provides an antidote to ethnocentrism (the biased tendency to consider one's own culture as the universal standard from which to judge all other cultures) and reveals the complexity of human existence in all its variations and manifestations, giving insight into one's own particular culture as an invention of human intention and social construction. In other words, making the strange familiar contributes to making the familiar strange, thus highlighting the extent to which cultural understandings shape human universes and vice versa.

A common misperception is that cultural relativism entails "moral relativism" (the nihilistic proposition that there is no such thing as "right" or "wrong" in absolute terms, and that any attempt to judge another's actions is a form of ethical imperialism – an imposition of one's own moral standards upon others who may not share those same standards). Social scientists that embrace cultural relativism in their theories and methods attempt to "suspend" moral judgment in order to make sense of diverse socio-cultural practices; however, taking a cultural relativist stance does not necessarily translate into adopting a moral relativist one. In fact, postmodern critics have questioned the perception of "culture" as a static, bounded, and homogeneous entity, and have fostered more complex understandings of "culture" as dynamic and fluid webs of both shared and contested meanings. Within each "culture" exists a range of ethical positions to which many social scientists have aligned themselves as culturally sensitive allies in the various political, social, and economic struggles of the people they study – an engagement propelled by, not in spite of, the tenets of cultural relativism.

SEE ALSO: Cultural Imperialism; Culture; Ethnocentrism; Multiculturalism; Sociocultural Relativism

SUGGESTED READINGS

Boas, F. (1963) [1938] *The Mind of Primitive Man*, rev. edn. with a new foreword by M. J. Herskovits. Free Press, New York.

Geertz, C. (1973) *The Interpretation of Cultures*. Basic Books, New York.

DIANA SANTILLÁN

cultural studies

Cultural studies is an interdisciplinary field that explores the linkages between society, politics, identity (or the person), and the full range of what is called "culture," from high culture and the popular arts or mass entertainment, to beliefs, discourses, and communicative practices. Cultural studies has drawn on different national traditions of inquiry into these connections – from the Frankfurt School's studies of the mass culture industry, and of the psychological processes that undercut democracy in liberal and affluent societies, to French structuralist and poststructuralist critiques of ideology, constraining categorical frames, and a monadic and unified concept of the self. The branch of cultural studies that early drew the most attention from sociologists was that articulated by the Birmingham Centre for Contemporary Cultural Studies, perhaps in part because Birmingham scholars were inspired by some aspects of American sociology, especially the Chicago School tradition, which gave their work a recognizably social dimension.

Taking Birmingham as an example is instructive in pointing out some characteristics of cultural studies as a field. Conventionalized intellectual genealogies often begin with the work of Raymond Williams, Richard Hoggart, and E. P. Thompson. All three challenged dominant traditions in the humanities in post war England. Hoggart and Williams argued first that literary or "high" culture is just one expression of culture, in the more anthropological sense – the broad range of meanings and interactions that make up social life. Second, they argued that cultural expressions could only be understood in a broader social context of "institutions, power relations, and history" (Seidman 1997).

Concerned about the new ways social domination operated in a post war world that was, at least for many in Europe, both relatively affluent and at peace, a new generation of scholars investigated the culture/society connection as a promising location for understanding this process. Post war shifts in the social organization of cultural and communications media also gave popular forms of culture immense social power. This was particularly true of cultural forms and technologies developing in and exported from the USA, which was becoming a global force because of television, Coca-Cola, and rock and roll – and later, MTV, the shopping mall, music videos, and theme parks – as well as more traditional forms of economic and military power. This shift also required new ways of thinking that linked culture, as it was linked in people's lives, more closely to society and politics, especially in relation to critical questions about democracy and equality.

But more recently, gentrification, global hip-hop culture, planned communities, and theme parks have begun to provide other material for thinking through the connections between "community" and identity.

Yet, similar opportunities for cultural studies scholarship appear as new disciplinary formations emerge in response to social change. Social studies of science, for instance, have grown up in tandem with the enormous growth of "big science" in the recent past, and their critical take on science comes as much from public questions about an endeavor that has brought us nuclear weapons and environmental devastation alongside space flight and the Salk vaccine, as from purely academic developments. Other new areas of investigation that are attracting cultural studies scholars include visual studies, cybercultures, and communities (this has also spawned Internet-based research methodologies), new technologies of embodiment and possibilities for identity construction, and globalization, which has affected the whole range of what are sometimes called the human sciences.

While this scholarship has spurred some significant departmental or program-level institutionalization in American universities, it is most obviously present as a major paradigm in existing interdisciplinary programs, such as American studies, ethnic and women's studies, urban studies, and science and technology studies, and is an important intellectual force in publishers' offerings and conferences both in the Anglophone world and beyond. It is also what one scholar calls an "accent" in more entrenched academic fields, perhaps more welcome in traditionally interpretive disciplines or traditions of inquiry than in those underwritten by positivist epistemology. For this reason, much of sociology has seen cultural studies as a threat rather than an opportunity, yet one can clearly see openings toward cultural studies in cultural sociology, sociology of religion, gender/sexuality, and race/ethnicity, urban sociology, qualitative sociology, and some branches of social theory.

SEE ALSO: Critical Theory/Frankfurt School; Cultural Studies, British; Culture; Gramsci, Antonio; Popular Culture

REFERENCE

Seidman, S. (1997) Relativizing sociology: the challenge of cultural studies. In: Long, E. (ed.), *From Sociology to Cultural Studies: New Perspectives*. Blackwell, Oxford, pp. 37–61.

SUGGESTED READINGS

Hall, S. (1980) Cultural studies: two paradigms. *Media, Culture and Society* 2: 57–72.

Williams, R. (1958) *Culture and Society 1780–1950*. Penguin, London.

ELIZABETH LONG

cultural studies, British

British cultural studies argues that culture is where we live our relations to the material world; it is the shared meanings we make and encounter in our everyday lives. In this way, then, cultures are made from the production, circulation, and consumption of meanings. For example, if I pass a business card to someone in China, the polite way to do it is with two hands. If I pass it with one hand I may cause offense. This is clearly a matter of culture. However, the "culture" is not so much in the gesture, it is in the "meaning" of the gesture. In other words, there is nothing essentially polite about using two hands; using two hands has been made to signify politeness. Nevertheless, signification has become embodied in a material practice, which can, in turn, produce material effects.

This is not to reduce everything "upwards" to culture as a signifying system, but it is to insist that culture defined in this way should be understood "as essentially involved in *all* forms of social activity" (Williams 1981: 13). While there is more to life than signifying systems, it is nevertheless the case that "it would . . . be wrong to suppose that we can ever usefully discuss a social system without including, as a central part of its practice, its signifying systems, on which, as a system, it fundamentally depends" (p. 207).

According to British cultural studies, then, to share a culture is to interpret the world – make it meaningful and experience it – in recognizably similar ways. So-called "culture shock" happens when we encounter a radically different network of meanings; when our "natural" or "common sense" is confronted by someone else's "natural" or "common sense." However, cultures are never simply shifting networks of shared meanings. On the contrary, cultures are always both shared and contested networks of meanings. That is, culture is where we share and contest meanings of ourselves, of each other, and of the social worlds in which we live.

British cultural studies draws two conclusions from this way of thinking about culture. First, although the world exists in all its enabling and constraining materiality outside culture, it is only in culture that the world can be *made to mean*. In other words, culture constructs the realities it appears only to describe. Second, because different meanings can be ascribed to the same thing, meaning-making is always a potential site of struggle and negotiation. For example, masculinity has real material conditions of existence, but there are different ways of representing masculinity in culture and different ways of being "masculine." Therefore, although masculinity seems to be fixed by its biological conditions of existence, what it *means*, and the struggle over what it means, always takes place *in* culture. This is not simply an issue of semantic difference, a simple question of interpreting the world differently; it is about relations of culture and power; about who can claim the power and authority to define social reality; to *make the world (and the things in it) mean* in particular ways.

Meanings have a "material" existence in that they help organize practice; they help establish norms of behavior. My examples of different masculinities and the passing of business cards in China are both instances of where signification organizes practice. Those with power often seek to regulate the impact of meanings on practice. In other words, dominant ways of making the world meaningful, produced by those with the power to make their meanings circulate in the world, can generate "hegemonic truths," which may come to assume an authority over the ways in which we see, think, communicate, and act in the world: that is, become the "common sense" which organizes our actions (Gramsci 1971). Culture and power, therefore, are the primary object of study in British cultural studies.

SEE ALSO: Cultural Studies; Culture; Hegemony and the Media; Popular Culture

REFERENCES

Gramsci, A. (1971) *Selections from Prison Notebooks*. Lawrence and Wishart, London.

Williams, R. (1981) *Culture*. Fontana, London.

SUGGESTED READINGS

Storey, J. (2009) *Cultural Theory and Popular Culture*. Pearson, London.

Turner, G. (2002) *British Cultural Studies*. Routledge, London.

JOHN STOREY

culture

Cultural sociologists treat "culture" as all socially located forms and processes of human *meaning-making*, whether or not they occur in specialized institutions, and whether or not they are confined to one clearly bounded group.

Cultural sociology is an area of social inquiry into meaning-making, defined by its analytic perspective, rather than a particular empirical topic or institutional domain. Cultural sociologists investigate how meaning-making happens, why meanings vary, how meanings influence human action, and the ways meaning-making is important in generating solidarity and conflict. This analytic perspective applies to a wide range of substantive topics and social domains, contributing to the understanding of key sociological topics such as stratification, political institutions, social movements, and economic action, as well as to specialized domains of cultural production such as the arts, media, science, and religion. As a perspective, cultural sociology contrasts with sociological perspectives which focus on analyzing social structures regardless of the meanings attached to them, and with investigations which, although they might include information about norms, attitudes, and values, do not examine the contingent processes of their formation and change.

Sociological research on culture demonstrated significant intellectual and institutional growth as a well-recognized area of inquiry only in the last decades of the twentieth century. From the 1970s there were increasingly frequent calls for new sociological approaches to culture which avoided over-generalized assumptions about consensus or ideology, which avoided both idealism and reductionism, and which did not confine themselves either to the study of subcultures or to the study of expressive artifacts like art. Cultural theorists working from a variety of different starting points all rejected the contrasting alternatives which had previously shaped sociological approaches to culture, and introduced a variety of conceptual innovations which generated more particular accounts of meaning-making processes. These developments loosened old assumptions and shifted old debates, encouraging an unprecedented growth in sociological analyses of meaning-making processes and the institutionalization of cultural sociology.

Three mid-range reconceptualizations of "culture" then emerged in cultural sociology, although different approaches were often productively combined. First, drawing on the sociology of organizations, and on the sociology of knowledge, some scholars argued for a focus on specific contexts of cultural production, an examination of the ways particular meanings, values, and artifacts are generated in particular organizations, institutions, and networks, and how those social contexts influence emergent meanings. This approach challenged over-generalizations about cultural "reflection" of societies as wholes, drawing on theoretical resources from the sociology of knowledge and the sociology of organizations. Although many "production of culture" studies focused on specialized realms of mass media, the arts, and sciences, attention to particular institutional circumstances and constraints affecting meaning-making processes is also crucial for the study of more diffuse cultural phenomena such as national identity, social movements, collective memory, or religion.

Another mid-range approach to culture, influenced sometimes by pragmatism and sometimes by practice theory, focused attention on how interactions and social practices are themselves meaning-making processes, and on the context-dependent ways in which individuals and groups endow actions with meanings. Like production-of-culture approaches, this focus on meaning-making in action and interaction challenged overly general reflection models of the relation between culture and society; it also relaxed the assumption that meanings and values are entirely shared, coherent, or consistent for a given group or even an individual, providing a better understanding of diverse interpretations of common norms, values, and cognitive frames and analyzing how individuals and groups draw fluidly on different elements in symbolic repertoires ("toolkits") according to context. Culture, here, is a contingent and variable element of the ways action is framed. Applicable to understanding any sites of action and interaction, this approach has been applied to such diverse topics as corporate culture, the formation of racial and class identities, audience interpretations of mass media and artistic forms, and everyday engagement with politics.

Third, other sociologists, building on Durkheimian insights, have emphasized the importance of the deep formal structure of discourses for meaning-making. Analyses of culture-structures have built on two distinct traditions. First, discourse analysts have drawn on theories and concepts of textual structure derived from work in the humanities to analyze meaning-making. They investigate the deep internal structure of discourses in terms of their categories, codes, genre, and narrative, showing how signifiers derive meaning from their relations in systems of signs. Such analyses of culture as structured discourse introduce to sociology a previously neglected set of influences in processes of meaning-making, which provide a basis for constituting culture as a distinct object of inquiry that is analytically independent of, and sometimes causally efficacious for, both institutional and interactional dimensions of meaning-making. Second, other cultural sociologists explore links between meaning-making and social psychological processes of cognition, especially categorization. Analysts of cultural structures in sociology have investigated such topics as political discourse, media texts, and gender, but this approach may be adopted whenever the *underlying* cultural forms which are contingently mobilized in organized cultural production and informal interaction are of interest.

The idea of culture has long been both capacious and ambiguous, due to its complex historical origins and intellectual development, and cultural analysis was not generally considered central to sociological inquiry for much of the twentieth century. However, sociologists now think of culture as human processes of meaning-making generating artifacts, categories, norms, values, practices, rituals, symbols, worldviews, ideas, ideologies, and discourses. They currently identify and analyze three different types of influence on meaning-making: institutional production, interactional process, and textual structure, emphasizing each dimension to different degrees according to empirical topic and theoretical perspective, and often debating their relative importance. These analytic tools have helped avoid over-generalization about cultural processes – for instance, about consensus or conflict, about idealism or materialism, about macro- or micro-levels of analysis, or about structure and agency. In turn, this has encouraged an efflorescence of sociological studies of culture on such topics as identity and difference, group boundaries, political institutions and practices, and the mass media and arts and their audiences. Cultural perspectives are also frequently integrated into research on such standard sociological issues as stratification, religion, immigration, and social movements. Since new empirical topics and theoretical issues in the sociological study of meaning-making continue to emerge rapidly, the likelihood is that culture will become much more central to sociological analysis.

SEE ALSO: Bourdieu, Pierre; Critical Theory/Frankfurt School; Cultural Studies; Discourse; Hermeneutics; Semiotics; Symbolic Classification; Values

SUGGESTED READINGS

Alexander, J. (2004) *The Meanings of Social Life*. Oxford University Press, New York.

Friedland, R. & Mohr, J. (eds.) (2004) *Matters of Culture: Cultural Sociology in Practice*. Cambridge University Press, New York.

Jacobs, M. D. & Hanrahan, N. W. (eds.) (2005) *The Blackwell Companion to the Sociology of Culture.* Blackwell, Oxford.
Spillman, L. (ed.) (2002) *Cultural Sociology*. Blackwell, Oxford.

LYN SPILLMAN

culture: conceptual clarifications

Raymond Williams (1976) informs us that "culture is one of the two or three most complicated words in the English language," which is a good place to begin. Despite the contemporary upsurge of interest in the idea – what Chaney (1994) refers to as the "cultural turn" in the humanities and social sciences – culture is a concept with a history.

One compelling account is that the idea of culture emerged in the late eighteenth century and on into the nineteenth century as part of (and largely as a reaction to) the massive changes that were occurring in the structure and quality of social life – what we might also refer to as the advance of modernity. These changes at the social, political, and personal levels were both confusing and disorienting, and at least controversial. The machine was viewed as consuming the natural character of humankind and whereas we began with "culture" mediating between humankind and Nature, it can now be seen to mediate between humankind and Machine.

Another account looks back to classical society. *Civilization*, deriving from the Latin *civis*, is a term descriptive of a state of belonging to a collectivity that embodied certain qualities, albeit self-appointed, which distinguished it from the "mass" or more lowly state of being typified as that of the "barbarian." In this context the idea of culture is not so much descriptive as metaphoric, and derives philologically from the agricultural or horticultural processes of cultivating the soil and bringing fauna and flora into being through growth. Whereas the former concept, "civilization," is descriptive of a kind of stasis, a membership, a belonging, indeed a status once achieved not to be relinquished, the latter, "culture," is resonant with other ideas of emergence and change, perhaps even transformation. Thus we move to ideas of socialization as "cultivating" the person, education as "cultivating" the mind, and colonialization as "cultivating" the natives. All of these uses of culture, as process, imply not just a transition but also a goal in the form of "culture" itself.

Just as in many forms of discourse *culture* and *civilization* are used interchangeably, so in others *culture*, *society*, and *social structure* are conflated, though not necessarily confused. The idea of culture as a theory of social structure has given rise to the major division between "social" and "cultural" anthropologies, the former stressing universality and constraint and the latter emphasizing relativism and difference between societies. In contemporary cultural studies some would argue that the concept of social structure has been abandoned altogether and that culture has become the sole source of causal explanation.

Social theories that are based on a materialist interpretation of reality, such as the variety of Marxisms, see culture as essentially an ideological set of understandings that arise from the sometimes calculated but more often simply distorted representations of the basic set of power and economic relationships at the heart of the society. Contrasting with this body of thought are the interpretive social theorists who argue that culture is realized far more as an autonomous and self-sustaining realm of social experience: a repertoire and a fund of symbolic forms that although related to their time are nevertheless both generative and self-reproducing in a way that escapes the constraints of materiality. Here culture is liberating rather than constraining; here creativity exceeds replication as a causal force.

Culture to British and US social theorists tends to have been most usefully applied as a concept of differentiation within a collectivity. That is to say that the concept has become artfully employed in the manner of "subculture." A subculture is the way of defining and honoring the particular specification and demarcation of special or different interests of a group of people within a larger collectivity.

We can summarize some of the above accounts of the genesis of our concept "culture" through a four-fold typology. First, culture is a cerebral, or certainly a cognitive, category. Culture becomes intelligible as a general state of mind. Second, culture is a more embodied and collective category. Culture invokes a state of intellectual and/or moral development in society. Third, culture is a descriptive and concrete category: culture viewed as the collective body of arts and intellectual work within any one society. Fourth, culture is a social category: culture regarded as the whole way of life of a people.

SEE ALSO: Cultural Critique; Cultural Imperialism; Cultural Relativism; Cultural Studies; Culture; Gramsci, Antonio; Subculture

REFERENCES

Chaney, D. (1994) *The Cultural Turn: Scene-Setting Essays on Contemporary Social History*. Routledge, London.
Williams, R. (1976) *Keywords*. Fontana, London.

SUGGESTED READING

Geertz, C. (1975) *The Interpretation of Cultures.* Hutchinson, London.

CHRIS JENKS

culture, nature and

There is a movement among sociologists and social critics to include the built environment and physical bodies in social analysis, and to think seriously about the ways that locations and creatures (including people) matter to group life. Part of this comes from anthropological leanings in sociology, and the tradition of thick description that includes discussions of chickens and back streets as well as group life. Sociologists have had a long-term interest in describing the physical forms and social effects of cultural relations on the natural world. While relatively few ethnographic sociologists have paid serious attention to the physical settings for social life, those who have done community studies have sometimes illustrated the centrality of cultures of nature to collective life.

Urban sociologists have also written about nature, too – the persistence of natural forces in artificial worlds. Sharon Zukin (1995) describes cities as quasi-natures of living creatures and supposedly inanimate structures that nonetheless settle and move. The city may seem to be the opposite of nature, but it is better understood as a culture of nature that seeks its control.

Donna Haraway (2002), in quite a different move, looks at the companion species that live with human beings, sometimes known as pets, to meditate on domination of nature and the possibility of friendships with non-human beings. She asks whether cross-species companionship can be a model for human relations with the natural world.

SEE ALSO: Built Environment; Ecology; Materialism; Nature; Technology, Science, and Culture

REFERENCES

Haraway, D. (2002) *The Companion Species Manifesto.* Prickly Paradigm, Chicago, IL.
Zukin, S. (1995) *The Culture of Cities.* Blackwell, Cambridge, MA.

CHANDRA MUKERJI

culture industries

Culture industries is a term which performs both a descriptive and conceptual function. Since the term was coined by Horkheimer and Adorno in their 1947 essay "The culture industry: enlightenment as mass deception," both what the term designates and its theoretical implications have undergone a number of shifts.

In its original Frankfurt School usage the term was a polemical intervention into the mass society/mass culture debate and a development of the Marxist theory of ideology. On the one hand, the term culture referred to the superstructure – the social realm of meaning construction and circulation where symbolic forms of all types were produced and distributed – and to the German Idealist tradition of culture (or art) as a realm of freedom from material constraint and interests. Its linkage to the term industry (in the singular), on the other hand, was intended polemically to indicate the destruction of the relative autonomy of the superstructure and of the emancipatory possibilities of art by the economic dynamics of the base. The culture industry thus primarily referred to the industrialization and commodification of the process of symbolic production and circulation *in toto.* For Horkheimer and Adorno, the ideological domination of capitalism, and thus the suppression of revolutionary possibilities, was effected not by the overt content of cultural production, but by the deep structure of the cultural forms and the alienated relations between both producer (artist) and cultural work and between producers and audiences that the system of capitalist industrial cultural production produced.

The use of the term industry referred (drawing on Marx) to the domination of the cultural realm by competitive and increasingly monopolistic corporations driven by the search for profit through the exchange of cultural commodities, thus necessarily alienating. It also referred (drawing on Weber) to a process of organizational rationalization, whereby cultural production and consumption were increasingly planned, thus suppressing cultural and political alternatives. Importantly, this approach placed the analysis of advertising and marketing at the center of a general process the purpose and effect of which was to hold the audience in thrall (the new opiate of the people). This rationalization took place not just within the process of production, but within the cultural form. Cultural products were standardized and produced "pseudo-individuality" in consumption.

SEE ALSO: Commodities, Commodity Fetishism and Commodification; Critical Theory/Frankfurt School

SUGGESTED READING
Adorno, T. & Horkheimer, M. (1997) *Dialectic of Enlightenment*. Verso, London.

NICHOLAS GARNHAM

culture jamming

Culture jamming refers to a tactical effort by a consumer activist or activists to counter or subvert pro-consumption messages delivered through mass media or other cultural institutions. Culture jammers use tactics such as creating anti-advertising promotions, graffiti and underground street art, billboard defacing and alteration, holding events such as spontaneous street parties or flash mobs, as well as social parody and satire to attempt to raise consciousness and criticism about important social issues surrounding consumption.

The term was coined by Negativland, a band, in 1984, relating these activities to the disruptive, subversive "jamming" of pirated radio frequencies. American cultural critic Mark Dery (1990) influentially developed the term to refer to artists, musicians, and other social critics who sought to challenge the economy of consumption images. The critical Canadian magazine *Adbusters* began developing the idea and practice in the early 1990s. Lately, groups such as the Billboard Liberation Front and Reverend Billy and the Church of Stop Shopping have gained public attention. However, culture jamming is not a coherent movement, but more a series of common practices and overlapping anti-corporate activist stances. These practices are intellectually rooted in much earlier writing and works, such as critical theory, situationism, and surrealism.

Many of the consumer activists engaged in culture jamming are motivated to action by a common view that contemporary public space and discourse is distorted. They consider openness in public communication to have been eroded by corporate interests that intentionally affect everyday culture through their control of the mass media. Culture jammers view the media and corporate advertising as ideological propaganda that argues unceasingly for the logic of increasing consumption and what they do as an activist attempt to break through this wall of corporate controlled ideology.

The logic underlying culture jamming is grounded in the critical theory of the Frankfurt School. It also resembles Mikhail Bakhtin's ideas of the carnivalesque, and Hakim Bey's notions of poetic terrorism. Culture jammers resist the corporate engineering of culture by marketers who define behaviors and identities, inherently limiting human potential. This culture of consumption becomes reified, appearing natural, concrete, objective, and void of competing worldviews.

Culture jamming seeks to break through this oppressive ideology. First, culture jammers try to identify the contradictions beneath advertising and consumerist messages, thus undermining the way advertising naturalizes and utopianizes consumption. Culture jamming unveils consumption's economic, social, and environmental dark side. The second step seeks reflexive resistance in the mind of the average consumer. This awareness raising sets the stage for the ultimate objective: emancipation from the trance of consumer culture. Once emancipated, consumers can envision and adopt alternatives to contemporary consumer culture.

The perspective underlying culture jamming has come under scrutiny and often been critiqued. It assumes that consumers are dupes that have been hoodwinked by clever advertisers. Similarly, it assumes that consumers need to be emancipated by enlightened activists – despite, even, their own protestations to the contrary. Cultural studies of consumers have found that individual consumers can, on their own, be aware of consumer culture's contradictions. These consumers can see culture jamming itself as an attempt by yet another set of cultural elitists, in this case misguided and evangelical social activists, to control the social agenda.

SEE ALSO: Brand Culture; Consumption; Cultural Critique

REFERENCE
Dery, M. (1990) The merry pranksters and the art of the hoax. *New York Times*, December 23, H1, H36.

SUGGESTED READINGS
Kozinets, R. V. & Handelman, J. M. (2004) Adversaries of consumption: consumer movements, activism, and ideology. *Journal of Consumer Research* 31: 4.
Rumbo, J. D. (2002) Consumer resistance in a world of advertising clutter: the case of adbuster. *Psychology and Marketing* 19 (2): 127–48.

ROBERT KOZINETS

culture of poverty

In the mid-1960s, Oscar Lewis described the amalgamation of conditions perpetuating patterns of inequality and poverty in society as the "culture of poverty." Through his research on Puerto Ricans, Lewis showed how difficult it was for people to escape poverty which he attributed to the influence of cultural beliefs that supported behaviors that allowed people to stay in poverty.

The basic premise is that through the combination of one's inability to transcend poverty and feelings of alienation, a culture develops which supports choices that provide short-term gratification. People begin to think that impoverished conditions such as inadequate health care, long-term unemployment, dilapidated housing and poor nutrition are "normal." The response is to then live as if there is no future since people develop the conviction that it is impossible to improve their lives. These beliefs and behaviors are then instilled from one generation to the next, which eventually develops into a "culture of poverty."

One of the interesting points about this concept is that it has been used and often misused, to justify stereotypes and punitive policies aimed at the poor. The culture of poverty has been used as a rationale to both increase and decrease government support for the poor, ranging from individuals within the USA to debates about developing nations and the amount of aid they "deserve" from industrialized nations. Often it is used to place pressure on individuals for their impoverished conditions.

A conservative application of this concept would use the culture of poverty as an illustration of laziness; of lack of motivation of individual poor people. In mainstream US discourse this is often illustrated by stereotypes of "welfare queens" living off of the US government; that poor people reliant on welfare possess questionable moral standards and expect society to take care of them. In the social policy realm, this translates into a reduction of assistance for the poor and an expectation for individuals to rise above their situation without help from others.

A liberal interpretation of the culture of poverty would be to examine the structural barriers that make it difficult for people to move out of poverty. This includes lack of transportation, poor educational opportunities, inadequate health care, and absence of jobs. Often the policy solution is to provide financial support for the poor. Both the conservative and liberal understandings are incomplete and inadequate. Conservatives ignore the impact of macro-issues, of societal structures that create conditions which lead to poverty and liberals often dismiss the role of personal responsibility by placing the crux of the issue squarely on the macro level.

Also missing is an exploration of the relationships of gender, race, ethnicity, and other markers of difference which impact poverty as well as various interpretations of Lewis's concept. Often the culture of poverty is treated as a means to claim that a certain population has a "defective" culture thus making it politically justifiable to treat them differently than the mainstream population. Historically this is seen in policies such as the establishment of family caps or forced birth control to limit the number of low-income children who would probably be dependent on the state. It also has been used to justify inadequate health care and education facilities as well as inappropriate policing within poor communities. By focusing on individuals or specific populations as responsible for their impoverished state, social structures and practices that create barriers to success escape accountability.

SEE ALSO: Feminization of Poverty; Poverty; Welfare Dependency and Welfare Underuse

SUGGESTED READINGS

Edin, K. & Lein, L. (1997) *Making Ends Meet: How Single Mothers Survive Welfare and Low Wage Work.* Russell Sage Foundation, New York.

Gans, H. (1995). *The War Against the Poor: The Underclass and Antipoverty Policy*. Basic Books, New York.

Lewis, O. (1965) *La Vida: A Puerto Rican Family in the Culture of Poverty – San Juan and New York*. Random House, New York.

KRISTINA B. WOLFF

cybercrime

Cybercrime refers to criminal acts that target or use computers as a criminal instrument, or transmit illegal information using computers. Cybercrime targets or uses computers. Hackers gain access to computers to damage databases or software by introducing viruses or "denial of service" attacks (i.e., viruses or worms that multiply computer transactions to the extent entire systems slow significantly or shut down).

One objective of cybercrimes is to destroy or interrupt the flow of computerized services. Another includes break-ins to protected computers or networks to steal data or services. Cybercrimes include theft, sale or counterfeiting of debit/credit card numbers from protected databases, child pornography, unauthorized computer access, identity theft, cyberstalking, and larceny of intellectual property. Child pornography is a major globalized cybercrime using computer networks, email, and encryption techniques. Cyberstalking is use of electronic communications to transmit threats of violence. Cyberterrorism describes criminal acts involving interference with public computer networks and automated operations of critical infrastructure.

Cybercrime involves three elements of crime: *actus reus*, *mens rea*, and concurrence. *Actus reus* involves illegal entrance into computer systems and actions taken in pursuit of electronic properties. The *mens rea* of cybercrime involves motivations including power, greed, dominance, revenge, or satisfaction of prurient interest. Concurrence of the criminal act and motive is more complicated because cybercrimes might not be detected for lengthy periods.

Many cybercrimes are perpetrated by small groups that affect the electronic property of many persons or organizations in different global locales. For any single victim, costs of cybercrimes are often too low to report, but total costs for all victims are high. Because computer networks are globalized, cybercrimes raise questions about jurisdictional authority. Effective cybercrime law enforcement requires interjurisdictional task forces to conduct investigations in different countries across different time zones. Many local police agencies now employ cybercrime units.

SEE ALSO: Consumption and the Internet; Crime; Crime, White-Collar; Internet

SUGGESTED READING

Wall, D. S. (2005) The Internet as a conduit for criminal activity. In: Pattavina, A. (ed.), *Information Technology and the Criminal Justice System*. Sage, Thousand Oaks, CA.

SAMUEL NUNN

cyberculture

Cyberculture is most commonly used to refer to forms of cultural expression and activity that take place in cyberspace, i.e. on the Internet, the world wide web, or other forms of digital environment. While some commentators limit the remit of the term to emerging "subcultures" and marginal cultural activities online, amongst academics and commentators cyberculture is usually read more widely, and used to describe many forms of human-digital interaction, digital-mediated communication, virtual worlds, and so on. As an academic topic, therefore, cyberculture combines insights from cross-disciplinary studies of how people and digital technologies live together. Hence, the -culture suffix refers to culture as ways of life, rather than narrower understandings of cultural activities as analogous to the arts. In this fully expanded sense, cyberculture represents a field of study centred on social and cultural understandings of the interrelationships between humans and digital technologies.

The development of cyberculture studies has, since the early 1990s, passed through a number of inter related phases, and at the same time witnessed diversification and proliferation. Scholars with backgrounds in computing, anthropology, psychology, media studies, architecture, philosophy, neuroscience, sociology, geography, lingustics and cultural studies – among many others – have developed research agendas exploring the still-emerging realms of cyberculture. For example, early academic studies investigated how online forms of communicating and socializing were rescripting key sociolo cultural concepts as identity and community. Studies of early experiments in cyberculture, such as multi-user domains (MUDs) or email bulletin boards sought to understand the relationship between "real" and "virtual" identities and communities, and to use conceptual tools such as poststructuralist understandings of identity to theorize new cultural formations in cyberspace. Predictions about future developments in both cybertechnologies and uses of those technologies contributed to a mushrooming of academic and journalistic work – for example the vast amounts of commentary on virtual reality, much of it speculating from early and somewhat limited experiments in creating interactive and immersive virtual worlds.

Later studies have kept pace empirically and conceptually with changing technologies and advances in theory, such that cyberculture studies now considers much more than human-computer interaction. As digital technologies have migrated into ever more aspects of everyday life, from computer-generated imagery in films to portable and mobile devices, so the focus of enquiry and the theoretical resources have co-evolved with the technologies and their uses. Insights from science and technology studies (STS), for example, have provided frameworks to understand cyberculture as a process whereby humans and digital technologies exist in cohabitation – a theoretical position challenging the "commonsense" notion of technological determinism, which suggests that technologies have a determining impact on shaping users' behavior. Instead, STS-based studies emphasize a two-way process, or "co-configuration" of technologies and users. Another major development has been the related field of new media studies, where the various forms of digital media content, and processes of media production and consumption, are explored. Again, given the rapid diversification of media content and devices, this field is continually moving, and drawing on a wide array of theories and methods.

Methodological innovation has, in fact, been a signature of cyberculture studies. A growing interest in in-depth ethnographic enquiry, in particular, has produced landmark studies but also provoked debate about the redefining of this technique in a digital age. As a way of exploring the cultures of cyberculture, virtual ethnography has arguably achieved a dominant position in the academic's toolkit. At the same time, novel and experimental forms of research practice have developed.

SEE ALSO: Cybersexualities and Virtual Sexuality; Internet; Web 2.0

SUGGESTED READINGS

Bell, D. (2007) *Cyberculture Theorists: Manual Castells and Donna Haraway*. London, Routledge.

Bell, D. & Kennedy, B. M. (eds.) (2007) *The Cybercultures Reader*, 2nd edn. London, Routledge.

Marshall, P. D. (2004) *New Media Cultures*. London, Arnold.

DAVID BELL

cybersexualities and virtual sexuality

Just as when photography and film were first introduced they generated the pornographic photograph and film, so as soon as the newer information technologies appeared, an erotic world of cybersex and intimacy appeared alongside and embedded within it. New information technologies are used in ways that can facilitate new patterns of sexualities and intimacies. Surfing the Internet gives access to a medium full of intimate words and images: from guidance pages on infertility (over a million sites on sperm banks), to sites engaged in bride-mail ordering; from images of the most "extreme" sexual fetishes ("Extreme" is indeed the name given to one such site), to access to potentially endless partners on email.

These new technologies have generated multiple new forms of intimacy: sex messaging, sex chat rooms, sex news groups and bulletin boards, email discussion groups, camcorder sex, new forms of porn, access to relationships of all kinds, new social movement campaigns around sexuality, even so-called cyborg sex, teledildonics, virtual sex, and new approaches to the body and emergent "techno-identities" and "techno-cultures." Along with this a new language has emerged that mirrors new forms of sexualities: cyberporn, cyberqueer, cyberstalking, cyberrape, cybervictim, cybersex. Although such new forms can result in people meeting in real space for "real sex," there is also a great deal of masturbatory sex being generated through these media, as well as virtual sex taking place in these virtual spaces.

Cybersexualities, then, are becoming increasingly an important means of sexual communication in the twenty-first century. And they have both positive and negative impacts. They reveal changing spaces and boundaries for new forms of sexualities and suggest key shifts in public/private dimensions. Through both webcams and the global nature of communications the old boundaries in sexual relations break down. The body starts to change its contours – no longer simply fixed and corporeal, but fluid, boundary-less and "virtual."

SEE ALSO: Body and Sexuality; Consumption and the Internet

SUGGESTED READING

Waskful, D. D. (ed.) (2004) Net.SeXXX: readings on sex, pornography and the Internet. *Digital Formations* 23.

KEN PLUMMER

D

Darwin, Charles (1809–82)

Charles Robert Darwin was an English naturalist most famous for having developed the theory of evolution by natural selection. After finishing his degree at Cambridge in 1831, Darwin signed on as a naturalist aboard the HMS *Beagle*, a ship that would sail along both coasts of South America with the purpose of measuring the coastline. His five years aboard the *Beagle* played a tremendous role in the development of his theory. Darwin became an evolutionist shortly after the completion of this voyage, when he began to reflect on the significance of the data he had collected in South America and the Galapagos Islands. Darwin apparently discovered his principle of natural selection in 1838 while reflecting on the significance of Malthus's "struggle for existence," but he did not publish his great book, *On the Origin of Species by Means of Natural Selection*, until 1859.

Darwin's central question was that of adaptation, or how species come to be adjusted to their environments. He outlined his explanatory mechanism, natural selection, in chapter 4, which is remarkable for its elegant simplicity: nature always produces more organisms than have resources available for survival; there arises a struggle for existence, and those organisms that have the most "fit" characteristics, i.e., that best allow them to survive in a given environment, are favored in this struggle; the differential survival of the fitter organisms is followed by their differential reproduction, i.e., the more fit leave more offspring, including their fitter traits, and as a result those traits over time spread throughout a population and come to characterize it.

Many scientists readily accepted Darwin's claim for the fact of evolution, but most balked at the causal mechanism proposed to explain it. It was not until the 1930s, with the emergence of the new field of population genetics, that an empirical basis was established for accepting it. The new population genetics showed how natural selection could work, and final resistance was thus overcome. Population genetics and Darwinian natural selection were combined into what came to be called "the modern synthesis."

SEE ALSO: Evolution

SUGGESTED READING

Watson, J. D. (ed.) (2005) *Darwin: The Indelible Stamp*. Running Press, Philadelphia.

STEPHEN K. SANDERSON

Davis, Kingsley (1908–97)

Kingsley Davis, a grand-nephew of Confederate President Jefferson Davis, earned a Ph.D. from Harvard University studying with Talcott Parsons, Pitrim Sorokin, W. Lloyd Warner, and Carle Zimmerman. As one of the most influential and eminent sociologists of the twentieth century, he made major contributions to sociology, anthropology, and demography. A pioneer of sociological theory as it emerged during the 1930s and 1940s, he published prominent papers on the social and normative foundations of legitimate and illicit sexual behavior, marriage, and divorce in contemporary societies, intermarriage in caste societies, and the place of children in the family and the broader social structure. Writing on issues central to the structure and functioning of society, and therefore ideologically, morally, and emotionally charged, Davis's analyses were illuminating, but often, perforce, subject to extensive debate and controversy, sometimes the focus of challenge from conservatives and other times confounding liberals.

Beyond his contributions to family sociology during the 1940s, Davis published (with Wilbert Moore in 1945) the most systematic and fully developed functional theory of social stratification, explaining the inequality found across social positions in all societies as the necessary consequence of their diverse positive contributions to the survival of the larger social system. Fierce debate followed as some critics took the theory to be an attack on the value position that equality is a virtue. Important subsequent contributions advancing theoretical sociology were his lucid synthesis in *Human Society* (1949) of fundamental sociological concepts and principles using ethnographic data, and his controversial Presidential Address to the American Sociological Association (1959) arguing that sociological analysis cannot be distinguished from functional analysis.

Davis's creativity and the breadth of his influence in academia, in the Washington policy community, and the discourse of the general public are reflected in the terms *demographic transition*, *population explosion*, and *zero population growth* which he coined, and in the honor bestowed upon him as the first sociologist to be elected to the US National Academy of Sciences. As one of the giants among twentieth-century social scientists, Kingsley Davis's legacy to scholarly and public discourse will endure for generations to come.

SEE ALSO: Demographic Transition Theory; Stratification and Inequality, Theories of; Structural Functional Theory; Urbanization

SUGGESTED READINGS

Davis, K. (1963) The theory of change and response in modern demographic history. *Population Index* 29 (4): 345–66.

Heer, D.M. (2004) *Kingsley Davis: A Biography and Selections from his Writings*. Transaction Publishers, London.

DONALD J. HERNANDEZ

death and dying

Sociology of death and dying is the study of the ways that beliefs, behavior, and institutional arrangements concerning death are structured by social contexts. Although death is a universal human experience, societal responses to death vary according to cultural values, and contextual factors including the primary causes of death, and normative age at which death occurs.

Conceptualizations of and practices surrounding death in the USA have come full circle over the past two centuries. In the eighteenth century, death was public and visible. Death tended to occur at a young age, at home, and due to incurable infectious diseases. Survivors expressed their grief in dramatic ways, and made elaborate efforts to memorialize the dead. Throughout the late nineteenth and most of the twentieth century, death became "invisible" (Aries 1981) and "bureaucratized" (Blauner 1966). Physicians and hospitals assumed control over dying, death and mourning became private, funeral rites were transferred from private homes to funeral parlors, and people were encouraged to deny death and to believe in life-extending medical technologies.

In the late twentieth and early twenty-first centuries, death is again becoming visible and managed by the dying and their families. Patients' and care providers' recognition that dying is often a socially isolated, physician-controlled experience has triggered several movements aimed at placing control of the dying process in the hands of patients and their families. The Patient Self-Determination Act, which encourages the use of living wills, was passed by Congress in 1990. The expanded use of palliative care at the end of life promotes pain management rather than life extension. As the experience of death has become more public and controlled by laypersons, sociological research on death and dying has flourished as well, culminating in a multivolume *Handbook of Death and Dying* edited by C. D. Bryant (2003).

SEE ALSO: Health and Culture; Life Course; Socioeconomic Status, Health, and Mortality

REFERENCES

Aries, P. (1981). *The Hour of Our Death*, trans. H. Weaver. Alfred A. Knopf, New York.

Blauner, R. (1966) Death and social structure. *Psychiatry* 29: 378–94.

DEBORAH CARR

death penalty as a social problem

The death penalty is the sentence of death after conviction following due process of law. The death penalty has been sanctioned by major juridical and religious traditions. It was defended during the Renaissance and Reformation by many Enlightenment thinkers such as Hobbes, Locke, and Rousseau. This same period first saw the emergence of the movement to abolish the death penalty with the seminal work of Cesare Beccaria (1764), an end which was advocated in the nineteenth century by the jurists Jeremy Bentham and Samuel Romilly.

The practice has undergone two key transformations in modern times: a restriction on the crimes and categories of offender punishable by death; and a transformation from public displays of excess to private, medicalized executions. These shifts have been explained either by the cultural dynamic of the privatization of disturbing events or by the transformation in technologies of power from punishment as a public and violent spectacle inflicting pain on the body to the emergence of disciplinary power and surveillance of the soul.

A number of international and regional treaties restrict and regulate the practice or provide for the abolition of the death penalty (Universal Declaration of Human Rights 1948, The Second Optional Protocol to the International Covenant on Civil and Political Rights 1989, Article 6 of the International

Covenant on Civil and Political Rights 1989). Protocol No. 6 to the European Convention of Human Rights abolished the death penalty in peacetime and since 1998 abolition became a condition for entry to the European Union. International courts and tribunals such as the International Criminal Court (1998) do not provide for the use of the death penalty.

Debates about the death penalty raise philosophical questions about its justice or morality and pragmatic questions about its usefulness, discriminatory or capricious distribution among the guilty, and the risk of executing the innocent. Arguments in support are usually framed by the principle of retribution and a presumption of a deterrent effect. It is argued that it has a deterrent effect especially where the threat of imprisonment is not a sufficient restraint. Arguments against the death penalty challenge empirical evidence on deterrence, arguing it constitutes a violation of human rights and the sanctity of life. There is at the moment no conclusive and undisputed evidence that executing offenders is more effective deterrence than life imprisonment.

The risks of error, arbitrariness, and discrimination are endemic even in sophisticated legislations. The risk of mistake (accurate determination of who deserves to die or botched executions) in capital cases is often used to challenge the legitimacy of this sanction.

SEE ALSO: Capital Punishment; Criminal Justice System; Death and Dying

SUGGESTED READINGS

Hood, R. (2002) *The Death Penalty: A Worldwide Perspective*. Oxford University Press, Oxford.

Schabas, W. A. (2003) *The Abolition of the Death Penalty in International Law*. Cambridge University Press, Cambridge.

EVI GIRLING

decolonization

Decolonization typically refers to a shift in a society's political status from colony to autonomous state or independent nation. It can also refer to a shift from colonial status to full incorporation into the dominant polity such that it is no longer subordinate to the latter. While decolonization has occurred in many different places and times, typical usage of the term in the modern period refers to the decolonization by western colonial powers of dependencies in Asia, Africa, or the Americas. It is strongly associated with the fall of modern empires and the spread of nationalism and the nation-state around the world. Decolonization has also been used to refer to a cultural or psychological process that may or may not correlate with formal political decolonization.

The first major period of decolonization in the modern era occurred in the late eighteenth and early nineteenth centuries. In this period, colonies of England, France, Portugal, and Spain emerged as independent nations. The period began with the revolution of Britain's continental colonies and the formation of the USA and the emergence of independent Haiti, formerly the French colony of Saint Domingue. Thereafter, in the early nineteenth century, colonies of Spain and Portugal in Latin America obtained independence in the wake of the occupation of Spain by Napoleon in 1808. The second major era of decolonization occurred in the mid-twentieth century. This period saw a far-reaching, global spread of decolonization. Most colonies in the Indian subcontinent, the Pacific, Southeast Asia, Africa, the Caribbean, and the Middle East obtained independence. The process began after World War I but was accelerated after World War II. From 1945 to 1981, approximately 105 new nations emerged as a direct or indirect result of decolonization. Most of these nations then joined the United Nations, such that the number of members in the United Nations expanded from 56 members to 156 in this period.

The two periods of decolonization differ in several respects, in part due to the character of the colonies involved. In the first period, decolonization was led by revolts among creoles and settlers who sought independence from their former mother country. In the second period, decolonization was led by indigenous groups rather than settlers or creoles.

There is little consensus on the causes of decolonization, but several classes of causation can be discerned. One includes factors internal to the colony, such as the emergence of nationalism among local populations and associated resistance to the metropolitan power. A second includes the relative capacity or willingness on the part of metropolitan powers. The third includes larger systemic factors in the global system of international politics, which might in turn shape the metropolitan powers' willingness to decolonize. Some theories suggest, for example, that when an imperial state is "hegemonic" in the world system, it prefers global free trade and therefore becomes more supportive of decolonization. A related factor is global political culture. After World War II, for example, colonial empires began to lose legitimacy and the ideal of the nation-state became most pronounced, in part because the USA lent support to anti-colonial sentiment.

One of the most significant consequences of decolonization is the emergence of the nation-state as the dominant form for organizing societies and the related realization of the modern interstate system around the world.

SEE ALSO: Colonialism (Neocolonialism); Dependency and World-Systems Theories; Nation-State

SUGGESTED READINGS

Betts, R. (2004) *Decolonization*. Routledge, New York.

Strang, D. (1990) From dependency to sovereignty: an event history analysis of decolonization. *American Sociological Review* 55: 846–60.

JULIAN GO

deconstruction

Associated with the French writer Jacques Derrida, deconstruction appears alongside several neologisms he initially created to read, yet reach beyond, the Platonic auspices of western metaphysics. Key among those auspices are oppositions that distinguish between appearance and reality, matter and form, temporal manifestation and essential principle. As well, metaphysical writing privileges logical arguments (*logocentrism*), formulating them as the center and marginalizing all other aspects of the text. So, the real, formal, and essential is assumed to be apodictic; logic within language faithfully represents, names, or classifies what is already there.

But what precisely is deconstruction? Although this question is not unproblematic in context, one might say that deconstruction has to do with opening up given linguistic arrangements to the mostly silent, background suppositions and aporias that enable their particular patterns of deferral. Its opening gambit, "guardrail," is to read a classic text closely (never abandoning it or rejecting it out of hand), surveying especially what it eclipses, ignores, rejects, expels, dismisses, marginalizes, renders supplemental, excludes, and eliminates. Deconstruction pores over these delegitimated elements of a text to make room for alternate interpretations that open up a reading to what is completely unforeseeable from the vantage of its meaning horizons. Through such openings, deconstruction seeks to reorganize a given language use by realigning conventional oppositions, creating space for unexpected linguistic possibilities and being.

From here, the waters get muddy for those in search of singular definitions that expect one to decide definitively about deconstruction. The very question "what is . . . ?" poses a unique problem: while it appears to open discussion, the *is* commits respondents to the existence of the very thing placed in question. Yet, as Derrida repeatedly indicates, deconstruction is not a finite being (a presence) that can be defined universally, once and for all. Indeed, formulating an essential, fixed definition of deconstruction would replicate the very "metaphysics of presence" that he challenges. Instead, a different approach to language is required, and one that immediately faces a definitional intricacy: the word "deconstruction" cannot be defined once and for all, with any fixed unity, because any meaning or feature attributed to it is always, in its turn, deconstructable (see Derrida 1988: 4).

Several further things may be said about deconstructive analysis. Each such analysis is subject to further deconstruction – the process is unending and without final decision. There is never a point at which deconstruction ends, for every emergent meaning horizon is traced through deconstructible grammars. Moreover, attempts at deconstruction do not approximate a sustained method, methodology, procedure, or unified strategy. Rather, their emergence is as diverse as the contexts in which they are located, and in each case a close familiarity with the analyzed text is required. Its contingent path is, however, never determined or predictable.

SEE ALSO: Derrida, Jacques; Poststructuralism; Postmodern Social Theory

REFERENCE

Derrida, J. (1988) Letter to a Japanese friend. In: Wood, D. & Bernasconi, R. (eds.), *Derrida and Difference*. Northwestern University Press. Evanston, IL, pp.1–5.

SUGGESTED READING

Derrida, J. (1976) *Of Grammatology*. Johns Hopkins University Press, Baltimore, MD.

GEORGE PAVLICH

definition of the situation

The term "definition of the situation" has come to signify the "Thomas theorem," the idea expressed by W. I. Thomas as follows: "If men define situations as real, they are real in their consequences" (Thomas & Thomas 1928: 571–2). That is, when the phrase is used, it usually carries with it the connotation of the whole theorem. However, the phrase "definition of the situation" predates Thomas's famous theorem. The more general conceptualization seems to be closely related to the concept of norms and culture. The interpretation of collective norms is important for all social action. It is only in certain situations where the agent chooses to redefine the norms. Park and Burgess (1921: 763–9) cite a Carnegie study (1919) where the term is used to discuss the topic of assimilation to American society, especially in terms of "Americanization": "common participation in common activities implies a common 'definition of the situation.' In fact, every single act, and eventually all moral life, is dependent upon the definition of the situation. A definition of the situation precedes and limits any possible action, and a redefinition of the situation changes the character of the action." Clearly the theorem, as it is often interpreted, applies more to the "redefinition" of a situation than to the norms defined by the collectivity.

Merton's (1948) self-fulfilling prophecy focuses on the false definition of the situation which evokes behavior that then makes the original false belief seem true. In that way, the self-fulfilling prophecy is a subset of the definition of the situation, not the other way around, as is often held. The Thomas theorem can also be interpreted as a contribution to general sociology. Thomas clearly did not mean that all human choice is limited to social constructions; there is an "obdurate" reality and many definitions are real due to group pressures. Thomas's contribution is valuable as a reminder that there are indeed times when the objective consequences of holding a false belief can be very real. Moreover, his ideas are not restricted to symbolic interaction; his sociological and anthropological "social psychological" interest in cognition and motivation overlaps with other approaches.

SEE ALSO: Thomas, William I.; Self-Fulfilling Prophecy; Social Psychology

REFERENCES

Carnegie Corporation (1919) Memorandum on Americanization: division of immigrant heritages, New York. Extract in Park & Burgess (eds.) (1921: 763–9).

Merton, R. K. (1948) The self-fulfilling prophecy. *Antioch Review* 8: 193–210.

Park, R. E. & Burgess, E. W. (eds. and comps.) (1921) *Introduction to the Science of Sociology*. University of Chicago Press, Chicago, IL.

Thomas, W. I. & Thomas, D. S. (1928) *The Child in America: Behavior Problems and Programs*. Alfred A. Knopf, New York.

J. I. (HANS) BAKKER

deinstitutionalization

In 1955 there were 559,000 patients in public mental hospitals in the USA, the highest there had ever been. At that time, patients were largely committed involuntarily and had long hospital stays. For more than a century, the number of patients at state institutions, historically the primary facilities for the treatment of psychiatric disorders, had been rising steadily. By 1980, however, this number had declined to just over 132,000, despite the fact that the national population grew considerably. In 2003, fewer than 53,000 remained. The 93 percent drop in the resident census of state hospitals was accompanied by the growth of outpatient clinics and community mental health centers as primary care facilities, the sharp reduction in patients' average length of hospitalization, and the shift to policies emphasizing more voluntary admissions.

These statistics, however, did not reflect a precipitous reduction in the number of seriously mentally ill persons. What took place, especially from 1965 to 1980, was a *transfer* of patients from state institutions to a range of institutional settings such as nursing homes, board-and-care facilities, halfway houses, and community treatment centers. This massive and unprecedented patient relocation from hospital to community, termed "deinstitutionalization" by both social scientists and the mass media, was supported by certain ideologies and political actions.

In the 1980s and 1990s, one of the most important unintended consequences of deinstitutionalization was the dramatic increase in the homeless population. Inexpensive housing in large cities was unavailable and many discharged mental patients simply had no place to go and ended up living on the streets, in alleyways, or in subway caverns with other homeless people. As early as 1984, the American Psychiatric Association proclaimed that deinstitutionalization was a failure and a major social tragedy.

SEE ALSO: Institution; Madness; Mental Disorder

SUGGESTED READING

Bachrach, L. L. (1996) Deinstitutionalization: promises, problems, and prospects. In: Knudsen, H. C. & Thornicroft, G. (eds.), *Mental Health Service Evaluation*. Cambridge University Press, Cambridge, pp. 3–18.

RAYMOND M. WEINSTEIN

democracy

It is only within the past two centuries – and mostly within the past century – that genuinely democratic governments have flourished. What is democracy? Rueschemeyer et al. (1992) identify four main characteristics of the most fully developed democracies:

- Parliamentary or congressional bodies with a power base independent of presidents or prime ministers.
- The regular, free, and fair election of government officials, with the entire adult population having the right to vote.
- Responsibility of other divisions of government to the parliament or legislature.
- Individual rights and freedoms pertaining to the entire population and their general honoring.

It is important to distinguish between *formal* democracies, in which the formal apparatus of democracy exists but democratic principles are usually not upheld in practice, and *substantive* democracies, which have not only the formal machinery of democratic government, but generally consistently implement this machinery. Another important distinction is that between *restricted* democracies, or those in which the right to vote is limited to certain segments of the adult population (such as men, property owners, or whites), and *unrestricted* democracies, or those in which the entire adult population has the right to vote. Democracy is not an all-or-none process, but rather a matter of degree.

In an exceptionally detailed cross-national study of democracy using 172 countries and covering the entire period from 1850 to the early 1990s, Vanhanen (1997) argues that democracy emerges when the large mass of the population acquires resources it can use to force autocratic states to open themselves up to mass suffrage and political rights. Vanhanen identifies six types of resources that contribute to democratization: size of the nonagricultural population, size of the urban population, the degree to which farms are owned by independent families, the literacy rate, the enrollment rate in higher education, and the deconcentration of nonagricultural economic resources.

Sanderson (2004) reanalyzed Vanhanen's data by looking at his six subcomponents separately. He consistently found that the best predictor of the level of democratization was the literacy rate, with the deconcentration of nonagricultural resources an important secondary predictor. Size of the nonagricultural population and size of the urban population turned out to be essentially unpredictive.

These last findings seem to contradict the conclusions of the comparative-historical (nonquantitative) study of democracy undertaken by Rueschemeyer et al. (1992). They found that the factor most critical to democracy was the level of industrialization and thus the size of the working class, which became an organized political force that struggled to establish democratic institutions, especially the right to vote. Democracy developed earliest and most fully in those societies with the largest working classes and latest and least in those societies with the smallest working classes.

SEE ALSO: Citizenship; Social Movements, Participatory Democracy in

REFERENCES

Rueschemeyer, D., Stephens, E. H., & Stephens, J. D. (1992) *Capitalist Development and Democracy*. University of Chicago Press, Chicago, IL.

Sanderson, S. K. (2004) World democratization, 1850–2000: a cross-national test of modernization and power resource theories. Paper presented at the annual meeting of the American Sociological Association, San Francisco, August.

Vanhanen, T. (1997) *Prospects of Democracy: A Study of 172 Countries*. Routledge, London.

STEPHEN K. SANDERSON

demographic data: censuses, registers, surveys

Population censuses, registers, and surveys are the primary sources of demographic data, including information about the size, composition, and characteristics of a population or population subgroups.

CENSUSES

A census is an enumeration of all households in a well-defined territory at a given point in time. In the USA, data from the decennial census are used to apportion Congressional seats in the US House of Representatives, draw new boundaries for legislative districts, and allocate billions of dollars in federal funds to states and local areas. Census data are also widely used by researchers, business groups, and local planners, who use them to monitor population trends, the demand for goods and services, and social and economic inequalities between groups.

Census questionnaires are typically completed by the household head or "reference" person and may include questions about age, gender, marital status, place of birth, relationship, educational level, occupation, religion, race/ethnicity, or other demographic characteristics.

REGISTERS

Countries with national population registers keep records of individuals from the time of birth (or immigration) to death (or emigration) and update the record over time with life events. In general, population registers are used to record four basic demographic events: births, deaths, marriages, and migration.

Population registers can also be used to monitor changes in a country's population size and composition, keep track of trends in fertility and mortality, or select random samples of individuals from the population. Data from pre-industrial registers in Europe have been used for historical demographic research on family structure, fertility, and mortality.

The main advantage of a national register is timeliness; demographic events are recorded on a continuous basis, rather than once every 5 or 10 years. Population registers are expensive to maintain, however, and require a high level of cooperation in order to produce high-quality data.

VITAL REGISTRATION SYSTEMS

Like population registers, vital registration systems collect data on a continuous basis, but are generally limited to information about births, deaths, marriages, and divorces. Data on vital events are drawn from birth certificates and other forms that are completed at the time the events occur. Along with basic statistics about the number of vital events that occur in a given month or year, vital registration systems often collect more detailed information on age, racial and ethnic composition, marital status, and other characteristics.

SURVEYS

Unlike censuses and registers, which enumerate the entire population, a survey is conducted for a sample or subset of the population. Surveys are generally used to collect detailed information about a specific topic, such as labor force trends. Surveys can also be used as a source of demographic data in countries without a regular national census. While most census data are collected by the government, surveys are collected by a variety of governmental and private organizations.

Surveys are often administered using a "probability" or random sample of the population, so that findings can be generalized to the population as a whole. Data based on a probability sample are subject to "sampling error," which indicates the extent to which sample estimates might differ from actual population characteristics.

Surveys are generally divided into two types: cross-sectional and longitudinal. Cross-sectional surveys provide a snapshot of the population and are best for descriptive analyses, while longitudinal surveys ask questions of people at two points in time and are more suitable for measuring causal relationships between variables.

SEE ALSO: Age, Period, and Cohort Effects; Demography; Survey Research

SUGGESTED READINGS

Bryan, T. (2004) Basic sources of statistics. In: Siegal, J. S. & Swanson, D. A. (eds.), *The Methods and Materials of Demography*. Elsevier Academic Press, San Diego, CA, pp. 9–41.

McFalls, J. A. (2007) Population: a lively introduction, 5th edn. *Population Bulletin* 62: 1.

Weeks, J. R. (2005) *Population: An Introduction to Concepts and Issues*, 9th edn. Wadsworth/Thomson Learning, Belmont, CA.

MARK MATHER

demographic techniques: population pyramids and age/sex structure

Age and sex are among the most fundamental demographic characteristics of individuals. Viewed in the aggregate, age/sex composition forms the basic structure of human populations. It tells us the relative numbers of young and old as well as the balance of men and women at different ages. By characterizing the "raw materials" of human populations, the age/sex structure indicates the numbers of people "at risk" or "available" to engage in a wide range of behaviors that vary by age (e.g., going to school, getting a job, committing a crime, getting married, starting a family, buying a home, getting divorced, retiring, getting sick and dying). By itself, it does not tell us who will engage in any of these behaviors, yet it does help determine overall patterns and trends.

Population aging is one of the most universal demographic trends characterizing early twenty-first-century populations. The age of a population simply refers to the relative numbers of people in different age groups. Populations around the world vary from being quite youthful (e.g., Uganda, where 51 percent of the population is under age 15 as of 2004), to being much older on average (e.g., Germany, where only 15 percent of the population is under age 15). The trend toward increasingly older populations is directly linked to declines in both fertility and mortality. With fewer births, the proportion of children declines, thereby raising the proportions at older ages; similarly, declines in adult mortality imply greater longevity and hence a larger proportion surviving to older ages. Trends in population aging are most evident in the more industrialized countries of Europe, North America, and Japan, where the percentage of the population over age 65 is projected to surpass 20 percent by 2030. However, a great many less developed countries can also anticipate rapid population aging in the near future as a result of their recent steep declines in both fertility and mortality.

The most common measure of the sex composition of a population is the sex ratio, which is simply the ratio of males to females (multiplied by 100). It is often assumed that populations are fairly balanced between men and women, but in most countries women outnumber men overall, though not necessarily at all ages. The sex ratio often declines with age because of progressively higher male than female mortality rates at older ages. In the USA, for example, the overall sex ratio is about 95 males for every 100 females; however, at birth, there are about 105 males for every 100 females, and by ages 85 and over, there are only about 40 males for every 100 females.

The dependency ratio is a summary measure of the age structure and is typically defined as the ratio of economically inactive to economically active persons. Since the economically inactive tend to be the young and the old, the dependency ratio is simply measured as the ratio of age groups (i.e. Children + Elderly/Working Ages). The precise ages used depends on the population being studied as well as the availability of data broken down by specific ages. In the USA for example, the dependency ratio is often measured as the ratio of "persons under age 15 and over age 65" to "persons of ages 15–64." While it is recognized that many persons over age 15 are not yet economically active, and many persons over age 65 are still economically active, the dependency ratio approximates the number of inactive persons whom each active person must support. Given the different needs of children and elders, it is often useful to look separately at the child dependency ratio (Children/Working Ages) and the aged dependency ratio (Elderly/Working Ages).

Data on age/sex structure are typically presented graphically in the form of an age pyramid, also known as a population pyramid. The pyramid can be thought of as two histograms placed on their sides and facing back to back, showing the age distributions for males on the left and females on the right. The vertical axis is age, coded in single years, or in 5-year age categories, with the youngest at the bottom. Each bar of the pyramid shows either the number or proportion of the population who are males or females in a given age group.

Since each bar is determined by past demographic patterns, it follows that the overall shape of the pyramid does as well. Rapidly growing populations, in which births far exceed deaths, are typically characterized by a wide base and a classic "pyramid-like" shape (i.e., each new cohort is larger than the previous one). In contrast, a population which is neither growing nor declining has a more rectangular shape whereby each new cohort entering at the bottom is roughly the same size as the preceding cohort. A population which is declining due to an excess of deaths over births would have an age pyramid which is narrower at the base than at older ages.

SEE ALSO: Age, Period, and Cohort Effects

SUGGESTED READING

Rowland, D. T. (2003) *Demographic Methods and Concepts*. Oxford University Press, Oxford.

JOAN R. KAHN

demographic techniques: time use

Time allocation is a major indicator of social differentiation and stratification. People with high levels of human capital may be better able to trade paid work time for leisure time and purchase time-saving goods and services than people with lower levels of human capital. Moreover, time use decisions have important implications for people's health, financial security, and general life satisfaction. In addition to personal preferences, myriad norms govern how people should use their time, such as how much time is appropriate to spend at work and how much time is needed to care for family. Thus, at the social level, people's time use patterns reflect how societies value categories such as work, family, and leisure.

MEASUREMENT

There are three primary ways to measure people's time use: (1) asking respondents to indicate on questionnaires how much time they spend in various activities; (2) observing people in their daily routines; and (3) prompting respondents to recount their day in a time diary. The time diary has become the preferred methodology because of its accuracy relative to estimates based on questionnaires and cost-effectiveness relative to observational methods.

Time diary methodology requires respondents to provide an account of one or more of their days, or even a week. Because respondents are constrained to a 24-hour period in each day and must recount their activities sequentially (i.e., in the order they occurred throughout the day), it is more difficult to exaggerate time expenditures. It prompts respondents to remember things more precisely than if they are asked to sum all time spent in a single activity, like market work, in a day and is less mentally taxing than responding to survey questions that ask respondents to quickly add up time in various activities. Time diaries also capture the complexity of time use. They indicate multitasking, or when people engage in more than one activity simultaneously, as well as the location and people present for each reported activity. At the same time, diaries are not perfect measures of time use as people may be reluctant to report socially deviant or embarrassing behaviors.

HISTORY OF TIME USE DATA COLLECTION

Although the history of time diary methodology extends back to the mid-1920s, the most comprehensive and well-known time diary study is the 1965 Multinational Comparative Time-Budget Research Project. In this study, 2,000 respondents from 12 countries completed single-day diaries. The Harmonized European Time Use Study was developed between 1996 and 1998 and captured time use data on 20 countries. To date, time diary studies have been administered in over 60 countries spanning North America, South America, Europe, Australia, Africa, and Asia.

In the US, a series of cross-sectional time diary studies based out of the Universities of Michigan and Maryland have been conducted at roughly 10-year intervals since the 1960s. Time diary methodology has become so popular that in January 2003, the Bureau of Labor Statistics launched the American Time Use Survey, which is now the largest time use survey ever conducted in the world.

FUTURE DIRECTIONS: SUBJECTIVE FEELINGS ABOUT TIME

Time use data tends to capture the objective measures of people's time use: what they are doing, where they are doing it, who is accompanying them, and how long they are engaging in their various activities. The sense of pressure and or enjoyment associated with activities is not a major component of most time diary collections, and therefore the field is moving to incorporate methodologies that evaluate the subjective dimensions of time use. One example of this includes experiential sampling studies, or "beeper" studies where respondents are randomly "beeped" and asked to report not only what they are doing, but how they feel about their selected activity.

SEE ALSO: Demography; Time

SUGGESTED READINGS

Bianchi, S. M., Robinson, J. P., & Milkie, M. A. (2006) *Changing Rhythms of American Family Life*. Russell Sage, New York.

Larson, R. & Richards, M. (1994) *Divergent Realities: The Emotional Lives of Mothers, Fathers, and Adolescents*. Basic Books, New York.

Robinson, J. & Godbey, G. (1999) *Time for Life*, 2nd edn. Penn State Press, State College, Philadelphia.

SARA RALEY

demographic transition

The demographic transition theory began as a description of the demographic changes that had taken place over time in the advanced nations: The transition from high birth and death rates to low birth and death rates, with an interstitial spurt in growth rates leading to a larger population at the end of the transition than there had been at the start. The idea emerged from work done by Warren Thompson (1929). In 1945, following the end of World War II, there was a growing concern about population growth and Frank Notestein (1945) and Kingsley Davis (1945) separately picked up the threads of Thompson's thesis and named the process "the demographic transition."

Modernization theory allowed the demographic transition to move from a mere description of events to a demographic perspective. Death rates declined as the standard of living improved, and birth rates almost always declined a few decades later, eventually dropping to low levels, although rarely as low as the death rate. It was argued that the decline in the birth rate typically lagged behind the decline in the death rate because it takes time for a population to adjust to the fact that mortality really is lower, and because the social and economic institutions that favored high fertility require time to adjust to new norms of lower fertility that are more consistent with the lower levels of mortality. Since most people value the prolongation of life, it is not hard to lower mortality, but the reduction of fertility is contrary to the established norms of societies that have required high birth rates to keep pace with high death rates. Such norms are not easily changed, even in the face of poverty. Birth rates eventually declined, it was argued, as the importance of family life was diminished by industrial and urban life, thus weakening the pressure for large families.

Over time it has become obvious that the demographic transition is too complex to be explained by simple reference to the modernization theory. The work of the European Fertility Project focused on explaining regional differences in fertility declines and gave rise to theories of the diffusion of the innovation of fertility control. This was a very important theoretical development, but not a comprehensive one because it only partially dealt with a central issue of the demographic transition theory: How (and under what conditions) can a mortality decline lead to a fertility decline? To answer that question, Kingsley Davis (1963) asked what happens to individuals when mortality declines. The answer, which came to be known as the *theory of demographic change and response*, is that more children survive through adulthood, putting greater pressure on family resources, and people have to reorganize their lives in an attempt to relieve that pressure; that is, people respond to the demographic change.

A shortcoming of all of the explanations of the demographic transition has been that they have focused largely on the causes of the mortality and fertility declines, without paying close attention to the other changes that are predictably put into motion as the rate of natural increase changes in a society. Interaction between population change and societal change is, in fact, at the heart of the realization that the demographic transition is really a whole set of transitions, rather than simply being one big transition. These transitions include the health and mortality (also known as the epidemiological) transition, the fertility transition, the age transition, the migration transition, the urban transition, and the family and household transition.

SEE ALSO: Davis, Kingsley; Family Demography; Malthus, Thomas Robert; Modernization; Mortality: Transitions and Measures

REFERENCES

Davis, K. (1945) The world demographic transition. *Annals of the American Academy of Political and Social Science* 237 (January): 1–11.

Davis, K. (1963) The theory of change and response in modern demographic history. *Population Index* 29 (4): 345–66.

Notestein, F. W. (1945) Population: the long view. In: Schultz, T. W. (ed.), *Food for the World*. University of Chicago Press, Chicago.

Thompson, W. (1929) Population. *American Journal of Sociology* 34 (6): 959–75.

JOHN R. WEEKS

demography

WHAT IS DEMOGRAPHY?

Demography is the scientific study of human population and its processes, such as fertility, mortality, and migration, and how these factors change over time and affect population size, growth, structure and composition, and the natural environment. The field of demography typically has been organized in terms of two strands of scholarship: *formal* and *social* demography.

POPULATION CHANGE AND DEMOGRAPHIC PROCESSES

The change observed in any population over a period of time is a function of the difference in the number of births ($B_{(t)}$) and deaths ($D_{(t)}$) plus the difference in the number of people moving in to ($IM_{(t)}$) and out of ($OM_{(t)}$) the population. It is expressed in the *basic demographic equation*:

$$P_{t+1} = P_t + B_t - D_t + IM_t - OM_t$$

Demographic processes accounting for population change are *fertility*, *mortality*, and *migration*. *Fertility* refers to actual reproduction measured as the *crude birth rate* (CBR), *age-specific fertility rates* (ASFR), and the *total fertility rate* (TFR):

$$CBR = \frac{\#\ of\ births}{Total\ Pop} \times 1000$$

$$ASFR = \frac{\#\ of\ births\ to\ women\ age_i}{Total\ women\ age_i} \times 1000$$

$$TFR = \sum ASFR$$

Mortality is the study of deaths within a population, estimated using a *crude death rate* or *age-specific death rates*. A commonly used age-specific death rate is the *infant mortality rate (IMR)*:

$$IMR = \frac{\#\ of\ deaths\ to\ children\ under\ age\ one\ in\ a\ given\ year}{\#\ of\ live\ births\ in\ the\ given\ year} \times 1000$$

Life expectancy is also used to assess mortality and represents the average number of years, typically measured at birth, that a person can be expected to live.

Demographers who study *migration* focus on the movement of people. Migration is typically estimated using an *intercensal component method*:

$$\textit{if}\ P_{t+1} = P_t + B_t - D_t + IM_t - OM_t \ \ \textit{then}$$
$$IM_t - OM_t = P_{t+1} - P_t - B_t - D_t$$

SOURCES OF DEMOGRAPHIC INFORMATION

One source of demographic information is a *census*, which provides a count of the number of people in a given area at a given point in time. Another source is a *vital register*, which documents population events, such as births, deaths, marriages, and divorce. *Sample surveys* provide information helpful for assessing population events in the context of broader social and economic change.

DEMOGRAPHIC PERSPECTIVES: THEORIES OF POPULATION CHANGE

In one of the earliest theories of population change, Malthus (1798) argued that the world would expand at a rate that could not be supported by the environment. Demographic evidence today indicates that this has not happened and the global society makes food at a tempo far above Malthus's original projections (Weeks 2004).

More than a century after Malthus, the *theory of demographic transition* emerged. The basic premise is that societies move through three stages of population growth: (1) a period of high mortality and fertility; (2) a period of mortality decline as the standard of living improved; and (3) a final stage when fertility declined.

The subtle assumption of demographic transition theory was that economic development created the preconditions for declines in mortality and fertility. Evidence from the European Fertility Project (Coale 1973) indicated a high level of regional variation in *when* fertility declined, suggesting that economic development was not enough to explain change in population growth. As a result, a series of reformulations emerged. Some argued that ideational components giving meaning to the costs and benefits of children were important. Similarly, Caldwell (1976) argued that fertility would not decline until the flow of wealth, which had been from children to parents, was reversed.

In response to the baby boom birth cohort of the 1950s and 1960s, Robert Easterlin (1978) argued that economic *well-being* was important in explaining fertility declines. Individuals will marry earlier and have higher birth rates if they can achieve a level of economic well-being similar to their parents'. If it is more difficult to achieve a standard of living similar to what was experienced as a child, individuals will delay marriage and childbearing.

Recent demographic trends suggest a deceleration in population growth on a global scale due to widespread declines in fertility. Some argue that these demographic changes characterize a "second demographic transition," also described in three stages (Lesthaeghe 1995). The first stage (1955–70), is marked by acceleration in divorce rates and an increase in the age of marriage. Increases in cohabitation and childbearing outside of marriage characterized the second stage (1975–80). In the third stage (mid-1980s and onwards), divorce rates flattened, cohabitation largely replaced remarriage, and delays in fertility were recouped after age 30. These changes are attributed to increasing individual autonomy and gender symmetry and a greater focus on the relationship between adult partners than in the past.

Many of the original theories, however, focused on developed countries. Yet, research revealed that the pace of transition was faster in developing than developed countries. Thus, other factors related to fertility behavior, such as control over family planning funds and the distribution of methods, and the diffusion of westernized family values, have been used to explain fertility decline in developing countries.

SEE ALSO: Age, Period, and Cohort Effects; Demographic Transition Theory; Fertility Transitions and Measures; Migration; Mortality; Second Demographic Transition

REFERENCES

Caldwell, J. C. (1976) Toward a restatement of demographic transition theory. *Population and Development Review* 2: 321–66.

Coale, A. J. (1973) The demographic transition. *Proceedings of the IUSSP International Population Conference*. Liege, pp. 53–71.

Easterlin, R. (1978) What will 1984 be like? Socioeconomic implications of recent twists in age structure. *Demography* 15: 397–432.

Lesthaeghe, R. (1995) The second demographic transition in Western countries: an interpretation. In: Mason, K. & Jensen, A. (eds.), *Gender and Family Change in Industrialized Countries*. Clarendon Press, Oxford, pp. 17–62.

Malthus, T. (1798). *An Essay on the Principle of Population*. J. Johnson, in St. Paul's Church-Yard, London.

Weeks, J. R. (2004) *Population: an Introduction to Concepts and Issues*. Wadsworth Publishing Company, Belmont, CA.

VANESSA R. WIGHT

dependency and world-systems theories

Dependency approaches emerged out of Latin America in the 1960s in reaction to modernization theories of development. *Dependentistas* attributed the difficulties of development in the global South to the legacies of the long history of colonialism, as well as contemporary international power relations. This approach suggested that international inequalities were socially structured and that hierarchy is a central feature of the global system of societies.

The world-systems perspective is a strategy for explaining social change that focuses on whole intersocietal systems rather than single societies. The main insight is that important interaction networks (trade, information flows, alliances, and fighting) have woven polities and cultures together since the beginning of human social evolution. Explanations of social change need to take intersocietal systems (world-systems) as the units that evolve. However, intersocietal interaction networks were rather small when transportation was mainly a matter of hiking with a pack. Globalization, in the sense of the expansion and intensification of larger interaction networks, has been increasing for millennia, albeit unevenly and in waves.

The idea of the *whole system* ought to mean that all the human interaction networks, small and large, from the household to global trade, constitute the world-system. It is not just a matter of "international relations" or global-scale institutions such as the World Bank. Rather, at the present time, the world-system is all the people of the earth and all their cultural, economic, and political institutions and the interactions and connections among them. The world-systems perspective looks at human institutions over long periods of time and employs the spatial scales that are required for comprehending these whole interaction systems.

The modern world-system can be understood structurally as a stratification system composed of economically, culturally, and militarily dominant core societies (themselves in competition with one another), and dependent peripheral and semiperipheral regions. Some dependent regions have been successful in improving their positions in the larger core/periphery hierarchy, while most have simply maintained their peripheral and semiperipheral positions. This structural perspective on world history allows us to analyze the cyclical features of social change and the long-term patterns of development in historical and comparative perspective. We can see the development of the modern world-system as driven primarily by capitalist accumulation and geopolitics in which businesses and states compete with one another for power and wealth. Competition among states and capitals is conditioned by the dynamics of struggle among classes and by the resistance of peripheral and semiperipheral peoples to domination and exploitation from the core. In the modern world-system, the semiperiphery is composed of large and powerful countries in the third world (e.g., Mexico, India, Brazil, China) as well as smaller countries that have intermediate levels of economic development (e.g., the newly industrializing countries of East Asia). It is not possible to understand the history of social change without taking into account both the strategies and technologies of the winners, and the strategies and forms of struggle of those who have resisted domination and exploitation.

Most world-systems scholars contend that leaving out the core/periphery dimension or treating the periphery as inert are grave mistakes, not only for reasons of completeness, but also because the ability of core capitalists and their states to exploit peripheral resources and labor has been a major factor in deciding the winners of the competition among core contenders. And the resistance to exploitation and domination mounted by peripheral peoples has played a powerful role in shaping the historical development of world orders. Thus world history cannot be properly understood without attention to the core/periphery hierarchy.

SEE ALSO: Capitalism; Colonialism (Neocolonialism); Development: Political Economy; Empire; Global Economy; Global Justice as a Social Movement; Global Politics; International Gender Division of Labor; Modernization

SUGGESTED READINGS

Cardoso, F. H. & Faletto, E. (1979) *Dependency and Development in Latin America*. University of California Press, Berkeley, CA.

Chase-Dunn, C. & Hall, T. D. (1997) *Rise and Demise: Comparing World-Systems*. Westview, Boulder, CO.

Shannon, T. R. (1996) *An Introduction to the World-Systems Perspective*. Westview, Boulder, CO.

Wallerstein, I. (2000) *The Essential Wallerstein*. New Press, New York.

CHRISTOPHER CHASE-DUNN

Derrida, Jacques (1930–2005)

Jacques Derrida was an Algerian-born philosopher remembered for his development of deconstruction, an approach to thinking that seeks to carefully analyze signifying objects in terms of the differences that are constitutive of those objects. Typically, this deconstructive approach proceeds through a close analysis of the ambivalent and marginal terms that help secure the bounded understanding of a text, concept, or phenomenon, but which resist a final, stable meaning intended by the author or by orthodox interpretation.

Derrida worked hard to counter the common conception that deconstruction entails a kind of textual free play that inevitably leads to a moral and intellectual relativism. In fact, his work represents a scrupulous commitment to the practice of carefully reading any text (written or otherwise), which, above all, respects the probity of the text under consideration. Thus, though his work offers a general strategy for thinking about conditions of knowledge and representation, the power of that approach is derived from its attentiveness to how those conditions are manifested in specific contexts. Derrida brought this practice of close reading to bear on examinations of an impressive variety of subjects, ranging across considerations of major figures in the western philosophical canon (e.g., Plato, Kant, Hegel, Husserl, Heidegger, Nietzsche, and Freud), literary productions (including the works of Ponge, Genet, Joyce, and Mallarmé), and a wide array of social and political themes (education, internationalism, telecommunications, political economy, and the death penalty, to offer a partial list).

In contrast to popular characterizations of deconstruction as positing the impossibility of coherent interpretations, Derrida sought to show how the possible coherence of any interpretation is derived within a specific semantic code and is thus premised upon the possibility of repeating that code, its "iterability." In the temporal and spatial movement of a repetition, there is always the possibility of slippage, and thus the recurring possibility of the new and the unforeseen, the possibility that any text might be grafted into new contexts that would begin to reshape its meaning. For Derrida, this iterative inevitability suggests a certain continuity and stability, but it also points to the inherently open-ended status of any text, phenomenon, or representation. Derrida's thinking does not seek to destroy the conceptual traditions from which it emerges (they are, in fact, its very condition of possibility); rather, it seeks to solicit them in a way that denaturalizes that which might otherwise seem natural and already decided.

Derrida's approach to reading, therefore, has epistemological, political, and ethical implications, linking an insistence on careful descriptive work with an always present normative orientation. Descriptively, this line of thinking has helped complicate working concepts within a broad range of intellectual disciplines, opening those concepts to an ongoing reconsideration and thus stressing a kind of scientific and intellectual practice that remains open to new perspectives and events. To take but one example, Derrida's work has provided tools and enacted a disposition for productively troubling liberal, Marxist, structuralist, feminist, and psychoanalytic understandings of the "human subject" and its relation to its social environment. Normatively, Derrida's general approach emphasizes a respect for the "other" that comes from outside of our previously consecrated and currently present understandings, resisting the tendency to reduce that which is different from the interpretive grids that we have inherited. Deconstruction, then, carries an ethical imperative that productively complicates our other-regarding orientations, and it is in this sense that Derrida would insist that deconstruction is always, in the very movement of its critical posture, an affirmative gesture that is capable of saying "yes" to that which is yet to come.

SEE ALSO: Deconstruction; Foucault, Michel; Postmodern Feminism; Poststructuralism; Semiotics

SUGGESTED READINGS

Derrida, J. (1974) *Of Grammatology*, trans. G. C. Spivak. Johns Hopkins University Press, Baltimore, MD.

Derrida, J. (1978) *Writing and Difference*, trans. A. Bass. University of Chicago Press, Chicago, IL.

MICHAEL LIPSCOMB

descriptive statistics

Descriptive statistics are used to illustrate the distribution of a variable or variables in a sample. Their purpose is to summarize data in a simple and understandable way. They are typically used only for describing the data rather than testing for significance and describe the central tendency and the dispersion of data. Measures of central tendency – mean, median, and mode – attempt to provide a snapshot of the center of a distribution. Measures of dispersion – range, variance, and standard deviation – attempt to provide a snapshot of how a distribution of the observed scores of a variable varies around the mean.

Before we begin to understand the measures of central tendency and dispersion, it is important to understand a distribution and an array. The distribution of a variable is the value of each individual score or category (for example: 70, 35, 32, 18, 45, 55, 43, 55, 17 could be the ages of individuals participating in a survey). An array is when these scores are sorted in an ascending manner (example: 17, 18, 32, 35, 43, 45, 55, 55, 70).

MEASURES OF CENTRAL TENDENCY

The *mode* is the most frequently occurring score in a distribution. In the above example, two participants are of the age 55, making it the mode. The *median* is the exact center of an array of variables.

In this example, the ages of four participants are below 43 and the ages of four participants are above 43. This makes 43 the median age of this sample. When mathematically calculating the median for a sample where there are an even number of participants, the median is the two middle scores in an array divided by two. The *mean* is the average score in the distribution of a variable. In this example, adding up all of the ages of the participants and then dividing it by the number of participants or the sample size $n = 9$ (example: $17 + 18 + 32 + 35 + 43 + 45 + 55 + 55 + 70 = 370$, now divide 370 by $n = 9$ to get the mean age of this sample: 41.11 years).

MEASURES OF DISPERSION

The *range* of a set of data is the difference between the highest and lowest values in the set. In the above example, the lowest age of any participant is 17 and the highest is 70 ($70 - 17 = 53$) making the range of this sample 53. The *variance* of a set of data is computed as the average squared deviation of each number from its mean. The notation for variance in a sample is $S^2 = \frac{\Sigma X - M^2}{N}$ where M is the mean of the sample. The variance is not as commonly discussed as a measure of dispersion as standard deviation. *Standard deviation* is the square root of variance or in simpler terms the average difference of scores from the mean.

The standard deviation is considered an important measure of spread. This is because, if the mean and standard deviation of a normal distribution are known, it is possible to compute the percentile rank associated with any given score. In a normal distribution, about 68 percent of the scores are within one standard deviation of the mean and about 95 percent of the scores are within two standard deviations of the mean.

SEE ALSO: Measures of Centrality; Statistical Significance Testing; Statistics; Validity, Quantitative

SUGGESTED READINGS

Healey, J. (2009) *Statistics: A Tool for Social Research*, 8th edn. Wadsworth, New York.

Larson, R. & Farber, E. (2005) *Elementary Statistics: Picturing the World*, 3rd edn. Prentice Hall, Englewood Cliffs, NJ.

SHEETAL RANJAN

deterrence theory

Deterrence occurs when people refrain from crime because of fear of legal punishment. Whereas specific deterrence pertains to people who have personally experienced legal punishment, general deterrence involves people who have observed or otherwise learned about others' punishment experiences. The relevant properties of legal punishment for deterrence theory are certainty, severity, and celerity, with certainty being the probability that a type of crime will be legally punished (e.g., by imprisonment), severity being the punishment's magnitude, and celerity being its swiftness. The actions of legal officials affect the actual certainty, severity, and celerity of legal punishment, for example by making arrests and convicting offenders. However, there is a distinction between actual legal punishments and people's perceptions of them, which is important because, according to deterrence theory, actual legal punishments deter only to the extent that people perceive them as certain, severe, and celeritous. The distinction between actual and perceived punishments is reflected in these three deterrence propositions, the third of which is deducible from the first two:

1. The greater the actual certainty, severity, and celerity of legal punishment for a type of crime, the greater the perceived certainty, severity, and celerity of legal punishment for that crime.
2. The greater the perceived certainty, severity, and celerity of legal punishment for a type of crime, the less the rate of that crime.
3. The greater the actual certainty, severity, and celerity of legal punishment for a type of crime, the less the rate of that crime.

SEE ALSO: Crime, Broken Windows Theory of; Crime, Social Control Theory of

SUGGESTED READING

Gibbs, J. D. (1975) *Crime, Punishment, and Deterrence*. Elsevier, New York.

MARK STAFFORD

development: political economy

The emergence of the idea of development in western culture is closely linked to the evolutionary worldview that began to gain ground in Europe in the eighteenth century. Their common denominator can be seen in the idea of continuous social change usually proceeding in distinct stages and entailing an improvement of living conditions.

In the eighteenth and nineteenth centuries, major political upheavals throughout the world and the spread of industrialization in the west made social and political change the norm. Unlike static and undifferentiated "traditional" societies, "modern" society was increasingly seen as the product of progress resulting from such constant change. Both western sociology and anthropology embraced an evolutionary perspective and set themselves the task to identify the stages of development through which each society must pass in order to reach the western standard of civilization. Classical political economy concurred in this view by conceiving of modes of production as chronologically structured and nationally determined. In this understanding, development represented the outcome of an immanent historical process to be traversed by individual social organisms on their way to maturity – i.e., modern society.

In the 1950s, the multidisciplinary US modernization school identified the problem of third world countries in their "traditionalism" and advocated modernization – a stage-by-stage replication of the economic development of Western Europe and North America – as a solution. Modernization theory saw societies as becoming increasingly similar in the course of a process of social change considered unidirectional, progressive, and irreversible, thus reviving basic premises of nineteenth-century evolutionary theory. In this variant, development became coterminous with planned economic growth and political modernization, to be implemented with the help of development agencies and foreign aid projects.

Rejecting both the main theoretical assumptions and the policy implications of the modernization school with respect to development, the neo-Marxist Latin American dependency theory focused instead on underdevelopment. Dependency theorists claimed that the modern world's center-periphery structure mirrored an underlying international division of labor, established during the European colonial expansion and currently maintained through economic domination. In this view, the economies of the colonized regions had been reorganized so as to meet the needs of the colonizer countries, and ended up producing raw materials that served the latter's interests. Unlike modernization theory, dependency theorists did not view underdevelopment as a "stage" previous to development, but as a distinct historical process that industrialized economies had not experienced. In this view, development and underdevelopment are different aspects of the same phenomenon, not different stages in an evolutionary continuum.

World-systems analysis expanded on this criticism of modernization studies and claimed that it was the current capitalist world system as a whole, not individual societies, that should constitute the basic unit of analysis. Reifying political-cultural units – i.e., states – into autonomously evolving entities led to ahistorical models of social transformation, as in the "traditional" vs. "modern" distinction. As with dependency theory, underdevelopment was viewed as a product of the international division of labor underlying the capitalist world economy. Upward mobility within the system (e.g., a semiperiphery's rise to core status) was not considered development, but merely successful expropriation of world surplus. Both the dependency school and world-systems analysis retained a notion of development in which progress was represented by the transition to (world) socialism.

By the end of the twentieth century, development as a theme of academic research had lost ground. Treatment of the political and economic factors of macrostructural change increasingly occurred within the theoretical framework of globalization. In conceptual terms, this translated as a shift in the process of development from nationally organized economic growth to globally managed economic growth. At the same time, the notion of globalization as liberalization of market economies, democratization, or transition from the second to the first world, revealed the same teleological understanding of world history on which nineteenth-century evolutionary models were premised. The search for alternative developments included "ethnodevelopment," focusing on indigenous peoples and ethnic minorities, "sustainable development," targeting the preservation of resources, and feminist development economics centered on gender-sensitive development policies, but also alternatives *to* development, fundamentally questioning the principle of economic growth and the model of modernity that has been based on it.

SEE ALSO: Dependency and World Systems Theories; Globalization; Modernization; Political Economy

SUGGESTED READINGS

Escobar, A. (1995) *Encountering Development: The Making and Unmaking of the Third World*. Princeton University Press, Princeton, NJ.

Frank, A. G. (1967) *Capitalism and Underdevelopment in Latin America: Historical Studies of Chile and Brazil*. Monthly Review Press, New York.

McMichael, P. (2005) *Development and Social Change: A Global Perspective*. Pine Forge Press, Thousand Oaks, CA.

Wallerstein, I. (1979) *The Capitalist World-Economy: Essays*. Cambridge University Press, Cambridge.

MANUELA BOATCĂ

deviance

Sociologists define deviance as the violation of a social norm which is likely to result in condemnation or punishment for the violator. Most sociologists who teach a course on deviance divide the field into two distinctly different perspectives: explanatory or *positivistic* theories, and constructionist approaches. Explanatory theories regard deviance as "objectively given," that is, a syndrome-like entity with more or less clear-cut, identifiable properties whose causal etiology can be discovered and explicated by the social scientist. In contrast, the *constructionist* approach sees deviance as "subjectively problematic," that is, "in the eye of the beholder," and takes as its primary task an understanding of how judgments of deviance are put together, applied, and with what consequences. Each perspective has its own mission, agenda, enterprise, and methodology. Though these two approaches define deviance in superficially similar ways, their definitions point to divergent universes of meaning. The enterprises in which these perspectives are engaged are linked only by the objectively similar nature of their subject matter; conceptually and theoretically, they are worlds apart.

The majority of sociologists of deviance are constructionists: they argue that their mission is to understand how deviance is created or defined subjectively and culturally. They argue that the dynamics and consequences of the social construction of deviance constitute what's most important about the concept rather than its objectivistic or essentialistic reality or its causal origin. The proponents of constructionism tend to adopt symbolic interactionism as their theoretical inspiration, use participant observation as their principal methodology, and typically focus on "soft" or low-consensus deviance – that is, acts that may or may not be crimes, but if they are, stand a low likelihood of arrest and incarceration, behavior that tends to be punished predominantly through the mechanism of informal social control. Constructionism seeks to shift the focus of deviance researchers away from the objective nature and causes of deviant behavior per se to the processes by which phenomena and persons come to be defined as deviant.

To the constructionist, the deviance concept is defined or *constituted by* particular reactions from observers or "audiences," real or potential, *inferred* as a result of what persons *do* or *say* when they discuss or discover something they regard as reprehensible. In other words, it is a "definition in use." According to this definition, deviance is implicit in all social interaction; one does not have to name it to see it in action. And the reactions that constitute deviance are universal, trans-historical and trans-cultural; they are found everywhere humans congregate. Hence, the fact that laypeople do not use the term "deviance" says nothing about its sociological purchase. Deviance is a fundamental sociological process, as essential to human existence as identity, social structure, status, and culture. All human collectivities establish and enforce norms; in all collectivities, these norms are violated; as a consequence, the enforcement of norms ("social control") constitutes the life-blood of all social life.

All sociological definitions of deviance regard the reactions of specific, identifiable *audiences* or onlookers, bystanders, evaluators – any and all cognate social collectivities – as the central, defining feature of deviance. The issue of audiences addresses the question, "*Deviant to whom?*" The "to whom?" question indicates that definitions of what constitutes a normative violation vary from one collectivity to another. Audiences need not literally witness the violation in question; they may be told about it or they may be potential audiences whose reactions may be inferred from their ongoing talk and values, that is, stated beliefs and attitudes.

To the constructionist, persons violate norms not only by engaging in certain forms of behavior but also by holding unacceptable attitudes or beliefs and possessing undesirable characteristics; attitudes, behavior, and characteristics constitute the "ABCs" of deviance (Adler and Adler 2003: 8). In addition, in certain collectivities, the presence of a "tribal" outsider, that is, one who possesses what is considered in those circles an "unacceptable" or "inappropriate" racial, or national background, or religious membership, will elicit hostile or other negative reactions (Goffman 1963: 4). Constructionist sociologists also study false accusations of deviance, since that generates condemnation, a defining element in their definition of deviance (Becker 1963: 20). The fact that the person who elicits negative reactions is not "at fault" or "to blame" is irrelevant to a sociological definition of deviance. The fact is, people can be, and are, punished for entirely involuntary – or nonexistent – normative violations, over which they had no control or choice.

To the advocates of the constructionist approach, *social control* is the core of any sociological understanding of deviance. Social control is defined as any and all efforts to ensure conformity to a norm. Humans are irrepressible; all of us have a tendency to violate some norms. To engage in normative violations is tempting both because such violations usually more surely than conformity obtain for us what we value, and because many of the things we have been told that we can't have are intrinsically rewarding. Hence, efforts to ensure conformity to the norms may be found in all collectivities, both historically and trans-societally. These include positive efforts such as rewards, and negative efforts such as punishment; formal efforts such as arrest, and informal efforts such as an insult or a slap in the face; and internal efforts, through the process of socialization, as well as external ones, such as censuring someone for engaging in a non-normative act. Hence, while the state plays a major role in social control, it is only one of a wide range of agents dedicated to ensuring conformity. The many faces of social control represent the flip side of deviance; social control is an effort to deal with and suppress normative violations, as well as encourage by rewarding normative conformity. And it is the many efforts of social control that *define* and *constitute* deviance.

Nearly all constructionist definitions of deviance and social control include the component of power. Collectivities that control more of society's resources tend to have relatively more power to influence deviance-defining social institutions, including the law and its enforcement. Members of relatively low-status collectivities are more likely to find their behavior, beliefs, and traits defined and reacted to as deviant than those who have higher status and more power. Collectivities that have more power tend to have more influence on, in addition to the law, the content of the media as well as the educational, religious, and political institutions all of which, in turn, influence definitions of right and wrong and hence, what's considered deviant. Power over subordinate collectivities does not, however, ensure their conformity or agreement among members of those collectivities that dominant definitions of right and wrong are just or righteous. As we saw, humans are rebellious and irrepressible; smaller, non-mainstream collectivities everywhere construct their own rules of right and wrong, independent of those of the most powerful strata of society. In all societies, the dominant institutions, regardless of how hegemonic they may seem, are incapable of intruding into each and every aspect of the lives of all human collectivities and groups within their scope. Still, power is a factor in the social construction of norms – and hence, in defining what's deviant.

SEE ALSO: Conflict Theory; Deviance, Constructivist Perspectives; Deviance, Theories of; Identity, Deviant; Labeling; Labeling Theory; Social Control

REFERENCES

Adler, P. A. & Adler, P. (eds.) (2009) *Constructions of Deviance: Social Power, Context, and Interaction*, 6th edn. Thompson Wadsworth, Belmont, CA.

Becker, H. S. (1963) *Outsiders: Studies in the Sociology of Deviance*. Free Press, New York.

Goffman, E. (1963) *Stigma: Notes on the Management of a Spoiled Identity*. Prentice Hall/Spectrum, Englewood Cliffs, NJ.

ERICH GOODE

deviance, academic

Since all organizations and occupations entail normative structures, they also present opportunities for legal and ethical violations. In the university setting, students may break rules (e.g., through cheating or plagiarism) as might administrators (e.g., through unlawful firing). But, the main focus in the study of academic deviance has been on the misbehavior of college and university faculty members. As central figures in the teaching/learning mission of higher education, faculty are both professionals within disciplines and employees of a college or university. Either role can involve openings for deviant behavior.

Two dimensions of activities are helpful in delineating the nature of academic deviance. First, one can distinguish between professional and occupational forms of deviance. A profession generally espouses a set of ethics, which can be violated, while an occupation offers possibilities for crime that people commit in their usual line of work. The second dimension has to do with the deviance being directed toward property or toward persons.

The forms of occupational deviance among academics do not differ greatly from those in other occupations. Much as white-collar workers or laborers pilfer property belonging to the organization which employs them, so also do some professors. When the occupational deviance operates on the interpersonal level, we might see among faculty members such behavior as the sexual harassment of colleagues or the exploitation of human subjects in research.

Professional deviance reflects the distinctive features of university and disciplinary organizations, especially their reward structures and constitutive roles. Where property offenses occur, they are more likely to involve the misappropriating of intellectual property. Two well-known and serious forms of this type of deviance are plagiarism and the fabrication or misrepresentation of research findings. These offenses are essentially acts of theft and fraud.

Where professional deviance is interpersonal, it entails evaluations of the work of others in the academic roles of scholar, teacher, and colleague. Such evaluations are evident in refereeing journal articles and grant proposals, grading student work, and evaluating faculty colleagues who are candidates for promotion or tenure. Deviance in these contexts involves breaches of an expected impartiality.

SEE ALSO: Deviance; Education; Educational Inequality

SUGGESTED READING

Heeren, J. W. & Shichor, D. (1993) Faculty malfeasance: understanding academic deviance. *Sociological Inquiry* 63: 49–63.

JOHN HEEREN

deviance, constructionist perspectives

Constructionist perspectives are ways of viewing reality as a human cognitive or social production. Social constructionism explains how people interactively make sense of, and order, their world by defining it and categorizing it, by representing it through language, symbols, maps, etc., and by acting toward the representations as though they were real. The extent to which reality is seen as having an independent existence outside the human mind or social processes distinguishes different versions. Strong constructionism argues that we cannot objectively verify the existence of reality; we can only observe the world from different positions and make "truth claims" about constructions of that world. Weak constructionism believes that some underlying reality exists; by selecting from and classifying this basic reality humans build social constructions having different appearances, and meaning depending upon the social and cultural context.

Constructionists see deviance as the consequence of humans attempting to create a moral order by defining and classifying selected behaviors, appearance, or statuses as normal, ethical and acceptable, and creating rules that ban, censure, and/or sanction norm violators. Deviance is seen as a variation from social norms that is perceived as different, judged as significant, and negatively evaluated as threatening. Social reaction by control agencies toward those designated as deviant can result in a labeling effect or "self-fulfilling prophesy" that amplifies the original deviant behavior or appearance, entrenches the incumbent in a deviant role, and produces additional deviance as a result of their pursuit of secrecy. Ultimately this can result in an identity transformation into "career deviance" as the norm violator becomes engulfed coping with the associated stigma that comes with their transformed social identity. Social constructionist perspectives toward deviance tend to focus on the practices of authoritative agents in creating moral panics about feared behavior and those who engage in it.

According to Goode and Ben-Yehuda (1994) moral panics are societal reactions to perceived threat characterized by: (1) their sudden appearance and rapid spread among large sections of the population via mass media and other means of communications, followed by a rapid decline in further instances of the problem; (2) the growth of experts who are claimed authorities in discerning cases of the said feared behavior; (3) an increased identification of cases that build into a "wave;" (4) hostility and persecution of the accused as enemies of society; (5) measurement of society's concern; (6) consensus about the seriousness of the threat; (7) disproportionality of the fear relative to actual harm; (8) a backlash against the persecution; and (9) exposure of the flaws in identifying the problem.

Social constructionists of deviance share a concern to examine how interest groups, moral entrepreneurs and social movements create claims about deviant behavior. Claims making involves a process of first assembling and diagnosing claims about behavior or conditions seen as morally problematic. Second, it involves presenting these claims as legitimate to significant audiences such as the news media. Third, framing a moral problem involves the prognosis of how to address the problem to bring about a desired outcome by defining strategies, tactics, and policy. Fourth, claims making involves contesting counter claims and mobilizing the support of key groups.

Critics of social constructionism have challenged each others' epistemological position. Pro-realists accuse constructionists of being nihilistic and unscientific; for implying that crime and deviance are merely fabrications. Anti-realists ridicule science as just another truth claim using scientific ideology to claim legitimacy for political ends. The point of constructionism is that by revealing how what is taken to be real is constituted, it can be deconstructed, enabling its reconstruction and, thereby, changing social reality.

SEE ALSO: Deviance; Essentialism and Constructionism

REFERENCE

Goode, E. & Ben-Yehuda, N. (1994). *Moral Panics: The Social Construction of Deviance*. Blackwell, Oxford.

SUGGESTED READINGS

Adler, P. A. & Adler, P. (eds.) (2006) *Constructions of Deviance: Power, Context and Interaction*.Thompson, Belmont, CA.

Burr, V. (1995) *An Introduction to Social Constructionism*. Routledge, London.

Gergen, K. (1999) *An Invitation to Social Construction*. Sage, London.

STUART HENRY

deviance, crime and

All societies and social collectivities exercise *social control*: They expect their members to conform to certain normative expectations and punish, condemn, or reproach persons who fail to meet them. Although the layperson rarely uses the term, the sociologist refers to a society's member's departure from the norms as "deviance." By exercising social control, society's members define or *constitute* deviance.

Sociologically, four components constitute deviance: One, the existence of a norm or rule or law. Two, someone who violates that norm. Three, an audience that observes or learns about the violation and the violator. And four, a negative reaction to the violation: a snub, punishment, condemnation, arrest, denunciation, ridicule, gossip, social isolation, reproach. Clearly, negative reactions range from slightly to strongly negative, which means that deviance is a spectrum, a matter of degree.

Social control may be *formal* or *informal*. Some actions are crimes, or violations of the formal norms we refer to as laws, and call for punishment by the state or government. Whenever the state arrests, prosecutes, and imprisons a miscreant, it exercises "formal" social control. By definition, a crime is an action the violation of which activates formal social control. A crime is a specific type of deviance. While all crime is a type of deviance, not all deviance is crime; obesity, full body tattooing, and believing that one has been kidnapped by extraterrestrials exemplify serious but not illegal deviance. Nonetheless, crimes are typically regarded as more serious violations of society's norms and usually generate a higher level of public consensus as to their "wrongness." Crime is studied by criminologists; criminology studies violations of the law, usually from a positivistic or explanatory perspective, in addition to the exercise of formal social control, while the sociology of deviance more often studies low-consensus normative violations, usually by means of ethnographic or qualitative methods.

The degree to which a given act, belief, or physical or mental condition is regarded as deviant is evaluated by diverse audiences; the standards that one audience applies as to whether a norm has been violated and deserving of condemnation may be quite different from those applied by a different audience. Thus, we see two very different species of deviance.

"Societal" deviance is made up of acts, beliefs, and traits that are regarded as objectionable on a widespread basis, in the society taken as a whole. The standard by which the unacceptability of the act, belief, or trait is judged is *vertical* and *hierarchical*: the norm is promulgated in major institutions such as education, the law, the media, politics, religion, and the family. Violations of such standards may be referred to as "high-consensus" deviance, and include murder, rape, robbery, incest, theft, alcoholism, adultery, and drug addiction. While some such practices do find endorsement in certain social circles, the individuals who embrace or endorse them tend to be exceptional, marginal, and themselves deviant. Discovery that someone engages in such practices is likely to result in arrest or, if they are not crimes, reproach, ridicule, avoidance, and social isolation.

In contrast, "situational" deviance is made up of those actions, beliefs, and traits that are endorsed or tolerated in some contexts, settings, locales, or social sectors that are elsewhere regarded as normative violations. Here, we find "low-consensus" deviance, the judgment of which is "horizontal" rather than vertical; with respect to deviance, society can be likened to a "mosaic" rather than a hierarchy. As we move from one group, stratum, or social circle to another, what's considered wrong or right, good or bad, deviant or conventional, likewise shifts around. For instance, evolution as a scientific fact is taught in most schools, colleges, and universities in the USA, but creationists constitute nearly half the population, and are rarely referred to as "deviants." Having a small number of inconspicuous tattoos, engaging in sex with more than a specific number of partners, smoking marijuana occasionally, and visiting nude beaches represent examples of "situational" or "low consensus" deviance. Again, since deviance is a matter of degree, the line between "societal" and "situational" deviance is blurry and in flux.

Social control will be applied to normative violations as long as humans organize themselves into collectivities, and as long as sociologists study human behavior, the concept of deviance will remain a vital subject of study.

SEE ALSO: Crime; Deviance; Deviance, Theories of; Labeling Theory; Social Control;

SUGGESTED READINGS

Adler, P. A., and Adler, P. (eds.) (2009) *Constructions of Deviance: Social Power, Context, and Interaction*. Thompson Wadsworth, Belmont, CA.

Dotter, D. (2004) *Creating deviance: an Interactionist Approach*. Altamira Press, Walnut Creek, CA.

Downes, D. & Rock, P. (2007) *Understanding Deviance*, 5th edn. Oxford University Press, New York & Oxford.

ERICH GOODE

deviance, criminalization of

Imputations of deviance occur whenever there is stigmatization, condemnation, segregation, retribution, or rehabilitation. Criminalization refers to the process of applying the criminal law to certain behaviors. Criminalization reinforces the dominant standards in a society through threatened criminal penalties, criminal prosecution, and punishment. Not all deviant behaviors are criminal. Many scholars study the processes through which, and conditions under which, the criminal sanction is applied to particular deviance categories.

To change the status of a deviant category to a crime requires collective action. Thus studies of the criminalization of deviance reveal the links between deviance, political action, and social change. The dominant approaches to studying criminalization are the deviance and social control viewpoint, which asks whether criminalization is a neutral process or if it serves the interests of the powerful, and the social problems viewpoint, which looks at the social meanings, or collective definitions of crime. Of course, not all demands to criminalize deviant behaviors and conditions are successful – many are ignored; others are overshadowed by new demands.

Jenness (2004) presents an authoritative review and evaluation of criminalization scholarship. Organizing this massive literature both chronologically and thematically, she examines three lines of inquiry. The first is classic work examining criminal laws that emerge in response to demographic changes that upset the balance between powerful interest groups and those they control. Classic work demonstrates the roles of both instrumental and symbolic politics in deviance defining and the emergence of criminal law. The second, contemporary line of inquiry "unpacks" the relative influences of organizational, social movement, and state-related factors involved in efforts to criminalize deviance. The focus is less on changes in structural conditions than on the specific strategies for producing criminal law. The third, more recent line of inquiry looks to connect local criminal law formation politics with broader processes of institutionalization, globalization, and modernization. This line of inquiry asks whether deviantization and criminalization at the local level (i.e., county, region, state, country, etc.) intersect with some larger social, political, or cultural system.

The study of when and how deviant behaviors and statuses become defined as criminal has expanded in many directions since Edwin Sutherland's groundbreaking and now classic study of the origins and diffusion of sexual psychopath laws (Sutherland 1950). Theoretical accounts of criminalization have moved away from traditional consensus and conflict models and toward integrative models which point to multiple factors, including individual activists, interest groups, the media, and organized social movements; the tactics, power, and motivations of these social forces, entities, and actors; and the political opportunities and structural conditions that make the criminalization of deviance possible. Contemporary work includes more sophisticated analyses of combinations of these factors, as well as how they operate across time. Very recent work is beginning to examine criminalization as a social process operating across geopolitical units.

Methods for studying criminalization have progressed as well. Assessments of the field argued that research on the emergence of criminal law suffered from a tendency to unconsciously vacillate between description and explanation, to focus on historically grounded case studies rather than general processes of criminalization, to substitute moral prejudgments for empirical inquiry, and to bog down in the stale debate between consensus and conflict theories. In response to these critiques, scholars began to inject other areas of sociological inquiry, to examine multiple case studies, and to create general models of the criminal law formation process. The literature now reflects the work of criminologists, sociologists, political scientists, and sociolegal scholars. Very recent research, theory, and methodology include linking research on the criminalization of deviance to the policy studies literature.

SEE ALSO: Crime; Criminology; Deviance; Deviance, Crime and; Social Control

REFERENCES

Jenness, V. (2004) Explaining criminalization: from demography and status to globalization and modernization. *Annual Review of Sociology* 30: 147–71.

Sutherland, E. H. (1950) The diffusion of sexual psychopath laws. *American Journal of Sociology* 56: 142–8.

SUGGESTED READING

Hagan, J. (1980) The legislation of crime and delinquency: a review of theory, method, and research. *Law and Society Review* 14: 603–28.

DANIEL HILLYARD

deviance, explanatory theories of

Sociologists define deviance as the violation of a norm that would, if discovered, result in the punishment or condemnation of the violator. A crime is a norm whose violation is punished by the state. This definition opens two radically different missions or lines of inquiry: *positivism*, or the attempt to explain the cause of the normative violations, and *constructionism*, or the exploration of the dynamics of the creation, maintenance, and enforcement of the norms.

Positivist or explanatory theories of deviance and crime are made up of the following postulates: *objectivism* (phenomena possess a pre-given reality, independent of human definition of construction); *empiricism* (we can know the world through our five senses); and *determinism* (the phenomena of the material world, including the social world, are linked in a cause-and-effect fashion).

The most influential explanatory sociological theories of deviant behavior and crime include: social disorganization theory; anomie theory; learning theory and the theory of differential association; social control theory; self-control theory; and routine activities theory.

Social disorganization theory argues that people who live in communities where residents are socially and geographically mobile and have low emotional investments in the community are more likely to engage in illegal and non-normative behaviors than persons residing in more stable communities. Members of such communities tend not to monitor or sanction the behavior of wrongdoers in their midst. Thus, residents can commit infractions of the law and the social norms without consequence, and so they tend to do so with greater frequency than in communities in which co-residents monitor and sanction one another's behavior.

Anomie theory explains the cause of deviance by the malintegration between a society's culture – what members learn to value, what they are motivated to want and seek, mainly material success – and its social and economic structure, which places limits on some of its members' ability to succeed. This disjunction subjects the members of the society who fail to achieve to strain, which in turn, results in deviant "modes of adaptation," or behavioral consequences of this failure to achieve.

Differential association theory argues that definitions favorable to committing criminal and deviant behavior is learned in face-to-face interaction between and among people who are close or intimate with one another. This theory argues that people who engage in criminal acts *differentially associate* with persons who endorse violations of the law. A person becomes criminal or delinquent as a result of an excess of definitions favorable to the violation of the law over definitions unfavorable to the violation of the law.

Social control theory turns the traditional question, "Why do they do it?" around and asks, "Why *don't* they do it?" If left to our own devices, most of us would deviate from society's rules, and cheat, lie, and steal. It is the *absence* of social control that causes deviant behavior. To the extent that persons have a stake in conformity – jobs, an education, a house, a relationship, a family – they will conform to the norms of the society and not risk losing that stake. To the extent that persons lack that stake in conformity, they are more willing to violate the law.

Self-control theory argues that crime ("force or fraud in pursuit of self-interest") does not need to be motivated or learned. A lack of self-control causes crime, as well as getting drunk or high, and engaging in all manner of risky, predatory sexual behavior. And what causes a lack of self-control is inconsistent and ineffective parenting. Parents who fail to monitor or sanction wrongdoing in their children produce offspring who lack self-control and engage in criminal, deviant, delinquent, and high-risk behavior. All such behaviors have one thing in common: They are impulsive and intended to seize short-term gratification without concern for long-run risk to the actor or harm to the victim.

Routine activity theory argues that crime takes place when there is a conjunction of a *motivated offender*, a *suitable target* (something of value worth seizing), and *the lack of a capable guardian*, or a protector of the "target." The theory is not an explanation of the propensity to commit crime, but a theory of *crime*, the likelihood of the commission of criminal acts.

SEE ALSO: Anomie; Crime, Social Control Theory of; Crime, Social Learning Theories of; Deviance

SUGGESTED READING
Akers, R. A. & Sellers, C. S. (2008) *Criminological Theories*, 5th edn. Oxford University Press, New York.

ERICH GOODE

deviance, medicalization of

Medicalization is the process whereby previously non-medical aspects of life come to be seen in medical terms, usually as disorders or illnesses. A wide range of phenomena has been *medicalized*, including normal life events (birth, death), biological processes (aging, menstruation), common human problems (learning and sexual difficulties), and forms of deviance. The medicalization of deviance thus refers to the process whereby non-normative or morally condemned appearance (obesity, unattractiveness, shortness), belief (mental disorder, racism), or conduct (drinking, gambling, sexual practices) come under medical jurisdiction.

Medicalization is a collective and political achievement that requires moral entrepreneurs who champion a medical framing of a problem. With levels and degrees we see that medicalization is not an either/or phenomenon. Nor is medicalization a one-way process. Just as deviance may become medical, the medical framing of deviance may be undone (in part or in full). As medical meaning is diluted or replaced, medical terminology and intervention are deemed inappropriate. Masturbation is the classic example of near total *demedicalization*; in the nineteenth century, masturbation was medicalized as "onanism," a disease in itself, as well as a gateway perversion that rendered those of weak constitutions more susceptible to other forms of sexual deviation. Another example is the removal of homosexuality from the third edition of the American Psychiatric Association's *Diagnostic and Statistical Manual of Mental Disorders* (DSM-III). But whereas earlier medical framing of masturbation now seems absurd to many, the reclassification of homosexuality illustrates *contested* demedicalization. Despite the 1973 decision by the American Psychiatric Association to remove homosexuality from the roster of mental disorders, a small but vocal psychiatric minority provides reparative or conversion therapy, and a portion of the public still views homosexuality as deviance (but not necessarily as illness). Homosexuality thus also illustrates that demedicalization does not automatically mean a form of deviance has or will become conventional, only that the official medical framing has ended.

The consequences of medicalization may be positive or negative – oftentimes both. The therapeutic ethos of medicine changes the moral status of both deviance and deviant. Extension of the sick role to the deviant diminishes stigma and culpability, both of which may increase the likelihood that a pedophile, batterer, or addict for example might seek treatment. Medical explanations for inchoate or diffuse difficulties can provide coherence to symptoms, validate and legitimate troubles, and support their self-management. In addition, medical recognition may facilitate insurance coverage of medical treatment, thereby transforming potential deviants into disease sufferers seen worthy of care and compassion.

Despite these benefits, many analysts are wary of medicalization and its potential negative consequences. The sick role, for example, may provide a "medical excuse" for deviance; certainly, it diminishes individual responsibility. As the medical model becomes more attuned to physiological and genetic "causes" of behavior, blame shifts from the person to the body, further displacing responsibility. Medicalization allows for the use of powerful forms of social control, such as psychoactive drugs or surgical procedures. But the guise of medical-scientific neutrality and/or a therapeutic modality means medicalization may be an insidious expansion of social control. Tendencies to individualize and depoliticize social problems are also linked to medicalization. Both obscure insight that deviance may be a reflection of or adaptation to the social organization of a situation; focus on the individual symptoms of gender identity disorder or battery, for example, deflects attention from the heteronormative gender order, gender inequality, and patriarchal values.

Medicalization appears to be on the increase, but how much depends in part on what is measured. One approach looks at the growing number of people diagnosed. Another considers the increasing number of diagnostic categories. In addition to the proliferation of categories, medicalization increases through expansion of extant categories. That is, diagnostic categories themselves may be stretched, encompassing more behavior within their bounds over time. Psychiatric categories, especially the functional disorders, seem especially prone to such expansion. The emergence of adult attention deficit hyperactivity disorder (ADHD), the extension of the uses of the PTSD diagnosis, and the widespread use of psychoactive medications like Prozac for unspecified psychological discomfort are examples of this.

SEE ALSO: Deviance, Constructionist Perspectives; Homophobia and Heterosexism;

Medical Sociology and Genetics; Mental Disorder; Moral Panics; Social Control

SUGGESTED READINGS

Conrad, P. (1992) Medicalization and social control. *Annual Review of Sociology* 19: 209–32.

Horwitz, A. (2002) *Creating Mental Illness*. University of Chicago Press, Chicago, IL.

PJ MCGANN AND PETER CONRAD

deviance, normative definitions of

A normative definition identifies deviance as a violation of a norm held in certain groups or by a majority of the members of the society at large. A norm is a standard about "what human beings should or should not think, say, or do under given circumstances" (Blake & Kingsley 1964). Put another way, a norm is a social expectation concerning thought or behavior in particular situations. To the normative definition, what defines something as deviance is a formal violation of social expectations.

Norms evaluate conduct; recognizing that some acts (including beliefs and the expression of beliefs) ought or ought not to occur, either in specific situations (e.g., no smoking in public elevators) or at any time or place (e.g., no armed robbery, ever). The use of proper etiquette reflects deliberate decisions to adhere to norms of respect and consideration for others. The norms that comprise etiquette are also situational, but are more likely to be codified than norms in many social situations.

The conception of norms as expectations highlights regularities of behavior based on habit or traditional customs. People expect a child, for example, to act a certain way in church, another way on the playground. This raises another dimension of norms: they are situationally bound. Running and yelling of children is appropriate for the playground, but not in church. Laughing is expected behavior in a comedy club, but not at a funeral.

Norms are not necessarily clear-cut rules because they are social properties. They are shared group evaluations or guidelines, and many of them are learned implicitly in the more general process of socialization. Norms are an absolutely essential component of the social order.

There is an enormous number of possible situations in which norms regulate behavior. There is, for example, a norm that guides people's behavior in elevators: one is expected to face the door. Sometimes the rationale for norms is vague. In this example, everyone facing the same direction avoids invading someone else's "personal space," the distance between two strangers that feels most comfortable. This distance varies from culture to culture. Italians are comfortable with less distance between them than are people in the USA.

People risk being labeled as deviant by audiences when they express unacceptable beliefs (such as worshiping devils), violate behavioral norms (such as engaging in proscribed sexual acts), or possessing certain physical traits widely regarded as undesirable, which include physical handicaps (being confined to a wheelchair) and violations of appearance norms (e.g., obesity). The normative sociologist does not have to wait until condemnation takes place to know that something is deviant. It is the violation of what the norms of a society or group say about proper and improper behavior, beliefs, and characteristics that defines them as deviant. For instance, we know in advance that it is a violation of society's norms to walk down the street nude (Gibbs 1972), and hence, that that act is deviant.

SEE ALSO: Deviance, Constructionist Perspectives; Deviance, Positivist Theories of; Deviance, Reactivist Definitions of; Deviant Beliefs/Cognitive Deviance; Norms

REFERENCES

Blake, J. & Kingsley, D. (1964) Norms, values, and sanctions. In: Faris, R. E. L. (ed.), *Handbook of Modern Sociology*. Rand McNally, Chicago, IL.

Gibbs, J. P. (1972) Issues in defining deviant behavior. In: Scott, R. A. & Douglas, J. D. (eds.), *Theoretical Perspectives on Deviance*. Basic Books, New York, pp. 39–68.

ROBERT F. MEIER

deviance, positivist theories of

Sociologists define deviance as the violation of a norm that, if discovered, typically results in punishment, scorn, or stigmatization of the offender. The normative violation can include acts, beliefs, and traits or characteristics. In the social sciences, positivism is usually defined as the natural science approach to social life. This means that the methods by which scientists study the world of biology, chemistry, and physics can be applied – taking their different subject matter into account, of course – to the social and political worlds.

The *sociological* positivist theories that attempt to explain or account for normative violations include but are not limited to social disorganization theory; anomie theory; learning theory; social control theory; and self-control theory.

SOCIAL DISORGANIZATION THEORY

During the 1920s, the sociology faculty at the University of Chicago developed a perspective that has come to be called the Chicago School, or social disorganization theory. These researchers thought the cause of deviance to be the instability of entire neighborhoods and communities. Regardless of their individual characteristics, people who live in such communities have higher rates of non-normative behaviors than persons residing in more stable communities. What makes for unstable or disorganized communities is a lack of social control. By the 1940s, the Chicago School had become regarded as obsolete. But by the late 1980s, social disorganization theory experienced a rebirth of interest, and is now a major perspective in the study of deviance.

ANOMIE THEORY

Closely associated with the early work of Robert Merton (1968), the anomie perspective was a structural theory of crime and delinquency. Modern societies, Merton reasoned, especially the United States, offered their residents substantial opportunities. But while status goals, like materialism and wealth, are stressed, access to these goals is limited and legitimate ways to achieve those goals are not stressed. So while some groups will be successful in achieving goals, others will be frustrated in their search for success. As a result, some will turn to illegitimate means by which to reach their success goals.

LEARNING THEORY

There are a number of learning theories of deviance, but one of the most respected is criminologist Edwin Sutherland's (1947) theory of differential association. Crime and other forms of deviance are the result of learning criminal norms. Sutherland, like other learning theorists, believed that the most powerful learning takes place in small, intimate groups among people who know one another well, such as close friends. Sutherland called the content of most of this learning "definitions favorable to violation of law." In other words, the content of the learning was a justification or motivation to commit a crime. Crime is neither inherited nor inevitable. Rather, it is acquired from others in a process of communication and interaction.

SOCIAL CONTROL THEORY

Social control theory, or more conventionally just control theory, asserts that deviance is not so much learned or the result of societal pressure as simply not controlled (Hirschi 1969). Most of the control in this theory is the individual's bond with society. The closer the bond, the less likely that person will commit a deviant act. There are several elements of the bond, including attachment, commitment, involvement, and belief. Control theory generated a good deal of research and was a leading positivist theory in the 1970s and 1980s.

SELF-CONTROL THEORY

Self-control theory, developed by Michael Gottfredson and Travis Hirschi (1990), is a theory with both learning and control elements. Self-control theory posits that through the general socialization process, some people fail to develop self-control over their behavior. They are therefore more likely to engage in risky acts, including crime, and other behavior that overlooks or neglects the long-term consequences of continuing to engage in that behavior.

SEE ALSO: Anomie; Criminology; Deviance, Crime and; Objectivity; Social Control; Deviance, Normative Definitions of

REFERENCES

Gottfredson, M. & Hirschi, T. (1990) *A General Theory of Crime*. Stanford University Press, Palo Alto, CA.

Hirschi, T. (1969) *Causes of Delinquency*. University of California Press, Berkeley, CA.

Merton, R. K. (1968) *Social Theory and Social Structure*. Free Press, New York.

Sutherland, E. H. (1947) *Criminology*, 4th edn. Lippincott, Philadelphia.

ROBERT F. MEIER

deviance, reactivist definitions of

The sociology of deviance entails two major perspectives, both of which emphasize the relative nature of the phenomenon. The normative perspective, which most sociologists adhere to, views deviance as being located in customs and rules; deviance is the formal violation of one or more norms. The reactivist perspective, which has been associated with the labeling theory of deviance, takes a more radical approach to the relative nature of deviance, and views the existence and characteristics of deviance in how real behaviors, beliefs, or conditions are actually judged by relevant audiences.

The reactivist perspective is commonly traced to the writings of historian Frank Tannenbaum (1938), who highlighted the nature of community reactions to juvenile delinquency as the "dramatization of evil," whereby the social definition of the behavior was attached instead to the people who behaved that way, making them more prone to take on a deviant (evil) role. A little over a decade later, sociologist Edwin M. Lemert (1951) greatly expanded upon this general idea, including broader conceptualizations that related symbolic interactionism to the study of deviance. His classic distinction between primary deviance (related to the original causes of deviant behavior, which he termed "polygenetic," or due to a wide range of causes) and secondary deviance (related to the effective causes, after labeling took place, and a person formed a deviant identity), and his insistence that reactions form the essential quality of the social reality of deviance, formed the basis for the reactivist definition of deviance.

"Strict" reactivists claim that in order for deviance to exist, the act, condition, or belief must first be heard about or witnessed, and second, must be met with concrete social disapproval, condemnation, or punishment. If these conditions are not satisfied, according to strict reactivists, deviance does not socially exist. If acts, beliefs, or conditions are known about and not reacted to as deviant, or if they remain hidden, makes no difference to strict reactivists. Real responses by audiences to concrete phenomena are what matter, and not the act, belief, or condition. Strict reactivists deny that audiences react to phenomena "in the abstract," that is, as *classes* of acts, beliefs, or conditions (Gibbs 1972). It is the real-life expression of some disapproval or condemnation of a specific act that defines deviance, according to strict reactivists.

Although Lemert's work was among the most influential in what became known as the labeling perspective, it is quite clear that he was not a "strict" reactivist. In his landmark work *Social Pathology* (1951), he acknowledges deviant acts that are "clandestine," have "low visibility," and "escape the public eye." That is, deviant forms can exist without actual reactions of audiences. What he does draw major intellectual attention to, however, is that socially visible deviations can attract a wide range of expressions and attitudes from a conforming majority. This entails an important dynamic process between *doing* deviance (for whatever reasons) and *becoming* a deviant (forming a deviant identity) that comprises the heart of the reactivist definition of deviance and the labeling perspective. He wrote that "older sociology ... tended to rest heavily upon the idea that deviance leads to social control. I have come to believe that the reverse idea, i.e., social control leads to deviance, is equally tenable and the potentially richer premise for studying deviance in modern society"(Lemert 1967: v).

Others theorists, most notably Howard Becker and Kai Erikson – the latter of whose work can also be placed within the functionalist school of thought – can be considered moderate reactivists. Unlike strict reactivists, they do not view deviance as simply residing in a concrete negative reaction to an actual behavior. Rather, moderate reactivists believe that the labeling process is crucial to understanding deviance as a social phenomenon and cannot be ignored scientifically.

Their approach centers on the problems inherent in the origins and consequences of labeling, which behaviors are condemned at different times and in different places, selectivity issues, the role and consequences of stigmatization, and the differences between known and secret deviants. In other words, the "soft" or moderate reactivist argues that *categories* of deviance exist, even if *specific* actors, believers, and possessors of non-normative characteristics have not been *concretely* punished or labeled.

SEE ALSO: Deviance; Deviant Beliefs/Cognitive Deviance; Deviance, Normative Definitions of; Symbolic Interaction

REFERENCES

Gibbs, J. P. (1972) Issues in Defining Deviance. In: Scott, R. A. & Douglas, J. D. (eds.), *Theoretical Perspectives on Deviance*. Basic Books, New York, pp. 39–68.

Lemert, E. M. (1951) *Social Pathology: A Systematic Approach to the Study of Sociopathic Behavior*. McGraw-Hill, New York.

Lemert, E. M. (1967) *Human Deviance, Social Problems, and Social Control*. Prentice Hall, Englewood Cliffs, NJ.

Tannenbaum, F. (1938) *Crime and the Community*. Ginn, New York.

HENRY N. PONTELL

deviance, theories of

The term *deviance* is at once denotative and connotative. It points, on the one hand, to thinking about an ill-assorted range of behavior with fuzzy boundaries and indeterminate definition. It attends to the way in which the meaning of deviance is contingent on a politics of power and authority, and, where control becomes a variable, it has been argued, crime is but one of a number of possible outcomes. Theories of deviance were thus potentially wider by far in their reach than criminology and they made the criminal law, criminalization, and the facts of crime newly and interestingly problematic. Indeed, Lemert (1967) and others came to propose that attention should shift away from deviant acts and people towards the phenomena of control. And where control was the variable, rule-making, policing, and regulation came newly into view, no longer to be taken for granted as the backdrop of criminology, but occupying center stage.

But theories of deviance were also importantly connotative. Institutionally anchored in the British National Deviancy Symposium, which flourished for almost a decade from 1968, and in the American Society for the Study of Social Problems and its journal, *Social Problems*, they advertised for many that there had been a conceptual, indeed, for some, political, break with past work whose errors and omissions were sometimes caricatured for dramatic effect.

By and large the new theories succeeded in their object. Criminology is more fully sociological than before. It is now more responsive to the argument that deviant phenomena are emergent, political, negotiated, contingent, and meaningful. And it has moved on. Theories of deviance are still being advanced, and the ethnographic mapping of deviance is still vigorous. They may no longer hold sway as in the past, but their obituary has proved decidedly premature.

Deviance could be represented by the structural-functionalist Talcott Parsons (1951) as the temporary or longer-lasting failure of individual or group adjustment in social systems undergoing change. It could be said by other functionalists to play the unintended role of acting as an illicit support to conventional institutions. It could, by extension, present the dialectical contrasts by which the respectable, normal, and conventional would be recognized and strengthened. And there were those who argued that deviance is manufactured precisely to support the moral order. In structuralist anthropology and sociology it could be a property of classification systems where the deviant was a worrying anomalous phenomenon that did not fit neatly into existing categories, and so posed a threat to the project of collective sense-making and social order. It could recapitulate the symbolic workings of systems of social stratification, where some symmetry may be expected between authority, wealth, and moral esteem, and where deviants are typically to be found among the lowest and least-valued strata or, indeed, outcast altogether. It could thereby refract the capacity of some effectively to assign to others a devalued social status, although such assignments could be, and were, frequently challenged. And it was that link with signifying processes that was perhaps most strongly to promote its elective affinity with the ideas of symbolic interactionism, phenomenology, and ethnomethodology. That bundle of ideas was probably the most distinctive theory of deviance of all, and it entailed a preference for certain methods, notably the ethnographic, and somewhat devalued quantitative approaches. What came to be called labeling theory, methodically explored the symbolic work undertaken when attempts are made to affix the deviant "label" to some person or group of persons, event, process, or phenomenon, encouraging power, "signification," and moral passages to become central topics.

SEE ALSO: Criminology; Deviance; Deviance, Positivist Theories of; Deviant Careers

REFERENCES

Lemert, E. (1967) *Human Deviance, Social Problems, and Social Control*. Prentice Hall, Englewood Cliffs, NJ.

Parsons, T. (1951) *The Social System*. Free Press, New York.

SUGGESTED READINGS

Matza, D. (1969) *Becoming Deviant*. Prentice Hall, Englewood Cliffs, NJ.

Scott, R. & Douglas, J. (eds.) (1972), *Theoretical Perspectives on Deviance*. Basic Books, New York.

PAUL ROCK AND DAVID DOWNES

deviance, women and

Often missing from discussions of deviance and crime is the notion of gender. Gender can be defined as the social positions, attitudes, traits, and behaviors that a society assigns to females and males. A close examination of theories of deviance reveals an androcentric perspective. Barring examinations of a few deviant behaviors (e.g., prostitution), there were, and still are, few serious considerations of female deviance.

Feminists have made a few strides with respect to introducing notions of gender into theories of deviance. While a single theory is still missing from the literature, there are four main schools of thought: (1) the chivalry perspective, (2) patriarchal considerations, (3) women's liberation, and (4) victimization.

The chivalry perspective proposes that girls and women are not seen as deviant because male members of society protect them from the label. Male police officers, prosecutors, and judges have a traditionally chivalrous attitude toward women and treat them with more leniency than men. This theory, regardless of its potential accuracy, perpetuates the cycle of male-centered perspectives, attempting to explain female behavior by examining male attitudes and behaviors.

Patriarchal explanations posit that male-dominated social institutions, especially the family, are designed to prevent girls and women from engaging in deviance and crime. Socialization controls girls more than boys, teaching boys to be risk takers while teaching girls to avoid risk. According to the theory, the behaviors of girls and women are more closely monitored and controlled, resulting in less delinquency.

The remaining two perspectives, the women's liberation hypothesis and the theory of victimization, attempt to explain the deviant behavior of girls and women apart from the attitudes/behavior of males. The women's liberation hypothesis proposes that as the gap between women's and men's social equality decreases, the gap between women's and men's deviant behavior decreases as well. The "liberation" hypothesis, however, has not received much empirical support. Though increasingly represented in the labor force, women continue to be concentrated in traditional "pink-collar" work that reflects a persistence of traditional gender roles. Therefore, this theory would not explain an increase in female crime rates.

One of the most persuasive theories regarding girls' and women's deviance proposes that they are deviants in part because of their status as victims. Chesney-Lind and Pasko (2004) recognize that girls are much more likely to be the victims of childhood sexual abuse than are boys. Additionally, women offenders frequently report abuse/violence in their life histories. Empirical research suggests that exposure to abuse and violence could compel girls/women to engage in various types of deviance (e.g., running away) and crime.

Contemporary research reflects a need to take female deviance and crime much more seriously. There is an increasing body of research examining girls and women engaged in deviance and crime (e.g., female gang members), but most of the contemporary research continues to examine girls and women engaged in traditional deviant and criminal behaviors (e.g., status offenses, prostitution) and/or limits discussions of women and deviance to women's status as victims.

SEE ALSO: Crime; Deviance, Crime and; Deviance, Theories of; Victimization

REFERENCES

Chesney-Lind, M. & Pasko, L. (2004) *The Female Offender: Girls, Women and Crime*. Sage, Walnut Creek, CA.

SUGGESTED READINGS

Hagan, J. (1989) Micro- and macro-structures of delinquency causation and a power-control theory of gender and delinquency. In: Messner, S., Krohn, M., & Liska, A. (eds.), *Theoretical Integration in the Study of Deviance and Crime*. SUNY Press, Albany, NY, pp. 213–28.

Thorne, B. (1994) *Gender Play: Girls and Boys in School*. Rutgers University Press, Piscataway, NJ.

GLORIA GADSDEN

deviant beliefs/cognitive deviance

Sociological discussions of deviance typically focus on non-normative *behaviors*. Cognitive deviance, on the other hand, refers to deviant *beliefs*. Beliefs are deviant if they fall outside the norms of acceptability and are deemed wrong, irrational, eccentric, or dangerous. Deviant beliefs are important to study because they reveal basic social processes and affirm the belief structure on which a society is built. In addition, the study of deviant beliefs is important because deviance is often the first step toward social change. Today's deviant idea may well be tomorrow's norm. The study of deviant beliefs reveals to the sociologist the social construction of all knowledge (Berger & Luckmann 1966).

Deviant beliefs are not always, or necessarily, minority beliefs. In fact, many widespread beliefs are rejected by society's dominant social institutions. Nor are deviant beliefs necessarily wrong or misguided. The empirical, objective, or scientific erroneousness of a belief is not what makes it deviant. What makes a belief deviant is the negative reaction it evokes.

What members of the society, or of specific social collectivities, take to be real and true has momentous consequences for the nature of the society. Beliefs that challenge these collective understandings may be reacted to negatively. Since the costs can be significant, deviant beliefs are difficult to maintain. Occasionally, the fringe may become the mainstream, blasphemy the inspiration, or the nutcase the prophet. Yet more commonly they remain fringe and lunatic. Most deviant beliefs, in fact, come and go with hardly a notice.

SEE ALSO: Belief; Deviance

REFERENCES AND SUGGESTED READINGS

Berger, P. L. & Luckmann, T. (1966) *The Social Construction of Reality: A Treatise in the Sociology of Knowledge*. Doubleday, Garden City, NY.

Goode, E. (2000) *Paranormal Beliefs: A Sociological Introduction*. Waveland Press, Prospect Heights, IL.

ROBIN D. PERRIN

deviant careers

The concept of career has its origin in the sociology of professions, where it has been used since the 1950s with different meanings. The common frame of the career concept is the construction of a related sequence of stages and positions that have to be passed through one after the other. Preceding stages and positions constitute specific preconditions for succeeding stages or positions, but changes of positions as "turning points" or "transitions" between stages have to be explained each by stage-specific social conditions and processes.

The sociology of deviance first adopted a perspective of career within analyses of deviant biographies in the context of the Chicago School of sociology and in the perspective of the "theory of differential association." Also, the multifactor approach of Eleanor and Sheldon Gluck used the concept of career, but only to order variables in a temporal sequence. Synonymous with the career concept, very often the term "natural history" has been employed. Individual developments in deviant behavior normally do not follow institutionalized or organized sequences. Nevertheless, in a retrospective view there can be constructed typical patterns and sequences of development, organized around the deviant behavior itself, by patterns of problematic social conditions in the life course seen as causes of the deviant behavior, or by a sequence of consecutive institutions that have reacted to the deviant behavior.

As a critique of etiological theories looking for uniform causes of deviant behavior within the person, the labeling approach in the 1960s demands explicit analyses of the dynamic processes by which the labels of deviant behavior are constructed, applied to specific persons, and adopted by them. Classical works from this perspective include Becker's analyses of the learning processes of "Becoming a marihuana smoker" (1953), Erving Goffman's (1961) description of individual adaptations and processes of identity development in the context of the total institution, and Scheff's (1966) theory of psychic disorders. Since then the notion of deviant career has spread into everyday meaning in different connections, such as drug career, criminal career, illness career, and poverty career.

SEE ALSO: Crime; Deviance; Drugs, Drug Abuse, and Drug Policy; Labeling; Labeling Theory

REFERENCES

Becker, H. S. (1953) Becoming a marihuana user. *American Journal of Sociology* 59 (2): 235–42.

Goffman, E. (1961) *Asylums*. Doubleday, New York.

Scheff, T. J. (1966) *Being Mentally Ill: A Sociological Theory*. University of Chicago Press, Chicago, IL.

AXEL GROENEMEYER

dialectic

The exact origin of dialectic – change generated by an internal dynamic of contradiction, negation and transcendence – is unclear. Whatever its origin, using Socratic Method in his dialogues – the continual questioning of existing knowledge which leads to the negation or overturning of previously held notions and produces increasingly refined ideas – Plato began to formalize dialectic. Aristotle continued the process, locating dialectic between rhetoric and logic. Dialectic revealed contradictions in argument and facilitated higher syntheses by demonstrating how two incompatible positions shared common truth although it was only non-contradictory logic that produced true knowledge.

By conceptualizing logic itself as dialectical, Hegel made dialectic critical to attaining Absolute Reason. The history of philosophy, Hegel (1971: 83) maintained, was more than "an accumulation of knowledge ordered in a certain manner" – it was the "in and for itself necessary development of thought." Philosophy was thought "brought to consciousness, occupied with itself, made into its own object" using its own, specific capacities and mechanisms for development (Hegel 1971: 82). Hegel's (1991: 133) *Logic* followed the "the doctrine of thought" beginning with "its *immediacy* – the doctrine of the *Concept in-itself*," progressing to thought's "*reflection* and *mediation* – [the doctrine of] the *being-for-itself* and *semblance* of the Concept," ultimately reaching "*being-returned-into-itself* and *its developed being-with-itself*"– that is, the Concept "*in-* and *for-itself*." As critical reflection, dialectic is "the *immanent* transcending [force], in which the one-sidedness and restrictedness of the determinations of the understanding displays itself as what it is, i.e., as their negation" and thereby progresses to grasp their "*immanent coherence*" (Hegel 1991: 128). Through dialectic – using the contradictions found within existing knowledge to transcend it through negation and incorporation into a higher form – philosophy progressed from immediate, partial, one-dimensional forms of understanding (*Verstand*) to a fully mediated, integrated, comprehensive Reason (*Vernunft*).

With Marx, dialectic is more complex because it informs two different facets of his work. First, by "inverting" Hegel, Marx located the dialectic of history in real, existing, "material" social relations. To capture and explain that reality, Marx's presentation had to be able to lay bare the dialectic of social history. The result was a massive (almost 5,000 pages of text), unfinished analysis of capitalism as a complex, dynamic, internally unstable, dialectical whole – and so was the presentation itself.

Marx transcended Hegel in his 1844 manuscripts. Hegel's greatness – "the dialectic of negativity as the moving and producing principle" – arose because he grasped "the self-production of humankind as a process, objectification as loss of the object [*Vergegenständlichung als Entgegenständlichung*], as alienation [*Entäußerung*] and overcoming that alienation" (Marx and Engels 1982: 404–5). Thus Hegel grasped "the essence of *labor*" and understood "objectifying humankind" as "the result of its *own labor*." Marx located the fundamental, generative dynamic of class-divided societies in real, actual labor where, in the process-of-objectification [*Vergegenständlichung*], the product/object stands opposite, confronts and is separated from [*Entgegenständlichung*] the worker. The creative process that should affirm and actualize humankind alienates and "deactualizes" it. This dialectical contradiction creates the dynamic struggle to overcome alienated existence.

To comprehend the dialectic of capitalism, Marx moved "downwards" analytically from the capitalist system as a whole to increasingly specific relations of contradiction. However, to present his analysis, Marx began with the "economic cell-form" of capitalism – the commodity-form of the product of labor and the specific, dialectically opposed value-forms (use-value, value, and exchange-value) and the commensurate forms of labor. Marx progressed toward the concrete whole by explaining the exchange process, then money and its transformation into capital, followed by the labor process, valorization process, manufacture and machinofacture, leading to analyses of absolute and relative surplus value. *Capital*'s three volumes were to reveal – comprehensively – the immanent dialectic leading beyond capitalist social relations.

Caricatured and distorted by Stalin as "dialectical materialism," dialectic was revitalized by Alexander Kojev, Henri Lefebvre, Karl Korsch, Georg Lukács, Herbert Marcuse, Theodor Adorno, and others as they reestablished the true Hegel-Marx connection to dialectic.

SEE ALSO: Critical Theory/Frankfurt School; Dialectical Materialism; Engels, Friedrich; Hegel, G. W. F.; Marx, Karl

REFERENCES

Hegel, G. W. F. (1971) [1805] Introduction to the history of philosophy. In: Lauer, Q. (ed.), *Hegel's Idea of Philosophy*. Fordham University Press, New York, pp. 67–142.

Hegel, G. (1991) [1817] *The Encyclopedia: Logic*, trans. T. F. Geraets, W. A. Suchting, & H. S. Harris. Hackett Publishing Co., Cambridge.

Marx, K. & Engels, F. (1982) *Marx–Engels Gesamtausgabe* (*Marx–Engels Complete Works*) part 1, vol. 2. Dietz, Berlin.

SUGGESTED READING

Marx, K. (1976) [1890] *Capital*, 4th edn., vol. (1), trans. B. Fowkes. Pelican Books, Harmondsworth.

ROB BEAMISH

dialectical materialism

Dialectical materialism became the dominant philosophy of Marxism during the Second International (1889–1917) and, in a different form, the official, formulaic philosophy of all Communist Parties during Joseph Stalin's dictatorship (1929–53).

Marx never used the term dialectical materialism. Nor did he write a comprehensive statement of ontology creating the opportunity to "finish" his incomplete project even though Marx had resisted attempts to convert his "materialist conception" into a totalizing philosophy.

Marx's materialism centered on the labor process as the mediating activity between humankind and nature and the real departure point for understanding social formations and social change. As a result, the ownership of the material conditions of production was a critical focal point. While Marx's "guiding thread" focused on key elements of material production, it did not represent a comprehensive ontology of the natural and social worlds. Marx's works attended to nuance and detail and were not consistent with the dialectical materialism that would emerge.

Engels had intermittently worked on a "dialectics of nature" that incorporated Hegel's dialectic into an eighteenth-century inspired materialism. To bring coherence to "Marxism," Engels used *Anti-Dühring* to link his work on nature with Marx's work to produce a single, comprehensive ontology. Seeking the credibility of "science," other Second International Marxists sought to develop Engels' "dialectical materialism" further.

Soviet theorist Georgi Plekhanov and Lenin pursued their own Engelsian-inspired materialist philosophy which Stalin, as Lenin's heir, instituted as the official philosophy of Marxism-Leninism. Dialectical Materialism (Diamat) brought together a simplistic notion of Hegel's dialectic with a crude materialism to constitute a single, allegedly coherent science that applied to all material, biological, historical, social, and political phenomena.

Maintaining that the social and natural worlds follow the same laws of motion, Diamat's three fundamental laws "explained" change: the transformation of quantity into quality (small quantitative changes lead to abrupt "leaps" of qualitative transformation), the unity of opposites (all phenomena are comprised of opposites which internally "struggle" with each other), and the negation of the negation (in the "struggle of opposites," one negates the other but it is later negated, leading to a higher, more developed unity). All change, according to Diamat, resulted from the crude dialectical triad of thesis–antithesis–synthesis inherent in all social and natural phenomena.

Diamat's significance was political rather than philosophical or scientific. By maintaining that nature and society followed the same laws, human consciousness and initiative became largely incidental aspects of the dialectically materialist totality. Moreover, Diamat's laws held little predictive capacity, leaving the Communist Party as the authoritative interpreter of social history and the guide to further social change. Through Diamat, the Party served as both the ruling intellectual and political force in the USSR.

Karl Korsch's ([1923] 1970) *Marxism and Philosophy* and Georg Lukács's ([1923] 1971) *History and Class Consciousness* fundamentally undermined Diamat's claims. Emphasizing the role of consciousness in history, Korsch and Lukács stimulated later western Marxists to focus on questions of epistemology, ontology, and a renewed understanding of Marx's critique of Hegel. The ensuing focus on the active, mediated engagement of humankind with the "material world" was buttressed by the 1932 publication of Marx's 1844 manuscripts, and the 1940s publication of the *Grundrisse*. Both texts undermined Diamat as a credible legacy to Marx's materialist conception of history.

SEE ALSO: Base and Superstructure; Dialectic; Marx, Karl; Materialism

SUGGESTED READINGS

Central Committee of the Communist Party of the Soviet Union (eds.) (1939) *History of the Communist Party of the Soviet Union (Bolsheviks): Short Course*. Foreign Languages Publishing House, Moscow.

Lichtheim, G. (1961) *Marxism: An Historical and Critical Study*. F. Praeger Publishers, New York.

ROB BEAMISH

diaspora

The term "diaspora" originates from the Greek "dia" (over) and "speiro" (to sow). The Greeks understood diaspora as migration and colonization of new lands. In modern parlance the term diaspora usually refers to ethnic groups whose sizeable parts have lived outside their country of origin for at least several generations, while maintaining some ties (even if purely symbolic or sentimental) to the historic homeland. The "classic" diasporas in terms of the oldest history of dispersion are Jewish, Armenian, and Greek; the more modern (and also more numerous) diasporas include African ("black American") diaspora resulting from forced migration of slaves to the Americas; Irish, Italian, Polish, Chinese, and Indian diasporas resulting from voluntary migrations.

Today the word diaspora is applied to a broad range of migrant populations whose current or historic uprooting was politically or economically motivated, including political refugees, voluntary migrants, guest workers, expatriates, stable ethnic minorities, and other dispersed groups. Modern political and social thinkers put forward several criteria for defining ethnic communities as diasporas: a history of dispersal (often forced or motivated by harsh living conditions), myths and memories of homeland, alienation in the host country, desire for eventual return (which can be ambivalent, eschatological or utopian), ongoing support of the homeland, and a collective identity (often including common linguistic and cultural practices). Thus, German diaspora embraces many generations of ethnic Germans in Eastern Europe and the former Soviet Union (most of whom returned to unified Germany over the 1990s); Turkish/Kurdish diaspora includes at least two generations of guest workers in Germany; Filipino diaspora embraces two generations of women and men working in nursing and personal services across the western world.

Some communities that used to have strong diasporic consciousness during the initial two or three generations upon resettlement, later on assimilated in the receiving societies and lost active ties with their homelands – the examples include Irish and Italian immigrants in North America and Australia. Other diasporas continued to exist for centuries without an actual homeland (e.g., 1,500 years of living in *galut* – dispersion – in the case of the Jews) or even without a tangible concept of a homeland, like Gypsies, or Roma, scattered across Europe and Asia. Indeed, the term diaspora has acquired metaphoric implications and is often used as a generic description of displaced people who feel, maintain, invent or revive a connection with a prior home, real or imagined.

SEE ALSO: Globalization, Culture and; Immigration; Migration: International

SUGGESTED READING

Cohen, R. (1997). *Global Diasporas: An Introduction*. University College of London Press, London.

LARISSA REMENNICK

disability as a social problem

Common sense takes disability as a simple natural fact, but the sociology of disability emphasizes that disability has to be differentiated from impairment. Not every chronic health condition is acknowledged as disability. There are cultures in which the social fact of disability does not exist. Disability as a social problem has evolved as a product of the modern welfare state. With the beginning of modernity and, above all, during the period of industrialization, a line was drawn between "the disabled" and other poor and unemployed people. In the course of the twentieth century disability became a horizontal category of social stratification. Even today the ascription process is ambivalent: it includes rights and benefits as well as discrimination and segregation.

Despite many efforts, an internationally accepted definition of disability does not exist. Nonetheless, on the national level classifications that constitute disability as social fact are in operation. Pedagogical diagnostics defining special educational needs are of great significance for establishing individual positions, not only in the school system but also in later life. Medical experts serve as gatekeepers to the rehabilitation system and have great influence on disability categories, while legislation and courts serve as agencies to control disability as a social problem.

The World Health Organization (WHO) made special efforts to find a universal disability concept on an international level. In 1980 it published the Classification of Impairments, Disabilities, and Handicaps (ICIDH). It was based on a threefold model: "impairment" denoted a defect or disorder in the medical sense, "disability" meant functional limitations, and "handicap" indicated the individual inability to fulfill normal social roles. More than 20 years later, the WHO (2001) revised this classification scheme. The topical Classification of Functioning, Disability, and Health (ICF) uses a multidimensional approach. Its first part, "functioning and disability," differentiates between "body functions and structures" and "activities and participation." The second part consists of "contextual factors" and contains "environmental" and "personal" factors. The use of the participation concept as well as the reference to environmental factors are important novelties in contrast to the ICIDH. Additionally, terminology was changed. The term disability now comprises medically defined impairments as well as activity limitations and participation restrictions. The term handicap was completely given up. Despite these innovations disability studies scholars criticize the ICF because the social model of disability was only half-heartedly implemented.

Since the 1960s, Goffman's (1963) stigma theory has been dominant in the sociology of disability. This microsociological approach views disability as constituted in social interaction. If a person has a highly visible bodily feature or behaves in a peculiar way and is therefore negatively valued by interaction partners, he or she becomes stigmatized. The stigma will result in social distance, but at the same time interaction rules demand "quasi-normalcy" to be maintained. For this reason, "mixed" social situations are typically characterized by feelings of ambivalence and insecurity about how to act. Stigma theory makes it possible to analyze disability not as an inner personal characteristic, but as a product of social relations.

SEE ALSO: Body and Society; Social Epidemiology; Social Exclusion; Concept and Perspectives; Sociology in Medicine; Stigma

REFERENCES

Goffman, E. (1963) *Stigma: Notes on the Management of Spoiled Identity*. Prentice Hall, Englewood Cliffs, NJ.

World Health Organization (2001) *International Classification of Functioning, Disability and Health: ICF.* World Health Organization, Geneva.

SUGGESTED READING

Albrecht, G. L., Seelman, K. D., & Bury, M. (eds.) (2001) *Handbook of Disability Studies.* Sage, Thousand Oaks, CA.

ANNE WALDSCHMIDT

discourse

The primary definition of discourse denotes a method of communication that conforms to particular structural and ethnographic norms and marks a particular social group by providing a means of solidarity for its members and a means of differentiating that group from other groups. It is more accurate and useful to regard this concept in the plural, that is, as *discourses*, thus encompassing its capacity not only for marking boundaries (using linguistic borders philosopher Kenneth Burke called "terministic screens," which are essentially the points at which one discourse becomes distinct from another), but also as a method in many disciplines.

Discourses come to be in different ways. One discourse may be chosen by the group to specifically designate its identity and membership (called a discourse community). Another discourse also may be imposed or identified by others as a means of stratification or "othering" a group, such as a pidgin language or other "non-standard language variety." Yet other discourses develop more natively, determined by cultural, technological, or other factors.

A second definition of discourse lies within the field of linguistics and underlies the metatheory discourse analysis, a term brought into use in 1952 by linguist Z. S. Harris. This definition, which to some degree defines and therefore precedes the others, holds that discourse describes extra-grammatical linguistic units, variably described as speech acts, speech events, exchanges, utterances, conversations, adjacency pairs, or combinations of these and other language chunks. The basic distinction ascribed to this definition is its extra-sentential status. Thus, to the linguist, discourse is often referred to as the study of language above the sentence.

The term discourse also functions as a way of identifying an approach to a subject (as in analyzing a discourse community or terministic screen), a way of identifying the methodology used to extract information (as in therapeutic analysis), or a way of identifying a subject in itself (as in of extra-grammatical analyses of linguistic phenomena). Further, the number of graduate-level discourse studies programs is growing in English-speaking countries, promising an interest in the subject of discourse now and well into the future. The omnipresence of the term confirms its inherent interdisciplinary and cross-disciplinary value. That said, the term may also be in danger of overuse. Appropriating the term to describe virtually any use of language diminishes its capacity to function as shown above.

SEE ALSO: Conversation Analysis; Language; Sociolinguistics

REFERENCE

Harris, Z. S. (1952) Discourse analysis. *Language* 28: 1–30.

SUGGESTED READINGS

Burke, K. (1966) Terministic screens. In: *Language as Symbolic Action.* University of California Press, Berkeley, CA, pp. 44–62.
Gumperz, J. (1982) *Discourse Strategies.* Cambridge University Press, Cambridge.
Schiffrin, D. (1994) *Approaches to Discourse.* Blackwell, Oxford.

MARTIN M. JACOBSEN

discrimination

Discrimination refers to the differential, and often unequal, treatment of people who have been either formally or informally grouped into a particular class of persons. There are many forms of discrimination that are specified according to the ways in which particular groups are identified, including race, ethnicity, gender, sexual orientation, marital status, class, age, disability, nationality, religion, or language. The United Nations Charter (1954) declared in article 55 that the UN will promote human rights and freedoms for all, "without distinction as to race, sex, language, and religion." Later in 1958, the Universal Declaration of Human Rights added eight further grounds for possible discrimination, which were color, political or other opinion, national or social origin, property, birth, or other status.

Banton (1994) notes that the family, the ethnic group, and the state are all based on acts of discrimination. In families, different individuals have differing roles and obligations that require particular types of behavior, for example husband and wife and parent and child. Members of ethnic groups may differentiate in their association with or exclusion of other people depending on the identification of their ethnic origins. States frequently discriminate between citizens and non-citizens in conferring rights and responsibilities. Although discrimination is often an individual action, it is also a social pattern of aggregate behavior. So, structures of inequality may be reproduced over generations through repeated patterns of differential treatment. Here, individuals are denied opportunities and resources for reasons that are not related to their merits, capacities, or behavior but primarily because of their membership of an identifiable group.

Discrimination takes many forms. Marger (2000) identifies a "spectrum of discrimination," which includes wide variations in both its forms and severity. Broadly, three categories of discrimination are identified as comprising this spectrum. Firstly, the most severe acts of discrimination involve mass societal aggression such as the annihilation of native peoples in North America, South Africa, and Australia, the Nazi Holocaust, plantation slavery, or more recent massacres of ethnic groups in Rwanda and Bosnia. Violent racism and domestic violence are two further examples of widespread discriminatory aggression. Secondly, discrimination involves denial of access to societal opportunities and rewards, for example in employment, education, housing, health, and justice. Thirdly, use of derogatory, abusive verbal language that is felt to be offensive (e.g., "Paki," "nigger"), which, together with racist jokes, use of Nazi insignia, and unwitting stereotyping and pejorative phrases, may all constitute lesser forms of discrimination. Dualistic notions of degradation and desire, love and hate, purity and disease, and inferiority and superiority may be involved in discursive strategies through which forms of discrimination are expressed. Explanations for discrimination require complex accounts that are able to embrace micropsychological processes, individual and group experiences, competition and socialization, together with structural power relations and aspects of globalization.

Poststructuralist and postmodernist directions in contemporary sociological theory have nurtured an increasing focus on the complexity of interactions between different forms of discrimination. The critique of the conceptual inflation of racism, which warns against labeling institutional practices as racist as they may have exclusionary effects on other groups, further supports the building of sociological complexity into the study of how discrimination works. This shift is also apparent in the development of international and national protections and remedies. Here, development of human rights approaches that emphasize particularly freedom from discrimination and respect for the dignity of individuals and their ways of life and personal development seek to build a collective agenda that encompasses the needs and interests of all individuals and groups. The shift toward the creation of general equality commissions in the UK and in Europe and the dismantling of institutions concerned with separate forms of discrimination such as race or disability further exemplifies this process. In future research, focus on the interactions between different structures of discrimination is likely to be key.

SEE ALSO: Gender Bias; Homophobia; Race (Racism); Racism, Structural and Institutional; Stereotyping and Stereotypes

REFERENCES

Banton, M. (1994) *Discrimination*. Open University Press, Buckingham.

Marger, M. N. (2000) *Race and Ethnic Relations*. Wadsworth, Stamford, CT.

SUGGESTED READINGS

Hepple, B. & Szyszczak, E. M. (eds.) (1992) *Discrimination: The Limits of Law*. Mansell, London.

Law, I. (1996) *Racism, Ethnicity, and Social Policy*. Harvester Wheatsheaf/Prentice Hall, Hemel Hempstead.

IAN LAW

distanciation and disembedding

Distanciation and disembedding are core elements of Anthony Giddens' structuration theory. Distanciation captures the ways in which societies are embedded within a particular context. As a social system experiences a gradual separation of space and time in the course of modernization, and intensified by globalization, particular forms of social practice become disembedded, or lifted out, from the immediate milieu within which they originated.

At the turn of the twentieth century, Simmel spoke acutely of how the spatial helped determine and symbolize social relationships and how the arrival of "a firmly fixed framework of time ... transcends all subjective elements" (1972/1903: 328). Polanyi's hugely influential corpus, especially *The Great Transformation* (1944), described how in non-market societies redistributive and reciprocal exchanges were "embedded" in particular sociocultural nexuses. With the development of market economies production and distribution became unfixed, or "disembedded," from local institutional norms and values. Social relations are then re-embedded in market economies.

Giddens attempts to expose limitations in functionalist and evolutionary social theories by revealing an over-emphasis on the distinction between synchrony and diachrony. Drawing on philosopher Heidegger and geographer Hägerstrand, Giddens claims that time and space are constitutive of social structure and consequently all social action. First, to respect human agency as embodied is to recognize its occupation of a physical space at a particular time; any human interaction is permeated by its specific spatio-temporal position. Moreover, social systems can be conceptualized according to their extension across time–space. In the premodern world, interaction with those physically absent was minimal so that, according to Giddens, time and space were intertwined. The question of "when" was generally meaningful through its association to a particular place. The arrival of mechanized time was significant since it allowed the sharing of a "space" by those not physically present to each other. Thus, social relations became ever more "phantasmagoric," that is, moulded by influences distant from them.

This decoupling of time and space permits processes of disembedding. As social relations are stretched across time–space they can be detached from the local circumstances which gave rise to them. Two central disembedding mechanisms are symbolic tokens (e.g. money) and expert systems (e.g. law). These two "abstract systems" provide impersonal guarantees across time–space of expectations that are validated external to the interaction. Hence, they reinforce time–space distanciation. This simultaneously widens the scope of possibilities for the self by reducing place's constraints while encouraging "reflexive monitoring," that is, the continuous and conscious evaluation of social interactions.

SEE ALSO: Globalization; New Institutional Theory; Polanyi, Karl; Risk; Simmel, Georg; Space; Structuration Theory; Time-Space

REFERENCES

Simmel, G. (1972) [1903] The metropolis and mental life. In: *On Individuality and Social Forms*. University of Chicago Press, Chicago, IL.

Simmel, G. (1972) *On Individuality and Social Forms*. University of Chicago Press, Chicago, IL.

SUGGESTED READINGS

Giddens, A. (1991) *The Consequences of Modernity*. Stanford University Press: Stanford, CA.

Giddens, A. (1981) *A Contemporary Critique of Historical Materialism*, vol. 1. Macmillan Press: London.

JOSEPH BURKE

distinction

Distinction references the social consequences of expressions of taste. When people consume – whether it be popular culture, leisure, fine arts, the home, vacations, or fashion – these actions, among other things, act to express tastes. And tastes are not innocuous. Rather, what and how people consume can act as a social reproduction mechanism. So expressions of taste are acts of distinction to the extent that they signal, and help to reproduce, differences in social class. Distinction can be distinguished from other important class reproduction mechanisms such as educational credentials, the accumulation of financial assets, and membership in clubs and associations.

Pierre Bourdieu in his seminal *Distinction: A Social Critique of the Judgment of Taste* (1984) makes three major contributions to the idea of distinction. First, he carefully unpacks and details the independent contributions of economic capital and what he terms cultural capital. Economic capital allows one to express tastes for luxurious and scarce goods, much like Veblen describes. Cultural capital is different in that it consists of the socialized tastes that come from "good breeding": growing up among educated parents and peers. Cultural elites express tastes that are conceptual, distanced, ironic, and idiosyncratic. So rather than a unidimensional social class hierarchy, Bourdieu is able to specify carefully how class fractions are composed (and often clash) due to differences in their relative amounts of economic and cultural capital.

Second, he specifies a materialist theory that explains why different class fractions tend toward particular tastes. He traces the causal linkages between social conditions and tastes; for example, the economic deprivations of the working class lead to the "taste for necessity." Rather than a consensus model, with Bourdieu's theory, one is able to predict the kinds of cultural products different class fractions will like and the ways in which they will consume them.

Third, what is most notable about Bourdieu's book, and least commented upon, is his nuanced eye for the subtle distinguishing practices that pervade everyday life. Much like Erving Goffman, Bourdieu is able to pick apart the micro details – how one dresses, how one vacations, the way in which one justifies aesthetic preferences – to reveal their broader sociological impact.

Bourdieu's research has stimulated a variety of empirical studies that have sought to test the relationship between tastes and social reproduction.

The results of these studies have been inconclusive. One of the inherent problems in such studies is that cultural practices that communicate distinction are often quite subtle. Many of these practices are not easily captured by conventional social science constructs, nor by survey measures, the primary method for follow-up studies to date.

SEE ALSO: Bourdieu, Pierre; Capital: Economic, Cultural, and Social; Cultural Capital

REFERENCE

Bourdieu, P. (1984) *Distinction: A Social Critique of the Judgment of Taste*. Harvard University Press, Cambridge, MA.

DOUGLAS B. HOLT

diversity

When applied to social phenomena, the term "diversity" generally refers to the distribution of units of analysis (e.g., people, students, families) in a specific social environment (e.g., workplace, classroom, nation-state) along a dimension (e.g., mother tongue, social class, political orientation). Measures of levels of diversity, such as the Index of Dissimilarity, usually define the maximum level of diversity as occurring when the units of analysis (e.g., people) are distributed evenly across the social dimension (e.g., racial categories). However, it is also common for a political ideal to serve as the benchmark in the assessment of levels of diversity. An American work setting may be considered to be appropriately diverse with respect to gender, for example, if the proportion of workers who are women is comparable to the proportion of applicants who are women.

Levels of racial and ethnic diversity are a particularly important issue in many societies because race and ethnicity are strongly related to issues of power, social inequality, and access to societal resources. Low levels of racial and ethnic diversity within a nation's major social institutions, such as its labor force, educational system, and political system, often lead to studies of discrimination and processes of exclusion, and social policies designed to redress these inequities. Diversity can also be assessed within and across physical space. This approach leads to studies of residential segregation. Studies of phenomena such as inter-religious marriages and interracial adoption highlight the presumption that the more intimate social domains such as the family are expected to be homogeneous, i.e., not diverse, along important dimensions such as race and religion.

Levels of diversity in a specific social setting are important not just because the causes may lie in social inequality, but because levels of diversity in one dimension can lead to group-specific levels of inequality in another dimension. For example, high levels of occupational segregation by sex and race (i.e., low levels of diversity within occupations) help produce sex-specific and race-specific differentials in earnings. High (or increases in) levels of diversity can also lead to interpersonal discomfort, cultural misunderstandings, and at worst, result in intergroup conflict. Groups in power may therefore seek to maintain low levels of diversity.

High levels of diversity along many social dimensions, however, can have positive social connotations. Highly diverse settings provide numerous opportunities for intergroup interactions and therefore opportunities for the clearing of misunderstandings and the dissolving of cultural barriers. In racially diverse schools, for example, children are more likely to form interracial friendships. Levels of interracial marriage are higher in geographical areas that are racially diverse. The rationale for affirmative action policies in the USA includes the presumptive positive effects of diversity on intergroup relations as well as the issue of equity of opportunity for minority group members. Highly diverse settings, by virtue of including people with a wide variety of characteristics, can also result in a more equitable representation of opinions and sharing of resources.

SEE ALSO: Affirmative Action; Family Diversity; Segregation

SUGGESTED READINGS

Blau, P. M., Blum, T. C., & Schwartz, J. E. (1982) Heterogeneity and intermarriage. *American Sociological Review* 47: 45–62.
Greenberg, J. H. (1956) The measurement of linguistic diversity. *Language* 32: 109–15.

GILLIAN STEVENS

division of labor

The concept of the division of labor is used by both structural functionalists, the students of Durkheim, and conflict theorists, the students of Marx, but the meaning of the concept differs. For Durkheim it means the occupational structure, and it also includes a new form of social solidarity – organic solidarity – that integrates the members of industrial societies in contrast to the mechanical solidarity of traditional societies. Durkheim saw this as a weaker, more precarious form of solidarity that was still in the process of development in the early twentieth century. For Marx it means a double division of labor: the technical division of labor in the enterprise that broke down the production process into a sequence of tasks, and the social division of labor among enterprises, industries and social classes that was mediated through commodity exchanges in market relations. While the social labor of the enterprise was rationally organized, Marx saw contradictions and class exploitation and domination in the social division of labor.

Durkheim saw the problems in terms of both the tendency to anomie, or normlessness, and the "forced division of labor." He thought that a new corporate order constituted by professional and occupational organizations would create a new moral order which would address the first problem. These organizations would mediate between the level of the state and the level of employers and workers. He thought the abolition of inherited wealth would address the second problem and allow those with natural talent to assume appropriate positions in the division of labor regardless of their social locations. On the other hand, Marx saw the problems as rooted in alienated labor and the exploitation of living labor by capital in the social division of labor. When the working class sells its labor power, its only commodity, to the capitalist class, it alienates control of the labor process and the wealth created in that process to the class that owns and/or controls private property. Further, the capitalist class takes advantage of the fact that during the labor process the working class creates more value than is returned to it in the form of the wage. The transformation of value is a metamorphic process that renders exploitation opaque to the members of the working class in contrast to the transparent process of exploitation in the production and property relations based on slavery, caste, or serfdom. Marx saw class conflict and a social revolution led by a class conscious working class as the agent of societal transformation.

Henri Lefebvre has extended Marx's analysis of production relations in the social division of labor to consumption and the reproduction of the relations of production by incorporating cultural processes as well as relations of domination and subordination that are not reduced to the mode of production as orthodox Marxists do. According to Lefebvre capitalism has undergone a mutation from its classical nineteenth-century form, the bureaucratic society of controlled consumption. When the working class failed to become a revolutionary agent, the technocrats brought stability and cohesion to a society that lacked both through their deployment of bureaucratic forms of organization and the ideology of technological modernism – the introduction of trivial technological changes on the surface of this society while the capitalist relations of production remained fundamentally unchanged. Class relations in the social division of labor do not have a life of their own; they do not persist due to inertia; they need to be reproduced in everyday life. For Lefebvre, culture is a means of distribution, especially the advertising form. Further, Lefebvre conceptualizes a new "state mode of production" where the state plays a critical role in promoting economic growth and in reproducing the relations of production. Lefebvre calls for an urban revolution and a revolution in everyday life. Production relations would be reoriented to the production of social needs and "rights to the city" that would be extensions of citizenship rights.

Current research is focusing on the globalization of the division of labor with new topics: information technologies, the deskilling of labor, automation, the transformation of production from manufacturing to services, and the outsourcing of production to developing nations. The students of Durkheim often see these developments as the inevitable consequences of technological change, a relentless force that escapes human agency. Whereas the students of Marx see these developments as an extension of alienated labor (Braverman) and class exploitation to a higher level through neocolonialism (Wallerstein), or through the colonization of everyday life (Debord).

SEE ALSO: Durkheim, Émile; Marx, Karl; Solidarity: Mechanical and Organic

SUGGESTED READINGS

Braverman, H. (1974) *Labor and Monopoly Capital*. Monthly Review Press, New York & London.

Durkheim, É. (1984) *The Division of Labor in Society*. Free Press, New York.

Lefebvre, H. (1976) *The Survival of Capitalism*. Allison and Busby, London.

Marx, K. (1977) *Capital*, vol. 1, 1st edn. Vintage, New York.

Wallerstein, I. (1976) *The Modern World System*. Academic Press, New York.

MICHAEL T. RYAN

divisions of household labor

Prior to the Industrial Revolution, economic production was organized around the home, and households were relatively self-sufficient. Households were multifunctional, acting, among other things, as eating establishment, educational institution, factory, and infirmary. Everyone belonging to the household, including family members, servants, and apprentices, did their part in the household's productive labor. The word "housework," first used in 1841 in England and in 1871 in the USA, would have made little sense prior to that time, since *all* work was focused in and around the home.

Over the course of the nineteenth century, however, the Industrial Revolution severed the workplace from the place of residence. Coinciding with this process, the ideology of separate spheres emerged, reflecting an increasing tendency for men to seek work in urban factories while women stayed home to look after the family. This ideology defined not only separate spheres, but different personality characteristics and divergent family roles for men and women, as well. In doing so, it naturalized the notion that men, strong and unemotional, should occupy the status of family breadwinner. Conversely, women, frail, pure, and living under the spell of the "cult of true womanhood," should aspire to nothing more profound than being good wives, mothers, and homemakers.

Thus, as men and single women ventured forth to work in the impersonal factories and workplaces of urban centers, married women, particularly those of the middle classes, stayed home to cook, clean, and raise the children. Production and productive activities moved out of these households into the industrializing workplace. Concurrently, the value and status of men's labor went up, while that of women's household labor went down. Previously an integral part of the home-centered production process, middle-class women found themselves with less "productive" work to do. As a result, their energies became more focused on reproductive work, which included making sure that their husbands and children were clean, well-fed, clothed, and nurtured. Although economic necessity continued to force working-class wives and women of color to seek employment outside of the home, the pattern of separate spheres reflected an ideal that most families desired to emulate. Toward the end of the nineteenth century, as households were increasingly motivated to purchase industrially produced necessities, women also became the family household consumption experts. As such, they orchestrated the family's purchase of food, clothing, soap, candles, and other material necessities that they had once helped produce in the home.

Today, in the USA and much of the industrialized world, household labor continues to be performed mostly by women, with chores themselves also segregated by gender. Women are still doing the majority of "routine" tasks, including cooking and meal preparation, meal clean-up and dish washing, laundry, house cleaning, and grocery shopping. Men, on the other hand, do the occasional chores such as lawn mowing, household repairs, car maintenance, and, less often, bill paying. Characteristically, routine chores tend to be more repetitious, time consuming, time sensitive, and boring than occasional chores, which are less tedious and can usually be completed when convenient. While studies of household labor tend to separately analyze routine and occasional housework, they often omit childcare or, alternatively, include it as a separate category of family work. Nevertheless, the presence of children also substantially increases the amount of routine housework that needs to be done, so the amount of household labor that women perform tends to go up when children are born. Men, on the other hand, spend more time in paid labor when children arrive, but often reduce their household labor participation. Some studies suggest that when men do more childcare, they may also increase their contributions to housework.

International trends largely appear to reflect those occurring in the USA. Women in most developed countries do the majority of the routine housework, although their contributions are declining while those of their male partners are increasing slightly. Japanese wives, for instance, continue to report doing a large majority of housework. On the other hand, wives in many formerly Soviet countries more often report that their husbands share housework equally than do women in the USA. Still, women in most countries devote well over half of their work time to unpaid labor while men devote one-third of their work time or less. The presence of young children increases women's unpaid labor time substantially more than that of men, while, in many countries, women whose education level exceeds that of their husbands do relatively less housework. Moreover, women worldwide are balancing their unpaid family work with increased time spent in the paid labor force, and while men's economic activity rates have decreased in many areas, women's rates have generally increased.

SEE ALSO: Gender Ideology and Gender Role Ideology; Gender, Work, and Family

SUGGESTED READINGS

Baxter, J. (1997) Gender equality and participation in housework: a cross-national perspective. *Journal of Comparative Family Studies* 28: 220–47.

Bianchi, S. M., Milkie, M. A., Sayer, L. C., & Robinson, J. P. (2000) Is anyone doing the housework? Trends in the gender division of household labor. *Social Forces* 79: 191–228.

MICHELE ADAMS

divorce

A major social trend during the past century has been a global increase in the divorce rate. During the second half of the twentieth century divorce rates increased in most industrialized countries. Some of the social characteristics that appear to have contributed to the increase in the divorce rate are increased individualism, increasing marital expectations, the economic independence of women, and no-fault divorce laws. During the past 30 years there has been a gradual decrease in the US divorce rate.

Divorce is a complex process influenced by many social and individual characteristics. Factors that have been found to be associated with the risk of divorce include age at marriage, premarital cohabitation, parental divorce, infidelity, alcohol and drug abuse, poor financial management, and domestic violence.

Numerous researchers have found that compared with married persons, divorced persons tend to have more economic hardship, higher levels of poverty, lower levels of psychological well-being, less happiness, more health problems, and a greater risk of mortality. Cross-national data have confirmed similar findings in 20 countries across the world. One of the ongoing questions among social scientists is whether the differences between married and divorced individuals are due to selection or the stress of divorce. Recent research indicates that divorce appears to have a significant impact on well-being that is not explained by selection.

Four key factors tend to be associated with adjustment following divorce. First, those with adequate financial resources are more likely to adjust to the divorce. Second, those with a new intimate relationship (dating regularly, cohabiting, or remarried) are better adjusted. Third, divorce adjustment is more difficult for older than younger individuals. Fourth, social networks provide encouragement, support, and other resources.

SEE ALSO: Cohabitation; Family Demography; Marriage

SUGGESTED READINGS

Amato, P. R. (2000) The consequences of divorce for adults and children. *Journal of Marriage and the Family* 62: 1269–87.

Wang, H. & Amato, P. R. (2000) Predictors of divorce adjustment: stressors, resources, and definitions. *Journal of Marriage and the Family* 62: 655–68.

STEPHEN J. BAHR, CHAO-CHIN LU, AND JONATHAN H. WESTOVER

doing gender

Candace West and Don Zimmerman introduced the concept "doing gender" in an article of the same title in 1987. They were the first to articulate an *ethnomethodological* perspective on the creation and affirmation of gender inequality between males and females in western society. The purview of ethnomethodology includes the study of the socially managed accomplishments of all aspects of life that are treated as objective, unchanging, and transsituational. West and Zimmerman's treatment of gender began by making problematic the prevailing cultural perspective: (1) female and male represent naturally defined categories of being that are derived from mutually exclusive (and easily distinguished) reproductive functions, and which result in distinctively different psychological and behavioral proclivities; (2) such divisions are rooted in that biological nature, which makes them both fundamental and enduring; (3) these essential differences between masculine and feminine are adequately reflected in the myriad differences observed between women and men and the social arrangements that solidify around them.

In clear contradiction to these notions, West and Zimmerman asserted that sex is founded on the socially agreed-upon biological criteria for initial assignment to sex category, but that classification typically has little to do with the everyday and commonsense sex categorization engaged in by members of a social group. They argued that it is not a rigid set of criteria that is applied to establish confidence that someone is male *or* female, but a seamless application of an "if–can" test. If someone *can be seen* as a member of an appropriate category, then he or she *should* be categorized accordingly. Following this assertion, West and Zimmerman were obliged to describe the process by which sex categorization is construed, created, and reaffirmed. They did this through the concept of "doing gender."

This concept challenged the current thinking about gender as an attribute, an individual set of performative displays (largely separate from the ongoing affairs of social life), or a response to vaguely defined role expectations. They completed what Dorothy Smith (2002: x) deemed "a ruthless but invaluable surgery" by distinguishing among sex, sex category, and gender. Under this new formulation, gender could no longer be seen as a social "variable" or individual "characteristic" but as a socially situated accomplishment. West and Zimmerman argued that the implication of such ubiquity is that the design and interpretation of social conduct can at any time be made subject to concerns about sex category. Thus individuals and their behavior – *in virtually any course of action* – can be evaluated in relation to a womanly or manly nature and character.

ELABORATIONS

Following the initial formulation in *Gender and Society*, Candace West and Sarah Fenstermaker clarified and extended the concept of "doing gender." Their interest widened to focus on the implications of the concept for explicating practices of inequality and on the application of the concept to empirical work. The subsequent theoretical commentary of West and Fenstermaker focused primarily on the relevance of gender to various forms of interpersonal and institutional inequality and to the extension of the concept to include race and class. They were motivated by an interest in the *social mechanisms* by which the various outcomes of social inequality (e.g., job discrimination, sexual harassment, violence against women, hate crime, differential treatment by gender in school, church, and government) are created and legitimated.

In their article "Doing difference" (1995), West and Fenstermaker posed a theoretical problem that took them well beyond their earlier preoccupation with gender. At the time, feminist sociological theory was beginning to pose questions about the categorical "intersectionality" of social life. West and Fenstermaker observed that there was little in the existing literature on gender that provided for an understanding of how race, class, and gender could operate *simultaneously* to shape and ultimately determine the outcomes of inequality. If such "intersections" or "interlocking categories" could go beyond metaphor, what was needed was a conceptual mechanism that illuminated "the relations between individual and institutional practice and among forms of domination" (West & Fenstermaker 1995: 19).

To adapt the argument offered in "Doing gender," West and Fenstermaker asserted that while the *resulting manifestations* of sexism, class oppression, and racism are certainly different, the mechanism by which such inequalities unfold are the same. That is, "difference" is done (invidious distinctions justified on grounds of race, class, or gender) within individual and institutional domains to produce social inequalities. These practices are influenced by existing social structure, but also serve to reinscribe the rightness of such practices over time.

SEE ALSO: Ethnomethodology; Femininities/Masculinities; Gender Ideology and Gender Role Ideology; Sex and Gender; Socialization, Gender

REFERENCES

Fenstermaker, S. & West, C. (2002) *Doing Gender, Doing Difference: Inequality, Power, and Institutional Change.* Routledge, New York.

Smith, D. (2002) Foreword. In: Fenstermaker, S. & West, C. (eds.), *Doing Difference, Doing Gender*. Routledge, New York, pp. ix–xii.

West, C. & Fenstermaker, S. (1995) Doing difference. *Gender and Society* 9 (1): 8–37.

West, C. & Zimmerman, D. (1987) Doing gender. *Gender and Society* 1 (2): 125–51.

SARAH FENSTERMAKER

domestic violence

Domestic violence is a pattern of coercive behavior designed to exert power and control over a person in an intimate relationship through the use of intimidating, threatening, harmful, or harassing behavior. Victims of domestic violence are primarily female. Bachman and Saltzman (1995) found that women are up to six times as likely to be assaulted by a partner or ex-partner than by a stranger and they are more likely to suffer an injury when their assailant is an intimate (Bachman and Carmody 1994). Domestic violence is one of the leading causes of injury to women in the USA. Domestic violence rates also vary by age and economic status, with highest victimization rates among the poor and females between the ages of 16 and 24 years.

SEE ALSO: Violence

REFERENCES

Bachman, R. & Carmody, D. C. (1994) Fighting fire with fire: the effects of self-protective behavior utilized by female victims of intimate versus stranger perpetrated assaults. *Journal of Family Violence* 9 (4): 319–31.

Bachman, R. & Saltzman, R. E. (1995) Violence against women: estimates from the redesigned survey. *Special Report*. US Department of Justice, Office of Justice Programs, Bureau of Justice Statistics, Washington, DC.

DIANNE CYR CARMODY

double consciousness

When W. E. B. Du Bois introduced the concept of "double consciousness" in his literary and autobiographical masterpiece, *The Souls of Black Folk* (1903), the idea of doubleness was already a major motif in the literary works of many notable authors. A restatement of the salient features of Du Bois' views on double consciousness permits us to focus on both the origins and consequences of this doubleness. In addition, a reassessment permits us to approach the concept from contemporary sociological perspectives in order to focus on its possible utility in the current era. The core of Du Bois on double consciousness is as follows: (1) it denies an objective consciousness; (2) the "other" becomes the eye through which the world is viewed; (3) it creates an internal warfare between black and white values and norms; (4) ultimately, the black and white selves may merge into a more creative and unique self; and (5) the struggle to appease black and white strivings has greatly handicapped an already distraught and oppressed black population.

Du Bois' metaphor of the double as "two souls, two thoughts, two unreconciled strivings; two warring ideals in one dark body" has been taken by many to refer to the hopelessness of the task facing blacks. The reality was far different from the picture painted by Du Bois. There was nothing in the black body or mind which mitigated against freedom for itself, hence, Du Bois led us sociologically into a blind alley by explaining the issue primarily as an internal battle, an internal war in which the black body was warring against itself. In reality, the war was external to the black body and stitched into fabric of the social structure.

As problematic as double consciousness might be, Du Bois, when one reads the social contexts in which the concept is used, situated the concept in a sociology of black life, though he did not draw the obvious conclusions when he used the term. What must be asserted, however, is the reality that consciousness of whatever type, must emerge from the lived experiences of the people. One part of Du Bois' logic is correct: Consciousness must originate in the economic and social relations within the society. One of the difficulties of tracing double consciousness is that, like so many examples in Du Bois' sociology, he does not consistently utilize the same terms throughout his empirical and theoretical works. And he does not delineate or even hint at the concept elsewhere in *Souls of Black Folk* outside of chapters one and ten. Nor does he use the concept in his subsequent works. This may mean that he really did not consider the concept as a major definer of black life in America. The question must be raised as to the term's sociological relevance, theoretically and methodically. Was the term merely of metaphorical value to Du Bois, and does it raise more questions than it answers or resolves? Though the concept is widely used today to refer to groups other than blacks – women, homosexuals, and other ethnic and racial groups – we might be faced with the reality that the Du Boisian idea of the double consciousness may best be observed and understood as a legacy developed out of literary works and the legacy of psychology as a discipline which analyzes the internal dynamics of the self. In this manner, the term can be closely allied to the concept of individual and group identity.

SEE ALSO: Acculturation; Critical Race Theory; Du Bois, W. E. B.; Marginalization, Outsiders;

SUGGESTED READING

Dennis, R. M. (2003) Du Bois and double consciousness: myth or reality. In: Stone, J. & Dennis, R. M. (eds) *Race and Ethnicity: Comparative and Theoretical Approaches.* Blackwell, Malden, MA.

RUTLEDGE M. DENNIS

drag queens and drag kings

Drag queens and drag kings are men, women, and transgendered people who perform femininity, masculinity, or something in between. Drag queens have long been part of gay life, but drag kings are a relatively recent phenomenon. Drag in various forms can be found in almost all parts of the world, and increasingly a transnational drag culture is evolving. Gender theorists have been very interested in cross-dressing and transgender performances for what they reveal about the social construction and performativity of gender and sexuality.

"Female impersonators" generally keep the illusion of being women, in contrast to drag queens, who regularly break it by speaking in their male voices, referring to themselves as men, or discussing their tucked penises. Drag king troupes, influenced by feminism and queer theory, tend consciously to deconstruct masculinity and femininity in performances, including by "bio queens," women who perform femininity, as well as by women performing masculinity. Ballroom, a cultural phenomenon in communities of color made famous by the film *Paris is Burning*, encompasses a variety of categories: "butch queens" (gay or bisexual men who are masculine, hypermasculine, or effeminate), "femme queens" (male-to-female transsexuals at various stages), "butch queens up in drags" (gay men in drag), "butches" (female-to-male transsexuals, butch lesbians, or any woman dressing as a man), "women," and "men" (straight men).

SEE ALSO: Doing Gender; Gay and Lesbian Movement; Homosexuality; Transgender, Transvestism, and Transsexualism

SUGGESTED READINGS

Rupp, L. J. & Taylor, V. (2003) *Drag Queens at the 801 Cabaret*. University of Chicago Press, Chicago, IL.

Shapiro, E. (2007) Drag kinging and the transformation of gender identities. *Gender & Society* 21: 250–71.

LEILA J. RUPP AND VERTA TAYLOR

dramaturgy

Dramaturgy points to a family of terms associated with the idea of analyzing selectively symbolized action – whether this be textual, prose or poetry, or social action. In social science, dramaturgy is a perspective that makes sense of action at several levels whether it is carried out by organizations, groups or individual actors. Dramaturgy concerns how a performance becomes the basis for order and ordering, and connotes *analysis* of the social by use of the theatric metaphor. How are performances enacted? With what effect(s)? What symbols are used to convey this action? It assumes feedback and reciprocity from an audience, a process by which claims are validated (verbal or non-verbal, written or electronic), and modes of remedy are advanced. Failure to produce feedback and reciprocity requires repair, apology, or an explanation. It is likely that the appeal of dramaturgy is its applicability to the increasing number of situations in mass society in which strangers must negotiate in the absence of shared values, beliefs, kin or ethnic ties.

Erving Goffman has most consistently and systematically employed dramaturgical analysis. Goffman's twin concerns from the beginning were the interaction order and the presentation of a performance in that context. He states (1959: ix) "I shall consider the ways in which the individual in ordinary work situations presents himself and his activities, the ways in which he guides and controls the impression they form of him, and the kinds of things he may or may not do while sustaining his performance before them." Here, dramaturgy is about the actor's impression management. This might be called the impression management aspect of dramaturgy. His strong connection to dramaturgy is signaled best by the organizing metaphors he employs, many of them taken from the theatre, front and back stage, script, role, audience, et al. It is likely that the range of concepts he uses are designed to shift emphases while illuminating the interaction order itself. There is also an emotional aspect of dramaturgy – the contingencies that arise in performing. Goffman's dramaturgy is powerful because it features the impression management of performances that are emotionally loaded and mutually recognizable. Goffman's aim is to see how interaction permits order by sanctioning performances and sustaining collaboration. Order is revealed in and through interaction, not via *a priori* concepts such as personality, values, norms, or social systems. Goffman struggled to show how actors display order and ordering conventions in many situations, with an eye always to ways humans adapt, interpret, read off and make sense of others' behavior. Life is not scripted, but it is performative. This does not assume life-as-chaos, nor does it require positing people as "puppets" with attributed feelings, aims, goals and a repertoire of strategies and tactics. Even an insincere performance is a performance.

SEE ALSO: Goffman, Erving; Interaction

REFERENCE

Goffman, E. (1959) *Presentation of Self in Everyday Life*. Doubleday Anchor, Garden City, NY.

SUGGESTED READINGS

Goffman, E. (1983a) The interaction order. *American Sociological Review* 48: 1–17.

Goffman, E. (1983b) Felicity's condition. *American Journal of Sociology* 89 (1): 1–53.

PETER MANNING

drug use

Drug addiction and abuse constitute a major social problem that is interlaced throughout our society. Each year it costs billions of dollars in terms of interdiction, prevention, enforcement, treatment, and lost productivity. Moreover, the drug problem exacerbates a number of other social problems including poverty, homelessness, crime, and family discord.

Society is bombarded constantly by all sorts of messages advocating the use of drugs. Pharmaceutical companies and vendors have inundated society with drug advertising. Few people can open their email accounts without having at least one message that attempts to sell some type of drug. Many of these vendors have their own physicians who can prescribe drugs in absentia. A significant proportion of television advertising is now devoted to prescription drugs, and they all end by urging viewers to ask their physician about some drug that will enhance their lives by making them feel better, look better, or have enhanced sexuality. There are approximately 3 billion prescriptions written annually, and the Center for Disease Control and Prevention (CDC) notes that each year physicians write about 1.5 prescriptions per office visit, demonstrating a substantial amount of medicating in the USA (NIDA 2004).

Nicotine and alcohol are the two most widely used drugs in society, but because of their legal status most people do not see them as such, although this has been moderated somewhat as government and public groups have attempted to negatively label their use and abuse.

Although compulsive drug use begins with experimentation, it is not true that all drug experimenters end up as compulsive drug users. In 2002, The National Survey on Drug Use and Health found that 46 percent of the population in the USA aged 12 or older had used an illicit drug in their lifetimes, but only 8.3 percent had used an illicit drug in the past month. The survey also found that approximately 19.5 million people in the USA were current drug users. The most widely used drug was marijuana with a use rate of 6.2 percent.

As noted above, drug use is interlaced with a variety of problems. The relationship between drugs and crime is of most importance and drives a substantial proportion of the concerns with drug abuse. Although drug use is attributable to some crime, many experts agree that the drug problem commingles with the crime problem and that criminals reside in a culture that is conducive to drug use. These experts argue that it is not a clear-cut causal relationship.

If drug usage statistics were examined in detail for a period of several years, it would reveal that there is an ebb and flow of drug problems. Drugs of choice, to some extent, vary by region of the country, age of the population, and city. Historically, society and government have not recognized that there are multiple drug problems, and for the most part have developed prevention, suppression, and treatment programs that may be applicable to one part of the country or one type of drug, but have less utility for other parts of the country and other drugs. The drug problems must be fully understood in terms of patterns of usage, and more effective programs must be fashioned that address specific populations and types of drugs.

SEE ALSO: Addiction and Dependency; Alcoholism and Alcohol Abuse; Deviance, Crime and; Drugs, Drug Abuse, and Drug Policy

REFERENCE

National Institute on Drug Abuse (NIDA) (2004) Nida.nih.gov/ResearchReports/Prescription/prescriptions.

SUGGESTED READINGS

Department of Health and Human Services (DHHS) (2003) *Results from the 2002 National Survey on Drug Use and Health: National Findings*. Department of Health and Human Services, Washington, DC.

Goode, E. (2005) *Drugs in American Society*, 6th edn. McGraw-Hill, New York.

LARRY GAINES

drugs, drug abuse, and drug policy

The term "drug" has been both broadly and narrowly defined. At its simplest, it is reserved for substances which are prohibited under criminal law. Deploying this definition, the range of substances classified as drugs varies across time and across jurisdictions. However, typically, it refers to substances such as heroin, (crack) cocaine, ecstasy, and amphetamines.

The terms "drug abuse" and "misuse" are frequently used in policy documents to describe the most harmful forms of drug use which warrant attention. However, there is an emerging consensus that these terms should be avoided because they are highly subjective and judgmental descriptions of patterns of drug use. Instead, the term "problem drug use" is preferred, which typically describes patterns of use which create social, psychological, physical, or legal problems for an individual drug user.

Problem drug use has been defined as a law and order, medical, public health and social problem. Defined as a law and order problem, policy attention is likely to be focused on strategies to reduce the supply of drugs through tackling drug markets or to decrease the demand for drugs through attempts to break the link between drugs and crime through the provision of treatment.

Approaching problem drug use as a medical problem involves equating it with a disease. The development of a medical model for understanding problem drug use was influential in moving understanding away from moral failure. Policies which flow from conceptualizing problem drug use in this way emphasize particular forms of treatment, and have been criticized for failing to appreciate the social causes and consequences of problem drug use.

Perceiving problem drug use as a public health problem stems from a concern about its effects on health and well-being for communities drug users live in. For example, community members may be exposed to used drug paraphernalia. Consequently, advocates of this approach suggest the need to pursue a harm-reduction strategy, which includes practices such as operating needle-exchange schemes and prescribed substitute medication.

Contemporary drug policy is often based upon a range of different conceptualizations of the type of problem drug use poses, which results in a wide range of policies being adopted. These policies are implemented by a varied group of organizations (e.g., criminal justice, health care, and social work agencies). In reality, this may mean that drug users are exposed to seemingly contradictory policies; for instance, policies which have the effect of criminalizing growing numbers of drug users can be pursued alongside policies which increase opportunities for drug users to give up drug use or to use drugs in a less harmful manner.

Problem drug use has also been understood as a social problem. A challenge for sociologists is to explore why problem drug use has been defined in this way and who has done the defining.

SEE ALSO: Addiction and Dependency; Deviance, Crime and Drug Use

SUGGESTED READINGS

Barton, A. (2003) *Illicit Drugs: Use and Control.* Routledge, London.

Blackman, S. (2004) *Chilling Out: The Cultural Politics of Substance, Consumption, Youth and Drug Policy.* Open University Press, Buckingham.

Hughes, R., Lart, R., & Higate, P. (eds.) (2006) *Drugs: Policy and Politics.* Open University Press, Buckingham.

EMMA WINCUP

Du Bois, W. E. B. (1868–1963)

W. E. B. Du Bois was a sociologist and historian, born in Great Barrington, Massachusetts. Though he wanted to attend Harvard after high school, the lack of funds and the advice of a few of his teachers dissuaded him, so, instead, he attended Fisk, where he received his BA in 1888. He received a second BA from Harvard University in 1890, where he was also awarded an MA (1891) and a PhD (1895) with the dissertation "The suppression of the African slave trade to the United States of America, 1638–1870." Between 1892 and 1894 Du Bois was a graduate student at the University of Berlin, made possible by a combination gift/loan from the Slater Fund. This experience would have enduring consequences on both his personality and his scholarship, though, as he stated in his classic *Souls of Black Folk* (1903), his experiences at both Fisk and Harvard had already shaped some of his views on race, class, and philosophy.

Du Bois' sociological significance rests on three major themes: (1) his role as one of the early sociology pioneers; (2) his role as a sociologist of race; and (3) his role as a scholar-activist. As one of the early modern pioneers, along with Durkheim, Weber, and Simmel, Du Bois viewed the connection between theory and research as inextricably linked to the alleviation of social problems and as contributors to overall societal reform. This was important to Du Bois because so little data had been collected in areas in which scholars allegedly knew so much.

Even as Du Bois fought mightily to believe that science and objectivity would make a difference in matters of race, class, and social justice, his scholarly and sociopolitical activities illustrated that he would be the Great Dialectician, whose mind, interests, and concerns might reflect shifting intellectual modes and themes. So, even as theme (1), science and research, was in operation, as a good dialectician he was already into theme (2) with its focus on a sociology of race. For example, his paper "The conservation of races" (1897) was a justification for maintaining certain racial/cultural values, even as blacks sought greater entry into the larger society. Today, such a claim is understandable under the rubric of social and cultural pluralism. This article and a later one, "The study of the Negro problem" (1898), but especially *The Souls of Black Folk*, would make race analysis, its shape, depth, and contours, as important for many as Marx's class analysis had been and continues to be. It is here as sociologists of race that later generations of scholars and students would find sociological richness in concepts such as the talented tenth, double consciousness, the color line, the veil, racial solidarity, and masking.

Du Bois' prescient assertion in *Souls* that "the problem of the twentieth century is the problem of the color-line" was a bold prediction for what was in store for the western world, but also presaged a lifetime struggle for himself, as he vowed to lend a hand in the destruction of that color line. The very title, *The Souls of Black Folk*, would be an exploratory search and revelation as Du Bois would lay bare, for whites to see, the heart and soul of a people. What was also patently visible was the heart and soul of the young scholar Du Bois, for even before C. Wright Mills asserted his version of a sociological imagination, Du Bois, in *Souls* (p. 87), had inserted himself personally into a larger national and international sociology and history.

The more one researches the life of Du Bois, the more it becomes abundantly clear that neither his life nor his intellectual and scholarly activities can be neatly compartmentalized, and his ideas are found in so many intellectual niches and corners. With the increasing loss of faith in science Du Bois began to define himself as a scholar-activist – he uses the term "propagandist" – and would become, as the chief "propagandist for the race," the scholar as organizer: organizer of four Pan-African Congresses; founder and general secretary of the Niagara Movement; one of the founders of the NAACP; founder and editor of *The Moon*; founder and editor of *The Horizon*; founder and editor of *The Crisis*; founder and editor of *Phylon*. And during this same period he writes sociologically significant books, books reflecting his markedly leftward political shift: *John Brown* (1909), *Black Reconstruction* (1935), *Dusk of Dawn* (1940), and *The World and Africa* (1947). *In Battle for Peace* (1952) was written after he had been indicted, placed on trial, and acquitted for being an unregistered foreign agent of the Soviet Union, as a result of his leadership in various peace movements and organizations. Given his pronounced political preferences and pronouncements throughout the 1940s and 1950s, it was not surprising to many when in 1961 Du Bois joined the Communist Party of the United States. In a masterful stroke marking him as a true dialectician, Du Bois, that same year, accepted an invitation from President Nkrumah to go to Ghana to complete his Encyclopedia Africana Project, a project which would be a version of the Encyclopedia of the Negro, which Du Bois initiated in 1909. In 1963 he renounced his United States citizenship and became a citizen of Ghana. He died on August 27, 1963, on the eve of the historic March On Washington.

SEE ALSO: Accommodation; Critical Race Theory; Double Consciousness; Race; Stratification, Race/Ethnicity and

SUGGESTED READINGS

Dennis, R. M. (1975) The sociology of W. E. B. Du Bois. Dissertation, Washington State University, Pullman, WA.

Dennis, R. M. (1996) *W. E. B. Du Bois: The Scholar as Activist*. JAI Press, Greenwich, CT.

RUTLEDGE M. DENNIS

dual labor markets

Dual labor markets was a concept developed to address the organizational structuring of labor markets, as white male workers were preferentially recruited to jobs offering training, pay gains, promotion and job security within internal labor markets. Meanwhile women and minority groups were often confined to insecure, low-paid, dead-end jobs in the external labour market. This contested standard economic models of the allocation of workers to jobs according to individual skills and preferences, as organizational structures and management decisions generated a division between primary and secondary labor markets which operated according to different logics. There were, however, different analyses of the sources of dualism. Some emphasized contrasting policies of large employers and small competitive enterprises. Some suggested managers constructed primary labor markets to retain relatively skilled workers with firm-specific training. Others suggested dualism was the result of management tactics of divide and rule, rather than calculations about protecting investment in training.

These analyses were designed to explain the *persistence* of labor market dualism, rather than to explain change. However, recent organizational restructuring has involved a reduction in stable routes of career progression and a growth in less secure forms of employment, while skills shortages and equal opportunities policies have opened *some* doors for qualified but hitherto excluded groups. These developments have prompted more complex analyses of labor market *segmentation*. This has involved identifying multiple and shifting labor market segments characterized by changing clusters of opportunities and insecurities, rather than a stable dualism or a uniform movement towards flux and insecurity. Such segmentation models have been underpinned by analyses of the varied and changing social organization of both the demand for labor and the supply of labor. While management decisions are pivotal on the demand side, changing family and household relations are central to the supply side, while state policies help to structure both.

SEE ALSO: International Gender Division of Labor; Labor Markets

SUGGESTED READING

Peck, J. (1996) *Work-Place: The Social Regulation of Labor Markets*. Guilford Press, New York.

TONY ELGER

Durkheim, Émile (1858–1917)

Émile Durkheim, often referred to as the founder of Sociology, was born April 15, 1858, in France. Appointed to the first professorship of Sociology in the world, he worked tirelessly over three decades as a lecturer and writer to establish Sociology as a distinct discipline with its own unique theoretical and methodological foundation. After an illustrious career, first in Bordeaux and then after 1902 in Paris at the Sorbonne, Durkheim died in November 1917, still a relatively young man, never having recovered from grief after most of the young sociologists he had trained, including his own son André, were killed in World War I.

Durkheim's basic argument was that the human rational being is a creation of social relations. His related arguments against individualism, and for a distinct sociological object and method, stand at the heart of Sociology as a discipline. Motivated by a recognition that the organization, rationality and morality of modern societies is different from traditional belief based social forms in fundamental ways, he argued that these differences pose serious challenges to contemporary society which has developed a practice based form of solidarity. He credited Rousseau and Montesquieu with inspiring his emphasis on justice and the social origin of the individual, which he holds in common with other classical social thinkers (e.g. Comte, Marx, Weber, and Mead). The individual as a social production, and the centrality of social phenomena in all aspects of human experience, are ideas that distinguish Sociology from other disciplines' approaches to social order, social action, modernity, economic exchange, mutual intelligibility, and justice.

Durkheim's arguments have played a central role in the development of almost every aspect of Sociology since its inception. His position was popularized as functionalism by Talcott Parsons in the late 1930s, and as a focus on symbolic systems by Lucien Levy-Bruhl and Claude Levi-Strauss from the 1920s to the 1960s. Postmodernism and poststructuralism, which developed in the 1960s and remained popular through the turn of the century, are both reactions to the way these two earlier conflicting interpretations of Durkheim's arguments developed over time.

MAJOR SUBSTANTIVE CONTRIBUTIONS

According to Durkheim the transformation of the individual biological being into a social being cannot be explained by either individual biology or psychology. Biological capacities exist, but require redirection and reformation by social processes. Reason, he argued, is a result of social processes and particular forms of association, or social bonding, are required to create and maintain social individuals which cannot exist except in the context of particular social configurations. Consequently, any position that begins with the individual, such as psychology, economics, or philosophy, and tries to explain social phenomena on the basis of aggregations of individual actions, will miss exactly what is important about society.

Durkheim elaborated these ideas in four major works, *The Division of Labor in Society* (1893), *The Rules of the Sociological Method* (1895), *Suicide* (1897), and *The Elementary Forms of Religious Life* (1912). Each was designed to illustrate a different point. In addition, Durkheim wrote a thesis on Montesquieu, countless articles for *l'Annee sociologique* (which he also edited), and lectured on Pragmatism, Socialism, Moral Education and Rousseau. Taken together these substantively different sociological studies make up a unified, empirically based theoretical view.

Durkheim's innovative use of statistics to demonstrate different forms of association in *Suicide* and his articulation of a sociological method of measuring what he called "social facts" in *Rules*, remain a foundation for sociological methodology today. His arguments with regard to the social origin of ideas in *Elementary Forms* inspired the development of the sociology of knowledge and, more recently, cultural sociology. His arguments regarding universes of discourse have also been taken up by the sociology of science where they rival Wittgenstein in their importance with regard to various sociologies of practice.

Durkheim's position was modern in crucial ways. For instance, whereas Freud's (1913) *Totem and Taboo* reflected the prejudices of the times by likening the primitive mind to the mentally ill, Durkheim's *Elementary Forms*, published a year earlier, insisted that aboriginal social forms and their corresponding beliefs were as rational as their modern counterparts. This was a surprisingly modern stand against the ethnocentrism of Durkheim's time. He regarded *reason* as a social product, rendering distinctions such as mental inferiority or superiority nonsensical, and infusing his sociology with a fundamental egalitarianism – a new moral philosophy grounded in social facts, and a new sociological epistemology with universal applicability.

METHODOLOGY

Durkheim used various qualitative and archival methods, particularly in his research on law and religion. Durkheim's method, whether statistical or qualitative, focused on the character of forms of association and on the consequences of those associations for the health of the social individual and/ or group. By contrast, statistics in contemporary

Sociology are generally used to measure relationships between the demographic character of individual actions and various institutional constraints (values, goals, sanctions). This has been the predominant sociological method since the 1940s and is often equated with "macro" sociological concerns. It is, however, a later interpretation of Durkheim's method, influenced by structuralism and not entirely consistent with his own approach.

Durkheim used statistics as indicators of social facts. For Durkheim, social facts in a modern differentiated society consist of forms and patterns of association, not beliefs and values. What matters are the ways in which members of various groups are associated with one another, not their orientation toward valued courses of action, which had been important in earlier social forms. Where statistics such as suicide rates provide indicators of these associations, they may be of use to sociologists.

Durkheim's approach did not correlate individual characteristics with value oriented behavior, however. It was Durkheim's position that social processes create entirely new dimensions of persons and associations between persons, creating social configurations in ways that add up to more than the sum of the individual parts. He used statistics to indicate the strength and character of various forms of association. For instance, if the forms of association in a group were very weak, then people in the group could be expected to have a greater number of moral and psychological problems. If the forms of association in a group were too strong, then people could be expected to sacrifice themselves for the group whenever necessary. The tricky part is specifying the ideal forms of association. Durkheim argued that this varies across societies. *The Division of Labor* worked out the difference between two forms of social solidarity whose forms of association were entirely different, and *Suicide* demonstrated that the conditions under which ties to the group would be too weak or too strong also differ. Suicide in traditional and modern societies would therefore have to be understood in entirely different terms – for Durkheim, more proof that suicide was a function of social relations.

It was Durkheim's position in *Rules* that sociologists should focus on the social facts of recurrent institutional and orderly social forms. He treated social order as a central topic for Sociology and argued that methods should treat the social as primary, avoid individualism, and be broadly scientific (i.e. consist of practices recognizable to other scientists). He did not argue for methodological hegemony and in Durkheim's work the character of particular social facts, and not some *a priori* prescription, seems to have determined the methods he used.

RELEVANCE TO THE HISTORY OF CONTEMPORARY SOCIOLOGY

Durkheim created a blueprint for the discipline of Sociology that defined it in entirely new terms. Understanding social theory, and engaging in the practice of Sociology without contradiction, entails giving up philosophical positions like individualism from which the sociological object, as Durkheim defined it, is rendered absurd.

As Sociology has struggled over the decades to define itself against philosophical individualism and to establish the social at its center point, Durkheim has always been the inspiration. Structural functionalism, cultural anthropology, cultural sociology, postmodernism, post-structuralism, sociological studies of science, sociology of knowledge, and legal studies were all inspired by Durkheim's arguments, some negatively and some positively. The work of Garfinkel, Goffman, Symbolic Interaction, and social constructivism, are similarly indebted. Durkheim's arguments with regard to social character of the individual self, the importance of concrete forms of association between people, and the special characteristics of self-regulating practices in modern social contexts are an important foundation of these contemporary arguments.

The true importance of Sociology as Durkheim envisioned it was not to play handmaiden to philosophy. He envisioned a sociology that evaluated social facts on its own terms. He rejected the idea that social facts were contingent and wanted to establish that certain social forms and processes were necessary or, put another way, that certain social needs must be fulfilled in order for society to go on. Once this is established, those necessities become the non-contingent social facts against which arguments can be anchored.

Feminists sometimes argue that Durkheim's work ignored women, or adopted an insensitive stance toward them. He certainly did not theorize about women in any depth, but very few men were aware of women's issues at all in the 1890s. Even so, it is significant that Durkheim not only argued for the rational status of aboriginal people, but also had some awareness of the position of women. For instance, in *Suicide* he noted that there seemed to be a fourth form of suicide which he called "fatalistic," that was particularly prevalent among women. While noting that he lacked sufficient evidence, he suggested that marriage, while beneficial to men, may have a negative effect on women.

Durkheim also noted in *The Division of Labor* that studies of aboriginal people suggest women were once as strong as men and that the development of society, and the positions women hold in modern societies, have made women weaker. Given the turn-of-the-century tendency to view women as innately gentle and weak, Durkheim's opinion in this regard is noteworthy.

Durkheim would have resisted allowing individualistic perspectives or disciplines to judge the validity of sociological arguments. He also would have disagreed with the currently popular position that the problem with Sociology is that it does not focus enough on individuals and on individual reason. Other disciplines would regard Sociology more favorably if it did so, but the point of Sociology from the beginning has been to challenge them in this regard. Sociology begins with the premise that individualism is wrong. There would be no Sociology if the individualism of philosophy, economics and psychology were accepted. Only if the social is primary does Sociology have a reason to exist as a discipline in the first place. On this foundation Durkheim hoped to ground a sociological understanding of the requirements for justice in modern society.

SEE ALSO: Anomie; Collective Conscience; Individualism; Law, Sociology of; Parsons, Talcott; Religion, Sociology of; Solidarity, Mechanical and Organic; Structural Functionalism; Suicide; Theory and Methods

SUGGESTED READINGS

Alexander, J. C. (ed.) (1988) *Durkheimian Sociology: Cultural Studies.* Cambridge University Press, Cambridge.

Giddens, A. (1971) *Capitalism and Modern Social Theory.* Cambridge University Press, Cambridge.

Lukes, S. (1973). *Emile Durkheim: His Life and Work, a Historical and Critical Study.* Stanford University Press, Stanford, CA.

Parsons, T. (1937) *The Structure of Social Action.* Free Press, New York.

ANNE WARFIELD RAWLS

dyads/triads

The smallest and most elementary social unit, a dyad is a social group composed of two members while a triad is a social group composed of three members. Most structural conditions and social processes are found in dyadic and triadic interaction. The analysis of dyads and triads clearly demonstrates the poverty of strict psychological reductionism.

A dyad is more fragile and precarious than other social units. If one person leaves or if one's attention is diverted, the dyad dissolves. The intensity of interaction required in dyads creates the conditions in which intimacy can develop.

Three distinct types of dyads can be identified. In *pure dyads* each is responsible only to the other for the maintenance of the relationship. The world external to the dyad, including the passage of time, tends to evaporate in pure dyadic interaction. With *representative dyads* one or both members have allegiances to other social units. How they act and respond to the other is, in part, based on their allegiances. Dyads (and triads for that matter) need not be made up of individuals. *Supra-individual dyads* are comprised of larger social units such as families, organizations, tribes, or societies. In this way we can understand how two businesses compete and political party coalitions form.

In a triad a new array of possible social relationships emerges. With triads, if one member leaves, the group continues. But, with a third person the intimate character of the dyad is lost. No matter how civilly inattentive the third party behaves, the dyad has acquired an audience that at once inhibits certain actions and alters others.

Triads forming one-to-two situations are commonplace. In one-to-two triads differentiation is established identifying the "one" as distinct from the others – as a leader or representative. The "one" defines and acts toward the others as a unit – as an audience, as students, as followers, or as captives. In one-to-two situations responsibility for the actions within the triad falls to the "one."

SEE ALSO: Simmel, Georg

SUGGESTED READING

Simmel, G. (1950) *The Sociology of Georg Simmel*, trans. and ed. K. Wolff. Free Press, New York.

DAN E. MILLER

E

ecological problems

Sociology devoted to local and global ecological problems (like air pollution in cities, the greenhouse effect, or overfishing of the oceans) is active in at least three areas of research: theories of the emergence of ecological problems, environmental attitudes and behavior of the general public, and environmental behavior of corporate actors (business firms, environmental movement organizations, and the state).

Theories of ecological problems fit into the four general paradigms of sociological theory: functionalism/system theory, conflict theory/the political economy perspective, rational choice theory, and interactionist/constructivist approaches. Proponents of functionalism/system theory locate the reasons for ecological problems in the complexities of systems, both eco- and social systems; human beings have difficulty perceiving and predicting the dynamic system effects of their actions, so they destroy the equilibrium of well-adapted natural and social systems. The conflict theory/political economy perspective blames the logic of the capitalist and neoliberal economy for the environmental crisis; capitalist economies are based not only on the exploitation of workers, but to an even greater extent on that of natural resources. Rational choice theory states that ecological problems often have the structure of a social dilemma such as a "commons dilemma" or a "prisoner's dilemma"; in a social dilemma, the rational individual strategy is non-cooperation and free-riding, i.e., pursuing one's own interests at the expense of the environment. Interactionist/constructivist approaches emphasize that environmental problems – like other societal problems – are socially defined and culturally patterned; given this focus, they are interested primarily in social and political processes through which ecological problems are placed and kept on the problem agenda.

Starting from the premise that ecological problems are finally caused by maladaptive individual behavior, much research focuses on environmental attitudes and behavior in the general public. Judging by the results of surveys in different countries, environmental concern increased to a peak around 1990, but has since decreased or at least stagnated. Citizens with a higher level of environmental concern are usually more likely to be young, female, highly educated, have a higher income, and hold a progressive/liberal political worldview. Comparing different countries, a higher GNP is associated with more widespread environmental awareness. This finding has often been interpreted as an indication that the quality of the environment is a luxury good, important primarily to the rich. There are two opposing schools of thought on the issue of how to change environmentally harmful behavior of individual citizens: attitudinal approaches give priority to moral suasion, value change, and environmental education; structural approaches have a preference for legal restrictions, financial rewards, and more convenient opportunities for ecological behavior.

The interests and behaviors of corporate actors are as important for the quality of the environment as those of individual citizens. The activities of business firms have tremendous effects on the state of the environment, both direct and indirect. Sociologists investigate which industries cause serious environmental damage, under what conditions firms are motivated to improve their ecological performance, which instruments they use to do so, and what barriers prevent a successful implementation of devices developed to reduce negative environmental impacts. Corporate actors directly fighting for an improvement of environmental conditions have grown out of the so-called environmental movement that began at the end of the 1960s. Sociologists have established a separate line of inquiry called social movement research, which is also dedicated to the environmental movement and to environmental NGOs. Many claims and proposals originally articulated by environmental organizations have found acceptance in the conventional political system and are now part of the programs of mainstream political parties and governmental agencies. This means that corporate actors in the political arena have become the dominant players in the field of ecological problems. On the national level, governments have founded their own ministries for the environment, enacted numerous environmental laws, and initiated other policies aimed at the protection of natural resources. Despite disagreement over strategies and measures of success, most governments today declare "sustainable development" to be the guiding principle behind their environmental policies. According to the well-known Brundtland Report (1987) which elaborated the idea of sustainable development on the international stage, such a development should guarantee that future generations will have a chance to fulfill their basic needs in a sound and healthy environment. More than two decades after the release of this report, it is safe to say more remains to be done in order to narrow the gap between sustainability goals and the actual condition of the environment.

SEE ALSO: Ecology; Environmental Movements; Social Problems, Politics of

SUGGESTED READINGS

Gardner, G. T. & Stern, P. C. (1996) *Environmental Problems and Human Behavior*. Allyn & Bacon, Boston, MA.

Meadows, D. H., Meadows, D. L., & Randers, J. (1992) *Beyond the Limits*. Post Mills, Chelsea Green.

Ostrom, E. (1990) *Governing the Commons: The Evolution of Institutions for Collective Action*. Cambridge University Press, Cambridge.

PETER PREISENDÖRFER AND ANDREAS DIEKMANN

ecology

Ecology generally refers to the scientific study of an organism or community of organisms and their relationship to each other as well as to the environment. The ecological framework is used in biological sciences, social sciences, botany, zoological sciences, and other research areas and is applied to myriad subareas including human ecology, cultural ecology, organizational ecology, plant ecology, population ecology, spatial ecology, and more. Early writings on ecology were influenced by the works of Malthus and Darwin. This can be seen in ecology's use of natural selection and the presence of other competing species in the race for survival.

Social scientists borrowed the ecological framework directly from the biological and plant sciences. Ecology's quantitative approach influenced both the conceptual approach to the human community and the methodological one. The term "human ecology" was used in the social sciences by Charles C. Adams in 1913. However, ecology as a social scientific approach received systematic formulation around 1915 from Robert Park. The classical human ecologists writing in the 1920s and 1930s applied to the interrelations of human beings a type of analysis previously applied to the interrelations of plants and animals. The human ecologists claimed that although the conditions that affect and control the movement and numbers of populations are more complex in human societies than in plant and animal communities, they exhibit extraordinary similarities.

Criticisms of the ecological approach within the social sciences include whether change can originate from within the socio-ecological system and whether communities and environments can be analyzed as truly being closed systems. Furthermore, recent use of the ecological framework in the social sciences is scarcely influenced by the original biological analogy. Despite the wide variation in the use of the term "ecology," the term for sociologists often becomes a synonym for "spatial" and loses much of the systematic interplay between environment and community.

SEE ALSO: Ecological Problems; Organization Theory; Urban Ecology

SUGGESTED READINGS

Michaels, J. W. (1974) On the relation between human ecology and behavioral social psychology. *Social Forces* 52 (3): 313–21.

Park, R. E. (1936) Human ecology. *American Journal of Sociology* 42 (1): 1–15.

MARC M. SANFORD

economic determinism

The concept of economic determinism refers to monocausal determinism by material, economic factors. The idea is often associated with Karl Marx's "historical materialism," but it is not clear that Marx himself was a strict economic determinist, or even a materialist. The Romantic strain in the work of the early Marx did not disappear entirely, which is evident in terms of his view of species being and the teleology of communism. Some commentators differentiate between economic determinism and dialectical materialism, where dialectical materialism allows for more flexibility and may even include a feedback mechanism. Rigid versions of economic determinism are often associated with Marxist-Leninism and Stalinism. In Marxist parlance, the forces of production determine the relations of production in any mode of production. Sometimes that statement is modified to include the disclaimer that such economic determinism is only true in the final analysis.

But precisely what "in the final analysis" means is rarely specified exactly.

Closely related is the concept of economic reductionism (Robertson & White 2005: 355–7), where emphasis is placed on the idea that the economy is closely intertwined with all forms of the culture of consumerism. Thus, for example, advertising images can be viewed as ideological constructs that are the product of economic forces working on decision-makers in corporations. Concern with capitalist globalization has been premised in part on the theory that economic globalization is determinative of all aspects of civil society, not just consumption. Studies of the origins of the "capitalist world system" have moved the classical Marxist argument about economic determinism from relations of production within nation-states to a global arena that involves the interaction among societies. Wallerstein (1974; 1980; 1989) "emphasized the causal significance of economic-material factors, relegating other aspects of epiphenomenal status" (Robertson & White 2005: 357). There are also counterarguments which stress "civilizational" or "cultural" factors as determinative. Weber's 1904–6 thesis (2002: 125) concerning the Protestant ethic is often misinterpreted as a one-sided idealist argument, but he explicitly points out that it is not his intention to replace a one-sided economic determinism with an equally misleading, one-sided idealist (ideological-cultural) determinism.

SEE ALSO: Base and Superstructure; Dialectical Materialism; Marx, Karl

REFERENCES

Robertson, R. & White, K. E. (2005) Globalization: sociology and cross-disciplinarity. In: Calhoun, C., Rojek, C., & Turner, B. (eds.), *The Sage Handbook of Sociology*. Sage, London, pp. 345–66.

Wallerstein, I. (1974, 1980, 1989) *The Modern World System*, 3 vols. Cambridge University Press, New York.

Weber, M. (2002) [1904] *The Protestant Ethic and the Spirit of Capitalism*, trans. S. Kalberg. Roxbury, Los Angeles, CA.

J. I. (HANS) BAKKER

economic development

Economic development studies are concerned with how societies have, could, and should pursue improvement in the quality and quantity of life for their inhabitants. Since the decades following World War II when development studies began and were implemented as policies, there has been neither consensus on how to pursue the goal of economic and social improvement nor unqualified improvement in the quality of life for most of the world's population. Nonetheless, the politically and socially important pursuit of economic development continues and involves academics, nation-states, regional and international organizations, non-governmental organizations, and philanthropic foundations.

Development scholarship arose out of the major social, political, and economic changes that accompanied the end of World War II and the restructuring of the global geopolitical map. As a consequence of the war, there was both a felt need to reconstruct the destroyed economies of Europe and Japan, and to supply financial assistance to the newly freed colonial possessions of losing states. Early efforts focused on the construction of critical industrial goods and state-owned infrastructures, and the overall modernization of political and economic institutions. Rebuilding activities were based on assumptions of social and economic "convergence": a belief that all societies progress in a stepwise fashion from traditional social orders toward increasingly modern social and economic systems as manifest by western industrial states.

During the early period, economic development theories were largely based on the belief that all societies developed through a set of stages that ultimately would lead to a modern nation-state and industrial economy. This evolutionist approach urged political and social reforms that would develop "primitive" or "backward" societies into modern economic systems like those in the west.

By the mid-1960s ideas about evolutionary progress and convergence toward a single model had been formalized in scholarly research and development policy such as modernization theory. Modernization theory (Rostow 1969) reflected three geopolitical trends that characterized this period: (1) the rise of the US as a superpower and with it Anglo-American style capitalism; (2) the simultaneous rise of the Soviet Union and its influence over Eastern Europe, China, and North Korea; and (3) the disintegration of the European colonial empires in Asia, Africa, and Latin America.

By the 1970s, another state-centric view of development emerged to counter the modernist view. An outcome of the turbulent experiences of Central and South America, Asia, and Africa as states there attempted to mimic first-world economies and states, scholars noted, was that developing countries, far from improving their economic circumstances, continued to be both dependent on and increasingly impoverished because of their relationship with western industrial states. Called dependency theory, these theorists pointed out that the underdeveloped world reflected colonial pasts that had not been substantially changed despite decades of development attempts to alter institutions and practices through economic loans and subsidies.

By the early 1980s, however, it became increasingly evident that state-centric ideas, whether of the modernization or dependency schools, could not entirely capture the whole of development outcomes for the rich and especially the poorer parts of the world. Attention by Wallerstein (1980) and others to global exchange structures painted a picture of a capitalist world economic system where economic outcomes are not determined by the actions of any one state. All states are part of a networked capitalist system and the prospects of any one state are influenced by its place in that system and its relation to other states.

During the 1980s and continuing into the 1990s, a resurgence in economic theorizing had an especially strong influence over global development institutions, especially lending institutions and donor countries. The World Bank and International Monetary Fund promoted neoclassical economic precepts, including laissez-faire trade policies such as low tariffs, few import controls, no export subsidies, and free labor markets through loan conditions and repayment terms. Taken together as a neoliberal policy agenda, these practices are known as the Washington Consensus and include the willingness of a developing nation to conform to fiscal discipline, lower taxes, a competitive exchange rate, liberalized foreign direct investment policies, privatization, property rights, and deregulation. These conditions have been a prerequisite for developing nations receiving funds from global development bodies.

Critics of the Washington Consensus point out that these policies and programs create an environment favorable to transnational firms wanting to do business in developing countries, and do not place the social and economic needs of those countries first.

Economic growth typically has been measured in terms of an increase in the size of a nation's material output. Gross domestic product, which supplanted the use of gross national product in the 1990s, is the most frequently used index of both the size and health of a domestic economy. Calculating a nation's GDP involves adding domestic consumption rates with investment, government purchases, and net exports. Increasingly, consumption has become the largest component in this measure.

While GDP details gains of economic significance, according to development scholars critical of this metric, it masks declines in the quality of life experienced by a good portion of the world's population, instead mostly capturing gains for elite countries and specifically the elites within those countries. Critics have devised a number of more inclusive measures of "well-being," such as the United Nations Development Program's Human Development Index (HDI) (UNDP 2001), among a growing list of such efforts. In addition to the traditional economic indicators of growth, "Quality of Life Indexes" typically try to move toward a fuller representation of both economic and non-economic well-being and include measures of "social health" such as education rates, income distribution, and national health. In some instances, indexes go so far as to include crime rates, measures of social benefits and safety nets, and rates of pollution, resource depletion, and long-term environmental damage. Advocates contend that these metrics better assess the overall health of a nation, not just the state of its material economy.

SEE ALSO: Dependency and World-Systems Theories; Economy (Sociological Approach); Global Economy; Modernization

REFERENCES

Rostow, W. W. (1969) *The Stages of Economic Growth.* Cambridge University Press, Cambridge.

United Nations Development Program (2001) *Human Development Report, 2001.* Oxford University Press, New York.

Wallerstein, I. (1980) *The Modern World-System II: Mercantilism and the Consolidation of the European World-Economy, 1600–1750.* Academic Press, New York.

THOMAS D. BEAMISH AND
NICOLE WOOLSEY BIGGART

economic sociology: classical political economic perspective

Classical political economy is the phase of economics from the late eighteenth century to the second half of the nineteenth century since Adam Smith. In addition to Smith, as the founder, its other key members include David Ricardo, Jean-Baptiste Say, William Senior, John S. Mill, Karl Marx and John Cairnes. Classical political economy is defined as the science of the production, distribution, exchange and consumption of wealth. It is divided into two intertwined branches: pure economics as the theory of the market economy and social economics or economic sociology as an analysis of the social-institutional conditions of the economy, including markets.

Classical political economy's perspective on economic sociology examines the influence of social conditions on economic life. In particular, it emphasizes that social institutions greatly affect the economy. Smith identifies certain political and legal institutions that ameliorate the "public welfare," such as civil government tending either to "promote or to disturb the happiness both of the individual and of the society." Say proposes the state can supply a "powerful stimulus" to individual economic activities and well-being. Senior recognizes that the "peculiar institutions of particular Countries," including slavery, legal monopolies, and poor laws, condition wealth distribution. Mill considers wealth distribution a "matter of human institution only" in virtue of its dependence on the "laws and customs of society," while characterizing private property as the "primary and fundamental" institution which underpins the "economic arrangements of society." Both Smith and Mill recognize that prices and markets are subject to institutional and political influences, including the "influence of fixed customs."

Classical political economy also analyzes the class structure of the economy. Smith identifies "different ranks and conditions of men in society," specifically "three great, original, and constituent orders of every civilised society" such as landowners, workers, and capitalists. He finds that "whenever the legislature attempts to regulate the difference between masters and their workmen, its counselors are always the masters." Ricardo regards wealth as distributed among "three classes of the community" and discovering the laws of its distribution as the "main problem" of political economy. For Marx, class – property relations form the "economic structure of society – the real foundation, on which legal and political superstructures arise and to which definite forms of social consciousness correspond."

Classical political economy also examines the social conditions of production and consumption, such as the impact of the division of labor on economic productivity. In a famous statement, Smith states that the division of labor generates the "greatest improvements" in productivity and individuals are "at all times in the need of cooperation" in civilized society. Generally, Cairnes acknowledges that social (and natural) conditions operate as the causes of the production and distribution of wealth. Further, Marx defines material production as a "social relationship" between workers and owners establishing "definite social and political relations" and showing that a certain "mode of production" relates to a certain "social stage." In particular, Marx redefines economic capital as a "social relation of production," such as "a relation of production of bourgeois society."

Some classical economists also recognize the social and cultural conditions of human preferences or tastes and wants and their variety and change. Mill suggests that "a plurality of motives," not just the "mere desire of wealth," motivates economic actors and their actions. Cairnes identifies both the variety of motives and their social conditions in that the "desires, passions and propensities" motivating actors in their pursuit of wealth are "almost infinite" and "may be developed in the progress of society" (invoking the effect of customs on "modifying human conduct"). Marx traces human wants and pleasures to the process of societal formation and historical evolution in that they have their sources in society endowing them with a social nature.

SEE ALSO: Markets; Marx, Karl; Political Economy; Smith, Adam

SUGGESTED READINGS

Marx, K. (1967) [1867] *Capital.* International Publishers, New York.

Mill, J. S. (1884) [1848] *Principles of Political Economy.* Appleton, New York.

Ricardo, D. (1975) [1817] *Principles of Political Economy and Taxation.* Cambridge University Press, Cambridge.

Say, J. (1964) [1803] *A Treatise on Political Economy.* Kelley, New York.

Smith, A (1976) [1776] *An Inquiry into the Nature and Causes of the Wealth of Nations.* Clarendon Press, Oxford.

MILAN ZAFIROVSKI

economic sociology: neoclassical economic perspective

Neoclassical economics is the phase of economic science from the 1870s to the 1930s and later. It resulted from the "marginalist revolution" in economics during the 1870s to the 1890s, above all, the marginal utility theory of value in reaction to classical political economy's labor-based version. Marginalism's founders were William Jevons, Carl Menger, and Leon Walras, simultaneously in 1871–4 "discovering" marginal utility theory to substitute for the labor version. "Neoclassical economics" was coined in the 1900s by Thorstein Veblen suggesting that marginalism was, with its utilitarianism and hedonism, continuous with and "scarcely distinguishable" from classical political economy. Subsequent neoclassical figures were Philip Wicksteed, Eugen Böhm-Bawerk, Friedrich Wieser, Knut Wicksell, Francis Edgeworth, Vilfredo Pareto, Alfred Marshall, Irving Fisher, John B. Clark, etc. Like classical political economy, neoclassical economics involved two branches: pure economic theory and social economics or economic sociology, while being narrower in scope and more mathematical in method.

Jevons coined the term "economic sociology" suggesting its inclusion into economics. He even suggested that "it is only by subdivision, by recognizing a branch of Economic Sociology [etc.], that we can rescue our [economic] science from its confused state." His economic sociology is defined as the "Science of the Evolution of Social Relations" in connection with the economy. Wicksteed advised that economics "must be the handmaid" of sociology. Edgeworth projected mathematical sociology of which marginal utility theory was the "most sublime branch" and considered economics the branch "most applicable" to sociology.

Walras adopted the idea of "social economy" redefined as the "theory of the distribution of social wealth" and integrated with "pure" political economy as the "theory of price determination under the hypothetical regime of absolutely free competition". Wicksell also embraced "social economy" as defined in conjunction with pure and applied economics. Clark considered "Social Economic Dynamics economics" to be "third division" integrated with its other "natural divisions" based on "sociological evolution". Pareto suggested that economists "have to consider not just the economic phenomenon taken by itself, but also the whole social situation, of which the economic situation is only a phase." Wieser advocated social economics studying the "social relations of the economy", or economic sociology addressing the "sociological problems of economic theory".

For much of neoclassical economics, the economy is implicated in society, thus a social phenomenon. Walras recognized that market and other economic transactions by necessity occurred within society. Pareto observed that the "states" of the economy formed "particular cases of the general states of the sociological system" which were "much more complicated," inferring that economics was an "integral" part of sociology in which "complications are greater still and by far." Menger described economic processes as instances of "concrete social phenomena" and the national economy as a social economy, the "social form" of economic activity. Wieser remarked that every economic agent interpreted the marginal principle of the highest total utility at the lowest cost "in the light of his social environment." For Wicksteed the economy is a social phenomenon because it "compels the individual to relate himself to others", making economic laws the "laws of human conduct", thus psycho-social rather than physical phenomena. According to Clark, through arranging producers and consumers into differentiated and unequal social groups the "socialization" of the economy results in societal differentiation, while a special case of "sociological evolution" is economic change.

For these neoclassical economists the influence of society on economic life is evident and strong. In Clark's view, many economic phenomena depend on "social organization." Walras conceded that without "interference" from political authority even a "laissez faire" economy could not function adequately. According to Wicksteed, the market "never has been left to itself" because of social interference, and it "never must be." Also, Marshall identified the adverse impact of customs on the "methods of production and the character of producers."

SEE ALSO: Economic Sociology: Classical Political Economic Perspective; Markets

SUGGESTED READINGS

Jevons, W. S. (1965) [1879] *The Theory of Political Economy*. Kelley, New York.

Pareto, V. (1963) [1916] *The Mind and Society*. Dover Publications, New York.

Schumpeter, J. (1954) *History of Economic Analysis*. New York: Oxford University Press.

Walras, L. (1936) [1896] Etudes d'économie sociale. Pichon et Durand Auzias, Paris.

Wicksteed, P. (1933) [1910] *The Common Sense of Political Economy*. Routledge and Kegan Paul, London.

MILAN ZAFIROVSKI

economics

Economics as a modern discipline focuses primarily on money-coordinated exchange and wage-based production. It is dominated by a US-centered tradition that uses mathematical models and quantitative data to explore *markets*, i.e. the aggregate outcomes of individual actors' decisions to buy and sell various *commodities*. It is probably the most influential of the social sciences because of its connection to the policies of *nation states*, and its role has become increasingly international during the era of *neoliberalism* and *globalization* at the end of the twentieth century. Its market-based explanations have been applied in a number of sociological subfields, but sociologists typically find its approach too narrow and unrealistic in the way it brackets the institutional contexts of actors' decisions.

MODERN MATHEMATICAL ECONOMICS

Economics mainly analyzes the material production of goods in societies with industrial technology, an extensive division of labor, and monetary means of exchange. From the early twentieth century onwards it has increasingly focused on mathematical models of rational decisions and market coordination. It is often presented as consisting of micro and macro branches, the former focusing on business, employee, and consumer-level decisions, the latter analyzing national and international systems of production, finance, and employment. Theories in both branches generally consist of precise stylized models involving graphs, equations summed over multiple dimensions, calculus-based solutions to maximization problems, and topological proofs of the possibility of complex equilibria. These models are typically tested using quantitative data and a wide variety of *regression*-based statistical techniques ("econometrics").

Economics does not typically attempt to explain cultural or other institutional contexts, nor does it examine the detailed structures of organizations or other social groups. With the exception of some experimental and psychology-based subfields it simply treats individual and collective actors "as if" they routinely make complex maximizing calculations in the appropriate markets. When it explains major macroeconomic shifts it does so in terms of exogenous developments in politics, technology, and attitudes, or changes in amounts of *human capital*. It does not focus on explaining the political, cultural, and environmental origins or consequences of such developments.

HISTORY AND SOCIAL ROLE

Western economics has always been closely tied to the policies of nation states. Early modern approaches focused on active governmental support of commerce and agriculture, while eighteenth-century "classical" ideas of markets and labor-based values implied that the material wealth of nations was best promoted by liberal, hands-off policies. *Laissez-faire* policies were also supported by late nineteenth-century "neoclassical" microeconomics, which began to use graphs and calculus-based models to explore how prices responded to demand as well as labor input, and how decisions were made in terms of marginal rather than average costs. During the *Great Depression* the macroeconomic models of John Maynard Keynes were much more in line with interventionist policies, and after World War II these flourished alongside new developments in constrained optimization modeling and econometrics. As neoliberal policy regimes began to increase in influence from the 1970s onwards, economics continued to combine a wide range of ideas and promote the further adoption of mathematical techniques, most notably in financial pricing models and *game theory*.

The post-war period was also when the discipline's center of gravity moved decisively towards the USA, where it was increasingly institutionalized as a *profession* with multiple representatives in business, government, and *transnational organizations*. The long-term significance of this – and of its subsequent spread to other countries – is hard to gauge. On the one hand it is clear that the scientific authority of mathematical market models is a potentially powerful discursive resource for justifying *neoliberal* policy regimes. It is also clear that economic theories have in many ways become embedded in modern institutions, for example in basic measures such as "gross national product," in complex financial trading algorithms, and even in the very notion of "the economy" as a distinct entity. On the other hand many orthodox economists are critical of extreme neoliberalism, and their influence in practical settings seems to depend greatly on the pre-existing interests and authority of decision-makers. Furthermore it must be remembered that most neoliberal ideology came from outside the professional mainstream, and that the math-based authority of economic knowledge was largely the same during the previous era of Keynesian interventionism.

RELATIONSHIP TO SOCIOLOGY

Economics and sociology tend to be institutionally and intellectually separate despite the clear overlap in subject matter. Comprehensive syntheses have not proved popular, and most interactions have involved economists attempting to bring scientific rigor to a supposedly inferior discipline, or sociologists arguing that market-based explanations of economic and other phenomena are hopelessly narrow, if not ideologically biased.

Major attempts by economists to explain ostensibly non-economic phenomena include public choice theory (analyzing voting patterns and the self-interested behavior of lobbyists, politicians, and bureaucrats), new institutional economics (modeling the effects of different institutionalized incentives on various levels of organizational structure), and Gary S. Becker's *rational choice* program (presenting utility maximization and human capital as the key to understanding all social interaction). While ideas from these lines of research have been selectively adopted in related sociological subfields, sociologists have generally remained unconvinced that choice or market models can ever adequately take account of broader social, cultural, and political factors.

Applications of sociology to economics have generally centered on this same issue of narrowness of focus. Examples of this are *Marxist* critiques of capitalism (including *world systems* and *dependency theories*) and other approaches to *stratification* which look at how apparently fair market allocations of wealth are in fact biased by historical, political, and cultural factors outside the scope of economic analysis. Analyses of *work*, *consumer* behavior, and the meanings of particular commodities similarly suggest that apparently simple market decisions actually depend on complex cultural and social factors. Finally, the field of *economic sociology* has developed very consciously as a counterpoint to economics, arguing that market processes can only be understood by examining their *embeddedness* in broader social contexts.

SEE ALSO: Economic Development; Economic Sociology: Classical Political Economic Perspective; Economic Sociology: Neoclassical Economic Perspective

SUGGESTED READINGS

Backhouse, R. E. (1985) *A History of Modern Economic Analysis*. Blackwell, Cambridge, MA.

Becker, G. S. (1978) *The Economic Approach to Human Behavior*. University of Chicago Press, Chicago, IL.

Bernstein, M. A. (2001) *A Perilous Progress: Economists and Public Purpose in Twentieth-Century America*. Princeton University Press, Princeton, NJ.

Fourcade-Gourinchas, M. (2006) The construction of a global profession: the transnationalization of economics. *American Journal of Sociology* 112: 145–94.

MacKenzie, D., Muniesa, F., & Siu, L. (eds.) (2007) *Do Economists Make Markets? On the Performativity of Economics*. Princeton University Press, Princeton, NJ.

MICHAEL REAY

economy, culture and

In traditional academic discourse, "culture" and "economy" have long been regarded as separate analytical spheres: on the one hand, the realm of shared cognitions, norms, and symbols, studied by anthropologists; on the other, the realm of self-interest, where economists reign supreme. Though the two disciplines overlap occasionally (in economic anthropology mainly), radical differences in the conceptual and methodological routes each field followed during the twentieth century have prevented any sort of meaningful interaction.

By contrast, the interaction between culture and the economy has always been a central component of sociological analysis. All the founding fathers of sociology were, one way or another, interested in the relationship between people's economic conditions and their moral universe. In his famous presentation in the *Preface to a Contribution to the Critique of Political Economy*, for instance, Marx described "forms of social consciousness" essentially as an epiphenomenon of material relations. Later interpretations, however, have suggested that even for Marx and Engels the relationships between "material base" and "superstructure" were far from deterministic. The "western" Marxist traditions that developed in Europe after World War I proposed a somewhat more sophisticated analysis that emphasized the integration of culture into the apparatus of domination – either because the hegemony exerted by bourgeois culture induces the masses into implicitly consenting to their own economic oppression, or because the incorporation of culture into the commercial nexus of capitalism leads to uniformity of spirit and behavior and the absence of critical thinking. Still, in these formulations, culture remains wedded to its material origins in capitalist relations of production.

Partly reacting against what they perceived to be a one-sided understanding of the relationships between base and superstructure in Marxist writings, Weber and Durkheim both sought to demonstrate the greater autonomy of the cultural realm, albeit in quite different ways. Both insisted that people's behavior is always infused with a meaning that is not reducible to their material positions. Weber, more than anyone else, demonstrated the influence of preexisting ideas and, in particular, religious worldviews on the economic conduct of individuals. For instance, even though their actions may look rational from the outside, the behavior of early Protestant capitalists was quite illogical from the inside: anxiety about salvation, rather than self-interest, motivated them to accumulate. In other words, their search for profit was not based on instrumental rationality, but it made *psychological* sense given the religious (cultural) universe in which they lived. In fact, Weber considered that all religions condition individual attitudes toward the world and therefore influence involvement in practical affairs – but they, of course, all do it differently, so that the "economic ethics" of individuals varies substantially across social contexts.

It is Durkheim, however, who best articulated the *collective* basis of our meaning-making orientation: groups of individuals share certain understandings that they come to take for granted in their routine dealings with each other. Hence how people behave, including in economic settings, is not a priori reducible to a set of predetermined individual preferences and the interests they support. Rather, most of people's actions are motivated by habit and routine; and preferences, as well as the institutions they support, are informed by cultural norms. In each society, then, culture and institutions act in tandem to shape individual consciousness and thereby representations of what is understood to be "rational."

As a system of representations that exists separately and independently of individuals, culture may shape economic behavior in many different ways. It may be more or less institutionalized. Corporate cultures, for instance, are often highly formalized, even bureaucratized, but the rules that underlie bazaar interactions, though obviously codified, remain very informal. Second, the effect of culture may be more or less profound: Meyer and Rowan (1977), for instance, have famously suggested that many organizational rules are adopted in a purely ceremonial way but have little impact on actual practice – a claim that has been notably supported by research on educational institutions and hospitals. On the other hand, substantial evidence has come out of cross-national studies of a deep patterning, not only of economic values and norms but also of economic institutions and organizations.

Biernacki (1995) illustrates particularly well the fact that we should think about the role of culture primarily through its inscription in *practices*. Economic settings, therefore, do not simply display, or reflect, preexisting cultural understandings, but should be regarded as places where distinctive local cultures are formed and carried out. There are two main ways in which this point has been articulated in the sociological literature. The first emphasizes the social meanings people produce (whether voluntarily or involuntarily) through their use of economic settings and economic objects, and is best illustrated by consumption studies. The second suggests that some form of social order – i.e., regulating norms and practices – emerges out of the interpersonal interactions that take place within economic settings, particularly formal organizations and markets.

SEE ALSO: Consumption; Culture; Globalization; Globalization, Culture and; McDonaldization

REFERENCES

Biernacki, R. (1995) *The Fabrication of Labor: Germany and Britain, 1640–1914*. University of California Press, Berkeley, CA.

Meyer, J. & Rowan, B. (1977) Institutionalized organizations: formal structure as myth and ceremony. *American Journal of Sociology* 83 (2): 340–63.

SUGGESTED READINGS

Amin, A. & Thrift, N. (eds.) (2004) *The Cultural Economy Reader*. Blackwell, Oxford.

Polanyi, K. (2001) [1944] *The Great Transformation*. Beacon Press, Boston, MA.

MARION FOURCADE-GOURINCHAS

economy (sociological approach)

The general problem of how to conceptualize and explain the relations of the economy to wider contexts of human behavior has been one of the main themes of major theorists in the sociological tradition. In the classical phase of the tradition, Marx, Weber, and Durkheim each treated the problem. Marx postulates that the economy as the base or foundation of social life that gives rise to social classes is rooted in the social relations of production, as in his analysis of capitalism. Weber took a more multidimensional approach that, for example, showed how cultural orientations and legal systems have an impact on economic phenomena, including capitalism. Durkheim took up Adam Smith's analysis of how the division of labor enhanced economic productivity and supplemented it with a corresponding analysis of how social differentiation led to an organic form of integration of modern societies through webs of interdependence of units.

Two successive developments or phases characterize later sociological analysis of the economy. The central contribution in the first phase occurred in the 1950s, an era in which functionalism was the dominant theoretical paradigm in sociology and Talcott Parsons was its leading advocate. In *Economy and Society* (1956), Parsons and his collaborator built on prior sociological and economic theoretical analyses to set out a functional systems analysis of the economy in relation to its various conceptualized environments. The basic idea is that any system of human behavior must have social structures and processes that perform four functions, namely, adaptation to environment, attainment of system goals, integration of parts, and maintenance of common meanings. For a societal system, these are identified as, respectively, the economic, the political, the social integration, and the culture maintenance (e.g., education) function. In many tribal societies these functions are all performed by the kinship system. But in more differentiated societies, there are structures and processes that tend to be specialized by function. This leads to the model of society as a system of four interrelated function subsystems. The economy is the subsystem that accomplishes the societal adaptation function in terms of provision of primary and acquired human needs in a particular habitat. Similarly, a polity or political subsystem consists of social organization that deals with societal goal attainment, interpreted as the need for collective decisions. There are input-output or "interchange" relations among the four function subsystems, through which each pair of subsystems obtains resources from the other, more or less adequate to perform its function for society under the given conditions. The notion of interchange makes it clear that the state of the economy is dependent upon the state of the other subsystems that constitute its societal environment.

Given its conceptual complexity involving, for instance, nested series of functional analyses of subsystems within subsystems, the model was difficult for other sociologists to grasp. As a consequence it did stimulate much research and when functionalism declined as a theoretical paradigm in sociology, economic sociology went into a kind of hibernation until the mid-1980s when a second phase emerged. Initially it was termed "the new economic sociology" to distinguish it from the earlier approach. Its key theme is the embeddedness of economic phenomena in culture and social structure, including interpersonal relations in social networks. By contrast with the earlier approach, the new phase has many more empirical investigators and a variety of specific lines of research and theory.

Sociologists have generalized the concept of capital to employ such notions as social capital in reference to the use of social connections as in the above example, and cultural capital, defined in terms of knowledge (e.g., art and music) and education. In empirical studies, Bourdieu (1984) proposes that economic and cultural capital are two dimensions of a space, called a field, such that consumer lifestyle choices depend upon position in the space and "habitus," an internal structure of dispositions acquired in socialization. Bourdieu claims this field-and-habitus model overcomes the limitations of both the rational choice assumption of standard economic theory (choice comes from the habitus) and the Marxian reduction of class conflict to economics (competitive struggles arise in a multi-dimensional field).

SEE ALSO: Bourdieu, Pierre; Economic Sociology: Classical Political Economic Perspective; Economic Sociology: Neoclassical Economic Perspective; Marx, Karl; Parsons, Talcott; Weber, Max

REFERENCES

Bourdieu, P. (1984) *Distinction: A Social Critique of the Judgment of Taste*. Harvard University Press, Cambridge, MA.

SUGGESTED READINGS

Dobbin, F. (ed.) (2004) *The New Economic Sociology: A Reader*. Princeton University Press, Princeton, NJ.

Granovetter, M. (1985) Economic action and social structure: the problem of embeddedness. *American Journal of Sociology* 91: 481–510.

Smelser, N. & Swedberg, R. (eds.) (2003) *Handbook of Economic Sociology*, 2nd edn. Russell Sage Foundation and Princeton University Press, Princeton, NJ.

THOMAS J. FARARO

education

After the Industrial Revolution, the responsibility for educating youth shifted from families to schools in developed nations. Schools are now a major social institution, educating the majority of children and youth in the developed world and functioning as a primary engine of change in developing countries. Sociology of education has sought to understand the central role that schools play in society from a variety of perspectives, with great emphasis on issues pertaining to equality and opportunity. Sociologists have two broad theoretical approaches to studying education's role in society: the functionalist and conflict paradigms. The functionalist paradigm emphasizes the role that education plays for society, while the conflict paradigm focuses on divisions within society that education maintains or reinforces.

The structure of a country's educational system is closely linked to its economic and political history. Though all developed nations provide universal education, some countries' school systems are run by the central government that ensures standardized curricula and funding, while others are more decentralized. In the developing world, many countries do not have a history of stability and this affects developing countries' ability to provide universal education. In many developing countries the school system is inherited in a large part from the former colonial power and is heavily shaped by the policies of the World Bank. Education systems are closely related to economic growth and having a disciplined and educated labor force is an important step in economic development.

Though commonalities in the structure of schooling exist across countries, each country is generally unique in its development of its schools. Systems of education not only reflect national values, but also play a major role in shaping national society. In the USA, the idea of public schooling – or the common school – developed in the early nineteenth century as a response to political and economic shifts in American society. Prior to common schooling, only children from wealthier families could afford formal schooling. As the USA moved from a barter-and-trade to a market economy, the fragmented and informal system of schooling was no longer adequate preparation for children to be competitive in the market-driven economy. The end result was the development of the common school. Common schools had two main goals: first, to provide knowledge and skills necessary to be an active member of civic life; and second, to create Americans who value the same things: patriotism, achievement, competition, and Protestant values. Though common schools provided more equitable access to education for white children than the previous informal system, these schools still reflected the values of the ruling elite – white Protestants.

When common schools finally included African-American children, after the US Civil War, they were educated in separate facilities. By 1896 "separate but equal" schools were officially sanctioned by the Supreme Court (in *Plessy v. Ferguson*). Racially-segregated schools became the norm across the USA, and white schools received substantially more financial and academic resources. In 1954, "Separate but equal" schools were finally declared inherently unequal in the Supreme Court decision *Brown v. Board of Education of Topeka* (1954), and schools were ordered to desegregate "with all deliberate speed."

Though *Brown* is perhaps one of the most widely-celebrated Supreme Court decisions, schools in the USA have failed to reflect the ideals of educational equality put forth in the ruling. Early research in sociology of education, such as the influential *Coleman Report* (1966), recognized that stratification in educational attainment was strongly related to students' family background, particularly in terms of race or ethnicity. This suggests that inequalities in education are deeply intertwined with inequalities in the structure of US society and that educational inequalities potentially begin before children ever set foot in kindergarten. Since *the Coleman Report*, educational researchers and policy makers have struggled to know how to provide equality of educational opportunity within a national context of socioeconomic inequality.

Beginning around 1980, sociologists of education turned their attention to stratification systems at work *within* schools. Secondary schools tend to group students in courses or "tracks" (such as academic, general, or vocational), and these groupings often reinforce the relationship between family background and attainment. Schools tend to provide more resources, such as higher quality instruction, to students in higher-level tracks which can have serious consequences for students in other tracks.

Though sociology of education has focused on how school processes affect achievement and equality, families play an important role in education that has received significant attention. For example, families from the middle and upper socioeconomic statuses (SES) may provide their children with more *cultural capital* – or dispositions, attitudes, and manners of speech that are recognized as elite – than parents from lower SES. Parents with higher levels of SES tend to actively foster children's growth through adult-organized activities that encourage critical and original thinking and provide children with *cultural capital* which they can then use to take advantage of opportunities at school. Working-class and poor parents, on the other hand, support their children's "natural growth" by providing the conditions necessary for their child's development, but leaving the structure of leisure activities to the children (Lareau 1987). Families can also transmit advantages to their children through *social capital*, or the "the norms, the social networks, and the relationships between adults and children that are of value for the child's growing up" (Coleman 1987: 334). The relationships can help monitor children's development, communicate norms (such as staying in school), and help deter bad behavior (such as cutting class).

SEE ALSO: Cultural Capital; Educational Inequality; Self-Fulfilling Prophecy; Sex Education

REFERENCES

Coleman, J. S. (1987) Families and schools. *Educational Researcher* 16 (6): 32–8.

Coleman, J. S., Campbell, E. Q., Hobson, C. J., McPartland, J., Mood, A. M., Weinfall, F. D., & York, R. L. (1966) *Equality of Educational Opportunity*. Department of Health, Education, and Welfare, Washington, DC.

Lareau, A. (1987) Social class differences in family–school relationships: the importance of cultural capital. *Sociology of Education* 60: 73–85.

ANNA S. MUELLER

educational inequality

Educational attainment is affected by effort and ability which, in turn, are affected by the characteristics of students' families of origin. Students raised by educated parents are more likely to exhibit higher levels of scholastic ability and motivation than those raised by less educated parents. It has been argued (Bourdieu et al. 1977) that children raised in the privileged social strata internalize the values of the dominant culture effortlessly and enjoy an advantage in the educational attainment process. Recent studies show that the main component of cultural capital that affects educational achievement is exposure to books and reading. Studies have also shown that children raised in small families benefit from a larger share of the family's resources, including parental attention which, in turn, enhances their cognitive development and educational attainment. In some societies, nuclear families are embedded in extended families in supportive communities whose assistance mitigates the negative effects of large sibships. Educational attainment is also affected by the social cohesion of families and communities. Sociologists refer to social cohesion as social capital. Children's educational attainment is also affected by their family's income because high-income families can afford the costs of education. Moreover, children raised in poverty are less likely to develop the cognitive skills necessary for subsequent educational success.

Most of the explained variance in students' educational achievements is due to individual and family characteristics of the kind discussed above. However, some variance is also explained by characteristics of the schools that students attend. Students benefit from attending schools that are attended by peers from privileged social origin. In addition, many educational systems place students into distinct curricular tracks. The most common distinction is between the tracks that prepare students for higher education, and tracks that prepare them for immediate entry into the labor force. Students from less privileged strata are more likely to attend the latter tracks, which restricts subsequent educational attainment. Thus, tracking transmits inequality between generations.

Historically, when the rates of labor-force participation by women were low, daughters were expected to function primarily in the private sphere: marry, bear children, and perform housework, activities not deemed to require an education above the very basic levels. More recently, women's educational levels have caught up and, in some countries, surpassed those of men. However, women are still more likely than men to attend lower-tier institutions such as two-year or less prestigious colleges and are less likely to study the exact sciences and engineering.

SEE ALSO: Education; Meritocracy; Stratification and Inequality, Theories of; Tracking

REFERENCES

Bourdieu, P., Passeron, J.-C., & Nice, R. (1977) *Reproduction in Education, Society and Culture*. Sage, London.

Bradley, K. (2000) The incorporation of women higher education: paradoxical outcomes? *Sociology of Education* 73: 1–18.

YOSSI SHAVIT

elections, the sociology of

The sociological theories of elections date back to the 1940s, when Paul Lazarsfeld developed the *Opinion Leaders Model* – also known as the *two-step hypothesis*. According to this theory, voters rely on an "opinion leader" when making political choices. An "opinion leader" is an individual in a "primary group" whose views are trusted on a subject. Instead of being swayed by the media, voters rely on the opinion-leader, who may rely on the media's coverage of the election. The process goes as follows:

Mass media → Opinion leaders → Citizens

The Michigan model, developed by Angus Campbell in *The American Voter* (1960), is the main alternative. The central concept is *party-identification*. Some voters are socialised to identify with one of the major political parties. Citizens who identify with a party (*party-identifiers*) will tend to vote in every election – and tend to vote for *their* party. Non-party identifiers, by contrast, will tend not to vote (unless prompted by short-term factors). Campbell distinguished between, respectively: "Maintaining elections" and "Deviating elections." In a "maintaining election," the campaign will typically be dull and devoid of "short-term factors." The outcome is determined by party-identifiers, as the party with the highest number of party-identifiers can rely on them to cast their vote. The result will converge towards the so-called "normal vote." In a "deviating" election, by contrast, short term factors (e.g. a charismatic candidate), will prompt non party-identifiers to turn out to vote (thus increasing turnout) and may tempt weaker party identifiers to shift party.

While fewer people are party identifiers now (some have talked about *dealignment*), the model is still used both in the USA and in other western democracies.

SEE ALSO: Democracy; Political Parties; Political Sociology; Politics; Politics and Media

SUGGESTED READING

Lazarsfeld, P. F., Berelson, B., & Gaudet, H. (1988) *The People's Choice*. Columbia University Press, New York.

MATT QVORTRUP

elective affinity

The term elective affinity is currently associated with Weber's thesis concerning modern capitalism. A key aspect concerns the linkage, attraction, or inner "affinity" between "the Protestant Ethic/Protestant sects" and the "spirit" of modern capitalism. The idea of an affinity could be indicated by any two factors seeming to go together – to be "connected." Weber argues that there is an "inner affinity" (*innere Verwandtschaft*) between several things, especially between (1) a this-worldly asceticism of sects (e.g., Quakers, Mennonites) and (2) the underlying "spirit" (*Geist*) of modern capitalism. Rather than hedonism, among Protestants there is an ascetic outlook, an estrangement from joy, as indicated by Benjamin Franklin's maxims. The lack of possibility of a temporal causal argument is already emphasized in Weber's 1905 statement (Weber 2002a), published at the same time as his famous methodological essay on "Objectivity." Since statistical terminology was not widely used there was no universally agreed term to represent the notion of an "association" or non-causal "co-relationship" between two factors or "variables" (Howe 1978).

SEE ALSO: Weber, Max

REFERENCES

Howe, R. (1978) Max Weber's elective affinities: sociology within the bounds of pure reason. *American Journal of Sociology* 84: 366–85.

Weber, M. (2002) [1905] *The Protestant Ethic and the Spirit of Capitalism: The Version of 1905, together with Weber's Rebuttals of Fischer and Rachfahl and Other Essays on Protestantism and Society*. Penguin, New York.

J. I. (HANS) BAKKER

Elias, Norbert (1897–1990)

Norbert Elias was born in Breslau, Germany in 1897. He was the son of a small manufacturer and was brought up in comfortable surroundings. Elias received his PhD in 1924 and then went to Heidelberg, where he became very actively involved in sociology circles, most notably one headed by Marianne Weber. He also became friend and assistant to Karl Mannheim. This relationship led Elias to follow Mannheim as his official assistant to the University of Frankfurt in 1930.

Elias proposed the concept of figuration as an alternative to thinking of the "individual" and "society" as different or antagonistic. Figurations are not static, but instead are social processes. In fact, during the latter part of his career, Elias chose the label *process sociology* to describe his work (Mennell 1992: 252). Figurations involve the "interweaving" of people. They describe the relationships between people rather than describing a type of structure which is external to or coercive over people. In other words, individuals are viewed as open and their relationships with one another compose figurations. Figurations are in a state of constant flux because of the changing nature of power, which is central to their understanding. They develop in largely unforeseeable ways.

The idea of a figuration is a broad one in that it can be used to apply to the micro and the macro, and to every social phenomenon in between. This image is best represented by Elias's notion of "chains of interdependence," which constitute the real focus of his work.

In addition to figurations and chains of interdependence, Elias's work is largely concerned with the "sociogenesis" of civilization, especially in the Occident (Bogner et al. 1992). In particular, Elias is interested in what he perceives to be the gradual changes that have occurred in the behavioral and psychological makeup of those living in the west. In his study of the history of manners, for example, Elias is concerned with the historical transformation of a wide array of rather mundane behaviors which have culminated in what we would now call civilized behavior. Some of the behaviors which most interest Elias include what embarrasses us, and how we have grown increasingly observant of others.

In *Power and Civility* (1994b) Elias is concerned with changes in social constraint that are associated with the rise of self-restraint, the real key to the civilizing process. The most important of these social constraints is the macrostructural phenomena of the lengthening of interdependency chains. This also contributes to the corresponding need for individuals to moderate their emotions by developing the "habit of connecting events in terms of chains of cause and effect" (p. 236). Thus, the ever-increasing differentiation of social functions plays a central role in the process of civilization. In addition and in conjunction with this differentiation is the importance of "a total reorganization of the social fabric" (p. 231). This is how Elias describes the historical process of the emergence of increasingly stable central organs of society that monopolize the means of physical force and taxation. Central to this development is the emergence of a king with absolute status, as well as of a court society.

The king and his court were of particular importance to Elias because it was here that changes took place that would eventually affect the rest of society. The court noble was forced to be increasingly sensitive to others while simultaneously curbing his own emotions because, unlike the warrior, his dependency chains were relatively long. The nobles play an important role in the civilizing process because they carry the changes from the court to the rest of society. Further, changes in the west are eventually spread to other parts of the world. Despite the importance of the king, the nobles, and the court, the ultimate cause of the most decisive changes is related to the changes in the entire figuration of the time. In other words, the real importance of change is found in the changing relationships between groups, as well as those between individuals in those groups.

SEE ALSO: Civilizations; Civilizing Process; Figurational Sociology; Micro–Macro Links

REFERENCES

Bogner, A., Baker, A., & Kilminster, R. (1992) The theory of the civilizing process: an idiographic theory of modernization. *Theory, Culture, and Society* 9: 23–52.

Elias, N. (1994b) [1939] *The Civilizing Process, Part 2: Power and Civility*. Pantheon, New York.

Mennell, S. (1992) *Norbert Elias: An Introduction*. Blackwell, Oxford.

SUGGESTED READING

Elias, N. (1994a) [1939] *The Civilizing Process*. Blackwell, Oxford.

GEORGE RITZER AND J. MICHAEL RYAN

elites

The classic work on elites was done in the nineteenth and early twentieth centuries by the Italians Vilfredo Pareto and his contemporary Gaetano Mosca. To them, the circulation of elites was paramount. A seminal study in this tradition is C. Wright Mills's *The Power Elite* (1956), which shows that the United States governmental, military, and business elites are highly interconnected. Today, the degree of openness of institutions and the chance that a particular person with certain characteristics will occupy an elite position are at the top of the research agenda. Thus, the French sociologist Pierre Bourdieu emphasizes the process of *reproduction* of elites through scholarly and cultural capital. In the German educational system, for example, while openness has increased, this is not true for the chances of obtaining an elite position (Hartmann 2002). While such groups have been studied, little data are available on how these elites make decisions in (in)formal settings.

Members of families sometimes show a great ability to stay in top positions, creating an almost dynastic continuity. For instance, the ability to obtain an elite position in the Dutch nobility, a characteristic based on birth, has not declined much during the twentieth century (Schijf et al. 2004). During the twentieth century local elites were incorporated into national elites. Today, one can see the rapid development of a global economy. Nevertheless, there are few indications of an international business elite. In the boards of executives in countries like France, Germany, Great Britain, and the US, the overwhelming majority of the executives have the same nationality as the countries where the corporations are located.

SEE ALSO: Bourdieu, Pierre; Mills, C. Wright; Power Elite

REFERENCES

Hartmann, M. (2002) *Der Mythos von den Leistungseliten. Spitzenkarrieren und soziale Herkunft in Wirtschaft. Politik, Justiz und Wissenschaft*. Campus, Frankfurt.

Schijf, H., Dronkers, J., & van den Broeke-George, J. (2004) Recruitment of members of Dutch noble and high-bourgeois families to elite positions in the 20th century. *Social Science Information* 43 (3): 435–77.

JAAP DRONKERS AND HUIBERT SCHIJF

emic/etic

"Emic" and "etic" have become shorthand terms, especially in anthropology, for an "insider" versus an "outsider" view of a particular social world. For example, an outsider view of an economic exchange might hold that a seller's goal is to maximize profit. An insider view from people actually involved in the exchange might show that profit was not the concern. Kinship ties, a long relationship history, previous social favors, earlier non-cash trades, a desire to curry favor – such social threads in a relationship might result in an exchange that, to an outsider, would look "irrational," while to an insider it would make perfect sense.

The distinction between emic and etic, insider and outsider, originated in the linguistics of the 1950s, most famously in the work of Kenneth Pike (1967). In the 1960s, anthropology borrowed and shortened the linguist's distinction between phonetic and phonemic and began talking about "etic" and "emic." But the abbreviated concepts were applied to ethnography as a whole, not just to language.

Because of debates between "materialist" or etic and "symbolic" or emic approaches to anthropology, "etic" and "emic" turned into labels for competing kinds of ethnographic descriptions. This was a fundamental error, since neither the original linguistic concepts nor their development in cognitive anthropology had defined an "either/or" use of the terms. The shift to etic/emic as a partition of the ethnographic space rather than a dialectic process by which it was explored introduced distortion into the use of the terms that continues to this day. The question should not be, does one do emic or etic ethnography? The question should be, how does one tack back and forth between human universals and the shape of a particular social world at the time an ethnographer encounters it. That was the original sense of emic and etic in phonology.

SEE ALSO: Culture; Ethnography; Observation, Participant and Non-Participant

REFERENCE

Pike, K. L. (1967) *Language in Relation to a Unified Theory of Human Behavior*. Mouton, The Hague.

SUGGESTED READING

D'Andrade, R. G. (1995) *The Development of Cognitive Anthropology*. Cambridge University Press, Cambridge.

MICHAEL AGAR

emotion: cultural aspects

The relationship between emotions and culture has been discussed ever since there was interest in what it means to be human, and since then that relationship has been contrastingly characterized as either inimical or reconcilable. Culture can be understood as the defining values, meanings, and thoughts of a local, national, or supranational community. When emotions are conceived in terms of psychological feelings and physical sensations, then they appear inimical to culture. This is because such a perspective suggests the involuntary nature and disorganizing consequence of emotions.

The majority of sociologists and anthropologists and large numbers of psychologists and philosophers who have written on emotions since the 1980s believe that emotions are constructed by cultural factors. The constructionist position holds that emotional experiences depend on cultural cues and interpretations, and therefore that linguistic practices, values, norms, and currents of belief constitute the substance of experience of emotions. Biological and even social structural factors are irrelevant for this approach. A corollary of constructionism is that persons can voluntarily determine the emotions they experience, that the cultural construction of emotions entails emotions management. The constructionist approach has enlivened discussion of emotions and drawn attention to the ways in which emotions are differentially experienced across societal divisions and through historical time. The object of any emotion will be influenced by prevailing meanings and values, as will the way emotions are expressed; thus what is feared and how people show fear, indeed how they may experience fear, will necessarily vary from culture to culture. The strength of this perspective is demonstrated by the fact that emotions attract cultural labels or names. In this way emotions become integrated into the broader conceptual repertoire of a culture and prevailing implicit cultural values and beliefs are infused into the meaning of named emotions. Thus the notorious difficulty of translating emotion words from one language to another.

The role of emotions in the construction of culture points not only to the composition of emotion but also significantly to its function. Emotions alert individuals to changes in and elements of their environment that are of concern to them, provide focus to situations in which these things are integral, and facilitate appropriate strategies to normalize these situations. That is, emotions both define the situations of persons and indicate what their interests are or intentions might be within them. It is a short step from this statement of the function of emotion to one concerning the emotional contribution to culture. The cultural regulation of emotion occurs through elaboration of cognitive-situational feelings. It is likely that this process can be understood as emotional reaction to emotional experience, and that much cultural variation can be understood in this way. Jealousy, for example, is a widespread if not universal emotion. But in "traditional" or "Mediterranean" societies people are proud of their jealousy, whereas in "modern" or "western" societies people may be ashamed of it. Even the apparent absence of certain emotions from particular cultures can be explained in this way, as with Simmel's "blasé feeling," the emotional antidote to self-regarding emotions under conditions of metropolitan life.

SEE ALSO: Affect Control Theory; Emotion: Social Psychological Aspects; Emotion Work

SUGGESTED READING

Barbalet, J. M. (1998) *Emotion, Social Theory, and Social Structure*. Cambridge University Press, Cambridge.

Turner, J. (2000) *On the Origins of Human Emotions*. Stanford University Press, Stanford, CA.

JACK BARBALET

emotions: social psychological aspects

The sociological study of emotion rests on a two-stage theory. The first stage is an internal state of biological arousal, and the second is a reflexive process using situational cues to interpret or identify which emotion is an appropriate response in that situation (Rosenberg 1990: "Reflexivity and emotions"). There may also be a third process of negotiation with others as to the emotional definition of the situation.

The sociology of emotions literature demonstrates many analytical and theoretical differences common to much of sociology as a whole. The most important theoretical or analytical differences are as follows: determinism vs. constructionism, cognition vs. emotion, structure vs. interaction, biology vs. socialization or political economy (e.g. gender), the social control of emotions vs. emotional forms of social control, and physiology vs. phenomenology. Similarly, the chief methodological debates center on questions of quantitative vs. qualitative methods of analysis, and prediction vs. description. A convenient way to characterize the sociology of emotions is in terms of symbolic interactionist and social psychological approaches.

Traditional sociological examinations of the self have generally left open the question of emotion. Emotion has been mentioned in passing, relegated to the discipline of psychology, or carefully skirted in treatises on motivation or motive. Social psychological research on emotions had until recently focused extensively on the use and recognition of physiological cues connected to emotional states, primarily under experimental conditions.

Through internalization of emotion norms in early socialization, individuals learn what emotions are appropriate to types of situations, and are therefore equipped to manage situated emotional identities. The development of the "looking glass self" (Cooley 1902) allows the growing social actor to experience sympathy or empathy, which may be a prerequisite for the adoption of the "role-taking" emotions of pride, shame, or envy.

A figurative or virtual audience, which Mead (1934) might have identified as the "generalized other," serves an internal regulative function similar to that provided by the literal social audience. Feeling rules and the consequent emotion work are the media through which the self learns to control his or her own behavior and feelings (Hochschild 1979: "Emotion work, feeling rules, and social structure"). Shott (1979: "Emotion and social life: a symbolic interactionist analysis") asserts that emotional social control becomes articulated in adult society as emotional self-control. In 1962, Schachter and Singer ("Cognitive, social, and physiological determinants of emotional state") injected their subjects with substances that stimulated states of physiological arousal for which there were no affective cues in the situation. Subjects were then provided with cognitive cues toward one or another emotion. Schachter and Singer concluded that situational cues or definitions indicated the appropriate emotion label for the participants.

Gross and Stone's (1964) pioneering article on the emotion of embarrassment proposed a theoretical justification for the treatment of embarrassment (and, by association, emotions in general) as a social phenomenon. Gross and Stone contributed two key ideas. First, they commented on the social nature of embarrassment, that certain situations are more prone to the effects of embarrassment than others (i.e., situations requiring "continuous and coordinated role performance" (1964: 116)). Second, certain situated identities are more precarious than others, and are therefore more prone to embarrassment, such as the identity of the adolescent.

SEE ALSO: Emotions: Cultural Aspects; Emotion Work; Identity: Social Psychological Aspects

REFERENCES

Cooley, C. H. (1902) *Human Nature and the Social Order*. Scribner's, New York.

Gross, E. and Stone, G. P. (1964) Embarrassment and the analysis of role requirements. *American Journal of Sociology* 70 (July): 1–15.

Hochschild, A. R. (1979) Emotion work, feeling rules, and social structure. *American Journal of Sociology* 85: 551–75.

Mead, G. H. (1934) *Mind, Self, and Society*. University of Chicago Press, Chicago, IL.

Rosenberg, M. (1990) Reflexivity and emotions. *Social Psychology Quarterly* 53: 3–12.

Schachter, S. and Singer, J. (1962) Cognitive, social, and physiological determinants of emotional state. *Psychological Review* 69: 379–99.

Shott, S. (1979) Emotion and social life: a symbolic interactionist analysis. *American Journal of Sociology* 84 (6): 1317–34.

LESLIE WASSON

emotion work

Emotion work refers to the management and regulation of one's own feelings, or the personal effort expended to maintain equilibrium in relationship, through the production, transformation or inhibition of feelings. The term "emotional labor" is sometimes used interchangeably with "emotion work," which can be confusing. To differentiate the terms, emotional labor takes place in a paid, public work environment, while emotion work is unpaid and engaged in a private or public setting within the context of personal relationships. Emotional labor requires workers to display certain emotions to customers or co-workers, as part of their job duties in order to promote specific organizational goals. Emotion work does not have specific requirements; it is an interactive process that occurs to preserve or sustain personal relationships. Emotion management refers to the complex process of managing oneself and others; it is another term used synonymously with emotion work.

Closely related to emotion work as a critical aspect of interpersonal communication in the social domain are affect control and display theories, social exchange theories, and ability and concept models of emotional intelligence. Each of these concepts focuses upon various aspects of the process, context, and outcomes of emotion work. Symbolic interactionists examine emotions by exploring ways that individuals use their agency to navigate their feelings among various cultural constraints. A sense of correct response to situations is rooted in "feeling rules," which are culturally and socially determined norms for how one is supposed to feel in a given situation (Hochschild 2003). For example, it is the norm to feel sad about tragic events and happy about achievements. Expressions of emotion work vary immensely within cultures, and may be displayed in various external manners ranging from a discreet facial expression to a profuse body gesture.

Sociologists have included emotion work in their research for decades. Early classical thinkers including Durkheim, Mead, Marx, and Weber addressed emotion in the larger context of their analyses of society. However, in the late 1970s, Arlie Hochschild introduced the concept of emotional labor in the workplace as the actual process a person engages in an effort to follow feeling rules.

Drawing upon the legacy of Erving Goffman's theory of facework, Hochschild states that emotions are managed through situational and cultural feeling rules and display dictums that constitute the emotion culture. Individuals may engage in either surface acting or deep acting in order to comply with feeling and display rules. Surface acting involves simply adapting one's outward expressions and presentation to deceive others about one's true feelings. In contrast, deep acting requires that an individual must not only change one's expressions, but also modify the personal experience of emotions by deceiving oneself about the nature or extent of one's feelings in order to match the emotional display required by an organization. Such acting can result in feeling inauthentic, as well as alienated, stressed, and depressed. Hochschild highlights the gendered nature of emotional work and labor, noting that women have handled the bulk of it in both the workforce and household.

While much research has been conducted in business organizations about the conceptualizations, linkages and operations of emotion work, much remains to explore regarding in-depth examinations of cross-cultural features of emotion work, and emotion work in children.

SEE ALSO: Affect Control Theory; Erving Goffman; Emotion: Cultural Aspects; Emotion: Social Psychological Aspects; Symbolic Interaction.

REFERENCE

Hochschild, A. R. (2003) *The Managed Heart: Commercialization of Human Feeling*, 20th anniv. edn. University of California Press, Berkeley, CA.

SUGGESTED READING

Goleman, D. (2005) *Emotional Intelligence*, 10th anniv. edn. Bantam Books, New York.

DIANNE FABII

empire

With etymological roots in the Latin *imperium*, empire refers to a large-scale, multi-ethnic political unit that rules over smaller political units, peoples and territory that have been aggregated through conquest. Hence, empire always involves relations of domination and subordination, which may be formal or informal. Understood in this way, empires and imperialism appear contemporaneously with civilization, beginning 5,000–6,000 years ago.

Empires first emerge in the Near East (Assyrian, Babylonian, Egyptian), and are followed by more expansive empires in the centuries immediately surrounding the beginning of the Christian era (Macedonian, Greek, Roman, Persian, and Chinese). It is not until the dawn of European modernity, however, that imperial expansion takes on a globalizing form.

The establishment of modern European empires can be divided into three periods. The first runs from the late fifteenth to the middle of the seventeenth century, and is marked by Portuguese and Spanish conquest of the New World. The second runs from the middle of the seventeenth to the middle of the nineteenth century, and was initiated by successful challenges to Spanish/Habsburg hegemony by Holland, Britain, and France, and by their own establishment of maritime empires. The third and final period, representing the zenith of European imperialism, begins in the second half of the nineteenth century and is not concluded until decolonization in the decades following World War II. Empire during this period is married with nationalism and racism in an era of intensifying inter-imperialist rivalry.

While the decades following World War II marked the denouement of formal empires, they did not mark the end of theorizing about empire. A new generation of radical thinkers insisted that formal imperial rule had simply been replaced by new forms of informal economic and political subjugation in the capitalist world system. More recently, such thinking has informed discussions of whether or not the contemporary USA is, or is moving towards, becoming an empire, given its most recent global projection of power.

SEE ALSO: Civilizations; Globalization; Global Politics

SUGGESTED READINGS

Hardt, M. & Negri, A. (2000) *Empire*. Harvard University Press, Cambridge, MA.

Lenin, V. I. (1950) [1917] *Imperialism, the Highest Stage of Capitalism*. In: *Selected Works*, vol. 1. Foreign Languages Publishing House, Moscow.

LLOYD COX

empiricism

The term empiricism refers to both a philosophical approach toward understanding the world and the principles and methods that ground modern scientific practices. The philosophy of empiricism, which was first stated by Aristotle and other classical philosophers, came to fruition in the writings of Enlightenment-era scholars including David Hume and John Locke. A key philosophical question at the time was whether knowledge should be generated based on experience, as the empiricists argued, or on a combination of intellect and intuition, as proposed by rationalists such as René Descartes. An increased acceptance of the empirical approach to understanding the world fostered the growth both of modern science and the Industrial Revolution.

Empiricist philosophy has become codified as modern principles of scientific inquiry which include the formulation of verifiable hypotheses that are tested through unbiased and repeatable experiments. While physical sciences allow for precise measurement of phenomena of interest, this is more difficult in the social sciences for several reasons, including the "observer effect," where people who are aware they are under scientific observation may change their behaviors to conform with or thwart researcher expectations, and the fact that the effects of social pressures cannot be measured directly. The founders of sociology, including Émile Durkheim and Max Weber, helped create an empirical approach to studying society when they addressed these issues.

Durkheim helped found the scientific approach to the study of society with his publication *Rules of Sociological Method* in 1895, which explains that sociology rests on the observation and measurement of the effects of social forces on people through measurable phenomena such as crime and suicide rates. The hermeneutic approach to sociology provides an alternative approach toward understanding the effects of society on human behavior, by using methods such as interviews, textual analysis, and self-observation to understand social phenomena. Max Weber is considered a foundational researcher in this approach primarily as a result of his study *The Protestant Ethic*, which argued that the Protestant belief system provided a strong foundation for the growth of capitalism.

The scientific approach to sociology popularized by Durkheim and the hermeneutic approach roughly correspond to the modern quantitative and qualitative approaches to sociology. Within each of these camps there is a further division over the role that social theory should play in driving social research. Researchers who support the deductive or "theory-driven" approach argue that studies should focus on testing existing social theories, while supporters of the inductive or "data-driven" approach argue that researchers should approach social phenomena with few preconceived notions and then allow their theories and research questions to evolve over the course of their research.

SEE ALSO: Hermeneutics; Methods; Theory and Methods

SUGGESTED READINGS

Durkheim, É. (1982) [1895] *Rules of Sociological Method*. Free Press, New York.

Weber, M. (2001) [1905] *The Protestant Ethic and the Spirit of Capitalism*. Routledge, New York.

CHARLES MCCORMICK

encoding/decoding

Stuart Hall employed the terms "encoding" and "decoding" in an influential article first drafted in 1973 as a stenciled paper published by the University of Birmingham's Centre for Contemporary Cultural Studies. CCCS, of which Hall was director from 1968 to 1979, was committed to developing new methods and models for the study of culture. Hall's rethinking of communication and mass media studies contributed enormously to a reformulation of the study of popular culture. Unlike those conventional mass media studies that view communication as a uni-directional circuit comprised of sender–message–receiver, Hall suggests that communication is an ongoing and ultimately unstable process marked by feedback, struggle, exchange, and negotiation. Importantly, in his encoding/decoding paper, he insists that the content of mass media must not be viewed as input that gives rise to predetermined effects. Instead, Hall invokes the language and logic of semiotics, focusing less on the presumed effectiveness of a particular instance of media communication and emphasizing the discursive production – by way of cultural *codes* – of the "media sign." No matter how transparent or natural the meaning of a media sign might seem, its intelligibility is always secured through the deployment of conventional (or *hegemonic*) codes.

Hall points out that successful communication doesn't come naturally; it depends upon the effective use of discursive codes to compel a meaningful decoding activity. Communication, on Hall's view, is an active process that requires work on the part of both producers (described as *encoders*) and viewers (described as *decoders*). On Hall's view, mass media messages are both carefully structured through the use of conventional codes and fundamentally polysemic, that is, open to a variety of readings.

The most analytically productive component of Hall's application of semiotic models to thinking about mass media is to be found in his careful discussion of three possible decoding positions. Meaningful media signs – signs that make sense – are those in which there is some measure of symmetry between the processes of encoding and decoding. The most symmetrical is the dominant-hegemonic position. Here, the viewer interprets the media sign according to the same logic used by encoder-producers. Often described as a "preferred reading," in this framework, the viewer's decoding strategies proceed along the same logic as the producers' encoding strategies. Without conflict, the meaning of the sign is secured hegemonically. By contrast, the least symmetrical decoding position is described as oppositional. Here, the viewer recognizes the preferred reading that has been constructed by producers, but rejects it in its totality. If in the dominant-hegemonic mode, signs are accepted and viewed as natural, in the oppositional mode, signs and the codes that produce them are viewed as misleading distortions of reality. More common than either the dominant-hegemonic or oppositional decoding position is the negotiated position, in which a viewer accepts portions of the preferred reading of the media sign while rejecting others.

The impact of Hall's short paper on the field of cultural studies cannot be underestimated. The invocation of semiotic models had a lasting impact upon the practice of cultural studies in Britain and North America. Hall endorsed a shift in this field towards a theoretically sophisticated form of audience studies, which was taken up most notably by David Morley (1980) in his analyses of *Nationwide* and by Janice Radway (1984) in *Reading the Romance*. Although it remains a significant model in the field of cultural studies, Hall's encoding/decoding has been displaced by poststructuralist approaches to making sense of communication.

SEE ALSO: Cultural studies, British Cultural Studies; Semiotics; Hegemony; Hegemony and the Media

SUGGESTED READINGS

Hall, S. (1973) Encoding and decoding in the media discourse. *CCCS Stencilled Paper* 7.

Hall, S. (1980) Encoding/decoding. In: Hobson, D., Lowe, A., & Willis, P. (eds.), *Culture, Media, Language*. Hutchinson, London.

MICHELLE MEAGHER

endogenous development

Endogenous development was presented as an alternative perspective on development that reconsidered modernization theory, which had until the 1960s been the dominant analytical paradigm of social change. The notion of "endogenous development" originates in two sources. One was the Dag Hammarskjöld report *Another Development*, presented to the Seventh Special Session of the United Nations General Assembly in 1975. The other original contribution came from a Japanese sociologist, Kazuko Tsurumi. She first used the term "endogenous development" in 1976, critically examining western theories of social change and modernization in light of non-western experiences.

The goal of endogenous development is for all humans and their groups to meet basic needs in food, clothing, shelter, and medical care as well as to create conditions in which individuals can fully utilize their potentialities. Paths to the goal follow diverse processes of social change. Individuals and groups in each region must autonomously create social visions and ways forward to the goal by adapting to their own ecological systems and basing development programs on their own cultural heritage and traditions.

The notion of endogenous development began to be employed extensively in the late 1970s by organizations, including the United Nations and UNESCO, as well as by individual researchers in various countries and regions. It was an attempt to explore an alternative route to development in a world faced with dangerous and seemingly intractable global problems, such as disruption of ecosystems, poverty, and famine.

SEE ALSO: Dependency and World-Systems Theories; Development: Political Economy; Globalization; Modernization

SUGGESTED READINGS

Dag Hammarskjöld Foundation (1975) *What Now: Another Development*. The 1975 Dag Hammarskjöld Report on Development and International Cooperation. Prepared for the Seventh Special Session of the United Nations General Assembly, New York, September 1–12.

Tsurumi, K. (1979) *Aspects of Endogenous Development in Modern Japan*. Research Papers, Series A-36. Institute of International Relations, Sophia University, Tokyo.

KOSAKU YOSHINO

Engels, Friedrich (1820–95)

Without Karl Marx, of course, few people today would know the name of Friedrich Engels; but without Engels we might have heard much less from Karl Marx.

Engels was born into a wealthy, devout, Protestant family in the industrial town of Barmen (now Wuppertal), in the Rhineland region of what is now Germany. The industrialist father wished his eldest son to follow in his footsteps, and so in 1838, before he could even finish high school, Engels was sent to clerk for a business in Bremen. Critically, neither his privileged family background nor his own eventual success as a capitalist prevented him from devoting his life to destroying capitalism. He also had a natural talent with languages – a skill he would put to good use in his later years as an international political figure and organizer.

In 1842, after completing his military service, Engels traveled to Cologne where he met with Karl Marx and Moses Hess, both of whom were editors at the *Rheinische Zeitung*, a radical newspaper for which Engels had written. Hess saw England as the country most likely to produce his hoped-for communist revolution. As it happened, Engels's father had significant financial interests in a large textile factory in Manchester, and so Engels, now a communist himself, went for two years to Manchester to work in the factory as a clerk. In 1845 he would publish a book entitled *The Condition of the Working-Class in England, 1844* based on his fieldwork in Manchester, and his work on the English political economists would point Marx toward the material for *Capital*.

On his way home to Barmen, Engels made a brief stop in Paris and again met with Marx. As Engels later wrote, "When I visited Marx in Paris in the summer of 1844 we found ourselves in complete agreement on questions of theory and our collaboration began at that time." He and Marx would collaborate on several manuscripts, including *The Holy Family*, and *The German Ideology* in which they would make some attempt to flesh out their philosophical and political positions and distinguish themselves from a number of rivals. And it was out of this collaboration, and at the request of the London-based League of the Just, that perhaps the world's most famous political pamphlet, *The Communist Manifesto*, was written.

After Marx's death in 1883 Engels devoted the rest of his life to Marx and Marxism, largely at the expense of his own work. Although he did manage to publish *The Origins of the Family, Private Property, and the State* in 1884, his *Dialectics of Nature* was published long after his death in 1925. His first priority was to see to it that the remaining volumes of *Capital* were published. No simple task given the disorganized state in which Marx left his papers; volume 2 was published in 1885 and volume 3 appeared nine years later in 1894. His second priority was leading the international socialist movement, which he did by continuing his worldwide correspondence, writing articles for and advising the leaders of the Second International, and meeting with visiting intellectuals and revolutionaries, such as Georgi Plekhanov, one of Russia's first Marxists. Vigorous until the end, Engels died of throat cancer in 1895.

SEE ALSO: Communism; Dialectical Materialism; Feminism; Marx, Karl; Marxism and Sociology

SUGGESTED READING

Marx, K. & Engels, F. (1975–2005) *Collected Works*, vols. 1–50. Lawrence and Wishart, London.

CLIFFORD L. STAPLES

environmental movements

Environmental movements are loose, uninstitutionalized networks of individuals and groups engaged in collective action motivated by shared concern about environmental issues. They are identical neither with organizations nor with protest. Less visible local action and interactions with governments and corporations are also important.

Although environmental concern has a long history, modern environmentalism dates from the 1970s, informed by increasing scientific knowledge and influenced by New left and counter cultural critiques. In North America and Western Europe, increasing concern and impatience with the timidity of conservationist organizations produced new, more radical internationalist environmental movement organizations (EMOs) that embraced nonviolent direct action: skilful exploitation of mass media made Friends of the Earth (FoE) and Greenpeace the fastest growing EMOs during the 1980s.

Their rise encouraged innovation in the tactics and agenda of conservation organizations. Soon, networking among older and newer organizations was common. Environmentalism developed through successive waves of critique, innovation, and incorporation. Radical ecological groupings and the environmental justice movement grew out of dissatisfaction with increasingly institutionalized reform environmentalism. EMOs increasingly embrace social justice and their networks extend to human rights and development NGOs.

Environmentalism is frequently explained as a dimension of post-materialism. But environmental concerns are held both by highly educated "post-materialistists," less fearful for their own security than concerned about global impacts of environmental change, and by less well educated people fearful for their own security.

Post-materialism better predicts environmental *activism*. Environmental activists and members of EMOs are disproportionately highly-educated, employed in teaching, creative, welfare, or caring professions. Because locally unwanted land uses more often impact upon the poor, grassroots environmental movements are more broadly inclusive, especially of women.

Traditionally, "success" for a social movement meant institutionalization, usually as a political party. Viewed thus, the institutionalization of a movement is a contradiction in terms. Environmental movements may have squared the circle. Measured by size, income, formality of organizations, number and professionalization of employees, and interaction with established institutional actors, EMOs in industrialized countries have, since the late 1980s, become institutionalized. Yet institutionalization did not simply entail deradicalization. Despite worries that institutionalization has turned EMOs into "protest businesses" incapable of mobilizing supporters for action, in western Europe in the 1990s reported environmental protest increased and became more confrontational. Even radical "disorganizations" committed to direct action were connected by networks of advice and support to more established organizations as groups realized the advantages of cooperation and practiced a division of labor. Thus environmental movements may retain many characteristics of an emergent movement whilst taking advantage of institutionalization. The "self-limiting radicalism" of green parties is less striking than the "self-limiting institutionalization" of environmental movements.

Environmental movements vary according to material differences in their environments. In North America, Australasia and Nordic countries, wilderness issues have been salient. In western Europe, where the physical environment is more obviously a human product, concern to protect landscapes more readily combines with concerns about the human consequences of environmental degradation.

In the global South, environmental issues are bound up with struggles over distribution of power and resources, and rarely sustain environmental movements. Impeded by lack of democratic rights and judicial protection, successful campaigns often depend upon support from Northern environmental or human rights organizations.

Deliberately informal networks rather than formal organization have been preferred in recent waves of environmental activism, but the relationship of local protests to movements is problematic. Most local protests are NIMBY (not in my backyard) in origin; although some are transformed into universalist campaigns, others remain particularistic. Only rarely do local campaign groups grow into general EMOs, but they may nevertheless serve as sources of innovation and renewal within national environmental movements, by "discovering" new issues, initiating new activists, and devising new tactics.

The absence of a developed global polity presents obstacles to the formation of a global environmental movement. Although international agreements and agencies encourage development of transnational environmental NGOs, these are not mass participatory organizations and, outside the North, rarely have deep roots in civil society. However, better and cheaper communications erode distance just as increasing participation in higher education gives more people the skills and resources to operate transnationally.

SEE ALSO: Ecological Problems; Environmental Sociology; Global Justice as a Social Movement; Social Movements; Social Movements, Networks and; Social Movements, Nonviolent

SUGGESTED READINGS

Rootes, C. (ed.) (1999) *Environmental Movements: Local, National and Global.* Frank Cass, London and Portland, OR.

Rootes, C. (ed.) (2003) *Environmental Protest in Western Europe*. Oxford University Press, Oxford.

Rootes, C. (2004) Environmental movements. In Snow, D. A., Soule, S. A., & Kriesi, H. (eds.), *The Blackwell Companion to Social Movements*. Blackwell, Oxford and Malden, MA, pp. 608–40.

CHRISTOPHER ROOTES

environmental problems

Humans have faced poor environmental conditions throughout history, but what we think of as "environmental problems" became more common and apparent with urbanization. In the USA urban air and water pollution attracted growing attention throughout the last century, and by the 1960s became recognized as significant problems. Celebration of the first "Earth Day" on April 22, 1970, helped transform "environmental quality" into a major social concern, and a wide range of environmental conditions from pollution to declining wilderness and wildlife became major social problems. Examining the socio economic processes that generate environmental problems is beyond the scope of this essay, but the nature of such problems can be clarified via use of an ecological perspective.

Ecologists note that the environment provides many "services" for human beings (and all other species), but we can simplify these into three general types of functions that it performs for human societies. First, the environment provides us with the resources necessary for life, from clean air and water to food and shelter, as well as the natural resources used in industrial economies. In providing what ecologists term the "sustenance base" for human societies, the environment is serving a "supply depot" function. It supplies us with both renewable and non-renewable resources, and overuse of the former (e.g. water) may result in shortages and the latter (e.g. fossil fuels) in potential scarcities.

Second, in the process of consuming resources humans produce "waste" products; indeed, we produce a vastly greater quantity and variety of waste products than any other species. The environment must serve as a "sink" or "waste repository" for these wastes, either absorbing or recycling them into useful or at least harmless substances. When the waste products (e.g., city sewage or factory emissions) exceed the environment's ability to absorb them, the result is pollution.

Finally, like all other species, humans must also have a place to live, and the environment provides our "habitat" – where we live, work, play, and travel (e.g., our vast transportation systems and recreational areas). Thus, the third function of the environment is to provide "living space" for human populations. When we overuse a given living space – from a city to the entire Earth – overcrowding and/or overpopulation occurs.

In sum, when humans overuse an environment's ability to fulfill any single function, "environmental problems" in the form of pollution, resource shortages and overcrowding and/or overpopulation are the result. Yet, not only must the environment serve all three functions, but when a given environment is used for one function its ability to fulfill the other two can be impaired. Functional incompatibilities between the living-space and waste-repository functions are apparent, for example, when using an area for a waste site makes it unsuitable for living space. Similarly, if hazardous materials escape from a waste repository and contaminate the soil or water, the area can no longer serve as a supply depot for drinking water or agricultural products. Finally, converting farmland or forests into housing subdivisions creates more living space for people, but means that the land can no longer function as a supply depot for food or timber or habitat for wildlife.

Separating these three functions and analyzing our conflicting uses of them provides insight into the evolution of environmental problems over time. In the 1960s and early 1970s, when awareness of environmental problems was growing rapidly in the USA, air and water pollution and the protection of areas of natural beauty and recreational value were major concerns. The "energy crisis" of 1973–4 highlighted the dependence of modern industrialized nations on fossil fuels, and thus our vulnerability to energy shortages. The living space function came to the fore in the late 1970s when it was discovered that the Love Canal neighborhood in upstate New York was built on an abandoned chemical waste site that was leaking toxic materials, the first of a rapidly growing number of contaminated sites continually discovered (but seldom fully remediated).

More recently, problems stemming from functional incompatibilities at larger geographical scales have become common. The quest for living space and agricultural land leads to tropical deforestation and loss of biodiversity, while use of the atmosphere as a waste site for aerosols and greenhouse gases produces ozone depletion and global warming.

Analysts use the "ecological footprint," a measure which captures all three functions of the environment, to measure the "load" which humans place on the global ecosystem, and results suggest that the current world population is unsustainable. However, the footprints of poorer nations are vastly lower than those of wealthy nations. Furthermore, wealthy nations are able to protect their living spaces in part by using poorer nations as supply depots (importing resources from them) and waste repositories (exporting pollution and polluting industries to them). Efforts to solve global environmental problems such as human-induced climate change thus encounter major equity issues.

Whereas historically the notion that human societies face "limits to growth" was based on the assumption that we may run out of food supplies or natural resources such as oil, contemporary "ecological limits" refers to the finite ability of the global ecosystem to serve all three functions simultaneously without having its own functioning impaired. The limited ability of the Earth's atmosphere to absorb greenhouse gas emissions without producing deleterious changes in climate may prove the most significant ecological limit of all, making prevention of global warming a critical challenge.

SEE ALSO: Ecological Problems; Ecology; Environmental Movements; Environmental Sociology; Global Warming

SUGGESTED READINGS:

Dunlap, R. E. & Catton, W. R., Jr. (2002) Which functions of the environment do we study? A comparison of environmental and natural resource sociology. *Society and Natural Resources* 14: 239–49.

Kitzes, J., Wackernagel, M., Loh, J., Peller, A., Goldfinger, S., Cheng, D., & Tea, K. (2008) Shrink and share: humanity's present and future footprint. *Philosophical Transactions of the Royal Society* 363: 467–75.

Millennium Ecosystem Assessment (2005) *Ecosystems and Human Well-Being: Synthesis*. Island Press, Washington, DC.

RILEY E. DUNLAP

environmental sociology

Environmental sociology emerged in the 1970s, largely in response to widespread societal awareness of environmental problems and mobilization of support for environmental protection symbolized by celebration of the first "Earth Day" in 1970. Early sociological research on environmental topics involved analyses of public opinion toward environmental issues; environmental activism at both the individual and organizational levels; governmental agencies responsible for natural resource management and environmental protection; and the roles of activists, media, scientists and public officials in generating attention to environmental problems. This research applied perspectives from established sociological fields such as social psychology, social movements, political sociology, and organizational sociology to environmental topics, constituting a "sociology of environmental issues."

The 1973–4 energy crisis highlighting the dependence of industrialized societies on fossil fuels, and increasing awareness of the seriousness of air and water pollution throughout the 1970s, ushered in a new strand of sociological research – examining how societies affect their environments and in turn are affected by changing environmental conditions such as pollution and resource scarcity. This concern with societal-environmental relationships reflected the emergence of a true "environmental sociology," and by the late 1970s it was a small but vigorous field. Its focus on the relationships between modern societies and their environments represented a major departure from disciplinary norms, however, putting environmental sociology on the margins of the larger discipline.

Sociology became a distinct discipline over a century ago by emphasizing the social – as opposed to biological, geographical and psychological – causes of human behavior. It developed during an era of general resource abundance, technological progress and economic growth. As a result, sociology became grounded in a cultural worldview which assumed that sophisticated social organization (e.g., complex division of labor) and scientific and technological advances had freed industrial societies from environmental influences such as resource constraints. This assumption reinforced negative reactions to earlier excesses of "environmental determinism" such as geographers' efforts to explain cultural differences via climatic variation. The result was that mid-twentieth-century sociology largely ignored the physical environment, and sociological references to "the environment" typically meant the social context of the phenomenon being investigated.

Sociological analyses of the societal impacts of energy shortages and possibility of ecological "limits to growth" constituted a significant disciplinary development in the 1970s. This work was quickly supplemented by research on the social impacts of toxic contamination and other forms of pollution, as well as examinations of the societal factors generating environmental degradation. By the 1980s a growing number of environmental sociologists were ignoring disciplinary norms by analyzing the societal causes and impacts of environmental problems.

The evolution of this work since the 1980s has turned environmental sociology into an intellectually vibrant field. It has achieved legitimacy in the larger discipline and credibility in academia and society at large due to realization that environmental problems are "social problems." They are caused by human behavior, have harmful impacts on humans (and other species) and their solution requires collective action. Moreover, environmental conditions do not become "problems" until they are defined and recognized as such. These aspects of environmental problems led to four major emphases in contemporary environmental sociology: analyses of (1) the "social construction" of environmental problems, (2) the causes of such problems, (3) the potential and actual impacts of the problems, and (4) societal efforts to solve the problems.

Noting that phenomena such as industrial wastes may be ignored in one era and/or locale but viewed as "pollution" later on or in other locations, environmental sociologists analyze how environmental conditions come to be viewed as "problematic." Researchers examine the roles of activists, government officials, scientists and the media in defining conditions as problematic; the techniques employed to legitimize the claims; and the challenges faced in gaining widespread acceptance of the claims. These analyses demonstrate that environmental problems do not simply emerge from "objective" conditions, but must be socially constructed as problematic by key actors and then become widely accepted as such.

Once environmental problems are recognized, their sources can be studied. Since environmental problems are frequently created by human behavior, environmental sociologists analyze the social forces generating such problems – from local toxic contamination to tropical deforestation and greenhouse gas emissions. Some studies investigate the roles of particular industries or government agencies in creating the problems, while others employ cross-national data to sort out the relative impacts of population, affluence and other national characteristics on indicators of environmental degradation such as CO_2 emissions or deforestation. Current cross-national research examines the relative importance of population size and growth, national affluence, consumption levels and economic factors such as trade patterns in generating environmental degradation.

Environmental problems are typically viewed as problematic because they pose threats to humans, and many environmental sociologists investigate the wide-ranging social impacts of these problems. The discovery of toxic wastes at Love Canal in the late 1970s stimulated numerous studies of "contaminated communities," and interest in the social impacts of a range of environmentally undesirable conditions from leaking landfills to air pollution. A common finding is that racial minorities and lower socioeconomic strata are disproportionately exposed to environmental hazards, and "environmental justice" research has become a major theme in environmental sociology. Recent analyses of how wealthy nations use poorer nations as resource providers and pollution dumps demonstrate environmental injustice at the global level.

Lastly, environmental sociologists examine efforts to solve or prevent environmental problems, often by evaluating existing and potential environmental policies. They demonstrate how environmentally relevant behaviors are embedded in structural conditions, and that promoting pro-environmental behavior therefore requires more than appealing for voluntary changes in lifestyle. Developing effective mass transit systems and providing community-wide collection of recyclables, for example, are more effective than simply asking people to drive less and recycle more. Likewise, promoting energy-efficient building standards is more efficacious than appealing for household conservation. At the macro level, environmental sociologists examine characteristics of industries and nation-states associated with environmental performance in order to determine the potential for improvements, as well as the roles of governments, corporations, and non-governmental organizations in promoting such improvements.

SEE ALSO: Consumption, Green/Sustainable; Ecological Problems; Ecology; Environmental Movements; Environmental Problems; Global Warming

SUGGESTED READINGS

Dietz, T. & Stern, P. C. (eds.) (2002) *New Tools for Environmental Policy*. National Academies Press, Washington, DC.

Dunlap, R. E. & Marshall, B. M. (2007) Environmental sociology. In: Bryant, C. D. & Peck, D. L. (eds.), *21st Century Sociology: A Reference Volume*. Sage, Thousand Oaks, CA, pp. 329–40.

Hannigan, J. (2006) *Environmental Sociology: A Social Constructivist Perspective*, 2nd edn. Routledge, New York.

Harper, C. L. (2008) *Environment and Society*, 4th edn. Prentice Hall, Upper Saddle River, NJ.

Pellow, D. N. & Brulle, R. J. (2005) *Power, Justice, and the Environment: A Critical Appraisal of the Environ-mental Justice Movement*. MIT Press, Cambridge, MA.

RILEY E. DUNLAP

epidemiology

Epidemiology is the study of the distribution of disease as well as its determinants and consequences in human populations. It uses statistical methods to answer questions on how much disease there is, what specific factors put individuals at risk, and how severe disease outcomes are in patient populations to inform public health policy-making. The term "disease" encompasses not only physical or mental illnesses but also behavioral patterns with negative health consequences such as substance abuse or violence.

The measurement of disease occurrence begins with the estimation of incidence and prevalence. Disease incidence is the number of new cases in a population within a specific period of time. First-ever incidence picks up only first-ever onsets; in contrast, episode incidence records all onsets of disease events, including those of recurrent episodes. Cumulative incidence expresses the risk of contracting a disease as the proportion of the population who would experience the onset over a specific time period.

Prevalence is the number of people in a population with a specific disease. Point prevalence counts all diseased individuals at a point in time, whereas period prevalence records those with the disease during a stated time period. Cumulative prevalence includes all those with the disease during their lives or between two specific time points. The nature of the disease itself determines the appropriate choice of measure. For example, for single-episode conditions with a clearly defined onset such as chickenpox, first-ever and cumulative incidence rates are most useful, but for recurrent conditions with ill-defined onsets such as allergy, period and cumulative prevalence rates are most often analyzed.

Population epidemiology attempts to unravel causal mechanisms of disease with a view to prevention. Since most diseases are determined by multiple genetic and environmental factors, exposures to single risk factors are usually neither sufficient nor necessary causes of a disease. Consequently, efforts are devoted to quantify the level of increased risk when exposed to a particular risk factor. Risk is normally measured as either a ratio of the prevalence of disease in two populations or the ratio of the odds of exposure to a particular risk factor between two groups. Clinical epidemiology, in turn, aims at the identification of disease outcomes with the goal to control the damage done to the patients.

Since the 1980s epidemiological methods have been successfully applied to the study of social maladies (e.g., divorce, homicide, drug addiction, etc.) and a new subfield known as social epidemiology has emerged to use sociological constructs (e.g., social inequalities, racial discrimination, sexism, residential segregation, etc.) in the analysis of disease. Knowledge derived from these cross-disciplinary fecundations is widely adopted by grassroots activists and policy makers for the empowerment of marginalized at-risk populations. In 2005 the World Health Organization established the Commission on the Social Determinants of Health to assist developing countries to combat social injustices leading to ill-health and premature deaths. The growing consensus that interpersonal interactions, collective activities, and social institutions affect and are affected by health will herald an even closer collaboration between epidemiologists and sociologists in the coming years.

SEE ALSO: Epidemiology; Health and Race; Socioeconomic Status, Health, and Mortality

SUGGESTED READINGS

Berkman, L. F., Kawachi, I. (eds.) (2000) *Social Epidemiology*. Oxford University Press, New York.

Bhopal, R. S. (2002) *Concepts of Epidemiology: An Integrated Introduction to the Ideas, Theories,*

Principles, and Methods of Epidemiology. Oxford University Press, New York.
Cwikel, J. G. (2006) *Social Epidemiology: Strategies for Public Health Activism*. Columbia University Press, New York.

HUNG-EN SUNG

epistemology

The Greek words for knowledge and explanation are *episteme* and *logos*, respectively. Epistemology is the study of the nature (theory) of knowledge and justification. Epistemology is the kind of philosophy (or the primary role assigned to philosophy) valued in the scientific view of the world. In such a world, significant emphasis is placed on providing evidence for our claims to know, and philosophy has the task of examining the logic and methods involved in questions of *how* we know and what gives knowledge the property of being valid. The phrase "after epistemology" or "overcoming epistemology" often heard in philosophical circles is, in part, a reaction to restricting philosophy to epistemological concerns, to matters of "knowing about knowing." The tradition of continental philosophy (hermeneutics, existentialism, critical theory, phenomenology, etc.) that inspires much thinking in the social sciences today, expands the concern with knowing to "knowing about being and doing." In other words its concerns are not strictly epistemological, but also metaphysical and aesthetic.

Debates between the two great classical modern philosophies of rationalism and empiricism that developed in the seventeenth and eighteenth centuries form the backdrop for understanding the emergence of social science methodologies. Empiricist epistemology (Locke, Hume, Berkeley) argued that knowledge is derived from sense experience; genuine, legitimate knowledge consists of beliefs that can be justified by observation. Rationalist epistemology (Descartes, Spinoza) held that reason is the sure path to knowledge. Rationalists may claim that sense experiences are an effect of external causes; that a priori ideas (concepts, theories, etc.) provide a structure for making sense of experience; and/or that reason provides a kind of certainty that the senses cannot provide. Kant's philosophy is recognized for (among other things) its grand synthesis and reconciliation of the key insights of these two theories of knowledge.

Empiricism as an epistemology continues to occupy a central place in thinking about methodology, particularly in Anglo-American traditions. It is one of the cornerstones of the naturalistic interpretation of the social sciences – the view that the explanatory and predictive methods of the natural sciences, as well as the aim of developing a theory of the way the natural world works, ought to be extended to the social (human or moral) sciences.

Rationalist and empiricist epistemologies are foundationalist; that is, they hold that any claim labeled as "knowledge" must rest on a secure (i.e., permanent, indisputable) foundation. The rationalist locates this foundation in reason; the empiricist, in sense experience. While acknowledging that reason and experience are important in understanding the nature of knowledge, much contemporary epistemology is nonfoundationalist – it rejects the view that knowledge must be erected on an absolutely secure foundation. Nonfoundationalists argue there simply are no such things as secure foundations; hence, our knowledge is always conjectural and subject to revision. This distinction between foundationalist and nonfoundationalist epistemologies is one way of marking the difference between philosophies of positivism and postpositivism. The former believe in the possibility (and necessity) of unassailable ground for any claim to knowledge; the latter abandon this idea. However, postpositivism does not discard the idea that knowledge is built up from (relatively) neutral observations of the "way things are." It simply acknowledges that, at any given time, our understanding of the way things are might be mistaken. Postpositivists are thus fallibilists with respect to knowledge – the presumption is that current knowledge is correct given the best available procedures, evidence, and arguments, yet current understandings can be revised in light of new criticism or evidence.

SEE ALSO: Feminism and Science, Feminist Epistemology; Knowledge, Sociology of; Objectivity; Positivism; Postpositivism; Social Epistemology

SUGGESTED READINGS

Grayling, A. C. (1996) Epistemology. In: Bunnin, N. & Tsui-James, E. P. (eds.), *The Blackwell Companion to Philosophy*. Blackwell, Oxford, pp. 38–63.
Taylor, C. (1995) Overcoming epistemology. In: *Philosophical Arguments*. Harvard University Press, Cambridge, MA.
Turner, S. P. & Roth, P. A. (2003) *The Blackwell Guide to the Philosophy of the Social Sciences*. Blackwell, Oxford.

THOMAS A. SCHWANDT

essentialism and constructionism

The debate over constructionism and essentialism is a longstanding philosophical argument, from Plato and Aristotle to contemporary debates over deconstruction in literary theory. Broadly and simply, essentialism suggests that qualities are inherent in objects of study, with little reference to contexts, ambiguities, and relativities. It is a "belief in the real, true essence of things" (Fuss 1989: xi). By contrast, constructionism (and its allied concept deconstruction, as put forward by Derrida) suggests qualities are always bound up with historically produced, contextually bound meanings or discourses. They are always open to change and never fixed. Many terms are allied antimonies such as absolutism and relativism, realism and interpretivism, and holism and methodological individualism. Other terms, such as humanism, can be used by either camp.

Essentialist theories of sexual identities suggest that an inner sense of self unfolds through biological or psychic processes, and the task is to uncover the "true" meaning of who one is sexually. A classic reading of Freud would suggest that although one is born of "polymorphous perversity" and potential bisexuality, that is channeled into a relatively stable and repressed sexual and gender identity through the resolution of the Oedipal complex. Through inner struggles with feelings towards the mother and father, children assemble a (largely unconscious) libidinal structure which helps to define then as male and female, homosexual and heterosexual.

Constructionist theories of sexual identities are concerned with locating oneself within a framework of sexual categorizations. Most commonly, identities are seen as heterosexual, homosexual, bisexual. But there are many others, such as sado-masochistic, sex worker, pedophiliac, or person with AIDS (PWA). Such terms, once invented, can be seen to characterize a person. But many of these are new; they are historically produced. Thus, Ned Katz in *The Invention of Heterosexuality* (1995) suggests that the idea of the heterosexual was not invented until the late nineteenth century, and that indeed the identity of homosexual was invented prior to this. This was also a period of clear sexual polarization – identities of being sexual were divided into a clear binary system that did not exist before.

Several problems have been identified with this debate. The first suggests that the debate tends to erect a false dualism or binary tension, in which each term actually comes to depend on the other. Without essentialism, constructionism would not make sense. Secondly, it is suggested that the debate is frequently drawn too starkly and sharply and that there are in fact "different degrees of social construction," ranging from those who more modestly suggest historical and cultural variability of meanings to those who suggest "there is no essential ... sexual impulse" (Vance 1989). Thirdly, it has been suggested that ideas of constructionism when taken in their simplest form create ways of thinking that are almost commonplace. And finally, the political implications of the debates are unclear. Constructionists can be radical and conservative; and so can essentialists. Spivak (1984–5) suggests that strategic essentialism champions essentialism even if it is not fully believed in because it is needed in the fighting of conflicts, intellectual arguments, and political battles. It can be a useful shorthand.

SEE ALSO: Homosexuality; Lesbianism; Symbolic Interaction

REFERENCES

Fuss, D. (1989) *Essentially Speaking*. Routledge, London.

Vance, C. S. (1989) Social construction theory: problems in the history of sexuality. In: Van Nierkerk, K. & Van Der Meer, T. (eds.), *Homosexuality? Which Homosexuality?* An Dekker, Amsterdam, pp. 13–34.

Spivak, G. C. (1984–5) Criticism, feminism and the institution. *Thesis Eleven* 10–11: 175–87.

KEN PLUMMER

ethics, fieldwork

Ethics in fieldwork draws on the perspectives of philosophy, law, and psychology to guide moral decisions. Consciously or otherwise, field researchers make ethical decisions whenever they gather, interpret, or present their data. However, ethical practice in fieldwork cannot simply rely on the guidelines for laboratory research.

Notorious abuses of human participants in twentieth-century biomedical studies led to mandated review of most academic research in the USA and (increasingly) elsewhere in the world. This process has been adapted by schools and public agencies and extended across the social sciences. While ethical reviews prevent many abuses, they pose problems for qualitative fieldwork. Two classic principles – "informed consent" and "anonymity" – illustrate the dilemma.

Informed consent has been the core of ethical review. Yet researchers launching a qualitative study cannot fully predict the course of the inquiry. Broad consent documents in legal language may baffle or frighten the uninitiated. For "consent" to be "informed," people must know the kind of text, the audience(s), and the context for their words, names, or pseudonyms.

Anonymity offers equally dubious protection in fieldwork. If a sociologist publishes a study of dating practices at a small college, there may be lively speculation on campus. If a vivid case study appears under a teacher-author's name, students may be recognized under their pseudonyms from cafeteria to school board. Research in online groups presents further dilemmas in that privacy and consent must be redefined in electronic "communities."

Most ethical risks arise in dissemination, where findings may harm reputations and relationships. Conversely, stakeholders who collaborate with a scholar may want credit more than anonymity. "Voice" is an ethical choice. While scholarly dialect can facilitate conversation among researchers, it usually excludes the researched. Some fieldworkers provide a summary report in everyday language while others invite participants to review drafts, adding their interpretations to create multivoiced reports.

Ethical decisions call for analyzing the local situation as well as global principles. Fieldworkers can start by examining the researcher and the researched – how each is constructed, their roles, and their relationships. The *researcher* may range from traditional "outsider" to "participant observer" to "insider." Moving along the continuum foregrounds certain ethical issues while resolving others. Today's field researchers tend toward self-representation, a sense of "being there" (Geertz 1988), and an analysis of their own lenses. The true "insiders" (action research/teacher research) have primary commitments to stakeholders and view research as an aspect of professionalism. The roles of the *researched* suggest a parallel continuum, from "human subjects" to the more engaged "human participants" to full collaborators, each with its own ethical risks. Because more researchers "study down" (families in poverty, college students) than "up" (elites), their challenge is to practice respect while acknowledging their power.

Ethical review of fieldwork is more (not less) complex than what is mandated for laboratory experiments, calling for dialogue among insiders and outsiders. Adopting an inquiry stance helps researchers ask more nuanced questions, such as:

- What question am I exploring? Why?
- To whom am I professionally accountable?
- How have I prepared myself culturally to understand the "other"?
- Should my report include the voices of participants whose views differ from mine?

Dialogue and inquiry throughout the fieldwork process can move "ethics" beyond the legalistic into the personal, the relational, and the covenantal.

SEE ALSO: Ethics, Research; Ethnography; Institutional Review Boards and Sociological Research; Observation, Participant and Non-Participant

REFERENCE

Geertz, C. (1988) *Works and Lives: The Anthropologist as Author*. Stanford University Press, Stanford, CA.

SUGGESTED READINGS

House, E. & Howe, K. (1999) *Values in Evaluation and Social Research*. Sage, Thousand Oaks, CA.

Kirsch, G. (1999) *Ethical Dilemmas in Feminist Research: The Politics of Location, Interpretation, and Publication*. SUNY Press, Albany, NY.

Zeni, J. (ed.) (2001) *Ethical Issues in Practitioner Research*. Teachers College Press, New York.

JANE ZENI

ethics, research

There has been very little consideration of the context in which discussion of ethics occurs; societal "frames" and sets of such frames are often unstated assumptions which do not have conceptual or operational definitions outside of very specific times and places. Generally, humanist, neo-Kantian, pragmatist, or other secular ethical systems are most common. The principle of the separation of church and state makes it difficult to adopt religiously based notions of the sacredness of the individual, but Kant's secular version, emphasizing respect for individual human dignity and autonomy, results in a similar awareness of the importance of not violating human dignity. While the philosophical questions concerning ethics are not frequently asked, there nevertheless are implied ethical standards that can be traced to ancient Greek and Enlightenment ethical viewpoints. A commonsense version of respect for human dignity and civil liberties is usually in the forefront. The general notion of utility is also frequently mentioned, with beneficence outweighing any possible harm.

Recent approaches which stress the way in which different models of science lead to different kinds of considerations concerning "values and objectivity" (Lacey 2005) are frequently left out of consideration. For example, a phenomenological approach to sociology can involve "ethnomethodological" research. In attempting to study nuances of expectations in everyday situations it would be deeply disturbing to announce ahead of time what is happening. For example, the study of a "breach" in normal expectations requires that participants not be informed before the fact.

The primary ethical concern is most often with research participants. Indeed, the move away from using the word "subjects" is probably indicative of the greater awareness of the importance of ethics, an awareness prompted by certain extreme cases of abuse. Of course, much social science research is relatively harmless, or would appear to be so on the surface. Some is not. Nevertheless, all research has to be vetted by Institutional Review Boards (IRBs) in the USA. In Canada a similar approach is maintained by Research Ethics Boards (REBs), with similar concerns. Confidentiality involves the data only being used for the explicit purposes for which permission had been granted and further consent prior to disclosure to third parties.

A pragmatic balance between methodological and practical concerns continues to be an elusive goal and the enormous variety of types of research undertaken make straightforward generalizations highly problematic and sometimes contested.

SEE ALSO: Ethics, Fieldwork; Institutional Review Boards and Sociological Research; Sexuality Research: Ethics

REFERENCE

Lacey, H. (2005) *Values and Objectivitiy in Science*. Rowman & Littlefield, Lanham, MD.

SUGGESTED READINGS

Hoonaard, W. C. van den (2002) *Walking the Tightrope: Ethical Issues for Qualitative Researchers*. University of Toronto Press, Toronto.

Office for Human Research Protections (OHRP) (2005) *Federal Policy for the Protection of Human Subjects ("the Common Rule")*. US Government, Washington, DC.

J. I. (HANS) BAKKER

ethnic enclaves

The ethnic enclave is a sub-economy that offers protected access to labor and markets, informal sources of credit, and business information for immigrant businesses and workers. It presents a route for economic and social mobility by promoting positive returns on human capital for immigrants in the labor market. Ethnic enclaves of Latin American and Asian immigrants are proliferating in contemporary gateway cities such as New York, Miami, Houston, and Los Angeles. There are costs as well as benefits that accrue to immigrants working in ethnic enclaves.

Pathbreaking research in the early 1980s on the concept of the enclave economy initially made a contrast between the Cuban enclave and the black economy of Miami. The Cuban-owned firms of the Miami area were found to comprise a dynamic sub-economy of construction, manufacturing, retail and wholesale trade, and banking firms that recirculated and multiplied income through inter-industry and consumption linkages. The economy of black neighborhoods, by contrast, was impoverished and capital-scarce, with income constantly leaking out of the community into factories and chain stores owned by whites and large corporations.

Investment capital is commonly raised in ethnic enclaves through kinship networks and rotating credit associations. These ethnic enclaves offer a protected sector for immigrants newly arrived without English language skills, good education, or official papers. The dynamism of the ethnic enclave economy is based in large part upon the multiplier effect, by which export earnings are spent and recirculated among co-ethnic enterprises throughout the remainder of the protected sector.

Research has also determined social costs of ethnic enclaves, chiefly that immigrant employers profited from their ability to exploit co-ethnic workers in a "sweatshop" sector under poor working conditions and poor labor rights. Positive returns for men were to some degree derived from negative returns to women as subordinate workers.

SEE ALSO: Ethnic/Informal Economy; Ethnic Groups

SUGGESTED READING

Logan, J. R., Alba, R. D., & McNulty, T. L. (1994) Ethnic economies in metropolitan regions: Miami and beyond. *Social Forces* 72 (3): 691–724.

JAN LIN

ethnic groups

Ethnic groups are fundamental units of social organization which consist of members who define themselves by a sense of common historical origins that may also include religious beliefs, a distinct language or a shared culture. Max Weber provided one of the most important modern definitions of ethnic groups as "human groups (other than kinship groups) which cherish a belief in their common origins of such a kind that it provides the basis for the creation of a community" (Weber 1922; cited in

Runciman 1978: 364). The boundaries of ethnic groups often overlap with similar categories such as "races" or nations.

In those societies that have been influenced by large scale immigration, like the USA, Argentina, Australia, and Canada, ethnic groups form a central theme of their social, economic and political life. Systematic research on American ethnic groups can be traced to the sociologists of the Chicago School (1920s to 1940s) led by W. I. Thomas and Robert Park, who were concerned with the processes of ethnic group assimilation into the dominant white mainstream. Park's (inaccurately named) *race relations cycle* outlined a sequence of stages consisting of "contact, competition, accommodation and assimilation," and implied that successive immigrant groups would be gradually absorbed into a relatively homogeneous core society. The underlying assumption of ethnic group theory was that these long-term trends would result in the disappearance of separate ethnic communities.

This uni-linear model gave way to more pluralistic conceptions of ethnicity in the USA in which various dimensions of assimilation were identified by sociologists like Milton Gordon (1964). Gordon distinguished between cultural assimilation (*acculturation*) and structural assimilation, the former signifying the adoption of the language, values and ideals of the dominant society, while the latter reflected the incorporation of ethnic groups into the institutions of mainstream society. While cultural assimilation did not necessarily result in an ethnic group's inclusion within the principal institutions of society, structural assimilation invariably meant that assimilation on all other dimensions – from personal identification to intermarriage – had already taken place.

Scholarly concern with ethnicity and ethnic conflict became increasingly salient in the second half of the twentieth century. Inadequate assumptions about the nature of modernization and modernity have been demonstrated by the pattern of social change under capitalism, socialism and in the developing world. The expectation that modernity would result in a smooth transition from *gemeinschaft* (community) to *gesellschaft* (association), accompanied by the gradual dissolution of ethnic affiliations, simply did not fit the facts. Some social scientists argued that there was a primordial basis to ethnic attachments, while others explained the apparent persistence of ethnicity in more instrumental terms, as a political resource to be mobilized in appropriate situations which may be activated by power and guided by cultural factors. Not only has ethnicity failed to recede in industrial and post-industrial societies, but ethnic divisions have continued to frustrate the efforts at democratization and economic growth in large sectors of the developing world. The collapse of the political regimes of the Communist bloc unleashed an upsurge in ethnic and national identity, some of which filled the void created by the demise of Marxism, while other elements of the same development, notably in the former Yugoslavia, generated bloody ethnonational conflicts and ethnic cleansing.

The focus of research on ethnic groups has shifted away from studies of specific groups to the broad processes of the creation of ethnicity (ethnogenesis), the construction and perpetuation of ethnic boundaries, the meaning of ethnic identity, and the impact of globalization and transnationalism. A wide variety of theoretical perspectives can be found supporting contemporary studies of ethnicity and ethnic groups. These include social psychological discussions of prejudice and discrimination; rational choice models based on individual costs and benefits; socio biological perspectives involving "selfish genes" and kin selection; and, most commonly, differential power analyses creating types of ethnic stratification, whether in the neo-Marxist form or in the more pluralistic tradition of the followers of Weber.

SEE ALSO: Ethnic Enclaves; Ethnicity; Race

REFERENCES

Gordon, M. (1964) *Assimilation in American Life: The Role of Race, Religion and National Origins*. Oxford University Press, New York.

Runciman, W. (ed.) (1978) *Max Weber: Selections in Translation*. Cambridge University Press, Cambridge.

SUGGESTED READING

Stone, J. & R. Dennis (eds.) (2003) *Race and Ethnicity: Comparative and Theoretical Approaches*. Blackwell, Malden, MA and Oxford.

JOHN STONE AND CATARINA FRITZ

ethnic/informal economy

Ethnic/informal economies are inconsistently defined by scholars. But fortunately, there is a common theme to the definitions one finds in the literature. All variants convey a sense of economic action embedded in solidaristic, co-ethnic social relations. Economic behavior is influenced by informal rules and practices that govern the normative behavior of group members.

An informative literature has emerged despite the lack of consistency in defining ethnic/informal economies. Researchers concentrate on how foreign-born groups establish and maintain economic niches that are usually accentuated by a profusion of small businesses. The field examines how limited acculturation and structural assimilation in the immigrant generation gives rise to collective action that promotes enterprising economic action. A substantial body of research documents how immigrant minorities draw on social ties in order to facilitate the development of informal economic relations. Family ties and ethnic group membership typically provide the social underpinnings of these economic relations.

The ability to draw on social connections in order to gain access to resources that are useful for economic action is an example of what scholars refer to as social capital. The literature describes many ways in which immigrants make use of family- and ethnic-based interpersonal connections in gaining access to resources such as business related information and financial credit. Economic activities, embedded in social relations, necessitate a sense of interdependence among in-group members that engenders trust and solidarity, and allows for sanctions to be imposed on those who violate the trust of others. Understanding such practices, which are steeped in informal institutionalized arrangements, is essential for understanding the origins and maintenance of ethnic/informal economies.

Interest in ethnic/informal economies is part of a larger scholarly examination of economic segmentation. This view conceives of the labor market as divided into a primary market where opportunities for advancement are prevalent and a low-wage secondary market with little opportunity for advancement. Most studies of ethnic/informal economies explore how immigrants draw on family- and ethnic-based social networks in an effort to build economic relationships and institutions that improve group members' job opportunities and facilitate the growth of self-employment within the group.

What has the literature taught us about the social bases of ethnic/informal economies? Researchers have revealed a number of informal mechanisms based on social relations that facilitate economic action. The most important outcomes of these mechanisms are the dissemination of employment and business related information, and providing access to informal financial institutions. Normative use of these resources and the repayment of debts are encouraged by enforcing trustful behavior under the threat of sanctions. Informal social bases of economic action tend to emerge among groups as members try to overcome limited economic options due to language barriers, poor human capital, or non-fungible foreign-earned human capital. And immigrant groups often face discrimination and prejudice. A tendency for group members to react to these problems by looking within their group for practical and emotional support encourages ethnic solidarity, which in turn encourages informal group practices that provide access to resources. Internally generated resources contribute to the growth of self-employment and this leads to increased opportunities for getting ahead. But there are winners and losers in the ethnic community. People seeking to better their lives and that of their family are involved in the rough and tumble environment of market economics. Even a modicum of success in small business usually requires out performing some competitors and matching the performance of others. This is a daunting task because ethnic/informal economies tend to be hotbeds of competition between small businesses.

SEE ALSO: Ethnicity; Economic Sociology: Neoclassical Economic Perspective; Ethnic Enclaves

SUGGESTED READINGS

Portes A. & Sensenbrenner J. (1993) Embeddedness and immigration: notes on the social determinants of economic action. *American Journal of Sociology* 98: 1320–50

Sanders J. and Nee, V. (1996) Immigrant self-employment: the family as social capital and the value of human capital. *American Sociological Review* 61: 231–49.

JIMY M. SANDERS

ethnicity

The ancient Greek word *ethnos* referred to a group of people who lived together, sharing a common way of life. After kinship, ethnicity may be the most ubiquitous way of classifying and organizing human collectivities; it is "the social organization of culture difference" (Barth 1969) and "the cultural organization of social difference" (Geertz 1973). How the nuanced complexities of culture are socially organized into ethnicity is not, however, obvious or straightforward. People who may appear to differ culturally may identify themselves as ethnic fellows; witness, for example, the global diversity that is "Jewishness." On the other hand, apparent cultural similarity does not preclude ethnic differentiation. An anthropologist from Mars might perceive Danes and Norwegians, for example, as co-ethnics; they, however, would not agree.

So our understanding of ethnicity cannot depend upon a crude model of discrete cultures, seen "in the round." What's more, some cultural themes seem to offer more scope for ethnic identification than others: language, notions of shared descent, myths and historical narratives, locality and co-residence, and religion are all potent ethnic markers. Even so, shared language or religious beliefs and practices, for example, are not necessarily sufficient in themselves to "create" ethnicity. Nor are shared space and place: living together is as likely to divide people in competition as to bring them together to exploit resources together cooperatively. Ethnicity is not, therefore, a matter of checklists with which to determine whether group A is *really* ethnically different from group B, or whether group C is *really* an ethnic group. Enumerating cultural traits – estimating distance and difference – cannot help us to understand or identify ethnicity.

The base line is always whether a group is perceived by its members to be cohesive and different. Self-definition isn't *all* that matters, however. It is also necessary that a group should be categorized as distinctive and cohesive by others. This means that power – whose definition counts – may be very important. It also means that ethnicity cannot be unilateral: a sense of ethnicity can only arise in the context of relationships and interaction with others. Which in turn means that without difference there can be no sense of similarity: defining *us* also defines *them* (and vice versa). It is difficult to imagine a meaningful identification, whether ethnic or whatever, that is not at least acknowledged by others.

In the contemporary world ethnic identification emerges across a long spectrum of "cultural scale": kinship ties, neighborhood and community, regional identity, or the "imagined community" of the nation, can all foster a sense of shared ethnic identification and belonging. However, because descent and kinship may be important in imaginings of the nation, we are also required to attend to "race," the supposedly "obvious" and distinctive biological "natures" of populations that are believed (by some) to shape, if not determine, lifestyles and cultures. Although "racial" categories depend on visible embodied difference to assert their "naturalness," it cannot be emphasized too often or too vigorously that "race" is historically and culturally – and thus arbitrarily – defined. Communal, local, regional, national, and "racial" identities are all culturally and historically specific variations on the generic principle of collective identification that is ethnicity. Each says something about "the social organization of culture difference" and "the cultural organization of social difference."

This broad understanding of ethnicity acknowledges that ethnic identification is a contextually variable and relative process. However, that ethnicity may be negotiable, flexible and variable in its significance, from one situation to another, also means that ethnicity may not *always* be negotiable. When ethnicity matters to people, it has the capacity to *really* matter, to move them to action and awaken powerful emotions.

There is no consistency with respect to the strength and consequences of ethnic identification (although that humans form ethnic attachments seems to be fairly universal). When ethnic attachments do seem to matter to people, we do not need to invoke notions of "primordial essence" to explain why. Local differences with respect to primary socialization, the power of rituals and symbols, the implacability of history, and the everyday consequences of identification, are sufficient to account for the variable strength of the "ethnic ties that bind." And while ethnic attachments may not *determine* what people do, they matter, and they cannot be ignored.

SEE ALSO: Conflict (Racial/Ethnic); Ethnic Enclaves; Ethnic Groups; Ethnic/Informal Economy; Race; Stratification, Race/Ethnicity and

REFERENCES

Barth, F. (1969) Introduction. In: Barth, F. (ed.), *Ethnic Groups and Boundaries: The Social Organization of Culture Difference*. Universitetsforlaget, Oslo, pp. 9–38.
Geertz, C. (1973) *The Interpretation of Culture*. Basic Books, New York.

SUGGESTED READING

Cornell, S. E. and Hartmann, D. (2007) *Ethnicity and Race: Making Identities in a Changing World*, 2nd edn. Pine Forge, Thousand Oaks, CA.
Jenkins, R. (2008) *Rethinking Ethnicity: Arguments and Explorations*, 2nd edn. Sage, London.

RICHARD JENKINS

ethnocentrism

Coined by William Graham Sumner in 1906, ethnocentrism is a type of bias that results from viewing one's own ethnic group and culture as superior to others. In contrast to cultural relativism, an ethnocentric perspective holds its own ethnic group and culture as the universal standard by which to judge all other cultures.

At times, an ethnocentric sense of superiority is a conscious, arrogant attitude with respect to "foreign" and "strange" customs, norms, beliefs, values, and ideas – a self-righteous conviction that one's cultural way of seeing and doing is the only way and the best way. Other times, ethnocentrism is an unconscious worldview that blinds one to alternative ways of living, thinking, acting, and being in the world, limiting one's imagination about the scope of human possibilities.

In many cases, ethnocentrism is an unintended product of a cultural upbringing with little exposure to ethnic and cultural diversity. Often, it is compounded by xenophobia, which fears the unfamiliar and leads to prejudice and discrimination toward out-groups. Throughout human history, ethnocentrism in its extreme forms has led to violent conflicts and genocide.

Postmodern critics have discussed the ways in which ethnocentrism pervades many "western" ideals of the Enlightenment and its faith in rationality and human evolutionary progress, coupled with the doctrine of Social Darwinism, which proposes that biological natural selection (misunderstood as "survival of the fittest") should be applied to human societies. According to this ethnocentric viewpoint, the strongest human societies should allow the weakest peoples to die out, or even kill them, to relieve the strain of a quickly multiplying human population on increasingly scarce resources.

"Orientalism," discussed by Edward Said, is a particular kind of ethnocentrism that feminizes non-western cultures as "exotic," "irrational," "emotional," and everything that the west is not, in order to justify western colonial and imperial interventions. To be sure, ethnocentric elements have saturated the field of international development policies, programs, and practices, with "first world" nation-states being held up as social, political, and economic models for the rest of the world to follow and imitate regardless of the diversity of cultural settings, histories, realities, and visions of what "development" might mean to it.

SEE ALSO: Cultural Relativism; Diversity; Ethnicity; Prejudice; Racism

SUGGESTED READINGS

Sumner, W. G. (1906) *Folkways: A Study of the Sociological Importance of Usages, Manners, Customs, Mores, and Morals.* Ginn, Boston, MA.

Escobar, A. (1995) *Encountering Development: The Making and Unmaking of the Third World.* Princeton University Press, Princeton, NJ.

Said, E. (1978) *Orientalism.* Pantheon, New York.

DIANA SANTILLÁN

ethnography

Ethnography was initially developed in anthropology in the early twentieth century. Here it generally involved the researcher living with a group of people for an extended period, perhaps a year or several years, in order to document their distinctive way of life, beliefs and values. Within sociology today, the term is normally used in a broader way to refer to studies that rely on participant observation and/or in-depth, relatively unstructured interviewing. In this more recent usage, there is considerable overlap in meaning with other labels for research approaches, whose meanings are also somewhat vague, such as "qualitative research," "fieldwork," "interpretive method," and "case study."

In more detailed practical terms, as a method, ethnography usually involves most of the following features:

- People's actions are studied primarily in everyday contexts rather than under conditions created by the researcher – such as in experiments or highly structured interview situations. In other words, research takes place "in the field."
- Data are gathered from a range of sources: while participant observation and/or relatively informal interviews are usually the main ones, others are also often employed – including documents or artifacts that are personal and/or official, physical and/or virtual.
- Data collection is "unstructured" in two senses. First, it does not involve following through a fixed and detailed research plan set up at the beginning, but is more flexible in design. Secondly, the categories to be used for interpreting the data are not built into the data collection process.
- The focus is normally on a small number of cases, perhaps a single setting or group of people, typically small-scale, with these being studied in depth.
- Analysis of the data involves interpretation of the meanings and functions of human actions, and how these are implicated in local and wider contexts; quantification and statistical analysis usually play a subordinate role at most.

As a set of methods, ethnography is not far removed from the means that we all use in everyday life to make sense of our surroundings. However, it involves a more deliberate and systematic approach and, also, a distinctive mentality. This can perhaps best be summarized as seeking to make the strange familiar, in the sense of finding intelligibility and rationality within it; and viewing the familiar as strange, by suspending some of those background assumptions that immediately give apparent sense to what we experience.

Over the course of its development, ethnography has been influenced by a range of methodological and theoretical movements. Early on, within anthropology, it was shaped by German ideas about the distinctive character of history and the human sciences, by Wundt's folk psychology, and even by positivism. Subsequently, in the form of the case-study approach of the Chicago School, it was also influenced by philosophical pragmatism, while in more recent times Marxism, phenomenology, hermeneutics, structuralism, "critical" theory, feminism, and poststructuralism have all informed its character.

While these influences have led to a diversification in approach, ethnography still tends to be characterized by a number of key methodological ideas about the nature of the social world and how it can be understood:

- Human behavior is not an automatic product of either internal or external stimuli. It is constructed and reconstructed over time, and across space, in ways that reflect the biographies and sociocultural locations of actors, and how they interpret the situations they face.
- There are diverse cultures that can inform human behavior, and these operate not just between societies or local communities but also within them; and sometimes even within individual actors.
- Human social life is not structured in terms of fixed, law-like patterns, but displays emergent processes of various kinds that involve a high degree of contingency.

To a large extent, ethnography shares these commitments with some other kinds of qualitative research, such as narrative and discourse analysis, but it applies them in distinctive ways through the kinds of data and forms of analysis it employs.

SEE ALSO: Ethics, Fieldwork; Interviewing, Structured, Unstructured, and Postmodern; Observation, Participant and Non-Participant

SUGGESTED READINGS

Atkinson, P. A., Delamont, S., Coffey, A. J., Lofland, J., & Lofland, L. H. (eds.) (2007) *Handbook of Ethnography*. 2nd edn. Sage, London.

Hammersley, M. & Atkinson, P. (2007) *Ethnography: Principles in Practice*. 3rd edn. Routledge, London.

O'Reilly, K. (2004) *Ethnographic Methods*. Routledge, London.

Wolcott, H. F. (1999) *Ethnography: A Way of Seeing*. Alta Mira Press, Walnut Creek, CA.

MARTYN HAMMERSLEY

ethnomethodology

Ethnomethodology (EM) is the study of people's methods of producing and reproducing recognizable orders and phenomena in social life. This program gained significant attention in sociology following the publication of Harold Garfinkel's *Studies in Ethnomethodology* in 1967 (see Garfinkel & Rawls 2010 [1967]). The prefix "ethno-" refers to "social members" or "members of a local social scene"; "method" refers to the procedures and actions people take to accomplish certain ends; the suffix "-ology" means "the study of." Together, ethnomethodology can be simply understood as "the study of the methods people use for producing recognizable social orders" (Rawls 2002: 6).

EM researchers have utilized different kinds of data, including organizational documents, personal interviews, participant observation, ethnography, and audio or video recordings of events and interactions. One historical connection between EM and classical sociology is EM's orientation toward specifying how people enact *social things* (or Durkheimian "social facts") that put social orders into work. The procedures by which people's methodical practices constitute social orders are extremely subtle and complex, involving the dynamic deployment of language, categories, institutions, communicative acts, ideas, rituals, and laws in local settings. While such processes are pervasive, they are often unintelligible and unclear even to the people who take part in, and are influenced by, them every day and every moment.

Therefore, many EM practitioners are involved in creating *accounts* about such processes, rendering them *discoverable* and *intelligible* to readers. Some EM researchers draw on first-person accounts from people engaging in normatively exceptional activities while others partake in them and "become" the social members that they study. Some EM investigators study mundane, routine practices – such as ordinary people walking on a crowded street, teachers conducting lessons, scientists representing their findings – to unearth the social processes that are normally taken for granted or taken as legitimate. A well-known strategy is the use of conversation analysis, the practitioners of which use audio- or video-tape data to go into incredible details to describe turn taking, utterance paring, nonverbal acts, and other local social actions employed by people on a moment-to-moment basis in talk-in-interaction. Another widely known strategy is the breaching method, the practitioners of which actively disrupt social scenes in order to demonstrate their (re)assembling processes, or the methods of (re)assembly.

Despite the diversity of approaches, enthomethodologists generally share several methodological commitments in common. First of all, EM investigators take seriously the role of human agency in producing social orders and phenomena. All social realities – including those that are seemingly mundane, extraordinary, or chaotic – are treated as the results of reflexive, artful practices done by people in interaction.

Secondly, because it is ingrained in the EM program that human agency is important and each phenomenon is unique, most ethnomethodologists do not seek to theorize the relationships between generic causes and generic social phenomena, as practiced in variable-based research. Instead, EM investigations create accounts for different states of affairs by *exhibiting* the complexity and fineness of social orders' constitution processes, demonstrating the methodical procedures involved.

Thirdly, EM investigators dedicate their attention to the issue of *practice*. This focus is distinct from some other approaches (e.g., phenomenology) that place emphasis on meaning or the mind, which embed a different philosophy about the manners by which the social world is ordered. "Meaning" would be analyzed as local, meaning-making *practices* in EM.

Ethnomethodology has been a diverse enterprise since its inception and has been selectively appropriated and applied into different disciplines and programs of study. It has noticeably contributed to path-breaking works in the studies of classroom processes, legal processes, the medical profession, workplace and organizations, gender, science and technology, discourse, social cognition and behavior, esoteric experience, and everyday life. Additionally, ethnomethodology has made important contributions to theoretical debates in philosophy and sociology surrounding the topics of justice, social order, knowledge/epistemology, reflexivity, and agency-structure relations.

SEE ALSO: Accounts; Conversation Analysis; Everyday Life; Practice Theory; Qualitative Methods

REFERENCES

Garfinkel, H. & Rawls, A. (2010) [1967] *Studies in Ethnomethodology: Expanded and Updated Edition.* Paradigm Publishers, Boulder, CO.

Rawls, A. (2002) Editor's introduction. In: Garfinkel, H. (ed.), *Ethnomethodology's Program: Working Out Durkheim's Aphorism.* Roman & Littlefield Publishers, Lanham, MD, pp. 1–64.

SUGGESTED READINGS

Maynard, D. W. & Clayman, S. E. (1991) The diversity of ethnomethodology. *Annual Review of Sociology* 17: 385–418.

GORDON C. CHANG

eugenics

"Eugenics" derives from the Greek word *eugenes* meaning "good in birth" or "noble in heredity." Eugenics was developed in the late nineteenth century and means ideologies and activities aiming to improve the quality of the human race by selecting the "genetically fit." It can entail (1) "positive" strategies to manipulate the heredity or breeding practices of "genetically superior" or "fit" people, or (2) "negative" strategies to exterminate the "genetically inferior."

Eugenics combines genetics as a scientific discipline with ideas from social planning and rational management developed during the industrial revolution. Eugenic "science" was considered to be the application of human genetic knowledge to social problems such as pauperism, alcoholism, criminality, violence, prostitution, mental illness, etc. In the early twentieth century, eugenics became a social movement first in Europe and then also in the United States. Public policies were developed which were rooted in eugenic ideology and justified on grounds of societal or state interests: those deemed "genetically unfit" were stigmatized as an *economic* and *moral* burden. Eugenics was supported across the political spectrum. There was, however, disagreement between conservatives, progressives and leftists regarding specific policies, means and political aims (e.g. the role of coercion; social change). In general, European eugenicists were preoccupied with class issues, while the focus of eugenic policies in the USA was on racial and ethnic minorities. The most radical eugenic programme was implemented by German Fascism leading to the fall of eugenics into disrepute after World War II. With the advance of new

human reproductive techn
with genetics in the 1980s,
of a "new" eugenics. Th
is based on individual rig
interests; in liberal eugenic
(especially prospective pare
criteria.

SEE ALSO: Genetic Engineering as a Social Problem; Medical Sociology and Genetics

SUGGESTED READINGS

Agar, N. (2004) *Liberal Eugenics: In Defence of Human Enhancement*. Blackwell, Oxford.

Duster, T. (1990) *Backdoor to Eugencis*. Routledge, New York.

Kevles, D. J. (1985) *In the Nature of Eugenics: Genetics and the Use of Human Heredity*. Alfred A. Knopf, New York.

GABRIELE ABELS

euthanasia

The dictionary defines euthanasia as an "act or method of causing death painlessly so as to end suffering: advocated by some as a way to deal with victims of incurable diseases." This is something of an over-simplification, however. The practice of euthanasia has long been a contentious issue and a matter of disputatious debate. Some have termed euthanasia "mercy killing" (Vernon 1970: 310), but others have reported that some critics have labeled it as murder.

While euthanasia has generally taken place within a medical context, historically, euthanasia, as a humanitarian act, has also occurred within other contexts, such as war. There are historical accounts (from all wars) of soldiers encountering badly wounded fellow soldiers or wounded enemy soldiers. If their wounds were severe and it appeared they would not survive and they could not be transported to a medical facility, the soldiers sometimes killed the wounded individual out of compassion, administering the "coup de grace" – in effect, putting the wounded man out of his misery (Leming & Dickinson 2002: 283). Euthanasia most frequently, however, has occurred within a medical context, and this term has come to be associated with terminal illness and the medical setting. The discomfort of terminal illness is not the only motivating factor in euthanasia.

There are two distinctly different modes of operationalizing euthanasia: *positive* euthanasia and *negative* euthanasia (Charmaz 1980: 112). Positive euthanasia refers to the practice of deliberately

hrough active means
verdose of sedatives,
he individual). This
hemistically termed
ia describes the prac-
ntive treatment, or
withholding some life-sustaining "drugs, medical devices, or procedures" (DeSpelder & Srickland 1999: 200). Charmaz (1980: 113) describes positive euthanasia as an act of *commission* and negative euthanasia as an act of *omission*. DeSpelder and Srickland (1999: 200) indicate that "this distinction is sometimes characterized as the difference between 'killing' and 'letting die.'"

Euthanasia, whether active or passive, voluntary or involuntary, or nonvoluntary, is socially (and legally) controversial. Assertive and persuasive arguments concerning euthanasia have been advanced by both proponents and opponents. According to Charmaz (1980: 112) there are "three interrelated ethical questions constituent to the controversy." First, should individuals have the right to *elect* and *control* death? Second, at what *point* might an individual legitimately exert these rights? Third, whose *interests* are going to be given priority, those of the individual or those of the society?

SEE ALSO: Abortion as a Social Problem; Death and Dying; Suicide

REFERENCES

Charmaz, K. (1980) *The Social Realities of Death*. Addison-Wesley, Reading, MA.

Vernon, G. M. (1970) *Sociology of Death: An Analysis of Death-Related Behavior*. Ronald Press, New York.

DeSpelder, L. A. & Strickland, A. L. (1999) *The Last Dance: Encountering Death and Dying*, 5th edn. Mayfield, Mountain View, CA.

Leming, M. R. & Dickinson, G. E. (2002) *Understanding Dying, Death & Bereavement*, 5th edn. Wadsworth, Belmont, CA.

CLIFTON D. BRYANT

everyday life

Everyday life, in the field of sociology, has been positioned as a condition, a social space, a political goal, and a methodological analytic. Its meaning has shifted with time, and its potential consequences have shifted with its meaning. One thing that has not changed has been the home of the concept, under the wing of the conflict school of theory. But while everyday life started its move into theory as a negative extension of Marx's idea of alienation, it has evolved into a celebrated realm for modern-day feminist sociology.

Henri Lefebvre, one of the most important French Marxist sociologists of the mid-century, first wrote of everyday life as a mind-numbing, alienating set of social conditions. His book, *Critique of Everyday Life*, was published in 1947. In it he linked what he called "everydayness" to Marx's theory of alienation. According to Lefebvre, everydayness was a modern-day extension of the grip of alienation, part of the consequence of the rise of a modern form of capitalism. Lefebvre argued that capitalism had gotten so powerful that it had grown beyond organizing our productive and social relations in society; it also actually sucked the meaning out of everyday life. Alienation, the feeling of exhaustion, stress, and poverty consequential from the act of being forced to sell one's labor, was experienced more painfully under modern capitalism precisely because the experiences of everyday life outside of work had been invaded by capitalism. Without the genuine meaning and connection that had once taken place in everyday life outside of work, modern workers turned to consumption to fill the gap. The lifestyle of consumption grew stronger and stronger under modern capitalism, and everyday life was marked by the purchase of commodities, which furthered the cycle of alienation.

Everyday life got a new set of meanings in the 1960s along with the reemergence of arguments about the public sphere and the private sphere. As the concept of the public sphere began to be increasingly defined as the world of work, politics, and the service of citizenship, the private sphere began to be seen as the space of everything else, or the space of everyday life. This loaded the idea of everyday life with the content of all that was seen as somehow being personal and private: love, family, sex, relationships, housework, emotions, etc.

It was in this context that feminist sociologists retrieved the idea of everyday life, and reinterpreted it as a social space that primarily contained that which was seen as belonging to women. The public sphere was the world of men, while the private sphere (and everyday life) was the realm of women. Feminist sociologists argued that the world of women and the social relations of everyday life should be celebrated and valued. Some also argued that the line between the public and private sphere should be obliterated, allowing women into the public realm and, more important, removing value judgment from the assessment of the realms in which people pursue social interaction. In other words, the obligations of everyday life – like helping a child with homework – are just as important as the work of the public realm – like participating in the work of a political party.

The women's movement politicized the idea of everyday life. Home, and the private world, were sites for battle over the work and role of women. "The personal is political" was a key theme for analysis and activism, and everyday life became a battleground.

By the 1970s, feminist sociologists such as Dorothy E. Smith had added an important new dimension to the concept of everyday life. They argued that the social reproduction of inequality could be seen in the normal interactions of everyday life. This analytical insight helped reshape the focus for feminist research. As a topic of analysis, the social relationships of everyday life became increasingly important. New empirical research during this time period began to focus on topics that had formerly been seen as banal, or unimportant, or too "everyday." Topics such as domestic violence, housework, mental illness, and childrearing emerged as critical – and controversial – areas for research. Everyday life was not just what was left over from the important work of the public realm, but was in itself a set of social relations that created and reproduced social inequalities. The experiences of everyday life are important pieces of knowledge about our social world, and everyday life became a key focus of empirical study.

SEE ALSO: Alienation; Capitalism; Feminist Pedagogy; Public and Private; Public Sphere

SUGGESTED READINGS

Lefebvre, H. (1992) [1947] *Critique of Everyday Life*. Verso, London.

Smith, D. E. (1987) *The Everyday World as Problematic: A Feminist Sociology*. Northeastern University Press, Lebanon, NH.

MARTHA EASTON

exchange network theory

An exchange network is a system of two or more connected exchange relations (Emerson 1962). Two exchange relations are connected if exchange in one relation affects exchange in the other. Exchange network theories explain how network structures affect power distributions, power exercise, and the benefits network members gain in exchanges.

NETWORK CONNECTIONS

Power-dependence (PD) theorists use the direction (unilateral or bilateral) and valence (negative or positive) of influence to describe network connections. A network, A–B–C is *unilaterally* connected at B if A–B exchange affects B–C exchange but B–C exchange does not affect A–B exchange. It is *bilaterally* connected if A–B and B–C exchanges have reciprocal effects. The network is *positively* connected if A–B exchange increases the likelihood of B–C exchange and *negatively* connected if A–B exchange reduces the possibility of B–C exchange (Emerson 1962).

Network Exchange Theory (NET) (Willer 1999) classifies connection types according to N, the number of positions connected to a position, i; M, the maximum number of relations from which i can benefit; and Q, the minimum number of relations within which i must exchange before it can gain any benefit (Willer 1999). Five connection types have been studied (see Table 1).

Table 1 Five connection types

1	*inclusive* connection:	$N_i = M_i = Q_i > 1$
2	*exclusive* connection:	$N_i > M_i \geq Q_i = 1$
3	*null* connection:	$N_i = M_i > Q_i = 1$
4	*inclusive-exclusive* connection:	$N_i > M_i \geq Q_i > 1$
5	*exclusive-null* connection:	$N_i = M_i > Q_i > 1$

An A–B–C network is inclusively connected if B can benefit from exchanges with A *and* C and must exchange with both before gaining any benefit ($N = 2 = M = 2 = Q = 2 > 1$). The network is exclusively connected if B can benefit from exchange with either A *or* C (but not both), and *must* exchange with one in order to gain any benefit ($2 > 1 \geq 1$), and similarly for the remaining connection types. Dyads are a special connection type (*singularly connected*) where $N_i = M_i = Q_i = 1$.

PROCEDURES FOR LOCATING POWER

PD theorists initially used graph-theoretic measures of *vulnerability* as indicators of dependence. Reduction in Maximum Flow (RMF) measures the degree to which a network is disrupted by removing a position. A revised procedure, CRMF, removes a line. Neither measure has proved adequate for testing hypotheses. Today PD researchers calculate B's dependence on A as the resources B gains from exchanges with A minus the resources B can gain from alternative exchange partners (e.g., C in the A–B–C network).

Coleman (1973) introduced r_i, a system-level measure of power, that gives precise values for N actors and resources *iff* actors' interests (X) in and control (C) of resources are known. The benefits actors gain in exchanges are a positive function of r_i. Only a limited number of experiments and simulations have tested Coleman's ideas. However, they include a variety of connection types and findings generally support Coleman's theory.

NET theorists use Elementary Theory and its Law of Resistance to predict power distributions (Willer and Anderson 1981). The law asserts that exchanges occur when actors are equally resistant to a proposed exchange. NET uses an *iterative seek* procedure in which actors are presumed to negotiate exchanges in high-benefit relations before turning to lower-benefit relations. The Resistance Law is general and has been applied successfully to several types of network connections.

Friedkin's (1992) Expected Value model uses a five-step process to calculate payoffs in exchange networks. Analysts identify: (1) the network structure, (2) *every* possible exchange, (3) the probable frequency of occurrence for every possible exchange, (4) the resources that can be acquired by each network position, and (5) the expected values of payoffs. Power distributions are inferred from expected payoffs. Research in this tradition was the first to apply exchange network procedures to a variety of networks with unequally valued resource pools.

Finally, game theorists (Bienenstock and Bonacich 1992) use the core solution for cooperative games to locate power. The approach is organized around the characteristic function, v. For every subset of positions in a network, $v(S)$ is the total payoff members can gain no matter what other positions do. The core solution is the set of all payoffs that satisfies individual, coalition, and group rationality. Individual rationality exists when no position in a coalition will accept a payoff less than it could gain on its own. Coalition rationality occurs when no set of actors will accept total benefits that are less than they could earn in a coalition and the condition is met for every coalition in the network. Finally, group rationality exists when a grand coalition of all members maximizes its total reward. Game Theory implies that networks for which there is a core solution have stable outcomes. Those without a core have unstable outcomes because some positions can improve their payoffs by joining a coalition. The core solution has been applied to exclusively connected networks but the method can be applied to a range of situations including many that fall outside the scope of exchange network theories.

SEE ALSO: Game Theory; Power, Theories of; Power-Dependence Theory; Social Exchange Theory

REFERENCES

Bienenstock, E. J. & Bonacich, P. (1992) The core as a solution to exclusionary networks. *Social Networks* 14: 231–43.

Coleman, J. S. (1973) *The Mathematics of Collective Action*. Aldine, Chicago, IL.

Emerson, R. M. (1962) Power-dependence relations. *American Sociological Review* 27: 31–41.

Friedkin, N. (1992) An expected value model of social power: predictions for selected exchange networks. *Social Networks* 14: 213–29.

Willer, D. (1999) *Network Exchange Theory*. Prager, Westport, CT.

Willer, D. & Anderson, B. (1981) *Networks, Exchange and Coercion*. Elsevier, New York.

HENRY A. WALKER

exchange-value

Exchange-value – the most misunderstood concept in Marx's analysis of the commodity – must be distinguished from the closely related but significantly different concept, value.

A commodity to be exchanged has a value – its sum of congealed, socially necessary, simple, abstract labor time. One cannot immediately see, touch, taste, smell, or hear value; its immediate reality is invisible. That substance must achieve a recognized, manifest form of expression to be exchanged. Value is the abstract substance of a commodity; exchange-value its social form and expression of the value substance.

Historically and conceptually, exchange-value has taken four forms. Value first becomes manifest in simple exchange. The value of 20 yards of linen is represented in a concrete "equivalent form of value" such as one coat. The coat is the linen's visibly manifest, equivalent form of value – the linen's exchange-value.

In a context of expanded exchange, the social form of value changes. The "expanded, relative form of value" exists when several commodities manifest each other's value (e.g., 1 coat = 10 pounds of coffee = 1 pound of iron = 200 yards of linen).

The "general form of value" arises as one commodity habitually represents the abstract value of others (e.g., a specific measure of iron represents a specific measure of yards of linen, a number of coats, or pounds of coffee). Finally, as one commodity – usually a precious metal – becomes the general form the "money form of value" arises. Money is the mature, social expression of exchange-value.

SEE ALSO: Marx, Karl; Money; Surplus Value; Use-Value; Value

SUGGESTED READING

Marx, K. (1976) *Capital*, vol. 1, trans. B. Fowkes. Penguin, London.

ROB BEAMISH

existential sociology

Existential sociology emerged in the late 1970s as the most recent version of everyday life sociology. Writers in this perspective have attempted to integrate symbolic interactionism's powerful concepts of the self and the situation, phenomenological sociology's emphasis on the social construction of reality, and ethnomethodology's telling critique of conventional sociological theory and methods, with an innovative argument for the centrality of embodiment and feelings to human agency. Thus, *existential sociology can be defined descriptively as the study of human experience-in-the-world (or existence) in all its forms.* A key feature of experience-in-the-(contemporary)-world is change. Existential sociologists expect, if not assume, change to be a constant feature of people's lives, their sense of self, their experience of the social world, the other people that populate the social world, and the culture that provides meaning for life. Everyday life is more than merely situational and problematic, a point on which all the varieties of everyday life sociology generally agree. Everyday life is *dramatic* – in an aesthetic sense – and experienced as such. In contrast to Erving Goffman's dramaturgical model of social life, the drama that existential sociologists see in everyday life does not follow anyone else's script. The actor is simultaneously writer, producer, and actor on a stage not necessarily of his or her choosing, but one that cannot simply be exited without confrontation with the producer/director (e.g., agents of social control).

Existentialist ideas began influencing the social sciences more than four decades ago. In 1962, Edward Tiryakian published *Sociologism and Existentialism*, an influential work of sociological theory, which sought to resolve two very different ways of thinking about human social life and existence: "sociologism," which sees society as preeminent over the individual; and "existentialism," which places a much greater emphasis on individuals, their choices, their responsibilities, their passions, their decisions, their cowardice, their virtues, and so on.

The concept of the existential self is concerned with the experience of individuality – through the perspective of the subject – as it unfolds, adapts, and copes in concrete, everyday life situations. *The existential self refers to an individual's unique experience of being within the context of contemporary social conditions, an experience most notably marked by an incessant sense of becoming and an active participation in social change.* The first major feature of the existential self is *embodiment*. Being-within-the-world means that feelings and primordial perception precede rationality and symbol use and, in fact, activate them. The second major feature is that the *existential self is becoming*. Our becoming must be grounded in the real, social world if we have any intention of being effective in coping with the given world. Existential sociology examines the various social activities in which people engage to preclude or escape meaninglessness including, for example, religion, spirituality, recreational drugs, music, dance, art, sex, athletics, self-actualization, and intellectual endeavors.

SEE ALSO: Emotion: Social Psychological Aspects; Everyday Life

SUGGESTED READINGS

Kotarba, J. A. & Fontana, A. (eds.) (1984) *The Existential Self in Society*. University of Chicago Press, Chicago, IL.

Kotarba, J. A. & Johnson, J. M. (eds.) (2002) *Postmodern Existential Sociology*. Alta Mira, Walnut Creek, CA.

JOSEPH A. KOTARBA

expectation states theory

Expectation states theory is a set of related theories concerned with processes by which *actors* draw information from their social and cultural environment and organize that information into expectation states that determine their interaction with others. Together with research testing these theories and other research applying them to problems in everyday interaction (such as interracial interaction in schools), expectation states theory constitutes a *theoretical research program*.

The earliest work in the program (called *power and prestige theory*) considers how actors develop expectations in groups where there are no significant social or cultural differences among the group members. However, the largest branch of the program is status characteristics theory, which is concerned with groups in which actors initially differ on such status distinctions as gender, race, or occupational positions. *Status characteristics theory* explains how such status distinctions consistently determine expectations and power and prestige behaviors in task groups, whether or not the distinction is related to the group's task.

Basically, the theory argues that the powerful effect of such statuses is based on the activation in the group of cultural beliefs about these status distinctions. A coherent set of such beliefs defines a *diffuse status characteristic* (D). For example, gender may be a D for an actor if, for that actor: (1) men are in general more highly valued than women, (2) men are seen as more mechanically skilled than women, and (3) men are seen as more capable at tasks in general than women. These beliefs become *salient* in a group if D is relevant to the group's task (e.g., the task is believed to favor males or females) or if D is a basis of discrimination in the group (as in a mixed-gender group). Even a D that is initially *not* relevant to the task will normally become *relevant*, unless its relevance is challenged or it is dissociated from the task. Status advantages thus tend to generalize from situation to situation. If new actors enter the group, the original group members add status information about the new actor to their previously processed information. If multiple status characteristics become relevant to the group's task, actors *combine* the information in these characteristics (i.e. whether they imply success or failure at the task and how relevant they are to the task) in forming expectations for themselves and the others. Finally, once actors have formed expectations for self and others, their observable power and prestige behaviors (i.e. initiation and receipt of interaction, evaluations of performance, and influence) are determined by these expectations.

The arguments and consequences of status characteristics theory have been supported by extensive empirical studies. In addition, the theory has been applied to a broad range of status distinctions including gender, race, ethnic identities, educational attainment, occupational position, sexual orientation, physical attractiveness, and the status structures of work teams.

Over the years the expectation states program has grown in a variety of different ways. Table 1 presents a summary of the major current branches of the program.

SEE ALSO: Legitimacy; Power, Theories of; Social Influence; Status Construction Theory; Theoretical Research Programs; Theory Construction

Table 1 Expectation states theory

Theory	*Phenomenon of concern*
Power and prestige	Emergence and maintenance of differentiated behavior in status-undifferentiated groups
Status characteristics and expectation states	Formation of expectation states based on socially established status characteristics; maintenance of behavioral hierarchies in status-differentiated groups
Distributive justice	Reward expectations and justice norms arising from the relation of reward expectations to actual reward allocations
Sources of evaluation	Formation of expectations and their effects on behavior based on evaluations of actors with legitimated rights to evaluate others
Evolution of status expectations	Evolution of status expectations as actors move through different task situations with different others
Status cues	Role of verbal and nonverbal cues in attributions of performance capacities and status categories; their dependence on actors' established status positions
Reward expectations	Interrelation of status, task, and reward expectations and the inequalities created by these interrelations
Behavior-status	Integrates research from the power and prestige and the status characteristics branches
Evaluations-expectations	Integrates research from status characteristics and source theory branches
Status legitimation	Legitimation and delegitimation of hierarchies
Sentiments and status	Interrelation of affect and sentiment processes with status and expectation state processes
Multiple standards	How multiple standards maintain prevailing status distinctions
Status construction	How institutionalized status characteristics are socially constructed and diffused through society

Source: Wagner, D. G. & Berger, J. (2002) Expectation states theory: an evolving research program. In: Berger, J. & Zelditch, M., Jr. (eds.), *New Directions in Contemporary Sociological Theory*. Rowman & Littlefield, Lanham, MD, pp. 41–76; the table appears on pp. 44–5.

SUGGESTED READINGS

Berger, J., Fisek, M. H., Norman, R. Z., & Zelditch, M., Jr. (1977) *Status Characteristics and Social Interaction: An Expectation States Approach*. Elsevier, New York.

JOSEPH BERGER AND DAVID G. WAGNER

experiment

An experiment is a highly controlled research scenario. It entails the intentional manipulation of one variable (the independent) in order to assess its causal impact on another variable (the dependent or outcome variable). The experiment is considered the best research design for examining cause and effect relationships. The strength of the experiment is found in its ability to control key study conditions – i.e. the deliberate creation of experimental and control groups, the intentional manipulation of the independent variable(s) and the careful measurement of the dependent variable.

The experimental group is exposed or subjected to the "experimental condition" – i.e. the independent variable being investigated for its alleged causal impact. The control group is not exposed to the independent variable and thus serves as a base for critical comparison in assessing any causal impact. The experimental and control groups are configured to be virtually identical – i.e. they should resemble each other in all significant ways. This condition is best achieved via a random assignment process. Random assignment requires that chance and chance alone determines who is assigned to each group. For example, the names of all volunteers for an experiment might be placed in a hat. The first name drawn from the hat might be assigned to the experimental group, the second to the control group, and so on.

Once the experimental and control groups are established, the intentional manipulation of the independent variable takes place. After the independent variable has been introduced into the experimental group, the dependent variable is then measured in both groups. If the observed outcome on the dependent variable is not the same in the two groups, the difference can be attributed to the independent variable, the only condition that differs between the two groups. Consider the following example: A researcher wants to see if there is a causal connection between chewing nicotine gum and a reduction in smoking. Smokers are randomly assigned to the experimental and the control groups. The experimental group is given nicotine gum to chew; the control group does not receive the nicotine gum. At the end of the study period, smoking activity is measured in both groups. If members of the experimental group are smoking less than members of the control group, the reduction is attributed to the nicotine gum.

The experimental design is superior to other research designs with regard to the issue of internal validity – i.e. the ability to correctly assess the causal connections between variables. The experiment is particularly strong in its ability to control or eliminate many known *threats to internal validity* – i.e. conditions that undermine our ability to say if one variable causally impacts another. For instance, events that coincide with the timing of a non-experimental study might confound the study's causal analysis. Consider for instance a simple before/after study trying to assess the impact of a driver's ed program on students' driving practices. The study's causal analysis would be compromised if a celebrity were involved in a serious car accident during the study period. This is known as a *history* threat to internal validity. The experiment, with its use of both an experimental and a control group, is able to "eliminate" the history threat when assessing any causal connections. History occurs to both groups and thus becomes an irrelevant factor in any causal assessment. There is a downside to the experiment – its contrived nature makes it weak on *external validity* – the ability to accurately generalize findings from experimental to nonexperimental conditions.

SEE ALSO: Asch Experiments; Experimental Design; Milgram, Stanley (Experiments); Zimbardo Prison Experiment; Validity, Qualitative; Validity, Quantitative

SUGGESTED READINGS

Frankfort-Nachmias, C. & Nachmias, D. (2000) *Research Methods in the Social Sciences*. Worth, New York.

Ruane, J. (2005) *Essentials of Research Methods: A Guide to Social Science Research*. Blackwell, Malden, MA.

JANET M. RUANE

experimental design

An experimental design is a plan for assigning experimental units to treatment levels and the statistical analysis associated with the plan (Kirk 1995: 1). An experimental design identifies the: (1) independent and dependent variables, (2) extraneous conditions that must be controlled (nuisance variables), and (3) indicates the way in which the randomization and statistical analysis of an experiment are to be carried out. Carefully designed and executed experiments are one of science's most powerful methods for discovering causal relationships.

The seminal ideas about experimental design can be traced to Ronald A. Fisher, a statistician, biologist, and geneticist. Fisher vigorously championed three key principles of experimental design: randomization, replication, and blocking or local control. *Random assignment* has three important benefits. First, it helps to distribute the idiosyncratic characteristics of experimental units over the treatment levels so that they do not selectively bias the outcome of an experiment. Second, random assignment permits the researcher to compute an unbiased estimate of *error effects* – those effects not attributable to the manipulation of the independent variable. Finally, random assignment helps to ensure that the error effects are statistically independent. Through random assignment, a researcher creates two or more groups of experimental units that at the time of assignment are probabilistically similar on the average.

Replication is the observation of two or more experimental units under the same conditions. Replication enables a researcher to estimate error effects and obtain a more precise estimate of treatment effects. *Blocking* or *local control* removes variation attributable to a nuisance variable from the error effects. By removing a nuisance variable from the numerator and denominator of the test statistic, a researcher is rewarded with a more powerful test of a false null hypothesis. Two simple experimental designs that illustrate these principles are described next.

One of the simplest experimental designs is the randomization and analysis plan that is used with a t statistic for independent samples. Consider an experiment to compare the effectiveness of two ways of presenting nutritional information – newspapers and television – in getting obese teenage boys to follow a more nutritious diet. The dependent variable is a measure of improvement in each boy's diet 1 month after the presentation. Assume that 30 boys are available to participate in the experiment. The researcher randomly assigns the boys to the 2 treatment levels with the restriction that

15 boys are assigned to each level. An independent samples t statistic is used to test the researcher's statistical hypothesis.

In this experimental design, the nuisance variable of gender is held constant: only boys are used. Other nuisance variables such as initial obesity and age are probabilistically controlled by random assignment. The design described next uses an additional procedure, blocking or local control, to remove the nuisance variable of preexisting differences in obesity from the error effects.

It is reasonable to assume that responsiveness to nutritional information is related to the amount by which a boy is overweight. The design of the experiment can be improved by isolating this nuisance variable and removing it from the error effects. This can be accomplished by using a dependent samples t statistic design. Suppose that instead of randomly assigning 30 boys to the treatment levels, the researcher formed 15 blocks each containing two boys who are overweight by about the same amount. After all the blocks have been formed, the two boys in a block are randomly assigned to the media presentations. This design is more likely to detect any differences in diet improvement than the independent samples t statistic design.

SEE ALSO: Experiment; Experimental Methods; Hypotheses; Statistical Significance Testing

REFERENCES

Kirk, R. E. (1995) *Experimental Design: Procedures for the Behavioral Sciences*, 3rd edn. Brooks/Cole, Pacific Grove, CA.

SUGGESTED READINGS

Keppel, G. (1991) *Design and Analysis: A Researcher's Handbook*, 3rd edn. Prentice Hall, Upper Saddle River, NJ.

Maxwell, S. E. & Delaney, H. D. (2004) *Designing Experiments and Analyzing Data: A Model Comparison Perspective*, 2nd edn. Lawrence Erlbaum, Mahwah, NJ.

ROGER E. KIRK

experimental methods (social psychology)

An experiment is a research method for which an investigator plans, builds or otherwise controls the conditions under which phenomena are observed. Experiments are used rarely in sociology where they are concentrated in the subfields of group processes and social psychology.

There are two distinct types of experiments – empiricist and theory-driven experiments (Willer and Walker 2007). Empiricist experiments are excellent tools for discovering phenomena and relations between phenomena. Empiricist designs (1) identify an event (X) that is presumed to "cause" another event (Y), (2) build experimental conditions in which X is present and control conditions in which X is absent, (3) randomly assign subjects to treatments, and (4) observe occurrences of Y.

Theory-driven experiments (1) build models of structures and processes described by theory, (2) translate theory-based models into experimental designs, and (3) find outcomes predicted by theory.

EXPERIMENTAL CONTROL

Sociology experiments are conducted in a variety of settings and experimental control varies substantially across them. Natural experiments are characterized by the *absence* of experimental control and laboratory experiments offer maximum possible control.

Vietnam-era draft lotteries created conditions for natural experiments. Days of the year were drawn randomly and used to order men's draft eligibility. The procedure established "natural" experimental groups including (1) certain draftees (i.e., men born on dates with low numbers) and (2) men with uncertain but calculable odds of being drafted (i.e., those with higher numbers). Subsequent research showed that men with low draft numbers had higher long-term, non-military mortality rates than those with higher numbers (Hearst et al. 1986).

Field experiments are conducted in natural settings and usually have limited experimental control. Massey and Lundy (2001) studied landlords' reactions to race-identified language by controlling speech characteristics of putative renters. They had no control of their subjects' characteristics; all of them had placed ads in local publications.

Survey experiments conduct studies with large samples, control the selection of participants and randomly assign participants to treatments (i.e., survey questions or forms of questions). The result is a powerful tool for discovering important social relationships or for testing theory.

Laboratory experiments offer maximum control. Researchers select participants and control the conditions under which they are studied. Moore (1968) studied women who attended the same community college and gave them information that their simulated partners differed from them on a single characteristic – the school she attended. The high degree of control was important because one scope restriction on the theory under test required group members to differ on a single characteristic.

THE FUTURE OF SOCIOLOGY EXPERIMENTS

The future of experiments in sociology is not clear. Perhaps, the spread of experimental techniques to other social and behavioral sciences will increase their visibility in sociology and create greater demand for sociologists trained in experimental methods.

SEE ALSO: Experiment; Experimental Design; Social Psychology

REFERENCES

Hearst, N., Newman, T. B., & Hulley, S. B. (1986) Delayed effects of the military draft on mortality: a randomized natural experiment. *New England Journal of Medicine* 314: 620–4.

Massey, D. S. & Lundy, G. (2001) Use of black English and discrimination in urban housing markets: new methods and findings. *Urban Affairs Review* 36: 452–69.

Moore, J. C. (1968) Status and influence in small group interactions. *Sociometry* 31: 47–63.

Willer, D. and Walker, H. A. (2007) *Building Experiments: Testing Social Theory*. Stanford University Press, Stanford, CA.

HENRY A. WALKER

exploitation

Exploitation occurs when someone or something (a material resource, an opportunity, etc.) is used or taken advantage of. Social scientists are chiefly concerned with the exploitation of people and classes, who are considered exploited if they are required, by force or by circumstances, to contribute more to some process than they receive in return. Crucially important to Marxian thought, the concept of exploitation is also employed in neoclassical economics and related sociological work. Yet the concept is controversial; many sociologists eschew it entirely.

Karl Marx held that working people in all class-divided societies are exploited because they are compelled to perform surplus labor – labor for which they receive no equivalent. He argued that this occurs because they lack access to land and other means of production, and must therefore work for others. Marx's definition of class, and his theories of class interests and antagonisms, are rooted in this idea, and he argued that a society's other economic and political relationships are based upon and correspond to its specific system of surplus-labor extraction.

He also argued that surplus labor is the exclusive source of profit under capitalism. Although capitalists seemingly pay for labor, Marx held that they actually purchase *labor-power* – workers' capacity to work. The wage contract therefore does not determine the actual amount of labor that workers perform. Profit arises because they are made to work longer than the period during which their labor adds an amount of new value that "replaces" their wages.

Critics have persistently claimed that Marx's demonstration of this proposition has been proven internally inconsistent, so that his argument must be rejected. In response to these claims, the "Fundamental Marxian Theorem" was put forward. It supposedly proved that surplus labor is the exclusive source of profit without relying on Marx's allegedly inconsistent value concepts. However, a new school of Marx-interpretation calls this theorem into question while also claiming to refute the proofs of inconsistency. It maintains that the inconsistencies are not features of Marx's original value theory, but are created by misinterpretation.

Unequal exchange theory begins from the observation that the prices of less developed countries' exports tend to be low relative to the amounts of labor used in their production, while the prices of developed countries' exports tend to be relatively high. Proponents of the theory thus regard international trade as a process of unequal exchange of labor. Many also regard it as exploitative, but Emmanuel (1972), who pioneered unequal exchange theory, did not.

In contrast to Marx's theory, neoclassical economics implies that exploitation of capitalists by workers (through, for instance, the formation of unions) is as likely as the exploitation of workers by capitalists. All people who provide productive inputs are considered exploited if they are paid less, or exploiters if they are paid more, than what neoclassical theory regards as the input's contribution to production. Sørensen (2000) seeks to make the neoclassical concept of exploitation the basis for sociological class analysis. He defines exploiting classes as groups that can exact payments for their inputs which exceed the minimum amounts needed to make the inputs available.

SEE ALSO: Dependency and World-Systems Theories; Economic Sociology: Neoclassical Economic Perspective; Labor Process; Marx, Karl

REFERENCES

Emmanuel, A. (1972) *Unequal Exchange: A Study of the Imperialism of Trade*. Monthly Review Press, New York.

Sørensen, A. B. (2000) Toward a sounder basis for class analysis. *American Journal of Sociology* 105 (6): 1523–58.

ANDREW KLIMAN

F

facework

The concept of "facework" was articulated by Erving Goffman (1967/1955). He provides a model of human interaction in which individuals' subjective perceptions are central. It is a matter of self-regulation and the ritual recreation of "face."

He defines "face" as "the positive social value a person effectively claims for himself." If a person makes "a good showing," then the image of him or her is perceived by that social actor as approved by members of the reference group. If there is a mismatch, there is likely to be a negative emotional reaction. In conventionalized encounters there is little choice about which face to "be in" or "maintain." A person can be said to be "in wrong face" or "out of face" when she cannot integrate the situation or deal with it in expected ways. When one is out of face there may be a sense of shame, while being "in face" tends to be associated with pride.

An interaction involves people trying to follow expected patterns. Expected signs such as glances and gestures are either given or withheld (Collins 1988: 16). Greetings and farewells are ritualized ceremonies which compensate for previous or future separations. The tendency, according to Goffman, is for all actors to support one another's face. Encounters help one to construct a sense of one's own face, or "self-image." People tend to try to protect their own inner idea of themselves even when they may rebel in open or hidden ways.

SEE ALSO: Goffman, Erving; Self-Concept

REFERENCES

Collins, R. (1988) Theoretical continuities in Goffman's work. In: Drew, P. & Wootton, A. (eds.), *Erving Goffman: Exploring the Interaction Order*. Northeastern University Press, Boston, MA, pp. 41–63.

Goffman, E. (1967) [1955] *Interaction Ritual*. Anchor, Garden City, NY.

J. I. (HANS) BAKKER

fact, theory and hypothesis including the history of the scientific fact

The terms "theory," "fact," and "hypothesis" are sometimes treated as though they have clear meanings and clear relations with one another, but the histories and uses of these are more complex and diverse than might be expected.

The usual sense of these words places them in a relationship of increasing uncertainty. A fact is usually thought of as a described state of affairs in which the descriptions are true or highly supported.

A highly corroborated or supported hypothesis is also a fact; a less well corroborated one is still a hypothesis. A hypothesis which is not supported by or corroborated by other evidence would not be a fact, but could become a fact if it came to be corroborated to a high degree of certainty by other evidence. Similarly, a theory, which is a logically connected set of hypotheses, could come to be a fact if the hypotheses in the theory were to be highly corroborated by the evidence.

When we collect data we have already described them or have a conceptual category for them. Since the "data" are already in a predefined category, we are not dealing directly with the world but with an already categorized world.

The methodological understanding of science that fits best the insight that facts are already conceptual is hypothetico-deductivism, which contrasts to a different view of methodology called inductivism.

Inductivism was the traditional understanding that science consists of generalizations which can be built up on the basis of the collection of data which can then be arranged into generalizations. The problem with inductivism is that there is no logical way to get from a collection of finite singular pieces of information to a generalization which goes beyond the particulars that have been collected.

Hypothetico-deductivism deals with this limitation by turning the problem upside down by beginning with hypotheses that are generalizations and asking whether the observable particulars are consistent with (because they are implied by) the generalization.

Hypothetico-deductivism has an advantage over inductivism as a method in that hypothetico-deductivism can be used to corroborate theories where the concepts in the theories are not themselves directly observable. This is an especially important possibility in sociology because many of the concepts in sociology do not directly apply to observable facts in the world, but instead to grounding concepts such as "society," or "role," or "attitude." These concepts can be understood as having observable manifestations, but are not limited to or equivalent to observable manifestations.

SENSE-MAKING IN THEORIES

The major difference between sociological and physical theory is that the concepts in sociology are typically sense-making: they serve to enable a fact described in its terms to be more fully intelligible.

Making a fact more intelligible will usually make its consequences more predictable. If one does something as simple as characterizing an action as a product of the agent's beliefs and positive attitudes towards some outcome specified by the agent's beliefs, one has improved the prediction over alternative descriptions or over chance.

If the sociologist can add to this simple situation of explaining in terms of beliefs and attitudes by characterizing the set of beliefs that support the particular belief that relates directly to the action, for example by understanding a religiously motivated action in terms of a typology of religious belief, and if the sociologist can explain how those beliefs come to be distributed in particular groups, she will have something that begins to look like a theory that explains those actions sociologically, that is to say at some level beyond the level of the individual.

SEE ALSO: Science, Social Construction of; Theory; Theory and Methods

SUGGESTED READINGS

Apel, K.-O. (1984) *Explanation and Understanding: A Transcendental-Pragmatic Perspective*. MIT Press, Cambridge, MA.

Giddens, A. (1993) *New Rules of Sociological Method*, 2nd edn. Stanford University Press, Palo Alto, CA.

STEPHEN TURNER

factor analysis

Factor analysis, a statistical technique introduced by British psychologist Charles Spearman, belongs to the general linear model (GLM) set of procedures, hence requiring many of the same assumptions as multiple regressions. The two types of factor analysis are *exploratory factor analysis* (EFA) that is most commonly used and *confirmatory factor analysis* (CFA).

Often, direct measurement of underlying concepts (or latent variables) such as "women's empowerment," "IQ," or "leadership" is difficult. Instead, they are best approximated through other *intercorrelated* and quantifiable variables using factor analysis. In this approach, a large set of variables that tap into a latent concept are condensed into a smaller coherent array of variables that, even if correlated with the original variables, are orthogonal (or non-overlapping) with each other. To do so, factor analysis uses only the variance that a variable shares with the other variables, and divides it into *factors* that focus on what is *common* to all variables, with minimum loss of information. Thus, highly correlated variables (whether positively or negatively) are influenced by the same factor and thus, have high *factor loading*, while relatively uncorrelated ones may be influenced by other factors.

Factor analysis generates a table where rows consist of the original set of variables, columns are the factors, and table cells consist of factor loadings or the correlation coefficients between the variables and factors. Analogous to Pearson's r, the squared factor loading is the percentage of variance in the variable explained by a factor and is the basis for imputing a *label*. Because computers do not automatically label underlying factors, they must be tagged by a statistician, often making the process vulnerable to researcher subjectivity. Factor loadings may also be *rotated* to obtain a new factor structure. Finally, a factor's *eigenvalue* is the sum of its squared factor loadings for all the variables, with a low eigenvalue indicating little contribution to the explanation of variances in the variables by the factor.

SEE ALSO: Descriptive Statistics; General Linear Model; Statistical Significance Testing; Statistics

SUGGESTED READING

Thompson, B. (2004) *Exploratory and Confirmatory Factor Analysis: Understanding Concepts and Applications*. American Psychological Association, Washington, DC.

SANGEETA PARASHAR

false consciousness

As an imperfect (or false) consciousness, this term begins with Hegel's *Phenomenology of Mind*. Hegel maintained that the human mind moves dialectically from understanding (a naïve, sense-based perception of the world which seems separated or alienated from it) to Reason (a fully mediated, true consciousness which grasps the world and the mind itself as a unified, complex totality).

Marx argued Hegel's philosophy represented an inverted, false representation of humankind's relationship to consciousness. Being determines consciousness and humankind's being centres on actual, material life-processes. The first step to overcoming false consciousness requires the transcendence of Hegel's phenomenology. In class societies, true consciousness also requires seeing through the mystifications that enshroud the real causes of exploitation.

Lukács (1971) provided a precise, detailed explication/elaboration of Marx's conceptions of false consciousness under capitalism. Through commodity fetishism, the social character of commodities "becomes imperceptible to the senses" and the relation between men assumes "the fantastic form of a relation between things" (p. 86). A process of reification (*Verdinglichung* – thingification) "sinks more fatefully, more definitively into the consciousness of man" (p. 93). As the individuals most subjected to reification, "the concrete dialectic between the social existence of the worker and the forms of his consciousness force them out of their pure immediacy" leading to a clearer, mediated conception of how to cause social change (p. 168).

Lukes develops false consciousness outside a Marxist framework. False consciousness exists in situations where grievances concerning real, empirically identifiable interests (e.g. clean drinking water, environmentally sound production techniques) are curtailed (or even absent) because people cannot imagine alternatives or accept things as natural and inevitable.

SEE ALSO: Capitalism; Commodities, Commodity Fetishism, and Commodification; Ideology; Marx, Karl

REFERENCE

Lukács, G. (1971) [1923] *History and Class Consciousness*, trans. R. Livingstone. Merlin Press, London.

SUGGESTED READINGS

Lukes, S. (1974) *Power: A Radical View*. Macmillan, London.

ROB BEAMISH

family, history of

European societies during the nineteenth century underwent massive changes. The old social order anchored in kinship, the village, the community, religion, and old regimes was attacked and fell to the twin forces of industrialism and revolutionary democracy. The sweeping changes had particular effect on the family. There was a dramatic increase in such conditions as poverty, child labor, desertions, prostitution, illegitimacy, and the abuse of women and children. These conditions were particularly evident in the newly emerging industrial cities.

The industrial revolution dramatically changed the nature of economic and social life. The factory system developed, and, with its development, there was a transformation from home industries in rural areas to factories in towns and cities of Europe and America. Rural people were lured by the novelty of city life and the prospects of greater economic opportunity. The domestic economy of the preindustrial family disappeared. The rural and village-based family system no longer served as a productive unit. The domestic economy had enabled the family to combine economic activities with the supervision and training of its children; the development of the factory system led to a major change in the division of labor in family roles.

The separation of work from the home had important implications for family members. Increasingly, the man became the sole provider for the family and the women and children developed a life comprised solely of concerns centered on the family, the home, and the school. Their contacts with the outside world diminished and they were removed from community involvements.

Sociological interest in the study of the history of the family was very strong in the mid-nineteenth century in Western Europe. Prior to the nineteenth century, western thought generally held to a biblical belief in the origins of the family stemming from God's creation of the world, including Adam and Eve. Although there was recognition of relatively minor familial changes over time, the biblical family form and its underlying patriarchal ideological precepts were seen as continuing intact into the nineteenth century.

Friedrich Engels' (1972) evolutionary theory saw economic factors as the primary determinants of social change and linked particular technological forms with particular family forms. He depicted a stage of savagery as one with no economic inequalities and no private ownership of property. The family form was group marriage based on matriarchy. During the stage of barbarism, men gained economic control over the means of production. In civilization, the last stage, women became subjugated to the male-dominated economic system and monogamy. This stage, in Engels's view, rather than representing the apex of marital and familial forms, represented the victory of private property over common ownership and group marriage. Engels speculated that the coming of socialist revolution would usher in a new evolutionary stage marked by gender equality and by common ownership of property. Engels' main achievement was in defining the family as an economic unit. This has become a major focus in much of the subsequent historical research on the family and is of great theoretical importance in the sociology of the family.

In traditional societies, the family (following the argument of Chicago School sociologists William Ogburn and Ernest Burgess) performed economic, educational, recreational, religious, and protective functions. In modern society most of these functions have been taken over as a consequence of the increased participation of government, economic enterprises, and education. The cornerstone of family life was its companionship and emotional functions. This shift in family functions led to Burgess's famous classification of family types as moving from "institution to companionship." According to Burgess, the institutional family is sustained by external community pressures and involvements; the companionate family, on the other hand, is sustained by the emotional attachments among its members.

Talcott Parsons emphasized the importance of the nuclear family – in the absence of extended kinship ties – in that it meets two major societal needs: the socialization of children and the satisfaction of the affectional and emotional demands of husbands, wives, and their children. Further, the isolated nuclear family, which is not handicapped by conflicting obligations to extended relatives, can best take advantage of occupational opportunities and is best able to cope with the demands of modern industrial urban life.

The classic statement of modernization theory, centering on the family and change, is William J. Goode's *World Revolution and Family Patterns* (1963). This work has had a profound impact on the comparative study of social change and the family. Goode's major contribution is the comprehensive and systematic gathering and analyses of cross-cultural and historical data to attack the notion that industrial and economic development was the principal reason that the family is changing. Goode concluded that changes in industrialization and the family are parallel processes, both being influenced by changing social and personal ideologies – the ideologies of economic progress, the conjugal family, and egalitarianism. Finally, Goode proposes that in the "world revolution" toward industrialization and urbanization there is a convergence of diverse types of extended family forms to some type of conjugal family system.

Globalization theory has become another perspective in examining family change. Here the emphasis is on an examination of the transnational processes that have an impact on families. Rather than focusing solely on families in the modernized countries or on families in third world societies, of paramount importance are relationships that exist and are experienced by individuals who have family members living in both rich and poor countries.

SEE ALSO: Family Diversity; Family Structure; Family Theory

SUGGESTED READINGS

Coleman, M. & Ganong, L. H. (2004) *Handbook of Contemporary Families*. Sage, Thousand Oaks, CA.

Engels, F. (1972) [1884] *The Origins of the Family, Private Property, and the State*. Pathfinder Press, New York.

Trost, J. & Adams, B. (eds.) (2005) *Handbook of World Families*. Sage, Thousand Oaks, CA.

MARK HUTTER

family demography

Family demography is a subfield of demography that focuses on explaining the causes and consequences of population trends related to the family. These trends include changing gender relations within households; the formation, dissolution and reformation of romantic unions; fertility; and changes in household size and composition. Family demographers are made up of researchers from a wide range of disciplines, including sociology, economics, anthropology, family studies, psychology, and public health. These researchers rely on theoretical frameworks to interpret trends in the family, such as the life course theory, demographic transition theories, developmental idealism, and theories that take gender dynamics and cultural contexts into account.

Family demographers employ demographic strategies of analysis to study the family. They depend on the use of large-scale surveys that produce representative data of household and family members. They also tend to study rates of people experiencing an event, with the denominator being those "at risk" of experiencing the event of interest (e.g., those "at risk" of marriage includes those who are currently unmarried). It is important to pay attention to effects that are attributable to age, period, *or* cohort that might influence family trends. For example, fertility rates are higher during certain *ages* of the reproductive life span. Fertility may also change due to *period* effects, such as an economic recession. On the other hand, a characteristic intrinsic to a *cohort*, such as higher levels of education than preceding cohorts, may cause women to have later or fewer births.

Families have undergone enormous changes in the last century. In the USA and other western countries there has been a decline in marriage due to people marrying later, spending more time in cohabiting unions, and divorcing more often. Yet, the majority of people still intend to and do marry at some point in their lives. For those marrying in the USA, divorce became more common in the second half of the twentieth century, though divorce rates have plateaued since the 1980s. Still, the USA maintains one of the highest divorce rates in the world. In conjunction with this high divorce rate, there has been an increase in remarriage, resulting in a greater number of step and blended family homes. Similarly, there has been an increase in single-parent households, with most of these households being headed by women.

In addition to these changes in marital patterns, western countries have seen an increase in separation of childbearing and marriage. There has been a rise in nonmarital births, both as a result of a declining proportion of births to married couples as well as a rising proportion of births to nonmarried couples. Many of these nonmarital births occur within cohabiting unions, although having children in these kinds of unions is less common in the USA than in other western nations. The rise in cohabitation has sparked interest among family demographers, who often seek to understand the differences between cohabitors in the USA versus in other western countries. In other countries, cohabitation is more commonly treated as an alternative to marriage and the line between marriage and cohabitation is blurred. In the USA, on the other hand, cohabitors are distinct from married couples in many ways including education, fertility, and pooling of income.

The study of fertility is closely linked to family demography, as reproduction is central to the family. Fertility rates are linked to family and household size and have implications for intergenerational relationships. The global fertility decline has been an ongoing focus of family demographers. In non-western countries, fertility decline was considered desirable to prevent rapid population growth, whereas in some western countries the concern is that fertility is too low, leading to population decline and concerns with support of the elderly. Related to the global fertility decline, family demographers also study the decreasing size of households and the move toward nuclear rather than extended households. Just as family dynamics change in response to fertility decline, the global decline in mortality and increase in life expectancy has also led to changes in family composition and intergenerational relationships. For example, an increased life expectancy means that people are spending more years in marital unions, leaving more opportunity for marriages to dissolve.

As family demography looks to the future there is more work to be done in understanding the unique situation of cohabitors and whether cohabitation in the USA is expected to become more like marriage. Another ongoing focus is likely to be on changing population structures in countries around the world. Populations around the world are becoming more concentrated in the older ages, leading to undesirable ratios between the working population and the elderly. The significance of this age distribution for family processes and intergenerational relationships is likely to become central in family demography.

SEE ALSO: Demographic Transition Theory; Family Diversity; Family Theory; Fertility: Transitions and Measures; Households; Lesbian and Gay Families; Marriage; Second Demographic Transition

SUGGESTED READING

Bianchi, S. M. & Casper, L. M. (2000) American families. *Population Bulletin* 55 (4).

Jayakody, R. Thornton, A., & Axinn, W. (2008) *International Family Change*. Lawrence Erlbaum Associates, New Jersey.

Thornton, A. T., Axinn, W. G. & Xie, Y. (2007) *Marriage and Cohabitation*. University of Chicago Press, Chicago, IL.

ELYSE JENNINGS

family diversity

Historically, the term family diversity referred to variations from a traditional family. This implied that there was one best type of family, and that all other family types were dysfunctional and deviant. In a more contemporary view, family diversity refers to a broad range of characteristics or dimensions on which families vary, along with a recognition that there are a multitude of different family types that function effectively. Family diversity thus refers to variations along structural or demographic dimensions (e.g., race/ethnicity, socioeconomic status), as well as in family processes (e.g., communication and parenting behaviors).

Family living arrangements in the USA and throughout much of the world are considerably more diverse, pluralistic, and fluid than they were just a few decades ago. We have witnessed profound demographic changes, including longer life expectancy, postponed marriage and childbearing, dramatic increases in both childbearing and childrearing outside of marriage, and substantial growth of singlehood, cohabitation, divorce, and remarriage. As a result, there has been a sharp increase in the visibility of diverse family forms such as single-parent (mostly single-mother) families, stepfamilies, households headed by gays and lesbians, and families living in poverty. These changes have stirred considerable debate surrounding the definition of family. For example, do two cohabiting adults and their dependent children constitute a family? Are they still a family without the presence of children in the household? What if the two adults are gay or lesbian?

Beginning in the middle of the twentieth century, a strong value was attached to a "benchmark" family type in the United States, or what is commonly termed the "traditional" nuclear family. Following World War II, rapid social changes including men returning to the labor force, a post-war economic boom, an increasing standard of living, increases in marriage and birth rates, and a decline in the divorce rate supported a set of values and beliefs that privileged the two biological parent, male breadwinner, female homemaker family. Although families of the 1950s often are viewed with nostalgia, evidence shows that many traditional families were characterized by severe inequities, male dominance, men's overinvolvement in work and underinvolvement in family activities, wife abuse, and alcoholism. Since then, changing historical contexts and powerful social movements (e.g., civil rights, women's rights, gay and lesbian liberation, and men's movements) have been associated with the establishment of a wide variety of family forms, making the diversity of families more visible and normative, and spurring debates over the future of marriage and whether there is one best type of family.

SEE ALSO: Cohabitation; Divorce; Family Structure; Lesbian and Gay Families; Lone Parent Families

SUGGESTED READINGS

Fine, M. A. (eds.), *Handbook of Family Diversity*. Oxford University Press, New York, pp. 15–31.

Patterson, C. J. (2000) Family relationships of lesbians and gay men. *Journal of Marriage and the Family* 62: 1052–69.

BRAD VAN EEDEN-MOOREFIELD AND DAVID H. DEMO

family poverty

Social scientists have had a long standing interest in family poverty for at least three major reasons. First, there has been a concern regarding the role that families play in the intergenerational transmission of poverty. Second, the importance of family structure as a causal factor leading to poverty, and in particular understanding the relationship between single parent families and the risk of poverty, has been of interest. Finally, researchers have been concerned about the detrimental effects that poverty exerts upon family well-being and functioning.

Early work addressing family poverty frequently assumed that poverty was chronic and handed down from generation to generation. One argument to explain this pattern was that it resulted from the larger economic reproduction of social class. Families with few resources were unable to provide their offspring with the types of advantages necessary for getting ahead economically, resulting in a perpetuation of poverty from one generation to the next. An important variation of this perspective was the culture of poverty framework derived from the ethnographic work of Oscar Lewis in the 1950s and 1960s.

With the advent of several large, longitudinal data sets in the late 1960s and 1970s, the assumption that family poverty was chronic, long lasting, and intergenerational could be empirically examined. Research indicated that households were typically impoverished for one or two years and then managed to get above the poverty line, perhaps experiencing an additional spell of poverty at some later point in their lives. This work showed a much more fluid and dynamic picture of family poverty than had frequently been assumed, yet at the same time, recent research has also demonstrated a strong correlation between parents' and children's overall socioeconomic status.

The rise in the number of female headed families with children during the latter third of the twentieth century (fueled by the high rate of divorce and an increasing number of out-of-wedlock births), led to a second major area of research among US sociologists and social scientists studying the patterns and causes of family poverty. This body of work demonstrated that female headed families with children were at a significant risk of encountering poverty and economic destitution. Various studies showed that following a divorce, the standard of living for women and their children declined sharply. Many women worked at lower paying jobs and lacked child support payments. The result was that female headed families with children had substantially higher rates of poverty than other types of families, and experienced poverty for longer periods of time.

These and other research findings spotlighting the significance of family structure have led to an academic and political debate regarding the importance of encouraging marriage as a strategy for alleviating family poverty. Recent welfare reform legislation in the USA has placed a strong emphasis on policies and programs to encourage marriage and to discourage out-of-wedlock births. Others have argued that a more reasonable and effective policy approach is to provide the supports necessary for all families and children to succeed, not just those in married-couple families.

A third area of research has examined the effect that poverty has had upon family well-being and functioning. Poverty has been shown to exert a profound negative influence upon the health and development of family members. For example, poor infants and young children are likely to have far lower levels of physical and mental growth (as measured in a variety of ways) than their non-poor counterparts. Both the duration and the depth of poverty intensify these negative outcomes. The result is that poverty can have long-lasting physical and mental consequences as children become adults. Poverty has also been shown to detrimentally impact various aspects of family well-being, such as the likelihood of violence, stress, and dissolution.

SEE ALSO: Family; Feminization of Poverty; Income Inequality and Income Mobility; Poverty; Welfare Dependency and Welfare Underuse

SUGGESTED READINGS

Rank, M. R. (2004). *One Nation, Underprivileged: Why American Poverty Affects Us All*. Oxford University Press, New York.

MARK R. RANK

family structure

Within any society there are more or less common ways of "doing" family relationships which are broadly accepted as appropriate in that society. This does not mean that all family relationships follow the same societal "rules." There are always variations and alternative practices. Moreover the more complex and diverse a society, the more variation there will be in the family practices given legitimacy by different social groupings within it. Indeed, the degree of social tolerance given to divergent patterns of family relationships is itself one element of family structure. More commonly, family structure is concerned with such issues as the boundaries of family membership; the distribution of power and authority within families; the patterns of solidarity and obligation that arise between different family members; and the differential access to resources different family members have. Much mid-twentieth-century family theorizing addressed these issues, focusing particularly on a shift from an extended family structure to a nuclear family one under the impact of industrialization, with Parsons (1943) providing the classic analysis.

Although heavily criticized, aspects of Parsons' arguments about the structural priority of what he terms the "conjugal" family continue to have strong salience. In particular, the increased emphasis placed on "the couple" reflects the centrality of nuclear families over wider kinship ties. This points to the continuing shift from marriage as an institution to marriage as a relationship. Similarly, the emphasis placed on the rights and needs of children, the increased responsibilities of care, and the growth of child- and adolescent-centered markets highlights the level of priority given to dependent children within contemporary family systems.

However family structure has also been altering in ways which are less compatible with the "nuclear family" model. Two issues are particularly significant. First, while the division of labor and responsibilities between spouses remains gendered, there is now less rigidity about this than there was for much of the twentieth century. Second, there is now far greater acceptance of diversity in family practices than there used to be. Patterns that were previously understood to be problematic, if not pathological, are now accepted as legitimate alternative family forms. Obvious examples include lone-parent families, step-families, cohabitation, and gay partnerships. Life course trajectories are now also more diverse than they were. With new forms of partnership, increasing levels of separation and divorce, and what can be termed "serial commitment" (i.e. an individual being involved in a series of committed relationships), the patterning of people's family lives over time has become increasingly variable.

This greater diversity within the family relationships people construct makes the specification of family structure within contemporary developed societies more problematic than previously. No single form of family organization or pattern of constructing family relationships holds normatively or experientially in the way Parsons' nuclear family model did in the mid-twentieth century. Nonetheless certain structuring principles remain important. Three warrant highlighting. First, gender remains a primary organizational principal within most families. Second, people normally prioritize their commitment to their partner and dependent children above those to other family members. And third, albeit with some ethnic diversity, love as a personal and emotional commitment is generally understood as the prime basis for contemporary partnership, whether or not this involves marriage.

SEE ALSO: Cohabitation; Divisions of Household Labor; Family Diversity.

REFERENCE

Parsons, T. (1943) The kinship system of the contemporary United States. *American Anthropologist* 43: 22–38.

SUGGESTED READINGS

Cherlin, A. (2004) The deinstitutionalization of American marriage. *Journal of Marriage and Family* 66: 848–61.

Gillis, J. (1997) *A World of Their Own Making*. Oxford University Press, Oxford.

GRAHAM ALLAN

family theory

There are many different theories in family theory. The following article will therefore set out some of the more influential approaches.

Exchange Theory

Individuals are seen as making choices about behavior based on the balance of rewards and costs that the behavior has for them. Behavior becomes exchange when the actions of one individual enter into the rewards and costs of another individual. Applications of exchange theory include the study of the choice of marriage partner, the quality of the marriage relationship, marriage bargaining, and separation and divorce.

Symbolic Interactionism

Here, the family is seen as a unity of interacting personalities. Whatever unity exists in family life can only be the result of interactions between family members. Interactionist work on family life includes studies of how behavior is negotiated and renegotiated among family members.

Family Life Course Development

The family life course development framework focuses on the systematic and patterned changes experienced by families as they move through stages and events of their family life course. More recently, the focus is upon the individual life course, and on how it affects and is affected by the life courses of other individuals.

Systems Theory

In systems theory, family processes are understood as the product of the entire family system. The systems approach to the family has therefore been welcomed by some scholars and practitioners as a way to understand family problems and intervene in family processes without blaming any one family member.

Conflict Theory

Conflict is a normal part of family life. Sources of conflict include the competition for scarce resources, and incompatible goals. The resources that are available within families are not only the subject of competition, but they are also the means by which one individual may gain power over others.

Feminist Theory

Feminist theory of family life holds three premises. First, there is thought to be an internal stratification of family life, in which men receive more benefits than do women. Second, relations between husbands and wives are identified as power relations, in which men dominate over women. Third, ideological legitimations of gender inequality are held to be responsible for the acceptance by women of their own subjection.

Family Ecology

A concern with individuals and their environment is at the heart of the ecological approach. One of the most popular ways of thinking about this is to conceive of the nested ecosystems in which the individual human being develops. Individuals develop within the family microsystem, which is influenced by the surrounding society.

CURRENT EMPHASES

The main current emphasis in family theorizing is on the deinstitutionalization of family life. Beck and Beck-Gernsheim have advanced individualization theory. This states that changes occurring in families are the result of a long-term trend in modern societies to accord more autonomy to individuals. Giddens argues that traditional family ties have been replaced by the pure relationship. A pure relationship is one based upon emotional communication, where the rewards derived from such communication are the main basis for the relationship to continue.

SEE ALSO: Conflict Theory; Family, Sociology of; Symbolic Interaction Theory

SUGGESTED READINGS

Beck, U. & Beck-Gernsheim, E. (2002) *Individualization: Institutionalized Individualism and Its Social and Political Consequences*. Sage, London.

Bengtson, V. L., Acock, A. C., Allen, K. R., Dilworth-Anderson, P., & Klein, D. M. (eds.) (2005) *Sourcebook of Family Theory and Research*. Sage, Thousand Oaks, CA.

Cheal, D. (1991) *Family and the State of Theory*. University of Toronto Press, Toronto.

Giddens, A. (1992) *The Transformation of Intimacy*. Polity, Cambridge.

White, J. M. & Klein, D. M. (2002) *Family Theories*, 2nd edn. Sage, Thousand Oaks, CA.

DAVID CHEAL

fascism

Fascism as a historical entity began in 1922 when Mussolini came to power in Italy. As a political ideology, fascism defines many of the movements that were present in post-World War I Europe from the British Union of Fascists to the Romanian Iron Guard. Fascism could have remained simply a characteristic of a group of historically specific political formations, but the term rather quickly developed a life of its own. Today, it serves as what Alexander (2003) has described as a bridging metaphor, that is, a term that one uses independently of historical or definitional context when confronted with acts of arbitrary violence or authoritarianism in political and, in some instances, social life.

The death-knell of fascism has not sounded either in the real world of political practice or in the relatively cloistered world of the academy. For example, Griffin (1991: 26) begins where earlier studies left off. He argues that the term fascism has undergone an "unacceptable loss of precision" and proposes a new "ideal type" of fascism based on the following definition: "Fascism is a genus of political ideology whose mythic core in its various permutations is a palingenetic form of populist ultra-nationalism." The collapse of communism in 1989, the electoral success of European right-wing populist parties that began in the early 1990s coupled with a resurgence of neo-Nazi violence, and the more recent rise of Islamic fundamentalism have reawakened social science interest in historical fascism.

Existing studies of fascism fall into two schools that may be broadly categorized as follows. The first tries to answer the "what" or definitional question. Frequently, this is articulated in a discussion of whether or not fascism is a "generic" concept or a national variation of historically specific political instances. For those who try to define fascism, the central theme is the impossibility of definition. The second approach bypasses definition and tries to establish the characteristics of regimes and constituencies. Lipset's (1981) classic account of the class composition of fascist movements attributes fascism's success to the political disaffection of the middle classes. Fascism, for Linz, was a peculiar combination of law and violence.

A central weakness in much of the writing on fascism, past and present, has been a failure to draw a sharp distinction between fascist movements and regimes, between fascism as ideology and fascism as state, between political impulse and political institution.

SEE ALSO: Authoritarianism; Communism; Democracy; Ideology; Socialism

REFERENCES

Griffin, R. (1991) *The Nature of Fascism*. St. Martin's Press, New York.

Lipset, S. M. (1981) *Political Man*. Johns Hopkins University Press, Baltimore, MD.

SUGGESTED READING

Alexander, J. C. (2003) *The Meanings of Social Life*. Oxford University Press, New York.

MABEL BEREZIN

fatherhood

Fatherhood is a social institution and includes the rights, responsibilities and statuses associated with being a father. It also refers to general ideologies and public meanings. There is general agreement that fatherhood has altered over recent decades but less consensus over the extent of change.

The breadth and depth of research on fatherhood has developed exponentially since the 1970s along with recognition of the heterogeneity of fathers' social situations. The significance of biological fatherhood has increased since it has been possible to identify the genetic parent. Perhaps paradoxically, social fatherhood is also gaining more attention. High levels of divorce and remarriage have led to many men entering fatherhood through formal and informal adoptive and step relationships. Variations in the experiences and ideals of fatherhood due to differences in residency, age, class, sexuality, and ethnicity are also increasingly the subject of study.

Within the social sciences, researchers working from a developmental perspective use quantitative techniques to explore the effect of paternal influence and father–child relations on the well-being of children and fathers. Qualitative approaches are adopted by scholars interested in exploring individuals' perceptions and experiences of fatherhood. Discourses of fatherhood are also examined, using images of fatherhood in policy documents and the popular media. In these latter two arenas key questions are the degree to which being the financial provider remains important and the extent to which nurturing and "caring for" children has become a significant component of fathering.

SEE ALSO: Motherhood; Gender, Work, and Family

SUGGESTED READING

Dermott, E. (2008) *Intimate Fatherhood*. Routledge, New York and London.

ESTHER DERMOTT

female genital cutting

Female genital cutting (FGC) is the ancient cultural practice of removing portions of a girl's genitalia. It occurs extensively in Africa on girls from infancy to puberty and is also known as female circumcision (FC) or female genital mutilation (FGM). In Arabic, the language of many proponents of genital cutting, the custom is known as *tahara*, cleanliness or purification. While practitioners affirm its value as an important and long-standing part of cultural identity, critics decry the practice as a violation of human rights that damages women's health and perpetuates violence against girls.

The practice of genital cutting is a significant rite of passage for girls in the regions where it is observed. Girls must be cut to be accepted as responsible adult members of their communities and suitable marriage partners. The procedure is thought to make girls beautiful and clean and to enhance male sexual pleasure, increasing marital stability. Since it typically reduces female sexual desire, it is believed to ensure girls' virginity and prevent infidelity among adult women. Celebrations often follow the procedure and girls are given gifts and public recognition of their new status. Parents who do not cut their daughters are seen as inexcusably neglectful. For practicing communities, genital cutting of girls is an important part of cultural and ethnic identity. Many Muslims believe that female circumcision is a religious duty stipulated in the Qur'an, though prominent Muslim scholars have strongly condemned female genital cutting. Other religions engage in female cutting in Africa as well, including Protestants, Catholics, Coptic Christians, and Ethiopian Jews.

Female genital cutting occurs in several patterns, ranging from removal of part of the clitoris (Sunnah circumcision) to excision of all external genitalia leaving a small opening for the passage of urine and menstrual blood (infibulation or Pharaonic circumcision). The practice occurs most frequently in Egypt, Somalia, Djibouti, Sudan, Mali, and Guinea, where over 90 percent of all adult women have been circumcised. Other countries with genital cutting include Ethiopia, Eritrea, Sierra Leone, Gambia, Burkina Faso, and Nigeria. The practice has been carried to Europe and North America by African immigrants. The most common age for genital cutting is four to eight years old, though in some areas girls are cut at the marriageable age of fourteen to sixteen years old. Worldwide, as many as 140 million women or 5 percent of the world's female population have been circumcised and an estimated three million additional girls are cut every year.

SEE ALSO: Culture; Gender, the Body and; Health and Culture; Patriarchy; Women's Health; Women, Sexuality and

SUGGESTED READING

Gruenbaum, E. (2001) *The Female Circumcision Controversy: An Anthropological Perspective*. University of Pennsylvania Press, Philadelphia.

SUSAN HAGOOD LEE

female masculinity

Female masculinity refers to a range of masculine-inflected identities and identifications. Debates over the status and meaning of female masculinity and the bodies and selves to whom the terms may be ascribed emerge in the context of analyses of sex, gender, and sexuality.

Social and cultural history has documented the lives of individual women who defied the gendered conventions of their times, adopted masculine clothing and/or engaged in gendered non-conformist behaviour in Anglo-American and European contexts from the eighteenth to the early twentieth century. Rigorous scholarly approaches to archival material have tended to challenge trans-historical claims of stable forms of female masculinity across time. Assumed relations of equivalence and translatability between and across culturally specific practices relating to female masculinity have also appeared suspect.

Key to the development of innovative conceptual trajectories on female masculinity in interdisciplinary academic gender studies are critical readings and sociocultural analyses of Radclyffe Hall's novel *The Well of Loneliness* (1928). In a pioneering essay, anthropologist Esther Newton (2000 [1984]) notes that Hall's novel constitutes a central reference for paradigmatic imaginings of female masculinity in the twentieth century, and the ground for the entrenchment and popularization of a relation between female masculinity and lesbianism.

In a groundbreaking study, Halberstam (1998) challenges psychoanalytic readings and proposes instead that unhinging the relation between masculinity and men may yield important insights into the social and cultural production of masculinity. This theoretical move reveals a spectrum of female masculine-inflected subject positions that historically have included the Androgyne, the Tribade and the Female Husband and that in mid- to late twentieth-century Anglo-American contexts comprise soft butch, butch, stone butch and transbutch identities, the youthful exuberance of tomboys and the parodic performances of drag kings (Halberstam 1998). In urban lesbian of color gender-non-conformist communities in the USA, "stud" and "aggressive" are terms which currently refer to masculine identifications which may or may not be coextensive with a lesbian identity.

Building on Rubin's (1992: 467) classic definition of butch as "a category of lesbian gender that is constituted through the deployment and manipulation of masculine gender codes and symbols," Halberstam (1998) aligns her spectrum of gender identifications of female masculinities firmly with lesbianism.

In relation to the future of female masculinity studies, queer theory and critical race studies perspectives should be noted. They hold great potential, as they can trouble academic and popular associations between female masculinity and lesbianism analytically, leading to an understanding of trans, genderqueer and female "nonlesbian" (Carter 2005) masculinities. A sustained consideration of the ways in which imaginings, practices and experiences of female masculinity are mediated by class, race and, crucially, racism is long overdue, as is an analysis that addresses the ways in which aesthetic, social and cultural categories may function ethnographically. This confirms the importance of investigating the complexities of social taxonomies of female virility and masculine experience, their contexts and meanings in everyday life.

SEE ALSO: Feminities/Masculinities; Lesbianism; Queer Theory

REFERENCES

Carter, J. (2005) On mother-love: history, queer theory, and nonlesbian identity. *Journal of the History of Sexuality* 14 (1/2): 107–38.

Halberstam, J. (1998) *Female Masculinity*. Duke University Press, Durham, NC, and London.

Newton, E. (2000) *Margaret Mead Made Me Gay: Personal Essays, Public Ideas*. Duke University Press, Durham, NC, and London.

Rubin, G. (1992) Of catamites and kings: reflections on butch, gender, and boundaries. In Nestle, J. (ed.), *The Persistent Desire: A Femme-Butch Reader*. Alyson Publications, Boston, MA.

SILVIA POSOCCO

femininities/masculinities

Femininities and masculinities are acquired social identities: as individuals become socialized they develop a gender identity, an understanding of what it means to be a "man" or a "woman." How individuals develop an understanding of their gender identity, including whether or not they fit into these prescribed gender roles, depends upon the context within which they are socialized and how they view themselves in relation to societal gender norms. Class, racial, ethnic, sexual, and national factors play heavily into how individuals construct their gender identities and how they are perceived externally. Gender identities are often naturalized; that is, they rely on a notion of biological difference, "so that 'natural' femininity [in a white, European, middle-class context] encompasses, for example, motherhood, being nurturing, a desire for pretty clothes and the exhibition of emotions" (Laurie et al. 1999: 3). "Natural" masculinity, in contrast, may encompass fatherhood, acting "tough," a desire for sports and competition, and hiding emotions. In both cases, these constructions of gender identity are based on stereotypes that fall within the range of normative femininities and masculinities. Yet, as many sociologists have pointed out, not all individuals fit within these prescribed norms and as such, masculinities and femininities must be recognized as socially constituted, fluid, wide-ranging, and historically and geographically differentiated.

Feminist scholars have long addressed the social construction of femininities, particularly in the context of gender inequality and power. Early feminist scholars such as Simone de Beauvoir (1980) argued that women's subordinated status in western societies was due to socialization rather than to any essential biological gender difference, as evidenced in her often-cited phrase, "One is not born, but rather becomes, a woman."

Since the 1980s, at least three areas of research on gender identity have helped shift the debate on femininities and masculinities: (1) masculinity studies, which emerged primarily in the 1980s and 1990s; (2) queer studies and lesbian, gay, bisexual, and transgender (LGBT) studies; and (3) gender, race, ethnic, and postcolonial studies.

In contrast to feminist scholarship that focused primarily on women's experiences with femininity, Connell's (1987) research on "hegemonic masculinity and emphasized femininity" was among the first to systematically analyze both sets of constructions as they contribute to global gender inequality. Connell argues that "hegemonic masculinity," a type of masculinity oriented toward accommodating the interests and desires of men, forms the basis of patriarchal social orders. Similarly, "emphasized femininity," a hegemonic form of femininity, is "defined around compliance with [female] subordination and is oriented to accommodating the interests and desires of men" (23). He argues that hegemonic masculinity is always constructed in relation to various subordinated masculinities as well as in relation to women. Thus, for example, non-European, poor, non-white, and/or gay men tend to experience subordinated masculinities, whereas men of middle-class European, white, and/or heterosexual backgrounds tend to benefit from the privileges of hegemonic masculinity.

Judith Butler's research on gender performativity has opened space for discussion about the naturalized linking of gender identity, the body, and sexual desire. Butler (1990) argues feminism has made a mistake by trying to assert that "women" are a group with common characteristics and interests. Like sociobiologists, feminists who rely exclusively on a sociocultural explanation of gender identity construction also fall prey to essentialism. Many individuals, especially those who define as "queer" or as lesbian, gay, bisexual, or transgendered, do not experience gender identity, embodiment, and sexual desire through the dominant norms of gender and heterosexuality. Like Connell, Butler suggests that certain cultural configurations of gender have seized a hegemonic hold. She calls for subversive action in the present: "gender trouble," the mobilization, subversive confusion, and proliferation of genders, and therefore identity. This idea of identity as free-floating and not connected to an "essence" is one of the key ideas expressed in queer theory.

Similarly, Halberstam's (1998) research addresses constructions of "female masculinity" and argues that scholars must separate discussions of gender identity (e.g., masculinities, femininities) from discussions of the body. Women can "act masculine" just as men can "act feminine"; how individuals identify in terms of their gender is not and should not be linked to their biological anatomies, however defined. Other scholars have examined how medical and scientific institutions have managed normative gender (and sexual) identities through psychological protocols and surgical intervention. This type of research points toward a broader understanding of gender that places dualistic conceptions of "masculine" vs. "feminine" and "male" vs. "female" into question.

Scholars of race, ethnic, and postcolonial studies have addressed how normative femininities and masculinities, which tend to benefit those with racial/ethnic privilege, help reinforce a racialized social order in which subordinated groups are demasculinized or feminized in ways that maintain their racial/ethnic subordination in society. One example involves the stereotyping of African American men as unruly and hypersexual. Similarly, postcolonial studies scholars have demonstrated how poor women in developing regions (particularly non-white women) have been simultaneously sexualized and exoticized, and also seen as passive, all notions based on stereotypes.

Critics have defended normative femininity and masculinity on religious, moral, and/or biological grounds. Some, for example, have argued that these social norms are "naturally" aligned with men's and women's assumed biological roles in reproduction and/or with their assumed heterosexual desire. Some women have joined feminist movements and challenged traditional notions of femininity; whereas other women have joined right-wing women's movements that embrace traditional gender roles and identities (e.g., Concerned Women for America). Men have formed feminist men's movements, as well as movements to embrace traditional notions of fatherhood, as in the divergent examples of the Christian-based (and largely white, middle-class) Promise Keepers and the Million

Man Marches, part of a movement to reclaim black masculinity.

SEE ALSO: Doing Gender; Female Masculinity; Feminism; Hegemonic Masculinity; Gender Oppression; Sex and Gender; Sexuality, Masculinity and; Socialization, Gender

REFERENCES

Butler, J. (1990) *Gender Trouble: Feminism and the Subversion of Identity*. Routledge, New York.

Connell, R. W. (1987) *Gender and Power: Society, the Person and Sexual Politics*. Stanford University Press, Palo Alto, CA.

de Beauvoir, S. (1980) [1952] *The Second Sex*. Random House/Alfred Knopf, New York.

Halberstam, J. (1998) *Female Masculinity*. Duke University Press, Durham, NC.

Laurie, N., Dwyer, C., Holloway, S., & Smith, F. (1999) *Geographies of New Femininities*. Longman, London.

SUGGESTED READING

Davis, A. (2001) Rape, racism and the myth of the black rapist. In: Bhavnani, K.-K. (ed.), *Feminism and "Race."* Oxford University Press, Oxford, pp. 50–64.

AMY LIND

feminism

Feminism is the system of ideas and political practices based on the principle that women are human beings equal to men. As a system of ideas, feminism includes several alternative discourses – liberal, cultural, materialist or socialist, radical, psychoanalytic, womanist, and postmodernist – of which liberal and materialist have been most important to sociology. Liberal feminism argues that women are equal to men and works to obtain equal rights through political and economic action while basically accepting the capitalist organization of society. Materialist feminism incorporates Marxist or socialist ideas and focuses on social production as the social process key to achieving equality.

As political practice, feminism is understood as a social movement with two periods of high mobilization – a "first wave," 1792–1920 and a "second wave," 1960–2008. Between first and second wave feminism, there is a period of relative quiet, a seeming "hiatus." "Third wave feminism" refers to the ideas and actions of feminists who will spend the majority of their lives in the twenty-first century.

Three main understandings of gender have emerged from the engagement of feminism and sociology: gender as a role performance across institutions (and as an institution in its own right, as a product of ongoing individual activities in which social actors hold each other accountable for "doing gender" (West and Zimmerman 1987), and as a stratificational category or an arrangement of gender classes. Central to all three approaches is the study of gender socialization, of how a person learns to conduct themselves and to configure their identities around the socially constructed categories of masculine and feminine.

The standpoint of women is the epistemological claim that a complete sociological knowledge requires an analysis of the world from the perspective of women. The idea of the standpoint of women has been refined by Patricia Hill Collins (1998) to reflect the fact of *intersectionality*, the lived experience in an individual biography of the daily workings of social power as multifaceted, involving, besides gender, inequalities of race, class, geosocial location, age, and sexuality.

Feminist sociology's model of society builds on a view of social production from the standpoint of women. *Social production* includes all the labor necessary to maintain human life-paid work in the economy, unpaid work in the home, the production of material goods, emotional goods, order in time and space and the reproduction of the worker both biologically and daily in the activities of maintenance. *Patriarchal ideology* divides this work into *public and private spheres* and assigns to women of every class responsibility in the private sphere. The public sphere is organized around the unacknowledged assumption of ongoing, uncompensated private sphere labor by women. These spheres overlap so that an individual's position in one sphere affects their position in the other. Feminist studies of the gendering of work have produced a vocabulary that has entered the everyday world: i.e., the second shift, sexual harassment, equal pay, pay equity, comparable worth, municipal housekeeping, the glass ceiling, the ideal worker norm, juggling work and family.

In *The Everyday World as Problematic* (1987), Dorothy E. Smith divides social production into *the local actualities of lived experience*, where the material work of production occurs and *the extra-local relations of ruling*, the interconnections of power which control and appropriate that production. All women are part of the local actualities of lived experience as are non-privileged men; the extra-local relations of ruling is a masculine domain, operating on what might be seen as the ethic of hegemonic masculinity (R. W. Connell 1987) control. For Smith, this control is exercised through impersonal, generalized *texts* – documents that prescribe who can legitimately do what.

Feminism's successes in sociology have turned on women sociologists of each generation finding ways to form as a class for itself, as people who understand and act on their common interests. In the Classical generation of sociology (1830–1930), this commonality was achieved through the social settlement movement, a practice of applied sociology in which educated young people lived in settlements located in the poorest urban areas, building a neighborly relation with the people there and working to alleviate social problems; women were a numerical majority of settlement residents and from this base women sociologists like Jane Addams rose to national and international prominence. In second wave feminism, women sociologists in the USA organized both within established professional associations and outside them as Sociologists for Women in Society (SWS); they demanded and achieved equity in the hiring of women and the support of women graduate students, a journal devoted to gender, *Gender & Society*, and power within the American Sociological Association, establishing the Section on Sex and Gender and promoting the election of eleven women as Association presidents since 1972.

SEE ALSO: Addams, Jane; Liberal Feminism; Inequality/Stratification, Gender; Feminism, First, Second, and Third Waves

REFERENCES

Collins, P. H. (1998) *Fighting Words: Black Women and the Search for Justice*. University of Minnesota Press, Minneapolis, MN.

Connell, R. W. (1987) *Gender and Power*. Stanford University Press, Stanford, CA.

Smith, D. E. (1987) *The Everyday World as Problematic: A Feminist Sociology*. Northeastern University Press, Boston, MA.

West, C. & Zimmerman, D. (1987) Doing gender. *Gender and Society* 2: 125–51.

SUGGESTED READING

Lengermann, P. & Niebrugge, G. (1998) *The Women Founders: Sociology and Social Theory, 1830–1930*. Waveland Press, Long Grove, IL.

PATRICIA LENGERMANN AND GILLIAN NIEBRUGGE

feminism, first, second, and third waves

The women's movement in the USA is generally broken into waves of protest, each set in different time periods with diverse tactics, ideologies, and goals. The waves are divided into a first wave, starting in the 1840s; a second wave, beginning in the late 1960s; and the third wave, emerging in the mid-1990s. Each wave is characterized by a period of mass mobilization when women of different backgrounds united on common issues, followed by periods of fragmentation, when women searched for ways to acknowledge their differences and to work on a variety of issues, including those pertaining to race/ethnicity, class, and sexual identity. Studies of the first wave tend to focus on the structural and organizational aspects of the movement. Therefore scholarship on the first wave investigates the organizations that emerged, activists' and organizations' relations with the political environment, and the larger social climate (e.g., demographic shifts). While these aspects continue to define the second and third waves of the movement, scholars also incorporate more cultural analyses to capture how individuals act politically, the role of identity and community, and multiplicity of oppression.

THE FIRST WAVE

The first wave of the US women's movement emerged in a time of great social change due to industrialization, national expansion, and a public discussion on individuals' rights. The issue of slavery drew many women into the public sphere and in the early 1800s, women were instrumental in organizing and participating in the Abolition Movement. When denied the right to speak and visibly participate at anti-slavery and temperance conventions, women reformers organized the first women's rights convention. The Seneca Falls Women's Rights Convention, held July 14, 1848, was organized by abolitionists Lucretia Mott and Elizabeth Cady Stanton and focused on multiple issues, including education rights, property reforms, and women's restrictive roles within the family. The convention attendees drew up a Declaration of Sentiments, modeled after the Declaration of Independence, which detailed how men had denied women their rights. It was only after much deliberation that the 300 attendees decided also to address the controversial issue of women's suffrage.

The first wave of the movement has been characterized as seeking national-level policy and legislative change, populated mostly by white upper- and middle-class women within organizational contexts, and subject to factions, divisiveness, and dwindling mobilization after the suffrage victory. By the 1950s, despite the traditional images of women, more and more middle-class white women were entering the labor force, and single motherhood and divorce rates were beginning to rise. The strain between societal expectations of domesticity and women's experiences in education and the workforce, along with other factors such as the rise of the cycle of new social movements that swept the United States and Western Europe, led to the reemergence of the movement in the 1960s and 1970s.

THE SECOND WAVE

The emergence of the second wave drew on activist networks from the first wave as well as other movements, particularly the New Left and the Civil Rights Movement. In addition, the publication of books such as Simone de Beauvoir's *The Second Sex* in 1952 and Betty Friedan's *The Feminine Mystique* in 1962 sparked primarily white middle-class women's dissatisfaction with the roles of men and women.

From the years 1972 to 1982, the second wave was in what has been characterized as its heyday. Women's liberation groups continued to recruit women to feminism and caused cultural shock waves with their critiques of femininity, gender roles, and heterosexuality. In the meantime, women's rights groups won legislative victories with the 1972 passage of Title IX directed at ending sex discrimination in publicly funded education and the 1973 *Roe v. Wade* decision by the Supreme Court legalizing abortion. One result of this heightened activity in the United States and abroad was that in 1975 the United Nations sponsored the First International Conference on Women in Mexico City.

Although these years were times of success for feminists, it was also a period of conflict, fragmentation, and growing discord in the movement. Lesbians, working-class women, and women of color critiqued white middle-class women's control of both branches of the movement. Informed by the discord in the first and second waves, feminists and feminist scholars, such as the Combahee River Collective and, later, Patricia Hill Collins, conceptualized an intersectional feminist paradigm that views race/ethnicity, class, gender, and sexuality as interlocking systems of oppression, forming a "matrix of domination."

THE THIRD WAVE

The popular media and some political pundits have repeatedly declared feminism dead or in decline. Scholars and activists respond to these obituaries in different ways. Some argue that these "premature" death notices serve a larger goal, preserving the status quo by erasing women's activism. Some argue that feminism diffused into the larger culture, bringing about a "post-feminist" era where feminist goals and ideology are alive but submerged into the broader culture. Others view the movement as fragmented, particularly because of issues of homophobia, classism, and racism, yet insist that it still remains active and vital. Related to this view, others argue that feminism has changed form and is now done in a different way by a new generation of activists.

Adopting the view that the movement has changed form and tactics, some scholars and participants refer to this phase of the women's movement as "the third wave." The idea of a third wave comes from the concept of a political generation, a period when common historical experiences form a political frame of reference for a group. Young women and men in the twenty-first century enter into feminism in a society dramatically shaped by the movement's first two waves. In addition, feminism is embedded in the institutions in which third wave feminists spend their lives. Their families, schools, health-care providers, and political representatives have been influenced by the beliefs and values of first and second wave feminism.

SEE ALSO: Black Feminist Thought; Cultural Feminism; Feminism; Feminist Pedagogy; Liberal Feminism; Radical Feminism; Socialist Feminism; Third World and Postcolonial Feminisms/Subaltern

SUGGESTED READINGS

Collins, P. H. (1990) *Black Feminist Thought.* Routledge, New York.

Reger, J. & Taylor, V. (2002) Women's movement research and social movement theory: a symbiotic relationship. *Research in Political Sociology, Sociological Views on Political Participation in the 21st Century* 10: 85–121.

Roth, B. (2004) *Separate Roads to Feminism: Black, Chicana, and White Feminist Movements in America's Second Wave.* Cambridge University Press, New York.

Taylor, V. (1989) Sources of continuity in social movements: the women's movement in abeyance. *American Sociological Review* 54: 761–75.

JO REGER

feminist methodology

Feminist methodology has been developed in response to concerns by feminist scholars about the limits of traditional methodology. Feminist social scientists have raised questions about separation of theory and method, gendered biases inherent in positivism, and hierarchies that limit who can be considered the most appropriate producers of theoretical knowledge. Feminist methodology includes an array of methods, approaches, and research strategies and offers a broad vision of research practice that can be used to study a wide range of topics, to analyze both men's and women's lives, and to explore both local and transnational or global processes.

Beginning in the 1970s, feminist scholars critiqued positivist scientific methods that reduce lived experiences to disconnected variables that do not do justice to the complexities of social life. They argued for the importance of starting analysis from the lived experiences of women and others who have been left out of the knowledge production process rather than start inquiry with the abstract categories and a priori assumptions of traditional academic disciplines. Feminist scholars also stress the importance of intersectional analysis, an approach that highlights the intersection of race, class, gender, and sexuality in women's lives.

In a follow-up to an assessment of feminist methods in 1991, Fonow and Cook (2005) found that concerns about researcher reflexivity, transparency of the research process, and women's empowerment remained central concerns in contemporary feminist methodology. The call for reflective practice has also been informed by critiques of the traditional research practices by third world and postcolonial feminist scholars.

A consistent goal expressed of feminist methodology is to create knowledge for social change purposes. Emphasis on social action has influenced the type of methods utilized by feminist researchers as well as the topics chosen for study. For example, feminists have utilized participatory action research to help empower subjects of research as well as to ensure that the research is responsive to the needs of specific communities or to social movements. This approach is also designed to diminish the power differentials between the researcher and those who are the subjects of the research. In an effort to democratize the research process, many activist researchers argue for adopting participatory strategies that involve community residents or other participants in the design, implementation, and analysis of the research. Collaborative writing also broadens the perspectives represented in the final product.

Feminist reconceptualizations of knowledge production processes contributed to a shift in research practices in many disciplines and to calls for more diverse methodological and self-reflective strategies than in traditional methodological approaches. Some feminist scholars question whether or not it is possible to develop a reflexive practice that can fully attend to all the different manifestations of power. However, since feminist methodology is open to critique and responsive to changing dynamics of power that shape women's lives and those of others who have been marginalized within academia, feminist researchers often act as innovators who are quick to develop new research approaches and frameworks.

SEE ALSO: Black Feminist Thought; Intersectionality; Feminist Pedagogy; Feminist Standpoint Theory; Methods

REFERENCES

Fonow, M. M. & Cook, J. A. (2005) Feminist methodology: new applications in the academy and public policy. *Signs: Journal of Women in Culture and Society* 30 (4): 221–36.

SUGGESTED READINGS

Fonow, M. M. & Cook, J. A. (eds.) (1991) *Beyond Methodology: Feminist Scholarship as Lived Research.* Indiana University Press, Bloomington, IN.

Harding, S. P. (ed.) (1987) *Feminism and Methodology.* Indiana University Press, Bloomington, IN.

NANCY A. NAPLES

feminist pedagogy

Feminist pedagogy begins with the premise that gender and the social inequality it represents in the wider society are often reproduced in the classroom. Existing curricula and classroom practices contain sexist biases and patriarchal assumptions as reflected in the fact that the contributions of women are often absent from textbooks; girls and women are portrayed in stereotypic ways in much of the literature of all disciplines; girls and women are often directed to certain fields of study and are directed away from others; and teaching practices typically favor the learning styles of boys and men. Teachers informed by principles of feminist pedagogy seek to express feminist values and goals in the classroom and to challenge traditional knowledge, seeking to advance the status and education of women and girls by providing them with educational experiences that encourage consciousness raising, empowerment, and voice through innovative educational strategies.

There are at least three distinctive variants of feminist pedagogical models: psychological, liberatory, and positional. The *psychologically oriented model* emphasizes the importance of relational connectivity in developmental learning and seeks to create non-combative and nurturing interaction dynamics in the classroom and between teacher and student. This approach to teaching seeks to create safe and non-intimidating classroom environments for interaction, exchange, and instructor evaluation. A familial language of caring and responsibility replaces the more sterile techno-scientific language of objectivity. In this context, a teacher's central authority is subtly redefined as facilitation; the teacher becomes a guide from the side and facilitates the creation of a cooperative learning environment that features collaboration, mutual responsibility, and sharing.

The *liberatory model* focuses on difference in the intersections of relationships of power, not only in terms of social position such as race, ethnicity, class, and gender, but also important intersections in the personal, political, and the pedagogical. The focus is on the emancipation and empowerment of girls and women as a historically oppressed group. Liberatory models typically address the production of knowledge, assuming that knowledge that is valued is associated with valued identities or groups in a culture. Traditional school curricula rely on bases of knowledge that are often biased or exclude or marginalize the contributions of women. This approach claims that women and other minorities must be included in the design of curriculum and instruction. Recognition of differences and of exclusions also informs pedagogical practices that seek to transform social relationships through raising critical consciousness and advocating equitable policies and programs.

Positional feminist pedagogy has been influenced by poststructural feminism with its emphasis on the intersecting social locations of race, ethnicity, class, and gender. Positional pedagogies seek to construct a multi-perspective discourse of interrogation, disruption, and intervention in order to resist patriarchal control of knowledge, theory, and pedagogy. Aware that institutional discourses as well as persons holding positions of authority coordinate knowledge, poststructural feminists value and address the multiplicity of intersections of power. Explorations of meaning and power are particularly explored from margin to center. The aim is to develop feminist projects of *standpoint* that locate women in relation to one another and in relation to men. In the classroom this is translated to mean that pedagogical experience and texts are both politically significant and historically contingent. The feminist agenda is to confront masculinist language, theory, and cultural constructions that maintain the status quo; it seeks in the process to shift viewpoints by building a pedagogy of possibility. Central to this approach is the belief that knowledge is actively constructed in relationships of difference and position. Differences of authority and other variables brought to the classroom are not "fixed identities" needing bridging, but rather serve as important markers for shifting power relationships. Rather than seeking to replicate power relationships, the goal is to challenge and to change them.

SEE ALSO: Critical Pedagogy; Feminism; Pedagogy

SUGGESTED READINGS

Luke, C. & Gore, J. (eds.) (1992) *Feminisms and Critical Pedagogy*. Routledge, New York.

Maher, F. & Tetreault, M. (1994) *The Feminist Classroom*. Basic Books, New York.

VICKY M. MACLEAN

feminist standpoint theory

Feminist standpoint theory is a broad categorization that includes somewhat diverse theories ranging from Hartsock's (1983) *feminist historical materialist* perspective, Haraway's (1988) analysis of *situated knowledges*, Collins's (1990) *black feminist thought*, Sandoval's (2000) explication of third world feminists = *differential oppositional consciousness*, and Smith's (1987) *everyday world* sociology for women. Harding (1986) first named feminist standpoint theory as a general approach within feminism to refer to the many different theorists who argued for the importance of situating knowledge in women's experiences. Standpoint theorists are found in a wide variety of disciplines and continue to raise important questions about the way power influences knowledge in a variety of fields.

Feminist standpoint theory was initially developed in response to debates surrounding Marxist feminism and socialist feminism in the 1970s and early 1980s. In reworking Marx's historical materialism from a feminist perspective, standpoint theorists' stated goal is to explicate how relations of domination are gendered in particular ways. Standpoint theory also developed in the context of third world and postcolonial feminist challenges to the so-called dual systems of patriarchy and capitalism. The dual systems approach was an attempt to merge feminist analyses of patriarchy and Marxist analyses of class to create a more complex socialist feminist theory of women's oppression. Critics of the dual systems approach pointed out the lack of attention paid by socialist feminist analyses to racism, white supremacy, and colonialism. In contrast, feminist standpoint theory offers an intersectional analysis of gender, race, ethnicity, class, and other social structural aspects of social life without privileging one dimension or adopting an additive formulation (for example, gender plus race). Standpoint theory retains elements of Marxist historical materialism for its central premise: knowledge develops in a complicated and contradictory way from lived experiences and social historical context.

Despite the diverse perspectives that are identified with standpoint epistemology, all standpoint theorists emphasize the importance of experience for feminist theorizing. In this regard, many point out the significance of standpoint analysis's connection to consciousness raising, the women's movement's knowledge production method. The consciousness-raising group process enabled women to share their experiences, identify and analyze the social and political mechanisms by which women are oppressed, and develop strategies for social change.

Standpoint theorists assert a link between the development of standpoint theory and feminist political goals of transformative social, political, and economic change. Standpoint theorists typically resist focusing their analyses on individual women removed from their social context. Knowledge generated from embodied standpoints of subordinates is powerful in that it can help transform traditional categories of analyses that originate from dominant groups. However, as many standpoint theorists argue, it remains only a partial perspective. Given standpoint theory's emphasis on a process of dialogue, analysis, and reflexivity, the approach has proven extremely vibrant and open to reassessment and revision. As a consequence, standpoint theory remains an extremely important approach within feminist theory.

SEE ALSO: Black Feminist Thought; Feminist Methodology; Feminist Pedagogy; Intersectionality; Matrix of Domination; Outsider-Within

REFERENCES

Collins, P. H. (1990) *Black Feminist Thought: Knowledge, Consciousness, and the Politics of Empowerment*. Unwin Hyman, Boston, MA.

Harding, S. (1986) *The Science Question in Feminism*. Cornell University Press, Ithaca, NY.

Haraway, D. (1988) Situated knowledges: the science question in feminism and the privilege of partial perspective. *Feminist Studies* 14 (3): 575–99.

Hartsock, N. (1983) *Money, Sex and Power: Toward a Feminist Historical Materialism*. Longman, New York.

Sandoval, C. (2000) *Methodology of the Oppressed*. University of Minnesota Press, St. Paul, MN.

Smith, Dorothy E. (1987) *The Everyday World as Problematic: A Feminist Sociology*. University of Toronto Press, Toronto.

NANCY A. NAPLES

feminization of poverty

Diana Pearce (1978) coined the term "feminization of poverty" in the late 1970s to describe the increasing overrepresentation of women and children among the poor in the United States. Since then the gender gap in poverty has increased, although some evidence suggests that improvements in women's earnings are beginning to close the poverty gap between women and men. Of householders, 12.4 percent of men are living in poverty compared with 18.9 percent of women (US Census Bureau, 2008). The disparity is sharper for African Americans: 20.2 percent of householder men live in poverty, compared to 35 percent of householder women (US Census Bureau 2008). However, the economic disadvantage of women is not a uniquely US experience, and scholarship in recent years highlights the need for a more global perspective on the feminization of poverty.

As Pearce (1978) noted in her now classic article, explanations for the feminization of poverty in the United States center on work and welfare. Currently, full-time women workers earn 77 percent of what full-time men workers earn (US Census Bureau, 2008), and the pay gap is attenuated but still holds within educational-level and occupational status. In addition, women are underrepresented among the beneficiaries of the more generous, work-related social insurance benefits, but overrepresented as recipients of public assistance, a far less generous, means-tested program. In short, the dualistic structure of the US social welfare system works against women (Fraser 1993). The "masculine" social welfare programs are social insurance schemes (unemployment insurance, Social Security, Medicare, SSSI) primarily benefiting men as rights bearers and rewarding productive labor. The "feminine" social welfare programs (TANF, formerly AFDC, food stamps, Medicaid, public housing assistance) are less generous, have a heavy surveillance component, and devalue reproductive labor. In her analysis of the impact of the economic meltdown on older women, Estes (2009) argues that ageism and sexism have resulted in social policies (namely, Social Security and Medicare) that put older women at risk for high rates of poverty, morbidity and mortality.

A cross-national picture of the feminization of poverty must be segmented into an examination of other Economic North (or industrialized) countries and countries of the Economic South.

Cross-national comparisons with other industrialized countries prove particularly illuminating for understanding potential solutions for the US situation. In short, labor market and social welfare policies together can be significant deterrents to the feminization of poverty. As Goldberg and Kremen (1990: 36) note, "Cross-national data reinforce the conclusion that one of the world's wealthiest nations is not generous to single mothers and their children."

What is the global evidence for the feminization of poverty among Economic South nations? Standardized poverty measures are difficult to obtain, but the United Nations reports issued for the Fourth World Conference on Women (Beijing) in 1995 indicated that of the 1.3 billion people in poverty, 70 percent are women. The Platform for Action adopted at the conference called for the eradication of the persistent and increasing burden of poverty on women. However, according to a 2005 report from the Women's Environment and Development Organization, since Beijing women's livelihoods have worsened, with increasing insecure employment and reduced access to social protection and public services. In general, women's economic contributions are undervalued (to the tune of $11 trillion per year in 1995) and women work longer hours than men, yet share less in the economic rewards.

SEE ALSO: Culture of Poverty; Family Poverty; Gender, Development and; Gender Oppression; Income Inequality, Global; Inequality/Stratification, Gender; Poverty

REFERENCES

Estes, C. (2009) The economic meltdown: older women and the politics of aging. SWS Feminist Activist presentation at Case Western Reserve University, Cleveland, OH.

Fraser, N. (1993) Women, welfare and the politics of need interpretation. In: Richardson, L. & Taylor, V. (eds.), *Feminist Frontiers III*. McGraw-Hill, New York, pp. 447–58.

Goldberg, G. S. & Kremen, E. (1990) *The Feminization of Poverty: Only in America?* Praeger, New York.

Pearce, D. (1978) The feminization of poverty: women, work, and welfare. *Urban and Social Change Review* 11: 28–36.

SUSAN W. HINZE AND DAWN ALIBERTI

fertility and public policy

Fertility levels vary widely among contemporary populations, from a high of 7.2 births per woman in Niger to a low of 0.9 in Macao (United Nations 2007). These levels are largely the result of decisions made by individual couples who are trying to maximize their families' welfare. The fertility that results from this individual decision-making is not necessarily optimal from a societal point of view, thus suggesting a potential role for government intervention.

POLICY RESPONSES TO HIGH FERTILITY IN THE DEVELOPING WORLD

High fertility and rapid population growth have a number of adverse health and socio-economic effects. In response, governments have attempted to reduce high birth rates through the implementation of voluntary family planning programs. The aim of these programs was to provide information about and access to contraception to permit women and men to take control of their reproductive lives and avoid unwanted childbearing. Only in rare cases, most notably in China, has coercion been used. The choice of voluntary family planning programs as the principal policy instrument to reduce fertility is based on the documentation of a substantial level of unwanted childbearing and unsatisfied demand for contraception. A sizable proportion of women who do not want to become pregnant are not protected from the risk of pregnancy by practicing effective contraception (including sterilization) and, as a result, unintended pregnancies are common. Women in the developing world have an estimated 76 million unplanned pregnancies every year, mostly due to non-use of contraception (Alan Guttmacher Institute 2003).

There is little doubt that family planning programs have made a substantial contribution to fertility declines in the developing countries. The most effective public policies to reduce high fertility not only strengthen the family planning program but also encourage human development (in particular the education of girls). The former is aimed primarily at reducing unplanned pregnancy and the latter at reducing the demand for children.

POLICY RESPONSES TO LOW FERTILITY IN THE DEVELOPED WORLD

Fertility in virtually all modern societies has dropped below the replacement level of 2.1 births per woman (United Nations 2007).This low fertility has become a concern because a continuation of current levels will lead to rapid population aging which threatens the sustainability of public pension and health care systems (OECD 1998). Governments are considering a range of options: reduced benefits, increased taxes, higher labor force participation, delayed retirement, privatization of pension systems, etc. Until recently, pronatalist measures have been largely absent from this debate. Governments are reluctant to support such measures because of a disinclination to interfere with personal decision-making regarding family size, or because of the apparent inconsistency of advocating pronatalism at home while supporting efforts to reduce fertility in poor developing countries; in addition, they may hope that fertility will soon increase again without intervention. But interest in efforts to encourage higher fertility directly or indirectly is growing. For example, family support measures such as subsidized child care, reduced taxes for families with children, and paid parental leaves are widely acceptable and could be expanded. The fact that desired family size in most developed countries is still around two indicates that actual fertility is lower than desired and strongly suggests that birth rates can be raised by policies that reduce the cost of childbearing and help women to combine a career with childbearing.

SEE ALSO: Fertility: Transitions and Measures

REFERENCES

Alan Guttmacher Institute (2003) *Adding It Up: The Benefits of Investing in Sexual and Reproductive Health Care*. Alan Guttmacher Institute, New York.

OECD (1998) *Maintaining Prosperity in an Ageing Society*. OECD, Paris.

United Nations (2007) *World Population Prospects: The 2006 Revision*. United Nations Population Division, New York.

SUGGESTED READINGS

Bongaarts, J. (1997) The role of family planning programmes in contemporary fertility transitions. In: Jones, G. W., Caldwell, J. C., Douglas, R. M., & D'Souza, R. M. (eds.), *The Continuing Demographic Transition*. Clarendon Press, Oxford, pp. 422–44.

Caldwell, J. C., Caldwell, P., & McDonald, P. (2002) Policy responses to low fertility and its consequences: a global survey. *Journal of Population Research* 19 (1): 1–24.

JOHN BONGAARTS

fertility: transitions and measures

Childbearing, or the fertility of human populations, has changed profoundly in the last several centuries. Four aspects are basic for measuring and studying human fertility: *age*, *parity* (number of children ever born), length of *birth interval*, and *population reproductivity*. Additionally, there are cross-cutting issues of time perspective and of fertility dimensions. The variety of fertility measures at a given time is both a result of the data available and a precondition to expansions in data collection efforts.

Fertility measures are expressed to reflect childbearing either in the time period in which they occur, or at the end of the (reproductive) lifetime of a cohort. *Period fertility* rates and analyses are cross-sectional and give a "snapshot" of a population for a short period of time. A major advantage of period rates is that they are immediately calculable. A second is that they provide the annual contribution to population growth through fertility. *Cohort fertility* rates and analyses concern a group of persons with a common temporal experience, such as a birth or marriage date. They take into account the events occurring to women (or men) until the end of their reproductive years. More stable than period rates, they provide the means to evaluate long-term population evolution. The main disadvantage in calculating cohort measures is that they require, at minimum, 30 years of data.

Direct measures of fertility are classically obtained from vital registration records, which provide the numerators (births), and from censuses, projections, or continuous registration systems, which provide the population denominators. The *crude birth rate* (CBR) provides the number of live births per 1,000 population in a given time period. The CBR is a measure of a population's overall growth, but it can mask – or exaggerate – fertility differences between two populations which have very different age structures. The *general fertility rate* (GFR) is the number of live births in a time period to women of reproductive age, usually expressed per 1,000 women aged 15 to 44 or 15 to 49. The *age-specific fertility rate* (ASFR) is the number of births to women of a certain age divided by the number of women in that age group (e.g., women aged 25 to 29). The *total fertility rate* (TFR) represents the average number of children ever born to a woman if she were to move through her reproductive years maintaining ASFRs of the current time period.

From the 1960s through the 1980s, a plethora of *indirect measures* was generated which estimated primarily TFRs and secondarily ASFRs in developing countries. This was due to the dual conditions of data deficiency – censuses being then the primary data source – and the nationally and internationally funded family planning and development programs which needed fertility measures to track outcomes. Indirect measures are necessary when vital statistics and large surveys are not available for calculating ASFRs and TFRs – the case when only census data are available. Also, other data are often incomplete, of dubious quality (especially in reference to age), or are based on small sample size; hence indirect measures may provide better estimates than would direct measures. Similarly, indirect measures can aid in data quality evaluation.

Birth interval analysis has not been given as much attention as age-based analysis. But with the growth of large surveys containing many covariates, the study of birth intervals provides information on the dynamics of family growth, control of reproduction, health consequences for mothers and infants, as well as tempo measures for formal demographic analysis.

Particular attention to measures of population replacement, or *reproductivity*, came into play during the fertility nadirs experienced by Europe and North America between the world wars and in the last decade of the twentieth century. Also, the sustained high fertility rates of many parts of the "third world" – particularly in the 1970s and 1980s – generated concern about long-run population growth. A set of measures made it possible to map where a country was in terms of replacing itself, and what that portended in the long run.

SEE ALSO: Age, Period, and Cohort Effects; Demographic Data: Censuses, Registers, Surveys; Demographic Techniques: Population Projections and Estimates; Demographic Transition Theory; Fertility and Public Policy; Infertility; Second Demographic Transition

SUGGESTED READINGS

Bogue, D., Arriaga, E., & Anderton, A. (eds.) (1993) *Readings in Population Research Methodology*. United Nations Population Fund, Chicago, IL.

Siegel, J. S., Swanson, D. A. (eds.) (2004) *The Methods and Materials of Demography*, 2nd edn. Elsevier Academic Press, San Diego, CA.

SHARON KIRMEYER

Feuerbach, Ludwig (1804–72)

Ludwig Feuerbach was born into a large, prominent, academic family in Landshut, Bavaria. His father was a distinguished professor of jurisprudence, and three of Ludwig's four brothers went on to noteworthy careers in mathematics, law, and archeology. Some social theorists and sociologists are familiar with Feuerbach's writings on religion, but most sociologists know Feuerbach primarily because of his influence on the young Karl Marx – a central figure within the sociological tradition. Feuerbach's critique of Hegel provided Marx with the occasion to, in turn, critique Feuerbach, and in the process Marx worked his way toward a thoroughly sociological approach to such core topics as history, ideology, and social evolution.

The Essence of Christianity (1841) made Feuerbach famous in Germany and established him as a leader, along with Bruno Bauer and eventually Karl Marx, of the "Young Hegelians" – students of Hegel who sought to realize the master's idealism by grounding it in social and political realities. What Feuerbach had to say about Christianity is less important, for the sociologist, than the paradigm shift he initiated with respect to how we might think about and understand religion and, more generally, ideology. Feuerbach viewed religion as a projection of human needs and desires. Feuerbach, like Marx after him, wants us to see that religious striving represents an alienation of man from himself, and it is only through the proper understanding of man's relationship to himself that he will find the liberation he is seeking in God. It is this turning away from the supernatural to the natural, material, and the human that marks Feuerbach's contribution to social thought and social analysis.

SEE ALSO: Hegel, G. W. F.; Ideology; Marx, Karl; Materialism; Religion, Sociology of

REFERENCE

Wartofsky, M. (1977) *Feuerbach*. Cambridge University Press, Cambridge.

CLIFFORD L. STAPLES

figurational sociology

Stemming from the work of Norbert Elias (1897–1990), figurational sociology offers a radical way of seeing the social world. Elias's work was informed by an engagement with Alfred Weber, Karl Mannheim and the Frankfurt School, and entailed a synthesis of elements of Comte, Durkheim, Marx, Simmel, Weber, and Freud. Based on this synthesis, figurational sociology studies how people cope with the problems of interdependence, and rests on several interrelated premises: that human beings are interdependent; that their lives develop in the figurations that they form with each other; that these figurations are continually in flux, undergoing changes of different orders, some quick and superficial, others slower but perhaps more enduring; and that the long-term developments taking place in figurations have been and continue to be largely unplanned and unforeseen. The concept of figuration is used to refer to the webs of interdependence that link individuals, and both constrain and enable their actions. Though produced and reproduced by acting individuals, the long-term structure and dynamics of figurations cannot be explained solely in terms of the properties of individuals. This approach is intended to overcome the dichotomies that characterize sociological research, including individual/society, agency/structure, freedom/determinism, micro/macro, and synchronic/diachronic.

In order to capture the scale and scope of the interconnections that constitute figurations, one must abandon thinking and language rooted in *homo clausus* (the individual closed off, or separate from society), and instead view people as *homines aperti*: "open human beings" living in interdependence with others. Functionalist models that isolate individuals from society and reduce processes to mono-causal, static and non-relational variables are replaced by an emphasis on probing the emergent and contingent, yet structured and patterned, nature of social relations. Hence, the alternative name of this approach: process sociology. An example *par excellence* of this approach is Elias's theory of civilizing processes: an investigation of how struggles for power and status permeate the habitus of the individual and the social structures of societies over the long term of human history.

Figurational sociology offers a non-relativist theory of science, which raises issues of involvement and detachment in the production of reality-congruent knowledge, and a theory of power, which focuses on the relations between established and outsider groups at local, national and global levels of interdependence. Four other key concepts assist in capturing human interdependence: functional democratization (the process, neither planned nor intended, whereby power ratios among people become relatively equal); monopoly mechanism (the structured processes of increasing concentration of power, accompanying social differentiation and integration); and the twin concepts of diminishing contrasts and increasing varieties (the non-dichotomous tendencies towards homogeneity and heterogeneity).

Figurational sociological research has explored such topics as the embodied emotions, sport and gender relations; globalization, civilizing/decivilizing processes and international relations; nations, nationalism and ethnicity and race relations; violence, crime, and punishment; and the nature of sociology as a science. Figurational sociology provides a highly sophisticated theoretical and methodological approach, offering a potential reorientation of the subject, and promise of further rich empirical insight into the human condition.

SEE ALSO: Civilizing Process; Critical Theory/Frankfurt School; Elias, Norbert; Habitus; Mannheim, Karl

SUGGESTED READINGS

Elias, N. (2000) [1939] *The Civilising Process*, rev. edn. Blackwell, Oxford.

Goudsblom, J. and Mennell, S. (eds) (1998) *The Norbert Elias Reader*. Blackwell, Oxford.

JOSEPH MAGUIRE AND JENNIFER SMITH MAGUIRE

Fordism and Post-Fordism

Taylorism and other forms of scientific management were implemented in many industries in the late nineteenth and early twentieth centuries to control the labor process. Control over the labor process was accelerated when Henry Ford and his engineers applied the principles of scientific management to the assembly line. Whereas Taylorism developed work rules to standardize the production of parts, Fordism brought these standardized parts to the worker and specified how the assembly of parts was to be done.

By creating more precise control over the labor process and the pace of work, Ford was able to extract more labor from workers. Some of the high profits that Ford's system generated were passed onto workers in the form of higher wages, which allowed him to be more selective when hiring workers and impose stricter work standards without generating labor unrest. Ford also created internal labor markets by establishing job classifications and hierarchies that allowed workers to be upwardly mobile within the company. These internal labor markets created competition among workers, which divided workers and undermined worker solidarity.

Fordism is also associated with other social changes. Most notably, the mass production of inexpensive commodities established the foundation for the culture of mass consumption. Fordism also entails a mode of state regulation that attempts to institutionalize economic growth and stability, create a welfare state, and limit workers' rights.

The limitations of Fordism became apparent in the mid-1970s when the energy crisis and the economic downturn resulted in an abrupt halt to economic growth and stability. This transition to *post-Fordism* represented a new phase of capitalist development characterized by an acceleration of global competition, the increased role of the state in balancing production with consumption, restructuring the production process, and the emergence of giant global financial and manufacturing corporations.

Despite agreement that a transition occurred, there is considerable debate over how to characterize post-Fordism. Whereas some scholars characterize post-Fordism as global corporate dominance, others view it as a flexible form of economic organization that increases opportunities for individualism and pluralistic lifestyles. Still others challenge the broad generalizations in post-Fordist theory for denying the complex and heterogeneous causal processes that operate in different places in the global economy.

One dimension of post-Fordism that has been the subject of considerable debate is the use of information. Post-Fordism suggests that access to more information creates the organizational capability for instant data analysis that is essential to flexible manufacturing, the manufacture of specialized products, and the coordination of diverse corporate interests. Whereas some research suggests that information fosters decentralization and autonomy at lower levels of the organizational hierarchy, others maintain that access to information contributes to centralization.

Despite agreement in some areas, there are many unsettled debates in the post-Fordist literature. Resolution of these debates will require more precise theorizing and empirical research focusing on the organizational and political-legal arrangements in which economic activity is embedded.

SEE ALSO: Labor Process; Post-Industrial Society; Postmodern Culture; Taylorism

SUGGESTED READINGS

Amin, A. (ed.) (1994) *Post-Fordism*. Blackwell, Oxford.

Dohse, K., Jurgens, U., & Malsch, T. (1985) From "Fordism" to "Toyotism"? The social organization of the labor process in the Japanese automobile industry. *Politics and Society*, 14: 115–46.

Harvey, D. (1991). *The Condition of Postmodernity*. Basil Blackwell, Cambridge, MA.

Prechel, H. (2000) *Big Business and the State: Historical Transitions and Corporate Transformations, 1880s–1990s*. SUNY Press, Albany, NY.

HARLAND PRECHEL

Foucauldian archaeology and genealogy

Michel Foucault's interpretors have generally broken down his thought into two phases. The early works, *Madness and Civilization*, *The Birth of the Clinic*, *The Order of Things*, and *The Archaeology of Knowledge* are identified as archaeological, while *Discipline and Punish* and *The History of Sexuality* are identified as genealogical. Foucault himself rejected this binary characterization of his work, yet the words "genealogy" and "archaeology" are his own. So, what distinguishes these two modes of analysis, and why did Foucault perceive them as being coterminous in his latter works?

Foucault (1969/1972: 21, 31–9) most fully articulates his early methodological program in *The Archaeology of Knowledge*, where he adopts the epistemological position that the history of human society must be understood through "discontinuity, rupture, threshold, limit, series, and transformation," which perforate the social discourses that span history, creating distinct historical epochs called "discursive regimes." By focusing on discontinuity, archaeology opposes itself to any totalizing form of analysis which presents history as a uniform narrative or as subject to a progressive teleological convergence. Moreover, archaeology avoids grounding history in essentializing origins such as human nature. Similar to the traditional image of the archaeologist in the field who unearths the great monuments of the past and attempts to reconstruct the complex circumstances owing to their existence, Foucault suggests that we examine the ordinary documents of a particular period to reconstruct the complex political processes concealed by the dominant discourses which emerged out of that period.

Ultimately, the radical potential of archaeology manifests when we compare previous discursive formations with our own – it is this deployment of the fruits of archaeology as a tactic for critical evaluation that defines genealogical inquiry. Thus, genealogy is more an extension of archaeology than a break with it. Foucault (1976/1980: 84) explains that his genealogy aims to resist the hegemony of scientific knowledge and to produce an "insurrection of knowledges that are opposed primarily [. . .] to the effects of the centralizing powers which are linked to the institution and functioning of an organized scientific discourse within a society such as ours." However, the genealogical project is always made difficult because subjects are so deeply embedded in the social logic which produced them that fully objective critical evaluations of the present are impossible.

In his genealogical works, Foucault becomes increasingly concerned with uncovering the (often mundane) practices responsible for the transition between history's disparate epochs. Importantly, the outcomes of these processes are not assumed to be historically necessary, so that, unlike Marxian theorists, Foucault does not propose that any of these stages were inevitable or that they occurred in a determined order. He also more rigorously elaborates the role of power in producing the subjects, institutions, knowledge, and practices of a given period. Foucault comes to view power and knowledge as co-determining. For this reason, the term "discursive regime" is abandoned in favor of "power-knowledge regime" (1976/1990: 11). In "Nietzsche, genealogy, history," Foucault (1971/1998) explicitly reflects on the theoretical evolution of his program and illustrates the profound influence of Friedrich Nietzsche on his later thought.

SEE ALSO: Foucault, Michel; Nietzsche, Friedrich; Marx, Karl; Poststructuralism

REFERENCES

Foucault, M. (1969/1972) *The Archaeology of Knowledge*, trans. A. M. Sheridan Smith. Pantheon, New York.
Foucault, M. (1971/1998) Nietzsche, genealogy, history. In: Faubion, J. & Rabinow, P. (eds.), *Aesthetic, Method, and Epistemology*. New Press, New York.
Foucault, M. (1976/1980) Two Lectures. *Power/Knowledge*, ed. C. Gordon. Pantheon, New York.
Foucault, M. (1976/1990) *The History of Sexuality: An Introduction*, vol. 1, trans. R. Hurley. Vintage Books, New York.

PJ REY

Foucault, Michel (1926–84)

Michel Foucault was a French philosopher whose work has greatly influenced sociologists, particularly in the areas of crime and deviance, gender and sexuality, health and illness, organizational theory, and social welfare.

Foucault was born in Poitiers, France. He received his Doctorat ès lettres in 1960 for *Folie et dé raison: Histoire de la folie à l'âge classique*, a history of mental illness that focused on the relationship between madness and reason (this would be published in English as *Madness and Civilization* in 1961). In 1966, his book *Le Mots et les choses* (published in English as *The Order of Things*) became a bestseller in France, launching Foucault to international prominence. In 1969 Foucault was elected to the College de France, where he became Professor and Chair of the History of Systems of Thought. Foucault published perhaps his most influential and overtly political book, *Surveiller et punir: Naissance de la prison*, in 1975 (translated into English as *Discipline and Punish* in 1977). Soon after, he began his multi-volume history of sexuality: *Histoire de la sexualité*, 1: *la volonte de savoir* was published in France in 1976, and is considered one of the founding texts in queer theory. The second and third volumes were translated into English shortly before Foucault's death in 1984.

THEMES IN FOUCAULT'S WORK

Foucault once explained that the goal of his work was "to create a history of the different modes by which ... human beings are made subjects" (Foucault 1983: 208). The first way that Foucault's work accomplishes this is through the lens of power-knowledge. The human sciences, Foucault argues, are disciplines in both senses: they are fields of expertise (i.e., in the sociological sense, they are "professions"), but they also are implicated in a particularly insidious form of power, whereby man becomes "the enslaved sovereign, the observed spectator" in the production of knowledge (Goldstein 1984). Heavily influenced by and indebted to Nietzsche, Foucault's work critiques the will to knowledge inherent in the human endeavor to understand ourselves. Foucault's illumination of the power-knowledge dynamic challenges linear narratives that regard advances in knowledge as part of a clear path to emancipation. As a result, Foucault is frequently characterized as a "postmodern" thinker, although he rejected that description of his work.

A second theme in Foucault's work is the concept of normalization, in which a field of study functions to enact a normative divide between one half of a binary (for example: healthy, sane, law-abiding, heterosexual) and the other (sick, insane, criminal, and homosexual). In his studies on human sexuality, for instance, Foucault contends that as the human sciences make sex an object of study, they serve to normalize various forms of sexual behavior, and thus produce and police the limits of our understanding of ourselves as sexual beings.

Perhaps the most compelling aspect of Foucault's work for sociologists is disciplinary power. In *Discipline and Punish* Foucault famously described Bentham's unrealized and yet enormously influential design for prisons, the Panopticon. In contrast to earlier forms of power, the Panopticon was organized so that a maximum number of people can be observed at a minimum cost. In its ideal form, all the prisoners require is the possibility of being watched in order to monitor their own behavior; that is, the Panopticon fashions subjects who internalize the force of an authoritative gaze. Panopticism is not limited to prisons and prisoners; according to Foucault, the kind of power exemplified in the Panopticon has been replicated across the modern world in all kinds of institutions.

CRITIQUE

Some of the most energetic critiques of Foucault have been directed at his account of power and agency. Foucault rejects what he calls an "economic" model of power, whereby power is something that some "have" and others do not. Instead, Foucault sees power as "something which circulates . . . never localized here or there, never in anybody's hands, never appraised as a commodity or piece of wealth" (Foucault 1980: 98). For Foucault, power is a field in which we are all implicated. Sangren (1995) argues this conception of power reduces people and institutions to mere objects (rather than subjects) in Foucault's analyses; power thus assumes the status of an explanatory telos. For this reason, Foucault has been taken to task for either being too deterministic (and thus incapable of providing an account of resistance to power) or not deterministic enough.

The second critique asks if social science is even possible if we take Foucault's work seriously. Foucault's work challenges the very assumptions that make social science possible. For Foucault, the difficulty with the social sciences lies in the fact that modern "man" comes to know himself both as the empirical object and the transcendental subject of knowledge. This leads Foucault to make one of his most controversial claims: that the era of "man" is drawing to a close, and eventually man will disappear, "like a face drawn in sand at the edge of the sea" (Foucault 1972: 387). As his supporters argue that his work helps pave the way for a new kind of social science, perhaps Foucault's greatest influence may be felt in debates about the future of the discipline itself.

SEE ALSO: Discourse; Foucauldian Archeological Analyses; Poststructuralism; Power, Theories of

REFERENCES

Foucault, M. (1972) *The Archaeology of Knowledge and the Discourse on Language*, trans. A. M. Sheridan Smith. Pantheon, New York.

Foucault, M. (1980) *Power/Knowledge: Selected Interviews and Other Writings 1972–1977*, ed. C. Gordon. Pantheon, New York.

Foucault, M. (1983) The subject and power. In: Dreyfus, H. & Rabinow, P. (eds.), *Michel Foucault: Beyond Structuralism and Hermeneutics*. University of Chicago Press, Chicago, pp. 208–26.

Goldstein, J. (1984) Foucault among the sociologists: the "disciplines" and the history of the professions. *History and Theory* 23 (2): 170–92.

Sangren, P. S. (1995) "Power" against ideology: a critique of Foucaultian usage. *Cultural Anthropology* 10 (February): 3–40.

SUGGESTED READING

Alford, C. (2000) What would it matter if everything Foucault said about prison were wrong? *Discipline and Punish* after twenty years. *Theory and Society* 29: 125–46.

Berdayes, V. (2002) Traditional management theory as panoptic discourse: language and the constitution of somatic flows. *Culture and Organization* 8 (1): 35–49.

Dreyfus, H. & Rabinow, P. (eds.) (1983) *Michel Foucault: Beyond Structuralism and Hermeneutics*. University of Chicago Press, Chicago, IL.

Epstein, S. (2003) An incitement to discourse: sociology and the history of sexuality. *Sociological Forum* 18 (3): 485–502.

MARGARET E. FARRAR

frame

The concept of frame designates interpretive structures that render events and occurrences subjectively meaningful, and thereby function to organize experience and guide action. Within sociology, the concept is derived primarily from the work of Erving Goffman, which is beholden in part to the earlier work of Gregory Bateson. For these scholars, as well as others who use the concept analytically, frames provide answers to such questions as: What is going on here? What is being said? What does this mean? According to Goffman, frames essentially enable individuals "to locate, perceive, identify, and label a seemingly infinite number of occurrences" within their immediate life situations or spaces.

Frames do this interpretive work by performing three core functions. First, like picture frames, they *focus attention* by punctuating or bracketing what in our sensual field is relevant and what is irrelevant, what is "in-frame" and what is "out-of-frame," in relation to the object of orientation. Second, they function as *articulation mechanisms* in the sense of tying together the various punctuated elements of the scene so that one set of meanings rather than another is conveyed, or, in the language of narrativity, one story rather than another is told. Third, frames perform a *transformative function* by reconstituting the way in which some objects of attention are seen or understood as relating to one another or to the actor. Examples of this transformative function abound, as in the deeroticization of the sexual in the physician's office, the transformation or reconfiguration of aspects of one's biography, as commonly occurs in contexts of religious conversion, and in the transformation of routine grievances or misfortunes into injustices or mobilizing grievances in the context of social movements.

SEE ALSO: Collective Action; Culture; Goffman, Erving; Ideology; Narrative

SUGGESTED READING

Benford, R. D. & Snow, D. A. (2000) Framing processes and social movements: an overview and assessment. *Annual Review of Sociology* 26: 611–39.

Goffman, E. (1974) *Frame Analysis: An Essay on the Organization of Experience*. Harper Colophon, New York.

DAVID A. SNOW

Freud, Sigmund (1856–1930)

Sigmund Freud's pioneering focus on unconscious motives arising from infant experiences offers a distinctive approach to understanding human motives. His focus on how the super-ego internalizes societal demands offered a way of understanding how social norms affect individuals. His approach has had an enduring influence in sociology, shaping important research especially in gender, family, and religion.

Freud was born to a middle-class Jewish family in Moravia. Freud, who had two half-brothers from his father's previous marriage, was the favored first son of his mother, to whom he was strongly attracted. Freud recalled strong jealousies toward his younger brothers and contempt for his father, who was two decades older than his mother and whom Freud perceived to be intellectually weak and unable to confront anti-Semitism. Freud spent most of his life in Vienna, where his family moved when he was four. After studying medicine, philosophy, and science at university, he worked as a physician studying neurology. In the late nineteenth century he rejected the medical emphasis on chemical imbalances as the cause of hysteria, focusing instead on how mental processes cause physical problems. For the rest of his life, he used his psychoanalytic work with patients to develop a theory of the mind that is his lasting contribution.

Freud emphasized that the motives that impel action are unconscious. Behind every sociological theory rests some understanding of human motives. Symbolic interactionists focus on how meanings drive action; rational-choice theorists focus on individuals' conscious weighing of costs and benefits; and ethnomethodologists see action as driven by habit and taken-for-granted knowledge. Freud insisted, based on his psychoanalytic work with his patients, that unconscious motives drive human action. He discovered the unconscious through his analysis of dreams, mental illness, jokes, and slips of the tongue. His psychoanalytic work suggested that unconscious desires arise from childhood relations with parents For Freud, the self so represses infantile and childhood desires that they cannot enter the self's consciousness. Yet they nonetheless drive adults' actions.

Freud's account of psychic structure recognizes how cultural norms root themselves in the human psyche. For Freud, the "id" or "it" represents the unconscious drives that demand satisfaction. The psychic structure's "super-ego" or "over-I" represents the internalization of cultural norms espoused by parents. The super-ego is an ego-ideal in which part of the psyche (unconsciously) takes on the parents' admonishing role, punishing other parts of the self. For Freud, the "ego" is the "I" which mediates between the demands of id, super-ego, and external reality. One of Freud's fundamental contributions to sociology is the recognition that the psyche itself internalizes social demands. The super-ego, he says, is the "special agency" in which "parental influence is prolonged" (Freud 1969: 3).

Freud applied his psychoanalytic insights to understanding social phenomena. In considering religion, he argued that "in all believers . . . the motives impelling them to religious practices are unknown or are replaced in consciousness by others which are advanced in their stead" (Freud 1963: 22). For Freud, it is the "infant's helplessness and the longing for the father aroused by it" that is the ultimate source of "religious needs" (p. 19). This focus on unconscious motives that derive from childhood experience is Freud's fundamental contribution to sociology, which continues to have influence in fields as diverse as the sociology of religion, the sociology of gender, and the sociology of family.

SEE ALSO: Family Theory; Mental Disorder; Psychoanalysis; Religion, Sociology of

REFERENCES

Freud, S. (1963) [1907] Obsessive acts and religious practices. In: Rieff, P. (ed.), *Character and Culture*. Collier, New York, pp. 17–26.

Freud, S. (1969) [1940] *Outline of Psychoanalysis*, trans. J. Strachey. Norton, New York.

STEVE DERNÉ

Friedan, Betty (1921–2006)

Betty Friedan was born Bettye Naomi Goldstein in Peoria, Illinois, on February 4, 1921. She left the Midwest's conservatism to attend Smith College in 1938. At Smith, Friedan concentrated her energy on academics as well as her involvement in the school newspaper. After graduating summa cum laude from Smith in 1942 with a degree in psychology, Friedan pursued graduate studies at the University of California, Berkeley. She took her first job as a journalist and later met and married Carl Friedan (whom she divorced in 1969).

Friedan was a feminist writer and activist in the post-World War II women's movement for over forty years. She was best known for her first and most popular work, *The Feminine Mystique* (1963), which exposed the ill-effects of rigid postwar gender roles that implored women to forgo careers and return or stay home to be housewives and mothers. To substantiate claims that women were fundamentally dissatisfied with these roles, she employed social scientific methodology and queried her Smith College cohort. The cause of women's discontent, Freidan suggested, resided in the legal, political, social, economic, and educational factors that mandated strict and polarized gender roles in American culture.

Friedan's text was instrumental to the resurgence in feminism in the revolutionary climate of the 1960s. Women participating in various social movements in the Untied States at this time were beginning to think seriously about their position in society. Her book, then, gave voice to feelings of women's secondary status relative to men at a time when women were paying more attention to their own experiences and relationships. The combination of these factors coupled with the release and success of *The Feminine Mystique* helped launch Friedan's career as an early figurehead of the second wave of the women's movement. Building on the success of her book she went on to become one of the founders, as well as the first president, of the National Organization for Women (NOW) in 1966.

Friedan went on to publish *It Changed My Life: Writings on the Women's Movement*, 1976; *The Second Stage*, 1981; *The Fountain of Age*, 1993; *Beyond Gender: the New Politics of Work and Family*, 1997; and her personal memoir, *Life So Far*, 2000.

SEE ALSO: Feminism, First, Second, and Third Waves; Women's Movements

REFERENCES

Friedan, B. (1963) *The Feminine Mystique*. Norton Books, New York.

LYNDSEY STULTS AND STEPHANIE GILMORE

friendship

Friendship refers to a broad category of positively disposed interpersonal relationships with equality, mutual goodwill, affection, and/or assistance varying according to social circumstances.

Friendships are characteristically voluntary, personal, equal, mutual, and affective. While social structural factors place people in functional proximity enabling friendships to develop, individuals voluntarily negotiate their mutual treatment as friends. Friendship's voluntary quality contrasts with blood ties to kin, the legal and religious sanctions of marital bonds, and the economic contracts regulating work relationships. Second, friends are personally valued as particular individuals rather than occupants of roles or categorically. Third, friends communicate and treat each other as equals despite personal attributes and social statuses that otherwise create hierarchical relationships. Fourth, friendship requires fairly symmetrical mutual inputs into the relationship and to each others' welfare. Fifth, friendship's affections range from positive concern for the other's well-being to heartfelt liking or love. The love of friendship is usually distinguished from sexual or romantic loving, with their possessive and exclusive overtones – though such relationships may include attributes of friendship.

Through the 1970s little social scientific work addressed friendship, primarily in social attraction studies emphasizing personality variables or residential propinquity, or in demographic and sociometric studies contrasting friendships as a residual category with family and work relationships. Subsequent work identified four dialectical tensions of interpersonal communication in forming, maintaining, and dissolving friendships across the life course. The tension between the freedom to be independent and the freedom to be dependent describes patterns of autonomy and obligation of friendships within embracing social configurations. The tension between affection and instrumentality describes the concerns of caring for a friend as an end in itself versus a means to an end. The tension between judgment and acceptance involves the dilemmas in friendship between objective appraisals of a friend's activities versus unconditional support. Finally, the tension between expressiveness and protectiveness addresses the tendencies to speak candidly with a friend and relate private thoughts and feelings, and the need to restrain one's disclosures to preserve privacy and avoid burdening one's friend.

Scholars disagree about the gender-linked patterns of friendship. Some argue the emotionally involved and interdependent friendships modally associated with females are more fulfilling than males' activity-based and independent friendships. Others argue these patterns describe qualitatively different forms of friendship with equivalent satisfaction. Second, depending on actual practices and circumstances, either gender's specific friendships may deviate from modal patterns and resemble the other gender. Third, contrasts diminish in women's and men's closer friendships. Fourth, these patterns primarily describe white, North American, middle-class participants. Robert Brain's *Friends and Lovers* (1976) notably surveys cross-cultural variations of friendship.

Women friends tend to value interdependence in reconciling their freedoms to be independent and dependent while men enact more independence. Women friends experience cross-pressures between affection and instrumentality, describing more emotional involvement than men. Juggling multiple household, employment, and recreational activities, expectations of caring and mutual reliance occasions strain in women's friendships. Men's friendships seem less emotionally charged and overtly affectionate, offering and receiving instrumental assistance while maintaining independence through reciprocity. Potentially volatile interplay between judgment and acceptance energizes women's friendships. Caring and expecting much from friends, women more typically communicate evaluations. Men seem less concerned and more accepting of friends' behaviors. Finally, women tend to be more expressive with friends and trust them with confidences. Avoiding vulnerability or burdening friends with personal concerns, men are more reserved and protective.

Emerging inquiries address friendships facilitating moral growth during youth, contributing ethically to adult life, and providing a basis for community development and political participation. Investigations are spanning and enriched by differences of religion, ethnicity, socioeconomic status, race, age, gender, and sexual orientation. Scholars probe friendship in educational and work settings, and the interplay among friendship, romance, and marriage. Gerontologists assess the comparative value of intimate friends versus companions for relieving loneliness and serving life satisfaction.

SEE ALSO: Interaction; Interpersonal Relationships

SUGGESTED READINGS

Rawlins, W. K. (1992) *Friendship Matters: Communication, Dialectics, and the Life Course*. Aldine de Gruyter, New York.

Rawlins, W. K. (2009) *The Compass of Friendship: Narratives, Identities, and Dialogues*. Sage, Thousand Oaks, CA.

Werking, K. J. (1997) *We're Just Good Friends: Women and Men in Nonromantic Relationships*. Guilford Press, New York.

WILLIAM K. RAWLINS

function

Function has been an important idea within specific sociological paradigms and in sociology more generally. Analyzing the function(s) of social practices has been central ever since Émile Durkheim, in *Division of Labor in Society* (1893), defined function as consequence, and exhorted sociologists to distinguish functions of social phenomena from their causes while examining both.

Examining functions of social practices need not imply viewing society as an interdependent set of differentiated structures functioning together to promote societal maintenance and well-being. However, these two ideas intertwined in the post-World War II US structural functionalist paradigm. Like Durkheim, structural functionalists examined how social order is maintained and reproduced. More recently, a metatheoretical movement called neofunctionalism tried to retain structural functionalism's core while extending it to address issues of social change and microfoundations.

Structural functionalism dominated US sociology in the period after World War II. Kingsley Davis, in his 1959 Presidential address to the American Sociological Association, went so far as to argue that structural functionalism was neither a special theory nor a special method, but synonymous with *all* sociology.

For Parsons, all systems, including biological, psychological, social, and cultural, must perform four functions to meet systemic needs. These functions are adaptation (adjusting to the environment), goal attainment (defining and achieving objectives), integration (coordinating and regulating interrelationships among parts), and pattern maintenance or latency (providing or maintaining motivation or cultural patterns sustaining motivation). In social systems, adaptation is primarily associated with the economy, goal attainment with the polity, integration with law and custom, and pattern maintenance with schools, families, and churches.

Merton noted that social practices could be functional for some organizations and groups, and dysfunctional for others. Instead of presuming that a social practice with a particular function in one setting was universally associated with that function and thus indispensable, Merton argued that there could be functional alternatives. Even if some function were required for system survival, there likely would be alternative practices that could fulfill this function. Finally, Merton highlighted unintended consequences of social practices. Intended versus unintended consequence is one dimension of Merton's (1968) famous contrast between manifest and latent functions.

SEE ALSO: Davis, Kingsley; Durkheim, Émile; Functionalism/Neofunctionalism; Merton, Robert K.; Parsons, Talcott; Structural Functional Theory

REFERENCES

Davis, K. (1959) The myth of functional analysis as a special method in sociology and anthropology. *American Sociological Review* 24: 757–73.

Merton, R. K. (1968) *Social Theory and Social Structure*. Free Press, New York.

ROBIN STRYKER

functionalism/neo-functionalism

Functionalism is a theoretical perspective emphasizing the contributions made by social arrangements (e.g. institutions, cultural values, norms, rites) to the maintenance and reproduction of society and culture. It often rests on an analogy between societies and biological organisms (e.g. in early functionalists like Herbert Spencer and Emile Durkheim), although later functionalist social anthropologists (e.g. A. R. Radcliffe-Brown, Bronislaw Malinowski) often jettisoned the organic analogy. Functionalists frequently emphasize the scientific nature of their work and adopt a positivist philosophical standpoint.

Durkheim's functionalist method appeared first in *The Division of Labor in Society* (1893). He argued that the complex division of labor in modern society normally promoted organic solidarity through the mutual dependence of differing forms of labor. This discussion had a strong influence on Radcliffe-Brown's structural functional analysis. Durkheim also thought deviant behavior provided opportunities for the expression of the collective consciousness of society through the execution of rituals of punishment. In the *Elementary Forms of Religious Life* (1912), Durkheim argued religion was a unified system of beliefs and practices concerning the sacred and its primary function was to integrate individuals into a moral community.

After World War II, these earlier functionalist perspectives were adapted and modified by Parsons and Robert K. Merton. They both created schools of thought, Parsons at Harvard and Merton at Columbia, where each trained a new generation of sociologists. Functionalism became the dominant theoretical perspective in the post-war period through their work and that of their students. In *The Social System* (1951), Parsons developed a systematic theory of society focused on the four functional problems of social systems: adaptation to their environment, goal attainment, integration, and cultural pattern maintenance. Parsons emphasized the exchanges and equilibrium among institutions fulfilling these functions (e.g. the economy, government, law, education, religion, the family). Disequilibria among these various institutions helped explain social change. Parsons emphasized the relations between culture and society and the integrative role of common values in creating social consensus. He developed a theory of social evolution focused on increasing social differentiation and the development of universalistic cultural values. Parsons's macro-functionalism was adopted in various ways by Marion Levy, Robert N. Bellah, and Neil Smelser, who applied its framework to the comparative study of societies such as England, China, Japan, and others. Kingsley Davis and Wilbert Moore used functionalist methods for the study of social stratification and argued that functionalism was largely identical with sociological analysis.

By contrast, in *Social Theory and Social Structure* (1949), Merton forged a more flexible "paradigm" of functional analysis with empirical applications. He rejected the functional necessity of particular social arrangements and argued for the idea of functional equivalence, in which differing concrete social arrangements could satisfy particular social functions. Merton emphasized negative dysfunctions along with positive functions and argued that social institutions have both positive and negative consequences for a society or some segment of it. He especially emphasized the "latent" character of social functions and dysfunctions, their largely unrecognized and unintended quality. Merton promoted "middle range" analysis, linking focused theorizing with empirical research on bureaucracy, deviance, reference groups, public opinion, propaganda, and others topics, thus avoiding the pitfalls of both of Parsons' "grand theory" and theoretically ungrounded empiricism.

Functionalism, particularly its Parsonian variety, came under increasing criticism by conflict theorists, symbolic interactionists, and others unpersuaded by functionalists' claims. Ralf Dahrendorf, C. Wright Mills, Barrington Moore, and others drew on Marx and Weber to emphasize the problems of political power, class conflict and bureaucratic organization. In their view, functionalism not only avoided such realities, but also had conservative political implications. In the 1960s, movements of national liberation, intergenerational revolt, civil rights, black nationalism, women's rights, and the anti-Vietnam war movement placed power, inequality, and conflict on the sociological agenda. Functionalism seemed out of touch with these explosive social changes. In response, Parsons addressed the problem of power by treating it (along with money) as a generalized medium of communication in society. In related efforts to address the issues of conflict and change, Parsons' collaborator, Neil Smelser, wrote his *Theory of Collective Behavior* (1962), while Merton's student, Lewis Coser wrote *The Social Functions of Conflict* (1956), drawing ideas from Georg Simmel's work.

Herbert Blumer's symbolic interactionism, Erving Goffman's sociology of everyday life, and various forms of social constructionism offered other critiques of functionalism. In their view, the functionalist emphasis on macro structures, institutions, and culture reified complex processes of social interaction among individuals whose mutually oriented actions created "society" and "culture". Another influential critic, George Homans, in his 1964 Presidential Address to the *American Sociological Association*, made a plea for "bringing men back in" and in *Social Behavior: Its Elementary Forms* (1961) developed an individualistic social theory rooted in social behaviorism and focused on exchange. In a different vein, Peter Berger and Thomas Luckmann, in *The Social Construction of Reality* (1966), merged ideas from Marx, Durkheim, Weber, phenomenology, and symbolic interactionism to attack functionalism on its own ground by offering an alternative theory of society and culture at both micro and micro levels.

In recent decades, functionalism was revived by a new wave of "neo-functionalists" such as Jeffrey Alexander, Niklas Luhmann, Jürgen Habermas, and others who have linked functionalism to conflict theory, systems theory, social evolutionism, and political theorizing. Despite their innovations, these neo-functionalist theoretical amalgams draw heavily on one or another element of Parsons' structural functional theory and his efforts to forge a "grand theory" of society and culture has provided them with a decisive impetus, despite their considerable modification of his ideas.

SEE ALSO: Durkhéim, Émile; Merton, Robert K.; Parsons, Talcott

SUGGESTED READING

Alexander, J. (1998) *Neo-functionalism and After*. Blackwell, Malden, MA.

DONALD A. NIELSEN

fundamentalism

Fundamentalism is a label that refers to the modern tendency to claim the unerring nature of a sacred text and to deduce from that a rational strategy for social action. The final goal is to achieve the utopia of a regime of the Truth, gain political power and rebuild organic solidarity. Many scholars hold the view that this is a modern global phenomenon involving the historic religions, for the most part. There are five common features characterizing fundamentalist movements, according to Marty and Appleby's research.

First of all, the type of social action dominated by the attitude of *fighting back*. The social actors claim to be restoring a mythical and sacred order of the past in contrast to the modern idea of atomized individuals in a fragmented society. The second element – *fighting for* – is implicit in the foregoing: the ultimate goal of the movement is political, despite the furious and intense religious motivations. The third feature – *fight with* – refers to a specific repository of symbolic resources of use in the crusade for restoring identity and gaining political power. They actually interpret the text, whilst pretending to claim its inerrancy, its a-historicity, and generally, its structural refractoriness to any rational hermeneutics. The fourth element is the *fight against*. There is a link between the fundamentalist mentality and the need for an enemy. The fifth feature – *fight under God* – refers to the intensity of the militants' conviction that they are "on the right path". They are certain they are called directly by a god to carry on with radical determination the struggle against the enemy. Thus, the symbolic and physical violence are legitimized.

The social scientists who accept the notion of fundamentalism in a comparative and global approach are divided whether the phenomenon should be interpreted as the quintessence of modernity or as a simple reaction to it. In a first approach, fundamentalism is a clear reaction to modernity, against the individualization of belief and socio-religious identity. The second orientation argues that fundamentalism is a direct consequence of modernity; using the advantages of modernity (i.e. the modern means of communication). A third approach stresses the relation between fundamentalism and secularization: the former witnesses the countertendency to gradual eclipse of the sacred.

SEE ALSO: Globalization, Religion and; Religion, Sociology of

SUGGESTED READING

Marty, M. E. and Appleby S. R. (eds.) (1995) *Fundamentalism Comprehended*. University of Chicago Press, Chicago, IL.

ENZO PACE

G

Galbraith, John Kenneth (1908–2006)

John Kenneth Galbraith was an influential Canadian-born American economist, professor, and diplomat. After being trained in Agricultural Economics at University of Toronto and University of California, Berkeley, Galbraith accepted a fellowship at Cambridge University, England, where he studied the theories of John Maynard Keynes. Besides an editorship at *Fortune* magazine and several government appointments, Galbraith taught at Princeton University and Harvard University, where he was the Paul W. Warburg Professor of Economics from 1949 to 1975. A political liberal, he served on the administration of several presidents including John F. Kennedy, who appointed him US ambassador to India from 1961 to 1963 and Lyndon Johnson, under whom Galbraith helped conceive the Great Society program. Galbraith was honored with the Presidential Medal of Freedom (1946 and 2000), Order of Canada (1997), and India's Padma Vibhusan (2001).

Besides several works of fiction, Galbraith published 33 books in economics spanning a wide and complex range of issues. His best known works include *American Capitalism* (1952), *The Great Crash* (1955), *The Affluent Society* (1958), *The Liberal Hour* (1960), *The New Industrial State* (1967), *The Triumph* (1968), *Ambassador's Journal* (1969), *Economics, Peace and Laughter* (1972), *Money* (1975), *The Age of Uncertainty* (1979), *Annals of an Abiding Liberal* (1979), *A Life of Our Time* (1981), *The Tenured Professor* (1990), and *The Good Society: The Human Agenda* (1996). In fact, Galbraith coined and popularized phrases such as "the affluent society," "conventional wisdom," and "countervailing power."

In *American Capitalism*, Galbraith debunked myths about the socially optimal effects of free markets and critiqued an increasingly oligopolistic economy characterized by power concentration. A nation's economy would stabilize if countervailing forces keep corporations and unions in equilibrium as they exert pressures on each other for profits and wages. In *The New Industrial State*, Galbraith expanded his theory of corporations and argued that the notion of a perfectly competitive firm must be replaced by one vying for market shares (and not profit maximization) via conventional (vertical integration, advertising, and product differentiation) and unconventional means (bureaucratization and capture of political favor).

In his most famous book, *The Affluent Society*, Galbraith attacked the culturally hegemonic "American way of life" and contrasted private-sector affluence with public-sector poverty that exacerbated income disparities. According to him, post-World War II America will thrive if the government spent public taxes on infrastructure and education, a move that political commentators feel contributed to the failure of the War on Poverty. In an updated version, *The Good Society*, Galbraith argued that America had become a "democracy of the fortunate" where overproduction of consumer goods had increased the perils of both inflation and recession.

Galbraith remained a staunch Kenyesian and institutionalist throughout his life and believed in the importance of public education, the political process, and the provision of public goods. a sentiment best expressed from *The Affluent Society*: "Let there be a coalition of the concerned ... The affluent would still be affluent, the comfortable still comfortable, but the poor would be part of the political system."

SEE ALSO: Economics; Economy (Sociological Approach); Economy, Culture and; State and Economy; Welfare State

SUGGESTED READING

Parker, R. (2006) *John Kenneth Galbraith: His Life, His Politics, His Economics*. University of Chicago Press, Chicago, IL.

SANGEETA PARASHAR

gambling as a social problem

While gambling is widely accepted today as a source of entertainment and recreation, a growing tendency to highlight problematic aspects is also to be noticed. Traditionally, heavy gamblers who sustained repeated losses and other adverse consequences were considered derelict, immoral, or criminal and for much of the twentieth century the prevailing view of excessive gambling continued to define that behavior as morally and legally reprehensible. A few decades ago, a new perspective emerged in which gambling is seen as pathological – as a form of addictive behavior in need of therapeutic treatment. The disease-concept (at least partly) replaced former deviance-definitions as a kind of willful norm violation, and excessive gambling increasingly is considered to be an expression of a mental disorder resembling the substance-related addictions. Since 1980, this change in perception has been strongly stimulated by – and reflected in – the evolving clinical classification and description of pathological gambling in the various editions of the *Diagnostic and Statistical Manual of Mental Disorders* (DSM) published by the American Psychiatric Association.

The medicalization-process was initiated in the USA by a self-help group named Gamblers Anonymous (GA). Soon, GA formed alliances with medical experts and a small circle of problem gamblers and professional claims-makers started to bring public attention to the problem. The National Council on Compulsive Gambling (since 1989: Problem Gambling) served as a model for similar organizations in other countries, and researchers and politicians became further influential actors in the social construction of the new disease.

SEE ALSO: Addiction and Dependency; Medicalization of Deviance

SUGGESTED READING

Schmidt, L. (1999) *Psychische Krankheit als soziales Problem. Die Konstruktion des Pathologischen Glücksspiels* (*Mental Disorder as Social Problem: The Construction of Pathological Gambling*). Leske & Budrich, Opladen.

LUCIA SCHMIDT

game theory

Game theory is used to model conflict and co-operation. A non-cooperative game consists of two or more players, each with a set of strategies and a utility function that assigns an individual payoff to each combination of strategies. In zero-sum games, a gain for one player is always a loss for the other, which precludes the possibility of cooperation for mutual gain. In variable-sum games, some players can be better off without making others worse off. In cooperative games, the problem is to negotiate the distribution of resources among a coalition of players. Sociologists use cooperative game theory to study the effects of network structure on power inequality in social exchange. Variable-sum non-cooperative games can be used to model social dilemmas in which individual rationality leads to collective irrational outcomes. This can include games in which there is a Pareto Deficient Nash Equilibrium (NE). A NE obtains when every strategy is a "best reply" to the other strategies played, hence, no player has an incentive to unilaterally change strategy. The equilibrium is Pareto Deficient when the outcome is preferred by no one while one or more players prefer some other outcome.

Knowing that an outcome is a NE means that if this state should obtain, the system will remain there forever, even in the absence of an enforceable contract. However, even when there is a unique NE, this does not tell us whether this state will ever be reached or what will happen if the equilibrium should be disturbed. Moreover, in most games, NE cannot identify a unique solution. In games that model on going interactions among players who care about future payoffs, the number of NE becomes indefinitely large, even in games that have a unique equilibrium in one-shot play. When games have multiple equlibria, NE cannot tell us which will obtain or how a population of players can move from one equilibrium to another.

Another limitation is the forward-looking analytical simplification that players have unlimited cognitive capacity with which to calculate the best response to any potential combination of strategies by other players. However, laboratory research on human behavior in experimental games reveals widespread and consistent deviations from best-response assumptions.

These limitations have led game theorists to explore backward-looking alternatives based on evolution and learning. Evolution alters the frequency distribution of strategies at the population level, while learning alters the probability distribution of strategies at the level of the individual player. In both, the outcomes that matter are those that have already occurred, not those that an analytical actor might expect to obtain in the future. This avoids the need to assume players have the ability to calculate future payoffs in advance, thereby extending applications to games played by highly routinized players, such as bureaucratic organizations or boundedly rational individuals whose behavior is based on heuristics, habits, or norms.

Sociology has lagged behind other social sciences in embracing game theory, in part because of skepticism about the heroic behavioral assumptions in the analytical approach. However, these backward-looking alternatives show that the key assumption in game theory is not rationality, it is instead what ought to be most compelling to sociology, the interdependence of the actors. The game paradigm obtains its theoretical leverage by modeling the social fabric as a matrix of interconnected agents guided by outcomes of their interaction with others, where the actions of each depend on, as well as shape, the behavior of those with whom they are linked. Viewed with that lens, game theory appears most relevant to the social science that has been most reluctant to embrace it.

SEE ALSO: Exchange Network Theory; Interaction; Power-Dependence Theory; Rational Choice Theories

SUGGESTED READINGS

Maynard-Smith, J. (1982). *Evolution and the Theory of Games*. Cambridge University Press, Cambridge.

Nash, J. F. (1950) *Non-Cooperative Games*. Princeton University Press, Princeton, NJ.

MICHAEL MACY AND ARNOUT VAN DE RIJT

gay and lesbian movement

Since the 1980s sociologists who have studied the gay and lesbian movement have focused on five sets of issues. The first set involves research on the structural conditions that led to the emergence of an organized movement. This research has stressed the importance of the rise of industrial capitalism, changes in the nature of the family accompanying capitalism, the impact of bureaucracy on intimacy among men, and the rise of medical science.

A second set of issues involves research on the goals of the movement. The initial impulse of the movement had been the desire to change the way the culture views homosexuality: the movement emerged in a society that saw homosexuality as sin, sickness, or crime. Later, the movement shifted to working for civil rights through the state and other social institutions. This dual emphasis on changing culture and changing laws and policies allows an analysis of issues of reform versus structural change, assimilation versus transformation.

The third set of research issues involves the ways that the movement constructs collective identity. Collective identity refers to the "shared definition of a group that derives from members' common interests, experiences and solidarity" (Taylor & Whittier 1992: 172). A unique feature of the gay and lesbian movement is its concern with defining who is the "we" that the movement represents and who gets to decide the boundaries of inclusion and exclusion.

Related to this set of issues is a fourth focus on framing. Framing refers to an interpretive schemata that distills the message or messages of the movement for several purposes: to recruit a constituency, create a collective identity, craft strategy, and gain outside support. For the gay and lesbian movement framing is challenging for several reasons: it is both a political and cultural movement, the fractious nature of the collective identity, and the strength of the countermovement.

A fifth focus is the impact of queer theory on the study of the movement. Queer theory has called attention to the instability of sex and gender categories and stresses the performative and provisional nature of identities. Queer theory asserts that the identity-based strategies of the movement deny the fluidity inherent in sexuality and invalidate the experiences of others with non-normative sexuality who may not easily fit the class and race or western inflected definition of the identity. In addition, identity-based strategies reinforce the boundaries between gay and straight, man and woman, and thus reproduce the hierarchical relationship between the dominant and the subordinate terms of the sex/gender system.

SEE ALSO: Homophobia and Heterosexism; Homosexuality; Lesbianism; Lesbian and Gay Families

SUGGESTED READINGS

D'Emilio, J. (1983) *Sexual Politics, Sexual Communities: The Making of a Homosexual Minority in the United States, 1940–1970*. University of Chicago Press, Chicago, IL.

Taylor, V. & Whittier, N. E. (1992) Collective identity in social movement communities: lesbian feminist mobilization. In: Morris A. D. & McClurg Mueller, C. (eds.), *Frontiers in Social Movement Theory*. Yale University Press, New Haven, CT, and London, pp. 104–29.

STEPHEN VALOCCHI

Geertz, Clifford (1926–2006)

Clifford Geertz is widely considered to be one of the most important cultural theorists of the latter part of the twentieth century. Working in the field of anthropology, Geertz conducted ethnographic fieldwork in Morocco and Indonesia. Yet he is best known not for his empirical contributions, but rather for the essays collected under the title

The Interpretation of Cultures (1973). These provided a hugely influential manifesto for a hermeneutic approach to social inquiry, one that has had a reach across the human sciences and that has made Geertz himself an iconic figure.

In *The Interpretation of Cultures*, Geertz argued against structuralism, functionalism, Marxism and in fact any effort towards a general theory. These were seen as too arrogant and as too insensitive to the play of situated, local meanings. He insisted that human action took place in rich symbolic environments and that it was primarily expressive and communicative. A good social science would be attuned to such complexities, taking social life as being somewhat like a text that needed to be interpreted. What was required was a method that would allow us to capture all the subtlety and ambiguity of the meaningful environments of action. For example, we needed to be able to decipher which of many possible meanings any particular wink might be conveying (conspiracy, ironic distance, or involuntary action). Drawing on literary theory and on ordinary language philosophy Geertz developed the influential idea of "thick description." This demanded that anthropologists and other interpreters offer detailed, nuanced and textured accounts of social life on the page. In a hugely influential essay on the Balinese cockfight Geertz offers some indication of what a thick description might look like. He refutes narrow and more utilitarian understandings of the cockfight as an activity aimed primarily at status competition or gambling. In a stylistic tour de force he insists that it is more than just a sport too. Rather it is a profound drama in which various symbol systems, contradictions and dilemmas of the Balinese culture collide: Masculinity, rage, death, and so forth.

Geertz's work has been pivotal for the cultural turn, but it has also been subject to critique. Many have been frustrated by Geertz's turn away from theory, his insistence that actions can be explained in terms of the logic of their local settings, and his emphasis on representation through writing. They see this as the first step towards relativism. Others, particularly in post-structural anthropology, see Geertz as inattentive to the tie of writing and interpretation to power. A related argument has suggested that Geertz did not practice what he preached. By the standards of contemporary ethnography his interpretations are not really accountable "thick descriptions" where we hear people speaking for themselves. Rather they are magisterial but somewhat idiosyncratic readings by a master writer, one who re-describes and trumps multiple indigenous realities and worldviews using bits and pieces of western theory. For all this, at the end of the day Geertz remains today the leading advocate for the close interpretation of symbolic actions and webs of meaning.

SEE ALSO: Ethnography; Hermeneutics

SUGGESTED READING

Geertz, C. (1973) *The Interpretation of Cultures*. Basic Books, New York.

PHILIP SMITH

gender, the body and

Feminist thinkers have long focused on the body as an expression of power and a site of social control. As early as 1792, Mary Wollstonecraft proclaimed that "genteel women are slaves to their bodies" and that "beauty is woman's scepter" (Wollstonecraft 1988). Second and third wave US feminists have transformed our thinking on gender and the body through their writings on rape, sexual assault, domestic violence, reproductive rights, beauty contests, eating disorders, sports, disabilities, cosmetic surgery, and more.

Western discourses on the dualism of the mind and body evolved along with other polarities such as male/female and culture/nature. On one axis, the mind, culture, and the masculine have been located and on an opposing axis the body, nature, and the feminine are positioned. Euro-American societies in particular have constructed the male body as the standard and the female body as an inadequate deviation from the norm. Sexist ideas about bodies advanced by early philosophers and theologians were strengthened by medical and scientific discourses of the industrial and post-industrial eras.

The "nature versus nurture" debate on the source of sex differences has greatly shaped the scholarship on gender and the body. Feminist thinking has developed in direct relation to dominant gender ideologies that posit gender differences as biologically determined and women's subordination and men's dominance as natural. Recent feminist scholarship critiques the terms of the nature versus nurture debate and offers a new paradigm that recognizes the inherent interaction of biological and social systems.

Corresponding with the development of new technologies, the basis of "scientific" theories about bodily and behavioral sex differences moved from genitals to gonads to chromosomes to hormones to brains. Fausto-Sterling (2000) challenges the binary construction of sex by arguing that sex is more of a continuum and that the body is changeable over the life course rather than fixed at birth. She theorizes an interactive biosocial model in which internal reproductive structures and external social, historical, and environmental factors are inseparable – interacting over time and circumstance. In a similar vein, Kessler (1998) shows how the medical management of intersexuality (repeated surgeries and hormone treatments) contributes to the construction of dichotomized, idealized genitals and normalizing beliefs about gender and sexuality. She also argues that acceptance of genital and gender variability will mean the subversion of the equation that genitals equal gender.

The emergence of the second wave women's movement sparked a wealth of new research on gender and the body that focused on how women's bodies were regulated, controlled, or violated. The body at this stage was viewed as a site through which masculine power operated rather than as an object of study in and of itself. The desire to counter theories of biological determinism and promote theories of social constructionism led feminists to sidestep theorizing the body. The recent "discursive turn" in feminist theory and the development of poststructural challenges to binary constructs and dualistic thinking have encouraged new theorizing that views bodies as texts which can be read as a statement of gender relations.

The emergent field of feminist disability studies contributes to our understanding of gender and the body by drawing attention to bodies culturally identified as sick, impaired, deformed, or malfunctioning and interrogating normalizing discourses of gendered/sexed bodies. The sociology of sport contributes to our understanding of gender and the body by examining the relationships between the symbolic representations of the body and embodied experiences within the sociohistorical contexts of competitive sports. Recent feminist theorizing on the body and embodiment has encouraged social movement scholars to focus attention on the role of the body in collective social action. As the diverse and lengthy history of embodied social protest suggests and the various theoretical frameworks on gender and the body illustrate, the body has been and seems will remain a central nexus to our understanding of gendered experiences, ideologies, and practices.

SEE ALSO: Body and Sexuality; Body and Society; Femininities/Masculinities; Rape Culture; Sex and Gender

REFERENCES

Fausto-Sterling, A. (2000) *Sexing the Body: Gender Politics and the Construction of Sexuality*. Basic Books, New York.

Kessler, S. (1998) *Lessons for the Intersexed*. Rutgers University Press, New Brunswick, NJ.

Wollstonecraft, M. (1988) *A Vindication of the Rights of Woman*. In: Rossi, A. (ed.), *The Feminist Papers*. Northeastern University Press, Boston, MA, pp. 40–85.

CYNTHIA FABRIZIO PELAK

gender, development and

Development refers to changes that advanced capitalist nations frequently measure using a country's gross domestic product (GDP) and its degree of industrialization, urbanization, technological sophistication, export capability, and consumer orientation. In contrast, countries of the global south view development as addressing survival issues like hunger and malnutrition, refugee displacement and homelessness, unemployment and underemployment, health services and disease, the destruction of the environment, and political repression and violence. Many of these survival problems result from the cumulative effects of unequal and dependent relationships that were established during colonization and are recreated in the present using structural adjustment programs and other strategies promulgated by supra-national agencies like the International Monetary Fund (IMF) and the World Bank.

Although early international development programs ignored their needs, usage of women's unpaid or underpaid labor has been crucial to many development programs and policies. In the mid-twentieth century, modernization approaches to development were most common. They assumed that developing nations needed to industrialize rapidly in order to gain economic strength, and that democracy, gender equity, and national prosperity would follow from industrialization. Such programs relied on manufacturing for export and foreign investment, and did not encourage self-sufficiency in the global south.

By the 1960s and 1970s, dependency theorists argued that this form of modernization allowed industrial nations to exploit developing ones. Other scholars noted that modernization theorists paid little attention to women's particular needs and had incorrectly assumed they would benefit in a "trickle-down" fashion as economies improved. Therefore, by the 1970s these male-focused arguments were largely supplanted by women in development (WID) ones, and more recently by gender and development (GAD) approaches, which try to incorporate strategies to enhance women's position.

WOMEN IN DEVELOPMENT (WID)

Until Boserup's work (1970), women were considered only as dependents who pursued reproductive roles; little attention was paid to women's economic contributions in the agricultural or informal economies of various global south nations. Her research fostered a conceptual shift from modernization theory to women in development approaches, resulting in increased research on previously ignored sectors of working women who are essential to developing economies, including domestics, tourist workers, women traders and street sellers, craft producers, and sex workers, as well as to families headed by women, who are often landless. Supporting this shift, the United Nations proclaimed 1975 as the first International Women's Year and then 1975–85 as the "Decade for Women," acknowledging that women had been active participants in the development process from the beginning, and should now become visible in development agencies and policies.

Several types of WID-based development projects began in the 1980s. The most common were income-generating programs that focused on traditional women's skills like sewing and handcrafts. Yet, these projects rarely were successful because of the low profit in these areas. Another approach, which has achieved international popularity over time, is to give women micro-entrepreneurs access to small loans with reasonable interest rates and low collateral requirements, allowing women to attain more autonomy and their small businesses to grow.

GENDER AND DEVELOPMENT (GAD)

Many development projects based on the WID philosophy helped women economically. However, few if any of these projects were intended to change the power relationships between women and men. In response to these limitations, a new approach, Gender and Development (GAD), was discussed by feminists and in women-focused NGOs during the 1980s, with the goal of improving women's rights and increasing gender equity. Many have called GAD an "empowerment" approach (Moser 1989) because its goals are to create development projects based on the needs of grassroots women, and to challenge women's subordination in households and in societies, not only to provide services.

Among the strategies used in the urban global south are organizing collective meals, health cooperatives, or neighborhood water-rights groups, while indigenous and peasant women in rural areas create projects around agricultural issues such as land tenure or plantation working conditions. Rather than privatizing their survival problems, women collectivize them and often place demands on the state for rights related to family survival.

By the 1990s international development agencies were adopting GAD rhetoric in their mission statements, but GAD was used more as an analytic framework than as a development strategy – possibly because it is easier to discuss empowerment than to implement it. Recently, such agencies have used the European model called "gender mainstreaming," which requires that a gender analysis occur within all bureaus and agencies to make sure that gender equality is considered in government policies. As an activist alternative, there also are many grassroots feminist groups (e.g., Development Alternatives with Women for a New Era, DAWN) developing transnational linkages with a GAD perspective.

SEE ALSO: Development; Political Economy; International Gendered Division of Labor; Global Economy

REFERENCES

Boserup, E. (1970) *Woman's Role in Economic Development*. St. Martin's Press, New York.

Moser, C. (1989) Gender planning in the third world: meeting practical and strategic gender needs. *World Development* 17: 1799–1825.

CHRISTINE E. BOSE

gender, education and

Social scientists and educational researchers paid relatively little attention to issues of gender in education until the 1970s, when questions emerged concerning equity in girls' and women's access to education across the world. Increasing female representation in primary and secondary education was cited as an important factor in promoting national economic development, and therefore seen as a vehicle for social change.

As the feminist movement increased awareness of widespread gender inequality within US society, researchers began to focus on the educational system as a site of and explanation for women's subordinated status. Feminist scholars documented sex discrimination in educational experiences and outcomes, and this early work led to the passage of Title IX in 1972, legislation that prohibited discrimination on the basis of sex in federally funded educational programs. During the 1970s and 1980s, women gained access to higher education and their share of college degrees climbed. Now women earn more undergraduate degrees than men. Despite this female advantage in college completion, women remain behind men in economic and social status, and a significant gender gap in pay remains. This paradox has led researchers to shift their focus from women's educational access to their academic experiences and outcomes.

Sex segregation within the educational system persists (England and Li 2006). Research following Title IX documented a wide gender gap in course-taking during high school: girls took fewer advanced math and science courses than boys, and these course-taking patterns left them unprepared to pursue these fields in higher education. Recent research suggests that these gaps are closing, and girls and boys now take similar numbers of math and science courses in high school. In addition, girls are now taking advanced courses such as calculus at comparable rates to boys. However, girls are still less likely to take physics, and technology and computer courses remain highly gendered. Conversely, girls are more highly concentrated in literature and foreign language courses, and they tend to score higher than boys on verbal skills on standardized tests.

Course-taking patterns in high school foreshadow gender differences in higher education, where a high degree of sex segregation remains in terms of degrees and specializations. In the United States, women are concentrated in education, English, nursing, and some social sciences, and they are less likely than men to pursue degrees in science, math, engineering, and technology. As these male-dominated fields are highly valued and highly salaried, women's absence from them accounts for a great deal of the gender gap in pay. Research suggests that cultural beliefs contribute to sex segregation by limiting what women (and men) see as possible or appropriate options (Correll 2004). Math, science, and technology are regarded as masculine subjects, and women are seen as ill-equipped for these fields. Conversely, subjects such as language arts and nursing are perceived as feminine subjects. Though sex typing in education appears to be a worldwide phenomenon, it varies in degree and scope. In countries where educational access is limited and reserved for members of the elite, women are often as likely as men to have access to all parts of the curriculum (Hanson 1996). However, in countries with more extensive educational systems, women have lower rates of participation in science and technology, fields greatly valued because of their link to development and modernity.

Recently, some educational researchers have suggested that concern for girls' education overshadows boys' disadvantages. They stress that boys remain behind in verbal skills, are overrepresented in remedial and special education classes, and are more likely to drop out of school. However, these negative outcomes tend to be concentrated among working-class boys and boys of color, suggesting that these problems may reflect race and class inequality rather than disadvantages affecting all boys (AAUW 2008). Research on how the intersection of race, class, and gender shapes educational experiences and outcomes is thus an important direction for the future of the sociology of education.

SEE ALSO: Gender, Development and; Inequality/Stratification, Gender; Socialization, Gender

REFERENCES

American Association of University Women (2008) *Where the Girls Are: The Facts about Gender Equity in Education*. Washington, DC.

Correll, S. (2004) Constraints into preferences: gender, status and emerging career aspirations. *American Sociological Review* (69): 93–113.

England, P. & Su Li (2006) Desegregation stalled: the changing gender composition of college majors, 1971–2002. *Gender & Society* 20: 657–77.

Hanson, S. L. (1996) Gender stratification in the science pipeline: a comparative analysis of seven countries. *Gender and Society* (10): 271–90.

JENNIFER PEARSON AND
CATHERINE RIEGLE-CRUMB

gender bias

Gender bias is behavior that shows favoritism toward one gender over another. Most often, gender bias is the act of favoring men and/or boys over women and/or girls. However, this is not always the case. In order to define gender bias completely, we first must make a distinction between the terms "gender" and "sex." When we use the term "gender," we mean socially constructed expectations and roles for women and men, and for girls and boys. Specifically, girls and women are expected to demonstrate feminine behavior, and boys and men are expected to act masculine. By sex, we mean biological differences assigned to females and males in order to distinguish between the two. The biological characteristics assigned to females and males often consist of primary or secondary sex characteristics.

The term "gender bias" is often (wrongly) used interchangeably with the term "sexism." Sexism is typically defined as the subordination of one sex, usually female, based on the assumed superiority of the other sex or an ideology that defines females as different from and inferior to males. Sex is the basis for the prejudice and presumed inferiority implicit in the term "sexism." The term "gender bias" is more inclusive than the term "sexism," as it includes both prejudice (attitudes) and discrimination (behavior) in its definition. Studies of gender bias also focus on gender, rather than on sex. Furthermore, the term gender bias could include instances of bias against boys and men in addition to bias against girls and women. This raises an important question: Are boys and men harmed by gender bias? While individual boys and men may suffer at the hands of gender bias, boys and men as groups benefit from gender bias embedded in our social institutions. The narrow benefits of gender bias for some are outweighed by much broader losses for all. And if gender roles and expectations constrain both girls and boys and both women and men, it can be said that gender bias limits the overall development of contemporary societies.

Gender bias is part of almost every aspect of life. The most common areas of gender bias are found in the social institutions of families, education, the economy, and health. Gender bias is also embedded in the media, sports, the state/government, and other social institutions. Gender is so pervasive in contemporary society that we often do not notice gender bias in our everyday lives. However, gender itself is not a variable that stands alone. Our race, ethnicity, social class, sexual orientation, and other social positions affect our everyday gendered experiences. Therefore, gender bias regularly intersects with other forms of bias such as ethnocentrism, racism, classism, and homophobia.

While it may appear gender bias disadvantages girls and women the most, gender bias, as well as other forms of bias, shortchanges all of us.

SEE ALSO: Inequality/Stratification, Gender; Sex and Gender

SUGGESTED READINGS

Andersen, M. (2006) *Thinking about Women: Sociological Perspectives on Sex and Gender*, 7th edn. Allyn & Bacon, Boston, MA.

Renzetti, C. M. & Curran, D. J. (2003) *Women, Men, and Society*. Allyn & Bacon, Boston, MA.

JENNIFER ROTHCHILD

gender ideology/gender role ideology

Both gender ideology and gender role ideology refer to attitudes regarding the appropriate roles, rights, and responsibilities of women and men in society. The concept can reflect these attitudes generally or in a specific domain, such as an economic, familial, legal, political, and/or social domain. Most gender ideology constructs are unidimensional and range from traditional, conservative, or anti-feminist to egalitarian, liberal, or feminist. Traditional gender ideologies emphasize the value of distinctive roles for women and men. According to a traditional gender ideology about the family, for example, men fulfill their family roles through instrumental, breadwinning activities and women fulfill their roles through nurturant, homemaker, and parenting activities. Egalitarian ideologies regarding the family, by contrast, endorse and value men's and women's shared breadwinning and nurturant family roles.

Gender ideology also sometimes refers to widespread societal beliefs that legitimate gender inequality. Used in this way, gender ideology is not a variable that ranges from liberal to conservative; instead it refers to a specific type of belief – those that support gender stratification. Gender ideology in the remainder of this summary refers to the first sense of the concept – attitudes that vary from conservative to liberal.

Sociologists' interest in measuring gender ideology can be traced at least as far back as the 1930s, with the development of instruments such as Kirkpatrick's 1936 Attitudes Toward Feminism scale. Interest continues today, and currently most major national surveys in the USA, such as the General Social Survey (GSS) and the National Survey of Families and Households, include gender ideology scales. The most common technique for measuring gender ideology is a summated rating scale in which respondents are presented with a statement and given three to seven response options that vary from strong agreement to strong disagreement. The following statement from the GSS is illustrative: "It is much better for everyone involved if the man is the achiever outside the home and the woman takes care of the home and family."

Researchers have examined the correlates, causes, and consequences of individuals' gender ideology. Within the USA, the documented antecedents include gender and birth cohort, with males and earlier cohorts reporting more conservative attitudes than females and later cohorts. Among women, labor force participation and educational attainment decrease conservatism. More generally, conservative gender ideologies are positively related to church attendance, fundamentalism, literal interpretations of the Bible and are negatively related to education, family income, parents' gender liberalism, and women's labor force participation (whether self, spouse, or mother). In addition, liberalism is positively related to married men's housework and child care contributions and negatively related to women's housework contributions.

Cross-national research has also shown that gender ideology is related to women's political representation. Using the *World Values Survey*, which includes individual level information on gender attitudes in 46 countries in 1995, Paxton and Kunovich (2003) showed that a conservative gender ideology is negatively related to the percentage of female members in the national legislature of a country even when controlling for political and social-structural factors.

SEE ALSO: Division of Household Labor; Gender, Work, and Family

SUGGESTED READINGS

Beere, C. A. (1990) *Gender Roles: A Handbook of Tests and Measures.* Greenwood Press, New York.

Brooks, C. & Bolzendahl, C. (2004). The transformation of US gender role attitudes: cohort replacement, social-structural change, and ideological learning. *Social Science Research* 33, 106–33.

Paxton, P. & Kunovich, S. (2003). Women's political representation: the importance of ideology. *Social Forces* 82: 87–114.

AMY KROSKA

gender oppression

Gender oppression is defined as oppression associated with the gender norms, relations, and stratification of a given society. Modern norms of gender in western societies consist of the dichotomous, mutually exclusive categories of masculinity and femininity. Developing in tandem with industrial capitalism and the nation-state, they had particular consequences for women and men. While masculinity was to consist of rationality, autonomy, activity, aggression, and competitiveness (all qualities that made men the ideal participants in the emerging public sphere of economy and polity), femininity was defined in contrast as emotionality, dependency, passivity and nurturance – all qualities that deemed women's "place" in the private sphere. These naturalized views of gender categories were embedded in burgeoning disciplines such as biology and sociology. However, not only were they premised on a dichotomous conception of sex and gender, they were also premised on heterosexuality, middle-class status, and European ethnic origin. As such, the gender oppression embedded therein is associated not only with the category with less power in the binary (femininity), but also with subjects that somehow deviate from either category.

Mainstream sociology initially ignored gender as well as gender oppression, marginalizing feminist sociologists in the early years. The subsequent period of structural functionalism excused and even supported dichotomous gender norms and their oppression, arguing that gender roles and identities served some functions in society. Sociological recognition and theorization of gender oppression thus required the denaturalization of the concept of gender itself within the discipline. A first step occurred in the 1970s, with debates regarding the extent to which "differences between the sexes" were biological. While this exchange enabled a limited discussion of gender oppression, the next set of debates allowed a greater role for the "social" – moving from sex differences to sex roles and socialization

Studies of gender relations in societies around the world have demonstrated that almost everywhere in the modern era, though in culturally specific ways, femininity is associated with a domestic sphere while masculinity is associated with a public sphere. At the macro level, dichotomous and naturalized views of gender are evident in the gendering of economic, political, and other institutions, where especially elite men dominate every major institution in most societies around the world. Ultimately, this gendering shapes the experiences of different groups of women globally and is expressed in higher levels of poverty; lower levels of formal political power; trivialization and sexual objectification in media; gender-specific health issues such as eating disorders, greater risk of AIDS, inadequate food/health care, and ongoing challenges to reproductive autonomy; greater levels of fear; and greater risk of interpersonal violence, to name a few.

Presently, the sociological approach to gender is even more "socialized," and gender is now recognized as a thoroughly social entity as well as a central organizing principle in all social systems, including work, politics, family, science, etc. As such, understanding of its complexity and scope has increased as well. Hence, a central area of interest in recent years has been the intersection of gender with other dimensions of experience and oppression, including race, class, culture, sex, and sexuality. Otherwise stated, while the above perspective elaborated the gender oppression of those who "fit" the dichotomous gender categories of masculinity and femininity, this lens is particularly useful for understanding the gender oppression of those who "do not or cannot fit" these categories. For example, the static and mutually exclusive norms of sex and gender that emerged in modernity denied the existence or personhood of the intersexed and the transgendered. Premised on heterosexuality, they denied the personhood of gays, lesbians, and bisexuals. Further premised on a masculine public sphere, working-class women who necessarily transgressed this space have also been made deviant. Moreover, these norms are fundamentally racialized in that they emerged in the context of the conflict-ridden contact between different peoples from the sixteenth century onwards. As European travelers in this period especially encountered racial and cultural "others," with their varying gender practices, European gender norms became a symbol of civilization, the deviation from which became a sign of racial and cultural inferiority. In this fashion, gender became a central vehicle for constructing racial and cultural hierarchy.

SEE ALSO: Feminism; Gender Bias; Inequality/Stratification, Gender; Intersectionality; Patriarchy

SUGGESTED READING

Ferree, M. M., Lorber, J., & Hess, B. B. (eds.) (2000) *Revisioning Gender*. Altamira Press, Oxford.

Peterson, V. S. & Runyan, A. (1999) *Global Gender Issues*. Westview Press, Oxford.

VRUSHALI PATIL

gender, work, and family

Gender, work, and family is the study of the intersection of work and family, with a focus on how those intersections vary by gender. This research is motivated in large part by the tremendous growth in labor force participation among women in their childbearing years during the second half of the twentieth century. This influx of wives and mothers – including single mothers – into the workforce has raised questions about the division of labor in the family and whether state and corporate policies are sufficient to support new family types. Researchers also examine the causes of the divergent outcomes men and women experience in the workplace, as well as the effects labor force participation has on family formation, dissolution, and carework. These questions are most frequently researched quantitatively, but qualitative and theoretical work also contributes to the understanding of gender, work, and family.

Rosabeth Moss Kanter's pivotal book *Work and Family in the United States* (1977) laid much of the groundwork for the study of gender, work, and family. Kanter made the case that changing family structures and increasing labor force participation among women were creating a new and complex set of interactions that were not being sufficiently studied in the traditional domains of the sociology of the family and the sociology of the labor force. Social scientists, Kanter claimed, subscribed to the "myth of separate worlds," a belief that work and family are separate and non-overlapping spheres, each of which operates free from the influence of the other and can be studied independently. Kanter' made a case that the structures of work are actually quite crucial in shaping family life, and that family life, in turn, affects the workplace.

One of the intersections of work and family Kanter identified is the time and timing of work. Work and family responsibilities are both quite time consuming. As more and more women joined the labor force, researchers became increasingly curious about how families manage to find the time for paid employment, unpaid work in the home, and leisure. Most research has found striking and persistent differences in time allocation by gender. Hochschild's (Hochschild with Machung 2003) ethnographic study of dual-earner households with children living at home found that mothers were working what amounted to a "second shift" of housework and childcare when they got home from their paid jobs, while their husbands shouldered a much lighter load. Time diary research, however, suggests that the imbalance is not in the number of hours worked, but in the distribution of hours. Mothers do tend to do more child care and housework, but fathers spend more time in paid employment.

Another approach is to look at the time use of families, rather than that of men and women as individuals. Family structures have changed considerably since the middle of the twentieth century. Today's families are much more likely to have two employed parents or be single-parent families than in the middle of the twentieth century. It is in these families in which all adults are employed that work–family conflict – in this case a "time crunch" – is most likely to be felt (Jacobs & Gerson 2004). Dual-earner families with children find it particularly difficult to balance the requirements of work and family. At the same time, however, there are also many families whose members are not able to find enough hours of paid work. It is also important to consider *when* family members work. Non-standard work schedules are associated with lower marital quality, especially among parents (Presser 2003).

SEE ALSO: Family Demography; Family Poverty; Gender Ideology and Gender Role Ideology

REFERENCES

Hochschild, A. R. with Machung, A. (2003) *The Second Shift*. Penguin Books, New York.

Jacobs, J. A. & Gerson, K. (2004) *The Time Divide: Work, Family, and Gender Inequality*. Harvard University Press, Cambridge, MA.

Presser, H. B. (2003) *Working in a 24/7 Economy: Challenges for American Families*. Russell Sage, New York.

ELIZABETH THORN

genealogy

The appeal to "genealogy" as a general historical method is usually attributed to Michel Foucault, who contrasted it with both teleology and his own preferred "archaeology," which suspends the search for causation altogether in favor of treating socio-epistemic structures (or *epistèmes*) as superimposed space-time strata, each of roughly coexistent events. (The palimpsest was thus Foucault's model for historiography.) Foucault's foil was Friedrich Nietzsche, whose *Genealogy of Morals* resurrected worries of legitimate lineage that had dominated the reproduction of social life prior to the modern nation-state. Replacing traditional legal concerns that political succession might be based on fraudulent documents, Nietzsche argued that contemporary morality might rest on forgotten etymologies, whereby "obligations" turn out to be strategies for making the strong feel guilty.

The contingency of origins is crucial for the genealogical method. Nietzsche wrote at a time – the final quarter of the nineteenth century – when the inexorability of human progress was a default position among intellectuals. Today the shock value of the genealogical method is not so strong, since under the influence of postmodernism, relatively few intellectuals take seriously Nietzsche's teleological foil.

What led Nietzsche to think that a defunct method for establishing right to rule should provide the basis for a deep understanding of society? Here the appeal to biology is crucial. Ernst Haeckel, Darwin's staunchest German defender, famously declared, "Ontogeny recapitulates phylogeny," by which he meant the biological development of the individual organism repeats the stages undergone in the evolution of all organisms. Nietzsche cleverly reworded Haeckel's slogan for his own purposes: "Ontology recapitulates philology." Nietzsche, a prodigy in the study of classical languages, found Haeckel's slogan appealing, especially when associated with a Darwinian sense of the arbitrary origin of life itself.

SEE ALSO: Foucault, Michel; Nietzsche, Friedrich

SUGGESTED READINGS

Foucault, M. (1970). *The Order of Things: An Archaeology of the Human Sciences*. Random House, New York.

Richards, R. (1987). *Darwin and the Emergence of Evolutionary Theories of Mind and Behavior*. University of Chicago Press, Chicago, IL.

STEVE FULLER

general linear model

In the social and behavioral sciences, traditionally, techniques involving categorical independent variables (e.g., *t*-test, ANOVA) and those involving continuous variables (e.g., correlation, regression) used to be treated as distinctly different data analysis systems "intended for types of research that differed fundamentally in design, goals, and types of variables" (Cohen et al. 2003: xxv). Despite the superficial differences, these and many other statistical techniques share one thing in common: they are designed to analyze linear relationships among variables. Cohen (1968) demonstrated that ANOVA-type techniques and regression-type techniques were statistically equivalent. Because of this, many techniques can be conceptualized as belonging to a general statistical model called the general linear model (GLM).

The GLM underlies most of the statistical techniques used in social science research. In the conventional (and narrower) sense, GLM may be conceptualized as a regression-based model. In regression analysis, the independent variable is assumed to be a continuous variable. In ANOVA-type methods, the independent variable is a categorical variable representing group membership (either naturally occurring groups such as gender or ethnic groups, or groups based on manipulated variables such as treatment vs. control groups in an experimental design). However, it is easy to extend the regression technique to subsume ANOVA-type methods (e.g., *t*-test, ANOVA, ANCOVA,

MANOVA) by converting the group membership categories to some form of "pseudo" quantitative coding. "Dummy coding" and "effect coding" are the two most popular coding schemes for this purpose. This conceptualization of GLM is currently implemented in the major statistical software packages (e.g., SPSS, SAS).

SEE ALSO: ANOVA (Analysis of Variance); Regression and Regression Analysis; Statistics

REFERENCE

Cohen, J., Cohen, P., West, S. G., & Aiken, L. S. (2003) *Applied Multiple Regression/Correlation Analysis for the Behavioral Sciences*, 3rd edn. Lawrence Erlbaum, Mahwah, NJ.

XITAO FAN

generalized other

The *generalized other* is a concept developed by George Herbert Mead to describe how the human personality develops by incorporating the perspectives of other persons and the community in which one interacts. The generalized others become parts of the self that reflect the standards and rules of the various communities in which one plays a role, as well as an understanding of the goals associated with given situations. The generalized other is developed through the child's engagement in what Mead terms the *play and game stages* of development. The generalized other is only possible because of the human capacity for language which allows for an internal dialogue of self-reflection, the ability to inhibit responses and to be controlled by the standards of the culture.

In the play stage the child engages in *taking the role* of *particular others*. For Mead children do not imitate others but begin to recognize how their actions produce particular responses in others. This ability depends on the idea that the identical response is provoked in the self as will be provoked in the other. This ability allows the child to anticipate others' responses and to gear activity to achieve goals in interaction.

The game stage, where the child engages in more complicated interactions with multiple others playing different roles, introduces not just complexity, but also an engagement with the abstract character of differentiating statuses, such as pitcher, catcher, and outfielder in the game of baseball, and the different roles, rules, and goals arising within that context. For Mead the vivid experience of playing the game requires the child to adopt complex perspectives into the self. The child will repeat this experience with a variety of games and interactional contexts where multiple statuses and perspectives must be engaged. This introduces an organization into the self where situations and contexts become predictable and one has learned the rules and the goals for multiple interactions.

As these experiences broaden, the child eventually incorporates the communal goals and meanings of their social environment as the generalized other introduces abstract ideas made possible through language use. By adopting these understandings of rules and goals, one allows oneself to be controlled by communal meanings of the various communities and the wider social groups to which one belongs. Ultimately, the widest social group is that constructed by the use of communal language and the adoption of rules of logic as governing one's thinking.

SEE ALSO: Game Stage; Mead, George Herbert; Play Stage; Role-taking; Self

SUGGESTED READING

Mead, G. H. (1934) *Mind, Self, and Society: From the Standpoint of a Behaviorist*. University of Chicago Press, Chicago, IL.

ALLISON CARTER

genetic engineering as a social problem

Genetic engineering (GE; often also called biotechnology) is the technique and science of intervention into the genetic mechanisms of a biological organism. For sociologists of risk (e.g. Ulrich Beck) GE it is a paradigmatic case for risk society. There are two main applications: agriculture and food production, and medical genetics; furthermore, GE is used in different fields of industrial production. GE is one of the most contested technologies, especially in the medical field. Critics claim that there is a general trend towards "geneticization," i.e. explaining social behaviour with genetics (e.g. homosexuality, criminality, alcoholism). Since people cannot change their "genetic outfit" and genetics has prognostic power also for families and future generations, the status of and access to genetic information are important issues in legal regulation. "Genetic privacy" refers to third party access to genetic information. Further topics are: the combination of genetics and reproductive technologies (pre-implantation and prenatal diagnosis), research on human embryos and stem cells, human cloning, gene therapy and human enhancement.

The sociological and philosophical debates focus on questions of genetic discrimination and the rise of a new eugenics, on changing concepts of health, sickness, and disability and their social implications, on the meaning of human identity, and "biopolitics" as an instrument for social (self-) control. Regarding the agricultural sector, major contested issues are the right to interfere into nature, environmental protection and animal health, food safety issues, trade issues and the relation between industrialized and developing countries. While there is currently an international regulatory regime in place concerning agricultural GE (e.g. Biosafety Protocol, European legislation), there is less binding international regulation regarding the medical field (e.g. UN Declaration on Human Genome and on Human Cloning).

SEE ALSO: Eugenics; Medical Sociology and Genetics

SUGGESTED READINGS

Bernard, G. (2001) Genetic engineering. In: Becker, L. & Becker, C. (eds.), *Encyclopedia of Ethics*, 2nd edn., vol. 1. Routledge, London, pp. 602–6.

Fukuyama, F. (2002) *Our Posthuman Future: Consequences of the Biotechnology Revolution*. Picador, New York.

GABRIELE ABELS

genocide

The term genocide was coined by Raphael Lemkin, a lawyer of Polish-Jewish origin, in 1944. It was legally defined in the United Nations Convention on the Prevention and Punishment of the Crime of Genocide in 1948. The Convention states that "genocide means ... acts committed with intent to destroy, in whole or in part, a national, ethnical, racial or religious group." Such acts as detailed in the Convention include: killing members of the group; causing serious bodily or mental harm to them; deliberately inflicting conditions of life calculated to bring about their physical destruction in whole or in part; imposing measures intended to prevent births within a group; and forcibly transferring children of the group to another one. This definition excludes groups defined by class and political affiliation. Contemporary human rights lawyers include these groups and count, e.g. the genocide of its own people by the Khmer Rouge in Cambodia as genocide.

Rubinstein (2004: 6) identifies five distinct types and periods in the history of genocide: in pre-literate societies, in the age of empires and religions (from 500 BC to 1492), colonial genocides from 1492 to 1914, in the age of totalitarianism (1914 to 1979), and contemporary ethnic cleansing and genocide since 1945. Estimates for the victims of genocide and mass killings as distinguished from war deaths range from 60 to 150 million for the twentieth century alone, with most estimates at about 80 million. For the second half of the twentieth century since 1945, estimates range between 9 and 20 million in more than 40 episodes of genocide. The perpetrators in contrast are comparably small in numbers. The figure of Germans who directly participated in the Holocaust is estimated at between 100,000 and 200,000. An estimate of immediate involvement in the Rwandan genocide suggests that the military forces that did most of the killing numbered about 10,000.

Genocide involves three distinct elements, which provide the basis for all attempts to explain why and how genocides happen: (1) the "identification of a social group as an enemy ... against which it is justified to use physical violence in a systematic way"; (2) "the intention to destroy the real or imputed power" of this group; and (3) "the actual deployment of violence ... through killing ... and other measures" (Shaw 2003: 37). Genocidal mass killings can be grouped into two general categories: "Dispossessive" mass killings result from policies that strip large groups of the population of their possessions, their homes, their way of life and finally their lives. "Coercive mass killings" occur in major armed conflicts, when political and military leaders use massive violence to coerce large numbers of civilians and their leaders into submission (Valentino 2004).

Three explanatory approaches have been most influential: (1) Genocide as the product of *modernity*, with Baumann (1989) as the most prominent proponent. (2) The *structural and psychosocial perspective*, focusing on broad social, cultural, and political factors, e.g. deep cleavages between social and ethnic groups; social crises which increase competition between groups; moral disengagement such as the erosion of norms of social responsibility and solidarity; and a cultural pattern of authoritarian and obedient attitudes. (3) The *strategic perspective*, according to which specific goals and strategies of political and military leaders are decisive for the precipitation of genocide. The Milgram Experiments and later Zimbardo's Stanford Prison experiment were influential in explaining the involvement of ordinary people in mass killings.

SEE ALSO: Authoritarian Personality; Fascism; Milgram, Stanley (Experiments); Violence; War

REFERENCES

Bauman, Z. (1989) *Modernity and the Holocaust*. Cornell University Press, Ithaca, NY.

Rubinstein, W. D. (2004) *Genocide*. Pearson Longman, London.

Shaw, M. (2003) *War and Genocide. Organized Killing in Modern Society*. Polity, Cambridge.

Valentino, B. A. (2004) *Final Solutions. Mass Killing and Genocide in the Twentieth Century*. Cornell University Press, Ithaca and London.

SUSANNE KARSTEDT

gentrification

Gentrification is the investment of commercial or residential capital in less affluent neighborhoods to encourage redevelopment for middle- and high-income inhabitants. Traditionally, the term "gentrification" refers to the displacement of working class residents from inner-city zones and the gradual entry of new "gentry" of well-off professionals. Early work explored the role of gentrification in accelerating the displacement of blue-collar jobs from the urban core during the 1950s and 1960s. Since the 1960s and 1970s, scholars have noted that processes of gentrification have become more widespread throughout US and European cities, especially, following the global economic recession of the 1970s, as capitalists sought new opportunities for profitable investment in the real estate sector. Thus, between the late 1970s and the early 1990s, a second phase of gentrification unfolded. During this period, inner-city reinvestment articulated with extra-local socio economic processes such as deindustrialization, globalization, and the rise of the so-called "FIRE" (finance, insurance and real estate) industrial cluster as an important engine of urban economic growth. The intense recession of the early 1990s witnessed predictions of an "end to gentrification" as investor capital evaporated. By the mid-1990s, however, a third wave of gentrification had began to crystallize, as additional neighborhoods, located ever further from the urban core, experienced significant capital-led redevelopment. In the US context, government mortgage policies, securitization, and globalization of finance supported and encouraged this third-wave gentrification (Smith 1996).

In a comprehensive survey of the literature, Hackworth (2002) argues that four novel changes distinguish third-wave gentrification: corporate developers are now the leading initiators of gentrification, federal and local governments are more open and assertive in facilitating gentrification; anti-gentrification movements have become more marginalized than in earlier decades; and, gentrification is diffusing to more remote neighborhoods. Overall, according to Hackworth (2002: 839), gentrification now is "more corporate, more state facilitated, and less resisted than ever before."

In elaborating on the third wave of gentrification, Gotham (2005) has developed and applied the concept of tourism gentrification as a heuristic device to explain the transformation of a middle-class neighborhood into a relatively affluent and exclusive enclave marked by a proliferation of corporate entertainment and tourism venues. As local elites use tourism as a strategy of economic revitalization, tourism services and facilities are incorporated into redevelopment zones and gentrifying areas. In this new urban landscape, gentrification and tourism amalgamate with other consumption-oriented activities such as shopping, restaurants, cultural facilities and entertainment venues. This blurring of entertainment, commercial activity and residential space suggests an implosion of culture and economics in the production and consumption of urban space.

More recently, the crisis of the subprime mortgage sector and the global recession have dampened investor confidence in real estate investment thus slowing down gentrification in many US and European cities. Nevertheless, a key feature of recent research on gentrification is the attempt to situate gentrification within larger economic and political processes, including the deregulation of national markets, shifting patterns of global finance and the power of transnational corporations (TNCs) and global production networks. Simply identifying a transition in housing stock or class composition of a neighborhood is, of course, no longer novel given the variety of causes and multilevel processes affecting gentrification. As many scholars have pointed out, gentrification is not an outcome of group preferences nor a reflection of market laws of supply and demand. Consumer taste for gentrified spaces is, instead, created and marketed, and depends on the alternatives offered by powerful capitalists who are primarily interested in producing the built environment from which they can extract the highest profit. Furthermore, gentrification reflects and is a product of an intricate intertwining of state and financial institutions.

SEE ALSO: Class; Economic Development; Urban Renewal and Redevelopment; Urban Tourism

REFERENCES

Gotham, K. F. (2005) Tourism gentrification: the case of New Orleans's Vieux Carre (French Quarter). *Urban Studies* 42 (7): 1099–1121.

Hackworth, J. (2002) Postrecession gentrification in New York City. *Urban Affairs Review* 37 (6): 815–43.
Smith, N. (1996) *The New Urban Frontier: Gentrification and the Revanchist City*. Routledge, New York.

KEVIN FOX GOTHAM

Gini coefficient

The Gini coefficient is the most commonly used measure of inequality. The coefficient is named after the Italian statistician and demographer Corrado Gini (1884–1965), who invented the measure in 1912. While the Gini coefficient is often used to measure income and wealth inequality, it is also widely employed to indicate uneven distribution in other social issues, such as industrial location and development, health care, and racial segregation. The coefficient ranges from 0 to 1, with 0 representing perfect equality (i.e., everyone has the same income) and 1 perfect inequality (i.e., a single person has all the income). An extension of the Gini coefficient is the Gini index, which equals the Gini coefficient multiplied by 100.

The Gini coefficient is calculated based on the Lorenz curve (Lorenz 1905) of income distribution. The graphical depiction of the Gini coefficient is shown in Figure 1. The Lorenz curve is plotted showing the relationship between the cumulative percentage of population and the cumulative percentage of income. The diagonal or 45 degree line indicates a perfect distribution of population and income (e.g., 30 percent of the population earns 30 percent of the income and 80 percent of the population earns 80 percent of the income).

The Gini coefficient is the ratio of the area between the Lorenz curve of income distribution and the diagonal line of perfect equality (the shaded area or area A in Figure 1) to the total area underneath the line of perfect equality. Putting it into an equation: the Gini coefficient = area A/(area A + area B). The further the Lorenz curve is below the line of perfect equality, the greater the inequality in the distribution of income.

Countries with Gini coefficients between 0.2 and 0.35 are generally viewed as having equitable distribution of income, whereas countries with Gini coefficients from 0.5 to 0.7 are considered to have high inequality in income distribution. Most European countries and Canada have Gini coefficients varying from 0.2 to 0.36, while many African and Latin American countries have high values of Gini coefficients exceeding 0.45. Most Asian nations have Gini coefficients between 0.25 and 0.45 (United Nations 2005). Income inequality in the United States showed an upward trend over the past three decades, increasing from a Gini of 0.39 in 1970 to 0.46 in 2000.

One needs to be cautious about the national measures of Gini coefficients for they may obscure great variations in income inequality across sectors of the population within a country. In the United States, for example, minorities (African Americans

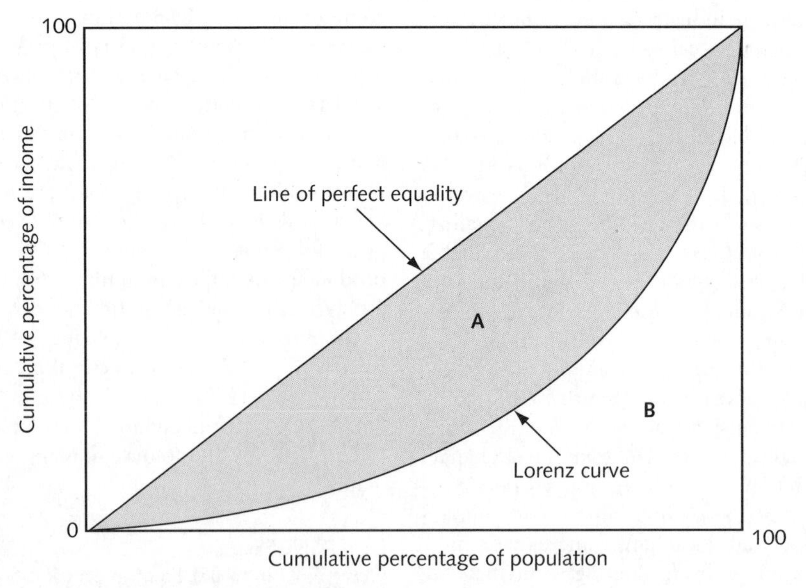

Figure 1 Graphical depiction of the Gini coefficient (A/A + B)

and Latinos) have higher levels of income inequality than non-Hispanic whites (US Census Bureau 2005). The Gini coefficient is also useful in understanding the impact of economic development. For example, a nation may experience rapid economic growth and an increasing Gini coefficient simultaneously, indicating that income becomes less evenly distributed and thus inequality and poverty are not necessarily improving.

SEE ALSO: Income Inequality, Global; Income Inequality and Income Mobility; Inequality, Wealth

REFERENCES

Lorenz, M. C. (1905) Methods of measuring the concentration of wealth. *Journal of the American Statistical Association* 9: 209–19.

United Nations (2005) *Human Development Reports*: hdr.undp.org/reports/global/2005/.

United States Census Bureau (2005) *Historical Income Inequality Tables*: www.census.gov/hhes/income/histinc/ineqtoc.html.

IVAN Y. SUN

global economy

The global economy refers to the sum of all the commercial relations between economic agents whether they are state or private or of other mixed forms. This distinctive concept of the global economy comes from globalization theorists and researchers who have identified globalizing corporations and their local affiliates, not states, as the dominant economic forces in the world today. Theory and research on the global economy has focused on several interrelated phenomena, increasingly significant since the 1960s. The transnational corporations (TNCs) have attracted an unprecedented level of attention in this period, not only from academic researchers but also from activists in the fields of human rights in general and child labour, sweatshops, and environmental justice in particular.

The novelty of theories of the global economy, in the sense used here, originates in the proposition that capitalism entered a new, global phase in the second half of the twentieth century. By the new millennium the largest TNCs had assets and annual sales far in excess of the Gross National Products of most of the countries in the world. The global scope of TNCs and the formal ownership (though not control) of their share capital through pension funds etc. have also expanded dramatically.

The globalization of cross-border finance and trading can be fruitfully analyzed in terms of the progressive weakening of the nation-state and the growing recognition that major institutions in the global economy, notably transnational financial and trading organizations, are setting the agenda for these weakened nation-states. Since the disintegration of the Soviet empire from the late 1980s, the struggle between capitalism and communism has been largely replaced by the struggle between the advocates of capitalist triumphalism and the opponents of capitalist globalization. Many theorists have discussed these issues within the triadic framework of states, TNCs and international economic institutions. From this perspective, the global economy is dominated by the relations between the major states and state-systems (USA, the EU and Japan), the major corporations, and the international financial institutions (World Bank, IMF, WTO, supplemented in some versions by other international bodies, major regional institutions, and so on). This has stimulated interest in who runs the global economy.

State-centrists argue that the global economy is a myth because most major TNCs are legally domiciled in the USA, Japan and Europe, and because they trade and invest mainly between themselves. Against this conclusion, proponents of the global economy argue that an increasing number of corporations operating outside their countries of origin are actively engaged in developing global strategies of various types, as is obvious from the contents of their annual reports and other corporate publications. While Marxist and Marx-inspired theories of the inevitability of a fatal economic crisis of the capitalist global economy appear to have lost most of their adherents, at least two related crises have been identified. The first is the simultaneous creation of increasing poverty and increasing wealth within and between societies (the class polarization crisis), not to be confused with Marx's emiseration thesis which failed to predict significant increases in wealth for rapidly expanding minorities all over the world. The second is the unsustainability of the global economy as it is presently organized (the ecological crisis).

SEE ALSO: Economy (Sociological Approach); Globalization; Globalization, Consumption and; Income Inequality, Global

REFERENCES

Dicken, P. (2007) *Global Shift*, 5th edn. Sage, London.

Sklair, L. (2001) *The Transnational Capitalist Class*. Blackwell, Oxford.

Sklair, L. (2002) *Globalization: Capitalism and Its Alternatives*, 3rd edn. Oxford University Press, Oxford.

Strange, S. (1996) *The Retreat of the State*. Cambridge University Press, Cambridge.

LESLIE SKLAIR

global justice as a social movement

The global justice movement is a transnational social movement rooted in the confluence of the human rights, labor, environmental, indigenous, peasant, and feminist movements' shared opposition to neoliberal globalization and vision of a more democratic, equitable, ecologically sustainable world. Neoliberal globalization refers to those structural changes in the global economy carried out by elites under a discourse of free markets that weaken or eliminate policies that protect the environment and vulnerable populations, such as workers and indigenous people, while creating a regulatory apparatus that favors transnational corporations (TNCs); accompanying cultural changes, such as the promotion of consumerism and an ideology emphasizing market-oriented solutions, including micro-credit and privatizing basic services, to social ills also comprise such globalization. The global justice movement is truly global in scope, with its membership ranging from non-profits and small volunteer collectives in the global north (first world), to large, grassroots labor, peasant and indigenous organizations in the global south (third world).

Often referred to, rather inaccurately, as the anti-globalization movement, global justice activists oppose only the current form of economic globalization – neoliberalism – and favor what they call globalization from below. They critique neoliberalism for taking critical economic decisions out of the democratic, public sphere and placing them in the hands of either TNCs or multilateral organizations with little democratic accountability, particularly the International Monetary Fund (IMF), World Bank, and World Trade Organization (WTO). Critics charge that, under neoliberalism, decisions are made primarily on the basis of short-term profit-maximization, resulting in growing poverty and ecological degradation. In response, global justice activists stress the importance of strengthening democracy. Their vision of democracy also goes beyond limited, mainstream understandings that focus on elections and lobbying, instead embracing a more grassroots, participatory model. They also advocate increased economic democracy, which might include stronger environmental and labor protection laws, guaranteeing basic needs such as food and healthcare as human rights, worker cooperatives, nationalization of key industries, and supporting indigenous traditions of collective property.

The global justice movement emerged in response to the rise of global neoliberalism in the 1970s and 1980s. In the 1980s, environmental and indigenous activists began to target the World Bank, charging that many of the development projects it funded, such as large dams and oil pipelines, were environmentally destructive and displaced indigenous people. As TNCs increasingly moved production (and therefore jobs) between countries in an effort to cut labor costs, labor unions began to create transnational organizing campaigns in response. As the movement grew, activists began holding regular international conferences focusing on confronting neoliberalism and envisioning a better world; most importantly, these included the *encuentros* (encounters) organized by the Zapatistas (an indigenous rebel group in Chiapas, Mexico), starting in 1996, and the World Social Forum, starting in 2001. The 1990s also saw the creation of several transnational coalitions, including Fifty Years is Enough, dedicated to either fundamentally reforming or eliminating the IMF and World Bank; Jubilee 2000, a network founded to abolish third-world debt; and Via Campesina, an international peasants' alliance. Reflecting the values of the movement, these networks have striven to maintain democratic relations internally, though this has not always been easy.

As a consequence of these networks, the late 1990s and early twenty-first century saw a dramatic expansion of global justice activism. In the north, this originally took the form of protests, such as those against the WTO in Seattle, in which activists attempted to shut down or disrupt high-level meetings of international political and business leaders. Increasingly, these protests have become less important, and there is more of an emphasis on grassroots organizing against local manifestations of neoliberalism, such as cutbacks in welfare programs, the gentrification of cities, and the privatization of local water supplies. There has also been a wave of successful activism in the south, particularly Latin America, where mass protests, road blockades and other such actions have forced governments to reverse neoliberal initiatives. In a number of Latin American countries, activists have also helped left-of-center governments get elected, although their willingness and ability to successfully implement significant reforms has varied. Parts of Africa and Asia have also seen waves of militant global justice activism.

This activism has born significant fruit. In 2005, after years of advocacy work by activists, the leading countries of the north agreed to require the IMF and World Bank to cancel the unpayable debts of many of the poorest countries of the south, dramatically reducing the power of these two organizations to pressure these countries into adopting neoliberal policies. As of 2010, talks to expand the scope of the WTO appear to have completely broken down, a result of both widespread grassroots protest and the frustration of many southern governments, who feel that northern governments are not dealing fairly with them. Nonetheless, neoliberal policies remain firmly in place in most countries, and other problems, such as environmental degradation, the scarcity of affordable food for much of the world's poor, and increasing economic instability, have grown worse.

SEE ALSO: Environmental Movements; Global Economy; Globalization; Globalization and Global Justice; Indigenous Movements; Neoliberalism; Transnational Movements.

SUGGESTED READINGS

Brandy, J. & Smith, J. (eds.) (2005). *Coalitions across Borders*. Rowman & Littlefield, Lanham, MD.

della Porta, D., & Tarrow, S. (eds.) (2005). *Transnational Protest and Global Activism*. Rowman & Littlefield, Lanham, MD.

Mertes, T. (ed.) (2004). *A Movement of Movements*. Verso, New York.

MATTHEW WILLIAMS

global politics

Global politics refers to political relations and activities that stretch across state borders, and whose consequences are worldwide in scope. As such, global politics includes but is not limited to inter-state relations. The latter has traditionally been the focus of the dominant realist tradition of International Relations (IR). This has routinely assumed the primacy of sovereign, bounded territorial states, which act in their own national interest in a sharply demarcated "external" political environment defined by zero-sum power equations. Many contemporary scholars of global politics argue that such realist views do not accurately reflect the new realities of what some have referred to as a *post-Westphalian* or *post-international* world, where the boundaries separating domestic and foreign policy are increasingly blurred.

Although the discourse on global politics only really takes off in the 1980s, it is traceable to many earlier intimations of a global political awareness. Karl Marx, for instance, had argued that capitalism is predisposed to expand beyond its geographical point of origin, to "nestle everywhere, settle everywhere, establish connexions everywhere" across the entire planet. For Marx and subsequent Marxists, such globalizing processes are inherently political. In more mainstream Political Science and IR, there were similar trends amongst scholars dissatisfied with the dominant realist paradigm. Modelski's (1972) treatise on world politics was particularly significant in this respect, as it was one of the first works in the social sciences to deploy the concept of globalization. This was followed by Richard Falk's (1975) appeal for mainstream Political Science and IR to take a more "global approach," and Keohane and Nye's (1977) important contribution on "complex interdependence." These and associated analyses were premised on the view that world politics could no longer (if indeed it ever could) be understood exclusively with reference to the interests of competing states within a largely anarchic interstate order.

These new perspectives on politics were a response to several developments. One was the explosive growth of international non-governmental organizations (INGOs) and intergovernmental organizations (IGOs) over the past century. These have arisen in response to economic, technological, environmental and security challenges that transcend the capacities of individual states, and thus demand new forms of transnational regulation and cooperation. There has also been a parallel growth of military and trading blocs that are widely viewed as being more than the sum of their national parts. Finally, the development of multi-layered governance, based on structures of overlapping and divided authority, is perhaps the key development to which theories of global politics has been a response.

Scholars who argue that such a new global political universe now exists typically emphasize four related points: (1) that state capacities and *de facto* sovereignty have been compromised in various ways by the globalization of economic, political and cultural processes; (2) that national borders are increasingly porous with respect to the movement of information, commodities and people across them, which contributes to 1 and problematizes the clear demarcation of domestic and foreign politics; (3) that politics has been partially "deterritorialized" as a result of 1 and 2; (4) that taken together 1, 2, and 3 represent a qualitative break from the state-centric, international world order that is assumed to have characterized world politics for the 300 or so years following the Peace of Westphalia (1648). The latter concluded the Thirty Years War in Europe and is often taken to have initiated the modern era of state sovereignty, with its presumptions of absolute and indivisible territorial authority, and rights to non-interference by external actors. It has now, proponent of global politics argue, been transcended.

Many critics dispute these claims, and reject the whole idea of a post-international, global political environment. They point out that so-called Westphalian sovereignty was always more of a normative ideal than it was a political reality, with states throughout the "Westphalian period" frequently having had their claims to absolute authority constrained and subverted by other states and non-state actors. Furthermore, the suggestion that state capacities have been uniformly eroded neglects the massive power discrepancies between different states, and glosses over the strengthening of some state capacities (the policing of immigration) even as others are eroded (the capacity to autonomously determine some aspects of economic policy). Given this, the idea that there has been a de-territorialization of politics is said to be out of step with both the past (where clearly not all political phenomena could be explained with reference to relations between territorial states) and with the present (where politics still has a demonstrable territorial dimension, as reflected in the continued salience of territorialized nationalist conflicts). In this view, global politics is, and will always remain, filtered through the prism of national institutions.

SEE ALSO: Global Justice as a Social Movement; Globalization; Globalization, Culture and; Politics

REFERENCES

Keohane, R. O. & Nye, J. (1977) *Power and Interdependence*. Little Brown, Boston, MA.

Modelski, G. (1972) *Principles of World Politics*. Free Press, New York.

SUGGESTED READING

Falk, R. (1975) *A Global Approach to National Policy*. Harvard University Press, Cambridge, MA.

LLOYD COX

global warming

Global warming is the increase of average temperatures in the lower atmosphere (near the Earth's surface and oceans). Global warming is not the same thing as climate change, which refers to a change in climate lasting for an extended period of time. The effects of global warming are numerous, from the melting of Arctic ice sheets, the loss of biodiversity, species extinction and changes in flora and fauna, rainfall amounts, ocean salinity and wind patterns and increases in extreme weather, such as droughts, flooding, heatwaves, and the intensification of tropical storms (e.g. Hurricane Katrina).

Global warming has been the subject of much debate and controversy. Much of the controversy deals with whether human actions and behaviors cause global warming. The Intergovernmental Panel on Climate Change (IPCC) makes the case that human activity is a major contributor primarily because of fossil fuel use and changes in land use (especially related to methane and nitrous oxide use in agriculture). Pre-industrial levels (determined from ice core samples) suggest that increases in carbon dioxide, methane, and nitrous oxide have increased significantly as a result of human activities since 1750.

Scientists, politicians, economists, and policymakers have all weighed in on global warming, its causes, effects and possible solutions. Even though global warming deniers and skeptics still make headlines, much of the scientific community accepts its actuality. The year 2005 has been identified as the point when conversations about global warming and climate change tipped towards certainty (Lever-Tracey 2008). The 2007 IPCC Report asserted that global warming is evident and uncontestable. Global temperatures have risen over 0.74°C in the last century as a consequence of greenhouses gases trapped in the Earth's atmosphere.

Along with threats to the environment, there is also a threat to social organization and patterns of human life. The 2007 IPCC Report identifies changes to agriculture, increased forest fires and increased health-related mortality due to malnutrition, respiratory diseases and infectious diseases. Human settlements are at risk due to deleterious effects on food and water supplies, desertification as well as flooding, thereby making areas increasingly uninhabitable and forcing community relocation. Poor areas and marginalized communities are especially vulnerable to these effects (often lying in flood-prone regions, for example).

The twentieth century has seen an increase in energy dependent patterns of living, especially transportation, electricity generation and the rise in mass production and consumption. Increased mobility, excess capitalism, and neoliberalism are explanatory factors underpinning these actions and behaviors. And while sociology takes these tenets as central to many analyses, sociology has been late to the conversation on global warming and its impact on society. Why? (1) Sociology privileges views of society as socially constructed and addressing global warming requires taking natural determinism seriously; and (2) thinking about global warming and its effects requires projecting into the future. Thinking about the future, about linear streams of progress, has become outdated as thinkers move away from narratives embedded in modernity.

Literature within sociology, especially within environmental sociology, examines how and why people negatively impact the environment and how these actions get institutionalized. Two schools of thought have emerged addressing these questions. First, the Ecological Modernization School posits that capitalism will provide solutions to global warming by merging capitalist production with ecological principles. Along with this idea is the search for alternative sources of energy to reduce reliance on fossil fuels. Second, eco-Marxists deem that capitalism will create the conditions of its own downfall because capitalist production cannot keep expanding on a planet with finite resources.

Global warming is an international problem. A 1°C increase is projected to cause 300,000 climate-related deaths from disease. A 2°C change will increase coastal flooding and affect up to 10 million people. The Kyoto Protocol, an international agreement among already-industrialized nations to cut emissions a few percentage points lower than their 1990 levels, is one such attempt to combat the problem across nation-states. However, not all countries have agreed to the Protocol, most notably the USA, claiming it is unfair to penalize the US economy when India and China are unregulated.

The Kyoto Protocol introduced the idea of market-related measures, which have been touted as the solution to curbing greenhouse gas emissions. One such proposal is emissions trading, also known as cap and trade. This approach has companies or other organizations purchase licenses to emit a certain, specified amount of pollutants. Companies that need to emit more have to buy licenses from companies that pollute less. Although this is one of many proposed solutions, the debate in the years ahead will concern how, and in what ways, global warming and the projected effects can be mitigated and if possible, reversed.

SEE ALSO: Ecological Problems; Environmental Movements; Environmental Problems; Environmental Sociology; Social Problems, Politics of

REFERENCE

Lever-Tracy, C. (2008) Global warming and sociology. *Current Sociology* 56: 445–66.

SUGGESTED READING

IPCC (2007) *Fourth Assessment Report: Climate Change 2007*: www.ipcc.ch/publications_and_data/publications_and_data_reports.htm.

McCright, A. M. & Dunlap, R. E. (2000) Challenging global warming as a social problem: an analysis of the conservative movement's counter-claims. *Social Problems* 47 (4): 499–522.

Urry, J. (2009) Sociology and climate change. *Sociological Review* 2 (57): 84–100.

HEATHER MARSH

global/world cities

The term "global city" was popularized by sociologist Sassen in 1991; however, the origins of the discourse on global/world cities began decades before. Hall's 1966 *The World Cities* was a pioneering study that investigated world cities in a broad context, including economics, demographics, culture, management, etc. He was among the first to define the role and formation of world cities. By the late 1960s and early 1970s Lefebvre, Castells and Harvey were advancing critical urban theories that linked the processes of city formation to historical capitalist development and free market forces. By the 1980s Friedmann introduced his "world cities hypothesis" and became among the first to describe urbanization in a specifically global context. As mentioned, in the 1990s Sassen designated certain world cities as "global cities" and leading urban scholars such as Taylor, Brenner, and others continued the discourse. The analysis made famous by Friedmann, Sassen, and others is sometimes called the "market-driven approach" because it views global city formation as resulting from the global expansion of capitalist relations. This concept of a global city is primarily economic, with the term "world" or "global" city applied to urban areas that are central to the accumulation, control and organization of international finance, trade, and production services, such cities as New York,

London, and Tokyo. This conventional discussion of global/world cities has been challenged on occasion and there is a growing consensus that in the new millennium the discourse of the 1980s and 1990s is increasingly too narrow. While most scholars of global/world cities acknowledge the central importance of this perspective, there is mounting agreement that other viewpoints should be considered and jointly employed. A more recently proposed "agency-driven approach" views global city development as resulting from the active and knowledgeable actions of human agents, whether operating in state, corporate or civil society sectors, and views all major urban centers as being affected by globalization. Therefore, the discourse on global/world cities should increasingly encompass a broader array of important urban areas around the world in order to arrive at a fuller understanding of globalization. It is argued that this can be achieved by examining locales in varying stages of development, not just the economically prominent cities. Global/world cities literature enhances the globalization discourse by analyzing its spatial causes, manifestations, and requirements. It sheds light on the spatial dimensions of globalization and serves as an important contribution to the study of both globalization and contemporary urbanism, as it facilitates the understanding of actual global forces operating through and producing spaces and places in relation to real social actors and institutions.

SEE ALSO: Chicago School; Globalization, Inequality and the City; Urban; Urban Space; Urbanism/Urban Culture, Urbanization

SUGGESTED READINGS

Amen, M. M., Archer, K., & Bosman, M. M. (eds.) (2006) *Relocating Global Cities: From the Center to the Margins*. Rowman and Littlefield Publishers, Lanham, MD.

Brenner, N. & Kiel, R. (eds.) (2006) *The Global Cities Reader*. Routledge, London.

Sassen, S. (2001). *The Global City*, Princeton University Press, Princeton, NJ.

The Globalization and World Cities Research Network, GAWC: www.lboro.ac.uk/gawc.

MARCOS BURGOS

globalization

Appearing first in the 1960s, "globalization" has become a central but contested sociological concept. Although the origins of globalization can be found in the distant past, the concept was used widely after the end of the cold war, after which it was possible at least to imagine a "borderless" world in which people, goods, ideas, and images would flow with relative ease. The global division between capitalism and state socialism gave way to a more uncertain world in which capitalism was the dominant economic and social system. This coincided with the development of digital communication technologies from the late 1980s and their dramatic consequences for socioeconomic organization and interpersonal interaction. Global restructuring of states, financial systems, production technologies and the politics of neoliberalism in turn accompanied these developments, creating previously unprecedented levels of transnational interdependence.

Globalization is not a single process. Economic globalization refers to such things as the global dominance of transnational corporations, global finance, flexible production and assembly, and the rise of information and service economies. Political globalization refers to the growth of international organizations, subnational regional autonomy, post-welfare public policies, and global social movements. Globalization is a cultural process, exemplified by the growth of global consumption cultures, migration, tourism, media and information flows, and transnational identities. Digital communication facilitates the experience of spatially distant events at the same time (sometimes called "instantaneity"), while creating a complex range of social interconnections along with a partial collapse of boundaries within national, cultural, and political spaces. However, the meaning and significance of globalization remains far from clear. There are globalization optimists such as Friedman (2000) and Ohmae (2005) who see a "borderless world" increasing human potential, but others are more pessimistic and critical of globalization's consequences (e.g., Falk 1999). Some such as Urry (2003) and Giddens (1999) regard globalization as an emergent process *sui generis*, while Rosenberg (2000) rejects this view arguing that what is called "globalization" is the *effect* of complex social, economic, cultural and political changes.

Globalization does not simply refer to increasing global interconnections but also to socio-spatial restructuring. For example through privatization and deregulation during the 1980s and 1990s various governance functions shifted from governments to the corporate world. Global financial cities then become strategic sites for the acceleration of capital and information flows, and increased in importance and power relative to nation-states. There have emerged new "corridors" and zones around nodal cities that are increasingly independent from their environs (Sassen 1996). But there remains considerable debate over the relationship between states and globalization (Ray 2007).

There are many theories of globalization. Robertson emphasizes "global consciousness," referring to "the compression of the world and the intensification of consciousness of the world as a whole" (1992: 8). This provokes new cultural conflicts for example between universalism and particularism. Religious traditions can be mobilized to provide an ultimate justification for one's view of the world – thus "fundamentalist" groups combine traditionalism with a global agenda. A globalized world is thus integrated but not harmonious.

For Giddens the concept of time–space distantiation is central. Locales are increasingly shaped by events far away and vice versa, while social relations are disembedded, or "lifted out" from locales. For example, peasant households in traditional societies were largely self-sufficient and money was of limited value. Modernization replaced local exchange with universal money exchange, which simplifies otherwise impossibly complex transitions and enables the circulation of complex forms of information and value in abstract and symbolic forms. Money exchange establishes social relations across time and space, which get intensified with globalization. Similarly, expert cultures arise as a result of the scientific revolutions bringing increases in technical knowledge and specialization. Specialist knowledge is then globally organized while increased social distance is created between professionals and their clients. As expert knowledge dominates globally, local perspectives become devalued and modern societies are reliant on expert systems. Trust is increasingly crucial to both monetary and expert systems and is the "glue" that holds modern societies together. But where trust is undermined, individuals experience ontological insecurity and a sense of insecurity with regard to their social reality.

Giddens (1999) also describes globalization as a "runaway world" which "is emerging in an anarchic, haphazard fashion." The global order is the result of an intersection of four processes – capitalism (economic logic), the interstate system (world order), militarism (world security and threats), and industrialism (the division of labor and lifestyles). However, Giddens does not say what the weight of each of these factors is and whether they change historically.

Similarly, David Harvey emphasizes the ways in which globalization revolutionizes the qualities of space and time. As space appears to shrink to a "global village" of telecommunications and ecological interdependencies and as time horizons shorten to the point where the present is all there is, so we have to learn how to cope with an overwhelming sense of *compression* of our spatial and temporal worlds (1990: 240–2). Time–space compression is driven by flexible accumulation and new technologies, the production of signs and images, just-in-time delivery, reduced turnover times and speeding up, and both de- and reskilling. Harvey points for support to the ephemerality of fashions, products, production techniques, speedup and vertical disintegration, financial markets and computerized trading, instantaneity and disposability, and regional competitiveness.

For Urry the changes associated with globalization are so far-reaching that we should now talk of "sociology beyond societies." The alleged decline of the nation-state in a globalized world results in the redundancy of the concept of "society" as a territorially bounded entity, which in turn shakes the foundations of the discipline. In its place Urry proposes new socialities of space (social topologies), regions (interregional competition), networks (new social morphology), and fluids (global enterprises). Mobility is central to this thesis since globalization involves the complex movement of people, images, goods, finances, and so on that constitutes a process across regions in faster and unpredictable shapes, all with no clear point of arrival or departure.

Despite the contrasting theoretical understandings of globalization, there is some measure of agreement that it poses new opportunities and threats. For example, globalization offers new forms of cosmopolitanism and economic growth but also increased global risks such as ecological crisis, global pandemics, and international crime and terrorism (Beck 2000). Globalization may be seen as encroachment and colonization as global corporations and technologies erode local customs and ways of life, which in turn engenders new forms of protest and assertion of local cultural identity. By contrast with globalization enthusiasts it can be argued that global patterns of inequality have become increasingly polarized. The global "war on terror" further dents the idea of a "borderless world."

Globalization has been the focus of extensive social movement activism, especially to neoliberal globalism represented by bodies such as the WTO. Such activists include churches, nationalist parties, leftist parties, environmentalists, peasant unions, anti-racism groups, anarchists and some charities. Glasius et al. (2002) identify the emergence of a "global civil society" exemplified by the growth of "parallel summits" such as the 2001 Porto Alegre meeting in Brazil to protest against the Davos (Switzerland) World Economic Forum. These are organized through multiple networks of social actors and NGOs operating on local and international levels. Many activists are not necessarily opposed to globalization as such but to economic neoliberalism intent on constricting local lifestyles in the pursuit of profit. For anti-globalization critics, globalization creates a "borderless" world for capital and finance but not for labor, since increasingly severe immigration controls exist in most developed countries while labor often lacks basic rights. If we take a broad view of globalization, though, these movements are themselves part of the process by which global solidarities (albeit rather weak and transitory ones) come to be formed.

SEE ALSO: Global Justice as a Social Movement; Global/World Cities; Glocalization; Grobalization; Neoliberalism

REFERENCES

Beck, U. (2000) *What Is Globalization?* Polity Press, Cambridge.

Falk, R. (1999) *Predatory Globalization: A Critique.* Polity Press, Cambridge.

Friedman, T. (2000) *The Lexus and the Olive Tree.* Anchor Books, New York.

Giddens, A. (1999) *Runaway World.* Polity Press, Cambridge.

Glasius, M., Kaldor, M., & Anheier, H. (eds.) (2002) *Global Civil Society 2002.* Oxford University Press, Oxford.

Harvey, D. (1990) *The Condition of Postmodernity.* Blackwell, Oxford.

Ohmae, K. (2005) *The Next Global Stage: Challenges and Opportunities in our Borderless World.* Warton School Publishing, Philadelphia.

Ray, L. (2007) *Globalization and Everyday Life.* London, Routledge.

Robertson, R. (1992) *Globalization.* Sage, London.

Rosenberg, R. (2000) *Follies of Globalization Theory.* Verso, London.

Sassen, S. (1996) Cities and communities in the global economy: rethinking our concepts. *American Behavioral Scientist* 39 (5): 629–39.

Urry, J. (2003) *Global Complexity.* Polity Press, Cambridge.

LARRY RAY

globalization, consumption and

"Globalization" and "consumption" emerged as key concepts in social theory in the last decades of the twentieth century, and combined with reference to the emergence of a "global consumer culture": the same products, services, and entertainment sold in the same kinds of retail and leisure spaces to consumers around the world. Product availability is less tied to specific places, first because the same global brands are on sale at the same time throughout the world and second because deterritorialized immigrants recreate the retail environment of their homeland by importing familiar products. New technologies accelerated the flow of information, money, people, and goods across national borders, creating a world market with a global division of labor and global consumers. These developments challenged sociology's implicit understanding of "society" in terms of bounded cultures within nation-states, and shifted the locus of social identity from class position and work to consumption and lifestyle.

Globalization of consumption is often equated with Americanization, an argument reinforced by the number of prominent global brands with corporate headquarters in the USA, including Coca-Cola, Disney, McDonald's, Nike, and Microsoft. Coca-Cola is in that sense iconic, with the term "Coca-Colanization" used to signify economic and cultural domination by the USA (Wagnleitner 1994). So, too, McDonald's, its golden arches metonyms of American culture and its restaurants regular targets for anti-American protest (Ritzer 2004). From this perspective, "global culture" is in fact "American culture" and its consumers are "Coca-colonials." Critics of this view point out that the sources of global culture are not all American, arguing that Ikea furniture, Indian ("Bollywood") movies and food, Japanese animation, electronics, and sushi – not to mention the global audience for soccer, a sport in which the USA is an inconsequential player – all point to more complex processes of global cultural flow. In addition, global products are consumed in culturally specific contexts which inflect them with different meaning.

Globalization has contradictory implications for consumption. The idea that consuming global products involves interplay between global and local rather than cultural homogenization gives rise to the terms "glocal" and "glocalization" (Robertson 1995) to describe what happens when consumers incorporate global culture into local practice and meaning to produce culture that is neither fully global nor strictly local. By implication, globalization of consumption increases cultural diversity, adding "glocal" hybrids to the existing pool of local cultures. A less optimistic view would see "glocal" cultures as replacing rather than coexisting with "local" cultures, with the balance between global and local shifting inexorably in favor of the global as what's left of the local in "glocal" decreases over time.

SEE ALSO: Consumption, Green/Sustainable; Consumption, Mass Consumption and Consumer Culture; Globalization; Grobalization; McDonaldization

REFERENCES

Ritzer, G. (2004) *The McDonaldization of Society*, rev. edn. Pine Forge Press, Thousand Oaks, CA.

Robertson, R. (1995) Glocalization: time–space and homogeneity–heterogeneity. In: Featherstone, M. (ed.), *Global Culture*. Sage, London.

Wagnleitner, R. (1994) *Coca-Colonization and the Cold War: The Cultural Mission of the United States in Austria after the Second World War*. University of North Carolina Press, Chapel Hill, NC.

BERYL LANGER

globalization, culture and

As the debate about globalization has rapidly expanded and become more, rather than less, contentious, there has emerged what might be called a "negative consensus" concerning the idea of global culture. While there is most definitely no widespread agreement, either "globally" or "locally," about what we might mean by the term global culture(s), there is – for many, a seemingly reluctant – confirmation of the proposition that the issue of global culture is of paramount significance.

Consideration of culture in global or at least transnational terms has led to much rethinking of the concept of culture and its part in social life, not least because practitioners of the metadiscipline of cultural studies have made major interventions in the discussion of globalization, globality, transnationality, global modernities, and so on. Thus, the oft-called cultural turn has had a major part in elevating culture to a position of significance in the globalization debate. This is not to say, however, that the cultural factor is totally accepted as central to the thinking of those working on matters global.

Almost certainly, the most controversial question in the general, non-reductionist discussion of globalization concerns whether the world as a whole is being swept by homogenizing cultural forces, at one extreme, or whether the world is, on the other hand, becoming increasingly marked by variety and difference. Insofar as the globalization-equals-homogenization thesis has been so much in evidence in recent years, often in tandem with the conceptually unacceptable claim that Americanization is the same as globalization, the emphasis here is more on heterogeneity than homogeneity. Globalization – conceived, of necessity, as *glocalization* (Robertson 1992: 173–4) – is a self-limiting process. In the light of the idea of glocality, globalization can only take hold if globalizing forces can find or produce a niche in relation to the local and the particular. This is to be seen in the maxim that it is the particular which makes the universal work.

The circulation of practices, ideas, and institutional forms around the world is a central aspect of global culture. This has in the past often been indicated by the term cultural diffusion. But the latter term in itself lacks explicit sensitivity to the glocalizing character of the circulation of sociocultural phenomena. The same is true of what are frequently cast as flows from one context to others. In recent times non-governmental organizations (NGOs) have played as big a part in this as they have in the promotion and sustaining of diasporic relations with the "homeland." In this case the multiplication of loyalties via population movements has become a crucial element of global culture. In particular, the assimilation of immigrants in the fully fledged sense is rapidly declining, so much so that the vast question of national societal membership and citizenship is a central and increasingly controversial problem of our time. Thus, the increasing significance of transnational communities with their own cultures, the prominence of these being greatly facilitated by the new and still expanding forms of electronic communication, the relative cheapness of air travel, and the growth of the illicit traffic in human beings.

It would be perfectly plausible to insist that global culture is much richer and "thicker" than the culture of any given nation-state. It is indeed more than a pity that so much intellectual energy has been expended in debating the homogenization-cum-Americanization thesis, as well as in arguing about the degree to which global (or any other) culture should, if at all, be considered epiphenomenally, when there is so much to address with respect to the diversity of global culture or cultures.

SEE ALSO: Civilizations; Culture; Globalization; Glocalization; Grobalization; Ideological Hegemony; McDonaldization; Nation-State; NGO/INGO

REFERENCE

Robertson, R. (1992) *Globalization: Social Theory and Global Culture*. Sage, London.

SUGGESTED READINGS

Beck, U., Sznaider, N., & Winter, R. (eds.) (2003) *Global America? The Cultural Consequences of Globalization*. Liverpool University Press, Liverpool.

Lechner, F. J. & Boli, J. (2005) *World Culture: Origins and Consequences*. Blackwell, Oxford.
Tomlinson, J. (1999) *Globalization and Culture*. University of Chicago Press, Chicago, IL.

ROLAND ROBERTSON

globalization, religion and

Globalization describes the historical process by which all the world's people come to live in a single social unit. Religion constitutes an important dimension of globalization through its worldwide institutional presence, its importance in structuring individual and collective cultural difference, and as an effective resource for local and global social mobilization for various goals. Religion is a highly contested, occasionally powerful, and often conflictual domain of some consequence in the global social system.

Although explicitly religious institutions are the foundation of religion's global social presence, it is the implication of religion in other social, but especially political, movements that has thus far received the most attention in social scientific literature. It is no mere coincidence that the political impact of religion in developments ranging from the Islamic revolution in Iran and the New Christian Right in the USA to the Hindu nationalism of the Bharatiya Janata Party in India and the religiously defined cleavages of Orthodox, Catholic, and Muslim in the former Yugoslavia, appeared on the global scene at roughly the same time as the notion of globalization. The often invidious term fundamentalism has gained a corresponding popularity, referring to religious movements like these, ones that advocate the public enforcement of religious precepts or the exclusive religious identification of state collectivities. Characteristic of such movements is that they seek to enforce highly particular and frequently absolutist visions of the world in their countries, but with explicit reference to the globalizing context which they deem to be the prime threat under such epithets as "global arrogance" (Iran) or "one-worldism" (USA). The religious visions that inform them are the basis for this combination of a claim to universal validity with being centered in a particular part of the world among a particular people. Thus does religion serve as a globally present way of making cultural difference a prime structural feature of a globalized world that also relativizes all such differences by incorporating everyone in a single social system.

The explicit study of religion in the context of globalization is only in its beginnings. The sociological neglect of this topic may be due to the fact that religions usually ground themselves in tradition as opposed to contemporary developments, to the close relation between religion and local and regional culture, and perhaps to the lingering effect of secularization perspectives which have led many social scientists to expect religion to be irrelevant in the modern world. Be that as it may, a now rapidly growing literature that sees religion as an important player in today's global context heralds a much needed new direction in this regard.

SEE ALSO: Fundamentalism; Globalization, Culture and; Religion, Sociology of

SUGGESTED READINGS

Beyer, P. (ed.) (2001) *Religion in the Process of Globalization* (*Religion im Prozess der Globalisierung*). Ergon Verlag, Wurzburg.
Esposito, J. L. & Watson, M. (eds.) (2000) *Religion and Global Order*. University of Wales Press, Cardiff.

PETER BEYER

globalization, sexuality and

The globalization of sexuality refers to the sexualized and embodied nature of processes associated with the movement of people, capital, and goods across national boundaries. It also refers to how the consciousness of the world as a single place is sexualized. The globalization of sexuality is manifest in a range of processes and phenomena that are often couched and approached in highly emotive terms (e.g., the trafficking of women into prostitution, mail-order brides, the development of the sex industry, and sex tourism). It is also characterized by the AIDS pandemic, mass international tourism, and the development of cyberspace. Each of these has in turn intensified consciousness of the status of sexual minorities and the unevenness of their treatment across the globe.

One of the main vectors of the globalization of sexuality is the global AIDS pandemic. Indeed, AIDS has often been seen as a metaphor for globalization itself, as it has brought into sharp relief how lives on the planet are interconnected with the impotence of nation-states to control flows of people with HIV across national borders. While helping to shape our consciousness of the world as a single place, the AIDS pandemic has impacted disproportionately on specific localities – the impact of the pandemic is experienced unevenly. Policy responses to the AIDS pandemic have been held responsible for the promotion of modern western models of gay identity as opposed to indigenous or folk models of sexual identity in developing countries.

A considerable body of work has been produced on the globalization of gay identity. We have witnessed the growth of a global gay consciousness and an associated activism and politics. For instance, the International Lesbian and Gay Association founded in 1978 now represents 370 organizations in 90 countries. The Internet is also playing a major role in facilitating the intensification of transnational activism around the rights of sexual dissidents. At the same time, global gay tourism has become visible through the development of global mega-events such as the Gay Games and pride events such as Sydney's Mardi Gras.

Debates on the globalization of gay identity have focused on whether the export of a western model of gay identity reflects the imposition of cultural imperialism, or whether the development of a global gay consciousness is a positive and empowering example of a cosmopolitan cultural politics which is forging transnational solidarities against homophobic policies and regimes. At the same time, it should be noted that groups and organizations such as the Christian Right that are hostile towards sexual dissidents also operate on a global scale.

Technological change is driving the acceleration of the globalization of sexuality. The development of the Internet in particular is significant in facilitating globalizing processes at a mundane level – for instance in aiding men's search for mail-order brides, but also enabling those involved in campaigning against the trafficking in women to maintain and develop transnational activist networks.

SEE ALSO: Globalization; HIV/AIDS and Population; Sex Tourism; Sexual Citizenship; Third World and Postcolonial Feminisms/ Subaltern

SUGGESTED READINGS

Altman, D. (2001) *Global Sex*. Chicago University Press, Chicago, IL.

Binnie, J. (2004) *The Globalization of Sexuality*. Sage, London.

Patton, C. (2002) *Globalizing AIDS*. University of Minnesota Press, Minneapolis, MN.

JON BINNIE

globalization, sport and

The emergence and diffusion of modern sport is bound up in a global network marked by power relations and global flows. The development of national and international sports organizations, the growth of competition between national teams, the worldwide acceptance of rules governing specific (western) sport forms, and the establishment of global competitions are all indicative of the globalization of sport. Global sport is connected, but not reducible, to the ideological practices and intentions of specific groups of people from particular countries. The receptivity of national popular cultures to non-indigenous sport products is active and heterogeneous; however, there is a political economy at work in the production and consumption of global sport products. In the past, and continuing in the present, some male members of western societies have acted as a form of established group on a world level. Their tastes and conduct, including their sports, were part of this, and these practices acted and act as signs of distinction, prestige, and power. Given this growth in the multiplicity of linkages and networks that transcend nation-states, some argue that we may be at the earliest stages of the development of a "global culture," of which sport is a part. This process entails a shift from ethnic or national cultures to "supranational" forms based upon a combination of the culture of a superpower and of cosmopolitan communication and migrant networks. However, there is considerable debate as to whether global sport is leading to a homogenized body culture – specifically, along western or American lines. Yet global flows are simultaneously increasing the varieties of body cultures and identities available to people in local cultures. Global sport, then, seems to be leading to the reduction in contrasts between societies, but also to the emergence of new varieties of body cultures and identities.

SEE ALSO: Sport and Culture

SUGGESTED READING

Maguire, J. (2005) *Power and Global Sport: Zones of Prestige, Emulation and Resistance*. Routledge, London.

JOSEPH MAGUIRE

globalization and global justice

Globalization has brought about enormous changes in structural and interpersonal relations such that mechanisms of power distribution are in a state of flux. Sociology offers both descriptive and critical accounts of how shifting micro-interactions and macro-structures negotiate material, legal, and political benefits, thereby reshaping identities. These transformations can assist, improve or worsen the well-being of individuals, groups, and the environment in potentially unjust ways. Globalization augments traditional spatio-temporal boundaries of fairness, introducing concerns of intergenerational and transnational justice, for instance climate change and financial debt. The normative content of sociological research on global justice is sometimes implicit, sometimes explicit reflecting the perceived role of the discipline. Core sociological concerns here are the emergence of an international civil society, universal human rights in a world of globalized risk and the effect of enhanced communication technologies on how we understand "globalization" itself.

Karl Polanyi's (1944) *The Great Transformation* introduced the concept of "double movement" to describe societal reaction to the changes resulting from the growth of market economies in the nineteenth century. It has been adopted by many contemporary sociologists to explain the current proliferation of civil society organizations as a counter-balance to the perceived weakening of the nation-state and a swell of corporate influence. They are understood as rejecting a depoliticized mechanical conception of globalization that serves the interests of transnational elites and causes environmental degradation, economic crises and social insecurity. There has been a documented fall in membership of political parties (50.4 percent decline between 1980 and 1998 in the USA). Nevertheless, the World Social Forum attracted some 150,000 people in 2005, on February 15, 2003, an estimated 30 million people gathered across the globe to protest against the Iraq war and in 2007 Earth Day enjoyed one billion participants.

The biological essentialism underpinning much universal rights theory is difficult to accept for many sociologists. Bryan S. Turner influentially proposed a sociological theory of human rights based on human frailty, collective sympathy and, crucially, "the historical implications of technological change for human existence and the increasingly risky nature of social life with globalisation" (1993: 508). There is a paradox of justice for a society of such globalized risk. On the one hand it is capable of producing new and extreme forms of social exclusion and inequality, where all characteristics of a group can be reduced to its level of risk. Nonetheless, it provides unprecedented opportunities for collective action amongst groups usually differentiated according to traditional identity types as they become aware of a common risk.

Ultimately, who defines "globalization" is of fundamental sociological interest with the ability to affect this understanding itself an issue of justice. The proliferation of cheap communication technologies has created the potential for nonpersons, those excluded by conventional media and political processes, to have a voice. Power relationships in this age are characterized by two features of these new technologies: (1) locally grounded while globally connected and (2) organized around networks not individual units (Castells 2009). Nevertheless, as more importance is invested in these technologies the threat of exclusion becomes more potent, especially as state control, processes of commodification and legal frameworks are only beginning to grapple with the wide-ranging effects of these modes of globalized communication.

SEE ALSO: Globalization; Global Justice as a Social Movement; Human Rights; Polanyi Karl; Social Justice, Theories of; Social Movement Organizations; Social Network Theory

REFERENCES

Castells, M. (2009) *Communication Power*. Oxford University Press, Oxford.

Turner, B. S. (1993) Outline of a theory on human rights. *Sociology* 27 (3): 489–512.

SUGGESTED READING

Beck, U. (2009) Critical theory of a world risk society: a cosmopolitan vision. *Constellations* 16 (1): 3–22.

JOSEPH PATRICK BURKE

glocalization

The neologism "glocalization" has emerged in recent years in economic, sociological, and cultural theories in response to the proliferation of writings about globalization and its local implications. It might best be described as the relationship between global and local processes, which are increasingly viewed as two sides to the same coin rather than being diametrically opposed.

Glocalization represents the intersection of political economics and sociocultural concerns, with its emphasis on the local and community impacts of global structures and processes. Ritzer (2004: 73) defines glocalization as "the integration of the global and the local resulting in unique outcomes in different geographic areas." Glocalization can thus represent the consequences (both tangible and intangible) of globalization, e.g., the creation of heterogeneous or hybridized cultures, communities, and identities.

Nevertheless, glocalization could also be viewed somewhat negatively. For example, Bauman (1998) suggests that the term glocalization is best thought of as a restratification of society based on the free mobility of some and the place-bound existence of others. Tourist flows, for example, are mainly unidirectional (e.g., west to east, or developed to less developed countries). For this reason, tourism has sometimes been described as a new form of imperialism, which causes acculturation and radical social change rather than hybridization (the inevitable consequence of sustained foreign influence over time). Similarly, global economic and business developments are often deemed "imperialistic," even where they have a local orientation.

Ritzer (2004) suggests that this dominance of capitalist nations and organizations might be termed "grobalization" rather than "glocalization." He argues, like Robertson (1994), that the key characteristics of glocalization are sensitivity to differences, the embracing of cosmopolitanism, and respect for the autonomy and creativity of individuals and groups. Overall, therefore, glocalization could be seen as a positive interpretation of the local impacts of globalization, that is, a process by which communities represent and assert their unique cultures globally, often through new media.

SEE ALSO: Cultural Imperialism; Globalization; Globalization, Culture and; Grobalization

REFERENCES

Bauman, Z. (1998) *Globalization: The Human Consequences.* Polity Press, Cambridge.

Ritzer, G. (2004) *The Globalization of Nothing.* Sage, London.

Robertson, R. (1994) Globalization or glocalization? *Journal of International Communication* 1: 33–52.

MELANIE SMITH

Goffman, Erving (1922–82)

Born in Mannville, Alberta, Canada, to Jewish migrants from the Ukraine, Goffman obtained degrees from the universities of Toronto (BA 1945) and Chicago (MA 1949; PhD 1953). His doctoral studies included fieldwork on the remote Shetland island of Unst. Following research posts at Chicago and at St. Elizabeth's Hospital, Washington, DC, he taught at the University of California, Berkeley from 1958 to 1968. Goffman then relocated to the University of Pennsylvania, where his work became increasingly sensitized to sociolinguistic and gender issues. He remained there until his death in 1982 from cancer.

Goffman demonstrated how the elements of the interaction order – the talk, gestures, expressions, and postures that humans constantly produce and readily recognize – were responsive not to individual psychology or social structural constraints but to the locally specific demands of the face-to-face social situation. This analytic aim was pursued through a number of papers and widely read books, including *The Presentation of Self in Everyday Life* (1959), *Asylums* (1961), *Stigma* (1963), and *Frame Analysis* (1974).

Goffman's sociological project bore the imprint of his training at the University of Chicago's famed sociology department. While Blumer was busy codifying "symbolic interactionism," Goffman critically absorbed its sources, often showing more regard for the thought of C. H. Cooley and J. Dewey than the ideas of G. H. Mead. Simmel's pioneering "sociational" conception of society that prioritized interactions between persons over large-scale structures and institutions was taken up by Goffman, as was his core method of extracting the "formal" features of sociation, which translated into analyses of a variety of forms of the interaction order, such as "face-work," the forms of alienation from interaction, or the stages of remedial interchange. Goffman creatively adapted the "symbolic" Durkheim of *The Elementary Forms of the Religious Life* (1912) to identify the "interaction rituals" everywhere present in social life. At Chicago Goffman was also influenced by literary theorist Kenneth Burke's method of "perspective by incongruity," evident in the many irreverent comparisons and unexpected contrasts that became a Goffman trademark.

Goffman saw his project as exploratory and provisional. Interaction analysis was at a stage where key conceptual distinctions were needed to chart this sociologically unexplored territory. While his writings displayed clear systematic intent, the drive to build a single system was absent.

Goffman burst onto the scene with the 1959 US publication of *Presentation of Self*, a book that breathed new life into the "all the world's a stage" metaphor. Goffman brilliantly analyzed the "dramaturgical" aspects of the expressions humans constantly "give" (through talk) and "give off" or exude (through tone, posture, gesture, and facial expression) when in the presence of others. Using a wide range of illustrative materials – ethnographies, histories, memoirs, popular journalism, novels and his own acute observations of human conduct – Goffman showed how interactional details could be sociologically understood as "performances" fostered on an "audience" requiring cooperative "teamwork" among performers to bring off a desired definition of the situation. A recurrent theme in his writings was that successful interaction needs not Parsonsian role-players but rather "interactants" skilled in "the arts of impression management."

The social self was for Goffman an abiding sociological referent. Critics sometimes complained of Goffman's "cynical" or "Machiavellian" view of human nature. Yet his ritual model, a secularized version of Durkheim's theory of religion, offered contrasting imagery centered upon the expression and control of the interactant's feelings towards both self and others. Here Goffman showed how greetings and farewells, apologies and avoidance practices all illustrated the need for persons to monitor their conduct when in the presence of that sacred deity, the self.

Goffman's analyses constantly distinguished out-of-awareness features of encounters that, once identified, become instantly recognizable. For example, a rule of "civil inattention" governs the conduct of unacquainted others on the street, persons silently walking past each other being likened to passing cars dipping their lights. Civil inattention belongs to a special class of social rules that regulate interaction known as "situational proprieties," departures from which Goffman found especially instructive. Situational *im*proprieties were less a matter of psychopathology as they were an expression of alienation from social establishments, social relationships, and encounters.

Goffman arrived at this conclusion following his monumental study of the plight of mental patients in *Asylums*, and his psychologically astute analysis of the identity implications of departures from normality in *Stigma*. The mental hospital belonged to a larger class of "total institutions" that included prisons, concentration camps, and monasteries. Social processes of "mortification" were common to them all. Mental patients underwent shared changes in self-conception – a shared "moral career" that was at once cause and consequence of their current predicament as they were sucked into a "betrayal funnel." Patients developed an underlife, rich in "secondary adjustments," which created space for conceptions of self at odds with those officially prescribed. *Asylums*, however, was not simply an influential critique of mental hospitals. It remains a vivid exploration of resistance to authority and the social sources of selfhood under extreme conditions.

Stigma also drew acclaim from outside academic sociology. It provided a careful analysis of normality and those temporarily or more extensively excluded from full social acceptance. The book anticipated contemporary identity politics and presented a powerful moral message.

Goffman deepened his perspective in his longest book, *Frame Analysis*, which provided a modulated phenomenological dimension to his sociology. Frames are perceptual principles that order events, sustained in both mind and activity. The theme reappeared in his last book, *Forms of Talk* (1981), where the concept of "footing" captured the shifting alignments of persons to their own and others' talk.

One of the more readable – and certainly one of the most quotable – of sociologists, Goffman's deceptively accessible writings can be understood in many ways. His sociology attracted extremes of assessment from extravagant commendation to outright dismissal. Goffman's writings conveyed a novel analytic attitude, a spirit of inquiry, and a highly distinctive voice that marked him out as one of the great figures of twentieth-century sociology.

SEE ALSO: Dramaturgy; Frame; Symbolic Interaction; Total Institutions

SUGGESTED READINGS

Branaman, A. & Lemert, C. (eds.) (1997) *The Goffman Reader*. Blackwell, Oxford.

Fine, G. A. & Smith, G. W. H. (eds.) (2000) *Erving Goffman*. Sage Masters of Modern Social Thought, 4 vols. Sage, London.

Smith, G. W. H. (2005) *Erving Goffman*. Routledge, London.

Waksler, F. (ed.) (1989) *Human Studies* 12 (1–2). Special Issue: Erving Goffman's Sociology.

GREGORY W. H. SMITH

Gramsci, Antonio (1891–1937)

Antonio Gramsci was leader of the Italian Communist Party and Italy's leading Marxist theorist. While jailed by fascism (1927–37) he filled 29 notebooks with fragmentary comments on many subjects.

Gramsci was provoked by Bukharin's *Historical Materialism: A Popular Textbook of Marxist Sociology* (1921), which stated that historical materialism was a sociology, thus departing from the Marxist-Leninist orthodoxy that sociology was simply a bourgeois science and relying heavily on the sociological masters, particularly Pareto's equilibrium theory. Gramsci critiqued this theory and the converse views of Henri de Man. He developed an understanding of sociology and its limits, denied that historical materialism is a sociology and yet intimated that it might contain one.

Asking "What is sociology?" Gramsci stated that it had been an attempt to create a scientific method for explaining history and politics based on evolutionary positivism. It could not grasp any social transformation that was qualitative. He regarded technological determinism as nonsense. To the calculable material presence there must be added that complex of passions and imperious sentiment that lead to action. He had great reservations about the "laws of large numbers" and statistical series, while admitting that when social groups and structures are relatively unchanging and "passive," statistical inquiry might have some validity. Scientific historical theory has no force until taken up by great masses and made "practical," meaning that foresight is made true only because great masses of humans act as if it were.

Gramsci wished to study "popular belief," which brought him closest to the traditional concerns of some Italian and European sociology. What concerned him was how the common sense of the "passive" group could become "good sense." On this, he regarded de Man as inferior to both Proudhon and Sorel because he took the position of a determinist scientist – a zoologist studying a world of insects – who studied popular feelings and did not feel *with* them to guide and lead them to catharsis. Yet de Man's *Il superamento di Marx* stimulated us to inform ourselves about the real feelings of groups and individuals and not the feelings that sociological laws suggest exist. To accept as eternal what was thought by the mass would be the worst form of fatalism. De Man's work resulted in a commonplace based on the error that theory and practice can be separate and not act on each other constantly.

SUGGESTED READINGS

Buttigieg, J. (ed.) (1992) *Antonio Gramsci: Prison Notebooks*. Columbia University Press, New York.
Gramsci, A. (1971) *Lettere dal carcere*. Einaudi, Turin.
Gramsci, A. (2001) *Quaderni del carcere*, 4 vols. Einaudi, Turin.
Hoare, Q. & Nowell-Smith, G. (eds.) (1973) *Selections from the Prison Notebooks of Antonio Gramsci*. International Publishers, New York.

ALASTAIR DAVIDSON

grobalization

Grobalization is a term coined by sociologist George Ritzer (2004) in his book *The Globalization of Nothing*. It is meant to serve as a companion to the widely employed concept of glocalization. While glocalization represents the unique combinations resulting from the interpenetration of the global and the local, grobalization represents "the imperialistic ambitions of nations, corporations, organizations, and the like and their desire, indeed need, to impose themselves on various geographic areas" (p. 73). Thus, glocalization would be most closely associated with postmodern, pluralistic ideas of heterogeneity, whereas grobalization represents a more modern, imperialistic, and homogenizing perspective.

Grobalization theorists would generally argue that the world is becoming increasingly less diverse as transnational economic, cultural, political, and social entities seek to impose their influence throughout the world. The agent in this perspective has relatively little power to maneuver within, between, or around structures. Their ability to construct their own identity and world is seriously impinged on by the growing forces of grobal powers, particularly commodities and the media. Social processes are deterministic and overwhelm the local, limiting its ability to interact with, much less act back against, the global.

Although grobalization encompasses a number of subprocesses, the main three are Americanization, McDonaldization, and capitalism (Ritzer & Ryan 2003). The quest for profits under capitalism, the most powerful of the subprocesses, has led corporations to seek ever-expanding global markets. The process of McDonaldization has facilitated the expansion of corporate entities and cultural patterns. Americanization can be closely tied to the dominant influence of the USA in the world today. Taken together, these three subprocesses constitute some of the main drivers of grobalization.

SEE ALSO: Globalization; Globalization, Consumption and; Glocalization; McDonaldization

REFERENCES

Ritzer, G. (2004) *The Globalization of Nothing*. Pine Forge Press, Thousand Oaks, CA.
Ritzer, G. & Ryan, J. M. (2003) Toward a richer understanding of global commodification: glocalization and grobalization. *Hedgehog Review* 5 (2): 66–76.

J. MICHAEL RYAN

grounded theory

The term grounded theory refers to systematic guidelines for data gathering, coding, synthesizing, categorizing, and integrating concepts to generate middle-range theory. Data collection and analysis proceed simultaneously and each informs the other. In their cutting-edge book, *The Discovery of Grounded Theory* (1967), Barney G. Glaser and

Anselm L. Strauss proposed that: (1) qualitative inquiry could make significant theoretical and empirical contributions, rather than merely serve as a precursor to quantitative research; (2) researchers could codify qualitative analysis in systematic ways; and (3) the divide between theory and methods was artificial.

Glaser built on his quantitative training at Columbia University with its underpinnings in positivism and assumptions about discovery, externality, neutrality, and parsimony. Strauss brought Chicago School traditions of ethnographic fieldwork, pragmatist philosophy, and symbolic interactionism to grounded theory. Later divisions between Glaser and Strauss, their separate versions of grounded theory, and a new variant of it make grounded theory a contested method. Despite epistemological and practice differences, all grounded theorists assume that: (1) theory construction is a major objective of grounded theory, (2) the logic of grounded theory differs from quantitative research, and (3) the grounded theory emerges from rigorous data analysis, not from adopting preconceived theories. When involved in conducting their studies, diverse grounded theorists agree on the following strategies: (1) collecting and analyzing data simultaneously; (2) using comparative methods during each analytic stage; (3) devising analytic categories early in the research process; (4) engaging in analytic writing throughout; and (5) sampling for the purpose of developing ideas.

Coding in grounded theory is at least a two-phased process: *initial* and *focused*. During initial coding, researchers ask: "What category does this incident indicate? What is actually happening in the data?" (Glaser 1978: 57). Close examination of data combined with comparisons between data prompts researchers to see their data in new ways. Initial coding also alerts the researcher to potential *in vivo* codes given in the setting or in participants' direct statements. As researchers engage in comparing and coding data, certain codes assume greater analytic power than other codes and often appear more frequently. They select these codes as focused codes to sift through large batches of data. This coding also provides the grist to interrogate the data and to contemplate what's missing in it.

Memowriting is the pivotal intermediate strategy that bridges coding and report writing. Memos are analytic notes covering all the researcher's ideas and questions about the codes that occur at the moment. In early memos, grounded theorists raise certain codes to preliminary categories and then explore them. In later memos, they develop specific categories through making incisive comparisons, and begin to integrate their categories. Hence, they compare category with category, as well as compare data with the relevant category.

After establishing analytic categories, researchers typically need to seek more data to fill out these categories through *theoretical sampling*, a selective, systematic, and strategic way of gathering specific additional data. Theoretical sampling increases the definitiveness, generality, and usefulness of the emerging theory.

Strauss and Corbin's *Basics of Qualitative Research* (1990) revised grounded theory. They introduced new techniques, treated grounded theory as a set of procedures, and advocated verification. Glaser (1992) repudiated their approach. He viewed grounded theory as a method of theory construction, not of verification, and saw their innovations as forcing data into preconceived categories.

The next major revision of grounded theory emerged when Charmaz (2006) distinguished between constructivist grounded theory and the earlier versions. Constructivist grounded theory: (1) places priority on the studied phenomenon rather than techniques of studying it; (2) takes reflexivity and research relationships into account; (3) assumes that both data and analyses are social constructions; (4) studies how participants create meanings and actions; (5) seeks an insider's view to the extent possible; and (6) acknowledges that analyses are contextually situated in time, place, culture, and situation.

SEE ALSO: Induction and Observation in Science; Interviewing: Structured, Unstructured, and Postmodern; Methods, Mixed; Theory Construction

REFERENCES

Charmaz, K. (2006) *Constructing Grounded Theory: A Practical Guide Through Qualitative Analysis.* Sage, London.

Glaser, B. G. (1978) *Theoretical Sensitivity.* Sociology Press, Mill Valley, CA.

Glaser, B. G. (1992) *Basics of Grounded Theory Analysis.* Sociology Press, Mill Valley, CA.

Strauss, A. L. & Corbin, J. (1990) *Basics of Qualitative Research: Grounded Theory Procedures and Techniques.* Sage, Newbury Park, CA.

KATHY CHARMAZ

group processes

Sociology's group processes perspective is characterized by theoretical development and basic research on fundamental social processes that occur in group contexts. Work in the group processes tradition dates to scholars who were interested in the interactions of individuals in small groups. As the perspective has developed, its focus has largely evolved to an interest in the processes that occur in group contexts rather than in groups themselves.

A focus on group processes, of course, implies an interest in two things – groups and processes. As the group processes perspective has developed, the focus of the area has shifted to a greater interest in processes than in the groups in which the processes occur. In large part because of the perspective's roots in the classification of behavior in small groups, however, sociologists not in the group processes perspective will frequently treat studying "small groups" and studying "group processes" as interchangeable.

What interests those in the group processes perspective is how various social processes operate in groups. The groups in which the processes operate need not be small. Two of the processes that dominate work in the perspective are power and status. These processes occur in groups both large and small, and they provide examples of the perspective's major focus on processes that occur in groups rather than on the groups in which processes occur.

Power, in simple terms, is the ability to control resources that people value. Your boss, for example, has the ability to fire you from your job. If you value your job, this ability gives your boss power. Early treatments of power generally focused on the characteristics of powerful people that made them powerful. This research was limited by the fact that almost anyone put in the right position can be powerful. In other words, nothing about your boss herself gives her power over you. Your boss's power comes not from individual traits but instead from a position in a structure. Group processes scholars focus their efforts on discovering the conditions of groups rather than of people that give rise to power differences. Note that the groups in which these conditions arise need not be small. The president of a university, for example, has power (the ability to control resources) over a group (the university's employees and students) because of her structural position.

Status is a position in a group based on esteem or respect. Perhaps the most well-developed group processes theory is a theory of status named *status characteristics theory* (Berger et al. 1977). Status, like power, is relative; in other words, people do not have status or power in and of themselves, but instead only in relation to other people. It is meaningless to say that medical doctors are high in status, for example, except in the context of other, lower-status occupations.

Status characteristics theory specifies the processes that lead some people to have more status in groups than others. According to the theory, status orders in groups develop out of the characteristics held by group members. Examples of status characteristics include gender, age, appearance, race, and education. Status characteristics theory proposes that individuals act as though they develop performance expectations consistent with larger cultural beliefs about the characteristics held by themselves and other group members. Members with characteristics accorded higher expectations have higher-status positions in the group and are likely to be evaluated more highly than others and to have more influence.

SEE ALSO: Exchange Network Theory; Groups; Power; Social Psychology; Status

REFERENCE

Berger, J., Hamit Fisek, M., Norman, R. Z., & Zelditch, M., Jr. (1977) *Status Characteristics and Social Interaction: An Expectation States Approach.* Elsevier, New York.

SUGGESTED READING

Bales, R. F. (1950) *Interaction Process Analysis: A Method for the Study of Small Groups.* Addison-Wesley, Reading, MA.

JEFFREY W. LUCAS

groups

The term "group" can refer to small, face-to-face groups or large, formal organizations. Collectivities, a third type of group, are defined by observable attributes (such as race or age), or by common interests (such as hunting or farming). Crowds are a special type of collectivity that brings individuals together in the same location at the same time. Some crowds can share a focus of attention that can produce a temporary feeling of cohesion. Workers, shoppers, and tourists who overflow city street at closing time are a crowd whose members display a rudimentary form of social organization in which individuals will generally keep both bodily and eye contact to a respectful minimum as they maneuver along crowded sidewalks.

Georg Simmel called attention to the significance between a group of two persons, and a group of three persons. If one person leaves a two-person group, the group ceases to exist. In three-person groups, one person may leave, and the remaining two may still constitute a group. In principle, a small group can last indefinitely if old members are replaced by new ones. The potential for a group to persist has been used to investigate the way group practices turn to norms as groups change over time.

In the 1930s and 1940s there were several innovations in the study of groups. Lewin, Lippitt, and White invigorated the field of social psychology in an experimental study with obvious references to the threat posed by Hitler to democratic regimes. At the same time, W. W. Whyte published his path breaking study of a small, street-corner gang exposing the gang's internal structure as it was related to the larger community. J. L. Moreno asked members of small groups simple questions, such as "Who are the persons in this group who are your three best friends and who are your three favored co-workers?" He plotted the results in a sociogram where each individual is represented by a dot on a piece of paper, and lines connecting the dots display a visual pattern of friendship and work relations within the group. The graphing of subjective preferences has now been transformed into mathematical theories that capture unsuspected regularities in contacts across the world wide web.

In the 1950s R. F. Bales, particularly in his collaboration with the dominant sociological theorist of the time, Talcott Parsons, created a short-lived synthesis of self, society and small groups. George Homans provided a major alternative to Parson-Bales' structural-functional orientation when he explained the interpersonal dynamics of a professional work group in terms of "social behavior as exchange." Homans observed that less competent workers in the group continually asked for help from a more accomplished co-worker, and in return the co-worker received deferential treatment. This study enlarged the theoretical boundaries of economic exchanges to encompass accounts of social exchanges.

George Herbert Mead shifted the emphasis from groups as foundational social units by proposing that human relations form when individuals learn to "take the role of the other." Later theorists would embrace the perspective of interaction-as-communication without paying particular attention to the structure of concrete groups in which interactions take place. Erving Goffman began a series of publications on what he was later to call the "interaction order." Inspired by anthropological accounts of ritual behavior, he saw repair work in everyday life as having a ritual quality that restored social order when everyday disputes threatened a group's functional cohesion. At the same time, Howard Garfinkel rejected the concept of social norms claiming that ordinary practices create and recreate social order as a living, ongoing achievement of everyday life. Dorothy Smith found Garfunkel's studies congenial to the problems faced by women who lived in a world of concepts developed by men who had conceptually marginalized women in everyday life.

SEE ALSO: Dyad/Triad; Goffman, Erving; Group Processes; In-Groups and Out-Groups; Mead, George Herbert; Parsons, Talcott

SUGGESTED READINGS

Goffman, E. (1967) *Interaction Ritual: Essays on Face-To-Face Interaction*. Doubleday-Anchor, Garden City, NY.

Whyte, W. W. (1943) *Street Corner Society*. University of Chicago Press, Chicago, IL.

WILLIAM BEZDEK

gun control, gun crime

Gun crimes – or firearms offenses – are never far away from the headlines in the USA – and other countries with high levels of gun ownership. Incidents such as the Virginia Tech Shootings in 2007, and the Columbine High School shootings in 1999 are examples of what some have called "the firearm epidemic" (Cukier and Sidel 2006: 3).

Overall, research has been divided into two schools – those who believe that guns deter crime and those who argue that more guns increase the risk of being a victim of a firearm offense. Criminologists subscribing to the latter view argue that there is a positive and numerical correlation between the number of firearm offenses and the availability of guns. Thus, the number of deaths caused by gunshots is consistently higher in countries with high rates of gun ownership. For example, in the USA there were 8,259 homicides in 2006 (roughly 10 to every 1,000 people) in a country where 85 percent of people own a gun. By comparison there were only 62 homicides in England and Wales (1 to every 1,000 people) in a country where only 3 percent own a gun and where all handguns are banned. This relationship has been corroborated by more detailed studies. A study (which examined the link between gun ownership rates in Canada, the USA, England and Wales, and Australia) concluded that 92 percent of the variance in death rates could be explained by differences in access to firearms (Killias 1993). However, one must be cautious not to make simple comparisons as the methods of data reporting and collection differ between countries. Gun control is a controversial issue and different groups have vested interests in making the figures appear, respectively, higher or lower. For example, figures from the National Rifle Association differ from those reported by the Gun-Control Network.

Another school of thought rejects this and argues that it is the other way round. In *More Guns. Less Crime*, John Lott (2000) has proposed that, if an increasing number of private citizens carry firearms this will deter crime as criminals are not keen on the possibility of being shot by their victims. This research has, however, been criticized on methodological grounds (Black and Nagin 1998: 218).

Gun crime also has social and economic costs. It has been estimated that the economic cost of every non-fatal gun crime is $30,500 for every injured person (Cook and Ludwig 2000).

SEE ALSO: Crime; Law, Sociology of; Violent Crime

REFERENCES

Black, D. & Nagin, D. (1998) Do right-to-carry laws deter violent crime? *Journal of Legal Studies* 27 (1): 209–19.

Cook, P. & Ludwig, J. (2000) *Gun Violence: The Real Costs*. Oxford University Press, London.

Cukier, W. & Sidel, V. W. (2006) *The Global Gun Epidemic: From Saturday Night Specials to AK-47s*. Praeger International, Westport, CT.

Killias, M. (1993) International correlations between gun ownership and rates of homicide and suicide. *Canadian Medical Association Journal* 148 (May): 1721–5.

Lott, J. R., Jr. (2000) *More Guns. Less Crime: Understanding Crime and Gun Control Laws*. University of Chicago Press, Chicago, IL.

MATT QVORTRUP

H

habitus/field

In the first chapter of *Outline of a Theory of Practice* (1977) Bourdieu explicitly addresses the problems inherent in limiting our understanding of human society to the false distinctions that represent typical sociological explanations – particularly, the distinctions between objective versus subjective and structure versus agency. He argues that the structure of society (as represented by social institutions and macro-structures) is far more dynamic than is normally portrayed, and that human agency has far more input in shaping social structures and social institutions than is normally discussed by sociologists. This discussion provides a natural segue to his discussion of habitus in the second chapter. Habitus epitomizes Bourdieu's interest in linking phenomenological and symbolic interactionist perspectives (sometimes equated with the subjectivist view) with the more structuralist approach (sometimes equated with the objectivist view) of American and some European sociologists. Additionally, habitus also illustrates the intimate connection between structure and agency as represented in the social actor, where the social actor can be an individual, a group, or any large collectivity.

Bourdieu defines habitus as the way in which actors calculate and determine future actions based on existing norms, rules, and values representing existing conditions. It is important to understand key aspects of habitus. One key element of this definition is that Bourdieu argues that existing norms, rules, and values have been mentally and cognitively integrated into the actor's frame of reference, and that they represent general social standards as well as specific situational and personal experiences. This illustrates his way of integrating the macro-elements of a structured social world that imposes its will on actors with the dynamic agency that enables actors to engage in individually determined actions. Additionally, this illustrates the integration of an objective reality created by existing structural elements in society with the subjective reality of the social actor. A second key element of habitus is that "future" actions refer to a range of possible actions, from what you do immediately upon reading this entry to what you might plan to do on your next vacation. Bourdieu states that social actors engage in a continuously dynamic interaction with their environment and other actors such that they are aware of negotiating from a range of possible actions to take. A third key element associated with his definition of habitus is that, in identifying actors' agency in calculating actions, Bourdieu explains that this process is rational in that it takes into account potential outcomes for any specific action as well as something other than rational in that it also takes into account subjective motivations. In other words, habitus reflects actors' emotional and spontaneous reactions to particular situations and the other actors involved. The final key element of the idea of habitus is that it represents a fluid set of guiding principles for the social actor. While actors in similar positions in society may share similar habitus, as their environment and the other actors in the environment change, so does the habitus. It is consistent across actors, which allows us to understand particular settings and cultures as well as what is unique to each individual.

Bourdieu's idea of field also serves to demonstrate the intimate connection between objective and subjective realities as well as between structure and agency. His discussion of fields also integrates a Marxist focus on conflictual relations with a Weberian focus on formal hierarchies. Fields represent the network of relations between and among positions actors hold within particular structural or organizational systems. For example, Bourdieu examines artistic or literary fields and he describes them in terms of the positions actors hold relative to one another. Additionally, he argues that there are several hierarchies of fields as well as hierarchies within each field. The specific positions held by actors linked in terms of similar structural or organizational systems are embedded in fields of power, which are then embedded in fields of class relations. The connection to Marxist and Weberian ideas is immediately evident when you view the field as a set of interconnecting positions that occur on several different levels – similar to 3-D chess, where the players must be aware of not only the first board, but also how the chess pieces on two other levels of boards are interacting with, and affecting, the primary or first board.

SEE ALSO: Agency (and Intention); Bourdieu, Pierre; Structure and Agency

REFERENCE

Bourdieu, P. (1977) *Outline of a Theory of Practice*. Cambridge University Press, New York.

ANNE F. EISENBERG

hate crimes

The term *hate crimes* has been employed since the mid-1980s to identify criminal acts motivated either entirely or in part by the fact or perception that a victim is different from the perpetrator in socially significant ways. In legal terms, the groups protected by hate crime laws differ from state to state. Some statutes prohibit hate crime behavior directly; others increase the penalty for committing a particular offense. In 2009, consistency was achieved by the expansion of a federal hate crimes statute, allowing federal prosecution of crimes based not only on race, religion, and national origin but also sexual orientation, gender, gender identity, and disability status.

In terms of offender motivation, hate crimes can be categorized as four major types (Levin & McDevitt 2001): (1) *thrill* which are recreational attacks committed by youngsters – usually groups of teenagers or young adults – who seek excitement as well as "bragging rights" with their friends; (2) *defensive* which are designed to protect an individual's neighborhood, workplace, school, or women from those who are considered to be outsiders; (3) *retaliatory* which are motivated by an individual's need for revenge as a result of a hate attack directed against his or her own group members; and (4) *mission* which are usually committed by the members of an organized hate group.

Actually, no more than 5 percent of all hate crimes nationally are committed by the members of organizations like the Ku Klux Klan or the White Aryan Resistance. Yet through their presence on the Internet, organized hate groups continue behind the scenes to support much larger numbers of violent offenses committed by non-members who may be unsophisticated with respect to the ideology of hate, but are looking to feel important and a sense of belonging.

SEE ALSO: Deviance, Crime and; Homophobia; Violent Crime

REFERENCE

Levin, J. & McDevitt, J. (2001) *Hate Crimes Revisited*. Westview Press, Boulder, CO.

SUGGESTED READINGS

Levin, J. & Nolan, J. (2010) *The Violence of Hate*. Allyn and Bacon, Boston, MA.

JACK LEVIN

Hawthorne effect

The Hawthorne effect refers to the possibility that subjects in a research project may modify their behavior in a positive manner simply as a result of being aware of being studied. This concept takes its name from studies conducted from 1924 to 1933 at the Western Electric Company's Hawthorne plant near Chicago. The specific research associated with the Hawthorne effect was the first step among several and was conducted by engineers at the plant from 1924 to 1927. This experiment involved increasing the lighting within a work area, using both experimental and control groups. Measuring worker output before and after the change in lighting showed an increase in productivity in *both* the experimental and control groups. Additional experiments with results along these lines led the researchers to conclude that increased worker output occurred simply because of increased attention directed toward the workers. It was at this point that Elton Mayo of Harvard University entered the research, and the focus moved from simple variation in illumination to a variety of alterations in actual worker activity. As a whole, the research provided the initial grounding for Mayo to create the *human relations movement*, particularly in complex organizations.

Later research has raised considerable doubts about whether the conclusions drawn across the studies as a whole are supported from the data. Subsequent studies show that the Hawthorne effect has a variety of limits and may also have been influenced by its novelty at the time. Nevertheless, the implications associated with the Hawthorne effect have been extended beyond classical experimental designs, which are relatively rare in sociology, to issues within survey research and to applied sociology by being incorporated into consultative approaches to labor management and productivity.

SEE ALSO: Experimental Design; Work, Sociology of

SUGGESTED READINGS

Franke, R. H. & Kaul, J. D. (1978) The Hawthorne experiments. *American Sociological Review* 43: 623–43.

Roethlisberger, F. J. & Dickson, W. J. (1939) *Management and the Worker*. Harvard University Press, Cambridge, MA.

WILLIAM H. SWATOS, JR.

health and culture

Health is generally defined as a state of well-being (physical and/or psychological), but sociological theories differ in their interpretation of the social meaning of illness. For example, as Gerhardt (1989) pointed out, structural-functionalism assigns responsibility for one's health to the individual; symbolic interaction theory sees illness in terms of stigmatization and proposes that societal and cultural influences impinge upon individuals' perception of health, self-determination, and ability to negotiate their situation; phenomenology sees the situation as "trouble-trust dialectics"; and conflict theory addresses the questions of power and domination and associates illness with a surfacing of the everyday conflict that results from social, "political, and economic inequity," an argument also pursued by Marxist and neo-Marxist approaches. Of these theories, symbolic interaction incorporates culture most directly, mainly in the form of socially constructed and subjectively perceived meanings of illness, definitions of illness severity, and labeling. Health behavior studies using social psychology theories (such as the health belief model, protection motivation theory, self-efficacy theory, and the theory of reasoned action) and approaches on social networks and help-seeking behavior (e.g., Levy and Pescosolido 2002) are now paying more attention to the relevance of culture.

The inclusion of culture (subjects' values, beliefs, and customs) in research designs means asking how culture impinges upon people's subjective perception of health, illness, power, and stigma; upon the meaning they attach to illness and health; upon their sense of trust, normality, and deviance; and upon their health behavior. Increased interest in the cultural dimension of health has been prompted since the 1940s by socio-political upheavals; major movements of populations as the result of forced and free migration (leading to higher rates of ethnic minorities in the developed world); substantial changes in people's lifestyle (such as diet, rate of physical activity, leisure activities, and high stress levels); demographic trends including the incidence of chronic diseases (e.g., cardiovascular diseases); and epidemics affecting a multitude of culturally diverse communities, for example HIV/AIDS and outbreaks of infectious diseases like SARS (severe acute respiratory syndrome).

Based on their principal unit of inquiry, studies of culture and health are of three types. The first type includes studies on the sources of illness as well as people's health-related behavior, attitudes, and beliefs through the health–illness trajectory: preventive health behavior, illness behavior, and sick-role behavior. The second type includes studies on the sources of healing, addressing the role of healers, groups, networks, and organizations whose main objective is helping the sick or safeguarding the health of others. The third category includes studies using the comparative pragmatic acculturation perspective (the borrowing of ideas and procedures from other cultures to solve specific problems) whereby both the users and the providers of healing are the focus of analysis. Pragmatic acculturation studies (Quah 2003) suggest that comparative research can provide more effective understanding of the permeability of cultural boundaries and its effect on health; of the permanent or temporary transformation in belief systems; and of the ways in which cultural beliefs and norms influence accounts of disease incidence and prevalence across communities and countries.

SEE ALSO: Health and Medicine; Health, Neighborhood Disadvantage; Health and Race

REFERENCES

Gerhardt, U. (1989) *Ideas about Illness: An Intellectual and Political History of Medical Sociology*. New York University Press, New York.
Levy, J. & Pescosolido, B. (eds.) (2002) *Social Networks and Health*. JAI Press, New York.
Quah, S. R. (2003) Traditional healing systems and the ethos of science. *Social Science and Medicine* 57: 1997–2012.

SUGGESTED READING

Stone, J. & Dennis, R. (2003) *Race and Ethnicity: Comparative and Theoretical Approaches*. Blackwell, Oxford.

STELLA QUAH

health and medicine

The origins of a sociology of medicine can be traced back to German physician Rudolf Virchow, who maintained that medicine was a social science and should be used to improve social conditions. Many years ago, medical historian Henry Sigerist (1946: 130) advocated incorporation of social science into medical curricula, arguing that "Social medicine is not so much a technique as rather an attitude and approach to the problems of medicine."

While there is a growing awareness that patient care decisions are not purely medical, the coming together of sociology and medicine remains elusory. There seems to be little application of social knowledge, despite the fact that sociology clearly can inform the clinician's view of the problem. However, applicable sociology still largely is thought to be too abstract and uncertain to be helpful.

Although we know much about the volume and cost of medical care utilization, there is less explanation of its cause and variation. The relationship between patients' health and their use of medical services is influenced by class, race, and other social variables.

Previous work mostly includes "users" of health care services when testing health care-seeking patterns. But this means that studies focusing on only users of health services are really measuring *frequency of use* rather than the broader issue of who is using and *not* using health services. The decision to go to a doctor is the result of an interpretive process, taking place within the social structural parameters. Factors other than need are important in health care utilization.

Health behaviors are ultimately influenced by how people think about their health. Individuals who place greater value on health potentially have different utilization patterns than those who attach less value. Indeed, individuals with greater confidence in their ability to influence their own health and those who are somewhat skeptical of medical science or distrust doctors are less likely to consult professionals. Moreover, sociological studies have primarily utilized self-reported measures, which may or may not correspond with actual health behavior. The latter is an important area of future inquiry.

Material considerations such as socioeconomic status and the lack of access to care that attends particular class strata are critical for understanding contemporary health disparities. But also, symbolic and cultural definitions of health are salient and vary by social structural context such as race and class. These too are critical to understanding how patients and providers do or do not connect and in turn to understanding differences in health perceptions, behaviors, and care. The presentation of health information must take into account patients' knowledge and values or it may create misunderstandings about treatment and prevention strategies. Moreover, patients may further aggravate their health by failing to follow treatment plans.

We may expect to see increasing use of home health care services as the "baby boomer" generation ages. This will necessitate the integration of formal and informal health care structures. Home-based formal support services may be the critical link to reducing burden of family members, but such services should also enhance those informal support systems. Formal care providers may have to take responsibility for what goes on outside the clinic. Current drives for universal health care are based on the premise that traditional biocentric medicine must expand its domain to include health promotion and prevention to be effective. Similarly, the scope of services can be broadened to include meaningful assistance to informal caregivers.

Proponents of alternative orientations toward the practice of medicine (and medical sociology) would like to see the emergence of new approaches and broadening conceptualizations of health and medicine, based on both traditional scientific methodology and new ways of knowing. Sociology can be at the center of an integrative network of health and illness. However, it will fall on sociologists to find ways of dealing with differences in our conceptual languages in order to infiltrate medicine and other physical and mental health settings, since invitations are not abundantly forthcoming.

SEE ALSO: Complementary and Alternative Medicine; Health Care Delivery Systems; Health and Culture; Health and Race; Medical Sociology; Medicine, Sociology of; Sociology in Medicine

REFERENCE

Sigerist, H. E. (1946) *The University at the Crossroads*. Henry Shuman, New York.

SUGGESTED READINGS

Clair, J. M. & Allman, R. M. (eds.) (1993) *Sociomedical Perspectives on Patient Care*. University Press of Kentucky, Lexington, KY.

Cockerham, W. (2007) *Medical Sociology*. Prentice Hall, Upper Saddle River, NJ.

JEFFREY MICHAEL CLAIR AND JASON WASSERMAN

health care delivery systems

A health care delivery system is the organized response of a society to the health problems of its inhabitants. Longitudinally, widespread kinship-based arrangements for survival were gradually supplemented and replaced by collective arrangements. This culminated in a *demographic transition* consisting of the reduction of a population's fertility. In modern societies it was no longer imperative to have many children as a provision against old-age poverty. In the course of this modernization process, the *epidemiological transition* took place that reflected a gradual shift from the sheer necessity to overcome infectious diseases (mainly affecting infants) toward dealing with chronic diseases (primarily affecting the late middle aged and elderly). Modern health care delivery systems require extensive financial resources which only advanced economies are able to put aside. Evidently, there is a strong association between health and wealth. In low-income countries hygiene, sanitation, vaccination, nutrition, and immunization are the important objectives for health care. Modern societies, with higher average levels of income, largely have to cope with rising costs due to the increasing demand for chronic care, as a consequence of an aging population.

In typifying a nation's health system the role of the state in funding is decisive:

- *Largely absent*: the state propagates non-interventionism, leaving room primarily for private insurance to fill this role.
- *In-between*: the state harmonizes the arrangements that developed between groups of citizens (e.g., employers, employees).
- *Central*: the state controls funding, *with* or *without* the provision of health care.

The *free market* model applies when the state conducts a policy of non-interventionism and restricts its interference in health care matters to the bare essentials, leaving all other expenses to private funding and corporate provision (HMOs). This is the typical situation in the USA, except for Medicaid (indigent) and Medicare (elderly) state interventions. Private insurance fills the gap to some degree, however, leaving about 15 percent of the US population uninsured for health care costs or loss of income due to illness and disability.

In the *social insurance system* patients pay an insurance premium to a sickness fund which has a contract with first-line (GP) and second-line (hospital and specialist) providers. The role of the state is confined to setting the overall terms of contracts between patients, providers, and insurers. Founded in Germany, the social insurance system still exists in a modified fashion in Germany, the Netherlands, Belgium, France, Austria, Switzerland, Luxembourg, and Japan.

The third model, typically found in the UK, is the tax-based *National Health Service (NHS) model*. It was first introduced in 1948, is also centralized and is funded by means of taxation, while the state is responsible for the provision of institution-based care (hospitals). The medical profession has a rather independent position. Self-employed GPs are the gatekeepers in primary health care. Currently the NHS model applies to the UK, Ireland, Denmark, Norway, Sweden, Finland, Iceland, and outside Europe to Australia and New Zealand. Four Southern European countries (Spain, Italy, Portugal, and Greece) have also adopted this tax-based model.

The fourth, most centralized health care delivery system model, the *Soviet model*, dates from 1920. It is characterized by a strong position of the state, guaranteeing full and free access to health care for everyone. This is realized by state ownership of health care facilities, by funding from the state budget (taxes), and by geographical distribution and provision of services throughout the country. Health services are fully hierarchically organized. They are provided by state employees, planned by hierarchical provision, and organized as a hierarchy of hospitals, with outpatient clinics (polyclinics) as lowest levels of entrance. Among the nations that, at least until recently, had a health care system based on the Soviet model were Russia, Belarus, the Central Asian republics of the former USSR, and some countries in Central and Eastern Europe. Many former Soviet Republics, however, are in a process of transition toward a social insurance-based system. Outside Europe the socialized Cuban health-care system remained largely intact, due to the government's support and grassroots organizations-based networks of solidarity. Also China used to have the now largely extinct twentieth-century communist health care system but moved to a private one (and its typical failures).

The four models make up a continuum in terms of their "system" character, with state interventionism and centralized health care at one end, and non-interventionism at the other. Centralized systems provide the best mechanisms for cost control, while absence of state intervention does not appear to be fruitful, as soaring costs in the USA evidently show. The four health delivery system models also reflect stages and outcomes of a historical process. Consequently, system models that came into existence in highly developed economies in the first half of the twentieth century can now still provide useful options to choose from in low-income countries or transitional economies like in Eastern European societies.

Contingencies like increasing health care costs, an aging population, changing disease patterns, technological developments, growing public demand, and so forth impose a common logic in terms of institutional performance and the structuring of modern health care. Yet the convergence of modern health care delivery systems is not undisputed. Differences exist in degree and similarity of these developments. National health delivery systems are the outcome of a dialectical tension between universal aspects of technology and medicine on the one hand, and particularistic cultural characteristics of each nation on the other. Health care institutions are still largely country specific. Such country specific elements would include social, economic, institutional, and ideological structures, the dominant belief system, the role of the state versus the market, patterns of health care coverage, and centralization or decentralization of political authority.

SEE ALSO: Health and Culture; Health Maintenance Organization; Socialist Medicine; Socialized Medicine

SUGGESTED READINGS

Stevens, F. C. J. and van der Zee, J. (2008) Health system organization models (including targets and goals for health systems). In: Heggenhougen, K. and Quah, S. (eds.), *International Encyclopedia of Public Health*, vol. 3. Academic Press, San Diego, CA, pp. 247–56.

Stevens, F. C. J. (2009) The convergence and divergence of modern health care systems. In: Cockerham, W. C. (ed.), *The New Blackwell Companion to Medical Sociology*. Wiley-Blackwell, Oxford.

Van der Zee J., Boerma, W. G. W., and Kroneman, M. W. (2004) Health care systems: understanding the stages of development. In: Jones, R., Britten, N., Culpepper, L., et al. (eds.), *Oxford Textbook of Primary Medical Care*, vol. 1. Oxford University Press, Oxford, pp. 51–5.

FRED STEVENS AND JOUKE VAN DER ZEE

Hegel, G. W. F. (1770–1831)

Seeking to overcome the barriers to Absolute Knowledge that Descartes and Kant erected, Georg Hegel's key works – the *Phenomenology of Spirit* (1804), *Science of Logic* (1812–16) and *Encyclopedia of Philosophy* (1817) – made him Prussia's foremost post-Kantian, idealist philosopher.

Hegel served as a critical foil to Marx's most important intellectual developments beginning with Marx's critique of Hegel's *Philosophy of Right*. Hegel argued that a constitutional state, with an impartial civil service, using the principles of Reason, would act in the interests of all and create a stable, historically evolving, social order. Marx criticized Hegel's oversight of class interests and his presentation of the real subject of history – human actors – as a passive predicate and the real predicate – the state and civil society – as the acting force. This critique, which identified the proletariat as the real revolutionary subject of bourgeois society, began to distance Marx from his Hegelian roots.

In the *Phenomenology*, Hegel argued that through self-reflexive interaction with the external, phenomenal world, the human mind/Spirit develops through several stages – consciousness, self-consciousness, Reason, Spirit, and Religion – to ultimately achieve Absolute Knowledge. Accepting Hegel's conception of history as the self-creation of humankind overcoming its alienated existence, Marx redirected the focus from thought-entities to real human labor. The creativity and ontological significance of labor in Marx's work developed at this time.

The Science of Logic, Hegel's systematic account of dialectical method, was the methodological inspiration for Marx's critique of political economy; it remains essential to genuinely understanding Marx's overall critique and method of presentation.

SEE ALSO: Dialectic; Labor/Labor Power; Marx, Karl

SUGGESTED READINGS

Kojève, A. (1969) [1947] *Introduction to the Reading of Hegel*, trans. J. Nichols. Basic Books, New York.

Lukács, G. (1975) [1948] *The Young Hegel*, trans. R. Livingstone. Merlin Press, London.

ROB BEAMISH

hegemonic masculinity

Developed in the 1980s to provide a relational and socially constructed conception of men and masculinities, hegemonic masculinity describes the hierarchical interaction between multiple masculinities and explains how some men make it appear normal and necessary that they dominate most women and other men (Connell 1987).

Hegemonic masculinity describes a position in the system of gender relations, the system itself, and the current ideology that serves to reproduce masculine domination.

Connell posits four types of masculinities, more as positions in relation to one another than as personality types: hegemonic, complicit, subordinated, and marginalized. The hegemonic position is the currently accepted male ideal within a particular culture at a particular time. Connell notes that this image changes over time and place, as well as being subject to contestation within a particular culture.

Most men fall within the second category, complicit. These men accept and participate in the system of hegemonic masculinity so as to enjoy the material, physical, and symbolic benefits of the subordination of women and, through fantasy, experience the sense of hegemony and learn to take pleasure in it, and avoid subordination.

The relations among the four positions are hierarchical. A man in the subordinated position suffers that fate despite appearing to possess the physical attributes necessary to aspire to hegemony. Men run the risk of subordination when they do not practice gender consistent with the hegemonic system and ideology. Marginalized men are those who cannot even aspire to hegemony – most often, men of color and men with disabilities.

Secondly, Connell uses hegemonic masculinity to describe the current system of gender relations: "configurations of practice" organize social relations and structures to the overall benefit of men in relation to women and of some men in relation to other men. These configurations of practice take place across four dimensions: power, the division of labor, emotional relations, and the symbolic. Hegemonic masculinity as a system becomes built into social institutions so as to make it appear normal and natural for men's superordinate position to be maintained.

The third usage of hegemonic masculinity, as an ideology, provides the justification through which patriarchy is legitimated and maintained. Hegemonic masculinity structures the manner in which all people experience and thereby know their world, although those experiences vary as both men and women are differentially situated by race, class, and sexuality. This ideology, referred to as hegemonic complicity, can be measured across four dimensions: ideal-type masculinity, hierarchical ranking of self and others, subordination of women, and the subordination of woman-like behavior (Levy 2005).

Those who criticize the concept of hegemonic masculinity for confusion, reification, colonialism or elitism fail to recognize its multiple usages and see that those allegations have merit only if the critic refuses to consider simultaneously the three understandings of hegemonic masculinity: position, system, and ideology. Given the ubiquity of hegemonic masculinity as both a system of gender relations and as a justificatory ideology, resistance can be expressed politically or interactionally; that is, rather than contesting the hegemonic position, resistance seeks to alter the configuration of gender practice that reproduces the system of hegemonic masculinity.

SEE ALSO: Doing Gender; Femininities/Masculinities; Gendered Organizations/Institutions; Homophobia; Patriarchy; Sex and Gender

REFERENCES

Connell, R. W. (1987) *Gender and Power*. Stanford University Press, Stanford, CA.

Levy, D. P. (2005) Hegemonic complicity, friendship and comradeship: validation and causal processes among white, middle-class, middle-aged men. *Journal of Men's Studies* 13 (2): 199–224.

SUGGESTED READINGS

Carrigan, T., Connell, R. W., & Lee, J. (1985) Toward a new sociology of masculinity. *Theory and Society* 14: 551–604.

Lorber, J. (1998) Symposium on R. W. Connell's *Masculinities*. *Gender and Society* 12: 469–72.

DON LEVY

hegemony and the media

In media analysis, "hegemony" refers to the ways in which film and television help to represent political and social issues. These represntations favor the interests of dominant groups, and help keep the rest of the population consenting to political and social systems.

Even entertainment media are seen as "political." None is suggesting that films or TV offer direct propaganda messages upholding government foreign policy, masculinity, or nationalism, but support for all of these views can be found in popular examples, nevertheless, often from the ways stories are told and characters managed.

For example, some substantial early analysis suggested that the James Bond movie offers us all sorts of constructions about other "races" and nationalities. North Koreans are sinister totalitarians in *Die Another Day*; Afro-Caribbeans are excitable and superstitious in *Dr No*; Central American dictators run the drug trade in *Licence to Kill*. In British popular opinion and in Bond films, the Americans are well intentioned, well resourced but lacking finesse, the Russians puritanical, bureaucratic and ruthless. As Bennett and Woollacott (1987) say, this enables the British to appear as resourceful, intelligent, and able to claim some imaginary post-imperial role as offering a "middle way" in international conflicts.

James Bond also features strong views about women. Some are exotic and expendable, and some are ambiguous sexually. In the latter case, Bond restores them to conventional sexuality and political loyalty simultaneously by displaying vigorous heterosexual masculinity.

Television examples in the same tradition have focused on newspapers, documentary and current affairs programs. These programs apparently follow a code of neutrality and balance, for example by letting each political party have equal time. However, this very debate legitimizes the overall political system which gets depicted as the only feasible form of "democracy." Radical alternatives that might lie outside the inter-party consensus are never considered as serious politics.

Brasfield (2006) offers a typical and more feminist version of the analysis, reading *Sex and the City*. The characters are feisty, independent individuals, but in the end they do nothing to challenge a society that supports the dominant position of white middle-class women. In popular media, women can challenge their place in the social order to a limited extent, and only in a way that leaves intact its main shape.

The critics might see mostly political implications, but ordinary members of the viewing public might not even be aware of them. Perhaps this failure to "read" films or programs in this way could mean that the analysis is exaggerated and partial. Defenders of the approach might suggest instead that viewers have been unconsciously influenced so deeply that they are not aware of it: the problem with that defense is that it makes the analysis immune to virtually any criticism.

Work on the actual responses of "active viewers" also suggests that people are often capable of "seeing through" dominant readings, sometimes drawing upon other sources of information about the world, and from their own everyday experiences of domination and resistance.

SEE ALSO: Ideological Hegemony; Politics and Media

REFERENCES

Bennett, T. and Woollacott, J. (1987) *Bond and Beyond: The Political Career of a Popular Hero*. Macmillan, London.

Brasfield R. (2006) Rereading *Sex and the City*: exposing the feminist hegemonic narrative. *Journal of Popular Film and Television* 34 (3): 130–9.

DAVE HARRIS

hermeneutics

Hermeneutics is a branch of sociology concerned with human understanding and interpretation. Originally applied solely to texts, sociologists have applied hermeneutics to social events by examining participants' understandings of the events from the standpoint of their specific historical and cultural context. Hermeneutics is opposed to the view that social phenomena can be grasped adequately by reference to invariant laws of cause and effect or statistical regularities, as with positivist and behaviorist approaches and some elements of functionalist theory. Hermeneutics is one among a range of approaches to meaning, symbolization, and representation in social life that includes semiotics, structuralism, deconstruction, and discourse analysis.

Hermeneutics initially focused on interpreting the Bible in order to understand the word of God. Writing during the early nineteenth century, theologian and philosopher Friedrich Schleiermacher favored broadening the focus of hermeneutics beyond religious texts. Schleiermacher proposed a radically different position from earlier traditions of hermeneutics that theorized a reader would understand intended meanings of a text until encountering incongruous or illogical passages. He, instead, argued that understanding is a process in which readers understand the text's context, its particular genre, and its historical circumstances.

As subsequent theorists applied Schleiermacher's work to other areas of study, hermeneutics flourished in German academia. Wilhelm Dilthey extended Schleiermacher's theory of interpretation to the human sciences, claiming that whereas the natural sciences seek *erklären*, the explanation of phenomena according to laws of regular correspondence between cause and effect, the goal of the human sciences is *verstehen*, the understanding of human action based on intention and context.

Conceived of as an attempt to understand the most appropriate way to study human life, hermeneutics became focused largely on method. In addition to influencing current sociological thought, the hermeneutic tradition's attention to textuality and interpretation informs related scholarship in a range of academic disciplines, including philosophy and rhetoric.

SEE ALSO: Behaviorism; Phenomenology; Positivism; Semiotics; Structuralism; *Verstehen*

SUGGESTED READINGS

Bauman, Z. (1981) *Hermeneutics and Social Science*. Hutchinson, London.

Harrington, A. (2001) *Hermeneutic Dialogue and Social Science*. Routledge, London.

WENDY HILTON-MORROW AND AUSTIN HARRINGTON

heterosexuality

In everyday terms "heterosexuality" is taken for granted as the "normal" form of sexuality. It is only since the 1970s that sociologists began to challenge this commonsense view and to reconceptualize heterosexuality as an institutional arrangement implicated in the social exclusion of sexual "others" and the perpetuation of gender divisions.

One impetus for this critical approach to heterosexuality was the development of social constructionism, exemplified by Gagnon and Simon's *Sexual Conduct* (1973), in which they argued that human sexuality, far from being ordained by nature, was the product of social scripts. At the same time a new generation of sociologists, inspired by the feminist and gay movements, began to question male dominated heterosexuality. While gay scholars emphasized heterosexuality's marginalization and oppression of homosexuality, feminists focused on gender inequality within heterosexual relationships. The most significant contributions came from lesbian feminists, particularly Monique Wittig in France and Adrienne Rich in the USA. In a series of articles published between 1976 and 1981, Wittig analysed the social categories "women" and "men" as products of men's appropriation of women's bodies and labour through the heterosexual marriage contract. Rich (1980) coined the term "compulsory heterosexuality" to capture the idea that heterosexuality was imposed upon women through the erasure of lesbianism from history and by a range of social practices that constrained women into subjection to men.

In the 1980s debates on sexuality were increasingly influenced by Michel Foucault (1978). For Foucault, power produces sexuality rather than repressing it. Concepts such as homosexuality and heterosexuality do not name pre-existing categories; rather they bring those categories into being as an effect of discourse/power. By the 1990s, Foucault's ideas had become incorporated into queer theory, which seeks to destabilize the boundaries between heterosexuality and homosexuality, interrogate the binaries of gay/straight and man/woman and to bring to light the instability and contingency of sexual identities. While queer theory and feminism have differing priorities, both question the naturalness of sexuality and both, to some extent at least, link the binary divide of gender with that between heterosexuality and homosexuality. This is particularly evident in Judith Butler's *Gender Trouble* (1990), a text that is both feminist and queer. The object of Butler's critique is the heterosexual matrix, the regulatory fictions that link sex, gender, and heterosexuality together as a seemingly natural, compulsory order.

Butler, like other queer theorists, says little about what goes on *within* heterosexual relations. Other feminists, however, continued to be concerned with gender inequality within heterosexuality, defined broadly not just as a form of sexual desire and conduct, but as involving wider social relations between women and men. Much feminist work since the 1990s, rather than treating heterosexuality as a monolithic oppressive entity, addresses its different facets: as institution, identity, experience, and practice. This enabled more nuanced understandings of the ways in which heterosexuality shapes sexual and non-sexual lives and acknowledges variability in heterosexual experience and practice. The appreciation of diversity in personal and domestic lives, along with advances in lesbian and gay rights in many countries, has led some to question whether heterosexuality is losing its hegemonic status. Most sociologists are more cautious, however, arguing that heterosexuality may have become less compulsory, but it is nonetheless still institutionalized.

SEE ALSO: Gender Oppression; Homophobia and Heterosexism; Homosexuality; Lesbian Feminism; Queer Theory; Sex and Gender; Sexuality.

REFERENCES

Foucault, M. (1979) *The History of Sexuality*, vol. 1. Allen Lane, London.

Rich, A. (1980) Compulsory heterosexuality and lesbian existence. *Signs* 5 (4): 631–60.

SUGGESTED READINGS

Ingraham, C. (ed.) (2004) *Thinking Straight: The Power, the Promise and the Paradox of Heterosexuality*. Routledge, New York.

Richardson, D. (ed.) (1996) *Theorising Heterosexuality*. Open University Press, Buckingham.

STEVI JACKSON

hidden curriculum

The term hidden curriculum refers to the unofficial rules, routines, and structures of schools through which students learn behaviors, values, beliefs, and attitudes. Elements of the hidden curriculum do not appear in schools' written goals, formal lesson plans, or learning objectives although they may reflect culturally dominant social values and ideas about what schools should teach. Of the three major approaches to the hidden curriculum, the functionalist orientation is most concerned with how hidden curricula reproduce unified societies, the conflict perspective focuses on the reproduction of stratified societies, and symbolic interactionism more fully incorporates interactional context with our understanding of the hidden curriculum.

Some scholars posit that the hidden curricula carry powerful class-based and race-based messages. Pierre Bourdieu and Basil Berstein, for example, suggest that schools also create social environments that better match with the class backgrounds of middle and upper class students. Through the hidden curriculum, students get the message that middle and upper class cultural values, norms, and attitudes are the standard by which all else is measured. Schools reward conformity to these cultural norms and certify certain methods of learning as the standard. These learning methods are likely to better match middle and upper class styles of interaction and penalize lower- or working-class students.

SEE ALSO: Educational Inequality; Gender, Education and; Self-Fulfilling Prophecy; Stratification: Functional and Conflict Theories

SUGGESTED READING

Bourdieu, P. & Passeron, J. (1977) *Reproduction in Education, Society, and Culture*. Sage, Beverly Hills, CA.

LAURA HAMILTON AND BRIAN POWELL

historical and comparative methods

Among the classical figures, Max Weber stands out from the others in his devotion to comparative historical sociology. His lifelong quest was to find through the study of "rationalization processes" what sets the west off from the non-western civilizations. Concretely, the concern was with modern, rational or bourgeois capitalism, its origins and development. Weber's series of studies is "macro" and it deals with changes over long stretches of time. These characteristics are shared by the genre of comparative historical sociology today.

Weber, a leading inspiration of comparative historical sociology, came closest among the classical writers to making major use of John Stuart Mill's method of (indirect) difference. Of Mill's two principal procedures, the method of difference is the one that usually features in explicitly comparative research; it is the most powerful of the "logics" he identified and studies usually try to approximate it as closely as possible.

Mill's method of agreement works as follows: (1) several cases are found to have the phenomenon to be explained (y); (2) they also share the hypothesized causal factors (x) (this is the crucial similarity); but (3) in other ways that might seem causally relevant according to alternative hypotheses, they vary (i.e., *overall* there are differences). Mill's method of difference, on the other hand, requires that the investigator take (positive) cases in which the *explanandum* and the *explanans* are present ($x - y$); these are then to be contrasted to other (negative) cases in which the *explanandum* and the *explanans* are absent (not x – not y). These negative cases are as similar as possible to the positive cases in other respects. Comparative historical sociologists, in particular, can supplement the method of agreement by introducing into their analyses the method of difference; in short, a research design combining elements of both is possible. Or the method of agreement can be applied twice over so as to approximate the method of difference.

Max Weber did this in his comparative studies of civilizations. Essentially, he conducted two sets of studies, of European societies that developed capitalism and non-western ones that did not. Weber thought he could see a number of factors linked to the former which the latter set of societies did not possess. But what if other factors he had not identified were operating? By comparing the two sets of societies, stressing as much as possible their likenesses, Weber was able to strengthen the presumption in favor of his selected factors as the cause of capitalism in the west, their absence as leading to its absence in China and India. Logically, differences among each set of societies, the European and the non-western, were reduced, i.e., made parametric, in order to highlight crucial similarities in each in the independent variable, the type of religion, and the dependent one, respectively the occurrence and non-occurrence of economic rationality (a "this-worldly asceticism"). Placing the two sets side by side – the differences again being reduced (made parametric) – amounts logically to displaying the crucial difference between east and west.

Research in the social sciences is restricted by the relatively small number of societies in which the investigator is interested for theoretical and substantive reasons. This means that the investigator has, usually with theoretical models of any degree of sophistication and realism, far more variables than cases in which to study them. The relative paucity of cases rules out often the use of sophisticated statistical techniques, such as multivariate analysis that permits study of the simultaneous relations of different kinds among a number of significant independent variables.

In addition to being historical, most monographs by historical sociologists study one, two or three cases. Why is there this tendency to a limited number? The argument for such a limitation is: (1) that the cases are intrinsically interesting (they may even exhaust the phenomenon in question); or (2) that they are the most representative (multivariate analysis is by contrast sometimes possible with large data sets but these are not historical). Unravelling complex compacted causes can only be attempted in a small number of cases treated as wholes. With respect to (1) (inherent interest), one can say that these cases matter to people generally, not just to statistically-minded social scientists pursuing autonomous, expert or specialized questions. In respect of the practical problem of complexity, any increase in the cases will so expand the number of relevant variables that the complexity becomes unmanageable. Or if resort is had to statistical methods contact with the detail of empirical case material must be sacrificed.

SEE ALSO: Ideal Type; Methods; Multivariate Analysis; Social Change; Variables; Weber, Max

SUGGESTED READING

Bendix, R. (1963) Concepts and generalizations in comparative sociological studies. *American Sociological Review* 28: 532–9.

Mahoney, J. (2003) Strategies of causal assessment in comparative historical analysis. In: Mahoney, J. & Rueschemeyer, D. (eds.), *Comparative Historical Analysis in the Social Sciences*. Cambridge University Press, Cambridge, pp. 337–72.

Ragin, C. C. (1987) *The Comparative Method: Moving Beyond Qualitative and Quantitative Strategies*. University of California Press, Berkeley, CA.

IAN VARCOE

HIV/AIDS and population

The connections between human immunodeficiency virus (HIV) and population features are vast. While HIV has its largest impacts on population size and structure by increasing mortality among young adults, it also affects and interacts with the other key components of population make-up and change, namely, sexual behavior and fertility, and migration. Impacts on these key components in turn affect the well-being of populations in profound ways.

The HIV/AIDS pandemic is likely to surpass all previously recorded epidemics regarding numbers of deaths. Within less than three decades since its introduction, HIV has infected over 60 million persons worldwide, killing more than 25 million of them through the various complications associated with acquired immune deficiency syndrome (AIDS). AIDS ranks fourth among the leading causes of death worldwide and first in sub-Saharan Africa. Unlike earlier epidemics that spread their misfortune across the age distribution, AIDS affects primarily young adults, at the precise ages when childrearing and economic responsibilities are highest. It is not just the epidemiological transition paradigm that was uprooted by the spread of HIV, but also the demographic transition paradigm, which predicted a steady decline of mortality and fertility in the developing world, and a gradual shift from a very young age structure to an older population with a much more evenly distributed age structure. The epidemic has reversed decades of progress in increasing life expectancy and distorted the population pyramids in several hardest-hit sub-Saharan countries. In highly affected countries, population size may decline.

Prevalence of HIV also affects current and future levels of fertility, primarily by increasing mortality among adults of child bearing age, which may reduce the number of births. Other effects of HIV on fertility are mediated through one or more of the classic proximate determinants of fertility. First, widespread widowhood will leave many young adult survivors without child-producing and child-rearing partners. Second, HIV-induced morbidity reduces sexual activity among the infected – in proximate determinants parlance, these first and second mechanisms decrease exposure to intercourse. Third, HIV may increase condom use at the expense of more effective contraceptives, such as the pill, thereby increasing exposure to conception. Fourth, HIV appears to increase fetal loss among infected women; affecting gestation. In addition, HIV may change fertility desires. A wish to compensate for HIV-related child mortality may increase fertility desires; fear of having an infected child and of leaving behind orphans may reduce them.

Migration patterns can be a cause or consequence of HIV transmission. Demographers speculate that migration patterns could facilitate HIV transmission among migrants, and facilitate the spread of HIV across regions. Migration exposes migrants, many of whom are young adults at reproductive age, to new opportunities for sexual experimentation, provides them the discretionary income with which to do so, removes them from the oversight and control of extended kin, and may lead to extended periods of spousal separation. Those conditions potentially increase the likelihood that they visit sex workers or engage in other types of high-risk sexual behavior. Hence, mobile populations often have above-average rates of HIV infection, and may transmit the virus to more permanent partners upon their return. Less studied but also important are patterns of migration that result from AIDS. Urban migrants who are infected often move back home to their villages for care-taking. While the implications for population distribution of such return migrations may not be major, the implications of such widespread moves on intergenerational exchanges (both monetary and in-kind) and the welfare of their parental caregivers are likely to be significant.

HIV also affects other key features of population well-being. The severe morbidity associated with HIV-infection severely diminishes the productivity of those infected, and diminishes scarce labor and financial resources that would have otherwise been available for family investment or consumption. In high-prevalence societies, the loss of highly-trained individuals such as teachers, nurses, and physicians to AIDS will affect critical social institutions such as education and health care. Clinics and hospitals may also become overwhelmed with AIDS patients seeking expensive and sophisticated treatments that the staff are ill-positioned to provide. And traditional patterns of care for children and the elderly, both of whom are dependent upon working age adults for their support, are also being disrupted. Because the use of AZT and other drugs is not yet widespread in some hard-hit countries, the disruption that HIV causes will rival, and perhaps even surpass, the plagues that ravaged Europe in previous centuries and the worldwide influenza epidemic in the most recent one.

SEE ALSO: AIDS, Sociology of; Sex Tourism; Sexual Health; Sexuality, Globalization and; Sexuality Research: Methods; Stigma

SUGGESTED READINGS

Knodel J. & VanLandingham, M. (2002) The impact of the AIDS epidemic on older persons. *AIDS* 16 (suppl. 4): S77–S83.

Stanecki, K. (2004) *The AIDS Pandemic in the 21st Century*. The Census Bureau, Washington, DC.

United Nations AIDS (UNAIDS) website: www.unaids.org.

MARK J. VANLANDINGHAM, HONGYUN FU, AND DOMINIQUE MEEKERS

Homans, George (1910–89)

George Caspar Homans was a major theoretical sociologist whose lucid writings helped to shape major developments in sociological theory and research. He was a lifelong Harvard faculty member, teaching both sociology and medieval history. In 1964, he was elected president of the American Sociological Association. Homans' theoretical work was dedicated to synthesis and explanation, understood in terms of the role of theory in natural science.

The synthesis objective first appeared in his most influential book, *The Human Group* (1950), which used published field studies of varied groups as evidence for a system of hypotheses describing group processes. The explanatory objective is paramount in his later publications, which are based upon methodological individualism. As he frames it, the idea is that fundamental explanatory principles in social science are to be true of individuals as members of the human species, not as members of particular groups or cultures (Homans 1967). This directive is implemented in an influential article (Homans 1958) that stimulated the rise of exchange theory and especially in *Social Behavior: Its Elementary Forms* (1961, rev. 1974), his second major book, which sets out a deductive theory grounded in behavioral psychology. The book was met with considerable theoretical criticism of the behaviorist foundation but it also stimulated research on particular topics, notably distributive justice. Today we can appreciate his explanatory focus on the emergence of spontaneous social order despite the limitations of his theory (Fararo 2001).

SEE ALSO: Group Processes; Social Exchange Theory; Theory and Method

REFERENCES

Fararo, T. J. (2001) *Social Action Systems: Foundation and Synthesis in Sociological Theory*. Praeger, Westport, CT.

Homans, G. C. (1958) Social behavior as exchange. *American Journal of Sociology* 63: 597–606.

Homans, G. C. (1967) *The Nature of Social Science*. Harcourt, Brace Jovanovich, New York.

THOMAS J. FARARO

homelessness

During the 1980s and 1990s, scholarship on homelessness focused on documenting the growing number of people sleeping in public places or public and private shelters. Scholars debated the reasons why so many lacked access to conventional dwelling and puzzled over whom and how many people lived precariously, invisibly and sometimes illegally with friends and family. Researchers investigated this continuum of residential instability and improvisational strategies and questioned whether, and to what extent, homelessness was a product of structural failings in job and housing markets; organizational inertia (perhaps incompetence) of agencies entrusted to help the homeless; or mental illness, drug and/or alcohol problems. Such inquiries inspired copious studies into the causes and persistence of homelessness.

In the past, the "old homeless" were romanticized as rugged individualists in studies of hoboes and tramps during the 1920s; families of the Great Depression in the 1930s whose misfortune earned our compassion, or disaffiliated adults whose presence in flophouses, single room occupancies and bars defined skid row sections of American cities until the 1970s. The "old homeless" were primarily single white males whose marginal relationship to employment implied their inability to form social connections with family and friends, which, it was argued, further isolated them from mainstream social institutions, norms and values. In contrast, current definitions of homelessness focus less on social disaffiliation and more on homelessness as a housing market condition while at the same time linking homelessness to broader structural and organizational problems facing those who live in extreme poverty. Peter H. Rossi's 1989 distinction between the *literally homeless* and the *marginally or precariously housed* discussed in *Down and Out in America*, resonates with HUD's McKinney–Vento Homeless Assistance Act, first enacted in 1987 and subsequently reauthorized, which defines homeless persons as lacking access to adequate nighttime residence, including shelters, institutional settings, and places not intended for human habitation. The Homeless Emergency Assistance and Rapid Transition to Housing Act develop programs that address the residential instability, heterogeneity, size, composition and geographic distribution of the homeless. Accommodating the diverse needs of sub-populations by age, mental illness, substance abuse; veteran and family (mostly female headed) status; and noting the disproportionate number of homeless Blacks, are all part of research and policy.

Current homeless policy falls under two models, both of which depend upon organizations to carry out policy objectives. *Housing readiness* models provide homeless families and individuals with a continuum of housing options. Clients temporarily reside in a series of structured housing programs, with the aim of eventually "graduating" into more permanent supportive housing. Moving up is contingent upon their ability and willingness to obey a set of rules and participate in a variety of supportive services, such as substance abuse and job readiness programs. These programs are designed to help homeless persons learn to live as "*independently as possible*," and are contingent upon the client's ability to *demonstrate* housing readiness.

In contrast, *Housing First* models emphasize providing housing irrespective of whether clients participate in supportive service programs. Intended for the chronically homeless – individuals with disabilities who have been continuously homeless for one year or have experienced at least four episodes of homelessness over the past three years – this model espouses the rapid placement of individuals into permanent, independent housing. Since housing and treatment services are separated, housing is not contingent on a client's ability to maintain sobriety, remain medicated, or meet with case managers on a monitored basis. Treatment is a choice.

However, policy goals are not the same as implementation, or *policy-in-action*. We need more in-depth and comparative ethnographic and qualitative studies of organizations and their fields to understand how the above housing program models operate in practice. We need to understand how organizational cultures and imperatives frame and execute policy goals. Such studies would provide useful information for policymakers and substantiate how organizations mediate homelessness.

SEE ALSO: Culture of Poverty; Ethnography; Organization Theory; Organizations; Poverty; Qualitative Methods

SUGGESTED READINGS

Dordick, G. (2002) Recovering from homelessness: determining the "quality of sobriety" in a transitional housing program, qualitative *Sociology* 25 (2): 7–32.

Lee, B. A.,Tyler, K., & Wright, J. (2010) The new homeless revisited. *Annual Review of Sociology* 36.

O'Flaherty, B. (1996) *Making Room: The Economics of Homelessness.* Harvard University Press, Cambridge, MA, and London.

US Department of Housing and Urban Development Office of Policy Development and Research (2007) *The Applicability of Housing First Models to Homeless Persons with Serious Mental Illness.* Washington, DC.

GWENDOLYN DORDICK

homophobia

Three important areas of research have emerged on homophobia since the 1970s. Since Weinberg (1972) first popularized the term homophobia in his book *Society and the Healthy Homosexual*, where he defined it as "the dread of being in close quarters with homosexuals," we have seen the emergence of sophisticated psychological instruments, a vast array of surveys and qualitative studies that explore the attitudes, feelings and social practices that constitute homophobia.

While scholars such as Sears and Williams (1997) now define homophobia more broadly as "prejudice, discrimination, harassment, or acts of violence against sexual minorities, including lesbians, gay men, bisexuals and transgendered persons," psychological instruments also differentiate between homophobic attitudes and feelings. For example, MacDonald and Games' (1974) 30-item instrument, Modified Attitudes Toward Homosexuality, and Hudson and Rickett's (1980) Index of Homophobia, which uses a scale to measure reactions to homosexual individuals, have become standard ways to assess homophobia. Although these psychological instruments are able to differentiate between attitudes as cognitive beliefs and feelings as deeply seated emotional responses, they do not capture how attitudes and feelings affect social practices.

The second and largest area of research on homophobia is the development of a huge variety of surveys on homophobic attitudes among adults. The general findings of these surveys in the USA show that the demographic characteristics of those who hold negative attitudes about homosexuals are more likely to live in the Midwest, the South or small towns and rural areas. Moreover, negative attitudes are more likely to be held by men who are older and less well educated. Increases in college-educated Americans and a general liberalizing of attitudes towards homosexuality since the 1970s but particularly salient during the 1990s has been supported by survey research in general. These surveys also show that men have stronger homophobic attitudes or feelings than women, and that men evidence a stronger dislike for gay male homosexuality than lesbianism.

Nayak and Kehily (1997) argue that identities are always constructed, and gain their meanings, through cultural oppositions. Hence, masculine identities are constructed through their opposition to feminine ones, gaining their meaning through excluding feminine identities but at the same time depending upon them for definition. This understanding, they argue, explains why young men are not necessarily against homosexuality itself but rather its associations with femininity and the lack of a masculine self-identity that it implies. They thus view homophobia as a practice that establishes boundaries of purity and pollution between pure heterosexual masculine men and polluted non-heterosexual feminine ones.

An even more violent heterosexual masculine identity, which depends on homophobia for its constitution, is analyzed by Sanday (1990) in her study of fraternity gang rape. Sanday shows that fraternity brothers promote compulsory heterosexuality in acts of gang rape by using homophobic social sanctions which deride those brothers who do not participate as homosexual or unmanly. At the same time, however, a sublimated homosexuality is expressed by the fact that the frat brothers are having sex with one another through the woman being gang raped. Homosexual desire is expunged out of the act of gang rape through homophobic and compulsory heterosexual discourses that construct masculine heterosexual brothers who "pull train," that is, gang rape a woman, as exclusively heterosexual.

In sum, homophobia has become an important topic in social science research. The growing sophistication of psychological instruments, the increasing number of surveys, and the numerous qualitative studies analyzing homophobia help us to better understand this complex phenomenon and its conceptualization as a form of deviance. Future quantitative and qualitative research on homophobia is still needed to fill in the literature, especially on men who consciously and behaviorally identify as heterosexual and commit the largest number of hate crimes against gays and lesbians. Similarly, more research on the most effective strategies for reducing homophobia is warranted. This research would help policymakers and others in mitigating the pernicious effects of this social problem.

SEE ALSO: Heterosexuality; Homosexuality; Sexual Deviance; Sexual Politics

REFERENCES

Nayak, A. and Kehily, M. (1997) Masculinities and schooling: why are young men so homophobic? In: Steinberg, D., Epstein, D. & Johnson, R. (eds.), *Border Patrols: Policing the Boundaries of Heterosexuality*. Cassell, London.

Sanday, P. (1990) *Fraternity Gang Rape: Sex, Brotherhood, and Privilege on Campus*. New York University Press, New York.

Sears, J. and Williams, W. (eds.) (1997) *Overcoming Heterosexism and Homophobia: Strategies that Work*. Columbia University Press, New York.

SUGGESTED READINGS

Adam, B. (1998) Theorizing homophobia. *Sexualities* 1 (4): 387–404.

Herek, G. and Glunt, E. (1993) Interpersonal contact and heterosexuals' attitudes toward gay men. *Journal of Sex Research* 30 (3): 239–44.

JAMES JOSEPH DEAN

homophobia and heterosexism

Homophobia is a widely understood term to refer to anti-homosexual attitudes and practices, but comparison of such terms as homophobia, heterosexism, and heteronormativity reveals how these terms rely on different ideas of what homosexual means and where opposition to same-sex relations originates. Homophobia typically denotes an irrational fear or a set of mistaken ideas held by prejudiced individuals; its alleviation therefore likely comes through therapy or education. Its use tends to focus attention on individuals, to locate its origins in childhood socialization, and to conceive of it as a prejudice directed against homosexual persons. Heterosexism offers a more sociological notion that shifts analysis to the ways in which government, workplace, religion, family, and media are organized to exclude or disadvantage same-sex relations. Finally, heteronormativity arises from analysis of how distinctions like heterosexual–homosexual are reproduced. For queer theory, the issue is not one of appealing for tolerance or acceptance for a quasi-ethnic community of lesbians and gay men, but of shaking up the entire heterosexual–homosexual binary that fuels the distinction in the first place.

There are several leading theories that lend credence to each of these conceptions. Gayle Rubin's influential essay on "The traffic in women" built on Claude Lévi-Strauss's work on how heterosexuality is recreated each generation through a system of fraternal interest groups that exercise control over women's reproductive power in families. Because homosexuality among men transgresses this fundamental social "game plan," it comes to be identified with the betrayal of masculinity and the inability to assert male domination over women. Lesbianism, as Monique Wittig (1992) argues in *The Straight Mind*, amounts to a "revolt of the trade goods" in the "traffic in women." Adrienne Rich (1980) also characterizes lesbianism as an assertion of women's self-determination and a direct challenge to patriarchy. Anti-lesbianism for Rich is a variant of misogyny, a means of enforcing "compulsory heterosexuality," and a system of keeping women subservient to male domination. Still, it must be noted that anti-homosexuality is not the inevitable consequence of kinship organization. In many societies around the world, same-sex bonding is accepted and valued.

Gender panic theory focuses particularly on homophobia as an effect of gender. Masculinity, this theory contends, is an achieved and insecure status. Defensiveness against losing male privilege generates homophobia. Psychological research shows how homophobia appears to be particularly strong among gender conservatives and adolescent males who feel insecure in their access to masculine status. The queer theory of Judith Butler and Eve Sedgwick extends gender panic theory, contending that heterosexual masculinity builds itself on the simultaneous exploitation and denial of homosexuality. Since heterosexual masculinity can never constitute itself as secure and unassailable, and homosexuality is a default subject location against which heterosexuality defines itself, then homosexual possibilities can never be fully repressed and remain necessary for the masculine self. While gender panic theory offers a strong explanation for homophobia in western and other patriarchal societies, it does not work for societies where same-sex bonding is itself regarded as masculine, and makes up a part of the socialization process to masculinize youths.

Sociohistorical theories are particularly interested in the social factors that fuel, or diminish, homophobia. These theories investigate why campaigns of persecution against homosexual relations break out in certain places and times and among particular social constituencies. Homophobia in western societies is associated with the symbolic value of disenfranchised and "upstart" social groups. In nineteenth- and twentieth-century Europe and North America, the adherents of anti-homosexual worldviews have typically come from a range of social groups disturbed or threatened by modernity – usually traditional elites fearful of change and declining social classes resentful of groups on the rise. Status defense theories note that people fearful of declining living standards are especially susceptible to a politics of resentment, and have a tendency to strike out against those they see as "undeserving." Anti-gay persecution has often run parallel to campaigns of persecution directed against other disenfranchised groups. Despite important gains in human rights legislation protecting the equality rights of LGBT people in many countries, homophobic attitudes and practices remain widespread.

SEE ALSO: Compulsory Heterosexuality; Gay and Lesbian Movement; Hate Crimes; Homophobia; Queer Theory

REFERENCE

Rich, A. (1980) Compulsory heterosexuality and lesbian existence. *Signs* 10 (4): 741–61.

Rubin, G. (1975) The traffic in women. In: Reiter, R. (ed.), *Toward an Anthropology of Women*. Monthly Review Press, New York, pp. 157–210.

Wittig, M. (1992) *The Straight Mind*. Harvester Wheatsheaf, New York.

SUGGESTED READING

Adam, B. D. (1998) Theorizing homophobia. *Sexualities* 1 (4): 387–404.

Butler, J. (1990) *Gender Trouble*. Routledge, New York.

Herek, G. (1998) *Stigma and Sexual Orientation*. Sage, Thousand Oaks, CA.

BARRY D. ADAM

homosexuality

Homosexuality refers to sexual behaviors and desires between males or between females. *Gay* refers to self-identification with such practices and desires. Gay and homosexual are terms mostly used only for men. Definitions have run into major problems, and nowadays the gender-inclusive concept *queer* indicates the fluency of sexual practices and gender performances. Since the 1970s, gay and lesbian, queer or LGBT studies (Lesbian, Gay, Bisexual, and Transgender) is an interdisciplinary specialization, connecting sociology to history, anthropology, and cultural studies. Sociology itself had a late start, although some of the key figures in the field were sociologists.

The term homosexual was first used in 1869 for political claims. Most of the early scholarly work on homosexuality was focused on psychiatry until the sociological breakthrough with Alfred Kinsey. He became the founder of the sociology of (homo)sexuality through his two books on sexual behavior of males and females (*Sexual Behavior in the Human Male*, 1948; *Sexual Behavior in the Human Female*, 1953). He produced the first sexual statistics. He found 37 percent of US men have had homosexual experiences and 4 percent exclusively and lifelong. This work changed the focus from the aberrant homosexual with gender identity problems to the society discriminating against homosexuals.

The Chicago School started in the same period to study sexual variation in urban gay subcultures. In 1979 the concept of "gay ghetto" was introduced by Martin Levine. After the queer turn of the 1990s, books on space and sexuality appeared. Gay urban histories boomed with George Chauncey's *Gay New York* (1994) and David Higgs' collection *Queer Sites* (1999). The symbolic-interactionist concept stigma was added to urban sociology, fitting the change from psychology to sociology, from pathology to activism. Gay men went on from psychiatrists into streets and finally to same-sex marriages. Gagnon and Simon (1973) developed "sexual scripting," later named narrative or story (Plummer 1995). Others engaged with the stages of homosexual "coming out": sensitization, resistance, acceptance, integration.

From the late 1970s the research became historical-sociological with Michel Foucault's 3-volume *Histoire de la sexualité* (1976, 1984, 1984). The first volume was the founding work of "social constructionism." Herein he remarks on the change from the legal concept of sodomy, an act, to the medical one of homosexuality, an identity that will be insistently researched as part of the politics of the body. He showed how discourses of sexual liberation had been around for two centuries and mainly contributed to normalization and stricter control of sexuality.

The rise of AIDS stimulated research on gay life, especially on sexual and preventive practices. The main aim was to impede risky behaviors and the method surveying sexual behavior. The outcome surprised because numbers of gay men were everywhere lower than those found by Kinsey. Specialized topics came to the forefront ranging from male prostitution, suicide, ethnic and age diversity to bisexuality, transgenderism, and SM (sadism and masochism). Recent issues are same-sex marriage and parenthood, homosexuals in the army, antigay violence, or discrimination.

The main question in gay research is the definition of the object of study. Most research is dependent on self-identification of interviewees, who may be unwilling to disclose their preferences. There are no objective criteria to define homosexuals. Kinsey therefore developed a homo-heterosexual scale from 0–6 of practices and fantasies. Other authors created layered scales that included more facets.

Biology often equates effeminacy and sexual passivity in males with homosexuality, while sociology should study the repercussions of such attributions. The research advice should be to learn the terminologies the respondents themselves use and clarify those. Classifications of homosexualities have been proposed based on gender, age, and class differences.

The new concept of sexual citizenship highlights the social aspects of sexuality. Such elements were hidden by the traditional relegation of sexuality to the natural and private. This terminology draws attention to the intimate or sexual side of citizenship. It is about body politics that are ruled by heteronormativity. These codes pervade all societal institutions and deserve more attention.

SEE ALSO: Gay and Lesbian Movement; Heterosexuality; Homophobia; Homophobia and Heterosexism; Lesbianism; Queer Theory; Sexuality, Masculinity and

REFERENCES

Gagnon, J. & Simon, W. (1973) *Sexual Conduct: The Social Sources of Sexual Meaning*. Aldine, Chicago, IL.

Plummer, K. (1995) *Telling Sexual Stories*. Routledge, London.

SUGGESTED READING

Bell, D. & Binnie, J. (2000) *The Sexual Citizen: Queer Politics and Beyond*. Polity Press, Cambridge.

GERT HEKMA

households

Defining who belongs to a household appears relatively straightforward, and for many people it is. Usually at any time there exists a clear-cut group of one or more individuals who eat together, share a common housekeeping and sleep in the same dwelling. As a result of recent demographic trends though, household patterns have been altering significantly in western societies. Three features are particularly important. First, household composition has been changing. With such factors as later marriage, high divorce rates and increases in lone parenthood, fewer people are now living in standard nuclear family households; equally, household size has been decreasing, and more households consist of individuals living alone. Second, people's household careers are now more diverse than they were for much of the twentieth century, reflecting greater variation in people's partnership and family commitments. For example, while as mentioned more people now live alone, the routes into single person households, the life phases involved and the length of time spent in them varies significantly. Third, household boundaries are becoming more diffuse, as increasing numbers of people are regularly spending time in different residences. Some people, for example, do weekly commutes to work; a growing number of couples are choosing to "live apart together," with each maintaining a separate home but also regularly spending time together; many children whose separated parents share care of them belong to both parents' households; and young adults often construct flexible living arrangements, moving out and then back into the parental home as circumstances in their lives – changing employment, relationship break-up, financial pressures – alter. These and other associated demographic changes are having an impact on household patterns throughout the developed world, resulting in the living arrangements people construct being more flexible and less "ordered." They are also creating new challenges for social analysts seeking to understand the structuring of contemporary domestic life.

SEE ALSO: Cohabitation; Family Structure

SUGGESTED READINGS

Allan, G. & Crow, G. (2001) *Families, Households and Society*. Palgrave, Basingstoke.

Buzan, S., Ogden, P., & Hall, R. (2005) Households matter: the quiet demography of urban transformation. *Progress in Human Geography* 29: 413–36.

Rybczynski, W. (1986) *Home: A Short History of an Idea*. Viking, New York.

GRAHAM ALLAN

housework

Housework refers to all unpaid labor performed to maintain family members and/or a home including cleaning, buying groceries, meal preparation, and laundry. In most studies, housework is defined by its measurement and often excludes childcare, emotion work, and other invisible types of labor. However, sociologists do acknowledge that the construction of "housework" as a concept is a historical process and is contingent upon other factors.

During industrialization "housework" was seen as separate from "work." With industrial capitalism, the household unit was no longer the source of production and by the nineteenth century a division of labor emerged based on the ideology of separate spheres. These boundaries were institutionalized and gendered, especially for the middle class, resulting in the "cult of true womanhood." This is further reflected in the dominant paradigms in sociology throughout the 1960s to 1980s. Functionalists argued that the family is based on complementary "sex roles," where men are seen as more instrumental and women have an expressive role which makes housework naturally suitable. "New home economics" provides another specialization model that conceptualizes housework as women's work based on the allocation of time and less investment in human capital in comparison to men.

Empirical research on housework became a topic of sociological study during the 1960s and 1970s. Blood and Wolfe's (1960) index of housework illustrates that divisions in labor vary based on relative employment. Oakely's (1974) research on housework was one of the first studies to approach the topic from a woman's perspective. However, most of this early empirical research was descriptive in nature and did not challenge the assumption that housework is women's work. This was further complicated by scholarly debates questioning whether housework and women who perform the majority of it produce value and/or surplus value.

By the 1990s, empirical research on housework proliferated along with the development of new theoretical perspectives. Much of the sociological research on housework starts from the assumption that nobody wants to do it, so the division of household labor may reflect power differentials in households or families. As such, research has focused explicitly on explaining the division of household labor and the consequences of this division. Time diaries and survey questions that specifically address housework and qualitative research such as Hochschild and Machung's *The Second Shift* (1989) detail the contributions men and women make to household labor.

Housework is fundamental to the well-being of families, the construction of gender, and the reproduction of society. Although fewer women today are full-time homemakers, housework remains women's responsibility. Women are still more likely to do housework themselves or to hire a domestic worker who is also more likely to be a woman. Modernization and labor-saving devices have had little effect on the structural changes that are needed to elevate housework from its devalued status. Housework is a shared experience of most women and is crucial to a sociological analysis of gender inequality.

SEE ALSO: Divisions of Household Labor; Gender Ideology and Gender Role Ideology; Gender, Work, and Family

REFERENCES

Blood, R. O., Jr. & Wolfe, D. M. (1960). *Husbands & Wives: The Dynamics of Married Living*. Free Press, Glencoe, IL.

Oakely, A. (1974) *Woman's Work: The Housewife, Past and Present*. Pantheon Books, New York.

SUGGESTED READING

Sayer, L. G. (2005) Gender, time and inequality: trends in women's and men's paid work, unpaid work and free time. *Social Forces* 84 (1): 285–303.

ANDREA N. HUNT

human genome and the science of life

Although the double helix structure of DNA was discovered in 1953 by James Watson, Francis Crick, Maurice Wilkins, and Rosalind Franklin, it was not until the 1980s that powerful sequencing and information technologies were developed that enabled scientists to identify particular genes associated with hereditary diseases and to begin to map all of the genes in human DNA: the so-called human genome. The human genome project was a massive international mapping exercise which began in the 1990s and culminated in the publication of a draft sequence by the International Human Genome Sequencing Consortium of the entire human genome in 2001, which is freely available on the Internet.

In the same period a broader range of biomedical knowledge was also developing, particularly in the fields of assisted conception. More recently, research into stem cells and tissue engineering, alongside the so-called "postgenomic sciences" of pharmacogenomics and proteomics, has also developed. This "science of life" involves detailed understanding of the basic cellular mechanisms involved in human development, as well as a focus upon copying and ultimately manipulating these processes in the laboratory. This is linked to a number of biomedical developments in the diagnosis and treatment of disease, particularly the move towards more targeted individualized treatments tailored to individuals' particular genetic makeup, and perhaps, in the future, utilizing cells and tissues taken from people's own bodies to develop treatments for them.

Sociological work on these developments covers a wide remit. The early days of the human genome project saw sociologists, in common with their colleagues in the ethical and legal disciplines, exploring the implications of greater knowledge about individuals' genetic makeup, particularly the dangers of eugenics and genetic determinism. Others focused upon the political economy of the project, especially patenting (notably, indigenous people's DNA) and access to genetic information by the state (primarily with respect to large-scale genetic databases). As Waldby (2002) noted, this was part of a growing trend of "biovalue" in which bodily parts and processes were commodified.

SEE ALSO: Eugenics; Genetic Engineering as a Social Problem; New Reproductive Technologies

SUGGESTED READINGS

Kerr, A. & Shakespeare, T. (2002) *Genetic Politics: From Eugenics to Genome*. New Clarion Press, Cheltenham.

Waldby, C. (2002) Stem cells, tissue culture and the production of biovalue. *Health* 6: 301–23.

ANNE KERR

human rights

"Human rights are those liberties, immunities and benefits which, by accepted contemporary values, all human being should be able to claim 'as of right' of the society in which they live" (*Encyclopedia of Public International Law* 1995: 886). Human rights are constitutive for the contemporary discourse on the *moral nature* of society and individuals that is simultaneously a *legal discourse* on rights of individuals, and obligations and accountability of states and international organizations. As such they embody the "collective conscience" of a world community that is developing among citizens, judiciaries and legislatures still embedded in nation states.

The paradigm of contemporary human rights emerged with the modern nation state and has its philosophical roots in the Enlightenment tradition of Europe and the United States. The Petition of Right in 1628 and the Bill of Rights in 1689 in Britain were followed by the American Declaration of Independence (1776), the French Declaration of the Rights of Man and of the Citizen (1789), and the American Bill of Rights (1791).

The Universal Declaration of Human Rights (UDHR) adopted by the United Nations General Assembly in 1948 was the first of the four "instruments" of the International Bill of Rights, which in addition comprises the International Covenant on Civil and Political Rights (ICCPR), the Optional Protocol to the International Covenant on Civil and Political Rights (ICCPR-OP) and the International Covenant on Economic, Social and Cultural Rights (ICESCR), all adopted in 1966. The International Bill of Rights is enshrined in regional conventions like the European Convention on Human Rights (1953), the African Charter on Human and Peoples' Rights (1986) and the Managua Declaration of the Organization of American States (1993). It is complemented by other human rights instruments that cover specific violations such as e.g. racial discrimination, forced labor, genocide, and torture, or address and protect the rights of specific groups like children, women, or migrant workers.

Human Rights are often described in terms of first, second and third "generation" rights. The first generation comprises civil and political rights and liberties, mainly protecting against arbitrary interference and deprivation of life, liberty and security by the state. The major document is the ICCPR. The ICESCR details the second generation of social and economic rights such as health, housing and education. Both Covenants further include third generation rights comprising peoples' or collective rights, prominently the right to self-determination.

Operating in the international sphere of sovereign states, the UN had to rule out strict enforcement mechanisms in favor of encouraging and promoting human rights through a system of monitoring. This system is based on *Charter Bodies* like e.g. the Human Rights Council (since 2006) and *Treaty Bodies*, which are committees of independent experts. The contemporary human rights regime is complemented by Intergovernmental Organisations, transnational human rights NGOs, and advocacy networks.

The International Bill of Rights established individuals and groups as subject and legitimate preoccupation of international law besides sovereign states, and destroyed the myth that the way in which states treat their citizens is not the concern of anyone else. This gives rise to controversies and paradoxes that are innate to the paradigm of human rights, and its relation to international law. The first of these concerns the paradox of the role of the state in human rights regimes – "as both the guardian of basic rights and as the behemoth against which one's rights need to be defended" (Ishay 2004b: 363); closely related to this is the second paradox of "international accountability for the domestic practice of sovereign states" (An-Na'Im 2004: 86), and the problem of international intervention when gross human rights abuses occur; this raises questions as to the "anti-democratic character" of human rights; the third controversy concerns the claim for universality of human rights; culture, traditions and practices challenge the claim to universality, and in its most extreme cultural relativism and exceptionalism deny the idea of transcultural and transcendent rights, and the obligation of states to comply with all human rights.

SEE ALSO: Democracy; Law, Sociology of; NGO/INGO; Tolerance

REFERENCES

An-Na'Im, A. A. (2004) Human rights. In: Blau, J. R. (ed.), *The Blackwell Companion to Sociology*. Blackwell, Malden, MA.

Encyclopedia of Public International Law (1995) Human rights, vol. 2. Elsevier, Amsterdam.

Ishay, M. R. (2004b) What are human rights? Six historical controversies. *Journal of Human Rights* 3: 359–71.

SUGGESTED READING

Ishay, M. R. (2004a) *The History of Human Rights: From Ancient Times to the Globalization Era*. University of California Press, Berkeley, CA.

SUSANNE KARSTEDT

humanism

Humanism, a philosophical movement that affirms the dignity of the human being, originated in Italy in the second half of the fourteenth century. The early Humanists were Christians who believed that God ruled the world; a world which they saw in need of change that could be brought about by human reason. The ability to use the power of reason, they believed, would usher in a humane world.

Humanism spread throughout Europe over the next few centuries, culminating in the Enlightenment. It was a group of Scottish and French Enlightenment philosophers (or *philosophes*, as they are collectively known), influenced by Humanism who laid the foundation of what Auguste Come (1798–1857) called "sociology." The *philosophes* advocated a fusion of morals and science, a social science that sought to liberate the human spirit and ensure the fullest development of the person. Whereas these traditions of moral philosophy and empiricism are now seen by modern sociologists as separate, they were intertwined for the Enlightenment *philosophes*.

This tradition of a "moral science" has been overlooked by the majority of contemporary sociologists who instead focus on the empiricism of the *philosophes*. By their dismissal of the "moral science" tradition and by almost unquestioningly embracing the positivism that Comte, Spenser, Durkheim, and the other early founders of sociology advocated, sociology as it began in Scotland, France, and England strayed from its humanist roots.

Humanist sociology today is associated with a small group of sociologists who are members of the Association for Humanist Sociology. Humanist sociology is explicitly based on moral precepts – the foremost of which is that of *freedom*, "the maximization of alternatives" (Scimecca 1995: 1). This is assumed to be *the* most desirable state for human beings – and the goal of sociology is to work toward the realization of conditions that can guarantee this freedom. Humanist sociology is concerned with what type of society best ensures that the freedom of the individual is not thwarted by the institutions of the society. For the Humanist sociologist, there is "one basic purpose – to develop a society where the best potential of *all* humans is most likely to be realized; in short, to develop a humane society" (Hoult 1979: 88).

SEE ALSO: Comte, Auguste; Sociology

REFERENCES

Hoult, T. F. (1979) *Sociology for a New Day*, 2nd edn. Random House, New York.

Scimecca, J. A. (1995) *Society and Freedom*, 2nd edn. Nelson-Hall, Chicago, IL.

JOSEPH SCIMECCA

hybridity

Hybridity refers to the mixture of phenomena that are held to be distinct, separate. In consumer behavior and lifestyles cut-'n'-mix experiences have become increasingly common. The theme of hybridity matches a world of intensive intercultural communication, everyday multiculturalism, growing migration and diaspora lives, and the erosion of boundaries, at least in some spheres. New hybrid forms indicate profound changes that are taking place. However, hybridity thinking also concerns existing or, so to speak, old hybridity. Anthropologists studying the travel of customs and foodstuffs show that our foundations are profoundly mixed, and it could not be otherwise. Mixing is inherent in the evolution of the species. History is a collage. We can think of hybridity as *layered* in history, including pre-colonial, colonial, and postcolonial layers, each with distinct sets of hybridity, as a function of the boundaries that were prominent at the time and their pathos of difference. Superimposed upon deep strata of mixing in evolutionary time are historical episodes of long-distance cross-cultural trade, conquest and empire and episodes such as transatlantic slavery and the triangular trade.

Hybridization is as old as history, but the pace of mixing accelerates and its scope widens in the wake of major changes, such as technologies that enable new forms of intercultural contact. Contemporary accelerated globalization is such a new phase. However, if practices of mixing are as old as the hills, the thematization of mixing is relatively recent. It includes *bricolage* in culture and art. Dada made mixing objects and perspectives its hallmark and inspired the collage. Psychoanalysis brought together dreams, jokes, Freudian slips and symbols under new headings relevant to psychological diagnosis. While hybridity may be unremarkable in itself, its critical contribution is that it questions taken-for-granted boundaries.

SEE ALSO: Globalization, Culture and; Glocalization; Multiculturalism

SUGGESTED READING
Canclini, N. G. (1995) *Hybrid Cultures*. University of Minnesota Press, Minneapolis, MN.
Nederveen Pieterse, J. (2009) *Globalization and Culture: Global Mélange*. Rowman & Littlefield, Lanham, MD.

JAN NEDERVEEN PIETERSE

hyperreality

The capitalist mode of production has gone through some significant changes in the twentieth century. Cultural phenomena have become crucial forces in the moments of distribution, exchange and consumption of commodities. The heroic age of the revolutionary bourgeoisie ended around 1910 with the decline of all of the referentials of early capitalism: clock time, the vanishing point in art, the work ethic and productive values, etc. Class strategy has shifted from the organization of production to the bureaucratic organization of consumption and everyday life. The age of simulation begins with the liquidation of referentials according to Jean Baudrillard. Signs and signifiers have become detached from their referents, from reality, and now only refer to each other. For Baudrillard, the production and reproduction of the hyperreal is what material production is all about in our postmodern society, a fundamental break from neo-capitalism. Simulations, signs and codes now structure social relations and social practices rather than the capital/labor relation of classical capitalism.

While commodification and industrialization were seen as elements of an explosive process in early capitalism, Baudrillard, following Marshall McLuhan, sees an implosion of all binary distinctions and boundaries in neo-capitalism: high and low culture, past and present, good and evil, capital and labor, male and female, white and nonwhite, developed and underdeveloped nations, appearance and reality, urban and rural, representation and reality, true and false etc. The poles of every opposition have been absorbed into one another and have become undecidable; indifference and neutralization of all of these dialectical oppositions is the consequence. Capital is simply one sign among a multitude of signs that structure social experience and practices in everyday life. Lefebvre traces this process of implosion to the failure of the proletariat to take us beyond the contradictions of capitalism. While Lefebvre sees the implosion of this over-organized society as a dystopic possibility, Baudrillard sees it as an accomplished fact and offers us only one alternative, a return to symbolic exchange.

SEE ALSO: Baudrillard, Jean; Postmodern Social Theory; Symbolic Exchange

SUGGESTED READING
Baudrillard, J., (1994) *Simulacra and Simulation*. University of Michigan Press, Ann Arbor, MI.
Gottdiener, M. (2001) *The Theming of America*, 2nd edn. Westview Press, Boulder, CO.

MICHAEL T. RYAN

hypotheses

Hypotheses are predictions that specify the relationships among the variables. The role of hypotheses in scientific research is to provide explanations for certain phenomena and to guide the investigation of related others. The development of scientific knowledge hinges ultimately upon the results from hypothesis testing. Formalized hypotheses consist of two types of variables: the independent and dependent variables. The former is the cause and the latter is the outcome. A good and well-worded hypothesis should (1) indicate the specific relationship between the dependent and independent variables to be examined; (2) suggest the nature of the relationship; and (3) imply the nature of the research design.

Hypotheses, which are derived directly from a theory or theories, have to be testable. The hypothesis-testing process generally involves three steps. The first step is to formulate two hypothesis statements: a null hypothesis (often symbolized as H_0) that predicts no relationship between the variables in the population (e.g., H_0: Social class is unrelated to deviant behavior) and an alternative hypothesis (H_1) that predicts a relationship between the variables (e.g., H_1: Social class is related to deviant behavior). The null hypothesis should be mutually exclusive of the alternative hypothesis, meaning that there is no overlap between the two hypotheses. They are also exhaustive, representing all possible outcomes in reality. If the null hypothesis is not correct or rejected, then the alternative hypothesis may be correct or accepted.

The second step is to select the level of significance. In order to decide whether to reject or fail to reject the null hypothesis, researchers must select a significance level (i.e., the α level) for the null hypothesis, which is typically at 0.05 or 0.01. If the alternative hypothesis specifies a direction of the relationship between the variables (e.g., H_1: Social class is negatively related to deviant behavior), then the test is called a one-tailed or directional hypothesis test of significance, which looks for either the increase or decrease of the dependent variable. If the alternative hypothesis does not specify a direction of the relationship (H_1: Social class is related to deviant behavior), then the test is called a two-tailed or non-directional hypothesis test of significance, which examines any change in the dependent variable.

A final step is to calculate the value of the test statistic and compare the statistic to a critical value obtained from distribution tables (e.g., distribution of t or chi square or F) based upon the α level. If the test statistic falls beyond the critical value, then the null hypothesis is rejected and the finding is significant (e.g., People with high and low social class differ significantly in their deviant behavior). If the test statistic does not exceed the critical value, then the null hypothesis cannot be rejected and the finding is not significant (e.g., People with high and low social class do not differ significantly in their deviant behavior), meaning that the difference in deviant behavior between people with high and low social class only occurs by random chance.

SEE ALSO: Fact, Theory, and Hypothesis: Including the History of the Scientific Fact

SUGGESTED READING

Gravetter, F. & Wallnau, L. (2004) *Statistics for the Behavioral Sciences*. Wadsworth, Belmont, CA.

IVAN Y. SUN

I

ideal type

Max Weber designed his use of the ideal type to solve the problem of comparison. All historical events are unique. Forcing these into some overall framework would do violence to the integrity of local detail. Capturing the general abstract qualities of a phenomenon in a mental model enables the construction of a refined and general version of the specific cases that might be met in reality.

What an ideal type captures is meaning: what counts for history is always the meaning of the people concerned in its production and interpretation. As Weber conceived them, ideal types were hypothetical ideational types that serve as a mental model that analysts can agree captures some essential features of a phenomenon. The ideal type does not correspond to reality but seeks to condense essential features of it in the model so that one can better recognize its real characteristics when it is met. It is not an embodiment of one side or aspect but the synthetic ideational representation of complex phenomena from reality.

For instance, Weber's analysis took emergent terms and ideas that were current in actual bureaucracies at the time that he was writing and used them as the basis for theoretical construction of an ideal type of bureaucracy. Bureaucracy was identified by Weber with its development by the nineteenth-century German state. Thus, a historical conception of bureaucracy defined the ideal type of bureaucracy.

Schutz (1967) took issue with one aspect of Weber's approach to ideal types: were they a construct by the analysts or were they the analysts' account of the constructs in use by the members of the research setting in question? He thought that the construction of types out of the concepts of everyday life should be such that they were grounded in the members' usage.

Because any ideal type is a historically specific construct later, different realities will not correspond to it. When writers such as Gouldner (1954) investigated organizations, they compared the realities they found with the type that they had inherited. The type became reified, taking on a life of its own. Weber's famous ideal type of bureaucracy, which he developed in the early twentieth century, was widely used much later, in the 1950s and 1960s, as the basis both for case studies, such as Gouldner (1954), as well as for the development of what were heralded as taxonomic approaches to organizations, that saw bureaucracy as a necessary and contingent organization structure that would vary with elements such as its size or technology – that is, it would be "more" or "less" bureaucratic. Both uses froze and reified a historically transitory phase of bureaucratic development into something without history. However, as Martindale (1960: 383) suggested, we should "compare different empirical configurations, not empirical configurations and types" as any specific type is always historically bounded and "destined to be scrapped."

SEE ALSO: Bureaucracy; Weber, Max

REFERENCES

Gouldner, A. W. (1954) *Patterns of Industrial Bureaucracy*. Free Press, New York.

Martindale, D. (1960) *The Nature and Types of Sociological Theory*. Routledge and Kegan Paul, London.

Schutz, A. (1967) *The Phenomenology of the Social World*. Heinemann, London.

SUGGESTED READING

Weber, M. (1978) *Economy and Society: An Outline of Interpretative Sociology*. University of California Press, Berkeley, CA.

STEWART CLEGG

identities, lesbian and gay

Ever since its arrival in academia during the 1970s, lesbian and gay studies have been haunted by the identity problem. Without doubt, it has consistently been one of the big themes for understanding "lesbian and gay lives" historically, comparatively, and contemporaneously.

Broadly, research on gay identity has highlighted six questions:

1 What is the nature of the lesbian and gay identity? – the essentialist/phenomenalist question.

2 How did the identity of lesbian and gay emerge? – the historical question.
3 How do people come to acquire the lesbian/gay identity? – the question of stages and processes.
4 How do people manage the lesbian and gay identity? – the coming out/outing/passing problem.
5 How is the identity changing?
6 What are the political uses of lesbian and gay identities? – which highlights the politics of identity and the issue of citizenship rights.

During the 1970s, a social science literature emerged which suggested the processes in which a person came to build up different kinds of sexual identity. These writings often delineated stages. Plummer (1975), for example, suggested the stages of sensitization, signification, subculturalization, and stabilization. Nowadays, such models are seen as perhaps having relevance for the 1960s and the 1970s when homosexuality was heavily stigmatized; however, these days younger people are experiencing much more flexible ways of relating to the category of homosexual.

By the 1980s it became clear that many sexual and gender identities were coming to be political categories. Increasingly both the women's movement and the gay and lesbian movement came to center around a pivotal (and usually essentialized) identity. Indeed, without such identities becoming extant, much of the politics of the new social movements would not be possible.

Gay identity became a political tactic. It also allowed rights to be attached to the identity.

But there have also been a number of countermovements to this. First, critics suggest that categories have oversimplified – even stereotyped and essentialized – complex experiences. Sexual and gender identities, for example, lie at the intersections of many other axes: ethnicity, nationality, age, disablement. These can readily hyphenate identities into "Asian gay identity" or "working-class, Native American lesbian identity."

Second, critics suggest that postmodern times have brought very different and largely unstable identities, as we have seen above: there is no fixed way of being sexual or gendered. These more radical tendencies in identity theory have since the late 1980s been linked to "queer." "Queer" is most definitely meant to take us beyond the boundaries and borders of heteronormativity. Identity is thus seriously questioned. Whether we can live with deconstructed identities in the future remains to be seen.

SEE ALSO: Coming Out/Closets; Gay and Lesbian Movement; Identity Politics/Relational Politics; Postmodern Sexualities; Queer Theory; Transgender, Transvestism, and Transsexualism

REFERENCE

Plummer, K. (1975) *Sexual Stigma: An Interactionist Account*. Routledge & Kegan Paul, London.

SUGGESTED READINGS

Plummer, K. (ed.) (1981) *The Making of the Modern Homosexual*. Hutchinson, London.
Troiden, R. R. (1988) *Gay and Lesbian Identity: A Sociological Study*. General Hall, Dix Hills, NY.

KEN PLUMMER

identity, deviant

Identities refer to the way people think of themselves. This is important in the field of deviance because if people conceive of themselves as deviant, they are more likely to engage in further deviant behavior. Central themes in the study of deviant identities include the ways that they develop, factors that foster their development, and consequences of having them.

The process of acquiring a deviant identity unfolds through seven stages. The point of departure, Becker (1963) suggested in *Outsiders*, is getting caught and publicly identified. Second, others begin to think of them differently. In light of this new information, others may engage in what Kitsuse (1962) called "retrospective interpretation," reflecting back onto individuals' pasts to see if their current and earlier behavior can be recast differently. Third, as this news spreads, either informally or through official agencies of social control, individuals develop "spoiled identities" (Goffman 1963: *Stigma*), where their reputations become tarnished. In *Wayward Puritans*, Erikson (1966) noted that once people's identities are spoiled they are hard to socially rehabilitate. Individuals may thus find it hard to recover from the lasting effect of such identity labeling, and often find that society expects them to commit further deviance.

Fourth, Lemert (1951) noted in *Social Pathology* that the dynamics of exclusion then set in, where certain groups of people may not want to associate with the newly labeled deviants, who become ostracized from participation and membership with them. Fifth, Lemert discussed the dynamics of inclusion, which make people labeled as deviant more attractive to others. Their very acts may lead individuals interested or engaged in similar forms of deviance to seek them out. Thus, as people move down the pathway of their deviant careers, they shift friendship circles, being pushed away from the company of some and welcomed into the others' company.

Sixth, others usually begin to treat those defined as deviant differently, often in a negative sense. Seventh, and finally, people react to this treatment using what Cooley (1902) referred to as their "looking glass selves." In the culminating stage of the identity career, they internalize the deviant label and come to think of themselves differently. This is likely to affect their future behavior. Although not all people who get caught in deviance progress completely through this full set of stages, Becker (1963) described this process as the effects of labeling.

While we all juggle a range of identities and social selves, Hughes (1945) asserted that a known deviant identity often assumes the position of a "master status," taking precedence over all others. Many social statuses fade in and out of relevance as people move through various situations, but a master status accompanies people into all their contexts, forming the key identity through which others see them. Master statuses are linked in society to auxiliary traits, the common social preconceptions that people associate with these. The relationship between master statuses and their auxiliary traits in society is reciprocal. When people learn that others have a certain deviant master status, they may impute the associated auxiliary traits onto them. Inversely, when people begin to recognize a few traits that they can put together to form the pattern of auxiliary traits associated with a particular deviant master status, they are likely to attribute that master status to others.

Exiting a deviant identity is considerably more problematic than assuming one in the first place. Avenues of opportunity, as Pager (2003: "The mark of a criminal record") showed, often close for those negatively marked. The route out of deviance, then, is often more gradual than precipitous, more solitary than social, more ascetic than pleasurable, and not easily attained.

SEE ALSO: Deviance; Deviant Careers; Identity Theory

REFERENCES

Cooley, C. H. (1902) *Human Nature and Social Order*. Scribner's, New York.

Hughes, E. (1945) Dilemmas and contradictions of statements. *American Journal of Sociology* 50: 353–9.

Kitsuse, J. (1962) Societal reactions to deviant behavior: problems of theory and method. *Social Problems* 9: 247–56.

PATRICIA A. ADLER AND PETER ADLER

identity: social psychological aspects

Identity is often thought of as a permanent feature of a person, connected to their bodily integrity, consciousness of time through memory, and sense of themselves as an individual with particular characteristics. Sociologists locate identity as a *social construction of reality* with relevance for both self and others. Social identities identify persons as members of groups or categories of persons, whether through statuses such as race, gender, sexuality, ability or disability, age, family, and kinship, which are commonly thought of as based in biology, as well as statuses such as nationality, ethnic group, religion, occupation, and other group memberships which are thought of as cultural. For sociologists, all of these statuses are understood as social constructions, including their characterization as rooted in biology.

Membership in an identity group or category confers expectations and meanings on the individual, orientations which are meaningful and influence both self and others. Sociologists recognize both multiple identities for any given individual and their *intersectionality*; for example, the intersectionality of race, gender and class means that each of these statuses influences the positionality of the person in social structure, as well as the meaning of each status and its impact on identity. Many statuses are associated with meanings that sociologists define as *stereotypes* which can be either negative or positive. These stereotyping attributions have been associated with the creation of spoiled identity or *stigma* by Erving Goffman, in which the self is disparaged by others for identities such as disabilities or racial/ethnic status. In postmodern theory the sense of difference engendered by stereotyping identity is characterized as the construction of *otherness* or *othering*, where others are characterized as inferior by members of a dominant group and are subject to dehumanization by those within the in-group.

Despite these issues, sociologists see social identities as allowing persons to interact with each other on the basis of typifications. Beginning with George Herbert Mead, the self has been characterized by its ability to anticipate the responses of others by placing them in situational context. Goffman built on and popularized the idea of situational identity, given by one's position in particular interactional contexts, such as student and teacher or doctor and patient. While these statuses are considered situational and temporary, to engage in such interactions one must be aware of the social expectations of appropriate behavior in each situation. Mead and Goffman emphasized both cultural influences and the emergent quality of such interactional moments, where individuals must construct appropriate behavior in order to meet their interactional goals. Behavior is influenced, but not determined, by situational requirements. For Goffman, individuals engage in *impression management* whereby they take up and maintain *lines* by means of which they make claims for identity and its associated social honor and must manage issues of credibility as they attempt to *maintain face* throughout interactions.

Questions about identity have been debated since the classic positions of Karl Marx and Max Weber on the issue of *class consciousness*. For Marx, identification with the working class was the essential ingredient of class or revolutionary consciousness. Weber understood identification with class as closer to social psychological constructions such as Bourdieu's notion of *habitus*, where the individual's experiences in a social position such as class status confers on the self an identity based on *cultural capital* acquired through everyday experience. *Identity politics* refers to self-conscious organization on the part of individuals who identify with interest groups to achieve political ends.

Sociologists share the idea of identity as a social construct, often citing the role of *narrative* as when individuals learn to narrate usable identities for particular contexts, such as when the self is problematized. Sociologists are divided on whether to be troubled by the social construction of identity. While some seem not to lament a loss of authenticity to the construction of identity, others do. For example, Arlie Hochschild voices concern about the *emotion management* required by employment in the service economy which intentionally echoes Marx's concerns about *alienation* from oneself and others.

For Kenneth Gergen the postmodern era is characterized by a *saturated self* arising out of the omnipresent influence of media, as well as the multiplicity of opportunities for interaction characterizing urban existence. These result in a *multiphrenic self* which senses its own inadequacy to meet the multitude of social and cultural obligations which it incurs. Unlike Mead who saw a rationality and logic emerging from one's immersion in the shared generalized others of one's society, Gergen sees the postmodern self as juggling not only a host of obligations, but a conflict of rationalities represented by those differing aspects of identity.

SEE ALSO: Freud, Sigmund; Goffman, Erving; Identity; Mead, George Herbert; Self; Stigma

SUGGESTED READINGS

Burke, P. J. & Stets, J. E. (2009) *Identity Theory*. Oxford University Press, Oxford.

Gergen, K. J. (1991) *The Saturated Self*. Basic Books, New York.

Goffman, E. (1963) *Stigma: Notes on the Management of Spoiled Identity*. Simon & Schuster, New York.

ALLISON CARTER

identity control theory

Identity control theory (ICT) is that part of *identity* theory that focuses on the relationships among a person's identities, their behavior, and their emotions. An *identity* is a set of meanings used to define the self as a group member (e.g., American), as a role occupant (e.g., student), or as a unique individual (e.g., honest). While people possess multiple identities, each identity is made up of meanings that are understood and shared by members of society.

In ICT, a stimulus in a situation evokes meaning or a response in an individual. When people share common responses to a stimulus, they understand each other through these shared meanings. For example, thinking about oneself as a student (stimulus) calls up a set of responses (meanings) similar to those called up in others who understand what it means to be a student, e.g., being studious, responsible, or social. These common responses lead to common expectations and understandings about what a student is, does, and the position of a student in the university – what it means to be a student.

Each identity is viewed as a *control system* with four components: an identity standard, perceptions, a comparator, and behavioral outputs. The *identity standard* is the set of meanings defining the identity. *Input perceptions* are of meanings in the situation that are relevant to an identity (mostly feedback from others about how we are coming across). The *comparator* is a mechanism that compares the input perceptions with the meanings in the identity standard and emits any difference as a discrepancy. *Behavior* is a function of the *discrepancy*.

In situations, persons enact behaviors that convey meanings consistent with their identity meanings, but modified by the discrepancy. If there is no discrepancy, people continue acting as they have been. If there is a disturbance to meanings in the situation and the discrepancy moves away from zero, people feel negative emotions including distress, and they change their behavior to counteract the disturbance and reduce the discrepancy toward zero. By changing their behavior, people change meanings in the situation that are again perceived and compared to the meanings in the identity standard in a continuous cycle.

When perceived self-relevant meanings in the situation are congruent with the meanings in the identity standard, the identity is verified and people feel good. The meanings in the identity standard represent goals or the way the situation is "supposed to be." People behave in the situation to realize these goals by creating and maintaining the situation in the way it is supposed to be. By verifying identities, people create and maintain the social structure in which the identities are embedded. Note that by controlling perceived situational meanings people are bringing about and maintaining perceptions of the situation, not behaviors. It is the outcome that is important, not the means that accomplishes the outcome.

ICT distinguishes between three identity bases. These are *role identities*, based on roles such as father, *social identities*, based on groups or categories such as American, and *person identities*, based on characteristics of the individual such as being honest. Identities formed on each of these bases operate in the same way, adjusting situations to seek verification. Verification of a role identity leads to feelings of efficacy; verification of a social identity leads to feeling of worthiness; verification of a person identity leads to feelings of authenticity.

In ICT, the multiple identities a person has are arranged into a control hierarchy. Higher-level identities act as general principles that guide the programs of lower-level identities. Higher-level identities include such master statuses as one's gender, race, or class, and many person identities that are enacted across situations, roles, and groups.

Identities act quickly counteracting disturbances to meanings in the situation. However, when people are in situations in which they cannot change their behavior to fix a discrepancy, ICT recognizes that the identity standard itself will also change slowly to match the meanings in the situation thereby reducing the discrepancy to zero. Both processes occur simultaneously to verify identities.

SEE ALSO: Affect Control Theory; Identity Theory; Social Identity Theory

SUGGESTED READINGS

Burke, P. J. (2004) Identity and social structure: the 2003 Cooley-Mead Award Address. *Social Psychology Quarterly* 67: 5–15.

Burke, P. J. and Stets, J. E. (2009) *Identity Theory*. Oxford University Press, Oxford.

Stryker, S., & Burke, P. J. (2000). The past, present, and future of an identity theory. *Social Psychology Quarterly Special Issue: The State of Sociological Social Psychology* 63 (4): 284–97.

PETER J. BURKE

identity politics/relational politics

Human society abounds with exercises of interpersonal power and identity politics. Power is the ability to get what you want with or without the consent or cooperation of others. Effects of deployed power are observable at the structural and institutional levels of society, and in face-to-face interactions. A discussion of identity politics (sometimes also called relational politics) may focus on either the class or group level or at the level of personal interactions. The subject of interpersonal politics rests within a set of related concepts, such as the distribution of social power, social location and status, and a stratified system in which these interpersonal resources may be valued and utilized for purposes of individual or group advantage over other individuals or groups.

Groups in a stratified system contend for advantage among themselves. Each group seeks to utilize group-level resources in addition to individual characteristics to secure a better or stronger position vis-à-vis the members of other groups. This may not be a result of actual conspiracy: often people acting in their own perceived self-interest serve the desires of others in a similar social position.

In the struggle for relative advantage, winning groups succeed in marketing the notion that their group members are the legitimate holders of a higher social position than members of other social groups. One example from recent American history was the successful claim by men that group characteristics associated with maleness and masculinity were more valuable to society and thereby more deserving of monetary compensation for paid labor than the group attributes of females in equivalent positions.

While some identity politics plays out at the level of the political order and public discourse, individuals also engage in identity politics in face-to-face encounters. Goffman (1959) notes: "an individual may find himself [sic] making a claim or an assumption which he knows the audience may well reject ... when the unguarded request is refused to the individual's face, he suffers what is called humiliation." Later (1963) he calls the resulting damage to identity a "stigma" that is then managed well or poorly by the individual in succeeding interactions.

Blumer (1986 [1969]: *Symbolic Interactionism: Perspective and Method*) describes how these patterned social interactions are real to their participants and result in mutual expectations for behavior in wider contexts.

One set of themes in the academic literature regarding identity politics involves the practices of identity claiming on the one hand, and altercasting on the other. In identity claiming, an individual seeks to portray herself or himself as a certain kind of person, which portrayal may or may not be met with agreement from others. Altercasting occurs when another or others attempt to impute an identity to an individual, which the individual may or may not embrace. These processes may also operate with groups.

A second theme in research and theory about identity politics is the ongoing debate between essentialist models of identity and social constructionism, also referred to as antiessentialist positions. Debating whether group level characteristics are innate (essential) or socially constructed obscures a basic misunderstanding about the difference between diversity and inequality. Over time, identity politics has shifted somewhat from demands for equality of opportunity toward demands for recognition of and structural access for persons and groups of diverse views and practices.

A third theme that may be observed in the literature on identity and relational politics is the relationship between individual experience, personal status, or social roles and political stance. For example, one might examine the expectation that part of being gay is being political, or that only members of oppressed minorities can legitimately "belong" in their movements for equality, such as an African-American rights group that only accepts European-American members in "auxiliary" roles.

SEE ALSO: Essentialism and Constructionism; Goffman, Erving; Social Identity Theory; Status

SUGGESTED READINGS

Bernstein, M. (2005) Identity politics. *Annual Review of Sociology* 31 (1): 47–74.

Warnke, G. (2005) Race, gender, and antiessentialist politics. *Signs: Journal of Women in Culture & Society* 31 (1): 93–116.

Goffman, E. (1959) *The Presentation of Self in Everyday Life*. Doubleday, New York.

Goffman, E. (1963) *Stigma: Notes on the Management of Spoiled Identity*. Prentice Hall, Englewood Cliffs, NJ.

LESLIE WASSON

identity theory

Identity Theory is a social psychological theory based on structural symbolic interactionism. The theory posits that identities are embedded in social structures, i.e. that what it means to be someone (or something) is directly affected by one's relationship and interactions with others. It assumes society is stable – the result of repeated, patterned behaviors of individuals. Identity theory is aligned with George Herbert Mead's theory of self concerning the reflexive nature between self and society, and conceives the self as comprised of multiple identities which determine how an actor behaves when alone, while engaged in a role, or when part of a group.

An identity is an *internal positional designation* which defines who one is in relation to others in the social structure. There are different types of identities: *role identities*, *social identities,* and *person identities. Role identities* (e.g. student, worker) are a combination of shared and idiosyncratic meanings actors attribute to themselves while performing a role. These meanings emerge from socialization and through culture, and from the unique, individual assessment of what playing a role means to an actor. *Social identities* (e.g. Republican, American) represent one's identification with a group. Social identities operate as an in-group/out-group dynamic, with in-group members categorized as similar and out-group members categorized as different. Social identities allow actors to create and maintain a sense of unity with others under a common theme and provide meanings to act in ways expected and approved by other in-group members. *Person identities* (e.g. moral, competitive) are unique characteristics that define an actor as an individual. Person identities can be viewed as master identities as they are often invoked and influence a wide range of behavior. All three types of identities can potentially operate simultaneously to influence perceptions, behavior, and emotions during social interactions.

There are three lines of research which have emerged within identity theory, following the work of Sheldon Stryker, Peter J. Burke, and George J. McCall and J. L. Simmons. Stryker's hierarchical approach to identity seeks to explain how an actor will behave in a situation based on how often and strongly identities are invoked. Behavior is a function of how *salient* and *committed* identities are for actors as they interact with others in the social structure. *Identity salience* refers to the probability an identity will be invoked in social situations; *identity commitment* refers to the degree to which actors' relationships to others depend on playing specific roles and maintaining identities. Stryker's work emphasizes how one's identity salience hierarchy determines behavior: the higher the identity is in the hierarchy, the higher the probability the identity will be activated, and the more the identity will impact behavior across contexts.

Burke et al.'s work in Identity Theory addresses internal dynamics of the self that influence behavior and emotions. Early work focused on how identity and behavior are linked by common meanings – by knowing an individual's identity meanings one can better understand the meanings of an individual's action. For Burke, the identity process is a perpetual control system where identities serve as standards that influence behavior. The perpetual control system is a circular process that explains how an actor's self-defined identity meanings are reflexively attached to experiences in the social structure. Basically, when an identity is activated in a situation, an internal feedback loop comes under an individual's conscious control. Actors seek to verify their identities by controlling perceptions of self and others during an interaction. Actors feel positive emotions when they verify their identities; they feel negative emotions when they cannot verify their identities. Burke's version of identity theory is also referred to as Identity Control Theory.

McCall and Simmons's (1978) version of identity theory mostly concerns role identities – an actor's subjective interpretation as an occupant of a social position. Role identities have a *conventional dimension*, which refers to expectations actors internalize concerning social positions within the greater social structure, and an *idiosyncratic dimension*, which regards the unique interpretations actors have for specific roles. McCall and Simmons define an identity *prominence hierarchy* which represents one's *ideal self*. An identity's location in the prominence hierarchy depends on the degree of support an individual obtains from others for an identity, the degree of commitment an individual has for an identity, and the rewards one receives by invoking an identity. As with Stryker, McCall and Simmons also identify a salience hierarchy, which reflects more the *situational* self rather than the *ideal* self. An identity's location in the salience hierarchy is a function of the identity's prominence, need for support, an actor's need for the kinds and amounts of intrinsic and extrinsic rewards achieved by the identity, and the perceived degree of opportunity for its profitable enactment in the situation. Actors have expectations for their roles as well as the roles of others; when interchanges go smoothly relationships are maintained and prominence hierarchies are supported.

Research in Identity Theory incorporates both quantitative and qualitative methods. Surveys and interviews have been used to examine identity meanings, identity commitment, and identity salience. Such methods allow researchers to discover the importance a subject places on an identity and how often an identity is salient for an actor across situations, and to measure the amount and type of people a subject is connected to through an identity. Laboratory experiments have also been used to measure identity processes. The corpus of work produced by scholars from all areas of identity theory has furthered the understanding of micro-level phenomena, both within sociological social psychology as well as sociology in general.

SEE ALSO: Identity Control Theory; Social Identity Theory; Social Psychology; Symbolic Interaction

REFERENCE

McCall, G. & Simmons, J. S. (1978) *Identities and Interaction*, rev. edn. Free Press, New York.

SUGGESTED READINGS

Burke, P. J. (1991) Identity processes and social stress. *American Sociological Review* 56: 836–49.

Stets, J. E. (2006) Identity theory. In: Burke, P. J. (ed.), *Contemporary Social Psychological Theories*. Stanford University Press, Palo Alto, CA.

Stryker, S. (1980) *Symbolic Interactionism: A Social Structural Version*. Benjamin/Cummings, Menlo Park, CA.

Stryker, S. and Burke, P. J. (2000) The past, present, and future of an identity theory. *Social Psychology Quarterly* 63: 284–97.

MICHAEL J. CARTER

ideological hegemony

Ideological hegemony explains relationships of domination and exploitation as embedded in socioculture. Its roots are in early twentieth-century Marxism, which had the task of explaining the absence or failure of worldwide communist revolutions. It suggests that to the extent that dominant class ideas are internalized by the dominated, they induce consent.

One of the earliest works to develop these ideas was *History and Class Consciousness* (Lukacs [1923] 1971), which drew a distinction between *objective* and *subjective* class consciousness. Objective class consciousness refers to workers' material interests whereas subjective class consciousness refers to workers' ideas and attitudes. "False consciousness" is the gap between workers' objective class interests and their awareness of them. This distinction moves away from "pure economism," which suggests that the inherent contradictions in capitalism make communism inevitable.

Antonio Gramsci (1891–1937) coined the term ideological hegemony while in prison in Fascist Italy between 1927 and 1935. *The Prison Notebooks* took aim at the Marxists of the Second International, who believed that universal suffrage in industrialized countries would naturally lead to the "dictatorship of the proletariat." Gramsci argued that ideational processes come between material forces and the meanings connected to them. The realm of ideas, or what Marx called the "superstructure" (religion, legal structures, the family, etc.), normalizes the interests of the ruling class so that they appear natural and justified. Exploited people unwittingly adopt ideas and ways of life that are consistent with their continued exploitation.

How is hegemony achieved? Gramsci proposed that the dominant group exercises hegemony in "civil society," which represents all that we consider private, whereas it utilizes the state to directly dominate "political society." But ideological hegemony is not automatic; it is a project that the ruling class must accomplish. Therefore, its level varies between societies. Where it is strong, capitalists rely on popular consensus, where it is weak, physical coercion becomes more necessary. Workers' revolutionary potential is higher in the latter, but they must develop counterhegemonies (the main political task of the socialist movement) to successfully accomplish their potential (Boggs 1978). Marcuse (1964) added the advertising industry, industrial management, and the very act of consumption to Gramsci's modes of hegemony. Mass consumption weds lower classes to an exploitative system, and mitigates oppositional behavior and critical thinking. Moreover, media scholars argue that the format of television creates a reified view of reality impervious to radical change by proposing character themes that are fixed rather than developing. Furthermore, the very act of consuming mainstream cultural transmission – watching television – precludes public discourse and encourages passive absorption of dominant ideologies. Finally, these scholars point to the profit logic driving media dissemination, which create appetites for sensationalism, rather than the redress of everyday problems.

Hegemony has limits because the economic/political structure of society is constantly changing, and hegemonic ideology must change to naturalize evolving social relations. Indeed, for Habermas, while "advanced capitalism" evolved past the pure wage labor/capital dichotomy and can therefore avert a terminal economic crisis, it does produce a series of distinct crises that can lead to a "legitimation crisis" (Habermas 1973), in which the system no longer produces the motivation for consent. Moreover, Todd Gitlin argues that television in the 1950s was able to exclude voices of dissent because of the relatively calm era of smooth economic expansion. By the 1970s, however, themes dealing with racism, sexism, and poverty entered the mainstream. Television culture attempted to domesticate feminist and ethnic resistance by delegitimizing "radical" views in favor of those that were easily co-opted.

SEE ALSO: Civil Society; Critical Theory/Frankfurt School; False Consciousness; Gramsci, Antonio; Hegemony and the Media; Ideology

REFERENCES

Boggs, C. (1978) *Gramsci's Marxism*. Pluto Press, London.

Habermas, J. (1973) *Legitimation Crisis*. Beacon Press, Boston, MA.

Marcuse, H. (1964) *One-Dimensional Man: Studies in the Ideology of Advanced Industrial Society*. Beacon Press, Boston, MA.

MATTHEW C. MAHUTGA
AND JUDITH STEPAN-NORRIS

ideology

Proposing a science of ideas which would empirically analyze the human mind, Antoine Destutt de Tracy's *Eléments d'idéologie* (1801) introduced the concept and gave ideology its first meaning. Consistent with Enlightenment rationalism, ideology would demonstrate that once the basis of ideas was understood, one could constitute society in harmony with human nature. Comte's *Cours de philosophie positive* is one culmination of this conception of ideology – achieving the positivist stage, the development of the human mind would indicate how all historical phenomena are subject to invariable, natural laws. Reason would allow true order to reign.

Initially supported by Napoleon Bonaparte, after he reconciled with the Roman Catholic Church Bonaparte denounced Destutt and other *savants* in the Institut de France for advocating a politically motivated, simplified body of ideas that distorted the truth. This gave ideology a second, politicized meaning.

In contrast to French positivism and British empiricism, Hegel's philosophy centred on the primacy of mind over matter. The history of philosophy was Mind progressively grasping the true rationality that underlies the sensible world. Thinking individuals are the medium through which Mind becomes the active, generating force leading towards absolute, comprehensive truth. Although Hegel's *Philosophy of Right* buttressed the conservative Prussian monarchy, his left-Hegelian interpreters emphasized the ongoing critical potential of individual, critical minds continuing Mind's development towards Absolute Reason. Hegel's ideology – his systematic study of ideas and their impact – dominated conservative and radical German thought in the mid-nineteenth century.

"Humankind has, up to now, always created false representations [*falsche Vorstellungen*] about itself and thus what it is and ought to be" Karl Marx and Friedrich Engels (1932: 3) argued. Humankind has endowed ideas with ultimate power and subsumed itself under its own creations; consciousness appears to determine being. *The German Ideology* (1845) criticized the "German ideologues" for failing to expose Hegel's fundamental errors and not recognizing the true origin of ideas. One must begin with "actual individuals, their actions and their material conditions of life" which give rise to "a definite way to express [*äußern*] their life" (pp. 10–11). "Consciousness [*Bewußtsein*] can never be anything else than conscious being [*bewußte Sein*], and the being of humanity is its actual life-process" (p. 15).

This perspective introduced new dimensions to ideology. It remained the systematic account of the basis for ideas but now claimed that there were "false conceptions" which arose because, like the *camera obscura*, reality is passively accepted in an inverted manner (ideas appear to govern people). By overturning this misperception, one would overcome an existing "false consciousness," discover the true origin of ideas, transcend a condition in which a human product, separated from its producers confronts and dominates its creators – a particular form of alienation – and recognize the real basis for social change.

Marx and Engels also used ideology to denote a partial, distorting perspective representing particular, vested interests – "The ideas of the ruling class are in every epoch the ruling ideas: i.e. the class which is the ruling *material* force of society is at the same time its ruling *intellectual* force."

In *History and Class Consciousness* (1923), criticizing "vulgar Marxists" for ignoring consciousness, Georg Lukács emphasized the Hegel–Marx connection to explore knowledge, ideology, reification and false consciousness in detail. He argued that the proletariat's unique, objective conditions would lead it beyond a reified, ideologically distorted, false consciousness to a true, universal consciousness. Lukács's subsequent disavowal of the work helped legitimize Stalin's Dialectical Materialism as official Soviet ideology – negating his great intellectual accomplishment.

Karl Mannheim wrote *Ideology and Utopia* (1929) to disentangle ideology from its Marxist roots. Ideologies, Mannheim argued, arose from social experiences and expressed a particular *Weltanschauung* (worldview). Detailing how knowledge was based on social practice, Mannheim initiated the sociology of knowledge as a sub-discipline within sociology. Mannheim also suggested that intellectuals could produce impartial worldviews to replace the distorting, total ideologies that were guiding political life.

For various reasons, sociologists have largely abandoned ideology to conceptualize how governing powers create consent to their rule and now use Antonio Gramsci's concept of hegemony. By including culture and various social practices within it, hegemony is conceptually more inclusive than ideology. Through "the war of position," hegemony also suggests that a dominant ideology competes against alternative worldviews, cultural perceptions, and other counter-hegemonic forces.

SEE ALSO: False Consciousness; Gender Ideology and Gender Role Ideology; Gramsci, Antonio; Knowledge, Sociology of; Mannheim, Karl;

REFERENCE

Marx, K. & Engels, F. (1932) *Marx–Engels Gesamtausgabe* (*Marx–Engels Complete Works*), part 1, vol. 5. Marx–Engels–Verlag, Berlin.

SUGGESTED READING

Eagleton, T. (2007) *Ideology*, 2nd edn. Verso, London.

ROB BEAMISH

imagined communities

"Imagined community" is a term coined by Benedict Anderson (1983) in *Imagined Communities: Reflections on the Origin and Spread of Nationalism*, an influential book on the emergence and persistence of nations. The concept addresses the relationship between states, capitalism, and cultural belonging.

Anderson defines the nation as *imagined* "because the members of even the smallest nation will never know most of their fellow-members ... yet in the minds of each lives the image of their communion" (1983: 6), and as a *community* because "regardless of the actual inequality and exploitation that may prevail . . . the nation is always conceived as a deep, horizontal comradeship" (1983: 7).

"Imagined community" positions national identities and nationalism as social constructs. Anderson emphasizes the dynamic coincidence of the development of printing technologies, industrial capitalism, and increased literacy as crucial in this regard, as this allowed the idea of the nation to be disseminated within national-linguistic markets to an emergent bourgeoisie (who could "imagine" themselves in national cultural communities outside of family structures and religious institutions).

For Anderson then, the promise of the nation as "imagined community" is in the social integration of strangers; the impression, albeit an illusion, is of a coherent group moving together through history and into a common future. In questioning how such narratives are constructed and maintained through culture, the concept of "imagined community" has become important to much sociological research on nationalism, ethnicity, and identity.

SEE ALSO: Community; Culture; Nationalism; State

REFERENCE

Anderson, B. (1983) *Imagined Communities: Reflections on the Origin and Spread of Nationalism.* Verso, London.

SUGGESTED READING

Billig, M. (1995) *Banal Nationalism.* Sage, London.

PAUL JONES

immigration

Sociologists look at migration as a social phenomenon. Their research is focused not on individual immigrants but on immigrant populations and their characteristics, because the characteristics of immigrant flows and immigrant populations are essential for understanding migration processes and the reaction to these processes from the receiving societies. The volume of the migration flow, its demographic structure (only young males, or whole families e.g.), the homogeneity or heterogeneity of the immigrant population according to educational attainments for instance, this kind of variable is relevant for the description of immigration as a social phenomenon.

A second decision relates to the societal context of our field of study. Because migration is such a ubiquitous phenomenon it has occurred and still occurs under very different circumstances. The world counts to date millions and millions of people who have migrated out of their own free will or as compelled by ethnic cleansing, civil wars or natural disasters. The receiving societies differ fundamentally in nature and stability of state formation to mention only one important characteristic. (Documentation of present-day world migration is available on the website: www.migrationinformation.org/GlobalData/.)

The most important historical development impinging on migration processes has been the rise of the modern state, at least in the western world. Government by the people for the people implied a distinction between citizens and non-citizens. With the rise of the state as the dominant social institution state borders have become the main impediments for migration flows. The distinction between internal and external migration became accepted as a fundamental distinction for the analysis and assessment of migration processes. Modern welfare states have developed a system of migration regulation controlling entry, residence and access to the labor market. The aim of these regulations is to select immigrants who are expected to contribute to society and to prevent immigrants, who are expected to become a burden, to settle in the country. However, the practical application of these mechanisms of migration control proves to be far from easy. In all states migration control has become a political issue and studies around the regulation of migration and the links to other aspects of social traditions, definitions and interests show a kaleidoscope of situations even within the category of welfare states, let alone in very different states such as the emirates around the Gulf. To make control over migration flows even more complicated all western states have signed the Convention of Geneva (1951) and thereby recognized the rights of refugees on settlement in a country, regardless of the interests of the host country. No government is in practice prepared to accept such an open-ended regulation. Hence we see governments continuously specifying the definitions and rules around the rights of asylum seekers.

The migration process does not end with the entry of immigrants in the receiving society. The relation between immigrant and host society has been, under various headings (assimilation, integration, incorporation), a main theme in the sociology of migration, especially in the USA. It was soon clear that the massive immigration of the late nineteenth century would change US society and that not all immigrants would become White Anglo-Saxon Protestants. Immigrants became on one hand Americanized, but on the other hand changed American society by introducing new religions, customs and lifestyles.

Recently the question has also come to the fore of what the impact is, or can be, of the modern means of transport and communication on the relation between immigrants and their new surroundings. Alba and Nee (2003) summarize the classical American studies and scrutinize the evidence with regard to the assimilation of modern immigrant communities. They point out that the rapid changes in the economy and the concomitant labor market indeed affect the ways immigrants adapt to the new society. The US mainstream, as in many other countries, now looks different from the mainstream in the industrial era, but that is not to say that there is no mainstream and that immigrants are not assimilating to it.

SEE ALSO: Immigration Policy; Migration and the Labor Force; Migration: International

REFERENCE

Alba, R. & Nee, V. (2003) *Remaking the American Mainstream: Assimilation and Contemporary Immigration*. Harvard University Press, Cambridge, MA, and London.

SUGGESTED READING

Brochmann, G. & Hammar, T. (eds.) (1999) *Mechanisms of Immigration Control: A Comparative Analysis of European Regulation Practices*. Berg, Oxford and New York.

Cornelius, W. A., Martin, P. A., & Hollifield, J. A. (eds.) (1994) *Controlling Migration: A Global Perspective*. Stanford University Press, Stanford, CA.

HANS VAN AMERSFOORT

immigration policy

Immigration policy specifies the laws and practices that allow persons to move permanently to other countries and petition for citizenship or to enter and stay for delimited lengths of time without the right to apply for citizenship. In developed countries, such policies include not only voluntary work and occupation-based and family-based migration but also the admission of refugees and the acceptance of asylum seekers. In its most comprehensive form, immigration policy not only involves the admission of immigrants, but also endeavors to coordinate labor needs with the control of migrant flows, affect international policies that might alleviate the need for some migration, and integrate newcomers into the socioeconomic fabric of the destination society. Immigration policies also often cover non-immigrants, such as those who cross borders to travel, conduct business, work temporarily, visit, or study. Such policies also extend to the treatment of unauthorized immigrants, or those who enter a country without a visa or who overstay a visa, although the presence of such persons in the country does not directly result from admissions policies.

Immigration policies vary across countries, although relatively few countries receive many international migrants and have formal migration policies in place. Traditional migrant-receiving countries such as the United States or Canada have tended to try to control who enters their borders through visa systems. Continental countries, such as Germany, that had not considered themselves migrant destinations despite decades of in-migration, have tended over the years to control migration through residence and work permits, the parameters of which might become more favorable the longer migrants stayed. While such distinctions of policy emphasis have blurred in recent years, policy conceptions between the traditional immigrant-receiving countries still perceive policy differently from new immigrant destinations.

Until the late nineteenth century, none of the major immigrant-receiving countries sought to adopt laws and practices to regulate migration, nor did they mount substantial efforts to control the magnitude of immigrant flows. To a considerable extent, this owed to the relative absence of political forces compelling such restriction. Nativism was a relatively small cultural current in early nineteenth-century America; most Americans at the time – as well as Canadians and Australians – understood that they needed to populate and settle their countries. After decades of flows of settlers, however, anti-immigrant activity began to arise in the United States in the mid-nineteenth century, first against Catholics, particularly the Irish but also the Germans; then against Asians, starting with the Chinese and moving on to Japanese and Filipinos; and then against all immigrants, particularly as immigrant flows were increasing from southern and eastern Europe.

SEE ALSO: Immigration; Migration: International; Migration: Undocumented/Illegal; Transnationalism

SUGGESTED READING

Cornelius, W., Martin, P., & Hollifield, J. (eds.) (2004) *Controlling Immigration: A Global Perspective*. Stanford University Press, Stanford, CA.

Lynch, J. P. & Simon, R. J. (2003) *Immigration the World Over: Statutes, Policies, and Practices*. Rowman & Littlefield, Lanham, MD.

SUSAN K. BROWN AND FRANK D. BEAN

imperialism

Imperialism designates the historical phenomenon in which certain political entities have sought to exert control over and extract resources from others, whether through formal conquest, informal coercion or a host of intermediate solutions. It also denotes the concepts or theories of imperialism. Initially coined to designate the existence and expansion of empires, the notion of imperialism gained prominence in the late nineteenth century, where it came to identify the reality of European colonialism. The ensuing history of the concept registers a distinction between purely political definitions of imperialism, which reduce it to an instance of power politics and foreground the issue of territorial gain, and socio-economic analyses, which, while not discounting the significance of physical expansion, emphasize the underlying and systemic causes of imperialist policies. The penchant for a given theory of imperialism will determine which processes and events count as cases of imperialism, so that analytical definitions are here inseparable from historical judgments.

The acceleration in colonizing ventures during what Eric Hobsbawm (1987) has termed "the age of empire" gave rise to the first great debates on imperialism. Liberal opposition to imperialism attacked what it regarded as a jingoistic manipulation of mass sentiment for irrational ends or petty interests. In Schumpeter's analysis, this led to a focus on the use of irrational and "objectless" nationalist tendencies to condition the masses. Where Schumpeter defined the causes of imperialism as primarily socio-political in character, Hobson's *Imperialism* opened the way for its structural analysis as a necessary correlate of a particular socio-economic order. Hobson contended that imperialism was driven by the needs of financial elites and monopolies which, failing to get sufficiently profitable returns on their investments in a saturated market constrained by the low purchasing power of workers, pushed for the forcible opening of overseas opportunities.

Hobson's ideas were of great import for what is certainly the most read and influential tract on the subject, Lenin's (1917) *Imperialism, the Highest Stage of Capitalism*. Compensating for the insufficient theorization of imperialism in Marx's own works, Lenin followed Hobson in seeing finance and monopoly capital as the key factor. In the midst of World War I, Lenin tried to understand that conflagration as an effect of the conflict between great capitalist powers, now held captive by increasingly parasitic financial oligarchies. Rosa Luxemburg (1913), in *The Accumulation of Capital*, also attempted to integrate a political critique of the age of empire with an economic analysis – founded on the idea of underconsumption and capitalism's constant need to expand to non-capitalist zones to create markets and realize surplus-value. She also introduced the analysis of "militarism" both as an ideological tool and as a component (in the guise of the arms industry) of capital accumulation under conditions of imperialism.

Marxist theories of imperialism grew in political significance and conceptual variety in the postwar period, in the contexts of the cold war and decolonization. The ebb of theories of imperialism in the 1980s seemed terminal, especially as the analysis of the political economy of the world market came under the aegis of globalization theories. Even from the Left, namely in Hardt and Negri's (2000) theory of "Empire" as a new form of virtual, decentered capitalist sovereignty, the notion of imperialism appeared to be relegated to another era. However, the recent wars in Iraq and Afghanistan have triggered a resurgence in thinking on imperialism.

One of the key questions has been whether the USA's form of primarily non-territorial economic power and influence should be defined as imperialism. David Harvey (2005) has argued that the "new imperialism" must be understood in terms of two conjoined but irreducible logics: a territorial logic of political power and a molecular logic of capital accumulation. He regards the war as a means of securing US hegemony over energy resources and thus bolstering its economic primacy. Ellen Wood (2005) has instead defined capitalist imperialism – as opposed to previous "empires of property" and "empires of commerce" – in terms of the detachment of economic from political power. However, this economic power demands for its hegemony and expansion the presence of a system of multiple states, and the more globally integrated the system, the greater the tendency to the hegemony of one of these states (e.g., the US "empire") over the task of maintaining the capitalist system. Updating the methods of historical materialism, Wood thus returns to the key theme already broached by Luxemburg: the intimate correlation between capital accumulation and expansionist militarism.

SEE ALSO: Capitalism; Colonialism (Neocolonialism); Cultural Imperialism; Dependency and World-Systems Theories

REFERENCES

Hardt, M. & Negri, A. (2000) *Empire*. Harvard University Press, Cambridge, MA.

Harvey, D. (2005) *The New Imperialism*. Oxford University Press, Oxford.

Hobsbawm, E. (1987) *The Age of Empire: 1875–1914*. Weidenfeld & Nicolson, London.

Wood, E. M. (2005) *Empire of Capital*. Verso, London.

ALBERTO TOSCANO

implosion

French postmodernist critic Jean Baudrillard's implosion theory is one of social entropy, wherein the consumer age of information, media, and mass media has ushered in an accelerated and coercive hyper-production of meaning and information to the "irrational" and "terroristic" extent that all meaning, knowledge, and subjectivity, the social, and thus social inquiry, are neutralized and ultimately collapse. All that is left is an imploding "mass ... an in vacuo aggregation of individual particles, refuse of the social and of media impulses; an opaque nebula whose growing density absorbs all the surrounding energy and light rays, to collapse finally under its own weight" (Baudrillard 1983: 3–4). Amid ubiquitous and proliferating media-generated information in a consumer society of simulacra and simulation, information ceases to be productive, or capable of transformation by human subjects. It produces merely destructive energy, more implosive density, more mass. The obliteration of the social collapses distinctions between "classes, political ideologies, cultural forms, and between media semiurgy and the real itself ... society in its entirety is implosive" (Best and Kellner 1991: 121).

The only "imaginary referent" remaining in Baudrillard's world of simulacra and semiurgy are the non-subject, non-object "silent majorities," or the purely "crystal ball" statistical morbid remains of status groupings. The "singular function" of the silent majorities is to absorb meaning, not refract or transform it. The only non-conscious "strategic resistance" to the present phase of the system for the inert, indifferent, passive masses is that of a "refusal of meaning ... the hyperconformist simulation of the very mechanisms of the system, which is a form of refusal and non-reception" (Baudrillard 1983: 108). Forestalling any interpretations of the defiantly apolitical, or theories of oppression or repression, Baudrillard claims ultimately, "the denial of meaning has no meaning" (Baudrillard 1983: 40–1).

SEE ALSO: Postmodern Social Theory; Mass Media; Consumer Society; Consumption; Spectacle; Simulation

REFERENCES

Best, S. and Kellner, D. (1991) *Postmodern Theory: Critical Interrogations*. Guilford Press, New York.

Baudrillard, J. (1983) *In the Shadow of the Silent Majorities Or, the End of the Social and Other Essays*. Semiotext(e), New York.

KAREN BETTEZ HALNON

impression formation

Impression formation is the process by which individuals perceive, organize, and ultimately integrate information to form impressions of others. Internalized expectations condition what information individuals deem is worthy of their attention, as well as how it is interpreted. In face-to-face interaction, social cues including physical appearance, verbal and non-verbal behavior, and the social setting combine with information in perceivers' memories to influence the ways in which they initially form impressions of others and themselves. These initial impressions serve as the basis for subsequent attributions. Research in social cognition provides explanations of general information gathering and processing, expectation states theory offers insights about information integration, while affect control theory provides a mathematical calculus designed in part to predict impression formation outcomes.

Due to limitations in our capacity to both perceive and process information, we rely on cognitive shortcuts to manage information. In addition, our social experiences provide a basis for preexisting expectations for events which further condition what we notice and how we then interpret it. For example, it is important to make "good first impressions" on those we meet because the temporal ordering of events influences the information processing. Specifically, examinations of the *primacy effect* and *recency effect* suggest that individuals weight information acquired first and most recently, respectively, more than that learned in between.

Research using expectation states theory suggests that multiple items of social information are aggregated into organized subsets to form impressions of self and others (Berger et al. 1992). In general, the effects of the salient multiple pieces of (sometimes contradictory) information are combined to form an aggregated expectation state about a social object/person. New information is likely to have a greater independent effect on status outcomes when presented in opposition to a field of contrary information than if it were presented alone and an attenuation function operates with respect to additional pieces of supporting information such that at some point there is a diminishing independent effect for each additional piece of information.

Affect control theory (ACT) offers a mathematical formalization of the impression formation process that synthesizes elements of symbolic interactionism and role theory. According to ACT, individuals see themselves and the others around them as participating in situations by enacting social roles. Individuals form definitions of the situations by assigning identity labels to self and other(s) after comparing the readily observable characteristics that each possesses with internalized cultural expectations for what identities are appropriate given the setting they are in. Once they have defined the setting and the others(s) in it, cultural rules pertaining to these definitions provide the basis from which they can form expectations for the events (behaviors) that are likely to occur.

SEE ALSO: Affect Control Theory; Attribution Theory; Expectation States Theory; Social Cognition

REFERENCES

Berger, J., Norman, R. Z., Balkwell, J. W. & Smith, R. F. (1992) Status inconsistency in task situations: a test of four status processing principles. *American Sociological Review* 57: 843–55.

SUGGESTED READING

Asch, S. E. (1946) Forming impressions of personality. *Journal of Abnormal and Social Psychology* 41: 258–90.

CHRISTOPHER D. MOORE

income inequality, global

Income inequality refers to the unequal distribution of income across units (usually individuals or households). *Global* income inequality refers to the unequal distribution of income across the world's citizens.

Global income inequality consists of two components, *between-nation income inequality* – the unequal distribution of *average income* across nations – and *within-nation income inequality* – the unequal distribution of income across individuals or households within countries. Sociological studies of inequality very often focus on inequality within nations. Most of the inequality in the distribution of the world's income, however, lies between nations. Average incomes in the world's richest and poorest nations vary by a factor of 30 or more, so the average person in a rich country receives as much in a single day as the average person in a poor country does in a month. As a result, even if we eliminated all inequality within countries – so citizens in every country earned the average income for their country – the majority of global income inequality would remain.

Global income inequality is massive today largely because of the highly uneven growth of regional and national incomes in the nineteenth and early twentieth centuries. During this period the world divided roughly into three income camps as the industrializing west surged ahead economically and Asia and Africa lagged badly behind. Incomes in a middle group, consisting of most of Latin America and Eastern Europe (including the former Soviet Union), grew at very roughly the world average. Because it was the richer regions that were growing faster, this unevenness in growth rates resulted in the great inequality in income across regions and nations that we see today. The legacy of the Industrial Revolution, then, is that of a world where incomes are much higher (on average) but also much more unevenly distributed.

Today, however, richer regions are no longer the growth leaders. Large poor countries such as China and India are experiencing faster income growth than rich nations. Although incomes continue to decline relatively (and in some instances absolutely) in many poor nations in sub-Saharan Africa, many more poor *individuals* live in poor nations where incomes are growing faster than the world average than in poor nations where incomes are growing slower than average. The result is declining income inequality across countries.

At the same time, inequality is rising within many, but not all, countries in the west and elsewhere. This new pattern of uneven income growth – declining inequality across nations, rising inequality within the average nation – reflects the reversal of a longstanding trend of rising inequality across nations and constant or declining inequality within nations. This reversal has been called the "new geography of global income inequality" (Firebaugh 2003).

What most social scientists, policy makers, and activists want to know is whether the decline in inequality across nations more than offsets the rising inequality within nations. Is global income inequality now declining, or is it still growing as it did over the nineteenth century and first half of the twentieth century? Studies give mixed results: Some find evidence that global income inequality continues to rise and others find that it is falling. This ambiguity is not surprising, given the difficulty of comparing income levels across countries. Despite heroic data collection efforts, with current data it is difficult to determine authoritatively whether global income inequality is trending up or down. What we can ascertain from the data is that global inequality is not moving rapidly in either direction, so concerns of rapidly worsening global income inequality are misplaced.

The major challenge for future research on global inequality, then, is data reliability. The measurement issues are pretty well settled: There is general consensus on the best ways to measure income, and on how to measure and decompose income inequality. But our measurements and decompositions are only as reliable as the data we input, and that is where much of the effort should be expended in future research on global income inequality.

SEE ALSO: Income Inequality and Income Mobility; Inequality, Wealth; Stratification and Inequality, Theories of

REFERENCES

Firebaugh, G. (2003) *The New Geography of Global Income Inequality*. Harvard University Press, Cambridge, MA.

SUGGESTED READINGS

Anand, S. and Segal, P. (2008) What do we know about global income inequality? *Journal of Economic Literature* 46: 57–94.

Milanovic, B. (2005) *Worlds Apart: Measuring International and Global Inequality*. Princeton University Press, Princeton, NJ.

Website: http://ucatlas.ucsc.edu/index.php.

GLENN FIREBAUGH

income inequality and income mobility

Research on income inequality within the social sciences took off as a byproduct of income taxation. Lists were published showing how many tax-paying units during a tax year had an income of a certain size. The distribution did not look like a bell-shaped curve, but was skewed at the upper end. The description of the distribution by one parameter started with Vilfredo Pareto, and his results led to the hypothesis that this statistic was more or less the same for all times and places. Later results, using better measures like the Gini coefficient, found differences between countries, leading to a hunt for explanations.

Sociologists proposed basically two explanations for country-level differences in income inequality. The first invokes economic factors, the second political ones. It has been held that in more economically developed countries income inequalities are smaller. Similarly, it has also been proposed that countries with a more peripheral (as opposed to central) place in the world economy have larger income inequalities. As to political factors, it has been maintained that in highly industrialized societies a long democratic history as well as a social democratic government, by way of various policies, have diminished income inequalities. Among these policies are progressive taxation, free secondary and tertiary education for all, and collective insurance against such matters as unemployment, work-related disabilities, and old age.

By way of quite simple comparisons and more sophisticated statistical techniques, these hypotheses have generally proved their mettle. An important issue is exactly how income inequalities are measured. If it is to be tested, an overall measure for income inequality in a country (like the Gini coefficient) will not do. Data on the income share of, say, the poorest and the richest 10 percent and 20 percent of the population are also necessary.

Sociologists have studied data on intergenerational mobility along a scale of occupational status. Blau and Duncan (1967) examined data from the USA and found a correlation between father and son's occupational status of 0.4 (with zero indicating no correlation and unity full correlation and the strongest possible determination of son's by father's occupational status). When reviewing Blau and Duncan's results, an economist suggested that occupational status as measured by sociologists is a reasonably good indicator of permanent income: not a person's income during one particular year, but a person's income calculated over a longer period. The interesting question is to what extent occupational correlations agree with data from long-running income panels.

Apart from depicting the USA as a much less mobile society than earlier income mobility data indicated, comparisons of US intergenerational income mobility data with those of other countries do not seem to show particularly low correlations for the USA. Research on Finland and Sweden using 3-year annual average earnings for fathers and sons found correlations closer to 0.1. Strict comparisons of a large number of countries remain a promise for the future, but it does seem that, for highly industrialized countries, low inequality in yearly income goes together with high income mobility.

SEE ALSO: Educational Attainment; Income Inequality, Global; Inequality, Wealth; Mobility, Horizontal and Vertical

SUGGESTED READINGS

Blau, P. & Duncan, O. D. (1967) *The American Occupational Structure*. Wiley, New York.

Solon, G. (2002) Cross-country differences in intergenerational earnings mobility. *Journal of Economic Perspectives* 16 (3): 59–66.

WOUT ULTEE

indigenous movements

Struggles for indigenous self-determination have become a major worldwide human rights movement. Throughout the Americas and in settler colonies such as Australia and Aotearoa/New Zealand, as well as across the Pacific and in Asia and Africa and the Caribbean, indigenous peoples reject their treatment as disadvantaged citizens of settler states and instead demand to be recognized as political communities with distinctive rights. The proliferation of indigenous mobilizations – irreducible to a single, unified movement – reflects a shifting terrain of struggle. New strategies, operating simultaneously on multiple scales, have been deployed to confront new and evolving threats to the individual and collective rights of indigenous peoples. Despite noteworthy gains, indigenous peoples, in many cases, still are losing control over lands, water and other resources, and access to sacred sites. Market-driven global processes, underwritten by dominant settler colonies such as the United States, are deepening environmental deterioration and increasing poverty, limiting the hope of sustainable futures for indigenous *and* non-indigenous people everywhere.

In response to overt settler violence and subtle coercion (e.g., subordination to states within liberal multicultural frameworks), indigenous peoples continue to fight old fights as well as mount new forms of resistance. While often concerned with defending recently re-acquired autonomy in local contexts ripe with racial tensions, the political and economic conjuncture brought on by global capitalism and its unprecedented demands for resources (e.g., forests, minerals, oil, water) has forced indigenous peoples to engage in new fights for survival. Generally speaking, indigenous movements employ a variety of strategies and operate from multiple locations in order to challenge the authority and question the legitimacy of the state and capital. Indigenous movements thus occupy a fluid position vis-à-vis the state and struggle for freedom both within *and* against structures of domination by taking power *and* making power.

Thus, indigenous movements emerge transhemispherically and transoceanically to challenge settler states' claims of absolute sovereignty. These multifaceted mobilizations stress self-determination and autonomy, often calling for restructuring states, territorial rights, control over economic development, and reforms of police powers over them. Everywhere, indigenous peoples remain as concerned as ever with safeguarding distinctive forms of government and governing, wrestling control of natural and cultural resources away from states and corporations, protecting sacred sites, and revitalizing indigenous languages and cultures.

SEE ALSO: Colonialism (Neo-Colonialism); Indigenous Peoples; Decolonization

SUGGESTED READINGS

Duncan I., Patton, P. & Sanders, W. (eds.) (2000). *Political Theory and the Rights of Indigenous Peoples*. Cambridge University Press, Cambridge.

Stuart-Harawira, M. (2005) *The New Imperial Order: Indigenous Responses to Globalization*. Zed Books, London.

D. ANTHONY TYEEME CLARK
AND NICHOLAS BROWN

indigenous peoples

"Indigenous peoples" refers to those peoples who either live or have lived within the past several centuries in nonstate societies, though now nearly all have been absorbed into state societies. For North America, we alternate among Native Americans, American Indians, native, or Indian. Many groups have reasserted their traditional names: Diné for Navajo, Ho-Chunk for Winnebago, or Tohono O'odham for Papago. The modern organization of many indigenous cultures has arisen from efforts to change or destroy them. Much ethnographic and ethnohistorical research shows that the symbolic, demographic, and social boundaries of indigenous groups have been quite flexible. The presumption of fixed or clear boundaries grew from the needs of European negotiators to identify "leaders" for purposes of treaty-making.

The study of indigenous peoples is invaluable to understanding social change because they exhibit a wide range in variation. It is erroneous to assume, however, that indigenous people are "living artifacts" of earlier times even though they have survived centuries of contact and interaction with state societies. The processes that brought first-hand accounts of indigenous societies also engendered rapid social change, thus, even the earliest accounts of Indian–European encounters cannot be presumed to reliably describe precontact situations. Global patterns of urbanization, industrialization, and resource extraction have led to a reduction in the number of indigenous people. Despite this trend there has been a global resurgence in indigenous political mobilization and cultural renewal in recent several decades. Indigenous peoples who are making land claims, petitioning for political rights, and demanding control of resources have had remarkable success given their limited resources. Many indigenous groups have a strong Internet presence.

CONTEMPORARY INDIGENOUS AMERICAN ISSUES AND TRENDS

A complex politics of numbers permeates the demography of indigenous peoples, and a desire to minimize the destruction due to European contact has led to a tendency to underestimate the precontact population of North America which ranges from one million to thirty million with seven million considered a conservative estimate. Native populations in the USA reached a nadir of about one-quarter million around the turn of the twentieth century. The decline from early contact resulted from diseases, land policies, forced population removals, and wars. Since then the Native American population has grown to well over two million. Population growth was greatest from 1960 to 2000 due to improved enumeration techniques, decreased death rates, and changes in self-identification. Because of high rates of intermarriage and changes in identity, questions about who is and is not "Indian" have continued, especially where gaming profits or natural resources may have important economic consequences.

Urbanization, education, participation in the paid labor force since World War II have facilitated political activity and formation of activist organizations such as the American Indian Movement, Women of All Red Nations, Native American Rights Fund, National Congress of American Indians, and National Tribal Chairmen's Association. Since the 1960s American Indians have staged a variety of protest events: "fish-ins" in the Pacific northwest in the mid-1960s, the 19-month occupation of Alcatraz Island beginning in 1969, the 71-day siege at Wounded Knee on the Pine Ridge Reservation in South Dakota in 1973, the occupation of Camp Yellow Thunder in the Black Hills in the 1980s, and protests against Indian athletic mascots since the 1980s. The resulting increased awareness of "Indian issues" led to more autonomy for Indian groups, and to more individuals reclaiming their Indian heritage (Nagel 1996).

A challenge for Native American groups has been how to participate in economic development without undermining traditional Indian values. The tension is central to debates in many indigenous communities globally. Indian successes have spawned social movements that are often anti-Indian movements, further increasing identity politics. Ironically, such controversies have generated a new interest in indigenous peoples around the world.

SEE ALSO: Indigenous Movements

REFERENCE

Nagel, J. (1996) *American Indian Ethnic Renewal: Red Power and the Resurgence of Identity and Culture.* Oxford University Press, New York.

SUGGESTED READING

Gedicks, A. (2001) *Resource Rebels: Native Challenges to Mining and Oil orporations.* South End Press, Cambridge, MA.

Hall, T. D. and Fenelon, J. V. (2008) Indigenous movements and globalization: what is different? What is the same? *Globalizations* 5 (1): 1–11.

Mann, C. C. (2005) *1491: New Revelations of the Americans before Columbus.* Alfred A. Knopf, New York.

Wilmer, F. (1993) *The Indigenous Voice in World Politics: Since Time Immemorial.* Sage, Newbury Park, CA.

THOMAS D. HALL AND JOANE NAGEL

individualism

Individualism emphasizes the importance of the individual, for example the individual's freedom, interests, rights, needs, or beliefs against the predominance of other institutions in regulating the individual's behavior, such as the state or the church. A range of theories in different societal domains contributes to the dissemination of individualistic ideas in society. In particular, economic and political liberalism are vehicles of individualism.

The term individualism was introduced by de Tocqueville. Even though he distinguished individualism from egotism, his distinction is essentially one of degree, but individualism would in the long run lead to "downright egotism."

A strong impact on the development of individualistic thinking in Western Europe can be traced to religion. The Reformation and the development of Protestantism indicated a shift to more individualistic thinking. This can be linked to Luther's claim that a personal relationship with God cannot be mediated by the interpretation of the church.

Another important contribution to individualistic thinking was given in economics by Adam Smith's development of a system of economic liberalism. He assumed that a simple system of natural liberty and exchange of goods and services in free and competitive markets, with as few interventions by the state as possible, would best support societal development and welfare.

A growing political individualism became most influential with the French Revolution and the emphasis on individual rights, referring to the idea of natural justice in contrast to the absolutist state. Several of these developments came together in the bourgeois Enlightenment in the seventeenth and eighteenth centuries.

In Anglophone discourse there is a tendency to interpret individualism as egoistic and selfish behavior. For example, Bellah et al. (1985) prominently argued that the prevalence of individualistic behavior would destroy the moral integrity of American society, though this view was contested. More positively, individualism is interpreted in Beck's (1992) theorizing on the risk society. Here, *individualization* indicates liberation from traditional bonds. Thus, it opens up more options from which to choose, but at the same time forces people to choose.

Methodological individualism emphasizes that sociological phenomena can only be explained by the characteristics of individuals. It was developed in opposition to methodological collectivism or holism. For example, Durkheim justified a specific sociological contribution to the examination of the human being by claiming that social phenomena can only be explained socially, and thereby proposed a holistic approach.

Today, this fundamental contradiction is rather outdated. Sociologists are much more concerned with questions of how sociocultural and sociostructural factors on the one hand and individuals, their actions or characteristics, on the other hand, are mutually linked or constitute each other. Instead of stating extreme positions, today's research is more often engaged with how both aspects combine in social reality.

SEE ALSO: Durkheim, Émile; Liberalism; Tocqueville, Alexis de

REFERENCES

Beck, U. (1992) *Risk Society: Towards a New Modernity.* Sage, Newbury Park, CA.

Bellah, R. N. et al. (1985) *Habits of the Heart: Middle America Observed.* Hutchinson Education, London.

JENS O. ZINN

induction and observation in science

One of the most persistent views of science is that in which scientists are understood to assemble observations and arrive at generalizations based upon them. Sometimes, wrongly, this simple inductive-empiricist view is laid at the door of Francis Bacon (1561–1626) and dubbed "Baconian inductivism." In fact, Bacon's views were considerably more complex than this, but the hare that he set running – inductive inference as the heart of scientific method – has subsequently been pursued by all manner of hounds. David Hume (1711–76) was pre-eminent among the early pursuers, and to this day "Hume's Problem" continues to preoccupy philosophy of science. In the mid-twentieth century there was a period when the seemingly more powerful deductive models of scientific inquiry appeared to have run inductivism and Hume's Problem to exhaustion. However, it rapidly became apparent that the issues surrounding inductive inference had a peculiar capacity to re-emerge from the coverts of deductive certainty, not least where the nature of observation itself was questioned. Into the space thus created have hastened newer, more relativistic epistemologies and, in full cry, the sociology of science.

Although Bacon was by no means a naïve inductivist, he did insist on the necessity of ridding the mind of certain kinds of preconceptions when examining the facts. In its period this was a bold formulation, but it immediately raised difficulties for those eager to underwrite scientific method in such inductive terms. For while deductive reasoning had a lengthy logical pedigree, inductive inference was to prove far more slippery. It was Hume who presented the central problem of inductivism in its most influential form: that however many instances we may find of a specific phenomenon this gives us no reason in logic to expect that observed pattern to continue in the future. In other words, we have no justification for making any reliable inference from past evidence. The future will hold surprises.

Faced with this difficulty inductivism gave way to more deductively inclined models of science. Rather than seeing science as founded on generalizations from data, these approaches emphasized the relative autonomy of theory. Their interest lay, rather, with deducing predictive hypotheses from theory which could then be subjected to (experimental) test. However, at the heart of any process of testing lay "observation" – which apparently relied upon some form of inductive inference from experience to the observation statements describing that experience, thus re-raising a variation of Hume's problem.

So, even where induction is not the defining element in the so-called Scientific Method it remains an important feature of actual scientific practice. Scientists make inductive inferences, albeit within a context of inquiry which also involves deduction, intuition, and competition. Accordingly, philosophers of science have continued to seek ways of bypassing the Humean difficulties.

SEE ALSO: Science; Science, Social Construction of

SUGGESTED READINGS

Hume, D. (1999) *An Enquiry Concerning Human Understanding*. Oxford University Press, Oxford.

Rescher, N. (1980) *Induction: An Essay on the Justification of Inductive Reasoning*. Basil Blackwell, Oxford.

ANDREW TUDOR

Industrial Revolution

The Industrial Revolution (IR) is the rapid increase in the use of machines powered by inanimate forms of energy (waterfalls, wind, coal, oil, or electricity) that began in England in about 1750. The term also refers to the totality of the resulting technological, economic, and social transformations that have conditioned the lives and worldviews of people in industrial societies today.

ORIGINS AND SHORT-TERM CONSEQUENCES

The IR resulted from the general accumulation of technological information in agrarian societies of western Europe in the preceding centuries. Innovations in shipbuilding and navigation made possible transoceanic travel and the discovery of the New World, increasing trade activity and infusing the European economy with large quantities of gold and silver. Resulting inflation favored commercial classes relative to the landed aristocracy, motivating the latter to greatly improve agricultural production. The mid-fifteenth-century invention of the printing press facilitated the IR by helping the spread of literacy, the rationalism of the Enlightenment, and perhaps an ethic of frugality and hard work associated with the Protestant Reformation, according to Max Weber.

During early industrialization successive technological improvements in the textile industry led to complex machines too heavy to be operated by muscle power alone. Factory-based production arose from the need to organize work activities near machines connected to a central source of power, such as a steam engine, leading to a decline in home-based production ("cottage industry") and precipitating an influx of rural population to towns and cities, causing crowding, pollution, and poverty. Despite employment of all household members (including children as young as 6), the average living standards of the population declined, consistent with the belief of many contemporaries, including Karl Marx, that the development of capitalism would result in impoverishment of the working class.

LONG-TERM DEVELOPMENTS

The proportion of the labor force employed in farming dwindled from an overwhelming majority prior to the IR to less than 5 percent by the close of the twentieth century. Employment in manufacturing peaked at a third of the total labor force early in the second half of the twentieth century. Employment in services rose steadily up to some three-quarters of the labor force.

The changing nature of economic firms from predominantly family-owned businesses to corporations run on bureaucratic principles emphasizing technical competence, and increasingly systematic application of science to industrial production resulted in rising demand for skills, from simple literacy to advanced engineering or legal training, and the development of formal education systems. Primary education was well developed by the late 1800s, often with compulsory attendance, but secondary and tertiary (college-level) education would not involve majority proportions of the target age cohorts until the second half of the twentieth century.

Economies of scale entail that a firm producing more units can reduce unit production costs by further subdividing fixed costs (costs of machinery, product development, and advertising). An initial market share advantage thus permits further reducing production costs and capturing an even larger market, resulting in an inherent tendency toward industrial concentration, a trend evident by the late 1800s. As corporations grew in size and complexity they became increasingly controlled by the appointed executives (who had the expertise needed to run the organization) as opposed to stockholders.

Industrializing societies experienced the *demographic transition* marked by a decline in the death rate followed by a delayed decline in the birth rate. The decline in deaths was due to improved food distribution facilitated by better transportation networks (canals and railroads), better sanitation (sewers and water treatment), and public health measures (vaccination). The decline in births was largely due to a decline in the desire for large families. As the decline in births lagged behind the decline in deaths, industrializing societies experienced rapid population growth followed by stabilization. Rising productivity of labor combined with tapering population growth eventually produced a remarkable rise in living standards for a majority of the population of industrial societies.

SEE ALSO: Capitalism; Industrialization; Labor/Labor Power; Post-Industrial Society; Urbanization

SUGGESTED READINGS

Davies, N. (1998) *Europe: A History*. HarperPerennial, New York.

Esping-Andersen, G. (1990) *The Three Worlds of Welfare Capitalism*. Polity Press, Cambridge.

Nolan, P. & Lenski, G. (2004) *Human Societies: An Introduction to Macrosociology*, 9th edn. Paradigm, Boulder, CO.

FRANÇOIS NIELSEN

industrialization

Industrialization is the process by which an economy shifts from an agricultural to a manufacturing base during a period of sustained change and growth, eventually creating a higher standard of living. Sociology's founders sought to link the causes, correlates and consequences of industrialization to broader social changes producing modern society.

For much of the twentieth century, however, sociology deferred to narrow economistic accounts of a single path of industrialization. Sociologists compiled profiles of *industrial society* featuring miscellaneous traits (e.g., division of labor, rationalization, urbanization, increased life expectancy, and democracy). More recently, the rise of newly industrialized countries (NICs) has fanned interest in multiple paths that industrialization may take in different institutional contexts.

A key influence on discussions of industrialization was Adam Smith's view that a specialized division of labor is more efficient and increases a nation's wealth if the state adopted a laissez faire stance. Another was provided by French writers who spoke of an *Industrial Revolution*, citing parallels with the French Revolution. Placing industrialism within the development of capitalism, Marx argued that a detailed division of labor abetted mechanization that subordinated and replaced workers. Victorian reformers redefined the problem as rapid technological change. Most sociologists, eschewing radicalism, favored Durkheim's argument that the division of labor temporarily made solidarity problematic or Weber's culturalist account of the Protestant Ethic. They largely ignored Weber's comprehensive analysis of how cultural, political, and economic factors interacted to produce *rational capitalism* as well as Marx's dialectical treatment.

A reform inclination in the early twentieth century was evident in the Chicago School's exploration of the industrial city's social problems and in *industrial sociology*'s study of industrial relations and organizations. Although celebrations by economic historians of the Industrial Revolution's technological achievements were muted by the 1930s, victory in World War II restored Anglo-American confidence that industrializing countries would converge around a common path. Many accepted Rostow's *modernization* thesis that all developing societies would have to pass through five stages of development with industrialization as the take-off stage. Yet, a new wave in economic history in the 1960s argued that industrialization had been a gradual, not revolutionary, process. Moreover, neo-Marxians tied it to injustice and inequality. Labor process studies revealed social control agendas behind efforts to subdivide and deskill factory work while dependency and world systems theorists proposed that unequal relations among nations constrained development.

In the 1980s the rise of East Asian industry stimulated sociologists to challenge economistic accounts. Piore and Sabel's comparison of mass and flexible production (1984) rekindled debate on paths of development. Some cite the role of *developmental states* in East Asia in helping entire segments move into higher-value sectors: such states devise national strategies, encourage the formation of business groups and guide capital into targeted sectors. Others explain varying paths of industrialization among NICs as resulting from the particular positions that their industries hold in global divisions of labor (e.g., *commodity chains*).

SEE ALSO: Capitalism; Division of Labor; Industrial Revolution; Post-Industrial Society

REFERENCE

Piore, M. J. and Sabel, C. F. (1984) *The Second Industrial Divide: Possibilities for Prosperity*. Basic Books, New York.

SUGGESTED READINGS

Coleman, D. C. (1992) *Myth, History and the Industrial Revolution*. Hambledon Press, London.

Gereffi, G. & Wyman, D. L. (eds.) (1990) *Manufacturing Miracles: Paths of Industrialization in Latin America and East Asia*. Princeton University Press.

MICHAEL INDERGAARD

inequality, wealth

In all human societies beyond a certain minimum size, material possessions (such as land, animals, houses, tools, and consumption goods) are distributed unequally among individuals and groups. Insofar as these possessions have a monetary or exchange value, this unequal distribution can be described as inequality of wealth. Besides, and related to, income inequality, wealth inequality is an aspect of economic inequality which in turn is a dimension of social inequality in the wide sense. *Wealth* can be defined as the monetary value of the sum total of assets or goods belonging to a certain unit. This unit may vary from a national society (national wealth) to an individual person (individual wealth). *Personal wealth* is the wealth owned by an individual person or a consumption unit consisting of more than one person (a household or family). *Wealth inequality* is usually understood as the unequal distribution of personal wealth in a society.

Wealth gives the owner certain advantages; in other words, it has functions for the owner. These functions vary with the relative amount of wealth, its composition (the specific goods that make up the wealth), and its institutional context (including laws of property). In general terms, three economic or material functions can be distinguished: wealth is a source of: (1) income (profits, interest, rent, dividend as well as capital gains), (2) material comfort and consumption (the ownership of a house and various durable consumption goods), and (3) material security. This latter function is particularly important when collective arrangements that guarantee some minimum income (pension rights, life insurances, social insurance, welfare payments) are lacking. Personal wealth can also have wider functions for its owners: it is a basis of (4) relative freedom and autonomy, (5) status, and (6) power. It contributes to individual freedom to the extent that it widens the scope of alternatives in consumption and leisure, and gives the possibility to postpone work, or not to work at all. Finally, personal wealth is (7) an important vehicle for keeping privileges within the family as it is transferred to the next generation through inheritance. On all these accounts, wealth inequality is at the basis of, and connected to, various dimensions of social inequality.

Several empirical studies have attempted to assess the degree of wealth inequality in a given society and trends over time on the basis of tax data.

Several conclusions can be drawn from these studies.

1. The degree of inequality in the distribution of personal wealth is much higher than that of income. The shares of the top 1 percent or 5 percent in total personal wealth are normally more than twice the shares of the top 1 percent or 5 percent in total disposable income.
2. During the first three-quarters of the twentieth century, wealth inequality in western countries tended to diminish, though this tendency was much less clear and outspoken for the USA than for the UK and Sweden. The same trend has been observed for several other western countries as well, such as France, Belgium, (West) Germany, Canada, and the Netherlands.
3. Since the last 15 to 25 years of the twentieth century, this trend stopped or even reversed: wealth inequality increased in many western societies.

SEE ALSO: Capital: Economic, Cultural, and Social; Class, Status, and Power; Income Inequality and Income Mobility; Stratification and Inequality, Theories of

SUGGESTED READINGS

Lindert, P. H. (2000) Three centuries of inequality in Britain and America. In: Atkinson, A. B. & Bourguignon, F. (eds.), *Handbook of Income Distribution*, vol. 1. Elsevier, Amsterdam.

NICO WILTERDINK

inequality/stratification, gender

Gender stratification refers to the level of inequality in society based on gender, the social characteristics associated with sex. Specifically, gender stratification refers to the differential ability of men and women to access society's resources and to receive its privileges. As gender stratification increases, so does the level of gender inequality, reflecting greater differences between men's and women's access to power. Because historically men have garnered greater social power, gender inequality has systematically disadvantaged women. Gender inequality is complicated, moreover, by the intersection of gender with race/ethnicity, social class, age, and sexuality.

Original applications of the terms sex and gender tended to confuse the two, which were often used interchangeably. More recently, most sociologists have begun to distinguish between them, agreeing that the terms should apply to different, but related, concepts. While sex is defined in terms of biology and the reproductive organs one is born with, gender is typically seen in more social terms, as society's idea of how people should be, based on their biological sex. Gender, that is, is socially constructed to reflect society's expectations about how men and women should act, dress, move, and comport themselves in the context of everyday social interaction.

Under what conditions did gender inequality originate and under what conditions has it been maintained? Early answers to this question drew on biological differences between men and women and their associated reproductive functions to posit a "natural" division of labor between the two. Accordingly, men were seen as having evolved from hunters to family breadwinners and providers, with women as childbearing, childrearing, and domestic experts. More sophisticated study of premodern societies, however, has discredited many of these assumptions, pointing to more diversity and fluidity in men's and women's roles than a natural division of labor could explain.

The women's movement has been instrumental in reducing gender inequality. In the USA, the first wave of the movement emerged in the mid-nineteenth century as a reaction to women's lack of power in both the public and private spheres. Elizabeth Cady Stanton and Susan B. Anthony are well-known as initiators of the movement, which ultimately turned its sights toward women's suffrage. After gaining the vote in 1920, the women's movement in the US became relatively inactive for the next 50 years, only to reemerge in the 1970s. This second wave of feminism reinvigorated the quest for women's empowerment in marriage and family and sought to equalize women's involvement and opportunity in institutions such as the labor force, education, law, and politics. While the struggle for women's equality is far from over, second wave feminism was able to mobilize many women (and men) on behalf of women's rights, overturning a number of institutionalized inequities embedded in law and promoting women's involvement in professional occupations and politics at the highest levels.

Nevertheless, both in the USA and globally, women continue to be negatively affected by gender stratification. Although inroads have been made, gender persists as a core organizing structure around which inequality is arranged. In the workplace, occupations remain gender segregated overall, with "women's work" providing lower pay, fewer benefits, and less security than "men's work," even if comparable in form or content. At home, women continue to shoulder the lion's share of household labor, child care, and domestic responsibility, even when employed in the paid labor force. These trends, moreover, extend globally, such that while women now constitute over a third of the world's labor force, they also, according to the Population Crisis Committee (1988), constitute 70 percent of the world's poor.

In some arenas, gender stratification appears to be declining; in others, it does not. Evidence of the former comes in the form of men's increasing participation in household labor and child care, once thought to be exclusively women's work. Evidence of the latter can be seen in the intractability of the gender wage gap and the glass ceiling that women bump up against in the paid labor force. Moreover, while men are, in fact, sharing more labor in the home, most of the increase can be explained by women who do less rather than by men who do substantially more. Nevertheless, as women continue to press for equality and men recognize the benefits that shared parenting and involved partnering have for them, gender equality is more likely than not to become the norm rather than the exception.

SEE ALSO: Gender, Development and; Gender Ideology and Gender Role Ideology; International Gender Division of Labor; Stratification, Gender and; Women's Movements

SUGGESTED READING

Chafetz, J. S. (1990) *Gender Equity: An Integrated Theory of Stability and Change*. Sage, Newbury Park, CA.

Coltrane, S. & Collins, R. (2001) *Sociology of Marriage and the Family: Gender, Love, and Property*. Wadsworth, Belmont, CA.

MICHELE ADAMS

infertility

Infertility is the physical inability to conceive a child or to successfully carry a child to term. Most medical professionals consider a couple to be infertile if they have failed to conceive after twelve months of unprotected intercourse. Either partner or both may have the reproductive impairment. Between 8 and 12 percent of couples – or between 50 and 80 million people worldwide – are affected by infertility. Perhaps twenty to forty percent of couples in any given society have been affected by infertility at some point in their lives. Infertility is particularly prevalent in sub-Saharan Africa.

Infertility can have far-reaching effects on life satisfaction, well-being, and psychological adjustment, especially for women. Because of the great importance attached to childbearing and parenting roles, women often experience infertility as a catastrophic role-failure, which can come to permeate every aspect of life. McQuillan et al. (2003) conclude that infertility distress is found primarily among infertile women who remain childless. Since female fertility declines with increasing age, the current trend in industrialized societies toward delayed child-bearing means that a larger percentage of infertile couples than before are childless when they discover their infertility. Suffering from infertility may be more pronounced in developing societies, where parenting is culturally mandatory and where alternative roles for women may be less available.

About half of infertile women in industrialized societies report that they have been to a physician or a clinic to seek treatment. It is in the developing world, where demand for infertility services is greatest, that access to infertility treatment in general is most limited. Treatment of infertility is often expensive, time-consuming, and invasive.

SEE ALSO: Fertility and Public Policy; Fertility: Transitions and Measures; New Reproductive Technologies;

REFERENCE

McQuillan, J., Greil, A. L., White, L., & Jacob, M. C. (2003) Frustrated fertility: infertility and psychological distress among women. *Journal of Marriage and the Family* 65: 1007–18.

SUGGESTED READING

Inhorn, M. C. & van Balen, F. (eds.) (2002) *Infertility around the Globe: New Thinking on Childlessness, Gender, and Reproductive Technologies*. University of California Press, Berkeley, CA.

ARTHUR L. GREIL

in-groups and out-groups

The terms in-group and out-group were coined by William Graham Sumner in his classic study, *Folkways* (1906). Similar to Charles Horton Cooley's (1909) notion of primary groups, in-groups are understood as those with which one is intimately connected and toward which one feels a particular sense of association and loyalty. Out-groups, on the other hand, are those from which one distances oneself and in opposition to which one defines one's group identity. For example, women might be understood as an in-group differentiated from men as an out-group. However, in-groups and out-groups are not necessarily distinguished based on socially ascribed statuses. Indeed, following this same logic, sociologists (in-group) might be distinguished from psychologists (out-group) or people wearing pink shirts (in-group) might be contrasted with those wearing white shirts (out-group).

As far back as Émile Durkheim (1893), social scientists have suggested that social solidarity – or, in-group cohesion – is reinforced by the presence of an out-group. The presence of deviance, for example, has been interpreted as creating a situation in which people can come together and identify themselves in an "us" versus "them" dichotomy, and, in this sense the (physical or symbolic) presence of an out-group is said to help articulate the boundaries of group membership and to sharpen and reinforce group norms. Such concepts are not restricted to the study of deviance, per se. They also have been applied to discuss a range of (social and symbolic) boundaries related to class, ethnicity and race, gender and sexuality. Because of the ways group identities are understood as constructed and maintained relative to other groups, the concept of in-group/out-group also has been applied to explain social stratification, prejudice, discrimination, and privilege.

More broadly, the in-group/out-group distinction has been applied to talk about the sociology of knowledge. In this vein, Nancy Naples (1996) has suggested, for example, "rather than one 'insider' or 'outsider' position, we all begin our work with different relationships to shifting aspects of social life." In other words, a number of more recent scholarship has served to complicate Sumner's early claims concerning the durability and permanence of in-groups and out-groups and the purported necessary relationship between in-group cohesion and out-group hostility.

SEE ALSO: Group Processes; Groups; Primary Groups; Reference Groups; Secondary Groups

REFERENCES

Cooley, C. H. (1909) *Social Organization: A Study of the Larger Mind*. Charles Scribner's Sons, New York.

Durkheim, É. (1893) *De la division du travail social*. Les Presses Universitaires de France, Paris.

Naples, N. A. (1996) A feminist revisiting of the insider/outsider debate: the "outsider phenomenon" in rural Iowa. *Qualitative Sociology* 19: 83–106.

JULIE GREGORY

institution

An institution is a set of behaviours patterned according to one or more variously codified and differentially enforced rules whose development can be evolved or constructed or both. Durability and modes of justification allow for comparability between social systems. A society can range on a theoretical spectrum from full institutionalization to *anomie*.

Mauss and Faconnet took institution to be those acts and ideas that individuals encounter and find somewhat impressed upon them. They declared that "the science of society is the science of institutions" (*Sociology* 1901: 11). Durkheim later concurred and suggested that since institutions exhibit more or less "crystallization" they are apt as a focus for sociology.

Institutions refer not to brute physical facts but to what Searle calls "institutional facts." They take the form "*X* counts as *Y* in context *C*" where *X* stands for some physical object or event and *Y* assigns a special status to the *X* in question (status function) implying certain obligations (deontic power). This is sustained due to the nature of human action as rule-following. Rules are necessarily intersubjective since a community of rule-followers is required to establish "rightness" and provide perpetual verification. Hence, institutions are never static and exist only through the continual interaction of a plurality, as noted in Bloor's (1997) *Wittgenstein, Rules and Institutions*.

This inherent rule-based fluidity, even in spite of apparent stability, brings to the fore the question of legitimacy for institutions. Social change can be viewed according to the predominance of particular forms of institutional justification over time. One can consider the main modes of institutional justification varying according to Weber's rationality types: practical, theoretical, substantive, and formal. The premodern era is thought of as emphasizing legitimacy of institutions according to tradition (substantive rationality). However, arguably, with the onset of industrialization institutions increasingly derive their authority from principles of efficiency and calculability (formal rationality). Post-World War II justification of institutions, especially at the macro-level, progressively require satisfaction of contested conditions of justice including fairness, non-interference and discourse compatibility. Alternatively, micro-level research of institutions, especially by symbolic interactionists, have found that symbolically loaded micro-level interactions legitimate various institutional types. An important example is Goffman's (1961) *Asylums* which characterized the "total institution" as a large number of people who live and work together in a shared, enclosed and formally administered space. These total institutions, for instance convents, prisons and residential hospitals, are legitimated by a coerced or compliant but always heavily symbolic undermining of the remnants of the pre-total institution self.

Institutions are potentially enabling as well as restricting. While institutions employ various prohibitive sanctions, they also provide the solutions to collective decision problems. Parsons (*The Social System*, 1951: 39) saw institutions as "a complex of institutionalized role integrates which is of strategic structural significance in the social system in question." The roles adopted can fall into five typical broad categories of institution: economic (good and service production and distribution), political (power designation), cultural (symbolic and scientific action), kinship (reproduction control and socialization of the young), stratificational (social status attribution).

The genesis of any institution is key to understanding it. Evolutionary game theoretical models have been used to show how the emergence of an institution can be endogenous to spontaneous and repetitive interactions. However, many institutions, particularly at the macro-level, are consciously designed and constructed in response to perceived needs and often according to normative ideals. How both these processes of institution formation interrelate is uncertain, as is what mixture is most desirable in what circumstances.

Much of today's research focusing on institutions revolves around extraordinarily influential work in the sociology of organizations and economic sociology. In the former, a distinct sociological new institutionalism has emerged following notable work by Meyer & Rowan and Di Maggio & Powell in which it became apparent that organizations were operating in a complex institutional environment of normative, regulative and cultural cognitive features. Meanwhile, Granovetter, particularly in his (1985) "Economic action and social structure: the problem of embeddedness," has critiqued how both over-socialized and under-socialized representations of actors fail to understand that economic institutions are embedded in networks of interpersonal relations.

SEE ALSO: Anomie; Institutional Theory, New; Organization Theory; Rationalization; Total Institutions

REFERENCES

Goffman, E. (1991) [1961] *Asylums: Essays on the Conditions of the Social Situations of Mental Patients and Other Inmates*. Penguin, London.

Mauss, M. & Faconnet, P. (1901) Sociologie: objet et methode. *Année Sociologique* 30: 165–76.
Parsons, T. (1951) *The Social System*. Routledge, London.

SUGGESTED READINGS

Durkheim, É. (1982) [1901] *The Rules of Sociological Method*. Free Press, Cambridge.
Powell, W. & Di Maggio, P. (1991) *The New Institutionalism of Organizational Analysis*. University of Chicago Press, Chicago, IL.
Searle, J. (1995) *The Construction of Social Reality*. Free Press, New York.

JOSEPH BURKE

Institutional Review Boards and sociological research

Conceived in response to the negligence of researchers conducting the Tuskegee syphilis experiments (1932–72) in the USA and to abusive experimentation by Nazis on prisoners during World War II, human subject review was implemented to deter possible abuses in biomedical research and has expanded due to research in the social sciences. The first major effort to establish Institutional review boards (IRBs) at universities occurred in 1974 in the USA. A national Commission was charged to determine the various distinctions between biomedical and behavioral research, establish a way to assess the risks and benefits of conducting research, outline the guidelines for subject selection, and define the boundaries of informed consent. The Commission's central policy document, the Belmont Report (1979), outlined three ethical principles to guide research: (1) respect for persons, (2) beneficence, and (3) justice. Today IRBs are charged with ensuring the rights of volunteers who participate in research conducted through a university. IRBs are responsible for translating federal, state, and local regulations into institutional practice and are mandated to approve, require modifications, or disprove of research activities related to human subjects and funded by federal resources.

The role of IRBs in research is not without controversy, especially as it pertains to sociological studies. Tension centers on how to interpret what constitutes research and the effects of IRB regulation on research. IRBs have the potential to share resources and expertise with scholars, as well as highlight the importance of reflexivity in research. Yet researchers complain that vague definitions and varying interpretations of research pose unique challenges to sociological work, that applying a biomedical model to social science research is ineffective, and that the implementation of IRB review inhibits academic freedom and restricts productivity. Further, many scholars perceive IRBs as increasingly more concerned with the protection of the university from lawsuits than with the protection of human subjects.

SEE ALSO: Ethics, Research

SUGGESTED READINGS

American Association of University Professors (1995) Protecting human beings: Institutional Review Boards and social science research. *Academe* 87 (3): 55–67.
Oakes, J. M. (2002) Risks and wrongs in social science research: an evaluator's guide to the IRB. *Evaluation Review* 26 (5): 443–79.
Tierney, W. G. & Corwin, Z. B. (2007) The tensions between academic freedom and Institutional Review Boards. *Qualitative Inquiry* 13 (3): 388–98.

ZOË BLUMBERG CORWIN AND WILLIAM G. TIERNEY

institutional theory, new

Emerging from the sociology of education in the 1970s, new institutional theory (NIT) has become one of the foremost positions within the mainstream of US management studies. It seeks to explain the ways in which institutions are created, sustained, and diffused. Adherents of NIT are keen to draw a distinction between "new" and "old" institutionalism. While old institutionalism emphasized politics and the role of conflict, NIT took legitimacy as its master concept. The old institutionalism focused on the existence of a negotiated order between different interest groups, while in its place NIT sought to understand the way in which the quest for legitimacy is a driving force behind the isomorphism of organizations. NIT is interested in understanding the means through which the socially constructed external environment enters the organization by "creating the lens through which actors view the world and the very categories of structure, action, and thought" (Powell & DiMaggio 1991).

Works by Meyer and Rowan (1977) and DiMaggio and Powell (1983) are generally held up as foundational or seminal statements of NIT. Constituting the two branches of NIT, they remain widely cited to this day. Meyer and Rowan examined why particular phenomena became institutionalized; that is, why certain forms were repeatedly enacted over time while the DiMaggio and Powell branch of NIT seeks to understand why it is that organizations are increasingly coming to resemble each other.

Despite its limitations, NIT remains a popular position and it has the capacity to help understand aspects of the intersubjective relationship between an organization and its field. It can help us understand the adoption of innovations, long-term shifts in organization fields, and variation among nation-states, an issue that is also addressed by the closely related societal effects school. Indeed, with the latter we may say that a separate European New Institutional School, more attuned to the classical sociological concerns of power, has been established. Recent important developments in new institutional theory include looking at practice variation and the sociology of translation.

SEE ALSO: Institution; Institutionalism; Management; Management, Theories of

REFERENCES

DiMaggio, P. J. & Powell, W. W. (1983) The iron cage revisited: institutional isomorphism and collective rationality in organizational fields. *American Sociological Review* 48: 147–60.

Meyer, J. W. & Rowan, B. (1977) Institutionalized organizations: formal structure as myth and ceremony. *American Journal of Sociology* 83: 340–63.

Powell, W. W. & DiMaggio, P. J. (eds.) (1991) *The New Institutionalism in Organizational Analysis.* University of Chicago Press, Chicago, IL.

CHRIS CARTER AND STEWART CLEGG

institutionalism

Institutions are persistent social facts that regulate social behavior. Most targets of sociological study are institutions. At a minimum, organizations, the state, social norms, laws, cultural values and socially constructed knowledge are, or are enlivened by, institutions. Indeed, Durkheim (1982: 59) defined sociology as "the science of institutions, their genesis and their functioning."

Two dimensions can be used to categorize institutions. A public/private dimension identifies the subjects of the institution. Public institutions apply to all members of a nation, culture or general sphere of interaction such as an industry, whereas private institutions apply to members of an exclusive social structure, such as a group or an organization. A centralized/decentralized dimension refers to the source of institutional authority. Centralized institutions are those created and enforced by some designated agent, whereas decentralized institutions are emergent, and responsibility for their enforcement is diffuse. Archetypes of the four institutional forms identified by these two dimensions are laws (public-centralized), cultural values (public-decentralized), organizational rules (private-centralized) and social norms (private-decentralized). The social structures that house these institutional forms are, respectively, states, civil society, organizations and networks.

Different schools of institutionalism focus on the influence of different institutional forms and often slight the relevance of other institutional forms. Nevertheless, some of the most exciting institutional arguments highlight that the functioning of one institutional form, such as state regulation, depends on other institutions, such as norms derived from social cohesion.

The most pressing challenge for institutionalism is to explain the origin and change of institutions. As institutions stabilize social structure and constrain behavior, it is unsurprising that theories say more about the persistence of institutions than their change, and that theories of institutional change emphasize incremental change processes. New theories of institutional change draw from social movement theory and argue that institutional entrepreneurs may affect more radical institutional change by brokering between social sites and institutional ideas and framing potential institutions in ways that appeal to pre-existing institutions.

SEE ALSO: Institution; Institutional Theory, New

REFERENCE

Durkheim, E. (1982) *The Rules of Sociological Method.* Free Press, New York.

PAUL INGRAM

intellectual property

Any form of literature, science, music, film, or computer program can be protected by copyright to prevent third parties from making copies without written permission. Copyright is the law of authorship and dates back to the Statute of Anne (1709) passed in England to protect the rights of authors and publishers from piracy. The law has been progressively elaborated in Europe and North America to grant copyright for a fixed term to the estate of deceased authors and protect authors from the violation of their rights through new technologies of reproduction and exchange.

The balance between the rights of authors and freedom of information is a delicate one and is regularly subject to legal challenge. In the USA the First Amendment, which guarantees free speech and a free press, has been used by litigants as the basis to contest the reach of copyright. The issue has escalated in legal and popular culture as new electronic technologies of reproduction and file sharing, such as the photocopier, home audiotape, videotape machines, and computers, have become available.

The Internet vastly increases the flow of data exchange and creates unprecedented challenges for policing and the application of copyright. Without a commercially viable system of monitoring file exchange, the integrity of copyright relies on the probity of Internet users. In the late 1990s the development of peer to peer (P2P) file exchange systems such as Napster seriously eroded the market share of record companies. This provoked a protracted and as yet unresolved series of legal disputes between P2P providers and copyright holders. The development of legal, fee-based download systems such as the Apple Music Store has been a partial solution to the problem.

SEE ALSO: Internet; Modernity; Popular Culture

SUGGESTED READING

Goldstein, P. (2003) *Copyright's Highway*. Stanford University Press, Stanford, CA.

CHRIS ROJEK

interaction

"Interaction" describes particular kinds of social relationship that are different from, but constitutive of, groups, organizations and networks. Interaction occurs when two or more participants are in each others' perceptual range and orient to each other through their action and activity. It ends when the participants dissolve their mutual orientation and leave the social situation. Theories and studies of interaction largely focus on the possibility and conditions for the establishment of mutual orientation to situations and on the relationship between interaction and social structure and culture as well as organization and personality. A different strand of research considers mutual orientation as practical accomplishment and explores the social organization of actions through which participants ongoingly produce mutual orientation.

George Caspar Homans (1910–89) developed exchange theory as an alternative concept to Talcott Parsons' attempt to bring about a theory that strives to integrate all the social sciences. He argues that interaction emerges because actors are rational decision-makers who aim to maximize their rewards when engaging in an exchange with others. His theory has been advanced by Peter Blau (1918–2002) and Richard Emerson (1925–82). They attempt to integrate exchange theory with contemporary theories of social structure and power and begin to develop a theory of "exchange networks." This theory has had a great impact on very recent concepts of the "network society" and the role of "trust" in the emergence of long-lasting social and economic relationships.

A very different approach to studying interaction was suggested by Erving Goffman (1922–82), who uses the metaphor of the "theatre" to explore social life. His "dramaturgical approach" investigates the techniques participants employ to manage the impression others have of them.

Herbert Blumer (1900–87) drew on George Herbert Mead's (1863–1931) theory of action to develop Symbolic Interactionism as a subfield of sociology and social psychology. It argues that people act in situations according to the meaning these situations have for them. The "definition of the situation" is produced in interaction with others. Hence, symbolic interactionist research is particularly interested in the interpretive processes by virtue of which participants negotiate the definition of the situation. They explore how the self and identity as well as meaning emerge in interaction between people. Coupled with Mead and others' theoretical work at the University of Chicago Blumer's theory and empirical studies contributed to the emergence of the "Chicago School of Sociology." Whilst the influence of the Chicago School has diminished since the 1960s their work on social interaction still greatly impacts the discipline of sociology.

A different approach to studing the process and organization of interaction has been developed by the so-called Iowa School. Founded by such eminent symbolic interactionists as Carl Couch (1925–94) and Manford Kuhn (1911–63), research at University of Iowa initially strived to develop "scientific methods" to explore the structure of the self and since the mid-1960s has introduced experimental methods to develop "a set of universal social principles" explaining how social units such as dyads and triads coordinate their activities.

Another influential body of research has emerged from Harold Garfinkel's (1917–) development of Ethnomethodology. In offering a critique of his teacher, Parsons, and by radicalizing Alfred Schutz's social phenomenology, Garfinkel has initiated a program of research that considers mutual orientation as a practical and social accomplishment. He began by conducting so-called breaching experiments that challenged people's trust in everyday situations. By virtue of these experiments Garfinkel has elaborated on the knowledge and the methods that people bring to bear when they produce their actions. These "ethnomethods" allow participants to "fit in" in social situations and account for incongruities with accounts for what is going on. Garfinkel's ethnomethodological program has given rise to various strands of research that significantly influence developments in sociology. The most famous area of research deriving from ethnomethodology is probably conversation analysis (CA). CA, developed by Harvey Sacks (1935–75) and his colleagues, is concerned with revealing the methods and procedures that people bring to bear in "talk-in-interaction." It elaborates on the social and sequential organization of talk, and explores interaction. CA's preoccupation with talk explains why CA has gained a growing followership in linguistics and cognate disciplines whilst its influence on sociology is debatable.

Drawing on these developments in Ethnomethodology and CA more recently video-based studies of interaction have emerged. These scrutinize video-recordings of "naturalistic" social situations to reveal the interactional organization of talk, bodily and material action. It is particularly interested in the ways in which participants orient to and embed objects and artifacts as well as tools and technologies in their interaction with each other.

SEE ALSO: Conversation Analysis; Ethnomethodology; Goffman, Erving; Symbolic Interaction; Mediated Interaction

SUGGESTED READINGS

Cahill, S. (2003) *Inside Social Life: Readings in Sociological Psychology and Microsociology*. Oxford University Press, Oxford and New York.

Couch, C. J. & Hintz, R. A. (eds.) (1975) *Constructing Social Life: Readings in Behavioral Sociology from the Iowa School*. Stipes Publishing Company, Champaign, IL.

Heath, C. C., Hindmarsh, J., & Luff, P. K. (forthcoming). *Video in Qualitative Research: Analyzing Social Interaction in Everyday Life*. Sage, London.

DIRK VOM LEHN

international gendered division of labor

World systems theorists were among the first to use the concept of an international division of labor by illustrating how the production of goods and services for "core" or more developed countries relied on the material resources of "peripheral" or developing nations. Their work describes the changing political and economic relationships among nations over the last six centuries, beginning with the period of colonization. By the middle of the twentieth century, most colonies had gained their political freedom and titular control over their own resources, but were never able to break away from their economic dependence on highly industrialized countries.

In the twentieth century a new process, called global or economic restructuring, created a new form of international division of labor between the developed countries of the global North and the developing nations of the global South. Beginning in the 1970s, in order to lessen production costs and enabled by new information and production technologies, corporations began to "off shore" some of their production processes to the global South, often moving to export-processing zones (EPZs) that provided manufacturing infrastructure, tax reductions, low labor costs, lax environmental regulations, and other incentives.

Simultaneously, international development or funding agencies, such as the International Monetary Fund or the World Bank, influence global South economies when they loan money to these nations, because loans are often tied to austerity measures known as structural adjustment programs that require the debtor countries to reduce government expenditures on social services and increase production for export, rather than supporting independent local businesses that produce for local consumption, in order to earn more foreign currency to pay back these loans. A by-product of these two processes is that developing economies are indirectly controlled by transnational corporations and/or funding agencies located in developed nations, thus reinforcing a new international division of labor.

This international division of labor is gendered in at least four ways that Maria Mies, et al. (1988) named an international "housewifization" of all labor because jobs are taking on the characteristics of women's work and because women are the source of new labor, worldwide. First, paid work is becoming increasingly feminized, with new jobs in the service sector drawing more on women's than men's labor. Second, paid work is increasingly organized like women's housework – with jobs that require flexible schedules and are occupationally segregated. Such "flexibilization" of the world economy refers to the growth of part-time, temporary, or seasonal employment, as well as to the need for families to have multiple income sources. Third, many of these jobs, like market trading, factory outwork, or off-the-books childcare, are found in the informal sector of the global economy that is rapidly expanding but, like housework, is not regulated by national labor laws. Finally, since women's traditional tasks are stereotyped as unskilled – although they are not – employers can more easily pay less and provide less job security.

Recent scholarship illustrates that there also is an international division of reproductive or carework labor. Parreñas (2000) argues there is a labor chain, transferring white women's domestic and reproductive labor in developed countries to women of color, who migrate from developing nations for these jobs. This creates an international system of racial stratification in reproductive work in which temporary overseas "contract workers" become a new export commodity for some developing countries.

SEE ALSO: Development: Political Economy; Division of Labor

REFERENCES

Mies, M., Bennholdt-Thomson, V. & von Werlhof, C. (1988) *Women: The Last Colony*. Zed, London.

Parreñas, R. S. (2000). Migrant Filipina domestic workers and the international division of reproductive labor. *Gender & Society* 14 (4): 560–80.

CHRISTINE E. BOSE

International Monetary Fund

The International Monetary Fund (IMF) is a multilateral financial organization that provides short-term loans to governments, promotes free trade and fiscal austerity policies, and collects financial data on the world economy. Its 186 member states agree to follow fiscal and monetary policies conducive to international financial stability and to allow IMF supervision of their national policy regimes. IMF loans typically carry policy conditions such as reductions in government spending, lower trade barriers, elimination of subsidies, and higher interest rates. Critics have charged that these policies hurt the poor and protect the interests of western financial institutions at the expense of impoverished nations.

The IMF originated in the 1944 conference at Bretton Woods, New Hampshire, convened to stabilize the world's economy following the end of World War II. It was created to monitor an international monetary system of fixed exchange rates and to provide a reserve fund for countries having short-term balance of payments problems. In the early years of the IMF, 75 percent of its loans or drawings were made to European countries recovering from the devastation of World War II. The rise of oil prices in the 1970s led to a dramatic increase in loans to developing countries. To address the ballooning debt burden of low-income nations, the IMF introduced the Structural Adjustment Facility in 1986. Funding was contingent on policy conditions such as reducing government subsidies for food and fuel, cutting back on social services such as education and health care, and reducing tariff barriers. The IMF instituted these policy conditions in concert with the World Bank and the US Treasury. Because these three institutions were all headquartered in Washington, DC, structural adjustment policies became known as the Washington Consensus. The USA has the most influence in shaping IMF policies since voting is weighted by the size of a member state's quota or subscription required for membership. The USA has the largest quota and an effective veto on decisions of the IMF's Board of Executive Directors.

The IMF has three main loan categories. "Standby" loans involve large amounts of quick money for member states undergoing a capital crisis and carry short maturities, typically one to five years. The Extended Loan Facility with maturities of eight to ten years is for states with longer-term financial problems. The third loan category is concessional loans at very low rates of interest (0.5 percent) and terms of ten years. These loans are reserved for the poorest member states facing protracted balance of payments problems.

Given its global influence and financial power, the IMF has been the target of much criticism, mostly concerning policy conditions required for loans. Critics have charged that the IMF ignores the social and political costs of policy conditions that amount to economic shock treatment. A number of massive protests have erupted after governments agreed to IMF conditions. The most serious confrontation was in Indonesia in 1998 when its government cut subsidies on petroleum and food in exchange for a $40 billion bailout. Riots targeted the wealthy minority Chinese Indonesians and 12,000 people were killed. Despite widespread criticism, the IMF holds to an economic orthodoxy of privatization, reduced government spending, lower tariffs, and increased foreign investment with no consideration of alternative routes to economic development. A better approach would be to use IMF influence to persuade banks to forgive loans and give low-income countries a fresh start.

SEE ALSO: Colonialism; Economic Development; Global Economy; Neoliberalism; World Bank.

SUGGESTED READING

IMF (2006) *What is the International Monetary Fund?* IMF, Washington, DC.

Peet, R. (2003) *Unholy Trinity: The IMF, World Bank and WTO*. Zed: New York.

Woods, N. (2006) *The Globalizers: The IMF, the World Bank, and Their Borrowers*. Cornell University Press, Ithaca, NY.

SUSAN HAGOOD LEE

Internet

The Internet is a global network of interconnected computer hardware and software systems, making possible the storage, retrieval, circulation, and processing of information and communication across time and space. A sociological account encompasses the constituent Internet technologies and attends to these as social phenomena. It also includes the information and other content which is produced, transmitted, and received by individuals and organizations using the Internet. Finally, a sociological account of the Internet includes the socially and historically structured contexts and processes in which the production, transmission, and reception of information and communication are embedded.

The Internet deserves the attention of sociologists for three major reasons. First, the Internet facilitates a reorganization of information and social relationships across time and space. Second, in investigating and understanding the complex subject matter of sociology, the Internet is an important tool for collecting data and for accessing information relevant to such an endeavor. Third, the Internet deserves the attention of sociologists because it expands the opportunities for circulating research findings and for supporting critical reflection, learning, and debate. However, in staking out the relevance of the Internet for sociology, we need to be aware that as a social phenomenon, it is an expression of the radical interconnection of people, organizations, different sectors of society, and the problems that we take up for study. In this way, studying the Internet involves shifts and linkages to perspectives that might traditionally have been considered to lie beyond the disciplinary boundaries of sociology. A comprehensive understanding of the Internet can only be developed jointly, from a multidisciplinary approach.

Fundamental to a sociological account of the Internet is that its development and use are not accidental to a set of complex and contradictory changes that are taking place in our world today. As such, the Internet is in the midst of some of our most severe and exciting challenges. The world we live in is becoming increasingly globalized. As a global communication network, the Internet is transforming the complex relationships between local activities and interaction across distance. The world we live in confronts us with new opportunities and dilemmas as the certainties afforded by tradition, authority, and nature no longer direct our lives in the way that they once did. Internet use radicalizes this process by placing "horizontal" forms of communications center stage, by allowing the questioning and blurring over of authority, and by allowing the reordering and expansion of the built environment. The world we live in is increasingly reflexive and saturated with information. As a technology of communication, the Internet transforms our information environments by facilitating global attentiveness, visibility, and questioning. Moreover, as a technology of communication, the Internet does not simply impact on this set of complex and contradictory changes; it contributes to the construction, mediation, and disclosure of what these transformations are.

SEE ALSO: Consumption and the Internet; Cyberculture

SUGGESTED READINGS

Castells, M. (2001) *The Internet Galaxy*. Oxford University Press, Oxford.

Hamelink, C. J. (2000) *Ethics of Cyberspace*. Sage, London.

Miller, D. & Slater, D. (2000) *The Internet: An Ethnographic Approach*. Berg, Oxford and New York.

Slevin, J. (2000) *The Internet and Society*. Polity Press, Cambridge.

Wellman, B. & Haythornthwaite, C. (eds.) (2002) *The Internet and Everyday Life*. Blackwell, Oxford.

Woolgar, S. (ed.) (2002) *Virtual Society? Technology, Cyberbole, Reality*. Oxford University Press, Oxford.

JAMES SLEVIN

interpersonal relationships

In any relationship, two participants are interdependent, where the behavior of each affects the outcomes of the other. Most of the research on interpersonal relationships has focused on relationships that are close, intimate, and have high interdependence. In the 1960s the initial focus of interpersonal relationship research was on the interpersonal attraction process, primarily between strangers meeting for the first time. This research developed primarily out of mate-selection studies first begun by family sociologists in the 1930s and 1940s (Burgess & Cottrell 1939). Most of the early research on the interpersonal attraction process relied on self-report measures to assess the factors that lead a person (P) to be attracted to another person (O). In the 1980s researchers turned their attention to the more intense sentiments and phenomena that occur within actual interpersonal relationships, and to the social context of various kinds of specific relationships. The majority of research started to focus on the "pulse" or quality of these interpersonal relationships and its link to processes inside (e.g., depression, physical health) and outside (e.g., work satisfaction, financial strain) the individual.

NEW DIRECTIONS IN RESEARCH

Even more recently, relationships have received considerable attention in sociology and the other social sciences. Research since 1980 illuminates several themes. First, an expanding body of literature demonstrates that interpersonal relationships are vital to the physical and mental health of individuals. Studies show that individuals are likely to suffer from depression, ill health, and other physical problems if they lack interpersonal relationships of high quantity and quality. Second, the current research emphasizes specific relational processes that are relevant at various stages of the life course of a relationship. A third new direction has been to concentrate on making the dyad the unit of analysis rather than the individual. This change is both methodological and conceptual and has become an important contribution. Fourth, given the prominence of symbolic interactionism in sociology, another new direction has been to apply symbolic interactionist concepts to the study of relationship well-being and stability. The self is created out of the interactions and feedback from others, and the relational context is even more salient for how individuals view themselves. The fifth new direction has been to examine the construction of meaning within relationships for relationship quality and stability. There is an acknowledgment that individuals may construct meanings of their relationships, based on the social context of that relationship and individual, which in turn has significant influence on individuals' evaluations and status of those relationships. Sixth, the larger environment and structural conditions that can be harmful or beneficial for a couple's well-being have been examined (e.g., social networks, race/ethnicity).

SEE ALSO: Dyad/Triad; Friendship: Interpersonal Aspects; Interaction; Marriage

REFERENCE

Burgess, E. W. & Cottrell, L. S. (1939) *Predicting Success or Failure in Marriage*. Prentice Hall, New York.

SUGGESTED READINGS

Felmlee, D. & Sprecher, S. (2000) Close relationships and social psychology: intersections and future paths. *Social Psychology Quarterly* 63 (4): 365–76.

Orbuch, T. L., Veroff, J., Hassan, H. & Horrocks, J. (2002) Who will divorce: a 14-year longitudinal study of black couples and white couples. *Journal of Social and Personal Relationships* 19 (2): 179–202.

TERRI L. ORBUCH

intersectionality

An intersectionality framework emerged during the late 1980s with roots in socialist feminism, critical race and ethnic studies, and postcolonial feminisms. This evolving interdisciplinary body of theory and practice emphasizes the simultaneity of oppressions. Collins (2000: 18) asserts that "oppression cannot be reduced to one fundamental type, and that oppressions work together in producing injustice." Within this framework "there are no gender relations per se, but only gender relations as constructed by and between classes, races, and cultures" (Harding 1991: 79). By focusing on how systems of inequality are cross-cutting this framework draws attention to differences among women (or among men) rather than simply differences between women and men. This tradition understands systems of oppression as grounded in relational power differentials. Men's domination is thus related to (and dependent upon) women's subordination and the status of poor women of color is related to (and dependent upon) the status of affluent white women. Baca Zinn and Thornton Dill (1996) identify five basic assertions common to intersectionality approaches: the conceptualization of gender and race as structures and not simply individual traits, the rejection of an a priori assumption that women constitute a unified category, the existence of interlocking systems of inequality and oppression, the recognition of the interplay of social structure and human agency, and the necessity for historically specific, local analyses to understand interlocking inequalities.

Gender and race are understood as structures, discourses, or sets of enduring relations rather than simply individual characteristics. Gender and race are seen as social constructions rather than predetermined, transhistorical, biological or natural phenomena. The changing meanings of gender and racial categories across time and place substantiate the fluid, social character of gender and race.

The analytical category of "women" is not assumed to be a homogeneous, unified group of individuals who experience a common oppression and not assumed prior to an investigation. Women's shared structural location as women is not sufficient for understanding their experiences of gender inequality. Mohanty et al. (1991: 58) asserts that "sisterhood cannot be assumed on the basis of gender; it must be forged in concrete historical and political practice and analysis."

An intersectionality perspective assumes that individuals' lives are embedded within and affected by interlocking systems of inequalities based on race, gender, class, and sexuality. Individuals occupy multiple and often contradictory status positions that simultaneously advantage and disadvantage their lives. This "matrix of domination," as described by Collins (2000), embraces a both/and model of inequalities rather than an additive model of inequalities or binary oppositions. Interlocking inequalities operate at a macro-level that refers to the connections between institutional and organizational structures of race, class, and gender and a micro-level that refers to how interactions between individuals and groups are shaped simultaneously by race, gender, and class structures. A woman's gendered experiences are always framed in the context of her racial and class locations. Using this multi-lens approach allows researchers to (1) ground scholarship on gender in the histories of racism, classism, imperialism, and nationalism; (2) highlight how status positions are relational such that positions of privilege and disadvantage are connected; and (3) understand consequential differences among women (or among men) rather than simply differences between women and men.

Intersectionality highlights the interplay of social structures and human agency and thus allows for social change. The focus is often on the strategies of creative resistance that women employ to survive and thrive in oppressive situations rather than emphasizing women's powerlessness and dependency on men. Intersectionality scholars do not simply examine overt, public political activity, but focus on the less visible politicized activities that are taken up by subordinated groups.

The basic assumptions of intersectionality necessitate the need for historically specific, local analyses that allow for the specification of the complexities of particular modes of structured power relations. It is through such analyses that theoretical categories can be generated from within the context being analyzed. Intersectionality scholars reject universalizing and ahistorical approaches that try to explain, for example, patriarchal organization for all places at all times.

SEE ALSO: Black Feminist Thought; Matrix of Domination; Outsider-Within; Third World and Postcolonial Feminisms/Subaltern; Womanism

REFERENCES

Baca Zinn, M. & Thornton Dill, B. (1996) Theorizing difference from multiracial feminism. *Feminist Studies* 22: 321–31.

Collins, P. H. (2000) *Black Feminist Thought: Knowledge, Consciousness, and the Politics of Empowerment*, 2nd edn. Routledge, New York.

Harding, S. (1991) *Whose Science? Whose Knowledge? Thinking from Women's Lives.* Cornell University Press, Ithaca, NY.

Mohanty, C. T., Russo, A., & Torres, L. (eds.) (1991) *Third World Women and the Politics of Feminism.* Indiana University Press, Bloomington, IN.

CYNTHIA FABRIZIO PELAK

intersexuality

Intersex refers to a variety of inborn conditions whereby an individual's sexual or reproductive anatomy varies from social expectations about "normal" male or female anatomy. Because the standards are arbitrary, "intersex" is not a discrete category – what counts as intersex depends upon who's counting. That said, about 1/2,000 babies is born with obvious enough differences to come to medical attention. This biological variation creates direct challenges to binary constructs of sex and gender and to the cultural institutional systems designed around assumptions that discrete sex categories naturally yield complementary gender roles and heterosexuality.

Individuals with intersex conditions entered the arena of gender and sexual identity politics with the formation of the Intersex Society of North America (ISNA) in 1993. Building on strategies employed by gender and sexual minority rights movements of the late twentieth century, ISNA members have demanded an end to cosmetic genital surgery on infants, noting the absence of empirical evidence supporting the practice and ethical, medical, and human rights concerns (see the ISNA website, www.isna.org). Sex assignment at birth has critical legal and social implications including marital rights, certain constitutional protections, military service, athletic program participation, and leadership opportunities in religious organizations. People with intersex argue the existing medical treatment protocol must be changed to reduce the shame and secrecy around their condition and to allow people with "ambiguous genitalia" the right to make their own decisions about plastic surgeries.

SEE ALSO: Transgender, Transvestism, and Transsexualism

SUGGESTED READINGS

Fausto-Sterling, A. (1997) How to build a man. In: Rosario, V. A. (ed.), *Science and Homosexualities*. Routledge, New York.

Fausto-Sterling, A. (1999) *Sexing the Body: How Biologists Construct Sexuality*. Basic Boooks, New York.

Kessler, S. J. (1990) The medical construction of gender: case management of intersexed infants. *Journal of Women in Culture and Society* 16: 3–26.

LAURA M. MOORE

intersubjectivity

Intersubjectivity refers to a shared perception of reality among two or more individuals. The term is important in many aspects of sociology, from postpositivist research methods to studies of the lived experiences of individuals by ethnomethodologists and feminist scholars.

We, as human beings, cannot know reality except through our own senses: sight, hearing, smell, taste, or touch. Accordingly, each individual's reality is necessarily subjective. We may extend our senses through measuring devices (telescopes, scales, cameras, etc.) but ultimately each person's understanding of reality is individually subjective. One cannot see "blue" except through one's own senses. With social reality, we have even less certainty. It is easier to know that the sky is blue than it is to know that "James likes me."

However, most individuals also understand that we cannot change reality simply by thinking. If one were to wake up and decide that "blue" is "yellow," it would be clear that one could not make this change "real" for others. This duality presents a problem when studying people; neither objectivity nor subjectivity is sufficient to explain an individual's life experiences. Intersubjectivity is an intermediate position that sociologists use to solve this problem. At best, people may achieve a common understanding of what is going on.

Philosophers of science and social scientists have used intersubjectivity, or intersubjective testability, to discuss the day-to-day operations of social science. Social scientists attempt to explain and predict the outcomes of certain situations based on some initial information and a theory of how things work. People in a particular field of study come to agree first on the rules of evidence. They obtain specialized training in order to be able to conduct tests of "knowledge claims" using clear definitions, precise theories, and transparent research methods. Since the rules of evidence are agreed upon, different scientists looking at the same information can agree on its meaning, obtaining intersubjectivity on the results of research.

In a different vein, phenomenologists and ethnomethodologists have used the term intersubjectivity for the understandings people come to share in their everyday lives. Again, presuppose that objectivity is not possible in human understanding. Social meaning is malleable and differences of subjective view are ubiquitous. Intersubjectivity in this context refers to the shared perspectives people sometimes actually achieve, and often assume they have achieved. People take for granted that reality is obdurate. They may realize that there is no way objectively to know what is "real." But for day-to-day activity, this is treated as unimportant. People operate as if reality is knowable, as if people similar to themselves see things the same way, and assume that if reasonable people discuss matters, they will probably come to the same conclusions.

Intersubjectivity is most visible, and its importance is highlighted, when it is violated. When taken-for-granted behaviors do not occur, or unexpected behaviors do occur, they call into question assumptions about reality. The resulting breakdown in intersubjectivity can be most unsettling. This leads to an often repeated phrase among social constructionists that "reality is negotiated."

Feminist scholars highlight the power aspects of intersubjectivity. Low-power actors are often required to share the perspectives of high-power actors, coming to an intersubjective agreement on "what you want, what you think, what you need." High-power actors are afforded the right to concern themselves with "what I want, think, and need." As a value statement, higher power researchers should attempt to achieve an intersubjective view with lower power interviewees. Researchers who are too interested in what they want to know from their interviewees may miss the opportunity to learn what their interviewees want them to know.

SEE ALSO: Ethnomethodology; Everyday Life; Interaction; Phenomenology; Schütz, Alfred; Structure and Agency

SUGGESTED READINGS

Lengermann, P. M. & Niebrugge, J. (1995) Intersubjectivity and domination: a feminist investigation of the sociology of Alfred Schutz. *Sociological Theory* 13 (1): 25–36.

Schütz, A. (1967) *The Phenomenology of the Social World*, trans. G. Walsh & F. Lehnert. Northwestern University Press, Chicago, IL.

PAUL T. MUNROE

interviewing, structured, unstructured, and postmodern

Interviewing is a flexible methodology to acquire information by asking questions. Interviews are commonly employed in qualitative research: face-to-face meetings, small groups, and by telephone or Internet surveys and chat rooms. The researcher's ontological and epistemological assumptions influence the interviews questions, interpretations and structure.

- *Structured interviews* often take the form of surveys but can include face-to-face dialogue. There must be consistency of measurement for comparison: formally structured questions; the questions' order and wording unchanged for each respondent; responses are constrained by pre-defined numerically coded categories. Interviewers assume a position of neutrality; interaction is limited to asking questions in the same way to each respondent.
- *Unstructured interviews*, often used in field research, ethnography, and oral/life history studies, are loosely organized and open-ended: no formal interview schedule; variable questions; no predefined responses. Interviewers emphasize understanding and empathy, respondents determine what is relevant. Each interview is flexible and unique.
- *Focus group interviews* are informal interactive and highly flexible discussions with limited (5–8) participants. Moderators facilitate discussion, focusing on participant perceptions and interpretations. They are ideal for generating information quickly, for interviewing transient populations, the elderly, and children, and for examining sensitive or new research topics.
- *Postmodern interviews* are shaped by postmodern epistemologies, they are reflexive and interactive. Knowledge is created though collaboration with respondents. Questions are produced throughout the interview; the researcher's role is ambiguous with minimal influence over the interview. Emphasis is placed on empowering respondents. Examples of interviews oriented to postmodern sensibilities include the gendered interview (focuses on difference; advocates for oppressed groups), and the active interview (focuses on what is communicated; how knowledge is constructed and revealed).

SEE ALSO: Ethnography; Methods; Qualitative Methods

SUGGESTED READINGS

Berg, B. (2009) *Qualitative Research Methods for the Social Sciences*. Allyn & Bacon, Boston, MA.
Gubrium, J. and Holstein, J. (eds.) (2003) *Postmodern Interviewing*. Sage, London.

CATHERINE KRULL

intimacy

"Intimacy" is a quality of relationships associated with particular ways of behaving. It is sometimes defined narrowly to mean the familiarity resulting from close physical association or, more specifically, sexual contact. In current usage, intimacy is typically presumed to involve something more profound, such as emotional attachment, love and care. For popular and academic commentators, intimacy is increasingly understood as representing a very particular form of "closeness" and being "special" to another person founded on "disclosing intimacy," mutual self-disclosure leading to knowledge and understanding of inner selves. In *The Transformation of Intimacy* (1992) Anthony Giddens argued that equal and democratic relationships based on disclosing intimacy were ascendant as the ideal type of relationship in Euro-North American societies by the late twentieth century. His work was a counterclaim to more pessimistic accounts of private intimacy displacing civic and community engagement or of individualized intimacy undermining "family values."

Discussion continues of whether and why women's relationships appear to involve more disclosing intimacy than men's with some commentators suggesting women routinely do more emotional work in relationships than men. In *Intimacy: Personal Relationships in Modern Societies* (1998) Lynn Jamieson reviews research on couple relationships, sexual relationships, parent–child relationships, and friendship relationships, demonstrating the continuance of a wider repertoire of intimacy than "disclosing intimacy" and that self-perceived "good" relationships were often neither equal nor democratic. Moreover, equal relationships were often sustained by working hard to have fair divisions of labor and to mutually negotiate practical care rather than simply self-disclosure. This is not, however, to deny the significance of self-disclosing intimacy in popular culture, or the discursive power of this ideal of intimacy to influence everyday perceptions of how to construct good relationships. Studies of personal life beyond the Euro-North

American contexts suggest the pervasive reach of this discourse about intimacy.

SEE ALSO: Love and Commitment; Marriage; Sexuality

SUGGESTED READINGS

Bauman, Z. (2003) *Liquid Love: On the Frailty of Human Bonds*. Polity Press, Cambridge.

Bellah, R. N., Madsen, R., Sullivan, W. M., Swidler, A. & Tipton, S. M. (1985) *Habits of the Heart: Individualism and Commitment in American Life*. University of California Press, Berkeley, CA.

LYNN JAMIESON

Islam

The sociology of Islam covers a diverse set of religious and cultural groups and histories. With a global population estimated at more than 1.6 billion as of 2009, Muslims constituted the world's second largest religious tradition (after Christianity). Nearly a quarter of all Muslims live outside majority-Muslim countries, including tens of millions throughout eastern and western Europe. Practices and orientations within Islam vary considerably from the mystical-experiential emphasis of Sufis to the austere discipline of Salafists to various shades of mainstream Shi'a and Sunni Islam around the world.

As with other major traditions, aspects of Islam may be said to be secularized in everyday life, making it reasonable to speak of Islamic cultures and secular Muslims without necessarily signifying religious commitment. Indeed, some scholars prefer to describe the field as the "sociology of Muslims" to emphasize lived experiences rather than to suggest pure, unchanging theological ideals disconnected from social practice. However, sociologists are likewise increasingly sensitive to problems of uncritically applying concepts from the Western Christian context to Islam without reflecting first on their relevance. For instance, anthropologist Talal Asad traces the historical contingency of basic categories like "religion" and "secular" and insists that cultural and historical context be taken into account in order to interpret how such concepts might apply to Islam.

In recent years the role of politics in Islam has been examined widely. By both popular and academic observers, it is sometimes said that Islam is intrinsically political in ways that, for instance, Christianity is not. Close historical studies tend to explode this notion as inaccurate. Fazlur Rahman noted that as early as the Umayyad dynasty (661 to 750 CE) political leaders had lost religious prestige and important religious innovations were taking place outside the political structure. Moreover, as far back as 1258 CE, the rule of the caliphs, the traditional title used by leaders of several Islamic dynasties based in modern Syria, Iraq, Egypt, and Turkey, seldom extended to all the major Muslim population centers. Hence neither the religious credibility of political leaders nor the political integration of those following Islam could be taken for granted starting at an early date in Muslim history.

Since the 1970s a major development in Islam has been a large-scale piety movement known as the "calling" to Islam (*da'wa*). It is perhaps best understood as a cross-national religious revival and cultural movement. It has been intertwined with, yet is distinct from, the rise of Islamist political parties and social organizing in many Muslim-majority countries. While in fact a diverse set of political (and apolitical) orientations have emerged in connection with the revival, most visible to Western observers were so-called fundamentalist movements that drew criticism for their severe and sometimes violent policies, which their advocates claimed were sanctioned by authoritative texts of Islam. The most sweeping political movements peaked in the late 1970s and 1980s as displeasure registered with corrupt or ineffective secular governments in countries ranging from Algeria and Egypt to Sudan and Pakistan. In most cases the Islamists failed to win or maintain power, with the notable exception of Iran's 1979 revolution. Others have chronicled the moderate or progressive politics which has emerged alongside or in reaction to the radical groups including Asef Bayat, who has championed the term "post-Islamist" to describe a trend of moderation following a period of radicalism and idealism.

SEE ALSO: Globalization, Religion and; Historical and Comparative Methods; Religion, Sociology of; Secularization

SUGGESTED READINGS

Asad, T. (1993) *Genealogies of Religion*. Johns Hopkins University Press, Baltimore, MD.

Ernst, C. (2003) *Following Muhammad*. University of North Carolina Press, Chapel Hill, NC.

Rahman, F. (1998) *Islam*, 2nd edn. University of Chicago Press, Chicago, IL.

SCOTT HEIL

J

Jacobs, Jane (1916–2006)

Born in 1916 and raised in Scranton, Pennsylvania, in her teens Jacobs moved to New York City where she bought a small row house in West Greenwich Village, eventually met and married an architect, and raised her family. They remained in New York City until 1969 when, because of their opposition to the Vietnam War, they moved to Toronto, Canada. There Jacobs lived and wrote for the next several decades, a lively and major political presence until she died in 2006.

Jacobs was the consummate political activist. She not only treasured living in cities, but she also enjoyed puttering around with their politics. She took on the expressways in New York as well as the eminent "power broker," Robert Moses. In her writings as well as her everyday politics, she argued forcefully against high-rise apartment buildings as well as the public housing of New York City. In Toronto she worked in big and small ways on behalf of the city, here arguing for retaining locally owned stores, there for the construction of neighborhoods that contained mixed-use, medium-rise, and high pedestrian traffic areas.

In her classic work, *The Death and Life of Great American Cities* (1961/1992), Jacobs provided a view of cities that was, at once, a scathing attack on modern city planning and a vision of how people in cities actually live. Despite her lack of a sociological pedigree, it also furnished a fundamentally sociological view of the city, echoes of which can be found in many contemporary writings not only about cities but also about modern society in general.

Like a good sociologist, she argued that the best way to understand the urban world was to view it at street level through the eyes and with the ears of its residents. Here one could observe the comings-and-goings of people, their everyday greetings to one another, social stuff that made up the everyday world of its residents.

Cities worked, they were made safe and livable, because of the life of people on and near the streets, she argued, not because of the great, looming designs of their developers or architects.

The neighborhood, not the precinct or the house or the apartment building, was the center and beehive of social activity in the city. It was here that people passed one another, shared hellos and goodbyes, and helped to shape a community with one another. Our human feelings of trust, of privacy, and of security in our urban surroundings, Jacobs argued, were grounded in these everyday occurrences.

An astute observer of city planning, Jacobs insisted that there should be mixed uses of buildings and enterprises. Cities should be constructed so there is a regular flow of people on the sidewalks; this means that the spaces of cities should be designed to take account of the different rhythms of people during the day.

Jacobs later expanded on her concerns by arguing that cities and their regions are the true basis of the modern economy. She insisted that nations were regarded by economists and other figures as the actors in the economy but this was purely an artifact of their measures. When studied closely, it was the cities and regions that proved to be essential to the vitality of modern economies.

SEE ALSO: Civil Society; Urbanization

REFERENCE

Jacobs, J. (1961/1992) *The Death and Life of Great American Cities*. Random House, New York.

SUGGESTED READING

City & Community (2006) A retrospective on Jane Jacobs. 5 (3) (September).

ANTHONY ORUM

Japanese-style management

The term "Japanese-style management" (JSM) was coined in the 1970s to delineate a number of interrelated work practices in Japan: lifetime employment, seniority wages and enterprise unionism. These were seen as products of traditional values the Japanese placed on verticality in human relationships (e.g., seniority), being part of a group (e.g., long-term employment), and consensual relationships (e.g., enterprise unionism). An associated list of outcomes included low levels of industrial disputation, a commitment to working long hours, the provision of certain types of company welfare, and lower labor turnover. The concomitant values were seen in an emphasis on social cohesion, a culturally ordained work ethic, familial and paternalistic orientations and an innate sense of group loyalty. The model has lately come to incorporate features such as widespread bottom-up consultation, spontaneous and voluntary quality control circles, internal labor markets, joint labor-management consultations, the absence of a strong militant class, and highly integrated tiered production systems.

Most of the early literature on JSM emphasized its uniqueness as an arrangement ordained by peculiarly Japanese cultural orientations. By the 1980s this kind of cultural essentialism was codified in accounts of nearly every aspect of Japanese society. Known as *nihonjinron*, they colored the learn-from-Japan campaign that emerged from the late 1970s. As the interest in the export of JSM intensified, two debates developed in tandem. One concerned the extent to which JSM was unique to Japan. Closely related, the second concerned whether the supporting values were peculiar to Japan. As Japanese firms implemented JSM abroad, they came under increasing scrutiny, especially by labor unions and by those interested in labor process, and further debate focused on whether the practices associated with JSM were post-Fordist or merely better techniques for intensifying the use of labor and hence a form of ultra-Fordism. That debate shifted the emphasis from JSM's alleged cultural origins to the structural requisites and the bottom-line outcomes of JSM simply as a way of organizing work.

SEE ALSO: Management, Theories of; Unions

SUGGESTED READINGS

Mouer, R. & Kawanishi, H. (2005) *A Sociology of Work in Japan*. Cambridge University Press, Cambridge.

Rebick, M. (2005) *The Japanese Employment System: Adapting to a New Economic Environment*. Oxford University Press, New York.

ROSS MOUER

jihad

The word *jihad* (which derives from the verb *jahada*, meaning "to strive, to exert oneself, to struggle") is one of the most prominent Arabic terms in the western world owing to its vital influence in Muslim society and its significant political role there. It is also one of the most crucial concepts in political sociology for understanding contemporary Muslim society, particularly with the emerging trend of Islamist movements in many parts of the globe.

The origin of the concept dates back to the history of the Prophet Muhammad (570–632), as reflected and written in the Qur'an and the notes of his speeches, sayings, and behavior (*hadith* and *sunnah*). The word is generally used to denote an endeavor toward a praiseworthy aim. However, the term has various and ambiguous meanings, as reflected in its different interpretations. In religious contexts it can mean the struggle against one's evil inclinations ("interior *jihad*") or an endeavor for the sake of Islam and the *umma* (the Muslim society), for example, attempting to convert unbelievers or working for the moral uplift of Islamic society ("exterior *jihad*"). Although in the contemporary context the word *jihad* is more widely associated with acts of violence and terror ("holy war"), the "*jihad* of the sword" was originally called "the smaller *jihad*," in contrast to the peaceful form that is "the greater *jihad*," signifying the interior *jihad* or personal struggle to rid one's soul of greed, hatred, and egotism.

This is also the line of reasoning used by Osama bin Ladin and his companions in al-Qa'idah to justify activities such as the attacks on the Pentagon and the World Trade Center in New York on September 11, 2001. The asymmetrical power relations between them and their opponents, such as President George W. Bush, Jr., and his allies, became more evident when the latter launched a counterattack targeted at Afghanistan and Iraq. In the period of the global war against terrorism promoted by former President Bush and his allies, *jihad* was wrongly defined and constructed as being synonymous with "terrorism," and many groups associated with *jihad* thus mistakenly became categorized as "terrorists."

SEE ALSO: Islam; Knowledge, Sociology of

SUGGESTED READINGS

Devji, F. (2005) *Landscape of the Jihad, Militancy, Morality and Modernity*. Cornell University Press, Ithaca, NY.

Peters, R. (1999) *Jihad in Classical and Modern Islam: A Reader*. Markus Wiener, Princeton, NJ.

MUHAMMAD NAJIB AZCA

Judaism

Judaism is one of the world's oldest religions, characterized by a belief in one God (monotheism), and the belief that the Torah is the source of divine knowledge. The Shema, "Hear, O Israel, the Lord our God is One," affirms Judaism's monotheism.

The Torah is also referred to as the Holy Scriptures, and is the first five books of what Christians refer to as the Old Testament. Abraham (ca. 1600 BCE) is considered the founder of Judaism, although, similar for other religions, researchers today question the possible mixture of legend and fact. The Jewish calendar goes back 1,946 years before Abraham, based on the 19 generations listed inclusively from Adam and Eve to Abraham (Abram) in Genesis 5:3–32 and Genesis 11:10–26. The Christian year of 2010–11 equals the Jewish year of 5770–1. The Jewish day begins at sundown instead of at midnight.

From a cultural perspective, most Jews today are classified as Sephardic–Mizrahi (backgrounds from Iberia or mostly Muslim counties of North Africa, the Middle East, and the Near East) or Ashkenazim (backgrounds in Europe, except Iberia, mostly Christian lands). Judaism has changed over time and has developed different definitions, degrees of traditionalism, and practices. The patterns are different for Ashkenazim and Sephardim–Mizrahim.

In most Ashkenazi areas, there are two main divisions, Orthodox or Traditional Judaism, and Liberal or Progressive Judaism. Orthodox Judaism requires a strong degree of traditional belief and daily observance. It is divided into Modern Orthodox and Traditional Orthodox. Liberal Judaism has made significant changes in both beliefs and practices. The USA, over 90 percent Ashkenazi, has a three-fold division of Orthodox, Conservative, and Reform Judaism because of migration patterns which were not experienced in other countries. A fourth branch of Judaism in the United States, Reconstructionism, views Judaism as an evolving religious civilization, and generally follows modern practices. Intermarriage, and the loss of children from Judaism, is a major challenge to Judaism in many parts of the world today.

Sephardic–Mizrahi migration patterns are different from Ashkenazic patterns, and did not lead to a division like the Ashkenazim. All Sephardic-Mizrahi Judaism is Orthodox, but because it represents all Sephardim–Mizrahim, with various degrees of traditionalism and modernization, it has adjusted internally and tends to be more flexible than Ashkenazi Orthodoxy.

Judaism has several major holidays, and many minor holidays. Most important are Rosh Hashanah, the Jewish New Year, which begins a ten-day period of repentance, and Yom Kippur (the Day of Atonement), the holiest day of the Jewish year which ends the ten-day period. They occur in September or October. Other major Jewish holidays reflect Judaism's long religious and cultural history, including persecutions and victories. Purim (February–March) is a joyful holiday that celebrates the victory of the Jews over a plot to destroy them in ancient Persia. Pesach, or Passover (March–April) is a celebration of the Jewish escape from slavery in ancient Egypt in the thirteenth century BCE Sukkot (September–October) is a joyful festival symbolizing the return of Jews to Israel after escaping from Egyptian slavery. Simchat Torah is a joyful holiday which celebrates the completion of the annual reading of the Torah and the beginning of a new cycle. Hanukkah (usually December) lasts for eight days and celebrates the victory of the Maccabees over the Seleucid oppression in 165 BCE Historically, Hanukkah was a relatively minor holiday, but it has become more important in Christian countries partly to offset Christmas so that Jewish children do not feel left out.

There are about 13 million Jews in the world today, with about 40 percent living in Israel and about 60 percent living in the diaspora (i.e., the dispersion outside Israel, the original homeland). The USA alone accounts for about 40 percent. About 37 percent of world Jewry were killed in the Holocaust, drastically reducing the number of Jews. Israel is roughly divided evenly between Ashkenazim and Sephardim–Mizrahim.

SEE ALSO: Globalization, Religion and; Religion, Sociology of

SUGGESTED READINGS

Neusner, J. (1992) *A Short History of Judaism: Three Meals, Three Epochs.* Fortress Press, Minneapolis, MN.

Zohar, Z. (ed.) (2005) *Sephardic and Mizrahi Jewry: From the Golden Age of Spain to Modern Times.* New York University Press, New York.

ABRAHAM D. LAVENDER

K

Kant, Immanuel (1724–1804)

Immanuel Kant was born in Königsberg, East Prussia (now Kaliningrad), where he spent his entire life, first as a student and *Privatdozent*, later as Professor of Logic and Metaphysics at the University of Königsberg. Kant's trilogy of main works, the *Critique of Pure Reason* (1781), *Critique of Practical Reason* (1788) and *Critique of Judgment* (1790), has become an indispensable reference point for all subsequent philosophy, but his theories of experience, ontology and ethics were also instrumental in laying the foundations of the human sciences, and classical sociology in particular was inspired from Kantian roots.

Kant's epistemology and ontology were developed from his inversion of conventional thinking about the relationship between experience and reality. He suggested that experience does not simply adapt itself to the world, but determines the way the world appears to us. The forms of space and time, together with other fundamental features – the "categories" of quantity, quality, relation (which includes causality), and modality – are imposed on the world by the act of experience itself. Since knowledge is limited by the bounds of experience, human beings can know only appearances in the world, and have no access to things-in-themselves, that is, to objects as they exist independently of our apprehension of them.

A similar line of thinking underpins Kant's theories of free will, ethics, and action. The existence of individual free will is unknowable. However faith in its existence is necessary in order to make sense of the institutions of morality and law, as well as widely held principles that guide judgment in human affairs such as autonomy, duty, and responsibility. Freedom is a condition for those acts that flow from obedience to the moral law, or what Kant famously entitled the categorical imperative, which (among other elements) requires that human beings treat others as ends-in-themselves rather than as mere means to their own ends.

Kant's influence on Durkheim is most visible in his program for a sociology of knowledge developed in *The Elementary Forms of Religious Life*. Durkheim agreed with Kant as to the constitutive role of experience in determining reality, but took issue with Kant's claim that the categories of experience are innate and identical for all rational beings. Durkheim, by contrast, regarded them as variable across cultures and over the course of social evolution. This variation is visible in the divergent classification systems adopted by different cultures, and which Durkheim (with Marcel Mauss) undertook to enumerate in *Primitive Classification*.

Classical German sociology developed directly out of the neo-Kantian program of grounding the emerging social sciences in Kant's philosophy, and this is evident in the work of both Simmel and Weber. Simmel accepted Kant's theory of experience, as laid out in the *Critique of Pure Reason*, as valid for objects within the natural order of reality. However, he argued that the concept of "society" implies a world of subjects that is experienced differently from the natural order, and which is unknowable through the methods of the natural sciences. "Society" may be studied instead through the "forms of sociation" (*Vergesellschaftung*), such as conflict, exchange and group size, which structure and organize social life in a manner analogous to the actions of the categories on the data of experience.

Weber was drawn to Kant's understanding of action in terms of means and ends, which underpinned the latter's moral philosophy. Weber's theory of rational action, a key component of his general theory of social action, may be taken as an extension of Kant's contrast between hypothetical and categorical imperatives. Weber distinguished between instrumentally rational (*Zweckrational*) and value-rational (*Wertrational*) action, that is, between action oriented towards efficient means and strategic ends on the one hand, and action oriented towards achievement of ends that are valued and pursued for their own sake (or ends-in-themselves) on the other. The contrast between instrumental and value-rational action was taken up by the Frankfurt School in a self-consciously critical manner that combined Kantian elements with Marxism.

All these Kantian elements have found their way, via the classical traditions, into contemporary sociological thinking, and Kant's work remains an important source of ideas and inspiration within contemporary social theory.

SEE ALSO: Epistemology; Hegel, G. W. F.

SUGGESTED READING

Cassirer, E. (1981) *Kant's Life and Thought*. Yale University Press, New Haven, CT.

Caygill, H. (1995) *A Kant Dictionary*. Blackwell, Oxford.

PHILIP WALSH

Khaldūn, Ibn (732–808 AH/ 1332–1406)

Walī al-Dīn 'Abd al-Raḥmān ibn Muḥammad Ibn Khaldūn al-Tūnisī al-Ḥaḍramī was born in Tunis on 1 Ramadhan of the Muslim year. His *Muqaddimah*, a prolegomenon to the study of history, was completed in 1378 and introduces what he believed to be a new science he called *'ilm al-ijtimā ' al-insānī* (science of human society).

Ibn Khaldūn's *Muqaddimah* is a prolegomenon to his larger historical work on the Arabs and Berbers, the *Kitāb al- 'Ibar wa Dīwān al-Mubtadā' wa al-Khabar f ī Ayyām al-'Arab wa al-'Ajam wa al-Barbar* (*Book of Examples and the Collection of Origins of the History of the Arabs and Berbers*). He begins the *Muqaddimah* by problematizing the study of history, suggesting that the only way to distinguish true from false reports and to ascertain the probability and possibility of events is the investigation of the nature of human society (Ibn Khaldūn 1981 [1378]: 38 [1967: I.77]). It is this investigation that he refers to as *'ilm al-ijtimā' al-insānī*. Ibn Khaldūn made the distinction between the outer forms (*Ẓāhir*), that is, facts and reports, and the inner meaning (*bāṭin*), that is, causes, of history (Ibn Khaldūn 1981 [1378]: 1 [1967: I.6]). The new science is presented by Ibn Khaldūn as a tool for the study of history and is directed to uncovering the inner meaning of history.

Empirically, Ibn Khaldūn's interest was in the study of the rise and fall of the various North African states. Only a society with a strong *'aṣabiyyah* or group feeling could establish domination over one with a weak *'aṣabiyyah* (Ibn Khaldūn 1981 [1378]: 139, 154 [1967: I.284, 313]). Because of superior *'aṣabiyyah* among nomadic peoples, they could defeat sedentary people in urban areas and establish their own dynasties. Having done so, urbanization resulted in the diminution of their *'aṣabiyyah*. With this went their military strength and their ability to rule. This leaves them vulnerable to attack by fresh supplies of pre-urban nomads with stronger *'aṣabiyyah* who replaced the weaker urbanized ones. And so the cycle repeats itself.

Underlying the above substantive concerns is Ibn Khaldūn's interest in elaborating a new science of society, based on the application of Aristotle's four types of causes, the formal, material, efficient, and final cause (Mahdi 1957: ch. 5). Understanding the inner meaning of history is to know the nature of society, which in turn requires the study of its causes. The causes are what gives society its constitution (material cause), its definition (formal cause), the motive forces of society (efficient cause), and society's end (final cause) (Mahdi 1957: 233–4, 253, 270). This can be said to be the elements of Ibn Khaldūn's general sociology, applicable to all types of societies, nomadic or sedentary, feudal or prebendal, Muslim or non-Muslim.

Ibn Khaldūn has been recognized as a founder of sociology by earlier generations of western sociologists in the nineteenth century. However, this degree of recognition has not been accorded to Ibn Khaldūn in contemporary teaching and the writing of the history of sociology.

SEE ALSO: Islam; Sociology; Theory

SYED FARID ALATAS

REFERENCES

Ibn, Khaldūn, 'Abd, al-Raḥmān (1981) [1378] *Muqaddimat Ibn Khaldūn*. Dar al-Qalam, Beirut. Page numbers in square brackets refer to Franz, Rosenthal's (1967) English translation, *Ibn Khaldûn: The Muqadimmah – An Introduction to History*, 3 vols. Routledge & Kegan Paul, London.

Mahdi, M. (1957) *Ibn Khaldûn's Philosophy of History*. George Allen & Unwin, London.

Kinsey, Alfred (1892–1956)

Alfred Kinsey was not by training a sociologist, but a biologist (specializing in the taxonomy of gall wasps) at Indiana University, Bloomington. Believing there was a need for a course about marriage and sexual behavior, in 1938 he was concerned to find little data on which to base such study. According to one small study at that time, some 96 percent of young Americans did not know the word masturbation and many thought it was a form of insanity. In general there was widespread ignorance, and he decided to conduct his own study of the sexual behavior of the American female and male during the 1930s to 1950s – most prominently as *The Sexual Behavior of the Human Male* (1948) and *The Sexual Behavior of the Human Female*

(1953), and after his death, less well-known studies such as *Sex Offenders* (1965). Ultimately providing some 18,000 life stories of individuals (many of whom he interviewed himself), it was largely taxonomic – a "social book keeping" exercise showing who does what with whom, where, when, and how often. Using the interviews, he and his colleagues asked around 300 questions. When published, his work was a large statistical and scientific study, but curiously it became a national bestseller and played a prominent role in shaping US cultural life in the later part of the twentieth century.

His work was largely atheoretical, but his data showed dramatically how sexual behavior was related to social forces. The theoretical implications were later drawn out by John Gagnon and William Simon, especially in their theory of social scripting.

For Kinsey, matters such as social class, age, marriage, urban living, and religion seriously shaped social patterns of sexual behavior. His work documented significant differences between men and women, noting that "the range of variation in the female far exceeds the range of variation in the male" (Kinsey et al. 1953: 537–8, see tables in vol. 2), as well as across social classes. He also showed a wide range of variant sexual behavior; for example, finding very high rates of extramarital and premarital sex, high rates of masturbation, curiously high rates of zoophilia, and most famously of all very high rates of homosexual behavior. He found much higher rates of participation in homosexual acts than previously thought, and invented the heterosexual–homosexual continuum with a point scale ranging from "exclusively homosexual" (Kinsey 6) through to "exclusively heterosexual" (Kinsey 0) (Kinsey et al. 1953: 470).

Among his other major contributions was the refinement of interview research tools – a major appendix on research strategy is included in the first volume and it became required reading for many students of sociology during the 1950s and 1960s. His interviews required great sensitivity in eliciting material, and his sample depended upon volunteers. It remains one of the most detailed large sample studies to date, though it depended upon volunteers and did not use random sampling.

Kinsey's work has been much criticized. Apart from many moralists who condemned his work as obscene, there were others who argued that the focus on sexual behavior – of measuring who does what to whom, where, and when – managed to reduce sex to orgasm-counting while robbing it of meaningful humanity. The importance of love was minimized (but Kinsey argued that this was not measurable and this was his concern). Sociologists were later very critical of its methodology: it did not employ a random probability sample but depended on volunteers, and hence, although large, the sample was seen as very biased. Further, the sample was not representative, and the interviews were not very accurate.

But others have seen it as a trailblazing study. For its time, the study was actually a remarkable methodological achievement, not least due to Kinsey's pioneering, single-minded efforts. Some have suggested that the key contribution of Kinsey's work was its impact on society: it rendered sexuality more democratic and generated an "ideology of tolerance" around sexuality that has now permeated culture. This, in turn, was built "on Kinsey's discovery of the remarkable variety of human experience." Kinsey also established the Kinsey Institute (formally known as the Kinsey Institute for Research in Sex, Gender, and Reproduction), which exists to this day in Bloomington, Indiana. Part of its work became therapeutic training for practitioners, and as such it played a prominent role in the development of sex therapy and sexology.

SEE ALSO: Homosexuality; Scripting Theories; Sexuality; Sexuality Research

REFERENCES

Kinsey, A., Pomeroy, W. B., Martin, C. & Gebhard, P. (1948) *The Sexual Behavior of the Human Male*. W. B. Saunders, New York.

Kinsey, A., Pomeroy, W. B., Martin, C. & Gebhard, P. (1953) *The Sexual Behaviour of the Human Female*. W. B. Saunders, New York.

KEN PLUMMER

kinship

For much of the twentieth century debates around kinship in western societies focused largely on the impact of industrialization on family structure. Parsons's (1949) arguments that industrialization encourages a kinship system with relatively strong boundaries around the nuclear family were particularly influential, though other writers queried how strong these boundaries really were. Certainly, there is now ample evidence that in industrial societies primary kin – mothers, fathers, sons, daughters, siblings – generally remain significant throughout a person's life, and not just when they reside together as a nuclear family. Typically, though not invariably, these kin act as resources for one another, being part of an individual's personal support network for coping with different contingencies. In particular, a parent's concern for children does not end when the child becomes adult, and few adult children lack any sense of commitment to their parents.

Within western societies, however, the "rules" of kinship are not tightly framed; the ordering of these relationships are *permissive* rather than *obligatory*. In other words, individuals have relative freedom to work out or "negotiate" how their kinship relationships should be patterned, though some groups or subcultures (including many migrant and religious minority groups) have stronger social regulation of kinship ties than others. The permissive character of western kinship was highlighted by Finch and Mason (1993) who focused on the negotiation of kinship responsibilities. Their model emphasizes that such negotiations do not occur in isolation, but are framed by the biographical development of the relationships in question. In other words, previous kinship behavior, as well as knowledge of the personalities and commitments of those involved, form part of the context in which the negotiations occur.

The importance of Finch and Mason's analysis is that it highlights the role of agency as well as structure in kin behavior. While there are clear patterns in the ways kin behave toward one another (e.g., in the greater likelihood of daughters rather than sons providing parents with personal care in later old age) there is also a great deal of variation. This variation has been compounded since the late 1970s by significant changes in patterns of family formation and dissolution. Of themselves, these changes raise questions about the categorization and meaning of kinship. For example, are ex-spouses categorized as kin? When does a step-parent or a cohabitee become kin? Such questions do not have clear-cut answers. Instead, the nature of the relationships which develop and the extent to which they are understood as operating within a kinship framework are emergent, and in this sense "negotiated".

Moreover, kinship is not just about individual relationships. Kinship comprises a network of relationships which interact on one another. The effective boundaries of the network vary for different people and change over time. But typically news and gossip flow readily through the network, with some individuals, particularly mothers, acting as "kin-keepers." In part it is because kinship operates as a network that a focus on negotiation is so useful for understanding kinship processes. Similarly, the questions raised above about new partners or step-parents coming to be regarded as kin are not solely individual issues. It also matters whether others in the kinship network regard them as "family" too.

SEE ALSO: Family Diversity; Family Structure; Marriage

REFERENCES

Finch, J. & Mason, J. (1993) *Negotiating Family Relationships*. Routledge, London.

Parsons, T. (1949) The social structure of the family. In: Ashen, R. (ed.), *The Family*. Haynor, New York, pp. 241–74.

SUGGESTED READING

Allan, G. (1996) *Kinship and Friendship in Modern Britain*. Oxford University Press, Oxford.

GRAHAM ALLAN

knowledge

Knowledge is relevant to sociology as the principle that social relations can be organized in terms of the differential access that members have to a common reality.

Until the late eighteenth century, Plato's *Republic* epitomized the role of knowledge as a static principle of social stratification. However, the Enlightenment introduced a more dynamic conception, whereby different forms of knowledge could be ordered according to the degree of freedom permitted to their possessors. An individual or a society might then pass through these stages in a process of development. Thus, thinkers as otherwise diverse as Hegel, Comte, and Mill came to associate progress with the extension of knowledge to more people.

However, this dynamic conception of knowledge produced a paradox: The distribution of knowledge and the production of power seem to trade off against each other. The more who know, the less it matters. Knowledge only seems to beget power if relatively few people enjoy it. The distinctly sociological response to this paradox was to jettison Plato's original idea that a single vision of reality needs to be the basis for knowledge. This response, popularly associated with philosophical relativism, asserts simply that different forms of knowledge are appropriate to the needs and wants of its possessors. Much of what is called the "sociology of knowledge" takes this position as its starting point.

As the sociological tradition emerged in the nineteenth century, it became clear that some forms of knowledge enable its possessors to adapt to, if not outright overcome, obstacles in the environment, be they of natural or human origin.

Such knowledge was commonly called "ideological," implying a disjuncture between mind and reality. This meant that knowledge did not so much "represent" reality as strategically distort reality in favour of the knowledge possessors. Marxists associated "science" with an accurate representation of reality, the possession of which enabled the possibility of a form of knowledge that could benefit everyone, and hence be truly "emancipatory."

However, starting in the 1960s, science itself was subject to "ideology critique" by the Frankfurt School, and since the 1970s has been subject to many case studies in "science and technology studies" that have together served to challenge the intrinsic rationality of science. Were scientists judged in terms of all the consequences of their activities, both intended and unintended, might they not appear as "irrational" as, say, priests and politicians? How, then, should the socially and ecologically transformative, sometimes even destructive, character of science be taken into any overall assessment of its "rationality." This challenge has been taken up most directly by "social epistemology," which attempts to reconstruct a normative order for science in light of this socially expanded sense of consequences.

Perhaps the biggest challenge facing the sociology of knowledge today is science's tendency to become embedded in the technological structure of society. Under the circumstances, science's character as a form of knowledge is reduced to its sheer capacity to increase the possessor's sphere of action. Such a reduction characterizes the definition of "knowledge" used by sociologists who argue that we live in "knowledge societies." For them, knowledge is a commodity traded in many markets by many producers. In this emerging political economy, institutions traditionally dedicated to the pursuit of knowledge like universities no longer enjoy any special advantage.

SEE ALSO: Epistemology; Knowledge, Sociology of; Scientific Knowledge, Sociology of; Social Epistemology

SUGGESTED READINGS

Berger, P. & Luckmann, T. (1967) *The Social Construction of Reality*. Doubleday, Garden City, NY.

Fuller, S. (1988) *Social Epistemology*. Indiana University Press, Bloomington, IN.

Mannheim, K. (1936/1929) *Ideology and Utopia*. Harcourt Brace & World, New York.

Stehr, N. (1994) *Knowledge Societies*. Sage, London.

STEVE FULLER

knowledge, sociology of

The sociology of knowledge examines the social and group origin of ideas, arguing that the entire "ideational realm" ("knowledges," ideas, ideologies, mentalities) develops within the context of a society's groups and institutions. Its ideas address broad sociological questions about the extent and limits of social and group influence through an examination of the social and cultural foundations of cognition and perception. Despite significant changes over time, classical and contemporary studies in the sociology of knowledge share a common theme: the social foundations of thought. Ideas, concepts, and belief systems share an intrinsic sociality explained by the contexts in which they emerge.

From its origins in German sociology in the 1920s, sociology of knowledge has assumed that ideas (knowledge) emerge out of and are determined by the social contexts and positions (structural locations) of their proponents. Its major premise is that the entire ideational realm is functionally related to sociohistorical reality. Outlined in early statements by Max Scheler (1980) and Karl Mannheim (1952), the new discipline reflected the intellectual needs of an era, to bring both rationality and objectivity to bear on the problems of intellectual and ideological confusion. It was in this sense that the sociology of knowledge has been described as a discipline that reflected a new way of understanding "knowledge" within a modern and ideologically pluralistic setting. What we believe that we *know* varies with the cognitive operations of human minds and these vary by community, class, culture, nation, generation, and so forth. While Scheler's original essays provoked commentary and debate, it was Mannheim's formulation of the discipline in *Ideology and Utopia* that defined the subject matter of the field for years to come.

Mannheim's treatise begins with a review and critique of Marxism and proceeds toward a theory of ideology in the broader sense: the mental structure in its totality as it appears in different currents of thought and across different social groups. This "total conception of ideology" examines thought on the structural level, allowing the same object to take on different (group) aspects. This understanding of ideology refers to a person's, group's, or society's way of conceiving things situated within particular historical and social settings. Like ideologies, "utopias" arise out of particular social and political conditions, but are distinguished by their opposition to the prevailing order. Utopias are the embodiment of "wish images" in collective actions that shatter and transform social worlds.

Werner Stark's *The Sociology of Knowledge* (1991), first published in 1958, prompted a major advancement and redirection of the field. It argued for the embedding of sociology of knowledge within the larger field of cultural sociology. Stark's book clarified the principal themes of earlier writers, especially sociologists, who had addressed the problem of the social element in thinking. He also intended it to serve as an introduction to the field that would prepare the way for a detailed and comprehensive history of the sociology of knowledge and its most significant ideas: theories of ideology of Marx and Mannheim; philosophical speculations of the neo-Kantians Heinrich Rickert and Max Weber; views of the German phenomenological school of the 1920s, especially Scheler.

Berger and Luckmann's *The Social Construction of Reality* (1966) moved the field further away from theoretical knowledge or ideas and toward the (pre-theoretical) knowledge that social actors draw from in everyday life. Their treatise also redirected the traditional theory of social determination of ideas by social realities: social reality itself is a *construct*. It integrated the perspectives of classical European social thought (Marx, Durkheim, Weber) with the social psychology of the American pragmatist philosopher George Herbert Mead, thereby advancing Meadian social psychology as a theoretical complement to European sociology of knowledge. What the authors proposed was that knowledge and social reality exist in a reciprocal or dialectical relationship of mutual constitution, thereby subsuming *knowledges* within a framework of interpretation, a *hermeneutics* concerned with the symbolic and signifying operations of knowledges.

More recently, the "new sociology of knowledge" can be seen as part of this larger movement in the social sciences, distinguished by a turn away from materialism and social structure toward semiotic theories that focus on the ways in which a society's meanings are communicated and reproduced. Swidler and Arditi (1994) focus on how social organizations (e.g., the media) order knowledges, rather than examining social locations and group interests. In light of new theories of social power and practice (Michel Foucault and Pierre Bourdieu), they also examine how knowledges maintain social hierarchies and how techniques of power are simultaneously and historically linked to knowledges.

SEE ALSO: Ideology; Knowledge; Mannheim, Karl; Scientific Knowledge, Sociology of

REFERENCES

Berger, P. L. & Luckmann, T. (1966) *The Social Construction of Reality*. Doubleday, New York.

McCarthy, E. D. (1996) *Knowledge as Culture: The New Sociology of Knowledge*. Routledge, New York.

Mannheim, K. (1952) [1925] The problem of a sociology of knowledge. In: Mannheim, K., *Essays on the Sociology of Knowledge*, ed. P. Kecskemeti. Harcourt, Brace, & World, New York, pp. 134–90.

Scheler, M. (1980) [1924] *Problems of a Sociology of Knowledge*, trans. M. S. Frings. Routledge & Kegan Paul, London.

Stark, W. (1991) [1958] *The Sociology of Knowledge*, intro. E. D. McCarthy. Transaction, New Brunswick, NJ.

Swidler, A. & Arditi, J. (1994) The new sociology of knowledge. *Annual Review of Sociology* 20: 305–29.

E. DOYLE MCCARTHY

Kuhn, Manford (1911–1963)

Manford H. Kuhn founded the branch of sociological social psychology referred to as the Iowa School. This branch was labeled as such because Kuhn spent his career at the University of Iowa (called the State University of Iowa upon his appointment). Though Kuhn was trained alongside Herbert Blumer and by George Herbert Mead, Kuhn's epistemological stance differed in fundamental ways from that of his mentors and noteworthy contemporaries.

In terms of social psychology, the Chicago School was the social psychological camp of thought associated with Blumer. Its approach emphasized participant observation research in an attempt to understand both groups and individuals by identifying the process of meaning construction and the meanings themselves for the things that comprise their social environments. Unlike the Iowa School, the Chicago School was uninterested in discovering generalizable patterns of human behavior, instead focusing on the subjectivity of the individual actor.

The Iowa School inspired a number of outgrowths, such as the work of McCall and Simmons on social roles, and subsequently Stryker's structural theory of social identity.

Kuhn's approach, the early core of the Iowa School, put an emphasis on empirical techniques that could be used to investigate and generalize about human interaction and cognition. Among his most influential contributions to social psychology was the concept of the core self, the idea that every person has a stable set of components of the self that persist across different social situations. This became the foundation for his "self theory." This core self shapes and constrains the way we define situations. Humans seek and have continuity and predictability.

Where Blumer conceptualized behavior as situationally specific and emerging from potentially unique circumstances, Kuhn thought of behavior as being driven by existing elements of the self which were static and measurable. The Iowa School generated multiple, successful lines of research, among them Sheldon Stryker's structural social identity theory.

Furthermore, while Kuhn conceptualized social structure as being created, maintained, and altered through social interaction, he also thought of social structure as providing constraints on social action. His structural view of social psychology informed his leaning toward developing objective measures of the self in the attempt to analyze quantitatively how the self-concept motivated cognition and behavior.

Kuhn's structural perspective, combined with the understanding that the self is an enduring entity, resulted in the development of the often-used Twenty Statements Test (TST) in 1954 with Thomas McPartland. The TST equips social psychologists with a method for uncovering self-identifications which exist because of the social roles people embody. By responding to the question, "Who am I?," respondents report, in order of importance, the social roles they enact. The response patterns to this question provide insights regarding the structure of the self. These meanings associated with these roles can be used to explain and predict likely behaviors across social situations.

SEE ALSO: Blumer, Herbert; Chicago School; Self; Social Identity Theory; Social Psychology

SUGGESTED READINGS

Kuhn, M. (1964) Major trends in symbolic interaction theory in the past twenty-five years. *Sociological Quarterly* 5: 61–84.

Kuhn, M. & McPartland, T. (1954) An empirical investigation of self-attitudes. *American Sociological Review* 19 (1): 68–76.

REEF YOUNGREEN

Kuhn, Thomas and scientific paradigms

Thomas S. Kuhn (1922–96) made major contributions to the history and philosophy of science, especially in relation to the character and change of a discipline's scientific paradigm. He emphasized the social construction of scientific knowledge and the defining and disciplinary force of scientific paradigms. A paradigm is a worldview, a set of implicit and explicit guides or examples defining the world and the questions and methods for analyzing the world. Kuhn's most recognized and enduring work is *The Structure of Scientific Revolutions*, in which he described a discipline's paradigm articulation up to the point at which that paradigm is no longer capable of furnishing or resolving interesting problems. The ensuing crisis of normal science provokes extraordinary science and the possibility of scientific revolution in which the basic paradigm of a discipline is changed.

Kuhn's work indicates the importance of social structure in any discussion of a scientific community. A clear picture of socialization emerges from the discussion of the intergenerational process of recruitment and accreditation. Paradigm discipline to sustain an integral core of fundamental problems and methods is a social process, most visible in the structure and function of a penalty-reward and status system in the discipline's hierarchy of journals, departments, and associations. Less visible but no less important is the tacit knowledge of shared commitments and research guides. This emphasis on the social construction of science is part of a general movement, dating at least to Marx, toward a sociology of knowing. If a unification of scientific knowledge is in the offing near term, it will likely build upon this growing concern with the process of human cognition.

SEE ALSO: Science, Social Construction of; Scientific Knowledge, Sociology of

SUGGESTED READINGS

Kuhn, T. (1970) *The Structure of Scientific Revolutions*, 2nd edn. University of Chicago Press, Chicago, IL.

Nickles, T. (ed.) (2003) *Thomas Kuhn*. Cambridge University Press, Cambridge.

JAMES RONALD STANFIELD &
MICHAEL C. CARROLL

L

labeling

In sociology the concept of labeling is used in two interrelated ways. One involves the labeling of people as *deviants*. When people receive a negatively evaluated label – delinquent, cheat, pervert, etc. – it is assumed the individual did something to deserve the label; however, this is not always the case and people may be *falsely accused* for a number of reasons. Regardless of the accuracy of the label it has important psychological and sociological consequences. The negative attributes associated with the label are assumed by others to be true about the person with the label which in turn impacts the labelee's social interaction and self-concept.

The other is the labeling of actions as *deviance*. Sociologists struggled with an operative definition of deviance because normative definitions and their application vary widely across situations. Groups often differ in their normative definitions; an individual may move through several settings each day each with a unique set of norms, and normative definitions in groups and settings tend to change over time. For these reasons the *reactive definition* – deviance is defined by a negative social reaction to a behavior – is most often favored by sociologists. This definition allows sociologists to focus on the social processes that lead to an act being defined as deviant rather than on the validity of the moral arguments in favor of the label.

Several factors determine which behaviors are labeled deviant and who is more likely to be labeled. Behaviors are more likely to be labeled as *deviance* if they are actions more typical of less powerful actors in a society. This is true as well for *deviants*, as less powerful and lower status group members are more likely to be labeled, especially falsely. Social distance and visibility are other factors that affect labeling.

SEE ALSO: Deviance, Constructionist Perspectives; Essentialism and Constructionism;
Labeling Theory; Mental Illness, Social Construction of

SUGGESTED READINGS

Goffman, E. (1963) *Stigma: Notes on the Management of Spoiled Identity*. Prentice Hall, Englewood Cliffs, NJ.

Scheff, T. (1966) *Being Mentally Ill: A Sociological Theory*. Aldine, Chicago, IL.

THOMAS CALHOUN & MARK KONTY

labeling theory

Unlike most theories of crime and deviance, which emphasize the causes of deviant behavior, labeling theories focus on society's reaction to crime and deviance. Labeling theorists argue that society's reaction to deviance is fundamental for three reasons. First, individuals who are labeled as deviant by society often become stigmatized and isolated from society, leading them into a deviant lifestyle. Second, the very definition of deviance lies not in the objective behavior of "deviants," but in powerful groups' ability to define and label the behavior of the powerless as deviant or criminal. Thus, deviance is socially constructed. Third, society's reaction to deviance provides positive functions for society by defining the boundary between deviant and conventional behavior and by reaffirming social solidarity.

Lemert (1951) used the term primary deviance to refer to harmless initial acts of deviance, and secondary deviance to refer to deviance resulting from the negative effects of labeling. Labeling theorists have identified many examples of secondary deviance. For example, because of the stigma of their arrest records, ex-prisoners have difficulty getting jobs, finding affordable housing in good neighborhoods, and finding non-criminal companions, all of which impedes reentry into conventional society. Mental patients institutionalized in mental hospitals are stripped of their identities and forced to adapt to a custodial environment, which can hamper their attempts to recover. The poor are sometimes labeled as lazy and slothful, which can undermine their self-esteem and attempts to secure and maintain jobs.

Perhaps more than any other theory of deviance, labeling theory takes seriously a social constructionist view. Rather than assuming that deviance and crime are objective behaviors "out there" to be discovered, labeling theorists argue that deviance is socially constructed through an institutional process involving politics and the legal system, and an interactional process involving the powerful applying of labels to the powerless. As a social construction, then, deviance is relative to a given society and historical period. Out of the nearly limitless variety of human acts, societies settle on a small range of acts to label as deviant; most entail harm to others, but some entail little harm. The relativity of deviance is underscored by labeling theorists' definition of deviance.

A hallmark of labeling theory is the observation that labels are not distributed equally in society, but rather are disproportionately applied to the powerless, the disadvantaged, and the poor. This begins with the creation of rules that define deviance. Labeling theorists argued that generally the powerful succeed in creating rules and laws outlawing behavior that violates their self-interests. Thus, rule creation is a result of group conflict in society, in which the powerful have a distinct advantage. Becker (1963) showed how moral entrepreneurs, typically drawn from the ranks of the middle and upper classes, create moral crusades by mobilizing disparate interest groups to outlaw behaviors that violate their common interest. Classic examples include the Marihuana Tax Act, prohibition, sexual-psychopath laws, and the creation of the juvenile court.

In sum, labeling theory has shaped how we view deviance and crime in society by underscoring the importance of society's reactions to deviance, analyzing political power and deviant labels, and showing how labeling can amplify deviance. Left for dead in the 1980s by some researchers, labeling theory is enjoying a revival by researchers responding to Becker's (1973) call for an interactionist theory of all aspects of deviance, including primary deviance, labeling, and secondary deviance.

SEE ALSO: Deviance, Crime and; Deviance, Criminalization of; Deviance, Theories of; Labeling

REFERENCES

Becker, H. S. (1973) Labeling theory reconsidered. In: *Outsiders: Studies in the Sociology of Deviance*. Free Press, New York, pp. 177–212.

Lemert, E. M. (1951) *Social Pathology: A Systematic Approach to the Theory of Sociopathic Behavior*. McGraw-Hill, New York.

ROSS MATSUEDA

labor markets

In principle a labor market is the primary method of allocating people to paid work, of whatever nature, within capitalist economies/societies. Within capitalism, the separation of the producer of a good or service from the means of its production has rendered a situation where labor power (that is, the capacity of a person to work) has become a commodity to be bought and sold. In theory both buyers and sellers of labor power are free to choose from or to whom they would like to buy or sell. Thus, the "market" can be represented as an efficient, voluntary mechanism of exchange wherein the economic rules of efficiency, perfect competition, and supply and demand apply, and equilibrium will be achieved. From such a perspective market imperfections (or disequilibria) when they occur do so because interest groups within a market are, for example, able to strengthen their position, restrict entry to their group, or force pay changes. Actions or events such as these are regarded essentially as "glitches" and, over time, theory suggests, equilibrium will be reachieved.

From a general picture of labor markets within the context provided, we can hone our examination by considering the notion of both external and internal labor markets. The model of the dual labor market developed by Doeringer and Piore (1971) introduced the idea of the primary and secondary sectors. The primary sector represents core skill areas for which employers were prepared to pay higher levels of wages and provide better employment terms and conditions as a means of ensuring as far as possible a secure, committed, and competitive labor force. By contrast, workers in the secondary sector would not expect to have so secure a position. Indeed, it is this sector which facilitates flexibility for employers, as workers within this context would tend to have contracts based on, for example, seasonal requirements or part-time availability of or for work. Within this sector would be subcontracted workers or even businesses, and significant levels of labor turnover would be both expected and tolerated.

From a sociological perspective, focus is placed upon the relationship between those groups within the labor market and within individual workplaces and occupations. Broadly speaking there is a rejection of the economists' notion of market efficiency. The basis of this alternative position is the inequitable nature of the employment relationship. The root of such inequity is firmly planted in the nature of capitalism and the dispossession of workers from the means of production, of either goods or services, including their lack of ownership of raw materials, tools, and places of production.

Sociologists developed an ongoing theme which challenges the dominant economic perspective on labor markets, including the notion that buyers and sellers of labor power are free to choose to whom they would like to buy from or sell to. From this perspective, we can see that the concept of the efficient market, perfect competition, and the achievement of equilibrium is highly questionable. A more realistic position recognizes market imperfections, or disequilibria, and that they emerge because of the varying strengths of the numerous interest groups.

SEE ALSO: Labor/Labor Power; Labor Process; Unemployment; Work, Sociology of

REFERENCE

Doeringer, P. B. & Piore, M. J. (1971) *Internal Labour Markets and Manpower Analysis.* D. C. Heath, Lexington, MA.

SUGGESTED READING

Jenkins, R. (1986) *Racism and Recruitment: Managers, Organizations and Equality in the Labour Market.* Cambridge University Press, Cambridge.

ANNE FEARFULL

labor process

Critical labor process analysis began with Marx's (1976) distinction, in *Capital*, volume I (*The Production Process of Capital*) between "the labour process in general" and "the labor process combined with the process of creating value [*Wertbildungsprozess*]" – the "valorization process [*Verwertungsprozess*]" (pp. 283–306). Marx emphasized the ontological significance of the labor process: humanity must interact with nature to survive (cultivating crops, making clothes, building shelter, etc.). The labor process is simultaneously the foundation of creativity as ideas are externalized and objectified. Even in the industrial age, the laboring human is essential: "A machine which is not active in the labour process is useless." "Living labour must seize on [machinery and raw materials]" and "awaken them from the dead." "Bathed in the fire of labour . . . and infused with [its] vital energy" machinery and raw materials become consumable commodities or the materials for new labor processes (Marx 1976: 289).

Within the valorization process, the labor process is changed fundamentally. The worker and process are governed by the structures of capitalism and imperatives for profit maximization through ever-increasing efficiency.

In the early 1900s, Frederick Winslow Taylor and Henry Ford systematized, in theory and practice, key aspects of the *Wertbildungsprozess*. While Taylor (1911: 13–21) identified "natural soldiering" (the "natural instinct to take things easy") as a problem, "systematic soldiering" was of greater concern. Management relied too heavily on workers' knowledge and experience allowing them to systematically control the pace of work. Furthermore, workers moving from planning to execution wasted valuable time. Taylor's "task idea" separated planning (head labor) from execution (hand labor) with management controlling planning, assigning individual workers precisely detailed, simplified tasks. Scientific management created savings in labor costs through increased efficiency, deskilling labor processes, and placing the creative aspects of production and planning directly under managerial control.

Ford used Taylor's "task idea" to create an entire system of mechanized, mass production. Pioneering the development and use of simple-to-install, standardized, interchangeable parts and specialized tools, "Fordism" assigned each worker simple, easily performed tasks – eliminating expensive, skilled assemblers. Arranging those tasks sequentially along continuous, automated assembly lines, management controls work speed while mass-producing standardized products.

Studying the impact of globalization, advanced technology, and the computerization of production, Mandel, Braverman and Burawoy updated Marx and revitalized analyses of labor processes. Mandel examined differing forms of exploitation as monopoly capital protected heavy investments in mechanized production within the global north while locating labor intensive, resource extracting work in the global south. Braverman argued that the imperatives of capitalist production, shaped by Taylorism, led to the continuing "degradation of work." Under monopoly capitalism, the computerization of traditional blue-collar, clerical and service industry jobs made work experiences increasingly similar, homogenizing the class structure. Burawoy's work added important subtlety to Braverman's work by showing that in the midst of increasingly mindless production, workers, through "labor games" that keep things interesting, are unwittingly co-opted by capital's *Wertbildungsprozess* rather than resisting it.

Contemporary sociology, drawing from Foucault, emphasizes docile bodies, economy and technologies of power, disciplinary practices and surveillance in the labor process, eschewing Marx, Mandel and Braverman's grander narratives.

SEE ALSO: Alienation; Braverman, Harry; Fordism/Post-Fordism; Foucault, Michel; Labor/Labor Power; Taylorism

REFERENCE

Taylor, F. W. (1911) *The Principles of Scientific Management*. Harper and Brothers, New York.

SUGGESTED READING

Braverman, H. (1974) *Labor and Monopoly Capitalism*. Monthly Review Press, New York.

ROB BEAMISH

labor/labor power

In *The German Ideology*, Marx and Engels maintained that one may distinguish humans from other biological entities by consciousness, religion, or anything else one chooses but humankind fundamentally differentiated itself from other organisms when it began to produce its means of life through labor. Labor is an eternal, naturally imposed condition, common to all societies. While producing its means of life, humankind indirectly creates the material conditions for its ongoing existence.

In *Capital*, Marx (1976: 283) emphasized the ontological status of "labor in general." Labor is "a process between man and nature . . . a process by which man, through his own actions, mediates, regulates and controls the metabolism between himself and nature." Labor changes nature and changes humankind's nature. Ensuing scholarship in the physical, biological, and social sciences have refined, but not fundamentally altered, Marx's position on labor's ontological character.

Humankind is directly part of the material order of nature and inescapably bound to its laws (e.g., gravity, mitosis and meiosis, aging). As living creatures, humans have specific material needs they must meet (e.g., they must metabolize oxygen, water, and protein to live). Those needs are not all met immediately and directly. Through the evolution of the material order, the human order stands separated or alienated from the material order. Whereas the material order of nature is direct, concrete, and thingly, the human order is concurrently immediate and mediate, concrete and abstract, and objective and subjective. Labor in general is the activity through which humankind mediates itself with the material order and draws upon the concrete and abstract aspects of its being to create and recreate its existence.

Marx's critique of Hegel's *Phenomenology* led to his deepest and most perceptive analyses of labor as the material, ontological basis to human life. While Hegel correctly emphasized the creative aspects of humanity, he limited it to the active, self-conscious mind. Marx maintained that human self-development stemmed from labor – a form of action that was simultaneously concrete and abstract. Labor externalizes an idea in a material form; it creates something that is separate from the producer. This object stands opposite and outside the producer but simultaneously remains a part of the producer as it represents the culmination of creative activity. Twenty-three years later, in *Capital*, Marx celebrated labor as the fire that infuses energy into raw materials, tools, and machinery, turning them from moribund objects into new products to meet human needs and wants.

Subject to the laws of the material order, labor is simultaneously objective and subjective: in producing an object through the externalization of an idea, the producer also gains subjective knowledge associated with that productive act. Labor is an inescapably creative, concrete process. The labor process crosses through the cultural grid humankind creates and recreates between itself and the natural order.

If labor is the eternal, naturally imposed condition of human life, labor power is the eternal, active, mediating capacity bringing humankind into contact with the material order. While probing the capital/labor exchange in *Grundrisse*, Marx (1953: 201) first recognized that workers sold their *capacity to labor* (*Arbeitsfähigkeit*) to capitalists, not their labor. Marx used several terms to denote this capacity before settling on labor power (*Arbeitskraft*). Labor power is a complex conception of potential, ability, power, and force which can act on the material order and refashion it. Labor power is the unique human capacity to establish an interaction with the material world through an activity that is concurrently concrete and abstract, objective and subjective, immediate and mediate.

In class societies, labor power is the sole source of value creation. Because labor power is a capacity, the purchaser need only pay enough for the worker – the bearer of this potential – to meet his or her socially determined needs and thereby be able to return to work day after day. The expenditure of labor power over a full working day, however, may produce more value than the replacement value of labor power, giving rise to surplus value. The identification of labor power as the source of surplus in capitalist societies was among Marx's most significant discoveries.

SEE ALSO: Alienation; Hegel, G. W. F.; Marx, Karl; Surplus Value; Value

REFERENCES

Marx, K. (1976) [1890] *Capital*, 4th edn. vol. 1, trans. B. Fowkes. Penguin, London.

Marx, K. (1953) [1857–58] *Grundrisse*. Dietz, Berlin.

SUGGESTED READING

Lukacs, G. (1978) *The Ontology of Social Being: Labour*, trans. D. Fernbach. Merlin Press, London.

ROB BEAMISH

language

Language is a very important topic in its own right (Crystal 1987) and in terms of philosophical debates in the social sciences (Rorty 1967), yet, surprisingly, many sociologists pay scant attention to language. Recently there has been a reexamination of the work of outstanding linguists and logicians. The important debates between those who identify with Enlightenment modernism and those who adhere to postmodernism have forced many social scientists to reexamine long-held assumptions. Critical approaches to the study of gender, race, and class have often involved a rethinking of basic linguistic categories by scholars such as Chomsky, Foucault, Baudrillard, Derrida, Bauman, Pinker, and many others. The study of language is a window to all of the social sciences, especially as cutting-edge theory is shaping up in the early twenty-first century. For many, there has been a philosophical shift from Cartesian "subject-centered reason" and rational action, to Fichtean "communicative social action" and symbolic interaction. Many writers have discussed the "linguistic turn" in contemporary thought, a paradigm shift that may have started with "ordinary language philosophy" and other trends in the 1960s, or even earlier. Modernist, structuralist epistemologies stressing the Cartesian subject–object dichotomy have been confronted by postmodernist, poststructuralist epistemologies which stress the "habitus" and the "lifeworld."

An examination of the anthropological and sociological aspects of language includes the study of the creation of artificial languages with simplified grammars (e.g., Esperanto). Language affects social structures and social structures, in turn, affect language. What interest the social scientist are the complex patterns that emerge from the human use of language. This leads to ethnolinguistics and anthropological linguistics. In sociology the focus is on sociolinguistics.

Various poststructuralist scholars have indicated that the Dilthey-Weber use of *Verstehen* – and "romantic hermeneutics" in general – may still be too individualistic and may neglect the importance of the sociolinguistic "field," the conscious and unconscious coordination of a group due to its shared language. Hence, we move from the individual scholar to the social actor and then to the "bundle of habits."

In the discipline of linguistics the field of "pragmatics" concerns the ways in which language usage is linked to contextual background features. This has a recognized overlap with sociological ethnomethodology. How do people "accomplish talk"? Knowledge of the sociocultural context and the social psychological situation can help us, for example, to distinguish between angry and joking behavior. Conversation analysis examines the structure of human dialogues.

The study of "symbolic interaction" by sociologists who call themselves symbolic interactionists is based in part on George Herbert Mead's insight that in order for two or more people to interact they need to have "significant symbols" in common. A significant symbol is a symbol that all participants to the interaction understand fairly clearly in terms of its practical consequences.

Some authors, following clues found in Saussure and Peirce, have argued that there should be a shift from linguistics to a much more generalized approach that is sometimes called semiotics. Peirce (1923) argues that the aspect of reality that is being signified is something "represented" by an interpretive community and not by an isolated individual. The interpretive community always signifies "the representant" through the use of a system of signs. Hence, language is a semiotic system that allows for human *and* animal communication.

For some, it is not possible to study anthropological linguistics, ethnolinguistics, sociolinguistics, or psycholinguistics without evoking all aspects of human communication (anthropo-semiotics). The argument is also frequently extended to include communication among other animals. Thus, the study of "the language of bees" is a study in animal communication (zoo-semiotics). The underlying premise is that there is a high degree of continuity between other animals and the human animal in the way in which we communicate.

There are many kinds of signs that are important to human languages, but perhaps the most important are "symbols" such as words and phrases. A set of such symbols, perhaps supplemented by iconic or indexical signs, can constitute a "text." Any piece of recorded symbolic communication is a kind of text, but when we think of language we think primarily in terms of written language and the formal "ground" of such a language, what Saussure refers to as *la langue*.

The stronger form of the Sapir–Whorf hypothesis is rejected today, but it is widely recognized that a weaker form of that theory is valid. Complex hypothetical and deductive linguistic theories have been postulated by many thinkers, including those who have emphasized the importance of "semiotics." Writers such as A. J. Greimas have utilized insights from thinkers like Saussure, Merleau-Ponty, Lévi-Strauss, Dumezil, Barthes, Lacan, Propp, and Jakobson to develop arguments concerning the relationship between language and communicative symbols in general. Such "structural" views tend to postulate the existence of a narrated universe of "deep semantic structures" that are reflected in the underlying grammar of all human languages.

REFERENCES

Crystal, D. (1987) *The Cambridge Encyclopedia of Language*. Cambridge University Press, Cambridge.

Peirce, C. S. (1923) *Chance, Love and Logic: Philosophical Essays*. Harcourt Brace, New York.

Rorty, R. (ed.) (1967) *The Linguistic Turn: Recent Essays in Philosophical Method*. University of Chicago Press, Chicago, IL.

J. I. (HANS) BAKKER

langue and *parole*

Ferdinand de Saussure distinguishes between a "language" (*langue*) in its structural form and the spoken word (*parole*). Saussure's distinction is synchronic rather than diachronic; the actual utterance by a person is a product of that speaker's having been socialized into a language which is relatively fixed during his or her lifetime. The ontological status of Saussure's categories is disputed. For example, Walter Benjamin was opposed to Saussure's ontological assumptions concerning the arbitrariness of the signifier.

Chomsky makes a distinction, similar to Saussure's, between "competence" and "performance." It is possible to speak a *langue* in a grammatically correct manner without any knowledge of the discipline of linguistics in general, or even the application of linguistic rules to that specific language.

These distinctions are similar to the anthropological terms "etic" and "emic," which are taken by analogy from phonetics and phonemics. In linguistics, phonemics studies the phonemes, which are a class of phonetically similar "phones" or speech sounds (from the Greek word for voice), while phonetics is also concerned with patterns of sound changes in a language or group of languages.

The structuralist tradition in anthropology associated with Claude Lévi-Strauss uses Saussure's distinction. A structuralist approach to *langue* is compatible with "semiology," "signology," or – as it is usually called now – semiotics (Seung 1982).

SEE ALSO: Language; Saussure, Ferdinand de; Semiology

REFERENCES

Seung, T. K. (1982) *Structuralism and Hermeneutics*. Columbia University Press, New York.

SUGGESTED READING

Chomsky, N. (1957) *Syntactic Structures*. Mouton, The Hague.

J. I. (HANS) BAKKER

law, sociology of

The sociology of law extends criminology's concern with coercion to incorporate studies of the role of law in regulating and facilitating social order.

Early sociologists thought changes in the nature of law signaled the transition to capitalism. Maine (1861) described this as a movement from a society based on *status* to one based on *contract*. In traditional societies, law expressed a sovereign or collective will, imposing order through repressive sanctions and sustaining relationships based on inherited or ascribed positions. Modern law facilitated free, autonomous and episodic relationships. Contemporary legal anthropologists reject this representation of traditional law but the image has been influential. Durkheim saw modern law as a solution to the social and moral fragmentation generated by the division of labor. Marx viewed law primarily as an ideological tool, supplying legitimacy to the power imbalance between owner and laborer. Weber adopted Marx's recognition of the role of law in legitimizing state power but also emphasized its contribution to rationalization in modern societies.

The contemporary research agenda is summarized in the title of a classic paper: naming, blaming, and claiming (Felstiner et al. 1980–1). Naming is recognizing that a problem may have a legal response. Blaming is identifying who is responsible for the problem and seeing law as a way to compel them to make some redress. Claiming is the process of mobilization that brings the problem into the legal system.

Claims are the tip of an "iceberg": potential causes for litigation are endemic in everyday life, but are rarely named as such (Greenhouse et al.

1994). Although many people believe that a "compensation culture" has developed, with both citizens and corporations, stimulated by lawyers, increasingly resorting to litigation, there is no substantial empirical evidence to support this. This perception is partly the product of a popular imagery of law that massively overstates the role of trials. Whether criminal or civil, most legal outcomes are negotiated.

It is argued that law now contributes mainly to the social and economic integration of an elite. People who are excluded are offered two options: alternative dispute resolution (ADR) and regulation. ADR joins two very different interests: social programs intended to strengthen the capacity of poor neighborhoods to resolve their own disputes; and governmental actors trying to reduce public expenditure. ADR reduces legal access for poor people while telling them that it is morally preferable for them to solve their own problems.

Regulation involves the screening of social and economic activity by a bureaucracy empowered to administer legal penalties or to bring cases to court. It is particularly evident where harms are diffuse, where there are great economic inequalities between parties, or where there are great informational inequalities. As with ADR, private enforcement by individual litigants is held to be morally preferable to collective action by a "nanny state."

The field's founders observed a world of "small states," with limited spheres of action, and looked to develop replacements for traditional legal forms in response to emerging social and economic issues. A modern world required modern law, as part of its system of governmentality. The perceived crisis of that system has allowed its critics to roll back many state-based elements, returning individual legal mobilization to a position that it has not occupied for some generations.

SEE ALSO: Criminology; Sexuality and the Law; Social Control; Weber, Max

REFERENCES

Cotterell, R. (1992) *The Sociology of Law: An Introduction (Second Edition)*. Butterworths, London.

Felstiner, W. L. F., Abel, R., & Sarat, A. (1980–1) The emergence and transformation of disputes: naming, blaming, claiming. *Law and Society Review* 15: 631–54.

Greenhouse, C., Yngvesson, B., & Engel, D. (1994) *Law and Community in Three American Towns*. Cornell University Press, Ithaca, NY.

Maine, H. (1861) *Ancient Law*. Murray, London.

SUGGESTED READING

Cotterell, R. (1992) *The Sociology of Law: An Introduction*, 2nd edn. Butterworths, London.

ROBERT DINGWALL

leadership

Leadership is the process of inspiring, directing, coordinating, motivating, and mentoring individuals, groups, organizations, societies, and nations. Weber (1947) identified three typologies of leadership in bureaucracy: charismatic, traditional, and legal. Charismatic leaders were attributed powerful qualities by their followers; traditional leaders were powerful by virtue of hereditary wealth; legal leadership draws its power from professional knowledge and technical expertise. The authority of leadership was legitimized through roles in the bureaucratic hierarchy, and by subordinates' understanding and respecting the bureaucracy's rules.

Sociological approaches to leadership tend to be about how power structures allow domination and control over others. In contrast, early leadership research and theory is embedded in psychological trait theories of personality. Such approaches distinguish leaders from non-leaders by identifying specific biological and genetic personality traits. Research, however, has been quite mixed because leaders proved no more likely to possess special traits than did "non-leaders." As a result, the behavioral school gained strength over trait theorists. Behaviorists argued that what distinguished leaders from non-leaders were observable behaviors rather than traits. As with trait theory, behavioral theory also produced spurious results. In response, arguments emerged stating that effective leadership was contingent upon certain situational factors. Situational leadership theory moved away from individual difference psychology back to the social psychological and sociological notions of leadership. There was a return to Weber's idea that leadership is a function of the willingness of subordinates to be led, but also as a function of several situational contingencies.

More recently the study of charismatic, transformational, and transactional leadership has dominated. Charismatic leaders exhibit qualities that followers are attracted to, and have the ability to inspire and sell vision. Transactional leaders attend to the necessary functional aspects of management, such as coordination and control. The transformational leader was based on the sociological work of Burns (1978) who argued such leaders set examples through inspirational performance, inspired change and innovation. Bass (1985) and others now offer

Full range Leadership theory, which posits that effective leadership requires a combination of all styles of leadership – transformational, transactional, and laissez-faire (the ability to step back).

"Newer" approaches to leadership have emerged, most notably from a positive psychological perspective. Positive psychology has its roots in William James, Carl Rogers, and Abraham Maslow, and has been reinvigorated by Seligman (1999). Work on positive leadership concentrates on a person's ability to create social as well as psychological capital, and an ability to be "authentic" (Luthans & Youssef 2004).

Other area of leadership theory and research are those of leadership substitutes, dispersed leadership and servant leadership. Substitutes are those things that replace or make leaders obsolete (teams, empowerment, self-leadership). Dispersed leadership addresses how leadership power is transferred to structure, rules, procedures, and technologies. Some argue that leadership substitutes such as empowerment are advanced and ingeniously designed forms of power.

In some postmodern leadership perspectives, leaders are servants to the frontline people who are servants to customers. Consumers and consumerism is king and all are servants to consumption. In essence postmodern leaders provide running commentary on how the organization is doing, and how people fit within it; they construct the stories and rituals around life in organizations, where the organization will go and can go, and how one can become a better servant of the consumer. For others leadership is nothing but a social construction of our collective imagination, and the role and performance of leadership are overstated. An example is the global expectation on President Obama to solve the world's problems.

SEE ALSO: Power, Theories of; Weber, Max

REFERENCES

Bass, B. M. (1985) *Leadership and Performance Beyond Expectation*. Free Press, New York.

Burns, J. M. (1978) *Leadership*. Harper & Row, New York.

Luthans, F. & Youssef, C. (2004) Human, social, and now positive psychological capital management: investing in people for competitive advantage. *Organizational Dynamics* 33 (2): 143–60.

Seligman, M. E. P. (1999) The president's address. *American Psychologist* 54: 559–62.

Weber, M. (1947) *The Theory of Social and Economic Organization*, trans. T. Parsons & A. M. Henderson. Free Press, New York.

TYRONE S. PITSIS

legitimacy

Legitimacy is defined as a state of appropriateness ascribed to an actor, object, system, structure, process, or action resulting from its integration with institutionalized norms, values, and beliefs. It is a topic of longstanding interest across the spectrum of sociological phenomena and levels of analysis. Legitimacy is a multilevel concept, as implied by the term "actor," which may refer to individuals, groups, organizations, nation-states, and world systems. It appears as a core concept in diverse areas of sociological inquiry including (but not limited to) social psychology, stratification, deviance, collective action, organizations, political systems, law, and science.

At its core, legitimacy involves a sense of appropriateness that is accorded to an entity. That is, a legitimate entity is one that we view as suited to its social environment and, as a result, deserving of support by other entities in the environment. The sense that an entity is suited to its environment arises from its perceived consistency with the institutionalized norms, values, and beliefs in which the entity is embedded. Institutionalized criteria are beyond the discretion of single actors (although they are socially constructed), and thus they represent superordinate standards, uncontaminated by individual motives and preferences. Their superordinate status lends them a taken-for-grantedness and the sense that, irrespective of privately held views, others will uphold them in the social system. Consequently, an entity that is perceived as integrated with institutionalized norms, values, and beliefs is one that we believe is appropriate and thus deserving of support. That support may take the form of social approval, the investment of social capital, or material/financial rewards.

SEE ALSO: Institution

SUGGESTED READINGS

Habermas, J. (1975) *Legitimation Crisis*. Beacon Press, Boston, MA.

Meyer, J. W. & Rowan, B. (1977) Institutionalized organizations: formal structure as myth and ceremony. *American Journal of Sociology* 83: 340–63.

Walker, H. A., Rogers, L. & Zelditch, M., Jr. (2003) Acts, persons, positions, and institutions: legitimating multiple objects and compliance with authority. In Chew, S. C., & Knottnerus, J. D. (eds.), *Structure, Culture, and History: Recent Issues in Social Theory*. Littlefield Press, Lanham, MD.

LISA TROYER

leisure

Leisure is a notoriously difficult concept to define. The study of leisure has early origins stretching back to the 1920s and Veblen's *The Theory of the Leisure Class* (1925). However, it was in the 1960s and 1970s that the foundations of leisure studies as an academic area were laid. Early writers such as Dumazedier in *Towards a Society of Leisure* (1967) defined leisure as activity that is set apart from other obligations such as work and family and provides individuals with the opportunity for relaxation, the broadening of knowledge, and social participation. Dumazedier's definition highlights the notion that leisure involves pleasure and freedom of choice and that this sets it apart from paid work and everyday commitments. Leisure could be seen as *compensation*, a means of escape from the routines of daily labor, or as *residual time*, time left over when other commitments have taken place.

The definition of leisure as in opposition to work and other obligations has been very significant within the sociology of leisure. In the UK, Parker (1971) was a major contribution that explored in greater detail this relationship between work and leisure and argued that leisure is an important aspect of social life that demands rigorous sociological analysis alongside the more conventional areas of work, family, education, youth, and so on. He argued that it was with industrialization that leisure became viewed as a separate sphere of life as work became more clearly demarcated in terms of time and space. Therefore, leisure cannot be understood in isolation from work. Parker identified three aspects of the work–leisure relationship: extension, opposition, and neutrality. He viewed the *extension* pattern as showing little demarcation between work and leisure activities, giving the examples of social workers, teachers, and doctors as typical of those that experience work and leisure in this way. *Opposition*, as the name suggests, relies on an intentional dissimilarity between work and leisure and Parker highlighted people with tough physical jobs such as miners or oil-rig workers as typical within this category. His third pattern of *neutrality* is defined by an "average" demarcation of spheres. Workers whose jobs are neither fulfilling nor oppressive and who tend to be passive and uninvolved in both their work and leisure activities are defined by this pattern.

There were several criticisms of Parker's early typology of the work–leisure relationship that highlighted the limitations of this analysis for those outside of the paid workforce. The unemployed, the retired, students, and women working in the home as carers and undertaking domestic work were all identified as outside this work–leisure model as paid work is not central in their lives. However, the recognition of the importance of situating leisure within a social context, not as a separate, totally autonomous sphere of individual free choice, was an important contribution to the developing sociology of leisure. As leisure became analyzed within a social context, emerging definitions reflected the different emphases of competing theoretical perspectives within leisure studies.

Leisure contexts and activities are extremely broad and include sport, physical activity, tourism, media, the arts, countryside recreation, and new technologies, amongst others. Leisure continues to provide an important site through which sociological questions can be explored. Work–leisure–family balance remains crucial to achieving quality of life and is of increasing significance as paid work intensifies, becomes more flexible, and working life becomes extended. The place of leisure in achieving work–life balance remains an important sociological question, as do questions relating to retirement, "serious leisure," and volunteerism. However, the early emphasis on the work–leisure relationship is being replaced, at least to a certain extent, by questions relating to the depth and spread of consumer culture.

SEE ALSO: Leisure Class; Popular Culture; Sport; Work, Sociology of

REFERENCES

Parker, S. (1971) *The Future of Work and Leisure.* MacGibbon & Kee, London.

SUGGESTED READING

Rojek, C. (2000) *Leisure and Culture.* Palgrave, Basingstoke.

SHEILA SCRATON

leisure class

The concept of the leisure class has been introduced by Thorstein Veblen (1899) in his *The Theory of the Leisure Class.* It here consists of those people who, due to their social position, can afford to abstain from productive work and live on other people's labour. Confining themselves to non-industrial occupations like "government, warfare, religious observances, and sports," their income is sourced from exploitation of industrial classes that are subdued by the leisure class's superior "pecuniary prowess." Positional claims are asserted by wasteful "conspicuous leisure" and by "conspicuous consumption" of costly goods that have no immediate utility.

Veblen sees one main effect of the modern leisure class in the exertion of a cultural dominance, setting socially accepted standards of taste. Aspiring classes emulate leisure class patterns of behavior and especially consumption, while the emulated leisure class in turn is constantly developing its "pecuniary canons of taste" in order to spoil emulative efforts. The leisure class thus functions as a consumerist avant-garde. While it is commonly accepted that it is not adequate to think of contemporary upper classes in terms of a "leisure class," the idea of emulation is still widely held.

The term "leisure class" is hardly used in recent sociology, but it still is informative in approaching a variety of contemporary social phenomena. Although it is never applicable in full to those groups, the concept is useful to highlight aspects of celebrity culture, unemployment, old age, and tourism.

SEE ALSO: Conspicuous Consumption; Leisure

REFERENCE

Veblen, T. (1899) *The Theory of the Leisure Class.* Macmillan, New York.

MATTHIAS ZICK VARUL

lesbian and gay families

In the narrowest sense, the term "lesbian and gay family" refers to lesbian and gay individuals or same-sex couples and their children. The term is sometimes used to refer to same-sex partnerships or cohabiting relationships. In the broadest sense, the term can denote social networks that include lesbian or gay individuals and/or couples where some or all of the members self-define as "family." These latter arrangements have also been described as "surrogate," "friendship," or "chosen" families.

Lesbian and gay families have become high-profile social and political issues since the 1980s. They touch on a broad range of sociological themes to do with family life and social change, family diversity, and alternative family practices. The topics of lesbian and gay families and families of choice have played an important part in debates on the demise of traditional conceptions of family, the legitimacy of new family forms, and contemporary reconfigurations of family obligations, responsibilities, and care. Existing sociological work on the topics includes theorizing and research into the historical, social, and political forces that have facilitated the emergence of lesbian and gay families and families of choice; theoretical discussions of their social and political significance; and studies of the meanings, structures, and social practices associated with them at local levels.

Several theorists have argued that the emergence of AIDS in the 1980s and political responses to it were key factors in shaping the current emphasis in lesbian and gay politics on family issues in Europe and North America. Initially, Moral Right responses to AIDS reinforced the historical construction of lesbians and gay men as a threat to the family. In the United Kingdom, for example, legislation was introduced in the late 1980s (commonly known as Section 28) that explicitly sought to ban the promotion by local authorities of homosexuality "as a pretended family relationship." Such interventions, however, had the reverse effect of mobilizing a lesbian and gay family-oriented politics. Some theorists have further argued that community-based caring responses to AIDS were ultimately to underscore the importance of family-type relationships for lesbians and gay men. This view has been criticized on the basis that it undermines the existence of non-heterosexual caring relationships that preexisted AIDS.

While lesbian and gay families have long been of interest to scholars of sexualities, they have more recently come to the attention of sociologists of family life. This new interest is partly due to the current concern with family diversity and changing patterns of relating. Lesbian and gay families are now being explored for the insights they provide into the challenges and possibilities presented by detraditionalized family life. From this perspective, these family forms are studied for how they are structured and operate outside institutionalized norms and supports that have traditionally shaped "the" family. Because of the lack of gender-based differences in same-sex relationships, lesbian and gay families are also examined for the possibilities of organizing family without clearly defined gendered roles. A number of theorists have argued that because of the lack of gendered assumptions, lesbian and gay families are more likely to adopt a friendship model for relating, and operate according to an egalitarian ideal. Empirical studies that have set out to explore the meanings, structure, and practices of lesbian and gay families and families of choice suggest a complex picture.

A number of studies have explored the place, roles, and experience of children in lesbian and gay families. Until recently, such studies tended to be concerned with the implications of growing up in these family forms. Most of this research suggests that this experience is unlikely to have any discernible long-term impact on children's sense of well-being, social connectedness, or family or personal security. Because of the changing historical circumstances in which lesbians and gay men have become parents, most existing studies are of lesbian and gay families with children who were conceived through a parent's previous heterosexual relationship. Recent studies have, however, begun to focus on the experience of families with children, where same-sex couples, individuals, or friends have chosen to take advantage of recent opportunities to become parents through self- or assisted insemination, surrogacy, adoption, and fostering. Many of these studies have moved beyond the focus on children's experience to also explore the blurring of the boundaries between biological and social parenting and the negotiated nature of same-sex parenting.

SEE ALSO: Family Diversity; Gay and Lesbian Movement; Homosexuality; Same Sex Marriage/Civil Unions

SUGGESTED READINGS

Ali, T. (1996) *We Are Family: Testimonies of Lesbian and Gay Parents*. Cassell, London and New York.

Heaphy, B., Donovan, C., & Weeks, J. (1998) "That's like my life": researching stories of non-heterosexual relationships. *Sexualities* 1: 435–70.

Weeks, J., Heaphy, B., & Donovan, C. (2001) *Same-Sex Intimacies: Families of Choice and Other Life Experiments*. Routledge, London.

BRIAN HEAPHY

lesbian feminism

Lesbian feminism is a political and philosophical strand of feminism that emerged in the US, Canada, and Britain in the 1970s. It holds as central tenets that heterosexuality is the seat of patriarchal power; lesbianism is a political choice and not an essential identity; and lesbians occupy a unique and empowered position vis-à-vis sexism and patriarchy because they do not rely on men for emotional, financial, or sexual attention and support. Lesbian feminism developed out of radical feminism and in reaction to sexism within gay liberation movements and homophobia within feminist movements of the 1960s. In response to Betty Friedan's 1970 characterization of lesbians as the "lavender menace," lesbians began to advocate for recognition from feminist movements. Out of the ensuing debates, groups like the Washington, DC-based "Furies" formed. In "The Woman Identified Woman" (1970), the first political statement of the lesbian feminist movement, the New York Radicalesbians, originally known as "Lavender Menace," argued that "lesbian" as an identity was not just a sexual object choice, but rather a chosen identity.

Approaching lesbian as a political identity, not just a sexual one, required a radical redefinition. In "Compulsory heterosexuality and lesbian existence," Adrienne Rich (1980) argued that sexuality was a socially constructed tool of patriarchy. She asserted that there was a lesbian continuum that opened up space for *all* women to be lesbians, including women who identified themselves sexually, spiritually, emotionally, *or* politically with other women, and that this was the cornerstone of dismantling patriarchy. Two related but distinct branches of lesbian feminism emerged in the 1970s. Cultural feminists argued that the creation of counter-institutions (such as women's bookstores and music labels) was a way to resist the sexism implicit in dominant institutions. The other branch that emerged – lesbian separatism – took this a step further and argued for a complete withdrawal from men and male-dominated institutions in order to effect significant social change.

Many scholars like Adrienne Rich, Charlotte Bunch, and Lillian Faderman merged academic theorizing and lesbian feminist ideology in the late 1970s and early 1980s, providing gendered critiques of heterosexuality and patriarchy. For women of color and poor women who experienced gender, class, and race as interconnected identities and oppressions, however, lesbian feminism's emphasis on an essential shared womanhood erased and invalidated their experiences. More recently, notions of essential womanhood (and exclusion based on this) have also been challenged by transgender communities, which continue to argue for a place within lesbian feminist and separatist spaces like Michigan Women's Music Festival. The emergence of queer theory in the 1990s, characterized by the theoretical decentering of identity, has led to a dismissal of much of lesbian feminist research as outdated. As many feminists have argued, however, that identity politics have been and continue to be central to lesbian and feminist organizing. Despite these criticisms, lesbian feminism continues to influence contemporary feminist and lesbian movements and many of the institutions founded in the 1970s and 1980s by lesbian feminist communities continue to thrive.

SEE ALSO: Cultural Feminism; Lesbianism; Radical Feminism; Sexualities and Culture Wars

REFERENCE

Rich, A. (1980) Compulsory heterosexuality and lesbian existence. *Signs: Journal of Women in Culture and Society* 5 (4): 631–60.

SUGGESTED READINGS

Johnston, J. (1973) *Lesbian Nation: The Feminist Solution*. Simon & Schuster, New York.

Staggenborg, S., Eder, D. & Sudderth, L. (1995) The National Women's Music Festival: collective identity and diversity in a lesbian–feminist community. *Journal of Contemporary Ethnography* 23 (4): 485–515.

EVE SHAPIRO

lesbianism

Lesbians are female people who organize their private as well as public social, emotional, political and sexual energies, lives and resources around other female people. This does not exclude male persons (children, adolescent or men) from lesbian led spaces. Indeed many lesbians are parents of male children, wives or former partners of men and of course are daughters to fathers and sisters to brothers. What marks lesbians and lesbian lives as distinctive is the fact that lesbians, by societal standards, are women who, by virtue of living female centered lives, simultaneously violate gender, sexual, economic, political, and religious norms, to name a few of the key issues.

Lesbians violate gender and sexual norms in at least two ways. Depending upon the lesbian in question, gender norms may be challenged if the lesbian expresses *female masculinity* (Halberstam 1998). Female masculinity is manifested when people who are genetically female perform gender behaviorism commonly associated with masculinity. Such examples can be seen in lesbians whose wardrobes consist strictly of clothing originally designed for male consumers, or in the example of lesbians who routinely wear closely cropped haircuts with or without ball caps, cowboy hats, or knitted skull caps; or in the example of lesbians who prefer to own large working trucks, motorcycles, dirt bikes, or elite bicycles for racing, exercise, or daily commuting. Lesbians who do not violate gender norms are often identified by the lesbian gender category of "femme" and those that do violate gender norms are labeled "butch."

Lesbians, due to their uniqueness as females violating other important social norms, also violate economic, political, and religious norms. Lesbians violate economic norms by being the "women" most likely to be lifelong participants in the workforce structure of society. Lesbians, unlike their heterosexual female counterparts, are less likely to have time out of the labor market to be "stay at home moms" for example. However, they are more likely to be coupled with other lesbians (or with other female persons who *do not* utilize the politically charged identifier of lesbian to define how they express their sexual desire and pleasure), therefore; they are also less likely to emulate the heteronormative temporality commonly defining the stages of life defining the lives of women whose private as well as public, social, emotional, political and sexual energies and resources revolve around male people. Lesbians live politically precarious lives as their issues are oftentimes tied up with the concerns of gay men. Such a gendered entanglement ensures that the multiple specificities and particularities of being female as well as homosexual, often time stay uninvestigated, thus always entangled, ensuring continued lack of specification leading to greater understanding of why gender matters in queer politics. Finally, lesbians, be they believers themselves or not, violate the many dominant Judeo-Christian-Muslim religious norms that damn homosexuality as sinful.

Lesbians are as diverse as any other population. They vary by race, class, presentation of lesbian gender, educational attainment, religious or secular beliefs, and so forth. They are also similar. In general lesbians also experience society as women and regardless of the list of differences here, the similarities shared between heterosexual women and lesbians are just as far-reaching in consequence. Lesbians as well as heterosexual women, for example, experience a culture where there exists a permanent threat of physical as well as sexual violence against them as well as the same traditional labor market limitations – i.e., less pay relative to men, less benefits, and less occupational or social upward mobility.

SEE ALSO: Female Masculinity; Homophobia and Heterosexism; Homosexuality; Women, Sexuality and

REFERENCES

Halberstam, J. (1998) *Female Masculinity.* Duke University Press, Durham, NC.

SUGGESTED READINGS

Munt, S. R. (1998) *butch/femme: Inside Lesbian Gender.* Cassell, London.

Rich, A. (1980) [1982] Compulsory heterosexuality and lesbians' existence. *Signs* 5 (4): 631–60.

KIMBERLY BONNER

liberal feminism

Liberal feminism is a social movement based on the premise that women's subordinate position in society is due to unequal opportunities and segregation from men. Society is viewed as consisting of individuals who are equals and therefore everyone should have equal rights. Liberal feminists create change largely through assimilationist tactics; by working within existing social structures, seeking to change people's beliefs, and to eliminate gender inequality.

The seeds of US feminism, which now is largely categorized as liberal feminism, emerged out of the anti-slavery movement in the early 1800s. Early activists and women's groups boycotted businesses and churches that supported slavery, lobbied for changes in laws and engaged in public forums. Many of these early founders of the *suffrage movement* are viewed as the core of *first wave* feminism. Their activities in the abolitionist movement led to working for rights for women. For example, during the Seneca Falls Convention in 1848, activist Elizabeth Cady Stanton presented the *Declaration of Sentiments* which sought an end to the second-class status of women by establishing voting rights and eliminating sexist laws.

These tactics continued with the rise of the *second wave* of feminism in the early 1960s. The contemporary Women's Liberation Movement emerged seeking equal rights for women and ushering in modern liberal feminism. Women worked for reform in the areas of employment, health care, education and politics by lobbying politicians, giving speeches and again, marching in the streets. In the same vein as early feminists, when the National Organization for Women (NOW) held their first national convention in 1967, a "Bill of Rights" was adopted which demanded equal rights for women including equal opportunities for education and job training, maternity leave, reproductive rights and the creation of the Equal Rights Amendment to eliminate discrimination based on sex.

One of the results of these efforts was the establishment of women's studies curriculum and departments in colleges and universities, including the formal development of feminist sociology. There have been many cultural and political changes due to the efforts of liberal feminists. Many companies now offer maternity and paternity leave, some provide childcare for their employees, additionally many business and local governments have nondiscrimination policies based on sex or gender and laws stating that women are the property of their husbands have largely been eliminated.

One of the main tenets of liberal feminism is that it maintains a clear division between the role of the state (public) and individual freedom (private). One of the movement's greatest successes is the most controversial: the court cases of *Roe v. Wade* and *Dole v. Bolton*. In 1973 the US Supreme Court granted women the legal right to have access to safe abortions. The state's responsibility to provide funding or actual services is highly contested, as is the right to abortion itself. Due to critiques of the narrowness of the focus on abortion rather than reproductive rights and options, more recent efforts have been made to expand women's choices. This largely concerns lower income women and women of color who have historically been forced to bear children and have been the subject of medical experiments, and forced sterilization.

From the beginning of the women's movement, there has been strong criticism as to the elite nature of liberal feminism. The vast majority of positions of power and authority have been held by white women with privilege and women of color have been ignored for their contribution to the elimination of gender inequality. There is also a criticism of the absence of a systematic analysis of social structures that maintain inequality largely because liberal feminists seek entry into these institutions rather than to significantly change them.

SEE ALSO: Cultural Feminism; Radical Feminism; Socialist Feminism

SUGGESTED READINGS

Friedan, B. (1963) *The Feminine Mystique*. W. W. Norton, New York.

hooks, bell (2000) *Feminist Theory: From Margin to Center*. South End Press, Cambridge.

Morgan, R. (1970) *Sisterhood Is Powerful: An Anthology of Writings from the Women's Liberation Movement*. Vintage, New York.

KRISTINA B. WOLFF

liberalism

Liberalism is the leading ideology of the modern era. During the nineteenth century it came to signify adherence to the principles of individualism, liberty, limited government, progress and equality. It has been espoused by thinkers as diverse as Mill, Constant, Bentham, Tocqueville, Hobhouse, and Hayek. At its core is a particular conception of human nature, based on beliefs in the moral primacy of the individual as the starting point for thinking about politics and society; the equal moral worth of every individual, regardless of class, nation, gender or race; and the possibility of improving social conditions and reforming political institutions. Individuals are conceived as the bearers of rights which exist independently of government and which it is the task of government to protect. The legitimacy of any system of government depends on how well it protects the liberty of its citizens.

Liberalism was shaped by the American and French Revolutions, which marked a decisive break with the old order and set out new principles of government – life, liberty and the pursuit of happiness in the American version, and liberty, equality and fraternity in the French. Both these revolutions proclaimed in different ways that sovereignty should be popular sovereignty, that government should be based on the will of the people, and that for this purpose all members of a political community should be regarded as equal, and able to participate in their self-government. These revolutions were part of much broader social changes which shaped different conceptions of modernity, with liberalism coming to stand for progress, rationalism, science, secularism and capitalism, and opposition to obscurantism, tradition, privilege and prejudice. Liberals have tended to be optimistic about the prospects for human progress because of their faith in reason, their universalism, and their confidence in rational, scientific methods to discover the causes of things and to propose improvements.

SEE ALSO: Conservatism; Democracy; Individualism; Neoliberalism

SUGGESTED READING

Bellamy, R. (1992) *Liberalism and Modern Society*. Polity, Cambridge.

ANDREW GAMBLE

life course

The term life course refers to the idea that the course of one's life is not determined by a natural process of aging but is mainly shaped by social institutions and sociocultural values as well as by decisions and unexpected events. Thus the life course consists of life stages (e.g., childhood, youth, adulthood), status passages or transitions (e.g., from youth to adulthood, from student to professional), and life events (e.g., marriage, job loss, illness). Formal institutions such as the law and the welfare state ascribe rights and duties by age and formal status, and when, for example, to start a family and how to divide labor within the household are also structured by sociocultural norms and habits.

The term life course differs from concepts such as the lifecycle which is connected to developmental concepts in psychology. Such concepts imply that life is structured by a specific order of events where one built on the previous event, and that they represent a "natural" order.

The modern notion of the life course differs from concepts in small "primitive" societies as described in ethnographic research, where transitions are understood as determined by natural processes (such as first menses to indicate that girls can be married) or "rites of passage" (Gennep 1981 [1909]).

The modern notion of the life course also differs from its ancestors. During the Middle Ages in western Europe, the understanding of life was captured in religious and magical thinking. Life seemed to be determined mainly by external powers, such as God or fate which are uncontrollable and unforeseeable for the individual. With modernization, ongoing sociocultural and sociostructural changes shift the meaning of the life course.

The institutionalization of education and a social security system as well as the formal regulation of rights and duties by age created a new framework and understanding of the life course as to be shaped individually. Models of normative expectations about how men and women should shape their life were institutionalized, and societal institutions orient themselves to such models of a "normal" life. Additionally, the increase in medical knowledge and standards of hygiene supports a significant change in mortality, which was moved to and concentrated on old age. A predictable life course became a normal experience for an increasing part of the population.

Life course research is interested in specific sociostructural patterns and the individual's sense-making of life. Sometimes the whole life is examined, but many studies focus on specific transitions, such as from youth to adulthood, from single to husband or wife and to father or mother, from unemployed to employed.

How people manage their life systematically differs by sociostructural indicators such as gender, ethnicity, health/disability, or generation. It is expected, for example, that women marry younger than men and that they bear children before 30, while it is accepted that men father children in older age as well. It is also accepted that younger women marry older men, but the reverse is perceived as unusual or even deviant. Such norms are reflected in different life plans and expectations regarding the future.

Early research on the life course are for example, the study by Glen Elder, *Children of the Great Depression* (1974), which showed how families mediated the individual's management of the hardships of economic slowdown. Barney Glaser and Anselm Strauss (1968) showed how people cope with dying. Another stream in the tradition of sociostructural analysis focuses on formal factors influencing the life course (e.g., class, educational attainment, gender, marital status, age).

Recent research often assumes that growing processes of individualization would weaken the individual's embeddedness in traditional institutions. Individualization would set free new generations from traditional bonds and open spaces for new opportunities and decisions. More critical studies argue that although the semantics of life course decisions have changed, the idea of growing self-responsibility does not go along with a significant change in vertical social mobility or increasing individual control of one's life.

The life course encompasses an objective course of life and the individual's sense-making. At the center of biographical research is the individual's sense-making of his or her life. Sociostructural researchers focus on the life course patterns that are expressed in durations of working and employment status or marital status or divorce. While the biographical approach mainly works with qualitative methods and narrative interviewing techniques to explain current activities by the cumulated sense-making of one's former life, the sociostructural approach uses event history modeling, or optimal pattern matching techniques to examine and compare life course patterns and events.

SEE ALSO: Biography; Individualism; Rite of Passage

REFERENCES

Elder, G. H. (1974) *Children of the Great Depression: Social Change in Life Experience*. University of Chicago Press, Chicago, IL.

Gennep, A. von (1981 [1909]) *Les Rites de passage*. Picard, Paris.

Glaser, B. G. & Strauss, A. L. (1968) *Time for Dying*. Aldine, Chicago, IL.

JENS O. ZINN

lifestyle

Lifestyle involves the typical features of everyday life of an individual or a group. These features pertain to interests, opinions, behaviors, and behavioral orientations. For example, lifestyle relates to choice and allocation of leisure time; preferences in clothes and food; tastes in music, reading, art, and television programs; and choice of consumer goods and services.

At the individual level, lifestyle denotes self-expression, personal taste, and identity. At the group level, the concept refers to shared preferences and tastes that are reflected primarily in consumption patterns and in the possession of goods. Lifestyles give members of a group a sense of solidarity, and mirror the differentiation between groups in society. The distinctive lifestyles of specific groups may be hierarchically ordered to different degrees, depending on the extent to which a clear system of prestige exists that attaches value to lifestyles.

Building on Max Weber's (1946) work, which emphasizes lifestyle as a means of social differentiation that could be used to acquire or to maintain a certain social status, a body of research has developed, which adopted the view that lifestyle is a major form of social stratification that can be used to characterize contemporary society (Veblen 1994; Bourdieu 1984).

Lifestyle elements, in terms of specific cultural preferences, consumption, and behavior, can be studied one at a time or as stylistic unities. Stylistic unity is an internal cultural consistency in the elements comprising a lifestyle and in symbolic properties of those elements. It rests on shared perceptions that lifestyle elements are patterned in a manner that makes some sort of aesthetic or other sense. Stylistic unity can range from a tight system of expectations for particular tastes and preferences, all adhering to a clear set of cultural imperatives, to a system of blurred, eclectic components, loosely connected by symbolic meanings. A comprehensive lifestyle analysis will emphasize the way in which arrays of lifestyles evolve over time, the degree to which different lifestyles (associated with class, race, sexuality, etc.) are legitimized, and the way lifestyles are linked to changes in social and economic structures.

Research on the determinants of lifestyle differentiation has predominantly concentrated on those factors that Weber, Veblen, and Bourdieu emphasized in their theoretical accounts of the contours of lifestyles. Indeed, a significant body of research has shown that tastes and consumption patterns are influenced by individuals' education, financial resources, occupational characteristics, parental education, and parental lifestyle. In addition, other factors have been shown to matter, such as gender, age, and race/ethnicity. At the same time, there is evidence that in contemporary society lifestyle is becoming more volatile and less hierarchical so that the correlation with social divisions is no longer conclusive. This is explained by social conditions that are becoming increasingly fragmented, partly because of the proliferation of information and cultural repertoires. Since collective affiliations are multiple, fragmented, and often conflicted, the lifestyles associated with these affiliations are more fluid, unsettled, and cross-cutting.

SEE ALSO: Bourdieu, Pierre; Consumption; Everyday Life

REFERENCES

Bourdieu, P. (1984) *Distinction: A Social Critique of the Judgment of Taste*. Harvard University Press, Cambridge, MA.

Veblen, T. (1994) *The Theory of the Leisure Class*. Penguin Books, New York.
Weber, M. (1946) Class, status, party. In: *Max Weber: Essays in Sociology*. Oxford University Press, New York, pp. 180–95.

SUGGESTED READING

Featherstone, M. (1991) *Consumer Culture and Postmodernism*. Sage, London.

TALLY KATZ-GERRO

lifeworld

The notion of "lifeworld" emerged from Edmund Husserl's attempts to lay bare the essential nature and actions of pure consciousness. Consciousness, he argued, entails "intentionality" – the directedness of action to (and creation of) an object – and an inter subjectively shared lifeworld. Together, they unconsciously shape how people go about the world. Through "phenomenological reduction," one brackets "the natural attitude" to examine pure acts of consciousness.

Formulating a transcendental phenomenological critique of Weber's conception of subjective meaning and the *verstehende Ansatz* (interpretive position), Husserl's student, Alfred Schütz, recognized transcendental phenomenology's limitations for a phenomenology of the social world. Schütz then focused more intensively on the lifeworld: "The sciences that would interpret and explain human action and thought must begin with a description of the foundational structures of what is prescientific, the reality which seems self-evident to men remaining within the natural attitude. This reality is the everyday life-world" (Schütz and Luckmann 1973: 3–4). The lifeworld is intersubjective from the outset, existing "as a subjective meaning-context" that people master according to their particular interests and projects. The lifeworld is inhabited by "bodies endowed with consciousness" whose acts, like ours, are "imbedded in meaning contexts," "subjectively motivated" and proceed according to actors' particular interests and "what is feasible for them" (p. 15). People assume they can continue on "until proven otherwise."

Exploring the lifeworld's scope, complexities, problems and contradictions, Schutz and Luckmann's (1973) *Structures of the Life-World* is the foundation for contemporary social constructionist theories and analyses.

SEE ALSO: Intersubjectivity; Phenomenology; Schütz, Alfred; Weber, Max

REFERENCES

Schütz, A. & Luckmann, T. (1973; 1989) *The Structures of the Life-World, Vols. 1–2*. Northwestern University Press, Evanston, IL.

SUGGESTED READINGS

Husserl, E. (1999) [1905] *Idea of Phenomenology*, trans. L. Hardy. Kluwer Academic Publishers, Boston, MA.
Schütz, A. (1962, 1964, 1966) *Collected Papers*, vols. 1–3. Martinus Nijhoff, The Hague.

ROB BEAMISH

literacy/illiteracy

Traditionally, literacy has meant the ability to read and write. As the cognitive skill requirements of work and daily life have increased, the definition has expanded. In the National Literacy Act of 1991, the US Congress defined literacy as "an individual's ability to read, write, and speak in English and compute and solve problems at levels of proficiency necessary to function on the job and in society, to achieve one's goals, and to develop one's knowledge and potential." Consistent with this, the National Assessments of Adult Literacy, conducted by the National Center for Education Statistics, have measured literacy along three dimensions: prose literacy, document literacy, and quantitative literacy. Each was measured on a scale defined by the skills needed to succeed at daily and work tasks ordered from simple to complex.

Over time and across nations, higher literacy rates have been associated with higher levels of economic development. This is a well-documented pattern, which has been most thoroughly analyzed by economists under the topic of "investment and returns to human capital."

What explains individual and group differentials in literacy, as measured by tests of cognitive skill and self-reports of educational attainment (number of years of schooling completed)? Both qualitative and quantitative studies point to parent–child interaction and children's oral language development during the preschool period as crucial for the creation of differentials in school readiness that strongly predict performance in early elementary school. Thus, the child's early literacy skill – oral vocabulary, grammatical usage, letter knowledge, and phonemic awareness (the ability to hear and manipulate the separate sounds in spoken language) – are among the principal predictors of success in first grade reading. Since scores on these variables tend to be lower for children from lower social class, African American, and Latino backgrounds, lower preschool literacy among these students predicts lower first grade reading attainment.

Nor does the process of differential literacy development end at this point. Lower-performing children have a higher rate of school dropout, and those who graduate from high school often go straight into the labor market. There they may encounter employers who consider their literacy and mathematics skills to be inadequate for the requirements of the jobs available. By contrast, higher-performing students typically undertake four more years of academic skill development in college, often followed by graduate-level or professional training. Then, when these individuals enter the labor market, they take jobs which themselves have a strong component of continued learning and literacy development. The result is a society composed of adults who, at least when we compare the top and bottom of the occupational hierarchy, are strongly differentiated on the basis of their cognitive skills, which are in turn correlated with their earnings.

SEE ALSO: Educational Inequality; Status Attainment

SUGGESTED READINGS

Baker, D. & LeTendre, G. (2005) *National Differences, Global Similarities: World Culture and the Future of Schooling.* Stanford University Press, Stanford, CA.

Neuman, S. & Dickinson, D. (eds.) (2002) *Handbook of Early Literacy Research.* Guilford Press, New York.

GEORGE FARKAS

logocentrism

Logocentrism, associated with French philosopher Jacques Derrida, refers to western philosophy's partiality for order manifested in an idealization of truth, a prejudice for speaking over writing and binary oppositions.

Logos, Greek for law, word and reason, has from Heraclitus (d. after 480 BC) to the Stoics (ca. 300 BC) underpinned cosmic stability – organizing providence and fate. In Christian theology Jesus is logos embodied and for some logos persists in science's laws of nature. "Logocentrism" emerges with Carus' and Bachofen's nineteenth-century aesthetics but was subsequently adopted by German philosopher Klages, denoting a priority given to mind over unified body and soul.

Derrida, through Heidegger, sees logocentrism emanating from a philosophy that equates being with substance for an autonomous agent infused with an instrumental view of nature. Spoken language's immediacy is taken as more expressive of mind, and hence truth, than derivative text. Logocentrism is phonocentrism; privileging the spoken word over writing generates sets of binary oppositions (cause/effect, black/white, good/evil). Turning to the author for unequivocal meaning represents the logocentric reach for a solid centre.

Logocentrism permeates sociological concerns for gender and justice. Cixous' (1975) "The laugh of Medusa" illustrated how logocentrism aims to justify male rationale; logocentrism is phallogocentrism. Meanwhile, Young's (1990) *Justice and Politics of Difference* argues that logocentrism overlooks and excludes plurality. Searle (1983) in "The world turned upside down" views logocentrism as "a series of muddles and gimmicks" that imagines an incoherent threat to science, language, and common sense. Nevertheless, Rorty's separation of a more defensible narrow (anti-foundationalism) logocentrism from a wider version (condemnation of all manners of speaking) is helpful.

SEE ALSO: Deconstruction; Derrida, Jacques; Epistemology; Feminism; Postmodern Social Theory

SUGGESTED READINGS:

Derrida, J. (1976) *Of Grammatology.* Johns Hopkins University Press, Baltimore, MD.

Rorty, R. (1991) *Essays on Heidegger and others.* Cambridge University Press, London.

JOSEPH BURKE

lone parent families

The term "lone parent family" does not have an exact definition but broadly consists of a family where one parent lives alone with one or more dependent children. This then raises the question of what a "dependent child" is and what constitutes "living alone" and "living with." In the UK, "dependent children" are defined for many official purposes as children aged up to 16 years old or 17–18 and in full-time education but many "children" over this age still live with their parents. When parents separate, the children may live with their mother for half the time and their father for the other half and so the simple division between a "lone parent" and "non-resident" parent may not be clear. Lone parent families are defined as having only one adult but if a lone parent begins to form a cohabiting relationship with a new partner, the family will, at some point, transform into a "step-parent family." The point at which this happens is not necessarily clear-cut. The definition of a lone parent family is therefore complex.

In the 1960s and 1970s, there was an increase in the number of lone parent families across many advanced industrial countries due to increasing divorce among married couples. In the 1980s and 1990s, a growing number of young single women became mothers outside of marriage, particularly in the UK. But while the growth of lone parenthood is a common trend across many countries, rates of lone parenthood, and types of lone parenthood, vary across different countries. Countries that are generally rich, Protestant, and north European have had higher rates, particularly of single lone mothers, compared with countries that are generally poor, Catholic, and southern countries. Lone parent families tend to be headed by women in most countries and also tend to be poorer than other groups but, again, this varies depending on how welfare states in particular countries support lone parents.

SEE ALSO: Childhood; Family Diversity; Family Structure

SUGGESTED READING

Rowlingson, K. & McKay, S. (2002) *Lone Parent Families: Gender, Class and State*. Pearson Education, Harlow.

KAREN ROWLINGSON

looking-glass self

The looking-glass self is Charles Horton Cooley's conceptualization of the "social self." Cooley used the image of a mirror as a metaphor for the way in which our experience of self is an emotional response to the supposed evaluations of others, especially significant others. Cooley distinguished three "principal elements" of the looking-glass self: "the imagination of our appearance to the other person; the imagination of his [*sic*] judgment of that appearance; and some sort of self-feeling, such as pride or mortification" (Cooley 1922: 184). When learning the meaning of personal pronouns, which refer to different objects when used by different people, children must imagine themselves from the perspective of others. After coming to understand what others mean when they refer to themselves, that is, that "I" refers to self-feeling, children "sympathize" with these others and this empathetic process gives meaning to their own incipient self-feelings. "I" is social because when it is used it is always addressed to an audience, and its use thus indicates children's newly acquired ability to take the role of their audience. Once they begin to do this, they can also perform different selves for different audiences.

The self emerges in interaction, becomes meaningful only in contrast to that which is not of self (society), and is thus inextricable from society. Cooley's looking-glass self was elaborated by George Herbert Mead in the latter's development of the notion of taking the role of the other, especially the generalized other, as the mechanism through which a unified self emerges in interaction. Cooley also influenced Goffman's dramaturgical analysis of the self as a situated performance. There is a significant body of research on what is now commonly referred to as "reflected self appraisal" and its role in the development of self-concepts, and Cooley's ideas have influenced the sociology of emotions.

SEE ALSO: Cooley, Charles Horton; Identity: Social Psychological Aspects; Self

REFERENCE

Cooley, C. H. (1922) *Human Nature and the Social Order*. Scribner's, New York.

SUGGESTED READING

Cooley, C. H. (1930) *Sociological Theory and Social Research*. Henry Holt, New York.

JENNIFER DUNN

love and commitment

DEFINITIONS OF LOVE

Lee's Colors of Love

- *Eros*: an erotic, passionate love. Eros love can be love at first sight and can end suddenly, leaving the person wondering what they saw in their former beloved.
- *Mania*: the dark side of passionate love. Mania involves obsession with the beloved person and jealousy.
- *Storge*: friendship-based love that develops gradually over time. Even if the love relationship ends, the strong friendship associated with storge often means one continues to be friends with the former beloved.
- *Agape*: altruistic love. Agape love is associated with the desire to give to the beloved without asking anything in return.
- *Pragma*: a practical love that involves loving something about the person, such as being a good parent, respected in the community or wealthy.

- *Ludus*: love for the moment, without commitment. Ludus is associated with flirtation and the desire to seduce someone for a sexual encounter.

Love styles are assessed at one point in time. One's feelings can change over time or with another partner.

Passionate versus Companionate Love

Passionate love involves strong sexual arousal, fantasy, and idealization of the beloved. It occurs suddenly and does not last long. Companionate Love is affection or deep friendship that develops gradually.

COMMITMENT TO A RELATIONSHIP

There are three basic forms of attachment that develop during infancy based on interactions with the primary caretaker: secure, avoidant, and anxious. Securely attached infants become upset when the caretaker is absent and happy when the caretaker is present. Avoidant infants are not upset about the caretaker's absence and show little positive affect in the presence of the caretaker. Anxious infants appear clinging when caretakers are present, and upset when absent. As adults, these infant reactions to the caregiver are transferred to the romantic partner. Work by Shaver and others has indicated that those with secure attachments are more committed to their romantic partners, and feel more satisfaction about these relationships. Those with an avoidant pattern are less committed to their romantic partners and report less satisfaction. The anxious adults form relationships very quickly, but they do not appear to have long-term commitments.

SEE ALSO: Emotion: Cultural Aspects; Marriage

SUGGESTED READINGS

Adams, J. J. & Jones, W. H. (eds.) (1999) *Handbook of Interpersonal Commitment and Relationship Atability*. Kluwer, New York.

Lee, J. (1977). *Colors of love: An Exploration of the Ways of Loving*. New Press, Don Mills, Ontario.

IRENE HANSON FRIEZE

M

macrosociology

Macrosociology deals with large-scale, long-term social processes, phenomena, and structures, such as social change, stratification, or the capitalist world-economy. Conceptually, the term is meant to distinguish the broad level of sociological analysis from that of microsociology, which studies small-scale units and individual relationships, like social roles, interaction, or deviance. Methodologically, macrosociology employs the method of agreement and/or the method of difference to compare and contrast a variety of units of analysis such as nation-states, regions, civilizations, or world-systems with respect to causal relations.

Macrosociological comparative and historical studies of "society as a whole" were central concerns for both sociology and anthropology in the late nineteenth century. Both disciplines were theoretically premised on evolutionism, the search for broad historical patterns of social change, and methodologically on the focus on individual societies – in the case of sociology, national, western ones. The models of social evolution proposed by Comte, Marx, or Spencer all subscribed to this logic of linear progress from a less differentiated stage to a complex one.

Evolutionism and the concern with macro-level phenomena became marginal in the first decades of the twentieth century but made a comeback as of the 1950s with Talcott Parsons' structural functionalism and the modernization school, which drew equally from functionalism and evolutionism. Daniel Lerner's *The Passing of Traditional Society. Modernizing the Middle East* typically identified in the sequence of stages of urbanization, growth of literacy, and industrialization a normative modernization process by which Middle Eastern societies were supposed to replicate western developments.

Neo-Marxist dependency theory, developed in Latin America in the 1960s, in turn argued that modern capitalism was a center–periphery structure resulting from an international division of labor between western colonial powers and their (ex-)colonies. Development, therefore, was not the outcome of passing through several stages from traditional to modern society, but a function of the structural position within the hierarchy. Drawing on dependency theory and the French Annales School, world-systems analysis gave pride of place to the issue of the unit of analysis, contending that macrostructural analysis should take into account the entire world-system made up of core, semiperipheral, and peripheral regions.

As of the 1980s, a new theoretical agenda intended as a reprise of Max Weber's comparative civilizational studies was espoused by political sociologists such as Theda Skocpol, Peter B. Evans, and Michael Mann. Focused on revolutions, social movements, and democracy, it increasingly offered explanations of the uniqueness of Western modernity and capitalism using the framework of world history.

Explicit opposition to Marxist analysis prompted the development of approaches intended to overcome the micro-macro dualism. Starting from a criticism of structuralist approaches and Marxist class theory, both Pierre Bourdieu and Anthony Giddens emphasized the interdependence of the micro and the macro by dwelling on the role of individual actors' practices for the reproduction of social structures.

With the end of the cold war, revamped versions of the liberal modernization paradigm resurfaced in the form of globalization theories, comparative modernization studies, and transition research. Their evolutionist and nationalist assumptions reproduced *the convergence hypothesis* inherent in modernization theory by identifying western patterns of capitalist development, individualization, secularization, and democratization throughout the world.

The neo-Weberian approach of multiple modernities, taking as units of analysis axial civilizations, stood for *the divergence hypothesis*. It argued that the cultural program of western modernity had first been transformed with the expansion of modernity in the Americas, and later in Asia and Africa, where it produced multiple institutional and ideological patterns. Modernization, therefore, is not westernization, as modernization theory had claimed. Stressing the role of imperialism and colonialism in the making of western European modernity, the entangled modernities perspective (Therborn 2003) maintained that there is no universal modernity acting as a guiding reference to latecomers, but several paths to entangled modernities. Similarly, postcolonial approaches that highlight the history of the "black" Atlantic (Gilroy 1993) or the global structure of power relations linking first world modernity to third world coloniality (Quijano 2007) undermine the classical division of labor between sociology and anthropology along the lines of binary categories such as modern vs. non-modern society. They thus allow for a possibility toward theoretical synthesis in the form of a global – rather than universal – sociology.

SEE ALSO: Civilizations; Microsociology; Micro-Macro Links

REFERENCES

Gilroy, P. (1993) *Black Atlantic: Modernity and Double Consciousness*. Verso, London.

Quijano, A. (2007) Coloniality and modernity/rationality. *Cultural Studies* 21 (2/3): 168–78.

Therborn, G. (2003) Entangled modernities. *European Journal of Social Theory* 6 (3), 293–305.

SUGGESTED READINGS

Eisenstadt, S. N. (2003) *Comparative Civilizations and Multiple Modernities*. Brill, Leiden.

Parsons, T. (1966) *Societies: Evolutionary and Comparative Perspectives*. Prentice Hall, Englewood Cliffs.

Wallerstein, I. (1979) *The Capitalist World-Economy: Essays*. Cambridge, Cambridge University Press.

MANUELA BOATCĂ

madness

Madness is a layman's term for what psychiatrists and medical professionals call mental illness or psychiatric disorder. A mad person is characterized by psychopathology of one kind or another: a disordered mind, irrational or unintelligible behavior, extreme mood swings, disturbed emotions, bouts of anxiety, or a dysfunctional personality. Madness and mental illness are terms that are both distinct from "insanity," which is a legal concept. If a mentally disturbed individual comes before a court of law, the concern is whether he or she is insane (i.e., knew right from wrong, poses a danger to self or others, and/or is responsible for his or her actions).

Madness has been recognized throughout history in every known society. Primitive cultures turn to witch doctors or shamans to apply magic, herbal mixtures, or folk medicine to rid deranged persons of evil spirits or bizarre behavior. In ancient Israel it was widely believed that mental or emotional disturbances were caused by supernatural forces or an angry God as a punishment for sin or failure to follow the commandments. The Greeks replaced concepts of the supernatural with a secular view, insisting that afflictions of the mind were no different than diseases of the body. The Romans put forth the idea that strong emotions could lead to bodily ailments, the basis of today's theory of psychosomatic illness. The Romans also embraced the notion of humane treatment for the mentally ill and codified into law the principle of insanity as a mitigation of responsibility for a criminal act.

During the Middle Ages, with the overriding influence of the Catholic Church, there was a return to the belief that supernatural forces, the Devil and witches were causing troubled mental states in people. During the Renaissance, with the rise of monarchies and state responsibility for the poor and disabled, there was a growing tendency to house mad men and women in special institutions. At century's end, the abuses and sufferings of the mentally ill led to public outrage and a period of reform. A program of "moral treatment" was begun – institutional care based on kindness, sympathy, guidance, work, and recreation – the reeducation of patients to behave normally. In the mid-nineteenth century there was the decline of moral treatment and the emergence of the "medical model," the perspective that stresses mental illness is caused by biological factors and is incurable.

The twentieth century is noted for the ascendancy of a variety of different concepts and treatments in psychiatry. In the 1920s the theories of Sigmund Freud on childhood psychosexual development and the unconscious mind profoundly affected psychiatric thinking and practice. The 1930s saw the introduction of electroconvulsive therapy, insulin treatment, and lobotomies. In the 1940s the war years uncovered a new disorder, "battle fatigue," while the post-war period, with the creation of the National Institute of Mental Health in the USA, saw the beginning of the federal government's commitment to helping the mentally ill. In the USA during the 1950s the populations of state hospitals, growing for over a century, peaked and began a long period of decline. By the 1960s a "psychiatric revolution" began, with an emphasis on recently developed psychoactive drugs to maintain patients both in and out of the hospital. Deinstitutionalization was public policy and became a social movement, complete with ideology and political action. At the end of the twentieth century the trend in institutionalization reversed again. Many former mental patients were returned to an expanding state hospital system as they could not be treated effectively in the community, were rejected by their families, or ended up on the streets of every major city, homeless and often in need of medical attention.

The second half of the twentieth century was marked with intense debate as to what madness is and whether hospital treatment is appropriate. Psychiatrists generally assume the presence of an abnormal condition in the individual which is manifested in specific symptomatology, but Thomas Szasz broke ranks and led the anti-psychiatry movement in the 1960s by arguing that mental illness is a myth, nothing more than "problems of living." Sociologists, on the other hand, tend to view mental illness as a label attached to persons who engage in certain types of deviant activities. Thomas Scheff, chief among them, argued that the symptoms and disturbed behavior typical of the mentally ill are more the conformity to a set of role expectations, products of situations, than the result of some personal predisposition or specific psychopathology. Walter Gove, however, argued that from a psychiatric point of view hospitalization is thought of positively, as a site to both treat patients and shield them from the environment that is causing or contributing to their madness. The sociological position, articulated best by Erving Goffman, casts the mental hospital in a negative light, as a "total institution" that stigmatizes the patient and reinforces the very behavior it is supposed to correct.

The coming of the twenty-first century has not seen the end of the centuries-old controversies surrounding madness in people and its consequences for society. The causes of mental illness are still largely unknown. Whether disorders of the mind are due to organic, genetic, and biological factors or the result of developmental and environmental influences is part of the larger longstanding battle between "nature" and "nurture" among medical and social scientists.

SEE ALSO: Deinstitutionalization; Freud, Sigmund; Goffman, Erving; Labeling Theory; Mental Disorder; Mental Illness, Social Construction of; Psychoanalysis; Stigma

SUGGESTED READINGS

Goffman, E. (1961) *Asylums: Essays on the Social Situation of Mental Patients and Other Inmates*. Doubleday Anchor, New York.

Gove, W. R. (1970) Societal reaction as an explanation of mental illness: an evaluation. *American Sociological Review* 35: 873–84.

Scheff, T. J. (1966) *Being Mentally Ill: A Sociological Theory*. Aldine, Chicago, IL.

Szasz, T. S. (1961) *The Myth of Mental Illness: Foundations of a Theory of Personal Conduct*. Harper & Row, New York.

RAYMOND M. WEINSTEIN

male rape

Many legal codes define male rape as involving the non-consensual penile penetration of the mouth or anus of a male. Since the late 1980s there has been a significant growth in research examining the problem of adult male rape. As a result of this work we have a much better understanding of its prevalence, impact and dynamics. It has also become increasingly apparent that this is a phenomenon not limited to institutional settings. While both heterosexual and gay males can be victims of rape, epidemiological research suggests that homosexuality is a particular risk factor in cases of adult sexual victimization. Likewise, perpetrators of male rape can be gay or heterosexual, and on the limited evidence available appear to rape for reasons of power, anger and control. Further, studies of victim trauma suggest males suffer a range of negative reactions following rape. These reactions are similar, though not necessarily identical, to the reactions of female victims. In particular, many, though not all raped males question their sense of masculinity and sexuality following rape. Recent research indicates that some male rape victims who report their experiences to the attention of the criminal justice system are met with disbelief, victim-blaming and homophobia.

SEE ALSO: Child Abuse; Doing Gender; Homophobia; Rape Culture; Rape/Sexual Assault

SUGGESTED READINGS

Abdullah-Khan, N. (2008) *Male Rape: The Emergence of a Social and Legal Issue*. Palgrave Macmillan, London.

Rumney, P. (2008) Policing male rape and sexual assault. *Journal of Criminal Law* 71: 67–86.

Scarce, M. (1997) *Male on Male Rape: The Hidden Toll of Stigma and Shame*. Insight Books, New York.

PHILIP RUMNEY

Malthus, Thomas Robert (1766–1834)

Thomas Robert Malthus is one of the most influential writers in history on the topic of population, especially his book *Essay on the Principle of Population as it affects the future improvement of society; With remarks on the speculations of Mr. Godwin, M. Condorcet, and other writers*. Malthus believed that human beings are "impelled" to increase the population of the species by the urge to reproduce. Further, if there were no checks on population growth, human beings would multiply to an "incalculable" number, filling "millions of worlds in a few thousand years" (Malthus [1872] 1971). This does not happen, however, because of the checks to growth, especially lack of food (the "means of subsistence"). In turn, the means of subsistence are limited by the amount of land available, the technology that could be applied to the land, and land ownership patterns. A cornerstone of his argument is that populations tend to grow more rapidly than does the food supply since population has the potential for growing geometrically, whereas he believed that food production could be increased only arithmetically, by adding one acre at a time. Thus, in the natural order, population growth will outstrip the food supply, and the lack of food will ultimately put a stop to the increase of people.

SEE ALSO: Darwin, Charles; Demographic Transition Theory

REFERENCE

Malthus, T. R. (1971) [1872] *An Essay on the the Principle of Population*, 7th edn. Reeves & Turner, London.

SUGGESTED READING

Malthus, T. R. (1965) [1798] *An Essay on Population*. Augustus Kelley, New York.

JOHN R. WEEKS

managed care

Managed care refers to processes or techniques used by, or on behalf of, purchasers of health care to control or influence the quality, accessibility, utilization, and costs of health care. Managed care emphasizes cost containment, performance assessment, measurable outcomes and subjects the treatment actions of health care providers to external review. Treatment decisions are evaluated in light of measurable client level outcomes; consequently managed care has resulted in a greater emphasis on accountability. There is also an increased emphasis on standardization of clinical practices and reliance upon evidence based medicine. Because treatment is reimbursed when there is a valid medical diagnosis for which an efficacious treatment exists, managed care has resulted in a view of care in terms of a medical model and excludes the many forms of support needed by individuals with chronic conditions. There is also an increased reliance on medications as the sole form of medical care. The debate is whether managed care simply reduces costs (efficiency) or whether it enhances care (effectiveness).

Sociologists have examined managed care constraints on professional autonomy and conflict with bureaucratic control systems. Most of the existent research focuses on physicians and sociologists have found that decisions about clinical care continue to rely upon medical expertise. There needs to be more research on how managed care has affected the work of different groups of health care providers as well as patients. Sociologists also need to focus on ways in which managed care has changed access to health care for different populations. Managed care has the potential to widen access by distributing health care more equitably; it may also restrict access by limiting care to those with acute health care problems and hence neglecting the long term needs of patients with chronic problems, and enhancing inequalities in care.

SEE ALSO: Health and Medicine; Heath Care Delivery Systems; Socioeconomic Status, Health, and Mortality

SUGGESTED READINGS

Scheid, T. (2004) *Tie a Knot and Hang On: Providing Mental Health Care in a Turbulent Environment*. Aldine de Gruyter, New York.
Sullivan, K. (2000) On the efficiency of managed care plans. *Health Affairs* 19: 139–48.

TERESA L. SCHEID

management

On the eve of World War I, scientific management became the first big management fad, a source of innumerable new truths about work and its organization, all of which were oriented to the efficiency of the individual human body. At the same time a revolution in manufacturing also occurred when Henry Ford introduced the assembly line, modeled on the Chicago slaughterhouses. In the abattoirs each job was separated into a series of simple repetitive actions as the bodies moved down the line to be progressively dismembered; in Ford the car was built on the same principles that the hog was butchered.

Later studies changed the landscape of management from Taylor's engineering approach to the political economy of the body to a social sciences approach that focused on the interior life, the mental states, the consciousness and unconsciousness, which Follett termed the "soul" of the employees: "Coercive power is the curse of the universe; coactive power, the enrichment and advancement of every human soul" (Follett 1924: xii). Worker productivity would henceforth be interpreted predominantly in terms of patterns of culture, motivation, leadership, and human relations. The locus of expert power shifted from the engineering expert, designing the job, selecting and training the right worker, and rewarding performance, to the manager, responsible for leading, motivating, communicating, and counseling the individual employee as well as designing the social milieu in which work takes place. Human relations came to the fore, as did a concern with leadership and authority.

As management theory became increasingly institutionalized, especially in business schools, it began to develop the traits that we would expect of any institutionalized body of knowledge. Rival camps with competing claims to territory emerged. Definitions of the field became contested. What was regarded as holy writ differed within each citation cartel, centered on different fulcra, whether journals, theories, or theorists.

The years since the 1980s have witnessed an explosion of management initiatives. Replete with their careful styling and image intensity such initiatives are now widely characterized as management fashions. Examples of management fashion since the 1990s include total quality management, downsizing, business process re-engineering, enterprise resource planning, knowledge management, and shareholder value.

In some respects, early management theorists were situated too close to its practice to reflect overly on its theory. These early texts were embedded, precisely, in the strategies for making sense of management that the pioneers forged and the managerial techniques they advocated. The political and moral economy of the body, and the emergence of a concern with the soul of the employee, did not enter greatly into subsequent accounts. Management became ever more abstracted and sophisticated in its use of metaphors drawn from contingency and system theory, yet it still struggled with the obdurate *matériel* of the human subject at its base. Overwhelmingly, its tendency has been to rationalize and routinize this obduracy through designing systems that reduce the capacity for human inventiveness, creativity, and innovation of those within the systems designed, as Ritzer's (2005) work on McDonaldization suggests. It is through this prism that we should see the latest trends in management thinking, such as knowledge management.

SEE ALSO: Capitalism; Institutional Theory, New; Japanese-Style Management; Labor Process; Management, Theories of

REFERENCES

Follett, M. P. (1924) *Creative Experience*. Longman, Green, New York.

Ritzer, G. (2005) *The McDonaldization of Society*, 2nd edn. Pine Forge Press, Thousand Oaks, CA.

SUGGESTED READING

Mayo, E. (1975) *The Social Problems of an Industrial Civilization*. Routledge & Kegan Paul, London.

STEWART CLEGG AND CHRIS CARTER

management, theories of

Management is defined as a social process and a social figure. As a social process, it is defined by the ways in which an organization operates effectively and efficiently. Whereas effectiveness is related to the attainment of goals, efficiency is related to the optimization of resources in the pursuit of organizational goals. The resulting effectiveness-efficiency dilemna underpins much of management thought.

Historically, management thinking has been produced by three groups – practitioners, consultants and academics. The most popular and influential theories have come from practitioners and consultants. After World War II, the work of academics became increasingly influential, although there has been concern about the extent to which the academic literature is only read by academics rather than practitioners. While the theories of the first two groups are mostly normative and prescriptive, the theories of the third group are mostly analytical.The majority of the theories produced upto today come from North American practitioners, consultants and academics.

Theories of management have proved to be both numerous and very diverse.This variety is due in part to the type of producer, the intellectual background, the mental representation of what an organization is (machine, living organism, social system, . . .), the regional space of production (Europe, North America, Asia, etc.) and the social historical context in which it appears. The main classical influential figures are historically Taylor, Fayol, Ford, Follet, Weber, the Human Relations current, and Barnard.

From the end of World War II to the mid-1970s, several things played a major role in reshaping management thinking. From the Living Sciences came the idea of open system. Among other things, this meant that the organizations adaptations to their environment are contingent. Still other developments came from sociology and psychosociology. There is, for example, the development of organizational behavior, which integrates new developments coming from industrial psychology, group dynamics, socioanalysis, sociometry, social psychology, and sociology of work and organizations. They are at the base of the theories of work satisfaction, work motivation, leadership, and group dynamics.

More recent developments include the following: the US model was seen as not the only one to produce efficiency and wealth; international competition gives a great push to strategic management thinking; the creation of networks of all kinds, notably the Internet, reconfigures organizational forms; concern with workforce mobilization, especially the rise of a new working class attitude; and several strategies to respond to it such as industrial democracy giving more power to the workers and the unions and building of corporate culture.

The feminization of the work force and the rise of female managers led to numerous publications dealing with such issues as management theories as gender productions; managerial practices to diminish gender inequality (e.g. affirmative action and managing diversity more generally); and dealing with individual satisfaction and motivation (e.g. stress management programs).

The twenty-first century, notably the 2008 financial crisis, has shown the limits of some firm's behaviors and of a neoliberal agenda. According to many management analysts, we are going to see great changes in ethics (e.g. sustainability), culture (cultural embeddeness and a universalistic approach) and socioeconomic conditions (equity, training, wealth sharing, quality, innovation).

SEE ALSO: Japanese-Style Management; Management

SUGGESTED READING

Clegg, S., Pitsis, T., & Kornberger, M. (2005) *Managing and Organizations: An Introduction to Theory and Practice*. Sage, London.

JEAN-FRANÇOIS CHANLAT

Mannheim, Karl (1893–1947)

Karl Mannheim was born in Budapest, Hungary, but developed his academic career in Germany (in Heidelberg and Frankfurt) and England (at the London School of Economics). He was the earliest proponent of the *sociology of knowledge*, a branch of theory concerned with the influence of social context on our way of perceiving, interpreting, and forming claims about the world. Although Mannheim began his career as a philosopher with an interest in epistemology, he became increasingly fascinated by the impact of society on thought processes, with particular emphasis on culture, intellectual competition, and intergenerational dynamics. In his most influential book, *Ideology and Utopia* (1929 [1936]), Mannheim distinguished between two forms of belief systems: *ideological* systems, which seek to ensure inertia in beliefs through an emphasis on the past; and *utopian* systems, which embrace change in beliefs through an emphasis on the future. After being forced from Germany in 1933, Mannheim's writings turned toward the contemporary crisis generated by fascism, examining the role of planning and the possibility of a democratic society.

Mannheim's interest in sociological theory developed in the early 1920s, through an intensive study of Max Weber, Alfred Weber, Max Scheler, and Karl Marx. These efforts came to fruition in 1925 with the publication of an article on "The problem of a sociology of knowledge", which created a new subfield of the discipline. At the time, Mannheim accepted his first faculty position at the University of Heidelberg. His most widely read book, *Ideology and Utopia*, was published four years later and introduced the sociology of knowledge to a much broader audience. In the same year, Mannheim was offered a professorship at the University of Frankfurt, which he held until his dismissal by the Nazi regime in 1933.

Following his exile to England, Mannheim joined the London School of Economics and Political Science. In this third phase of his career, he became fascinated by the crisis of liberal democracy, as evidenced by the regime change in Germany. Mannheim expanded his existing scholarship on the role of the intelligentsia to address the problem of planning in a democratic society. This led to an interest in the sociology of education and an appointment to the chair in education at the University of London in 1945. In 1947, Mannheim was offered the job of directing the European division of UNESCO and appeared to have an opportunity to apply his theories on planning and education. Unfortunately, he died unexpectedly a few weeks later at the age of 53.

SEE ALSO: Democracy; Ideology; Knowledge; Knowledge, Sociology of

REFERENCE

Mannheim, K. (1936) [1929] *Ideology and Utopia: An Introduction to the Sociology of Knowledge*. Harcourt Brace, New York.

MARTIN RUEF

Marcuse, Herbert (1898–1979)

Herbert Marcuse, philosopher and social theorist, was a leading member of the Frankfurt School of Critical Theory and, with Jean-Paul Sartre, inspired 1960s student radicalism. Marcuse formulated a distinctive critical theory of society which combined Hegelian-Marxism with insights drawn from his many masterful studies of modern and twentieth-century philosophy and social theory.

Among these are *Reason and Revolution: Hegel and the Rise of Social Theory* (1941), which rescued Hegelian philosophy from its Nazi-propagated association with totalitarian ideology; *Eros and Civilization: A Philosophical Inquiry into Freud* (1955), which formulated a unique Marx/Freud synthesis; and *One-Dimensional Man: Studies in the Ideology of Advanced Industrial Society* (1964), which analyzed "a comfortable, smooth, reasonable, democratic unfreedom . . . in advanced industrial civilization," which, Marcuse immediately added, was "a token of technical progress."

Despite his prominence and the influence of such later books as *An Essay on Liberation* (1969), *Counterrevolution and Revolt* (1972), and *The Aesthetic Dimension* (1978), Marcuse's social and political thought has had little effect on professional sociology. This may be attributed to Marcuse's lifelong commitment to "negation" or "dialectical" forms of analysis, which places his otherwise rich oeuvre at loggerheads with positivist mainstream sociology. Likewise, as the generation of the 1960s fades into its golden years, it is doubtful that Marcuse's intellectual legacy will again significantly inform mass political sensibilities. Neglect of Marcuse is ironic since today's advanced industrial society appears no less "one-dimensional" – no less capable of imagining qualitative self-transformation – nor any less wedded to "repressive desublimation" – the process whereby pseudo-gratifications translate into pseudo-freedoms, much as Prole Feed, Hate Week, and the up-scale satisfactions symbolized by Victory Gin were just about enough to ensure happiness in Oceania. "Either there will be a catastrophe or things will get worse," Marcuse sometimes prophesized to his many students. The jury remains out on which it will be.

SEE ALSO: Dialectic; Critical Theory/Frankfurt School; Freud, Sigmund; Positivism

SUGGESTED READING

Kellner, D. (1984) *Herbert Marcuse and the Crisis of Marxism.* University of California Press, Berkeley, CA.

STEVEN DANDANEAU

marginalization, outsiders

Marginalization is a metaphor that refers to processes by which individuals or groups are kept at, or pushed beyond, the edges of society. The term outsiders may be used to refer to those individuals or groups who are marginalized.

The term marginalization is attributed to Park (1928) who coined the expression "marginal man" to characterize the lot of impoverished minority ethnic immigrants into a predominantly white Anglo-Saxon protestant USA. It later became popular, particularly in Latin America, as a term that captured the supposed "backwardness," not of immigrants in developed countries, but of people in developing countries who fail or are prevented from participating in the economic, political and cultural transition to modernity. Modernity makes the subordinate status and cultural differences of rural peoples and the urban poor anomalous. More recently the term marginalization has been largely superseded, especially in Europe, by the term "exclusion." None the less, marginalization often appears as a synonym for extreme poverty or for social exclusion and it may sometimes be difficult to distinguish between the concepts other than in terms of who is using them. People may be marginalized from economic production; from consumption (including the consumption of public services); from political participation; and/or from social or cultural interaction.

The nature of the capitalist production processes is such that not everybody will be employed by them and Marx famously referred to those who are rendered outsiders as the "reserve army of labour," who are pushed to the margins of the labor market. Those outside the formal economy may engage in marginalized forms of economic activity, for example in subsistence agriculture in the developing world, in informal or unregulated economic activity, or in street-level activities, such as hustling or begging. Equally important, especially in the context of a consumer society is that those who cannot afford to obtain access to goods or services may be marginalized: not only can they remain or become outsiders or strangers to the kinds of goods and facilities that others use, but they may inhabit marginalized neighborhoods that are poorly served by public services or which may, for example, have been "red-lined" by credit providers. Ultimately they may exist outside the parameters that define a customary lifestyle, as happens, for example, when people become homeless. Democratic systems may marginalize or ignore the interests of minority electoral groups, and those who are for whatever reason stigmatized or reviled may be marginalized from mainstream social networks and community life.

It is not only what people may be marginalized from, but why? The poor may become outsiders, but so too can the rich when they choose to live separately in gated communities. Disabled people may quite literally be outsiders if, because their needs are marginal to the interests of architects, builders and planners, they cannot obtain access to public buildings or housing accommodation. Minority and/or itinerant ethnic groups may be marginalized because of racism and so form outsider communities.

The most extreme form of marginalization is associated with criminalization, which occurs when individuals or groups are labelled as deviant (Becker 1963). This can occur when popular or media inspired "moral panics" stigmatize particular kinds of behavior (which may or may not be technically criminal) and when the offenders assume a marginalized identity.

SEE ALSO: Deviance, Criminalization of; Social Exclusion

REFERENCES

Becker, H. (1963) *Outsiders: Studies in the sociology of deviance*. Free Press, Glencoe, IL.

Park, R. (1928) Human migration and the marginal man. *American Journal of Sociology* 33: 881–93.

HARTLEY DEAN

markets

Markets are the foremost subject of economic science as market economics. Markets also are of interest for economic sociology, as indicated by the sociology of the market. Conventional economics and economic sociology treat markets in different ways, as economic mechanisms and as social creations, respectively.

In conventional economics, markets are mechanisms operating in various ways and forms. First and foremost, markets are mechanisms involving relations and laws of supply and demand. A similar conventional economic conception is that of markets as mechanisms and spheres of economic freedom, specifically free competition. Also, conventional economics conceives markets as almost automatic economic mechanisms operating with self-regulation and a tendency toward equilibrium and optimum. In a related conception, markets are spontaneous and impersonal mechanisms for economic coordination, originating in the concept of an "invisible hand" of market competition. In particular, markets are conceived as mechanisms for efficient resource allocation as well as objective wealth distribution. Markets are seen as impersonal mechanisms for the determination of exchange values or prices. Lastly, in conventional economics markets operate as mechanisms of natural selection in the economy, of rapid economic growth, and of improved material welfare.

Economic sociology treats markets as social creations, complementing their treatment as economic mechanisms in conventional economics. Generally, for economic sociology markets are special cases of social categories or facts existing and involved in society. Markets and their functions, as elements of the social economy, are necessarily embedded in social relations and institutions, as Comte emphasized. Durkheim considers markets and economies particular forms of social facts, the origin and substance of which is primarily society. According to Simmel, market exchanges are not just economic facts but social phenomena because of their non-economic conditions, especially culture.

In particular, economic sociology analyzes markets as social institutions. For Durkheim, markets are special cases of social or public institutions, specifically those involving exchange forming the subject of *economic sociology*, together with institutions related to the production and distribution of wealth. He identifies the institutional or normative (non-contractual) ingredients of market contracts in that the latter are far from self-sufficient and instead subject to social regulations. Tönnies observes that society is present in all market contracts and exchanges. Weber treats markets as normative-institutional arrangements in that group formation through market exchange is substantively equivalent to associations formed via rational agreement or imposition of norms. He classifies markets into the most developed economic institutions of modern capitalism. The classical treatment of markets as social institutions has been adopted and refined in contemporary economic sociology.

Also, in economic sociology markets are analyzed in terms of social interactions and relations. In Weber's view, the market is a sociological variable of the economy in virtue of being a set of social relations. Simmel describes market competition as a sociological condition and process involving social interaction. In contemporary economic sociology, social relations are crucial to markets viewed as embedded in networks of interpersonal ties and institutions (embeddedness).

Further, economic sociology considers markets social systems or structures. Durkheim characterizes markets and economies as social systems permeated by values. Pareto suggests that markets and the economy overall are integral elements of the social system but more general and complex. Contemporary economic sociology also approaches markets as special social structures. In addition, economic sociology treats markets as fields of power and conflict, as well as of cultural values.

SEE ALSO: Capitalism; Economy

SUGGESTED READING

Schumpeter, J. (1954) *History of Economic Analysis.* Oxford University Press, New York.

MILAN ZAFIROVSKI

marriage

Marriage is important to the individuals concerned, the others to whom they are connected, and to the society within which the marriage is recognized. Marriage will not necessarily be important in the same way across different societies or to the different individuals within these societies. Recognizing this qualification, the list here outlines some of the key ways in which sociologists have described the importance of marriage:

- Marriage is seen as a key element within a wider set of family relationships. It establishes links between different families and over different generations.
- Marriage is seen as a key element in the life course. It is seen as an important transition in the lives of individuals and of those to whom they are connected.
- Marriage is seen as a key element in the social ordering of gender and sexuality. This is the most widespread understanding of marriage (one man, one woman) and reaffirms distinctions between men and women and the dominant importance of heterosexuality.
- Marriage is seen as a key element in the wider social structure. This is because the parties involved in a marriage are not just gendered and sexualized individuals but have class, ethnic, religious, and other differently based identities.
- Marriage is important as an element in the mobilization of patterns of care and social support.
- Marriage is important in the formation of personal and social identity.

These are in addition to the key function which links marriage and parenthood and which sees marriage in terms of the production, legitimizing, and social placement of children. Research into marriage may be classified under two headings: the comparative and historical, and the study of its internal dynamics. The first considers how marriage differs between different societies or different historical periods and how it has changed over time. Earlier comparative research into marriage explored different marriage systems and the ways in which these were linked to wider aspects of social structure such as the division of societies into classes or castes, or the distribution of property. The emphasis was often a strongly functional one considering the part that a particular marriage system (polygyny, polyandry, arranged, and so on) played within the wider social structure. Comparative research might also be linked to a wider theory of social evolution, speculating on the ways in which marriage patterns and the wider social order together change over time.

More narrowly, attempts have been made to analyze changes in marriage in Britain, the United States, and other Anglophone societies together with much of western and northern Europe. Sometimes this might be expressed simply as a "decline" of marriage, as increasing numbers of people do not go through a formal marriage ceremony, have children outside wedlock, or divorce. Further, with the partial recognition of cohabiting and non-heterosexual partnerships, the privileged status of heterosexual marriage seems to be less secure.

Notions of the decline of marriage may be countered by showing that marriage continues to be an important, if frequently delayed, transition in the life course and pointing to the increasing demands for the recognition of gay and lesbian marriages. The issue here is one of change rather than decline, with researchers often accounting for these changes in terms of a broad historical process of "individualization." The emphasis here is on the ways in which individuals are increasingly called upon to shape their own relational biographies with little reference to the expectations of others or previously established patterns of behavior. This may sometimes be seen as the extension of democratic ideals into intimate relationships.

Yet another formulation is in terms of a long-term shift in marriage from institution to relationship. Marriage may be seen as moving from a social context where it was clearly embedded in a wider network of familial and kinship ties and obligations and where it constituted the major legitimate adult identity. As marriage becomes more of a relationship, there is greater emphasis on individual choice and the needs and satisfactions of the participants. Choice here includes the possibility of choosing not to get married.

Turning to the more "internal" aspects of marriage, we can look at gender divisions and questions of identity. It is widely believed that marriages have become more equal in terms of gender; the very idea of a relationship suggests some degree of mutuality and equality between the partners. At the same time, there has been a considerable body of research exploring gendered inequalities and differences within marriage. These include unequal participation in household and parental tasks; differences in the management of money within the home; and differences in patterns of paid employment and leisure activities outside the home. The sources of these persisting differences include men's and women's differential labor market participation and earning power; the persistence of deeply held assumptions about the nature of men and women; and inequalities in power within the household, including physical power and the potential for violence. Some have argued that we should consider the different balances between "love" and "power" within marriage.

SEE ALSO: Cohabitation; Divisions of Household Labor; Intimacy; Same-Sex Marriage/Civil Unions

SUGGESTED READING

Beck, U. & Beck-Gernsheim, E. (1995) *The Normal Chaos of Love*. Polity Press, Cambridge.
Therborn, G. (2004) *Between Sex and Power: Family in the World, 1900–2000*. Routledge, London.

DAVID H. J. MORGAN

Martineau, Harriet (1802–76)

Harriet Martineau's 25 volumes of short novels illustrating the principles of political economy outsold the works of her contemporary, Charles Dickens; Martineau's travel chronicles of nineteenth-century American society and its cultural beliefs are comparative historical accounts that have been likened to Tocqueville's *Democracy in America*; she authored sociology's first systematic treatment of methodology six decades before Durkheim's *Rules of the Sociological Method*; and Martineau translated and condensed Auguste Comte's *Cours de philosophie positive*, and introduced his attempt to establish a sociological science within the English-speaking world. However, the story of sociology's emergence has been a history of men and their contributions to the formation of the discipline.

Martineau's initial move into what would become sociology began in 1834 with her two-year travels to the USA. With *Society in America* (1836–7) and *Retrospect of Western Travel* (1838b) Martineau transformed travel writing into social scientific inquiry. In these works Martineau implemented the theories outlined in her yet-unpublished method's treatment, *How to Observe Morals and Manners* (1838a). She believed that any examination of society must take into account morals (i.e., cultural beliefs and values, and manners): social interaction. If a scientific observer of society seeks to understand the morals of a group, Martineau proposed that she examine the meanings of an activity for the social actor. Martineau did not propose value-neutrality on the part of the observer; however, she did propose that the researcher's biases be acknowledged. According to Martineau, sympathy toward the actor was a skill that separated the scientific study of society from the natural sciences. (The methodological approach is similar to Weber's *verstehen*.) *How to Observe Morals and Manners* is more than a methodological treatise; it sets social theoretical precedents. Before Marx, Weber, and Durkheim, "Martineau sociologically examined social class, forms of religion, types of suicide, national character, domestic relations and the status of women, delinquency and criminology, and the intricate interrelations between repressive social institutions and the individual" (Hill 1991: 292).

Martineau's approach to the study of American society dealt with the problem of ethnocentrism in comparative works written for a European male audience. She highlighted the importance of women's issues as an essential component to the study of a society. Although she presumed her readers to be male, Martineau directed their attention to the study of the household and the domestic role of women in culture as necessary for a sociological study. And instead of merely comparing the USA to England, she divided her work into three volumes: political structure, economy, and a category she called "civilization" that dealt with social mores and values. Martineau (1836–7) identified the moral principles that Americans claimed to hold dear, and then contrasted them to the everyday reality of life in the US to see "how far the people of the United States lived up to or fell below their own theory."

SEE ALSO: Comte, Auguste; Durkheim, Émile; Malthus, Thomas Robert

REFERENCES

Hill, M. R. (1991) Harriet Martineau. In: Deegan, M. J. (ed.), *Women in Sociology: A Bio-Bibliographical Sourcebook*. Greenwood Press, Westport, CT.
Martineau, H. (1836–7) *Society in America*, 2 vols. Saunders & Otley, New York.

CYNTHIA SIEMSEN

Marx, Karl (1818–83)

Karl Marx's critique of economic inequality and appeals for social justice inspired left-wing political parties, labor movements, and insurgencies worldwide. Post-World War II, North American theorists portrayed him as a founder of "conflict theory" or "critical sociology," declaring him part of modern social theory's founding troika (with Émile Durkheim and Max Weber). Critics countered that this canon was too narrow and Eurocentric and that communism's collapse rendered Marx irrelevant. Others held that globalization, neoliberal deregulation, and increased economic inequality made him more relevant than ever. Marx has influenced sociological work widely, including that aimed to disprove his theories. Questions and concepts which he framed have been deployed in diverse research and theory programs.

Marx's parents had Jewish origins, but their native Prussia's anti-Semitism led them to convert to Protestantism. As a university student, Marx joined a group of left-wing intellectuals, who embraced Hegel's philosophical vision of humanity making itself through labor. Marx finished his doctoral dissertation in 1841, but did not complete the second thesis required to enter German academe. His radicalism and Jewish roots precluded an academic career. Marx became a journalist and editor. His newspaper flourished, but Prussian officials shut it down in 1843 for criticizing the monarchy and state. That year Marx married Jenny von Westphalen, and left for Paris, where he learned about the industrial working class and communism.

Marx's collaborator, Friedrich Engels provided invaluable criticism, editorial assistance, and financial support. Engels understated his role, but contributed greatly to Marx's thought. Marx's and Engels' *The German Ideology* (1845–6) established "mode of production" and "class" as their core analytical categories. Their ideas about large firms, mechanized production, and globalization anticipated Marx's later work. Expressing lucidly and succinctly Marx's and Engels' materialist perspective, their *The Communist Manifesto* (1848) held that capitalism was spreading globally, revolutionizing its productive forces, overthrowing tradition, and creating a mass of impoverished industrial workers destined to overthrow capitalism. The *Manifesto* was the most widely read, politically important Marxist work. In 1849 Marx moved to London, bastion of modern capitalism. He participated in working-class politics, leading the First International 1864–72. He eventually gave full attention to his theoretical work. His *Capital* (1867) was the first of a planned six-volume magnum opus. Although writing thousands of pages and filling numerous notebooks, he never finished the work. After his death, Engels edited and assembled two unfinished core volumes, and Karl Kautsky edited three related volumes.

MARX'S ANALYSIS OF CAPITALISM

Marx held that the social relationship between capitalism's ruling class and direct producers – *capitalists* and *wage workers* – is *the* key to grasping the system as a whole. His masterwork's integrative *labor theory of value* held that a commodity's *value* manifests the "socially-necessary labor time" that it takes to find, mine, refine, fashion, assemble, or make it (assuming average efficiency relative to existing productive forces). Although acknowledging that supply and demand, monopoly, and other conditions cause "exchange values," or prices, to fluctuate, Marx argued that they gravitate toward an average determined by the crystallized labor time in commodities. He saw the contingent factors to be vital for success or failure of individual capitalists, but believed that variations cancel each other out and cannot explain accumulation as a whole. Most importantly, Marx held that the average worker is paid only for subsistence, or a fraction of the labor time that he or she transfers to the product; capitalists keep the unpaid portion and realize the "surplus value" when they sell it. Holding that "labor power" is the *only* commodity to produce regularly more value than it commands in exchange, he identified the unequal wage relationship as the source of profit and growth. He argued that, under capitalism, as in earlier modes of production, ruling classes appropriate direct producers' surplus and leave them only necessities (which vary with the level of production). Like slaves and serfs, he held, wage workers do not retain their surplus product or live off that of others. By contrast to slavery or serfdom, however, Marx claimed that capitalism's formally voluntary labor contract creates the illusion of freedom and equal exchange.

Marx held that capitalists make surplus profits when they are first to develop technical innovations that produce a commodity substantially below its socially necessary labor time (e.g., Henry Ford's assembly line). However, he contended that, eventually, other producers adopt the same innovation and socially necessary labor time is adjusted downward. He argued that, in the long run, mechanization and automation, driven by capitalist competition, will reduce sharply the proportion of "living labor" in the productive process, causing ever-increasing unemployment and falling profits. He thought that monopoly pricing, global expansion of capitalist production into low-wage countries, and other strategies would pump up profits and slow the decline, but could not avert an eventual, terminal capitalist crisis. Marx claimed that automated production, centralized productive organization, and applied science and technology, decoupled from capitalism and class would provide means to refine productive forces much more systematically, reducing their destructive impacts on people and nature, generating increased surplus, reducing unnecessary labor, and creating equitable distribution. However, Marx's vision of this transition to "communism" presumed prior spread of highly advanced, knowledge-based capitalism and automated production to the entire globe. Even Marx and Engels had doubts about this scenario.

MARX'S MATERIALIST MODEL

Marx saw *class* (people sharing a location in capitalism and similar material conditions) to be the most pervasive source of systematic social constraint. He held that class shapes typical superordinate and subordinate individuals, reproduced generation after generation. Depending on historical circumstances, he argued, classes can be fragmented aggregates, unaware of their common condition, or class conscious groups, which grasp their shared position and interests. Marx argued that the *mode of production*, or *base*, is society's primary structuring factor; it includes *productive forces* (natural resources, tools, labor power, technology, science, modes of cooperation), or factors contributing directly to creation of necessary and surplus product, and *property relations*, or class-based relationships that determine who has effective control over productive forces and disposition of product and who must do productive labor. Marx held that *superstructure* ("modes of intercourse" and "ideology") helps reproduce the mode of production. For example, he saw the state's military, police, legal, and administrative arms as perpetuating productive forces and property relations. He argued that other associations and organizations (e.g. families and voluntary groups) control, socialize, or fashion people to fit the mode of production. Marx did *not* claim that all organizations, associations, and cultures contribute equally to the process. For example, he knew that labor unions and political parties sometimes oppose capitalism, yet still participate in public life or operate at its borders. For Marx, ideology meant facets of culture that either play a direct role in justifying the mode of production or make an indirect, but determinate contribution (e.g., *capitalist* ideas of the state, economy, or culture).

Marx spoke of relations of *correspondence* reproducing the mode of production, and relations of *contradiction*, undermining it. For example, feudal laws and customs, which bound serfs to lords and journeymen to masters and forbade unrestricted sale of property, open-ended technical innovation, and market competition, corresponded to the manor's and guild's productive forces and property relations, but contradicted nascent capitalism. Capitalist development intensified the contradictions and generated class conflicts between the emergent bourgeoisie and opposed feudal aristocrats and guild masters. Victorious capitalists created administrative, legal, and sociocultural forms that upheld the new productive forces and class structure. Marx saw "class struggle" to be the immediate "motor" of such transformations, but held that new productive forces are the *ultimate* causal agent. Marx did *not* argue that all sociocultural change originates in this way. Moreover, he saw the "material" realm to be social as well as natural, which made causality a complicated matter. He often praised art and literature, and did *not* reduce them to materialist reflux. He held that social formations bear their mode of production's imprint, but considered their parts to be, at variable levels, relatively autonomous.

Twenty-first-century peoples still live in the wake of the world-historical transformation that Marx analyzed. His materialism provides heuristic tools, which pose penetrating sociological questions about social inequality, wealth, growth, ideology, and overall social development. Also, his social theory's ethical thrust, stressing just distribution of the sociomaterial means of participation, challenges us to rethink socioeconomic justice after twentieth-century communism and social democracy and to entertain fresh alternatives to unrestricted economic liberalism and its sharp inequalities. Marx's specter hangs over us.

SEE ALSO: Capitalism; Class; Class Consciousness; Communism; Conflict Theory; Economic Determinism; Engels, Freidrich; Globalization; Ideology; Dialectical Materialism, Neo-Marxism; Socialism

REFERENCES

Marx, K. (1867) *Capital: A Critique of Political Economy, Vol. 1. The Process of Capitalist Production*, ed. F. Engels. In: *Collected Works*, vol. 35, pp. 43–807.

Marx, K. & Engels, F. (1845–6) *The German Ideology*. In: *Collected Works*, vol. 5, pp. 19–608.

Marx, K & Engels, F. (1848) *The Communist Manifesto*. In *Collected Works*, vol. 6, pp. 477–519.

SUGGESTED READING

McLellan, D. (1973) *Karl Marx: His Life and Thought*. Harper & Row, New York.

ROBERT J. ANTONIO

Marxism and sociology

Marxists argue that capitalist societies are organized around social classes defined in terms of their unequal rights and powers over the means of production and over the products of economic production. Class relations are understood as relations of *exploitation*, meaning that the surplus created by the producing classes is appropriated by the owning classes. Capitalism is understood as an intrinsically volatile and unstable system. Investment decisions are oriented toward maximizing profits rather than human needs and established ways of life. Aggregate profit rates periodically plummet, leading to massive disinvestment, unemployment, the "creative destruction" of old infrastructure and productive spaces, and new forms of socioeconomic regulation that promise to undergird a new cycle of capital accumulation. Capitalism is restlessly expansionist, constantly seeking to incorporate and encompass new land and property and to shape practices that previously lay outside of it. At the same time capitalist history is characterized by repeated moments of *decommodification*, wherein entire practices, populations, or geographic regions are released into a non-capitalist state of being. Some argue that European colonial rulers sought to enhance political control and depress the cost of labor power by combining non-capitalist zones of "indirect rule" with directly ruled areas that were fully integrated into markets. Urban populations that were central to mid-twentieth-century Fordist production have become ever more distant from the central zones of capitalist vitality in many parts of the USA and Europe, frequently shunted off into a huge *prison-industrial complex* (Wacquant 2009).

Marxist theory has been challenged in various ways. Gender, ethnicity, race, and nationality have been shown to be as important as social class in accounting for people's self-understanding and social practices. Proletarian workers, seen by Marx as the bearers of progressive change, have often supported far-right parties and movements. The first anti-capitalist revolutions occurred not in the most developed parts of the capitalist world, as expected by Marx, but in semi-feudal Russia. The USSR and other socialist countries became politically repressive and economically stagnant.

Marxists have proposed various *neo-Marxist* alternatives in response to these problems. Some of them retain Marxism's insistence on the causal primacy of social class or the dynamics of capitalist accumulation and the value form. Others reframe the Marxist theory of capitalism at the global scale. Theorists of "dual systems" and "intersectionality" give equal weight to gender and/or race and ethnicity alongside class as axes of domination and exploitation. Adorno's (1990 [1966]: 10) "negative dialectics" moved beyond traditional Marxist assumptions of teleological progress. Althusser (1990 [1965]) acknowledged a plurality of semi-autonomous forms of practice and argued that significant social events resulted from contingent, unpredictable conjunctures rather than the regular unfolding of a single process. *Critical realist* philosophers urged Marxists and positivists to accept the existence of a "rainforestlike profusion" (Collier 2005) of social structures and practices that interact in unexpected ways to produce the flow of social events. Neo-Marxists acknowledged that the state and culture were semi-autonomous forces in their own right rather than simple epiphenomena of more fundamental capitalist structures. Bourdieu (1993), who sometimes described his sociology as a "generalized Marxism," argued that cultural practices could "invert" the economic world. Neo-Marxist theorists of imperialism describe international politics as driven also by irreducibly political geostrategic dynamics alongside capitalist profit seeking. The policies of modern states sometimes run directly against capitalist interests. In other cases state policies correspond to the needs of capitalist accumulation for reasons other than those described by Marxist theory. Neo-Marxist *regulation theory* (Boyer 1990) explores the stabilizing frameworks such as "Fordism" that are sometimes elaborated in response to capitalist crisis, but insists that longer-term crises of profitability and persistent "muddling through" are also possible since there is no omniscient agent or structural mechanism guaranteeing a solution. Capitalism is still seen as having powerful effects on the rest of society but Marxism is now construed as a *regional theory* of capitalism that no longer claims to explain the entirety of social life.

SEE ALSO: Capitalism; Commodities, Commodity Fetishism, and Commodification; Critical Theory/Frankfurt School; Dependency and World-Systems Theories; Marx, Karl; Neo-Marxism

REFERENCES

Adorno, T. W. (1990) [1966] *Negative Dialectics*. Continuum, New York.

Althusser, L. (1990) [1965] Contradiction and overdetermination. In: *For Marx*. Allen Lane, London, pp. 87–128.

Bourdieu, P. (1993) The field of cultural production, or: the economic world reversed. In: Johnson, R. (ed.),

The Field of Cultural Production. Polity Press, London, pp. 29–73.
Boyer, R. (1990) *The Regulation School: A Critical Introduction*. Columbia University Press, New York.
Collier, A. (2005) Critical realism. In: Steinmetz, G. (ed.), *The Politics of Method in the Human Sciences: Positivism and its Epistemological Others*. Duke University Press, Durham, NC, pp. 327–45.
Wacquant, L. (2009). *Punishing the Poor: The Neoliberal Government of Social Insecurity*. Duke University Press, Durham, NC.

GEORGE STEINMETZ

mass culture and mass society

Controversy and debate with respect to mass culture initially flourished between 1935 and 1955. Recognition of the mass media as a significant cultural force in democratic societies coincided with the development of totalitarian forms of control under Hitler and Stalin. The perceived affinities between these developments prompted concern about how best to defend the institutions of civil society, culture in general, and high culture in particular. For critical theorists such as Theodor Adorno, mass culture served interests that derived from the owners of capital, and expressed the exploitative expansion of modes of rationality that had hitherto been associated with industrial organization. This critical group's understanding of the attributes of a high modernist culture was that it was autonomous; experimental; adversarial; highly reflexive with respect to the media through which it is produced; and the product of individual genius. By contrast mass culture was seen as thoroughly commodified; employed conventional and formulaic aesthetic codes; was culturally and ideologically conformist; collectively produced but centrally controlled in accordance with the economic imperatives, organizational routines, and technological requirements of its media of transmission.

As against this contrast between mass culture and that of high modern*ism*, mass society theorists such as William Kornhauser and Arnold Rose interpreted mass culture as a social consequence of modern*ity*. Social relationships were interpreted as having been transformed by the growth of, and movement into, cities, by developments in both the means and the speed of transportation, the mechanization of production processes, the expansion of democracy, the rise of bureaucratic forms of organization, and the emergence of the mass media. It was argued that as a consequence of such changes, there is a waning of the primordial ties of primary group membership, kinship, community and locality. Conduct is neither sanctified by tradition nor the product of inner conviction, but rather is shaped by the mass media and contemporary social fashion.

SEE ALSO: Consumption, Mass Consumption, and Consumer Culture

SUGGESTED READINGS

Giner, S. (1976) *Mass Society*. Martin Robertson, London.
Huyssen, A. (1986) *After the Great Divide*. Macmillan, London.
Rosenberg, B. & White, D. M. (eds.) (1971) *Mass Culture Revisited*. Van Nostrand, London.

NICK PERRY

mass media and socialization

Socialization is a life-long process through which people learn the patterns of their culture, including behavioral expectations, values and "truths." Increasingly ubiquitous and ever divergent, the mass media is a major agent of socialization that shapes the way we see ourselves and the world around us.

Sociologists have studied and postulated media impacts for much of the last century. Early researchers theorized that the mass media destroys the individual's capacity to act autonomously. However, subsequent scholars posited a more complex interaction between the mass media and society. Elevating the role of human agency in the socialization process, this later work contended that individuals actively evaluate and interpret mass media narratives. Theories about media influence have evolved from those which emphasized direct and immediate influence (a "hypodermic needle" model) and those which suggested relatively little influence (a "minimal effects" model) through those that maintained a select influence (an "agenda setting" model) and long-term effects (a "cultivation" model). Recognizing the dynamic tension between human agency and social structure most contemporary media scholars address both the media as a process and also the relationships among the myriad elements of this process.

Certainly the mass media are vital sites of cultural and economic brokerage. Never fully shut out, mass media narratives serve as conduits through which society re-presents itself and ways by which social and personal identities are articulated and disseminated.

SEE ALSO: Socialization, Agents of; Hegemony and the Media

SUGGESTED READINGS
Fiske, J. (1994) *Media Matters*. University of Minnesota Press, Minneapolis, MN.
Potter, W. J. (2008) *Media Literacy*, 4th edn. Sage, Thousand Oaks, CA.

STEPHEN L. MUZZATTI

master status

The term master status denotes a perceived social standing that has exceptional significance for individual identity, frequently shaping a person's entire social experience. The concept is at least implied within the theoretical framework of structural functionalism, especially the work of Talcott Parsons who was predisposed toward using the expression in a normative sense. Here, master status is attached to the prestige relating to the individual's primary social role. However, in the disciplines of sociology and social psychology, master status is a concept used more specifically in the field of deviance.

The principal development of the notion of a master status is usually attributed to the theories of Howard Becker, especially through his work *Outsiders* (1963). For Becker, a master status usually implies a negative connotation. It is related to the potential effects upon an individual of being openly labeled as deviant. In Becker's analysis a deviant act only becomes deviant when social actors perceive and define it as such. It follows that deviants are those who are labeled as a result of these sociopsychological processes. A label is not neutral since it contains an evaluation of the person to whom it is attached. A major consequence of labeling is the formation of a master status surpassing and indeed contaminating all other statuses possessed by an individual. Other social actors subsequently appraise and respond to the labeled person in terms of the perceived attributes of the master status, thus assuming that he or she has the negative characteristics normally associated with such labels. Since individuals' self-concepts are largely derived from the response of others, they are inclined to see themselves in terms of the label, perhaps engendering a self-fulfilling prophecy whereby the deviant's identification with his or her master status becomes the controlling one.

The concept of master status has been further used in the area of deviance, including Jock Young's (1971) survey of the implications of labeling "hippie" marijuana users. However, it is probably in the seminal work of Erving Goffman where the concept has been used most effectively. The consequences of being labeled with a master status are analyzed by Goffman in terms of the effects of stigma upon self-conceptions. He focused, in particular, on the often vain struggle of the stigmatized to maintain self-respect and reputable public image by various coping strategies. This is taken further in his volume *Asylums* (1968), which explores the role of total institutions in the application of a stigmatized master status.

SEE ALSO: Goffman, Erving; Identity: Social Psychological Aspects; Labeling Theory; Stigma

REFERENCES
Becker, H. (1963) *Outsiders: Studies in the Sociology of Deviance*. Free Press, New York.
Goffman, E. (1968) *Stigma: Notes on the Management of Spoiled Identity*. Prentice Hall, Englewood Cliffs, NJ.
Young, J. (1971) The role of the police as amplifiers of deviancy, negotiators of reality, and the translators of fantasy. In: Cohen, S. (ed.), *Images of Deviance*. Harmondsworth, Penguin, pp. 27–61.

STEPHEN HUNT

material culture

The phrase "material culture" refers to the physical stuff that human beings surround themselves with and which has meaning for the members of a cultural group. Mostly this "stuff" is things that are made within a society but sometimes it is gathered directly from the natural world or recovered from past or distant cultures. It can be contrasted with other cultural forms such as ideas, images, practices, beliefs, and language that can be treated as independent from any specific material substance. The clothes, tools, utensils, gadgets, ornaments, pictures, furniture, buildings, and equipment of a group of people are its material culture and for disciplines such as archaeology and anthropology provide the raw data for understanding other societies. In recent years sociologists have begun to recognize that the ways that material things are incorporated into the culture shape the way that society works and communicate many of its features to individual members.

Jean Baudrillard's (1996) critique of Marx's analysis of production and exchange led him to explore how the "system of objects" circulates sign value within a society articulating cultural distinctions and meanings. The uses of different materials such as wood or glass to create the atmosphere of interior spaces, the embedding of technology within "gadgets" and tools, how things extend the form and actions of the human body, and the relations between objects that are unique and those that are parts of series, are all systems which shape the culture. The recent literature on the sociology of consumption has frequently recognized that material things are not only useful in themselves but can be signs of social status and cultural location. A motor car is much more than a functional transportation device because it encapsulates a set of cultural messages about the aesthetics, wealth and technological values of a culture as well as the status of the individual who drives it.

The consumption of material stuff may locate individual identities within a culture, but it also threatens the environment and uses up scarce resources. However as research by Christian Heath (2003) and his colleagues has shown, those material objects involved in the interactions between human beings provide a topic as well as a resource for constructing meaning. Developing research in a different direction, Elizabeth Shove (2003) argues that the material stuff of a culture "co-evolves" not only with other stuff but also with human practices and systems of action. And the emergence of new types of objects late in the twentieth century – such as computers, mobile phones, digital cameras and MP3 players – have expanded the possibilities for mediation while at the same time shifting the focus of material culture to blur even further what Robert Dourish (2004) identifies as the boundaries between the social and the technical and between meaning and function. But the embodied "material interaction" directly between individual humans and the stuff around them continues to depend on a socially acquired repertoire of gestures and practices to release the cultural meanings embedded in the materiality of stuff.

SEE ALSO: Materialism; Sociology of Consumption

REFERENCES

Baudrillard, J. (1996) *The System of Objects*. Verso, London.

Dourish, P. (2004) *Where the Action Is: The Foundation of Embodied Interaction*. MIT Press, Cambridge, MA.

Heath, H. J. & Heath, C. (2003) Transcending the object in embodied interaction. In: J. Coupland, J. & Gwyn, R. (eds.), *Discourse, the Body and Identity*. Palgrave, Basingstoke.

Shove, E. (2003) *Comfort, Cleanliness and Convenience*. Berg, Oxford.

TIM DANT

materialism

Materialism is the philosophy that explains the nature of reality and the world – physical, social, cultural, etc. – in terms of matter. It asserts that reality and the universe are first and foremost material; they exist outside of human thought and ideas and are independent of the human mind. The human intellect can come to know the world of matter through experience and sense perception and can interact and shape the material world; but the world of material existence is primary. Philosophical materialism stands in opposition to the philosophy of idealism that states that ideas, thought, and mind are the essential nature of all reality and the world of matter is a reflection of mind, thought, and ideas.

Materialism, the philosophical outlook of science, has been an important philosophy in eras of scientific development in ancient times as early as the fourth century BCE among Greek philosophers, and in modern times in the seventeenth and eighteenth centuries in Newton's scientific study of nature and the emerging social science of the Enlightenment *Philosophes*.

The centrality of materialism in shaping modern social theory emerged in the 1700s and 1800s. Several important streams of social thought informed by the materialist worldview and the scientific method developed, namely the mechanical materialism of Feuerbach, and the dialectical and historical materialism (i.e., historical materialism) of Marx and Engels. The empiricism and positivism of Saint-Simon, Comte, and Durkheim presented itself as science based in materialist methodology, but was actually rooted in philosophical idealism.

Mechanical materialism analyzes social life and even idea systems such as religion in terms of material conditions, but is static in its overall worldview and offers no theory of human agency or future beyond what was then emerging (i.e., industrial capitalism). Social theory and research in the mechanical materialist tradition remains an important tendency in sociology, and examines materially based social problems, especially various forms of social inequality and domination.

Historical materialism critically analyzes capitalism and its antecedents. It embodies a dialectical image of the social world and a dialectical method, and views the structures and processes of capitalism as a transient stage of human social development giving way to its negation through contradictions and antagonisms that give rise to socialism and communism. Historical materialism as a revolutionary theory and practice in the twentieth century has been located primarily in political struggles and building socialist states outside the academy.

Throughout history historical materialists have lifted up as their mantra in response to mechanical materialists Marx's famous eleventh thesis on Feuerbach: "The philosophers have only *interpreted* the world, in various ways; the point however is to *change* it" (Marx & Engels 1986: 30).

SEE ALSO: Marx, Karl; Marxism and Sociology

REFERENCE

Marx, K. & Engels, F. (1986) *Selected Works*. International Publishers, New York.

SUGGESTED READINGS

Hennessy, R. & Ingraham, C. (eds.) (1997) *Materialist Feminism: A Reader in Class*. Routledge, New York.
Oppenheimer, M., Murray, M., & Levine, R. (eds.) (1991) *Radical Sociologists and the Movement: Experiences, Lessons, and Legacies*. Temple University Press, Philadelphia.

WALDA KATZ-FISHMAN, RALPH GOMES, AND JEROME SCOTT

mathematical sociology

Many sociological theories are strong in substantive content but do not employ any formal language that would enable the deduction of testable predictions about the phenomena of interest. Aiming to improve this situation, since the middle of the twentieth century some sociologists have engaged in the construction of mathematical models, stating sociological assumptions in mathematical terms so that derived consequences can be empirically tested by comparison with appropriate empirical data. Such mathematical models can deal with social structures and/or social processes. For instance, a social network can be represented as a matrix in which rows and columns refer to social units and the entries pertain to the social relationship of each pair. Theoretical interest in social structure in this sense has led to the extensive use of mathematical methods with new work regularly published in the journal *Social Networks*. Various social processes, such as social influence and social mobility, have been treated in terms of the construction of mathematical models. Various fields of mathematics have proved useful, such as differential and difference equations, abstract algebra, probability theory and stochastic processes, and linear algebra. Examples may be found in the *Journal of Mathematical Sociology*, published since 1971. Where the analytical method tends to break down because of complexity, especially nonlinearity, more and more analysts have turned to computer simulation with the objective of deriving complex outcomes of processes described in terms of simple rules of interaction among agents. Fundamental problems relating to social emergence, social cooperation and social order are being studied with such computational models. Some of this work involves applications of concepts from game theory. See the special issue of the *American Journal of Sociology* (110 (4) 2005).

SEE ALSO: Game Theory; Social Network Analysis; Theory and Methods

SUGGESTED READINGS

Edling, C. R. (2002) Mathematics in sociology. *Annual Review of Sociology* 28: 197–220.
Fararo, T. J. (1973) *Mathematical Sociology*. Wiley, New York.
Wasserman, S. & Faust, K. (1994) *Social Network Analysis: Methods and Applications*. Cambridge University Press, New York.

THOMAS J. FARARO

matriarchy

Early ideas concerning what Linnaeus called *Homo sapiens* were biased in favor of "men's history." One aspect of matriarchy is the notion that some societies have been politically dominated by women. Bachhofen, a Swiss, argued that the earliest stage of human culture was characterized by general promiscuity. When people became aware of maternity, matriarchy started and the core of family life was the link between a mother and her children. The theory of matriarchical civilization, first articulated by Bachhofen in 1861 (1992), was once very popular and indirectly influenced Morgan, Engels, and others. He overgeneralized, based on limited data. Some writers took up the theme in the 1970s. Some argue that matriarchy not only preceded patriarchy but was superior to it. Many feminists still use the term patriarchy to describe all forms of male dominance. The idea of patriarchy succeeding matriarchy is largely discredited. Max Weber (1968 [1920]: 231–6) discusses "primary patriarchalism" as an elementary form of traditional "legitimate authority" (*Herrschaft*). "Gerontocracy and patriarchalism," he states, "are frequently found side by side." Obedience is owed to the individual male leader. The extension of patriarchal authority, according to Weber, leads to patrimonialism (e.g., sultanism).

SEE ALSO: Feminism; Kinship; Lesbianism; Myth; Patriarchy

REFERENCES

Bachhofen, J. J. (1992) *Myth, Religion, and Mother Right: Selected Writings*. Princeton University Press, Princeton, NJ.

Weber, M. (1968) [1920] *Economy and Society: An Outline of Interpretive Sociology*, ed. G. Roth & C. Wittich. University of California Press, Berkeley, CA.

J. I. (HANS) BAKKER

matrix of domination

The term matrix of domination is associated with the feminist thought of Patricia Hill Collins, who came to prominence in the academic movement that arose from women's activism in the 1960s and 1970s. Her project locates lived experiences of oppression within the social contexts that produce those experiences. Collins' term refers to the particular configurations of oppression and resistance (along varied lines of socially constructed difference) that shape life in specific communities and historical moments.

In an influential article, "Learning from the outsider within" (1986), and then a book titled *Black Feminist Thought* (1991; rev. 2000), Collins drew from diverse texts produced by black women to bring forward a body of subjugated knowledge. She emphasized the distinctiveness of black feminist thought in relation to undifferentiated feminist and race-based analyses, and she became a leader in the academic movement that began to challenge unitary gender or race analyses that did not account for the cross-cutting dynamics of these systems of oppression. Collins argued that these structures of inequality intersect, in any specific historical and community context, in a matrix of domination that produces distinctive experiences of oppression and resistance. That idea has been taken up and extended, by Collins and others, under the rubrics of "intersectionality" (Collins 1998) and "race, class, and gender" (a phrase sometimes used as a shorthand meant to include other dimensions of difference related to sexuality, ability, etc.).

Collins (2000) locates a standpoint associated with the lived experiences and community lives of African American women. Exploring the "standpoint" of this subjugated group allows her to sketch out their knowledge: a community-based "wisdom" that includes, for example, practices of resistance to dominant body ideals, and of "other mothering" or community care for African American children. While the first edition of the book emphasizes race, class, and gender, Collins's (2000) revision incorporates into her conceptualization of the matrix the dimensions of sexual orientation and nation, drawing from emergent social justice movements and scholarship focused on sexuality, citizenship, and transnationalism (see Collins 2004).

SEE ALSO: Black Feminist Thought; Consciousness Raising; Feminist Standpoint Theory

REFERENCES

Collins, P. H. (1986) Learning from the outsider within: the sociological significance of black feminist thought. *Social Problems* 33: S14–32.

Collins, P. H. (1998) *Fighting Words: Black Women and the Search for Justice*. University of Minnesota Press, Minneapolis, MN.

Collins, P. H. (2000) [1991] *Black Feminist Thought: Knowledge, Consciousness, and the Politics of Empowerment*. Routledge, New York.

Collins, P. H. (2004) *Black Sexual Politics: African Americans, Gender, and the New Racism*. Routledge, New York.

MARJORIE L. DE VAULT

Matthew effect

The *Matthew effect*, an expression coined by Merton in overt reference to St. Matthew's gospel, has become a milestone when referring to the cases of credit misallocation among scientists. The social mechanism that leads to this misallocation operates through the accruing of large increments of peer recognition to scientists of considerable repute for their past contributions, at the expense of less-known scientists of comparable performance. Indeed, having learned the value of attending to the work of certain scientists in the past, and faced with a literature of unmanageable proportions, scientists tend to notice the work of well-known scientists, take it more seriously, and ultimately use it more frequently. Thus, credit is conferred by the community on the basis of a scientist location within a highly stratified *social system* of science.

If *cumulative advantage* shapes the distribution of rewards in science and leads to increasing disparities among scientists over the course of their careers, the Matthew effect refers to a special case in which cumulative advantage gets reinforced as a result of a complex pattern of credit misallocation for scientific performance. The effect, therefore, enlarges differences in reputation and rewards over and above those merely attributable to differences in quality of scientific performance and to processes of accumulation of advantage. Because the social mechanism at work is based on personal attributes of individuals rather than on assessment of their role performance, the Matthew effect introduces its own variety of *particularism* into the social system of science.

Being an outcome of peer reviewing and communication processes in science, the effect was initially elaborated by looking at it in documented historical cases of multiple discovery and co-authorship. Further empirical and theoretical investigations have proposed that the effect takes place also over the entire communication system of science, as a generalized principle at work in society at large, and generating gender inequities.

SEE ALSO: Functionalism/Neo-Functionalism; Intellectual Property

SUGGESTED READING

Merton, R. K. (1968) The Matthew effect in science. *Science* 159: 56–63.

YURI JACK GÓMEZ MORALES

McDonaldization

McDonaldization is the process by which the principles of the fast-food restaurant are coming to dominate more and more spheres of US society and the world. Coined by George Ritzer, the term invokes the famous fast-food chain as a metaphor for a widespread change in the delivery of goods and services toward more instrumentally efficient means of distribution.

Ritzer derives five principles of McDonaldization from Weber's writings on rationalization. These are efficiency, calculability, predictability, control through the substitution of non-human for human technology, and the irrationality of rationality. Efficiency refers to the optimal means for achieving a given end. Efficiency is often achieved by the functional differentiation of tasks and the development of discrete routines that are engineered to save time and labor. Calculability places an emphasis on the quantifiable aspects of a product or process such as units sold, speed, size, or cost. Predictability means that the settings, procedure, and product of a McDonaldized system are consistent from one time or place to another. Control may be exercised through the substitution of non-human for human technology. Automation is also used to prompt workers to perform their specified routines, typically using a system of timers and blinking lights. The enlistment of customers as active participants contributes to the overall efficiency of the operation. The irrationality of rationality refers to the negative consequences of McDonaldized systems. McDonaldization has adverse effects on the environment because of the amount of disposable material it generates. It has had a negative effect on public health as the emphasis on quantity over quality has been identified as a contributor to an increase in obesity among Americans.

McDonaldized systems alienate consumers by submitting them to the dehumanizing controls of a rationalized environment. Operators are at pains to make their rational system more attractive settings for consumers by using themes and spectacles, but they remain a systematic threat to genuine human sociality and diminish the possibility of deriving meaning from consumer activities.

Ritzer worries that the success of McDonaldization has contributed to the decline of local and regional forms of consumer culture by subjecting less efficient forms of production and service delivery to intensive competition. The principles of McDonaldization have diffused primarily in two ways: first, through the competitive expansion of the franchise (now 30,000 outlets worldwide); second, by the emulative actions of competitors. Simplified products, low labor costs, and no-frills service are elements of a dominant paradigm that has spread to many sectors of the economy. Others have described the McDonaldization of non-commercial institutions, including higher education, the church, and the justice system.

The theory of McDonaldization has been subject to a variety of critiques. Critics have asked whether customers are truly alienated by McDonaldization. The moral objection of groups such as vegetarians has been cited as evidence of resistance to McDonaldization. Critics also question the scope of McDonaldization suggesting that it is an issue only for a relatively wealthy fraction of the world's population. Finally, counter-examples point to the limits of McDonaldization: for example, the diversity found in art markets suggests that streamlining is not incommensurate with creative and personal products.

SEE ALSO: Consumption; Disneyization; Globalization; Grobalization; Rationalization

SUGGESTED READINGS

Ritzer, G. (1998) *The McDonaldization Thesis.* Sage, London.

Ritzer, G. (ed.) (2006) *McDonaldization: The Reader.* Pine Forge Press, Thousand Oaks, CA.

Ritzer, G. (2007) *The McDonaldization of Society 5.* Pine Forge Press, Thousand Oaks, CA.

Ritzer, G. (2005) *Enchanting a Disenchanted World: Revolutionizing the Means of Consumption*, 2nd edn. Pine Forge Press, Thousand Oaks, CA.

Smart, B. (ed.) (1999) *Resisting McDonaldization.* Sage, London.

TODD STILLMAN

McLuhan, Marshall (1911–80)

Herbert Marshall McLuhan was born in Edmonton and passed away in Toronto on the cusp of the 1980s. He took his doctorate in English literature at Cambridge. McLuhan taught at the University of Toronto from 1946 until his death. McLuhan's name is associated with the imagined "Toronto School" of communications that includes Harold Innis and Eric Havelock.

McLuhan came to prominence with his book on popular American culture, *The Mechanical Bride* (1951). While this placed McLuhan in the global company of scholars as diverse as Roland Barthes, Richard Hoggart, and Reuel Denny all of whom worked in a nascent cultural studies, McLuhan felt that his early work was unduly critical and moralizing.

The tri-phasal civilizational change outlined in *The Gutenberg Galaxy* (1962) confirmed the label of technological determinist that has stuck. Massive historical swathes distinguish the passage from a multisensory, predominantly oral, universe which gave way with the invention of movable type to typographic culture marked by linearity, visuality and specialization; this phase is surpassed by the new tribalism of television and electric, ultimately electronic, communications in a new global village of simultaneity, non-linearity, and integrated cosmic consciousness.

McLuhan's *Understanding Media* (1964) is a key cultural text of the twentieth century that contains his most famous conceptual distinctions: hot and cool media (radio versus television); explosion and implosion (fragmented versus integrating); and "the medium is the message," a formalist statement that rejects content and the social scicnce research paradigm, and instead studies the social effects of media technologies the content of which is a previous medium. It is also a mystical book in which the human sensorium is outered into the wired world and worn as a universal skin in a collective harmony realized in the passage of pure informatic flows. This endeared McLuhan to cybercultural theorists and played a key role in his 1990s resurrection.

SEE ALSO: Cyberculture; Globalization; Media

SUGGESTED READING

Genosko, G. (2005) *Marshall McLuhan: Critical Evaluations in Cultural Theory*, vols. 1, 2, & 3. Routledge, London.

GARY GENOSKO

Mead, George Herbert (1863–1931)

Despite being a professor of philosophy, sociologists have come to appreciate George H. Mead's ideas far more than philosophers have. Today, he is recognized not only as one of the most important early sociological figures in the USA, but also in the entire world. Mead analyzes three ideas of significance to sociologists: (1) the social act, (2) the self, and (3) society. The starting point for understanding Mead's sociological views is not the self, as many sociologists have long mistakenly thought, but the social act. Without engaging in social acts, people could never have developed selves, and without selves, societies as we know them could have never arisen.

Mead defines a social act as any activity that requires at least one other person to complete. According to him, social acts are comprised of five basic components: (1) roles, (2) attitudes, (3) significant speech, (4) attitudinal assumption, and (5) social objects. For Mead, roles are the basic building blocks from which all social acts are assembled. More specifically, they are the individual acts that each participant must carry out to insure a social act's completion. Roles operate hand in hand with attitudes. Mead defines attitudes as the preparation or readiness to perform our specific roles within a larger unfolding social act. Because attitudes originate from vague bodily impulses, they unite our corporal and social existences. Mead uses his term "significant speech" as a synonym for language. It refers to our use of vocal or written gestures that have a similar meaning to us as they have to the other participants in a social act. For Mead, attitudinal assumption, which significant speech makes possible, refers to our assuming the attitudes of others so that we can anticipate the roles that they will perform in the social acts in which we are participants. Finally, according to Mead, a "social object" is the common attitude that participants assume toward the construction of a prospective social act. Thus, when participants form a social object of a social act, they simultaneously form what Mead called a "common plan of action" for its subsequent execution.

Mead speaks of the self, which for him inserts itself inside the social act, in two alternative ways. The most poetic way in which he speaks of it is as a conversation between an "I" and a "me." The "I" represents the impulse that excites our attitudes or preparation to perform our roles in a social act, as well as the later expression of that attitude in the actual performance of our role. Conversely, the "me" represents the attitudes of the other participants or society at large that we assume during the performance of our particular role in a social act. The "me" affects the expression of our "I" and thereby how we perform our roles in a social act, but not always in the same way. It can outright endorse, veto, or make major or minor alterations in our "I's" expression. On rare occasions, the "I" can simply ignore the "me" altogether.

Mead also speaks of the self more mundanely as an attitudinal assumption process. People assume each others' attitudes by telling each other what they plan to do and how and when they plan to do it. To have a self, he argues, we must not only assume the attitudes of the other participants in a social act. Our assumption of their attitudes must also affect our attitude and, thereby, how we actually perform our role in the social act. Whether viewed as a conversation between "I" and "me," or as an "attitudinal assumption" process, Mead views the key ingredient of the self as "reflexivity" – the ability to adjust your attitude toward the performance of your role in a social act on the basis of your assumption of the other participants' attitudes toward the performance of their roles in it. Thus, for Mead, reflexivity and, in turn, selfhood, require more than our merely being conscious or aware of others' attitudes; it also requires that this awareness change, however slightly, our attitudes toward our roles and, thereby, the subsequent performance of them in a social act.

According to Mead, the self not only inserts itself into the social act but, by its insertion, it makes society possible. He views society as a community organized on the basis of institutions and an institution as only a special form of social action. Institutionalized social acts are launched to satisfy recurrent socio-physiological impulses, such as communication, sex, parenting, bartering, etc. The recurrent impulses that launch institutional social acts stir in us attitudes to perform complementary roles in these acts, such as speaker and hearer, mother and father, and seller and buyer.

Mead believes that during institutionalized social acts, we always draw on common maxims to help us form a common social object of the unfolding social act and, in turn, construct a congruent plan of action for carrying out our particular roles in it. However, we cannot do this without assuming the attitude of our society which, in turn, requires that we must have selves. Institutionalized social acts are necessarily repetitive. Although our successful execution of a plan of action for the completion of an institutional social act satisfies the socio-physiological impulse that launched it, we will later need to satisfy this same impulse over and over again in future institutional social acts. Finally, for Mead, our social institutions are not immutable. Once made, they can be reinvented through individual ingenuity. The "I" can sometimes jump over the "me." We can invent new maxims to form novel social objects of our social acts and new congruent plans of action for their execution.

Without institutions, Mead believes that we would still be living in a disorganized mass. Mead explicitly identified only six basic societal institutions: (1) language, (2) family, (3) economy, (4) religion, (5) polity, and (6) science. Although he believes that all six of these institutions are of great importance not only to the development of human society, but also for its on-going operation, he believes that language is the single most important one. Because language makes it possible for human beings to assume the attitude of their society and, in turn, its common maxims of action, it is a requirement for the creation and subsequent operation of all the other institutions in society.

SEE ALSO: Attitudes and Behavior; Language; Self; Social Psychology

SUGGESTED READINGS

Mead, G. (1934) Mind. In: *Self and Society*, ed. C. Morris. University of Chicago Press, Chicago, IL.

Mead, G. (1964) *Mead: Selected Writings*, ed. A. Reck. Bobbs-Merrill, Indianapolis, IN.

LONNIE ATHENS

measures of centrality

Measures of centrality (or central tendency) are statistical indices of the "typical" or "average" score. They constitute one of three key characteristics of a set of scores: center, shape, and spread. There are three common measures of centrality: mode, median, and mean. Their applicability to a set of scores depends on the scale of measurement of the scores, as explained below.

The simplest index of centrality is the mode, or most frequently occurring score. Since the mode is found by counting the number of occurrences of each score, it can used for the categorical data of nominal scales, the lowest level of measurement, for which it is the only applicable index (Stevens 1946). Nominal measurement sorts things into different categories, such as Republican, Democrat, or Libertarian. If more voters were registered as Republicans than any other party, then Republican would be the modal party, even if Republicans did not constitute a majority of voters.

The median is the score that occurs in the middle of the set of scores when they are ranked from smallest to largest. It is the score at the fiftieth percentile, for which half of the scores are smaller and half larger. Identification of the median requires at least ordinal data (i.e., data that can be ranked).

The most statistically sophisticated measure of centrality is the mean: the sum of the scores divided by the number of scores. Calculation of a mean is appropriate only for interval or ratio scales (e.g., Fahrenheit vs. Kelvin temperatures, respectively), the common feature of which is that the differences between scores (e.g., $38° - 33° = 76° - 71°$) are meaningful and consistent for all scores. The mean is used to calculate the variance and standard deviation. These measures of variability, along with the mean, are the key ingredients of statistical analyses such as analysis of variance, correlation and regression, hierarchical linear modeling, and structural equation modeling.

For interval and ratio data, the shape of the distribution of scores influences relationships among the three measures of centrality. For some distributions, such as the bell curve (i.e., normal distribution), the mean, median, and mode all have the same value. However, for skewed distributions, their values differ. For example, in positively skewed distributions, where the scores pile up at the lower end of the scale and tail off to the upper end, the mean will have the highest value, followed by the median and mode, respectively. In negatively skewed distributions, the order is reversed. Thus, for example, if most household incomes in a community were under $30,000 but a few were $100,000 or higher, the mean income would be highest, and the mode would be lowest.

Outliers, or scores that fall well outside the range of the rest of the distribution, also differentially affect measures of centrality. Since the mean is the only measure of centrality that reflects the exact value of every score, it is the only one affected by outliers. For example, it would not affect the modal or median income in the community described above if the highest income was $300,000 or $300,000,000, but it would affect the mean. The impact of outliers on the mean is greatest when the number of scores in the distribution (e.g., households in the community) is small.

Thus, despite its utility in statistical analyses, the mean can be a misleading indicator of central tendency. For this reason, the median typically is used to depict the "average" score in skewed distributions such as personal income and cost of houses. In addition, outliers sometimes are excluded to avoid distortion of the mean (as well as standard deviation and variance) for higher level statistical analyses. When this is done, the researcher should report that fact, providing information about the number of outliers discarded and the rationale and rules for exclusion, so that readers can evaluate whether eliminating outliers biased the analyses in favor of confirming the researchers' hypotheses.

SEE ALSO: Bell Curve; Outliers; Statistical Significance Testing; Validity, Quantitative; Variance

REFERENCE

Stevens, S. S. (1946) On the theory of levels of measurement. *Science* 103: 677–80.

SUGGESTED READINGS

Glass, G. V. & Hopkins, K. D. (1996) *Statistical Methods in Education and Psychology*, 3rd edn. Allyn & Bacon, Boston, MA.

Shavelson, R. J. (1996). *Statistical Reasoning for the Behavioral Sciences*, 3rd edn. Allyn & Bacon, Boston, MA.

ERNEST GOETZ

media

Discussions of media in a social context are generally concerned with mass media and, more recently, new media. Mass media are defined as communication systems by which centralized providers use industrialized technologies to reach large and geographically scattered audiences, distributing content broadly classified as information and entertainment. Media reaching mass populations emerged in the late nineteenth century – newspapers, magazines, the film industry – and expanded to include radio from the 1920s and television broadcasting from the 1950s. A range of "new media" developed from the 1980s, including video, cable and pay TV, CD-ROMs, mobile/cellular phones, and the Internet. In twenty-first century societies media are pervasive and integral to modern life. Even in less developed societies they are widespread, although disparities in access remain. Economic profitability is also seen as a defining feature of modern media, reflecting the importance of commercial considerations to media institutions.

The newspaper press was the first "mass medium." In the late nineteenth century social and economic change (industrialization, growing urban populations, expanding education and rising literacy, changing patterns of work and leisure), technological developments (telegraph, telephone, printing technologies, the spread of railways), and policy changes such as the abolition of stamp duties that had restricted newspaper circulation, opened the way to development of newspapers attracting a mass readership. Changes in economic organization were crucial: the rise of advertising made it possible to sustain a cheap popular press; and the development of newspaper (and magazine) chains achieved economies of scale.

Film also emerged as a medium of mass entertainment in the late nineteenth century, drawing on inventions and technological developments in the USA, the UK, France, and Germany (the application of electricity, developments in photography and celluloid film, invention of the motion picture camera, new projection techniques). Initially an urban, working-class entertainment, in the early twentieth century film became "respectable," appealing to middle-class audiences as film's potential to tell stories was exploited, permanent movie theaters were built, and more efficient distribution methods introduced.

Radio developed as a mass medium in the 1920s. The US Navy was an early user of wireless telegraphy; technological developments contributed to the development of radio broadcasting, as did the pioneering work of individuals (Gugliemo Marconi from Italy, Lee De Forest in the USA) and enthusiastic experimentation by amateurs with crystal sets. Building on technical developments during World War I, radio rapidly gained popularity in the 1920s, bringing information and entertainment into the home at a time when there was increasing emphasis on the private sphere in industrialized societies, and when other changes such as the spread of electricity made it possible to use radio sets.

Limited television broadcasting began in the 1930s in Germany, the UK, and the USA, but the outbreak of war in 1939 delayed its development, and it was not until the 1950s that television developed as a mass medium. It too drew on various developments (in electricity, telegraphy, photography, motion pictures, radio) and the work of inventors (including John Logie Baird in the UK and the Russian-born Vladimir Zworykin in the USA on scanning devices). Television remains a powerful mass medium, although affected by changing contexts and patterns of ownership – the strength of free market ideologies, deregulation, and the quest for profits by the conglomerates that absorbed the networks. The influence of commercial interests has encouraged a blurring of the distinction between advertising and programs (product placement in entertainment programs is an example) and a proliferation of popular talk and "reality" shows with low production costs.

A range of new media developed from the 1980s. Again, technological innovation was essential, with the expansion of digital technologies allowing the convergence of previously separate media and more sophisticated links between traditional media and new information and communication technologies (ICTs). The expanding range of new media includes video recorders, home videotape players, pay TV delivered by cable and satellite, direct broadcasting by satellite, multimedia computers, CD-ROMs, digital video discs (DVDs), the Internet and World Wide Web, mobile/cellular phones, and various handheld devices (the latest "generation" of these technologies offers not only telephone and messaging services but also commercial and personal video, photographs, and graphical information services). These have revolutionized communication, introduced opportunities for convergence of media content, and expanded audience choice and opportunities for interactivity.

There has been debate about the relationship between media and society, especially since mass media developed in the late nineteenth century. Various theoretical approaches have been employed, drawing on different disciplines and areas of study. Fundamental to media research has been an understanding of human communication, with basic questions about who says what, using which "channel," to whom, with what effect, underpinning different perspectives.

"Mass society" approaches have been influential in media studies. Early critics (T. S. Eliot, F. R. Leavis) deplored the effects of mass media, seeing "packaged" popular culture as inferior; their views reflected "critical anxiety" about the media, apprehension about mass society that grew as media industries developed. The Marxist Frankfurt School (Adorno, Horkheimer, Marcuse) saw the mass media as industries used to control the masses. The media contributed to the survival of capitalism by encouraging the working class to be passive recipients of the dominant ideology, allowing social control and maintenance of capitalist values. Other advocates of an "ideological control" approach (for example, Louis Althusser) saw media or their messages as supporting those in power (conveying a false view of reality, encouraging passivity and acceptance of the status quo). Theorists have pointed to the use of media in totalitarian societies to gain support for the ideology of those in power, and in democratic states to foster powerful consumer cultures. Mass society approaches became less influential in the late twentieth century as the concept of mass society lost ground and media institutions and patterns of ownership changed. Nonetheless, notions of media and the reproduction of ideology, linked to analysis of audience interpretations and reception of media messages, remained influential in late twentieth-century cultural studies. "Effects research" (reflecting sociological and psychological interests) shifted attention from the impact of media on mass society to audiences and their "uses" of, and responses to, mass media.

Contemporary media studies has vast scope, and many examples illustrate interest in the ways media influence or reflect social or individual experiences. Examples include the relationship between media and politics; the relationship between media and military during war and (a related issue) the use of media as propaganda tools; and the impact of media on sport.

SEE ALSO: Hegemony and the Media; Information Technology; Internet; Mass Culture and Mass Society; Media and Globalization; Media Monopoly; Politics and Media; Propaganda

SUGGESTED READINGS

Briggs, A. & Burke, P. (2002) *A Social History of the Media: From Gutenberg to the Internet*. Polity Press, Cambridge.

Craig, G. (2004) *The Media, Politics and Public Life*. Allen & Unwin, Crows Nest.

Curran, J. & Gurevitch, M. (eds.) (2005) *Mass Media and Society*, 4th edn. Arnold, London.

Gorman, L. and McLean, D. (2009) *Media and Society into the 21st Century: A Historical Introduction*, 2nd edn. Wiley-Blackwell, Oxford.

LYN GORMAN

media and globalization

While in everyday language "globalization" usually refers to economic and political integration on a world scale, it also has a crucial cultural dimension in which the media have a central role. Indeed, in sociology and other disciplines that focus on the media, the concept of globalization has had to be adopted so as to take account of a new reality in which global institutions, especially the media, impact upon the structures and processes of the nation-state, including its national culture. In that sense, media globalization is about how most national media systems have become more internationalized, becoming more open to outside influences, both in their content and in their ownership and control. This is a cultural phenomenon, one with implications for our contemporary sense of identity, but it is closely linked also to the economic and political factors driving globalization, notably the deregulation of national markets and the liberalization of trade and investment, which in turn facilitate the inroads of global corporations.

There are some global media corporations, such as Sony, which began as communications hardware industries and then branched into content production, in Sony's case, film and recordings. However, others have been built upon the basis of the media industries themselves. Their rapid growth over the closing decades of the twentieth century was due to the ideological and structural shift toward privatization and economic liberalization of trade and investment which characterized this era, but also to a range of technological developments, particularly the trend to the convergence of media with telecommunications.

The globalization of the media has enabled vast sections of humanity to gain access as never before to the enormous output of information and entertainment which flows around the world. On occasion, they also can become spectators to global media events, ranging from regularly scheduled ones such as the Olympics, to unique and totally unexpected ones like those of September 11, 2001, in the USA. Yet it is important to appreciate that contemporary globalization theorists do not necessarily fear global culture as an irresistible force of homogenization, as their predecessors did.

One of the most influential theorists has been Arjun Appadurai (1990), who identifies a series of "flows" – of people, media, technology, capital, and ideas – which constitute globalization. These flows are "disjunctive," that is, they operate independently of one another, unlike in theories derived from Marx which see cultural phenomena as being conditioned by economic processes. Marxist theories have emphasized what they see as a trend to cultural "homogenization," that is, the similarities in media content found throughout the world, particularly in the form of "Americanization." Appadurai acknowledges this trend but argues that it exists in tension with a countertrend to "heterogenization," which is the hybrid cultural differences that occur when global influences become absorbed and adapted in various local settings. Heterogenization happens now that people are presented by global media with a mélange of cultural and consumption choices that they never had when their cultural imagining was defined by a dominant national culture.

Different media exhibit different patterns of globalization. The Hollywood blockbuster movie would most closely fit the notion in literal terms, being released and exhibited more or less simultaneously in the various national markets of the world, dubbed or subtitled as required. Television, arguably the most widely diffused and most influential of all the popular media, is different. In the 1960s and even the 1970s, the critics of cultural imperialism were alarmed to discover high levels of foreign content, mainly from the USA, on the television screens of the world. However, as television markets have matured and developed the capacity for their own production, they have moved away from this initial dependence. The evidence now indicates that audiences prefer television programming from their own country, and in their own language, when that is available, or if not, from other countries which are culturally and linguistically similar.

SEE ALSO: Globalization; Globalization, Culture and; Grobalization; Hegemony and the Media; Media

REFERENCE

Appadurai, A. (1990) Disjuncture and difference in the global cultural economy. In: Featherstone, M. (ed.), *Global Culture*. Sage, London, pp. 295–310.

SUGGESTED READINGS

Herman, E. & McChesney, R. (1997) *The Global Media: The New Missionaries of Corporate Capitalism*. Cassell, London and Washington, DC.

Sinclair, J. (1999) *Latin American Television: A Global View*. Oxford University Press, Oxford and New York.

JOHN SINCLAIR

mediated interaction

Face-to-face interaction is the canonical form of human social encounter against which mediated interaction is often found wanting. John Thompson (1995) draws a distinction between three forms of interaction in the modern age: face to face interaction, mediated interaction, and mediated quasi-interaction. The first requires co-presence with a shared sense of space and time; the second involves stretching communication between individuals via a technical medium (paper in the case of a letter, or fiber-optic cable in the case of the telephone or the Internet), thereby uncoupling the link between space and time; whilst the third, "quasi" mediated interaction, also involves time-space dislocation but is produced for an indefinite range of potential recipients which applies to forms of mass media like broadcasting.

The categories are helpful, but they are often used to imply a hierarchy. Face to face interaction relies on a full range of symbolic cues, gestures etc., that can be read into the co-present, fully dialogic (two-way) encounter. Mediated interaction (via the telephone or instant messaging) is reciprocal, but there is a limited range of symbolic cues on offer depending upon the technology, whilst the most impoverished form of interaction is "quasi" because encountering a television presenter is essentially monologic and can only *simulate* reciprocity – fueling debates about the linear (and ideological) imperative of mass communication.

However, forms of mediated interaction regularly employ new repertoires of expressive cues such as the use of emoticons in computer mediated messaging, and whilst there is no immediate back-channel to speak to the television presenter, viewers regularly call in, text in and shout back at the television set in interactions which are still "authentic" even if we accept them as "quasi." We should remind ourselves that power is enacted in most forms of communication, and therefore the challenge is to fully understand the *evolving* ways "in which we live amid exploded conversations [and] turns that never quite connect" (Durham Peters 2006: 120) without privileging face to face communication as some nostalgic humanist ideal.

SEE ALSO: Interaction; Media

REFERENCE

Durham Peters, J. (2006) Media as conversation: conversation as media. In: James Thompson, J. (ed.) *The Media and Modernity*. Polity, Cambridge.

HELEN WOOD

mediation

Conventionally the verb "mediate" has the meaning of interposing something as a means for connecting two things. Mediation, for instance, functions in the form of a third person in Christian theology, reconciling humanity with God, or in law, citizens with the state. In philosophy the structure of consciousness mediates the relation between the objects of sense and our perceptions to produce knowledge of things and others. In media studies mediation takes the form of means for transmitting messages between parties: the state and the citizen, and the market and the consumer. In each of these cases the processes of mediation involve the technological, institutional, or symbolic means for connecting things. Discussion on mediation thus tends to focus on the question of the adequacy and authority of these means. In the case of media, this question emerges in the representation and mediation of differences between social categories such as class, race, and gender. Metaphors such as mirror, reflection, window, and frame (McQuail 1994: 64–6) have been employed to explain this mediating function. And issues of media power, consensus, bias, distortion, ideology, hegemony, and agency of the media audience have emerged to critically engage with this mediating function. In each of these, the referential capacities of media texts, and the social power of the media industries and audiences are, in varying degrees, in question. Today the processes of mediation are inseparably linked to technologies of production, distribution, and consumption. Instantaneous networks, high-definition images and digital sound reproduction point to a technocapitalist society that desires pure communication, without noise or interference. The means for communication, however, are firmly entrenched in economic, technical, and political processes, and the question of mediation remains crucial for understanding the social world.

SEE ALSO: Media and Globalization; Mediated Interaction

REFERENCE

McQuail, D. (1994) *Mass Communication Theory: An Introduction*. Sage, London.

BRETT NICHOLLS

medical sociology

Medical sociology is a subdiscipline of sociology that studies the social causes and consequences of health and illness. Major areas of investigation include the social aspects of health and disease, the social behavior of health care workers and the people who utilize their services, the social functions of health organizations and institutions, the social patterns of health services, the relationship of health care delivery systems to other social systems, and health policy. What makes medical sociology important is the significant role social factors play in determining the health of individuals, groups, and the larger society.

In recognition of the broad impact of social factors on health, medical sociology is sometimes referred to as "health sociology" or the "sociology of health." Medical sociologists comprise one of the largest groups of sociologists in the world. They have employment opportunities both within and outside of academia. Medical sociologists work not only in university sociology departments, medical, nursing, and public health schools and various other health-related professional schools, but also in research organizations and government agencies.

Medical sociology is a relatively new sociological specialty. It came of age in the late 1940s and early 1950s in an intellectual climate far different from sociology's traditional specialties. Sociology's early theorists ignored medicine because it was not an institution shaping society. Medical sociology evolved as a specialty in sociology in response to funding agencies and policymakers after World War II who viewed it as an applied field that could produce knowledge useful for medical practice, public health campaigns, and health policy formulation. Ample funding for research to help solve the health problems of society during the post-World War II era stimulated its growth. A related problem in the early development of medical sociology was its potential to become dependent on medicine for its direction and research orientation. However, this did not happen, as medical sociologists adopted an independent course and made the practice of medicine one of its major subjects of inquiry.

A decisive event took place in medical sociology in 1951 that provided a theoretical direction to a formerly applied field. This was the appearance of Parsons' *The Social System*, written to explain a complex structural functionalist model of society that contained Parsons' concept of the sick role. Parsons had become the best-known sociologist in the world and having a theorist of his stature provide the first major theory in medical sociology called attention to the young subdiscipline. The next major area of research was medical education. Howard Becker and his associates published *Boys in White* (1961), a study of medical school socialization, conducted from a symbolic interactionist perspective, that became a sociological classic.

With the introduction of symbolic interaction into a field that had previously been dominated by structural functionalism, medical sociology became a significant arena of debate between two of sociology's major theoretical schools. This debate helped stimulate a virtual flood of publications in medical sociology in the 1960s. For example, Goffman's *Asylums* (1961), a study of life in a mental hospital, presented his concept of "total institutions" that stands as a significant sociological statement about social life in an externally controlled environment. An abundant literature emerged at this time that established the sociology of mental disorder as a major subfield within medical sociology.

Since1970, medical sociology emerged as a mature sociological subdiscipline. This period was marked by the publication of two especially important books, Eliot Friedson's *Professional Dominance* (1970) on the power of the medical profession and Paul Starr's Pulitzer Prize winning *The Social Transformation of American Medicine* (1982) on the decline of that power. Another major work was Bryan Turner's *Body and Society* (1984), which led to the development of the field of study that became the sociology of the body. The 1990s saw medical sociology move closer to its parent discipline of sociology, while sociology moved closer to medical sociology as the field remains one of the largest and most robust sociological specialties. Ultimately, what allows medical sociology to retain its unique character is (1) its utilization and mastery of sociological theory in the study of health and (2) the sociological perspective that accounts for collective causes and outcomes of health problems and issues. No other field is able to bring these skills to health-related research and analysis. As medical sociology continues on its present course, it is likely to emerge as one of sociology's core specialties as the pursuit of health increasingly becomes important in everyday social life.

SEE ALSO: Goffman, Erving; Health and Medicine; Medical Sociology and Genetics; Parsons, Talcott; Sociology in Medicine

SUGGESTED READINGS

Bloom, S. (2002) *The Word as Scalpel: A History of Medical Sociology*. Oxford University Press, New York.

Cockerham, W. (2007) *Social Causes of Health and Disease*. Polity Press, Cambridge.

Cockerham, W. (2010) *Medical Sociology*, 11th edn. Pearson Prentice Hall, Upper Saddle River, NJ.

WILLIAM C. COCKERHAM

medical sociology and genetics

Medical sociology looks at genetics in two ways: its explanations of human behavior, and its impact on the health sector.

Genetic science often assumes a determinate relationship between biology and society. However:

- Reproductive choice is not determined purely by biological fitness, but the availability of partners in an environment that is socially and culturally stratified.
- Genotypes cannot be labeled as "good" or "bad," but only as more or less adaptive in environments that are as much social and cultural as biological.
- Claims of a biological basis for deviance ignore the absence of inherent meaning in behavior, which makes this a matter of social context and cultural definition.

Medical sociologists ask why such naive accounts of human social behavior are taken seriously. Who wants this knowledge? Whose interests does it serve?

"Geneticization" describes the way in which differences between humans are reduced to differences in their genes. It has been associated with "genetic exceptionalism," the idea that genetic information is so radically novel that it requires an entirely new body of social analysis. This claim now looks like an acceptance by medical sociologists of the hyping of genetic research rather than a critical assessment. Many supposedly unique features of genetic medicine reincarnate well-established topics like professional–patient interaction, the nature of disease and its relation to other forms of deviance, the structuring of health services and the choice between public and private systems of funding. However, medical sociology and the sociology of science and technology do converge in new research lines, on the present impact of different imagined futures, on the balance between science, commerce, and regulation in R&D, and on the organization and ethics of trials.

SEE ALSO: Genetic Engineering as a Social Problem; Medical Sociology

SUGGESTED READING

Pilnick, A. (2002) *Genetics and Society: An Introduction*. Open University Press, Buckingham.

ROBERT DINGWALL

medicine, sociology of

Sociology of medicine is the sociological investigation of medicine as a subsystem of the social structure. This label is given to traditional study within medical sociology of the influences social forces have on the sciences, practices, and teachings of medicine, and how these components of medicine, in turn, affect society. Thus, the sociologist of medicine aspires to contribute to the development of basic sociological knowledge using medicine as a social institution worthy of study in itself. The sociologist of medicine is most often positioned outside the medical setting, in contrast to the position of the medical sociologist working in collaboration with medical organizations. The dichotomy of sociology of medicine and sociology in medicine was formalized by Robert Straus in 1957, in an effort to identify the affiliations and activities of medical sociologists in the United States for creation of a communication network among this newly institutionalized professional group. The distinction is, in part, based on the structural position of the scholar, on where the basic professional affiliation of the scholar is held. Sociologists of medicine are likely to hold academic appointments in conventional sociology departments.

Early in the institutionalization process of medical sociology, examination of the methodologies, organization, and structure of the medical institution was an obvious avenue of study, due to medicine's influence of as well as dependence on social forces. Organizational structure, role relationships, value systems, rituals, functions of medicine as a system of behavior, and social components of health and illness have been and still are predominant areas of study for the sociologist of medicine. During the 1950s and 1960s, however, sociology of medicine took a backseat to sociology in medicine. A majority of medical sociologists were involved in the applied side of the new discipline due to increases in research funding and expansion of medical schools, and well over half of the medical sociologists in the United States were positioned within medical or health organizations. Inadequate access to quality resources was a tremendous difficulty faced by sociologists of medicine who were operating from outside medicine. Sociology of medicine recovered substantially during the cold war as sociology in medicine's influence declined dramatically and medical sociologists were pushed back into conventional sociology departments.

The sociologist of medicine uses the basic research methods of sociology to generate insights into the properties and patterns of social relationships and social organization of health and medicine. Potential hazards in this pure pursuit of knowledge have, however, been thoroughly documented. Similar to any sociologist involved in scrutiny of organizational systems, a danger faced by sociologists of medicine is a loss of objectivity through identification with the medical organization. Retention of a sociological perspective to serve the basic interests of the discipline while studying health and medicine has proven difficult. This danger has been combated by the positioning of the sociologist of medicine outside of the medical organization. In a response to this positioning, it is argued that medicine's failure to respond to the sociological critique may be caused in large part by the failure of sociologists of medicine in becoming more actively involved in the social organization and culture of medicine. Thus, maintaining allegiance to the objective pursuit of knowledge for the sake of sociology has often restricted the voice of sociologists of medicine in potential influences of the medical system. This restriction, however, is experiencing change.

From the 1990s forward, sociologists of medicine have had increasing access to research opportunities, and emphasis in the parent discipline on applied sociological work has led to some convergence of sociology of and sociology in medicine. Sociology of medicine retains its focus on the organizational and professional structures, roles, values, rituals, and functions of medicine as a subsystem of the social structure, and on the social psychology of health and illness. The acceptance and pursuit of applicable studies in conventional sociology departments is increasingly pushing medical sociology to deliver a sociology with medicine rather than the dichotomous sociologies of and in medicine. A sociology with medicine contributes to a sociological understanding of medicine as a reflection of social life in general, as well as the opportunity to influence medical and health systems with applicable knowledge.

SEE ALSO: Medical Sociology; Sociology in Medicine

SUGGESTED READINGS

Cockerham, W. C. (2007) *Medical Sociology*, 10th edn. Prentice Hall, Englewood Cliffs, NJ.

Straus, R. (1957) The nature and status of medical sociology. *American Sociological Review* 22: 200–4.

Straus, R. (1999) Medical sociology: a personal fifty year perspective. *Journal of Health and Social Behavior* 40: 103–10.

CAREY L. USHER

mental disorder

Sociologists who study mental disorder work from a number of assumptions that define and distinguish their approach. They view mental disorder as a normal consequence of social life caused by structured inequality. They regard mental disorder as the outcome of social processes that include the labeling of deviant behavior and stigmatic societal reactions to those labels. They often define the object of study as general psychological distress rather than as specific psychiatric disorders. They may view the mental health treatment system as an institution for the social control of deviant behavior. Finally, the sociological perspective is concerned with properties of groups and populations and it is less informative regarding individual and clinical concerns.

Sociologists argue that disorder or distress arises from a *stress process* in which eventful, chronic, and traumatic stressors represent risks to well-being. Individuals can also mobilize resources to offset the effects of stressors. Both exposure to risk and the ability to mobilize protective resources are a function of social status. Race, class and gender, in particular, are related to risk exposure and access to protective resources. This accounts for differences in the rates of distress/disorder by race, class and gender. Over the life course individuals are exposed to stressors and have access to resources that consistently affect well-being as a direct function of socially structured access to resources and exposure to risk factors. Hence, both risk and protective resources that predict mental disorder arise in the normal day-to-day lives of persons as a function of social status.

Sociologists also view mental disorder as the outcome of a social process in which others evaluate and label deviant behavior. The labeling perspective represents an external causal explanation for disorder in which others confer a label on certain forms of deviant behavior. When an individual behaves in ways that others find deviant and unexplainable, that individual can be diagnosed (labeled) as having a mental disorder as a way of explaining the deviant behavior. The label has powerful effects for both those who encounter the labeled individual and the labeled individual. The mental illness label is stigmatic and it is associated among the general public with negative attributes of dangerousness, unpredictability, and lack of personal responsibility. Finally, labeling is a form of social control because it can be used to constrain behavior and because it reflects power relations in social systems.

Sociologists are not sure that psychiatric labels refer to real entities or diseases. There are strong theoretical and empirical grounds for believing that diagnostic categories of disorder can be arbitrary, value-laden, and normative. A review of official diagnostic categories suggests that many of the disorders described could also easily be labeled simply as non-normative behavior. The medicalization of deviance argument describes a social process that turns deviant behavior into illness symptoms.

The treatment of mental disorders can be understood as the social control of deviance. In this regard, sociologists view the mental health treatment system as a social control institution and they are interested in race and class patterns of mental health treatment including: differences between public and private treatment modalities, the goals of treatment, and differential access to mental health services in general.

The sociological study of mental disorder focuses on the mental health status of social groups and populations. Sociologists do not attempt to explain why a particular individual feels depressed but why persons with low socioeconomic status, for example, are more likely to feel depressed compared to persons with high socioeconomic status. The perspective has limited application to clinical concerns and is not especially useful for explaining individual cases of disorder.

SEE ALSO: Aging, Mental Health, and Well-Being; Deviance, Medicalization of; Labeling; Madness; Mental Illness, Social Construction of; Social Epidemiology; Stigma

SUGGESTED READINGS

Aneshensel, C. S. & Phelan, J. C. (eds.) (1999) *Handbook of the Sociology of Mental Health.* Kluwer Academic/Plenum, New York.

Horwitz, A.V. (2002) *Creating Mental Illness.* University of Chicago Press, Chicago, IL.

Kutchins, H. & Kirk, S. A. (1997) *Making Us Crazy: DSM: The Psychiatric Bible and the Creation of Mental Disorders.* Free Press, New York.

Scheff, T. J. (1984) *Being Mentally Ill.* Aldine, New York.

MARK TAUSIG

mental illness, social construction of

Social constructionist studies of mental illness examine how cultural conceptions of mental illness arise, are applied, and change. Such studies address questions of how conceptions of mental illness emerge in particular social circumstances, which groups have the power to enforce definitions of normality and abnormality, and what social and cultural forces are responsible for why these conceptions change.

Thomas Scheff's *Being Mentally Ill* (1966) was the first major social constructionist study of mental illness in American sociology. Scheff studied "residual rule-breaking" that refers to how observers categorize rule-violating behaviors that they cannot explain through other culturally recognizable categories. For example, while an adolescent who throws rocks at streetlights might be viewed as a vandal, no cultural category defines a middle-aged person who engages in the same behavior so that the latter is at risk of being labeled as mentally ill.

Another type of social constructionist study examines how particular types of disorder either succeed or fail to gain the psychiatric profession's recognition as official categories of mental disorder. For example, Scott (1990) shows how veterans of the Vietnam War successfully lobbied to have post-traumatic stress disorder considered as a mental disorder because of the therapeutic and financial benefits that would follow from such recognition. Conversely, other studies show how particular interest groups were able to have conditions previously considered as disorders such as homosexuality removed from the diagnostic manual or to prevent psychiatrists from incorporating new types of mental illness such as premenstrual syndrome into the manual.

Some research shows how the current system of psychiatric classification itself emerged from a variety of social factors. Since 1980 the psychiatric profession has relied upon definitions of several hundred specific types of mental illnesses. These definitions expanded the sorts of conditions that are considered to be legitimate objects of psychiatric concern. In addition, clinicians could use these diagnoses to justify reimbursement for the treatment of a broader range of patients than might otherwise qualify because insurers generally will pay to treat disorders but not problems of living. The drug industry also benefited from and promoted these symptom-based definitions. It relentlessly promoted the notion that common emotions such as depressed mood, agitation, anxiety, or inability to concentrate might be symptoms of mental illnesses.

The constructionist perspective has been subject to a number of criticisms. One, posed by the philosopher Ian Hacking (1999), asks: "The social construction of what?" That is, social constructionists typically have difficulty answering the question of exactly what it is that is being socially constructed. In the case of mental illness, this means that constructionists usually ignore any constraints that biological processes such as hallucinations and delusions or massive amounts of alcohol consumption create in the definition of mental symptoms.

A second difficulty stems from the assumption that mental disorders are whatever conditions any group defines as such. Yet, culturally-specific concepts of mental disorder provide no logical or scientific grounds for claiming that any view of mental illness is any better, or worse, than any other view. In addition, if definitions of mental illness are culturally specific so that there are no universal standards for mental disorders, then no basis for comparison of mental illnesses in different settings exists. Finally, constructionist studies tend to ignore the experiences of persons who receive labels of mental illness and to view such persons as passive victims of the labeling process. However, people often actively seek psychiatric labels and willingly embrace them or, conversely, aggressively reject the labels that professionals attempt to apply to them.

Despite these criticisms social constructionist studies can make a powerful contribution to the understanding of mental illness. Indeed, they might even show that the social and cultural variation that social constructionists stress could be even more influential determinants of definitions, responses, and rates of mental illness than the biological universals that current research emphasizes.

SEE ALSO: Essentialism and Constructionism; Madness; Mental Disorder

REFERENCES

Hacking, I. (1999) *The Social Construction of What?* Harvard University Press, Cambridge, MA.

Scheff, T. J. (1966) *Being Mentally Ill: A Sociological Theory*. Aldine, Chicago, IL.

Scott, W. (1990) PTSD in DSM-III: a case of the politics of diagnosis and disease. *Social Problems* 37: 294–310.

SUGGESTED READINGS

Bayer, R. (1987) *Homosexuality and American Psychiatry: The Politics of Diagnosis*. Princeton University Press, Princeton, NJ.

Figert, A. E. (1996) *Women and the Ownership of PMS: The Structuring of a Psychiatric Diagnosis*. Aldine de Gruyter, New York.

Horwitz, A. V. (2002) *Creating Mental Illness*. University of Chicago Press, Chicago.

Kirk, S. A. & Kutchins, H. (1992) *The Selling of DSM: The Rhetoric of Science in Psychiatry*. Aldine de Gruyter, New York.

ALLAN V. HORWITZ

meritocracy

The term "meritocracy" has three interrelated meanings. First, it refers to the type of social order where rewards are distributed to individuals in accordance with criteria of personal merit. Put differently, it denotes the "rule of the talented," a system of governance wherein the brightest and most conscientious individuals are accurately and efficiently assigned to occupy the most important positions, based on their talent and achievements. Second, the concept pertains to an elite social class, a definite group of people that enjoys high prestige because its select members proved to have merit based on their unique abilities and attainments (i.e., the aristocracy of merit as coined by Thomas

Jefferson). Third, the term touches upon the criteria of allocation of positions, roles, prestige, power, and economic reward, whereby excellent individuals are over-benefited in relation to others. These criteria are based on achieved rather than ascribed characteristics, and reflect the assumption that while achievements of merit are rare and difficult to attain, they are culturally valued.

In its elementary form, meritocracy is based on the allocation of rewards in congruence with human excellence, defined by Young (1958) as the sum of intelligence and effort ($M = I + E$, where M is merit, I is IQ, and E is effort). Practically, however, merit is usually equated with the achievement of educational qualifications, commonly measured by cognitive achievements and educational attainments. Meritocracy is also contrasted with systems that are based on selection by ascribed characteristics such as inherited wealth, social class, ethnicity, race, and, more generally, with any system of nepotism.

In essence, a meritocracy is based on inequality of outcome. Paradoxically, however, it refers to the prior arrangement of equal opportunities that – when operated fairly in free markets and open societies – should result in unequal but morally deserving outcomes. Like the *Theory of Justice* proposed by John Rawls (1971), the meritocracy justifies social inequality under conditions of antecedent equality. Based on a principle of equity (rather than equality or need), it states that individuals should be provided with equal opportunities to make the most of their intellectual potential and moral character. But since there are inherent inequalities in human potential (e.g., the bell curve of IQ distribution), and since individuals exhibit variable levels of motivation to excel, the social order should reflect the hierarchy of attained merit.

The meritocratic ideal states that – given that equality of opportunity is in place – the distribution of outcomes should be decided by open competition between individuals. Furthermore, the behavior of individuals during the preparatory stages of this competition is to rank them according to their merits. Intelligent individuals who invest effort in the competition (i.e., education) deserve to benefit. Others of lesser merit should be ranked lower. The resulting hierarchical rank order in the educational competition should then be transferred to the distribution of rewards in adult society.

SEE ALSO: School Segregation, Desegregation; Stratification and Inequality, Theories of

REFERENCE

Young, M. (1958) *The Rise of the Meritocracy, 1870–2033*. Thames & Hudson, London.

SUGGESTED READING

McNamee, S. J. & Miller, R. K. (2004) *The Meritocracy Myth*. Rowman & Littlefield, Lanham, MD.

GAD YAIR

Merton, Robert K. (1910–2003)

Robert K. Merton is one of those rare titanic figures that the discipline of sociology had the fortune to have at those crucial moments of its disciplinary break-through and expansion. Merton's works have not only steered sociology into new territories such as sociology of knowledge and studies of social time, but also deepened our theoretical grasp of social structures, group dynamics, culture, and the phenomenon of social ambivalence. Merton's insistent and persistent endeavor in working on theories of the middle range has undoubtedly bridged the often troubling gap between grand theories and empirical research. Today's sociologists (perhaps social scientists in general) are indebted to Merton for terms such as self-fulfilling prophecy, unanticipated consequences of social action, reference groups, and manifest and latent functions. In fact, these concepts have also entered into our everyday vernacular.

Merton was born to a first-generation immigrant family in urban Philadelphia. As a young passionate scholar of keen intellect, Merton received his training at Temple University and Harvard University under the mentorship of George E. Simpson and Pitirim Sorokin. Having taught at and chaired the sociology department at Tulane for two years, Merton moved to Colombia in the early 1940s and remained there during his 62-year tenure and career.

Often questionably associated with Parsonian functionalism, Merton's works have in fact showed much nuanced framework and analysis of social processes and social phenomena; and remained a subtle distance from Parsonian functionalism. In one of his most cited works, "Social structure and anomie" (1938), Merton, working in the middle range, proposed a framework on the interplays between social and cultural structures, which allows the sociologist to examine multiple social processes such as conformity, innovation, ritualism, retreatism, and rebellion, without entangling herself in an abstract language of action systems. Merton's works on reference groups and self-fulfilling prophecy not only laid a solid foundation for studies of group processes and dynamics but also pioneered the analysis of racial and ethnic structures and processes in US society. Consistently exhibited in Merton's works is his masterful shifting among multiple observational perspectives. His works on manifest and latent functions and his analysis of social dysfunctions draw clear distinctions among individual motivations, group goals-tasks, and their structural consequences-functions, which enables the sociologist to go beyond the ways in which individuals rationalize their actions and to inquire into the structural processes as consequences of individual and group actions. Merton's works on social status and role-set and sociological ambivalence bear clear and convincing witness to his penetratingly perceptive observation and exquisitely delicate construction of theoretical and analytical frameworks. For Merton, a social status often entails multiple roles (a role-set) for the social actor; and these roles often contradict one another. As a consequence, the individual person may experience affective, cognitive, and behavioral ambivalence, which in turn may be the cause of individual strain. This type of theoretical framework clearly locates the sources of social and individual strains in the social structural settings rather than in the gap between the individual's needs and structural constraints.

Another of Merton's lifelong pursuits was the sociology of knowledge, particularly the sociology of science. Critically working in the traditions of Manheim, Marx, Weber, and Sorokin, Merton examined the rise of modern scientific enterprise by locating it in the social contexts of English Puritanism and German pietism. Instead of constructing a linear narrative for modern science, Merton explores the paradoxes within the religious doctrines and the contradictions between religious doctrines and their social practice, showing that it was the social dynamics generated through structural contradictions that compelled the development of modern science.

In addition to being a great scholar and thinker, Merton is also remembered as a fascinating and inspiring mentor. Among his beneficiaries are such influential people in sociology as Peter Blau, James Coleman, Lewis and Roe Coser, Alvin Gouldner, Seymor Martin Lipset, and many others.

SEE ALSO: Anomie; Parsons, Talcott; Role Theory; Social Structure; Theory and Methods; Theory Construction

REFERENCE

Merton, R. K. (1938) Social structure and anomie. *American Sociological Review* 3: 672–82.

SUGGESTED READINGS

Merton, R. K. (1968) [1957] *Social Theory and Social Structure*, rev. and enlarged edn. Free Press, New York.

Hodges, P. C. & Merton, R. K. (1984) An interview with Robert K. Merton. *Teaching Sociology* 11 (4): 355–86.

YONG WANG

mesostructure

Mesostructure refers to the social processes that occur between the macro and micro levels of social organization. Mesostructure is the level of social analysis within which more macro structural or cultural arrangements shape and condition situations of interaction between individuals or groups, and within which the latter in turn maintain, modify, or change the former. David Maines (1982) and Peter Hall (1987) explicated the notion mesostructure as an answer to the "micro-macro problem." They argued that conventional treatments of the micro-macro issue reified a false dualism between the interaction processes on one hand, and large-scale social structure on the other.

Hall (1987) identifies six mesostructural categories of analysis:

1. *Process and temporality* focus attention on how past actions constrain decisions and activities in the present, and the ways in which actors project future scenarios and strategies.
2. *Conventions and practices* focus attention on the shared, habitual, taken for granted ground rules for action and interaction.
3. *Collective activity* draws attention to chains of joint actions by two or more individuals with regard to some social object.
4. *Networks* are the sets of transactions or relationships between actors.
5. *Resources and power* represent "any attribute, possession, or circumstance" at the disposal of collective or individual actors to achieve desired goals.
6. *Grounding* lodges micro level interaction in historical, cultural, and structural contexts.

SEE ALSO: Habitus/Field; Structuration Theory

REFERENCES

Hall, P. (1987) Interactionism and the study of social organization. *Sociological Quarterly* 28: 1–22.

Maines, D. R. (1982) In search of mesostructure: studies in the negotiated order. *Urban Life* 11: 267–79.

JEFFERY T. ULMER

meta-analysis

The term "meta-analysis" can be used to indicate: (1) a literature review of a body of empirical findings; (2) a summary of replication research on a specific topic; or (3) a theoretical or methodological analysis of philosophical problems associated with approaches like "methodological individualism" (Lukes 1994). The first usage is common in psychology while the second is often used in physical science. Involved in the third usage is, for example, Ritzer's (1975) emphasis on the importance of *paradigmatic* "metatheory." His schema for analyzing sociological theory involves a "meta-meta-analysis" of three kinds of metatheory: (1) a means for deeper *understanding*; (2) a *prelude* to theory construction; and (3) a source of *overarching perspectives* (Ritzer & Goodman 2004: A–1 to A–22).

All calls for "reflexive sociology" could be considered meta-analyses. There are disputes in metatheory as to whether theoretical or empirical commonalities should be emphasized. To take a bird's-eye view of a substantive field and decide on commonalities requires intimate knowledge and a philosophical grasp of fundamentals.

SEE ALSO: Content Analysis; Metatheory

REFERENCES

Lukes, S. (1994) Methodological individualism reconsidered. In: Martin, M. & McIntyre, M. C. (eds.), *Readings in the Philosophy of Science*. MIT Press, Cambridge, MA, pp. 451–8.

Ritzer, G. (1975) *Sociology: A Multiple Paradigm Science*. Allyn & Bacon, Boston, MA.

Ritzer, G. & Goodman, D. J. (2004) *Sociological Theory*, 6th edn. McGraw-Hill, Boston, MA.

J. I. (HANS) BAKKER

metatheory

A metatheory is a broad perspective that overarches two, or more, theories. There are many metatheories – positivism, postpositivism, hermeneutics, and so on – of importance in sociology and other social sciences. Two of the best known and most important are methodological holism and methodological individualism.

A particularly useful term to use in thinking about metatheories is Thomas Kuhn's famous notion of a paradigm. In fact, a paradigm is broader than a metatheory because it encompasses not only theories, but also methods, images of the subject matter of sociology, and a body of work that serves as an exemplar for those who work within the paradigm.

The social facts paradigm derives its name and orientation from the work of Émile Durkheim and his contention that sociology should involve the study of social facts that are external to and coercive over individuals. The two major theories subsumed under this heading are structural functionalism and conflict theory, and to a lesser extent systems theory. The social definition paradigm derives its name from W. I. Thomas's "definition of the situation." Symbolic interactionism is a theoretical component of the social definition paradigm, as is ethnomethodology. Finally, there is the social behavior paradigm, adopting a focus on behavior from the psychological behaviorists. Exchange theory and rational choice would be included in this paradigm.

The relatively narrow macro (social facts) and micro (social definition and social behavior) foci of extant paradigms led to the delineation of a more integrated sociological paradigm. Marx and his dialectical approach are taken as the exemplar of this approach and this paradigm can be seen as encompassing the micro–macro and agency–structure theories mentioned above.

Metatheorizing can be seen as a specific form of metasociology that examines sociological theory. While sociological theorizing attempts to make sense of the social world, metatheorizing attempts to make sense of sociological theorizing. As with other forms of metastudy, reflexivity is a crucial component of sociological metatheorizing. Metasociology encompasses not only metatheorizing, but also meta-methods and meta-data-analysis. A wide variety of work can be included under the heading of sociological metatheorizing. There are three varieties of metatheorizing, largely defined by differences in their end products – "metatheorizing as a means of attaining a deeper understanding of theory (Mu)," "metatheorizing as a prelude to theory development (Mp)," and "metatheorizing as a source of overarching theoretical perspectives (Mo)" (Ritzer 1975).

The prevalence of metatheorizing in sociology is rooted in the fact that sociologists deal with culturally diverse and historically specific subjects. The failure to discover universal truths and invariant laws of the social world has informed many metatheoretical efforts. The clashes of multiple paradigms competing in the realm of sociological theorizing create a perfect condition for the emergence of metatheoretical discourse.

The coming of age of metatheorizing in American sociology can be traced to the collapse of the dominant social facts paradigm during the 1960s. That paradigm, especially its major theoretical component, Parsonsian functionalism, had dominated

American sociology for more than two decades before it was seriously challenged by rival paradigms, as well as critics from a wide range of other perspectives. The emergence of a multiparadigmatic structure in sociology in the late 1960s reflected the growing disunity of the discipline and increasingly fragmented sociological research. There emerged a widespread feeling that sociology was facing a profound crisis. It was this sense of imminent disciplinary crisis that helped to invigorate meta-analyses of all types. A more recent challenge and spur to metatheorizing is the rise of postmodern social theory. Since the latter involves an assault on rationality and the modern orientation and metatheorizing is both modern and rational, it has come to be questioned by postmodernists. On the other hand, postmodernism has provided metatheorists with a whole series of new tools (e.g. deconstruction) and approaches with which to study theory.

SEE ALSO: Deconstruction; Durkhéim, Émile; Hermeneutics; Meta-Analysis; Positivism; Postpositivisim; Theory Construction

REFERENCE

Ritzer, G. (1975) *Sociology: A Multiple Paradigm Science.* Allyn & Bacon, Boston, MA.

SUGGESTED READINGS

Kuhn, T. (1970) *The Structure of Scientific Revolutions*, 2nd edn. University of Chicago Press, Chicago, IL.

Ritzer, G., Zhao, S., & Murphy, J. (2001) Metatheorizing in sociology: the basic parameters and the potential contributions of postmodernism. In: Turner, J. (ed.), *Handbook of Sociological Theory.* Kluwer, New York, pp. 113–31.

GEORGE RITZER

methods

We can distinguish between: (1) "methodology" as the theoretical understanding of basic principles, and (2) "method" as research techniques (Abbot 2001). The topics discussed under methods often include both. A classical experimental design (CED), with random assignment to an experimental group and a control group, is a basic aspect of methodology. In most sociological research there is a multivariant approach. It would be very difficult to actually carry out an experiment on such multivariable models, hence we rely on "path analysis" to simulate the logic of CED. The term methods is often used to primarily represent specific techniques of research, both quantitative and qualitative. All of the inferential statistics, parametric and nonparametric, may be studied as aspects of quantitative methods. Similarly, all aspects of ethnographic fieldwork, open-ended interviewing, and observation may be considered in the context of qualitative methods. There is also an interest in moving beyond the quantitative–qualitative distinction. There is a very vibrant literature on statistical techniques. For example, Karl Pearson's (1900) "product moment correlation coefficient" (rho, ρ) is based on a set of assumptions, including having data with a ratio or at least an interval "level of measurement." But much sociological data are categorical, numerically ordinal, or even nominal. So many researchers have attempted to use Pearson's ρ with ordinal- or even nominal-level data (Lyons's 1971 essay, "Techniques for using ordinal measures in regression and path analysis"). Similarly, in qualitative data analysis there has been a move away from intuitive scanning of a complex body of material to the use of computer software packages which allow for summaries of aspects of the information gathered, especially blocks of text files.

The logic of method tends to overlap with the philosophy of science. That, in turn, has been influenced by science and technology studies (S&TS). Work on what actually happens in a laboratory provides a window on methodology in the broader sense. One widely discussed typology differentiates among positivism, interpretivism, and criticalism. For the positivist social scientist, it is important to stress the epistemological questions related to conducting research in such a way that a truly scientific body of data will be collected. But there is considerable disagreement concerning the precise nature of science in the social sciences. Many conceive of methods in terms of "positivism and its epistemological others" (Steinmetz 2005). Until the late 1960s there was a strong trend within sociology to try to make the discipline "scientific." Sociology hit a "crisis" and a host of non-positivist methods were reiterated or invented. A great variety of methods became more acceptable. Pathbreaking was an inductive "grounded theory" approach (Glaser & Strauss 1967). But the epistemological stress on grounded theory eventually led to a wider discussion reminiscent of the struggle concerning methodology in German-speaking Europe.

The interpretive approach downplays epistemological concerns and takes distance from physical sciences. Interpretive sociologists accept that the study of human beings is likely to produce different methodologies. One strain can be traced to Wilhelm Dilthey in his *Introduction to the Human Sciences: Selected Works* (vol. 1, 1989). Another important root source for the interpretive meta-paradigm is Georg Simmel, whose work directly influenced the Chicago School. For the interpretive social scientist it is the question of "philosophical anthropology" that should be highlighted. How are human beings different? Are people different from rocks and stars? Are humans cognitively and emotionally different from other animals, even the higher apes? This sometimes leads to the conclusion that the best methodological approach is to study individual social actors and to regard all "functional" arguments about collective "structures" as ontologically suspect. The Chicago School of Sociology stresses the interpretive approach, as in the famous study of *The Polish Peasant in Europe and America* by Thomas and Znaniecki, which utilizes the kinds of documents of which Dilthey thought highly. Where both the positive and the interpretive meta-paradigms tend to agree is that questions of axiology (morals and ethics) as well as long-term, historical teleology (future end goals) are better left out. As Max Weber, following Heinrich Rickert, argued persuasively with regard to his own interpretive sociology (*verstehende Soziologie*), it is important to distinguish between the reasons we carry out research studies and the way in which we examine the evidence. A topic may have "value relevance" but the actual study, positive or interpretive, should strive to be as "value neutral" as possible.

The strong dissenting voice on this question of axiology and teleology is critical theory. The term is derived from the Frankfurt School but has gained wider coinage. Criticalists feel that some specific value or future end goal is of such importance that considerations of epistemology and ontology are less important. Those who hold to this position tend to emphasize the ways in which notions of value-free objectivity can be used to justify certain kinds of policy. Feminists also emphasize axiology and teleology, a society that has eliminated "patriarchy." Other forms of criticalism are environmentalism and Gandhianism.

Considerable debate continues to mark sociological research studies. The topic of triangulation has led to many different ways of conceiving a multimethod approach. The idea that it would be possible in principle to combine insights from positive, interpretive, and critical meta-paradigms is a key to Habermas's general theory. Bourdieu has utilized multiple correspondence analysis (MCA), a form of data reduction based on dual scaling.

This has led to acceptance by some of a fourth attitude toward methods which can be called the postmodernist meta-paradigm in sociology. The social science version of postmodernism is a rejection of all "foundationalisms." That lack of any methodological foundations does not, however, restrict postmodernist thinkers like Foucault, Baudrillard, Barthes, Lyotard, and Derrida from holding positions. A distinction needs to be made between postmodern epistemology and empirical study of the phenomena of late modernism. There have been modernist approaches to the study of postmodern societies.

There is some question as to whether the "incommensurability" of paradigms may be overstated. Nevertheless, those who adhere to a specific approach tend to continue to refine and adjust their own methods and invent new techniques. The move from cross-tabulation to regression and path analysis in sociology in the 1970s led to speculation concerning the possibility of a mathematical and statistical approach to sociology. Ragin (2000) has criticized the conventional approach to quantitative methods. He points out that researchers are often insensitive to the difficulty of determining a population. He also points out that we need to distinguish between necessary and sufficient conditions when making causal claims. He introduces a qualitative comparative analysis (QCA) that emphasizes the comparison of diverse cases. Ragin also indicates the usefulness of fuzzy sets versus crisp sets. There has been significant rethinking of fundamental assumptions once taken as axiomatic.

In the future it is likely that techniques such as partial least squares (PLS), singular value decomposition (SVD), penalized logistic regression (PLR), and recursive feature elimination (RFE) will lead to more sophisticated techniques for the study of complex sociological systems. Secondary data sets generate a large volume of sociological data. Bioinformatics will probably be extended to human social structures. Bayesian statistics will also be important.

SEE ALSO: Methods, Mixed; Qualitative Methods; Quantitative Methods; Theory and Methods

REFERENCES

Abbott, A. (2001) *Chaos of Disciplines.* University of Chicago Press, Chicago, IL.

Glaser, B. G. & Strauss, A. L. (1967) *The Discovery of Grounded Theory: Strategies for Qualitative Research.* Aldine de Gruyter, New York.

Lyons, M. (1971) Techniques for using ordinal measures in regressin and path analysis. In: Dostner, H. L. (ed.), *Sociological Methodology.* Jossey-Bass, San Francisco, CA, pp. 147–71.

Pearson, K. (1900) On the criterion that a given system of deviations from the probable in the case of a correlated system of variables is such that it can be reasonably supposed to have arisen from random sampling. *Philosophical Magazine*, series 5, 50: 157–75.
Ragin, C. (2000) *Fuzzy-Set Social Science*. University of Chicago Press, Chicago, IL.
Steinmetz, G. (ed.) (2005) *The Politics of Method in the Human Sciences: Positivism and Its Epistemological Others*. Duke University Press, Durham, NC.

J. I. (HANS) BAKKER

methods, mixed

Over the last several decades, numerous fields from the social and behavioral sciences, including the field of sociology, have undergone three methodological waves in research. The quantitative research paradigm, rooted in (logical) positivism, marked the first methodological wave, inasmuch as it was characterized by a comprehensive and formal set of assumptions and principles surrounding epistemology, ontology, axiology, methodology, and rhetoric.

The years 1900 to 1950 marked the second methodological wave, in which many researchers who rejected positivism embraced the qualitative research paradigm. Qualitative research is characterized by qualitative researchers attempting to write reliable, valid, and objective accounts of their field experiences.

The eclectic period (from 1998) gave way to the third methodological movement known as mixed methods research, which emerged from the publication of Tashakkori and Teddlie's (1998) book *Mixed Methodology: Combining Qualitative and Quantitative Approaches*. As noted by Johnson and Onwuegbuzie (2004), mixed methods research involves collecting, analyzing, and interpreting quantitative and qualitative data in a single study or series of studies that investigate the same underlying phenomenon. Mixed methods research has been distinguished by an integrated and interactive set of epistemological, ontological, methodological, and rhetorical assumptions that promote the compatibility thesis, which posited that quantitative and qualitative approaches were neither mutually exclusive nor interchangeable. This notion allows researchers from the social and behavioral science fields the ability to collect multiple data using different strategies, approaches, and methods resulting in "complementary strengths and nonoverlapping weaknesses" (Johnson & Turner 2003: 299).

SEE ALSO: Qualitative Methods; Quantitative Methods

REFERENCES

Johnson, R. B. & Onwuegbuzie, A. J. (2004) Mixed methods research: a research paradigm whose time has come. *Educational Researcher* 33 (7): 14–26.
Johnson, R. B. & Turner, L. A. (2003) Data collection strategies in mixed methods research. In: Tashakkori, A. & Teddlie, C. (eds.), *Handbook of Mixed Methods in Social and Behavioral Research*. Sage, Thousand Oaks, CA, pp. 297–319.

ANTHONY J. ONWUEGBUZIE AND MELISSA L. BURGESS

metropolis

Metropolis broadly refers to the largest, most powerful, and culturally influential city of an epoch or region. A succession of great metropolitan cities charts the course of western urban history.

Two features of the metropolis are revealed in the etymology of its Greek origins (*meter*/ mother + *polis*/ city). As population forced some city states in antiquity to found colonies, they became the "mother city" of those colonies. As polis, ancient metropolis was a relatively open political community attracting commercial and other forms of exchange, and offering opportunities for sophisticated living. In this way metropolis differed from other forms of the imperial city which were typically rigid, closed and hierarchical, affording residents few independent rights.

Ancient Athens is often considered the epitome of the Greek polis, its contributions to democracy, humanism and open inquiry central in shaping western values and culture. By the fifth century, however, Athens had grown to many times the size of the ideal polis. Despite the magnificence of its public buildings, most of the city's residents lived in poverty.

Imperial Rome also developed the metropolitan urban form. Here politics was understood more as public authority than self-ruling democracy. Yet management of empire emphasized practical arts – military organization, civil engineering and city planning. Roman power established many cities which shared features such as a *defined center*, a clear *boundary or perimeter* and an overall spatial distribution of buildings, functions and people where the core was systematically valued over more distant parts.

The modern metropolis is the foremost expression of the centralizing and accumulating tendencies of first mercantile, then industrial, now global capitalism. Growth of the market economy initially amplified the importance of the urban core. Modern metropolis grew up around a single center or business district. Locations at a distance from the hub were at a disadvantage. Thus city growth produced the distinctive patterns of urban development described by Frederick Engels, Ernest Burgess, and others.

Relentless growth has transformed the metropolis from a densely populated, bounded entity with a single center into a vast urbanized region. Early evidence of this shift is found in Victorian London where the term "metropolitan" first appears to describe services extending over the "whole city." As economic and technological forces consistently pushed development beyond the city, the metropolis became redefined as a geographic or statistical area composed of one or more established urban nuclei.

In the USA, in 1910 the Census Bureau devised *metropolitan district* – a central city with a population of at least 200,000 plus adjacent townships. In 1949, this measure was replaced by the *standard metropolitan area* – an area containing a city of at least 50,000 plus surrounding counties. Three principal types of metropolitan area are currently recognized. *Metropolitan Statistical Areas* (MSAs) are areas with populations of less than one million, regardless of the number of counties contained. If the metropolitan area exceeds one million, it is designated a *Consolidated Metropolitan Statistical Area* (CMSA). *Primary Metropolitan Statistical Areas* (PMSAs) are areas in their own right, but integrated with other adjacent PMSAs forming multi-centered CMSAs.

Such designations signal transformation of the metropolis into an urban region containing many centers of work, residence and shopping and sprawling across multiple administrative districts. New metropolitan regions are typically bifurcated into areas experiencing rapid growth or severe decline.

SEE ALSO: New Urbanism; Urban Revolution

SUGGESTED READINGS

Hall, P. (1998) *Cities in Civilization*. Weidenfeld & Nicolson, London.

LeGates, R. T. & Stout, F. (eds.) (2007) *The City Reader*. Routledge, New York.

Mumford, L. (1961) *The City in History: Its Origins, Its Transformations and Its Prospects*. Harcourt, Brace & World, New York.

JAMES DICKINSON

metrosexual

"Metrosexual" is a term that generally refers to a male whose lifestyle, spending habits, and concern for personal appearance are likened to stereotypes associated with homosexual men. Developed by British writer Mark Simpson in a 1994 article "Meet the metrosexual," the typical metrosexual is "a young man with money to spend living in or within easy reach of a metropolis – because that's where all the best shops, clubs, gyms, and hairdressers are. He might be officially gay, straight, or bisexual, but this is utterly immaterial because he has clearly taken himself as his own love object" (2002). While Simpson originally defined metrosexuality as neither heterosexual nor homosexual, its popular application has remained predominantly associated with heterosexual males.

Cultural and social changes associated with western masculinity are central to metrosexuality. As a product of consumer capitalism, the metrosexual denotes a progressive breakdown of boundaries between homosexual/heterosexual and masculine/feminine cultural signifiers and forms of expression. Thus, alterations in cultural meanings associated with heterosexual masculinity represent a challenge to traditional western masculine norms regarding proper forms of social conduct and expression.

In popular culture, metrosexuality has been associated with numerous male celebrities, and was most notably depicted in the Bravo network's program *Queer Eye for the Straight Guy* (2003–7), which portrayed the practices of stereotypically style- and culture-conscious gay men who gave advice to heterosexual counterparts on proper forms of consumption.

SEE ALSO: Heterosexuality; Homosexuality; Sexual Identities; Sexualities and Consumption

REFERENCE

Simpson, M. (2002) [1994] *Meet the Metrosexual*. Salon.com website: archive.salon.com/ent/feature/2002/07/22/metrosexual/.

SUGGESTED READING

Simpson, M. (1994) *Male Impersonators: Men Performing Masculinity*. Routledge, London.

MICHAEL YAKSICH

micro-macro links

"The sociological imagination," C. Wright Mills (1959: 6) emphasized, "enables us to grasp history and biography and the relations between the two within society. That is its task and promise." Any social study that fails "to come back to problems of biography, of history, and of their intersections within society," has not completed its intellectual journey. Mills' exhortation challenges sociologists to address the fundamental micro (actions at the personal level) and macro (the larger socio-historical context within which micro events transpire) link. Exploring, grasping and explaining social phenomena through that link is a key challenge and objective.

Over the course of sociology's history, emphases on the micro-macro link have varied. During the classical period, as Europe underwent broad institutional change, the emphasis tended towards the macro although key thinkers like Karl Marx and Emile Durkheim indicated, at various times, how individual agents internalized, resisted, and changed larger social forces. Rejecting organic analogies and the Orthodox Marxists' economism, Max Weber made meaningful social action central to his sociology but by emphasizing the uniformities of social action and typical modes of conduct, action was not conceptualized at the purely micro level, yielding a consciously constructed micro-macro linkage.

Talcott Parsons' work dominated sociology from the 1940s into the 1960s. The micro dynamics of Parsons' original theory of social action were, however, eclipsed by his shift in focus towards the social system and its requisites. The 1960s' turbulence and structural functionalism's analytical shortcomings initiated two responses. One maintained the macro focus while incorporating social conflict into the framework (e.g. Ralf Dahrendorf, Randall Collins). Conflict theory, like structural functionalism, continued to emphasize social structures, institutions, and broader socio-historical processes, leaving the micro level under-examined. The second response was a variety of micro perspectives, some with indigenous roots in US social thought – e.g. Charles Horton Cooley's or George Herbert Mead's symbolic interactionism, William James' or John Dewey's pragmatism, George Homans' or Peter Blau's exchange theory – while others arose in response to the heavy macro determination of US sociology – e.g. Alfred Schütz's, Thomas Luckmann's and Peter Berger's phenomenology (or social constructionism), and Aaron Cicourel's or Harold Garfinkel's ethnomethodology. These theorists focused intensely on interaction, meaning construction and individual action leaving the macro context as background.

While some maintain that micro and macro constitute separate levels of analysis, most theories tend towards one or the other due to the specific problems addressed or the theoretical question under consideration. There are five basic positions regarding the micro-macro relation: the macro social order is created through micro acts of free choice by rational, purposeful individuals; the macro order is created through the uniformity of individual's largely typified, interpretive actions at the micro level; self-reflexive, socialized individuals create/re-create society as a collective force through interpretively based micro-level action; through micro-level actions, socialized individuals reproduce the existing macro-social environment; due to external, social control, rational, purposeful actors acquiesce to macro forces.

The 1980s witnessed an intense interest in the micro-macro linkage. Jeffrey Alexander, for example, noted that the micro-macro dichotomy is an analytic distinction and any attempt to link it to concrete dichotomies – e.g. individual versus society – is misguided. Understanding the differentiation analytically enables interparadigmatic discourse, allowing theorists to conceptualize linkages rather than reducing one level to another. Alexander's work shifted from conceptualizing action and order as dichotomous polarities to one where contingent action has a more systematic element within it.

Pierre Bourdieu's (1990) theory of practice attempted to establish the dialectical relations between objective structures and the structured dispositions that exist within action and tend to reproduce those structures. The *habitus* – acquired patterns of thought, behavior and taste – constitutes the link between social structures and human agency.

Anthony Giddens (1984: 2) argued that sociology's basic domain "is neither the experience of the individual actor, nor the existence of any form of societal totality, but social practices across time and space." In his theory of structuration, the subject is de-centered slightly as situationally positioned, knowledgeable, reflexively monitoring human agents draw from existing rules and resources (structures) which enable and constrain their action, to engage in interactions that are largely routinized across space and time as they produce and reproduce systems of social action.

Jürgen Habermas's (1984: xl) theory of communicative action consciously sought to establish "a two-level concept of society that connects the 'lifeworld' and 'system' paradigms in more than a rhetorical fashion." Earlier, Habermas had identified three specific human interests – technical (knowing and controlling the natural environment giving rise to natural science), practical (understanding and working with one another, leading to hermeneutical knowledge), and emancipatory (the desire to end distorted communication and understanding leading to the critical sciences). It is within the lifeworld that micro-interaction, concerned with each interest, takes place, but that action occurs within a larger social system; action draws from existing knowledge systems related to technical, practical and emancipatory interests.

George Ritzer (1991: 151–8) maintained that despite some progress, a genuine micro-macro link could only arise through a thoroughgoing, overarching, metatheorization of sociological theory. Such theorization must explicitly address the conceptual integration of different levels of sociological analysis.

Finally, Johnathan Turner argued that social reality operates at the micro, meso and macro levels, with each "embedded" in the other. Embedding does not reduce one level to another; it emphasizes that processes operating at one level influence and are influenced by processes at another.

SEE ALSO: Bourdieu, Pierre; Habitus/Field; Macrosociology; Mesostructure; Microsociology; Structuration Theory; Structure and Agency; Theory Construction

REFERENCES

Alexander, J., Munch, R., & Smelser, N. J. (eds.) (1986) *The Micro-Macro Link*. University of California Press, Berkeley, CA.

Bourdieu, P. (1990) [1980] *The Logic of Practice*, trans. R. Nice. Stanford University Press, Stanford, CA.

Giddens, A. (1984) *The Constitution of Society*. University of California Press, Berkeley, CA.

Habermas, J. (1984; 1987) [1981] *The Theory of Communicative Action*, 2 vols., trans. T. McCarthy. Beacon Press, Boston, MA.

Mills, C. W. (1959) *The Sociological Imagination*. Oxford University Press, New York.

Ritzer, G. (1991) *Metatheorizing in Sociology*. Lexington Books, Lexington, MA.

Turner, J. (1988). *A Theory of Social Interaction*. Stanford University Press, Stanford, CA.

ROB BEAMISH

microsociology

Microsociology fills in details missing from abstract representations of human conduct by describing the structure/process of social life, the reciprocal relationship between these events and the nature of society.

There have been three main approaches: ethnographic, experimental, and linguistic. Ethnography uses close observations and reportage of behavior in context. For example, Edwin Lemert studied paranoia among executives in business organizations. By interviewing and observing, Lemert was able to make a contribution to the development of labeling theory.

Experimental studies by Asch represent the quantitative approach, showing how context influences conformity and non-conformity: a majority of subjects were inappropriately influenced by their conformity to the majority.

Finally, discourse and conversation analysis demonstrates regularities in linguistic sequences (such as questions and responses) that usually go unnoticed. Unlike the first two approaches, close reading of discourse reveals an otherwise invisible filigree.

However, each of the three approaches is specialized to the point that important aspects are omitted. In Milan Kundera's essay on the history of the novel he addresses the problem:

> Try to reconstruct a dialogue from your own life, the dialogue of a quarrel or a dialogue of love. The most precious, the most important situations are utterly gone. Their abstract sense remains (I took this point of view, he took that one. I was aggressive, he was defensive), perhaps a detail or two, but the acoustic-visual concreteness of the situation in all its continuity is lost. (Kundera 1995: 128–9)

How can a scientist or scholar capture reality, when we and the people whom we study usually cannot? Kundera suggests that only the greatest of novelists, such as Tolstoy and Proust, have come close, by reporting the evocative details that we usually ignore or forget.

Charles Horton Cooley provided an important step toward understanding social interaction. The *looking-glass self* has three parts: "the imagination of our appearance to the other person; the imagination of his judgment of that appearance, and some sort of self-feeling, such as pride or mortification."

Cooley's conjecture points to the basic components of social life. The first two involve the imagination of the other's view of self. The other component is made up of the emotional reactions that are real, not imagined, either pride or shame.

Cooley's focus on pride and shame is provocative. Western culture glorifies the isolated, self-contained individual. The pride/shame response implies that we are dependent on others. For this reason, mention of shame and its derivatives is usually taboo.

Goffman did not acknowledge a debt to Cooley, but his analysis of concrete examples led him to a deep exploration of the looking-glass self (Scheff 2006).

Indeed, Goffman's treatment implies a fourth step. Cooley stopped at the experience of pride or shame. Goffman's analyzes, especially of impression management, imply a fourth step: the management of emotion.

Goffman's examples suggest that actors seldom accept shame/embarrassment passively. Instead, they try to manage it, by avoidance, if possible. Most of the embarrassment/shame possibilities in Goffman's examples are not about the actual occurrence of emotions, but anticipations, and management based on these anticipations.

Goffman's examples further imply that if shame/embarrassment cannot be avoided, then his actors actively deny it, attempting to save face, on the one hand, and/or to avoid pain, on the other. It is Goffman's fourth step that brings his examples to life, because it touches on the dynamics of impression and emotion management that underlie everyday life.

The Cooley/Goffman looking-glass self provides an underlying model of structure/process of social life. Alienation/solidarity can be understood in terms of degree of attunement, on the one hand, and the emotional responses that follow from it, on the other. Pride signals and generates solidarity. Shame signals and generates alienation. Shame is a normal part of the process of social control; it becomes disruptive only when hidden or denied.

Denial of shame, especially when it takes the form of false pride (egoism), generates self-perpetuating cycles of alienation. Threats to a secure bond can come in two different formats: either the bond is too loose or too tight. Relationships in which the bond is too loose are *isolated*: there is mutual misunderstanding. Relationships in which the bond is too tight are *engulfed*: at least one of the parties in the relationship, say the subordinate, understands and embraces the standpoint of the other at the expense of the subordinate's own beliefs, values, or feelings.

This approach concerns both interpersonal and intergroup levels. The Kunderarian idea of the concrete reality of relationships can be implemented by close study of verbatim recordings at the interpersonal level, and by the close analysis of exchanges between leaders of groups at the collective level. Microsociology can be applied both to interpersonal and societal interaction in a way that may afford a path to linking the least parts (words and gestures) to the greatest wholes (abstract theories and social structures).

SEE ALSO: Conversation Analysis; Cooley, Charles Horton; Ethnography; Goffman, Erving; Looking-Glass Self; Mead, George Herbert; Micro-Macro Links; Social Psychology

REFERENCES

Kundera, M. (1995) *Testaments Betrayed.* Harper Collins, New York.

Scheff, T. J. (2006) *Goffman Unbound: Toward a New Paradigm.* Paradigm Publishers, Boulder, CO.

THOMAS J. SCHEFF

migration: internal

Internal migration is typically defined as the permanent residential relocation of an individual or population from one geographical unit to another within a particular country. Examples of internal migration include a move between regions of a country, between a rural area and a city, from one city to another, and between the neighborhoods of a city. Internal migration flows represent the redistribution of the existing population of a country and affect patterns of population growth and composition in both the sending and receiving areas. Thus, internal migration affects competition for food, housing, and other resources in both locations, helps to maintain equilibrium between the distribution of economic opportunities and the distribution of labor across areas of a country, and is a primary individual-level mechanism shaping broader population patterns, including regional growth trends, population decentralization, and residential segregation. The push–pull theory – viewing migration as a function of the relative economic and social attributes of various residential options and intervening factors related to the costs of making a move – remains the most widely used explanatory framework in the study of internal migration. Individual-level variations in the response to various push and pull factors and the strength of intervening obstacles help to shape migrant populations that are selective of certain characteristics, including race, socioeconomic status, age, and gender. As a result, migrants are rarely representative of the populations in either the sending or receiving areas so that patterns of migration have the potential to dramatically alter the composition of both sending and receiving locations. Depending on the type of move, internal migration may also have profound effects on migrants themselves, necessitating not only a change in residence, but also often a change in the range of economic opportunities, exposure to different social and environmental contexts, and the disruption of old personal networks.

SEE ALSO: Demographic Data: Censuses, Registers, Surveys; Migration: International

SUGGESTED READING

Bilsboro, R. E. (ed.) (1998) *Migration, Urbanization, and Development: New Directions and Issues.* UNFPA/ Kluwer, Norwell, MA.

KYLE CROWDER AND MATTHEW HALL

migration: international

International migration refers to the movement of people from one country to another on a permanent or semi-permanent basis. While people have migrated for centuries, international migration started with the carving up of the world into territorially bounded sovereign countries, a process that dates to the start of the Westphalian state system in the seventeenth century. Both country exits and entries of citizens and foreigners are part of the international migration process but government policy measures typically focus on regulating entries of foreigners rather than exits or return migrations of their own nationals.

The United Nations estimated that nearly 3 percent of the world's population – 191 million people – were international migrants in 2005. These numbers are growing rapidly, however, and include persons of all nations and creeds migrating along pathways that crisscross the globe. Today virtually every country in the world is a sender or receiver of international migrants and growing numbers are both senders and receivers.

Theories of international migration focus on demographic, economic, geographic, political, and social differentials between sending and receiving countries that "push" people to leave their homelands and that "pull" them to countries that migrants perceive as offering better opportunity. For instance, unskilled labor migrants are pushed from their homelands by unemployment and low wages. Persecution pushes political refugees into neighboring countries. Students are pulled to other countries in search of higher education. Retirees are pulled to countries with warm climates and low living costs. Skilled workers, migrant family members, and other types of migrants respond to different push/pull forces. While structural disparities, social and economic inequalities, and the ease and relatively low cost of international travel and communication set the stage for international migrations, cross-country networks of migrants and institutions enable growing numbers of migrants to find opportunities outside their countries in an increasingly interdependent world.

SEE ALSO: Immigration Policy; Migration: Internal

SUGGESTED READINGS

Castles, S. & Miller, M. J. (2009) *The Age of Migration: International Population Movements in the Modern World*, 4th edn. Guilford Press, New York.

Massey, D. S. & Taylor, E. J. (2004) *International Migration: Prospects and Policies in a Global Market (International Studies in Demography).* Oxford University Press, New York.

Zolberg, A. R. (2006) *A Nation by Design: Immigration Policy in the Fashioning of America.* Russell Sage Foundation and Harvard University Press, New York and Cambridge, MA.

MARY M. KRITZ

migration: undocumented/illegal

Illegal migration involves people moving away from a country of origin to another country in which they reside in violation of local citizenship laws. Entry into the receiving country can be legal (student, temporary work, or tourist visas) or illegal (crossing the border from places other than the legal entry ports). Illegal immigration has been studied widely and systematically only since the 1980s, partly because of the difficulties involved in obtaining information. The literature shows that illegal immigrants in most countries share certain characteristics closely related to their position of insecurity, fear, and precarious existence. Multiple reasons lead to people's movement from their country of origin to another illegally. Typically, illegal immigrants seek better livelihoods for themselves and their families, or seek to avoid persecution. Lack of and/or poor statistical recording systems and the illegal status and high spatial mobility of migrants make the measurement of numbers extremely unreliable.

Theoretical frameworks (such as classical migration theory based on push-pull factors and Marxist labor-market theory based on social class within capitalist expansionism) that have historically dominated international migration analyses have focused on men. Where mentioned, women are incorporated as a component of the male study respondents' "social capital," or network of social ties that influence potential costs, risks, and benefits associated with the men's migration (Massey & Espinosa 1997).

The growing selection of explicitly gendered field studies that took off during the 1980s reveals the great complexity of issues migrant women face, particularly as they intersect with the fate of children. Studies initially were concerned with how to "add" women to the migration field, where their presence was either peripheral or simply invisible.

They often appeared when issues of employment or reproductive rights were discussed. Numerous studies in the 1990s, however, placed women at the center of analysis as proper agents of structural and social change, thus reconceptualizing tools central to conventional models of migration, such as regulating the patterns of skill transfer, household decision-making, labor market segmentation dynamics, networking, and residential location choice. These studies debunk some of the myths on migration in general and illegal migration in particular by addressing issues pertinent to female migration, kinship relations, and the interconnections among gender, class, and race.

Thousands of people living without status in different parts of the world face the fear and very real threat of deportation or imprisonment. This situation prevents many people of low social status not only from obtaining decent employment, but also from using services such as social housing, education, health care, social assistance, and emergency services, including police protection. An example is the 1994 Proposition 187 in California, barring illegal immigrants from non-emergency health care and public schooling (the proposition was later found to be unconstitutional) and the various reports presented by undocumented women.

The DADT (Don't Ask Don't Tell) Toronto Campaign is a policy which presents a local solution to the problem by preventing city employees from inquiring about the immigration status of people accessing city services. Also, it prohibits city employees from sharing information with federal and provincial enforcement agencies, including the Department of Citizenship and Immigration Canada (CIC), on the immigration status of anyone accessing city services. This policy represents a recognition of some of the most pressing theoretical and practical concerns of transnational anti-racist feminist solidarity, which would provide all workers, including illegal workers, with a structure of dignity and societal inclusion.

SEE ALSO: Discrimination; Diversity; Globalization, Culture and; Inequality/ Stratification, Gender; Migration: International; Race

REFERENCE

Massey, D. & Espinosa, K. (1997) What's driving Mexico–US migration? A theoretical empirical and policy analysis. *American Journal of Sociology* 102: 939–99.

SUGGESTED READINGS

Kimer, J. T. (2005) A generation of migrants. *NACLA Report on the Americas* 39 (1): 31–7.

Massey, D., Durand, J., & Malone, N. (2002) *Beyond Smoke and Mirrors: Mexican Immigration in an Era of Economic Integration*. Russell Sage Foundation, New York.

JOANNA HADJICOSTANDI

migration and the labor force

How do migrants fare in the host labor market and how do they affect native labor?

Chiswick theorized that migrants often begin with low earnings because, lacking specific skills such as fluency in the host-country's language, their home-country education and experience is undervalued. As they acquire these skills, their earnings grow. Supporting Chiswick's theory, cross-sectional analyses of the USA and other countries revealed that immigrant earnings grow and approach the earnings of natives with similar years of schooling and experience.

This optimistic picture was shattered when Borjas showed that recent immigrants start at much lower earnings than their predecessors. Pairing the actual earnings growth of earlier immigrants with the low initial earnings of recent immigrants produced a bleak picture of immigrant economic assimilation in the USA and elsewhere.

Duleep and Regets questioned using the earnings growth of earlier cohorts to predict the earnings growth of recent cohorts. A low opportunity cost of immigrants' human capital combined with its value for learning new skills should promote high investment in human capital, particularly for immigrants with low initial earnings. Immigrants should experience higher earnings growth than natives and among immigrants there should be an inverse relationship between entry earnings and earnings growth. These expectations emerge in empirical analyses that follow cohorts and individuals. As entry earnings fell, earnings growth increased; the earnings growth of recent immigrants exceeds that of natives and earlier immigrants. The Duleep/Regets model and associated empirical findings caution against assuming inter-cohort stability in earnings growth when measuring immigrant earnings growth. A key prediction of the model is that immigrants have a high propensity to invest in all forms of human capital, thus injecting dynamism into the host economy.

How migration affects native-born labor also yields conflicting answers for several reasons. Immigrants move in time periods and to areas with better than average wages and employment opportunities, obfuscating potential effects on native labor in cross-sectional and time-series analyses. Natural experiments help in this regard. Immigrants also cluster: estimates of immigration's effect on natives' employment and wages may fluctuate with the economic circumstances of one principal immigration state. Combining time-series and cross-sectional data alleviates this problem.

Cross-sectional and historical comparisons may show no immigration effect if natives respond to immigration by moving. Note the south–north migration of blacks and the imposition and relaxation of immigration controls. The recent movement of low-educated natives out of and high-educated natives into areas with large immigrant flows provides circumstantial evidence that recently arrived immigrants are labor-market substitutes for low-educated natives and complements for high-educated natives. There are, however, alternative explanations for this migration pattern and causality is difficult to determine.

Consumption patterns will also affect how immigration affects native labor. Immigrants buy native-produced products. Production/consumption interactions also exist. If immigration makes one product cheaper, the demand for complementary (substitute) products rises (falls). The availability of immigrants to tend kids and clean homes allows middle-class women to work and spend money on goods and services that may be produced by low-educated natives.

Case-study evidence often shows an influx of unskilled immigrant labor displacing unskilled native labor, in contrast to statistical estimates of small immigration effects. Yet an estimated wage or employment effect, if causal, only suggests that, on balance, immigration positively or negatively affects natives' employment and wages, consistent with the existence of specific cases of displacement and immigration-induced wage declines. Case-study evidence can nevertheless elucidate how jobs traditionally filled by natives become dominated by immigrants and what happens to the natives who were formerly employed in these jobs. Turnovers from native to immigrant labor do not necessarily constitute evidence that displacement has occurred.

The theoretical expectation that increases in unskilled immigrant labor must harm native unskilled labor comes from models with only skilled and unskilled labor. Yet, within unskilled occupations immigrants and natives are differentiated by the nature of their work and the process by which they become employed, trained, and promoted. Moreover, businesses develop or persist, and industries change their use of labor, in response to immigration.

SEE ALSO: Immigration Policy; International Gender Division of Labor; Migration: Internal; Migration: International; Migration: Undocumented/Illegal

SUGGESTED READINGS

Chiswick, B. R. (1991) Review of international differences in the labor market performance of immigrants. *Industrial Labor Relations Review* 44 (3): 570–1.

Duleep, H. O. and Regets, M. (1999) Immigrants and human capital investment. *American Economic Review* 89: 186–91.

Gang, I. N. and Rivera-Batiz, F. L. (1994) Labor market effects of immigration in the United States and Europe: substitution vs. complementarity. *Journal of Population Economics* 7 (2): 157–75.

HARRIET ORCUTT DULEEP AND REGAN MAIN

Milgram, Stanley (experiments)

Stanley Milgram (1933–84) was one of the most influential social psychologists of the twentieth century. Born in New York, he received a Ph.D. from Harvard and subsequently held faculty positions in psychology at Yale University and the City University of New York. Milgram's work was focused on the social-psychological aspects of social structure. He proposed that the mass killings of the Holocaust were primarily the result of the hierarchical bureaucratic organizations and the willingness of people to submit to legitimate authority. Milgram is known for his famous obedience experiments (1960–1963). Milgram recruited unsuspecting male research participants for a study on the effect of punishment on memory, which, in reality, was a well-designed experimental ruse. Participants were asked by an experimenter to assume the role of a "teacher" who would read a series of word pairings, which a "learner" (in reality an actor) was supposed to memorize. Using an electric generator, the experimenter instructed the teacher to apply punishing electric shocks and steadily increase the voltage each time the learner made a new mistake. As mistakes and the voltage of the shocks increased, the learner would increasingly complain and eventually stop responding altogether. Facing the learner's reaction all teachers were agonizing over whether to proceed, repeatedly turning to the experimenter for direction. The experimenter replied with a scripted sequence of verbal prods encouraging the teacher to go on. Indeed, typically a majority of participants (65 percent in the first experiment) continued all the way to 450 volts, which would have likely electrocuted the learner had the generator been real. Milgram's experiments illustrate the powerful effect of the social structure: by accepting the role of teacher in the experiment, participants had agreed to accept the legitimate authority of the experimenter and carry out his instructions even when they had doubts. Though providing important insights, Milgram's obedience studies are generally considered unethical because they exposed research participants to unacceptable levels of stress.

SEE ALSO: Authority and Conformity; Zimbardo Prison Experiment

SUGGESTED READING

Milgram, S. (1974) *Obedience to Authority: An Experimental View*. Harper & Row, New York.

MARKUS KEMMELMEIER

military sociology

Military sociology employs sociological concepts, theories, and methods to analyze the internal organization, practices, and perceptions of the armed forces and the relationships between the military and other social institutions. Some of the topics of investigation include small group processes related to race/ethnicity, gender, and sexual orientation, leadership, policy, veterans, combat, historical cases, the USA and foreign military organization, international affairs, manpower models, the transition from conscription to all-volunteer forces, the social legitimacy of military organization, the military as a form of industrial organization, and civil–military relations.

The military and its members have been an abundant source of information to address a broad range of sociological subfields. Military sociologists often use the differences and similarities between the military and society in conducting their analysis. Military sociology has been used to understand the military and its relationship to other social institutions and also social institutions in and of themselves.

Military sociology can roughly be divided into three distinct time periods corresponding roughly to World War II (1941–50), the cold war (1950–89), and the post-cold war (1989–present) eras. During each of these periods there have been general topics of study which have driven analysis, debate, and study within the field.

Early military sociology was dominated by people in the USA. Some of the early pioneers were Samuel Stouffer, Edward Shils, Morris Janowitz, and S. L. A. Marshall. Their studies used an applied research approach, applicable at the individual and group levels of analysis, to understand soldier adjustment, motivation, and small group processes during World War II.

Military sociology rapidly expanded during the cold war. The cold war caused many to think about how to control large standing forces and ensure that they remained subservient to civil authority. This is referred to as the civil–military relations debate which was spearheaded by Samuel Huntington (1957) and Morris Janowitz (1960).

In 1960 Janowitz founded the Inter-University Seminar on Armed Forces and Society (IUS), which began publishing its own journal, *Armed Forces and Society*, in 1972. In 1965 Charles C. Coates and Roland J. Pellegrin published the first major military sociology textbook, *Military Sociology: A Study of American Military Institutions and Military Life*. The topics that they presented are still generally regarded as the focal points of military sociology.

In the late 1960s and early 1970s military sociology moved toward understanding the social implications of the Vietnam War on both the military and society. In the USA political, social and economic strife were manifested in the US military in the form of increased use of illicit drugs, fragging incidents, absenteeism, draft evasion, and race riots within the ranks of the US Armed Forces.

The establishment of the All-Volunteer Force in 1973 produced an onslaught of military sociological thought and debate. The *Journal of Political and Military Science*, founded in 1973 at Northern Illinois University, and *Armed Forces and Society* were the two major journals that provided a forum for these debates.

In the early 1970s Charles C. Moskos developed the institutional/occupational (I/O) model, which suggested that military service was moving away from being a calling towards becoming an occupation. This theoretical model was the impetus for much of the debate within the field throughout the 1970s and early 1980s. During the 1980s the field continued to grow and became more internationally focused. The number of international sociologists studying within the field increased substantially during this decade.

The end of the cold war changed the nature of war and how states viewed the use of their militaries. Military sociology has attempted to understand how these changes have impacted the relationship between the military and society. Throughout this period there was also a concern that a culture gap existed between civil society and the military. The ensuing debate, originated by Peter Feaver and Richard Kohn, produced large volumes of work. Recently, the events of September 11, 2001 and the subsequent conflicts in Iraq and Afghanistan have added a new chapter to military sociology

SEE ALSO: Anti-War and Peace Movements; War; World Conflict

REFERENCES

Huntington, S. P. (1957) *The Soldier and the State: The Theory and Politics of Civil–Military Relations*. Harvard University Press, Cambridge, MA.

Janowitz, M. (1960) *The Professional Soldier: A Social and Political Portrait*. Free Press, Glencoe, IL.

SUGGESTED READINGS

Booth, B., Kestnbaum, M., & Segal, D. R. (2001) Are post-cold war militaries postmodern? *Armed Forces and Society* 27: 319.

Eric, O. (ed.). (2005) *New Directions in Military Sociology*: de Sitter Publications, Ontario.

IRVING SMITH

Mills, C. Wright (1916–62)

C. Wright Mills is perhaps the most recognized figure in the history of sociology in the USA. He authored three of US sociology's most influential books – *White Collar* (1951), *The Power Elite* (1956), and *The Sociological Imagination* (1959) – and did much else to define US sociology's distinctive character.

C. Wright Mills was born Charles Wright Mills in Waco, Texas, on August 28, 1916. He earned a BA in sociology and an MA in philosophy from the University of Texas at Austin in 1939 and his doctorate in sociology from the University of Wisconsin at Madison in 1942. Mills served as a professor of sociology at the University of Maryland at College Park before accepting appointments at the Bureau of Applied Social Research and, in 1946, a faculty position in the Department of Sociology at Columbia University, which Mills held until his death at the age of 45 on March 20, 1962.

Mills' critical sociology fused American pragmatist philosophy and European social theory into a parallel to Frankfurt School-style critical theory. Mills regarded this work as a continuation of "the classic tradition" of sociology, which was founded most of all in the work of Max Weber and Karl Marx (see his books *From Max Weber* [1946] and *Images of Man* [1960]). Mills's particular contribution to this style stemmed from the fact that he was among the first to glimpse the rise of what he called "post-modern society," which he analyzed, on the one hand, in terms of mass society's self-reproduction (*The New Men of Power* [1948], *White Collar* [1951]), and the advent of the nuclear state on the other (*The Power Elite* [1956], *The Causes of World War Three* [1958], *Listen, Yankee* [1960]). In the above as well as in such political documents as his "Letter to the new left" (1960), Mills also engaged in partisan opposition to these dominant tendencies of his age. A "new left" was needed, he argued, because postmodernity rendered reason and freedom moot in everyday human affairs, and was geared structurally to end in the destruction of humankind as such.

When Dwight D. Eisenhower delivered his famous farewell address to the nation in 1961 in which he warned of the pernicious development of a "military-industrial complex," he gave C. Wright Mills's *The Power Elite* perhaps the best de facto book review in the history of US sociology. When President John F. Kennedy defended his policy toward Castro's Cuba by explaining that he was President of the USA, "not some sociologist," he suggested the public importance of Mills' timely and urgent interventions into the crises of his times. And when it is recalled that Mills passed away only a months prior to the Cuban Missile Crisis, it is not difficult to appreciate the urgency and passion which Mills infused in his later work, what, in a relatively light-hearted moment one imagines, Mills called his "preachings."

Mills's legacy continues to be assessed. New studies of Mills's sociology, his politics, and even his biography compete for shelf-space with new editions of his most enduring books, publication of his letters and autobiographical writings, and new collections of his many scholarly articles and essays. Mills's currency is only partly explained by the intrinsic value and attraction of his engaging style, as documented both in his writings and in the often exaggerated, no doubt, remembrance of his larger-than-life persona. More significant, and more consistent with Mills's own historically-grounded sociological project, Mills's legacy remains debated because the everyday denizens of postmodernity – Mills' primary audience – continue to struggle to gain perspective and self-understanding and the means to face down new threats to their well-being and survival.

SEE ALSO: Critical Theory/Frankfurt School; Power Elite; Pragmatism; Sociological Imagination

SUGGESTED READINGS

Aronowitz, S. (ed.) (2004) *C. Wright Mills*, 3 vols. Sage, Thousand Oaks, CA.

Summers, J. (ed.) (2008) *The Politics of Truth: Selected Writings of C. Wright Mills*. Oxford University Press, Oxford.

STEVEN P. DANDANEAU

mind

Mind is often thought of as located in the brain as the site of human reason, intelligence, and the experience of consciousness. George Herbert Mead put forth a version of mind as rooted beyond the individual in social experience, formed through interaction with the environment through attempts to manipulate it, and resulting in a conception of mind as essentially self-reflective. Both social adaptation and self-consciousness are achieved through the human capacity for language.

For Mead the origins of thinking are social and related to the organism's interaction with the environment. Mead is not a sensationalist; the human capacity to select an object or particular characteristics of an object to attend to is rooted in the goals of potential human conduct toward that object, what Mead refers to as the *act*. The mind is not a blank slate that impartially takes in all objects; nor are individuals' concerns in the environment given by a priori interests and structures. The individual develops a history of interactions with the environment of inanimate objects and others that develops connections in the central nervous system between images and language (significant symbols), creating memories that are invoked when similar situations arise. The individual, unlike the animal, has a history of significant memories that are invoked in the brain as responses to certain stimuli in the environment. Humans differ from animals in the capacity to provide internal stimuli to the self.

Beginning with a *conversation of gestures*, humans develop language or shared *significant symbols* that relate to significant objects in the human environment and these eventually lead to the development of abstractions. Language allows an individual to communicate with oneself as well as with others. Unlike animals, human consciousness has the capacity for delay between stimulus and response; this delay coupled with the ability to use symbols to communicate with oneself, creates the human capacity for thought, as well as freedom from determination by external stimuli. Humans can both invoke their own stimuli, using imagery or significant symbols, and resist external stimuli.

Influenced by Watson's behaviorism which focused on observable behavior but rejected consciousness as an object of study, Mead's social behaviorism posits the objective character of consciousness in the capacity for shared meaning. The capacity for thought develops in social interaction by means of the acquisition of shared significant symbols which arouse the same responses in self as others. Meaning resides in this shared significance; through their capacity of being shareable, significant symbols are universal and objective. The contents of the mind are neither subjective nor private, but, rather, objective.

The capacity for conscious thought arises when an obstacle prevents an habitual response to a stimulus and where several alternative courses of action present themselves for potential conduct. When this involves others, the goal for the individual is one of adjustment, fitting one's actions to the environment in ways that allow one to predict or control the responses of others. This capacity for *role-taking* or *taking the role of the other* is premised on the idea that one can anticipate others' reactions to possible courses of action by means of the shared, objective meanings one has developed. One incorporates into the process of role-taking the perspectives of *particular others* and eventually, the more abstract perspectives of *generalized others* which reflect the shared meanings of the various communities to which one belongs.

Yet the individual is not captive to the meanings of the community. Mead's notion of *the I and the me* reflects the mind's interior dialogue, both its capacity for self-reflection and ability to make an object of itself and its capacity for spontaneity and creativity. Acts and cooperative social behavior must be constructed anew; the ability to think through significant symbols not only allows one to create new social constructs but allows individuals to develop new social structures.

SEE ALSO: Behaviorism; Generalized Other; Mead, George Herbert; Reflexivity; Role-Taking; Self; Significant Symbol; Symbolic Interaction

REFERENCES

Joas, H. (1997) *G.H. Mead: A Contemporary Re-examination of His Thought*. MIT Press, Cambridge, MA.

Mead, G. H. (1934) *Mind, Self, and Society*. University of Chicago Press, Chicago, IL.

ALLISON CARTER

mobility, horizontal and vertical

The notion that in contemporary highly industrialized societies persons may climb up or slide down the social ladder presupposed some scale with an upper end and a lower end and the possibility of ranking people on it. Individual income can be taken as such a scale, and if this is used it is possible to speak of upward and downward mobility and to quantify the extent to which a person is upwardly or downwardly mobile. Occupational status, as indicated by the prestige accorded to occupations in surveys involving representative samples from a country's population, also makes it possible to ascertain mobility. In these cases a sociologist speaks of *vertical* mobility.

Sometimes sociologists also speak of *horizontal* mobility. In that case, they do not avail themselves of a scale allowing a full ranking of persons. A case in point are class schemas, for instance the one developed by Erikson and Goldthorpe (1992) for research on social mobility involving a comparison of countries. This schema has a "top": the persons belonging to what they call the service class. It has a "bottom," too: the unskilled and semi-skilled manual workers in industry, together with agricultural workers. However, the schema does not rank the intermediate categories, such as those for skilled manual workers, routine non-manual workers, farmers, and small proprietors. Movement from these categories to the service class is upward mobility, and movement to the class of unskilled manual workers is downward mobility, but movement from one of these intermediate categories to another of these intermediate categories is horizontal mobility.

Of course, it is possible to rank the various intermediate categories according to the average income of their members, but class schemas are not about income. They refer to the work relations of persons (and the hypothesis for further research is that work relations affect income). Persons in some jobs follow commands, persons in other jobs give commands, and some persons have a business all their own that involves neither supervision nor being commanded. The labor contract of some persons stipulates that they can be laid off immediately in slack periods, while other contracts do not allow for this. The output of some persons is easily monitored and of others not at all. This multiplicity of work relations makes for classes that can be ranked below other classes and above yet other classes, but not among each other.

According to Erikson and Goldthorpe, horizontal mobility is as interesting to study as vertical mobility. A case in point is the contraction of the agricultural sector in industrial societies. Farm laborers left their jobs, mainly going to unskilled manual jobs in the industrial sector, and farmers often became self-employed in small businesses connected to the agrarian sector. Thus, this sectorial transformation of a country's economy did not lead to upward mobility, as some theories of modernization have held, but only to horizontal mobility.

SEE ALSO: Income Inequality and Income Mobility; Income Inequality, Global; Inequality, Wealth

REFERENCE

Erikson, R. & Goldthorpe, J. H. (1992) *The Constant Flux*. Oxford University Press, Oxford.

WOUT ULTEE

modernity

The idea of modernity concerns the interpretation of the present time in light of historical reinterpretation. It refers too to the confluence of the cultural, social, and political currents in modern society. The term signals a tension within modern society between its various dynamics and suggests a process by which society constantly renews itself.

The term modernity as opposed to modern did not arise until the nineteenth century. One of the most famous uses of the term was in 1864, when the French poet Baudelaire (1964: 13) gave it the most well-known definition: "By modernity I mean the transitory, the fugitive, the contingent." Baudelaire's definition of modernity was reflected in part in modernism to indicate a particular cultural current in modern society that captured the sense of renewal and cosmopolitanism of modern life. It signaled a spirit of creativity and renewal that was most radically expressed in the avant-garde movement. But the term had a wider social and political resonance in the spirit of revolution and social reconstruction that was a feature of the nineteenth century. Marx and Engels in the *Communist Manifesto* invoked the spirit of modernity with their description of modern society and capitalism as the condition "all that is solid melts into air."

Within classical sociology, Georg Simmel is generally regarded as the figure who first gave a more rigorous sociological interpretation of modernity, with his account of social life in the modern city. For Simmel, as for Benjamin, modernity is expressed in diverse "momentary images" or "snapshots." The fragmentation of modern society, on the one side, and on the other new technologies such as the camera and the cinema led to more and more such moments and the feeling that there is nothing durable and solid.

Modernity may thus be described simply as the loss of certainty and the realization that certainty can never be established once and for all. It is a term that also can simply refer to reflection on the age and in particular to movements within modern society that lead to the emergence of new modes of thought and consciousness.

Developments within postmodern thought gave additional weight to modernity as containing autonomous logics of development and unfulfilled potential. Several theorists argued that the postmodern moment should be seen to be merely modernity in a new key. What has emerged out of these developments is a new interest in "cultural modernity" as a countermovement in modern society. Rather than dispensing with modernity, postmodernism and postcolonialism have given a new significance to the idea of modernity which now lies at the center of many debates in sociology and other related disciplines in the social and human sciences.

Anthony Giddens and Ulrich Beck, in different but related ways, have highlighted the reflexivity of modernity. The notion of reflexive modernization, or reflexive modernity, is aimed to capture the ways in which much of the movement of modernity acts upon itself. Beck has introduced the notion of late modernity as a "second modernity," while Giddens characterized modernity in terms of "disembedding" processes such as the separation of time and space. Such approaches to the question of modernity have been principally responding to the challenge of globalization. Globalization can be seen as a process that intensifies connections between many parts of the world, and as such it is one of the primary mechanisms of modernity today. This has led some theorists to refer to global modernity, for modernity today is global.

On the one side, modernity is indeed global, but on the other there is a diversity of routes to modernity. The problem thus becomes one of how to reconcile the diversity of societal forms with a conception of modernity that acknowledges the consequences of globalization. It is in this context that the term multiple modernities can be introduced. Originally advocated by S. N. Eisenstadt (2003), this has grown out of the debate on globalization, comparative civilizational analysis, and the postcolonial concern with "alternative modernities" (Gaonkar 2001). Central to this approach is a conceptualization of modernity as plural condition. Associated with this turn in the theory of modernity is a gradual movement away from the exclusive concern with western modernity to a more cosmopolitan perspective.

SEE ALSO: Capitalism; Civilizations; Globalization; Modernization; Postmodern Social Theory; Postmodernism; Reflexive Modernization

REFERENCE

Baudelaire, C. (1964) The painter of modern life. In: *The Painter of Modern Life and Other Essays*. Phaidon Press, London.

SUGGESTED READINGS

Bauman, Z. (1987) *Legislators and Interpreters: On Modernity, Postmodernity, and Intellectuals*. Polity Press, Cambridge.
Beck, U., Giddens, A., & Lash, S. (1994) *Reflexive Modernization*. Polity Press, Cambridge.
Eisenstadt, S. N. (2003) *Comparative Civilizations and Multiple Modernities*, vols. 1 and 2. Brill, Leiden.
Gaonkar, D. P. (ed.) (2001) *Alternative Modernities*. Duke University Press, Durham, NC.

GERARD DELANTY

modernization

Modernization is an encompassing process of massive social changes that, once set in motion, tends to penetrate all domains of life, from economic activities to social life to political institutions, in a self-reinforcing process. Modernization brings an intense awareness of change and innovation, linked with the idea that human societies are progressing.

Historically, the idea of human progress is relatively new. As long as societies did not exert significant control over their environment and were helplessly exposed to the vagaries of natural forces, and as long as agrarian economies were trapped in a steady-state equilibrium where no growth in mass living standards took place, the idea of human progress seemed unrealistic. The situation began to change only when sustained economic growth began to occur.

However, the idea of human progress was contested from the beginning by opposing ideas that considered ongoing societal changes as a sign of human decay. Thus, modernization theory was doomed to make a career swinging between wholehearted appreciation and fierce rejection, depending on whether the dominant mood of the time was rather optimistic or pessimistic. The history of modernization theory is thus the history of antimodernization theory. Both are ideological reflections of far-ranging dynamics that continue to accelerate the pace of social change since the rise of pre-industrial capitalism.

The term modernization connotes first of all changes in production technology inducing major economic transitions from pre-industrial to industrial societies and from industrial to postindustrial societies. All these changes originate in humans' intellectual achievements in the sciences, which manifest themselves in an ever-increasing technological control over various mechanical, chemical, electronic, and biological processes. The social transformations initiated by these technological changes have various massive consequences on the societies' outlook, such as the growth of mass-based human resources, occupational diversification, organizational differentiation, state capacity growth and state activity extension, mass political involvement, and rationalization and secularization. The common denominator of all these aspects of modernization is the growing complexity, knowledge intensity, and sophistication of performed human activities.

Modernization theory emerged in the Enlightenment era with the belief that technological progress would give humanity increasing control over nature. Adam Smith and Karl Marx propagated competing versions of modernization, with Smith advocating a capitalist vision, and Marx advocating communism. Competing versions of modernization theory enjoyed a new resurgence after World War II when the capitalist and communist superpowers espoused opposing ideologies as guidelines for the best route to modernity. Although they competed fiercely, both ideologies were committed to economic growth, social progress, and modernization, and they both brought broader mass participation in politics (Moore 1966).

Modernization theory's career is closely linked with theories of underdevelopment. In the post-war USA, a version of modernization theory emerged that viewed underdevelopment as a direct consequence of a country's internal characteristics, especially its traditional psychological and cultural traits. This perspective was strongly influenced by Max Weber's theory of the cultural origins of capitalism, which viewed underdevelopment as a function of traditionally irrational, spiritual, and communal values – values that discourage human achievement motivation. From this perspective, traditional values were not only mutable but could – and should – also be replaced by modern values, enabling these societies to follow the path of capitalist development. The causal agents in this developmental process were seen as the rich developed nations that stimulated the modernization of "backward" nations through economic, cultural, and military assistance.

This version of modernization theory was not merely criticized as patronizing, it was pronounced dead (Wallerstein 1976). Neo-Marxist and world-systems theorists argued that rich countries exploit poor countries, locking them in positions of powerlessness and structural dependence. This school of thought conveys the message to poor countries that poverty has nothing to do with their traditional values: it is the fault of global capitalism. In the 1970s and 1980s, modernization theory seemed discredited; dependency theory came into vogue (Cardoso & Faletto 1979). Adherents of dependency theory claimed that the third world nations could only escape from global exploitation if they withdrew from the world market and adopted import substitution policies.

Modernization theories have been criticized for their tendency toward technological and socioeconomic determinism. Usually these critiques cite Max Weber (1958 [1904]), who reversed the Marxian notion that technologically induced socioeconomic development determines cultural change. Indeed, in his explanation of the rise of capitalism, Weber turns causality in the opposite direction, arguing that the Calvinist variant of Protestantism (along with other factors) led to the rise of a capitalist economy rather than the other way round. Revised versions of modernization theory (Inglehart & Baker 2000) emphasize that both Marx and Weber were partly correct: on one hand, socioeconomic development brings predictable cultural changes in people's moral values; but on the other hand, these changes are path dependent, so that a society's initial starting position remains visible in its relative position to other societies, reflecting its cultural heritage. Nevertheless, recent evidence indicates that – even though the relationship between socioeconomic development and cultural change is reciprocal – the stronger causal arrow seems to run from socioeconomic development to cultural change (Inglehart & Welzel 2005).

SEE ALSO: Dependency and World-Systems Theories; Economic Development; Industrialization; Political Economy; Post-Industrial Society; Social Change; Solidarity, Mechanical and Organic

REFERENCES

Cardoso, F. H. & Faletto, E. (1979) *Dependency and Development in Latin America*. University of California Press, Berkeley, CA.

Inglehart, R. & Baker, W. E. (2000) Modernization, cultural change, and the persistence of traditional values. *American Sociological Review* 65 (February): 19–51.

Inglehart, R. & Welzel, C. (2005) *Modernization, Cultural Change, and Democracy*. Cambridge University Press, New York.

Moore, B. (1966) *The Social Origins of Democracy and Dictatorship: Lord and Peasant in the Making of the Modern World*. Beacon Press, Boston, MA.

Wallerstein, I. (1976) Modernization: requiescat in pace. In: Coser, L. A. & Larsen, O. N. (eds.), *The Uses of Controversy in Sociology*. Free Press, New York, pp. 131–5.
Weber, M. (1958) [1904] *The Protestant Ethic and the Spirit of Capitalism*. Charles Scribner's Sons, New York.

RONALD INGLEHART AND CHRISTIAN WELZEL

money

Significant theoretical contributions to a sociological understanding of money were made by Marx, Simmel and Weber, among others. According to Marx, money is a commodity, and its quantitative relationship to other commodities – its function as a "universal measure of value" – is made possible by the amount of labour-time that it contains. This is not only true of precious metals but of other forms of "credit" money, such as banknotes, which derive their value from a commodity such as gold. Thus to view exchange relations merely as "monetary" relations, or as a series of prices determined by supply and demand, is to overlook the social relations of production – and, of course, exploitation – on which they fundamentally depend. Weber focused primarily on the legal status of money, broadly agreeing with Knapp's characterization of money as a "creature of the state." Simmel took a quite different view of the value of money. By his reckoning, money represents an abstract idea of value that is underwritten by "society": its value, in other words, ultimately depends on a form of trust in society that Simmel likened to "quasi-religious faith." On the basis of the characterization, Simmel (1994) explored the roots and consequences of the development of the "mature money economy," whereby an increasing number of social relationships are mediated by money.

In economics, money is usually defined in terms of three main functions: money is a medium of exchange, a store of value, a unit of account. Classical sociologists were mainly concerned with money's role as a store of value. Marx explored the relationship between money and gold, for example, while Weber discussed the distinctiveness and viability of state issued "paper" money. Even Simmel, who used money as a means for a much wider philosophical investigation into the role of exchange in modern culture, began his study with the question of value.

At the beginning of the twenty-first century, sociologists are addressing a rather different set of concerns than their classical forebears. The central question no longer concerns the "value" of money once its connection with gold has been severed. Instead, sociologists, together with scholars in related disciplines, have been exploring an apparent decline in the relationship between money and the state. This development is not a straightforward process, and its implications remain contested.

Recently, however, a number of sociologists have produced major publications in which they sought to develop a systematic sociological treatment of money. Zelizer (1994) argued against an image of money as "neutral" and "impersonal" through an historical analysis that examined money in relation to the social context of its use. Dodd (1994) sought to elaborate Simmel's concept of money as a "pure instrument" by relating it to consumerism and the globalization of finance. More recently, Ingham (2004) has brought sociological arguments to bear on theories of money in orthodox and heterodox economics.

The present-day world of money is characterized by two countervailing trends. To some degree, these reflect contrasting approaches to the sociology of money. On the one hand, large-scale currencies such as the US dollar are increasingly circulating outside the borders of their issuing states, and in some cases are actually replacing smaller currencies. This process constitutes a trend towards increasing *homogeneity*. On the other hand, the range of monetary forms in circulation that are not state-issued currency is increasing, primarily through the development of e-money and complementary currencies. This constitutes a trend towards increasing *diversity*. For sociologists, these developments offer some exciting research opportunities.

SEE ALSO: Economy (Sociological Approach); Globalization; Markets; Simmel, Georg

REFERENCES

Dodd, N. (1994) *The Sociology of Money*. Polity Press, Cambridge.
Ingham, G. (2004) *The Nature of Money*. Polity Press, Cambridge.
Simmel, G. (1907) *The Philosophy of Money*
Zelizer, V. (1994) *The Social Meaning of Money*. Princeton University Press, Princeton, NJ.

NIGEL DODD

moral economy

Moral economy can be defined as a common notion of the just distribution of resources and social exchange. The concept has been developed and is used in the context of political and social analysis to understand, for example, various systems of social exchange or instances of rebellion. It is claimed that social communities tend to invoke a moral repertoire for all kinds of social exchanges and transfers that leads them to distinguish between legitimate and illegitimate social practices.

E. P. Thompson's (1971) study on the eighteenth-century food riots first popularized the term moral economy. He observes how the emergence of the market order seriously challenges traditional normative standards, and thereby evoked popular resistance and protest. According to his account, it was not "objective" forms of hardship that engendered social protest, but rather the violation of well-entrenched communal values. Since there is a widespread consensus about legitimate and illegitimate social practices people are ready to engage in a moral protest. Thompson's contribution has inspired a whole branch of anthropological and ethnographic studies dealing with diverse peasant societies. Their findings show that the marketization of traditional societies tends to violate well-entrenched norms and reciprocities and thereby triggers social and political unrest.

One of the key concepts of the moral economy approach is the idea of embeddedness, which highlights the notion that economic behavior in traditional societies takes place within the context of religious, social, and political institutions. Karl Polanyi's book *The Great Transformation* (1957) investigates the conditions and rationales of economic exchanges and distinguishes the embedded (traditional) and the disembedded or autonomous (modern) economies.

In the light of more recent evidence it has been suggested that the concept of the moral economy rests too heavily on the distinction between market and non-market-based societies. Also, modern societies are not devoid of forms of moral regulation. Thus, beyond the accounts that deal with the trajectory from traditional to modern societies, the moral economy framework has inspired a larger part of economic sociology challenging some of the propositions of economic and rational choice theory. Rather than conceiving the profit-seeking individual as *the* pivot of economic behavior, a closer understanding of the sociocultural components and determinants of behavior is needed. By the same token, the idea of autonomous, self-regulating markets needs critical revision in favor of revealing the institutional and political, but also normative prerequisites of how the market functions. Critics of the moral economy approach suggest that it "moralizes" and "over-socializes" individual actions. For some, the moral economic framework sticks to a rather generalized understanding of morality that is not prepared to construe and to identify the role of specific social relations.

SEE ALSO: Morality; Polanyi, Karl

REFERENCE

Thompson, E. P. (1971) The Moral economy of the English crowd in the eighteenth century. *Past and Present: A Journal of Historical Studies* 50: 79–136.

SUGGESTED READING

Booth, W. J. (1994) On the idea of the moral economy. *American Political Science Review* 88 (3): 653–67.

STEFFEN MAU

moral panics

Moral panic refers to a distinctive type of social deviance characterized by a heightened sense of threat in some segment of the population, sudden emergence and subsidence, attribution of the troubled condition to a "folk devil," and a disproportionate response relative to an objectively assessed threat level. The term moral panic was initially coined by Jock Young in Stanley Cohen's *Images of Deviance* (1971). Cohen subsequently employed the concept in his study of two 1960s British youth movements, *Folk Devils and Moral Panics* (1972). He defined a moral panic as a group or condition that is a response to a threat to established values or interests. The central actors in moral panics include the media, the public, law enforcement agencies, political officials, and action groups. The targets are "folk devils," individuals or groups who personify evil by engaging in harmful behavior that must be halted.

The most systematic theoretical formulation of the moral panics concept has been developed by Erich Goode and Nachman Ben-Yehuda in *Moral Panics: The Social Construction of Deviance* (1994). They enumerate a number of indicators of a moral panic focused on a group or category: heightened concern, increased hostility, consensus about the threat, disproportionality of the threat, and episode volatility. The concept of moral panics has been profitably applied to a number of episodes over the last several decades involving controversy over issues such as illicit drug use, the existence of religious and satanic cults, the vulnerability of young children, predatory crime, troublesome youth, and sexual exploitation and deviance.

Scholars also continue to debate whether moral panic constitutes a discrete, meaningful category of sociological analysis and the relative merit of functionalist and critical theory perspectives. These various critiques suggest a number of theoretical and methodological issues that have yet to be resolved.

SEE ALSO: Deviance, Constructionist Perspectives; Moral Economy; Morality

REFERENCE

Goode, E. & Ben-Yehuda, N. (1994) *Moral Panics: The Social Construction of Deviance*. Blackwell, Oxford.

DAVID G. BROMLEY

mortality: transitions and measures

In the course of human history, life expectancy at birth has increased from around 20–30 years during prehistoric times to 75–80 years in many low-mortality countries today. Nearly half of this increase has taken place during the twentieth century. The highest life expectancy has been recorded in Japan, a developed country where health improvements in the early part of the twentieth century lagged behind those of European countries, but where mortality declines have been particularly impressive since the 1950s. Life expectancy at birth in Japan reached 84.6 years for women and 77.6 years for men by the year 2000. Moreover, the United Nations' estimates show an average life expectancy of 74.8 years in the more developed regions of the world, with 56 percent of industrialized countries having life expectancies of over 75 years in 1995–2000. The lowest life expectancies in industrialized countries are found in Eastern Europe and the former Soviet Union, where health conditions stagnated during the late twentieth century, particularly for adult men.

By the middle of the twentieth century, life expectancy in the less developed regions of the world had reached 40.9 years and it had further increased to 62.5 years by the end of the century according to the United Nations' estimates. These gains are impressive and suggest that life expectancy more than doubled between 1900 and 2000 in most parts of the developing world. As a result, the gap in average life expectancy between more and less developed regions has narrowed over time – from about 26 years in 1950–5 to about 11 years in 1995–2000. The mortality decline in developing countries, however, has not been uniform, and the slower pace of improvement in the least developed regions relative to others has led to a greater disparity among developing countries over time. Estimates show an average life expectancy of only about 50 years in Africa, with only 21 percent of African countries having estimated life expectancies of 60 years or more. In contrast, the average life expectancy was estimated to be around 69 years in Latin America, with 64 percent of Latin American countries having life expectancies of 70 years or more.

The epidemiologic transition, a shift from infectious diseases to chronic degenerative diseases as leading causes of death, has been instrumental in shaping trends in human mortality and the age pattern of mortality decline. The fall in death rates from infectious diseases led to significant improvements in the survival chances of infants and young children and was largely responsible for the rise in life expectancy in the late nineteenth and early twentieth centuries in industrialized countries, and during the second half of the twentieth century in less developed regions of the world. These reductions in infant and child mortality, together with a decline in fertility, have contributed to a shift in the population age distribution toward an older population in both developed and developing countries. As a result, chronic degenerative diseases have become more common and today represent an ever-increasing percentage of all deaths even as adult mortality has continued to decline in most places. Future gains in life expectancy in industrialized nations will thus largely depend on trends in mortality from such leading chronic diseases as heart disease and cancer at older ages.

Many less developed countries have experienced an epidemiologic transition characterized by overlapping eras whereby chronic diseases of middle and older ages have become more common as populations have aged, at the time that childhood infectious diseases have continued to create a major health burden among the poor. The emergence of HIV/AIDS and drug-resistant varieties of tuberculosis and malaria is perhaps the best example of the continued impact of infectious diseases on mortality.

Many factors have influenced the mortality trends discussed above, including improvements in living standards, public health measures, cultural and behavioral factors, modern medical technologies, and the actions of governments and international agencies and organizations. Most notably, much of the mortality reduction at older ages in the latter decades of the twentieth century was due to decline in death rates from cardiovascular diseases. In addition, behavioral changes, most importantly reductions in smoking, have contributed to mortality decline, especially among men.

SEE ALSO: Biodemography; Demographic Data: Censuses, Registers, Surveys; Demographic Transition Theory; HIV/AIDS and Population; Socioeconomic Status

SUGGESTED READINGS

Omran, A. R. (1971) The epidemiologic transition: a theory of the epidemiology of population change. *Milbank Memorial Fund Quarterly* 49 (4): 509–37.

Preston, S. H. (1995) Human mortality throughout history and prehistory. In: Simon, J. L. (ed.),

The State of Humanity. Blackwell, Cambridge, MA, pp. 30–6.
United Nations (1999) *Health and Mortality Issues of Global Concern*. United Nations, New York.

IRMA T. ELO

motherhood

Motherhood is the word that sociologists use when referring to social experiences associated with being a mother. The term is meant to differentiate the biological fact of producing a baby (becoming a mother) and practices involved in taking care of children (mothering) from social norms linked to creating and caring for children. Theorists of motherhood treat its institutionalization as a social arrangement to explain, rather than as a biological given. They conceptualize why mothers mother as they do through psychoanalytic as well as economic and political lenses. They examine dominant ideologies of "good" mothering created in expert advice literature, interactions between women and men, and women's identities.

Although much scholarly work combines theoretical examination with empirical grounding, there remain gaps between what scholars think about motherhood and what they actually know through examination of mothers' actual experiences. Future research should seek to close these gaps as well as to embed the study of mothers in their social worlds. Mothers enact mothering with other people: children, and often, adult partners. Our understanding of motherhood will increase by studying mothers' interactions in the context of other institutions that intersect with motherhood: fatherhood, work, marriage, heterosexuality, and gender.

SEE ALSO: Fatherhood; Gender, Work, and Family

SUGGESTED READINGS

Arendell, T. (2000) Conceiving and investigating motherhood: the decade's scholarship. *Journal of Marriage and the Family* 62: 1192–1207.
Hays, S. (1996) *The Cultural Contradictions of Motherhood*. Yale University Press, New Haven, CT.

SUSAN WALZER

multiculturalism

The term "multiculturalism" emerged in the 1960s in Anglophone countries. The policy focus was often initially on schooling and the children of Asian/black/Hispanic post/neo-colonial immigrants, and multiculturalism meant the extension of the school, both in terms of curriculum and as an institution, to include features such as "mother-tongue" teaching, non-Christian religions and holidays, halal food, Asian dress, and so on. From such a starting point, the perspective can develop to meeting such cultural requirements in other or even all social spheres and the empowering of marginalized groups. In Canada and Australia the focus was much wider from the start and included, for example, constitutional and land issues and has been about the definition of the nation. Hence, even today, both in theoretical and policy discourses, multiculturalism means different things in different places. While in North America, language-based ethnicity is seen as the major political challenge, in western Europe, the conjunction of the terms "immigration" and "culture" now nearly always invoke the large, newly-settled Muslim populations. Central to multiculturalism and the politics of difference is the rejection of the idea that political concepts such as equality and citizenship can be colour-blind and culture-neutral, and the contention that ethnicity and culture cannot be confined to some so-called private sphere but shape political and opportunity structures in all societies. It is the basis for the conclusion that allegedly "neutral" liberal democracies have hegemonic cultures that systematically de-ethnicize or marginalize minorities. Hence, the claim that minority cultures, norms and symbols have as much right as their hegemonic counterparts to state provision and to be in the public space, to be "recognized" as groups and not just as culturally-neutered individuals.

One of the most fundamental divisions amongst scholars concerns the validity of "cultural groups" as a point of reference for multiculturalism. The dominant view in socio-cultural studies has become that groups always have internal differences, including hierarchies, gender inequality and dissent, and culture is always fluid and subject to varied influences, mixtures and change. To think otherwise is to "essentialize" groups such as blacks, Muslims, Asians, and so on. Political theorists, on the other hand, continue to think of cultural groups as socio-political actors who may bear rights and have needs that should be institutionally accommodated. This approach challenges the view of culture as radically unstable and primarily expressive by putting moral communities at the centre of a definition of "culture." Empirical studies, however, suggest that both these views have some substance. For while many young people, from majority and minority backgrounds, do not wish to be defined by a singular ethnicity but wish to actively mix and share several heritages, there is simultaneously a development of distinct communities, usually ethno-religious, and sometimes seeking corporate representation.

Since "9/11" and its aftermath it is Muslims that have become the focus of discourse about minorities in the west. This is partly an issue of security, but more generally is accompanied by a "multiculturalism is dead" rhetoric. This has led to, or reinforced, policy reversals in many countries and is marked by the fact that a new assimilationism is espoused not just on the political right but also on the centre-left and by erstwhile supporters of multiculturalism. Muslims in western Europe it is argued are disloyal to European states, prefer segregation and socio-cultural separatism to integration; they are illiberal on a range of issues, most notably on the personal freedom of women and on homosexuality; and they are challenging the secular character of European political culture by thrusting religious identities and communalism into the public space. The last charge marks the most serious theoretical reversal of multiculturalism as the non-privatization of minority identities is one of the core ideas of multiculturalism. Yet the emergence of Muslim political mobilization has led some multiculturalists to argue that religion is a feature of plural societies that is uniquely legitimate to confine to the private sphere. This prohibiting of Muslim identity in public space has so far been taken furthest in France, where in 2004 Parliament passed, with little debate but an overwhelming majority, a ban on the wearing of "ostentatious" religious symbols (primarily the *hijab* (headscarf)) in public schools.

SEE ALSO: Culture; Globalization, Culture and; Subculture

SUGGESTED READINGS

Modood, T. (2005) *Multicultural Politics: Racism, Ethnicity, and Muslims in Britain*. Minnesota and Edinburgh University Presses, Edinburgh.

Said, E. (1978) *Orientalism*. Routledge, London.

TARIQ MODOOD

multivariate analysis

Multivariate analysis involves, in the loose sense of the term, more than two variables and, in its strict sense, at least two dependent and two independent variables. Multivariate analysis procedures can be classified in different ways, and no classification is exhaustive, especially due to the dynamics of the field.

With increasing numbers of variables, statistical modeling becomes necessary and more complex. At the same time, these models are more appropriate for social sciences, since in social reality many variables are intertwined and there is rarely one central determination.

Once data are collected and read into a database processable by statistical software, the typical steps in a multivariate data analysis are the following.

1. *Framing the research question* in such a way that it can be modeled mathematically.
2. *Selecting the right statistical model*: every multivariate model searches for certain patterns in data. It might miss other patterns. Using different multivariate methods therefore may lead to different results. Among the theoretical questions multivariate analysis can address are: (a) identifying latent classes; (b) causal analysis; (c) identifying patterns in time; (d) network analysis; and (e) multilevel analysis. Most multivariate procedures can be viewed as a special case of general linear models (GLM).
3. *Verifying that assumptions and prerequisites* for the chosen statistical procedure are met.
4. *Preparing data for the specific analysis.*
5. *Computing the model* using a special statistical computer package such as SAS, SPSS, or Stata.
6. *The results of data analysis always have to be interpreted.*

SEE ALSO: ANOVA (Analysis of Variance); General Linear Model; Statistics

SUGGESTED READINGS

Quantitative Applications in the Social Sciences Series. Sage, London.

Scott, J., & Xie, Y. (eds.) (2005) *Quantitative Social Science*. Sage, London.

NINA BAUR AND SIEGFRIED LAMNEK

myth

A myth is a story with a parallel structure linking the past to the present and suggesting directions for the future. A myth may be a cautionary tale, a moral tale, or a tale of idealized behavioral standards, as in hero myths. As a sociological term the use of the word myth has been rather casual. Sociologists refer to the "myth" of masculinity, the "myth" of self-esteem or the "myth" of the mommy role. This use of the term imputes a less-than-factual status to the topic of reference and calls into question the veracity of others' accounts and theories. However, sociology currently lacks a clear concept of myth such as is found in anthropology or cultural studies.

Comparative evolutionary anthropology, of which Frazer's *The Golden Bough* (1890) is perhaps the most recognized example, links contemporary myths to primitive rituals in the search for meaning through mystical experiences. A more modern structural approach to the anthropology of myth derives primarily from the work of Lévi-Strauss (1978) in which he reexamines the dismissive attitude of western cultures toward the myths (cultural narratives) of nonindustrial societies and suggests the valuable purpose of myth in human culture and history.

SEE ALSO: Culture

REFERENCE

Frazer, J. G. [1890] (1995). *The Golden Bough: A Study in Magic and Religion*. Touchstone, Clearwater, FL.

LESLIE WASSON

N

nationalism

Nationalism is a complex social phenomenon with the nation as its object. Rooted in the Latin *natio*, denoting community of birth, the term *nationalismus* seems to have been coined by Johann Gottfried Herder as a part of his Romantic celebration of cultural diversity. Nevertheless, modern nationalism has its ideological roots in both the Enlightenment and the Romantic reaction to it. Definitions of "nationalism" as, indeed, of the "nation" vary. Anthony D. Smith's (1986) definition of nationalism is probably the most inclusive. It describes it as an ideological movement for attaining and maintaining, first, political and economic autonomy (or independence) and citizenship rights; second, ethnocultural identity; and third, social unity, on behalf of a population which is deemed by some of its members to constitute a nation. Scholars have also identified different types of nationalism. Two typologies of nationalism have been particularly influential since World War II. Those of Hans Kohn and Carlton J. H. Hayes recognize the existence of different kinds of nationalism and reconcile the division between political and cultural theorists. Kohn (1961 [1944]) distinguished between "west" and "east" (of the Rhine) European nationalisms. Kohn's two types of nationalism are now usually referred to as "civic" and "ethnic" nationalisms and are applicable outside European societies, to Asia and Africa, where they have been diffused. Civic nationalisms of the west European type are inspired by the political, democratic, rational, and classical values of the Enlightenment and the French Revolution: *liberté, égalité, fraternité*. Ethnic nationalisms of the East European type are inspired by the traditionalism, mysticism, historicism, and folklorism of Romanticism. Hayes (1960) distinguished between "political" and "cultural" nationalisms. Political nationalism is when a cultural group or "nationality" strives for a state of its own; cultural nationalism is when a nationality cherishes and extols its common language and traditions without political ends.

SEE ALSO: Multiculturalism; Nation-State

REFERENCES

Hayes, C. J. H. (1960) *Nationalism: A Religion*. Macmillan, New York.

Kohn, H. (1961) [1944] *The Idea of Nationalism*. Collier-Macmillan, New York.

Smith, A. D. (1986) *The Ethnic Origins of Nations*. Blackwell, Oxford.

ATHENA LEOUSSI

nation-state

The term nation-state was originally intended to describe a political unit (a state) whose borders coincided or roughly coincided with the territorial distribution of a nation, the latter in its pristine sense of a human grouping who share a conviction of being ancestrally related. The word nation derives from the Latin verb *nasci* (meaning to be born) and its noun form, *natio* (connoting breed or race). The very coining of the hyphenate, nation-state, illustrated an appreciation of the essential difference between its two components, but careless terminology has subsequently tended to obscure the difference. Today, nation is often used as a substitute for a state (as in "the United Nations") or as a synonym for the population of a state without regard to its ethnonational composition (e.g., "the British nation"). With the distinction between nation and state thus blurred, the term nation-state has lost much of its original value as a means of distinguishing among types of states. Although only some 10 percent of all states are sufficiently ethnically homogeneous to merit being described as nation-states, it has become an increasingly common practice to refer to all states as nation-states.

The confusing of nation with state would not be so troublesome were all states nation-states. In such cases, loyalty to nation (nationalism) and loyalty to the state (patriotism) reinforce one another in a seamless manner. The state is perceived as the political extension or expression of the nation, and appeals to the one trigger the same associations and emotions as do appeals to the other. The same blurring of the two loyalties is common in the case of a *staatvolk*, a nation which is sufficiently preeminent – politically, culturally, and usually numerically – that its members also popularly perceive the state in monopolistic terms as the state of our nation, even though other nations are present. (Examples include the Han Chinese, the Russians, and, at least prior to the very late twentieth century, the English.)

For people with their own nation-state and for *staatvolk*, then, nationalism and civic loyalty coincide and reinforce. But the overwhelming number of nations neither have their own state nor constitute a *staatvolk*. For them, civic and national loyalty do not coincide and may well conflict. And, as substantiated by the commonness of secessionist movements waged under the banner of national self-determination, when the two loyalties are perceived as being in irreconcilable conflict, nationalism has customarily proven the more powerful of the two loyalties.

In recognition of the unparalleled advantage that the nation-state enjoys over other forms of states for mobilizing the entire population under its jurisdiction, governments have adopted policies aimed at increasing national homogeneity. Although, in a very few cases, governments have permitted – in still rarer cases, even encouraged – a homeland-dwelling minority to secede, determination to maintain the territorial integrity of the state customarily places secession beyond governmental contemplation. More commonly, governments have pursued homogenization through what is currently called "ethnic cleansing." Genocide, expulsion, and population transfers, employed separately or in combination, are the usual means of achievement. Far more commonly, however, governments of heterogeneous states accept the current inhabitants of the state as a given and pursue homogenization through assimilationist programs. Such programs vary considerably in scope, complexity, intensity, ingenuity, degree of coerciveness/persuasion, envisaged timetable, and fervidity of the implementors. But programmed assimilation does not have an impressive record, as we are reminded by the history of the Soviet Union wherein national consciousness and resentment grew among non-Russian peoples despite 70 years of comprehensive and sophisticated governmental efforts to solve what was officially termed "the national question." As a result of such failures, an increasing number of governments have elected to shun the nation-state model in favor of programs seeking to peacefully accommodate national diversity through the granting of greater cultural and political autonomy to minority nations.

SEE ALSO: Assimilation; Genocide; Multiculturalism; Nationalism; State

REFERENCES

Connor, W. (1994) *Ethnonationalism: The Quest for Understanding*. Princeton University Press, Princeton, NJ.

Tilly, C. (ed.) (1975) *The Formation of National States in Western Europe*. Princeton University Press, Princeton, NJ.

WALKER CONNOR

nature

The sociological analysis of nature as it is used in the modern west (by specific cultures and space(s)) is fraught with definitional problems, notably the seemingly very different and overlapping senses of the word nature.

> It is relatively easy to distinguish three areas of meaning: (i) the essential quality and character *of* something; (ii) the inherent force which directs either the world or human beings or both; (iii) the material world itself, taken as including or not human beings. (Williams 1983: 219)

The first sense is a specific singular and was in use in the thirteenth century. The second and third senses are abstract singulars deriving from the fourteenth century to the seventeenth centuries. Williams relates this transformation to changes in religious and scientific thought where sense one derived from a plural, pantheistic worldview of gods and forces, and where sense (ii) derived from a more omnipotent singular directing force as a universal power, while sense three emerged later to describe the unity of the material world so ordered.

While Williams was able to tease out fascinating social constructions of nature it was not equally true that sociology took much notice of nature until very recently. By the time sociology emerged western humanity was increasingly urbanized, and the city was taken to be outside the natural world. Since the city was not governed or anchored in nature, natural rhythms or cycles it was cut loose to develop in opposed ways.

Despite the early work the work of sociologists Dunlap and Catton (1979), the call for a sociology of nature dates to 1995 when two influential articles emerged. Murphy's (1995) plea for "a sociology where nature mattered" argued that the immanent and irrefutable environmental and ecological crisis could not be ignored any longer by sociology; that the environmental and ecological movement required collaboration with sociology because the environmental crisis was composed of two challenges: to produce the right scientific diagnoses and responses to questions of sustainability and the right social responses that would be consistent with those.

In common with realist demands for more sociological participation in environmental issues and theory, Murphy preserved the ontologically separable status of society and nature and wished only to understand (and change) the exchanges between them. Critical realist thinkers theorized a dialectical relationship between humanity and nature such that both have agency conceived very abstractly as "causal powers." Such objects were not constituted by and through their on-going relations with heterogenous others, an ontology now preferred by Donna Haraway, Bruno Latour, John Law, and others.

Macnaghten and Urry's 1995 paper, for example, asserts a considerable social content *already* manifest in environmental agendas, scientific discourses, and natures and this became of interest to those working in many established fields of sociology: social movements; social justice; leisure and tourism; feminism, science and technology studies, neo-Durkheimian studies.

Since these debates, nature has become far more significant in a range of sociological work. It has moved away from a primary focus on the environment to embrace the relation between biology and society, biopolitics and "life itself"; the implications of dissolving the nature-culture difference; the fluid and commodified nature of "life itself" in post-genomic society and new ontological understandings of relations between humans and nonhumans.

SEE ALSO: Culture, Nature and Environmental Sociology

REFERENCES

Dunlap, R. and Catton, W. (1979) Environmental sociology. *Annual Review of Sociology* 5: 243–73.

Macnaghten, P. and Urry, J. (1995) Towards a sociology of nature. *Sociology* 29 (2): 124–37.

Williams, R. (1983) *Keywords*. Fontana, London.

SUGGESTED READING

Murphy, R. (1995) Sociology as if nature did not matter: an ecological critique. *British Journal of Sociology* 46 (4): 688–707.

ADRIAN FRANKLIN

neoliberalism

Neoliberalism as a distinctive strand of liberal ideology first appeared in the 1940s, but its period of major influence is usually dated from the 1970s. Neoliberalism is not a uniform doctrine and has many internal tensions, not least between a laissez-faire strand which believes that the best policy is to allow markets to operate with as few impediments as possible, and a social market strand which believes that for the free market to reach its full potential the state has to be active in creating and sustaining the institutions which make that possible.

The first people to call themselves neoliberals were the German Ordo liberals such as Alexander Rüstow. They became part of a wider movement of western liberals after 1945 seeking to reverse the long retreat of liberalism in the face of collectivist ideologies and reasserting what they saw as the basic principles of liberalism – the rule of law, the minimal state, individual liberty – against all forms of collectivism, including many versions of liberalism, such as New Liberalism and Keynesianism, which had sanctioned an expanding state to provide welfare programmes, full employment, and economic prosperity.

The classic statement of neoliberal principles was Hayek's *The Constitution of Liberty* published in 1960. This set out the political institutions and rules necessary for a liberal order, drawing on the classical liberal tradition, in particular the critical rationalism of Adam Smith. Hayek was keen to distinguish true liberalism from false liberalism, and to recapture the term liberal from its contamination by collectivist ideas. Neoliberal ideas began to gain ground in the 1970s. The adoption of basic neoliberal precepts by international agencies such as the IMF for containing inflation was key. The crisis of the 1970s made a new set of guiding principles to manage the global economy necessary, and this was supplied by neoliberalism, initially in the ideas of monetarism put forward by economists such as Milton Friedman to tackle inflation, but soon widened into a more general neoliberal political economy for removing the perceived wider institutional causes of inflation, which included trade union power, welfare states, taxation, regulation, and barriers to competition.

As an economic doctrine the core of neoliberalism has been an attempt to revive the case for reducing the role of government in the management of the economy as much as possible, giving primacy to markets and the free play of competition. It is axiomatic in neoliberalism that government solutions are inferior to market solutions because they are less efficient in economic terms and they harm individual liberty. The solution to every public policy problem is to take responsibility away from government and allow markets to function freely. Typical neoliberal policy prescriptions are therefore for deregulation of economic activity, privatization of assets owned by the state, and reduction of welfare spending except for the provision of a safety net for the very poorest. This combined with a more general withdrawal of the state from involvement in many other areas of social and economic life gives scope for large cuts in taxation and the share of state spending in national income.

The role of the state in the neoliberal programme is not a passive one. It has to be both active and forceful. The free economy requires a strong state in order to function properly. The state should not intervene directly in the workings of the market; instead its task is to guarantee the basic institutional requirements of a liberal market order. These include the minimal state functions of external defence and internal order, the rule of law, sound money, and the enforcement of property rights. Without these requirements individuals do not have the confidence or the incentive to produce and exchange freely. The market order is a natural spontaneous growth, but it is also very fragile and easily damaged by state intervention and state control, or by private monopolies which prevent free exchange. The state has to reform its own practices so as to minimize their harmful effects on the economy; at the same time it needs to remove all other obstacles to the free working of the economy. These may include restrictive practices of all kinds, by companies, trade unions, professions, and public bodies. The role of the state is to be the champion and defender of the free market, by enabling the institutions it requires and empowering its agents.

From being a heresy neoliberalism became an orthodoxy in the 1980s and 1990s, and many of its favourite nostrums were crystallized in the set of assumptions and prescriptions about the world and how it should be governed which became known as the Washington consensus. Neoliberalism shaped the policy prescriptions of globalization, setting out the conditions which countries had to meet in order to integrate fully into the global economy and be in good standing with the financial markets. To its critics, neoliberalism had become a form of market fundamentalism, which advocated the breaking down of obstacles to the commodification of social life and the penetration of market forces into all areas of economy, society and politics.

With the collapse of the Soviet Union the neoliberal message that there was no alternative to markets and private property in coordinating modern complex large-scale economies appeared unchallenged. All governments were forced to become in some sense neoliberal, since they were obliged to operate within a set of structures in the global economy which reflected, however imperfectly, neoliberal principles of global order. The ascendancy of neoliberalism however suffered a major setback in the great financial crash of 2008. Its belief in the superiority of market over government solutions, and in the ability of markets to be self-regulating and to price all risks encouraged the dismantling of regulatory controls over the financial sector in the 1980s and 1990s, and a rapid expansion of new forms of credit and financial instruments. Speculative asset bubbles developed, particularly in housing, which when they finally burst required crisis measures by governments to bail out the banks and stop the collapse of the financial system. Critics of neoliberalism argued that the events of 2007-8 demonstrated the limits and potential risks of deregulated markets, and the need for governments to be more interventionist.

SEE ALSO: Democracy; Global Politics; Liberalism; Markets; Privatization

SUGGESTED READINGS

Harvey, D. (2005) *A Brief History of Neoliberalism.* Oxford University Press, New York.

Hayek, F. A. (1960) *The Constitution of Liberty.* Routledge, London.

Skidelsky, R. (2009) *Keynes: The Return of the Master.* Allen Lane, London.

Turner, R. (2008) *Neo-Liberal Ideology: History, Concepts and Policies.* Edinburgh University Press, Edinburgh.

ANDREW GAMBLE

neo-Marxism

Neo-Marxism is a term designating the critical renaissance of Marxist thought in the post-war period. Though the label "neo-Marxist" is sometimes applied to thinkers who combined a fidelity to Marx's critical and political aims with a sense of the limitations of Marxism in the face of phenomena like fascism or mass culture, its main reference is to radical political economists (such as Joan Robinson, Paul A. Baran, and Paul M. Sweezy) who sought to renew Marx's project in a situation marked by the rise of global corporations, anti-colonial struggles for national liberation, and the politics of US imperialism.

Whereas the post-World War I Marxist concern with the cultural sphere and political subjectivity can be put under the aegis of "western Marxism" (as opposed to "classical Marxism"), neo-Marxism points to the attempt, during and after World War II, to reflect on the pertinence of Marxist categories for an understanding of the changed conditions of capital accumulation and the political realities that accompanied them. Having intersected the Frankfurt School (Baran was present at the Institute for Social Research in 1930), and later influencing some of its erstwhile members (*Monopoly Capital* was a considerable reference for Marcuse's *One-Dimensional Man*), neo-Marxists shared with them a conviction regarding the increasingly prominent role of the state within the capitalist system. Hence the influential use of the expression "state monopoly capitalism" to designate a situation where the state itself becomes a "collective capitalist" rather than the mere enforcer of the capitalist system of social relations.

The experience of Roosevelt's New Deal, as well as those of the Marshall Plan and the rise of the "military-industrial complex," suggested to neo-Marxists that the orthodox Marxist understanding of crisis and development within capitalism was insufficient to grasp post-war realities. Thus, they tended to give short thrift to the labor theory of value and to regard the tendency of the rate of profit to fall as an inadequate tool in the light of the long boom of an American-led capitalist system after 1945. Following Keynes, they replaced the notion of surplus value with a far broader one of "economic surplus."

With regard to their understanding of imperialism, Baran and Sweezy saw monopoly capital as a system unable to absorb surplus either in terms of effective demand or through productive investments. Moreover, they conceived of monopoly capitalism as fundamentally irrational, insofar as it subordinated all dimensions of social existence (from sexuality to art, body posture to religion) to the calculated, "rationalized" attempt to realize economic surplus. Even the capitalist rationality of *quid pro quo* breaks down. For Baran and Sweezy (1966): "Human and material resources remain idle because there is in the market no *quid* to exchange against the *quo* of their potential output."

The anti-imperialist bent of neo-Marxism, and specifically Baran's notion that monopoly capitalism led to the "development of underdevelopment" in peripheral settings, was a significant component in the formulation of dependency theory and the work of figures such as André Gunder Frank and Samir Amin. Its political influence on debates about socialism and national liberation in Cuba, Latin America and elsewhere, especially through the journal *The Monthly Review*, was massive.

In Anglo-American sociology, this renewed emphasis, from the standpoint of political economy, on questions of exploitation and imperialism in the new, "affluent" society, influenced a host of research programmes which have often been described as neo-Marxist. Thus, in the work of Willis, or Bowles and Gintis, we encounter a neo-Marxist sociology of education which seeks to analyze the reproduction of capitalist socioeconomic structures through curricula, as well as the forms of resistance and conflict that accompany these processes. In works by Braverman and Burawoy, the labour process and its ideological reproduction is subjected to neo-Marxist scrutiny. In the domain of class analysis, the work of Erik Olin Wright has sought to combine a Marxist analysis of class exploitation with a Weberian analysis of status and domination, crystallized in the notion of "contradictory class locations." Spurred by the work of Nicos Poulantzas, Bob Jessop and others synthesized a neo-Marxist analysis of the capitalist state, questioning any univocal correspondence between the form of the state and its economic function, and seeking to delve into the class relations and class fractions that traverse the state itself. In the field of political economy, the neo-Marxist label has also been applied to the French Regulation School – with its emphasis on the social and governmental "modes of regulation" that contingently govern the reproduction of "regimes of accumulation" – as well as to more orthodox Marxists seeking to analyze the transformations of "late capitalism" (Ernest Mandel).

Despite the absence of any single, coherent programme or statement of its departures from classical Marxism, neo-Marxism is best periodized and comprehended as an intellectual sensibility which tried to amalgamate a fidelity to certain guiding ideas of classical Marxism (economic exploitation, class struggle, the horizon of social emancipation) with an attention to the transformed conditions under which capitalist social relations were being reproduced in the post-war period. This entailed attending to the specificity and relative autonomy of the contemporary capitalist state, as well as to the political and economic consequences of militarism, imperialism. and the rise of the corporation as a social force. Many neo-Marxist authors felt compelled to inject non-Marxist ideas (from the likes of Keynes or Weber) into Marxism to cope with unprecedented transformations within capitalist society – whence the eclecticism that critics have often accused in their work. Politically, neo-Marxist ideas on power, the state and political subjectivities beyond the traditional working class fed into the development of the New Left in the 60s and 70s.

SEE ALSO: Class Conflict; Critical Theory/Frankfurt School; Dependency and World-Systems Theories; Imperialism; Marx, Karl; Marxism; Marxism and Sociology

REFERENCE

Baran, P. A. & Sweezy, P. M. (1966) *Monopoly Capital: An Essay on the American Economic and Social Order*. Penguin, London.

SUGGESTED READINGS

Bowles, S. & Gintis, H. (1976) *Schooling in Capitalist America: Educational Reform and the Contradictions of Economic Life*. Routledge, London.

Wright, E. O. (1990) *The Debate on Classes*. Verso, London.

ALBERTO TOSCANO

networks

The social units of network analysis can be persons or small groups (micro level), organizations or fields (meso level), and larger entities such as institutions, cities, nations, or even the entire globe (macro level).

A convention of network theory is to use the term node to refer to a position, that is, a network location occupied by an actor (whether an individual, group, or organization). Actors in this sense are "decision-making entities" that occupy positions (nodes) linked by relations (or ties; see Markovsky et al. 1988). Owing largely to the work of Linton Freeman (1979), one of the more important network concepts is centrality, namely, the extent to which an actor is centrally located within a network. Degree centrality is the number of direct links with other actors. Betweenness centrality is the extent to which an actor mediates, or falls between, any other two actors on the shortest path between those actors. In general, actors in central network positions have greater access to, and potential control over, valued resources. Actors who are able to control such resources are able to acquire power, largely as a result of increasing others' dependence on them.

Perhaps the single most influential contribution to network theory is Mark Granovetter's (1973) conceptual distinction between weak and strong ties. According to Granovetter, strong ties exist between persons who know one another very well (e.g., close friends and family members). Weak ties, on the other hand exist between persons who are merely acquaintances. Persons who are loosely associated may act as a bridge between clumps of densely tied friendship networks. These dense networks of strong ties would have no connections with other networks were it not for the occasional node weakly tied between them. Hence, in an ironic twist, Granovetter illustrates the strength of weak ties.

This idea has also been explored by Ronald Burt, with some modifications. Whereas the great majority of network analysis is concerned with the nature and strength of ties between nodes, Burt's (1992) concept of structural holes turns attention toward the *absence* of ties. Because nodes in densely clustered networks tend to receive redundant information, some actors may seek to invest in connections to diverse others in order to receive novel information. These nodes must be disconnected from other nodes in order to ensure information is non-redundant. It is these disconnections between diverse others that are structural holes. For example, expertise in a particular field (such as the position of journal editor) allows gatekeepers to monopolize information and maintain structural holes. Similarly, ideas which are endorsed by more distant contacts (such as external reviewers) are more likely to be considered good or important than those endorsed by friends or other close acquaintances.

SEE ALSO: Network Society; Social Network Analysis; Weak Ties (Strength of)

REFERENCES

Burt, R. S. (1992) *Structural Holes*. Harvard University Press, Cambridge, MA.

Burt, R. S. (2004) Structural holes and good ideas. *American Journal of Sociology* 110 (2): 349–99.

Granovetter, M. S. (1973) The strength of weak ties. *American Journal of Sociology* 78 (6): 1360–80.

Markovsky, B., Willer, D., & Patton, T. (1988) Power relations in exchange networks. *American Sociological Review* 53: 220–36.

JAMES J. CHRISS

new religious movements

The term new religious movement (NRM) refers both to various forms of Eastern spirituality brought to the west by immigrants, and to groups founded since World War II, and identified as "cults" or "sects" in popular parlance. The enormous diversity within the current wave of new religions cannot be over-emphasized, but in so far as they are first-generation movements, their membership of converts tends to consist disproportionately of enthusiastic young Caucasian adults from the better-educated middle classes. Founding leaders, often accorded a charismatic authority unbounded by rules or traditions, frequently encourage a dichotomous mindset, drawing clear distinctions between "true" and "false"; "Godly" and "satanic"; and "them" and "us."

A further characteristic of NRMs is that they change more fundamentally and rapidly than older religions: charismatic leaders die; unfulfilled prophecies, second and subsequent generations and a maturing membership may result in a relaxation of theological fervour and contribute to accommodation to the host society. Furthermore, external social changes can introduce radical transformations within the "cult scene," two obvious examples being the collapse of socialism, and the arrival of the Internet.

Throughout history, new religions have been greeted with suspicion, fear and even hatred by those to whom they pose an alternative, and from the 1970s a number of groups generically referred to as the anti-cult movement emerged in opposition to what they termed "destructive cults." Official responses to NRMs have ranged from their being completely outlawed to their being treated much like any other religion.

No one knows exactly how many NRMs there are, partly because of definitional variations. There are possibly around two thousand identifiable NRMs in Europe and North America, with several thousand more elsewhere. The number of members is, however, usually relatively small with a high turnover rate, many movements failing to survive much beyond two or three generations.

SEE ALSO: Religion, Sociology of

SUGGESTED READINGS

Barker, E. (2004) What are we studying? A sociological case for keeping the "Nova." *Nova Religio* 8 (1): 88-102.

Bromley, D. G. & Gordon Melton, J. (eds.) (2002) *Cults, Religion and Violence*. Cambridge University Press, Cambridge.

Dawson, L. L. (ed.) (2003) *Cults and New Religious Movements: A Reader*. Blackwell, Oxford.

EILEEN BARKER

new reproductive technologies

The new reproductive technologies constitute a broad constellation of technologies aimed at facilitating, preventing, or otherwise intervening in the process of reproduction. This includes, for example, contraception, abortion, antenatal testing, birth technologies, and conceptive technologies. These interventions focus predominantly, although not exclusively, on the female body and usually operate within the medical domain. The new reproductive technologies constitute a highly controversial and contested site. One of the key areas of debate is in relation to the disputed "life" status of embryos and fetuses. These debates lie at the heart of attempts to draw ethical, moral and legal boundaries around the conditions under which women are allowed to terminate pregnancies, and more recently, in relation to the creation and use of IVF embryos for stem cell research. Another site of contestation is the role of the new reproductive technologies in the production of novel, and often controversial, family structures, redefining relationships and kinship categories – for example, though the technologies of gamete donation, IVF and cryo-preservation. This signals for some a threat to "family values" and the "natural" reproductive order, while presenting exciting new family-building opportunities for others.

However, while high profile cases of novel family forms and high tech research are undoubtedly significant in sociological terms, they are not representative of the more mundane, everyday experience of the new reproductive technologies. In particular, the technologies themselves are inaccessible to many people, either through religious, social or cultural prescription, or because of prohibitive costs. Conversely, others may find themselves fighting for the right to *not* use particular technologies (for example, unwanted abortions or sterilizations). Race and class are therefore crucial dimensions to people's experiences of the new reproductive technologies, both within national contexts and internationally.

SEE ALSO: Human Genome and the Science of Life; Technology, Science, and Culture

SUGGESTED READINGS

Edwards, J., Franklin, S., Hirsch, E., Price, F., & Strathern, M. (1999) *Technologies of Procreation: Kinship in the Age of Assisted Conception*, 2nd edn. Routledge, London.

Williams, C., Kitzinger, J., & Henderson, L. (2003) Envisaging the embryo in stem cell research: rhetorical strategies and media reporting of the ethical debates. *Sociology of Health and Illness* 25 (7): 793–814.

KAREN THROSBY

new social movement theory

New social movement theory (NSMT) emerged in the 1980s in Europe to analyze new movements that appeared from the 1960s onward. They were "new" vis-a-vis the "old" working-class movement of Marxist theory. By contrast, new social movements are organized around race, ethnicity, youth, sexuality, countercultures, environmentalism, pacifism, human rights, and the like. NSMT is a distinctive approach, albeit with significant internal variations.

NSMT analyzed new social movements as historically specific responses to new social formations such as post-industrial or post-modern society. These theorists were as interested in the changing contours of the larger society as with the new movements that responded to them; the "newness" referred to social formations as well as protest forms. NSMT also reflected the cultural turn in social theory, emphasizing symbolic contests in the cultural arena over instrumental struggles in the political sphere.

NSMT's emphasis on collective identity has been popular in US social movement theory. For NSMT, no group identity (including class) is objectively given, and every collective identity must be socially constructed before collective action is possible. The "old" issue of cultivating class consciousness has been replaced with the "new" one of constructing collective identity itself. In fluid new social formations with multiple and transient identities, the construction of collective identity is a major accomplishment and a prerequisite for other movement objectives.

Additional themes in NSMT theory include their middle-class social base, their symbolic, post-material goals, their quest for autonomy, their politicization of everyday life, and their preferences for decentralized and participatory forms of movement organization.

The most common criticism of NSMT concerned its claim of a sharp disjuncture between old labor movements and new cultural movements. The most incisive critiques found that many of the supposedly distinctive features of new social movements were vital to the "old" labor movement, including cultural symbols, collective identity, and self-determination.

NSMT entered US sociology through selective cooptation. The grand theorizing of European NSMT couldn't take root in the pragmatic, positivist soil of US sociology. The latter ignored NSMT's most distinctive claims about links between social formations and types of movements. Instead, NSMT was reduced in elementarist fashion to new variables alongside familiar ones. A decontextualized concept of collective identity then became very popular in mainstream research alongside mobilizing structures and framing processes. For these reasons, the story of NSMT remains entangled with larger differences in theoretical style between European and US sociology.

SEE ALSO: Anti-War and Peace Movements; Collective Action; Environmental Movements; Gay and Lesbian Movement; Indigenous Movements; Social Movements; Student Movements

SUGGESTED READINGS

Buechler, S. (2000) *Social Movements in Advanced Capitalism*. Oxford University Press, New York.

Cohen, J. (1985) Strategy or identity? New theoretical paradigms and contemporary social movements. *Social Research* 52: 663–716.

Dalton, R. & Kuechler, M. (eds.) (1990) *Challenging the Political Order*. Oxford University Press, New York.

Klandermans, B. (1991) New social movements and resource mobilization: the European and American approaches revisited. In: Rucht, D. (ed.), *Research on Social Movements*. Westview, Boulder, CO.

Larana, E., Johnston, H., & Gusfield, J. (eds.) (1994) *New Social Movements: From Ideology to Identity*. Temple University Press, Philadelphia.

STEVEN M. BUECHLER

new urbanism

New urbanism is an architectural and city planning approach that emphasizes communities that are compact, multi or mixed use, economically and socially diverse, and pedestrian and public transportation friendly. Its principles have been used to both revitalize existing neighborhoods and create new ones. New urbanism gained popularity as a planning approach in the 1980s as a criticism of suburban sprawl and disinvestment in central cities. New urbanists advocate using planning strategies to revitalize declining urban areas, promote local culture, preserve limited natural resources, reduce dependency on automobiles, address social inequalities, and create spaces conducive to challenging social problems, such as crime. Given its broad range of concerns, new urbanism has garnered support amongst those concerned with environmental protection, historical preservation, smart growth, public transportation, and social justice. Critics of new urbanism argue that its goals are too malleable and agendas too elastic to provide meaningful guidance for planning, especially at the regional and corridor levels, and that attempts at new urbanism neighborhood projects continue to result in predominantly high-income, ethnically homogeneous suburban communities. Despite these criticisms, new urbanism has inspired renewed interest in the relationship between environment and behavior as well as using city planning to address pressing social problems such as environmental degradation and racial segregation.

SEE ALSO: Urban Renewal and Redevelopment; Urbanism/Urban Culture

SUGGESTED READINGS
Katz, P. (1994) *The New Urbanism.* McGraw Hill, New York.
Meredith, J. (2003) Sprawl and the new urbanist solution. *Virginia Law Review* 89: 447–503.

ELYSHIA ASELTINE

NGO/INGO

Non-governmental organizations (NGOs) and international non-governmental organizations (INGOs) are umbrella terms that refer to organizations not directly controlled by the state or governments, mostly concerned with human rights of various kinds (including civic and political, economic and social, and environmental rights), professional and occupational interests, and various other enthusiasms. They range from very large organizations with considerable budgets and international recognition, through national organizations with a strictly domestic agenda, to small, locally funded neighborhood groups. Many are connected and overlap with social and political movements. However, the existence of many domestically and internationally powerful QUANGOs (quasi-NGOs) and GONGOs (government-organized NGOs) suggests that, in practice, "non-governmental" is not as straightforward as it at first appears. The close involvement of many NGOs/INGOs with governments, intergovernmental bodies (notably the UN and the World Bank), and transnational corporations and other organs of big business is a constant source of controversy.

The most influential human rights INGO is Amnesty International, with around a million members in more than 160 countries and national sections in over 50 countries. Its budget of around US$25 million is raised from individual subscriptions and funding from private foundations. It does not accept money from governments, although most NGOs/INGOs do. The AI website is heavily used and the AI link with the UN Commission on Human Rights is particularly useful for studying the contradictions inherent for genuinely non-governmental INGOs forced to work with governments and intergovernmental agencies. Despite the work they do, many human rights INGOs have become rather elitist organizations and this has created difficulties for those they are dedicated to serve. The same can be said for the major environmental INGOS, notably Greenpeace and Friends of the Earth. The mainstream view of NGOs/INGOs is that their growth has paralleled the growth of global civil society (indeed, for many scholars in the field, this is a tautology). The success of the largest of them has led to the creation of a new class of activist-lobbyists, who command respect if not affection from governments and big business for their expertise (particularly their use of the media to highlight abuses of human rights and environmental justice). As a result, some prominent NGO/INGO leaders have taken up lucrative job offers in the state apparatus or in big business. This has led to splits between the large, powerful NGOs/INGOs and some of their smaller, more radical, anti-establishment counterparts, who came together in the meetings of the World Social Forum first in Porto Alegre, Brazil in 2001, and all over the world since then.

SEE ALSO: Civil Society; Global Justice as a Social Movement; Human Rights; Transnational Movements

SUGGESTED READINGS
Fisher, W. & Ponniah, T. (eds.) (2003) *Another World is Possible: Popular Alternatives to Globalization at the World Social Forum.* Zed Books, London.

LESLIE SKLAIR

Nietzsche, Friedrich (1844–1900)

At 25, Nietzsche was granted his doctorate from the University of Leipzig, without completing a dissertation, and was appointed to a position in classical philology at the University of Basel. His philosophical writing was brilliant, unorthodox, and controversial. He dispensed with formalities of academic writing and systemic philosophizing. Nietzsche was influenced by Arthur Schopenhauer's philosophy and Richard Wagner's music. Service as a medic in the Franco-Prussian war helped stir his critique of the state and patriotic fervor as the bane of all genuine culture. After ten years of teaching, poor health forced Nietzsche to leave academe. He wrote his major philosophical works in obscurity, but his fame grew meteorically shortly after madness ended his writing in 1889. Nietzsche's impacts are not easy to trace for they have been multifarious and diffuse. However, he has had enormous impact on many of the twentieth century's top writers, philosophers, cultural critics, and social theorists. Max Weber purportedly declared that Nietzsche, along with Marx, changed social thought so profoundly that all serious social theorists must engage the two thinkers, either directly or indirectly.

Although mostly indirect and unrecognized, Nietzsche's contribution to sociology and social theory is multifaceted and basic. His critique of Enlightenment rationality and arguments about modern science's limits have contributed to thought about the relation of facts to values, science and disenchantment, and meaning in post-traditional cultures. His stress on aesthetic, emotional, bodily sensibilities as a source of value and pivotal element in interpersonal relations counters overly rational, cognitive, conformist theories of socialization. His perspectivist critique of truth and connection of knowledge and values to situated cultural interests and, especially, his "genealogy of morals" contributed to the rise of the sociology of knowledge, critical theories, and standpoint theories. His views about the primacy of culture and its pivotal role in the formation and perpetuation of enduring civilizations anticipated the rise of comparative civilizational studies and cultural sociology. His argument about western "decadence" influenced widely later twentieth century critiques of Eurocentrism and postmodern cultural theories.

However, Nietzsche's argument about the *entwinement of morality and power* is arguably his greatest contribution to social theory; it provokes *fundamental questioning of the taken for granted identity of the moral with the good.* This core sociological facet of his "antisociology" has stimulated theorists to ponder the normative directions of social theory and modern culture and politics. Nietzsche held that moral claims often call for unreflective obedience and justify manipulation and violence. What Nietzsche feared came true; the twentieth century was marked by fanatical politics, fundamentalism, ethnic and religious struggles, bloodbaths, and genocide. Its mass warfare killed and maimed tens of millions of people, including enormous numbers of innocent noncombatants. Globalization, 9/11, resurgent fundamentalism, and rampant political invocation of the good versus evil make Nietzsche a most timely twenty-first century theorist. Nietzsche's linkage of morality to power stimulates provocative sociological questions.

SEE ALSO: Critical Theory/Frankfurt School; Culture; Modernity; Morality

SUGGESTED READINGS

Antonio, R. J. (1995) Nietzsche's antisociology: subjectified culture and the end of history. *American Journal of Sociology* 101: 1–43

Nietzsche, F. (1966) [1886] *Beyond Good and Evil: Prelude to a Philosophy of the Future*, trans. W. Kaufmann. Vintage Books, New York.

Nietzsche, F. (1969) [1887] *On the Genealogy of Morals*, trans. W. Kaufmann and R. J. Hollingdale, and [1888] *Ecce Homo*, trans. Walter Kaufmann. Vintage Books, New York.

ROBERT J. ANTONIO

norms

Norms are informal rules which guide social interaction. They are, as Cristina Bicchieri (2006) calls them, "the rules we live by." As the do's and don'ts of social life, norms are a critical component in the makeup of human culture and therefore play a highly significant role in determining what it means to be human. When codified, norms are laws or other types of institutionalized regulatory strictures. When conceived without moral consequence, the term can also refer to mere behavioral regularities. Variously defined even by sociologists themselves, there is perhaps no other sociological concept more regularly used nor one about which more has been written and discussed. It is therefore not surprising that a concept as vague as it is elemental to the sociological enterprise is also one that is oft-debated.

Rational choice theorists, for example, have looked to norms as potential explanation for otherwise seemingly irrational individual behavior. As Hechter and Opp (2001) argue, basic phenomena such as cooperation and collective action, not to mention social order itself, are difficult to explain using only "rational egoistic behavioral assumptions" of the sort typical of rational choice theory. In Bicchieri's (2006) account, the power of norms to constrain behavior is tested using game theory simulations such as Ultimatum, Dictator, Trust, and Social Dilemma. While computer simulation of normative behavior brings us considerable distance from William Graham Sumner's *Folkways: A Study of the Sociological Implications of Usages, Manners, Customs, Mores, and Morals* (1906) and Talcott Parsons's *The Social System* (1951), these works share the same interest in understanding the workings of a uniquely human moral order.

Human, yes, but from whence do norms originate? At one extreme is speculation as to whether certain fundamental norms are inherent and universal in human social life. Alvin Gouldner (1960) argued that "the norm of reciprocity," like the incest taboo, was very probably a cultural universal. He meant that guidelines were everywhere and always in some manner in effect which encouraged actors to help, and not harm, those who have helped them. This comes very close to positing a sociological Golden Rule. At the other extreme is attention to the power of actors to suppress, reject, alter, or spontaneously create norms, even with respect to those previously deemed sacred. For Bicchieri (2006), norms can even "endogenously emerge" as a result of nothing more than interaction among actors sharing prior dispositions.

Alan Wolfe's sociology seeks to merge these tendencies in a coherent analysis of contemporary norms. Drawing on classical theorists as divergent as Émile Durkheim and William James, Wolfe (2001) argues that ours will be "the century of moral freedom," which is to say that twenty-first-century individuals will increasingly choose their own norms from the plurality of normative systems characteristic of postmodern society, thus setting for themselves their own course toward the true, right, and good. While this proposition seems out of sync with Durkheim's nineteenth-century concern about modern society's tendency to weaken normative regulation, what Durkehim termed the pathology of "anomy," Wolfe emphasizes the individual's capacity for moral discernment and decision, which is consistent at least with Durkheim's advocacy for moral individualism. Indeed, attention to the "varieties of moral experience" à la James is consistent with cohesion in a pluralistic society which values its own pluralism.

SEE ALSO: Deviance, Theories of; Durkheim, Émile; Parsons, Talcott; Values

REFERENCES

Bicchieri, C. (2006) *The Grammar of Society: The Nature and Dynamics of Social Norms.* Cambridge University Press, Cambridge.

Gouldner, A. (1960) The norm of reciprocity. *American Sociological Review* 25 (2): 161–78.

Hechter, M. & Opp, K.-D. (eds.) (2001) *Social Norms.* Russell Sage Foundation, New York.

Wolfe, A. (2001) *Moral Freedom.* W. W. Norton, New York.

STEVEN P. DANDANEAU

O

objectivity

The term *objectivity* can refer to *a property or quality of a claim*: a claim or statement is objective if it is supported with reasons and evidence (or warrantable, supportable), and it is subjective if it is not so supported and only an expression of individual taste or preference. Objectivity can also refer to *a characteristic of a person*: the objective person is unbiased, unprejudiced, and evinces respect for the importance of evidence and argument. Finally, *an aspect or characteristic of a process* or means by which a claim is warranted can be called objective. Hence, some argue that the enterprise of science is objective because the claims of scientists are subject to public scrutiny and intersubjective criticism.

In the literatures on social science methodology and philosophy there are several interrelated but distinct senses of this term:

1. An absolute or ontological sense reflecting a belief in metaphysical realism. Thus, objectivity here refers to the idea of objectively perceiving an independently existing reality.
2. A disciplinary or critically intersubjective sense that associates objectivity with a particular aspect of the process of inquiry, specifically, the ability to reach consensus within some specialized disciplinary community through dialogue, debate, and reasoned argument.
3. A mechanical sense in which objectivity connotes following the rules or procedures because these are a check on subjectivity and restrain idiosyncrasy and personal judgment.
4. A moral-political sense in which to be objective means to be fair and impartial, and to avoid the kinds of self-interest or prejudice that distort judgment.

Objectivity has also been associated (for better or worse) with three other important notions in social science methodology: value neutrality, objectivism, and objectification. Value neutrality is an ideology that holds that politics and values should be external to the practice of scientific inquiry. Objectivism is a term that designates a complex set of interlocking beliefs about the nature of knowledge (foundationalist epistemology), the nature of reality (metaphysical realism), the manner in which that reality can be known and knowledge claims justified (logical positivist or representationalist epistemology), the role of the scientist (an axiology of disinterest), and the Enlightenment belief in the unquestioned power (and authority) of science to shape society. Objectification is a belief in a particular metaphysical and epistemological relation of subject to object often characterized by the ideas of disengagement from and yet an attempt to control the object of knowledge.

SEE ALSO: Epistemology; Intersubjectivity; Subjectivity

SUGGESTED READINGS

Megill, A. (ed.) (1994) *Rethinking Objectivity*. Duke University Press, Durham, NC.
Porter, T. M. (1995) *Trust in Numbers: The Pursuit of Objectivity in Science and Public Life*. Princeton University Press, Princeton, NJ.

THOMAS A. SCHWANDT

observation, participant and non-participant

As a method of inquiry, observation is an alternative or complement to the use of interview, documentary, or questionnaire data. It is usually conceived as taking place in "natural" rather than experimental situations; though, of course, in a broader sense experiments necessarily rely upon observation too. In brief, observation involves a researcher watching and listening to actions and events within some "natural" context over some period of time, and making a record of what has been witnessed. This may be done through writing open-ended fieldnotes, documenting the frequency and/or duration of various types of events on a schedule, and/or using audio- or videorecording.

The distinction between participant and non-participant observation draws attention to the fact that the role of an observer can vary greatly. In gross terms, he or she may take on a role in the setting being observed, or may play no explicit participant role. The primary concern motivating this distinction is reactivity; in other words, the extent to which and ways in which the behavior of the people being studied is likely to be shaped both by the fact of being researched in a given way (procedural reactivity) and by the particular characteristics of the researcher (personal reactivity). There are conflicting arguments about whether, in overt observation, taking on a participant role in the field is likely to increase or reduce reactivity. In many circumstances, it may decrease procedural reactivity but could increase personal reactivity. If observation is covert, procedural reactivity will be zero; but there may still be personal reactivity if a covert participant role is adopted.

Reactivity is widely regarded as a potential source of error: it may render inferences from observational data about what happens on other occasions and in other contexts false. Much depends upon the particular role taken on by an observer, and this can have other consequences too. Some participant roles will allow note-taking at the time events are happening, and perhaps even the use of recording devices, while others will not. Similarly, taking on different roles in the field will open up different sources of information, and perhaps close down others; for example, there will usually be restrictions on who will tell what to whom. Participation in a role in the setting can also provide first-hand experience that may enhance the researcher's understanding of how people feel and why they behave in the ways that they do; although it also involves the danger of "going native," of taking over biases from participants.

While useful, the distinction between participant and non-participant observation is complex, and can be misleading. This is partly because it involves several dimensions. These include whether or not the people researched are aware of being studied (or who among them is and is not aware), how central to the setting any role that a researcher adopts is, whether or not the researcher asks participants questions in the course of observation, and how long is spent observing in any particular location. Also occasionally implied in the distinction, and an important issue in itself, is whether or not the observational process is structured: whether it involves the assignment of events to pre-identified categories, rather than being open-ended and developmental in character.

There are, of course, ethical issues relevant to covert observational research, about which there has been considerable debate over the years, and there are also issues to do with personal safety. But important ethical problems are involved in overt research too, notably around what constitutes informed consent. Indeed, while covert research is often rejected because it entails deceit, potential invasion of privacy, etc., these issues are by no means absent where observation is open.

The significance of both the methodological and the ethical issues in any particular study will vary depending upon both what role the researcher adopts and the nature of the people and places being investigated, as well as on the form that observation takes.

SEE ALSO: Ethics, Fieldwork; Ethics, Research; Ethnography

SUGGESTED READINGS

Foster, P. (1996) *Observing Schools: A Methodological Guide*. Paul Chapman, London.

McCall, G. J. (1978) *Observing the Law: Applications of Field Methods to the Study of the Criminal Justice System*. Free Press, New York.

McCall, G. J. & Simmons, J. L. (eds.) (1969) *Issues in Participant Observation*. Addison-Wesley, Reading, MA.

MARTYN HAMMERSLEY

online social networking

Online social networking is a phenomenon of the first decade of the twenty-first century. It refers to the use of social network sites (SNSs) – such as MySpace and Facebook – for online communication, the establishment and extension of friendships and personal networks. SNSs are defined as "web-based services that allow individuals to: (1) construct a public or semi-public profile within a bounded system, (2) articulate a list of other users with whom they share a connection, and (3) view and traverse their list of connections and those made by others within the system." These sites share properties of persistence, searchability, replicability, and invisible audiences (Boyd and Ellison 2007). Researchers differ over what counts as a social network site in the dynamic web environment. The following focuses on what are most commonly acknowledged as SNSs. It does not include photo and video sharing sites (such as Flickr and You Tube), virtual worlds (Second Life), microblogging (Twitter), social bookmarking (del.icio.us), or aggregating services (FriendFeed).

SNSs are among the features that characterize "Web 2.0"; others are blogs, wikis, podcasts, and vodcasts. While there is debate about the extent to which the World Wide Web has entered its second generation in technical terms, there is general agreement that there is now greater interactivity, user participation, data sharing, and networking. In the Internet environment users now create as well as consume content; and while Web 1.0 was primarily an information source, Web 2.0 is a participatory environment. Thus "user-generated content" is a defining feature of Web 2.0 – and one of the characteristics of SNSs.

The sites are based on users providing personal information – building profiles with information on background, interests, work, etc., uploading photographs, and in some cases music and videos – "making friends" with other users, perhaps joining site-based groups, or using the site to organize events. Sites may encourage activities in particular areas (for example, music sharing), and the extent of customization of individual sites varies.

The largest SNSs in the western world are now owned by large corporations. MySpace, established in 1999 by eUniverse (later Intermix), was acquired in July 2005 by News Corporation for $580 million. Facebook was originally developed for, and restricted to, students at Harvard College when launched in early 2004. (It is named after the facebooks issued to incoming college students and staff as a means of familiarizing them with the College.) By September 2006 Facebook had been open to anyone aged 13 or older and began to attract corporate world attention. Venture capital companies invested, and in October 2007 Microsoft purchased a 1.6 percent share (for $240 million); in the following month twelve global brands became involved with Facebook Ads (including Coca-Cola, Sony Pictures, and Blockbuster). In March 2008 Bebo, founded in early 2005 by Michael and Xochi Birch, was sold to AOL for $850 million.

While SNSs have created new communication, socializing and political opportunities, extended collaboration between the music industry and new media, and collaborative possibilities for old and new media, during the short time they have existed they have become controversial. While one might have predicted that scholarly interest in SNSs would reflect existing theoretical approaches – such as social network theory and Manuel Castells' work on networks in the "Information Age" – research to date has focused on the following aspects of online social networking: online relationships and online-offline connections, friendship and friendship management, profiles and impression management, privacy, trust, surveillance, and to a lesser extent commercialization, marketing, and commodification. Because SNSs are relatively new, there is an absence of longitudinal studies; research has also tended to be based on small samples (relevant to numbers of users reportedly engaged in online social networking); and despite their global scale, cross-cultural studies of SNSs are lacking. Thus scholarly understanding of SNS use and users is limited. It should not be forgotten that global inequalities of access to the Internet mean that, even in the first decade of the twenty-first century, there are areas of the world where online social networking is still not an option.

SEE ALSO: Cyberculture; Cybersexualities and Virtual Sexuality; Internet; Media and Globalization; Social Network Analysis; Surveillance

SUGGESTED READINGS

Boyd, D. M. and Ellison, N. B. (2007) Social network sites: definition, history, and scholarship. *Journal of Computer-Mediated Communication* 13 (1): article 11, http://jcmc.indiana.edu/vol13/issue1/boyd.illison.html.

List of Social Networking Websites: http://en.wikipedia.org/wiki/List_of_social_networking_websites, retrieved June 19, 2008.

LYN GORMAN

organizations

A broad definition of an organization could be said to be that of any purposeful arrangement of social activity that implies active control over human relations ordered for particular ends. In this sense, organizations involve patterns of relationships beyond primary group associations that are largely spontaneous, unplanned, and informal, and that are typified by kinship relations, peer groups, and localized community networks. There is, however, no generally accepted definition of an organization since its meaning may vary in terms of the different sociological approaches applied to the subject. Moreover, while organizations may be deliberately constructed or reconstructed for specific ends, the problem of definition founders on the specification of "organizational goals," since groups and individuals within organizations may hold a variety of different and competing goals and the level of compliance and cooperation displayed by subordinates may vary, thus leading to the distinction between "formal" and "informal" organizations.

There are numerous existing sociological frameworks of organizational analysis and many have sought to categorize their forms by recourse to various criteria. For example, by using a classification of motivation behind adhering to organizational authority, Amitai Etzioni (1975) identifies three types. Those who work for remuneration are members of a utilitarian organization. Large commercial enterprises, for instance, generate profits for their owners and offer remuneration in the form of salaries and wages for employees. Joining utilitarian organizations is usually a matter of individual choice, although the purpose is that of income. Individuals joining normative organizations do so not for remuneration but to pursue goals they consider morally worthwhile, perhaps typified by voluntary organizations, political parties, and numerous other confederations concerned with specific issues. Finally, in Etzioni's typology, coercive organizations are distinguished by involuntary membership which forces members to join by coercion or for punitive reasons.

Max Weber (1946 [1921]), to whom the first comprehensive sociological treatment of organizations is usually attributed, offered a distinction between modern bureaucracies and other forms of organization (*Verband*). Weber pointed out that patterns of authority in previous forms of organization did not conform to what he regarded as his typology of "legal-rational" authority that infused the modern bureaucracy. Formal organizations, however, as Weber accounts, dated back to antiquity. The elites who ruled early empires, ranging from Babylonian, Egyptian, to Chinese, relied on government officials to extend their domination over large subject populations and vast geographical areas. Formal organizations, and their attendant bureaucratic structures, consequently allowed rulers to administer through the collection of taxes, military campaigns, and construction projects.

Early critiques of organizational functionality did not, however, curtail the tendency for the discipline of sociology to view the organization as a central hallmark of modernity. This explains the normative appeal of particular schools of organization theory that dominated for so long within the discipline. A yardstick of such an attraction was inherent in the mid-twentieth-century analytical frameworks of the structural functionalist accounts of Talcott Parsons, who established an organizational typology that was underpinned by rational instrumentality (Parsons 1960). In short, functional imperatives and rules established a relationship between the needs of organizations as organic social systems and individual and collective roles and motivations.

In questioning the efficiency of formal rules and regulations, Blau (1963) insisted that unofficial practices are an established and vital part of the structure of all organizations, serving to increase internal efficiency. In particular, it is via informal networks that information and experience are shared and problem solving facilitated. Hence, knowledge of complex regulations is widened, leading to time saving and efficiency, while consultation transforms the organizational staff from a disparate collection of officials into a cohesive working group. Moreover, informality may help to legitimate needs sometimes overlooked by formal regulation, or may amount to "cutting corners" in the carrying out of duties in order to simplify the means to achieve specified goals. Thus, paradoxically, unofficial practices which are explicitly prohibited by official regulations may further the achievement of organizational objectives.

The postmodern approach to organizations is clearly currently increasingly influential. It has tended to deny the previous sociological preoccupation with organizational analysis. This is because postmodern accounts, which center on the application of literary and cultural theorizing, lead to the neglect or denial of structural theory in any shape or form. The increasing popularity of a postmodern approach, with its central concern of deconstructionism, has in turn added to a further development in organization study and theorizing: its increasing fragmentation and isolation. However, organizational analysis, especially in the USA, continues to focus on the intricacies of structure, systems, hierarchy, and technology. Thus there remains an enduring interest in the relationship between organizations and their wider environment, particularly with macroeconomic factors and the dynamics of the contemporary marketplace.

SEE ALSO: Institutional Theory, New; Organization Theory; Organizations as Coercive Institutions; Organizations as Social Structures

REFERENCES

Blau, P. (1963) *The Dynamics of Bureaucracy*. University of Chicago Press, Chicago, IL.

Etzioni, A. (1975) *A Comparative Analysis of Complex Organizations: On Power, Involvement, and Their Correlates*. Free Press, New York.

Parsons, T. (1960) *Structure and Process in Modern Societies*. Free Press, Glencoe, IL.

Weber, M. (1946) [1921] Bureaucracy. In: Gerth, H. & Mills, C. W. (eds.), *From Max Weber: Essays in Sociology*. Oxford University Press, New York, pp. 196–262.

SUGGESTED READING

Foucault, M. (1975) *Discipline and Punish: The Birth of the Prison*. Vintage, New York.

STEPHEN HUNT

organizations as social structures

Organizations as social structures is a perspective that focuses on the hardware of human association, the durable factors that govern people's ways of being together as they achieve common goals by coordinated means. As it has been understood in the literature, social structure is what permits the organization's persistence over time; it describes relations among differentiated positions, and references an agency or institutional will that transcends that of individuals. Structure implies wholeness rather than aggregates, predictable patterns of transformation, self-regulation, and closure. Structure itself is a term borrowed from architecture, hence the spatial emphasis on prescribed places that people can inhabit. Organizational studies would need to be devised to disclose the plans and patterns of the social edifice.

The possibility of identifying structure rested upon a positive disposition toward the nature of society; namely, that the interconnections among persons were an entity in their own right, but also that these fixtures bore the properties of reason. Society is rational, and structures are the register in which rules can be read. The anxieties swirling around the turbulence of market societies derived from the concern that those displaced from traditional beliefs and dispossessed from their ways of life constituted a mass that would devolve into a mob, threatening public order and property. The emerging sociological profile was Janus-faced: modern society was rule giving, but also generated its own forms of unreason; it normalized but engendered abnormality; it imposed association in common but was riven by conflict. As organizational studies coalesced in the twentieth century around the notion of social structure, they undertook the analysis of these societal antinomies in terms that could be either apologetic or critical.

The consolidation of organizations as a generalizable field of study corresponded less to the passage away from industrialization linked to the first half of the century than to a deepening and extension of the industrial model to domains of activity and association hitherto untouched by it. The resonance of structures across what were presented as functionally distinct domains of polity, culture, and economy made the case that society was becoming increasingly rationalized. At the same time, rationality was itself grounded in problems of labor control and inspired by models of decision-making derived from research and development in the military and the stock market. If the key conceptual turn that gave rise to the field of organizations was the use of structure to treat human association as a system, an architectural metaphor was being used to underwrite the idea that society worked like a machine. But if the system metaphor was to serve the legitimating perquisites of a modernizing society grounded in expanding opportunities for wealth and progressive opportunities for participation in general decision-making, it would need to attend some dynamic of change or morphogenesis in its structure.

The dialectic between fixity and contingency, continuity and change was expressed in the dualism of structure and process which oriented organizational sociology during its florescence from the 1950s to the mid-1970s. Over the past 30 years organizational studies have continued within sociology (and perhaps more robustly without). The idea of organizations as bounded entities containing discrete memberships and fixed structures has become untenable, both in concept and in practice. Structure and process have merged and internal and external adaptations have become intertwined. Appropriate to the times, the architectural metaphor that social structure had rested upon may shift its reference from buildings (the internal skeleton) to computers, where the term applies at once to hardware and software. Structure's future may lie in its ability to transit in between.

SEE ALSO: Organization Theory; Structure and Agency; System Theories

SUGGESTED READINGS

Ahrne, G. (1994) *Social Organization: Interaction Inside, Outside, and Between Organizations*. Sage, London.

Blau, P. & Schoenherr, R. (1971) *The Structure of Organizations*. Basic Books, New York.

Scott, W. R. (2004) Reflections on a half-century of organizational sociology. *Annual Review of Sociology* 30: 1–21.

RANDY MARTIN

organization theory

The ability of societies to respond to social and economic problems depends upon the availability of diverse *organizational forms*. Organization theorists are interested in the range of organizational forms, their capabilities and consequences, in how new organizational forms arise and become established, and in who controls them for what purposes.

Prior to the 1960s, and based on the work of Max Weber, "bureaucracy" was regarded as the most efficient organizational form because it imbued organizations with technical rationality. Beginning in the late 1950s, a series of studies showed that the relevance of the Weberian model was "contingent" upon the degree of task uncertainty, complexity, and organizational size.

A second foundational perspective is the behavioral theory of the firm. Cyert and March (1963) explored how individuals use simplifying decision rules to model and cope with complexity. Decision-making is thus "boundedly rational." Organizations are intendedly adaptive systems struggling to cope with complex and ambiguous information.

Weick (1995) offered a *sensemaking theory* of how organizations relate to their contexts. Managers build "mental models" that shape how they think about their industry and understand possible courses of action. Weick also introduced the idea that organizations *enact* their contexts. That is, sensemaking concurrently involves reflection (often retrospective) and action to "test out" tentative and incomplete understandings. But actions shape contexts, bringing them into being, thus "confirming" emergent mental models.

- *Transaction cost theory* points to market failures as the reason for organizations. Unanticipated disagreements and investments in specific assets are managed by incorporating activities into an organization, using hierarchy rather than markets as the governance mechanism.
- *Resource dependence theory* proposes that organizations seek to control their environments by not becoming over-dependent on other organizations for resources necessary for organizational survival, whilst creating and exploiting situations where organizations are dependent upon them. The relationship between context and organization is not unidirectional but reciprocal.
- *Neo-institutional theory* observes that within any given industry, organizations use similar organizational forms because social conventions prescribe socially acceptable ways of doing things. Organizations conform because doing so provides social legitimacy and enhances survival prospects. Organizations are not simply production systems but social and cultural systems embedded within an "institutional" context, comprising the state, professions, interest groups, and public opinion. Institutionalized prescriptions are enduring and often taken for granted.
- *Population ecology* regards organizational survival as the product of fit between organizational forms and, primarily, market forces. Ecological theories are interested in why organizational forms become established and survive or decline. Forms best aligned to given contextual locations flourish. Less well-aligned forms disappear. Changes in context pose survival challenges because managers are unable to change organizations quickly enough.
- *Evolutionary theory* emphasizes classification of organizational forms to identify their defining features; attention to the mechanisms by which organizational forms are "isolated" and retain their distinctiveness; and the interactions between organizations and their environments that enable them to explore new forms of adaptation.
- *Network theory* focuses upon the topography of links ("ties") connecting organizations. The network is a structure of resource opportunities which organizations differentially access by their connections and positions within the network. It also sees organizations not as taking advantage of a network but as being shaped by it. Networks are also seen as embedded relationships.
- *Critical theory* proposes that organizations be regarded as instruments of political exploitation with distributive consequences. Perrow (2002), for example, sees the large modern corporation not as a response to functional pressures but as the means by which elite interests preserve and enhance positions of privilege.

The range of perspectives within organization theory continues to grow. There is, thus, no organization theory per se, but a fertile array of complementary, competing, and enlightening insights into one of the most significant societal constructs: the modern organization.

SEE ALSO: Bureaucracy; Management, Theories of; Organizations; Organizations as Social Structures; Weber, Max

REFERENCES

Cyert, R. M. & March, J. G. (1963) *A Behavioral Theory of the Firm*. Prentice Hall, Englewood Cliffs, NJ.
Perrow, C. (2002) *Organizing America*. Princeton University Press, Princeton, NJ.
Weick, K. E. (1995) *Sensemaking in Organizations*. Sage, Thousand Oaks, CA.

ROYSTON GREENWOOD

Orientalism

Orientalism is the study of the "Orient" and its "eastern" arts, languages, sciences, histories, faiths, cultures, and peoples by Christian theological experts, humanist scholars, and natural and social scientists since the 1500s. Orientalist writers consider the "Orient" as consisting of societies geographically east of Christian Europe to be explored, acquired, and colonized for their raw materials, abundant labor, and pieces of seemingly opulent civilizations in decline. These colonial explorations resulted in man-made, imaginary geographies and political demarcations such as the Near East, the Middle East, Central Asia, the Far East, the Pacific Isles, the New World, and the "Dark Continent."

Since the 1950s, critics of Orientalist scholarship objected to the essentialization, exoticization and racialization enacted through imperialist projects. These critics object to their claims of validity and objectivity and to the authoritative statements and classroom materials on topics such as Islam, Middle Eastern affairs, Indian civilization, and Chinese philosophies. Moreover, they charge that Orientalism assists in the economic and political domination and restructuring of the "Orient" through its denials, distortions, and suppressions of lived experiences under western imperialism with its claims of western and Christian superiority in knowledge, commerce, gender relations, and ways of life.

Cultural theorist Edward Said offers, in his landmark *Orientalism* (1978), a sustained study of Eurocentric discourse representing itself as innocent, objective, and well-intentioned. He argues that it is never simply negative racial stereotyping and prejudice by those who never had contact with the orientalized "other." Instead, US, British, French, and other first world scholars often have had and needed direct contacts with their "others" to produce Orientalist knowledge in attempts to explain and justify imperialist projects during their respective periods of conquest and empire.

Said argues that US, British, and French Orientalisms produce racialized discourses in the arts, media, politics, and social science knowledge that are erroneous abstractions, in particular, of people of Islamic faith and from the Middle East. To legitimate and maintain western dominance since the late 1960s, US Orientalism, for instance, represents the Middle East as an Islamic place bursting with villains and terrorists and denies the historical, lived, and racially and religiously diverse realities of dispossessed Palestinians. These varying strategic deployments of Orientalist discourse produce a global politics and civic engagement tinted by a deeply distorted image of the social complexity of millions of people practicing Islam or residing in the third world.

Feminist scholars document how Orientalist constructions have been significantly sexualized and gendered. Prominent male scholars are not the exclusive producers of these constructions; some feminists and women's studies scholars historically have participated in Orientalism too. These feminists and women's studies scholars analyze the ways Orientalist scholars deploy problematic gendered, sexualized, and racialized discourses to further "the [western and liberal] Feminist Project" and to liberate women from seemingly "oppressive," "traditional" third world cultures.

Sociologists Bryan Turner and Stuart Hall contend that Orientalist discourse exists in the underlying assumptions, fundamental concepts, epistemological models, and methodological procedures of modern sociology. Turner, Hall, and others trace the origins of this discourse in the writings of early influential theorists in western European sociology and examine their varied legacies. Consequently, sociology has participated in fostering Orientalism, and unduly assists first world imperialist projects through its varied theoretical, research, and policy practices.

SEE ALSO: Empire; Islam; Third World and Postcolonial Feminisms/Subaltern

REFERENCE

Said, E. (1978) *Orientalism*. Vintage, New York.

SUGGESTED READINGS

Hall, S. (1996) The west and the rest. In: Hall, S., Held, D., Hubert, D., & Thomson, K. (eds.), *Modern Societies: An Introduction*. Blackwell, Malden, MA, pp. 184–227.

Lewis, R. (1996) *Gendering Orientalism: Race, Femininity, and Representation*. Routledge, London.

PETER CHUA

Orthodoxy

Orthodoxy is a major branch of Christianity, represented by the Eastern Orthodox Church, with an unbroken continuity to the apostolic tradition and a claim to curry the authentic Christian faith and practice. The term Orthodoxy (from the Greek *orthe doxa*), meaning both right faith and right worship, developed and came to usage during the fourth and fifth centuries in order to distinguish and protect the faith of the Church from a variety of heretical movements, Arianism and Nestorianism in particular. The early ecumenical councils produced the formal creeds of the Church and consolidated the notion of Orthodoxy which was Greek based and took a different theological and cultural ethos from the western church which was Latin based, the two churches eventually separating (1054).

Today, the Orthodox Church consists of the ancient patriarchates (Constantinople, Alexandria,

Antiochia, Jerusalem) and various national autocephalous Churches. The Patriarchate of Constantinople, also called Ecumenical, enjoys the primacy of honor among the other patriarchates and the rest of the Orthodox Churches without any administrative or other jurisdiction over them. The churches of Russia, Serbia, Romania, Bulgaria, and Georgia carry patriarchal status – being led by patriarchs. The Churches of Greece, Cyprus, and Albania are led by archbishops. There are also the smaller churches of Poland, Finland, and former Czechoslovakia, also led by archbishops. The Greek Orthodox diaspora in America, Europe, and Australia is under the jurisdiction of the Ecumenical Patriarchate and the Russian Orthodox diaspora everywhere is under the jurisdiction of the patriarchate of Moscow.

The Orthodox Churches are held together and are in communion with each other through common doctrine and practice of the sacraments. In all, the Orthodox populations (practicing in the broad sense) in the world today are estimated at around 180 million. Today, Orthodoxy plays a new spiritual, cultural and political role, especially in post-communist countries, and the world at large.

SEE ALSO: Church; Secularization

SUGGESTED READINGS

Gianolatos, A. (2001) *Globalisation and Orthodoxy*. Akritas, Athens.

Ware, K. (1963) *The Orthodox Church*. Penguin, London.

NIKOS KOKOSALAKIS

outliers

An outlier is an observation or measurement that is unusually large or small relative to the other values in a data set. Outliers occur for a variety of reasons. They can represent an error in measurement, data recording, or data entry, or a correct value that just happens to be extreme. Outliers can result in biased or distorted sample statistics and faulty conclusions. Alternatively, they can be the most interesting finding in the data. History records many scientific breakthroughs that have resulted from following up on extreme observations.

A number of rules have been suggested for identifying outliers. One rule identifies an outlier as any measurement or observation that falls outside of the interval given by $Mdn \pm 2(Q_3 - Q_1)$, where Mdn denotes the median and Q_3 and Q_1 denote, respectively, the third and first quartiles. Once an outlier has been identified, the next step is to determine whether the outlier is really a correct, extreme value or an error. If the outlier is an error, it should be corrected or deleted. If a correct, extreme value is included in an analysis, its impact can be softened by transforming the data using a square root or logarithmic transformation. Alternatively, distribution-free statistics or Winsorized measures can be selected that are robust in the presence of outliers. As a last resort, a correct, extreme value can be deleted in which case it is desirable to report the results both with and without the outlier.

SEE ALSO: Measures of Centrality; Statistics

SUGGESTED READING

Tukey, J. W. (1977) *Exploratory Data Analysis*. Addison-Wesley, Reading, MA.

ROGER E. KIRK

outsider-within

Patricia Hill Collins's idea of the outsider-within has quickly become a classic in feminist theories. The term was originally used to describe the location of individuals who find themselves in the border space between groups: that is, who no longer have clear membership in any one group. Dissatisfied with this usage because of its resemblance to early sociology's "marginal man," Collins later modified the term to "describe social locations or border spaces occupied by groups of unequal power" (1998: 5). Rather than static positions, these locations contain a number of contradictions for the individuals who occupy them. While individuals in these unique locations appear to be members of the dominant group based on possession of the necessary qualifications for, and apparent rights of, member standing, they do not necessarily enjoy all of the experiential benefits afforded to formal members. Collins uses the example of blacks in the United States; while they have basic citizenship rights, they are often treated as second-class citizens.

Knowledge production is also central to Collins' work. In a search for social justice, the outsider-within location describes not only a membership position but also a knowledge/power relationship. This unique location is one where members of a subordinated group can access information about the dominant group without being afforded the rights and privileges accorded to group members. It is this unique knowledge of both sides that distinguishes the outsider-within from both elite and oppositional locations.

SEE ALSO: Black Feminist Thought; Feminist Standpoint Theory

REFERENCE

Collins, P. H. (1998) *Fighting Words: Black Women and the Search for Justice*. University of Minnesota Press, Minneapolis, MN.

J. MICHAEL RYAN

outsourcing

Outsourcing refers to the fundamental decision to contract out specific activities that previously were undertaken internally. In other words, outsourcing involves the decision to reject the internalization of an activity and can be viewed as vertical disintegration. As it means to obtain by contract from an outside supplier, it is also called contracting out or subcontracting.

Outsourcing is not new. Contractual relationships dominated the economic organization of production prior to and during the Industrial Revolution. However, from the mid-nineteenth century until the 1980s, the internalization of transactions within organizations became the dominant trend. From the 1880s, there was a shift from a regime of *laissez-faire* production consisting of many small firms to a regime based on large, vertically integrated corporations, or what is called a shift from markets to hierarchies, which culminated in the large-scale public and private sector bureaucracies of the post-war era. Two reinforcing tendencies played an important part in this trend: the growth of direct government involvement in economic activity and the development of production technologies that favored large, vertically integrated organizations. Those same factors forced the retreat from outsourcing in the 1980s and 1990s. In the first years of this outsourcing trend, mainly non-core and less strategically important activities were subcontracted, such as cleaning, catering, and maintenance, also called blue-collar activities. Increasingly, however, organizations began to outsource white-collar, business services, which many might claim are strategic, such as IT and telecommunications. The offshore contracting out of manufacturing and especially of service activities to developing countries is the reason for a growing skepticism toward outsourcing in the developed countries.

A large number of studies are primarily engaged with the empirical proof of the existence of cost efficiencies from outsourcing. As a leading figure in this research, Domberger (1998) undertook several empirical studies of outsourcing in the UK and Australian public and private sector, reporting that, on the average, organizations realized 20 percent increases in efficiency and decreases in cost through outsourcing. These cost efficiencies result, for example, from the reduced capital intensity and lower fixed costs for the outsourcing companies and in the reduced costs of the outsourced activity due to the supplier's economies of scale and scope. Additionally, other positive effects have been proposed, such as higher flexibility through the choice between different suppliers and the easy switch between technologies, quick response to changes in the environment, increased managerial attention and resource allocation to tasks where the organization has its core competences, and increased quality and innovativeness of the purchased products or services due to specialization of the supplier and spreading of risk.

Despite the arguments that outsourcing firms often achieve better performance than vertically integrated firms, there is a lack of consistency as to the extent to which outsourcing improves the performance and the competitive situation of organizations. Several studies show that efficiency gains are often much smaller than claimed, or even that costs increased after services are contracted out. Additionally, it has been argued that using outsourcing merely as a defensive technique can cause long-term negative effects. Because of outsourcing, there is the danger for firms to enter the so-called "spiral of decline" (also called hollowing out of organizations): after contracting out, companies need to shift overhead allocation to those products and services that remain in-house. As a result, the remaining products and services become more expensive and less competitive, which raises their vulnerability to subsequent outsourcing. This process can lead to the loss of important knowledge and capabilities and, as a result, can threaten the long-term survival of organizations.

Some other important disadvantages that may result from outsourcing are a negative impact upon employees that remain in the company (e.g., lower employee commitment, drop in promotional opportunities, drop in job satisfaction, and changes in duties), declining innovation by the outsourcer, dependence on the supplier, and the provider's lack of necessary capabilities. Especially the social cost associated with loss of employment in the outsourcing organizations has been strongly criticized by opponents of outsourcing.

SEE ALSO: Institutionalism; Networks; Social Exchange Theory

REFERENCE

Domberger, S. (1998) *The Contracting Organization: A Strategic Guide to Outsourcing*. Oxford University Press, Oxford.

NATALIA NIKOLOVA

P

Panopticon

The Panopticon, designed by the English philosopher, Jeremy Bentham, in 1791, is a prison in which an observer positioned in a center tower has the ability to see into all of the cells across from the tower in an annular building. Backlighting allows the observer to see into the cells and observe the occupants. Since those inside the cells are unable to see into the center tower (its windows are covered), the prisoners can never tell if (and when) they are being observed.

Under the constant threat of being watched, the cell occupant begins to internalize this gaze and, in turn, begins to self-police and supervise his/her thoughts, behaviors, and actions whether or not anyone is actually watching. In this way, power is not imposed upon the corporeal body directly, such as through the use of torture, but rather, through an array of design and lighting features and through the distribution of bodies in cells.

The Panopticon, typically portrayed as a prison to control prisoners, was designed to serve as a modern solution to social problems. It could function as an asylum to control illness, a workhouse to control workers or even to control a school full of children. Through mechanisms of control, surveillance and self-discipline, the Panopticon became a way to deploy state power through various institutions. By turning the watcher's gaze inward, self-policing made the role of the state as a disciplinary body less visible since people were doing the work themselves.

The Panopticon was never actually built. However, it serves as a metaphor for surveillance society since the disciplinary techniques envisioned for the Panopticon inevitably spread throughout the social body. Thus, the Panopticon is more than a building spec; the Panopticon inspires mechanisms of control such as surveillance and self-policing, and in this way, helps us to think about how individuals constitute themselves as subjects in a disciplinary society.

SEE ALSO: Disciplinary Society; Foucault, Michel; Prisons; Surveillance

SUGGESTED READINGS

Bentham, J. (1995) *The Panopticon Writings*, ed. M. Božovič. Verso, London.

Foucault, M. (1995) [1978] *Discipline and Punish: The Birth of the Prison*, trans. A. Sheridan. Vintage Books, New York.

HEATHER MARSH

paradigms

Since the publication of Thomas Kuhn's (1962) *The Structure of Scientific Revolutions*, a paradigm has been considered a conglomeration of concepts, theories and methods which guide research and become dominant during particular historical epochs and/or within particular disciplines. Rohmann (1999: 296) highlights this dominant character by explaining that a paradigm "tends to become ingrained, influencing the very choice of questions deemed worthy of study, the methods used to study those questions, and the interpretations of the results." As unified and dominant worldviews which imply particular concerns and preferences related to ontology (the nature of reality), epistemology (theories about knowledge acquisition), and methodology (techniques used to acquire knowledge), paradigms have been described as in competition with one another. Paradigms need not be viewed as so homogenizing, however. Instead, some researchers encourage the choice of paradigm based on its *fit* with the particular phenomenon under investigation. More recently, scholars have begun to promote "greater spirituality within research efforts" via multiparadigmatic research endeavours (Lincoln & Guba 2003: 286).

SEE ALSO: Epistemology; Knowledge, Sociology of; Kuhn, Thomas and Scientific Paradigms; Theory Construction

REFERENCES

Rohmann, C. (1999) *The World of Ideas: A Dictionary of Important Theories, Concepts, Beliefs, and Thinkers*. Ballantine Books, New York.

Lincoln, Y. S. & Guba, E. G. (2003) Paradigmatic controversies, contradictions, and emerging confluences. In: Denzin, N. K. & Lincoln Y. S. (eds.), *The Landscape of Qualitative Research*, 2nd edn. Sage, Thousand Oaks, CA, pp. 253–91.

JULIE GREGORY

Park, Robert F. (1864–1944) and Burgess, Ernest W. (1886–1966)

Robert Ezra Park and Ernest Watson Burgess advanced American sociology during its formative period, making contributions to ethnic studies, urban sociology, and the study of collective behavior. They were the two central figures responsible for defining and shaping the "Chicago School" during its most influential period, when Park assumed the chairperson's position and Burgess became his assistant.

Born in Harveyville, Pennsylvania, Park attended the University of Michigan and Harvard. He spent time in studying in Germany. Upon returning home, Park worked as a muckraking journalist for the Congo Reform Association, where he met Booker T. Washington. After working for Washington at Tuskegee, he began his career at Chicago. Park chaired the department from 1918 until his retirement in 1933, after which time he taught at Fisk University. Burgess was born in Tilbury, Ontario, though his family moved to the USA early in his life. After completing his undergraduate studies at Kingfisher College, he obtained his PhD at the University of Chicago. After teaching elsewhere for a few years, he returned to Chicago, where he remained for the rest of his academic career.

The 1921 publication of their coauthored textbook, *Introduction to the Science of Sociology* served to codify their perspective on the discipline. Park and Burgess were simultaneously influenced by human ecology and by a perspective that was concerned with meaningful social action. Park and Burgess promoted a sociology that focused on the heterogeneous subgroups of urban dwellers. Of special interest were the ethnic and racial minorities migrating to cities.

Two central characteristics of the Chicago School approach to sociology that emerged out of this focus were: (1) a concern with the ecological patterns of urban life, and (2) attention to the patterns of adjustment and incorporation of newcomers. The ecological perspective borrowed from biology by focusing on competition for and conflict over resources and territory. Ecological sociology placed a premium on spatial dynamics, as is attested by the well-known concentric zone model that Burgess developed. Park and Burgess considered Chicago to be a laboratory for investigation. Given that the boundaries of inquiry were defined in terms of neighborhoods, the methodological approach that they favored was ethnography.

Park in particular was interested in delineating the processes of immigrant adjustment, which he did by developing a version of assimilation theory. Though often viewed as the canonical formulation of assimilation theory, Park's ideas have been badly misinterpreted. His perspective has been portrayed as the theoretical articulation of the melting pot thesis. However, a close reading of Park's writings on assimilation leads one to conclude that in fact it does not necessarily entail the eradication of ethnic attachments, but instead can be seen as occurring in a pluralist context where ethnic groups maintain their distinctive identities while also being committed to the larger society.

In their coauthored textbook, Park and Burgess make three points about assimilation. First, it occurs most rapidly and completely in situations where social contacts between newcomers and native-born occur in the realm of primary group life, whereas if contact is confined to secondary groups, accommodation is more likely to result. Second, a shared language is a prerequisite for assimilation. Third, rather than being a sign of like-mindedness, assimilation is a reflection of shared experiences and mental frameworks, out of which emerge a shared sense of collective purpose.

Park and Burgess' work had a marked impact on American sociology prior to World War II. Among their most prominent students were Herbert Blumer, E. Franklin Frazier, Everett Hughes, and Louis Wirth. However, after 1940 the center of gravity shifted from Chicago to Harvard. The Chicago School brand of sociology was frequently criticized for being atheoretical. Moreover, Park and Burgess were criticized for being inattentive to power and politics. Methodologically, advocates of survey research challenged their emphasis on ethnography. In the area of urban sociology, their ecological approach gave way to approaches more influenced by political economy.

In recent years there is evidence of a renewal of interest in their work. A number of publications have appeared seeking to revisit and reappropriate the legacy of the Chicago School. The general consensus is that they were more theoretically sophisticated than has been appreciated. Ethnographic research is now far more accepted than it was during the heyday of structural functionalism. At the same time, the ecological approach has largely been abandoned because of its theoretical shortcomings. Critics make a persuasive case that Park and Burgess were relatively inattentive to power. In short, what has emerged is a clearer portrait of this influential duo that reveals both the weaknesses and the strengths of their work.

SEE ALSO: Chicago School; Ethnography; Urban Ecology

SUGGESTED READINGS

Kivisto, P. (2004) What is the canonical theory of assimilation? Robert E. Park and his predecessors. *Journal of the History of the Behavioral Sciences* 40 (2): 1–15.

Matthews, F. H. (1977) *Robert E. Park and the Chicago School.* Montreal: McGill-Queen's University Press.

PETER KIVISTO

Parsons, Talcott (1902–79)

Talcott Parsons, sociological theorist and Harvard University professor, developed a "general theory of action," a conceptual scheme designed to apply to all aspects of human social organization in all times and places. Books and essays published over fifty years brought the theory to an unparalleled level of analytic complexity and detail.

Parsons' thought was shaped by many influences, including Kant and Whitehead in philosophy, Freud in psychoanalysis, Vilfredo Pareto's system theory, and Norbert Wiener's cybernetics. However, the greatest influences were Max Weber, whose works he encountered as a student at the University of Heidelberg, and Emile Durkheim, whose writings he studied intensively from the 1930s.

The Structure of Social Action (1937) presented Parsons's first formulation of his conceptual framework. It analyzed the "unit act," a conception of *any* instance of meaningful human conduct, into four essential elements, ends, means, norms, and conditions, and in some statements a fifth element, effort to implement action. Parsons argued that action is not possible unless an instance of each element is involved; conversely, all human action can be understood as combinations of these elements.

Parsons maintained that a sound conceptual framework is the logical starting point for a science, hence, sociological theories that do not recognize each of the basic elements of action are in principle flawed. He criticized utilitarian and behaviorist theories for overlooking the importance of norms, and idealist theories for overemphasizing ends and norms but underemphasizing conditions and means. Contemporary structuralism assimilates norms and conditions into its notion of structure, denying their independence, while underemphasizing ends and means.

In *The Social System* (1951), Parsons made systems of interaction and social relationships, social systems, his central concept, replacing the unit act. He then related social systems to cultural and personality systems, proposing that the three kinds of systems are integrated normatively. Norms gain moral authority from contexts of evaluative culture, are institutionalized in social systems, and are internalized in the superegos of personalities. In chapters on socialization and social control, *The Social System* explored the dynamics through which norms are institutionalized in social relationships. A chapter on medical practice analyzed the processes of social control embedded in the sick role and physician-patient relationship.

The revised conceptual scheme raised questions of how social systems sustain themselves over time. Parsons' eventual answer was the "four function paradigm." This was not an open-ended list of functional requisites, as in previous functional theories, but an analysis of the concept of action system into four general *dimensions* that can be identified in any empirical system. The four functions are:

- *Pattern maintenance*: the processes of generating attachment to basic principles that distinguish a system from its environment – in societies, through religion, education, family life, and socialization to common values.
- *Integration*: the processes of reciprocal adjustment among a system's units, promoting their interdependence – in societies, through civil and criminal law, community institutions, and strata formation.
- *Goal attainment*: the processes of changing a system's relations with its environments to align them with shared ends – in societies, through political institutions that set collective ends and mobilize resources for reaching them.
- *Adaptation*: the processes of developing generalized control over the environment by the creation and allocation of diverse resources – in societies, through economic production and market exchange.

Application of the four function paradigm yielded a theory of four functionally specialized subsystems of society: (1) the economy for the adaptive function, (2) the polity for the goal attainment function, (3) the societal community for the integrative function, and (4) the fiduciary system for the pattern maintenance function. In *Economy and Society* (1956), Parsons and Smelser integrated the sociology of economic institutions with Keynesian theory in economics. In *Politics and Social Structure* (1969) Parsons reviewed theories of power and authority and studies of electoral, executive, and administrative institutions to develop the idea of the polity. His writings on the fiduciary system codified previous research on religion, family, and socialization, while his conception of the societal community synthesized studies of reference groups, status and class systems, and legal institutions.

Parsons portrayed the societal subsystems as complex entities, organized in terms of differentiated institutions and as dynamically interdependent, exchanging resources at open boundaries. The idea of the boundary exchanges was a generalization of economists' treatment of the exchanges of wages for labor and consumer spending for goods and services between business firms and households. Noting that money mediates the boundary exchanges of economies, Parsons then sought to identify comparable "symbolic media" for the boundary exchanges of the other societal subsystems. Innovative essays followed on power as political medium, influence as medium of the societal community, and value-commitments as fiduciary medium.

Parsons wrote over one hundred essays that used theoretical ideas to illuminate specific empirical problems – the rise of Nazism, social stratification, the Joseph McCarthy movement, order in international relations, universities, and American religion and values. Often caricatured as a Grand Theorist advocating a closed system, Parsons was actually a pragmatic critic who sought to refine basic sociological concepts to enhance their empirical implications.

SEE ALSO: Culture; Durkheim, Emile; Functionalism/Neo-functionalism; Institution; Modernization; Social Control; Structural Functional Theory; Values; Weber, Max

REFERENCES

Parsons, T. (1949) [1937] *The Structure of Social Action*. Free Press, New York.

Parsons, T. (1951) *The Social System*. Free Press, New York.

Parsons, T. (1969) *Politics and Social Structure*. Free Press, New York.

Parsons, T. & Smelser, N. J. (1956) *Economy and Society*. Free Press, New York.

SUGGESTED READINGS

Bourricaud, F. (1981) *The Sociology of Talcott Parsons*. University of Chicago Pess, Chicago, IL.

Fox, R. C. (1997) Talcott Parsons, my teacher. *American Scholar* 66 (3): 395–410.

VICTOR LIDZ

passing

Passing is a process by which one's racial, sexual, religious, cultural, ethnic, and/or national identity crosses over from one culture or community into another undetected. Though generations the term has come to be applicable to many diverse communities, such as lesbian, gay, bisexual, and transgender populations (LGBT), as well as people of Muslim faith and/or Middle Eastern descent, as well as other ethnic groups. The historical connotation of the term is intimately connected with black America. "Passing," "crossing over," or "going over to the other side" typically refers to a black person whose appearance is such that they can *pass* for white. The profound structural roots of racism against blacks that led to the drastic choice for some to *pass,* is explained by centuries of abusive laws and policies that enslaved, segregated, and oppressed blacks. The historic 1896 *Plessy v. Ferguson* decision ushered in over 60 years of legally sanctioned segregation, commonly referred to as the Jim Crow era. Reinforcing a "separate but equal" ideology, that maintains separate realities for blacks and whites in the USA, this is a period of extreme oppression for blacks, socially, economically, and physically, as many were victims of mob violence and lived under the constant threat of lynching. Rather than endure the racist and segregated world that blacks were subjected to at this time, in some instances those who were able opted to *pass* for white. In the slave era preceding Jim Crow significant race mixing had occurred. Through rape, forced breeding, and a host of other coercive means, several generations later, the concept of "colored" had developed into a social construction which no longer strictly represented one's phenotype.

Though passing and segregation were not new developments of the twentieth century, the dawn of the 1900s saw a definite rise in the number of light-skinned "blacks" passing for white as they particularly felt the sting of segregation. In order to fully exploit economic, social, and educational opportunities, some blacks, who were able, generally passed into white society on three levels: basic, complex, and fundamental. At the *basic* level of passing, an individual might occasionally accept the mistaken assumption that she or he is in fact white. This allows black citizens certain freedoms that they would otherwise be denied, such as moving about the cities where they live without fear of violence, shopping in any store, and eating at any lunch counter. The *complex* level of passing is more purposefully planned. Individuals might work on one side of town under the premise of being white, where s/he could earn money and advancement, or even attend a university as a white student. Yet when they return home at night or during holidays, they resume their black lives. This level is quite complicated and dangerous. In order for individuals to navigate this dual reality, they must move seamlessly from one world into another, all the while keeping their two worlds – one black and one white – completely separate. The *fundamental* level of passing sees the black person actually casting off his or her entire black identity in favor of a white reality. The adjustments one makes for this level of commitment are not merely cosmetic. Instead, one must make profound changes to one's thoughts, memories, beliefs, history, culture, language, politics, ethics, and so on. Though the term passing is commonly used as a historical reference, it is important to note that in the multicultural polyethnic new millennium, color, and now culture, is as ambiguous as ever. Thus, one cannot ignore other populations for whom passing remains a viable option, such as LGBT communities, Latinos, and people of Middle Eastern descent. In a post-9/11 world, amid a culture of "don't ask, don't tell," many populations other than blacks are employing various elements of passing in order to navigate the rough waters of inequality.

SEE ALSO: Coming Out/Closets; Double Consciousness; Identity Formation; Race; Race (Racism); Segregation

SUGGESTED READINGS

Johnson, J. W. (1989) *The Autobiography of an Ex-Colored Man*. Vintage, New York.

Larsen, N. (1997 [1929]) *Passing*. Penguin, New York.

NICOLE ROUSSEAU

patriarchy

An analysis of patriarchal social formations is at the heart of feminist scholarship and informs scholarly discussions of gender in a variety of fields, including sociology. Sociologists and feminists alike have noted the presence of sex differentiation and attendant patterns of social stratification in virtually every known society. Patriarchy is a theory that attempts to explain this widespread gender stratification as an effect of social organization rather than the result of some natural or biological fact.

Originally used to describe autocratic rule by a male head of a family, patriarchy has been extended to describe a more general system in which power is secured in the hands of adult men. Canadian sociologist Dorothy E. Smith (1983) describes patriarchy as "the totality of male domination and its pervasiveness in women's lives." Others further point to the ways in which patriarchy secures economic and social privileges in the hands of men. Despite significant political, legal, and cultural gains, there remains a near total domination of women by men at both the micro level of intimate relationships and the macro level of government, law, and religion. Patriarchy offers a structural analysis of such sex-based inequality and offers a systemic explanation for the ongoing distribution of power and privilege according to gender lines.

Debate concerning the concept of patriarchy has taken two central forms. One, most pressing for second wave feminist scholars (those active in the period from the mid 1960s to early 1990s), concerns the roots of patriarchy and its relationship to other forms of oppression. Centrally, feminists were concerned to ascertain whether patriarchy was the primary form of oppression or simply derivative of some other form of domination. For some, it was understood to be a universal and trans-historical phenomenon that could only be overcome by way of radical and revolutionary means. Shulamith Firestone (1971), for instance, describes patriarchy as a primary form of oppression from which all other forms of domination are derived. For those feminists more closely inspired by Marxist and socialist projects, patriarchy is seen as an effect of a particular mode of production, an effect, in specific terms, of capitalism's class structure.

Contemporary debate on the usefulness of patriarchy as an analytic term turn on its ability to make sense of difference. From a poststructuralist perspective, the presumed universality of patriarchy falls into the trap of a grand narrative. Poststructural feminism calls for a nuanced theory of patriarchy, one that can explain the ways that patriarchal social formations work to construct gendered subject positions and attend to the ways in which power inequities are discursively produced and reproduced in historically specific contexts. Third wave feminist scholars (those active in the period post-1990 and typically associated with activism and youth movements) are similarly concerned with the theory's totalizing tendencies, with a specific critique laid toward its inability to adequately take account of the ways in which patriarchy is related to the intersecting axes of privilege, domination, and oppression. Unlike earlier debates over the question of which sort of oppression is prior to which, contemporary feminists point to the ways in which patriarchal oppression – oppression resulting from the distribution of power according to sex – is always linked into other systems of inequality and privilege, including but certainly not limited to age, ability, education, race, sexual orientation, class, and color. African American feminist activist and thinker, bell hooks, has described patriarchy as white supremacist and capitalist, insisting that attention be paid to the ways that patriarchy is associated with – and gains speed from – other unjust systems of power distribution.

Certainly, contemporary scholars are quick to view patriarchy as a system that impacts both women and men. In this context, patriarchy is understood to be a system in which economic, political, and ideological power is secured in the hands of *some* men (specifically: white, educated, heterosexual, financially secure, able-bodied adult men) and denied to others. In this way, an understanding of patriarchy contributes not just to an understanding of women's lives but to the ways in which power is distributed to all members of a family, group, organization, or society.

SEE ALSO: Feminism; Power; Privilege; Women's Movements; Class

REFERENCES

Firestone, S. (1971) *The Dialectic of Sex*. Bantam, London.
Smith, D. (1983) Women, the family and the productive process. In: Grayson, J. P. (ed.), *Introduction to Sociology*. Gage, Toronto, pp. 312–44.

SUGGESTED READINGS

hooks, b. (2000) *Feminism is for Everybody: Passionate Politics*, South End Press, Cambridge, MA.
Millett, K. (1969) *Sexual Politics*. Avon Books, New York.
De Beauvoir, S. (1952) *The Second Sex*. Alfred A Knopf, New York.

MICHELLE MEAGHER

pedagogy

In both conservative and progressive discourses pedagogy is often treated simply as a set of strategies and skills to use in order to teach prespecified subject matter. In this context, pedagogy becomes synonymous with teaching as a technique or the practice of a craft-like skill. Any viable notion of critical pedagogy must reject this definition and its endless slavish imitations even when they are claimed as part of a radical discourse or project. Pedagogy in the more critical sense illuminates the relationship among knowledge, authority, and power. It draws attention to questions concerning who has control over the conditions for the production of knowledge.

Moreover, it delineates the ways in which the circuit of power works through the various processes through which knowledge, identities, and authority are constructed within particular sets of social relations.

What critical pedagogy as a form of cultural politics refers to in this case is a deliberate attempt on the part of cultural workers to influence how and what knowledge and subjectivities are produced within particular sets of social relations. It draws attention to the ways in which knowledge, power, desire, and experience are produced under specific basic conditions of learning. This approach to critical pedagogy does not reduce educational practice to the mastery of methodologies, it stresses, instead, the importance of understanding what actually happens in classrooms and other educational settings by raising questions regarding what knowledge is of most worth, in what direction should one desire, and what it means to know. Of course, the language of critical pedagogy does something more. Pedagogy is simultaneously about the knowledge and practices that teachers, cultural workers, and students might engage in together and the cultural politics and visions such practices legitimate. It is in this sense that cultural workers need to be attentive to pedagogy as a political practice and the cultural practices of pedagogy.

SEE ALSO: Critical Pedagogy; Education; Feminist Pedagogy

SUGGESTED READINGS

Freire, P. (1998) *Pedagogy of the Oppressed*, new rev. 20th-anniversay edn. Continuum Publishing, New York.
Giroux, H. (2004) *The Giroux Reader*. Paradigm Publishers, Denver, CO.

HENRY A. GIROUX

phenomenology

In its philosophical guise phenomenology maintains that the pure meaning of phenomena are only to be subjectively apprehended and intuitively grasped in their essence. It became relevant to the social sciences within the tension between logical positivism and interpretivism, or, in nineteenth-century terms, between natural and cultural sciences. At the turn of the twentieth century the neo-Kantian insistence on a distinctive epistemology and methodology for the "cultural" sciences found a well-considered resonance in German sociological thought (Weber). The growth, explanatory force and extension of natural science's objective perspective and positivistic methodology to the domains of the cultural sciences were challenged by the philosopher Edmund Husserl who laid the foundation of the twentieth-century phenomenological movement.

He emphasized how humans relate subjectively and intersubjectively (with others) to the world meaningfully experienced – the "life-world" (*Lebenswelt*). This world is apprehended in the "natural attitude," in an unquestioning and pre-predicative way. The philosopher's task is to transcend this world of taken for granted meanings, of phenomena (appearances) in order to grasp its essence (*eidos*). Towards this end one has to engage in a form of reflection called "bracketing" (*epoché*), a procedure that exposes the self-evidence of the "natural attitude" as mere claims.

The grasp of "essences" proved less attractive to sociological thinkers. It was the concepts "life-world" and "bracketing" that were taken up by Alfred Schutz in his pioneering work, *Phenomenology of the Social World* (1967).

To him the perspective of the social actor (instead of the philosopher's "subject") is central and intersubjectively linked to others in a shared life-world. He concentrates on the meaningful construction of the *social world*. He thus re-conceptualizes Husserl's universal life-world more narrowly as the "social world." The actor experiences the (social) life-world from the "natural attitude," taking it for granted in an unquestioning way. The cognitive style of the life-world thus entails the "suspension of doubt." The social world is spatially and temporally structured from the point of view of the actor. Within this framework he/she creates or draws on typifications of situations, persons and recipes for action. Schutz calls the actor's typifications in everyday life "first order" constructs.

Schutz employs "bracketing" in order to explain "second order," i.e. (social) scientific constructs. Scientific constructs bracket the truth claims of the natural attitude. In transcending the life-world of the mundane, phenomenologically oriented scientists utilize a cognitive style that suspends belief rather than doubt. They "detach" themselves as disinterested observers. The typications they produce are not concrete but more abstract and generic. They are "ideal-types" in Weber's terms.

Peter Berger and Thomas Luckmann's *The Social Construction of Reality: A Treatise in the Sociology of Knowledge* (1972) focuses on the social construction of *reality* rather than of social reality. They "bracket" the ontological claims of society. In an ambitious integrative project they account for the intersubjective construction of reality, its institutionalization as structure and internalization in a dialectical fashion that portrays humans as both constructors and constructs.

Rather than employing phenomenology as a perspective or method other exponents view it as a paradigm in the form of phenomenological sociology. In 1971 the American Sociological Association recognized it as a specialization in this form. Phenomenology also inspired ethnomethodology's critical examination of the methods ordinary members of society employ to achieve a sense of normality in everyday situations. In recent decades its subjective emphasis guided a slew of qualitative research manuals. Its influence rapidly extended to Japan, Europe, and Latin America. Currently phenomenological description and analysis consolidate existing foci on religion, education, art, architecture and politics and widen its scope to medicine, nursing, health care, the environment, ethnicity, gender, embodiment, history, and technology.

SEE ALSO: Essentialism and Constructionism; Ethnomethodology; Intersubjectivity; Knowledge, Sociology of; Schutz, Alfred

SUGGESTED READING

Crowell, S., Embree, L., & Julian, S. J. (eds.) (2001) *The Reach of Reflection: Issues for Phenomenology's Second Century*. Electron Press.

GERHARD SCHUTTE

place

It would be possible to confuse the term place with the very similar term space. Place refers to a specific location in the physical or cultural world and the attributes of that setting or niche. Space refers to the amount of physical or social distance maintained among the social actors.

Goffman's (1961) dramaturgical treatment of social settings as staging areas for the enactment of social scripts demonstrated that place characteristics can have a profound effect on interaction. This insight has been influential in architecture and urban planning as well as in sociology. People's conception of identities they possess already or aspire to can drive the construction or location of the places they inhabit.

In the second sense of place, part of the individual's self-concept may derive from socialization or experiences in a particular geographic location. The individual may express nostalgia or homesickness for the prior location, and link its influence to elements of self or social character in the present.

In its third sense, place is a cultural or social location rather than a physical setting. Having a sense of social place is especially important when a society is highly stratified. Frequently there are elaborate rituals of deference, acknowledgement, and space use associated with the social place of the individual. The distribution of access or resources may hinge upon it.

SEE ALSO: Goffman, Erving; Space

REFERENCE

Goffman, E. (1961) *Encounters.* Bobbs-Merrill, Indianapolis, IN.

SUGGESTED READINGS

Creswell, T. (1996) *In Place/Out of Place: Geography, Ideology and Transgression.* University of Minnesota Press, Minneapolis, MN.
Milligan, M. (1998) Interactional past and potential: the social construction of place attachment, *Symbolic Interaction* 21 (1): 1–34.

LESLIE WASSON

play

Play is a pattern of individual behavior and social interaction, which features competition, improvisation, and fantasy. Sociologists have made important contributions to the study of play. Mead emphasized the importance of role play in his theory of self-development. Simmel discussed the ways in which social relationships can be expressed as play-forms. Veblen criticized the degree to which play activities have been used to display and reaffirm status differences among groups, a theme that was also developed by Bourdieu. Goffman articulated some of these themes in a more general view of social life as an "information game" or pattern of "strategic interaction." Following Weber's concern with the rationalization of experience in modernity, Elias described a centuries-old "civilizing process" and its countertheme, a "quest for excitement" that marks people's attempts to de-control their emotions in socially regulated settings.

More recent sociologists have highlighted the dialectical or interactional character of play itself, the social causes and consequences of playful activity, and the ways in which formal organization transforms play. Attention has been given to the processes by which cultures and subcultures channel playful expression; to variations in play resulting from gender, class, age, and ethnic differences; and to the distinctive roles of the playground. Play has also been identified as a central element of advanced industrial or postmodern societies that feature blending of work and leisure, risk management, consumerism, and personal experience. In that light, a special focus has been the sponsorship of play by large businesses, governments, and schools. Most of these studies, however, concentrate on play in specific settings – that is, on sport, music and art, sexuality, tourism, shopping, and electronic entertainment. Future studies must integrate these narrow accounts with a broader understanding of play as a fundamental pattern of human relating that has profound implications for the character of societies.

SEE ALSO: Leisure; Mead, George Herbert; Sport

SUGGESTED READINGS

Henricks, T. (2006) *Play Reconsidered: Sociological Perspectives on human expression.* University of Illinois Press, Urbana, IL.
Huizinga, J. (1955) *Homo Ludens: A Study of the Play Element in Culture.* Beacon, Boston, MA.

THOMAS HENRICKS

Polanyi, Karl (1886–1964)

Karl Polanyi was an interwar immigrant from Central Europe who was very influential in political economy, economic anthropology, economic sociology, and institutional economics. Influenced by Owen and Marx and his interwar experience of the cataclysm that a poorly instituted political economy can provoke, his central interest became the problem of lives and livelihood: the relation of individual and community life to the manner by which the community makes its living – the place of economy in society. Polanyi laid out these concerns in his classic book, *The Great Transformation,* and later co-directed (with Conrad Arensberg) the Columbia University project which resulted in the very influential volume, *Trade and Market in the Early Empires.*

Polanyi's analysis of market capitalism centered on the concept of a double movement. He considered the application of the self-regulating market mechanism to the necessary task of social provisioning to be profoundly disruptive of the social order. This social disruption induced a spontaneous socially protective response directed at limiting the self-regulating market system to contain its erosion of social and community life.

Polanyi's work in economic anthropology expanded his criticism of the market mentality by developing the contrast of its formalist methodology of rational choice to the substantive, provisioning view of economic life. He emphasized that market exchange was only one pattern of integrating the social division of labor and developed the concepts of socially structured reciprocity and redistribution transactions. He saw the market pattern to be ultimately receding in the face of the protective response, and formalist economics, an explicit expression of the market mentality, to be incapable of comprehending the past, and therefore unable to guide the imagination of the future.

Polanyi may be considered an early post-Marxian in that he emphasized the Marxian concern with lives and livelihood but presented a different conception of the tendencies of market capitalism. Polanyi's analysis suggests that the protective response interferes with Marx's laws of motion of capitalism. Polanyi is a forerunner of today's non-essentialist Marxism and has much in common with the postmodern deconstruction of metahistorical imperatives.

SEE ALSO: Economy (Sociological Approach); Marx, Karl; Political Economy

SUGGESTED READINGS

Levitt, K. P. (ed.) (1990) *The Life and Work of Karl Polanyi: A Budapest Celebration.* Black Rose Books, Montreal.

Stanfield, J. R. (1986) *The Economic Thought of Karl Polanyi: Lives and Livelihood.* Macmillan, London.

JAMES RONALD STANFIELD AND MICHAEL C. CARROLL

political economy

Political economy refers to a branch of the social sciences that analyzes how socio-economic activities are regulated in different institutional contexts, underlining the reciprocal influences among economic, social, and political factors. Over recent decades, this field of research has witnessed a remarkable revival, especially in economics, political science, and sociology. The origin of the term, however, is strictly connected to the birth of economics. Its first use is usually made to go back to the French economist Montchrétien who, in the *Traicté de l'oeconomie politique* (1615), made reference to it as "the science of the acquisition of wealth": a "political science" connected to public economy and state finances. This approach was in part modified by the classic economists, who affirmed the scientific autonomy of the new discipline with respect to politics. The denomination was nevertheless maintained. It was with the "marginalist revolution", at the end of the nineteenth century, that the term economics became increasingly used to indicate economic science in general. The advent of the neo-classical economics – with its focalization on the study of markets – also implied an increasing disciplinary specialization among the social sciences. The "recent rediscovery" of political economy signals an inversion in this tendency, and is characterized by two main aspects: a new attention – often in a comparative perspective – to the study of institutions, and a greater interdisciplinary activity. That said the use of the same denomination masks the existence of various analytical perspectives.

ECONOMICS

An important stimulus to political economy has come from *new institutional economics*, a theoretical perspective that reintroduces institutions into economic analyses. Unlike the old institutionalism, the new version does not introduce itself as an alternative to mainstream (neoclassical) economics. Nevertheless – thanks to the support of economic history – it widens the analytic perspective toward a comparative reflection on the different modes of organizing economic activities at both a macro and a micro level. This new approach consists of two distinct yet complementary currents. The first concentrates, above all, on the institutional environment of economies, whereas the second – developed by transaction cost economics – studies the governance of contractual relations between productive units.

In economics, other trends that favor interdisciplinary dialogue are also evident. First, there is a revival of *old economic institutionalism*, and the development of *evolutionary* and *regulation approaches*, which underline the role of institutions and of various coordination mechanisms in economic and technological change. There is a second current that, taking up Alfred Marshall's original formulations on *industrial districts*, concentrates on the spatial dimension of economic activities. Finally, at the boundary with political science, there is the growth of a *political economics* theory which combines institutions, policy choices and strategic interaction among rational individuals.

POLITICAL SCIENCE

In political science, the spread of political economy – mainly in the USA – has assumed the form of an extension of the economic paradigm to the study of political phenomena. The assumptions of methodological (neoclassical) individualism – with its corollaries of rational and maximizing behaviors – were developed in the formulations of game theory, rational choice, and public choice, giving birth to a variegated "economic approach to politics." Even though its diffusion has taken place primarily since the second half of the 1970s, the initiating models were developed in the 1950s and 1960s. However, in the second half of the 1980s, as a result of contamination with the neo-institutionalist current, there was a partial revision of this approach. Since then, while still maintaining many of the previous assumptions, the *new political economy* has placed greater emphasis upon institutions, decisional procedures, and the empirical verification of theoretical models.

SOCIOLOGY

In sociology a different orientation of political economy began to spread in the second half of the 1970s. The paradigm of rational choice gained little ground, especially in Europe. Instead, attention was directed toward the sociocultural, political and institutional factors influencing the instability of advanced economies. For example, a fruitful convergence of economic sociology and political studies developed, which focused on two different models of interests representation in the capitalist countries: neocorporatism and pluralism.

Beginning in the early 1980s, the sociological approach has dealt with post-Fordism models of production, the varieties of capitalism in advanced societies, and the different paths followed by the less developed countries. The first current analyzed the crisis experienced by many large, vertically integrated firms and the emergence of a new productive paradigm – denominated "flexible specialization" – based on network forms of organization concerned with the quality and diversification of products. The second current studied the variety of capitalist systems, connecting micro and macro level reflections on industrial readjustment and regulation models. In this way, two ideal types of contemporary capitalism have been identified: the Rhine model, or the coordinated market economies, and the Anglo-Saxon model of liberal market economies. Finally, with regard to sociology of modernization, the extraordinary growth in the Asian economies has stimulated a strong revival of comparative analysis focusing on the complex interrelations between the state and the economy in the development process.

SEE ALSO: Development: Political Economy; Economy (Sociological Approach); Urban Political Economy

REFERENCES

Alt, J. E. & Alesina, A. (1996) Political economy: an overview. In: Goodin, R. E. & Klingemann, H. D. (eds.), *A New Handbook of Political Science*. Oxford University Press, Oxford, pp. 645–74.

Monroe, K. R. (ed.) (1991) The *Economic Approach to Politics: A Critical Reassessment of the Theory of Rational Action*. HarperCollins, New York.

Peersson, T. & Tabellini, G. (2000) *Political Economics: Explaining Economic Policy*. MIT Press, Cambridge, MA.

Trigilia, C. (2002) *Economic Sociology: State, Market, and Society in Modern Capitalism*. Blackwell, Oxford.

FRANCESCO RAMELLA

political sociology

Political sociology analyzes the operation of power at all levels of social life: individual, organizational, communal, national, and international.

Although Aristotle, Ibn Khaldun, or Montesquieu could claim to have founded political sociology, most political sociologists trace their intellectual lineage to Marx or Weber. Political sociology emerged as a distinct subfield in the 1950s, especially in the debate between pluralists and elite theorists. In the 1980s and 1990s, political sociologists turned to social movements, the state, and institutions.

MARX AND WEBER

According to Marx and Engels, economic structure and class relations underpin all political activity. Under capitalism, the capitalist class controls the state, which helps perpetuate its domination. Instrumentalist Marxists portray the state as the tool of a unified capitalist class that controls both the economic and political spheres. Structural Marxists view the state, and politics more generally, as a relatively autonomous product of conflict between and sometimes within classes.

Weber recognized that political competition occurs among not only classes but also status groups, political parties, trade unions, bureaucracies, and powerful officeholders. The political sphere, although linked to other spheres, has its own logic of contestation. Against Marx's stress on the economy and class struggle, Weber emphasized the advance of rationality. Over time, the bases of political authority have shifted from traditional or charismatic forms to legal-rational ones. Contemporary states dominate society with expanded, bureaucratized coercive apparatuses. Mass citizenship legitimizes this "iron cage."

ELITE THEORY, PLURALISM, AND THE THIRD WORLD

Weber argued that political power always concentrates in small groups, but he believed that popular support provides the authority behind institutions that grant this power. Elite theorists, such as Pareto and Mosca, posited the reverse: power makes authority, law, and political culture possible.

According to Michels' "iron law of oligarchy" (1966), all organizations come to be led by a few.

Mills (1956) produced a radical version of elite theory. He described a "power elite" of families that dominated America's political, military, and business sectors. Radical elite theory presumed that mass politics is passive. Radical elite theory responded to pluralism, which was influential in the two decades after World War II, when American liberal democracy seemed stable.

Pluralism's basic assumption is that in modern democracies, no single group dominates. Power is dispersed because it has many sources, including wealth, office, social status, social connections, and popular legitimacy. Individuals subscribe to multiple groups and interests, creating stability. The state merely arbitrates among competing interests.

The cold war highlighted democratization, industrialization, and anti-colonialism in the "third world." Modernization theory posits that societies follow a stage-by-stage trajectory of political, economic, and social evolution. Dependency theory responded that developing societies' problems arise from their structural positions in the capitalist world-economy, not from evolutionary backwardness (Cardoso and Faletto 1979: *Dependency and Development in Latin America*). By presenting distinct paths of political development, Moore (1966: *Social Origins of Dictatorship and Democracy*) also critiqued modernization theory and laid the foundations for historically oriented political sociology.

SOCIAL MOVEMENTS, THE STATE, AND THE NEW INSTITUTIONALISMS

In the 1960s and 1970s, protests shook the industrialized world, undermining pluralism's claims. Anti-colonial movements in Africa and Southeast Asia raised questions about the conditions for resistance and revolution. Social movements gained scholarly attention.

McAdam (1982: *Political Process and the Development of Black Insurgency*) identifies three models of social movements. The pluralist-friendly classical model portrays them as abnormalities, occurring when structural pathologies cause psychological strain. The resource-mobilization model retorts that they are natural political phenomena; rational individuals join based on a cost-benefit calculus. Finally, the political-process model stresses the interplay between activist strategy, skill, and intensity on the one hand and resource availability and political-opportunity structures on the other.

In the late 1970s, social scientists began arguing that pluralist, elite, and Marxist theory underemphasized the state as an autonomous entity. "State-centered" approaches sought to remedy a "society-centered" bias in scholarship. Skocpol (1985) remarked that state goals do not simply reflect "the demands or interests of social groups, classes, or society." This state-centered movement has included research on how the modern state arose: how states became centralized, developed differentiated structures, increased coercive power over their populations, and developed national identities superseding class and religion.

Scholars soon recognized that "the state" is a broad concept best analyzed in terms of institutions that compose and shape it. Three "new institutionalisms" emerged, each defining institutions differently. Rational-choice institutionalism defines institutions as the formal rules, historical institutionalism defines them as formal and informal rules and procedures, and organizational institutionalism includes not just rules but also habits, rituals, and other cognitive frameworks.

REDIRECTING POLITICAL SOCIOLOGY

Changing national and international political environments have taken political sociology in new directions. It participates in the proliferating globalization literature and increasingly addresses the "sub-politics" lying outside politics' traditional realm of contestation for state power (Beck 1992).

Theoretically, there are serious challenges to the foundations of political sociology. Rational-choice models assume actors in political contexts seek to maximize utility. This de-emphasizes politics' social dimensions. From different perspectives, Unger (1997: *Politics*, 3 vols.), who argues for the autonomy of politics, and Foucault (1977: *Discipline and Punish*), who probed the microphysics of power, bypass traditional sociological concerns with groups and institutions. For Unger and Foucault, political sociology misrecognizes the very nature of power.

Political sociology's evolution has mirrored modern history's political movements. Class-based models have risen and fallen with socialism's cachet. Conservative elite theory linked itself to Italian fascism in the 1920s. Pluralist models have been fellow-travelers of liberal democracy's credibility. Social-movements theory interrogated upheavals of the 1960s and 1970s. Today, as boundaries and identities change in a global age, political sociology continues to expand its horizons, investigating new configurations of power.

SEE ALSO: Institutional Theory, New; Politics; Power Elite; Social Movements; State

REFERENCES

Beck, U. (1992) *Risk Society*, trans. Mark Ritter. Sage, Newbury Park, CA.

Michels, R. (1966) *Political Parties: A Sociological Study of the Oligarchical Tendencies of Modern Democracy*. Free Press, New York.

Mills, C. W. (1956) *The Power Elite*. Oxford University Press, New York.

Skocpol, T. (1985) Bringing the state back in: strategies of analysis in current research. In: Evans, P., Rueschemeyer, D., & Skocpol, T. (eds.), *Bringing the State Back In*. Cambridge University Press, Cambridge.

RYAN CALDER AND JOHN LIE

politics

The discipline of sociology has generated few outright political classics. One of the sociology classics, Max Weber's *Economy and Society*, contributed a great deal to the understanding of political behavior. Yet it is not a political work in the sense that Aristotle's *Politics* or Hobbes' *Leviathan* is. *Economy and Society* sometimes hints at but it never enumerates the "best practical" regime. Aristotle and Hobbes had no doubt that such a regime existed – even if they disagreed about what it was. Weber's comparison of traditional, charismatic and procedural authority bears a passing resemblance to the comparison of monarchy, aristocracy and democracy perennially made by the great political thinkers, but the resemblance is limited.

The discipline of politics persistently asks "what is the best type of state?" Answers vary, but the question is constant. The prime object of sociological inquiry is not the state but society. Even Weber, who was politically astute, preferred terms like "authority" and "domination" to "the state." Sociological categories have a much broader application than expressly political categories like "democracy" or "monarchy". Weber's discussion of legitimate authority was a major and enduring contribution to understanding the consensual foundations of power, but it did not replace the older and equally enduring topic of political regime. A democracy can be traditional, charismatic or procedural, depending on time and circumstance. Even if we can resolve which one of these types of legitimate authority we favor, and which we think would be most feasible for a country in a given period or situation, larger questions still remain. Is democracy preferable to monarchy or military rule? Which regime – stratocracy or democracy, oligarchy or monarchy – is most compatible with tradition, charisma and procedure?

Sociology is not political science reborn. Yet sociology does have a political resonance, because it emerges out of the disintegration of hierarchical societies. At its core, sociology is an answer to the question: how is society possible without the binding agent of hierarchy? This is a political question insofar as, until the beginning of the nineteenth century, all states – whether they were city states, monarchies or empires – were built around social hierarchies. Political forms turned on the social orders of master and servant, noble and commoner, tribute receiver and giver, citizen and free person, slave owner and slave. A threshold was crossed in the late eighteenth century. The traditional social authority of hierarchy started to be replaced. The drive to explain what it was that was replacing hierarchies created sociology. This had a political spin-off. Anyone who tried to explain the post-hierarchical social condition also had to hypothesize about the nature of post-hierarchical states. One of the best hypotheses was Weber's idea that traditional authority was being replaced by legal-rational authority. This, though, applied as much to the business corporation as it did to the state.

Rational-legal bureaucracy produced its own kind of hierarchy – organizational hierarchy – that was different from traditional social hierarchy. As traditional hierarchies crumbled, organizational ties replaced personal relations as the backbone of state and society. Sociology sometimes ascribed cooperation in these organizations to positive knowledge (Comte) and sometimes to the vocational ethics of the professionals who ran them (Durkheim, Weber). Scientific knowledge and professional norms both eviscerated the loyalty and faith of traditional social orders. Sociology viewed post-hierarchical society as the product of an epochal transition – from metaphysical to positive knowledge, militant to industrial society, consumer to producer society, status to contract, mechanical to organic solidarity, community to society, class to classless society, uniformity to differentiation, producer to consumer society, ascription to achievement, martial to pacific power, local to territorial power, and so on. Each of these models was obliquely political. Each one assumed that the evolution from martial to industrial society also transformed state, law and justice. The end of this transformation was a society that would be just, fair, equal, enlightened or authentic – a goal that sociology was always disappointed never arrived.

SEE ALSO: Democracy; Political Sociology; State

SUGGESTED READINGS

Aristotle (1998) *Politics*. Oxford University Press, Oxford.

Comte, A. (1988) *Introduction to Positive Philosophy*. Hackett, Indianapolis, IN.
Marx, K. (1993) *Grundrisse*. Penguin, Harmondsworth.
Weber, M. (1978) *Economy and Society*. University of California Press, Berkeley, CA.
Durkheim, E. (1984) *The Division of Labor in Society*. Macmillan: Basingstoke.

PETER MURPHY

politics and media

In 1922 the American journalist and social commentator Walter Lippmann wrote that "the significant revolution of modern times is the revolution taking place in the art of creating consent among the governed" (Lippmann 1954). From his vantage point in the early twentieth century, just four years after the end of World War I, Lippmann was drawing attention to the fact that politicians were entering a new era in which the role of the media was going to be central to effective government. Henceforth, they would have to know and understand how the media impacted on public opinion. Such knowledge, he predicted, would "alter every political premise." And so it has turned out. Politics in the twenty-first century is inconceivable without the part played by media institutions. As reporters, analysts, and interpreters of events to mass electorates the media are integral to the democratic process and no politician, party, or government can afford to ignore or dismiss them.

Since the invention of the printing press by Gutenberg in the late fifteenth century, media have driven politics. Early correspondents were employed by monarchs, bishops, aristocrats, and other elites in feudal societies as sources of information, be it from the far reaches of the kingdom, or from overseas. The first journalists provided a form of surveillance for political elites, making available information on the state of markets and commodity prices, or the progress of wars and court intrigues.

The rise of recognizably free media accompanied the rise of democracy from the ashes of feudalism in the seventeenth century, and was indeed an essential part of that process. The English Civil War saw the relaxation of feudal censorship and the emergence of the first independent newspapers, free to take sides in political disputes. Between them, the English, French, and American revolutions defined the modern role of the media in democracy as active, interventionist, and adversarial. The journalist was to be a constraint on the exercise of political power, one of the checks and balances without which democratic government could so easily slip back into authoritarian habits.

The growing importance of public opinion in the twentieth century propelled the growth of a new kind of communication, expressly intended to influence media output and through it public opinion. Lippmann and other pioneers of what we now know as public relations called it "press counseling," meaning the effort to influence what media organizations wrote and said about politics. Practicing this new form of communication were press counselors, skilled in the techniques of making media amenable to the wishes of politicians.

Public relations in the modern sense is a direct response to the growth of mass democracy on the one hand, and mass media on the other. Both make necessary an intermediate communicative class, a Fifth Estate operating in the space between politics and journalism, whose professional role is to manage, shape, and manipulate public opinion through managing, shaping, and manipulating the output of the media. Today, it is often called spin, a term which carries a negative connotation, but which quite accurately conveys the notion that this form of political communication aims to put a "spin" on the meaning of events as they appear in the public sphere. Events happen, and they are reported. Spin, and spin doctors, strive to ensure that the reportage, as well as the analysis and commentary which make up so much of contemporary political journalism, are advantageous to their political clients.

SEE ALSO: Political Sociology; Politics; Public Opinion; Public Sphere

SUGGESTED READINGS

Franklin, B. (2004) *Packaging Politics*. Arnold, London.
Lippmann, W. (1954) *Public Opinion*. Macmillan, New York.
Lloyd, J. (2004) *What the Media Are Doing to Our Politics*. Constable, London.

BRIAN MCNAIR

popular culture

The word "popular" denotes "of the people," "by the people," and "for the people." "The popular" is made up of *subjects*, whom it textualizes via drama, sport, and information; *workers*, who do that textualization through performances and recording; and *audiences*, who receive the ensuing texts.

Three discourses determine the direction sociologists have taken towards this topic. A discourse about art sees it elevating people above ordinary life, transcending body, time, and place. Conversely, a discourse about folk-life expects it to settle us into society through the wellsprings of community, as part of daily existence. And a discourse about pop idealizes fun, offering transcendence through joy, but doing so by referring to the everyday.

The concept of culture derives from tending and developing agriculture. With the emergence of capitalism, culture came both to embody instrumentalism and to abjure it, via the industrialization of farming, on the one hand, and the cultivation of individual taste, on the other. Culture has usually been understood in two registers, via the social sciences and the humanities – truth versus beauty. This was a heuristic distinction in the sixteenth century, but it became substantive as time passed. Culture is now a marker of differences and similarities in taste and status within groups, as explored interpretively or methodically. In today's humanities, theater, film, television, radio, art, craft, writing, music, dance, and electronic gaming are judged by criteria of quality, as framed by practices of cultural criticism and history. The social sciences focus on the languages, religions, customs, times, and spaces of different groups, as explored ethnographically or statistically.

"Popular culture" clearly relates to markets. Neoclassical economics assumes that expressions of the desire and capacity to pay for services stimulate the provision of entertainment and hence determine what is "popular." Value is decided through competition between providers to obtain the favor of consumers, with the conflictual rationality of the parties producing value to society. The connection of markets to new identities leads to a variety of sociological reactions. During the Industrial Revolution, anxieties about a suddenly urbanized and educated population saw theorists from both right and left arguing that newly literate publics would be vulnerable to manipulation by demagogues. The subsequent emergence of public schooling in the west took as its project empowering, and hence disciplining, the working class.

This notion of the suddenly enfranchised being bamboozled by the unscrupulously fluent has recurred throughout the modern period. It inevitably leads to a primary emphasis on the number and conduct of audiences to popular culture: where they came from, how many there were, and what they did as a consequence of being present. These audiences are conceived as empirical entities that can be known via research instruments derived from sociology, demography, psychology, and marketing. Such concerns are coupled with a secondary concentration on content: *what* were audiences watching when they ... And so texts, too, are conceived as empirical entities that can be known, via research instruments derived from sociology, psychology, and literary criticism. Classical Marxism views the popular as a means to false consciousness that diverts the working class from recognizing its economic oppression; feminist approaches vary between a condemnation of the popular as a similar diversion from gendered consciousness and its celebration as a distinctive part of women's culture; and cultural studies regards the popular as a key location for symbolic resistance of class and gender oppression alike.

Antonio Gramsci maintains that each social group creates "organically, one or more strata of intellectuals which give it homogeneity and an awareness of its own function not only in the economic but also in the social and political fields": the industrial technology, law, economy, and culture of each group. They comprise the " 'hegemony' which the dominant group exercises throughout society" as well as the " 'direct domination' or command exercised through the State and 'juridical' government." Ordinary people give " 'spontaneous' consent" to the "general direction imposed on social life by the dominant fundamental group." In other words, popular culture legitimizes sociopolitical arrangements in the public mind and can be the site of struggle as well as domination.

SEE ALSO: Critical Theory/Frankfurt School; Culture; Gramsci, Antonio; Popular Culture Forms: Jazz; Popular Culture Forms: Reality TV

SUGGESTED READINGS

Adorno, T. W. & Horkheimer, M. (1977) The culture industry: enlightenment as mass deception. In: Curran, J., Gurevitch, M., & Woollacott, J. (eds.), *Mass Communication and Society*. Edward Arnold, London, pp. 349–83.

Gramsci, A. (1978) *Selections from the Prison Notebooks of Antonio Gramsci*, trans. Q. Hoare & G. Nowell-Smith. International Publishers, New York.

Hebdige, D. (1979) *Subculture: The Meaning of Style*. Methuen, London.

TOBY MILLER

popular culture forms: hip hop

Hip hop originated in 1974 in the South Bronx, New York City with Kingston, Jamaica-born Clive Campell, the founding "Father of hip hop."(Chang and Herc 2005). Its main subcultural elements include DJing (cutting and scratching with two turntables, and performing with the microphone); B-Boying / B-Girling (breaking or break dancing); Emceeing (rapping, or talking in rhyme to the rhyme of the beat); and Tagging and Graffiti Art. Aided by commercialization, hip hop is also a style of dress (designer baggy shirts and pants, silver and gold chains, backwards baseball caps, scullies, bright white sneakers, and/or Timberlands). Other elements include distinctive urban "street" language and the spirit of "keepin it real" (or keeping the style reflective of the everyday realities of black urban life, and minimizing the distorting forces of commercialism). However, the "bling, bling" and flashy "cribs" of successful rappers are a central staple of success and are made explicit to the point of parody in New Orleans rapper band Cash Money Millionaires and the 2000s music and dress style "Ghetto Fabulous."

By the 2000s hip hop culture had become a billion dollar industry that included famous women rappers such at Lil Kim, Foxy Brown, and Trina and white rapper Eminem, the most economically successful rapper of all time. Hip hop has also achieved cultural recognition via the application of much serious scholarly inquiry and being the object of several noted national museum exhibits. Debates often center on racial ownership of the subculture and its sexist, misogynistic, homophobic, and violent elements. While debates ensue, pop rap endures as the dominant sound over many radio airwaves and pervades youth culture in language, style of dress, cultural and artistic aesthetics, and musical preferences.

SEE ALSO: Counterculture; Popular Culture; Race

REFERENCE

Chang, J. and Herc, D. J. (Intro.) (2005). *Can't Stop Won't Stop: A History of the hip hop Generation*. St. Martin's Press, New York.

SUGGESTED READING

Halnon, K. B. (2005) Alienation incorporated: "F*** the mainstream music" in the mainstream. *Current Sociology* 53 (4): 441–64.

KAREN BETTEZ HALNON

popular culture forms: jazz

Jazz is a musical style that developed from both African and European traditions emerging around the beginning of the twentieth century in African American communities, particularly in New Orleans. Most jazz styles share some or many of the following musical qualities: syncopation, swing, improvisation, "blue notes," call and response, sound innovation such as growls and stretched notes and polyrhythmic structure.

Ragtime (where brass instruments and African rhythm and beat fused to form "raggedy" music) was quickly absorbed into early twentieth century mainstream white musical cultures. As the New Orleans ragtime moved north through California to Chicago and New York, new variants appeared: "big band" in the 1930s, "swing" in the 1940s and "bebop" in the 1940s and 1950s. Then there were new styles and fusions from the avant-garde sound of Keith Jarrett and Eberhard Weber through jazz funk and acid jazz to jazz house and nu jazz.

Jazz clubs emerged in the days of alcohol prohibition as sites away from surveillance and the policing of alcohol and drugs. It then became synonymous with a variety of counter cultures (black, gangster, immigrant, youth) in which individual freedom and Dionysian values were cultivated. Critically, jazz opened up spaces of cultural transition: "jazz was welcoming, inclusive, open. It replaced minstrelsy with a cultural site where all Americans could participate, speak to one another, override or ignore or challenge or slide by the society's fixations on racial and ethnic stereotypes. Black Americans (and other ethnic outsiders) could use it to enter mainstream society, white Americans could flee to it from mainstream society, and the transactions created a flux and flow that powered American cultural syntheses" (Santano 2001).

SEE ALSO: Popular Culture; Popular Culture Forms: Hip-Hop

REFERENCE

Santano, G. (2001) All that jazz. *The Nation*, January 29.

ADRIAN FRANKLIN

popular culture forms: reality TV

Reality TV is a catchall category that includes a wide range of popular factual programs located in border territories between information and entertainment, documentary and drama. Reality TV has become the success story of television in the 1990s and 2000s. There are three main strands to the development of reality TV, and these relate to three distinct, yet overlapping, areas of media production: tabloid journalism, documentary television, and popular entertainment. There are a variety of styles and techniques associated with reality TV, such as non-professional actors, unscripted dialogue, surveillance footage. The main formats include infotainment (on-scene footage of emergency services, e.g., *Rescue 911*), docusoap (popular observational documentary, e.g., *Airport*), lifestyle (home and personal makeovers, e.g., *What Not to Wear*), and reality gameshow (experiments that place ordinary people in controlled environments, e.g., *Big Brother*). These formats draw on existing popular genres, such as game shows, to create hybrid programs, and focus on telling stories in an entertaining style. Reality TV has been the motor of primetime throughout the 1990s and 2000s, and formats such as *Pop Idol* are international bestsellers, with local versions appearing all over the world.

Critics have attacked the genre for being voyeuristic, cheap, sensational television. Such criticism is based on general concerns about quality standards within public service and commercial television, the influence of television on viewers, and the ethics of popular television. Academic work suggests reality TV is a rich site for analysis and debate on issues such as genre, audiences, gender, class, and identity, performance and authenticity, celebrities, and new media. Reality TV has repositioned factual and entertainment programming within popular culture. And this shift between information and entertainment is irreversible, blurring the boundaries of fact and fiction for a new generation of television viewers.

SEE ALSO: Popular Culture

SUGGESTED READING

Hill, A. (2005) *Reality TV: Audiences and Popular Factual Television*. Routledge, London and New York.

ANNETTE HILL

popular culture icons: *Star Trek*

Star Trek is the most successful "brand" in the history of US television science fiction. The first version ran from 1966 to 1969 with several other series to follow (an animated children's series, *The Next Generation*, *Deep Space Nine*, *Voyager*, and *Enterprise*). A movie spin off *Star Trek: The Motion Picture* was released in 1979, with ten further movie sequels to follow. Both TV series and films acquired a worldwide fan base.

Commentary on ideology tends to situate *Star Trek* in relation to 1960s US liberalism. So its quasi-utopian optimism about technological and social progress is reminiscent of the official enthusiasm for the space race and social reform under the Democratic administrations of Presidents Kennedy and Johnson. *Star Trek*'s initial successes and those of the NASA space programme were roughly contemporaneous. Eventually, what began as temporal overlap evolved into institutional symbiosis: the first NASA space shuttle was named after the Enterprise; and the fourth *Star Trek* movie was dedicated to the astronauts killed in the shuttle Challenger. Penley describes how the Agency and the TV show merged symbolically to "form a powerful cultural icon ... 'NASA/TREK'," which "shapes our popular and institutional imaginings about space" (Penley 1997: 16).

Star Trek's fan base is exceptionally active. When the NBC network threatened to cancel the series in 1967, a "Save *Star Trek*" campaign produced over 114,667 letters of protest and finally secured its renewal. This mass "movement" of "Trekkers" has since become a semi-permanent accompaniment to the franchise. For *Star Trek*, as for science fiction more generally, the convention, where fans meet with each other and with actors, directors and writers, has become a crucial fan institution.

SEE ALSO: Culture Industries; Popular Culture

REFERENCE

Penley, C. (1997) *NASA/TREK: Popular Science and Sex in America*. Verso, London.

ANDREW MILNER

population and development

While development can include a wide range of meanings, here, development is taken to mean economic development defined to refer narrowly to economic growth and then more broadly to the economic transformations leading to the emergence of modern economic institutions and practices and the disappearance of traditional forms.

The relationship between population and economic development is highly contested and has been so for centuries. Adam Smith saw population growth as a stimulus to economic growth because it enlarged the size of the market and provided opportunities for economies of scale and hence more efficient production. This was contested by Thomas Malthus and David Ricardo who argued that there was a law of diminishing returns to scale. Their view was that population growth would eventually lead to natural resource constraints, especially a shortage of cultivatable land. The subsequent advance of technology and the associated rise in human capital through education has served to prolong the debate. Since the nineteenth century, according to Angus Maddison, gross production has risen considerably faster than population and has continued to do so until today.

Debate about the negative effects of rapid population growth on economic development arose again in the post-colonial era. In 1958, Coale and Hoover argued that a reduction in fertility would reduce the number of children that a country needed to support while, at the same time, having little or no impact on the size of the labor force for the following two decades. This reduction in dependency would reduce consumption and increase savings and investment and, hence, stimulate economic growth. The result was the funding and implementation of government family planning programs in many developing countries from the 1960s onwards that have contributed to dramatic declines in fertility rates in most developing countries. This argument was broadened at the beginning of the 1970s into a global argument in the writings of Paul Ehrlich and the Club of Rome. They argued that global resources would be depleted if population growth was above zero.

In reaction to these claims, Simon Kuznets and Julian Simon re-asserted the eighteenth-century view of Adam Smith that population growth stimulated economic growth. They argued that a growing population leads to increases in the supply of labor preventing wage inflation and promoting mobility, productivity and innovation. Notably, Ester Boserup argued that population growth provided a stimulus to technological progress through the innovative character of a young labor force, through increased competition in the labor force and through economies of scale in technological research and development.

As more empirical evidence has been examined on the relationship between population and economic development, conclusions have become increasingly indefinite. This is evidenced by the progression across three nationally commissioned reports from 1971 to 1995. The US National Academy of Sciences Report of 1971 concluded, in keeping with the conventional wisdom of the time, that, in general, rapid population growth had a negative impact on economic development. By the time of the 1986 Report of the US National Academy of Sciences, the conclusion was consistent with the 1971 report but was couched in caveats that left the conclusion in heavy doubt. A report commissioned by the Australian Government in 1994 was almost totally agnostic, concluding that population growth is likely to produce both positive and negative impacts on economic development and the size of the net effect cannot be determined from existing evidence.

SEE ALSO: Economic Development; Malthus, Thomas Robert

SUGGESTED READINGS

Ahlburg, D., Kelley, A., & Mason, K. (eds.) (1996) *The Impact of Population Growth and Well-Being in Developing Countries*. Springer-Verlag, Berlin (based on a report to the Australian Government in 1994).

Bloom, D., Canning, D., & Sevilla, J. (2003) *The Demographic Dividend: A New Perspective on the Economic Consequences of Population Change*. RAND, Santa Monica, CA.

US National Academy of Sciences (1986) *Population Growth and Economic Development: Policy Questions*. National Research Council, National Academy Press, Washington, DC.

PETER MCDONALD

population and gender

Gender is socially constructed and represents the roles, rights, and obligations that culture and society attach to individuals according to whether they are born male or female. Gender:

- is not "value" neutral. Male roles and rights are valued more highly than female roles and rights socially, culturally, economically, and legally. This translates into a greater value being placed on the health and survival of males than of females;
- involves differences in power, both *power to* and *power over*. Differences in "*power to*" encompass legal and informal rights, resource access, and pursuit of knowledge and personal goals; differences in "*power over*" encompass issues of control, including control of household and societal resources and decisions, cultural and religious ideology, and own and others' bodies. In general, men have greater power than women in most domains and, in some domains, even have power over *women*;
- is not static or immutable. Being socially constructed, gender roles, rights, and expectations change as societal needs, opportunities, and mores change.

Gender affects the main building blocks of population – fertility, mortality, and migration. Gender norms that value women mainly in the role of mothers, value sons more than daughters, and emphasize women's dependence on men promote high fertility and excess female mortality and limit female mobility. Under such gender regimes, parents have little to gain from educating daughters and delaying their marriage, and adults have little incentive to limit their number of children. For men, the non-substitutability of gender roles ensures that the non-economic costs of bearing and rearing children are largely borne by women; for women, children, particularly sons, are a major source of status and a form of insurance. Strong son preference manifests in excessively male sex ratios at birth through the use of sex-selective technologies and abortions and higher female than male childhood mortality through female infanticide and neglect of the female child.

With limited education and exposure, women are unlikely to have the knowledge, means, or authority to control their fertility or avoid infant mortality. Polygamy, dowry, bride price, and domestic violence reinforce gender inequality, thereby providing indirect support to higher fertility and infant mortality. Very early ages at marriage contribute to higher mortality because both maternal and infant mortality have a U-shaped relationship with maternal age at birth. Maternal mortality is also higher where women's access to proper nutrition, effective means to space births, and timely and appropriate antenatal, delivery, and postnatal care are limited. While poverty curtails the availability of resources, the amount that societies and households invest in keeping women and girls alive is reflective of the roles, rights, and perceived worth of women. Gender norms that condone marriages between young girls and much older, sexually experienced men, emphasize women's subservience to the sexual needs of their husbands, and tolerate physical and sexual abuse of women reduce the likelihood that women will seek care for infections such as HIV, leave an infected partner, or insist on condom use or other ways to protect themselves. Because the social construction of "manhood" is consistent with male risk-taking and violence, gender can also adversely affect men's health and mortality.

Finally, traditional gender roles, by limiting women's mobility and marketable skills, decrease the likelihood that women will migrate for jobs or education, but are consistent with women's forced migration to their husbands' homes at the time of marriage and female trafficking. However, changes in gender roles, increases in female access to education, delays in marriage and childbearing, and the gradual whittling down of occupational barriers are changing the sex composition of even voluntary migratory streams to include more women.

SEE ALSO: Gender Ideology and Gender Role Ideology; Stratification, Gender and

SUGGESTED READING

Presser, H. B. & Sen, G. (eds.) (2000) *Women's Empowerment and Demographic Processes.* Oxford University Press, New York.

SUNITA KISHOR

populism

Populism is a concept that is used in a variety of ways (as an economic, social and/or political term, a version of democracy or authoritarianism, etc.), to describe a variety of phenomena (governments, leaders, ideologies, economic systems, a type of discourse) in a variety of historical moments (most notably since the 1940s but with notable cases before as well). The concept of populism, therefore, is highly problematic to define as the same word is used to define a great variety of phenomena that have many important differences.

Despite the problems in solidifying a definition of populism, there are a number of key characteristics common to most usages of the term – the presence of a charismatic leader (for this reason participants in populist movements are often referred to as "-istas" of the leader. For example, Peronistas in Argentina, Chavistas in Venezuela, and Correistas in Ecuador), the construction of an us/them dichotomy (the "us" and the "them" changes in each instance but the division of society into two opposing groups is relatively constant), and a general reorganization of the economic system (for example a shift to import substitution industrialization with Peron in Argentina, to neoliberalism with Fujimori in Peru, and to twenty-first century socialism with Chavez in Venezuela).

Above all, populism is characterized by a focus on "the people" understood as the ordinary collective whose values are seen as more virtuous than those of the opposing elites. Such a loose definition, however, has been used to characterize extreme left, extreme right, and a variety of governments in-between.

Although populism has been used to describe phenomena ranging from movements of intellectuals in late nineteenth-century Russia to farmers in early twentieth-century USA, to scattered movements throughout Europe, it is most commonly used to characterize different political regimes and social movements in Latin America. For this reason, most of the prominent scholarship on populism has come out of, or been based on, Latin America.

In an effort to more clearly define the concept of populism, some authors have taken to differentiating various forms using terms such as neo-populism or radical populism to describe populist instanciations in various historical moments.

SEE ALSO: Charisma; Political Economy; Politics; Politics and Media

SUGGESTED READINGS

Faletto, E. & Cardoso, F. H. (1979) *Dependency and Development in Latin America*, trans. M. M. Urquidi. University of California Press, Berkeley, CA.
Laclau, E. (2005) *On Populist Reason*. Verso, New York.
de la Torre, C. (2000) *Populist Seduction in Latin America*. Ohio University Press, Athens, OH.

J. MICHAEL RYAN

pornography and erotica

There is no universally accepted definition of either term "pornography" or "erotica": mediated communication depicting sexually explicit subject matter. "Erotica" was first coined to differentiate more elevated and exclusive material and is now often used in reference to material produced by and for women and gays. A range of other distinctions have been made; pornography is designed only to induce sexual arousal, whereas erotica combines sexual with emotional and aesthetic responses; pornography stimulates solitary masturbation whereas erotica inspires interpersonal sex. Another approach is to see the category of pornography as a function of censorship: the "hard-core" left once erotic material with artistic or scientific value has been redeemed. Another way of drawing the distinction between erotica and hard-core, is to class the former as the creative representation of sexual subject matter and the latter as the direct visual documentation of sexual acts.

Until the 1960s, when many western states began to ease restrictions, the concern of political and moral authorities was that pornography would deprave and corrupt what they regarded as the more susceptible parts of the population, such as the young or uneducated. The process of liberalization culminated with the *Johnson Commission* (1970), which drew the majority conclusion that the social effects of pornography were, if anything, "benign." Although these findings were rejected by President Nixon, this marks the end of any consensus behind the effort to control pornography on moral grounds. But soon a new concern began to be expressed by feminists, such as Andrea Dworkin, who saw pornography as inciting sexual violence against women. In the 1980s Dworkin and Catherine MacKinnon introduced anti-porn ordinances in American cities. These were ruled unconstitutional by the Supreme Court but the furore inspired President Reagan to establish the Meese Commission (1986), which condemned pornography as a cause of harm to women. In response a second body of feminist opinion began to organize anti-censorship campaigns. These feminists agreed that much existing pornography was sexist but argued that the best way to bring about change was through a diversification of erotic representation involving the creative participation of lesbians, gay men and straight women.

Since 1970 a great deal of social science research has tested the harmful effects of pornography on men's conduct towards women. The data can be divided into three categories: survey, experimental and testimonial. However such research has usually been framed in behaviorist terms, which fail to recognize that the subjectivity of the social actor intervenes between stimuli and response, so that responses to pornography are not objectively determinate. In recent years the political debate and the research effort have diminished, while restrictions have further relaxed and the Internet has extended access to unregulated material. The porn industry has continued to grow and now operates on a massive scale. Yet this significant part of modern mass-culture now goes virtually unnoticed by the social sciences.

The current scope for research can be divided into two broad areas concerning the industry/production and audiences/cultural impact. As far as the industry is concerned there are issues about the health and exploitation of performers. We should also ask how far porn reflects the full gamut of human sexual diversity or simply the commercial homogenization of desire. As regards audiences and cultural impact, qualitative data can greatly enhance our understanding of the experiences and subjective responses of those who view pornography. In this way researchers are beginning to address neglected questions about the impact of pornography, such as the role it plays in the development of young people's sexuality. Finally, we must ask how far new media technologies have broken down the division between producer and consumer, or contributed to the growth of radical new pornographies that challenge the conventions of the genre.

SEE ALSO: Sexualities and Culture Wars; Sexuality

SUGGESTED READINGS

Dworkin, A. (1981) *Pornography: Men Possessing Women*. The Women's Press, London.

Williams, L. (ed.) (2004) *Porn Studies*. Duke University Press, London.

SIMON HARDY

positive deviance

Dodge (1985: 17) formally introduced positive deviance into the sociology of deviant behaviour to broaden the field beyond simply negative deviance – the "offensive, disgusting, contemptible, annoying or threatening." Sagarin (1985) immediately contested the term, calling it an oxymoron, initiating a "fiery debate" over the concept's viability, leading to "at least nine different ways" in which the term was portrayed (West 2003).

The key issues centre on positive deviance's normative and reactivist dimensions. If conforming to normative expectations is a continuum of social behaviour, then negative (under-conformity) and positive (over-conformity) deviance are the outliers. For Dodge (1985: 18) positive deviance encompassed "those persons and acts that are evaluated as superior because they surpass conventional expectations."

In reactivist terms, under-conformist behaviour receiving reactions of condemnation (e.g. theft, terrorism) is negative deviance while the same action gaining supportive responses (e.g. theft by Robin Hood, liberationist struggle) connotes positive deviance.

Positive deviance also described over-commitment to positively valued behaviours resulting in negatively perceived practices (e.g. fully committed to athletic training – using steroids, striving for a svelte body – turning to bulimia).

Sagarin (1985: 169) was also concerned that positive deviance collapsed together two ends of a continuum with "nothing in common" and would so broaden studies of deviance that they would lose coherence and specific focus. Others countered that even when studies in deviance stay with traditional issues, positive deviance (over-conformity and/or positive reactivist) provides a necessary interrelated, analytic counter-point that sheds critical light on negative deviance.

SEE ALSO: Deviance; Deviance, Normative Definitions of; Deviance, Reactivist Definitions of

REFERENCES

Dodge, D. L. (1985) The over-negativized conceptualization of deviance: a programmatic exploration. *Deviant Behavior* (6): 17–37.

Sagarin, E. (1985) Positive deviance: an oxymoron. *Deviant Behavior* 6: 169–81.

West, B. (2003) Synergies in deviance: revisiting the positive deviance debate. Online: *Electronic Journal of Sociology*.

ROB BEAMISH

positivism

While it has been customary to distinguish between the quasi-political movement called "positivism" originated by Auguste Comte in the 1830s and the more strictly philosophical movement called "logical positivism" associated with the Vienna Circle of the 1930s, both held that the unchecked exercise of reason can have disastrous practical consequences. Thus, reason needs "foundations" to structure its development so as not to fall prey to a self-destructive scepticism. The history of positivism can be neatly captured as three moments in a Hegelian dialectic epitomized by the work of Auguste Comte (thesis), Ernst Mach (antithesis), and the Vienna Circle (synthesis).

Comte, an early graduate of the Ecole Polytechnique, believed that its Napoleonic mission of rendering research a vehicle for societal transformation had been betrayed, once he failed to achieve an academic post. Mach was a politically active physicist on the losing side of so many of the leading scientific debates of his day that his famous chair in Vienna, from which the logical positivists sprang, was awarded for his critical-historical studies, *not* his experimental work. Finally, the intellectual leader of the Vienna Circle, Rudolf Carnap, abandoned physics for philosophy because his doctoral dissertation topic was seen as too "metatheoretical" for a properly empirical discipline. For Carnap, physics had devolved into another specialized field of study, rather than – as it had still been for Einstein – natural philosophy pursued by more exact means.

Positivism's appeal to organized reason, or "science," in the public sphere is fundamentally ambiguous. On the one hand, it implies that it is in everyone's interest to pursue their ends by scientific means, so as to economize on effort and hence allow more time for the fruits of their labour to be enjoyed. On the other hand, science can unify the polity by authoritatively resolving, containing or circumventing social conflict. Here a well-established procedure or a decisive set of facts is supposed to replace more "primitive" and volatile forms of conflict resolution. A scientific politics should not merely satisfy the parties concerned: it should arrive at the "correct" solution.

Positivist social researchers have put a democratic spin on such politics by presenting survey data from parties whose voices are unlikely to be heard in an open assembly. But exactly who reaps the political benefits of these newly articulated voices: the people under investigation; the investigators themselves; or the investigators' clients?

After the leading members of the Vienna Circle migrated to the USA in the 1930s, logical positivism seeded the analytic philosophy establishment for the second half of the twentieth century. However, this is the only context in which positivism possibly dominated an established discipline. Otherwise positivism has been embraced by disciplines that have yet to achieve academic respectability, not least the social sciences. Thomas Kuhn's *The Structure of Scientific Revolutions*, published in 1962 as the final instalment of the logical positivists' International Encyclopedia of Unified Science, substantially altered all this. Unlike previous positivist accounts, Kuhn's was explicitly a model of knowledge production within particular scientific disciplines (or "paradigms") that did not presume that science as a whole is heading toward a unified understanding of reality. Kuhn's approach anticipated what is now called the "postmodern condition." However, if positivism has a future, it lies in rekindling a sense of "Science" that transcends the boundaries of particular scientific disciplines. This was how Comte originally thought about the discipline he called "sociology."

SEE ALSO: Comte, Auguste; Deviance, Positivist Theories of; Kuhn, Thomas and Scientific Paradigms; Postpositivism

SUGGESTED READINGS

Adorno, T. (ed.) (1976) *The Positivist Dispute in German Sociology*. Heinemann, London.

Fuller, S. (2006) *The Philosophy of Science and Technology Studies*. University of Chicago Press, Chicago, IL.

Kolakowski, L. (1972) *Positivist Philosophy*. Penguin, Harmondsworth.

Proctor, R. (1991) *Value-Free Science? Purity and Power in Modern Knowledge*. Harvard University Press, Cambridge, MA.

STEVE FULLER

post-industrial society

Following the Keynesian response to the Great Depression, the Allies' defeat of fascism, the Marshall Plan and the reconstruction of western Europe and sustained economic growth in the western bloc from 1945 into the 1960s, Raymond Aron (1967), Daniel Bell (1960), Ralf Dahrendorf (1959) and John Goldthorpe et al. (1969), among others, argued that western capitalist societies had developed into industrial societies.

Industrial societies' chief characteristics, its proponents argued, included an open, meritocratic stratification system; improved standards of living offering access to a wide range of consumer goods; growing diversity in share ownership; professionally trained managers running trans-national firms; human relations strategies to improve productivity and working conditions; a diversified division of labor emphasizing skill and education; the systematic application of science and technology in production; the institutionalization of class conflict in collective bargaining; and the end of ideology.

Bell's (1973) extremely influential *The Coming of Post-Industrial Society* built on those claims. Bell argued that technology and information processing would define post-industrial societies. The coming order would feature economies centred on telecommunications, information and computer technology, differentiating them from pre-industrial, extraction-based or industrial, fabrication-based societies. The centrality of theoretical knowledge; creation of new intellectual technologies; growing influence of a knowledge class; growth of services; changing nature of work; and greater inclusion of women in the labor force would characterize post-industrial societies. Manuel Castells' (1996; 1997; 1998) *The Information Age* built on Bell's analysis.

SEE ALSO: Fordism/Post-Fordism; Industrialization; Postmodern Culture

REFERENCES

Aron, R. (1967) *18 Lectures on Industrial Society*. Weidenfeld and Nicolson, London.

Bell, D. (1960) *The End of Ideology*. Free Press, Glencoe, IL.

Dahrendorf, R. (1959) *Class and Class Conflict in Industrial Society*. Stanford University Press, Stanford, CA.

Goldthorpe, J., Lockwood, D., Bechhofer, F., & Platt, J. (1969) *The Affluent Worker in the Class Structure*. Cambridge University Press, Cambridge.

ROB BEAMISH

postmodern culture

Postmodern culture is a far-reaching term describing a range of activities, events, and perspectives relating to art, architecture, the humanities, and the social sciences beginning in the second half of the twentieth century. In contrast to modern culture, with its emphasis on social progress, coherence, and universality, postmodern culture represents instances of dramatic historical and ideological change in which modernist narratives of progress and social holism are viewed as incomplete, elastic, and contradictory. In conjunction with the end of modernist progress narratives, an insistence on coherence gives way to diversity and the dominance of universality is subverted by difference within a postmodern condition. Additionally, postmodern culture stands for more than the current state of society. Postmodern culture is characterized by the valuing of activities, events, and perspectives that emphasize the particular over the global or the fragment over the whole. This reversal of a modernist ideology necessitates a valuation of variation and flexibility in the cultural sphere. Primarily through the writings of Jean-François Lyotard, whose seminal book *The Postmodern Condition: A Report on Knowledge* (1984) remains the definitive exposition of the term and its significance to society, postmodern culture has come to be identified with a radical critique of the relationship between the particular and the universal in art, culture, and politics.

The "postmodern condition" is a disruption in the claim to totality found in the Enlightenment. According to postmodernists, the western worldview, with its commitment to universality in all things related to being human, gives way under the weight of its own contradictions and repressions. The comprehensive grand theories or grand narratives subsequently fail in a postmodern era insofar as the plurality of human existence emerges within a wider cultural space. Postmodern knowledge of the world must take into account the multiplicity of experience or "phrasings" (Lyotard) and the possibility of new, unanticipated experiences that will assist in making sense of reality in ways either not permitted or not imagined by a modernist ideology. The content of knowledge we presently possess is continually being transformed by technology. Culture, as it pertains to postmodernism, is more than a repository of data; it is the activity that shapes and gives meaning to the world, constructing reality rather than presenting it.

Postmodern culture, as a valorization of the multiplicity found in "little narratives," exhibits anti-modernist tendencies, with art and politics rejecting calls to narrative totalization. Frederick Jameson (1984), referring to the social theorist Jürgen Habermas, states that "postmodernism involves the explicit repudiation of the modernist tradition – the return of the middle-class philistine or *Spießbürger* (bourgeois) rejection of modernist forms and values – and as such the expression of a new social conservatism." While an emphasis on the particular over the universal captures the revolutionary impulse found in the political and aesthetic sentiments of Lyotardian postmodernism, it runs counter to a lengthy critique of postmodernism by social theorists, mainly Marxists, who view this turn to the particularity of "little narratives" as a symptom of late capitalism, with its valuation on proliferating commodities and flexible corporate organizational models. The characteristics of multiplicity, pastiche, and non-linearity, while viewed as offering new aesthetic, epistemological, and political possibilities by postmodern artists, architects, writers, filmmakers, and theorists, are understood by those who reject postmodernism as examples of the "logic of late capitalism" (Jameson 1984) in which commodities and consumers enter into rapid, undifferentiated exchange in ever-increasing and diversified markets.

SEE ALSO: Culture; Modernity; Postmodern Feminism; Postmodern Sexualities; Postmodern Social Theory

REFERENCE

Jameson, F. (1984) Foreword. In: Lyotard, J.-F., *The Postmodern Condition: A Report on Knowledge*. University of Minnesota Press, Minneapolis, MN, pp. vii–xxi.

SUGGESTED READING

Taylor, V. (2000) *Para/Inquiry: Postmodern Religion and Culture*. Routledge, London.

VICTOR E. TAYLOR

postmodern feminism

Postmodern feminism confronts and rejects essentialist practices, understandings and explanations of society as established in and by modernity. Merged with postmodern theory, this form of feminism challenges claims of a unified subject, such as one common definition of "woman"; and instead recognizes differences, of having all views and voices recognized. The combination of postmodernist thought and feminism allows for a questioning of essentialist approaches within and outside of feminism. The belief that there is a universal understanding of "female" and "male" is rejected; gender is viewed as fluid, temporary, and perhaps, non-existent. Central to postmodern thought is the importance of recognizing that all things being studied occur in specific historical, cultural and political moments.

Postmodern feminist theorists critique the fixed binary structure of gender and the impact this structure has on social, political and cultural institutions. Constructions of gender are viewed as multiple, through a variety of lenses, integrating in the complexities of race, ethnicity, class, sexual orientation, age and other differences. Our concepts of what gender and sexuality *are,* are actually social constructions and therefore there is no true meaning. Reality is seen as a fabrication.

By shifting from a dualistic approach to multifaceted examinations, the subject/object split in essentialism is challenged. One of the tasks of postmodern feminists is to reconstruct conceptualizations of the subject/object split into recognizing a recreation of self that has endless revolutionary potential. The push to move beyond dualistic thinking is far-reaching, particularly within academe. Postmodern feminist theorists have challenged and changed definitions of science and knowledge; seeking to move marginalized groups from the position of subject, that which is being studied, to more central positions, where they are advancing knowledge.

SEE ALSO: Cultural Feminism; Postmodern Social Theory

SUGGESTED READINGS

Butler, J. (1999) *Gender Trouble: Feminism and the Subversion of Identity*. Routledge, New York.

Nicholson, L. (ed.) (1990) *Feminism/Postmodernism*. Routledge, New York.

KRISTINA B. WOLFF

postmodern sexualities

Sexuality is often located within various epochs – classic, premodern, modern, and the like – and the most recent stage has been controversially identified as "postmodern." Here human sexualities are not seen as well-fashioned patterns, solid identities, grand truths, or essential natures. In contrast, new social accounts of sexualities usually offer up more modest, constructed, and fragmented narratives of sexualities. For example, those found in the modern sexological world – from Freud to sexology – try to develop scientifically a knowledge of sexuality. Such views have haunted much of the modern world's analysis of sexuality, seeing it as an autonomous sphere of reality. For postmoderns this is a deeply flawed idea: "sex" is no longer the source of a truth, as it was for the moderns with their strong belief in science. Instead, according to William Simon in *Postmodern Sexualities* (1996), human sexualities have become "destabilized, decentred and de-essentialized." Sexual life is no longer seen as harboring an essential unitary core locatable within a clear framework with an essential truth waiting to be discovered; instead it is partial and fragmented, with little grand design or form. Indeed, it is "accompanied by the problematic at every stage." As he argues: "all discourses of sexuality are inherently discourses about something else; sexuality, rather than serving as a constant thread that unifies the totality of human experience, is the ultimate dependent variable, requiring explanation more often than it provides explanation."

Human sexualities, then, are always more than "*just* human sexualities." They overlap with, and are omnipresent in, all of social life. At the simplest level, the proliferation of fragmented and diversifying sexualities is marked by rapid changes and fluidity. It is also marked by a high level of openness, or as Anthony Giddens, in *The Transformation of Society* (1992), calls it, a "plastic sexuality" in which it is no longer tied so strongly to biology. Sexualities are fluid; in the words of Zygmunt Bauman (2003), there is "liquid love."

SEE ALSO: Cybersexualities and Virtual Sexuality; Foucault, Michel; Postmodern Social Theory; Queer Theory; Sexual Identities

REFERENCE

Bauman, Z. (2003) *Liquid Love: On the Facility of Human Bonds*. Polity Press, Cambridge.

SUGGESTED READING

Queen, C. & Schimel, L. (1997) *Pomosexuals: Challenging Assumptions about Gender and Sexuality*. Cleis Press, San Francisco, CA.

KEN PLUMMER

postmodern social theory

Postmodern social theory is a field which is both difficult to define and rejects being defined. It is, in fact, a field that struggles against definitions, against norms, against protocols. Instead, it seeks to deconstruct, decenter, and delegitimize scientific claims to universal truths. With these characteristics in mind, it is easy to understand why defining such a field would be a difficult, if not counterproductive, task. Various authors have sought to overcome this difficulty by relying on common characteristics of various postmodern theories, others have defined the field by those who work in it, and still others – particularly those who work in the field itself – have avoided any attempts to define it at all. Regardless of which of these approaches one takes, however, there is no denying that something called postmodern social theory was at one time a flourishing presence in sociology (and elsewhere). There is also little denying that that time has passed and that now postmodern social theory is little more than a memory of a past epoch in social thought. Despite this "death" of postmodern theory, however, its short life has had profound effects on the way social theorists do theory, and will, no doubt, continue to have such an effect for a long time to come (Ritzer and Ryan 2007).

Few theories have had as meteoric a rise and fall in sociology as postmodern social theory. While it had various antecedents (most notably poststructuralism), it burst on the scene in sociology in the 1960s and within two or three decades observers were writing its obituary. In a sense it *is* dead because there have been few, if any, major contributions to it in the last few decades. The statement that postmodern social theory is dead is simultaneously controversial, clichéd, and meaningless. It is controversial because there are still a few who believe themselves to be doing work in this area. It is clichéd because it has been a taken-for-granted assumption by many for years, even among those who never realized it was born or what its life was like. It is also meaningless because many of those associated with postmodern thinking – Foucault, Baudrillard – would argue that such a theory has never existed to die.

Postmodern social thought shifts thinking from the center to the margins. It seeks to decenter, deconstruct, and delegitimize the center. Rather than seeking answers and the Truth, it seeks to keep the conversation going and denies the possibility of Truth. Above all, it represents the death of the grand narrative. It opposes theory (thus to speak of postmodern social theory is a bit paradoxical), is irrational, anti-science, and anti-essentialist. It directs attention toward consumption, the body, and signs. There is a loss of history, a disorienting sense of geography, and a breakdown between nature, culture, and society. Postmodernism emphasizes pastiche, the ephemeral, and play. Although not completely antithetical to modern social theory, postmodern social theory does present a radically different way of looking at the world.

In many ways the methodological ideas of the postmodern theorists were more important than their substantive contributions. Many of these methodological ideas were posed in critical terms. That is, the postmodernists were critical of the modernists' propensity to think in terms of truth, of "grand (or meta-) narratives," to offer totalizations, to search for origins, to try to find the center, to be foundational, to focus on the author, to be essentialistic, to be overly scientistic and rationalistic, and so on. Many of these things went to the heart of modern theorizing and, after reading the critiques, it became very difficult to theorize in that way, at least unself-consciously. But the postmodernists went beyond critiquing modern theory: they developed a variety of more positive ideas about how to theorize, including keeping the conversation going (instead of ending it with the "truth"), archeology, genealogy, decentering, deconstructing, pastiche, *différance*, and so on. Involved here were new ways to theorize, and these had a more positive impact on social theory. Thus, in both positive and negative ways, postmodern thinking affected and continues to affect social theorists.

Postmodern social theory has given rise to or at least has significantly helped to pave the way for, a number of other theoretical orientations. The newly privileged periphery that found itself center stage with postmodern considerations allowed for the meaningful development and academic institutionalization of feminist studies, queer studies, multicultural studies, and postcolonial studies, among others. Additionally, many of the basic ideas and concepts (consumer society, simulation, implosion, hyperreality, hyperspace, governmentality, panopticon, schizoanalysis, dromology, etc.) associated with postmodern social theory have made their way into the heart of contemporary social theory.

Postmodern social theory quickly came under several attacks. It was argued that the theory itself represented the kind of grand narrative that it sought to oppose. It was argued that its methods failed to live up to scientific standards and that it offered critiques without a normative basis for judgment. Its lack of alternative visions for the future made it highly pessimistic, and a sense of agency is difficult to uncover. Perhaps most troubling for modern thinkers were the unresolved questions and ambiguities postmodernism left in its path.

Zygmunt Bauman developed a well-known distinction between postmodern sociology and a sociology of postmodernity, the former being a new type of sociology and the latter being sociology as usual but with postmodernity as the topic. While Bauman has been more affected by postmodern ideas than most modern theorists, and while he is far more sensitized to the realities of the postmodern world, he is still a modernist. In that sense, he epitomizes the point that while in one way postmodern social theory might be dead, in another it lives on in the work of contemporary modern (or "late modern") theorists. Those who fail to understand the critiques of the postmodernists, and who fail to at least think through some of the alternatives they offer, are doomed to repeat the mistakes of the modern theorists.

SEE ALSO: Foucault, Michel; Modernity; Postmodern Culture; Postmodern Feminism; Postmodern Sexualities; Poststructuralism

REFERENCE

Ritzer, G. & Ryan, J. M. (2007) Postmodern social theory and sociology: on symbolic exchange with a "dead" theory. In: Powell, J. & Owen, T. (eds.), *Reconstructing Postmodernism: Critical Debates*. Nova Science Publishers, New York, pp. 41–57.

SUGGESTED READINGS

Baudrillard, J. (1983) *Simulations*, trans. P. F. P. Patton & P. Beitchman. Semiotext(e), New York.
Baudrillard, J. (1998) [1970] *The Consumer Society*. Sage, London.
Bauman, Z. (1993) *Postmodern Ethics*. Blackwell, Oxford.
Bauman, Z. (2000) *Liquid Modernity*. Polity Press, Cambridge.
Derrida, J. (1978) *Writing and Difference*, trans. A. Bass. University of Chicago Press, Chicago, IL.
Featherstone, M. (1991) *Consumer Culture and Postmodernism*. Sage, London.
Lyotard, J.-F. (1984) *The Postmodern Condition: A Report on Knowledge*, trans. R. Durand. University of Minnesota Press, Minneapolis, MN.

J. MICHAEL RYAN

postpositivism

In the twentieth century the heritage of positivism as a philosophy of science underwent major changes. Earlier intellectual developments in the century led to logical positivism (and, with some variation in ideas, logical empiricism). The continuity with classical positivism was maintained in terms of opposition to metaphysics, but other and more specific doctrines were elaborated. A scientific theory, for instance, was said to be a formal deductive system with an empirical interpretation that enabled verification by appeal to observations.

However, Popper (1959), while not disputing the deductive system formulation, argued that the universality of theoretical statements made them impossible to verify. Rather, a theory was credible to the extent that it "proved its mettle" by surviving falsification efforts. But Kuhn (1970) noted that scientists usually worked within a paradigm and resisted efforts to revise it until anomalies that could not be resolved led to a revolutionary change of paradigm. By the late 1970s there was consensus that a postpositivist era had emerged in the philosophy of science, in which the "received view" was replaced by a variety of critical reformulations concerning the nature of scientific knowledge and, in particular, the structure of scientific theories. In addition, philosophers formulated a more dynamic conception of sciences featuring such leading notions as research traditions and research programs. Even metaphysics has returned as contemporary analysts propose ideas about the relationships between theory and reality, as in variant forms of "scientific realism" as a philosophy of science.

These developments have had ramifications for sociology. Earlier, some sociological theorists looked to logical empiricism for guidance about theory construction, but more recently the favored ideas have been closer to scientific realism in outlook, favoring models and mechanisms in formulating theories. Theory development has been framed as a pluralistic and collective over-time process using a conception of theoretical research programs drawn from the postpositivist philosophy of science.

Other theorists have made quite different proposals in framing a postpositivist conception of sociological theory. For example, Alexander (1982) formulates an explicit contrast between postpositivism and positivism in philosophy as a prelude to his analysis of issues in sociological theory. Contrary to the positivist standpoint, for instance, postpositivism denies any radical break between empirical and non-empirical statements: all scientific data are theory-laden. Also contrary to positivism, postpositivism accepts the legitimacy of general intellectual issues in science.

Based on these and related ideas, Alexander argues that sociology has institutionalized what is an aberration in natural science, namely, presuppositional debates about the most general conceptual problems in the field. The function of theoretical logic in sociology, he maintains, is to make explicit the fundamental issues around which such enduring debates will continue, in particular those relating to rationality and to social order. Critics argue that such discursive debates perpetuate non-explanatory theorizing and are no substitute for the formulation of theories with logical consequences that can be tested empirically. However, one can accept a good part of Alexander's argument while also favoring the construction and empirical testing of theoretical models that embody generative rules or mechanisms.

SEE ALSO: Metatheory; Positivism; Theory and Method

REFERENCES

Alexander, J. C. (1982) *Positivism, Presuppositions, and Current Controversies*. University of California Press, Berkeley, CA.

Kuhn, T. S. (1970) [1962] *The Structure of Scientific Revolutions*. University of Chicago Press, Chicago, IL.
Popper, K. (1959) *The Logic of Scientific Discovery*. Hutchinson, London.

SUGGESTED READINGS

Berger, J. & Zelditch, M., Jr. (eds.) (2002) *New Directions in Contemporary Sociological Theory*. Rowman & Littlefield, Lanham, MD.
Fararo, T. J. (1989) *The Meaning of General Theoretical Sociology: Tradition and Formalization*. Cambridge University Press, New York.
Godfrey-Smith, P. (2003) *Theory and Reality: An Introduction to the Philosophy of Science*. University of Chicago Press, Chicago, IL.

THOMAS J. FARARO

poststructuralism

Like postmodernism, this relatively recent coinage encompasses a wide range of intellectual schools and levels of analysis. These approaches tend to cluster around two somewhat overlapping camps: the "literary" theorists interested in describing the structure of language and culture, and the "sociological" camp consisting of sociologists and anthropologists interested in describing the structure of society and human agency.

Linguistic and cultural uses of poststructuralism draw from linguistic and philosophical debates regarding whether the essential nature of language, and by extension human consciousness, is rooted in constantly shifting systems of meaning. The founder of linguistic structuralism, Ferdinand de Saussure, argued that language only has meaning in relation to a specific cultural framework. He argued that the system of meaning that underlies language or *signifiers* is always shifting and can only be studied synchronically (at a given moment in time). Signifiers only make sense in relation to other signifiers and have no fixed relationship to the real world they represent at a given time. To illustrate, consider how the terms "gay" and "queer" have shifted from their conventional meanings, to pejorative terms for people with alternate sexual orientations and, more recently, to a more contested positive connotation for identifying the same group.

While Saussure was primarily interested in studying the system of meaning that underlies language itself, the literary strain of poststructuralist thought argues that other human creations such as film, advertisements, and other cultural forms can be studied as systems of meaning that only make sense within a specific cultural framework and time period. Members of this camp agree with Saussure's assertion that language, and by extension culture, exists as a system of signifiers with no relation to the signs they represent, while rejecting his belief that this system of signs forms a well-defined and cohesive system of meanings that can be mapped through semiotics.

The first step towards literary poststructuralism was taken by Roland Barthes in his analysis of French popular culture. Barthes is notable for developing Saussure's link between the signified and signifier into the study of culture. In *Mythologies* (1972) he explored the meaning underlying many forms of popular culture, including the characters and performances that made professional wrestling meaningful to spectators of the time who, he argued, were more interested in the way that culturally meaningful dramas and characters such as "the clown" and "the traitor" interacted than they were in the athleticism involved. Barthes explained that myths acted to naturalize a society's values while cloaking this form of socialization behind entertainment or objectivity. His science of semiotics involves looking at various forms of literature and popular culture to uncover the social values they communicate and the practices they encourage.

Barthes was also interested in *intertextuality*, the idea that a work of art, such as a novel or performance, has a meaning that shifts according to the audience experiencing it and its relationship to other works of art. Barthes's ideas were further expanded by thinkers such as Derrida and Baudrillard who emphasize the constantly shifting nature of any system of signifiers. Signifiers only make sense as they are interpreted by a reader, viewer, or participant, and since the experience and interpretations of cultural systems vary widely between individuals and across time, there is a constant shifting of cultural meanings.

Through his concept of *différance*, Derrida explains that any given signifier only makes sense in relation to its opposition to other signifiers. Because these relationships are not linked to any specific real-world referent and shift across different works and the interpretation, the true meaning of a text is always "deferred." By extension, Derrida argues that attempts to close systems of meaning within literary or philosophical texts under the guise of accurately described real-world experiences, or providing a system of "ultimate truths," are power games masked as objectivity. Derrida's attempt to seek inconsistencies within these texts, to *deconstruct* the contingency of an author's belief system, parallels postmodernism's rejection of metanarratives which describe the world as a whole.

The second camp of poststructuralism – the sociological one – refers to a shift from structuralist models of agency, society, and power to a more general understanding of the way that social structures influence our behavior and identity. Like Derrida and other poststructuralists in the literary camp, these poststructuralists borrowed many of the methods of structuralism while reaching very different conclusions.

Social poststructuralists argue that human agency is shaped but not determined by a wide variety of social structures and cultural forces, including systems of belief and knowledge, disciplines of the body, and other systems of thought and action. This camp of poststructuralists is primarily interested in the way that culture and other "ideologies" shape human identities and act as unconscious systems of power over individuals.

Foucault, for example, uses the term *discourses* to emphasize that in modern society, power most often takes a moral form. New systems of moral control develop as a result of a compulsion to discuss and scientifically study issues that have been problematized. As a result, the academic disciplines, classifications, and practices that emerge from these discourses become systems of power.

Critics of both camps of poststructuralism provide two objections to these ideas: (1) a scientific study of culture or society is nearly impossible if these forces are viewed as situational and constantly shifting, and (2) there is little or no opportunity for resistance against social forces if they are internalized and invisible to individuals.As a result, it is argued that poststructuralist research and theory have no value for improving society because they cannot tell individuals how to escape from the yoke of social power.

SEE ALSO: Bourdieu, Pierre; Cultural Studies; Deconstruction; Derrida, Jacques; Discourse; Foucault, Michel; Postmodern Social Theory; Saussure, Ferdinard de; Semiotics; Structuralism

REFERENCE

Barthes, R. (1972) [1957] *Mythologies*. Hill & Wang, New York.

SUGGESTED READINGS

Bourdieu, P. (1984) *Distinction: A Social Critique of the Judgment of Taste*. Harvard University Press, Cambridge, MA.

Derrida, J. (1998) *Of Grammatology*. Johns Hopkins University Press, Baltimore, MD.

Foucault, M. (1990) *The History of Sexuality: An Introduction*. Vintage Press, New York.

CHARLES MCCORMICK

poverty

Poverty is often thought of as economic privation – a lack of resources such as food, shelter, clothing, and financial assets that contribute to material deprivation – but poverty can also be understood as a "diminished capacity" to engage in society – social relationships, cultural traditions, politics, the labor and consumer markets – which can lead to social dislocation, exclusion, and alienation. As an aspect of social stratification and unequal social relationships, poverty represents a fundamental inequality in the distribution of resources, opportunity, and exposure to risk; and the risk of being poor is not equal across groups. Income is stratified by race, ethnicity, and gender, making poverty most prevalent among those groups who are already socially disadvantaged.

Research consistently finds that poverty exposes individuals to a host of physical and psychological problems that have enduring effects on their life chances. The poor experience higher rates of mortality and poorer health as a result of stress, poor nutrition, hazardous jobs, limited access to health care, and low-quality housing; individuals report feelings of stress, powerlessness and shame at their inability to provide for themselves and the need to rely on others. Children raised in poverty experience an increased risk of lower educational/occupational attainment and higher rates of high school dropout, early sexual initiation, drug experimentation, and poverty, as adults.

As poverty is multi-dimensional, it can be measured in many ways; *income* poverty is most commonly measured by comparing household income to an *absolute* or *relative* measure of poverty. *Absolute* measures define a fixed threshold below which people are considered deprived; for example, the World Bank uses a threshold of $1 or $2 a day (for a family of three) to estimate poverty in much of the developing world. However, what it means to be poor varies over time and by location; therefore poverty thresholds used in developing areas do not meaningfully describe poverty in more developed areas. The US poverty standard, adopted in 1965, provides a long-standing gauge of absolute poverty in the USA; while it is updated yearly to reflect inflation, some researchers argue that the poverty standard has fallen out of step with what it means to be poor as costs and trends in consumption have changed over time.

Whereas absolute measures illustrate social stratification, relative measures highlight income inequality. Used widely in Europe, *relative* thresholds measure poverty as percentage of median income, e.g. 50 percent. Relative measures move in step with economic trends and reflect changes in the standard of living; however, defining poverty as a measure of *relative* disadvantage, there will always be a segment of the population that is considered poor, regardless of actual levels of wealth.

When compared cross-nationally, the USA has high rates of both absolute and relative poverty, signaling a wide income disparity and real income inadequacy. Three factors, demographic changes, economic activity, and government transfers contribute to the size of the poverty population. The number of single-mother (often minority) families has grown significantly since the 1960s and they have disproportionately high rates of poverty, leading to a so-called "feminization of poverty." While demographic changes have contributed to the widening income disparity, low wages and limited public benefits largely account for the size of the low-income population. The USA favors a market-based approach to poverty reduction in which policies enable individuals to "earn" their way out of poverty rather than to redistribute income, per se. The central ethos of a capitalist market is to maximize profits and minimize wages, so employment alone may not provide sufficient resources for low-wage workers to escape poverty; in Scandinavian countries, strong safety net policies are effective in bridging the gap between earned income and the poverty line.

The failure of the economic prosperity of the 1990s to dramatically reduce poverty has reinvigorated cultural theories of poverty that argue that there is an "underclass" culture which eschews mainstream values, and transmits poverty intergenerationally through the reliance on government support, reduced labor force participation, and single-mother households. While cultural theories focus on individual behavior, other models assert the importance of *structural* factors and societal stratification, such as discrimination, segregation, and the availability of jobs in limiting opportunities to escape poverty.

According to the World Bank (2001), there are five keys to reducing poverty: promoting opportunity by stimulating economic growth; making the market work for poor people; enabling poor people to build assets; making state and social institutions more responsive to poor people; protecting people against the shock of economic crises, natural disasters, war, and illness.

SEE ALSO: Culture of Poverty; Family Poverty; Feminization of Poverty; Income Inequality and Income Mobility; Income Inequality, Global; Urban Poverty

REFERENCE

World Bank (2001) *World Development Report 2000/2001: Attacking Poverty*. Oxford University Press, Oxford.

SUGGESTED READINGS

Danizer, S. & Haveman, R. (2001) *Understanding Poverty*. Harvard University Press, Cambridge, MA.

Iceland, J. (2003) *Poverty in America*. University of California Press, Berkeley, CA.

Sen, A. (1999) *Development as Freedom*. Alfred A. Knopf, New York.

TRACY ROBERTS

power

Power is an "essentially contested and complex term" (Lukes 1974: 7). Some theorists define power as the capacity to act ("power to"). Hobbes's (1985 [1641]: 150) definition of power as a person's "present means ... to obtain some future apparent Good" is a classic example of this understanding of power. Others define power as getting someone else to do what you want them to do ("power over"). Feminist authors, such as Stacey and Price (1983: *Women, Power and Politics*), define power in this manner when they view it as the more or less one-sided patriarchal ability to position women's lives through the actions of men over them. Alternatively, Foucault (1977) suggests power is "relational." One social actor may exercise power over others, but all individuals nevertheless possess power as they can engage in resistance.

Sociologists have focused primarily (but not exclusively) upon "power over" viewpoints. Marxism is a classic example. It argues power derives from economic ownership, with a ruling class (the bourgeoisie) controlling the means of production, distribution and exchange within capitalist society. Sociological discussion of "power over" is typical held to begin with Weber (1978). Weber distinguished between coercive power and power based upon three types of legitimate authority: charismatic, traditional, and legal-rational. People obey charismatic leaders, such as Jesus Christ, because of the personal qualities of the person doing the telling. Traditional authority involves acceptance of rules that symbolize ritual or ancient practice, such as religion. Weber held that modern societies are increasingly characterized by the growth of bureaucracies whose formal rules of procedure are legitimized by legal-rational authority.

Weber laid the foundation stones on which sociologists later developed "pluralist" and "elitist" viewpoints when discussing power. Pluralist theorists (e.g. Dahl 1961: *Who Governs?*) view power as being held by a variety of competing groups within society. Since no one group is able to dominate all others (because of checks and balances built into a democratic system of government) a "plurality" of competing interest groups, political parties, and so forth, is held to characterize democratic society. In contrast, elite theorists (e.g. Mills 1959: *The Power Elite*) argue that rather than there being a simple plurality of competing groups within society, there is instead a series of elites: powerful groups who are able to impose their will upon the rest of society.

Foucault's (1977) analysis contrasts with "pluralist" and "elitist" viewpoints by focusing upon the "microphysics" of power. Power does not lie in the hands of a sovereign ruler or the state, but rather lacks concrete form, occurring only at a locus of struggle (Foucault 1978: *The History of Sexuality*, vol. 1). Power is therefore not possessed, but rather is recognized in and through acts of resistance. Resistance through defiance defines power and hence becomes possible *through* power. Without resistance, power is absent.

SEE ALSO: Feminism; Foucault, Michel; Ideology; Marxism and Sociology; Mills, C. Wright; Power Elite; Power, Theories of; Weber, Max

REFERENCES

Foucault, M. (1977) *Discipline and Punish*. Penguin, London.

Hobbes, T. (1985) [1641] *Leviathan*. Penguin, New York.

Lukes, S. (1974) *Power: A Radical View*. Macmillan, London.

Weber, M. (1978) *Economy and Society: An Outline of Interpretive Sociology*, trans. E. Fischoff et al. University of California Press, Berkeley, CA.

JASON L. POWELL AND JOHN M. CHAMBERLAIN

power, theories of

In contemporary sociology, the term power is used in two distinct but interrelated ways. In the broadest usage power refers to a *structural capacity* for an actor A to cause any change in the behavior of another actor B. This meaning of power captures the potential for power to be exercised or not in social interaction. The second meaning refers to a *concrete event* in which one individual benefits at the expense of another. Modern theorists refer to such events as *power use* or *power exercise*. Importantly, both meanings imply that power is a relational phenomenon. Thus, theories of power focus on the relationship between two or more actors, and not the characteristics of actors themselves. Although the terms are sometimes conflated, power is distinct from other relational concepts such as *influence* (which is voluntarily accepted), *force* (wherein the target has no choice but to comply), and *authority* (which involves a request from a legitimate social position).

Perhaps the first formal theory of power was proposed by Thibaut and Kelley in *The Social Psychology of Groups* (1959). They asserted that individuals evaluate their current relationship against some standard, or comparison level (CL). The theory also claims that actors assess the attractiveness of a relationship by comparing their focal relationship to benefits expected from others (CL_{ALT}). The power of actor A over B is defined as "A's ability to affect the quality of outcomes attained by B." There are two ways that this can occur. *Fate control* exists when actor A affects actor B's outcome by changing her/his own behavior, independent of B's action. *Behavior control* exists when the rewards obtained by B are a function of both A and B's behavior. In either case, whether A has fate control or behavior control, B is dependent on A for rewards and thus A has a source of power over B.

A major theoretical shift occurred in the early 1970s, with the development of Richard Emerson's *Power Dependence Theory* (Emerson 1972a; 1972b). Emerson put forward the notion that relations between actors are part of a larger set of potential exchange relations, i.e., an exchange network. Thus, in analyzing a dyad, he asserted that it is important to consider its broader connection to other dyads – the larger network in which it is embedded. Emerson considered two kinds of connection. A *negative connection* exists when interaction in one dyad reduces interaction in another. A *positive connection* exists when interaction in one dyad promotes interaction in another. The attention to dyadic connectedness gave Emerson's theorizing a decidedly structural theme.

Power Dependence Theory claims that power emerges when some individuals are more dependent than others for the exchange of valued goods. Fomally, the theory asserts that the power of actor A over actor B is equal to the dependence of B on A, summarized by the equation $P_{AB} = D_{BA}$.

In turn, dependence is a function of two key factors: the availability of alternative exchange relations, and the extent to which the actors value those relations. Since the original formulation Power Dependence Theory has given rise to numerous other branches of theory. For instance, Molm (1990) has expanded the power dependence framework to include both reward-based power and punishment-based power. Lawler (1992) has developed a theory of power that includes both dependence-based power and punitive-based power. Both lines of work affirm the importance of dependence in generating power.

An alternative approach to power is found in David Willer's *Elementary Theory*, which anchors power in the ability of some actors to *exclude* others from valued goods. The theory identifies three kinds of social relations – conflict, coercion, and exchange – defined by the value of the sanctions transmitted in each. Within exchange the theory identifies three kinds of power structures. *Strong power* structures are those that only contain two kinds of positions: high-power positions that can never be excluded and two or more low-power positions, one of which must always be excluded. The classic example is the three-person dating network in which B has two potential partners while either A or C must be excluded. *Equal power* networks contain only one set of structurally identical positions, such as dyads or triangles. In *weak power* networks no position is necessarily excluded, but some may be. At the heart of the theory is a resistance model that relates the distribution of profit when two actors exchange to the benefits lost when they do not. Tests find that the resistance model predicts power exercise in a range of settings.

SEE ALSO: Power-Dependence Theory; Power

REFERENCES

Emerson, R. (1972a) Exchange theory, part I: a psychological basis for social exchange. In: Berger, J., Zelditch, M., & Anderson, B. (eds.), *Sociological Theories in Progress*, vol 2. Houghton-Mifflin, Boston, MA, pp. 38–57.

Emerson, R. (1972b) Exchange theory, part II: exchange relations and networks. In Berger, J., Zelditch, M., & Anderson, B. (eds.), *Sociological Theories in Progress*, vol. 2. Houghton-Mifflin, Boston, MA, pp. 58–87.

Lawler, E. J. (1992) Power processes in bargaining. *Sociological Quarterly* 33: 17–34.

Molm, L. (1990) Structure, action and outcomes: the dynamics of power in social exchange. *American Sociological Review* 55: 427–47.

SUGGESTED READING

Willer, D. (ed.) (1999) *Network Exchange Theory*. Praeger, London.

SHANE THYE

power elite

The concept "power elite" was advanced by the American sociologist C. Wright Mills (1956). The "power elite" draws its membership from three areas: (1) political leaders and their close advisers; (2) major corporate owners and directors; (3) high-ranking military officers. Mills argues that through their control of governmental, financial, educational, civic and cultural institutions, the "power elite" hold a disproportionate amount of influence within society. He asserts that instead of initiating policy, or even controlling those who govern them, society's citizens have become mere passive spectators, cheering the heroes and booing the villains, but taking little or no direct part in the action. This leads them to become increasingly alienated and estranged from politics, as can be seen in the sharp decline in electoral participation over the last several decades. As a result, control over their destinies has fallen even further into the hands of the "power elite." Mills rejects "pluralist" assertions that within modern democracies various centers of power exist that serve as "checks and balances" on one another. Whereas "pluralists" are somewhat content with what they believe is a fair, if admittedly imperfect, system, "power elite" theorists decry the unequal and unjust distribution of power they find everywhere. However, by arguing that those at the top encounter no real opposition to their actions, "power elite" theory can be criticized for implying society is by and large homogenous and characterized by consensus.

SEE ALSO: Elites; Marxism and Sociology; Mills, C. Wright; Politics; Power, Theories of

REFERENCE

Mills, C. W. (1956) *The Power Elite*. Oxford University Press, New York.

JASON L POWELL AND JOHN M CHAMBERLAIN

power-dependence theory

Power-dependence theory is the name commonly given to the social exchange theory originally formulated by Richard Emerson (1972). The dynamics of the theory revolve around power, power use, and power-balancing operations, and rest on the central concept of dependence. Mutual dependence brings people together, increasing their likelihood of forming and maintaining exchange relationships, while inequalities in dependence create power imbalances that can lead to conflict and social change.

The publication of Emerson's theory in 1972 marked a turning point in the development of the social exchange framework in sociology. By integrating principles of behavioral psychology with the growing field of social network analysis, Emerson developed an exchange theory in which the structure of relations, rather than the motivations or skills of individuals, was the central focus. Power-dependence theory assumes that actors are self-interested, but this assumption is based on the backward-looking logic of operant psychology rather than on the forward-looking logic of rational choice. The smallest unit of analysis in the theory is the exchange relation, defined as a series of repeated exchanges between a pair of actors, rather than the individual actor or actions. Furthermore, exchange relations are typically embedded in exchange networks, defined as sets of connected exchange relations among actors. Two relations are connected if the frequency or value of exchange in one relation (e.g., A–B) affects the frequency or value of exchange in another relation (e.g., B–C), either positively (by increasing exchange in the other), or negatively (by decreasing exchange in the other). The actors in exchange relations can be either individual persons or corporate actors such as groups or organizations. The concepts of exchange networks and corporate actors allowed power-dependence theory to bridge micro- and macro-levels of analysis more successfully than its predecessors.

The theory's title derives from the basic insight that actors' mutual dependence on one another for valued resources provides the structural basis for their power over each other. A's power over B derives from, and is equal to, B's dependence on A, and vice versa. B's dependence on A increases with the value to B of the resources A controls, and decreases with B's alternative sources of those resources, both of which are influenced by the larger network in which the A–B relation resides. Thus, power is a structural attribute of an exchange relation or network, not a property of an actor. Power use is the behavioral exercise of that structural potential. Power in dyadic relations is described by two dimensions: cohesion – actors' absolute power over each other, and balance – actors' relative power over one another. If actors are equally dependent on one another, power in the relation is balanced; if B is more dependent on A, power is imbalanced, and A has a power advantage equal to the degree of imbalance.

Over time, the structure of power has predictable effects on the frequency and distribution of exchange as actors use power to maintain exchange or gain advantage. A's initiations of exchange with B increase with A's dependence on B, the frequency of exchange in a relation increases with cohesion, and in imbalanced relations, the ratio of exchange changes in favor of the more powerful, less dependent actor. Emerson also argued that imbalanced relations are unstable and lead to power-balancing processes that alter either the alternatives or values that govern power and dependence (e.g., coalition formation can balance power by reducing a powerful actor's alternatives).

Emerson's collaboration with Karen Cook and their students, beginning in the late 1970s, produced the first research program testing the basic tenets of power-dependence theory and extending its scope. The experimental setting that Cook and Emerson developed, in which subjects negotiated the terms of exchange through a series of offers and counteroffers, became the prototype for studying power in exchange networks and was adopted by numerous other scholars, including many who proposed competing theories to explain the distribution of power in exchange networks. After Emerson's untimely death in 1982, Cook's work with Toshio Yamagishi (and, more recently, with other students of Cook's) continued to modify and expand the theory, including development in 1992 of a new algorithm for predicting the distribution of power in the network as a whole, rather than within dyadic relations.

At the same time that Cook and Emerson were developing their research program, other scholars, particularly Edward Lawler and Linda Molm, were drawing on concepts from power-dependence theory to develop their own theories of power and related processes. Their work introduced ideas and concepts that were not part of Emerson's original formulation: greater attention to cognition and affect in exchange, consideration of punitive as well as rewarding actions in exchange, and analysis of different forms of exchange. In the late 1970s and early 1980s, Bacharach and Lawler integrated power-dependence theory's analysis of structural power with bargaining theories' analyses of tactical power. Traditional work on bargaining neglected the power structure within which parties negotiate; Lawler and Bacharach used ideas from power-dependence theory to fill that gap. Molm's (1997) work on coercion in exchange also focused more attention on strategic power use and expanded the theory to include punishment and coercion, arguing that both reward power and coercive power are derived from dependence on others, either for obtaining rewards or avoiding punishment, and potentially can be explained by the same principles.

The two most recent developments among power-dependence researchers are the shift from the study of power and inequality to the study of integrative outcomes such as commitment, trust, and affect, and the expansion of both theory and research to include different forms of exchange: reciprocal as well as negotiated direct exchange, generalized or indirect exchange, and productive exchange. Lawler's affect theory of exchange (and his earlier, related work with Jeongkoo Yoon and Shane Thye on relational cohesion) initiated the first line of work, and the work of Molm and her students on comparisons of negotiated and reciprocal exchange (and, most recently, generalized exchange) initiated the latter. Both lines of work are now continued by a growing number of power-dependence theorists.

SEE ALSO: Blau, Peter; Exchange Network Theory; Homans, George; Power, Theories of; Social Exchange Theory

REFERENCES

Emerson, R. M. (1972) Exchange theory, part I: a psychological basis for social exchange; Exchange theory, part II: exchange relations and network structures. In: Berger, J., Zelditch, M., Jr., & Anderson, B. (eds.), *Sociological Theories in Progress*, vol. 2. Houghton Mifflin, Boston, MA, pp. 38–87.

Molm, L. D. (1997) *Coercive Power in Social Exchange*. Cambridge University Press, Cambridge.

SUGGESTED READINGS

Cook, K. S. & Emerson, R. M. (1978) Power, equity and commitment in exchange networks. *American Sociological Review* 43: 721–39.

Lawler, E. J. (2001) An affect theory of social exchange. *American Journal of Sociology* 107: 321–52.

LINDA D. MOLM

practice theory

The label "practice theory" refers to a group of approaches in late twentieth-century social and cultural theory which highlights the routinized and performative character of action, its dependence on tacit knowledge and implicit understanding. Besides, these approaches emphasize the "material" character of action and culture as anchored in embodiment and networks of artifacts. Practice theory has its roots in anti-dualist social philosophy, above all in Ludwig Wittgenstein and Martin Heidegger. In contemporary social theory, Pierre Bourdieu, Theodore Schatzki, Anthony Giddens, and Harold Garfinkel contain diverse forms of practice theory. In a broad sense, Bruno Latour and Judith Butler, partly also Michel Foucault, comprise praxeological ideas as well.

It is Theodore Schatzki's (1996) book *Social Practices*, which gives the label "practice theory" a profile. However, the problematique of practice theory is considerably older and embraces an array of authors who have encouraged the social sciences to a turn to the "everyday," to its implicit and bodily foundations. Of special importance here is Pierre Bourdieu who in 1972 published his *Outline of a Theory of Practice*. Other authors such as Foucault, de Certeau or Garfinkel also coin the term "practices" at central places in their works.

Practice theory mainly directs its critique at intellectualist social theory, i.e. against those approaches which ascribe a basically intentional, rational and conscious character to human action. Instead, it participates in the broad movement of a cultural/interpretative turn in the social sciences. However, there are also distinct differences between practice theory and certain intellectualist tendencies of culturalism: Thus, practice theory is sceptical towards the inclination of structuralism to reduce culture to logical systems and towards the phenomenological focus on the intentionality of consciousness. Instead, for practice theorists the social consists of patterns of routinized action carried by embodied tacit knowledge. In this basic idea they follow radical attempts in twentieth-century social philosophy (cf. Wittgenstein, Heidegger) to overcome a series of classical dualisms: between the individual and the social, between consciousness and the unconscious, between subject and object, eventually between culture and materiality. For contemporary practice theory, thus the smallest unit of social and cultural analysis is neither an action nor a norm, neither an agent nor a sign, but a practice as a routinized type of bodily behaviour carried by an inherent form of practical knowledge. There are three basic elements of practices: the dependence of actions on tacit knowledge; the materiality of the social, deriving from the nexus of bodies and of artifacts; and finally, the tension of practices between repetitiveness and unpredictability.

Practice theory proceeds from the assumption that patterns of actions depend largely on a realm of prereflexive, taken-for-granted knowledge, less a "knowing that" than a "knowing how." In their understanding of action and the social, practice theorists ascribe a special place to the body. The body here cannot be reduced to an instrumental status; rather social practices appear as a repetition of bodily movements. Correspondingly, practice theorists regard practical knowledge less as a quality of minds than of bodies, as embodied knowledge.

As bodily movements social practices possess a specific materiality. However, also in a second respect practice theorists emphasize the materiality of practice: Practices often contain artifacts and form nexuses of bodies and things. Recent practice theory thus regards the constitutive role of artifacts as part of its analytical agenda, although the exact status of non-human "actants" (Latour) in relation to human bodies and their incorporated understanding remains contested.

The tension between the routine character of patterns of action on the one hand and their unpredictability and stubbornness on the other, forms a last complex of practice-theoretical interest. Generally, practice theory stresses the repetitive, recursive character of practices which enables a reproduction of the social world (cf. Bourdieu's habitus). On the other hand, practice theorists have often turned to the incalculability of practices, i.e. the latent possibilities of aberrations. Thus, Garfinkel refers to the context-dependence of all actions and Butler to subversions within repetitions. Again, practice theorists do no trace this unpredictability back to conscious agents, but rather to surprising effects which the application of routine movements and understanding in new contexts can bring about.

SEE ALSO: Actor-Network Theory; Bourdieu, Pierre

REFERENCE

Schatzki, T. R. (1996) *Social Practices: A Wittgensteinian Approach to Human Activity and the Social.* Cambridge University Press, Cambridge.

SUGGESTED READING

Reckwitz, A. (2002) Toward a theory of social practices: development in culturalist theorizing, *European Journal of Social Theory* 2: 245–65.

ANDREAS RECKWITZ

pragmatism

Pragmatism began in the USA in the 1870s, in the wake of the intellectual revolution touched off by Darwin, as a term for a method designed to clarify disputed, abstract intellectual concepts by defining them with reference to their concrete behavioral consequences. It later took on a broader meaning as the name for a comprehensive philosophical perspective which became widely known and influential from 1898 to its waning during the period of the cold war. Nevertheless, the perspective continued to influence sociology throughout the twentieth century and into the twenty-first, especially in the tradition of symbolic interaction. A resurgence of research and interest in pragmatism, beginning in the 1980s and accelerating since 1990, has been seen in general sociology in the work of such authors as Hans Joas, Mustafa Emirbayer, Dmitri Shalin, and David Maines.

Scottish psychologist Alexander Bain had defined a belief as that for which a person is willing and committed to act, even in the face of considerable risk. For Bain, the opposite of belief was doubt, a state of confusion, uncertainty, anxiety, or frustration about how to act next. Charles Peirce expanded on this theory of belief in his doubt-belief theory of inquiry. Peirce maintained that belief breaks down and doubt ensues when the requirements of human organisms and those of their environment fall out of step with each other. Human doubt triggers inquiry, the goal of which is the "fixation of belief." In Peirce's hands, belief became defined as habit, or a disposition to act in a certain way under certain circumstances.

According to Peirce's pragmatic maxim, as expressed in its 1906 revision, the best definition of a concept is "a description of the habit it will produce" (quoted in Short 1981: 218). Concepts defined in this way are empirically testable, and a concept can be tentatively considered true so long as it passes all such testing. Hence, Peirce's pragmatic maxim is a part of his theory of inquiry. The maxim is also part of his semeiotic or general theory of signs, which was Peirce's crowning achievement and which became the linchpin of his entire philosophy.

Although Peirce was justified in calling himself the father of pragmatism, William James was the first to use the term publicly, in an 1898 lecture (published the same year) at the University of California. It would also be James whose lectures and publications would popularize pragmatism and cause its wide dissemination throughout the world. However, James had already made his greatest contribution to the perspective in his 1890 *Principles of Psychology* because of the major influence this work would have on John Dewey and George Herbert Mead. In his *Principles*, James replaced traditional introspective, faculty, and associationist psychologies with a functional and processual psychology, in which the self and consciousness are seen not as entities but as functions that are actively engaged with the world.

SEE ALSO: Mead, George Herbert; Role-Taking; Semiotics; Symbolic Interaction

REFERENCE

Short, T. L. (1981) Semiosis and intentionality. *Transactions of the Charles S. Peirce Society* 17: 197–223.

SUGGESTED READINGS

Fisch, M. H. (1986) *Peirce, Semeiotic, and Pragmatism: Essays by Max H. Fisch.* Indiana University Press, Bloomington, IN.

Sleeper, R. W. (2001) [1986] *The Necessity of Pragmatism: John Dewey's Conception of Philosophy.* University of Illinois Press, Urbana, IL.

DAVID L. ELLIOTT

praxis

Praxis is a term most commonly associated with the ability of oppressed groups to change their economic, political, and social worlds through rationally informed reflection and deliberate social action. As advocated and critiqued by contemporary theorists, the term itself is often loosely associated with the melding of theory to liberatory human action.

In classical sociological theory, praxis is connected with Karl Marx and his emphasis on the revolutionary potential of the proletariat. Interpretations of Marx's usage of praxis vary, but most associate a Marxist-based praxis with societal transformation that involves a concomitant change in the proletariat's material activity, consciousness, and social relations. Hence, Marx is frequently quoted: "The philosophers have only *interpreted* the world, in various ways; the point, however, is to *change* it" (1978 [1844]: 145). Moreover, Marx and Friedrich Engels's *Communist Manifesto* lays out this theory and plan of praxis: the dual abolition of class and class exploitation in the forms of private property, the patriarchal nuclear family, traditional religion, and country and nation. At issue for Marx is holistic human and social transformation.

Contemporary theorists advocate praxis-based solutions to end the subaltern status of many oppressed groups, including, but not limited to, the colonized, the poor, women, people of color, and gays and lesbians. For many, the institution of education is fundamentally linked to praxis. For instance, Paulo Freire's (1972) theory of praxis specifically offers Brazilian *campesinos* as a mechanism that combines reflection and action to transform a psychological, social, political, and economic legacy of imperialism and colonialism. For Freire, praxis is the act of creativity and social change achieved through the oppressed's own experience and the creative process of education: that is, acquiring and developing literacy and reactive responses to the ruling social and political structures. Hence, praxis and its ends are not preordained, but are, instead, a creative process of becoming.

SEE ALSO: Marx, Karl; Social Change; Social Movements

REFERENCES

Freire, P. (1972) *Pedagogy of the Oppressed.* Harmondsworth, Penguin.

Marx, K. (1978) [1844] *Theses on Feuerbach.* In: Tucker, R. (ed.), *The Marx Engels Reader.* Norton, New York.

SUGGESTED READINGS

Gouldner, A. (1980) *The Two Marxisms.* Macmillan, London.

Vrankicki, P. (1965) On the problem of practice. *Praxis* 1: 41–8.

SUSAN WORTMANN

prejudice

Prejudice is the judging of a person or idea, without prior knowledge of the person or idea, on the basis of some perceived group membership. Prejudice can be negative or positive. Some writers, in defining prejudice, stress an irrational component; others maintain that it is incorrect to do so because prejudice is often rooted in quite rational self-interest.

Social scientists began to show great interest in prejudice in the early to mid-twentieth century when anti-immigrant and anti-Jewish sentiment was widespread and often erupted in violence. Gordon Allport (1954) described prejudice as the result of a psychological process of categorizing people into in-groups and out-groups. In-groups are considered desirable and in possession of positive attributes, while out-groups are seen as possessing negative or undesirable attributes and, thus, as appropriate targets for abuse.

Other works investigated the idea of a prejudiced personality type (the authoritarian personality) characterized by overly rigid thinking, acceptance of stereotypes, excessive conformity and submission to authority, discomfort with ambiguity, and highly conservative and/or fundamentalist beliefs.

In contrast to early theories of prejudice which treated it as a psychological phenomenon, Herbert Blumer advanced the notion of racial prejudice as "a sense of group position" in which the words and actions of influential public figures establish a public perception of social group hierarchy and of the positioning of one's own group relative to others. Prejudice is thus not merely an individual ideology but a social phenomenon rooted in intergroup relations and arising from specific historical contexts.

As social scientists began to uncover the structural foundations of racism and sexism, interest in prejudice as a research topic began to wane. Focusing attention on the individual ideological aspects of prejudice was thought to divert attention from its even more harmful structural counterpart: institutionalized racial and sexual discrimination and violence. The uncovering of the racist and sexist practices of the state, of business, of the legal justice system, of commerce and real estate and employers, of science and systems of higher education, seemed to render the beliefs of individual racists trivial. More recently, however, scholars are reemphasizing the importance of prejudice and the severity of its consequences; several prominent sociologists have urged that cumulative daily encounters with prejudice not be discounted in the rush to study structural factors.

Because of the research linking prejudice to stereotyping and to various other traits such as conformity and lower levels of education, some social scientists have suggested education as a cure for prejudice. Others have suggested that prejudice arises from ignorance about the group(s) in question and hence that the remedy lies in increased contact between members of various groups.

This contact theory, with its hypothesis that intergroup prejudice can be reduced by increasing the levels of contact between members of different groups, has been tested repeatedly, with mixed results. In some cases, increasing contact between groups actually results in higher levels of prejudice. Those situations in which contact does seem to result in lower levels of prejudice are those in which members of different groups have ample opportunity to interact in positive ways and to work together on cooperative tasks. Another essential element of successful contacts is that the participants are of equal status in the social situation(s) under study.

Because stereotypes often have widespread social support, people's attitudes and prejudices are not likely to change unless there is leadership support for change, and willingness among authority figures to impose rewards and sanctions to further change. This suggests that leaders who insist that prejudice and discrimination are no longer problems may actually help to preserve prejudice.

SEE ALSO: Authoritarian Personality; Discrimination; Homophobia and Heterosexism; In-Groups and Out-Groups; Stereotyping and Stereotypes

SUGGESTED READINGS

Allport, G. W. (1954) *The Nature of Prejudice.* Addison-Wesley, Reading, MA.

Blumer, H. (2000) *Selected Works of Herbert Blumer: A Public Philosophy for Mass Society.* University of Illinois Press, Urbana, IL.

Stangor, C. (2000) *Stereotypes and Prejudice: Essential Readings.* Psychology Press of Taylor & Francis, Philadelphia.

LAURA JENNINGS

primary groups

Cooley (1909) coined the term primary group to denote intimate, comparatively permanent, and solidarity associations of mutually identifying persons, and a century of sociological research has increased our understanding of primary groups in their variety of forms and multifaceted, contingent functions. According to Cooley, primary groups are primary in the sense of providing the first and (because of the greater openness and pliability of children) the most important socialization. The most important examples he cited in this sense are the family, children's play-groups, and the neighborhood or village community.

Primary groups are also primary in the sense of being the source out of which emerge both individuals and social institutions. Cooley agreed with George Herbert Mead that the self and its ideals emerge out of such primary relations. As examples of social institutions, Cooley cites democracy as an outgrowth of the village community and Christianity as an outgrowth of the family.

These groups are primary in the additional sense of providing primary human needs such as attachment, security, support, and recognition. Since these needs persist in some forms and to some degree throughout the lifecycle, primary relations never cease to be important. In Cooley's conceptualization, a primary group instills feelings in its members of sympathy and identification with the group, its goals, values, and members. All that is distinctively human is a product of this feeling of a "we," which constrains but does not eliminate people's animal passions of greed, conflict, and so forth.

SEE ALSO: Cooley, Charles Horton; Secondary Groups; Significant Others; Socialization, Primary

REFERENCE

Cooley, C. H. (1909) *Social Organization: A Study of the Larger Mind.* Charles Scribner's Sons, New York.

DAVID L. ELLIOTT

primitive religion

While there is no universally accepted definition of "primitive religion," typically it is understood to mean beliefs and practices in nonliterate, small-scale societies with limited technological and material culture. Nonetheless some contemporary social scientists are ill at ease with the label "primitive" because of its pejorative connotations and a legacy of western observers misreading the social and cultural patterns to which the term is supposed to refer. At times "primitive religion" appeared almost as a blank slate for developing theories ultimately to describe contemporary societies.

Some of the pioneering efforts in the sociology of religion were motivated by analyses of so-called primitive religions, often as part of a social evolution theory. Such early figures as British anthropologists Edward B. Tylor and James G. Frazer developed controversial theories that attempted to explain primitive cultures and at least implicitly contrast them to European patterns. Most famously, Durkheim in his *Elementary Forms of Religious Life* drew extensively on accounts of aboriginal Australians and Native Americans to advance his thesis about the nature of all religion.

However, problems became apparent with those theories. First, they sometimes equated present-day simple societies with historic or prehistoric times, even though such a claim rests on unproven assertions that present-day groups and patterns exist unchanged relative to a remote, often poorly understood past. Second, the theories tended to gloss over two important questions of context: whether western ideas of religion were meaningful in non-western societies and whether the contemporary images of religion were applicable to the distant past. Each case could represent an unwarranted projection of the researcher's cultural context onto the "primitive" sources. And third, by the mid-twentieth century, closer studies of cultures labeled as primitive revealed considerable complexity and adaptation which was overlooked before.

Thus subsequent scholars rejected the early theories as overly simplistic. Edward Evans-Pritchard derided the dualism that pitted "primitive" versus "modern," which he argued was rooted in a colonial and even racial discourse of western societies. He and other scholars dismissed as speculative the quest for discovering the origin of religion by using "primitive" analogies. And Mary Douglas suggested that despite western scholars' conventional wisdom, if they looked closely they might find that the "primitives" were less religious than moderns.

Still, a variety of later and respected studies employ the notion of primitive religion. Robert Bellah wrote in an influential essay that the primitive was the first stage of religious evolution. Adopting Clifford Geertz's view of religion as a symbolic system, Bellah explains religious evolution as the rising complexity of religious symbolization. Hence "primitive" refers to the least complex and least differentiated stage. He writes that in its primitive form religion is fully integrated with other areas of social life and, as a result, does not cope well with social change or give rise to political alternatives. Bellah asserts his five stages could apply to present-day religions and required neither a strict chronological sequencing of the stages nor a value judgment favoring one over another.

In another example, French political scientist Marcel Gauchet argues that primordial religion consists of an attitude of absolute disempowerment of humans relative to the supernatural. Gauchet then uses this definition as a foil for arguing that Christianity, especially through the Reformation, provided the opposite attitude, absolute empowerment, which enables the "exit" from all religion – in other words, secularization. While Gauchet does not claim to be a specialist in primitive religion, his theory stakes out a new dimension for contemporary researchers to consider.

SEE ALSO: Durkheim, Émile; Historical and Comparative Methods; Religion, Sociology of; Secularization

SUGGESTED READINGS

Bellah, R. (1991) *Beyond Belief: Essays on Religion in a Post-Traditionalist World.* University of California Press, Berkeley, CA.

Evans-Pritchard, E. E. (1985) *Theories of Primitive Religion.* Greenwood Press, Westport, CT.

Gauchet, M. (1997) *The Disenchantment of the World: A Political History of Religion.* Princeton University Press, Princeton, NJ.

SCOTT HEIL

privatization

Privatization is a transfer of public services provided by various levels of governments in national states to the private sector of business. It is a relatively recent transformation of governance and markets in countries worldwide. In fact, it is an extraordinary, rapidly expanding phenomenon that is rising in global waves, transferring ownership from governments to private enterprises.

Rendering public services via private businesses creates important political, economic, and cultural changes. The actual methods for privatization are manifold; they can be outright purchases, leases, subsidies or other cooperative partnerships, or yet other approaches. However, they put the privatized public service into the hands of private managers. The concept of privacy is not identical with privatization, but it is a part of the cluster of values linked to other changing values for governance and for markets. Privacy of enterprises emphasizes autonomy, independence, secrecy, and profit for the owners; both governance and markets demand transparency, accountability, and benefits for the public good. Democracy can be benefited by the efficiencies of privatization if the provided service responds to public needs and sensitivities, but it may be harmed where the private owners of a function are alien to the public.

Early efforts to reduce the economic role of the state included Churchill's "denationalization" of the British steel industry and Adenauer's withdrawal of the West German government's major investment in Volkswagen in 1961. However, denationalization at the time was not very popular. The major movement toward privatization was energized much later by Margaret Thatcher. She also coined the concept of privatization. At that time (the early 1980s) a number of privatization goals were pursued by the British government: (1) provide new revenue through privatization of pubic enterprises; (2) improve economic efficiency; (3) limit the government's role in the economy; (4) encourage broader share ownership; (5) encourage competition; (6) require state-owned enterprises to aspire to market discipline. In the USA Ronald Reagan won a landslide victory in 1980 and easily won his second term in 1984. His policies were to reduce taxes, cut government programs, and finance an astounding defense buildup, resulting in a large budget deficit. Privatization in various forms was encouraged by Reagan. Reducing the role of government (except the military) was a high priority.

SEE ALSO: Capitalism; Neoliberalism; Public and Private; Public Sphere; Welfare State

SUGGESTED READINGS

Parker, D. & Saal, D. (eds.) (2003) *International Handbook on Privatization*. Edward Elgar, Cheltenham.

Yarrow, G. & Jasiński, P. (eds.) (1996) *Privatization: Critical Perspectives on the World Economy*, 4 vols. Routledge, New York.

BURKART HOLZNER

privilege

There is a historical and cultural tendency for dominant groups to institutionalize discrimination against subdominant groups. Discrimination is justified by arguing that members of the subdominant group are deficient in some way when compared to members of the dominant group. The idealized characteristics of the dominant group are intertwined in social, cultural, and legal institutions and ultimately work to advantage, or privilege, members of the dominant group and disadvantage those of the subdominant group. Sociologists most often discuss privilege in terms of gender (how women are subordinated to men), race/ethnicity (how people of color are subordinated to those with white skin), and sexuality (how homosexuals, bisexuals, and transsexuals are subordinated to heterosexuals).

In the USA, gender roles and expectations have been governed by the doctrine of the separate spheres. This ideology holds that women are virtuous, nurturing, and frail and therefore unable to contend with the demands of politics and commerce. Men, in contrast, are aggressive, competitive, and strong and, thus, better suited for public life. Even as these beliefs were challenged throughout the twentieth century, the inequities between men and women persisted. Sociologists identify male privilege as being both embedded in the structure of complex organizations and reproduced in social relations.

Sociologists note that male privilege also is reproduced through interactions in these structures. At work, women's jobs often require deference to and caregiving for a male authority. For example, secretaries, paralegals, and nurse assistants tend to the schedules and well-being of their (male) bosses. In school, teacher interactions with students often reinforce gender stereotypes about the fields in which boys and girls excel by giving boys more attention than girls in science and math classes and by differently praising their work (commending boys for content while commending girls for being neat).

Race and ethnicity, like gender, are social concepts. While race and ethnicity have different sociological meanings, they are often used interchangeably. Race and ethnic categories are given meaning through the social relations and within the historical context in which they are embedded.

While much of the early research on race and ethnicity tried to justify the subordination of people of color by citing biological and cultural differences, sociologists argue that white privilege, like male privilege, is embedded in institutional structures and interactions. Scholars specifically examine how institutional racism, or the system of beliefs and behavior by which a racial or ethnic group is defined and oppressed, affects the opportunities and realities of people of color. For example, many scholars have shown that the lack of access to decent jobs, adequate housing, high-quality education, and adequate health care in the USA has resulted in higher rates of poverty among African Americans.

Sexuality too is rooted in privilege. Sociologists have followed two different analytical threads in the study of sexuality. Some scholars linked research on race, ethnicity, gender, class, and sexuality together. These scholars conceptualize race, gender, class, and sexuality as interlocking systems and argue that an individual's location in the system determines the kinds of privilege and oppression he or she will face. For example, beliefs about African American sexuality are important to maintaining institutional racism. The stereotype of the "welfare queen" ignores white privilege and attributes the inability of African Americans to pull themselves out of poverty to promiscuity and laziness.

The second analytical thread conceptualizes sexuality as a system of oppression comparable to race, class, and gender. These sociologists argue that heterosexism, or the institutionalized structures and beliefs that define heterosexual behavior as normative, privileges heterosexuality and subordinates alternative definitions of sexuality and sexual expression. Thus, like gender and race, sexuality is a historically rooted social concept that privileges one set of social relations between the sexes.

In sum, beliefs about gender, race, and sexuality are embedded in social, cultural, and legal institutions and affect the realities and opportunities of dominant and subdominant members of these groups. Those in the dominant group (male, white, and heterosexual) are privileged and reap the benefits from their membership, while those in the subdominant group (female, non-white, and homosexual, bisexual, or transsexual) are disadvantaged and are intentionally and unintentionally discriminated against. That said, it is important to recognize that gender, race, ethnicity, and sexuality are interlocking systems, and that one's privilege varies according to one's status within these systems.

SEE ALSO: Discrimination; Gender Ideology and Gender Role Ideology; Homophobia and Heterosexism; Racism, Structural and Institutional

SUGGESTED READINGS

Collins, P. H. (1990) *Black Feminist Thought: Knowledge, Consciousness, and the Politics of Empowerment*. Unwin Hyman, Boston, MA.

Greenberg, D. (1988) *The Construction of Homosexuality*. University of Chicago Press, Chicago, IL.

Pharr, S. (1997) *Homophobia: A Weapon of Sexism*. Chardon Press, Berkeley, CA.

Sadker, M. & Sadker, D. (1994) *How America's Schools Cheat Girls*. Scribner's, New York.

DEANA A. ROHLINGER

propaganda

The word "propaganda" is used and understood, broadly speaking, in two different ways.

First, it is often understood, neutrally, in a sense related to the Latin word "propagare," meaning "to propagate." In this sense, propaganda can be defined as an organized attempt to affect the thinking, feelings and actions of a target audience in ways desired by the communicator. In line with this usage, propagating messages is not necessarily good or bad in itself; rather, the goodness or badness of the dissemination will depend on the goodness or badness of the messages and the intent of the communicator.

But the second, and more common, understanding of the word "propaganda" is negative.

Propaganda here becomes distinguished from ordinary attempts at persuasion by the use of means that are discreditable, including manipulating a target audience with a view to gaining or maintaining power over them. Typically, for propaganda in its negative sense, the interests of the audience are subordinated to those of the propagandist. Such things as truth, education, clarity of reasoning and adequacy of information sources become treated as secondary. Propaganda in this pejorative sense can be defined as an organized attempt, through communication, to affect beliefs, attitudes or actions of a target audience by means that circumvent or suppress the target's ability to understand and evaluate the truth of a pertinent matter.

Lies are an obvious form of propagandistic communication, but deception can often be achieved by one-sided, selective presentation of truths that, taken together and in isolation from other truths of contrary import, create a false impression. To mention one country's attack on another, without mentioning that the other was the first to attack, is an example. Censorship can be an important component of propaganda by suppressing facts that, in the minds of the target, would create discord with those beliefs or attitudes that the propagandist wishes to impart.

The goal of propaganda is not necessarily to create conviction. The intent may merely be to create uncertainty and inaction among those who would otherwise be staunch opponents of some political, economic, or military power. Falsehoods repeated endlessly can have this effect. A common goal is to encourage forgetfulness about some things and artificially stimulate attention to others. Music, pageantry, imagery, catch-phrases and slogans can all be utilized to capture and sustain the attention and impart feeling to a target audience, often without the target being conscious of any manipulation. To succeed, propaganda generally needs to escape detection.

A very common technique in propaganda is to disguise the source of messages designed to influence people. "Fake news" involves video material that resembles a TV station's news format, but is paid for and produced by an interested party, with no acknowledgement of this fact. As another example, so called "Astroturf" protest groups resemble spontaneously formed community groups but are secretly created and controlled by an interested party.

Practitioners and analysts of modern mass persuasion stress the importance of how an issue is framed in the public mind – health versus freedom of speech in the case of tobacco advertising, for example. Much ingenuity is spent in finding memorable catch phrases and enduring images to sustain the desired way of framing the issue.

Since it is well understood that in certain contexts of eristic (combative) discourse, such as in a courtroom or with electoral campaign literature, truth presentation will be selective, some greater leeway can be allowed before calling this discourse "propaganda," because the message recipients will be on guard and the other side will be presented. The case for this leeway collapses, though, when an eristic presentation is disguised as heuristic (truth discovery) discourse – for example, by concealing the true source.

SEE ALSO: Hegemony and the Media; Media

SUGGESTED READINGS

Ellul, J. (1965) *Propaganda*. Random House, London.

Walton, D. (2007) *Media Argumentation*. Cambridge University Press, Cambridge.

Marlin, R. (2002) *Propaganda and the Ethics of Persuasion*. Broadview, Peterborough, Ontario.

RANDAL MARLIN

property, private

Property implies ownership, to which rights attach. These rights may take usurpatory, moral, or legal form. The types of things that can be owned as property, and therefore subject to property rights, are enormously varied. Depending on the particular circumstances, they might include, for instance, a human person, a person's capacities (especially for labor), the products of another's labor, any material of use or exchange, land, options, patents, ideas, and so on. The structure of ownership is also variable. In ancient societies, classically described as the "indian village community" in Maine's *Ancient Law* (1861), co-ownership or communal property prevailed. In peasant societies, on the other hand, the household rather than the community is typically the unit which exercises controlling rights over productive possessions. From early capitalist societies private property arose as the dominant form of ownership in which individual persons exercise rights over their objects of possession. In late capitalist societies corporate and public property forms emerge, combining elements of both communal and private property. Corporate property is communal insofar as ownership rights are shared by a number of proprietors, each of whom can exercise or dispose of their rights as they choose as individuals without collective constraint, and similarly use the benefits of their ownership as they individually see fit. Public property excludes private ownership and only nominally involves co-ownership, as various forms of statutory authorities exercise such property rights, putatively on behalf of the public, subject to legal and political controls.

The concept of private property, at least since the seventeenth century in Europe, is central in political and social theory. This is because the issue of private property is fundamental to moral, political, psychological, and social principles and outcomes. Private property is closely associated with the concept of individual freedom, for instance, where other forms of property may curtail such freedom. Economic and industrial efficiency is also frequently regarded as optimized under conditions of private property and compromised – if not undermined – by communal or public property. Psychologically, however, private property is more than other forms of property held to promote an unhealthy regard for material possession and corrode ethical orientations, as well as undermine respect for the natural and social environment experienced in common. Similarly, private property is regarded as the source and consolidator of inequitable and unjust distributions of earnings and wealth.

Marxism, on the other hand, focuses not on rights but on the productive relationships constitutive of private property. In this sense private property is understood in terms of power relations rather than rights. Marx holds that ownership or possession of property is the principle of organization within relations of production and distribution. Those who possess private property have direct access to means of consumption; those who do not must offer their labor services to owners, who pay wages in exchange for activating their property productively. In this exchange the reciprocity between property owners and property-less workers is asymmetrical, with the material benefits being greater for owners and the opportunity costs being greater for non-owners. This relationship Marx characterizes as exploitation. In this manner Marx holds that there is a characteristic endogenous dynamic within each form of property, corresponding to historical stages of societal development, including primitive communism, Asiatic society, feudalism, and capitalism.

SEE ALSO: Capitalism; Capitalism, Social Institutions of; Communism; Exploitation; Socialism

SUGGESTED READINGS

Macpherson, C. B. (ed.) (1978) *Property: Mainstream and Critical Positions.* Toronto University Press, Toronto.

Ryan, A. (1984) *Property and Political Theory.* Oxford University Press, Oxford.

JACK BARBALET

prostitution

The term prostitution is popularly used to refer to the trade of sexual services for payment in cash or kind, and so to a form of social interaction that is simultaneously sexual and economic. This makes prostitution a difficult cultural category, for in most societies sexual and economic relations are imagined and regulated in very different ways. Prostitution therefore straddles two quite different symbolic domains. Since these domains are highly gendered, the female prostitute has long represented a troubling figure, disrupting what are traditionally deemed to be natural gender binaries (active/passive, public/private, etc.), and stigmatized as unnatural, immoral, and polluting.

Yet prostitution is often simultaneously viewed as an inevitable feature of all human societies, for it is held to meet the supposedly powerful and biologically given sexual impulses of men. Thus it is sometimes described as a "necessary evil" and considered to protect the virtue of "good" girls and women by "soaking up" excess male sexual urges which would otherwise lead to rape and marital breakdown. This traditional view of prostitution found sociological expression in a classic article by Kingsley Davis (1937), which explained the institution of prostitution as a necessary counterbalance to the reproductive institutions of society (such as the family) that placed a check upon men's sexual liberty.

Prostitution is part of a wider market for commercial sex that has expanded and diversified rapidly in both affluent and developing nations over the past two decades. Old forms of sex commerce, including prostitution, are taking place in more and different settings; new technologies have generated possibilities for entirely new forms of commercial sexual experience; women are now amongst consumers of commercial sex; the boundaries between commercial sex and other sectors, such as tourism, leisure, and entertainment, have shifted.

There is a strong relationship between colonialism, imperialism, nationalism, militarism, and war on the one hand, and prostitution on the other. The presence of international peacekeepers and police, civilian contractors and aid workers in post-conflict settings has acted as a stimulus for the rapid growth of a prostitution market in many regions.

Prostitution has commanded much attention from feminists in recent years, but has also highlighted deep theoretical and political divisions within feminism. On one side of the divide stand "radical feminists" or "feminist abolitionists" who foreground the sexual domination of women by men in their analyses of gender inequality, and view prostitution as the unambiguous embodiment of patriarchal oppression. All prostitution is a form of sexual violence and slavery that violates women's human right to dignity and bodily integrity, and buying sex is equivalent to the act of rape. This account rests on the assumption that no woman freely chooses or genuinely consents to prostitute. It leaves little room for women as agents within prostitution, and provides what critics deem to be a gender essentialist, totalizing, and reductive analysis of prostitution.

On the other side of the divide stand those who might loosely be described as "sex work feminists." They reject the assumption that prostitution is intrinsically degrading and, treating prostitution as a form of service work, make a strong distinction between "free choice" prostitution by adults and all forms of forced and child prostitution. Whilst the latter should be outlawed, the former can be an economic activity like any other, and should be legally and socially treated as such. This perspective emphasizes women's capacity (and right) to act as moral agents within prostitution.

Male sex workers rarely feature in such debates on the rights and wrongs of prostitution, and this may partly reflect an (untested) assumption that sexual transactions between men are inherently less exploitative than those involving a female seller and a male buyer. Research on male prostitutes' experience has largely been driven by concerns about sexual health and HIV/AIDS prevention, and to a lesser extent by interest in the relationship between male sex work and gay identities.

SEE ALSO: Globalization, Sexuality and; Sex and Gender; Sex Tourism; Sexual Politics; Sexualities and Consumption; Sexuality, Masculinity and

REFERENCE

Davis, K. (1937) The sociology of prostitution. *American Sociological Review* 2 (October): 746–55.

SUGGESTED READINGS

Aggleton, P. (ed.) (1999) *Men Who Sell Sex*. UCL Press, London.

O'Connell Davidson, J. (2005) *Children in the Global Sex Trade*. Polity Press, Cambridge.

JULIA O'CONNELL DAVIDSON

psychoanalysis

When sociologists speak about psychoanalysis, they usually refer to Freud's structural theory of id, ego, and superego. But that is by no means a defining feature of psychoanalysis. Psychoanalysis is a theoretical perspective that focuses on the unconscious mental processes. To Freud, the father of psychoanalysis, our thoughts, feelings and behavior are determined by factors that are outside of our conscious awareness. Freud defined psychoanalysis as a form of therapy, a mode of observation and inquiry, and a theoretical system. However, his passion lay primarily in psychoanalysis as a mode of scientific investigation. Psychoanalytic theory is based on Freud's image of the individual and his notion of psychic reality. The individual's perception and conception of the self, the other, and the world in which he or she resides are by and large illusory. The individual is presented as profane, irrational, self-deceptive, narcissistic, power hungry, and the slave of the most primitive desires. This is the image of the decentered man, and is perhaps one reason for Freud's popularity among postmodernists. According to psychoanalytic theory, the ground on which the individual stands is paved with uncertainty, and the reality to which he or she appeals is highly suspect. The past is a reconstruction, the memory is a perception, and the perception is a fantasy. The person's conviction of the validity of recall is much more important than its factual authenticity. As with symbolic interaction theory, Freud was concerned not with the "real" situation but with the individual's interpretations of it. Deconstructing such interpretations is the goal of psychoanalysis. Although psychoanalysis has gone through profound changes since Freud, it continues to remain an elegant mode of listening to a patient or reading a text. Contrary to other psychotherapeutic techniques, the analyst does not ask the patient to change, to give up his symptoms, to be normal, to adapt or behave in a particular way. The analyst is not to have any desire or plan for the patient but to help him discover his own desires rather than being the slave to others' demands. The desired outcome of a successful psychoanalytic treatment is a person who has few skeletons in his or her unconscious closet and is free to think, feel and act in the stage of life. Psychoanalytic treatment evolves primarily around the analysis of transference. Transference is what the patient brings to the analytic situation. It is the patient's characteristic mode of conflict, perception, expectation, object relation, or definitions of situations. These internalized patterns of conflict, object relation, and expectation tend to constrain the individual's external relations and to create problems that must be worked through.

The methodological debates in psychoanalysis today are reminiscent of those in psychology and sociology almost a half century ago. A lively debate is in progress in psychoanalysis between those who call themselves "natural" scientists and those who maintain that psychoanalysis is inherently interpretive and hermeneutic and should be studied with that fact in mind. There are also those who agree with the interpretive tradition, but maintain that psychoanalysis goes beyond the hermeneutic method in that the impact of interpretation can be subjected to empirical study. Since psychoanalytic data consist of emotional exchanges in the analytic situation, the primary method of investigation in psychoanalysis remains participant observation and case study.

SEE ALSO: Freud, Sigmund; Mind; Postmodernism

SUGGESTED READINGS

Freud, S. (1957) [1904] Psychoanalytic procedure. In: Strachey, J. (ed. and trans.), *Standard Edition of*

the Complete Psychological Works of Sigmund Freud, vol. 7. Hogarth Press, London, pp. 249–56.
Gill, M. (1994) *Psychoanalysis in Transition*. Analytic Press, Hillsdale, NJ.
Movahedi, S. and Wagner, A. (2005) The "voice" of the analysand and the "subject" of diagnosis. *Contemporary Psychoanalysis* 41 (2): 281–305.

SIAMAK MOVAHEDI

psychological social psychology

Psychological social psychology is concerned with social influences on individual behavior. In its century of modern history, psychological social psychology has addressed issues of attitude, perception, memory, prejudice, personality, emotion, conformity, learning, socialization, persuasion, and cognition. In topics, methods, and theory there has been minimal overlap with sociological social psychology primarily because of psychology's persistent emphasis on the individual as the most important unit of analysis.

One of the more foundational works was accomplished by Floyd Allport in his 1924 *Social Psychology*. Allport identified social psychology as an exclusive subfield of psychology, and as an experimental science of the individual, dismissing what he saw as sociology's reliance on imaginary social forces to explain human behavior. In casting social psychology as an experimental science, Allport invited the control and predictability of the laboratory. These central features of early social psychology created a divide between psychological and sociological social psychologies that has lasted to the present. The division becomes sharper in consideration of how Allport set the direction of causal analysis. Phenomena for sociology – contexts, conditions, or structures – in psychological study became relevant only insofar as they influenced individual behavior. Moreover, features of the individual could be formulated as dependent variables. So while sociologists were struggling with the self as dependent upon and determined by social relations, psychologists were able to investigate the impact of social variables on stable entities like personalities.

Survey research and psychological testing found places in social psychology as new, sophisticated tools were invented. Thurstone proposed attitude scaling measures by 1929 (the first publication year of the *Journal of Social Psychology*), and by 1932 Likert had perfected the simple 1 to 7 continuum of agreement and disagreement. The most memorable stagecraft in experimental social psychology was also a product of this era. A classic example of laboratory experiments in social influence is Sherif's study of group convergence in judging the movement of a light. Although the light in his laboratory was stationary, autokinetic effects produced the illusion of movement, and Sherif found that individuals tailored their reports about the distance a light moves to fit a group norm. This study was modeled by many researchers over the next 40 years, and the famous conformity studies of the 1940s and 1950s by Solomon Asch and the obedience studies of the 1960s by Stanley Milgram are often mentioned in tandem with Sherif's work.

Increasingly complex instances of social influence were managed in laboratories throughout the middle decades of the twentieth century. The acclaimed creative champion was the gestalt psychologist Kurt Lewin, whose influential field theories and group dynamics characterized psychology as a social science. Lewin felt that psychology should consider the total situation of an individual's "life spaces" by attending to environmental and social variables. The energizing work of Lewin and the influence of gestalt principles fostered a new family of cognitive social psychologies. These perspectives are linked by the observation of a basic urge to see consistency in and between thoughts and feelings. Fritz Heider's balance theories were the first in this generation of contemporary influences. Heider asserted that individuals confronted with incomplete information about others will pattern beliefs, attitudes, or motives of others in consistent and sensible ways. These can be familiar processes such as friends assuming they share attitudes, beliefs, or tastes about things they have not discussed. They can also be complex, as when an individual attributes motives to a stranger. Regardless of the relative accuracy of assumptions and attributions, people will try to balance their elements.

The touchstone for cognitive social psychologies is cognitive dissonance theory. As interest in the processing of conflicting information grew, Leon Festinger's observations of the consequences of holding contradictory thoughts and feelings were among the most discussed, cited, and developed findings in all of modern psychology. Festinger's initial assumptions were simple: two cognitive elements in relation to each other will produce consonance or dissonance. Opposing thoughts or feelings produce uncomfortable dissonance in individuals. They will try to reduce it.

In its present incarnation, psychological social psychology is mostly in the business of formalizing and mathematizing theories, and making incremental refinements in perspectives through controlled experimentation. Along with long-term adherence to the study of individuals and to strict scientific protocols, this provides a contrast to sociological social psychology – seen as absent controls, struggling with methods, and grappling with many versions of its basic unit of analysis. At present, social psychological research in the traditions of analyzing individual behavior has had the most impact on exchange, rational choice, and expectation states perspectives – the most psychological of the sociological social psychologies.

SEE ALSO: Asch Experiments; Cognitive Dissonance Theory (Festinger); Exchange Network Theory; Expectation States Theory; Milgram, Stanley (Experiments); Social Psychology

SUGGESTED READINGS

Boutilier, R. G., Roed, J. C., & Svendsen, A. C. (1980) Crises in the two social psychologies: a critical comparison. *Social Psychology Quarterly* 43 (1): 5–17.

House, J. S. (1977) The three faces of social psychology. *Sociometry* 40 (2): 161–77.

Lewin, K., Lippitt, R., & White, R. (1939) Patterns of aggressive behavior in experimentally created "social climates." *Journal of Social Psychology* 10: 271–99.

JOEL POWELL

Psychology

Psychology is the scientific study of individual behavior and mental processes. Psychologists divide their work into pure and applied fields. Pure researchers have adopted the investigative methods of the natural sciences (i.e. positivist empiricism and variants) and study the fundamental processes that are said to undergird human behavior. Applied practitioners have pursued "in the world" applications of psychological research such as clinical and counseling psychology.

Wilhelm Wundt (1832–1920) is considered the "father" of experimental psychology since he founded the first psychology laboratory in Leipzig, Germany in 1879. Wundt pioneered the method of introspection and gave rise to structuralist psychology. Structuralism assumed that psychological processes could be reduced to more basic elements. Introspection sought these elements by pairing the methods of psychophysics with rigorous self-observation of internal states. Recent debates over Wundt's legacy have questioned the centrality of experimental methods to his research program. Indeed, Wundt dedicated the last 20 years of his career to the development of a cultural psychology, published as the 10-volume *Völkerpsychologie* ("folk psychology") in which he argued that higher level psychological phenomena could only be understood through the comparative, historical, and interpretive methods of the human sciences.

Historians note two further influences on early psychological research (Danziger 1990). French clinical practice, exemplified in the work of Jean Martin Charcot (1825–93), provided the impetus for a psychology modeled on the medical relationship between doctor and patient. A third model was developed by Francis Galton (1822–1911) who drew on educational testing techniques from English and French schools to develop psychometric measures of, for example, intelligence.

In the late nineteenth and early twentieth century scientific psychology moved from Germany to America and emerged in two forms: functionalism and behaviorism. William James (1842–1910) introduced the "New Psychology" of functionalism which drew on Darwinian evolutionary theory, and conceived of human beings as entities always in relationship to their environments. John Watson (1878–1958) radicalized American functionalism through the introduction of behaviorist psychology. In his 1913 manifesto "Psychology as the Behaviorist Views It" Watson argued that psychologists should take as their objects of study only overt, directly visible phenomena such as the movements of organisms. The principles of behaviorism were further extended by Burrhus Frederic Skinner (1904–90) who developed the field of radical behaviorism and conducted research on "operant conditioning."

Despite the expectation that behaviorism would become the foundation for scientific psychology it was under heavy attack by the 1950s. Within psychology it became apparent that complex human behaviors could not be explained by reference to external conditioning processes alone. From outside of psychology, the linguist Noam Chomsky demonstrated the inadequacy of behaviorist concepts for the explanation of even the simplest verbal behaviors. Since the 1960s, cognitive psychology has been the dominant approach in experimental psychology. Encouraged by the invention of the electronic computer and research in cybernetic theory, cognitive psychologists took the computer as analogue for the human mind and cognitive processes. More recently cognitive psychology has allied itself with neuroscience to create the influential field of cognitive neuroscience.

Despite the dominance of scientifically based psychology, since its beginnings psychology has also been a contested field. Against the reductionist explanations offered by mainstream psychology, human science approaches advocate a holistic understanding of human beings. In turn of the century Germany this was represented by gestalt psychology, and later the social psychology of German-American immigrant Kurt Lewin. This alternative was also reflected in the humanist movement of the 1960s, and more recently in Amedeo Giorgi's phenomenological research program.

Reflecting a concern for sociological issues, other psychologists have addressed questions of exclusion and ideology. Marxist critics argue that mainstream psychology is a bourgeois enterprise that reflects the concerns and interests of capital, and promotes an American version of the human subject. In contrast, Marxist psychologies have offered conceptions of human psychology grounded in material-historic conditions. Since the 1970s we have also seen the development of feminist psychologies. Feminist critics argue that as it has been practiced scientific psychology reflects primarily male interests and thus its findings are irrelevant to the lives of women. While some feminists argue for greater equality within the discipline, others insist that the scientific method itself is antithetical to the interests of women. Feminist alternatives have been advanced under the umbrella of standpoint theory, which focuses on explicating the unique character of women's experience, and poststructuralist theory, which relies upon the methods of deconstruction to demonstrate the manner in which psychology is implicated in the constructions of femininity, masculinity, gender and sexuality. Psychology has also been shaped by work in postcolonial and anti-racist theory. Critics argue two points. First, by claiming relationships between race and psychological capacities like "intelligence" some psychologists (e.g. Francis Galton and Phillip Rushton) have advanced racist agendas. Second, even when not overtly racist, psychologists frequently impose western psychological constructs (intelligence, personality, attention) in their analysis of non-western subjects. As an alternative, postcolonial psychologists develop approaches grounded in the language and practices of indigenous communities.

Though these critical psychologies have remained for the most part on the periphery, recent years have seen the emergence of a formidable metatheoretical alternative to the positivist mainstream: social constructionism. This approach grows out of critiques of science offered by Thomas Kuhn, Paul Feyerabend, Peter Winch, Charles Taylor, and others. It draws upon French poststructuralism, pragmatism and ordinary language philosophy and places discourse and language use at the center of psychological analysis. It also offers a relational conception of persons to counter the individualism that dominates mainstream psychology. Though there is ongoing debate, with its focus on critique, the constructionist metatheory has united critical psychological alternatives. In this regard, as it moves into the twenty-first century psychology is well-equipped to provide normative, critical, and interdisciplinary knowledge.

SEE ALSO: Behaviorism; Freud, Sigmund; Madness; Milgram, Stanley (Experiments); Psychoanalysis; Psychological Social Psychology; Social Psychology

SUGGESTED READINGS

Danziger, K. (1990) *Constructing the Subject: Historical Origins of Psychological Research*. Cambridge University Press, New York.

Holzkamp, K. (1972) *Kritische Psychologie: Vobereitende Arbeiten* (*Critical Psychology: Preparatory Works*). Fischer, Frankfurt am Main.

Teo, T. (2005) *The Critique of Psychology: From Kant to Postcolonial Theory*. Springer, New York.

Wilkinson, S. & Kitzinger, C. (1996). *Feminism and Discourse: Psychological Perspectives*. Sage, London.

JEFF STEPNISKY

public opinion

Three distinct perspectives emerge in the literature on public opinion. From the individual level perspective public opinion is conceived as an aggregation of the preferences of a group of individuals. At the collective level public opinion is an emergent product of debate and discussion. Public opinion is also defined as a communication process that allows people to organize into publics within which opinions are formed and which enable them to exercise their influence.

Within these perspectives public opinion can be seen as rational or as a form of social control. In the rational model of public opinion, people are understood to develop their opinions during a public debate by listening to and presenting arguments in which their opinions are rationally sound judgments based on thoughtful consideration. Public opinion is also conceived, however, as a form of social control, where its role is to promote social integration and to ensure that there is a sufficient level of consensus on which actions and decisions may be based. Exposure to the media and participation in discussions allow people to assess the extent of consensus and controversy. It is this mutual awareness of the extent of consensus and controversy which ensures that public opinion can act as a social force.

To gauge public opinion one can attend to the mass media, communicate with colleagues and citizens, conduct focus groups, and monitor the behavior of citizens. The opinion poll, however, is the most ubiquitous and authoritative measurement instrument. Opinion polling has changed the essential nature of public opinion itself. The assumption implicit in all polls that everyone might have an opinion and that all opinions are equally important creates an impression of public opinion as the aggregate of opinions of individuals. In some situations one might even say that opinion polls have replaced public opinion. When heeding public opinion, politicians increasingly turn to opinion polls in order to validate and defend their positions on the issues of the day. This phenomenon is included in the following definition of public opinion (De Boer & 't Hart, 2007): "Public opinion is the collection of opinions about an issue within a public, which are expressed in communication and/or the opinions about the issue, which are ascribed to the public" (p. 49).

SEE ALSO: Hegemony and the Media; Media; Public Sphere

REFERENCE

De Boer, C & 't Hart, H. (2007). *Publieke opinie* (*Public Opinion*). Boom, Amsterdam.

CONNIE DE BOER

public and private

The distinction between public and private life has been a useful tool for charting long-term social change and comparing societies. In classical Greece the equivalent distinction was between participation in the (public) life of the polis and the management of one's (private) household, where the political life was higher and more self-sufficient (Aristotle) than the meeting of material needs; privacy here implies privation, falling short of a fully human life. This ideal of the polis has hovered over social and political thought ever since. But it began to fade with the emergence of modern industrial society. For if in feudal society political power is the source of wealth, mature industrial society makes possible the pursuit of wealth without recourse to politics, and the putting of self-interest before the public good. Politics in the form of the modern state then becomes either a framework for the pursuit of individual self-interest (liberalism) or a mechanism for the maximization of collective wealth (in modern welfare states or under socialism). In either case politics becomes a means with which something else can be achieved. A sustained assault on this development is found in the writings of Arendt, Oakeshott, and Wolin. Against this judgment stands the claim, popular with eighteenth-century political economy, that it is precisely the pursuit of private gain in commercial society which opens individuals to the variousness of human affairs and indirectly fosters the moral sentiments consistent with public virtue.

If classicist political theory equates public/private with politics/economics and laments the triumph of privacy, then sociology, social history, and philosophy introduce new distributions. In sociology, the pursuit of individual self-interest brings with it a more complex division of labor, the growth of new forms of refinement, and new marks of social distinction. Privacy begins to be equated not with the household economy but with the family as a source of individual labor. This individualization is fostered by a new organization of domestic space, and also by the growth of the city, with its possibilities of distance, reserve, and secrecy (Simmel); this is grafted on to already-existing ideas about the inwardness of the self found in Protestantism. Public/private implies external/internal to the self.

The tradition of philosophy which begins with Kant provides another sense of public and private. The fusion of eighteenth-century rationalism with German pietism led Kant to the "deontological" view of the self, in which individuals have the capacity to abstract from all of their determinate social and political relations. The fruit of such abstraction is not introspection or brooding, but the discovery of the individual's capacity for reason and judgment; at their most inward and private, individuals discover the moral law, a principle of duty which is the same for all. Individuals are also equipped with the capacity to make use of their unaided, autonomous reason in public. "Public" here is not the same as politics in the classical sense, but implies a republic of letters located between the private sphere and that of government and administration. For Habermas, the twentieth century sees the loss of the public sphere in this sense, as a result of the interpenetration of state and society under welfare regimes and political democracy. A series of partial publics dominated by large bureaucracies emerges, overlain with a thin veneer of publicity in the form of "public opinion," to be mobilized for demagogic as well as democratic purposes.

Alongside the idea of a loss of the public-as-polis, and of the public-as-republic-of-letters, lies a third theme: the loss of civility, that is, of civil behavior between strangers. Phrases such as the culture of narcissism, the triumph of the therapeutic (Rieff 1966) or the fall of public man (Sennett 1977) imply a triumph of individualism so complete that public questions are seen in private terms, the world is seen as a mirror of the self, and those forms of collectivity that do arise are forms of community based upon the private principle of resemblance-to-self rather than the public principle of communal purpose.

Curiously enough, in the 1960s this plea for civility, and for a distinction between private and public matters, ran up against the feminist slogan "the personal is political". Here, the neglect of power mechanisms in the sphere of personal relations is a major lacuna in modern thought; and the very tradition at whose heart is the polis, or the public sphere, is pervaded by masculinist reason. This viewpoint has had a significant effect, both on public and private life, and on scholarship.

SEE ALSO: Households; Politics; Public Opinion; Public Sphere; Welfare State

REFERENCES

Rieff, P. (1966) *The Triumph of the Therapeutic*. Chatto & Windus, London.
Sennett, R. (1977) *The Fall of Public Man*. Faber, London.

SUGGESTED READING

Habermas, J. (1982) [1962] *The Structural Transformation of the Public Sphere*. Polity Press, Cambridge.

CHARLES TURNER

public sphere

The concept of the public sphere has become a key term in sociology since it was introduced by Jürgen Habermas as a sociologically pertinent concept. The public sphere refers to the space that exists in modern societies between the state and society. It concerns a domain that is generally related to civil society, but goes beyond it to refer to the wider category of the public. The public sphere comes into existence with the formation of civil society and the forms of associational politics to which it led.

According to Habermas (1989), modern society from the seventeenth century to the early nineteenth century saw the emergence of a social domain distinct from court society, on the one side, and the absolute state, on the other. This was the space of the public, which was formed in new spaces such as the coffee house, public libraries, a free press, and wherever public debate took place outside formal institutions. One of its main features was public opinion. Initially, the public sphere was defined by opposition to the court society, but it also increasingly became defined by opposition to the private domain of domestic life. In Habermas's early theory of the public sphere, it was characteristically associated with the political and cultural world of the European Enlightenment.

SEE ALSO: Modernity; Privatization; Public and Private

REFERENCE

Habermas, J. (1989) *The Structural Transformation of the Public Sphere*. Polity Press, Cambridge.

GERARD DELANTY

Q

qualitative methods

Methodological debate is at the heart of much discourse about the state and direction of sociology. This article describes qualitative methods, exploring epistemic and practical features, often in contrast to quantitative approaches.

For any research question, there are a number of possible strategies for exploration. One may wish to know how mortality is affected by poverty. To answer this question, the researcher might collect data to see if these are statistically correlated. If as the rate of poverty increases the mortality rate also increases, we may have good reason to assert that mortality is predicted, at least partly, by poverty. However, another researcher may want to understand how death is understood among that population. Here, the question concerns what death means, rather than what predicts it. For these questions, one must gain an intimate knowledge of people and their culture, how they view death in particular and the world in general. While quantitative methods can answer the first question, qualitative methods better address the second.

Fluid dialogue and development of a partnership between the researcher and respondent highlight an important aspect of qualitative research: the researcher is a fundamental part of the research, not only the proctor of a questionnaire. Beyond the ostensible subject matter of the interview, qualitative researchers must pick up on markers such as subtle passing remarks, tone of voice, facial expressions, and body language. The ability to follow these lines of inquiry is partly what enables qualitative research to achieve depth.

Quantitative approaches can compare large numbers of people using structured techniques. Qualitative research is not usually able to make such concise comparisons, but rather the researcher must interpret individualized responses. Qualitative research is therefore seen as inductive. That is, there is nothing concrete to indicate what the data mean. For example, a quantitative researcher might ask how often someone had trouble paying bills and quantify responses. But the qualitative researcher would follow this same question with probing statements such as, "Tell me about that," in order to explore the intimate features of that experience. In the quantitative version, the respondents who "often" have trouble paying bills are assigned the number "4" and those who never do are assigned a "0". This type of data minimizes interpretation; four is greater than zero. Some assert that this controls researcher bias, which remains problematic for qualitative methodologists. However, many suggest that quantitative research is by no means deductive. The quantitative researcher still must ultimately speculate about whether one phenomenon *causes* another or whether they simply are correlated, and also whether the statistical measurements of a concept actually measure that phenomenon (e.g. whether trouble paying bills actually measures socioeconomic status).

Based on these fundamentally different approaches, quantitative and qualitative methods often are seen as resting on different epistemological foundations. Qualitative methods mostly are conceived as founded on interpretivism, the notion that all knowledge is fundamentally dependent on human observation and conceptualization. Quantitative methods often proceed from positivist foundations asserting that there is a reality independent of human observation that can be known using scientific methods. However, the interpretivist–positivist dichotomy does not neatly overlay the qualitative–quantitative one. For example, early ethnographic work (e.g., Malinowski, Evans-Pritchard) was based on decidedly positivist epistemology, interpretivism does not preclude the use of quantitative methods, properly contextualized.

The interpretivist underpinnings of qualitative methodology and its lack of structured research techniques are the focal point of criticism. Because the data collected cannot be easily compared between respondents in the study or between various different studies, nor can they be deductively generalized, critics charge that the results from qualitative work amount to little more than the researcher's subjective impressions.

Responses to these criticisms have been varied. Some researchers have quantified qualitative data, for example by counting up references to particular concepts. While this provides comparable data, it does little to address the subjectivity in the interview process, the coding process, or the interpretation of subsequently quantified data. Another response has been to use an experimental design for qualitative studies. Others simply have been unapologetic about their interpretive episteme. These researchers assert that quantitative work is equally plagued by subjectivity. While a valid retort, proactively addressing the question of bias seems to be the foremost challenge for qualitative research.

Even if subjective bias cannot be eliminated, perhaps it can be overcome by exposing it to the audience. This is the thrust of reflexive ethnography, where researchers actively analyze themselves as a fundamental part of the research. If these biases are exposed, they not only become less problematic, but can actually be informative. Some even locate the researcher as the central object of analysis, an approach labeled by Hayano (1979) as autoethnography.

Additionally, while the qualitative interview is relatively unstructured, qualitative researchers still utilize a conceptual framework. For example, Harrington (2003) asserts that various issues of population access and researcher-participant interaction can be organized under conceptual frameworks of social identity and self-presentation. If multiple studies were similarly organized, these frameworks could provide structure that would allow comparison of researcher narratives.

Grounded theory suggests a relatively formalized process for analyzing qualitative data, which does not rely on quantification. Grounded theory is a method for generating theory rather than testing it, which is the thrust of quantitative work, and it works by coding data into concepts in a hierarchical and dialogical fashion so that insights emerge from the data rather than being supposed in advance. This comparative transparency exposes biases in the analytical process.

Grounded theory provides a systematic method for deriving concepts, but not conceptual structures; we can delineate the concepts of health and poverty, but theory is produced by explicating their relationship not just their mutual existence. Researchers are beginning to address this by utilizing non-linear logic to understand and model the complex phenomenon of social life. Fractal logic for example illustrates how social systems can be investigated qualitatively in a systematic way, without dulling the depth and complexity that are the hallmarks of qualitative work.

Sociologists largely recognize that the split between qualitative and quantitative methodologies is dogmatic and somewhat arbitrary. Still, this dichotomy often frames disciplinary practices. Perhaps the most important future challenge for sociology as a whole will be overcoming its methodological divide, a goal often discussed and rarely acted upon.

SEE ALSO: Action Research; Content Analysis; Ethics, Fieldwork; Ethics, Research; Ethnography; Grounded Theory; Observation, Participant and Non-Participant; Quantitative Methods; Reflexivity

REFERENCES

Harrington, B. (2003) The social psychology of access in ethnographic research. *Journal of Contemporary Ethnography* (32): 592–625.

Hayano, D. (1979) Auto-ethnography: paradigms, problems, and prospects. *Human Organization* (38): 113–20.

SUGGESTED READINGS

Denzin, N. K. & Lincoln, Y. S. (2007) The discipline and practice of qualitative research. In: Denzin, N. K. & Lincoln, Y. S. (eds.), *Collecting and Interpreting Qualitative Materials*. Sage, Thousand Oaks, CA, pp. 1–44.

Glaser, B. G. & Strauss, A. L. (1967) *The Discovery of Grounded Theory, Strategies for Qualitative Research*. Aldine, New York.

JEFFREY MICHAEL CLAIR AND JASON WASSERMAN

quantitative methods

Quantitative methods in sociology pertain to research methods of collecting and analyzing data which will eventually lead to statistical analyses. These analyses, for the most part, use probability statistics to make generalizations applicable to the larger population using data gathered from a representative sample. This idea of generalization is the key concept driving quantitative research methods. Research using quantitative methods broadly includes four major parts: sampling, measurement, design and analysis.

Sampling is the process of selecting units from a population of interest so that by studying the sample we may be able to generalize the findings to the population. For example if your population of interest is female students at your university, then you first need to get a list of all female students at your university. This list is the sampling frame from which you will select the participants for your study. You can select participants for your study using a variety of sampling methods. For example, you can write the names on little pieces of paper and use a lottery method to pick out a sample of

100 participants from the sampling frame for your study. Using a random sample (such as the one in the example), ensures that you can generalize back to the population of interest. Other examples of sampling methods include stratified sampling, cluster sampling, and convenience sampling.

Measurement is the process by which you observe and record information collected as part of the research process. First in this process one has to decide how the information is going to be collected (questionnaire survey or interview) and at what level of measurement. Questionnaires either in the form or surveys or interviews are the most common methods of collecting data for quantitative research methods. The questionnaires can be mailed to individuals (example census) or these days they are more commonly collected web based forms (example: you can create an online survey using www.surveymoneky.com or similar services).

Whatever the method, the questionnaires are highly structured such that the same information is collected from each individual. Within the questionnaire, depending on the type of question different levels of measurement are used. The four levels of measurement are nominal, ordinal, interval and ratio. *Nominal* level measurement collects the "name" of the attribute (example: names of people, names of countries or cities). In *ordinal* level of measurement the attributes can be ordered (example: your rating of iTunes songs on a range of 0 to 5 stars, where more stars indicate a higher rating; but you are not able to say that the distance between 0 to 1 star is the same as the distance between 4 to 5 star meaning that the interval between values cannot be interpreted in an ordinal measure). In an *interval* level of measurement the distance between two attributes has meaning (example: when you measure temperature (in - Fahrenheit), the distance from 20 to 30 is the same as distance from 50 to 60. The interval between values is interpretable, but the "zero" value of temperature is not defined and therefore 60F is not twice as hot as 30F). In the *ratio* level of measurement there is always an absolute zero that is meaningful (example: an income of $50,000 is twice as much as $25,000 and an income of $0 means a person has no income). Using these methods, one collects data about a large number of individual variables from a sample of people. This type of quantitative data can then be tested for reliability (whether the same questionnaire used by a different person would give the same results?), validity (do you have evidence that what you did in the study caused what you observed to happen?), and representativeness (how generalizable is this study?) using statistical techniques.

Design is the process by which all parts of the research are pieced together to answer the specific research question. Designs could be experimental, quasi-experimental or cross-sectional in nature depending on the specific research question or hypotheses.

Regardless of the type of design used, the data collected needs to be analyzed using statistical methods to generate the findings of the study. There are numerous statistics computer programs such as SPSS (or PASW now), SAS, Stata etc, using which one can do simple or complex statistical analyses. The data that has been collected using the questionnaire need to be coded, entered into the program and appropriate statistical analyses conducted. Simple descriptive analyses such as mean, median, mode, variance and standard deviation provide basic information about the sample/population. Further, depending on the design of the study and the specific hypothesis, inferential analyses such as t-tests (to compare two groups), ANOVA (to compare multiple groups), Pearson's correlation (to compare the degree of relationship between two variables) etc. can be conducted. If the results of the analysis are statistically significant above a certain threshold, then the results of the research are not due to chance and the hypothesis is proven.

SEE ALSO: Descriptive Statistics; Statistical Significance Testing; Statistics; Survey Research; Variables; Variables, Dependent; Variables, Independent

SUGGESTED READINGS

Black, T. R. (1999). *Doing Quantitative Research in the Social Sciences: An Integrated Approach to Research Design, Measurement and Statistics.* Sage, London.

Field, A. (2009) *Discovering Statistics Using SPSS.* Sage, London.

SHEETAL RANJAN

queer theory

Queer theory is a loosely defined interdisciplinary set of critiques and perspectives which call into question those political, cultural, and social forces which traditionally naturalized categories of sexual orientation and gender identity. Queer theory often defines its position as existing in contrast to studies of "gay and lesbian" history or politics in that it emphasizes the non-assimilating aspect of queerness into such normalizing categories. While gay and lesbian studies theorists emphasize the need for a history of gay and lesbian lives, queer theory points to those lives and experiences which fail to fit these very categories, pointing to the cultural and historical specificity of such formations of gender and sexuality. Grounded in such accounts of the experience of being queer – of not fitting the available categories of sexual orientation – queer theory takes these subject positions seriously and theorizes from such a perspective. This allows queer theory to turn back upon the social field critically in order to attempt to expose the social forces which have organized knowledge practices such that equate heterosexuality with human nature.

Drawing from the social constructionist approach of feminist and post-structural critiques, queer theory has argued against the innate "naturalness" of heterosexuality. Queer theory criticizes the heterosexual/homosexual binary and the way it can exercise power to obscure those sexual experiences and identities which do not easily fit these categories. Instead of asking the proper categories which should organize sexuality, queer theory is critical of these very formations, tying them to the exercise of disciplinary, subjectivizing power. In this account, both homosexuality and heterosexuality are seen as socially constructed and produced by similar linguistic categories of power-knowledge formations. Michel Foucault's account (1978: *The History of Sexuality*, vol. 1) of the productive power of discourse has been a strong foundation of queer theory, offering both a means of understanding the social and historical specificity of the knowledge categories of sexual orientation and also the use of sexual orientation to normalize the population. Building on Foucault, theorist Judith Butler (1997) argues that one's sexual orientation becomes intelligible through the enactment of these categories on the body, and that their repetition is what gives them stability or power, that which makes them intelligible. Bodies "come to matter" when they fit these formations. The repetition of normative categories asserts their power and dominance. Materiality does not exist prior to epistemology, unmarked. The categories of sexual difference, are, therefore, not natural representations of material or scientific fact, but socially constructed formations of power-knowledge.

Queer theorists have been openly critical of gay and lesbian mainstream politics that seeks rights and acceptance through discourses of "normality." Such positioning both fails to recognize the exercise of power-knowledge through categories of normal and pathological, the same discursive structures which produced queer as a kind of perversion in history, and also re-essentializes the category of LGBT as stable and fixed. Michael Warner (1999: *The Trouble with Normal*) for example, has offered a critique of the cultural forces, pressures, discourses, and productions that have lead to the exercise of power through the normalization of heterosexuality (heteronormativity) and the related homosexual discourse of normality (homonormativity). In fact, whereas mainstream gay and lesbian politics seek equal rights and increased visibility, in contrast queer theory often embraces, celebrates, and theorizes its own invisibility. This is especially present in studies of queers in environments that are more distant from the reach of this emerging western homonormative rights-driven discourse.

Recent queer theory has moved farther and farther from identity politics toward problematizing the boundaries of queerness beyond its original connection to sexual orientation or gender, applying a queer analysis to not only boundaries of sexual orientation and identity, but to the boundaries between bodies, selves, and affect. The critique of borders and boundaries of queer theory has influenced other intellectual currents of thought, such as post-humanism and technology studies. Most recently, scholars have imported the "affective turn" (Clough 2007), a focus on the body's capacity to affect and be affected, with an emphasizing how queer organizes the body's felt sensations. Others have illustrated that queerness is intricately tied together with discourses and relations of race and disability.

SEE ALSO: Body and Sexuality; Compulsory Heterosexuality; Identity Politics/Relational Politics; Postmodern Sexualities; Sexual Politics; Sexualities and Culture Wars

REFERENCES

Butler, J. (1997) Critically queer. In: Phelan, S. (ed.), *Playing With Fire*. Routledge, New York, pp. 11–30.

Clough, P. T. & Halley, J. (eds.) (2007) *The Affective Turn: Theorizing the Social*. Duke University Press, Durham, NC, and London.

KIMBERLY JASPER CUNNINGHAM

R

race

To sociologists, race is a system of stratification based on physical differences ("phenotypes") that are seen as essential and permanent. These differences may be real or they may be imagined. Though individuals can and do come to identify in racial terms, race is most important as a system of categorization which is externally imposed. The fact that race is imposed externally is the major difference between it and the concept of ethnicity.

The concept of race emerged relatively recently in human history. Many historians of race believe that the concept of race emerged with modernity and was the consequence of two major developments in European society: first, the development of a capitalist ethos which blamed those who did not progress for their own fate; and second, the British experience of colonizing the Irish, which prepared them for future experiences in colonization and racial hierarchies. Others point to the important role of Christian religious thought, particularly the Myth of Ham, a biblical tale which tells how Noah's son Ham and his descendants were condemned to servitude because Ham "looked upon the nakedness of" his father. This story was used by some Christian religious authorities to justify the enslavement of black Africans, since they were seen as the racial descendants of Ham.

With the arrival of the Enlightenment and rational-scientific thought, people turned to scientific methods to seek an understanding of racial differences and to justify their conceptions of racial hierarchies. One of the first scientific projects for racial scholars was the development of comprehensive taxonomies of racial difference. First attempted by Carl Linnaeus in 1758, scholars developed classification schemes which specified the number and variety of human races, ranging from a low of 3 (African, European, and Mongolian) to a high of over 30. These taxonomies were generally based on ideas of the physical, but also included some attributes which we would not today think of as biologically-based, such as clothing and cultural behavior.

As the modern scientific method developed, scientists who studied human variation came to believe that it was not sufficient to label races based on classifiers' superstitions or beliefs. Instead, they pushed for the development of scientific techniques and experiments that were carefully designed to measure the degree of racial difference and inferiority. The earliest techniques, called craniometry, involved measuring skull capacity and other dimensions of the head. By the late 1800s, most of these techniques had been discredited or were in doubt. After the IQ test was invented in 1905, it was used to demonstrate racial difference and inferiority. IQ tests were successful at producing results that lined up with people's expectations about race and intelligence.

While most contemporary social and biological scientists do not believe that there is any biological or genetic evidence for racial difference, some geneticists have turned to the field of population genetics to look for patterns of genetic expression among supposed racial groups. These geneticists believe that the differences they find may be useful in medical and forensic applications. However, new evidence about the degree of mixing between people from different continents over time casts doubt on this conclusion. In fact, some researchers have suggested that as many as 80 percent or more of American blacks may have some white ancestors in their family tree.

The contemporary image of racial difference varies across national and cultural contexts. In particular, the conception of the dividing lines between racial groups is not the same everywhere. In the USA, race has traditionally been perceived through the lens of the "one-drop rule," meaning that anyone with any degree of black ancestry (even so little as one thirty-second of one's ancestry, and even when the individual appears white) is seen as black. This racial ideology is related to a history in the USA of cultural and legal barriers against miscegenation, or marital and sexual relationships across the color line. Though the rigidity of the one-drop rule has declined as interracial marriage has grown, it still shapes how Americans view racial classifications.

Not all nations and societies stick to such a rigid system of racial classification. In many Caribbean and Latin American societies, there are gradations of race between black and white. Individuals' own places on these scales can vary according to class, education, and skin color, not just ancestry. In many of these countries, miscegenation was not considered to be an especially big problem. Mixing between races and a less rigid color line do not mean that race is any less important in regulating the life chances of individuals in these nations, however. Another variation in the conception of racial difference could be found in South Africa during the time of Apartheid. South Africa's racial order was predicated upon restricting the mixing of races. However, instead of declaring all of those of mixed racial backgrounds to simply be black, in South Africa a new racial category called "colored" was created to take in those who were considered to be neither black nor white.

Race continues to play an important role in individuals' daily lives. According to the American Sociological Association's 2003 statement on race, the effects that it has can be classified into three major categories: sorting people into categories on the basis of which they chose appropriate family members and friends; stratifying people in terms of their access to resources; and organizing people into groups through which they seek to challenge or maintain the racial status quo.

SEE ALSO: Conflict (Racial/Ethnic); Health and Race; Race (Racism); Racism, Structural and Institutional; Stratification, Race/Ethnicity and; Whiteness

REFERENCE

American Sociological Association. (2003) *The Importance of Collecting Data and Doing Research on Race*. Washington, DC.

SUGGESTED READINGS

Bonilla-Silva, E. (2003) *Racism without Racists: Color-Blind Racism and the Persistence of Racial Inequality in the United States*. Rowman and Littlefield, New York.

Gould, S. J. (1996) *The Mismeasure of Man*, 2nd edn. W. W. Norton, New York.

Smedley, A. (1999) *Race in North America*, 2nd edn. Westview Press, Boulder, CO.

Winant, H. (2002) *The World is a Ghetto*. Basic Books, New York.

MIKAILA MARIEL LEMONIK ARTHUR

race and crime

The role of race in the production of criminal conduct has been an issue in US criminology for decades. The fact that African Americans are disproportionately involved as offenders in the criminal justice system in the USA is not in dispute. US public health statistics consistently show homicide is a leading cause of death for black males, and the FBI's Supplementary Homicide Reports suggest that black offenders are responsible for most homicides involving black victims. Black males have been over-represented in both victimization and offender figures for over 35 years. This has not been the case for American Indian, Asian, or "other race" males. Hispanic victims and offenders are not part of a separate racial group and may be counted as white, black, Asian, or American Indian.

Although explanations for these differences have ranged from biological to sociological, most of those trying to explain the differences in black and white arrest and incarceration rates focus on social, cultural, economic, or political factors. For these theorists, patterns of homicide rates by race suggest that the rates are primarily linked to exclusion and segregation – economic, racial, and ethnic – but especially to the separation and isolation of large segments of urban populations based on income and assets.

Sampson and Wilson called attention to the cultural and structural effects of racial and class segregation in 1990 ("A theory of race, crime and urban inequality"). They noted the existence of neighborhoods highly segregated by race, class, and level of family disruption that are isolated from mainstream culture and argued that these neighborhood characteristics were the result of policies of racial segregation, economic transformation, black male joblessness, class-linked out-migration and housing discrimination. They suggested that the structural and cultural disorganization that increased crime rates grew out of residential segregation and separation from work.

Not every criminologist believes that the differences by race found in official data are the result of real differences in behavior. Some criminologists argue that arrest and conviction statistics reflect the racial bias of those operating the system of justice. The strongest evidence for this position comes from studies of the use of drug laws and analyses of motorist stops. Although official definitions of crime are legislative, crime is also defined by administrative policies and enforcement practices. The police, for example, have wide discretion in decisions to arrest and charge. Given the history of race relations in the United States, it would be surprising to find that race does not play a role in some decisions to arrest and convict.

However, reviews of court studies from the 1960s to 2000 produce inconsistent evidence on sentencing disparity by race. Today, many researchers in this area think that it is important to examine context – asking, "When does race matter?" In their review of this literature, Walker et al. (2000) suggest there is evidence that race matters when the crime is less serious, when the victim is white and the accused is not, and when the accused is unemployed. Young black males may be "over arrested" for minor offenses and offenses involving drug possession or sale but a disproportionate number of young black males are involved in murders, rapes, robberies, and other forms of predatory crime. However, in the light of the sad history of race relations in the United States it is hard to identify the reasons for the differences in any of these arrest and offending rates. As in many areas of criminology, there is no shortage of theory, assertion, and speculation. But there is a serious shortage of well focused, dependable research on the relationship of race and crime.

SEE ALSO: Crime; Crime, White Collar; Hate Crimes; Race and the Criminal Justice System; Stratification, Race/Ethnicity and

REFERENCE

Walker, S., Spohn, C., & DeLone, M. (2000) The color of justice: race, ethnicity, and crime in America, 2nd edn. Wadsworth Thomson Learning, Belmont, CA.

SUGGESTED READING

Reiman, J. (2001) *The Rich Get Richer and the Poor Get Prison*. Allyn and Bacon, Boston, MA.

ROLAND CHILTON

race and the criminal justice system

As of 2010, 2 million residents in the USA reside in the country's prisons, more than in any other country. A disproportionately high percentage of these prisoners are minorities, who represent a larger share of the prison population than of the broader population. Blacks are incarcerated at 8.2 times the rate of whites which roughly translates into the incarceration of one in every 20 black men over the age of 18, compared to one in 180 white men.

Researchers explain this racial disparity in rates of incarceration as the result of: 1) the differential treatment of minority offenders in a racially biased criminal justice system; or 2) a higher rate of participation in criminal activity among minority individuals.

The first line of thought argues that the criminal justice system is inherently biased, from the police who disproportionately arrest minorities, to judges who hand down longer sentences, to lawmakers who favor policies that ensnare minority offenders rather than whites. The process from arrest to incarceration requires agents of the criminal justice system to broadly exercise their discretion; however, with discretion comes the possibility that personal beliefs concerning race and criminality affect behavior.

There may be a self-perpetuating cycle in which the perception that most crimes are committed by minorities can produce a reality in which most minorities commit crimes. While false, these perceptions can result in increased surveillance by the police, causing a disproportionate number of minorities to be arrested and incarcerated, thereby reinforcing initial perceptions that justify policies based on race. For example, stereotypes regarding race and crime contribute to practices such as racial profiling in which the police stop, question, and search minorities based on their race/ethnicity. Even if all racial groups committed crimes at the same rate, arrest rates for minority groups would be higher, simply as a result of the increased number of interactions with the police.

Researchers often refer to the drug policies enacted in the 1980s (the "War on drugs") as an example of the system's racial bias. The 100 to 1 disparity in prison arrests for crack, more often sold and used by blacks, versus powder cocaine, more often used by whites, has become a symbol of this bias. While scientists find no basis for distinguishing between the drugs, stiffer penalties for the possession of crack cocaine than for powder cocaine result in a drug-related incarceration rate for black men that is thirteen times greater than the rate for white men.

The second argument suggests that racial differences in patterns of offending and sentencing, and not a racial bias in the criminal justice system, explain the preponderance of minorities in prison. Researchers find that minorities are more likely to commit offenses that result in arrest, incarceration, and long prison sentences. This argument does not necessarily suggest that minorities are more prone to criminality, rather that the intersection of race, poverty, and urban dwelling exposes minority individuals to greater scrutiny by the police and that structural disadvantages increase both the need and the motivation to commit crime.

Spatial segregation contributes to the concentration of poor minorities in central cities which have higher crime and victimization rates while wealthier, white families are dispersed among outlying suburban areas where poverty and crime rates are lower. In poor black neighborhoods, drug transactions are more likely to be conducted on the streets, in public, and between strangers; in white neighborhoods – working class through upper class – drugs are more likely to be sold indoors, at private homes, and between trusted contacts. Statistical evidence indicates drug possession and selling cut across racial, socio-economic and geographic lines, yet because drug law enforcement resources have been concentrated in low-income, predominantly minority urban areas, drug offending whites have been relatively free from arrest.

Why do racial disparities in the criminal justice system matter? Incarceration has enduring effects on individuals, their families, and their communities; as minorities have a higher rate of incarceration and arrest than whites, these effects are predominantly concentrated in minority communities, thereby exacerbating structural disadvantages already present and making it more difficult to escape the problems that plague many of these communities – unemployment, poverty, substance use, and, criminal behavior. Upon release, ex-offenders often suffer reduced wages or unemployment furthering their families' economic instability and contributing to cycles of reoffending. As a consequence of incarceration, individuals can be disenfranchised, losing the right to vote and to receive various public benefits that might provide economic and social support to families and communities in need.

SEE ALSO: Criminal Justice System; Criminology; Race; Race and Crime; Racism, Structural and Institutional

SUGGESTED READINGS

Bobo, L. D. & Thompson, V. (2006) Unfair by design: the war on drugs race, and the legitimacy of the criminal justice system. *Social Research* 73: 445–72.

Robinson, M. (2000) The construction and reinforcement of myths of race and crime. *Journal of Contemporary Criminal Justice* 6: 133–56.

TRACY ROBERTS

race, definitions of

Of all the terms in the social science lexicon, few have generated more heat and less light than "race." It has variously meant:

1 an entire biological species (e.g. "the human race");
2 a biological sub-population within a species, however loosely defined (e.g. "the Caucasoid race");
3 a mixture of several such sub-groups (e.g. "the mestizo race");
4 a group socially defined by ancestry, irrespective of physical appearance (e.g. "the Jewish race");
5 a synonym for ethnic or linguistic group (e.g. "the French race").

Perhaps the term "race" would be best discarded altogether. Yet, many argue that race still matters, both those who believe in it, and those who do not. Perversely, some even claim that the ultimate form of "racism" is denying the significance of race.

What sense, if any, can one make of all this confusion? The general consensus among scientists is that the biological concept of race has little if any use for our species because:

1 there is not much genetic variation in our species;
2 there is more genetic variation within human groups than between them;
3 differences in gene frequencies between groups do not clearly co-vary, and, thus, do not distinguish the same groups;
4 whatever genetic differences may have developed over tens of thousands of years of climactic adaptation during our dispersal out of Africa (e.g. in skin pigmentation) have been extensively blurred by mass migrations and interbreeding in the last few centuries.

Thus, most scientists would conclude, "race" is a social construct, highly variable from culture to culture (e.g. the widely discrepant definition of "black" in, say, Brazil, the USA, India or the Sudan). Its only significance lies in what people in a given time and place make of it, with often serious consequences for the unequal distribution of resources in society.

That said, however, one cannot dismiss the importance of human biology. As a species, we evolved both genetically and culturally in a process of adaptation to a wide range of environments. Our biology and our culture complexly interact to produce genetic, somatic and cultural diversity between human groups. Sometimes a single mutation can have vast cultural consequences, such as the development of adult lactose tolerance and the milking of cattle. Human history is a tale of gene-culture co-evolution. But little if any of that complex process can be captured by the simplistic concept of race, however defined.

SEE ALSO: Critical Race Theory; Race

SUGGESTED READINGS
Banton, M. (1977) *The Idea of Race*. Tavistock, London.
Cashmere, E. E. (1984) *Dictionary of Race and Ethnic Relations*. Routledge and Kegan Paul, London.
van den Berghe, P. L. (1978) *Race and Racism, A Comparative Perspective*. Wiley, New York.

PIERRE L. VAN DEN BERGHE

racism, structural and institutional

When most people think about racism, they think about the concept of individual prejudice – in other words, negative thoughts or stereotypes about a particular racial group. However, racism can also be embedded in the institutions and structures of social life. This type of racism can be called structural or institutional racism (hereafter "institutional racism"), and it is significant in creating and maintaining the disparate outcomes that characterize the landscape of racial inequality. There are two main types of institutional racism. The first, which is called "direct," occurs when policies are consciously designed to have discriminatory effects. These policies can be maintained through the legal system (such as in the case of Jim Crow in the USA); or through conscious institutional practice (such as redlining in residential real estate). The second type, "indirect" institutional racism, includes practices that have disparate racial impacts even without any intent to discriminate (such as network hiring in workplaces).

Institutional racism affects many areas of life, in particular education, housing, economic life, imprisonment, and health care. Indirect institutional racism also continues to affect the lives of people of color, and because it is unconscious, those who maintain institutional structures and policies may not be aware of its existence unless it is challenged by activists or lawsuits. For instance, the Rockefeller drug laws in New York State, enacted in 1973, include very heavy penalties for those selling or possessing narcotics. These laws were enacted with the intent of protecting communities from the scourge of drug sales but have lead to disparate imprisonment of young black men. This is because though individuals of all races use drugs at similar rates, young black men are disproportionately likely to use the particular drugs targeted by the Rockefeller drug laws.

It is much harder for researchers to find evidence of institutional racism than of individual discrimination. This is because it is possible for a set of guidelines to disadvantage a particular racial group while being consistently and fairly applied to all individuals. One of the most powerful tools that has been used to uncover evidence of institutional racism is the audit study method, where testers are matched on all characteristics except for race and sent to apply for jobs or housing. These studies present powerful evidence of the continued effects of institutional racism. For instance, Pager (2003) showed that white men with prison records and black men without prison records who are matched on other characteristics such as education and prior work experience are about equally likely to be hired for entry-level jobs. Similar research has shown that black applicants for home loans or rental apartments are much less likely to be approved, and that people searching for residential real estate are likely to be steered to neighborhoods which match their skin color.

While civil rights legislation banning discrimination both in the public sphere (voting and *de jure* segregation) and the private sphere (universities and housing developments) was passed in the 1960s with the aim of outlawing direct institutional racism, lawsuits are of limited utility when it comes to enforcing such legislation in the absence of concrete evidence of harm to specific individuals. Instead, the best ways to combat institutional racism include becoming conscious of its existence, drafting formal regulations that challenge it, and developing policies that respond to the historical disadvantages faced by communities of color.

SEE ALSO: Discrimination; Prejudice; Privilege; Race; Race (Racism)

REFERENCE
Pager, D. (2003) The mark of a criminal record. *American Journal of Sociology* 108: 937–75.

SUGGESTED READINGS
Brown, M. K., Carnoy, M., Currie E., et al. (2003) *Whitewashing Race: The Myth of a Color-Blind Society*. University of California Press, Berkeley, CA.
Omi, M. & Winant, H. (1994) *Racial Formation in the United States*. Routledge, New York.

MIKAILA MARIEL LEMONIK ARTHUR

radical feminism

Radical feminism arose in the USA, Canada, and Britain out of young women's experiences within the civil rights, New Left, and anti-war movements of the 1960s. It was a revolutionary movement that called for fundamental institutional and cultural changes in society. There were three key beliefs guiding radical feminist activism. First, radical feminism argued that gender was the primary oppression all women face. Second, it asserted that women were fundamentally different from men. Third, it held that social institutions rely on women's subordination, and consequently are constructed to perpetuate gender inequality, including around deeply personal facets like reproduction. Radical feminism was the most dominant force in the development of feminist activism and scholarship through the mid-1970s.

Radical feminism was distinct from the surge in liberal feminist activism that also emerged in the late 1960s. Women formed radical feminist groups such as the London Women's Liberation Workshop, and the Redstockings, seemingly overnight in 1967 and 1968. One of the first protests was held at the opening of the US Congress in January 1968. The "Jeanette Rankin Brigade," named after the first woman elected to Congress and led by Rankin herself, brought 5,000 women affiliated with women's peace groups to demonstrate against the Vietnam War. It was at this protest that the phrase "sisterhood is powerful" was first used.

Radical feminists theorized that sex-class (women as a distinct class) was a social phenomenon maintained through violence and social sanctions. Out of this ideology developed critiques of all social institutions, including language, science, capitalism, family, violence, and law. One of the most important concepts to come out of radical feminism was the idea that the "personal is political," highlighting the belief that women's intimate experiences of oppression were not isolated events, but rather products of institutional inequality. Consciousness-raising (CR) groups – small gatherings where women shared their experiences of sexism and developed a collective feminist critique – originated with the New York Radical Women, and quickly became a staple of radical feminism. It was through these groups that issues such as rape, abortion, and sexuality became politicized issues for feminist movements.

Some of the most significant legacies of radical feminist organizing are the service organizations that grew out of women's liberation groups. Domestic violence shelters were founded in the early 1970s, as were rape crisis centers, feminist bookstores, and women's studies programs. By the end of the 1970s, differences between radical and liberal feminisms became less clear as liberal groups radicalized and radical feminism moved toward cultural and service organizations. Simultaneously, sparked by homophobia within feminist movements, and sexism within gay liberation movements, many lesbian-identified feminists split with radical feminism. Lesbian feminism extended radical feminist ideology and argued that gender and sexuality work together to reinforce patriarchal power.

The central critique of radical feminism has been that theorizing women as a sex-class obscures differences between women, especially in terms of race, class, and nation. In *Black Feminist Thought: Knowledge, Consciousness, and the Politics of Empowerment* (1990) Patricia Hill-Collins described the interrelationships of oppression as a "matrix of domination" and argued that radical feminism marginalized women of color and poor women. Regardless of these critiques radical feminist theorizing has continued to influence feminist activism and scholarship. The institutional legacies, in the form of cultural and political organizations, continue to thrive, and radical feminist ideology continues to shape contemporary feminist movements.

SEE ALSO: Black Feminist Thought; Cultural Feminism; Liberal Feminism; Matrix of Domination; Socialist Feminism

SUGGESTED READINGS

Crow, B. (ed.) (2000) *Radical Feminism: A Documentary Reader*. New York University Press, New York.

Moraga, C. & Anzaldua, G. (eds.) (1981) *This Bridge Called My Back: Writings by Radical Women of Color*. Kitchen Table Press, New York.

EVE SHAPIRO

random sample

A census, which is a survey of every unit in a population, is rarely used to gather information in the social sciences because it is often costly, time consuming, or impracticable. Instead, researchers gather the information from a simple random sample that is assumed to be representative of the population. Such a sample can be obtained by using a simple random sampling procedure. The procedure selects a sample of size n without replacement from a finite population of size $N > n$ such that each of the $N!/[n!(N-n)!]$ possible samples is equally likely to be selected. Simple random sampling has two advantages over non-random sampling. First, randomness avoids bias, that is, a systematic or long-run misrepresentation of the population. Second, randomness enables researchers to apply the laws of probability in determining the likely error of sample statistics. A particular random sample rarely yields a statistic that equals the population parameter. However, the expected value of the statistic over an indefinitely large number of samples will equal the population parameter.

A simple random sample can be obtained in a variety of ways. One method uses a table of random numbers that contains a sequence of digits with two properties: each digit is equally likely to be 0, 1, . . . , 9 and the digits are independent of each other. To select a simple random sample of n units from a population of N units, number the units 01, 02, . . . , N. If $N \leq 99$, select n successive, unique two-digit numbers from the table. If $N \leq 999$, select n three-digit numbers, and so on. The sample consists of the units corresponding to the n numbers selected.

SEE ALSO: Chance and Probability; Convenience Sample

SUGGESTED READING

Scheaffer, R. L., Mendenhall III, W., & Ott, L. O. (1996) *Elementary Survey Sampling*, 5th edn. Duxbury, North Scituate, MA.

ROGER E. KIRK

rape culture

The concept of rape culture links nonconsensual sex with the cultural fabric of a society. Using rape as descriptive of culture suggests a pattern of learned behavior created, organized, and transmitted from generation to generation as a part of the expectations associated with being male and being female. Rape culture is not an either-or phenomenon but exists in varying degrees, from the institutionalization of rape to its perfunctory punishment as crime. In the most strident form of rape culture women are the property of men who deny them respect and the right to control their own bodies.

A cultural explanation of rape moves causation from a micro to a macro level. Rape is not just the problem of an individual victim or of a sick perpetrator but a socially and culturally produced problem to be addressed at the societal level. A rape culture is a product of behaviors and attitudes as well as of the institutions supporting those behaviors and attitudes. Rape culture is generated and maintained by a social structure of gender inequality that allows and enables men, as arbiters of power, to exploit and abuse women – consciously and unconsciously. In a rape culture women are socialized to assume responsibility for controlling the "naturally aggressive" behavior of men in interpersonal relations and by restricting their own movements and behavior. A rape culture is a culture in which young girls internalize fear and role-restrictions simply because they are female. The major criticism of the concept of rape culture and of the feminist theory from which it emanates is its monolithic implication that ultimately all women are victimized by all men.

SEE ALSO: Rape/Sexual Assault; Sexual Politics

SUGGESTED READINGS

Brownmiller, S. (1975) *Against Our Will: Men, Women and Rape*. Fawcett Columbine, New York.

Buchwald, E., Fletcher, P. R., & Roth, M. (1993). *Transforming A Rape Culture*. Milkweed Editions, Minneapolis, MN.

JOYCE E. WILLIAMS

rape/sexual assault

Prior to the mid-1970s, the crime of rape was defined by most state statutes in terms of the British common law and involved the "carnal knowledge of a female, not his wife, forcibly and against her will" (Bienen 1983: 140). Legislative reforms, designed primarily to reduce rape case attrition, redefined the crime of rape in sex neutral language and replaced the single offense of rape with a series of calibrated sexual offenses and commensurate penalties. Definitional changes resulted in an expansive category of sexual offenses, relabeled in such terms as "sexual battery," "sexual assault," or "criminal sexual conduct" (Bienen 1983).

Although there are jurisdictional variations in criminal statutes, the crime of rape is typically categorized as a first degree sexual assault or battery. *Rape* refers to completed or attempted sexual intercourse with another person by the use of forcible compulsion. The concept of *forcible compulsion* may refer to physical force or psychological coercion. The act of forced sexual intercourse may involve vaginal, anal, or oral penetration by the offender, using either his/her body or an inanimate object. This crime may involve heterosexual or homosexual intercourse, as well as male or female victims.

Second and third degree sexual assaults incorporate a wide range of completed or attempted sexual victimizations which are distinct from the crime of rape. These assaults include unwanted sexual contact with another person and may or may not involve the use of force on the part of the perpetrator. Some behaviors that are common in these categories are inappropriate fondling or grabbing; however, these crimes may also involve the perpetrator's lewd or lascivious behavior or speech while in the presence of the victim.

Regardless of statutory classification, sexual victimizations are among the most highly under-reported crimes. Thus, given that victims may be unwilling to report their victimizations to strangers – police officers and researchers alike – determining the actual rates of sexual victimizations is highly problematic. Although there is no way to determine the exact number of sexual victimizations that are not reported to researchers, the most recent National Crime Victimization Survey data suggests that fewer than half (38 percent) of all victimizations are reported to police in the USA (Bureau of Justice Statistics 2008).

The issues surrounding under-reporting notwithstanding, there are two primary sources for data on sexual victimizations in the USA: The National Crime Victimization Survey (NCVS) and the Uniform Crime Reports (UCR). Whereas the NCVS is a collection of information from US households for all victims age 12 and older for sexual victimizations reported and not reported to the police, the UCR provides data on all completed and attempted forcible rapes and sexual assaults against female victims which have been reported to the police. The NCVS data suggest that there were an estimated 255,630 completed and attempted rapes and sexual assaults in 2006, resulting in a sexual victimization rate of 1.1 per 1,000 persons age twelve or older (BJS 2008). Comparable data from the UCR indicate that 90,427 sexual victimizations against female victims were reported to police in 2007, yielding a rate of 30 forcible rapes per 100,000 females (US Federal Bureau of Investigations 2008).

SEE ALSO: Male Rape; Rape Culture

REFERENCES

Bienen, L. (1983) Rape reform legislation in the United States: a look at some practical effects. *Victimology* 8: 139–51.

Bureau of Justice Statistics (2008) *National Crime Victimization Survey: Criminal Victimization, 2006*. US Department of Justice, Washington, DC.

United States Federal Bureau of Investigation (2008) *Uniform Crime Reports for the United States, 2007*. US Government Printing Office, Washington, DC.

DAWN BEICHNER

rational choice theories

Rational choice theories explain social behavior via the aggregated actions of *rational* or *purposive* actors. The actors are rational in the sense that, given a set of values and beliefs, they calculate the relative costs and benefits of alternative actions and, from these calculations, make a choice that maximizes their expected utility. Rational choice models assume that the range of alternatives open to actors is constrained by the environment or institutions within which actors make their decisions. In their purest form, these theories also assume that actors possess complete information about their values and the various courses of action through which they can pursue them. Actors collect, organize, and analyze this information prior to making a decision. Thus, rational choice theories are means-end theories. That is, they describe the means or rational calculus through which actors go about obtaining their desired ends, or values.

The theory received its first formal treatment in economics, where it has long been the dominant paradigm. More recently, it has become one of the dominant approaches in political science and has made a number of inroads into psychology and sociology.

The introduction of rational choice into sociology has generated a fair amount of controversy. The position sociologists take in these debates is determined in part by whether they subscribe to *methodological individualism* or *methodological holism*. For holists and many individualists, the objective of sociology is to explain macro-level social systems. (Other individualists seek to explain the workings of micro-level social systems.) The two disagree on whether these social systems can be explained solely with other social systems (holism), or whether the theorist must "come down" to the micro level to explain the effects of one social system on another via reference to individual actors that comprise these systems (individualism).

Almost all rational choice sociologists subscribe to some form of methodological individualism. The individualist position holds that a theory must begin by stating how a social system (e.g., law or religion) affects the options available to individuals and how this (limited) range of options, in turn, affects decisions. The theory must then build back up by describing how individuals' choices "aggregate" to impact a second system-level variable (e.g., economic development).

While virtually all rational choice theorists subscribe to some form of methodological individualism, not all methodological individualists are rational choice theorists. Some maintain that sociology needs a model of the actor, but oppose models based on rational choice principles. Others claim that rational choice theory's explicitness makes it the best choice for a scientific sociology. Debates generally center on either *means* (the rationality component), or the *ends* typically assumed in applications of the theory, that individuals are motivated by self-interest.

MEANS

One of the main criticisms of rational choice theory is the extensive cognitive and computational demand it places on actors. Rather than judiciously gathering and systematically processing data about all possible courses of action, as rational choice theory assumes, humans greatly simplify their social worlds. *Bounded rationality* models recognize that humans are only capable of gathering, organizing, and processing a finite amount of information, and that much of this activity is subject to cognitive biases. Thus, these models replace the complex calculations assumed in traditional (unbounded) rational choice models with heuristics or rules of thumb. But the increased realism is often accompanied by a decrease in precision. Thus, rational choice proponents often prefer to keep the theoretical precision by assuming that actors make decisions "as if" they are rational.

ENDS

While rational choice theory is officially silent on values, in practice, most applications assume actors are motivated by self-interest, narrowly defined. In fact, the assumption that actors seek to maximize their wealth and nothing else is so common in rational choice approaches that many mistakenly believe narrow self-interest to be axiomatic, rather than a "default" auxiliary assumption. Some justify the "typical value assumption" by noting that wealth can be exchanged for valued immanent goods. When it can, these scholars contend, rational choice theory can use wealth as a proxy for these other ends. Others justify the typical value assumption on the grounds that it works well when predicting macro-level outcomes. Although some lines of research in rational choice sociology have fared well employing the typical value assumption, many see a need to develop more realistic models of values.

SEE ALSO: Micro-macro Links; Microsociology

SUGGESTED READINGS

Coleman, J. S. (1990) *Foundations of Social Theory*. Harvard University Press, Harvard, CT.

Heckathorn, D. D. (1997) The paradoxical relationship between sociology and rational choice. *American Sociologist* 28: 6–15.

Udehn, L. (2001) *Methodological Individualism: Background, History and Meaning*. Routledge, London.

BRENT SIMPSON

rational legal authority

According to Max Weber, rational legal authority represents a form of legitimate domination, with domination being the "probability that certain commands (or all commands) from a given source will be obeyed by a given group of persons". While this probability implies a certain interest on the part of those obeying in the effects of their compliance, such interest can be diverse, and individuals may act upon calculated self-interest, habituation, affection, or idealistic orientations. For domination to endure, however, it depends on the belief in the legitimacy of the command and its source. Accordingly, Weber distinguishes three types of legitimate domination. Charismatic authority rests upon a belief in the extraordinary, sacred, and/or exemplary qualities of the person commanding, while traditional authority calls for submission to those who are privileged to rule by historical convention. In contrast, rational legal authority differs in its unique combination of impersonality, formality, and everyday profaneness. It rests upon "a belief in the 'legality' of patterns of normative rules and the right of those elevated to authority under such rules to issue commands (legal authority)."

The innate ambivalence of the principles that constitute rational legal authority provoke ambiguous and, occasionally, conflicting consequences. In Weber's conceptualization, rational legal administration is most effective and efficient the more it operates along the lines of formal rationality, thus excluding any substantive values and eradicating personal emotions, sentiments, or ideals.

Rational legal authority has changed its face, but it has not withered away. Rationalization of production, consumption, and life pursuit is still prevalent, as cathedrals of consumption, supranational institutions, and lateral careers demonstrate. In fact, where rational legal structures have retreated – be it in international disputes – brute power or even violence seems to prevail. Perhaps McDonaldization rather than bureaucratization is the dominant form these days; yet still, our saturated selves rely upon "civilization" within somewhat more "fancy" iron cages.

SEE ALSO: Authority and Legitimacy; Authority and Conformity; Bureaucratic Personality; McDonaldization; Weber, Max

SUGGESTED READINGS

Weber, M. (1968) *Economy and Society: An Outline of Interpretive Sociology*, ed. G. Roth & C. Wittich. Bedminster Press, New York.

Weber, M. (1988) [1920] *Gesammelte Aufsätze zur Religionssoziologie*. J. B. C. Mohr (Paul Siebeck), Tübingen.

DIRK BUNZEL

rationalization

The concept of rationalization is most often associated with the work of Max Weber and his followers. Weber's thinking on rationalization is based on his analysis of the basic types of rationality. In Weber's terms, *practical* rationality involves the utilization of pragmatic, calculating and means-ends strategies in order to pursue mundane ends. *Theoretical* rationality refers to the employment of abstract ideas and conceptual schemes to describe, elucidate and comprehend empirical reality. *Substantive* rationality is involved in decision making that is subject to the values and ethical norms of the particular society. *Formal* rationality involves decision-making in accordance with a set of universal rules, laws and regulations. It is only in the west that formal rationality emerged and became predominant. And it is that type of rationality that lies at the base of the rationalization process.

According to Weber, everyday life is rationalized and while that brings with it great advantages such as increased efficiency, it also leads to a variety of negative consequences such as disenchantment and alienation. Most generally, Weber feared the development of an "iron cage" of rationalization that would increasingly enslave people and from which it would be increasingly difficult to escape.

Bureaucracy plays a key role in Weber's sociology and can be seen as the paradigm of the rationalization process. The bureaucracy is an organizational form that is rationally designed to perform complex tasks in the most efficient way possible. Although Weber saw the ideal-typical bureaucracy as an efficient system, he did not fail to note the substantial irrationalities that are inherent in it. Bureaucracy, which is all but indissoluble once it is established, applies the same set of abstract rules to individual cases and limits the autonomy of the individual. Therefore, the domination of bureaucracy is likely to result in injustices. Moreover, as bureaucracy often suffers from inefficiencies, it often fails to accomplish the tasks that it exists to perform. Finally, of course, the bureaucracy can represent a clear case of the kind of "iron cage" Weber feared.

Georg Simmel also theorized about rationalization. In *The Philosophy of Money*, Simmel (1907) sets out to deal with money as an abstract and universal system that provides a fundamental model of the rationalization process. Money, as the symbol of abstract social relations, exemplifies the declining significance of the individual in the face of the expansion of objective culture, which is associated with intellectual rationality, mathematical calculability, abstraction, objectivity, anonymity, and leveling.

Also of note is Karl Mannheim's thinking on rationalization. Resembling formal rationality in his work is the concept of functional rationality which he sees as growing increasingly ubiquitous and coercive over people. Instead of substantive rationality, Mannheim deals with substantial rationality which fundamentally involves peoples' ability to think intelligently. He sees the latter as being undermined by the former.

Inspired by the work on the rationalization of the modern western society, critical theorists associated with the Frankfurt School criticized the consequences of the growth of rationality, or instrumental reason, for modern society. As elaborated by Adorno and Horkheimer, the rationality of capitalism is consolidated through the decline of individualism and that has made it more difficult to achieve the goals of the Enlightenment. Marcuse focused on the relationship between technology and rationalization. Marcuse contended that formally rational structures have replaced more substantially rational structures and capitalist society has become one-dimensional in the sense that it is dominated by organized forces that restrict opposition, choice and critique. Although there appears to be democracy, liberty, and freedom, society prevents radical change since it is able to absorb criticism and opposition, and to render these criticisms futile.

Habermas agrees with Weber that the development of modern society is driven by an underlying logic of rationalization, however, he maintains that this has a dual quality. Rejecting the pessimism of Weber, Adorno, and Horkheimer, Habermas argues that the development of both instrumental and communicative rationality can produce not only unprecedented technical achievements, but also the kind of humanity that can utilize those advancements to better itself rather than being enslaved by them.

The concept of rationalization has profoundly affected the direction of social theory, perhaps most notably theories of state formation, governmentality, organization, politics, and technology. The concept has also triggered debates regarding the central issues of the contemporary world such as the culture of consumption. Ritzer's McDonaldization thesis, in particular, illustrates the continuing importance of the Weberian notion of rationalization, as it extends it into many new domains, especially consumption, popular culture and everyday life.

SEE ALSO: Bureaucracy; Critical Theory/Frankfurt School; Mannheim, Karl; McDonaldization; Modernity; Rational-Legal Authority; Weber, Max

SUGGESTED READINGS

Habermas, J. (1971) *Toward a Rational Society*. London, Heinemann.

Marcuse, H. (1964) *One-Dimensional Man: The Ideology of Industrial Society*. Sphere Books, London.

Weber, M. (1958) *The Protestant Ethic and the Spirit of Capitalism*. Scribner's, New York.

ZEYNEP ATALAY

reference groups

The term reference group denotes a cluster of social psychological concepts pertaining to the relationship between individual identities, social norms, and social control. Reference groups may constitute a group into which individuals are members, as well as those groups to which one does not belong. The utility of the term lies in its ability to provide an explanation as to how social groups influence individual values, attitudes, and behavior.

Reference groups have also been useful in understanding the development of identity boundaries, particularly concerning ethnicity and adaptation among children of immigrants. Many scholars interested in second-generation immigration highlight the tensions that exist between the ideals of two conflicting reference groups, that of the immigrant culture and that of dominant American society. The values and behaviors of each reference group provide powerful socializing forces on the children of immigrants. Thus, inquiries into identity development often seek to determine to what extent each group serves as an audience in front of whom the second generation acts to achieve acceptance.

The use of reference groups has had enormous impact on the development and use of measures in the social sciences. Self-report measures of social, psychological, and biological phenomena including attitudes, behaviors, and physical well-being invariably are influenced within a context, by social comparison. For example, inequalities in society may be as much a product of subjective interpretation involving an individual comparing his or her situation to a group or category as they are a consequence of objective, observable differences. The reference group concept has furthermore served to highlight the potential confounding effects of group comparison research, especially concerning cross-cultural studies. Building off the awareness that most people's self-understanding results from how people compare themselves with others around them, and in particular others similar to them, the suggestion emerges that different groups have diverse standards by which evaluations are made. Moreover, shifting evaluations may occur depending on the context. Thus, analyses that seek to compare mean scores from different cultures (who invariably have different referents) risk the threat of misleading results.

SEE ALSO: Generalized Other; Looking-Glass Self; Role-Taking

SUGGESTED READING

Sherif, M. & Sherif, C. W. (1964) *Reference Groups: Exploration into Conformity and Deviation of Adolescents*. Harper, New York.

KRISTINE J. AJROUCH

reflexive modernization

Ulrich Beck introduced the term reflexive modernity (also called second modernity) by explicitly demarcating himself from postmodern approaches which would imply that current developments go beyond modernity (Beck et al. 2003).

He first outlined his argument in *Risk Society* (1992). The central thesis is that modernity has transformed itself by the radicalized application of the core concepts of modern industrialized society (also called first modernity or simple modernity). Central principles (e.g., the distinction between nature and culture or science and politics), as well as basic institutions (e.g., the gender division of labor, the traditional family, the normal model of the life course), have been transformed into a new modernity.

Since "reflexive" often causes misunderstandings Beck emphasizes that it does not mean that people in today's society are more self-conscious than in the past. It indicates rather a heightened awareness that mastery of nature, technique, the social, and so on is impossible.

Originally, Beck (1992) developed the concept of reflexive modernization referring to the occurrence of a risk society and growing institutional individualization. New risks would occur as unexpected side effects of industrialization that take place in nature (e.g., climate change, depleted ozone layer) and as technical catastrophes (e.g., accidents in Bhopal, Chernobyl). They would erode the belief in the manageability of nature by science and thereby politicize risk decisions. Additionally, individualization processes would release people from traditional institutions, which at the same time erode and became supplanted by secondary institutions (e.g., labor market, welfare state, the media). Individualization demands individual decisions where routines and traditions prevailed before.

Reflexive modernization resonates in the discourse on social change in Britain. Beck et al. (1994) critically discussed social change in modernity. While Lash emphasized the cultural aspects of these changes ("risk culture"), Giddens prefers the expression "institutional reflexivity" and emphasizes growing individual self-awareness and self-responsibility, which lead to more political considerations regarding a "Third Way". Beck developed his theoretical considerations into a general theory. He broadened the concept of social change from "risk" and "individualization" to a general change of central institutions and principles of first modernity into a reflexive modernity.

The multiplication of boundaries (or attempts to draw boundaries) is introduced as a central criterion to identify the change from first to reflexive modernity (Beck et al. 2003). For example, instead of one identity linked to a specific cultural background there is the possibility of several identities referring to different (often contradictory) backgrounds without the necessity to decide for one or the other. The result is in many respects a change from a so-called either-or society to a this-as-well-as-that world. Boundaries between nature and culture, life and death, knowledge and superstition, us and others, expert and laymen, for example, become blurred. In *World at Risk*, Beck (2008) published an overview about recent developments of his approach.

Although many of Beck's observations are acknowledged, the theory itself is still contested. It is criticized as often being too general to explain concrete behavior and its lack of empirical evidence.

SEE ALSO: Individualism; Modernity; Risk, Risk Society, Risk Behavior, and Social Problems

REFERENCES

Beck, U. (1992) *Risk Society: Towards a New Modernity*. Sage, Newbury Park, CA.

Beck, U., Giddens, A., & Lash, S. (1994) *Reflexive Modernization: Politics, Tradition and Aesthetics in the Modern Social Order*. Stanford University Press, Stanford, CA.

Beck, U., Bonß, W., & Lau, C. (2003) The theory of reflexive modernization: problematic, hypotheses and research programme. *Theory, Culture and Society* 20 (2): 1–33.

JENS O. ZINN

reflexivity

Reflexivity can be broadly defined to mean an understanding of the knowledge-making enterprise, including a consideration of the subjective, institutional, social, and political processes whereby research is conducted and knowledge is produced. The researcher is part of the social world that is studied and this calls for exploration and self-examination. A reflexive researcher "intentionally or self-consciously shares (whether in agreement or disagreement) with her or his audiences the underlying assumptions that occasion a set of questions" (Robertson 2002: 786).

The recent interest in reflexivity has been linked to the influence of postmodernism and poststructuralism whose insights have drawn attention to the problematic nature of research, the dubious position of the researcher, the crisis of representation, and the constructive nature of language, as well as an admission of the fact that there is no "one best way" of conducting either theoretical or empirical work. Reflexivity is about dealing with "a sense of uncertainty and crisis as increasingly complex questions are raised concerning the status, validity, basis and authority of knowledge claims" (Mauthner & Doucet 2003: 417).

Leading philosophers of science and intellectuals have struggled with issues similar to those brought forward by the "reflexive turn" for a long time. The work of Kuhn (1970) has been vital in raising questions around the limits of scientific rationality and progress. Postmodern thinking, critical studies, feminism, and interpretive and other qualitative work more generally all cast doubt on the idea that "competent observers" can "with objectivity, clarity, and precision report on their own observations of the social world." Informed by the linguistic turn, such researchers have increasingly stressed the ambiguous, unstable, and context-dependent character of language; noted the dependence of observers and data on interpretation and theory; and argued that interpretation-free, theory-neutral facts do not exist but, rather, that data and facts are constructions that result from interpretation.

There is a multitude of reflexivity – reflexivit*ies*. For some authors, the key theme is the researcher-self and the personal experiences of the research process: "reflexive ethnographies primarily focus on a culture or subculture, authors use their own experiences in the culture reflexively to bend back on self and look more deeply at self–other interactions" (Ellis & Bochner 2000: 741). For others, it concerns the cognitive aspects around construction processes in research. For still others, reflexivity revolves around language, inviting the investigator "into the fuller realm of shared languages. The reflexive attempt is thus relational, emphasizing the expansion of the languages of understanding" (Gergen & Gergen 1991: 79). Other versions of reflexivity revolve around the research text and authorship, theoretical perspectives and vocabularies and what they accomplish, or the empirical subjects "out there" and how their voices are being (mis-)represented.

For some authors, reflexivity is intimately connected to the broad intellectual stream of postmodernism and/or radical social constructionism. This may imply a broader set of considerations, for example, postmodernism is frequently associated with the indecidabilities of meaning, fragmented selves, power/knowledge connections, the problematic nature of master narratives, and problems of representation, providing an ambitious set of themes for reflexive work. Again, for others, reflexivity means the breaking of the logic associated with a particular stream – reflexivity involves confronting dataistic, interpretive, critical, and postmodern lines of reasoning and challenging the truths and emphasis following from each of these (Alvesson & Sköldberg 2009).

SEE ALSO: Essentialism and Constructionism; Knowledge; Knowledge, Sociology of; Methods; Poststructuralism

REFERENCES

Ellis, C. & Bochner, A. (2000) Autoethnography, personal narrative, reflexivity: researcher as subject. In: Denzin, N. & Lincoln, Y. (eds.), *Handbook of Qualitative Research*, 2nd edn. Sage, Thousand Oaks, CA, pp. 769–802.

Gergen, K. & Gergen, M. (1991) Toward reflexive methodologies. In: Steier, F. (ed.), *Research and Reflexitivity*. Sage, London.

Kuhn, T. S. (1970) *The Structure of Scientific Revolution*. University of Chicago Press, Chicago, IL.

Mauthner, N. & Doucet, A. (2003) Reflexive accounts and accounts of reflexivity in qualitative data analysis. *Sociology* 37: 413–31.

Robertson, J. (2002) Reflexivity redux: a pithy polemic on positionality. *Anthropological Quarterly* 75 (4): 785–93.

MATS ALVESSON

refugees

In international law "refugee" refers to individuals who are residing outside of their country of origin and who are unable or unwilling to return because of a well-founded fear of persecution on account of race, religion, nationality, membership of a particular social group or political opinion.

The term derives from the Latin *refugere* – to flee – and is believed to have first been applied to the Huguenots who fled France in the seventeenth century. Its modern legal usage follows the UN General Assembly's establishment of the United Nations High Commission on Refugees (UNHCR) in 1950. Within a system of nation-states with fixed borders, and a burgeoning cold war rivalry, the UNHCR's principal aim was to guarantee and provide international protection and assistance to individuals who had become displaced by World War II. By becoming signatories to the 1951 UN Convention, nation-states agreed to grant special protection on an international basis to citizens of a state that could not guarantee their human rights and physical security. This remit for protection was later extended beyond Europe to encompass refugees from all over the world, as the problem of displaced people became more global, with the signing of the 1967 Bellagio Protocol. There are currently 137 states that are signatories to both the 1951 Convention and Bellagio Protocol.

There are, however, a number of conceptual distinctions within refugee discourse. People who are forced from their homes for reasons outlined in the 1951 UN definition of a refugee, but who remain within the borders of their own country, are known as internally displaced persons (IDPs), of which the UN estimates the number to be 25 million. By contrast, those who seek refugee status outside of their own state of origin must make an application to the country where they arrive and are referred to as asylum seekers. Hence, an asylum seeker is a person who is seeking asylum on the basis of his or her claim to be a refugee. Refugee status may be granted to asylum seekers following a formal legal procedure in which the host country decides whether to grant refugee status or otherwise.

The rising numbers of asylum seekers and refugees, as a specific type of migration, has also raised problems concerning how to conceptualize processes of migration. In contrast to the dominant rational choice theories of migration, which postulate individuals rationally weighing the costs and benefits of leaving one area for another in order to maximize their utility, refugee movement is often conceptualized as "forced" or "impelled." Discussions concerning refugees refer to involuntary migrations that distinguish between the forced movements of refugees and the free movements of economic migrants. They also look to the political sphere rather than to economic forces as explanatory factors.

Such conceptualizations raise questions concerning agency and structure, as well as the very accounting practices that determine what is "chosen" or "forced."

SEE ALSO: Diaspora; Immigration; Transnationalism

SUGGESTED READING

United Nations High Commission on Refugees (2003) *Global Report 2003*. United Nations, New York.

STEVE LOYAL

regression and regression analysis

Regression is a statistical technique used to study the relation among quantitative variables. Both, in cases of two variables (simple regression) as in cases of more than two variables (multiple regression), regression analysis can be used for exploring and quantifying the relation among a so-called dependent variable (y) and one or more so-called independent variables ($x_1, x_2 \ldots, x_p$). In others words, to find out to what degree the dependent variable can be explained by the independent variable(s). Furthermore, we can write an equation that allows us to predict the values of a dependent (y) variable, knowing the values of one or more independent (x) variables.

The simplest way of expressing a relation among variables is through a mathematical equation, which allows us to describe the form as one variable changes with the other one. The regression equation is as follows:

$$Y = \text{alpha} + \text{beta}\ (X) + \text{epsilon}$$

Y is the dependent variable; the *alpha* parameter is a constant or value of "Y" when "X" is equal to 0; the *beta* coefficient determines the slope of the line; X is the independent variable (in multiple regression the equation is extended to include additional x variables"; and *epsilon* is the error comprised of variation in "Y" not accounted for by the remainder of the equation.

The problem is that in the social sciences it is difficult to find perfect linear associations among variables and therefore it is necessary to find the regression line that better adjusts to the data. The most used regression form is ordinary least squares linear regression. But even this line is not always a good summary of the existing relation in the data and so we usually resort to the coefficient of determination – R squared – to know the goodness of fit. This coefficient takes values between 0 (absence of relation among the variables) and 1 (perfect relation among the variables), and the value of R squared represents the degree of profit that is obtained when we predict a variable from the knowledge that we have of other variable(s). The higher the value of R squared, the better the fit of the equation and therefore the greater is our ability to predict the values of the dependent variable (y) knowing the values of the independent variable(s) (x).

SEE ALSO: General Linear Model; Statistical Significance Testing; Statistics

SUGGESTED READING

Allison, P. D. (1999) *Multiple Regression: A Primer*. Pine Forge Press, Thousand Oaks, CA.

GASPAR BRANDLE

reification

Sociologists from several perspectives have critically addressed reification. In general, reification refers to the act (or its result) of attributing to analytic or abstract concepts a material reality – it is a misplaced concreteness. Through reification people regard human relations, actions, and ideas as independent of themselves, sometimes governing them. The abstraction "society" is frequently reified into something that has the power to act. Society does not act – people do. Reification is an error of attribution; it is corrected by eliminating the hypostatization of abstractions into things or agents.

For phenomenologists, reification is a potential outcome of the social construction of reality. To enter the lifeworld, human expression and subjective intention are externalized through "objectivation" where they become part of a socially constructed reality. Language is the common vehicle although objectivation occurs through various symbolic forms.

Reification occurs when people understand objectivations as if they were non-human or supra-human things and act "*as if* they were something other than human products – such as facts of nature, results of cosmic laws, or manifestations of divine will." Reification indicates we have forgotten our "own authorship of the human world" (Berger & Luckmann 1966: 89). A reified world is a dehumanized one.

Marxist sociologists conceptualize reification as created by the "fetishism of commodities" where "the social character of labor appears as the objective (*gegenständliche*) character of the products themselves." To the producers, "the social relationships of their private labors appear as what they are, not as the immediate social relations of people in their labors but as thingly (*sachliche*) relations of people and the social relations of things" (Marx 1922: 39). The producers' own social movement "posses for them the form of a movement of things (*Sachen*) under the control of which they stand rather than the producers controlling it" (p. 41). Here, reification – *Verdinglichung* (*ver-* connoting a process; *dinglich* "thingly" – thus "thingification") – is a real social process whereby the social relations among producers do become "thingly." Their social relations really are those of commodities (and their value). Human characteristics matter little; one's "properties" as the bearer of commodities, especially labor power, do. This thing-like relation of commodity production dominates the workers engaged in production.

Reification links to Marx's early concern with alienation, where the products and production process under private property are separated from and stand against their human producers. It is a real social process that must be overturned to put social production under the control of its immediate producers.

Lukács (1971: *History and Class Consciousness*) argued that reification created false consciousness, thwarting a spontaneous, workers' class consciousness and thereby supported Lenin's argument about the need for a revolutionary, vanguard party. Other Marxists, like Gramsci and Korsch, argued that workers would, amid the contradictions of commodity production, break through reified, commodity fetishism and achieve the consciousness needed to struggle for social change.

SEE ALSO: Alienation; Commodity Fetishism, and Commodification; Marx, Karl; Phenomenology

REFERENCES

Berger, P. & Luckmann, T. (1966) *The Social Construction of Reality*. Doubleday, Garden City, NY.

Marx, K. (1922) [1890] *Das Kapital*, 4th edn., vol. 1. Otto Meissner, Hamburg.

ROB BEAMISH

reliability

Reliability refers, at a general level, to *consistency* of measurement. Consistency can be conceptualized differently for different forms of reliability estimation, but in all cases reliability is focused on whether a measurement yields consistent results.

Such consistency is critical to research practice, where variables must be operationalized and measured. For example, socioeconomic status can be measured as average family income, whether a child receives a reduced lunch rate, education level of parent, or by other variables. Regardless of method, the measurement must reflect dependable characterizations of the units of observation (e.g., people, families) on the variable. One head of household might guess at his or her annual family income while another provides an accurate amount. In such a case, the variable is not being consistently measured across the units of observation.

There are three dominant measurement theories that can be used to conceptualize reliability of scores: *classical test theory*, *generalizability theory*, and *item response theory*. In research practice, however, it is much more common for researchers to employ the classical test theory framework than the other two methods, at least in part due to ease of use and historical precedence.

In classical test theory, sometimes called *true score theory*, a score is perfectly reliable only when the obtained score is measured without error. Theoretically, then, the true score (T) is a function of both the obtained score (O) and some degree of error, as indicated by:

$$X_T = X_O + \text{error}.$$

Reliability can estimated in a variety of ways to account for different types of measurement error, including but not limited to, test-retest (stability), alternate forms, internal consistency, and interrater reliability.

The most common reliability statistic is coefficient alpha, as introduced by Lee Cronbach in 1951. The intraclass correlation (ICC) can also be valuable to estimate reliability in a number of situations.

SEE ALSO: Correlation; Descriptive Statistics; Validity, Qualitative

SUGGESTED READING

Henson, R. K. (2001) Understanding internal consistency reliability estimates: a conceptual primer on coefficient alpha. *Measurement and Evaluation in Counseling and Development* 34: 177–89.

ROBIN K. HENSON

religion, sociology of

The study of religion is a core component of sociology, from its substantive place in the classical theorizing of Max Weber and Émile Durkheim, to comprising one of the most vibrant areas of research among contemporary sociologists. The sociology of religion is not interested in speculating about the existence of God or in assessing the validity and coherence of religious belief. It is concerned, rather, with how individuals, social institutions, and cultures construe God or the sacred, how these ideas penetrate public culture and individual lives, and with the implications of these interpretations for individual, institutional, and societal processes. Thus sociologists of religion draw on the full range of research methodologies available to explore theoretically informed questions about the relevance, meaning, and implications of religion in local, national, and global socio-historical contexts. Standardized indicators include finely differentiated measures of religious affiliation and beliefs, frequency of church attendance, private prayer and religious reading, the self-perceived importance of religion in an individual's life, and personal images of God. In addition to quantitative indicators, there is also a strong tradition of ethnographic research documenting the multiple and varied ways in which religious meanings and identities evolve for particular religious collectivities (e.g., congregations) and in individual lives.

A dominant theme in the sociology of religion and vigorously engaged by scholars on both sides of the Atlantic is secularization. The term is conceptualized differently by various scholars, but for the most part, refers to the constellation of historical and social processes that allegedly bring about the declining significance of religious belief and authority in society. The secularization thesis has its roots in the writings of both Weber and Durkheim. Weber predicted that the increased rationalization of society – bureaucratization, scientific and technical progress, and the expanding pervasiveness of instrumental reason – would substantively attenuate the scope of religion, both through the specialization of institutional spheres (of family, economy, law, politics) and as a result of disenchantment in the face of competing rationalized value spheres (e.g., science). Durkheim, although a strong proponent of the centrality of the sacred in maintaining social cohesion, nonetheless predicted that the integrative functions performed by religious symbols and rituals in traditional societies would increasingly in modern societies be displaced by the emergence of differentiated professional and scientific membership communities.

Weber's secularization thesis was highly influential in the paradigm of social change articulated by Talcott Parsons and modernization scholars in the 1960s, predicting religion's loss of institutional and cultural authority in the face of economic and social development. Nonetheless, there was persistent empirical evidence (especially in the USA) that secularization was not an all-encompassing force. The scholarly reassessment of secularization was also prompted by the increased public visibility of religious-political movements (e.g., the Moral Majority in the USA, Solidarity in Poland, and the religious roots of the Iranian Revolution), theoretical challenges to modernization theory, and by greater scholarly awareness, largely driven by feminist sociologists, to the critical importance of nonrational sources of meaning and authority in everyday life (e.g., emotion, tradition). Advancing this paradigm reassessment, the application of rational choice theory to the study of religion resulted in an intense, empirically informed debate about the ways in which competitive (pluralistic) religious environments (religious economies) produce religious vitality and church growth. This approach rejected the assumptions of secularization theory, arguing that they were more appropriate for the historically monopolized religious contexts (markets) found in Europe, but at odds with the American context of religious pluralism and religion freedom. Today, any generalized assessment of secularization must be attentive to the large body of empirical data demonstrating the continuing significance of religion in the public domain and in individual lives, and the coexistence of these trends with equally valid empirical evidence indicating selectivity in, and reflexivity toward, the acceptance of religion's theological, moral, and political authority.

Much of the contemporary research on religion highlights the complexity and multidimensionality of religion as it is lived out across diverse contexts. The scope and cultural hold of religion is documented in research on the increased prominence of global religious movements such as Pentecostalism and Islam; the political legitimacy of faith-based social movements and organizations; the significant impact of religion on voting and on everyday health and social behavior independent of other social factors (e.g., ethnicity, social class); and the influential presence of religious worldviews in shaping public policy debates and activism (e.g., on abortion, gay rights, stem cell research). One of the newer areas of study is the attempt to systematically differentiate between, and investigate the social implications of, church-based religion and deinstitutionalized, individual spirituality. Increasingly too, the issue of religious diversity is coming to the fore, prompted especially by the emergence of public controversies, mostly in Europe, over the accommodation of Islamic religious symbols and practices in the allegedly secular public sphere. The resurgence of religion in western societies previously considered as secular (e.g., France,

England), is inspiring new intellectual debates about how the role of religion in civil society should be construed, and whether it is meaningful to talk of post-secular society.

The overarching methodological challenge in studying religion involves the ongoing monitoring of the validity of existing measures of religious and spiritual behavior across all levels of analysis (individual, institutional, and societal). Researchers need to be simultaneously attentive to the substantive content of religious and spiritual beliefs, the specific contexts in which religion and spirituality emerge and are practiced, and to identifying the mechanisms informing how different aspects of religion and spirituality impact social outcomes (e.g., voting, concern for others, violence).

Contemporary sociological theorists, on the other hand, should be cautioned that any theory of society that does not give due recognition to the nuanced diversity that characterizes contemporary forms of religion and spirituality will lack explanatory relevance in today's global society.

SEE ALSO: Durkheim, Émile; Globalization, Religion and; Sexuality, Religion and; Secularization

SUGGESTED READINGS

Dillon, M. & Wink, P. (2007). *In the Course of a Lifetime: Tracing Religious Belief, Practice, and Change*. Berkeley: University of California Press, CA.

Finke, R. & Stark, R. (2005) *The Churching of America*, 2nd edn. Rutgers University Press, New Brunswick, NJ.

Habermas, J. (2008) Notes on a post-secular society. *New Perspectives Quarterly* 25:4.

Warner, R. S. (1993) Work in progress toward a new paradigm for the sociological study of religion. *American Journal of Sociology* 98: 1044–93.

MICHELE DILLON

repressive hypothesis

The publication of Michel Foucault's first volume of the *The History of Sexuality* thoroughly transformed theoretical thinking around sexuality (1990). With this book, Foucault provides a history of sexuality "from the viewpoint of the history of discourses." Foucault's concept of discourse is intrinsically interwoven with what he perceived to be distinctively modern forms of power. Premodern forms of power were based on the idea of *power-sovereignty* or *power-law*. They were derived from monarchical techniques of government and drew upon the binary ruler/ruled. From within this paradigm, power is conceived as *negative*. It works through measures, such as censorship, prohibition, prevention, exclusion, or spectacular forms of punishment. In contradistinction, power as a modality of discourse is *positive* in that it is productive of social relationships, forms of knowledge and modes of subjectivity.

In volume I of the *History of Sexuality*, Foucault applies this understanding of power to the subject of sexuality in order to challenge what he calls the "repressive hypothesis." Whereas in the traditional understanding, power is exerted to repress, silence, censor or erase sexuality, Foucault starts to conceive of sexuality as being an immediate effect of power. From this point of view, the most significant strategies of power in modern societies are not the exclusion of sexuality from discourse, but its regulation through the production of public discourses on sexuality. Foucault identifies an institutional incitement to speak about sex at the heart of modern western culture(s). It is in the multiplication of discourses on sexuality and the assumption that sex would reveal the truth of our innermost selves that the power-sexuality relation is realized. Foucault thus refutes the supposition at the heart of sexual liberationism that it is possible to revolutionize society by freeing our natural sexual selves. Foucault's anti-essentialist arguments have been widely taken up by scholars working from within a constructionist point of view. They have further inspired the deconstructive endeavor of recent queer theorizing.

SEE ALSO: Discourse; Foucault, Michel

REFERENCE

Foucault, M. (1990) *The History of Sexuality*, vol. 1: *An Introduction*. Penguin, Harmondsworth.

CHRISTIAN KLESSE

resource mobilization theory

A renaissance of social movement research has occurred since the 1980s as scholars have sought to understand the emergence, significance and effects of social movements. Resource mobilization theory (RMT) contributes to our understanding by taking the analytical insights of organizational sociology and extending them by analogy to social movements. RMT views social movements as purposive collective action undertaken to pursue (or resist) social, political or cultural change. From this perspective a social movement is a set of preferences for social, political, or cultural change held by individuals within a society. Individuals who share those preferences are called *adherents,* while those who watch from the sidelines with no opinion are *bystanders*. A key analytical issue for RMT is how social movements turn bystanders into adherents and subsequently mobilize adherents to active participation. Such tasks of mobilization are undertaken most often by *social movement organizations* (SMOs) which figure prominently in RMT analyses. RMT argues that effective social movement mobilization depends, in large part, on how well SMOs access and utilize key resources. Five types of resources play important roles in mobilization: moral, cultural, human, social, and material. All but the very smallest social movement groups gain access to resources by multiple means including self-production; aggregation from adherents; appropriation and patronage. RMT emphasizes that all societies have an unequal distribution of resources. Therefore, they want to understand how social movement adherents and organizations overcome those patterns of resource inequality in order to redirect resources to aid social movements. Thus, RMT is at root a partial theory of how relatively disadvantaged individuals and groups overcome inequalities and mobilize resources to pursue their preferences for social, cultural or political change.

SEE ALSO: New Social Movement Theory; Social Movements; Social Movements, Networks and

SUGGESTED READING

Edwards, R. & McCarthy, J. D. (2004) Resources and social movement mobilization. In: Snow, D. A., Soule, S. A., & Kriesi, H. (eds.), *The Blackwell Companion to Social Movements*. Blackwell Publishing, Malden, MA, pp. 116–52.

BOB EDWARDS

revolutions

Revolutions have helped define the modern age, associated with the emergence of democracy, capitalism, and socialism. Inspiring attempts to make a better world, they have typically fallen short of the goals of their makers.

"*Social* revolutions are rapid, basic transformations of a society's state and class structures ... in part carried through by class-based revolts from below" (Skocpol 1979: 4). Thus the great revolutions combine deep political *and* socioeconomic change with mass participation, whether violently, with little violence, or even through elections. In *political* revolutions, social struggles change governments but not the underlying social structure.

Karl Marx saw revolutions as the product of class struggles leading to a new mode of production (feudalism to capitalism, and ultimately, to socialism). Since Marx, three main "generations" of approaches have arisen. The 1930s "Natural History School" identified stages through which all revolutions supposedly passed. In the 1960s, social scientists posited aggregate psychological states – frustration at relative deprivation – or rapid social changes compelling people to embrace radical ideologies. In the 1970s Theda Skocpol insisted that "Revolutions are not made; they come" (1979: 17); her structural approach argued that the French, Russian, and Chinese monarchies could not cope with military defeat or economic pressure because of a limited agricultural base.

Since the 1990s, a "fourth generation" of scholars has balanced structure and agency, and political, economic, and cultural factors in multicausal models of revolution. What the causes of social revolutions are is still not settled.

Who, precisely, makes revolutions, and why? Classically, the answer was a single key class: for Marx, industrial workers; for others, peasants. Contemporary scholarship stresses the significance of multi-class coalitions of most social classes, representing "the people."

Recently, scholars have acknowledged the roles of women and diverse ethnic and racial groups. Julie Shayne (2004) shows how women act as "gendered revolutionary bridges," bringing ordinary people into the movement. People of color have been active across revolutions too. In the twenty-first century, indigenous people are leading revolutionary struggles in Bolivia, Ecuador, and Mexico's Zapatista insurgency.

But why would people take great personal risks in revolutions that shatter the fabric of their everyday routines? Eric Selbin (2010: *Revolution, Resistance, Rebellion: The Power of Story*) stresses shared stories – folk tales, myths, and symbols extolling past or present resistance to oppression, turning Skocpol's aphorism on its head: revolutions do not come, they are made by people. Jean-Pierre Reed and John Foran (2002) emphasize "political cultures of opposition," an amalgam of lived experiences, common understandings, and effective social networks.

The great social revolutions produced stronger, more centralized states better capable of competing economically with their rivals. Many of the twentieth century's revolutions have considerably improved people's lives, especially in China and Cuba.

Measured against the hopes they unleash, revolutions have generally disappointed their makers, and virtually no revolution has delivered both long-lasting economic gains and political rights.

Two factors might explain these mixed outcomes: the pressure put on revolutionary societies by powerful external enemies (often the USA), compounded by fragmentation of revolutionary coalitions, concentrating authority in the state and military. This in turn undermines economic improvements.

National revolutions will persist, since neoliberal globalization exacerbates inequality and poverty. Radical reformers and revolutionaries may take electoral democratic routes to power, as in Latin America. Both armed and peaceful resistance to foreign occupations will continue. The Zapatistas have created new forms of community governance and local economy rather than seeking national-level power. The global justice movement, organized around climate activism, communal alternatives to capitalism, and deeper participation, seeks a new form of world revolution across borders, that may bring the old revolutionary dream of social justice closer to reality. Revolutions will be with us to the end of human time, offering hopeful possibilities for humanly-directed social change.

SEE ALSO: Global Justice as a Social Movement; Marx, Karl; Social Change; Social Movements, Participatory Democracy in

REFERENCES

Reed, J.-P. & Foran, J. (2002) Political cultures of opposition: exploring idioms, ideologies, and revolutionary agency in the case of Nicaragua. *Critical Sociology* 28 (3): 335–70.

Shayne, J. D. (2004) *The Revolution Question: Feminisms in El Salvador, Chile, and Cuba*. Rutgers University Press, New Brunswick.

Skocpol, T. (1979) *States and Social Revolutions: A Comparative Analysis of France, Russia, and China*. Cambridge University Press, Cambridge.

JOHN FORAN

risk

The term "risk" can be viewed from at least two different perspectives – the information approach and the decision approach.

INFORMATION APPROACH

The risk of a certain event ($R_{(E)}$) is defined as the probability of a dangerous event ($p_{(E)}$) multiplied by the amount of the expected damage (D) connected to this event: $R_{(E)} = p_{(E)} \times D$. In this conception, risk is a question of complete or incomplete knowledge. Risk management, in this perspective, has the task of dealing with an information problem, namely the problem to acquire as much information as possible about probability and damage. One critical issue of this approach is the quantification of possible benefits and damages. Many situations in technological decision-making, but also in everyday life, make it difficult to establish a uniform risk measure.

DECISION APPROACH

The central characteristic of a *risk decision* consists of the need to select between different options, which all may entail negative consequences for third parties and therefore will provoke the issue of responsibility. A decision is risky, because and insofar as three aspects are intertwined: (1) the knowledge that non-decision is impossible; even inactivity contains a decision; (2) the knowledge that unspecific knowledge is unavoidable; this knowledge makes us aware that consequences will appear later, which are epistemologically unknown when the decision is taken; and they will bear negative effects for others; (3) the knowledge that future consequences will be attributed to the decision and to the decision-maker's responsibility. This aspect of uncertainty entails a paradoxical moment, which Clausen and Dombrowsky (1984) called the warning paradox. It says that warning against possible dangers does not help to decide risky cases. The reason is that we only can learn whether the warning was reasonable if do *not* listen to it. If we follow the warning, we will never know whether it was well founded or not.

Whereas risk is related to the decision-making actor or institution, the concept of *danger* refers to the side of those affected by the consequences of the decision. Modern societies are fundamentally characterized by the difference between decision-makers and those affected by the decisions. Every person may usually take each of the two sides of this distinction in various social contexts.

Three groups of risk theory describe and explain aspects of risk in modern society:

- *Psychology and cognition theory* is focused on analyzing individual and collective attitudes toward risk behaviour and risk management under given situational conditions. It shows that risks which are taken voluntarily are viewed as much more acceptable than those which are forced. Moreover, the acceptance of a given risk depends on the amount of perceived control over the risk and/or over the source of the risk. The more distant the possible consequences seem to be, the lower will the risk of a decision be judged. Also, risk acceptance in particular depends on the perceived reversibility of the decision.

- *Cultural theory* looks at social groups as a decisive factor. It understands risk as a collective social construct, one which depends on the properties of the social group in which it occurs. Douglas and Wildavsky (1982), distinguish four types of social groups (*cultures*), each with a specific concept of risk: (1) *hierarchical* treats risks as manageable; (2) *individualistic* market culture attributes risks to the sphere of individual action frames and generally accepts them as calculable issues; (3) *egalitarian* culture is highly averse to risk and very sensitive to all kinds of danger; (4) *fatalist* culture conceives risks as imposed by others. In contrast to the psychological theories, cultural theory aims at, and allows for, an understanding of risk as a socially constructed phenomenon.
- Sociological *systems theory* also looks at risk as a social phenomenon by studying the characteristic features of risky decisions. The future more and more becomes a relevant dimension with respect to the legitimation of decisions. It is no longer seen as constitutively intransparent and incalculable. The issue of risk assessment becomes pervasive for all social systems which tend to externalize these risks and to shift the responsibility of risky decisions to other functional systems.

SEE ALSO: Information Society

REFERENCES

Clausen, L. & Dombrowsky, W. R. (1984) Warnpraxis und Warnlogik. *Zeitschrift für Soziologie* 13 (4): 293–307.

Collingridge, D. (1980) *The Social Control of Technology*. Frances Pinter, London.

Douglas, M. & Wildavsky, A. (1982) *Risk and Culture*. University of California Press, Berkeley, CA.

Luhmann, N. (1993) *Risk: A Sociological Theory*. De Gruyter, Berlin/New York.

SUGGESTED READING

Beck, U. (1999) *World Risk Society*. Polity Press, Cambridge.

ALFONS BORA

rite of passage

Pioneered by the Durkheimian anthropologist Arnold Van Gennep (1909: *Les Rites de Passage*), the term refers to ceremonies that mark individual changes of identity (e.g. childbirth, death) or collective celebrations of seasonal change (Easter, harvest). Van Gennep identified three phases in these rites: (1) separation, when the individual or the group is distanced from their former identities; (2) liminality, an intermediate phase; and (3) reaggregation (incorporation), during which the individual/group is readmitted to society as bearer of new status. Because rites of passage demarcate sacred from profane time (everyday life), their performance is formalized. Initiates are placed in symbolically subordinate positions vis-à-vis those who have already been initiated, undergoing elaborate "trials" (isolation, humiliation, fasting) before they are accepted back into the community.

Van Gennep influenced two important twentieth-century symbolic anthropologists, Victor Turner and Mary Douglas. Turner (1966) explored liminality as a dangerous phase for the initiate(s) and the whole community, which both challenges and sustains social order. Douglas (1966) suggests that liminality negotiates opposing structural situations: her analysis of "dirt" as a moral sign that enables societies to establish boundaries between social categories (clean and unclean, good and evil, dangerous and safe) echoes Van Gennep's tripartite analytical schema.

It was noted that the concept's inherent vagueness invites researchers to construct most transitional stages as rites of passage. Van Gennep also stressed that in such rites one phase may be ritualistically exaggerated at the expense of the other two (e.g. baptism as incorporation into society). This led to confusion concerning the classification of transitional rituals as rites of separation, liminality, or incorporation (e.g., marriage can be all three). The concept found various uses in the social sciences (e.g. in tourism/leisure studies).

SEE ALSO: Durkheim, Émile; Ritual

REFERENCES

Douglas, M. (1966) *Purity and Danger: An Analysis of the Concepts of Pollution and Taboo*. Routledge & Kegan Paul, London.

Turner, V. (1966) *The Ritual Process: Structure and Anti-Structure*. Cornell University Press, Ithaca, NY.

Van Gennep, A. (1960) [1909] *The Rites of Passage*. University of Chicago Press, Chicago, IL.

RODANTHI TZANELLI

ritual

Ritual involves conventionalized, stylized, communicative and meaningful human actions. Sometimes rituals are planned special occasions that generate powerful emotional responses among participants. Religious and political ritual is a case in point. By contrast other uses of the concept point to a low key presence in everyday life. Sometimes this is referred to as interaction ritual.

The canonical text for the study of ritual in social science is Durkheim's *Elementary Forms of Religious Life*. Here, Durkheim (1968 [1912]) drew upon ethnographic material about Aboriginal Australia to argue that societies needed periodically to renew social bonds and solidaristic ties. Tribal gatherings involving ritual activity performed this function. They involved the manipulation and invocation of sacred and profane symbols, totems, and supernatural forces; coordinated bodily motions and expressive actions; feasting and sexual activity; the enactment of myths and legends. The result was a heightened emotional sensibility and a sense of excitement that Durkheim called *collective effervescence*. Although he drew his material from what he thought of as a "primitive" society, Durkheim explicitly intended his insights on the characteristics and social functions of ritual to have universal relevance. Subsequent work by W. Lloyd Warner on American small-town life and by Edward Shils and Michael Young on the 1953 coronation of Queen Elizabeth II supported this contention. Robert Bellah, Mary Douglas, and Victor Turner developed slightly later arguments consistent with Durkheim's vision of a ritually integrated or ritually organized society. This approach has been criticized for assuming social consensus and normative integration.

The period extending through the 1970s and 1980s saw new visions of ritual as an instrumental political strategy emerging. Steven Lukes (1975) and David Kertzer argued that we needed to understand rituals as events with sponsors that were attempts at domination. Scholars like Stuart Hall in the emergent area of cultural studies read of youth subcultures as "rituals of resistance" characterized by stylized critique of the dominant social order. Michel Foucault spoke of the "spectacle of the scaffold" and the ways this reproduced systems of control. These perspectives have been critiqued for subordinating meaning to struggles for power or for having an overly purposive view of ritual action.

A second front against the Durkheimian mainstream emerged out of Erving Goffman's work on face-to-face interaction. What Goffman (1967) called *interaction rituals* were everyday encounters between people in which appropriate displays of deference and demeanor were expected. These offered mutual confirmation of the value of the self, of social status, and of role expectations, thus providing a sense of ontological security and allowing interactions to be successfully accomplished by more or less reflexive social agents. Recently Randall Collins has combined this line of thinking with conflict sociology. Collective identities and solidarities are built from the bottom up through "*interaction ritual chains*." These not only generate pro-social emotions, such as enthusiasm and esprit de corps, but also play a role in the formation of stratification hierarchies and exclusionary cliques. Some are inside the ritual interaction and derive psychological and network benefits, others are kept out.

SEE ALSO: Durkheim, Émile; Goffman, Erving; Religion; Religion, Sociology of

REFERENCES

Durkheim, É. (1968) [1912] *The Elementary Forms of Religious Life*. Allen & Unwin, London.

Goffman, E. (1967) *Interaction Ritual*. Aldine, Chicago, IL.

Lukes, S. (1975) Political ritual and social integration. *British Journal of Sociology* 9 (2): 289–308.

PHILIP SMITH

role

The term *role* derives from the french *rôle*, which refers to the part that an actor must learn for a theatrical performance. In an analogous way, in the field of sociology, this concept relates to the social role that an individual plays within a given society. Role, therefore, can be viewed as a model of behavior which arises concerning a certain social function and which refers to the set of expectations that the society has on the behavior of an individual occupying a particular social position.

The concept of role is narrowly linked to the concept of status. But whereas status is generally seen as a more static concept, since it indicates the social positioning of an individual in a certain moment, the concept of role is more dynamic referring to the different behaviors that an individual must carry out when he/she is occupying a particular social position.

In every culture there exists a set of well-defined roles, having a generalized agreement on the behavior expected from the individuals who exercise these roles (i.e. the role of a mother). Through the process of socialization, an individual learns and internalizes the norms of behavior associated with given social positions. However, the social assumption of every role is not absolutely determined, so that the behaviors prescribed for every social position are wide enough that each individual has a margin of freedom to adapt his/her behavior to his/her own personality.

All individuals play diverse roles, so many as groups to which he/she belongs. The sum of all the roles that the individual plays constitutes his/her social personality. Every person can accede to a role by means of the assignment, the role is given to him/her from outside (son's role), or by means of achievement, when it is applied by means of a personal decision (the role of a sociology student). The play of different social roles can derive in a conflict of incompatibility when the fulfillment of the expectations of one role prevents an individual from fulfilling the expectations of another. For example, playing the role of a professional can often interfere with playing the role of a family member.

The concept of social role has been studied from different theoretical approaches within sociology. The structural-functionalist approach, exemplified by Talcott Parsons and Robert Merton, considers roles as a standardized, stable and difficult to modify way of behavior that is associated with a particular social position. From this perspective, the individuals will have little freedom to modify their expected social behavior, provided that the role is firmly prescribed by the social norms. On the other hand, from the phenomenological perspective within sociology, exemplified by Peter Berger and Thomas Luckmann, roles are seen as guides to what is expected from the social actors in a particular situation. Thus, they grant a certain amount of freedom to the individual to represent the social role in his/her own way. Similarly, the dramaturgical model, exemplified by Erving Goffman, focuses on the different roles that individuals play in varying social contexts to interact with other persons.

SEE ALSO: Gender Ideology and Gender Role Ideology; Goffman, Erving; Role Theory; Role-Taking

SUGGESTED READINGS

Stryker, S. (1980) *Symbolic Interaction: A Structural Version*. University of California Press, Menlo Park, CA.

Turner, R. (1962) Role-taking: process versis conformity. In: Rose, A. (ed.), *Human Behavior and Social Processes*. Houghton Mifflin, Boston, MA, pp. 20–40.

GASPAR BRANDLE

role theory

Role theory is designed to explain how individuals who occupy particular social positions are expected to behave and how they expect others to behave. Role theory is based on the observation that people behave predictably and that an individual's behavior is context-specific, based on their social position and situation. Role theory is often described using the metaphor of the theater.

There has been substantial debate over the meaning of the key concept in role theory: that of role. A role can be defined as a social position, behavior associated with a social position, or a typical behavior. Some theorists have suggested that roles are expectations about how an individual ought to behave, while others consider how individuals actually behave in a given social position. Others have suggested that a role is a characteristic behavior or expected behavior, a part to be played, or a script for social conduct.

Theorists have used the term role to connote characteristic behaviors, social parts to be played, or social conduct, depending on the theorist's definition. While some agreement exists that the basic concerns of role theory are with characteristic behaviors, parts to be played, and scripts for behavior, theorists differ on whether roles are norms, beliefs, or preferences. Because the term is used in everyday language, imprecision in the sociological definition has led to misinterpretations of role theory itself and some disagreement concerning key aspects of role theory (e.g., whether expectations about behaviors associated with social positions are based on norms, beliefs, or preferences).

SEE ALSO: Mead, George Herbert; Role; Role-Taking

SUGGESTED READING

Turner, R. H. (2001) Role theory. In: Turner, J. H. (ed.), *Handbook of Sociological Theory*. Kluwer Academic/Plenum Publishers, New York.

MICHELLE J. HINDIN

role-taking

Role-taking refers to social interaction in which people adopt and act out a particular social role. If society is indeed a stage, then people may be thought of as social actors performing roles, each the other's fellow player. Rendered more clinically, and following Ralph H. Turner (1956; 1962), role-taking is the process of anticipating and viewing behavior as motivated by an imputed social role. From the child playing at being "a mother" to the adult who receives a paycheck for playing at being "a police officer," role-taking is a ubiquitous feature of social life.

The most influential conception of role-taking as an elementary feature of social life was given in the pragmatist social psychology of George Herbert Mead, who coined the phrase "taking the role of the other." In Mead's view, society is best understood as a symbolic universe created and recreated through ongoing, emergent, and ultimately indeterminate symbolic interaction. This constantly (even though usually subtly) changing symbolic universe mediates all major facets of human experience, as in the title of his most famous collection of lectures, *Mind, Self, and Society* (1934).

SEE ALSO: Dramaturgy; Goffman, Erving; Interaction; Komarovsky, Mirra; Mead, George Herbert; Role; Role Theory

REFERENCES

Turner, R. H. (1956) Role-taking, role standpoint, and reference-group behavior. *American Journal of Sociology* 61 (4): 316–28.

Turner, R. H. (1962) Role-taking: process versus conformity. In: Rose, A. M. (ed.), *Human Behavior and Social Process: An Interactionist Approach*. Houghton Mifflin, Boston, MA, pp. 20–40.

STEVEN P. DANDANEAU

rural sociology

Rural sociology grew out of the same historical era and ferment as sociology more broadly, but whereas the discipline from whence it sprang was rooted heavily in liberal arts colleges, rural sociology – in the USA – was heavily indebted institutionally to the rise of the land grant university. This was a uniquely US initiative, deeding land to states specifically for establishing universities that consciously sought to link teaching, research, and service – in this latter case, in the form of another institution, the Cooperative Extension Service.

Rural sociology's foci historically and contemporarily have followed closely what is generally meant by "rural". In general, the term was thought to have three meanings. First, "rural" often was a short-hand for areas with relatively low population density. The population emphasis was also true in US census categories, where people were sorted by such residential distinctions as farming, open land, small town, less than 2,500 total population, population 2,500–25,000 (or sometimes 50,000), and so on up to and including large cities. In time, this kind of categorization changed to be called non-metropolitan and metropolitan (among other schemes). A second way of characterizing rural areas was by occupation, giving great emphasis to farming both as activity and as industry. A third way of thinking about rural areas was one based on values. Where urban areas were heterogeneous (in all ways) and modern, rural areas were homogeneous and traditional. Early sociologists, including Redfield and Tönnies, among others, captured this difference with terms such as "folk" and "urban" or *Gemeinschaft* and *Gesellschaft*.

The first department of rural sociology was established in 1915 at Cornell University and in 1936 the Rural Sociological Society was established. Despite its size (in 2008, while the American Sociological Association had about 14,000 members, the Rural Sociological Society had about 700), rural sociology has had considerable impact, partly because it was fairly narrowly focused on issues such as population, community, family, economic development, and in recent years environment and agriculture/food systems. Some of the early rural sociologists (e.g., Dwight Sanderson, Charles Loomis, and William Sewell) were elected as president of both the Rural Sociological Society and the American Sociological Association

Coming out of World War II, rural sociology entered a period of both institutional and organizational growth. Virtually all states had either a department of rural sociology ensconced in their land grant universities or a strong rural sociology unit nested in their departments of sociology. Many universities awarded PhDs in rural sociology and jobs were plentiful in the land grant system, in government, and in an expanding network of non-governmental organizations States and federal funding for rural sociological research, along with funding for the social sciences in general, grew throughout the 1950s and 1960s. During the 1970s the organizational fabric of rural sociology came under scrutiny as states began to withdraw support from higher education in general and agricultural programs in particular. In the 1980s the field of rural sociology experienced a resurgence of sorts, in part to accommodate scholarship in the area of the environment. As the twentieth century ended and the twenty-first began, the sociology of agriculture and food systems emerged as a burgeoning area of scholarship and outreach in many rural sociology programs around the country. In the contemporary era, rural sociology has struggled to keep its competitive advantage – both broadly (in sociology) and narrowly (in "ag" schools).

SEE ALSO: Community; Metropolis; Urban Revolution

SUGGESTED READINGS

Falk, W. W. and Zhao, S. (1989) Paradigms, theories and methods in contemporary rural sociology: a partial replication and extension. *Rural Sociology* 54: 587–600.

Lyson, T. A. (2004) *Civic Agriculture: Reconnecting Farm, Food and Family*. Tufts University Press, Medford, MA.

WILLIAM W. FALK

S

sacred

The Latin word *sacer*, from which the term sacred is derived, denotes a distinction between what is and what is not pertaining to the gods. In not a dissimilar fashion, the Hebrew root of *k–d–sh*, which is usually translated as "Holy," is based on the idea of separation of the consecrated and desecrated in relation to the divine. Whatever the specific expression of the sacred, however, there is a fairly universal cultural division where the sacred constitutes phenomena which are set apart, revered, and distinguished from all other phenomena that constitute the profane or the mundane. However, in Hinduism there has long existed the belief that the sacred and the unclean both belong to a single linguistic category. Thus, the Hindu notion of pollution suggests that the sacred and the non-sacred need not be absolute opposites; they can be relative categories; what is clean in relation to one thing may be unclean in relation to another, and vice versa.

The interest of sociologists in the social significance of the sacred is largely derived from the concerns of the subdiscipline of the sociology of religion. However, considerable disagreement exists as to the precise social origins of that which is designated sacred. Hence, an understanding of the sacred is frequently intimately bound up with broad definitions of religion itself, the categorization of certain social activities as religious, and particular sociological approaches to the subject. Such concerns have subsequently ensured that sociological perceptions of what constitutes the sacred as a social manifestation are subject to constant change and have led to a divergence of thought as to its nature.

While early anthropological accounts of the nature of the sacred have informed sociological theorizing, it was in turn heavily influenced by the work of Durkheim. In the opening chapter to *The Elementary Forms of the Religious Life* (1915) Durkheim summarized and rejected earlier definitions of religion. Durkheim argued that by sacred things we should not understand simply those things which are called gods or spirits – a rock a tree, a river, a pebble, a building – which are frequently held as sacred, as displaying inherent sacred qualities. The totem is the emblem of the clan, but is also at once the symbol of the sacred and society, for the sacred and society are one. Thus, through worship of god or the totem, human beings worship society – the real object of religious veneration. It is a relationship of inferiority and dependency. Durkheim argued that it is easier for human beings to visualize and direct feelings of awe towards a symbol than such a complex thing as a clan. This is what gives the totem, hence society, its sacred quality.

SEE ALSO: Durkheim, Émile; Primitive Religion; Religion, Sociology of; Sacred/Profane

SUGGESTED READINGS

Berger, P. (1967) *The Sacred Canopy: Elements of a Sociological Theory of Religion*. Doubleday, New York.

Freud, S. (1938) *Totem and Taboo*. Penguin, London.

STEPHEN HUNT

sacred/profane

The significance of the sacred/profane distinction in sociology is to be most directly credited to Durkheim's *The Elementary Forms of the Religious Life*, where he defines religion as "a unified system of beliefs and practices relative to sacred things, that is to say, things set apart and forbidden – beliefs and practices which unite into one single moral community called a Church, all who adhere to them" (1915: 47). The sacred thus involves *things set apart and forbidden*. Everything else is profane. As a result, "profane" is always easy to define: it is anything within a society that is not sacred. To come to this conclusion about the sacred and its role in establishing a "single moral community," Durkheim read anthropological works, specifically on the Australian aborigines and particularly the role of totems among clans or tribes of what were considered "primitive" peoples. This is the significance of the word *elementary* in the title of his book. Durkheim, like many other early sociologists, believed that by studying the maintenance of social organization among these peoples significant insights could be obtained about core processes that enabled societies to develop and maintain themselves – and, as a corollary, what changes in the transition to modernity might explain the emerging social problems of his day. The distinction had an enormous direct effect in the sociology of religion, but also powerfully influenced the broader sociological theoretical paradigm of functionalism, especially through its integration into Talcott Parsons's *The Structure of Social Action* (1938).

In the Parsonian synthesis that popularized and standardized Durkheim's definition for an especially formative generation of sociologists, the notion of "church" in the original Durkheimian formulation of the definition of religion was gradually secularized into "society" – that is, whereas Durkheim spoke quite specifically of a moral community "called a Church," later generations came to identify the moral community with society or in other cases with virtually any other ongoing social group. Rather tautologically, in fact, social scientists began to look for "the sacred" in groupings and structures that one would not normally associate with religion – ranging across as wide a spectrum as the flag and related patriotic paraphernalia in the USA and the tombs of Lenin and Stalin in the Soviet Union to Babe Ruth's bat as sacred to baseball. This understanding of sacrality had a twofold effect on the study of both society and religion: On the one hand, it made religion an essential social institution: no religion, no society. On the other hand, it also said that while religion was good (functional), it was not true. That is, it reduced the end point of religion (the divine, in whatever name or form) to a social construction.

Durkheim's sacrality proposition led in at least two directions in the study of religion. The positive outcome was a corpus of work on political religion that flowed freely and broadly from a seminal essay by Parsons's former student Robert Bellah, "Civil religion in America" (1963). This concept refers to a "transcendent religion of the nation" and resonates well with the functionalism of both Durkheim and Parsons. A move away from functionalism generally in sociology beginning in the late 1960s brought in its wake first secularization theory, and then a reaction against the Parsonian-Durkheimian formulation as an adequate understanding of religion. Secularization theory hence led to anti-secularization theory, which amounted to a rethinking of both religion and sacrality in the Durkheimian context.

SEE ALSO: Durkheim, Émile; Sacred

REFERENCES

Bellah, R. (1963) Civil religion in America. *Dædalus* 96: 1–21.

Durkheim, E. (1915) *The Elementary Forms of Religious Life*. Allen & Unwin, London.

Parsons, T. (1937) *The Structure of Social Action*. New York: Free Press.

SUGGESTED READING

Swatos, W. H., Jr. (1999) Revisiting the sacred. *Implicit Religion* 2: 33–8.

WILLIAM H. SWATOS, JR.

safer sex

Safer sex emerged as a strategy to prevent the spread of disease with the advent of the AIDS epidemic in the early 1980s. Richard Berkowitz and Michael Callen, two gay New Yorkers, first outlined the theory and application of safer sex in their 1983 tract, "How to have sex in an epidemic." As an alternative to the confusing, all-or-nothing early approaches to HIV prevention, safer sex offered a practical strategy. People were going to have sex. As such, it was best to do it in a safe, mutually satisfying, caring manner. Berkowitz and Callen presented a harm-reduction approach now recognized around the world as a model that allows for both intimacy and protection. The result was a revolution allowing for personal and political protection, both for sex and for the movement that liberated it. With time, safer sex practices spread around the globe as a theoretical and practical approach to preventing the spread of HIV. Safer sex became the model for sex-positive discourses that rejected the politics of sexual shame, temperance, and prohibition.

Future research will need to contend with the problems of safer sex and explore alternative technologies, such as microbicides, which can serve as substitutes for latex. In the two and a half decades since the birth of safer sex, new practices of safer sexual activity have emerged. These include community-based approaches such as "jack off" clubs, where men meet to have the safest type of safe sex – mutual masturbation – and more distant approaches such as telephone sex and cybersex.

SEE ALSO: AIDS, Sociology of; Sex Education; Sexual Practices

SUGGESTED READING

Berkowitz, R. & Callen, M. (2001) [1983] How to have sex in an epidemic. In: Bull, C. (ed.), *Come Out Fighting: A Century of Essential Writing on Gay and Lesbian Liberation*. Thunder's Mouth Press, New York.

BENJAMIN SHEPARD

Saint-Simon, Claude Henri (1760–1825)

A self-taught philosopher, Claude Henri de Rouvroy, Comte de Saint-Simon, helped inspire sociology, socialism, technocratic approaches to social organization, and the idea of a united Europe. He called for the refounding of knowledge, including the study of society, on the basis of the sciences, which he believed held the key to intellectual order and thus social stability after the French Revolution and Napoleonic Wars. Based on his analysis of history, he predicted that society in the future would be scientific and industrial. It would be a workshop in which everyone would take up useful activities. A perceptive analyst of modernity, Saint-Simon left a significant legacy.

Taking a holistic approach to society, Saint-Simon was important for ascertaining that intellectual, moral, social, political, and economic developments were closely interrelated. He saw that society was undergoing a profound, all-encompassing transformation, going from a feudal, Christian system marked by the consumption needs of a privileged class to a scientific, industrial system characterized by production and the rise of new classes. He influenced Karl Marx and Friedrich Engels, who developed modern socialism from his ideas of tracing class conflict throughout history; organizing economic and social life for collective, non-militaristic ends; and reducing the role of government to meeting the needs of the poor. After Saint-Simon's death, Auguste Comte developed positivism (the scientific philosophy encompassing all knowledge) as well as sociology, which he viewed as a kind of social engineering in the interest of social stability and harmony. Many businessmen during the Second Empire were attracted to Saint-Simon's stress on industrial productivity, efficiency, utility, and technocracy. Others who were influenced by him and the Saint-Simonian movement include John Stuart Mill, Thomas Carlyle, Herbert Spencer, Heinrich Heine, Alexander Herzen, and Charles Lemonnier. The latter's work inspired the idea of the League of Nations.

SEE ALSO: Comte, Auguste; Marx, Karl; Socialism

SUGGESTED READINGS

de Saint-Simon, C. H. (1975) *Henri Saint-Simon, 1760–1825: Selected Writings on Science, Industry, and Social Organisation*, ed. and trans. K. Taylor. Holmes & Meier, New York.

de Saint-Simon, C. H. (1976) *The Political Thought of Saint-Simon*, ed. G. Ionescu, trans. V. Ionescu. Oxford University Press, London.

MARY PICKERING

same-sex marriage/civil unions

Same-sex marriage refers to a union by two people of the same sex that is legally sanctioned by the state, where identical rights and responsibilities are afforded same-sex and heterosexual married couples. The term "gay marriage" is popularly used to refer to same-sex partnerships or cohabiting relationships that are formally registered in some way as a "civil union" (variously known as civil partnerships, registered partnerships, and registered cohabitation), although the latter are in fact legally distinct from marriage. The term is also sometimes employed to talk about unregistered same-sex couple cohabitation or partnerships acknowledged through commitment ceremonies. A growing number of states currently afford same-sex couples the opportunity to participate in marriage. As of late 2010 these include Belgium, Spain, the Netherlands, Canada, South Africa, Norway, Sweden, Portugal, Iceland, and Argentina. In addition, same-sex marriages are recognized in Mexico City, Mexico and in the USA in Massachusetts, Vermont, Iowa, New Hampshire, Connecticut, and the District of Columbia. Same-sex marriages from other countries are honored (though not for domestic citizens) in Israel, Mexico (though they are performed in Mexico City), as well as in the USA in New York, Maryland, and Rhode Island (see the following websites for detailed information on changing status in different countries: www.marriageequality.org; www.samesexmarriage.ca; www.stonewall.org.uk). Civil unions, civil partnerships, and registered cohabitation, which include some exemptions from the automatic rights and responsibilities afforded heterosexual married couples, are the most common forms of legal recognition. They offer some of the symbolic and material advantages associated with marriage, but with more limited legal status. At a global level, most same-sex partners must currently rely on "do-it-yourself" affirmation and commitment ceremonies, or seek religious blessings where available.

Same-sex marriage and civil unions have become high-profile political issues in many countries since the early 1990s. In Europe the number of states that have extended, or are planning to extend, legal recognition to lesbian and gay relationships through civil unions has increased steadily since the first civil partnership legislation was passed in Denmark in 1989. Elsewhere, Australia, Argentina, Brazil,

New Zealand, South Africa, and other countries have either nationwide or regional legal facilities for the recognition of same-sex partnerships or cohabiting relationships. In the United States, the issue of same-sex marriage has been an especially contentious one. While some states have introduced legislation to recognize same-sex marriage or civil unions, other states have enacted constitutional amendments that explicitly forbid same-sex marriage, or have passed legislation that bars civil union-type recognition. This points to the strength of support and opposition that the issue of same-sex marriage can generate in the US and most other countries where the issue is debated. On the one hand, some constituencies see same-sex marriage and civil unions as an ultimate marker of social and political tolerance. On the other hand, some groups view the issue as indicative of the decline in religious and moral values in an increasingly secular world. Amongst conservative religious and social groups especially, same-sex marriage is often interpreted as an attack on the primacy and "naturalness" of the heterosexual married bond that is assumed to underpin a stable society.

A number of social developments have influenced the current focus of lesbian and gay politics on same-sex marriage. AIDS, some theorists argue, was a catalyst in mobilizing a new lesbian and gay relational politics in the 1980s. This was initially focused on the recognition of same-sex partners' caring commitments, and protecting "rights" in relation to property and next-of-kin issues. Community responses to AIDS facilitated the institution building and political confidence that made same-sex marriage seem like a realizable political objective. Since the 1980s new possibilities have opened up for lesbian and gay parenting (through self and assisted insemination, surrogacy, fostering, adoption, and so on) and a growing number of same-sex couples are choosing to parent. Same-sex marriage is seen as a crucial strategy for recognizing and protecting co-parenting commitments.

Another social development is the changing nature of heterosexual marriage itself. The separation of marriage from the needs of reproduction and women's increasing economic independence from men are transforming the meanings of heterosexual marriage. Some theorists cite statistics on divorce, cohabitation, single parenting, and solo living as an indication of the fragility of the institution of marriage. The recognition of same-sex marriage can therefore be interpreted as an attempt to reinvigorate or reinvent an ailing institution. A different perspective suggests that the changing role of welfare states can explain the political support that same-sex marriage has received from unexpected quarters. Some argue that as welfare states seek to shift social and care responsibilities back onto individuals and their families and communities, the recognition of same-sex marriage makes sense as it formalizes the responsibilities of lesbians and gay men for their partners and families.

SEE ALSO: Cohabitation; Family Diversity; Gay and Lesbian Movement; Identities, Lesbian and Gay; Lesbian and Gay Families; Marriage

SUGGESTED READINGS

Sullivan, A. (ed.) (1997) *Same-Sex Marriage: Pro and Con – A Reader*. Vintage Books, New York.

Weeks, J., Heaphy, B., & Donovan, C. (2001) *Same-Sex Intimacies: Families of Choice and Other Life Experiments*. Routledge, London.

BRIAN HEAPHY

sampling, qualitative (purposive)

Perhaps nothing better captures the difference between quantitative and qualitative methods than the different logics that undergird sampling approaches. Qualitative inquiry typically focuses in depth on relatively small samples, even single cases ($n = 1$), selected *purposefully*. Quantitative methods typically depend on larger samples selected randomly. Not only are the techniques for sampling different, but also the very logic of each approach is unique because the purpose of each strategy is different.

The logic and power of random sampling derives from statistical probability theory. In contrast, the logic and power of *purposive sampling* lies in selecting *information-rich cases* for study in depth. Information-rich cases are those from which one can learn a great deal about issues of central importance to the purpose of the inquiry, thus the term *purposive* sampling (or alternatively, purposeful sampling). What would be "bias" in statistical sampling, and therefore a weakness, becomes intended focus in qualitative sampling, and therefore a strength. Studying information-rich cases yields insights and in-depth understanding rather than empirical generalizations. For example, if the purpose of a program evaluation is to increase the effectiveness of a program in reaching lower-socioeconomic groups, one may learn a great deal more by studying in depth a small number of carefully selected poor families than by gathering standardized information from a large, statistically representative sample of the whole program. Purposive sampling focuses on selecting information-rich cases whose study will illuminate the questions under study. There are several different strategies for purposefully selecting information-rich cases. The logic of each strategy serves a particular purpose. Only one strategy is reviewed here.

Extreme or deviant case sampling involves selecting cases that are information-rich because they are unusual or special in some way, such as outstanding successes or notable failures. In the early days of AIDS research when HIV infections almost always resulted in death, a small number of cases of people infected with HIV who did not develop AIDS became crucial outlier cases that provided important insights into directions researchers should take in combating AIDS. In program evaluation, the logic of extreme-case sampling is that lessons may be learned from successes and failures that are relevant to improving more typical programs. Consider a national program with hundreds of local sites. Many programs are operating adequately based on reports from knowledgeable sources who have made site visits to enough programs to know what the variation is. But a few programs verge on being disasters and others are excelling. If one wanted to document precisely the natural variation among programs, a random sample would be appropriate, one of sufficient size to be representative and permit generalizations to the total population of programs. However, with limited resources and time, and with the priority being how to improve programs, an evaluator might learn more by intensively studying one or more examples of really poor programs and one or more examples of really excellent programs. The evaluation focus then becomes a question of understanding under what conditions programs get into trouble and under what conditions programs exemplify excellence. The researchers and intended users involved in the study think through *what cases they could learn the most from* and those are the cases that are selected for study.

SEE ALSO: Methods; Random Sample; Qualitative Methods

SUGGESTED READINGS

Bernard, H. R. (2000) Social research methods: qualitative and quantitative approaches. Sage, Thousand Oaks, CA.
Denzin, N. & Lincoln, Y. (eds.) (2000) *Handbook of Qualitative Research*, 2nd edn. Sage, Thousand Oaks, CA.
Patton, M. Q. (2002) *Qualitative Research and Evaluation Methods*, 3rd edn. Sage, Thousand Oaks, CA.

MICHAEL QUINN PATTON

Saussure, Ferdinand de (1857–1913)

Ferdinand de Saussure is an important linguist and, along with C. S. Peirce, one of the two main contributors to semiotics (Sanders 2004). His distinction between the signifier and the signified is central. The theory of signification, the idea that a sign (like, for example, a "word" or a mathematical plus sign) is an entirely arbitrary verbal or written phonemic and phonetic device, is attributed to him. For example, the relationships between the word "cat" and the same word in French ("chat") or German ("Katze") are different only linguistically; the signified "object" (a physical cat) remains the same. The verbal sound used to signify the animal is entirely arbitrary. The standard view of Saussure is based on posthumous publication of his lecture notes (1983). Like work by Max Weber and George Herbert Mead, the *Course in General Linguistics* is the product of other hands. Between 1906 and 1911, Saussure taught three courses on general linguistics. Saussure himself found many ideas in linguistics problematic. Readers should pay attention to all of the work that Saussure did during his lifetime and not just the final lectures.

SEE ALSO: Language; *Langue* and *Parole*; Semiotics

REFERENCES

Sanders, C. (ed.) (2004) *The Cambridge Companion to Saussure*. Cambridge University Press, Cambridge.
Saussure, F. de (1983) *Course in General Linguistics*, trans. R. Harris. Duckworth, London. (Translation based on Payot editions of 1916, 1922, 1931, 1949, and 1955.)

J. I. (HANS) BAKKER

school segregation, desegregation

The USA has a long history of providing racially segregated and unequal public education to its children. Racially separate and unequal public education was not an accident; it was created by public laws and policies enacted and enforced by state governments and local school systems. After a series of Supreme Court decisions eliminated the formal legal foundation for segregation, it was recreated through racially discriminatory practices in federal housing policies, lending for home purchases, employment, wages, and school assignment practices.

Desegregation is the process that removes the formal and informal barriers preventing students from diverse racial and ethnic backgrounds from learning in the same classrooms and schools. Since the middle of the twentieth century, various desegregation policies have been widely used to remedy *de jure* (by law) and *de facto* (by practice) segregation. Among the policies employed were mandatory and voluntary busing, pairing of white and minority schools, using magnet programs to attract diverse students to segregated schools, redrawing of school attendance boundaries, and siting new schools in areas between minority and white neighborhoods. Desegregation also involved creating racially diverse faculty and staff, employing multicultural curricula, and nurturing diversity in extra and cocurricular activities. These processes ensure that, once in desegregated schools, all children have equitable opportunities to learn.

The still-unfinished process of school desegregation commenced with the landmark 1954 *Brown* vs. *Board of Education* decision, in which the Supreme Court declared that "separate educational facilities are inherently unequal" and "a denial of the equal protection of the laws."

The *Brown* decision was a sea change, overturning the essence of the infamous *Plessy* vs. *Ferguson* case, which had legitimized racially "separate but equal" public spheres. However, *Brown* only addressed public actions, not private behaviors. This tension between legal mandates for racial justice in education and private actions to preserve white educational privileges slowed effective school desegregation for decades. Arguably, the most enduring legacy of the *Brown* decision is not desegregated public schools – especially in light of nationwide trends toward resegregation and the continuing struggle for educational equity. Rather, *Brown* enshrined in US law the concept that all people are citizens of this nation and that state-enforced racial segregation is unconstitutional.

Southern schools remained segregated well into the 1960s and northern schools until the 1970s. Nevertheless, since the *Brown* decision, some regions of the United States were more successful in desegregating their schools than others. Southern and border states eventually experienced the greatest degree of desegregation. In some southern school systems the percentage of blacks attending extremely segregated minority schools dropped from 78 percent in the late 1960s to 25 percent at its lowest in the mid-1980s. Other regions of the country, where *de facto* segregation was the norm, also desegregated to a large degree. In the middle of the 1980s the national trend toward greater interracial contact in public schools stalled and began a slow reversal by the decade's end.

There are a number of reasons that the significant strides toward desegregated public education began to reverse in the late 1980s. The convergence of white interests in economic growth through interracial tranquility with black interests in educational and occupational mobility that permitted desegregation in the first three quarters of the last century did not survive through the 1990s. Other reasons for resegregation trends include the lifting of federal court orders mandating desegregation, demographic shifts in the US population – especially the explosive growth in ethnic minority populations – and the suburbanization of US communities. As a result, school systems that were once relatively desegregated are now becoming resegregated. Much of current segregation is between districts – especially central cities and their metropolitan area suburbs – rather than among schools within a single district, as was historically the case. Some observers estimate that the levels of interracial contact in public schools will soon return to pre-*Brown* levels of racial isolation.

SEE ALSO: Education; Educational Inequality; Racism, Structural and Institutional; Tracking

SUGGESTED READINGS

Clotfelter, C. T. (2004) *After Brown: The Rise and Retreat of School Desegregation*. Harvard University Press, Cambridge, MA.

Rossell, C., Armor, D. J., & Walberg, H. J. (eds.) (2002) *School Desegregation in the 21st Century*. Praeger, Westport, CT.

ROSLYN ARLIN MICKELSON

Schumpeter, Joseph A. (1883–1950)

Schumpeter is generally acknowledged as one of the first-rank economists of the twentieth century, along with John Maynard Keynes. He was born in Třešt, a small Moravian town in the Austro-Hungarian Empire (now the Czech Republic). He was educated at the University of Vienna. He taught at some provincial universities (Czernowitz, Graz, and Bonn), and for a short period after World War I he held the post of finance minister under the Austrian socialist government. In 1932 Schumpeter moved to Harvard University, and stayed there until his death.

Schumpeter's central concern was the formulation of the evolution of the capitalist economic system. His wide-ranging project can be interpreted as consisting of a system of substantive theory, i.e., (1) economic statics, (2) economic dynamics, and (3) economic sociology, and a system of metatheory, i.e., (4) the philosophy of science, (5) the history of science, and (6) the sociology of science, and is called a three-layered, two-structure approach to mind and society (Shionoya 1997). The ambitious aim Schumpeter cherished throughout his academic life was a "comprehensive sociology," an approach to social phenomena as a whole. Its central idea is the *Soziologisierung* (sociologizing) of all social sciences. Schumpeter's two-structure approach was intended to replace Marx's social theory based on the economic interpretation of history.

Schumpeter's economic dynamics or theory of economic development is well known for its emphasis on entrepreneurial innovation in a capitalist economy that includes new products, new techniques, new markets, new sources of supply and new forms of organization. He called the process of economic development "creative destruction," referring to the destruction of existing economic order by the introduction of innovation.

Schumpeter defined economic sociology as "a sort of generalized or typified or stylized economic history." The core of economic sociology is the concept of an institution that can generalize, typify, or stylize the complexities of economic history consisting of a series of innovations. He identified economic sociology as the fourth basic technique of economic analysis besides theory, statistics, and history.

In *Capitalism, Socialism, and Democracy* (1942), Schumpeter presented his famous thesis on the demise of capitalism as the result of its success. The relevance of Schumpeter's idea of economic sociology is its impact on the growth of institutional economics and evolutionary economics after World War II.

SEE ALSO: Capitalism; Economic Development

REFERENCE

Schumpeter, J. A. (1950) [1942] *Capitalism, Socialism, and Democracy*, 3rd edn. Harper & Brothers, New York.

SUGGESTED READING

Shionoya, Y. (1997) *Schumpeter and the Idea of Social Science: A Metatheoretical Study*. Cambridge University Press, Cambridge.

YUICHI SHIONOYA

Schütz, Alfred (1899–1959)

Alfred Schütz pioneered social *phenomenology*. He provided a critique of Max Weber's interpretive sociology of meaningful action, published in 1932 (1967). Three volumes of his *Collected Papers* on philosophical, epistemological, and sociological topics were published posthumously (1962; 1964; 1966), as was *Structures of the Lifeworld* (1973), completed by Thomas Luckmann on the basis of Schütz's schema. Born in Vienna in 1899, the only child of well-to-do Austrian Jewish parents, and educated at the University of Vienna, Schütz emigrated with his family to New York in 1938, where he continued a banking career and subsequently became a professor at the New School for Social Research.

Schütz critiqued Weber for treating meaning from an *observer's* point of view without considering how it is constituted *subjectively*. Drawing on Edmund Husserl's transcendental phenomenology of the temporal flow of events experienced in the mind, Schütz connected subjective meaning to: (1) the flow of mental experience in the vivid present, (2) its sedimentation in memory (and recollection), and (3) anticipation of the future. Building from his critique, Schütz developed a lifeworldly phenomenology that describes transhistorical and transcultural structures of the social world. Critics wonder whether Schütz's ego-based phenomenology has any basis for moving from consciousness to society. However, intersubjectivity is central to his analysis, and he wrote descriptive phenomenological essays on actors and forms of interaction (e.g., the man on the street, the stranger, making music).

Schütz has been underutilized relative to the power of his ideas. Nevertheless, his phenomenology has percolated into wider currents, notably through the work of Harold Garfinkel, John O'Neill, Kurt Wolff, Peter Berger, and Thomas Luckman, Dorothy Smith, Pierre Bourdieu, and Jürgen Habermas. Overall, sociology as a whole has become more "phenomenological." However, we have yet to see a fully developed phenomenological analysis of society. Thus, the full potential of Schütz's work remains unrealized.

SEE ALSO: Everyday Life; Lifeworld; Phenomenology; Weber, Max

SUGGESTED READINGS

Barber, M. (2002) Alfred Schütz. In: Zalta, E. N. (ed.), *Stanford Encyclopedia of Philosophy*: www.plato.stanford.edu/archives/win2002/entries/schutz/.

Kurrild-Klitgaard, P. (2003) The Viennese connection: Alfred Schütz and the Austrian School. *Quarterly Journal of Austrian Economics* 6: 35–67.

Wagner, H. (1983) *Alfred Schütz: An Intellectual Biography*. University of Chicago Press, Chicago, IL.

JOHN R. HALL

science

"Science" is a contested concept. There is no consensus about what it is and some maintain that the question itself is mistaken since there is no "object," science. The two epistemological extremes between which sociological frameworks used in the study of "science" move are, first, that nature is recorded by science, provided that science is in a fit state as a social institution to do so, and, second, that science is a social construction and in this sense in principle no different than any other part of culture. If one is convinced of the first proposition one's interest will be directed towards the "goal" of science; the institutional norms that regulate the activity of the community of scientists; competition; and the reward structure of science operating through "recognition" (citation practices, Nobel prizes, peer review). If one is convinced of the second proposition one will be interested not so much in the institution and community of science but rather in scientific knowledge and the question of how scientists reach a point where it can be said to have been "made." One will be interested in the "negotiation" (including writing practices) through which a stable order of scientific objects is arrived at. Let us consider these two possibilities.

The US sociologist, Robert K. Merton, was certain that science had social underpinnings. It was not the product of timeless individual curiosity. Although twentieth-century experience showed that science could be affected by political ideology, in the west it seemed to retain its "autonomy." While located within capitalist society it was insulated from it, to a certain extent, by a set of distinctive norms. The upholding of these cemented the community of scientists, and functioned to allow the pursuit of reliable (or certified) knowledge to go on. Priority disputes demonstrated how important recognition was to scientists as their only reward. Scientists are expected to share their findings; to subject the claims of others to rigorous critical tests; to be disinterested; and to judge claims not by persons but by universal criteria. Merton's norms were subjected to severe criticism of both an empirical and a theoretical kind. To his credit Merton was concerned with the distinctiveness of science. He founded the sociology of science, initiating a program of research carried out mainly by followers in the United States.

A second research tradition grew up in opposition to the Mertonian. It was known generically as the sociology of scientific knowledge (SSK). Sociologists in Britain declared their intention to carry through Karl Mannheim's sociology of knowledge to its logical conclusion, not exempting scientific beliefs from its injunction to study the social bases of all beliefs. The aim should be to open what Merton and his followers had left as a "black box." Why, it was argued, should sociological analysis halt at the threshold of scientists' beliefs as if these could not be socially influenced? SSK was avowedly relativist in its approach to scientific knowledge. Two broad schools are identifiable.

The first to appear was the "interests" approach. Owing to "interpretive flexibility," replication is not a sure-fire, decisive way to close down uncertainty about the "results" of experiments; and the closure which stabilizes "knowledge" is brought about by a range of social factors rather than something in the data: the struggle is to define the data (or the "phenomenon").

To critics of this approach the idea that social interests cause interpretive behaviour represents a failure to carry the "interpretive" perspective through to its full logical conclusion, namely that there is *only* interpretation in scientific and social life generally. This point of view was backed up by the offering of an alternative, the ethnographic study of the laboratory through usually prolonged participant observation to see how science is "made" from the messy materials to be found therein. A second alternative was the analysis of scientists' discourse to see the devices by which they sustain their sense of reality "out there" and their own access to it, against their competitors. Both approaches call for a more thoroughgoing reflexivity than the interests approach practiced. Arguably, by claiming to be authoritative, interest-type studies fail in full reflexivity. They are not based on the empirical testing of deductive theory, but rather on the *post hoc* interpretation of the interview data. Interview material is used to construct a "story" of what was "really going on" in disputes. That is, interview material is taken at face value as a faithful account rather than rhetoric and some of it is favored over the rest by the sociologist as being closer than other parts to "what really happened."

Ethnographic study has also been criticized for failing to meet its own requirements: (1) by drawing on theory and thus not truly letting the discourse "speak" as far as possible without interpretation; (2) by having no way of recognizing the basis of differential authority in science, the *effect* of which the approach brings out; and (3) through acknowledging the role of rhetoric, allowing implicitly causal forces while denying them programmatically. Recent and current studies in the sociology of science have tended to move away from an epistemologically single-stranded approach and actor-network theory tried with limited success to combine interpretive flexibility – or in principle openness – with attention to real-world outcomes.

Turning to political economy, Merton's liberal view of science's autonomy in democratic societies was not shared by J. D. Bernal, who raised the question as to whether a people's science would be a different science from the one existing under capitalism. Analysts have divided on this issue, with some, like Bernal, adopting a relativist position similar to the sociologists of scientific knowledge. Herbert Marcuse took this position as later did some feminists (though in a somewhat different way). Freed from the existing relations of domination, human society would generate a new kind of science, different from the existing one, geared to emancipation. The alternative view to this one is that scientific knowledge is effectively neutral knowledge of nature, but the direction research takes and the uses of results that are fostered, are influenced by the social, political and economic relations of capitalism to the detriment of the freedom and enlightenment that science promises. Profit and military needs dictate the use to which a basically neutral science is put. This view tends to share with Merton the belief that nature speaks through science.

SEE ALSO: Actor-Network Theory; Epistemology; Induction and Observation in Science; Science, Social Construction of; Scientific Knowledge, Sociology of; Technology, Science, and Culture

SUGGESTED READINGS

Bernal, J. D. (1964) [1939] *The Social Function of Science*. MIT Press, Cambridge, MA.

Latour, B. & Woolgar, S. (1986) [1979] *Laboratory Life: The Construction of Scientific Facts*. Princeton University Press, Princeton, NJ.

Merton, R. K. (1973) *The Sociology of Science: Theoretical and Empirical Investigations*. University of Chicago Press, Chicago, IL.

Woolgar, S. (1986) *Science: The Very Idea*. Tavistock, London.

IAN VARCOE

science, social construction of

In its simplest form, the claim that science is socially constructed means that there is no direct link between nature and our ideas about nature – the products of science are not themselves natural. This claim can be taken to mean different things and a distinction is often made between strong and weak interpretations of social constructivism. The stronger claim would not recognize an independent reality or materiality outside of our perceptions of it, or at least dismiss it as of no relevance as we cannot access it. This stance is, however, not a very common one. A weaker social constructivism tends to leave ontological queries to one side and instead focus on epistemological matters – how we gain knowledge about the world. What we count as knowledge is dependent on, and shaped by, the contexts in which it is created. Knowledge is thus made by people drawing on available cultural material, not preexisting facts in a world outside of human action, waiting to be uncovered.

Whereas the idea of science and scientific knowledge as socially constructed can be traced to many a scholar, the very concept of social construction was introduced into mainstream social sciences by Peter L. Berger and Thomas Luckmann in their influential book *The Social Construction of Reality. A Treatise in the Sociology of Knowledge* (1966). In it, the authors combine ideas from Durkheim and Weber with perspectives from George Herbert Mead, to form a theory of social action. This theory would not only deal with plurality of knowledge and reality – for example what counts as knowledge in Borneo may make little sense in Bath and vice versa – but also study the ways in which realities are taken as known in human society. How is it that a concept such as gender is taken to be "natural" and "real" in every culture, while at the same time it is perceived and performed very differently in different cultures? Knowledge about the society in which we live is "a realization in the double sense of the word, in the sense of apprehending objectivated social reality, and in the sense of ongoingly producing this reality." An objectivated social reality is a reality that is not "private" to the person who produced it, but accessed and shared by others. As humans we are continuously creating and recreating reality, and the role of the sociologist is to analyze the process of how reality is constructed, that is, how knowledge becomes institutionally established as real.

One way of understanding science as socially constructed is to point to obvious and "external" social factors, such as funding structures or political influences. These affect the way in which science develops; business interests can determine which projects are pursued, policy decisions can effectively close down entire avenues of research, and so on. The way in which research is institutionally organized is another much-cited example of "external" social shaping of science – for example how heavy bureaucracy and strict disciplinary boundaries render the pursuit of trans-disciplinary science difficult. Another variety of this brand of social constructivism is the argument that only scientific knowledge deemed to be "relevant" or interesting will be pursued.

The definition of scientific problems and framing of hypotheses often come with an inbuilt gender bias. Male contraception is an under-researched area because reproductive responsibilities are firmly placed with women in our society and it is thus assumed that it is the female body that is to be manipulated. Such social values are also reflected in the very methods that scientists will use – most human trials of medicines are performed on young men between 18 and 20 years of age. The generic "human" is thus a young man, whereas elderly women are the more likely consumers of the medicines that are being trialled.

Scientists tend to insist that their *way* of arriving at knowledge makes their claims more true and more valuable than other groups' knowledge claims (who arrived at their conclusions by different means and on different grounds). They argue that while it may be the case that certain types of knowledge – such as ideas about morality – are socially constructed, scientific knowledge should be exempt from such a mode of analysis. Scientific knowledge has a special authority and status because of the way in which we arrive at such knowledge. The "scientific method" – rigorous and systematic examination, testing, and replication – thus guarantees the veracity of scientific claims. "Truthfulness" is taken to mean that the claim in question is a direct representation of a reality that exists outside of, and independent from, our perceptions of it. A social constructivist view of science instead holds that scientific knowledge is as "social" as other types of knowledge.

SEE ALSO: Actor-Network Theory; Nature; Science; Science and Culture; Scientific Knowledge, Sociology of

SUGGESTED READINGS

Hacking, I. (1999) *The Social Construction of What?* Harvard University Press, Cambridge, MA.

Harding, S. (1991) *Whose Science? Whose Knowledge?* Cornell University Press, Ithaca, NY.

Latour, B. & Woolgar, S. (1986) *Laboratory Life.* Princeton University Press, Princeton, NJ.

LENA ERIKSSON

scientific knowledge, sociology of

In the early 1970s, the sociology of scientific knowledge (SSK) started to dynamically emerge from a broad church of sociological, historical and philosophical reflections upon the very nature, direction, content and truth status of scientific knowledge itself, rather than merely upon the social relations between those who happen to be scientists.

Hence, even the heartland of rationality, namely logic and mathematics, should systematically be investigated and explained in terms of its social origin and underpinnings. According to the Strong Program, which originally took form on the basis of an acute critique against Robert Merton's sociological work, as well as of the post-Kuhnian problematic around the relationship between the sociology of science and the sociology of knowledge, this systematic investigation should, in principle, be causal, impartial, symmetrical, and reflexive.

Furthermore, ethnomethodological researchers, mainly inspired from the Nietzschean and Wittgensteinian philosophies of language and meaning, have adopted an *ethnographic approach* to the study of what Bruno Latour and Steve Woolgar (1986) perceptively called "Laboratory Life," which has eventually gone on to comprehensively include studies of conferences, journal management etc. That is, empirical access to the everyday lifeworldly experiences and negotiations at the "lab bench" is said to give an added dimension of insight into the very reality of social life inside technoscience.

These researchers have strategically pointed out the myriad ways in which "truth" and the idea (or impression) of "objectivity" are competently managed and creatively enacted in the everyday performative activities of technoscience – in particular, the myriad ways in which the inherently messy business of generating new data is "cleaned up" in its later presentation at scientific conferences and in academic publications.

A groundbreaking contribution, which has been closely related to the aforementioned "laboratory studies" and systematically attempted to develop new innovative directions within SSK, can be discerned in the original emphasis on *actor-network theory* (or the *sociology of translation*). Bruno Latour and others (Michel Callon, John Law, and Madeline Akrich) elaborated this theory by carefully giving up any received distinction between social/nature, social/technology, and human/nonhuman. Here, the "hardness" of scientific facts simply relies on changing networks of *heterogeneous* actors or "actants" (and their ongoing interactions).

The very notion of an ultra-activistic nature ultimately constituted a radical departure from our taken-for-granted anthropocentric worldviews assigning priority to the human and the social. Subsequently, old dualisms disappeared from the field of SSK, on the methodological basis of the supposedly universally applicable principles of agnosticism, generalized symmetry, and free association.

Since the 1980s, the parallel pragmatist reconsideration of the Strong Program's principle of reflexivity, derived from several intellectual movements such as post-structuralism, constructivism, feminism, discourse analysis, and ethnomethodology, has obviously served the goal of a generalized symmetry between science and the social world, aiming to self-consciously prevent sociology from pretending the detached and free-floating observer. But this profoundly calls for a *critical sociology of scientific knowledge* – that is, a critical broadening of SSK beyond the selective ontological focus on "substantive findings" and the subsequent exclusion of moral, political and policy questions.

SEE ALSO: Actor-Network Theory; Epistemology; Knowledge; Knowledge, Sociology of; Kuhn, Thomas and Scientific Paradigms; Merton, Robert K; Science; Science, Social Construction of; Technology, Science, and Culture

SUGGESTED READINGS

Latour, B. & Woolgar, S. (1986) *Laboratory Life: The Construction of Scientific Facts*. Princeton University Press, Princeton, NJ.

Woolgar, S. (1988) *Science: The Very Idea*. Tavistock, London.

CHARALAMBOS TSEKERIS

scientific revolution

The scientific revolution was the time when a new way of studying the natural, physical world became widely accepted by a small "community of scholars." But the specific status of that "new way" is hotly disputed and the precise historical steps involved in that development are extremely complex. Standard histories are those by Dampier (1966) and Cohen (2001). Cohen stresses the stages involved from initial creative insight to dissemination (orally or in letters, later on in print) and then widespread acceptance. In the seventeenth century there was a significant qualitative transformation in the approach to the study of natural philosophy and that major change is now often called the "scientific revolution," but it is clear that small-scale "revolutions" took place before and have happened since. It was at that time that the transition from undifferentiated "astronomy/astrology" and "alchemy/chemistry" first really got under way. Moreover, great advances were made in mathematics. Different natural philosophies changed at different rates and in different ways. For example, empirical and theoretical progress in astronomy and physics was different from progress in other physical sciences like chemistry (Goodman & Russell 1991: 387–414). However, it was between circa 1500 and 1800 that the distinction between true science and proto-science or pseudo-science (Shermer 2001: 22–65) became somewhat clearer. Many thinkers have seen the essence of the intellectual revolution as a leap beyond the tradition inherited from Aristotelianism and rationalism. But the notion that simple inductive empiricism, often identified with Francis Bacon's New "Organon" (*Novum organum*) of 1620, is the basis of the scientific method has been rejected. The idea of the importance of nuances of general theoretical assumptions concerning ontology and epistemology has been widely shared ever since the early 1960s. Indeed, the social sciences now also regularly use Kuhn's (1970) general theory of an oscillation between "normal science" and "paradigmatic revolutions." The seventeenth-century paradigmatic revolution associated with Descartes, Galileo, Copernicus, Kepler, and von Helmont laid the foundation for what was considered to be true science for the next four centuries. Newton's laws of gravitational attraction, motion, and force (i.e., inverse square law) in the *Principia Mathematica* (1687) led to British Newtonianism, which was widely exported throughout Europe, but Cartesianism in France was a rival for many years (Russell 1991). In the eighteenth century botany and zoology became more systematic with the use of binomial nomenclature, although Linnaeus's theories of nature and of society were deeply flawed (Koerner 1999). Einstein's theory of relativity did not reject Newtonian mechanics, but did make it clear that Newton's assumptions about space and time were too limited and that a true explanation of gravity required postulating "space–time." Similarly, discoveries in mathematics and statistics, particularly the invention of non-Euclidean geometry, revolutionized science in the twentieth century in somewhat the same way they had in earlier times (Newman 1956). The same can be said for Boolean and Fregean mathematical and symbolic logic (Bartley in Dodgson 1986: 3–42). Comte (1957) wrote that scientific thinking moves only gradually, but inevitably, from the study of distant objects, such as stars, to that which is closest to human life – society itself. The term *Wissenschaft* encompasses not only physical and natural sciences, but also social sciences and other disciplines such as history and jurisprudence.

SEE ALSO: Science; Scientific Knowledge, Sociology of

REFERENCES

Cohen, I. B. (2001) *Revolution in Science*. Belknap/Harvard University Press, Cambridge, MA.

Dampier, W. C. (1966) [1929] *A History of Science*, 4th edn. Cambridge University Press, Cambridge.

Dodgson, C. L. (1986) [1896] *Lewis Carroll's Symbolic Logic*, ed. W. W. Bartley, III. Clarkson N. Potter,

New York. (Dodgson is the author of *Symbolic Logic*, but he is better known by his pen name, Lewis Carroll.)
Koerner, L. (1999) *Linnaeus: Nature and Nation.* Harvard University Press, Cambridge, MA.
Kuhn, T. (1970) *The Structure of Scientific Revolutions*, 2nd edn. University of Chicago Press, Chicago, IL.
Newman, J. R. (ed.) (1956) *The World of Mathematics*, 4 vols. Simon & Schuster, New York.
Russell, C. A. (1991) The reception of Newtonianism in Europe. In: Goodman, D. & Russell, C. A. (eds.), *The Rise of Scientific Europe: 1500–1800.* Hodder & Stoughton, London, pp. 253–78.
Shermer, M. (2001) *The Borderlands of Science.* Oxford University Press, Oxford.

SEE ALSO: Kuhn, Thomas and Scientific Paradigms; Science; Scientific Knowledge, Sociology of; Technology, Science and Culture

SUGGESTED READINGS

Aristotle (1941) *Organon.* In: McKeon, R. (ed.), *The Basic Works of Aristotle.* Random House, New York, pp. 1–212.
Comte, A. (1957) *A General View of Positivism*, trans. J. H. Bridges. Robert Speller & Sons, New York.

J. I. (HANS) BAKKER

Scientology

Scientology, or officially the "Church of Scientology," was founded by adherents of Lafayette Ron Hubbard (1911–86) in 1954, but the movement behind Scientology dates back to Hubbard's publication of the book *Dianetics: The Modern Science of Mental health* in 1950. Dianetics was a therapeutic system which Hubbard claimed could cure psychosomatic illness. Dianetics can be described as an attack on what Hubbard considered to be the materialistic position of psychiatry. Hubbard stressed that he wanted to overcome the unspiritual therapeutic strategies he found in psychiatry. In his anthropology, man is basically good and strives for survival of various collectives termed "dynamics," in Dianetics from the individual to that of humanity, and in Scientology up to the "urge towards existence as infinity," termed the "God Dynamic". Scientology assumes that a person receives and stores painful memories from this or earlier lives up to billions of years ago, and that these memories lead the individuals to irrational acts.

Socially the movement which originated around Dianetics was loosely organised and public whereas the Church of Scientology is hierarchic, with control systems making the employees act in accordance with the organization. This system has been reshuffled and strengthened a number of times.

Scientology accepts dual religious membership, so the total membership is difficult to estimate. World-based estimates vary from about 1 million to the official figure of 9 million members in 2008. Besides the religious activities, Scientology runs a number of non-profit organizations working for drug habilitation, improvement of eductaion, and human rights.

The organizational development has been identified as one of the rare transformations from a so-called cult to a sect. The cult consists of open-minded seekers in a cultic milieu, whereas the sect claims to have a unique way of salvation which the adherents have to follow. Recent developments of canon formation, altruistic work, and extension to the surrounding society in other ways may point to Scientology's endeavour to be generally accepted as a church.

SEE ALSO: Globalization, Religion and; Religion, Sociology of

SUGGESTED READING

Lewis, J. R. (ed.) (2009) *Scientology.* Oxford: Oxford University Press

PETER B. ANDERSEN

second demographic transition

The first or "classic" demographic transition refers to the historical declines in mortality and fertility, as witnessed from the eighteenth century onward in several European populations, and continuing at present in most developing countries. The end point of the first demographic transition (FDT) was supposed to be an older stationary and stable population corresponding with replacement fertility (i.e. just over 2 children on average), zero population growth, and life expectancies higher that 70 years. As there would be an ultimate balance between deaths and births, there would be no "demographic" need for sustained immigration. Moreover, households in all parts of the world would converge toward the nuclear and conjugal types, composed of married couples and their offspring.

The second demographic transition (SDT), on the other hand, sees no such equilibrium as the end-point. Rather, new developments bring postponement of marriage and parenthood, sustained sub-replacement fertility, a multitude of living arrangements other than marriage, the disconnection between marriage and procreation, and no stationary population. Instead, populations would face declining sizes if not complemented by new migrants (i.e. "replacement migration"), and they will also be much older than envisaged by the FDT as a result of lower fertility and additional gains in longevity. Migration streams will not be capable of stemming aging altogether, but merely stabilize population sizes. Nonetheless, the outcome is still the further growth of "multicultural societies." On the whole, the SDT brings new social challenges, including those associated with further aging, integration of immigrants and other cultures, less stability of households, and high levels of poverty or exclusion among certain household types (e.g. single persons of all ages, lone mothers).

The idea of a distinct phase stems directly from Philippe Ariès's analysis of the history of childhood (1962) and his subsequent 1980 paper on "Two successive motivations for low fertility." In his view, during the FDT, the decline in fertility was "unleashed by an enormous sentimental and financial investment in the child." Ariès refers to this as the "Child-king era," and the fertility transition was carried by an altruistic investment in child quality (see also Arsène Dumont's "Social capillarity"). This motivation is no longer the dominant one. Within the SDT, the motivation for parenthood is adult self-realization, and the choice for just one particular life style in competition with several others. The altruistic element focusing on offspring has weakened and the adult dyadic relationship has gained prominence instead.

A second stepping stone of the SDT-theory has been Abraham Maslow's (1954) theory of changing needs, *Motivation and Personality*. As populations become more wealthy and more educated, the attention shifts away from needs associated with survival, security and solidarity. Instead greater weight is attached to individual self-realization, recognition, grassroots democracy and expressive work and education values. The SDT-theory is therefore closely related to Ron Inglehart's (1990) concept of "post-materialism" and its growing importance in political development. The direct consequence of this is also that the SDT predicts that the typical demographic outcomes (sustained sub-replacement fertility, growth of alternative living arrangements) are likely to emerge in non-western societies that equally develop in the direction of capitalist economies with multi-level democratic institutions, greater accentuation of Maslowian "higher order needs," and the unfolding of a plurality of life styles that is not merely associated with existing social class differences.

It should be stressed that the SDT-theory fully recognizes the effects of macro-level structural changes and of micro-level economic calculus. As such it is not at odds with the core arguments of neo-classic economic reasoning. Only, the SDT view does not consider these explanations as sufficient but merely as non-redundant. The SDT is therefore an overarching theory that spans both economic and sociological reasoning.

SEE ALSO: Demography; Family Demography

REFERENCES

Ariès, P. (1980) Two successive motivations for the declining birth rate in the west. *Population and Development Review* 6 (4): 645–50.

Inglehart, R. (1990) *Culture Shift in Advanced Industrial Society*. Princeton University Press, Princeton NJ.

RON J. LESTHAEGHE

secondary data analysis

Secondary data analysis is the method of using preexisting data to answer a new research question. Thousands of large-scale data sets are now available for the secondary data analyst. The decennial population census by the US Bureau of the Census is the single most important governmental data source in the United States, but many other data sets are collected by the Census and by other government agencies, including the US Census Bureau's Current Population Survey and its Survey of Manufactures or the Bureau of Labor Statistics' Consumer Expenditure Survey. These government data sets typically are quantitative; in fact, the term "statistics" – state-istics – is derived from this type of data. Surveys conducted by social scientists are another common source of secondary data.

The University of Michigan's Inter-University Consortium for Political and Social Research (ICPSR) maintains the largest collection of social science data sets in the world: more than 7,400 data sets from 130 countries. Government data, social surveys, political polls, research by international organizations are available online to individuals at the more than 500 colleges and universities around the world that have joined ICPSR. Qualitative datasets are also available at Yale University's Human Relations Area Files (over 800,000 pages of information on more than 365 different groups studied by anthropologists), at the Murray Research Center at Harvard's Radcliffe Institute for Advanced Study, and at the University of Southern Maine's Center for the Study of Lives.

Secondary data analysts face some unique challenges. Secondary data analysis cannot design data collection methods that are best suited to answer their research question; they cannot test and refine their methods on the basis of preliminary feedback from the population to be studied; and they cannot engage in the iterative process of making observations, developing concepts, making more observations, and refining the concepts that is the hallmark of much qualitative methodology. Secondary data analysis inevitably involves a tradeoff between the ease with which the research process can be initiated and the specific hypotheses that can be tested and methods that can be used. Hypotheses or even the research question itself may need to be modified in order to match the analytic possibilities presented by the available data. Secondary analysis of qualitative data must forgo the interaction with research participants that is a hallmark of this method. Data quality must always be evaluated. Government data collection efforts may be limited or incomplete due to limited funding or political considerations. International comparative research must take into account different data collection systems and definitions of key variables used in different countries.

These problems can be lessened by reviewing data features and quality before deciding to develop an analysis of secondary data and then developing analysis plans that maximize the value of the available data. Replicating key analyses with alternative indicators of key concepts, testing for the stability of relationships across theoretically meaningful subsets of the data, and examining findings of comparable studies conducted with other data sets can each strengthen confidence in the findings of a secondary analysis.

SEE ALSO: Demographic Data: Censuses, Registers, Surveys; Descriptive Statistics; Social Change; Survey Research

SUGGESTED READINGS

Heaton, J. (2004) *Reworking Qualitative Data*. Sage, Thousand Oaks, CA.

Riedel, M. (2000) *Research Strategies for Secondary Data: A Perspective for Criminology and Criminal Justice*. Sage, Thousand Oaks, CA.

RUSSELL K. SCHUTT

secondary groups

A secondary group is a form of social group that tends to be formally organized or highly structured and based on predominantly impersonal or role-based instrumental (task oriented) interactions that are of a nonpermanent nature. Examples of secondary groups include the impersonal relationship between salesclerk and customer in a department store; large lecture courses at popular universities; and complex organizations such as the American Sociological Association. Furthermore, the bureaucratically organized form of complex organization is commonly held up as the classic epitome of the secondary group.

The work of Charles Horton Cooley (1909) and Ferdinand Tönnies (1963) set the tone for the consistent application of the concept in sociology. In *Social Organization* (1909) Cooley presents the forms, functions, and attributes of the social units he called "primary groups." However, Cooley did not develop a term for those social units which were not primary groups. As a result, the conventionally accepted set of attributes and characteristics of secondary groups have simply been extrapolated from Cooley's expression of primary groups. Or in other words, knowing what primary groups are, secondary groups by corollary are that which primary groups are not. As a result, sociologists continue to define the concept of secondary group simply in relation to the associated concept of primary group. To Cooley's credit, both his explicit definition of primary groups and the associated implicit definition of secondary groups have withstood the test of time. In addition, Ferdinand Tönnies's (1963) expression of the dualistic conception of *Gemeinschaft* and *Gesellschaft* sought to explain the relationship between community and social organization. Accordingly, Tönnies's explanations and assumptions regarding the forms, attributes, and characteristics of *Gesellschaften* – including but not limited to short-term and impersonal relationships – have become closely associated with the conventional definition of secondary groups.

SEE ALSO: Cooley, Charles Horton; Primary Groups; Tönnies, Ferdinand

REFERENCES

Cooley, C. H. (1909) *Social Organization: A Study of the Larger Mind*. Scribner's, New York.

Tönnies, F. (1963) [1887] *Community and Society*. Harper & Row, New York.

PATRICK J. W. MCGINTY

secularization

Secularization is the result of the process of *functional differentiation*, which developed different sub-systems (e.g. economy, polity and family)

performing particular functions for modern societies (production and distribution of goods and services; taking binding decisions and procreation and mutual support). To guarantee these functions and to communicate with their environment, organizations have been established (enterprises; political parties and families). Each of these organizations functions on the basis of its own medium (money; power; and love) and according to the values of their sub-system and its specific norms. Regarding religion, these organizations affirm their autonomy rejecting religiously prescribed rules – e.g. the separation of church and state; the rejection of church prescriptions about birth control, abortion and euthanasia – which allowed the development of functional rationality. Consequently, the influence of institutional religion is increasingly being confined to the religious sub-system itself. We may the define secularization as a process by which the overarching and transcendent religious system is reduced in modern *functionally* differentiated societies to a sub-system alongside other sub-systems, losing in this process its overarching claims over them it had in pre-modern times. This definition points out that the religious authorities of institutionalized religion have lost control over the other sub-systems.

Secularization can be an "intended and recognized" consequence. Certain government policies are examples of such *manifest* secularization, which is called *laïcisation* in France. This country gives a paradigmatic example of manifest secularization: the "*laïque Republic*" is a constitutional principle, which implied the de-sacralization of authority, the separation of church and state and the autonomization of so-called secular institutions – e.g. medicine, law and education – vis-à-vis the Catholic Church in particular. Other examples are the secular Republic of Turkey and the establishment of secular Communist States in central and eastern Europe. However, secularization may also be an unintended and unrecognized consequence, i.e. a form of *latent* secularization. A good example of this is the introduction of the clock. at the turn of the fourteenth century. Time was no longer regulated by the time sequence of the monasteries which was based on bell ringing. The clock imposed a secular time order and time was also dissociated from God-given nature, which was provided by the sundial. Once the clock started regulating time it became controlled by humans (e.g. Daylight saving Time).

Consequently, secularization is not a mechanical evolutionary process, it is consciously or un-consciously human-made. Neither is it a straightforward process, the de-secularization of former communist regimes attests to this. To rebuild society after the collapse of the communist regimes in 1989, religion served as a substitute for the communist ideology, alliances between church and state were to a certain extent re-established (e.g. in Russia), and religious classes were also re-introduced in school curricula in many of these countries.

On the individual level there are two aspects to be studied: compartmentalization and, what is traditionally called, individual secularization. *Compartmentalization* measures the impact of societal secularization on the secularization in the minds of individuals. Do people *think* in terms of the separation of institutional religion and the so-called societal subsystems? In other words, do they think that religion should not inform these sub-systems, that they are autonomous and that any interference of institutional religion in these sub-systems should be eradicated and disallowed? *Individual secularization* rejects religious authority, like the autonomous sub-systems reject religiously prescribed rules and societal secularization reduces institutional religion to its sub-system. More and more individuals became unchurched and many of the remaining church members do not take the set menu of their church but select "à la carte" certain rituals, beliefs and moral prescriptions. However, individual secularization does not mean religious decline per se, since central in the definition is the reference to the lost power of the religious authorities of institutionalized religions to control individual religiousness. Consequently, a continuing individual religious sensitivity is not a falsification of secularization theory, but confirms it as does the use of the term spirituality in opposition to the term religion. Spirituality is non-dogmatic, it is flexible; it is a personal search, and God may not be the "radical other," nor the transcendent, but the immanent, the "God within."

SEE ALSO: Civil Religion; Religion, Sociology of; Church

SUGGESTED READINGS

Baubérot, J. (2005) *Histoire de la laïcité en France*, 3rd enlarged edn. Presses Universitaires de France, Collection Que sais-je, no. 3571, Paris.

Borowik, I. (ed.) (1999) *Church–State Relations in Central and Eastern Europe*. Nomos, Kraków.

Dobbelaere, K. (2002) *Secularization: An Analysis at Three Levels*. P. I. E. Peter Lang, Gods, Humans and Religions series, no. 1, Brussels.

KARL DOBBELAERE

segregation

Segregation is both the formal and informal separation of one group from another. This can occur, for example, according to class, gender, sexual orientation, or religious differences. These markers of difference are used as reasons for justifying a split between groups and populations. The repercussions of these separations are vast, creating and supporting structural inequality throughout all levels of society.

Segregation is often explained according to whether it is classified as *de facto* or *de jure*. The most common form is *de facto*, which is often viewed as self-segregation. Divisions occur between groups of people in specific areas of their social lives such as in schools, housing and in the workplace. People are seen as "naturally" self-selecting where they live and work. This is often visible when examining immigration patterns as people tend to move to areas where they know other people or where the population is similar to them. This kind of segregation is supported by a host of systemic practices such as discriminatory housing and lending policies. For example, historically the banking, insurance and real estate industries practiced *red lining*, which determines what neighborhoods are not eligible for mortgages, loans or other services due to their deteriorating conditions. Often these decisions were based on the ethnic, religious or racial characteristics of the residents. These practices continue today largely in the form of higher interest rates for loans and higher insurance premiums.

Legal segregation is labeled as *de jure*. This type of segregation takes the form of regulations that determine access to public services and accommodation, housing, property ownership and employment. Limits are also placed on individuals' rights to inheritance, adoption of children or choice in marriage partner. In the USA examples of this include "male-only" or "white-only" jobs, denial of housing based on sexuality, separate facilities for whites and blacks and barriers to same-sex marriage. These formalized practices reinforce *de facto* segregation. While many nations have eliminated *de jure* segregation, discrimination and isolation continue on many informal levels.

There are a variety of reasons why *de facto* segregation continues to exist. Living in communities where there are groups of people similar to oneself can help maintain common cultural practices while fostering a spirit of community. Residential segregation is also heavily influenced by economic class as well as race/ethnicity. Sociologists have found that the better groups and individuals can assimilate into society, particularly immigrants, the less likely they will face issues related to inequality. This reinforces a continual tension between living where and how someone chooses while attempting to have a society where difference is honored rather than used as a means of discrimination and separation.

Scholarship on the continuation of segregation in the USA splits between attributing it to racism or classism. This debate filters into the practices of segregation in the areas of work, education and health. While *de jure* segregation has been eliminated, cultural practices and the social institutions that have been framed according to these policies and ideologies remain slow to change. Contemporary research is finding that residential segregation is increasing, proportionally non-white groups make up a larger percentage of lower income individuals and Black Americans continue to have higher mortality rates and lower high school graduation rates. Research has shown that integration of workplace, schools and neighborhoods, on race, ethnic and economic class levels, significantly reduces crime and violence, improves academic performance, economic opportunities and reduces bias and discriminatory practices.

SEE ALSO: Assimilation; Racism, Structural and Institutional; School Segregation, Desegregation

SUGGESTED READINGS

Charles, C. (2003) The dynamics of racial residential segregation. *Annual Review of Sociology* 29.

Massey, D. & Denton, N. (1993). *American Apartheid: Segregation and the Making of the Underclass.* Harvard University Press: Cambridge, MA.

Wilson, W. J. (1991). *Another Look at The Truly Disadvantaged. Political Science Quarterly* 106: 4.

KRISTINA B. WOLFF

self

The concept of self refers to a person's experience of stability or consistency over time. To have a self is to experience and imagine oneself as the same person in the past, present, and future. The term is distinguished from related concepts such as mind (the center of cognitive activity), consciousness (the experience of self-awareness), and identity (the traits possessed by a self). In contrast to psychologists, who treat the self as an individual possession, sociologists generally view the self as a product of interpersonal relationship that is shaped by social and historical currents. As a consequence, for sociologists, the experience of self, and even the existence of selfhood, varies across cultures and historical periods.

Symbolic interactionism is the most influential sociological theory of self. This perspective grew out of the pragmatist social psychology of George Herbert Mead (1934). According to Mead, the self emerges as part of a developmental process that depends upon children's interaction with language using caregivers. It is in the back and forth of human exchange that children learn to see themselves as others see them. Once children internalize the view that others have of them, a two-part structure is created: the I and the Me. The self is the "conversation" between these two parts. The "I" refers to subjective, creative, and spontaneous aspects of the self. It initiates action, but also escapes full-fledged articulation. It can never be captured entirely or described; hence its unpredictability and creativity. The "Me" refers to objective, socially conditioned aspects of the self. This is the product of the internalization of the view of the other; the set of traits that make the self recognizable as a member of a society and community. Structural symbolic interactionists have studied these objective, and therefore measureable, aspects of the self. They have developed concepts like self-concept (the overall view a person has of herself), self-efficacy (the sense of control one has over one's self), and self-esteem (the feelings one has for one's self). Tests such as Manford Kuhn's Twenty Statements Test (TST) and Morris Rosenberg's Self-esteem Scale are used to measure these different aspects of self.

Erving Goffman (1959) further describes the relational character of selfhood through his dramaturgical theory. Selfhood, he argues, is the product of social performances akin to those in a theatrical production. In contrast to symbolic interactionism which, more or less, treats selves as stable and consistent over time, Goffman argues that there is no real or authentic self. Rather, selves are situationally contingent productions that depend upon the performances of others just as much as the performances of the social actor. Goffman summarizes this position with the following: "the self, then, as a performed character, is not an organic thing that has a specific location, whose fundamental fate is to be born, mature, and die; it is a dramatic effect arising diffusely from a scene that is presented" (1959: 252–3).

Postmodern theorists have emphasized the cultural origins of selfhood. Like Goffman, they insist that authentic selfhood is an illusion. Through the technique of deconstruction, they attempt to reveal the linguistic structures, and grand narratives, that generate the ideal of selfhood. Most notably, contemporary western constructions of self valorize the individual, self-contained, masculine self. This kind of self is critiqued because it reflects the interests and experiences of only a small subset of the human population. In opposition to these culturally sanctioned aspirations, postmodernists offer an alternative ethic of selfhood. Since selves are constituted through language, and in relationship, it is possible to renegotiate and reconstruct outmoded and potentially harmful constructions of self. Here the commitment to a stable self is replaced by an ongoing playful encounter between self and other. The obligation to self is replaced by an obligation to fruitful relationship, selfhood becoming a product constituted only insofar as it serves the needs of relationship (Gergen 1991).

At its most radical, the postmodern view suggests that selfhood is infinitely malleable and even dispensable. Several contemporary scholars have challenged this implication, even as they embrace the importance of language and culture to the constitution of selves. Most important here is the work of Charles Taylor (1989). For Taylor, it is precisely the weight of culture and history – especially when these are integrated into personal biography – that gives selves their solidity, objectivity, and indubitable reality. Taylor shares with numerous contemporaries the view that selves are constituted in narrative. In contrast to the postmodernists who deconstruct narrative, Taylor shows that humans cannot help but to think and live their lives within the framework of shared, overarching stories. Narratives give human life existential meaning by structuring the inevitable relationship to time and death. Stories also provide people with moral orientations; deeply felt relationships to higher goods. The problem for contemporary selves, Taylor suggests, is that western cultures have lost the overarching narratives that historically have provided personal depth. Ironically, even though the principles of self-development and self-fulfillment have become central ideals of contemporary consumer societies, these principles remain without significant mooring and therefore meaning.

The most recent scholarship on selfhood has turned to problems of the body and emotion. This is a correction to the historical dominance of the language based theories described above. With her work on emotion management, Arlie Hochschild uses Goffman's theory of self presentation to show that the management of situationally appropriate feeling is necessary for successful performances of selfhood. Thus, emotion is not only psychological, and biological, but also sociological. Scholars such as Norbert Elias, Michel Foucault, and Judith Butler have argued that the body is a social construction, disciplined through social norms and practices, rather than a natural fact. The achievement of selfhood depends upon the production of the kinds of bodies that align with the narratives and ideals that circulate within a culture.

Recent developments in the life sciences have lead sociologists like Patricia Clough to consider how biological processes, historically inaccessible to selves, have become central to the experience and production of selfhood. Here, "affect theory" is unique in how it integrates biological phenomena into sociological accounts. Rather than using biological theories to explain human behavior, affect theorists describe how contemporary technologies interact with biology to create and control life energies and affective flows. Antidepressant medications, for example, allow people to modify mood by altering neurotransmitter levels in the brain. In the current context, then, the self is relational not only in its linguistic and social constructions, but also in the way that it is affected by the technological manipulation of deep biological processes. Future research will have to account for selfhood at all of these levels.

SEE ALSO: Body and Society; Emotion: Social Psychological Aspects; Facework; Goffman, Erving; Identity: Social Psychological Aspects; Looking-Glass Self; Mead, George Herbert; Self-Concept; Self-Esteem, Theories of; Subjectivity

REFERENCES

Goffman, E. (1959) *The Presentation of Self in Everyday Life*. Anchor, New York.
Gergen, K. (1991) *The Saturated Self: Dilemmas of Identity in Contemporary Life*. Basic Books, New York.
Mead, G. H. (1934) *Mind, Self, and Society: From the Standpoint of a Social Behaviorist*. University of Chicago Press, Chicago, IL.
Taylor, C. (1989) *Sources of the Self: The Making of the Modern Identity*. Harvard University Press, Cambridge, MA.

SUGGESTED READING

Elliott, A. (2007) *Concepts of the Self*, 2nd edn. Polity, Cambridge.

JEFF STEPNISKY

self-concept

Sociological interest in the self-concept, rooted in the early writings of Cooley and Mead, has evolved into a multifaceted quest to describe the connections between social contexts and personal functioning. In his classic work, *Conceiving the Self* (1979), Rosenberg defines the self-concept as all of the thoughts and feelings that individuals maintain about the self as an object. Gecas and Burke (1995) have expanded on the definition: the self-concept "is composed of various identities, attitudes, beliefs, values, motives, and experiences, along with their evaluative and affective components (e.g., self-efficacy, self-esteem), in terms of which individuals define themselves" (42). These processes involve reflexivity and self-awareness; that is, a level of consciousness or awareness about one's self that emerges from the distinctly human capacity to be an object and a subject to one's self.

A substantial core of the content of the self-concept involves identities – the meanings that individuals attach to the self. Identities embody the answer to the question: "Who am I?" Often, but not always, identities are connected to the major institutionalized social roles of society such as "spouse," "parent," "worker," "student," "church member, "Muslim," and so on. In many respects, identity is the most "public" feature of the self-concept because it typically describes one's place or membership in structural arrangements and social organization. At a social event, for example, individuals will ask each other about their work, their interests, their neighborhoods, and other pieces of information that typically peel back the layers of their identities. However, there may be a cost to the public nature of identities. Goffman illustrated the "spoiled identity" as socially undesirable or stigmatized aspects of the self-concept. Spoiled identities contain discredited elements of the self-concept that the individual is encouraged to conceal or "manage." Failure to do so often exacts social costs. Collectively, these ideas underscore the highly *social* nature of the self-concept: other people have substantial influence on the form, content, consequences, and revelation of the self-concept.

Some of the most widely known research on the self-concept has focused on its evaluative and affective components, especially self-esteem and self-efficacy. Self-esteem is "the evaluation which the individual makes and customarily maintains with regard to himself or herself: it expresses an attitude of approval or disapproval toward oneself" (Rosenberg 1965: 5).

Survey researchers have sought to measure self-esteem with responses to statements that include: "I feel that I have a number of good qualities," "I feel that I'm a person of worth at least equal to others," "I am able to do things as well as most other people," "I take a positive attitude toward myself," and so on. By contrast, self-efficacy – also referred to as the sense of mastery or personal control – involves the extent to which one feels in control of events and outcomes in everyday life. Measures of the sense of mastery ask about agreement or disagreement with statements like: "I have little control over the things that happen to me," "There is really no way I can solve some of the problems I have," "What happens to me in the future mostly depends on me," "I can do just about anything I really set my mind to," and so on. Sociologists are interested in mastery and self-esteem for several reasons: because they are socially distributed, because their absence may erode well-being, and because of their potential as psychosocial resources that help people avoid or manage stressors. That is, what groups have higher or lower levels of self-esteem than others? How does a low sense of mastery influence psychological well-being? And, do people who possess more favorable self-evaluations have a different capacity to cope with the presence and consequences of stressful adversity?

The complexity of processes involving self-dynamics has also provided researchers with terrain for theoretical and empirical developments about the self-concept. For example, actors are often motivated to protect the self-concept from external threats. In broader terms, an array of socialization forces and social-structural arrangements shape the formation and content of the self-concept; thus, it is a *social product*. In terms of self-concept formation, the notion of personal or self-investment evokes the ideas of identity salience and the centrality of achieved statuses, such as education, for the emergence of positive self-evaluations. Analyses of the structural determinants of personal qualities, especially with respect to achieved statuses and dimensions of social stratification, have a long tradition in sociology.

SEE ALSO: Cooley, Charles Horton; Identity: Social Psychological Aspects; Identity Theory; Mead, George Herbert; Self

REFERENCES

Gecas, V. & Burke, P. J. (1995) Self and Identity. In: Cook, K., Fine, G. A., & House, J. S. (eds.), *Sociological Perspectives on Social Psychology*. Allyn & Bacon, Boston, MA, pp. 41–67.

Rosenberg, M. (1965) *Society and the Adolescent Self-Image*. Princeton University Press, Princeton, NJ.

SUGGESTED READING

Gecas, V. & Burke, P. J. (1995) Self and identity. In: Cook, K., Fine, G. A., & House, J. S. (eds.), *Sociological Perspectives on Social Psychology*. Allyn & Bacon, Boston, MA, pp. 41–67.

SCOTT SCHIEMAN

self-esteem, theories of

Self-esteem is the positive or negative attitude people take toward themselves. Yet to properly understand it requires seeing its relationship to associated superordinate and subordinate concepts (self, self-concept and global/specific self-esteem, respectively; see diagram) (Owens et al. forthcoming). The *self* is an organized and interactive system of thoughts, feelings, identities, drives, and dispositions that characterize a unique human being. *Self-concept* is the totality of a person's thoughts and feelings toward their self as an object of reflection. Through self-objectification, people (i.e., the subject, the knower – the "I") figuratively stand outside themselves and perceive and react to their self as an object of consideration (i.e., the object, the known – the "me"). Acknowledging the self's subject/object duality provides the philosophical basis for sociological studies of self-concept, and consequently self-esteem (see Figure 1).

The self is predicated on reflexivity and language. Reflexivity entails viewing oneself as others might (self-as-object) while labeling, categorizing, evaluating, and manipulating oneself (self-as-subject). Language – whether verbal/nonverbal or written/unwritten – drives reflexivity. The reflexive self is central to human abilities, including planning, worrying about personal problems, ruminating past actions, lamenting present circumstances, envying others.

James (1890) outlined the earliest formulation of self-esteem as individuals weighing their perceptions of "success" in some role or domain (e.g., sports, academics) versus their pretensions (desire) for success in the role or domain (e.g., being the top college debater).

$$\text{Self-esteem} = \frac{\text{Success}}{\text{Pretensions}}$$

Since James, many sociological theories of self-esteem have been posed, with most being indebted to symbolic interactionism and social comparisons. Rosenberg's (1979) four principles of self-concept formation, and by extension self-esteem, have garnered the most contemporary sociological attention. First, the principle of *reflected appraisals*, stemming

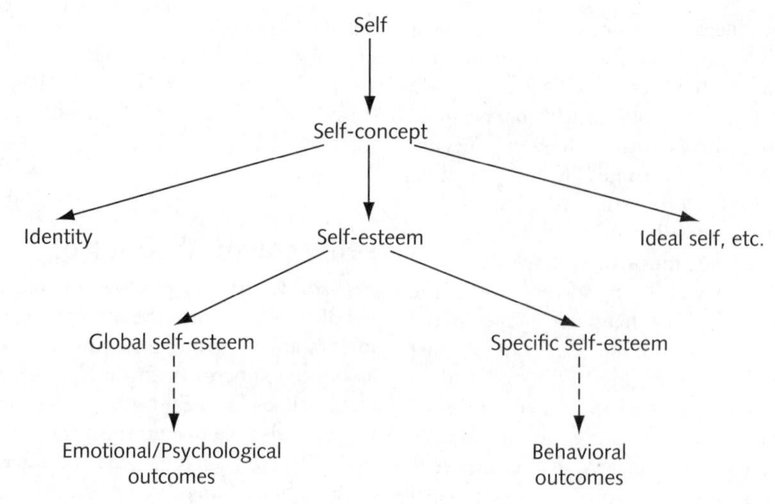

Figure 1 Hierarchical view of self, self-concept, and self-esteem

from Cooley's looking-glass self and Mead's role-taking, sees self-concept as a product of how we believe others perceive us. It includes three basic kinds of reflected appraisals: perceived selves, the most important, is ego's speculation on how specific alters cognize him/her; direct reflections are the actual, direct, responses that alter has toward ego; and the generalized other is ego's composite sense of what others think of him/her. Second, through *social comparisons*, people evaluate themselves with respect to particular individuals, groups, or social categories. Social comparisons can be criterion-based (i.e., superior/inferior, better/worse) or normative-based (i.e., deviance/conformity, same/different). Third, the principle of *self-attributions* has people observing their own behaviors and behavioral outcomes, then drawing some conclusion about themselves (e.g., funny, popular, intelligent). Finally, *psychological centrality* sees the self as an interrelated and hierarchically organized system of identities and attributes. It helps protect one's self-esteem by pushing potentially damaging self-attributes and identities to the periphery of the self system, while holding enhancing attributes closer to the center.

Self-esteem is also a social product and a social force. As a social product, its origins are investigated (as in the four self-concept principles above). As a social force, self-esteem is a vital gauge of a population's psychological and emotional well-being. It also contributes to our understanding of myriad social problems and issues such as prosocial behavior, participation in social movements, and deviant or risky behavior. These underscore the importance of the self-esteem motive, or the fundamental human desire to protect, and if possible, enhance one's self-esteem.

Failing to recognize the difference between specific and global self-esteem has led to considerable confusion and mischaracterization of this vital concept because each is associated with different outcomes (see earlier diagram). Specific self-esteem is tied to a person's particular roles, identities, activities, contexts or attributes (e.g., academic, physical, social, moral, family), and tends to predict behavioral and performance outcomes (e.g., grade point average). Global self-esteem is an *overall* characterization of one's self as worthy/worthless, good/bad, useful/useless, etc., without reference to specific social contexts, activities or identities. It tends to predict emotional and psychological outcomes (e.g., depression).

SEE ALSO: Looking-Glass Self; Self; Self-Concept; Self-Serving Bias

REFERENCES

James, W. (1890) *The Principles of Psychology*. Henry Holt, New York.

Rosenberg, M. (1979) *Conceiving the Self*. Basic Books, New York.

SUGGESTED READINGS

Festinger, L. (1954) A theory of social comparison processes. *Human Relations* 7: 117–40.

Owens, T. J., Stryker, S., & Goodman, N. (eds.) (2001) *Extending Self-Esteem Theory and Research: Sociological and Psychological Currents*. Cambridge University Press, New York.

Owens, T. J., Robinson, D. T., & Smith-Lovin, L. (in press) Three faces of identity. *Annual Review of Sociology* 36.

TIMOTHY J. OWENS

self-fulfilling prophecy

The self-fulfilling prophecy is the process by which one's expectations of other people lead those people to behave in ways that confirm those expectations. The term "self-fulfilling prophecy" was coined in 1948 by Robert K. Merton, who drew upon W. I. Thomas's well-known dictum: "if men define situations as real, they are real in their consequences" (Wineberg 1987). The Thomas theorem suggests that the meanings of human actions are not inherent merely in their actions. Rather people attribute meanings to those actions, and the meanings have consequences for future actions.

In education, the self-fulfilling prophecy illuminates the ways that teacher expectations influence students' behavior and academic outcomes. This is also known as the Pygmalion effect after the publication in 1968 of "Pygmalion in the Classroom" by Richard Rosenthal and Lenore Jacobson. In their study, Rosenthal and Jacobson created different teacher expectations and showed that students who were falsely identified as "spurters" – those who were expected to "show an academic spurt" (Rosenthal & Jacobson 1968: 66) – made significantly greater gains in IQ scores than did those who were not identified. Thus, *Pygmalion* established a positive relationship between teacher expectations and students' intelligence, confirming the existence of the educational self-fulfilling prophecy.

Ray Rist's ethnographic study in 1970 was the earliest sociological study of the educational self-fulfilling prophecy. A striking finding in Rist's study was that the teacher formed expectations during the first days of kindergarten. The teacher then assigned her students to groups based on student's socioeconomic (SES) backgrounds, not on their academic ability, and treated each group differently. She gave more freedom and encouragements to students in the highest SES group, but more criticisms and restrictions to students in the lowest SES group. Students in the highest SES group could get physically closer to the teacher, and eventually they received more instruction and showed better performance than did students in the lowest SES group.

Both *Pygmalion* and Rist's study sparked controversies as researchers searched for evidence to support or refute the prophecy. By the 1980s there were about 400 experiments and meta-analyses. However, many studies failed to replicate earlier findings, and this led other researchers to investigate *why* these studies did not observe the teacher expectancy effects. Later studies, for example, revealed that the timing of "expectancy induction" was critical for the formation of teacher expectations in experimental studies (Raudenbush 1984).

Since the 1970s, our knowledge about the self-fulfilling prophecy has greatly increased both in the US and abroad. Studies conducted in England, New Zealand, Australia, and South Korea, among others, support the notion of the educational self-fulfilling prophecy (Tauber 1997: *Self-Fulfillng Prophecy: A Practical Guide to Its Use in Education*). More recently, the concept of the self-fulfilling prophecy was also applied to the settings beyond the classroom. These include work organization, judicial settings, substance uses, delinquencies, and health care.

SEE ALSO: Educational Inequality; Merton, Robert K.; Self-Serving Bias

REFERENCES

Raudenbush, S. (1984) Magnitude of teacher expectancy effects on pupil IQ as a function of the credibility of expectancy induction: a synthesis of findings from 18 experiments. *Journal of Educational Psychology* 76: 85–97.

Rosenthal, R. & Jacobson, L. (1968) *Pygmalion in the Classroom*. Holt, Rinehart, & Winston, New York.

Wineberg, S. S. (1987) The self-fulfillment of the self-fulfilling prophecy. *Educational Researcher* 16, 28–44.

SUGGESTED READING

Rist, R. (1970) Student social class and teacher expectations: the self-fulfilling prophecy in ghetto education. *Harvard Educational Review* 40, 411–51.

TAKAKO NOMI AND SUET-LING PONG

self-serving bias

The "self-serving bias" refers to people's tendency to attribute positive outcomes or successes to internal or personal factors (such as effort or ability) and to attribute negative outcomes or failures to external or situational factors (such as task difficulty or luck). Variously labeled as "defensive," "egocentric," or "egotistic" attribution, the bias accounts for people's greater tendency to take credit for success than failure (e.g., having a perfect score on the SAT because of innate intelligence or hard work as opposed to having a low score on the test because of unfavorable test conditions; doing well in a boxing match because of exceptional strength and skills as opposed to doing poorly because of unfair rules). It is also evident in people's tendency to assess morally ambiguous situations in ways concordant with their interests; or in perceptions of fairness – arriving at judgments of what is fair or right that are biased in favor of self.

A more "systematic" form of the bias shows in the "above average effect" – people's tendency to rate themselves as above average in domains that are self-relevant (important to their self-esteem).

The phenomenon may also manifest itself at the group level. Known as the "ultimate attribution error," group-serving bias is the tendency for in-group members to attribute positive outcomes to causes internal to the group and negative ones to factors external to the group. Members of a football team, for example, might attribute a winning game to athletic prowess, while attributing a losing one to "bad refereeing."

SEE ALSO: Attribution Theory; Impression Management

MAMADI CORRA

SUGGESTED READING

Miller, D. T., & Ross, M. (1975) Self-serving biases in the attribution of causality: fact or fiction? *Psychological Bulletin* 82: 213–25.

semiotics

Put simply, semiotics is the study of signs. Although the study of signs has a history that goes back (at least) to the work of St. Augustine, modern semiotics has its origins in semiology, a science of signs developed by French linguist Ferdinand de Saussure, and in the work of US logician Charles Sanders Peirce. For Peirce, a sign is defined as "something which stands to somebody for something in some respect or capacity." Peirce develops a set of logical distinctions between iconic, indexical, and symbolic signs. Iconic signs function by way of likeness or resemblance (a portrait is an iconic sign that represents its sitter; an architectural model is an iconic sign that represents a building). Indexical signs function through direct connection or relationship (smoke is an index of fire; a knock on the door is an index of a visitor). Finally symbolic signs – which include language – function purely by convention. The connections between the word "rose" and the bloom of a thorny bush, or between a flashing red light and the requirement that one stop are arbitrary; they function symbolically and must be learned.

In his *Course in General Linguistics*, a set of lecture notes published posthumously in 1916 by his students, Saussure describes language as a sign system and words as signs. As signs, words are part of a larger structured totality that Saussure describes as "langue." Langue here is to be understood as a self-contained and essentially abstract system that must be differentiated from parole – the everyday usage of words. Saussure's science of signs is thus a structuralist study of the way that signs function within langue. Understanding signification – the process by which signs come to function within langue – requires analysis of the individual abstract components of language systems: sign, signifier, and signified. The sign is the complete whole that results from the association between a signified (a concept or idea) and a signifier (a sound, a collection of letters, a word).

Contemporary semiotics views the study of the linguistic sign as only one aspect of a much larger project – the study of signs in general. The broad definition of a sign as "something which stands to somebody for something," offered by Peirce, has been beneficial to a contemporary rethinking of the goals and objects of semiotic analysis to include a whole variety of meaningful signs: media texts, visual images, fashion, public performances, and the like. Perhaps the most influential figure in contemporary semiotics is French social and literary critic, Roland Barthes, who applied the semiotic method in a series of essays that analyzed the use of signs and perpetuation of myths in mid twentieth century French culture. In this text, titled Mythologies, Barthes famously analyzes the image of a black soldier saluting the French flag on the cover of a Paris-Match magazine. This image works denotatively, indicating a soldier who salutes his flag. However, the image may also be understood to function ideologically by way of connotation. In the context of French colonial history, the image does more than represent a black soldier; it represents the presumed loyalty of all black Algerians to French colonial power. Most importantly, this is a mythical representation that works to naturalize colonialism and to undermine criticism of French imperialism. In this and other examples, Barthes points to the ways in which signs are recruited to produce ideological meaning. Semiotic analysis thus permits the analyst to identify cultural value-systems (mythologies) that are embedded in signs and absorbed by readers.

The principles of semiotics have been widely employed by many of the most important thinkers of the twentieth century. Structuralists like anthropologist Claude Levi-Strauss and Louis Althusser employed semiotic principles to identify the underlying structures of social institutions and shared cultural stories or myths. Psychoanalytic thinker Jacques Lacan read Saussure alongside Freud in order to consider the ways in which the unconscious is structured like a language. Jacques

Derrida's enormously influential project of deconstruction turns on a rejection of Saussurean models of the sign.

In its capacity to identify the workings of ideological sign-systems, semiotics has been enormously influential in the field of cultural studies. For sociologists and social theorists, semiotics has been employed to understand social formations more generally. In the North American context, semiotics is closely linked to communications studies, with emphasis on the ways in which all human activities – and all human interactions – require the use of signs.

SEE ALSO: Saussure, Ferdinand de; Langue and Parole; Cultural Studies; Ideology; Signs

SUGGESTED READINGS

Barthes, R. (1972) [1957] *Mythologies*. Farrar Straus and Giroux, New York.
De Saussure, F. (1983) [1916] *Course in General Linguistics*. Duckworth, London.
Peirce, C. S. (1972) *Charles S. Peirce: The Essential Writings*. Harper and Row, New York.

MICHELLE MEAGHER

service work

The presence of a service-recipient within the labor process is the central definitional element of service work. Service work is increasingly moving toward center stage in the sociology of work. This is appropriate because "more Americans now work in physician's offices than in auto plants, in laundries and dry cleaners than in steel mills" (Herzenberg et al. 1998: 3). At the very least, the worker-service recipient relationship constitutes an aspect unique to the sociology of service work. The worker-service recipient relationship has been examined in terms of sexualization, of degrees of worker or service-recipient servility, of who controls the interaction, and of degrees of social embeddedness and economic instrumentalism. More profoundly, it has been argued that the addition of the customer in the social relations of production has crucial knock-on effects upon key aspects of work organization, and upon the subjective experience of work (Korczynski 2002). Hochschild's *The Managed Heart* (1983) with its exploration of emotional labor within service occupations constituted the first important step in this direction.

Notably, there is also an emerging current within macro-sociological theorizing to take an aspect of service work and to see in it a metaphor for the overall trajectory of society. George Ritzer's thesis of the McDonaldization of society and Alan Bryman's thesis of Disneyization of society have a shared provenance in that service firms serve as the basis for their root metaphors. At present, however, the movement to look across service jobs to create a macro-picture of service work per se remains an undeveloped process.

SEE ALSO: Emotion Work; Labor Markets; McDonaldization; Work, Sociology of

REFERENCES

Herzenberg, S., Alic, J., & Wial, H. (1998) *New Rules for a New Economy*. Cornell University Press, Ithaca, NY.
Korczynski, M. (2002) *Human Resource Management in Service Work*. Palgrave/Macmillan, Basingstoke.

MAREK KORCZYNSKI

sex and gender

Sex is related to the biological distinctions between males and females primarily found in relation to reproductive functions.

Gender is a social definition of expected behavior based on one's sex category. Because gender can be enacted in an infinite variety of ways, and indeed is, we know that gender is a social construction and, therefore, learned behavior.

Most people live their lives with unquestioned assumptions about men and women based on an overemphasis of the role of biology in shaping thoughts and actions. Yet, research has shown that there is a profound social influence on sex and gender with the effects of social interaction far overriding biology on human behavior. Differences among people primarily emerge through interaction and the social processes found in institutions such as religion, politics, economic positioning, and work relations. Gendered messages are everywhere and constant, beginning with the family. Over the life course, television and movies provide scripts on "doing gender" that model how to play our roles on the stage of life.

Sex and gender are related yet distinctive terms, both heavily imbued with definitions, restrictions, privileges, and misconceptions based on the ways they have been socially constructed in different societies around the world. Sex, the biological component, is often used as a justification to privilege men over women. Gender, which has the widest and deepest applications, is often treated as if it were a biological condition rather than a social categorization that can and is used for placement in stratification systems.

SEE ALSO: Intersexuality; Sexuality; Transgender, Transvestism, and Transsexualism; Socialization

SUGGESTED READINGS

Fenstermaker, S. & West, C. (eds.) (2002) *Doing Gender, Doing Difference*. Routledge, New York.

Kimmel, Michael S. (2004) *The Gendered Society*. Oxford University Press, New York.

BARBARA RYAN

sex education

Whilst often purporting to be the conveyance of a body of scientific knowledge, in fact "sex education" connotes and has always connoted hegemonic discourses relating to politics, morality, sexuality, and social control. As such, it is subject to a multitude of approaches, meanings, and pedagogical strategies and is highly contextual, with localized cultures and understandings making significant differences to both the purposes and practices involved. It is, therefore, often highly politicized.

Historically, and in the present, sex education has occupied an uneasy position, straddled between the perceived need to tell young people about the dangers of illness and pregnancy and the fear that talking about sex will make it even more attractive. In this respect, moral hygiene (avoiding talking about it) is counterposed to physical hygiene (preventing the spread of disease and pregnancy).

This simultaneous need for selective information about sex and the wish to control people, has determined sex education in the Anglophone world throughout the twentieth century. In the UK, the white (settler) colonies of the British Commonwealth and in the USA this was accompanied by an imperative to avoid "miscegenation" and "excessive breeding" by subjugated people. In this context "social purity" campaigners called for sex education in schools, while vice campaigners argued against it (Irvine 2002).

Contemporary approaches to sex education in Anglophone countries fall into three categories:

- the promotion of sexual abstinence (strongest in the USA)
- a focus on sexual reproduction and danger, with a nod in the direction of relationships (mainstream in most countries)
- emergent sociological, psychological and historical approaches (virtually non-existent in schools).

The first two approaches are rooted in the attempted social control of young people but have been proved unsuccessful in this regard – in the case of abstinence education, spectacularly so. Fine (1988) suggests that this is the result of the "missing discourse of desire".

In "developing" countries, sex education follows the first two approaches, often seen as a form of contraception, limiting population growth and aiding economies. In the context of HIV, particularly in sub-Saharan Africa, approaches often stress danger, instructing people to "Abstain, Be Faithful, Condomize" (ABC). These countries have also seen a growth of peer sex education with some limited evidence of success.

The third approach is barely in evidence anywhere, despite being advocated by a number of researchers in response to the failures of the first two approaches and the urgency of the HIV pandemic.

SEE ALSO: Gender, Education and; Moral Panics; Sex Panic; Sexuality

REFERENCE

Irvine, J. (2002) *Talk about Sex: The Battles over Sex Education in the United States*. University of California Press, Berkeley and Los Angeles, CA.

SUGGESTED READING

Epstein, D., O'Flynn, S., & Telford, D. (2003) *Silenced Sexualities in Schools and Universities*. Trentham Books, Stoke-on-Trent.

DEBBIE EPSTEIN

sex panics

Historian Allan Bérubé suggests the term sex panic refers to "a moral crusade that leads to crackdowns on sexual outsiders" (Wockner: 1997). "Sex panics, witch hunts, and red scares are staples of American history," writes Lisa Duggan (1989/1995). She elaborates: "While often promoted by relatively powerless but vocal minorities hostile to cultural difference, they have been enthusiastically taken up by powerful groups in an effort to impose rigid orthodoxy on the majority." They generally function to obscure "any responsibility to confront and address very real problems, that is poverty, militarism, sexism, and racism" (Duggan, 1989/95: 75).

Critics suggest panics take shape as a condemnation of queerness, public sexual culture, those on welfare, or women who have children out of wedlock. In response to a panic over queer sexuality in the 1990s, a group of scholars suggested:

> This is not the first time that officials have launched repressive measures against sex in the name of public

> good. Since the nineteenth century, it has been a recurrent pattern: Public morals and health have been invoked; scapegoats have been found in homosexuals, sex workers and others who are unlikely to fight back; and a fantasy of purity is held up as the norm. Historians have come to call this pattern a "sex panic." (Crimp et al. 1998)

The concept of sex panic is useful in that it helps explain collective behavior – including periods of "hysteria," "red scares," and "prohibition." Yet, just because something is stirred by irrational behavior does not necessarily mean it is a panic. Future research must highlight approaches to combat the dynamics of panic so reason can prevail over fear.

SEE ALSO: Moral Panics; Sex Education

REFERENCES

Crimp, D., Pelligrini, A., Pendleton, E., & Warner, M. (1998) This is a sexpanic! *Fountain* 6 (2): 22–4.

Duggan, L. (1989/1995) Sex panics. In: Duggan, L. & Hunter, N. (eds.), *Sex Wars: Sexual Dissent and Political Culture*. Routledge, New York, pp. 74–9.

Wockner, R. (1997) Sex-lib activists confront "SexPanic." *Gaywave* November 17.

BENJAMIN SHEPARD

sex tourism

Sex tourism is a multibillion dollar global industry wherein individuals (sex tourists) from industrialized, developed nations travel abroad with the distinct purpose of purchasing a variety of sexually associated services. Destinations vary, but most sex tourists seek the services of individuals from developing nations. Sex tourists' travel and consumption, facilitated by technology and an unequal and increasingly interconnected world system, have raised the profitability of this industry to a historically unprecedented level. Blending global race, ethnicity, class, gender, and age inequalities with capitalist consumption, sex tourism creates and perpetuates a range of problems for sex workers and host countries. A growing body of interdisciplinary studies reveals a complex blend of exploitation and agency involved in sex tourism, the links between local and global, the need for inclusive and further study of homosexual, transgendered and bisexual, as well as heterosexual sex tourism, and the importance of understanding rather than stereotyping workers and experiences.

Sex tourism is credited with both the creation and intensification of micro and macro social problems including, but not limited to, violence against individuals (workers and tourists); disease and morbidity; child prostitution; and social/environmental destruction. Sex workers often suffer abuse and exploitation from clients, including refusal to wear condoms, physical or emotional violence, and failure to pay. They are likely to experience harassment by club operators and law enforcement. In most countries the sex trade is illegal and sex workers are unlikely to be legally protected. AIDS and sexually transmitted diseases (STDs) are prevalent and can impact buyer, seller, or future and present sex partners and children. Paradoxically, the threat of AIDS is reported to appeal to some sex tourists who regard it as adventure and high-risk sport. Child prostitution, reported in many areas, has attracted international attention. International actions, such as passing legislation to make those who engage children as prostitutes liable abroad and in their own countries, may deflect attention and resources from adult workers and may make them scapegoats for the sex trade.

SEE ALSO: Globalization, Sexuality and; Imperialism; Prostitution

SUGGESTED READING

Ryan, C. (2000) Sex tourism. In: Clift, S. & Carter, S. (eds.), *Tourism and Sex Culture, Commerce and Coercion*. Continuum International, New York.

SUSAN L. WORTMANN

sexism

Sexism is discrimination on the basis of sex and/or gender. It occurs at various levels, from the individual to the institutional, and involves practices that promote gender-based prejudice and stereotyping. Most commonly, sexism refers to inequalities that exist among men and women, particularly where women are treated as unequal or inferior to men. Like other forms of discrimination, sexism can occur through blatant or covert actions, including outright displays of hatred or disdain for an individual or group; the privileging of one gender over another; or tokenism, where, for example, a woman is hired only because she is a woman, rather than because of her skills and experience. How sexism plays out varies according to the social location of the individual or group involved, particularly in regard to racial, ethnic, class, sexual, and/or religious background.

Beginning in the 1960s, sexism became a commonly used term by participants in feminist movements. In the USA, the National Organization for Women (NOW) fought for an Equal Rights

Amendment (ERA) which, had it passed, would have provided full equality to men and women under the law. The 1972 Education Amendment to the Civil Rights Act, or "Title IX," mandated that schools, colleges, and universities that received public funds must provide equality in funding for male and female students at all levels, including in sports. Globally, the United Nations Convention on the Elimination of All Forms of Discrimination against Women (CEDAW), adopted in 1979, urged governments to adopt legislation that promotes gender equality. As of 2009, more than 90 percent (186 member countries) have ratified the Convention.

The definition of sexism has changed over time, reflecting contemporary sociological debates on sex vs. gender and nature vs. nurture. While the nature–nurture debates continue, many feminist scholars continue to agree that the social context, rather than any assumed biological difference between men and women, is crucial to understanding how and why women are viewed as the "weaker sex" and therefore subject to sexism.

SEE ALSO: Discrimination; Gender Bias; Gender Ideology and Gender Role Ideology; Gender Oppression; Sex and Gender

SUGGESTED READINGS

England, P. (1992) *Comparable Worth: Theories and Evidence*. Aldine de Gruyter, New York.

Friedan, B. (2001) [1963] *The Feminine Mystique*. W. W. Norton, New York.

Lorber, J. (1994) *Paradoxes of Gender*. Yale University Press, New Haven, CT.

AMY LIND

sexual citizenship

Until the emergence of the concept of sexual citizenship, sociological explorations of human sexualities were limited by focusing on discrete forms of sexual "deviance," without critical reference to their emergence in patriarchal, heteronormative capitalism. Sexual citizenship focuses on the complex dynamic material (political, legal, economic) construction of sexualities through differential citizenship (civil, political, social rights), determined by divergent legal and moral judgements of sexual status within and outwith the ideological norm of the marital, monogamous, reproductive, heterosexual family. Differential sexual citizenship is determined by degrees of moral and legal inclusion and exclusion, from, for example, unmarried heterosexual relationships, single parenthood, surrogacy, adoption, homosexuality, lesbianism through to sex work, transvestism and transsexualism to the criminal: rapists and pedophiles. This construction of sexualities through statutory recognition (civil, political, social rights) modified by differential moral approbation, is also qualified by degrees of niche market access and lifestyle consumption. Sexual citizenship thus embraces such apparently "non-sexual" differentials as taxation, life insurance, health care, home ownership, inheritance rights, conditions of employment, use of "public" and "private" spaces, etc.

Sociological interest in general citizenship was stimulated in the 1980s by analyses of "disorganized" capitalism: fragmentation of economic interest groups with greater industrial flexibility in increasingly consumerist economies; breakdown of neo-corporatist state regulation; growing contradictions between state and capital; growth of fragmented and discrete social movements, with active citizens as reflexive consumers. Capital, culture, technology and politics developed beyond the regulatory power of the national state, which retreated from moralist to causalist principles of governance. Rather than appraising "deviant" sexualities as "immoral" and interfering in the private lives of citizens, the law concentrated on causal effects, preservation of public order and decency, and restriction of tolerated sexual "deviance" without "victims" to "private," i.e. "public" but discrete, increasingly leisure and lifestyle territories and markets. Despite this acknowledgement of sexual citizenship diversity, the ideal of "heteronormativity" within the family context, threatened by AIDS, child sex abuse, and other "immoral" dangers, remained pronounced.

This materialist formulation of "sexual citizenship" emerged simultaneously with a markedly different interpretation. Plummer (1992, 2003) interprets "disorganised capitalism" as symptomatic of postmodernity rather than adaptive capitalism, notable for a new "intimate" sexual citizenship, an empowering "radical, pluralistic ... participatory politics of human life choices and difference" (Plummer 2003), manifest through "communities" of sexual stories. Whilst Evans (1993) concentrates on the structural readjustments and consequences of the late modern state's deployment of citizenship to incorporate still "immoral" though legal sexual citizens, through the distractions of single-issue "rights" fetishized as "equal," "disorganized" conditions leading to crises in governance in the short term but resolved through further citizenship readjustments, Plummer (1992) asserts that " 'rights' campaigns around 'being gay' and 'lesbian' have had ... remarkable payoffs in the western world . . . [in which] being gay and lesbian . . . [brings] no more problems than any other way of living and loving." For Evans (1993) such claims demonstrate how effectively bourgeois citizenship reconstructs and contains sexual difference and dissent, imposing on sexual political movements the language of citizenship rather than of that of "liberation" as twenty years earlier. Thus, behind the rhetorical facade of "liberty" and "equality," the state fragments, neutralizes, and distracts sexual dissidents to sustain its own "moral authority" and the heteronormative ideal.

Potentially both interpretations provide complementary perspectives on the comparative analysis of the macro-dynamic structuration of sexualities in late capitalism and globally. In both hitherto discrete sexualities are grounded in the same material conditions of "disorganized" capitalism; all citizenship rights and duties are revealed as heteronormatively discriminating and hegemonic heteronormativity, so often left as an all-powerful nebulous organizing principle, is revealed in all its concrete complexity, inconsistency, and duplicity.

SEE ALSO: Citizenship; Gay and Lesbian Movement; Queer Theory; Sexual Identities

REFERENCES

Evans, D. T. (1993) *Sexual Citizenship: The Material Construction of Sexualities*. Routledge, London.

Plummer, K. (1992) Speaking its name: inventing a lesbian and gay studies. In: Plummer, K. (ed.), *Modern Homosexualities*. Routledge, London.

Plummer, K. (2003) Intimate citizenship and the culture of sexual story telling. In: Weeks, J., Holland, J., & Waites, S. (eds.), *Sexualities and Society*. Polity Press, Cambridge.

DAVID T. EVANS

sexual deviance

Sexual deviance, and what is defined as sexually deviant, is culturally and historically specific. This concept refers to behaviors that involve individuals seeking erotic gratification through means that are considered odd, different, or unacceptable to either most or influential persons in one's community. As with most forms of deviance, sexual deviance is something that is defined differently by persons of different backgrounds, beliefs, morals, and locations. However, sexual deviance is also an idea about which most persons hold very strong views, and react in stigmatizing and ostracizing ways.

Sexual deviance is a term that refers to behavior that has a sexual aspect to it and is considered a violation of either general societal norms or the expectations and/or limits of behavior for specific cultural settings. Defining some sexually oriented behavior as deviant means that the action meets at least one (or a combination) of four criteria: (1) degree of consent, (2) the nature of the persons/objects involved in the action, (3) the actual action and body parts involved, or (4) the setting in which the behavior is performed. Generally speaking, sexual behavior that is not fully consensual by all persons involved is considered deviant. Rape and exhibitionism (where the persons to whom sexual images are presented are unwilling recipients) are obvious examples of sexual deviance defined by degree of consent. Sexual behavior with children, animals, or "odd" objects (vegetables, firearms, kitchen appliances, etc.) would be considered deviant by most people because such persons and objects are not generally considered sexual. When we speak of sexual deviance based on the action or body parts involved as the defining elements we could think of individuals who receive sexual gratification from violence, setting fires, wearing opposite-gender clothing, or even for some people, masturbation. This category would also include sexual acts that include body parts not typically considered sexual, such as individuals' feet, ears, or noses. Finally, some settings, such as a courtroom, church, or an open field in a public park would be thought of by most people as inappropriate for sexual activities. Therefore, sexual acts performed in these locations (regardless of how "normal" the acts may be) would be considered deviant, simply because of where they were performed.

It is important to keep in mind that sexual deviance, as with all types of deviance, is not usually something that is inherently "wrong." Instead, sexual deviance is so determined by one of two approaches, both based on social conditions. The easier to see of these two approaches is the idea of statistical definitions. This means that sexual behaviors in which only a minority of persons engages would be considered deviant. In this view, behaviors in which a majority of persons participate would be normative, and those actions that only a "few" people do would be "different" (i.e., deviant). A more purely sociological approach to defining sexual deviance is to focus on the ways that society members react and respond to particular acts. In this approach, when others learn of an individual's sexual activities with farm animals and react by showing their distaste for the act and stigmatization of the persons involved, we know that sex with farm animals is considered deviant.

SEE ALSO: Deviance; Sexual Practices; Stigma

SUGGESTED READINGS

Gagnon, J. & Simon, W. (1967) *Sexual Deviance*. Harper & Row, New York.

Hensley, C. & Tewksbury, R. (2003) *Sexual Deviance*. Lynne Rienner Publishers, Boulder, CO.

RICHARD TEWKSBURY

sexual harassment

Sexual harassment refers to unwelcome sexual advances, requests for sexual favors, or other forms of unwanted attention of a sexual nature, in a workplace or elsewhere. Sexual harassment includes unwelcome (sexual) jokes, remarks with sexual connotations, gossip, repeated requests to go out, and any form of unwanted touching or invasion of personal space, as well as sexual advances or assault.

The overwhelming majority of victims are women, as well as adolescent and young workers. Perpetrators are most often individual men or groups of men. Same-sex harassment has also received attention, in particular, gender and sexual harassment among men. Besides consequences such as loss of a job or not being promoted, victims can experience adverse psychological effects such as confusion, discomfort, anxiety, anger, and stress.

The experiences, interpretations, and perceptions of sexual harassment vary not only by gender but also by age, social class, race/ethnicity, and sexual orientation. There are cross-national differences in individual, organizational, social, political, and legal interpretations of sexual harassment.

Feminist theories view sexual harassment primarily as rooted in unequal gender relations and the abuse of power of men over women. Sexual harassment is the product of a gender system that maintains a dominant, (hetero)normative form of masculinity. "Sex roles" or assumptions about male sexual aggression and female passivity spill over into the workplace.

For organizational theories sexual harassment is perpetuated through gendered organizational and institutional structures. The occupational status of the victim and supervisory authority of the perpetrator influence the perceptions and interpretations of sexual harassment. Women's lower status at work, sex segregation, gender gaps in authority, and other organizational factors contribute to and are perpetuated by sexual harassment.

SEE ALSO: Femininities/Masculinities; Sex and Gender; Sex Panics; Sexual Politics; Sexuality and the Law

SUGGESTED READING

MacKinnon, C. A. (1979) *Sexual Harassment of Working Women: A Case of Sex Discrimination*. Yale University Press, New Haven, CT.

KATHRIN ZIPPEL

sexual health

Sexual health is both a lay expression and a technical term defined in national and international legal and public policy documents. As employed by social scientists, sexual health generally refers to a state of physical and emotional well-being in which an individual enjoys freedom from sexually related disease, dysfunction, coercion, and shame, and thus the ability to enjoy and act on sexual feelings. Sociological studies of sexual health employ both quantitative and qualitative methods, with the former being more common, especially for issues deemed relevant to public health.

Although scholars and policy makers have treated sexuality as a public health issue since the mid-1800s, few used the expression "sexual health" before the mid-1990s. Originally, reproductive health and sexual health were treated as a single issue, with the emphasis on reproduction. In the 1960s, however, effective new contraceptives, increasing secularization, and social acceptance of nonmarital sexuality in many societies facilitated a sharper distinction. Leading sexologists' use of biomedical models to legitimize sex research and therapy also helped to construct sexuality as a health issue. The increasing popularity of the term "sexual health" among North American, Australian, European, and Latin American scholars may reflect attempts to circumvent increasing conservative opposition, insofar as research on sexuality is deemed more justifiable when focused on health.

In 1975, the World Health Organization (WHO) formally defined sexual health in fundamentally social, rather than biomedical, terms as entailing the "right to sexual information and...pleasure," the "capacity to ... control sexual and reproductive behaviour," "freedom from ... psychological factors inhibiting sexual response and ... relationship," and "freedom from organic disorders, diseases, and deficiencies that interfere with sexual and reproductive functions." These elements have been central components of all subsequent major definitions of sexual health, whether scholarly or lay.

In 2002, responding to concerns about social diversity and critiques from women's health and development NGOs, the WHO issued a revised definition of sexual health as:

> a state of physical, emotional, mental and social well-being related to sexuality ... Sexual health requires a positive and respectful approach to sexuality and sexual relationships, as well as the possibility of having pleasurable and safe sexual experiences, free of coercion, discrimination and violence.

The WHO further declared that attaining sexual health depended on having the "sexual rights of all persons ... respected, protected and fulfilled." The exact relationship among sexual health, reproductive health, and sexual rights remains contested, however.

For much of the twentieth century, prevailing moral codes/attitudes meant that most studies of sexual health focused on married couples of reproductive age or heterosexual adolescents (whose sexuality is presumed to be problematic) and tended to treat White middle-class people as paragons of health and normalcy while framing economically disadvantaged people and/or members of racial/ethnic minorities as deviant or unhealthy. Study populations have become increasingly diverse since the 1970s, as have the range of issues explored.

Feminism has inspired research into power, gendered expectations, reproduction, and rape; with studies of men's sexual health proliferating since the 1990s. GLBTQ activism has encouraged research on gay men's health, especially HIV/AIDS, lesbians' use of health services, and sexuality-related hate crimes. The aging of western societies and expanding pharmaceutical industry have drawn attention to sexual dysfunction and sexual activity after menopause/climacteric. Contemporary research also addresses female genital mutilation (FGM), sexuality and chronic illnesses, and sexuality education.

SEE ALSO: AIDS, Sociology of; Female Genital Mutilation; Safer Sex; Women's Health

SUGGESTED READINGS

Edwards, W. M., & Coleman, E. (2004) Defining sexual health: a descriptive overview. *Archives of Sexual Behavior* 33 (3): 189–95.

Giami, A. (2002) Sexual health: the emergence, development, and diversity of a concept. *Annual Review of Sex Research* 13: 1–35.

World Health Organization (2002) *Definition of Sexual Health*: www.who.int/reproductive-health/gender/sexual_health.html, accessed August 3, 2004.

LAURA M. CARPENTER

sexual politics

"Sexual politics" refers to the contestation of power relations with respect to sex, gender, and sexuality. The concept originates in the second-wave feminist movement which emerged from the 1960s in western societies. Its definitive textual origin is Kate Millett's *Sexual Politics*, first published in 1970, which analyzed "patriarchy" – the social system of rule by men. For Millett, "sexual politics" meant that "sex is a status category with political implications."

Sexual politics was revolutionary for sociology. Power relations between men and women became understood as products of society by feminists who initially sought to distinguish sex, as biological, from gender, as social. More recently the assumption of two pre-social sexes has been challenged by radical transgender and feminist theorists advocating a "new gender politics" (Butler, 2004). Sexual politics today encompasses activities by women, men, transgender people, lesbian, gay, bisexual, queer and heterosexual people, sadomasochists, pedophiles, pornography campaigners, and others.

In many wealthier states feminism has achieved a fundamental shift from the assumed model of the heterosexual nuclear family, with a male "breadwinner" and corresponding norms of femininity and masculinity, to legitimization of both partners having paid employment. Diverse heterosexual masculinities and femininities are more acceptable, while gay and lesbian movements have achieved a shift *Beyond the Closet* (Seidman 2004). The emergence of "queer politics" and "queer theory," influenced by poststructuralist Michel Foucault, challenges the heterosexual/homosexual dichotomy, "heteronormativity," and a liberal assimilationist gay politics. Transgender people in some states have experienced legal reforms such as the UK's *Gender Recognition Act* (2004). Meanwhile men's movements have emerged to campaign on fathers' rights. In the global south sexual politics is equally dynamic: HIV/AIDS interventions, post-colonial nationalisms and religious movements are everywhere structured by gender and sexuality.

SEE ALSO: Feminism; Feminism, First, Second, and Third Waves; Gay and Lesbian Movement; Sex and Gender; Sexualities and Culture Wars

REFERENCES
Butler, J. (2004) *Undoing Gender*. Routledge, London.
Seidman, S. (2004) *Beyond the Closet: The Transformation of Gay and Lesbian Life*. Routledge, London.

SUGGESTED READINGS
Millett, K. (1972) *Sexual Politics*. Abacus, London.
Weeks, J., Holland, J., & Waites, M. (eds.) (2003) *Sexualities and Society: A Reader*. Polity Press, Cambridge.

MATTHEW WAITES

sexual practices

Sexual practices have varied widely across time and space. Freud and the Freudians dominated the study of human sexuality for many years. For Freud, sex was an overpowering biological drive that was repressed by society in varying ways and degrees. Kinsey emerged onto the scene in the late 1940s, and Masters and Johnson in the 1960s. Their work had little theory and has been referred to as a kind of "radical empiricism" (Brake 1982).

The currently dominant approach to explaining sexual practices seems to be *social constructionism*, which downplays the biological nature of humans and emphasizes that sexual practices are socially and culturally created. Among the earliest sociologists to take this approach, specifically in the form of symbolic interactionism, were John Gagnon and William Simon, as well as Ken Plummer. Social constructionists oppose "essentialism," or the notion that sexuality is largely a matter of biologically pre-given drives. For the constructionists, sexual practices are less biologically given than determined by society through complex webs of social interaction and social definition. Gagnon and Simon emphasized the importance of "sexual scripts"; for them, sexual conduct "is acquired and assembled in human interaction, judged and performed in specific cultural and historical worlds" (Gagnon 1977: 2). And, as Plummer tells us, "Sexuality has no meaning other than that given to it in social situations. Thus the forms and the contents of sexual meanings are another cultural variable, and why certain meanings are learnt and not others is problematic" (1982: 233).

The leading alternative to social constructionism today is the *Darwinian* approach of sociobiologists and evolutionary psychologists. Donald Symons (1979), for example, has sought to show how Darwinian sexual selection has acted on human sexual desires by looking in particular at universal or extremely widespread sexual attitudes and practices. He points to such things as the overwhelming tendency of males everywhere to be aroused by visual sexual stimuli; to the apparently universal desire of men to mate with younger females; to copulation as primarily a service provided by females to males; and to the universal desire of males for a wide variety of sexual partners. The Darwinian approach has made little headway in sociology, but it has been highly influential in psychology and anthropology.

STEPHEN K. SANDERSON

SEE ALSO: Globalization, Sexuality and; Heterosexuality; Homosexuality; Lesbianism; Pornography and Erotica; Safer Sex; Sexuality

REFERENCES
Brake, M. (1982) Sexuality as praxis: a consideration of the contribution of sexual theory to the process of sexual being. In: Brake, M. (ed.), *Human Sexual Relations*. Pantheon, New York.
Gagnon, J. (1977) *Human Sexualities*. Scott, Foresman, Glenview, IL.
Plummer, K. (1982) Symbolic interactionism and sexual conduct: an emergent perspective. In: Brake, M. (ed.), *Human Sexual Relations*. Pantheon, New York.
Symons, D. (1979) *The Evolution of Human Sexuality*. Oxford University Press, New York.

sexualities and consumption

Sexuality and consumption are interlinked in powerful and significant ways, perhaps even more so in contemporary, even "postmodern," times, shaping various material and subjective possibilities and impossibilities, as sexuality is displayed and regulated via consumption. Consumption refers to a wide variety of spending patterns and behaviors and is typically equated with "choice"; what we choose to buy, where and when, and how we choose to use purchasable commodities, ranging from mundane everyday goods and services to extravagant "one-off " specials, which seemingly reinforce the uniqueness of our own individual consumer choice.

Yet to consume also implies a potential restriction in terms of what is being offered and to whom. Other market activities, such as employment, leisure activities, and citizenship, are related to consumption insofar as these afford possibilities for participating in certain markets, create and foreground certain "choices," while restricting and regulating individuals within multiple social domains. Heterosexuality is privileged, even expected, within many consumer spheres, but lesbian, gay, and bisexual sexualities are also increasingly affecting, and indeed affected by, marketization, as the notion of a ready, waiting, and willing "pink pound" implies (Chasin 2000; Hennessy 2000).

Chasin (2000) uncovers the linkage between the development of the "lesbian and gay movement" in the USA and the growth of lesbian and gay "niche markets" that promise inclusion into the marketplace and the nation itself – but at a price. Within her account, social recognition is dependent on ability to consume as identity becomes branded, commodified, and consumed. Lesbians and gays are integrated, even assimilated, as consumers rather than as citizens. Money then represents the prerequisite for participation as well as the boundary. Chasin's catchy (and cutting) title *Selling Out* conveys notions of failure and possible fraudulence, hinting at the ways in which sexual identities have been depoliticized, as they become only another consumer possibility.

SEE ALSO: Consumption; Globalization, Sexuality and; Homophobia and Heterosexism; Metrosexual; Postmodern Sexualities

REFERENCES

Chasin, A. (2000) *Selling Out: The Gay and Lesbian Movement Goes to Market*. Palgrave, Basingstoke.
Hennessy, R. (2000) *Profit and Pleasure: Sexual Identities in Late Capitalism*. Taylor & Francis, London.

YVETTE TAYLOR

sexualities and culture wars

The term "culture wars" came to prominence in the early 1990s, referring to conflicts in United States society over abortion, religion in schools, acceptance of homosexuals, pornography, the judiciary, and the arts. Many flashpoints in the culture war derived from competing assumptions about the body and sexuality. Sociologist James Davison Hunter (1991) depicted *elite* knowledge workers seeking to impose their competing understandings on the rest of society. In the contests over abortion, gay sexuality, and religion in the public sphere Hunter detected a realignment as Jewish, Protestant and Roman Catholic *elites* formed new alliances, cutting across old antagonisms.

Below the surface conflicts (liberal vs. conservative), knowledge workers clustered towards two poles of moral authority: the orthodox and the progressives. The orthodox moral universe is based on commitment to an external transcendent Being while the progressive moral universe entails a tendency to recast values and historic faiths in light of prevailing cultural assumptions. While diversity exists between the two poles, an impulse towards polarity occurs.

The orthodox perspective largely militated against gay marriage and abortion rights, seeing progressive efforts as assaults on the family and moral society. Progressives contended that the freedoms guaranteed by the US constitution, and enlightened thinking generally, meant extending full civil rights to gays and lesbians and maintaining a woman's right to choose in dealing with a pregnancy. Rooted in ultimate concerns, these competing perspectives did not share much common ground.

Three significant criticisms of the culture wars thesis emerged. One, public opinion really is not very polarized; two, the orthodox/progressive dichotomy is too simplistic to account for the diversity of positions in contested culture; three, the metaphor of "war" is overstated, sensationalistic and thus inappropriate. However, the 2000 and 2004 US elections and ballot initiatives about gay marriage revived the culture wars thesis.

SEE ALSO: Abortion as a Social Problem; Homophobia; Moral Panics; Power Elite

REFERENCE

Hunter, J. D. (1991) *Culture Wars: The Struggle to Define America*. Basic Books, New York.

GLENN LUCKE

sexuality

Approaches to understanding sexuality are categorized as either essentialist or social constructionist. Essentialism, focusing on the individual expression of human desire and pleasure, favours a biological explanation. Social constructionism, focusing on the relationship between individual and society, explores how sexuality is embedded in historical, political, and social practices. Attention is paid to the ways in which sexual desires, practices, identities, and attitudes are conceptualized, categorized, deployed, and regulated through the social institutions and practices of society.

HISTORY OF SEXUALITY

Foucault (1979) traces the history of the hetero-sexuality/homosexuality dichotomy to processes that began in the nineteenth century and the birth of sexology. Challenging essentialist conceptualizations of sex and sexuality as transhistorical and stable categories, Foucault claims that the discursive invention of sexuality as a biological instinct fundamental to understanding an individual's health, pathology and identity lead to biopower.

While sex denoted the sexual act, sexuality symbolized the true essence of the individual. Distortion or perversion of the natural instinct would lead to sexual abnormality and deviance. Sexual behaviour represented the true nature and identity of an individual. Same-sex sexual behaviour denoted a homosexual identity; opposite-sex behaviour a heterosexual one. For Foucault, this resulted in the connection of the body, the new human sciences, and the demands for regulation and surveillance, so that power and pleasure (knowledge and sex) meshed with each other. Homosexuality was constructed as a perversion, thus legitimating its regulation and surveillance alongside the institutional promotion of heterosexuality.

While the sexologists favored a biological explanation, Freud's psychoanalytic theory of sexual development led to the psychological construction of different sexual identities. The individual progresses from an initial polymorphous sexuality in early childhood through to the development of a mature stable heterosexual identity in adulthood; homosexuality is a temporary (adolescent) stage of development. Adults who identify as homosexual are either "fixated" on an earlier phase or have, due to psychological disturbance "regressed" backwards. Either way, homosexuality is located within a discourse of deviance, and psychopathology.

SOCIOLOGY OF HOMOSEXUALITY

Kinsey's large-scale studies (1948; 1953) on human sexual behaviour highlighted the discrepancy between the number of people who engage in same-sex behavior and the number who identify as homosexual. Kinsey developed a six-point continuum to encompass the variety of sexual behavior and feelings present, ranging from exclusively heterosexual (1) to exclusively homosexual (6); bisexuality is in the middle. Individuals might move between categories throughout their life, thus rendering invalid the use of discrete sexual identities.

Gay Liberation and the Women's Movement in the 1960s led to academic interest in oppressed groups. The Kinsey Reports and the development of the labeling perspective provided the theoretical catalyst for sociological interest in sexuality, initially focused mainly on sexual deviance. Sociologists suggest that people who engage in same-sex behavior are labeled deviant due to the reactions of a hostile society; there is nothing intrinsically deviant about a homosexual identity. McIntosh (1968) stated that the very conceptualization of homosexuality as an individual condition is a form of social control, deterring newcomers while isolating those identified as deviant.

GENDER AND SEXUALITY

Prioritizing the relationship between sex, gender, and sexuality radical feminists argue that women's sexuality and their reproductive capabilities are controlled and regulated by men through a patriarchal sex/gender system in which women are constructed as sexually passive, men as active. Deconstructing this "natural" relationship, radical feminists theorize both lesbianism and heterosexuality as political institutions aimed at regulating and controlling women's sexuality.

Other feminists, critical of the perceived essentialism and anti-sex thinking present in radical feminism have focused on heterosexuality as a "political regime" based on an artificial biologically based distinction between women and men, hence oppressive to both women and homosexuals. This analysis undermines the traditional understanding of the category of sex as being biologically defined and immutable and enables the examination of how sex difference contributes to the existing social order. Essentialist categories of woman, man, heterosexual, and homosexual are reconfigured as political categories to become critical sites of gender deconstruction.

More recently, sociologists have begun to examine the social construction of masculinity, its links to power and the social organization of sexuality. Key concepts include "hegemonic masculinity", "subordinated" and "complicit" masculinities. Heterosexuality is regarded as being central to hegemonic masculinity.

QUEER THEORY

Queer theory, drawing on the work of Foucault and Derrida, concentrates on the dynamic relationship between the dualism homosexuality/heterosexuality, thus permitting an examination of the heteronormative nature of all knowledge and social structures. Heterosexuality represents an axis of power and dominant model for conducting intimate gender normative relationships. Heteronormativity dominates both the legal and cultural systems, thus normalizing differential treatment of those who stand outside of the heterosexual regime. The concept increases our understanding of both the structural disadvantages of those who stand outside the heterosexual regime and the way in which institutionalized heterosexuality limits and constrains those who identify as heterosexual.

A focus on the borders that exist between sexual identities leads to the deconstruction of all sexual identities, including politicized ones. Although the construction of the homosexual enabled the struggle for civil rights, claiming the label homosexual simultaneously reinforces the centrality of heterosexuality. It is impossible to locate oneself "outside" of dominant discourses, for to define oneself as standing outside the sexual norm means first placing oneself within dominant definitions of sexuality. Thus, claiming a homosexual identity contributes to reinforcing the hetero/homo split (Namaste 1994).

Queer theory and practice signal important theoretical shifts, resulting in a critical distancing from the terms lesbian and gay; the term queer has become a catalyst for people disaffected by earlier work on sexual identity, which homogenized the experiences and interests of lesbian and gay men and assumed that sexual identity is both visible and static. Queer theory's poststructuralist approach challenges the foundationalist assumptions present in existing understandings of identity and uses this as a basis to question current notions of sexual identity, leading to a rejection of unifying concepts and an increasing emphasis on difference and plurality.

THEORY AND PRACTICE

Explanations for sexuality, regardless of origin, have a direct consequence at an individual, institutional and societal level. The stigmatization of homosexuality has a detrimental effect on people who find themselves attracted to members of the same sex, a situation that can be exacerbated by the social and legal sanctions surrounding same-sex lifestyles. Likewise, while feminists have exposed the complex relationship between gender and sexuality, women in many parts of the world remain legally and socially subordinate to men, sociological interest in sexuality provides a broader analysis of the social organization of sexuality in society.

SEE ALSO: Bisexuality; Essentialism and Constructionism; Foucault, Michel; Heterosexuality; Homosexuality; Queer Theory

REFERENCES

Foucault, M. (1979) *The History of Sexuality: An Introduction*, trans. R. Hurley. Penguin, London.

Kinsey, A. C., Gebhard, P., Pomeroy, W. B. & Martin, C. E. (1948) *Sexual Behaviour in the Human Male*. W. B. Saunders, Philadelphia.

Kinsey, A. C., Gebhard, P., Pomeroy, W. B. & Martin, C. E. (1953) *Sexual Behaviour in the Human Female*. W. B. Saunders, Philadelphia.

McIntosh, M. (1968) The homosexual role. *Social Problems* 16 (2): 182–92.

Namaste, K. (1994) The politics of inside/out: queer theory, poststructuralism, and a sociological approach to sexuality. *Sociological Theory* 12: 220–31.

SUGGESTED READINGS

Katz, J. N. (1996) *The Invention of Heterosexuality*. Plume Penguin, London.

Plummer, K. (ed.) (1981) *The Making of the Modern Homosexual*. Hutchinson, London.

Rich, A. (1980) Compulsory heterosexuality and lesbian existence. *Signs* 5 (4): 631–60.

Richardson, D. (ed.) (1996) *Theorizing Heterosexuality*. Open University Press, Milton Keynes.

ANN CRONIN

sexuality, masculinity and

Many people believe that sexuality is a simple reflection of biological differences. To sociologists, sexuality is derived from experiences constructed within social, cultural, and historical contexts. Sexual identities and behaviors develop herein; norms and cultural expectations guide individuals. western societies also privilege binary, dichotomized gender roles. Research suggests that in most of the world, action, autonomy, competition, and aggression are desirable masculine qualities. Sexuality is scripted to encourage men to initiate, be aggressive, and be sexually knowledgeable, especially in heterosex, from flirtation to foreplay and everything else. Masculine sexuality is thought to be powered by a libido that inhibits rationality and planning; condom use is believed to interfere with these spur-of-the-moment impulses.

Though hegemonic masculinities define racial, ethnic and class similarities, differences exist, especially in the USA. Caucasian men masturbate younger and Asian Americans have less sexual experience. Intercourse is the primary sexual expression for African Americans, while Latinos differ based on ethnicity and acculturation. Transgender men face other issues, including visibility.

Men's bodies are seen as mechanized, tool-like, exemplified by the occasional practice of referring to the penis as an object separate from a man's mind. Erections – "proof" of arousal – are given hundreds of slang terms denoting the importance and power of the phallus. This mind/body separation can lead to *recreational sex*, where feelings of intimacy, love, and tenderness are dissociated from partnered sex. Men are expected to master their bodies, thus experiencing *performance anxiety* when they "can't get the job done."

Pornography, sexually explicit materials intended to arouse, depicts men as powerful, lusty initiators with enormous, reliable phalluses. Via pornography, western men learn about sexualities in general and their own scripts in particular. *Coitus* (penile–vaginal intercourse) is assumed to be "the most natural" sexual behavior, reinforcing heterosexuality's dominance and making gay sex and sex between men invisible. Cultural acceptance of non-genital and solo sexual expression is limited, though masculine sexuality can include watching strippers, going to sex clubs, and engaging in domination and submission.

Patriarchy, when social power mostly rests in men's hands, can create gender hierarchies in which men dominate women. Rape, sexual assault, and child molestation are the darkest aspects of patriarchal societies. A complex mix of patriarchy and sexism, *homophobia* (the fear of anyone or anything defined as gay or lesbian) includes the misperception that to be gay is to be less than a man. The word *fag* and other terms are often used as a form of social control. Risky, emotionally circumscribed interactions showing sexual prowess are often employed to confer status and convey heterosexuality.

"Normative" men's sexuality has been constructed as non-relational, objectifying, and phallocentric, more amenable to paraphilia and fetishes, multiple partners, recreational sexuality and a strict separation of sex and love. Normative men's sexuality is all-too-often an embodiment of gender and societal inequalities. These norms ignore the everyday contexts in which sexualities are produced and individually experienced. Luckily, norms are more fungible in practice, and individual men still have large latitude in negotiating and developing different (and more equal) sexual expressions.

SEE ALSO: Femininities/Masculinities; Male Rape; Pornography and Erotica; Socialization, Gender

SUGGESTED READINGS

Herek, G. (2005) Beyond "homophobia": thinking about sexual prejudice and stigma in the twenty-first century. *Sexuality Research & Policy: Journal of NSRC* 1 (2): 6–24.

Laumann, E. O., Gagnon, J. H, Michael, R. T. & Michaels, S. (1994) *The Social Organization of Sexuality: Sexual Practices in the United States.* University of Chicago Press, Chicago, IL.

REBECCA F. PLANTE AND MICHAEL S. KIMMEL

sexuality, religion and

Long perceived as major sources of social, political, economic, and even esoteric power, sexuality and religion are logical partners for sociological study. The key connections between these two powerful social institutions lie in religious ritual, social structure and social control, and boundary creation and maintenance.

Although much of the study of religion has focused on belief, to individual members of a religion practice is often most central. This holds especially true in the context of sexuality, which is generally practiced – or not – depending on the teachings of a religious group and the practitioner's position within that group. Some religions practice rites that directly involve sexuality. More common than sexual rituals, though, are ritual restrictions on and purifications of sexuality, and important rituals regulate sexuality in the broader culture as well as within a religion – particularly marital rites and the religious practice of celibacy. Several religions consider either women or (more commonly) men to be better suited to abstinence and therefore to advanced spiritual development; religion thus becomes an important determinant of gender roles along with attitudes toward sexuality.

Religious beliefs and practices shape sexual practices, beliefs, roles, identities, and norms; they are a key factor in the social construction of desire. Religion can also provide a site for powerful challenges to an existing social-sexual order. In a number of societies sexual and gender norms are closely intertwined, with deviation from expected gender roles – especially on the part of men – implying an accompanying deviation from expected sexual roles. In most cases this has little to do with religion, but especially in cultures where religion is diffuse, there is often overlap. Marriage is also an important point of intersection for religion and sexuality. The most prominent of such intersections in most western countries currently may be the legalization and religious recognition of same-sex marriage, but questions of religious intermarriage and spousal conversion have been of concern in a number of religions for quite some time. Finally, political organizing by religious groups, both conservative and liberal, in the US has increasingly focused on sexuality issues since the 1960s.

Sexuality, politics, and religion intersect not only in secular spheres but also within religious organizations – and that intersection is increasingly global. As women, lesbians, gay men, and bisexuals demand inclusion and rise to leadership positions within an increasing number of religious groups, those groups with international membership are forced to grapple with questions of human sexuality whose answers are often culturally bound. Furthermore, the creation and violation of personal sexual boundaries becomes a religious issue not only when religions are responsible for defining those boundaries, but also when religious leaders use their power and prestige to gain illicit sexual access to followers. Religion and sexuality have also conspired in the creation of boundaries and the construction of Others in ways that fundamentally shape the processes of colonialism, decolonization, and globalization – such as the religious and, later, academic construction of colonized peoples through sexual and gendered metaphors and stereotypes. As countries around the world gained independence from European colonial powers, another important sexual and often religious symbol came to the fore: the use of the human body, and especially the bodies of women, as a metaphor for the nation.

Under conditions of globalization, the cultural tensions that arise between immigrant communities and their hosts also link religion and sexuality. Concerns over western sexual mores and sexual identities sometimes attend the immigration of westerners into non-western countries, and every immigrant community struggles some way with the differences in (often religiously based) sexual morality between the home culture and the host culture.

SEE ALSO: Globalization, Sexuality and; Sex and Gender; Sexual Identities; Sexual Politics

SUGGESTED READINGS

Machacek, D. W. & Wilcox, M. M. (2003) *Sexuality and the World's Religions.* ABC-CLIO, Goleta, CA.

Moon, D. (2004) *God, Sex, and Politics: Homosexuality and Everyday Theologies.* University of Chicago Press, Chicago, IL.

MELISSA M. WILCOX

sexuality and sport

Michel Foucault, one of the most influential historians of sexuality, argues that sex and sexuality became a pivot for the organization and control of life in modernity, and that sex and sexuality are increasingly central to human affairs to the extent that much of contemporary life has been organized around these concepts. Sport has long been a site for the reproduction of sexual difference, but sexuality occupied a somewhat "absent presence" in sport sociological research until the late 1980s and early 1990s. In early studies on sexuality and sport, feminist scholars identified the "conspiracy of silence" that led to the demonization and invisibility of lesbian athletes, while, concurrently, it was revealed that pervasive expectations of heterosexuality made it impossible for gay men to come out, legitimized homophobic violence, and resulted in displays of aggressive hyper-masculinity in male sports. These early studies served as strategic and anti-oppressive scholarship that brought the experiences of lesbian and gay athletes out of the sports closet. Since that time, scholars in the sociology of sport have continued to critique the ways in which sport serves as a site for: confirming the two sex/gender classification system, which codes lesbians as masculine and gay men as effeminate, constructing and policing sexualities, *and* resisting heterosexism and the heterosexualization of sport-related forms. Contemporary theorizing demonstrates an increasing awareness and application of postmodern, poststructuralist, queer, postcolonial, and cultural geography theories to the study of sexuality and sport. Although each of these "new" theories provides a unique approach, scholars using these theories focus their attention on: examining the intersectionalities of gender, sexuality, race, and class; critiquing the discourses that organize sexuality, the body, and the sex/gender dimorphic system; investigating the heteronormative spaces of sport.

While the homoerotic potential of men's sport has been explored, there is relatively little work on homoeroticism in women's sport. Women are usually represented as objects of desire rather than desiring subjects, and scholarship on lesbians and sport has tended to de-eroticize lesbian desire in order to present a non-threatening image of lesbians so as to promote full inclusion as athletes and coaches. Sport as a socio-cultural institution has established boundaries for experiencing the moving body, pleasure and erotic desire. Queer theorists seek to disrupt these boundaries by suggesting that sport is inherently erotic and sexual and imagine a physical culture that celebrates Eros, rather than rationality. However, the continued sexual objectification of women in sports; the sexual harassment of women, girls, and young boys in sport; the shame associated with homosexual abuse in men's sport; and the use of sexual games in ritualistic team hazing, which have been profiled in the media, continue to make people fearful of sexuality and the sexual and erotic potential of sport. A recent decision by the International Olympic Committee (IOC) that allows transsexual athletes to compete in Olympic Games appears to acknowledge a continuum of sexualities and desires in sport, and perhaps signals a move forward in human rights in relation to sexuality and sport. However, scholars are skeptical that these policies disrupt the heteronormative sports world. Sexuality and sport remains a site of contestation. Sport sociologists recognize the importance of *undoing gender* (Butler 2004) and continue to research the ways in which sport might celebrate sexuality and desire in ways that do not ethically exploit, oppress, or cause harm to other beings.

SEE ALSO: Foucault, Michel; Sex and Gender; Sexualities and Consumption; Sexuality; Sexuality, Masculinity and

REFERENCE

Butler, J. (2004) *Undoing Gender*. Routledge, New York.

SUGGESTED READINGS

Burstyn, V. (1999) *The Rites of Men: Manhood, Politics, and the Culture of Sport*. University of Toronto Press, Toronto.

Lenskyj, H. (2003) *Out on the Field*. Women's Press, Toronto.

CAROLINE FUSCO

sexuality research: ethics

Sexuality research and sex research differ in a number of important ways. Sex research focuses on the mechanics of sex and is dominated by biomedical discourses and most often framed from an "objective" stance. Sexuality research, on the other hand, recognizes power relations between women and men, between heterosexual and homosexual, and between cultures, and therefore is inherently political. Sexuality and the research of sexuality are embedded in cultural and historical contexts. Both are embodied experiences that consider the complex dynamic meanings and activities, cultural signs, politics, and ethics that impact on its realization or repression.

Power relations are embedded in every aspect of sexuality research. As Denzin in *The Research Act* (1989) has argued, when sociologists do research they inevitably take sides for or against particular values, political bodies, and society at large. This includes sexuality researchers, who focus on the most intimate aspects of people's lives. Within the divergent research traditions of sociology there are a number of approaches that reflect particular forms of knowledge about sexuality and ethics. These include functionalists such as Talcott Parsons, symbolic interactionists such as Gagnon and Simon, and Plummer, feminist theorists as diverse as Dworkin and Rubin, masculinity theorists such as Connell, and poststructuralist theorists such as Foucault. While each of these perspectives varies in how it conceptualizes sexuality and gender, they all reflect particular configurations of values, ethics, and society. How sexuality researchers frame their research projects will be influenced by their commitment to or rejection of these or other social theories.

Ethical considerations include the way the research question is constructed, the topic to be studied, and the people or issue being explored, the biography and relations among researchers, the values of the funding body and other actors, and the methodology chosen by the researcher. Ethics also includes which individuals or groups are excluded from research and whether they represent marginal or more powerful groups.

There are several ways that sexuality researchers can seek guidance to resolve research ethics. Reference to codes of ethical practice such as those of the British Sociological Association (2002) or the American Sociological Association (1999) may provide a general overview. However, much of the academic surveillance of research is carried out by university ethics committees or internal review boards (US). It appears to vary significantly between disciplines, universities, and countries.

In the face of these regulatory ethics bodies, sexuality researchers may have to defend their proposals against positivist and biomedical models of research that result in questioning the "objectivity" of qualitative methodology and sampling "bias" when sexual cultures or networks are the focus of study. There is danger in researchers feeling that all the ethical issues have been dealt with once ethics committee approval is obtained. Codes of practice assume a fixed position and deny the dynamic nature of research and a conception of ethics where meanings are subject to negotiation and redefinition. However, ethical issues confront researchers in a number of areas, including relationships in the field, informed consent, use of the Internet, representation of data, and support for researchers. The development of ethical practice in relation to sexuality research requires a much more dynamic and complex process than a purely regulatory approach. The sensitive and intimate nature of sexuality research and the multiple sites and cultural contexts in which it is carried out suggest the need to encourage ethical subjectivity in researchers.

SEE ALSO: Sexuality; Sexuality Research: History; Sexuality Research: Methods

SUGGESTED READINGS

Binik, Y. M., Mah, K., & Kiesler, S. (1999) Ethical issues in conducting sex research on the Internet. *Journal of Sex Research* 36 (1): 82–90.

Connell, R. W. & Dowsett, G. W. (eds.) (1993) *Rethinking Sex: Social Theory and Sexuality Research*. Temple University Press, Philadelphia.

Kulick, D. & Wilson, M. (eds.) (1995) *Taboo: Sex, Identity, Erotic Subjectivity in Anthropological Fieldwork*. Routledge, London.

MOIRA CARMODY

sexuality research: history

Research on sexuality began as a marginalized and stigmatized endeavour, responding to the topic's growing social resonance during the nineteenth century. Initially, specific problems were considered in isolation, the focus largely continuing to rest on those who were not "normal" privileged males, either by gender, race, or sexual orientation. A number of studies in different countries addressed prostitution as a problem, without engaging with the question of its male clientele. Debate on homosexuality was initiated by men trying to understand their own desires, but later work by psychiatrists such as Richard von Krafft-Ebing tended to develop a disease model on the basis of professional encounters with homosexual criminals or mental patients. Darwin's work on the importance of sexual selection was highly influential in developing the study of sexuality, and other phenomena which could not be assimilated to an evolutionary model of the role of sexual selection in reproduction were also analyzed.

From the 1890s several writers pulled together various developing strands into broader syntheses. British doctor Havelock Ellis produced the seven-volume *Studies in the Psychology of Sex*, 1897–1927. The German doctor Magnus Hirschfeld began as a homosexual law reformer, but as researcher, educator, and campaigner ranged more widely. He connected isolated individuals by establishing journals and facilitating international networks. These syntheses of diverse materials laid a foundation for further work. A very different approach, emphasizing the depths of the psyche, was evolved by Sigmund Freud and those he influenced.

Research into sex hormones lagged behind investigation into other endocrine secretions. Besides general taboo, the project was compromised by its association with "rejuvenation" treatments. Until the late 1920s, investigations were predicated on assumptions of gender-specific ovarian and testicular hormones. Biochemical investigations moved sex research into the laboratory, possibly increasing its scientific respectability and access to resources, but detaching it from a wider context.

Surveys of individual experiences of individuals were long hindered by societal taboos and legal strictures but gained a degree of legitimacy from arguments that studying sexual lives would facilitate the improvement of marriage. On that presumption Alfred Kinsey was able to undertake numerous interviews with human subjects, published as *Sexual Behaviour in the Human Male/Female* (1948; 1953). William Masters and Virginia Johnson broke a further taboo in the 1960s by mapping the processes of arousal and satisfaction in the laboratory.

Research into sexuality moved from the specific to the broadly synthetic, then bifurcated onto separate paths investigating distinct aspects. Lack of coordination between differing approaches has remained a problem.

SEE ALSO: Sexuality; Sexuality Research: Ethics; Sexuality Research: Methods

SUGGESTED READINGS

Bullough, V. (1994) *Science in the Bedroom: A History of Sex Research*. Basic Books, New York.

Robinson, P. (1976/1989) *The Modernization of Sex: Havelock Ellis, Alfred Kinsey, William Masters and Virginia Johnson*. Harper and Row, New York.

LESLEY A. HALL

sexuality research: methods

As Kinsey and others discovered to their cost, sex research is fraught with problems for researchers and must be managed carefully. In the USA, Congress has cut or threatened the funding in recent decades for two national surveys of sexual behavior: a study of massage parlor workers and a study of sexual risk-taking, among other topics. And those who publish research invite trouble, as the University of Minnesota Press found when it published Judith Levine's *Harmful to Minors*. Levine's book, a critique of the hysteria over pedophilia in American society, so offended the Minnesota board of trustees, that they cut funding to the university press even though Levine's book could in no way be seen as a defense of pedophilia.

Although researchers have been concerned about (these problems) for over 100 years, Kinsey was the first to discuss it explicitly. Worried about guarding the confidentiality of the thousands of respondents who agreed to share their sex histories, he trained his hand-picked interviewers to learn the questions and write the answers in carefully guarded code, and he kept locks on all the materials in his institute. Even so, in 1954, when Congress investigated the Rockefeller Foundation to punish it for opposing the House Un-American Activities Committee, the only issue raised was their funding of Kinsey's research. As a result, the funding ceased.

While sociologists argue that we become sexual just like we become anything else, those who engage in sexuality research recognize that their work differs from that of others, for the reasons outlined above. These researchers have responded to the perceived dangers by careful management. Many sociologists of sexuality write theoretical articles, or use small numbers of qualitative interviews with carefully selected volunteer respondents, or undertake historical research using texts as their data source. Problems of small samples and inconsistent questionnaires make it hard to generalize to larger populations. Researchers who undertake quantitative work on other topics justify their carefully picked topics by citing compelling social reasons.

In addition, researchers have ignored methodological problems associated with asking sensitive questions for fear of inviting criticism discrediting their results. As a result, they have claimed their research is more accurate than it is and have only recently faced such problems as the inconsistent responses between men and women in the number of reported sexual partners, or the difficulties of asking uniformly worded questions about masturbation when there is no term for this practice that is generally accepted and understood by all segments of the population. For example, there has been an enormous amount of research on voting behavior in the United States in response to the difficult problems associated with getting an accurate account of the vote and with predicting who will vote and how in forthcoming elections. Until recently, there has been no comparable body of research on sexual behavior surveys.

In the last decade or so the picture has changed, and major research centers have begun to undertake methodological research on sex surveys. In spite of Foucault's declaration that talk about sex led to self-policing, not to liberation, and even in the face of much discourse intended to control sexuality, most would agree that attitudes towards sexuality are more liberal and facilitate more open discussion of sexual behavior than previously. Surveys are one kind of open discussion about sex. In addition, the devastation caused by AIDS has provided ample justification for prying into the private lives of individuals.

SEE ALSO: AIDS, Sociology of; Kinsey, Alfred; Methods; Random Sample; Sexuality Research: Ethics; Sexuality Research: History

SUGGESTED READINGS

Ericksen, J. A. (1999) *Kiss and Tell: Surveying Sex in the Twentieth Century*. Harvard University Press, Cambridge, MA.

Laumann, E. O., Gagnon, J. H., Michael, R. T., & Michaels, S. (1994) *The Social Organization of Sexuality*, Appendix A. University of Chicago Press, Chicago, IL.

JULIA A. ERICKSEN AND EUGENE P. ERICKSEN

significant others

This term refers to those individuals who play an essential part in another's internalization of social norms and plays a formative role in his or her development of a concept of self. Most commonly associated with American pragmatist, George Herbert Mead's (1934) work on child socialization, the concept of significant other is an integral part of symbolic interactionism. It continues to play a key role in contemporary studies in social psychology and social cognition.

"Significant other" was coined by psychiatrist Henry Stack Sullivan in *Conceptions of Modern Psychiatry* (1940) to describe anyone, of whom one has specific knowledge, believed important to one's well-being. Mead's theory of child socialization involves three stages: preparatory stage, play stage and game stage. In the play stage, the newly linguistic child moves out of meaningless imitation (preparatory stage) and adopts the roles of certain significant others such as a parent, a sibling or a teacher. In doing so, the child is able to conceive of how they are perceived from the position of this significant other. Embodying this role in play is an indispensable part of the child's formation of selfhood as they are, as of yet, unable to form an abstract perspective (game stage).

Contemporary research has developed towards a "social-cognitive model of transference", which outlines how in the mind of an agent a hitherto unknown person can activate, and have applied to them, a mental representation of a significant other.

SEE ALSO: Mead, George Herbert; Generalized Other; Interpersonal Relationships; Socialization; Social Psychology; Symbolic Interaction

REFERENCE

Mead, G. H. (1934) *Mind, Self, and Society: From the Perspective of a Social Behaviorist*. University of Chicago Press, Chicago, IL.

SUGGESTED READING

Forgas, J. P., Williams, K. P., & Wheeler, L. (2003) *The Social Mind: Cognitive and Motivational Aspects of Interpersonal Behaviour*. Cambridge University Press, Cambridge.

JOSEPH BURKE

significant symbol

A "significant symbol" is anything with a shared meaning to a group of people or collectivity. It may be an object, gesture, sound, color, person, event, or any other thing; its distinctiveness lies in the fact that it means the same thing to members of a group or collectivity. For most citizens of the USA, for example, the American Flag is a significant symbol signifying country; it has a shared meaning of peoplehood. Among the People of the Gambia, West Africa, "kola nut" is a significant symbol denoting union: the union of a husband and a wife; the union of a newly born child and a couple; etc. Experts similarly employ significant symbols when they use language that is unique to their areas of expertise (i.e., attorneys arguing the legal merits of a "class action suit"; sociologists debating the "Marxian" versus "Weberian" approach to the study of society).

The uniqueness of a significant symbol, therefore, is that it arouses the same reaction in one member of a group as it does in all other members. Hence, it allows users to anticipate each others' reaction, thus coordinating their activities.

Consider, for example, a person that throws a ball to another. The person throwing the ball does so because he/she anticipates that the other will do exactly what he/she would have done had the ball been directed at him/herself (catch the ball). The throwing of the ball, therefore, is a significant symbol in that it evokes the same meaning in the sender of the ball as it does to the one to whom the ball is directed: it implies the catching of the ball, which, in turn, reveals the intentionality (meaning) of the initiating act (the throwing of the ball).

SEE ALSO: Language; Mead, George Herbert; Symbolic Interaction

SUGGESTED READING

Mead, G. H. (1934) *Mind, Self, and Society*, ed. C. W. Morris. University of Chicago Press, Chicago, IL.

MAMADI CORRA

signs

The term "sign" is used as a covering word for all forms of gestures, ciphers, tokens, marks, indices, and symbols that convey human meaning. Some thinkers trace the beginning of human cognition by the earliest *Homo sapiens* to the use of signs. Religious thinkers emphasized some supernatural indicators of the true nature of reality; they understood "signs" in nature as messages. This led to necromancy and other forms of divination. The Chinese *Yi Ching* was initially based on the reading of tortoise shells. In ancient times victory in battle was often seen as a sign of the whim of the gods. That which was not understood directly had to be conjectured. Greek physicians utilized somatic signs to diagnose disease. They called this process semiosis.

The idea of signs has been extended to cover more features of reality. Modernity has made the notion that signs come from supernatural forces less acceptable. Classicist and theologian Friederich Schleiermacher discovered that the way he carried out exegesis was no different for the pagan, secular texts than for the Christian, sacred texts. Hence, he postulated the possibility of a *general* hermeneutics. This idea was further developed by Wilhelm Dilthey. Dilthey's approach helped to provide a foundation for social sciences. His hermeneutics is based on the study of human beings as moral actors whose motivations could be understood (*Geisteswissenchaften* which used *Verstehen*).

But hermeneutics lacked a more general epistemological foundation. That semiotic foundation came with the work of Charles Sanders Peirce, founder of pragmatism. Peirce emphasized the way in which signs mediate the represented and the interpreted. Peirce's critique of Cartesian dualism makes it clear that an epistemology which focuses on the solitary individual "subject" as an interpreter of "objects" is severely misleading. The isolated individual never exists in reality but only as a thought experiment. In reality all scientific understanding is based on communities of scholars.

We do not see the world precisely as it is; we only interpret stimuli with the aid of signs. Peirce had a complex typology of signs but the most important for sociology are icons, indices, and symbols. Icons are very specific images. Indices are signs which point to a more abstract level of reality. All statistics are indices. The most complex type of human sign is the symbol. George Herbert Mead's concept of the "significant symbol" is an echo of Peirce's general theory of signs. Some philosophers (e.g., Wittgenstein) argue that the real meaning of a sign is in its use. Due to "intertextuality" we cannot escape a certain degree of circularity in examining signs (Eco 1999: 275–9).

Theories put forward by Ferdinand de Saussure and C. S. Peirce have been further developed by other semioticians. The key ingredient is awareness of the universal function of signs. There has been considerable attention paid to signs in models of the process of semiosis.

SEE ALSO: Language; Mead, George Herbert; Pragmatism; Saussure, Ferdinand de; Semiotics

REFERENCE

Eco, U. (1999) *Kant and the Platypus*. Harcourt Harvest, San Diego, CA.

SUGGESTED READINGS

Bouissac, P. (ed.) (1998) *Encyclopedia of Semiotics*. Oxford University Press, New York.

Petrilli, S. & Ponzio, A. (eds.) (2005) *Semiotics Unbounded: Interpretive Routes through the Open Network of Signs*. University of Toronto Press, Toronto.

J. I. (HANS) BAKKER

Simmel, Georg (1858–1918)

Georg Simmel (born Berlin, died Strasbourg) achieved importance as a sociologist in the second half of the twentieth century. He was a friend and contemporary of the German sociologist, Max Weber and a colleague of the renowned philosopher, Wilhelm Dilthey. Among those academicians influenced by Simmel, four major figures in American Sociology attended his Berlin lectures: Albion Small, founding editor of the *American Journal of Sociology*, George Herbert Mead, University of Chicago philosopher, W. I. Thomas, Chicago sociologist: and Robert Park, founder of the tradition known as Ethnography. In the 1921 *Introduction to Sociology*, Park and Burgess selected more contributions from Simmel than from any other European sociologist. His influence, although marred by his omission from Parsons's seminal *Structure of Social Action* (1937), further extends in the1960s with his rediscovery by Erving Goffman, Lewis Coser, and Kurt Wolff.

Born to a middle-class, Jewish family, Georg was the youngest of seven children. Georg married Gertrud Kinel in 1890 with one son, Hans, born 1891. A daughter, Angela was born in 1904 to Gertrud Kantorowicz, writer and art historian, Simmel's lover and former student. Originally Jewish, the Simmels converted to Evangelical Protestantism, a necessity in the Austro-Hungarian Empire for securing state employment, social and professional contacts or any form of royal patronage. This is particularly relevant in Simmel's biography, as many subsequent writers have attributed his lack of recognition in Germany in his lifetime to anti-Semitism. After schooling in Berlin, in 1876, Simmel studied History, Ethnology and Philosophy at the Berlin University given by the most eminent scholars of his day. Between 1881and 1885 he prepared two dissertations, on "Kant's physical monadology" (theory of substances) and "On the relationship between ethical ideals and the logical and aesthetic," to complete his doctorate.

His teaching included Ethics, New Philosophical Theory, Sociology and Social Psychology. As Associate Lecturer, Simmel was paid according to attendances, distinguishing registered students from paying guests. His attractive style, performance and topical content attracted a regular audience of around 200. It was this style and topicality that originates an approach to Sociology developed by later sociologists like Park, Blumer, and Erving Goffman although rejected by the positivist Structural Functionalists, notably Talcott Parsons.

With his wife's daytime *salon* and his at-home tutorials, Simmel's courses were fashionable among Berlin intellectuals and visiting students from America on their post-graduate European tour or roving students from other European countries who spread his ideas and approach around the modern world. His popularity and earnings were the envy of his senior fellows and colleagues and a source of much resentment. Frequent attempts to sponsor Simmel for appointment as full professor were defeated. His 1900 award of *ausserordentlicher* (Extraordinary) professorship allowed him to teach and adopt the title but not the full status. Otherwise, his importance in Sociology might have been established much earlier. There are three possible explanations for this exclusion: anti-Semitism within the university; jealousy and criticism of his popularity because he was seen as diminishing the status of science through promoting the emerging discipline of Sociology; or personal attacks directed at his "anti-scientific" presentation of Sociology with its radical and revolutionary potential. His flamboyant appeal to foreigners and to women, filling lecture halls, further weakened the case for Simmel as a serious academic. Finally, in 1914 aged 56, a full professorship in Strasbourg was secured. Dissatisfied and unfulfilled, his health and his motivation went into rapid decline and he died of liver cancer in September 1918.

Simmel's importance to Sociology lies in his answer to the question "How is *gesellschaft* (society) possible?" – the first chapter of his *Soziologie* (1908). His opening argument was that Sociology was not a science but a method for exploring society or the ongoing, continuous processes of *socialization*, or *social interaction*. The data of social life were drawn from other disciplines like Psychology and Economics. Sociology's task was to apply these data in describing and explaining processes of *sociation* occurring in different cultures. *Formen* or *lebensformen* are descriptions that allow those processes to be divided into the categories that are society.

The *dyad* is a unique form of *sociation* that necessitates the presence of two individuals whose associating makes up the process. One person cannot continue an argument if the other party leaves the room. Correspondingly, *triads* or larger groups can have a constantly changing or revolving membership. A local soccer game can change personnel several times without interruption but one, alone, cannot continue a game of chess. Simmel thus explains the *persistence of groups*, large and small, while also being able to examine the internal features, stability, and fragility of, for example, monogamous marriage.

"Superordination" and "subordination" describe both the simple leader-follower relation in a small group and larger processes that maintain stable relations between aristocracies and their people. Attending to the core sociological concept of "inequality," Simmel identifies the form, *social differentiation*. This describes exchanges between individuals, the total of these differences appearing as a fixed structure. Changing social interactions between individuals can radically transform apparently fixed social structures. The origin was always the individual-in-interaction "building" society from the bottom up. It was probably this radical individualism that critics saw as revolutionary and dangerous.

Simmel located *conflict* in the complex environment of work in the modern city. There forms of conflict like physical assault, war, or revolution were now institutionalized into contests between lawyers in courts. This brought to social conflict two new dimensions: regulation in a system of rules, norms, and laws, and normal "conflict" as an expected phase in any process of interaction, resolvable without destroying the relationship between parties.

Simmel's last book, *Lebensanschauung* (1922), returns to the theme of the individual-in-interaction as "self," as an aggregate process of the *forms* of sociation in which the individual engages. George Herbert Mead, in the USA, Martin Heidegger, the German philosopher and Alfred Schütz, a leading Phenomenologist, continued work on this original theme. Simmel, though rarely quoted in the development of the concept of *self*, was central to that development.

Simmel's rank in Sociology is probably below contemporaries like Max Weber or Emile Durkheim. His writings are not key texts for the modern student but few sociologists would deny some methodological or theoretical debt traceable to Simmel's *Soziologie*. The methodological stream, Qualitative Research, first appears in Simmel's teachings and writings. The focus on deviance, the outsider, the stranger, as they characterize urban and city life, gave rise to Urban Sociology, the Sociology of Deviance and of Mental Illness. Micro-Sociology, Symbolic Interactionism, Sociology in the Natural Attitude, all find their initial steps in Simmel's lectures and papers. Currently, Cultural Studies in its attention to fashion, art, sculpture, music and performance set in the modern or post-modern world draws most from Simmel's work.

SEE ALSO: City; Dyad/Triad; Interaction; Postmodern Social Theory; Qualitative Methods; Social Type (Simmel); Stranger, the; Urban

SUGGESTED READINGS

Park, R. E. & Burgess, E. W. (1921) *Introduction to the Science of Sociology*. Greenwood Press, New York.

Spykman, N. (1925) *The Social Theory of Georg Simmel*. University of Chicago Press, London.

Wolff, K. H. (ed.) (1950) *The Sociology of Georg Simmel*. Free Press, New York.

RUSSELL KELLY

simulation

For a number of social theorists the "postmodern" age, saturated by mass media, is dominated by an endless stream of simulations, imitations, and representations of reality where an original never existed. This world of dreams and images is largely a product of advertisers, marketers, and political consultants who create and disseminate the spectacles and simulations of "hyperreality."

For most of history, communication has attempted to describe or "re-present" reality, or at least a particular version of reality that describes the nature of the world. In 1967 (1986), Umberto Eco noted the proliferation of the artificial, the fake, the imitation and the replica was the new reality, a new "hyperreality" that was especially evident in Disneyland, Los Angeles, and Las Vegas, primary realms of recreations that were better than the real. In the magical realms of Disney, imitations of Main Streets, German castles, animatronic people, animals, and monsters, stood as prototypical expressions of an artificial realm of mass produced replicas and fantasies. The USA was a land of fake history, fake art, fake nature, and fake cities where imitations did not so much represent reality, but created a "better version" of history without oppression, art without flaws, jungles without danger and cities without crime, dirt, or even actual people.

For Jean Baudrillard, we now live in a new, postmodern, "semiurgical" society, based on semiotics, the production and interpretations of meanings in which acts and objects served as "signs" that have relationships to each other to produce "texts." "Postmodern society" consists of an unending stream of simulacra-signs, symbols and meanings, representations, detached from actual objects. Today, mass produced and mediated representations in newspapers, magazines, radio, film, and TV have transformed the way people experience themselves and their world.

There is no longer a distinction between the representation and reality. We now live in a world where mass mediated communication and mass produced simulations, fakes have "created" a new order of reality, a spectacular "hyperreality" of images, simulations, and mythologies that have no connection with actual reality. *The "real" has imploded and been replaced by codes of reality*. Nor does this simulated reality hide "truth" behind appearances; rather, there are no more "truths" other than the simulated images that now dominate our culture.

Producers of simulations such as advertisers, politicians, or celebrities attempt to manipulate the public by controlling the interpretive frameworks – the code. The code is an over-arching mode of sign organization that influences the "correct" or widely accepted interpretation. The masses get bombarded by images (simulations) and signs (simulacra) which encourage them to buy, vote, work, play, but eventually they become apathetic (i.e. cynical). "Public opinion" has become more "real" than actual people. For Hedges (2009), we now live in an "empire of illusion" were people are no longer concerned with knowing the truth – the image is sufficient. This creates a world in which consumerism leads to the "goods life," while congenial, photogenic, yet often inept leaders are elected, disastrous policies appear brilliant while a public exposed to thousands and thousands of media images show little concern or outrage.

Yet some critics worry. The endless images and meanings of consumer society has engendered "pseudo needs" to consume, that much like the drudgery of work under capitalism, have fostered alienation and in turn, powerlessness and passivity. The fetish of the commodity form has now colonized everyday life; subjective experiences were imitations of experience. Individuals have become simulations of self that are articulated in spectacular self-presentations. Being "human" has become equated with buying and "having" things, and "having" has been transformed into appearances. The domination of appearances, what seemed plausible, or even true, has isolated the present from history and maintained the status quo as an eternal today.

SEE ALSO: Baudrillard, Jean; Hyperreality; Mass Media and Socialization; Postmodern Social Theory

REFERENCES

Eco, U. (1967) [1986] *Travels in Hyperreality*. Harcourt Brace, New York.

Hedges, C. (2009) *Empire of Illusion: The End of Literacy and the Triumph of Spectacle*. Nation, New York.

SUGGESTED READINGS

Cubbit, S. (2000) *Simulation and Social Theory*. Sage, London.

Baudrillard, J. (1994) *Simulacra and Simulation*. University of Michigan Press, Ann Arbor, MI.

LAUREN LANGMAN

situationists

The situationists were a small but influential collective of anti-capitalist thinkers, active from the late 1950s to the early 1970s, which theorized the alienated character of modern consumer society and its revolutionary overcoming. Targeting the capitalist colonization of everyday life, the situationists sought to overcome the political limitations of the avant-gardes. Capitalist culture was to be undermined through a deliberate political and aesthetic practice of "constructing situations" that would rupture the alienation of the worker-consumer from their capacities and desires. The situationists advocated a "unitary urbanism" that would reactivate the sedimented potentials of the city, creating spatial experiences freed from the tyranny of commodities. They also practiced "détournement," the subversive usage of the materials of capitalist culture, from films to comic strips.

The principal theoretical contribution of the Situationist International is Debord's 1967 *The Society of the Spectacle*. Relying heavily on Hegel, Feuerbach, the early Marx and Lukács, this book proposed to update the categories of ideology critique to confront the novelty of advanced capitalism. Debord argued that the hegemony of capital over life had become virtually total, as capital was accumulated not just in the guise of material commodities but in that of "spectacles." According to Debord, the social relations underlying such spectacles were alienated in a manner far more severe than the one envisaged by Marx's account of commodity fetishism. In the spectacle, life itself vanishes into its separate or independent representation and capitalism perpetually celebrates its own existence. Even the most revolutionary of practices (situationist ones included) can be "recuperated" and made functional to the perpetuation of alienated life.

The situationists' theory of contemporary society was accompanied by a bleak estimation of the human sciences, which they regarded as forms of passivity deriving from the separation of intellectual from manual labor, collaborating with the reign of the spectacular economy.

SEE ALSO: Capitalism; Cultural Critique

SUGGESTED READING

McDonough, T. (ed.) (2002) *Guy Debord and the Situationist International.* MIT Press, Cambridge, MA.

ALBERTO TOSCANO

Smith, Adam (1723–90)

Adam Smith was born on June 5, 1723, in Kirkcaldy, Scotland. His father had been a Comptroller of Customs. He studied moral philosophy at the University of Glasgow, where his teacher, Francis Hutcheson, was emphasizing "the greatest happiness of the greatest number" even in the shadow of John Knox and Scottish Puritanism. Smith then spent six years at Oxford as a Snell Scholar. A crisis of faith, possibly brought on by an exposure to the epistemological skepticism of David Hume, led him to abandon his plan to become a clergyman.

Returning to Scotland in 1748, Smith lectured on literature (student notes have been published as *Lectures on Rhetoric and Belles Lettres*) and from 1751–63 was Professor of Moral Philosophy at the University of Glasgow. His *Theory of Moral Sentiments* appeared in 1759. In it he argues that there is a social consensus on right and wrong which the sensitive social actor both absorbs and replicates. His theory of the "impartial spectator" who serves as the sounding board recalls the later ideas of G. H. Mead, while his appeal to "sympathy" or empathy that give the individual a way into others' feelings and thoughts looks forward to Weber on *Verstehen*.

Smith spent the years 1754–6 accompanying the young Duke of Buccleuch on his "grand tour" to Paris, Toulouse, Geneva, and other centers of European culture and thought. Smith met the French *philosophes* (including Turgot, Helvétius, and Rousseau) and also absorbed the great lesson of Physiocratic economics that the whole is an interdependent and a nature-driven circular flow. France in the last years of the *ancien régime* must have been an object lesson to him of how liberty could be suppressed by the Bastille, economical statesmanship by Versailles, and optimal allocation by tariffs and taxes.

Smith spent the next ten years, in receipt of a pension from the duke, doing research in Kirkcaldy. It was then that he wrote his great work, *An Inquiry into the Nature and Causes of the Wealth of Nations*. Published in 1776, it was an immediate success. It seemed to be defending the "invisible hand" of the free market against mercantilist politicians and incompetent bureaucrats (including, significantly, the corporate hierarchy that Weber, Schumpeter, and Galbraith were to praise so highly) and to be saying that the instinctual drive to "truck, barter, and exchange" would be enough to produce rising living standards for all classes even without a Poor Law or a social welfare net.

Smith anticipates Marx in that he formulates a labor theory of value, implies that the class antagonisms of post-feudal industrialism would be based around the inputs of labor and capital, and demonstrates that the division of labor in the modern production-line system leaves the worker debased and alienated, "stupid and ignorant." His insights into conspicuous consumption resemble those of Veblen on the proof of status. They also demonstrate that he was envisaging a meritocratic, mobile society in which ascription would be challenged by achievement.

In 1778 Smith was appointed a Comptroller of Customs. He died in Edinburgh on July 17, 1790, aged 67, and is buried in the Canongate churchyard.

SEE ALSO: Economic Sociology: Neoclassical Economic Perspective; Liberalism; Moral Economy

SUGGESTED READINGS

Pack, S. J. (1991) *Capitalism as a Moral System: Adam Smith's Critique of the Free Market Economy*. Edward Elgar, Aldershot.

Reisman, D. A. (1976) *Adam Smith's Sociological Economics*. Croom Helm, London.

Smith, A. (1976) [1776] *An Inquiry into the Nature and Causes of the Wealth of Nations*. Clarendon Press, Oxford.

D. A. REISMAN

soccer

The game of association football, also known as soccer, involves two competing teams of 11 players. The players attempt to maneuver the football into the opposing team's goal, using any part of the body except the hands and arms. Only the goalkeeper is permitted to handle the ball, and then only within the penalty area surrounding the goal. The winning team scores most goals over a set time period, usually 90 minutes.

Association football is to be distinguished from those "football" codes that allow general ball handling and arm tackling, notably "American football," Australian Rules football, rugby union, and rugby league. Football is sometimes known as the "simplest game": its 17 basic laws and minimal equipment (a ball) ensure that games may be improvised and played in informal settings.

Football is the world's most popular team sport in participant and spectator numbers. The global governing body, the Fédération Internationale de Football Association (FIFA), estimated in 2000 that there are 250 million registered players, and over 1.4 billion people interested in football. At the time of writing, FIFA boasts 205 member states, more than the 191 members of the United Nations, and, as a global organization, is eclipsed only by the International Amateur Athletics Federation (IAAF) with 211 members.

The social and institutional aspects of football's global spread are of sociological interest. Football's international diffusion between the 1860s and 1914 was largely dependent upon British trade and educational influence overseas. In Europe, British migrant workers would form teams and attract challenges from local sides; or young local men would return from their education or peregrinations in Britain with a ball and rulebook to teach the game to their compatriots. In Latin America, British engineers, railway workers, sailors, teachers, and pupils were largely responsible for introducing local people to football. A similar story arises in Africa, though British soldiers also introduced football in occupied territories such as modern-day Nigeria and South Africa. Thus football became more firmly established in the "informal" British Empire (and where the game was introduced by working- and merchant-class colonizers), in contrast with other British sports like cricket and rugby, which became popular in those countries formally subject to British imperial rule (and where sports were introduced by colonizers who were public school educated and held elite administrative roles in the host societies). Football was thus probably seen by non-British peoples as more "neutral" culturally, less compromised by imperialistic mores, as well as the most materially accessible form of modern sport.

SEE ALSO: Globalization, Sport and; Sport and Culture

SUGGESTED READING

Giulianotti, R. (1999) *Football: A Sociology of the Global Game*. Polity Press, Cambridge.

RICHARD GIULIANOTTI AND DOMINIC MALCOLM

social capital

The concept of social capital refers to the ways people connect through social networks, and the common values, trust and reciprocity that constitute resources for members of the network and society more generally. Different theorists emphasize slightly different features within this broad definition.

Putnam's work (2000) poses social capital as a distinct form of "public good," embodied in civic engagement and having knock-on effects for democracy and economic prosperity. He highlights self-sustaining voluntary associations as generating the "bridging" form of social capital that enables people to "get ahead" – horizontal trust and reciprocal connections between people from different walks of life – as opposed to the "bonding" social capital among homogeneous people that allows them only to "get by." Woolcock (1998) has also added the notion of vertical "linking" social capital with formal organizations, with the state facilitating new local partnership networks. Coleman (1990) argues that the family is where children have their human capital (notably, educational success) developed and are socialized into the norms, values, and sanctions of society.

For these theorists, social capital is undermined, variously, by lone mother and dual earner families, youth culture and television, and migration and ethnic diversity. Bourdieu (1986), however, highlights social capital as intertwined with other capital assets: economic, cultural, and symbolic, which are transmitted and reproduced over time, sustaining class privilege and power. Dominant social capital understandings and processes are seen also as marginalizing or confining people on the basis of their ethnicity, gender, and age.

There is concern that both theoretical and policy engagement with social capital is suffused with liberal economic rationality. Other criticisms include its definitional and methodological shortcomings.

SEE ALSO: Capital: Economic, Cultural, and Social; Network Society; Social Network Theory

REFERENCES

Bourdieu, P. (1986) The forms of capital. In: Richardson, J. E. (ed.), *Handbook of Theory for Research in the Sociology of Education*. Greenwood Press, Westport, CT.

Coleman, J. S. (1990) *Foundations of Social Theory*. Harvard University Press, London.

Putnam, R. D. (2000) *Bowling Alone: The Collapse and Revival of American Community*. Simon & Schuster, New York.

Woolcock, M. (1998) Social capital and economic development: towards a theoretical synthesis and policy framework. *S* 27 (2): 151–208.

ROSALIND EDWARDS

social change

Change can be defined as a "succession of events which produce over time a modification or replacement of particular patterns or units by other novel ones" (Smith 1973: 1). Sociology as a discipline emerged in the middle of the nineteenth century as an attempt to explain the great waves of change sweeping Europe in the form of industrialization and democratization, and the observed gap between European and colonized societies.

The diagnosis of change or stability depends on the theoretical approach used to explain the causal mechanisms operating on the observed unit of analysis. Classical sociology was not only preoccupied with the explanation of the uniqueness of observed change, for example, the rise of capitalism in the west, but it was grounded on the assumption that some general principles and mechanisms producing all observed changes could be discovered. For Comte, such principles were the development of knowledge and ideas, for Marx dialectics of productive forces and productive relationships.

Theoretical approaches to the question of macro-societal change can be divided into two broad groups. In the first are theories starting from the assumption that underlying principles, general laws of social change, could be discovered. Although they differ in the acceptance of directionality or nonlinearity of change, they have in common the belief of "basic principles." On the other hand, we have theories rejecting this assumption and trying to explain particular historical events or configurations of factors characterizing group of events like revolutions or empires.

The first group of theories is based on the idea of evolution. According to that approach, the general mechanism of historical change can be described as going through certain stages driven by some inherent forces. These stages are the expression of some basic principle and are pointing in a certain direction. For Comte, societies go through three stages: a theological-military, a metaphysical-judicial and a scientific-industrial stage. Karl Marx can also be classified within the frames of classical evolutionary thinking. His evolutionism was of a particular kind, with class conflict being the main force producing change.

Another subgroup of evolutionary theories is based on the idea of close resemblance of biological and social evolution. Herbert Spencer developed an evolutionary scheme for explaining historical change. The evolution of society can be understood by comparing it to the growth of an organism. Both increase in size and in structure, from a few like parts to numerous interrelated unlike parts.

Modern evolutionary theory is less rigid in interpreting the stages of history. Nolan and Lenski in *Human Societies, An Introduction to Macrosociology* (1999) based their explanation of social change on the increased technological capacities of societies. New technologies of material production, as of information processing, send ripples of change through all aspects of social life. The evolution of societies is not predetermined but some general evolutionary patterns can be detected.

Another approach intertwined with evolutionism is functionalism. It regards change as the adaptation of a social system to its environment by the process of differentiation and increasing structural complexity. Society is viewed as a complex and interconnected pattern of functions, and change is explained as an epiphenomenon of the constant search for equilibrium. The dominant system structure is taken as the fixed point of reference against which other structures or latent consequences are seen as potentially disruptive. This means that deviance and strains of various kinds are residual in the model. They are not given full-fledged status as integral parts of the system as in the conflict model of social change.

Another group of theories emphasizes the cycles of growth and decay. The roots of this approach are in the works of philosophers like Arnold Toynbee and Oswald Spengler. The four volumes of *Social and Cultural Dynamics* (1937–41) by Pitirim Sorokin are a sociological version of philosophizers' cyclical analysis. He saw societies oscillating among three different types of mentalities; sensate, ideational, and idealistic.

The main position of modern historical sociology, which is another type of general theory, is that there can be no single explanation for all the important transitions in human history. Important contemporary work in that tradition includes Barrington Moore's *The Social Origins of Dictatorship and Democracy* (1966), Theda Skopcol's *States and Social Revolutions* (1979) and Randall Collins' *Weberian Sociological Theory* (1986) and *Macrohistory* (1999).

SEE ALSO: Functionalism/Neofunctionalism; Parsons, Talcot; Fordism and Post-Fordism; Postmodernism; Post-Industrial Society

REFERENCE

Smith, A. (1973) *The Concept of Social Change*. Routledge & Kegan Paul, London.

SUGGESTED READING

Vago, S. (2004) *Social Change*. Prentice Hall, Englewood Cliffs, NJ.

DUSKO SEKULIC

social cognition

Studies of social cognition attempt to explain how thought or cognitive problem solving takes places in groups. While scholars generally agree that learning can be a collective activity, many are reluctant to accept that thinking itself could have a social dimension. Psychologists and cognitive scientists tend to consider thought as an internal brain activity. Sociologists generally avoid the problem by focusing on social behavior. When sociologists look at consciousness, they generally study how internal psychological processes have been shaped by external social demands. Media scholars examine patterns of persuasion, and political sociologists look at ideology and hegemonic practices. All agree that collective life proceeds through the mind as well as the body, but few consider social cognition or how thinking might take place through interaction.

Scholars doing work in the sociology of scientific knowledge (SSK) have been the exception. Conducting fieldwork in laboratories, they have repeatedly found that ideas emerge through interaction. Researchers talk to one another about what they are seeing and how they understand their data. Their thinking takes place in conversation and this fact is documented in the long list of authors in many scientific publications.

According to Longino (1990), the reluctance to see cognition as social is grounded on the philosophical assumptions of Descartes and his followers that for centuries privileged the individual knower in the pursuit of truth. Descartes defined outside influences as a source of confusion to anyone seeking knowledge. He argued that authorities can proffer illusions rather than point to the truth, so thinking independently is necessary for the pursuit of knowledge. Longino breaks with this tradition and makes a philosophical argument in favor of social epistemology, using the laboratory from SSK as her guide. She argues that group problem solving can be just as progressive as individual thought. Individuals as well as groups can cultivate illusions, but in fact, she says, the shared professional skepticism of scientists is a better means of dispelling than individual contemplation.

Currently, those who study social cognition do not question whether such a thing exists or not. The evidence for it seems strong. But it is still difficult to differentiate a pattern of *social* thought from a chain of command. In the former, group members share their ideas and find common solutions to problems together. In the latter, information is fed from the bottom to the people at the top, who do the thinking. More research is needed to make more precise descriptions of this. And more precise theories are needed to distinguish social cognition or distributed thought from other patterns of solving problems.

What is most intriguing in current research are the efforts to clarify what difference it makes that human beings can talk with one another and stabilize common understandings of things. Clearly, groups can sometimes accomplish through distributed cognition what individuals could not do on their own. The question is when and how this capacity is employed and how much of social life is founded on this ability.

SEE ALSO: Knowledge, Sociology of; Mannheim, Karl; Scientific Knowledge, Sociology of

SUGGESTED READINGS

Hutchins, E. (1995) *Cognition in the Wild*. MIT Press, Cambridge, MA.
Longino, H. (1990) *Science as Social Knowledge*. Princeton University Press, Princeton, NJ.

CHANDRA MUKERJI

social comparison theory

Comparisons with other people play a significant role in social life, as they provide meaning and self-relevant knowledge. How people view their own circumstances, abilities, and behaviors varies according to the types of social comparisons they make. Although in his seminal work Leon Festinger

(1954) did not offer a precise definition of social comparison, it is generally conceptualized as the process of thinking about the self in relation to other people. Individuals frequently make social comparisons because no objective comparison information is available; however, when privy to both social and objective information, the social variety is often favored, as it is frequently more diagnostic. Comparisons may be with real or imagined others, and do not require personal contact or conscious thought. Although comparison information can be encountered naturally in one's environment, most research has focused on comparisons that people seek out intentionally.

Various motivations underlie the pursuit of social comparison information. For example, comparisons can provide information for self-evaluative, self-improvement, or self-enhancement purposes. They can also inform future behavior or be driven by a desire to affiliate with or gather information about others. In order to achieve the goal of the comparison, individuals can be selective in their choice of a comparison target and strategic in their interpreting, distorting, or disregarding of comparison information. Additionally, the presence of varying goals may lead to different types of comparisons. For example, cancer patients typically compare their coping and health with those less fortunate (i.e., a downward comparison), satisfying a need for positive self-evaluation. However, patients also seek interactions with patients who are doing better than the self (i.e., an upward comparison), satisfying the need for self-improvement.

Social comparisons evoke a variety of behavioral, cognitive, and affective reactions. Such reactions are largely thought to be brought about by a threat to the self-image, a sense of injustice, or some other uncomfortable state resulting from a comparison. For instance, a worker who learns that he gets paid more than a colleague may justify this inequity by either working harder or by reasoning that his work is more difficult than that of the lower-paid worker. As illustrated by this example, people often can choose between behavioral and cognitive responses. Affective responses have also been intensely studied. In general, a comparison with someone whose abilities, performance, or attributes are superior produces more negative affect and lower self-esteem than does a comparison with someone who is inferior. This general tendency is qualified, however, by a number of caveats, and an individual's response may be contingent upon such factors as the importance of the comparison domain to one's self image, the degree of similarity with the comparison other, and the control an individual feels over the comparison domain.

The diversity of motivations, reactions to, and characterizations of social comparison has led researchers to employ a variety of methods in their study of the topic. There are three general methodological approaches to social comparison research (Wood, 1996). The selection approach examines the processes underlying how individuals seek social information, including their selection of comparison other, while the narrative approach concentrates on participants' descriptions and reports of comparisons made in everyday life. The reaction approach focuses on the impact of provided social information and how the information affects variables such as mood, jealousy, self-esteem, self-evaluation, and performance.

SEE ALSO: Interaction; Self; Self-Esteem, Theories of; Social Psychology

REFERENCES

Festinger, L. (1954) A theory of social comparison processes. *Human Relations* (7): 117–40.

Wood, J. V. (1996) Theory and research concerning social comparisons of personal attributes. *Psychological Bulletin* 106 (2): 231–48.

SUGGESTED READING

Suls, J. & Wheeler, L. (eds.) (2000) *Handbook of Social Comparison: Theory and Research*. Kluwer/Plenum, New York.

DAVID M. FLORES AND MONICA K. MILLER

social control

The first sociological writings on social control took an expansive view, applying the concept to all the institutions and practices whereby societies maintain social order. These writings often contended that while social control is unavoidable, it need not be repressive. The concept figured prominently for the "Chicago School" of urban sociologists who argued that because cities are relatively anonymous, city dwellers feel less compelled to honor each others' rights or sanction each others' transgressions. Hence, cities must delegate the work of social control to professionals in place of the self-policing community found in small towns. They observed that because professional agencies of social control cannot be as ubiquitous, these agencies cannot as effectively maintain social order as can fuller community participation in this effort. The early Chicago School's approach to social control was later both refined and rivaled by the likes of C. Everett

Hughes, Talcott Parsons, and Harold Garfinkel each of whom focused in different ways on the collectively orchestrated aspects of social control and its role in creating and maintaining consensus, equilibrium, and collaborative activity.

In contrast, critical theories have insisted that because people inevitably disagree about what merits regulation, social control must entail stronger groups controlling weaker groups, not in the collective interest but in their own self-interest. Various research agendas emphasizing the coercive and exploitative dimensions of social control became prominent in the 1950s and 1960s. Labeling theory insisted that social control involves not only a *response* to deviance, but a definition as deviant of certain activities (e.g. drug use, homosexuality) that in other societies aren't defined as deviant or singled out for social control. Ultimately, labeling theorists were challenged by other, largely Marxist, critical theorists who see social control not just as the imposition of one group's morality upon another, but as a significant aspect of economic exploitation. Hence they emphasize efforts to: secure property through policing; debilitate unions through intimidation, scabs, and legal restrictions; discipline workers to make them both less threatening and more efficient; or diffuse working-class resentment through either a mass media that distracts and pacifies or social welfare programs. In sum, Marxist critical theorists see social control as a multifaceted project undertaken by elites to maintain or amass wealth and power.

Marxists often distinguish power as control by force from knowledge as control by persuasion. Michel Foucault argued this distinction fails to appreciate that all power requires knowledge regimes through which its goals are formulated, and methods for achieving those goals are devised and refined. Foucault described the fusion of power and knowledge in prisons, the military, hospitals, and bureaucracies more generally, arguing that each of these embodied a distinctive form of social control. He referred to these regimes as instances of "governmentality," a concept he applied broadly to all who engage in the "conduct of conduct." This is something that employers do with employees, parents do with children, teachers do with students, and that we as individuals do with our selves – as when we diet. Over the years, Foucault grew increasingly interested in the fact that we do, at some level, govern our own lives according to our own visions of the good. While these visions are heavily influenced by our place in history, they do not, for that, cease to be our own. He seemed to become more hopeful that social control could, in principle, be exercised democratically and compassionately rather than coercively and exploitatively. And along with many other students of social control, he was convinced that, while necessary as such, the regulation of society is, at present, considerably more coercive and exploitative than it has to be.

SEE ALSO: Crime, Social Control Theory of; Foucault, Michel; Labeling Theory

SUGGESTED READINGS

Becker, H. S. (1963) *Outsiders: Studies in the Sociolgy of Deviance*. Free Press, New York.

Meier, R. F. (1982) Perspectives on the concept of social control. *Annual Review of Sociology* 8: 35–55.

DARIN WEINBERG

social distance

The concept of social distance is based on social norms that differentiate individuals and groups on the basis of characteristics such as race, ethnicity, age, sex, social class, religion, or nationality. It was Emory Bogardus (1925) who first constructed a unidimensional and cumulative scale based on the assumption that respondents would accept members of the designated group to all steps below their highest level of acceptance. His initial work involved asking participants their willingness to admit members of different racial and ethnic groups to: close kinship by marriage, as fellow club members, as neighbors, as co-workers, to citizenship, as visitors only to their country, and as persons to be excluded from the country. Through the years social scientists have applied variations of the social distance scale to racial, religious, and other groups and have found it a reliable measure of the level of acceptance of one group by another.

Bogardus assumed that social nearness originates in favorable experiences and farness in unfavorable experiences, the result determined by either a lack of knowledge or by stereotypic knowledge about group differences such as appearance, beliefs, or behaviors. Typically the concept of social distance subsumes individual characteristics. Poole (1927) was the first to distinguish between social distance and personal distance, thereby offering an explanation of how individuals become "exceptions" to their groups. Social distance is dictated by social norms. Personal distance as in acquaintances, friendships, and love, on the other hand, is limited only by the possibilities of association between individuals or individuals and groups.

SEE ALSO: In-Groups and Out-Groups; Prejudice

REFERENCES

Bogardus, E. S. (1925) Measuring social distance. *Journal of Applied Sociology* 9: 299–308.

Poole, W. C. (1927) Social distance and personal distance. *Journal of Applied Sociology* 11: 114–20.

JOYCE E. WILLIAMS

social epidemiology

Social epidemiology lies at the intersection between the traditionally biomedical field of epidemiology, which is concerned with understanding the distribution, spread, and determinants of disease in populations, and the parts of sociology and other social sciences concerned with understanding the role of social factors, forces, and processes in the epidemiology of health and illness of individuals and populations. As a field, social epidemiology has been largely created since the 1950s by the combined efforts of persons trained in sociology and related social sciences to study the nature, etiology, and course of physical and mental health and illness in human populations.

The result has been the development and growth of a major new and vibrant interdisciplinary field and the transformation of scientific and popular understanding of the nature of determinants of physical health and illness. From a hegemonic paradigm that, for about a century through the 1950s, viewed physical health as largely a function of biomedical factors, physical health and illness are now understood by both scientists and lay persons as equally or more a function of social, psychological, and behavioral factors. Early understanding (e.g. Freudian) of mental health and illness as being as much or more psychosocial as biomedical in nature, contributed importantly to the development of the social epidemiology of physical health and illness. Mental health epidemiology and treatment, in contrast, have headed in a more biological direction.

SEE ALSO: Biosociological Theories; Disease, Social Causation

SUGGESTED READINGS

House, J. S. (2002) Understanding social factors and inequalities in health: 20th century progress and 21st century prospects. *Journal of Health and Social Behavior* 23: 125–42.

Link, B. G. & Phelan, J. C. (1995) Social conditions as fundamental causes of disease. *Journal of Health and Social Behavior* 35 (extra issue): 80–94.

JAMES HOUSE

social epistemology

Social epistemology addresses questions of the organization of knowledge processes and products. The field reflects an interdisciplinary gap between philosophy and sociology: Philosophy tends to stress normative approaches without considering their empirical realizability or political consequences. Sociology suffers the reverse problem of capturing the empirical and ideological character of knowledge, but without offering guidance on how knowledge policy should be conducted; hence the debilitating sense of "relativism" traditionally associated with the sociology of knowledge.

From the nineteenth century onward, epistemologies descended from French positivism and German idealism have consistently stressed the systematic and collective character of knowledge. In contrast, Anglo-American philosophy has remained wedded to the individual – be it Cartesian or Darwinian – as the paradigm case of the knower. In this context, "social epistemology" is explicitly designed to redress the balance.

Social epistemologies may be compared in terms of the presumptive answers they provide to the following research questions:

- Are the norms of inquiry autonomous from the norms governing the rest of society?
- Is there anything more to a "form of inquiry" than the manner in which inquirers are arranged?
- Do truth and the other normative aims of science remain unchanged as particular forms of inquiry come and go?
- Is there anything more to "the problem of knowledge" than a matter of *whose* actions are licensed on the basis of *which* claims made under *what* circumstances?
- Is the social character of knowledge reducible to the aggregated beliefs of some group of individuals?
- Is social epistemology's purview limited to the identification of mechanisms and institutions that meet conceptually satisfying definitions of knowledge?

SEE ALSO: Epistemology; Knowledge, Sociology of

SUGGESTED READINGS

Fuller, S. (1988) *Social Epistemology*. Indiana University Press, Bloomington, IN.

Harding, S. (1991) *Whose Science? Whose Knowledge?* Indiana University, Bloomington, IN.

STEVE FULLER

social exchange theory

Social exchange theory analyzes the nature and internal dynamics of individual acts of exchange as well as explaining the development of social systems emerging from exchange processes. Widely used in the 1960s, it was largely replaced by rational choice and social network theories although the revived interest in Georg Simmel has drawn attention again to social exchange.

The two major, early proponents of a systematically developed theory of social exchange were George Homans (1974) and Peter Blau (1964; 1995) although the concept of social exchange and its impact upon social formations predates them considerably. A sampling of earlier usage demonstrates the interest social exchange has held across time, cultures, and within vastly different social formations.

Aristotle's *Nichomachean Ethics* examines various forms of exchange, distinguishing economic – based upon precisely stated terms – from exchanges where A gives something to B as though it is a free gift but there is an underlying understanding/expectation of some later reciprocation. Most social exchanges are like loans with unspecified but mutually understood terms of gratitude, personal indebtedness, and expectation of repayment. Aristotle's interest was the breadth of exchange, its unspoken reciprocity and ethical parameters.

Adam Smith's *Wealth of Nations* suggested in 1776 that due to humankind's "natural propensity" to truck, barter and exchange, individuals, in the pursuit of their own particular interests, enter the market and, through the extended processes of social exchange, meet their needs and wants. The market's "unseen hand" ensures that everyone's needs and wants are met and exchange becomes the basis for a larger social dynamic. Smith's work emphasized how individual exchange created a larger system of exchange – the link to social network theory – and also suggested that people are rational, utility maximizers linking social exchange to rational choice theories.

Simmel's 1908 work, *Soziologie*, started from radically individualist premises but through concepts like dyad, triad, and "sociation" showed how a macro web of group affiliation emerged through exchange.

Social exchange theory also figured prominently in anthropology. The key works are Bronislaw Malinowski's 1922 study, *Argonauts of the Western Pacific*, which demonstrated how the *kula* exchange structured relationships extending from the interpersonal to alliances among tribes against distant enemies. Marcel Mauss's 1925, *Essai sur le don: Forme et raison de l'échange dans les societies archaïques* (*The Gift: Forms and Functions of Exchange in Archaic Societies*), explored the power relations of gift exchange as generous gifts pressure the recipient for an equivalent response or suffer losses in prestige, authority, and privilege.

While frequently confined to economic acts, social exchange theorists emphasize that exchange is ubiquitous in social life and ranges, for example, from the sharing of toys, tools and information to secrets, favors, sex, friendship, and love. Exchange presupposes differentiation among individuals through the uneven dispersion of resources that will help meet different needs and wants. Exchange begins through association whereby enough trust exists or develops for A to give something that B finds rewarding creating an unspoken "debt" that B will repay at a later time (or remain in A's debt). Through ongoing exchange, trust may grow and the intrinsic, personal value and nature of the exchange may deepen. Exchange will continue until one party no longer feels rewarded and the desire to continue fades. In social exchange, there is no specific debt or currency involved – a diffuse sense of obligation is created – and the benefits are usually tied to the source of the reward itself. Through exchange, an ongoing pattern of interaction emerges which may begin to form a network of social relations – a social system.

Although social exchange stems from trust and produces friendship bonds it also establishes power relations. A's power increases proportionate to the extent that each of the following conditions holds: A has a resource (e.g. toy, tool, idea, smile, loving disposition) that B needs or wants; B cannot get that resource elsewhere; B chooses exchange rather than force to receive the resource from A; B's need or want of the resource is ongoing.

Though broad in scope, social exchange theory does not cover all social action – e.g. eating when hungry, reading, or driving fast do not directly involve exchange.

SEE ALSO: Blau, Peter; Homans, George; Rational Choice Theories; Simmel, Georg; Smith, Adam; Social Network Theory

REFERENCES

Blau, P. M. (1964) *Exchange and Power in Social Life.* Wiley, New York.

Blau, P. M. (1995) A circuitous path to macrostructural theory. *Annual Review of Sociology* 21: 1–19.

Homans, G. C. (1974) *Social Behavior: Its Elementary Forms*, rev. edn. Harcourt, Brace, Jovanovich, New York.

MICHAEL LOVAGLIA

social fact

The concept of social fact is identified with Émile Durkheim, but is also relevant to social theories viewing society as an objective reality apart from the individual. In *The Rules of Sociological Method* (1895), Durkheim defined social facts as ways of feeling, thinking, and acting external to and exercising constraint over the individual. Sociology and psychology are independent levels of analysis. Durkheim thought social facts should be treated as things, realities in their own right, with their own laws of organization, apart from individual consciousness. For Durkheim, social facts include such phenomena as social institutions (e.g. religion, the state, kinship structures, legal codes) as well as more diffuse phenomena (e.g. mass behavior of crowds, collective trends such as suicide and crime rates). In classic studies such as *The Division of Labor in Society* (1893), *Suicide* (1897), and *Elementary Forms of the Religious Life* (1912), Durkheim examined a variety of social facts and explained them by reference to purely social causes. Durkheim's followers (e.g. Marcel Mauss, Robert Hertz, Maurice Halbwachs, and others) continued this approach in their studies of seasonal variations in social integration, gift exchange, religious polarity, and collective memory.

Other theorists have variously emphasized the facticity of social conditions. Karl Marx argued that individuals make history, but under conditions independent of their individual wills. Social existence conditions consciousness and individuals are primarily personifications of objective economic forces. Collective actors, especially social classes (e.g. bourgeoisie and the proletariat), are his central focus.

Functionalist and structuralist approaches emerged from these earlier treatments of the factuality of social existence. Talcott Parsons's mature work developed a systematic, structural-functional theory emphasizing four functional problems of social systems (i.e. adaptation, goal attainment, social integration, cultural pattern maintenance) and the interchanges among institutions serving these functions (e.g., economy, polity, household, school, law). In *Economy and Society* (1956) Parsons (and Neil Smelser) examined the economy as a social system and its relations with non-economic systems, while in *Family, Socialization and Interaction Process* (1955), Parsons and his collaborators discussed the family as a social system, including its structure of instrumental and integrative roles.

Modern French social thought produced several variations on Durkheim's sociological objectivism, including Claude Lévi-Strauss's structural anthropology, Michel Foucault's investigations, and the theorizing of Louis Althusser. Lévi-Strauss combined structural linguistics with ideas drawn from the Durkheim school, Marx, and Freud to create structural theories of kinship, myth, and culture which emphasized the centrality of enduring structures of human cognition and organization. Individual expressions and the actions represented variants within these established social and cultural structures. Foucault diminished the role of the subject in his studies of madness, the clinic, the prison, and changing systems of knowledge. Causal sequences rooted in the actions of individuals or groups are rejected and actors are seen as instantiating the words and deeds made possible by reigning discourses. These theoretical tendencies are most fully expressed in Althusser's work. He rejects Marx's early humanistic writings in favor of his later, objectivist scientific work and forges a structural theory of society eliminating human agency and viewing social change as a process of internal contradictions within dynamic socioeconomic, political, and legal structures.

Thinkers who see human agency as central to understanding social processes often oppose the idea of social facts. For example, Max Weber's social action theory, Herbert Blumer's symbolic interactionism, and Alfred Schutz's phenomenological sociology emphasize either "methodological individualism" (Weber), or society as a process of social interaction (Blumer), or the taken-for-granted conceptualizations of individuals in everyday situations (Schutz). Efforts by Peter Berger and Thomas Luckmann, Anthony Giddens, Pierre Bourdieu, and others to synthesize the tradition emphasizing social facts with a focus on social action, interaction, and agency have not always been fully successful in doing justice to both sides of what is evidently a perennial dilemma in social theory.

SEE ALSO: Durkheim, Émile; Foucault, Michel; Marx, Karl; Parsons, Talcott; Positivism; Structuralism

SUGGESTED READINGS

Althusser, L. (1970) *For Marx*, trans. B. Brewster. Vintage Books, New York.

Durkheim, É. (1982) [1895] *The Rules of Sociological Method*, trans. W. D. Halls. Free Press, New York.

Gilbert, M. (1992) *On Social Facts*. Princeton University Press, Princeton, NJ.

Nielsen, D. A. (1999) *Three Faces of God: Society, Religion and the Categories of Totality in the Philosophy*

of Émile Durkheim. State University of New York Press, Albany, NY.
Ritzer, G. (1980) *Sociology: A Multiple Paradigm Science*. Allyn & Bacon, Boston, MA.

DONALD A. NIELSEN

social identity theory

Social identity theory offers a social psychological explanation of intergroup prejudice, discrimination, and conflict. Its origins lie in the work of Henri Tajfel (Tajfel & Turner 1979) and his associates who have been instrumental in the development of a distinctly European approach to psychology. For Tajfel, the key to understanding prejudice, discrimination, and intergroup conflict is found in an individual's social identity as defined by group membership. Social identity theory rejects explanations based on individual defects of physiology, personality, or attitude. In this regard, it represents a challenge to more traditional psychological theories and has generated nascent interest among sociologists. Tajfel's experimental findings on group affiliation and personal bias were first published in the 1960s and, since then, social identity theory has generated an immense body of empirical research in support of its basic hypotheses. Over the years, social identity theory has been elaborated and extended to encompass issues of group leadership, organizational psychology, deviance, and political action. Today, social identity theory stands as one of the most influential theoretical perspectives within psychological social psychology.

The empirical starting point for understanding social identity theory is found in a series of laboratory experiments that have come to be known as the minimal group paradigm. The objective in this early research was to identify the minimal conditions required to produce favoritism toward one group and discrimination against another. In the minimal group design, subjects are randomly assigned to one of two groups that they believe were established on the basis of a trivial preliminary test (e.g., whether one underestimated or overestimated the number of dots on a screen). The conditions are such that there is no history or prior knowledge of the group or of other group members, there is no interaction among or between group members, other group members cannot be heard or seen, no competition of any sort is ever established, and the only differentiating factor is the perception that there are two distinct groups. Results from studies using the minimal group paradigm consistently show favoritism toward one's own group and bias against another group (usually measured in terms of reward distribution to group members and member attitudes toward the in-group and the out-group). Thus, on the basis of a purely cognitive discrimination of groups as defined by simple category distinctions, the seeds of intergroup conflict are sown.

Social identity refers to an individual's subjective understanding of group membership. It is a cognitive category that includes emotional and evaluative associations. Social identity can be as simple and fleeting as a label employed in a psychology experiment or as complex and encompassing as national, religious, or ethnic affiliations. While an enormous body of empirical research has established that the salience of a social identity (psychological commitment to a group) leads to prejudice, discrimination, and conflict between groups, we also know from this same research tradition that these basic associations are not universal. Not all group commitments for all individuals lead to the same type of bias. Perhaps the most valuable contribution of social identity theory is that it provides a framework for predicting when and how group bias occurs.

The distinguishing feature of social identity theory is its explanation of the psychological foundation of intergroup prejudice, discrimination and conflict. In contrast to the symbolic interactionist tradition in sociology where self, identity, and personhood are seen as inherently social at all levels, social identity theory argues that group identity is formed psychologically. In other words, the psychology of group behavior is assumed to be qualitatively different from the psychology of interpersonal behavior. While this ontological distinction provides social identity theory with the conceptual language needed to understand prejudice, discrimination, and conflict as ordinary, adaptive, and functional interactions of group behavior, critics have argued that it has led to the adoption of an overly restricted understanding of the social dimension of identity.

SEE ALSO: Discrimination; Identity Theory; In-Groups and Out-Groups; Prejudice; Psychological Social Psychology

REFERENCE

Tajfel, H. & Turner, J. C. (1979) An integrative theory of intergroup conflict. In: Austin, W. G. & Worchel, S. (eds.), *The Social Psychology of Intergroup Relations*. Brooks/Cole, Monterey, CA, pp. 33–47.

SUGGESTED READINGS

Brown, R. (2000) Social identity theory: past achievements, current problems, and future challenges. *European Journal of Social Psychology* 30: 745–78.

Ellemers, N., Spears, R., & Doosje, B. (1999) *Social Identity*. Blackwell, Oxford.
Hogg, M. A. (2006) Social identity theory. In: Burke, P. J. (ed.), *Contemporary Social Psychological Theories*. Stanford University Press, Stanford, CA.

PETER L. CALLERO

social influence

Social influence is the process by which individuals make *real* changes to their feelings and behaviors through interaction with others who are perceived to be similar, desirable or expert. Current research on social influence falls into five main areas: (1) minority influence, (2) research on persuasion, (3) Dynamic Social Impact Theory, (4) a structural approach to social influence, and (5) Expectation States Theory. *Minority influence* occurs when a minority subgroup attempts to change the majority. While some research has characterized the process of social influence as the majority riding roughshod over the minority, many scholars interested in minority influence believe that every member of a group can influence others. Current *research on persuasion*, defined as change in attitudes or beliefs based on information received from others, focuses on messages sent from source to recipient. This research assumes that individuals process messages carefully whenever they are motivated and able to do so. *Dynamic Social Impact Theory* describes and predicts the diffusion of beliefs through social systems. In this view, social structure is the result of individuals influencing each other in a dynamic and iterative way and society is a system in which individuals interact and impact each others' beliefs. The *structural approach* to social influence examines interpersonal influence that occurs within a larger network of influences. Social influence here is the process by which a group of actors will weigh and then integrate the opinions of others. *Expectation States Theory* provides another formal treatment of social influence. When group members are initially unequal in status, inequalities are imported to the group from the larger society such that, for example, age structures a hierarchy of influence.

SEE ALSO: Reference Groups; Expectation States Theory

SUGGESTED READINGS

Friedkin, N. (1998) *A Structural Theory of Social Influence*. Cambridge University Press, Cambridge.
Moscovici, S., Mucchi-Faina, A., & Maass, A. (eds.) (1994) *Minority Influence*. Nelson-Hall, Chicago, IL.

LISA RASHOTTE

social justice, theories of

Justice, in its many guises, is a fundamental principle ensuring order in social groups ranging from small, intimate circles of friends to large, diverse societies. Its counterpart, injustice, arises when expectations about distributions, procedures, or interactions are unmet. Such unmet expectations stimulate the potential for change, both trivial and profound. The study of social justice in social psychology has focused largely on individual perceptions and responses, while sociological concerns about social justice pertain to issues of income inequality, racism, sexism, etc.

Drawing on the work of philosophers, social psychologists examine three types of justice. *Distributive justice* pertains to the fairness of the allocation of rewards or burdens to a circle of recipients. Rules of distributive justice include equity, equality, and needs. *Procedural justice* captures the fairness of decision-making procedures, emphasizing rules about suppressing bias, ensuring consistency and accuracy, allowing for representation by or giving "voice" to those affected, and the like. *Interactional justice* refers to fairness in the treatment of individuals within a group. Demonstration of respect and truthfulness are key aspects of interactional justice. On an abstract level, all types of justice should reflect the impartiality of decision-makers, rely upon a consensus of those affected, and promote collective welfare. Formal definitions, however, ignore the subjectivity that characterizes what individuals perceive as fair, and that injustice responses depend on more than simply the experience of unfairness.

Focusing on perceptions of injustice, theories posit individual level and contextual factors that stimulate cognitive and comparison processes that give rise to evaluations of injustice. Perceived injustice is distressing, which motivates individuals to redress the injustice through actions or by changing cognitions about the situation. Models of responses to distributive injustice presume that material self-interests drive perceptions and reactions; subsequent formulations suggest other motivations, including (self-interested) social concerns with gaining the regard of group members and a moral sense of justice that captures concerns for others. Regardless of underlying motivations, empirical evidence generally demonstrates that individuals disadvantaged by some type of injustice are more likely to feel angry and to attempt to redress the injustice than are those advantaged by injustice. Yet how individuals react also depends upon the extent to which situational circumstances facilitate or inhibit responses to alter the distribution, procedure, or treatment.

A key factor quelling responses to distributive injustice is the perception that a distribution decision was made fairly, i.e., that procedural justice existed. The field of organizational justice, in particular, focuses on how the three types of justice combine to affect the perceptions and responses of workers within organizations. The organizational context also draws attention to the role of observers in assessing injustice that befalls another person, such as a co-worker. Skarlicki and Kulik (2005) argue that models appropriate for examining perceptions of and responses to personal injustice may be extended to understand how and why third parties may take action to rectify others' injustices.

Observers, people unaffected or even advantaged by an unequal distribution of societal resources or particular procedures, may act individually or collectively in a manner to ameliorate a situation that sorely disadvantages others. Their perceptions, like those who suffer injustice personally, are also subjective and underlie the potential for conflict between social groups. Social justice encompasses distributions of resources, opportunities, and rights based on promoting human dignity and collective welfare and disallows distributions, procedures, or treatments that are biased by the decision-maker or recipients' gender, race, sexual orientation, religion, or social class (wealth). Income inequality, sexism, racism, and the like raise the specter of injustice by highlighting the evaluation of the distribution of resources to a group or the treatment of group members based on their (subjectively devalued or presumed inferior) characteristics. Debates over the distribution of societal goods (e.g., health care, jobs, housing) and societal burdens (e.g., hazardous wastes, taxes) to different groups in society also constitute issues of social justice. Social movements, while caused by many factors and requiring resources and organization, may rally individuals with cries of injustice and signal actions to redress injustice. Social psychological theories contribute to an understanding of not just what disadvantaged individuals are likely to perceive, feel, and do, but also of the conditions under which people who benefit from current societal procedures and distributions are likely to step beyond their own self-interests to effect social change and ultimately create a more consensual notion of justice.

SEE ALSO: Criminal Justice System; Global Justice as a Social Movement; Globalization and Global Justice; Inequality/Stratification, Gender; Social Movements; Stratification and Inequality, Theories of

REFERENCE

Skarlicki, D. P, & Kulik, C. T. (2005) Third-party reactions to employee (mis)treatment: a justice perspective. *Research in Organizational Behavior* 26: 183–229.

SUGGESTED READINGS

Hegtvedt, K. A. (2005) Doing justice to the group: examining the roles of the group in justice research. *Annual Review of Sociology* 31: 25–45.

Skitka, L. J., Bauman, C. W., & Mullen, E. (2008) Morality and justice: an expanded theoretical perspective and empirical review. *Advances in Group Processes* 25: 1–27.

KAREN A. HEGTVEDT

social learning theory

Social learning theory was developed in the 1950s by Albert Bandura to explain the reciprocal influence of environmental cues on an individual's behavior, and the impact of the individual's behavior on the environment. In addition, social learning theory places an emphasis on individuals' cognitive processes as they decide upon future courses of action. Thus, social learning theory takes a middle-ground position between social psychological theories that stress either environmental or internal cognitive processes as the sole components of learning.

Social learning theory posits that people learn about their social worlds in two distinct ways. First, following in the tradition of behaviorism, individuals learn through direct experience with their environments, and the rewards and consequences that follow. *Reinforcement contingencies* encourage an individual to keep repeating a task. *Punishment contingencies* serve to diminish a particular behavior. Both behaviorism and social learning theory assume that individuals attempt to maximize their rewards and avoid punishments. For example, Carrie may learn that hitting her brother Bill is unacceptable when she is punished by her mother for that act. Here we would expect Carrie to stop hitting Bill to avoid the negative sanction (punishment contingency). Similarly, Carrie might learn that putting her clothes in the hamper is good when her mother praises her for that act. Here we would expect Carrie to keep putting her clothes in the hamper in order to continue receiving praise (reinforcement contingency).

In addition to recognizing the importance of direct experience on learning, social learning theory also stresses the importance of observational learning, or modeling the actions of others. Social learning theory posits that individuals do not have to experience consequences directly to determine the value of a particular action if they have been able to observe the consequences somebody else has received. Thus, in reference to the first example above, if Carrie watches her older sister Margaret get in trouble for hitting Bill, she will learn that hitting Bill has negative consequences without experiencing the negative consequences for herself. Given this information, Carrie will be less likely to hit Bill in the future unless the reward for hurting him is greater than the punishment she receives from her mother. In reference to the second example, if Carrie sees Margaret get rewarded for putting her clothes in the hamper, she may model Margaret's behavior and put *her* clothes in the hamper to get a reward. The concept of modeling is intrinsic to the discussion of observational learning. Whenever we learn by observing someone else's rewards/consequences, they become a model for that behavior, whether we choose to reenact that behavior ourselves or not.

Adding observational learning to behaviorism's focus on operant conditioning was a great advance for social learning theory. However, both direct and observational learning still emphasize the environment when predicting the behaviors of individuals. Social learning theory extends this to include individual cognitions as part of the learning process. Given the assumption that individuals desire to maximize rewards and minimize punishments, social learning theory posits that they learn to regulate themselves in order to obtain desired rewards; when observing the response consequences of others, individuals begin to understand the future consequences of various actions they could take, and plan for them.

SEE ALSO: Aggression; Psychological Social Psychology; Socialization

SUGGESTED READINGS

Akers, R. L. (1998) *Social Learning and Social Structure: A General Theory of Crime and Deviance*. Northeastern University Press, Boston, MA.

Bandura, A. (1977) *Social Learning Theory*. Prentice Hall, Englewood Cliffs, NJ.

LAURA AUF DER HEIDE

social movements

Although scholarly definitions vary, common usage portrays social movements as sustained and intentional efforts to foster or retard social changes, primarily outside the normal institutional channels encouraged by authorities. *Sustained* implies that movements differ from single events such as riots or rallies. Their persistence often allows them to develop formal organizations, but they may also operate through informal social networks. *Intentional* links movements to culture and strategy: people have ideas about what they want and how to get it, ideas that are filtered through culture as well as psychology. Movements have purposes, even when these have to do with transforming members themselves (as in many religious movements) rather than the world outside the movement. *Foster or retard*: although many scholars have a Whiggish tendency to view movements as progressive, dismissing regressive efforts as "countermovements," this distinction seems arbitrary and unsustainable (not to mention the unfortunate effect that different tools are then used to analyze the two types). *Noninstitutional* distinguishes movements from political parties and interest groups that are a more regular part of many political systems, even though movements frequently create these other entities and often maintain close relationships to them. Most movements today deploy some tactics within mainstream institutions – and "noninstitutional" protest is itself often quite institutionalized.

For most of recorded history, intellectual observers have feared and derided the action of the irrational "mob," a view which persisted in one form or another into the 1960s. At that point, scholars began to form more sympathetic views of the movements they saw around them, of African Americans, students, women, and others. In Europe and the United States, theories developed which saw social movements as a natural response to the rise of cities, nation states, and national political arenas (especially the work of Charles Tilly), or as an historical effort to control the distribution of material goods, cultural understandings, or the direction of social change (in Alain Touraine's work). Increasingly, protestors were portrayed as reasonable, pursuing normal political ends through noninstitutional means. The last several decades has seen, instead of dismissal, an explosion of fine-grained empirical research into just how they do so.

Several variables help explain who is recruited into emerging movements. One is "biographical availability": the lack of spouse, children, or demanding jobs that frees people for the time commitment of participation. More important is whether the potential recruit already knows someone in the movement. In many movements, a majority of participants are recruited this way. In "bloc recruitment," entire networks can be coopted for new purposes. The messages transmitted across networks are also important: recruiters and potential participants must "align" their "frames" to achieve a common definition of a problem and prescription for solving it. As important as this cognitive agreement are the moral visions and emotions that propel people into action. Fear and anger must be transformed into indignation and outrage.

In addition to people (both leaders and followers), an emerging movement usually needs some infrastructure to carry out its activities. It requires basic means of communication and transportation: a bullhorn to address a large crowd, a fax machine or Internet access to reach supporters, carpools to get people to a rally, a place to meet. Financial support allows organizers to purchase what they need.

What do movements do? Tilly suggests that a society contains a repertory of collective action, from which protestors inevitably draw, depending on local senses of justice, the daily routines and social organization of the participants, their prior experience with collective action, and the repression they are likely to face. Most social movements in a society will conduct the same activities, since that's what they have learned to do through trial and error. New tactics, outside the repertoire, may take opponents and authorities by surprise, but protestors themselves may bungle them due to lack of experience and know-how. At the extreme, those who face extreme surveillance and few legal rights, are restricted to "weapons of the weak" such as sabotage, pilfering, poaching, or even jokes and gossip.

Movements can have a variety of effects. Few attain their stated goals, but they may shift cultural understandings by bringing attention to new social problems or emerging constituencies. They may also affect policy makers, who try to mollify them by satisfying some of their demands. If nothing else, they may make a new issue respectable. And even when social movements have little impact on the world around them, they almost always affect their own members, shaping their political values and activities.

SEE ALSO: Global Justice as a Social Movement; New Social Movement Theory; Social Movements, Nonviolent; Social Movements, Participatory Democracy in

SUGGESTED READINGS

Alain T. (1981) *The Voice and the Eye*. Cambridge University Press, Cambridge.

Charles T. (1978) *From Mobilization to Revolution*. Addison-Wesley, Reading, MA.

Sidney T. (1998) *Power in Movement*. Cambridge University Press, Cambridge.

JAMES M. JASPER

social movements, networks and

Social movement analysts have treated networks either as important facilitators of individuals' decisions to become involved in collective action, or as the structure of the links between the actors committed to a certain cause. Movement networks may include both individual activists and organizations, connected through ties that do not just involve the exchange of resources or information, but also shared identities linked to deeper worldviews.

Still in the 1970s, many regarded movement participants as individuals lacking a proper social integration. By the 1980s, however, research had showed that social movements participants are usually well integrated in dense networks, consisting both of private ties and of links originated in the context of previous experiences of collective action. Individual networks may affect not only presence or absence of participation, but participation in specific types of activities, its continuation over time, and the amount of risk one is prepared to face. Networks may facilitate the development of cognitive skills and competences, provide the context for the socialization of individuals to specific sets of values, or represent the locus for the development of strong emotional feelings. In general, strong ties should matter more for participation in highly demanding activities, while weak ties might help the spread of movement ideas to broader constituencies.

Network perspectives also help analyzing movements as complex interaction fields including multiple actors. This had already been noticed in the 1970s by scholars interested in subcultural and countercultural dynamics, but has become most visible with the spread of transnational contention and coalition building on issues such as global justice. It is actually very difficult to think of movements as consisting of one organization. When this happens, as in the instance of the Bolshevik party in Russia, it usually means that the transition from movement to bureaucratic organization is complete. Sometimes, the relationships between groups and organizations active in a movement are frequent enough to enable analysts to identify distinctive "alliance" and "oppositional" structures; other times, *ad hoc*, shifting coalitions prevail. Movements differ from coalitions because their members share an identity which one cannot find in purely instrumental coalitions. As identity is not a given trait but is the product of incessant negotiations between social actors, which often involves ideological conflicts, movement boundaries are rarely stable. However, the segmentation of movement networks might also depend on the diversity of issue agendas between different organizations.

Sometimes, social movements are close to subcultural and countercultural networks, based on individual activists sharing in distinctive lifestyles and cultural models. Examples abound in both "new" social movements (e.g., gay and lesbian subcultures, alternative scenes, radical intellectual milieus) and traditional working class communities. Communitarian ties not only strengthen identity and solidarity among movement activists; they also represent a specific context for conflicts focusing on the symbolic side.

SEE ALSO: Counterculture; Resource Mobilization Theory; Social Movements

SUGGESTED READINGS

Diani, M. (2011) Social movements and collective action. In: Carrington, P. & Scott, J. (eds.), *Sage Handbook of Social Network Analysis*. Sage, London.

Diani, M. & McAdam, D. (eds.) (2003) *Social Movements and Networks*. Oxford University Press, Oxford.

MARIO DIANI

social movements, nonviolent

Nonviolent social movements are collective, organized, and sustained attempts to promote social change through methods of nonviolent action. That is, through actions that occur outside of conventional politics, but do not involve violence or the threat of violence against the opponent. Such actions include, but are not limited to, protest demonstrations, marches, boycotts, strikes, disruption, and civil disobedience.

Although most social movements concerned with personal transformation, lifestyle, and culture are nonviolent, those concerned with political, social, and economic change that directly challenge the interests of the elite may be violent, nonviolent, or a combination of the two. Of course, any social movement that directly challenges the interests of the elite, whether it is nonviolent or violent, may be met with violence.

Methods of nonviolent action have been used in struggles against oppression sporadically throughout history; however it was Mohandas Gandhi who was most influential in identifying nonviolent resistance as a unique form of struggle with power different from violence. Prior to Gandhi, people turned to methods of nonviolent action because their moral or religious beliefs prevented them from using violence, because they lacked the means of violence, or because nonviolent actions were simply part of the repertoire of contention that people spontaneously drew from when conflicts arose. Gandhi, however, was crucial in transforming nonviolent resistance into a conscious, reflective, and strategic method of struggle. During the first half of the twentieth century, Gandhi forged a strategy of collective nonviolent resistance during struggles against racism in South Africa and imperialism in India.

Increasingly over the course of the twentieth century, nonviolent social movements were organized and implemented. Although many of these movements were not Gandhian in a strict sense, they implemented mass-based methods of nonviolent action and many of them drew inspiration from Gandhi's example. Major episodes of twentieth century nonviolent resistance include the civil rights movement led by Martin Luther King Jr. that challenged racial discrimination in the US South (1955–68); numerous protest movements in more developed countries in the late 1960s – exemplified by the student and anti-Vietnam war movements in the USA and Australia, and the student-led insurrection in France in 1968; and a wave of "unarmed insurrections" throughout the "second" and "third" worlds from 1978 into the twenty-first century that challenged non-democratic regimes, including those in Iran, South Africa, Chile, the Philippines, Indonesia, Nepal, Burma, China, and Ukraine. Nonviolent social movements, beginning with the Solidarity movement in Poland in the early 1980s, contributed to the toppling of communist regimes in Eastern Europe. Moreover, these struggles contributed to the breakup of the Soviet empire and the end of the cold war.

Various issue-related social movements have been almost exclusively nonviolent. Women's movements have adopted nonviolent action as both a tactical choice and a framing element, and have cultivated a social critique of violence – from domestic violence to war making. Labor movements have historically depended on methods of noncooperation, especially the strike, to force concessions from capitalists and the state. The "new social movements" that emerged in western industrialized countries after World War II, such as the environmental and peace movements, have been almost exclusively nonviolent.

SEE ALSO: Anti-War and Peace Movements; Civil Rights Movement; Collective Action; Global Justice as a Social Movement;

Revolutions; Social Movements; Women's Movements

SUGGESTED READINGS

Ackerman, P. & DuVall, J. (2000) *A Force More Powerful: A Century of Nonviolent Conflict*. St. Martin's Press, New York.

Burrowes, R. J. (1996) *The Strategy of Nonviolent Defense: A Gandhian Approach*. State University of New York Press, Albany, NY.

Sharp, G. (1973) *The Politics of Nonviolent Action*, 3 vols. Porter Sargent Publishers, Boston, MA.

KURT SCHOCK

social movements, participatory democracy in

Participatory democracy refers to an organizational form in which decisionmaking is decentralized, nonhierarchical, and consensus-oriented. It can be contrasted with bureaucracy, in which decision-making is centralized, hierarchical, and based on a formal division of labor, as well as with majority vote.

Participatory democratic organizations today claim a diverse lineage, with precursors in ancient Athenian democracy, the New England town hall, Quaker meetings, Spanish civil war affinity groups, and the American post-World War II pacifist movement. The term itself was popularized in 1962 by the new left group, Students for a Democratic Society (SDS) and it soon became an organizational ethos for many in the new left and the student wing of the civil rights movement. "Collectives" run on participatory democratic principles proliferated in the radical feminist and antiwar movements of the late 1960s. By the end of the decade, many young activists perceived the political system as intransigent, and they turned to building alternative schools, health centers, food coops, and publishing guilds, thus contributing to an enduring cooperative movement. With the rise of the antinuclear movement in Europe and the USA in the late 1970s, activists put participatory democratic movement organizations to use once again in overtly challenging the state, developing institutions of "affinity groups" and "spokescouncils" to coordinate mass actions involving thousands of people. More recently, participatory democratic forms have been prominent in the anti-corporate globalization and global justice movements.

For sociologists writing about the surge of collectivist organizations in the 1960s, the participatory democratic impulse reflected a youthful repudiation of authority that was at odds with the demands of effective political reform. Since then, many scholars have instead adopted Breines's (1989) view of participatory democracy as animated by a *prefigurative* impulse. By enacting within the movement itself values of radical equality, freedom, and community, activists have sought to bring into being a society marked by those values. Far from anti-political, participatory democracy has been an attempt to transform what counts as politics.

Still, most scholars have seen participatory democracies as fragile. Earlier accounts emphasized the form's fundamental inefficiency, inequity, or its inability to reconcile competing interests. More recent accounts have sought instead to identify the factors that make participatory democracies more or less difficult to sustain. For example, participatory democracy is generally good at some movement tasks, such as fostering tactical innovation and leadership development and less good at others, such as coordinating large-scale protests and negotiating with authorities. Funders' requirements that organizations have formal job descriptions and conventional boards of directors has forced many movement organizations to adopt a more bureaucratic structure than they originally envisioned. A view of participatory democracy as middle class and white has sometimes discouraged its use among activists of color.

At the same time, scholars have recognized that the meanings of participatory democracy, equality, even consensus, have varied across organizations and over time. For example, contemporary feminist organizations with a formal hierarchy of offices but consultation across them, or with only some decisions made by consensus might not be recognized as "pure" participatory democracies by 1960s activists but their proponents say that they are participatory, democratic, and effective. Perhaps an even better example comes from the contemporary anti-corporate globalization movement. New digital technologies have not only made it possible to coordinate actions democratically across long distances and multiple organizations; they have also generated new conceptions of participatory democracies as horizontal networks.

SEE ALSO: Anarchism; Democracy; Leadership; Social Movement; Women's Movements

REFERENCES

Breines, W. (1989) *Community and Organization in the New Left, 1962–1968: The Great Refusal*. Rutgers University Press, New Brunswick, NJ.

SUGGESTED READINGS

Juris, J. S. (2008) *Networking Futures: The Movements Against Corporate Globalization.* Duke University Press, Durham, NC.

Polletta, F. (2002). *Freedom Is an Endless Meeting: Democracy in American Social Movements.* University of Chicago Press, Chicago, IL.

FRANCESCA POLLETTA

social movements, repression of

The repression of social movements involves attempts by state or private actors to increase the costs of participating in social movements or otherwise limiting social movement activity (e.g., surveillance, arrest, or imprisonment; violence; counterintelligence programs).

Major distinctions have been made between forms of repression. First, is the repression easily observable (e.g., covert counterintelligence programs versus the use of military force against civilians)? Second, is it coercion (i.e., violence, harassment, and surveillance) or channeling, which includes laws, policies, or actions rewarding protest movements for certain kinds of tactics (typically, more institutional and/or nonviolent tactics) while discouraging others (typically, more radical, non-institutional, or violent tactics)? Third, who is "doing" the repression: national governmental agents, more local governmental agents, or private actors?

All three of these distinctions bear on two fundamental questions about repression: (1) how can researchers explain the level and types of repressive actions taken against different activists and social movements? and (2) how can researchers explain the consequences, or effects, of repression on activists and social movements?

The vast majority of research that casts repression as a dependent variable has focused on explaining the level of particular types of repression without discussing trade-offs between different types of repression. Several causal explanations are featured in these models, including: (1) the threat model, which predicts that the more threatening a social movement, a social movement organization, or a protest activity is to the government and government elites, the more likely severe repressive action will be; (2) the weakness model, which predicts that states are interested in suppressing all challengers, but that weak/vulnerable challengers will quickly become targets of repressive action; and (3) police-centered models, or authority-centered models more generally, which predict that institutional and organizational imperatives of authorities independently influence repression.

In contrast, others have argued that such general theories are unhelpful because repression is situation-specific, resulting from the in situ interactions between insurgents and authorities. Still others focus on the relationships between authorities and insurgents over time, using predator-prey interaction models or other models of temporal feedback.

Repression has also been discussed by political process theorists as a type of "political opportunity." One of political process theory's fundamental propositions is that favorable political opportunities have a direct (or curvilinear, according to some) relationship with movement emergence, mobilization, and success. The prevalence of state repression at a given moment is often referred to as being a component of overall political opportunities, but is also sometimes argued to be a consequence of other political opportunities, such as the openness of the ruling party to protest.

Research has also examined the effects of repression on activists and social movements. Political process theorists tend to argue that repression dampens social movement mobilization and may encourage the use of more institutional, and less violent, social movement tactics. Rational choice theorists of collective action have agreed.

While supportive evidence of this claim has been found, evidence has also been found suggesting that repression radicalizes social movement participants. Instead of diminishing protest or deterring the use of particularly aggressive tactics, many scholars have argued that repression encourages further protest and the use of non-institutional tactics.

Still other scholars have argued that repression has a curvilinear (or, alternatively, an inverted-U) relationship to movement participation and the use of confrontational tactics.

This dizzying array of theoretical arguments is matched by a similarly large array of discordant findings: empirical evidence exists for direct, inverse, curvilinear, inverted-U, and null effects of repression on movement mobilization and tactical deployment.

SEE ALSO: New Social Movement Theory; Social Movements, Nonviolent; Social Movements, Participatory Democracy in

SUGGESTED READINGS

Davenport, C. (ed.) (2000) *Paths to State Repression: Human Rights Violations and Contentious Politics.* Rowman & Littlefield, Lanham, MD.

Earl, J., Soule, S. A., & McCarthy, J. D. (2003) Protests under fire? Explaining protest policing. *American Sociological Review* 69: 581–606.

JENNIFER EARL

social network analysis

Social network analysis developed from diverse sources, including anthropological accounts of detribalized urban migrants, surveys of people's long-distance communities, political upheavals, Internet connectivity, and trade relations among nations. The Internet, inherently network-like, has so popularized the approach that *Business Week* named social network analysis "the hottest new technology" of 2003, and membership in network analysis' professional organization has doubled in four years.

Social network analysts reason from whole to part; from structure to relation to individual; from behavior to attitude. They argue that their social structural explanations have more analytic power than individualistic analyses that do not take relational patterns into account and that interpret behavior in terms of the internalized norms of discrete individuals. The structure of a network, the relations among network members, and the location of a member within a network are critical factors in understanding social behavior. Analysts search for regular structures of ties underlying often incoherent surface appearances, and they study how these social structures constrain network members' behavior. Key concepts include network density, centrality, transitivity, tie strength, clustering, and structural equivalence.

Social networks are formally defined as a set of *nodes* (or *network members*) that are *tied* by one or more specific types of *relations*. In much research, these nodes are individual persons, but they can also be groups, corporations, households, blogs, nation-states, or other collectivities. Ties consist of one or more specific relations, such as financial exchange, friendship, hate, trade, web links, or airline routes. Ties vary in *quality* (whether the relation provides emotional aid or companionship), *quantity* (how much emotional aid; how frequent the companionship), *multiplexity* (sometimes called multistrandedness: ties containing only one relation or several), and *symmetry* (resources flowing in one direction or both). The non-random structure of ties channels resources to specific locations in social systems, fostering inequalities.

Several analytic tendencies distinguish network analysis. First, there is no assumption that groups are the building blocks of society. While social network analytic techniques can discover the empirical existence of groups, the approach is open to studying less-bounded social systems. For example, researchers have mapped the structure of the World Wide Web on the Internet, showing how superconnectors shorten distances between websites.

Second, although social network data often include information about the attributes of individuals, such as age, gender, and beliefs, individuals are not treated as discrete units of analysis. Instead, analysis focuses on how the networks affect the individuals and ties embedded in them.

Third, social network analysis contrasts with analyses which assume that socialization into norms determines behavior and social structure. By contrast, network analysis looks to see the extent to which patterns of social relations affect norms and values.

Social network analysts gather data in many ways, such as ethnography, surveys, archives, and simulations. Their data collection emphasizes ties and the problematic nature of boundaries. Although analysts often visualize networks as point and line graphs, they analyze them as matrices that are more amenable to statistical and mathematical manipulation.

SEE ALSO: Organization Theory; Social Network Theory; Weak Ties (Strength of)

SUGGESTED READINGS

Carrington, P., Scott, J., & Wasserman, S. (eds.) (2005) *Models and Methods in Social Network Analysis*. Cambridge University Press, Cambridge.

Freeman, L. (2004) *The Development of Social Network Analysis*. Empirical Press, Vancouver.

Scott, J. (ed.) (2002) *Social Networks: Critical Concepts in Sociology*, 4 vols. Routledge, London.

Wellman, B. (ed.) (1999) *Networks in the Global Village*. Westview Press, Boulder, CO.

BARRY WELLMAN

social network theory

The idea of social networks is prevalent in everyday vernacular language, ranging from the game "Six Degrees of Kevin Bacon" where players identify how any one actor is linked to the actor Kevin Bacon through no more than six different people, to the way in which people "network" with one another as an avenue through which they gain social capital, to how we describe our computers' ability to "talk" with other computers. The idea of social networks has an equally wide range of applications in sociology, from formal network theory to social network data analysis. The historical development of the sociological use of the idea of social networks originates with Durkheim and Simmel, and its breadth of use is reflected in contemporary theoretical and methodological developments and applications. In its different uses, from the vernacular to its historical development to its current developments, social network theory refers to the ways in which people are connected to one another and how these connections create and define human society on all levels: the individual, the group, and the institutional.

HISTORICAL DEVELOPMENT

The historical development of social networks as a sociologically important idea is represented by two main stages: its origins in the sociological work of Durkheim and Simmel, and its early development in the areas of social psychology. While Durkheim does not use the phrase social networks, it is obvious from his writings about religion, suicide, and the division of labor that he focused on how changes in the social world, such as those brought about by industrialization and capitalism, affected the connections between people. More to the point, he aptly illustrated how connections between people serve as the basis for human society. For example, in describing the shift from mechanical solidarity to organic solidarity he focused on several criteria, including the quality and quantity of individuals' connections to one another, as expressed by the idea of dynamic density, and by the level of the division of labor.

Simmel's work can generally be described as examining different aspects of individual lives and individuals' interactions. Similarly to Durkheim, while Simmel never directly used the phrase social networks, his writings focused on how interactions were affected by the way in which people are connected to one another in terms of an individual's social status, as well as the dynamics that occur as different people engage in interactions with one another. For example, in discussing how group size affected interactions, Simmel examined the qualitative change that occurs in interactions when the dyad becomes a triad. In the dyad, actors are connected by their total interdependence, while in a triad it is possible for a coalition to develop between two of the three actors. Simmel's focus on the different variables that affect our connections to one another is evident in a wide range of his discussions, from exchanges as a form of interactions, to group development, through a series of interactions among people, to the social characteristics (such as whether a person is a stranger) that affect the creation of connections between people.

The second stage in the historical development of social networks as a sociological idea occurs in the early work of sociologists specializing in social psychology. For example, George Homans highlighted the basic principles of exchange theory, which focused on how connections between people were based on the need for exchanges to occur to fulfill each actor's needs. Peter Blau and Richard Emerson and his colleagues further developed Homans's ideas by explicating the conditions under which exchanges proceed (for the former) and how such exchanges might then create collective action between actors through different types of exchange networks (the latter). While Emerson was the only early social psychologist explicitly using the phrase social networks, it is evident from the work of Homans and Blau that their underlying themes examined the creation and maintenance of connections between people. These themes, and the phrase social networks, are developed further by contemporary theorists and empirical research applications.

Cook and colleagues (1993), among others, extended Emerson's original formulation of exchange theory to examine issues such as the distribution of power in social exchange networks, how bargaining in social networks is affected by power distribution, commitment formation, and coalition formations. Each of these theoretical extensions of Emerson and Blau's work focuses on some aspect of social networks in terms of how connections between actors then affect further interactions and exchanges. Willer and colleagues (2002) developed network exchange theory (NET) to focus on exchange structures and power relations. NET provides explicit predictions about exchanges that may occur based on factors such as whether or not social networks are exclusively connected, the level of hierarchy and mobility that exists in any particular social network, and the order in which exchanges occur. These factors then allow Willer and colleagues to explore how collective action develops among actors in a social network.

Network theory is a broader term that represents theoretical developments in all areas of sociology by focusing on the key idea of actors and how they are connected, whereby actors can be individuals or groups or social institutions. In other words, network theory allows us to examine the objective pattern of interactions represented by how actors are connected to one another. By examining how actors are connected to one another, sociologists gain insight into the structure of social interactions on the individual level as well as the structure of groups and institutions. For example, Granovetter (1973) used social networks to explain the importance of weak ties among people and how these types of ties affected exchanges. His work served as the basis for further work in economic sociology, such as explaining organizational survival in particular economic environments.

SEE ALSO: Exchange Network Theory; Social Network Analysis; Weak Ties (Strength of)

REFERENCES

Cook, K. S., Molm, L. D., & Yamagishi, T. (1993) Exchange relations and exchange networks: recent developments in social exchange theory. In: Berger, J. & Zelditch, M., Jr. (eds.), *Theoretical Research Programs: Studies in the Growth of Theory*. Stanford University Press, Stanford, CA, pp. 296–322.

Granovetter, M. (1973) The strength of weak ties. *American Journal of Sociology* 91: 481–510.

Willer, D., Walker, H. A., Markovsky, B., Willer, R., Lovaglia, M., Thye, S., & Simpson, B. (2002) Network exchange theory. In: Berger, J. & Zelditch, M., Jr. (eds.), *New Directions in Contemporary Sociological Theory*. Rowman & Littlefield, New York, pp. 109–43.

ANNE F. EISENBERG AND JEFFREY HOUSER

social order

Social order is synonymous with society and social science. People do not regularly live in chaos, even when they are the denizens of postmodern societies which characteristically exacerbate the already chaotic tempo bequeathed by modernity. Regardless of whether it is edifying to accept, ritual and routine, not rebellion and revolution, absorb the lion's share of everyday energies. Likewise, apart from whether society is conceived theoretically as organism or system, language game or mode of production, interaction ritual or ethereal spectacle, the essential notion of "society" is scientifically and practically meaningful only when it refers to routinely observable phenomena about which lasting statements are possible. Without social order, social science would dissolve into the ephemeral study of ephemerality.

Probably no figure in the history of sociology more clearly represents the concern for theorizing the practical achievement of social order than Talcott Parsons. Parsons self-consciously built an integrated theory of social order through synthesis of previous ambitious attempts to grasp the totality of human society, including via the work of Herbert Spencer, Vilfredo Pareto, Émile Durkheim, Alfred Marshall, and Max Weber, the last four serving as the principal subjects of Parsons's *The Structure of Social Action* (1937). The "problem of order," as Parsons put it, is further systematized in the aptly titled *The Social System* (1951), which outlined a model of society as a functionally differentiated set of institutions and cultural patterns. In such a view, social order is conceived as the aggregate equilibrium which is achieved when subsystems adapt to meet a priori societal needs. As determinative as this model appears, Parsons (1977) emphasized that social order was always already "precarious" and "problematical," not an "imperative" to be associated with theoretical, much less actual, "fascism."

Parsons's critics, such as C. Wright Mills (1959), viewed his attempt to grasp an overarching social order as an instance of "grand theory," a pejorative highlighting the theory's ahistorical and empirically disconnected quality as well as usefulness as ideological buttress for the specific faults of the mid-century United States of America. Alvin W. Gouldner (1970) pushed this criticism further, assessing the conservative roots of Parsons's theoretical system in Platonic philosophy and announcing the need for a thorough rethinking of sociology's order-based self-conception. Harold Garfinkel's (1967) "ethnomethodology" rejected Parsons's airy theoretical approach in favor of empirical analysis of everyday rules (the ethnomethods) which actors use in creating social order.

Parsons's problem of social order remains an ongoing practical as well as theoretical problem. On the one hand, researchers' plates are full in pursuit of empirical analysis of postmodernity's acceleration, intensification, dispersal, and differentiation of social and cultural life, which may or may not ultimately facilitate the production of social order. Does the World Wide Web integrate globally, or divide humanity into disparate viewers of superficial information? Does the emergence of post-Fordist/Keynesian economic systems provide efficiency and facilitate meeting increasingly differentiated consumer demand, or globalize the crisis of overproduction without hope of an equally global Keynesian fix? Does the fact of planetary ecological crisis portend unprecedented forms of international cooperation, or will "the North" use its political, military, and economic power to suppress "the South's" demands for an equitable and democratically coordinated response? Will globalization result in genuinely pluralist societies, or will atavistic and ethnocentric responses undermine civility among culturally diverse populations? Will medical technologies result in the further amelioration of disease and mortality, or will social order be subverted by viral contagions, whether organic or computer, endemic or laboratory synthesized, unintentionally or by menacing design? The twenty-first century appears destined to challenge the achievement of social order on terms as particular and general as human experience provides.

SEE ALSO: Ethnomethodology; Mills, C. Wright; Parsons, Talcott

REFERENCES

Garfinkel, H. (1967) *Studies in Ethnomethodology*. Prentice Hall, Englewood Cliffs, NJ.

Gouldner, A. W. (1970) *The Coming Crisis of Western Sociology*. Basic Books, New York.

Mills, C. W. (1959) *The Sociological Imagination*. Oxford University Press, Oxford.

Parsons, T. (1977) *Social Systems and the Evolution of Action Theory*. Free Press, New York.

STEVEN P. DANDANEAU

social problems: concept and perspectives

"Social problems" have formed a specialized field within sociology, especially in the USA, at least since the end of the nineteenth century. The European context has always been marked by the concept of the "social question," which was one of the principal sources for the development of sociology as a scientific discipline apart from philosophy, history, political science, and political economy. Unlike US sociology, in the European tradition the concept of social problems was not disseminated in the sociological literature until the end of the 1960s, when it appeared first in books and articles about social work. While the concept today is institutionalized in special sections of sociological associations and in some journals and textbooks, and its use has been spread in public and political discourse, European sociology has always privileged the concept of the social question, with greater emphasis on social inequality and exclusion.

The term "social problem" is used in public and political discussions and refers to very different social situations, conditions, and forms of behavior, like crime, racism, drug use, unemployment, poverty, exclusion, alcoholism, sexual abuse, and madness. However, especially in textbooks and journal articles, it also refers to premenstrual syndrome, ecological problems, stalking, exploitation of natural resources, traffic accidents, or even war, terrorism, and genocide.

This diversity has been a challenge for sociological definitions and invites the question of identifying the feature that justifies classifying such phenomena under a common topic or theoretical perspective.

A quite formal and simple definition of social problems has been proposed by Merton (1976: 7): "social problems are a discrepancy between cultural standards, norms, or values and the actual conditions of social life, a discrepancy between what should be and what is." One of the main problems for a sociology of social problems arose from the question who decide about the standards in society, the actual social condition and the discrepancy and whether such a decision is even possible.

While typologies of theoretical positions are arbitrary and misleading, very often there can be found a differentiation between "objective" or "realist" approaches and "constructionist" perspectives. These labels are misleading because, on the one hand, they involve the danger of misinterpreting constructions of social problems as not being real social problems, and, on the other hand, they lead to the misinterpretation of "objectivist" approaches in assuming that there is still a methodological position of naïve objectivism in sociology. But these approaches signify two different sets of research questions, one starting with social problems as harm, asking about causes, epidemiology and social control, the other starting with social problems as constructions asking about the problematic character and the establishment of public discourses.

SOCIAL PROBLEMS AS SOCIAL HARM AND SOCIAL DISORDER

An early version of describing social problems as harm and social disorder are social pathology and social disorganization. These perspectives, still very common in political and popular discourse, are based on the idea of society as an organism. Social problems are indicators of a pathological state of society, caused by pathological individuals, or of disorganized social systems. The identification of social problems is not a problem, because the criteria underlying society as a well-functioning organism are seen as evident and based on commonsense normative and moral ideas, marking a normative or ideological perspective that nevertheless corresponds with applied sociology, where the problematic character of the issue has to be taken for granted. Beyond criticisms of its normative base, the social disorganization perspective has been criticized for failing to specify the difference between *cultural conflict* and social disorganization. Also, the problem of separating "normal" or even necessary and disorganizing social change is not solved.

With the supremacy of *structural functionalism*, the idea of anomic developments became one of the leading sociological perspectives on social problems in the 1950s and 1960s. The functioning of social systems and their stable reproduction became the central point of reference for identifying social problems as a "technical" analysis of the possibility of a better functioning of a social system, allowing criticisms of existing public definitions of issues as being ideological misconceptions, or diagnosing social developments as resulting in "latent social problems" not yet defined as social problems in public. But this concept has not been able to provide "technical" criteria for the healthy functioning of a social system without reference to values, interests, and power apart from the absence of conflict and deviant behavior. Implicit in this view is the misconception of social problems as being conditions that could and should be solved. Obviously, societies survive quite well even if they leave unsolved their major social problems, and typically the treatment or solution of one social problem means the creation of social problems in other fields of modern societies and they could fulfill important stabilizing functions for societies inasmuch as they provide sources of solidarity, mark limits of morality, symbolize examples of misconduct, or indicate necessary social change. This approach loses much of its power of persuasion when we ask why certain social harms or discriminations last over a long period without being identified as social problems by the public, or why definitions or interpretations of social problems change over time even if the social conditions seem to remain nearly unchanged.

SOCIAL PROBLEMS AS SOCIAL CONSTRUCTION

Whereas sociological perspectives that define and analyze social problems as social harm insist on the fact that social structures and developments could result in problematic life conditions and behavior, for constructionist perspectives these social conditions are merely "putative" and a more or less rhetorical means of "claims-making activities": social problems are constructions that successfully attract public and political attention. As a consequence, the main questions to be analyzed are no longer about causes and social conditions that might explain the existence and affection of specific groups, but concern the processes of how social problems are successful in attracting public attention and become public issues. The sociology of social problems consists in the reconstruction of activities and processes that explain the public mobilization for specific definitions of issues and themes within society and the establishment of social problem discourses. In its radical form, this approach is limited to the analysis of rhetoric and counter-rhetoric in public discourses. Today, especially in the US context, the sociology of social problems is identified with this constructionist perspective, and a vast amount of social problem research is devoted to case studies of many different issues that at one time or another attracted public attention.

Even if social problems are social constructions they are no less real in their consequences and effects; it makes no sense to talk about social problems as social constructions in opposition to "real" social problems. The central question within this perspective is nowadays whether and how the constructions are based on cultural and social resources that are rooted in social structures and embedded in social change in modern societies, i.e. whether constructionism rests in the scope of microsociological perspectives or can be earthed by macrosociological contexts.

SEE ALSO: Anomie; Deviance; Deviance, Constructionist Perspectives; Social Movements; Social Problems, Politics of

REFERENCE

Merton, R. K. (1976) The sociology of social problems. In: Merton, R. K. & Nisbet, R. A. (eds.) *Contemporary Social Problems*, 4th edn. Harcourt Brace Jovanovich, New York, pp. 3–43.

SUGGESTED READINGS

Best, J. (2008) *Social Problems*. W. W. Norton & Co., New York.

Ritzer, G. (ed.) (2004) *Handbook of Social Problems: A Comparative International Perspective*. Sage, Thousand Oaks, CA.

AXEL GROENEMEYER

social problems, politics of

The sociology of social problems always has to be a historical and sociological analysis of the politics of social problems and their social control. Whereas the constructionist perspective of sociology of social problems is concerned with the construction of social problems categories in society, the politics of social problems emphasizes the political processes in the development of social and political issues and its institutionalization within and by the political system. The politics of social problems refers to four interrelated dimensions and questions: (1) the social construction of social problems categories and problem discourses as a political process; (2) the establishment and institutionalization of social problems as political issues; (3) the transformation of social problems within the political system; and (4) the political use of social problems.

1 CLAIMS-MAKING AS POLITICAL PROCESS

The construction of social problems always is based on interests and values of social groups, collective actors or already established organizations making claims of social or political change. These processes always are shaped by social conflicts about definitions or constructions of a problem and about different solutions of a (putative) problem. Competing interpretations and discourses of a problem, but also different issues within the public, struggle for public attention and political influence. The social construction of social problems always is a struggle for hegemonic interpretations and discourses that is related to the distribution of material, political, and symbolic resources and power, a fundamental political process. Beyond this, politics as struggle for power always also is a struggle for meaning and symbols embedded in everyday life as well as in social institutions.

2 CLAIMS-MAKING AS AGENDA-SETTING WITHIN THE POLITICAL SYSTEM

Even if the treatment or claims of solutions for social problems sometimes are addressed to public associations or by private enterprises, the political system and the state are the main addressee and the ultimate arbiters of allocating valued goods and resources. The different forms of the political system constitute a political regime, institutionalized and organized within a nation-specific political system of representation, including established political parties, interest groups, and associations with institutionalized access processes of decision-making. The success of establishing a specific definition of social problems or claims in this perspective depends only on the capacity of mobilizing power and influence by social actors. Important advances have been made with ideas of political agenda setting as development of political opportunities set by an intersection of problem constructions, solutions, and political support within the political system.

3 SOCIAL PROBLEMS WITHIN THE POLITICAL PROCESS

The social issues and claims then are accepted, rejected, canalized, or redefined by specific mechanisms of selection and filters of the organizations within the political system. Even if a public claim is accepted as a political issue, the political arena in which it is placed is important, as are the political actors and the strategy by which it is placed. A network of organizations, professional associations and collective actors within society is established in processes of decision-making and implementation of programs, bargaining and transforming social issues into administrative categories with their own orientations and interests.

4 THE POLITICAL USE AND CONSEQUENCES OF SOCIAL PROBLEMS

Organizations of the political system are not only passive receivers of inputs from the society, but also are actively and strategically engaged in producing and constructing public issues and social problems according to the criteria of the system, like election strategies, gaining public support in interorganizational or party concurrence or accumulation of resources by presenting specific problem-solving capacities. Very often it is the political system, and not collective actors in societies, that play the central role in promoting mobilizations and moralizations of social problems. For the political system, social problems fulfill other purposes than being solved. The definitions of social problems could become the object of strategic politics, and the political restructuring and manipulation of the cultural and moral milieu of social problem constructions could ensure the regulation of social conflicts. Symbolic and rhetorical forms of political action assume central importance in the political system, signaling that something is done about the social problem. Political programs and the institutionalization of measures produce official definitions of social problems categories as legal and administrative categories that "entitle" specific social groups to claims or controls, and they constitute a cultural and social frame of reference for standards of normality and reasonableness relating to alternative social constructions. Very often, one solution for a social problem leads to other social problems and conflicts in other areas, or the institutionalization of one solution leads to increased political opportunities for new mobilizations and discourses on new problematic issues.

SEE ALSO: Politics; Power; Social Movements; Social Problems, Concept and Perspectives; State

SUGGESTED READINGS

Best, J. (2008) *Social Problems*. W.W. Norton, New York.

Rochefort, D. A. & Cobb, R. W. (eds.) (1994) *The Politics of Problem Definition. Shaping the Policy Agenda*. University Press of Kansas, Lawrence, KS.

Zahariadis, N. (2003) *Ambiguity and Choice in Public Policy: Political Decision Making in Modern Democracies*. Georgetown University Press, Washington, DC.

AXEL GROENEMEYER

social psychology

Social psychology is an approach to understanding human social relations that focuses on individuals and how their interactions impact social organizations and social institutions. Social psychological scholarship includes a wide range of theoretical perspectives, methodological tools, and substantive applications originating from diverse intellectual schools such as sociology, psychology, economics, education, and business. Contemporary social psychology is best understood by examining its range of theoretical perspectives, methodological tools, and substantive foci.

THEORETICAL PERSPECTIVES AND THEORETICAL IDEAS

In 1980 Sheldon Stryker articulated three "faces" of social psychology: psychological social psychology, sociological social psychology, and symbolic interactionism. All three perspectives share a focus on the individual and individual interactions as the explanatory factor for all aspects of social life, such as the creation of stable group structures and the formation of successful social movements. The three theoretical perspectives in social psychology are known more generally as cognitive and intrapersonal, symbolic interactionist, and structural.

Cognitive and intrapersonal social psychology focuses on understanding how internal processes affect an individual's ability to interact with others. The internal processes most studied in this perspective are cognitive and physiological. The cognitive approach examines how brain activity specifically associated with memory, perception, and decision-making processes affects an individual's ability to understand the information necessary for engaging in successful interactions. Additionally, this approach also explores how variations in cognitive processes lead to differences in individuals' ability to interact. The physiological approach explores the ways that specific biological and chemical processes affect individuals' ability to create adequate and useful schemas, use their memory, perceive things accurately, and then make relevant decisions.

Symbolic interactionism originated from the work of George Herbert Mead and his students at the University of Chicago as well as the work of pragmatic philosophers. One of the sociology students, Herbert Blumer, coined the term symbolic interactionism and other sociology students were instrumental in publishing Mead's ideas, after his death, concerning the individual. These ideas center on his discussions of the mind (what makes humans uniquely social creatures), self (how we become uniquely social creatures), and society (how our interactions are affected by social institutions). Generally, the symbolic interactionist perspective in social psychology focuses on studying the meanings that underlie social interactions in terms of how they are created, how they are maintained, and how we learn to understand such meanings. Additionally, theorists writing within this perspective argue that individual interactions lead to the creation of formal social organizations and social institutions. Therefore, to understand society, it is necessary to understand the interactions that shape it and maintain it. There are three main theoretical approaches in the symbolic interactionist perspective, symbolic interactionism, phenomenological, and life course.

- The symbolic interactionism approach is most closely related to Mead's original ideas concerning social psychology and focuses on exploring how meanings are created and maintained within social interactions with the self as the basis for such interactions. The underlying theme of this approach is that individuals create and manage meanings through the roles and identities they hold. It is important to note that each individual holds any number of roles and identities, depending on the people with whom they interact as well as the environment in which they find themselves.
- The phenomenological approach originated from European sociology and philosophy, emphasizing the meanings themselves and how such meanings reflect unstated normative expectations for interactions. The underlying theme of this approach is that language, verbal and non-verbal, represents the informal and formal rules and norms that guide social interactions and structure society.
- The life course approach in symbolic interactionism focuses on how humans learn the meanings associated with interactions throughout their lifetime and the stages that reflect such learning processes. The underlying theme of this approach is that the norms, rules, and values that guide interactions and shape society change throughout individuals' lives, especially as they move into different social positions and environments.

Structural social psychology originated with the work of economists, psychologists, and sociologists interested in explaining social interactions more formally and mathematically with the goal of creating testable hypotheses. Structural social psychology assumes that social actors are driven by rational concerns centered on maximizing rewards and minimizing punishments. Another related assumption is that interactions based on rational calculations result in formally structured individual, group, and institutional interactions. There are three main theoretical programs that represent this approach: power, exchange, and bargaining studies; social influence and authority studies; and status characteristics, expectation states theory, and social network studies.

- Power, exchange, and bargaining studies explore how social interactions can be described as exchanges between social actors with the assumption that individuals rationally calculate the costs and benefits associated with any particular interaction.
- Social influence and authority studies share an underlying theme that there are several factors that encourage people to be influenced by others, including the status or position others hold in comparison to themselves and group encouragement of conformity.
- Status characteristics, expectation states, and social network studies examine how social interactions are based on socially and culturally derived expectations for behavior that people have of one another. These socially and culturally derived expectations are associated with assumed predictions concerning how successfully any individual will contribute to an exchange, or interaction, process.

METHODOLOGICAL TOOLS

Social psychologists use a variety of research methods with which to explore and explain specific aspects of social interactions as well as test specific hypotheses concerning these social interactions.

- Interpretive methods, also known as "qualitative methods," are used to gain an in-depth understanding of social psychological phenomena, ranging from individuals to their interactions to the groups and environments in which such interactions occur. The type of interpretive research methods used by social psychologists include participant observation, unobtrusive research utilizing archival documents as representation of individuals and their interactions, and more extensive field research similar to ethnographic research commonly used by anthropologists.
- Experimental methods in social psychology serve as a way to test specific theoretical hypotheses as well as to explore particular aspects of interactions. There are a range of experimental methods, from the quasi-experimental study which has fewer strict controls to the fully experimental study with formal control and experimental groups, as well as full control of all variables associated with the study.
- Survey and interview methods used by social psychologists serve to test specific hypotheses as well as explore specific aspects of interactions, groups, and social institutions. Similarly to other areas in sociology, social psychologists use a range of survey tools and interview techniques including self-completing surveys, those conducted by the researcher, and in-depth interviews. It is worth noting that social psychologists often use surveys and interviews as the second approach as a way of engaging in methodological triangulation. For example, pre- and post-study surveys are used in experimental studies where the participant will either complete the survey without the researcher present or be asked a series of questions by the researcher.

SUBSTANTIVE FOCUS

Beginning students in social psychology are often surprised to learn the degree to which understanding the individual and her or his interactions allows them to also explain group dynamics, behavior in social organizations, whether a social movement will be successful, and the seeming durability of social institutions. Similar to the discussion of the methodological tools used by social psychologists, it is simplistic to describe the field as focused only on the individual. The substantive focus of social psychological theory and research ranges from individuals and their interactions to the groups in which they engage to the social organizations and social institutions that shape these interactions.

- The study of individuals and their interactions seeks to explore, understand, and explain different aspects of the unique social quality of people. The range of topics includes understanding why prejudice and discrimination exist, the best way to persuade and influence people, and those topics typically found in social psychology texts – interpersonal attraction, helping and altruism, and aggression.
- The study of groups highlights that the group environment affects individuals and their interactions. The range of topics for studying groups includes group conformity, group performance, and intergroup relations.
- In understanding individuals and their interactions, as well as how group membership affects those interactions, social psychologists are able to discuss and study social organizations and institutions. Some of the topics examined

include social movements and whether they are successful as well as the idea of deviance as a social institution.

SEE ALSO: Blumer, Herbert George; Ethnomethodology; Identity Theory; Interaction; Mead, George Herbert; Power, Theories of; Psychological Social Psychology; Role; Self; Social Cognition; Social Psychology; Symbolic Interaction

SUGGESTED READINGS

Blau, P. (1964) *Exchange and Power in Social Life*. Wiley, New York.

Blumer, H. (1969) *Symbolic Interactionism: Perspective and Method*. Prentice Hall, Englewood Cliffs, NJ.

Cook, K. (ed.) (1987) *Social Exchange Theory*. Sage, Thousand Oaks, CA.

Stryker, S. (1980) *Symbolic Interactionism: A Social Structural Version*. Benjamin Cummings, Menlo Park, CA.

ANNE F. EISENBERG

social services

Social services are provisions that society makes to support individuals in need. Developed in the west to supplement family care, social services are found across the world and delivered mainly by social workers in various settings (state, voluntary agencies and commercial enterprises) in a "mixed economy of care." Bureaucratized under the "new" managerialism and market forces, social services cover children, families, older people, disabled people, mentally ill people and offenders. Social workers care for and about people within a tension-filled environment that complicates delivery.

An important issue is what causes need – personal inadequacies or structural factors. The Settlement Movement favoured explanations involving structural causes. The Charity Organization Society (COS) originally popularized personal pathology, dividing claimants into deserving and undeserving ones. The former received stigmatized and inadequate services; the latter nothing. This tension continues as "welfare dependency." Other sources of tension are: care-control dilemmas; low professional status; charitable giving or societal entitlements; state or market providers; and public or personal responsibility. Professionals and claimants have challenged analyses based on individual pathologies and demanded change through radical social work. Legislative fiat and social policies constrain their aspirations through reduced public expenditures and shifting service boundaries. Social workers' remit is contested by other professionals who claim this territory and dominate interagency operations.

Marketization privileges private providers and leaves those unable to access the market with stigmatized and inadequate resources. Globalization and GATS (General Agreement on Trades and Services) have intensified the trend in health, social services and education to increase privatization, profit-making opportunities for multinational companies, and personal self-reliance. To divest the state of responsibility for service provision, claimants are increasingly forced to find work. This reflects persistent strains between family, state and community support. State failure in moving people into gainful employment continues under today's New Deal in the UK and Workfare in the USA. This traps social workers into stretching inadequate resources, balancing personal pathology with social causation, and apportioning responsibilities amongst stakeholders instead of practicing holistically to ensure individuals acquire a valued place in society and access to services.

SEE ALSO: Privitzation; Social Work: History and Institutions; Social Work: Theory and Methods

SUGGESTED READING

Dominelli, L. (2004) *Social Work: Theory and Practice for a Changing Profession*. Polity Press, Cambridge.

LENA DOMINELLI

social structure

The term social structure denotes a more or less enduring pattern of social arrangements within a particular society, group, or social organization. Nonetheless, despite its widespread usage, there is no single agreed concept of social structure that exists in sociology or related disciplines. An early attempt to theorize the notion of social structure was seen in the work of Lévi-Strauss, the French social anthropologist, who attempted to discover the universal rules that underpin everyday activities and custom through cultural systems (Lévi-Strauss 1967). Within sociology, however, the term has been employed in various ways according to the theoretical approach within which the concept is used.

Historically speaking, sociological theories exploring the concept of social structure are generally associated with macro or structural perspectives oriented to understanding the nature of social order, and in doing so stand in stark contrast to social action (or micro) approaches which seek meaning and motivation behind human social behavior. Social structural analysis has tended to be identified with two schools of thought. First, it is associated with the theoretical speculations of structural functionalists such as Talcott Parsons, for whom the major concern of the sociological enterprise was to explain how social life was possible. For Parsons (1951), the answer lay in the establishment of a certain degree of order and stability which is essential for the survival of the social system. Parsons identified cultural values as the key to stability. Value consensus provides the foundations for cooperation, since common values produce common goals. The value system permeated social structures which, in Parsons's schemata, constituted a fourfold system of functional prerequisites which give way to universal arrangements oriented towards adaptation, goal attainment, integration, and pattern maintenance. In Parsons's structuralist theory the notion of social structure also implied that human behavior and relationships are, to one degree or another, "structured," particularly in terms of rules, social status and roles, and normative values. Social behavior and relationships are thus patterned and recurrent. It follows that the structure of society can be seen as the sum total of normative behavior, as well as social relationships which are governed by norms.

In western Europe, in particular, functionalism has long been rivaled by Marxist schools of structuralism. Marx (1964) himself considered the importance of what he identified as the two dimensions of the social structure: the overarching economic substructure (or base) which for the most part determined the social superstructure comprised of the various institutions of society. In turn, the "hard" interpretation of Marxist thought came to identify the processes of dialectical and historical materialism as forging social structures concomitant with the economic base. In this elucidation the social superstructure was transformed into social structures that enforced class subjugation and exploitation.

Criticisms of macro-level structuralist theories were to lead to the intellectual movement of poststructuralism which developed from the 1960s. Although initially derived from structuralist schools, theorists challenged assumptions concerning society and language as signifying coherent "systems." Through major exponents such as Derrida, Foucault, and others associated with schools of postmodernism, even earlier poststructuralist theory was itself "deconstructed" in order to understand how knowledge, linguistics, and centers of power came into existence in the first place.

SEE ALSO: Merton, Robert K.; Mesostructure; Poststructuralism; Structural Functional Theory; Structure and Agency

REFERENCES

Lévi-Strauss, C. (1967) *The Scope of Anthropology*. Cape, London.

Marx, K. (1964) *The Economic and Philosophical Manuscripts*. International Manuscripts, New York.

Parsons, T. (1951) *The Social System*. Free Press, New York.

STEPHEN HUNT

social system

A "social system" may be defined as two or more people engaged in on-going social interaction. The aspect of interaction which makes it specifically a "system" is a high degree of regularity conducive to permanent structural arrangements. While this categorization of a social system is largely identified with mid-twentieth century structural functionalism, Herbert Spencer (1820–1903) earlier drew an analogy between the social system and biological organisms. Spencer's speculation that all social systems "evolved" led him to develop a three-fold scheme for categorizing societies based on complex or simple structures and their degree of stability. Firstly, a "simple" system is undifferentiated by sections, groups, or tribal formations. Secondly, a "compound" system amounts to an amalgamation of communities with a rudimentary hierarchy and division of labor. Thirdly, "doubly compound" systems are more complex still and united under one authority (Spencer 1971).

The major contributor to structural functionalism, Talcott Parsons (1902–97), drew a blueprint of the social system applicable universally while allowing for complexity as societies evolved from pre-industrial to industrial forms. For Parsons, the social system was constituted by interacting function "parts" that dealt with essential prerequisites and whose fulfillment ensured the survival of any society. Also ensuring the endurance of the system was the need of constituent parts to evolve through the differentiation that came with modernization.

In Parson's schemata, a four-fold system of functional prerequisites gave way to universal structural arrangements: adaptation, goal attainment, integration, and pattern maintenance. These universal "sub-systems" realized these prerequisites through the following: economic activity (control over the environment), political arrangements (establishing goals and priorities), integration (the adjustment of potential or actual conflict) and the maintenance of value patterns (kinship structures and socialization processes). Parsons identified cultural values as the key to stability since value consensus integrates the various institutions or subsystems and engenders common goals. In Parson's model both value consensus and sub-system formations structured patterned and recurrent human action and relationship in terms of rules, social status, roles, and norms.

For Parsons, the task of sociology was to analyze the institutionalization of the social system's value orientation. When values were institutionalized and behavior structured in terms of them, the result was a stable system. This "social equilibrium" was sustained by socialization – the means by which values are transmitted, alongside forms of social control encouraging conformity and discouraging deviance.

According to Parsons change in one constitutive part (adaptation, goal attainment, integration and pattern maintenance) was likely to bring change in another. Such evolution involved a general adaptive capacity as the social system increased its control over the environment. However, while economic adaptation might provide the initial stimulus for social evolution, it was changes in value consensus that ensured that such change was forthcoming.

In identifying the evolutionary state of any given social system, Parsons outlined five variables which he referred to as cultural patterns "A" and "B." The former were synonymous with more simple forms, while the latter constituted the cultural patterns of advanced societies. Firstly, the change from ascribed to "achieved" status allowed social mobility according to merit. Secondly, the move from the diffuse and organic nature of social relationships towards the more utilitarian relationships associated with modernity. Thirdly, "particularism" is transformed into social acts according to universal principles. Fourthly, the change from the affectivity of immediate gratification to deferred gratification. Finally, the evolution from a collective orientation towards self-orientation.

In attempting to develop functionalist theory, Robert Merton (1910–2003) focused upon the alleged efficacy of a number of underlying assumptions. In particular, Merton questioned whether any given sub-system or constituent element of the social system may be alternatively functional, dysfunctional, or non-functional. Thus, he advocated the necessity of evaluating their overall contribution to system survival. Secondly, he speculated whether the functional utility of the constituent elements of a social system are particularly integrative, especially in advanced industrial society.

A damaging criticism of the paradigm of a social system was derived from the teleology inherent in structural functionalism. While advancing the view that constituent parts of the social system existed because they have beneficial consequences, it effectively treated an effect as a cause. Moreover, assessing the positive effects of these elements is often unquantifiable. Subsequently, the biological analogy on which the paradigm was initially based became perceived as ultimately flawed.

SEE ALSO: Functionalism/Neofunctionalism; Social Structure; Structural Functional theory

REFERENCE

Spencer, H. (1971) *Structure, Function and Evolution*. Nelson, London.

SUGGESTED READINGS

Merton, R. (1949) *Social Theory and Social Structure*. Free Press, Glencoe, IL.

Parsons, T. (1951) *The Social System*. Free Press, NewYork.

STEPHEN HUNT

social theory and sport

Sport provides unique opportunities for understanding the complexities of everyday life ranging from the macro to the micro. Macro perspectives include sport as science, politics, class, media, and globalization. Micro orientations focus on preference and participation, socialization, social-psychological outcomes, and sense of self.

Coakley (2008) details dominant theoretical perspectives and their relation to the study of sports, which are summarized in Table 1.

As a young field, the areas in need of theoretical attention are vast. While attention to race, class, gender, and media studies have legitmated sport in the wider discipline, other intriguing substantive areas remain fertile ground for development. We suggest three fruitful areas are: (1) the political nature of sport, (2) sport as art, and (3) the moral assumptions embedded in sport.

POLITICAL NATURE OF SPORT

Viewing sports as politics is not new. This connection has been referred to as "war without weapons" (Coakley 2008). Strenk (1979) points out how Nazis under Hitler and Fascists under Mussolini propagandized sport. The globalization process seems to have only increased the prominence of sport in politics. The Olympics in particular have clearly intersected with politics as the losers of both world

Table 1 Summary of theoretical perspectives

Theoretical paradigm	*Focus in sport*
Functionalist	Sport as producing positive social outcomes
Conflict	Political-economic forces that drive sport and the class-based relations that define it
Interactionist	Relations of sport participants including the production of athlete identity the meaning and significance of sport for athletes and spectators
Critical	Power relations involved in sporting activities such as how sport reproduces advantage or disadvan-tage, the relationship of sports to images of health compared to sickness, etc.
Feminist	Gender relations embedded in sport such as the construction of gendered identities

Source: Adapted from Coakely (2008).

wars have been banned, countries frequently boycott for political reasons, and political protests are routinely a feature in host cities. Additionally, the results of sport contests have directly resulted in political conflict, for example where Gabon, Congo, Honduras, and El Salvador have gone to war over the outcome of soccer games. Finally, cold war politics weighed heavily on sporting contests between the USA and Russia, embodying contentions of the superiority of their political and economic systems. During the same period, the USA used table tennis to open relations with China.

Gender also links sport and war as masculine traits of physicality, power, and domination underlie both the good athlete and the good soldier. As sports are not simply the random interactional assertion of masculinity, but also structured expressions of it, gender provides a pathway that bridges the macro and micro perspectives of sport as politics.

SPORT AS ART

Athletes talk about a sense of effortless competency, a sense of play where training and skill unconsciously come together. This is referred to as, "being in the zone," where consciously learned skill melds with inner will. This creative action-rhythm is the very essence of the true athlete as artist.

A sporting contest is itself artistic expression (Young 1999). Our team reveals the multicultural mix of our community. While we still sit in hierarchical seating, we experience a union with one another, a manifest integrity of our community. We see our morality in the rules (e.g. fairness, earned accomplishment, etc). And with the final outcome, win or lose, we come to grips with being mortal. Social theory, particularly in the sociology of emotions, has much to contribute and gain from studying the creative, artistic, and emotional qualities of sport, and the meanings we find in it.

MORAL ASSUMPTIONS EMBEDDED IN SPORT

Sport both embodies and impresses particular assumptions about human nature and a moral order. In a cyclical fashion, sport both assumes competition as an innate human quality and in turn teaches that this is the case. Like much western social, political, and economic theory, implicit in sport is the ideological assumption of a human will to power. The extent to which this is innate rather than cultural, if it is at all, remains unclear. Many traditional societies often do not overtly reflect this will to power. Thus, one might claim that it is the structure of sports, and more broadly capitalist economic models, that produce competitive tendencies.

While emphasis on competition is still the pervasive ethos of sport, some youth organizations have increasingly and consciously resisted it. For example, many leagues provide participation trophies rather than distinguishing top teams and players. Coaches may be discouraged from emphasizing winning as a value, or even from showing too much enthusiasm for "successful" play. Social theory ought to be able to contribute to and gain from the study of youth development, attitudes, and mental health by comparing these different models of sport, which are polarized concerning the value of competition.

SEE ALSO: Alternative Sports; Globalization and Sport; Sport; Sports and culture

REFERENCES

Coakley, J. (2008) *Sports in Society: Issues and Controversies*. McGraw Hill, Boston, MA.

Strenk, A. (1979) What price victory? The world of international sports and politics. *Annals of the American Academy of Political and Social Science* 445: 128–40.

Young, J. (1999) Artwork and sportwork: Heideggerian reflections. *Journal of Aesthetics and Art Criticism* 57: 267–77.

JEFFREY MICHAEL CLAIR AND
JASON ADAM WASSERMAN

social type (Simmel)

Simmel's discussions of social types can be grouped into two categories: types defined on the basis of (1) their position in some interactional form, like the metropolitan or the stranger, or (2) their cultural orientations to the world, like the artist or the adventurer.

Simmel's sociology is concerned with the pure forms of interaction (such as urbanism), not with the specific contents of experience (in Berlin, Tokyo, or Chicago). Positions within these forms define social types. For example, in his famous discussion of "The Stranger" ("Exkurs über den Fremden," in Simmel 1908) Simmel argues that the Stranger is defined by a distinct position in spatial relations: simultaneous relations of nearness and distance, such as occur, for example, in the development of commerce when traders came from afar into unfamiliar groups. Strangers are close and far, insiders and outsiders, at once. Such positions are associated with certain general characteristics: strangers tend to become judges and emotional confidants and to be treated abstractly.

Simmel also defines some social types as individual personifications of certain cultural domains. For example, Simmel writes of "the artist" as typifying the orientation of the "world of art." All practical life involves some "seeing," where our visual field is constituted by selecting what is relevant to our practical needs. "The artist" emerges when seeing as such is taken up for itself and comes to creatively shape life in its own terms. Whereas non-artists see on the basis of all sorts of non-optical needs (e.g., looking for food), the artist's defining need is to determine the world purely in terms of how it can be seen (e.g., painting food). Articulating this sort of social type means describing in detail from the inside what it is like to inhabit a particular cultural world.

SEE ALSO: Schütz, Alfred; Simmel, Georg; Stranger, The

REFERENCE

Simmel, G. (1908) *Soziologie. Untersuchungen über die Formen der Vergesellschaftung*. Duncker & Humblot, Leipzig.

SUGGESTED READING

Levine, D. N. (ed.) (1971) *On Individuality and Social Forms: Selected Writings of Georg Simmel*. University of Chicago Press, Chicago, IL.

DANIEL SILVER

social work: history and institutions

Since the ideas of the Enlightenment and human rights as well as the negative social consequences of industrialization have given rise to a public discussion on the "social question," many different social activities could be noted.

The first international welfare conference as such took place in Paris in 1856, called "Congrès internationale de Bienfaisance." Nearly 300 participants from 20 countries came to the conclusion that there should be regular meetings in the future to create common standards of poor relief and charity. In the following proceedings until the end of the association in 1863, the discussion was dominated by questions about social insurance and social security as well as the principles of self help.

But national as well as international political conflicts hindered the development of international social welfare over several years. Not long before 1889, a new international association could be founded: The "Congrès d'Assistance publique et privée," which turned out to be the most important precursor of the International Council of Social Welfare (ICSW).

The last conference of the "Congrès" (held in Copenhagen in 1910) discussed the challenges of a modern welfare system based on three main principles: a balance between social insurance and social work, coordination of state and private welfare structures, and vocational training.

Although World War I furthered these challenges of welfare modernization, because all countries had to cope with an enormous amount of welfare needs, the international cooperation was severely disrupted again – until 1928. In this period the American welfare organizations became a larger influence in the field of social work. Therefore, the main starting signal for the "great" International Conference of Social Welfare (held in Paris in 1928), came from the USA. Besides these incentives, it was the merit of the International League of the Red Cross, that the by then largest welfare conference could take place.

The most important result of the conference was the foundation of the International Council of Social Welfare (ICSW) as a world wide platform for professional development and exchange.

The next conference of the ICSW was held in Frankfurt in 1932, focusing on "The Consequences of Unemployment for the Family," and the third conference on "Social Work and the Community" took place in London, in 1936. The most significant characteristic of this last pre-war meeting was the attempt of the fascist countries like Germany and Italy to functionalize the term "Community" for their idea of the "Volk."

The plans for next conferences were foiled by World War II – and it was not until August 1946 that the former presidents of the ICSW tried to reconstruct the organization. They had to take into account however, that a couple of social organizations had been established during the war, in order to give help to refugees and other needy persons: The "United Nations Relief and Rehabilitation Administration" (UNRRA), the "International Relief Organization" (IRO), the UNICEF and the WHO, all of them being – in contrast to the ICSW – well equipped with financial means and an enormous amount of helpers.

At the proceedings of the ICSW in Atlantic City (1948) two items turned out to be of greatest importance for the future: Firstly, it became obvious that "international" meant more than "Europe" and the "United States." The second item was related to the already mentioned increase of international social organizations and required an efficient way of labor division among them: The ICSW had to exclude the political mandate for social work (held by the UN), the representation of the profession (held by the International Association of Social Workers), and all items of vocational training (covered by the International Association of Schools of Social Work). Therefore the ICSW defined itself in relation to the multitude of international organizations in the field of welfare as a partner for theoretical and methodical discourses and as a coordinator for common incentives.

SEE ALSO: Human Rights; Social Problems, Politics of; Social Work: Theory and Methods

SUGGESTED READINGS

Friedlaender, W. A. (1975) *International Social Welfare*. Prentice Hall, Englewood Cliffs, NJ.

Lorenz, W. (1994) *Social Work in a Changing Europe*. Routledge, London.

Macdonald, J. (1975) *The International Council of Social Welfare: Yesterday, Today and Tomorrow*. International Council of Social Welfare, New York.

Première Conference international du Service Social (1928) July 3–13, Paris.

SABINE HERING

social work: theory and methods

Theory construction in social work as a discipline and profession grows out of (1) a theory of the individual and society and the interaction between them; (2) policy/action guidelines for changing problematic situations; and (3) clients, professionals, social services, social movements, etc. committed to carry this change through with the help of specific science-based methods.

An internationally consensual definition of social work is as follows: "The social work profession promotes social change, problem solving in human relationships and the empowerment and liberation of people to enhance well-being. Utilizing theories of human behavior and social systems, social work intervenes at the points where people interact with their environments. Principles of human rights and social justice are fundamental to social work" (supplement, *International Journal of Social Work*, 2007, p. 5).

After the first period of theory-building, *psychodynamic concepts* became the base for many practice concepts, first drawing from *psychoanalytic theory*. Notions of a sustaining relationship and techniques to reduce anxiety, low self-esteem, and lack of confidence were developed, adding procedures to work with the social environment. The role of the social worker is an interpreter of feelings, promoter of insights, helping to develop a realistic, anxiety-free, perspective of his or her situation and adapting to it.

- *Behavioral theories* derive from the work of experimental behavioral psychologists which criticized the untestable conceptions of psychoanalytic theory. Clients are coping with frustration and aggression in different role settings. The main goal is adequate role behavior as parent, pupil, employee etc., by techniques of classical conditioning and social learning.
- *Cognitive theories* work on the assumption that people construct their own versions of reality and problems. There can be thus conflicts between self-conceptions, perceiving self through others, and intentional self. The task is to confront the client with inconsistencies and to support strategies of rational problem solving, sustained by a diary and tasks (i.e. homework).
- *Task-centered social work* seeks to replace psychodynamic social work based on a "time-consuming" supportive relationship with a "short-term therapy" that has a clear time limit and starts with a contract. Central is what the client presents or accepts as problems and what he or she wants to change.

Theories and methods of interaction or networks between individuals are mostly focused on communication patterns, i.e. in relation to stigmatizing and scapegoating, within "people-processing organizations."

An approach in family treatment is *transaction analysis*, focusing on the ego states of persons (as child, parent, adult) interacting with those in other persons. When transactions involve different ego states, problems and misunderstandings arise. The social worker has to change communication patterns which make the other feel bad, incompetent, powerless, i.e. by reframing, family sculpting, role-playing, videotaping, or homework.

Social work with *groups* bases its interventions on the structure and dynamics of groups. The role of the social worker can be task oriented, supportive/therapeutic, or community-action oriented. He or she might construct supportive networks or organizations in a community, e.g. for the development of new jobs for minority members who have no chance of getting a job in the mainstream economy.

From the 1960s to the 1980s, neo-Marxist "radical social work" developed. It was accompanied by a radical critique of the social welfare system being a servant of the ruling, capitalist class. The general hypothesis was that service users would act rationally in their own interests once they understood that the true origins of their problems lay in exploitative and oppressive capitalistic structures. "Structural theory" extended the approach to all forms of overlapping and mutually reinforcing injustices in relation to class, gender, race, disability, sexual orientation, and religious and ethnic minority status. The role of social work was seen as: (1) transforming private troubles into public issues and (2) introducing human rights/social justice in the code of ethics and practice and promoting social change.

The *Ecosystems perspective* of Germain/Gitterman (1996) focuses on the poor fit of transactions between individuals and social systems. The main principles are partnership based on reciprocity, assessment of life stressors in passing from one system to another (family to school, school to work), and discussing with the client an "ecomap" as a pictorial representation of micro, meso, and macro systems in concentric circles and their resources. The goals are reinclusion or the management of the excluded.

The *systemic paradigm* of social work sees systems theory as a chance for a unifying (meta)theoretical, transdisciplinary foundation of social work. The main focus is on understanding the structure and dynamics/transactions of and between biological, psychic, and social/cultural systems. Social work practitioners face individuals with needs, cognitions, wants, hopes, plans, learning and behavioral capacities who are involved in destructive interactions, discriminating and oppressive sociocultural systems, from the family to world society. Social work works with science-based methods for the well-being of individuals, families etc. and the social reform/change of social systems, relying on human rights, especially social justice, as regulative ideas.

SEE ALSO: Social Problems, Politics of; Social Work: History and Institutions

REFERENCE

Germain, C. & Gitterman, A. (1996) *The Life Model of Social Work Practice: Advances in Theory and Practice*, 2nd edn. Columbia University Press, New York.

SUGGESTED READING

Staub-Bernasconi, S. (1991) Social action, empowerment, and social work: an integrative theoretical frame of reference for social work. *Journal of Community and Clinical Practice* 14 (3/4): 35–51.

SILVIA STAUB-BERNASCONI

social worlds

The term social world is used in two main ways. First as in a generic reference to the immediate milieu of the focus of research – the specific situation or social context (e.g., the social world of antique collectors, professional baseball, or surfing). Subcultures are similar, but (sub)cultural studies generally focus on the subculture itself (members, what they do, how and why, etc.), such as "Deadhead" or "Trekkie" fandoms. In contrast, the generic use of social world usually points outward from the individuals or collectivities being studied to their salient contexts to situate them in sociocultural space and time.

Second, in explicit social worlds/arenas theory in symbolic interactionism, a number of elaborating concepts form a theoretical/analytical framework useful in empirical research, developed by sociologists Anselm Strauss, Howard Becker, Tamotsu Shibutani, and Rue Bucher. Social worlds (e.g., a recreation group, an occupation, a theoretical tradition) generate shared perspectives that form the basis for collective action. Individual and collective identities are constituted through commitments to and active participation in social worlds. Social worlds are *universes of discourse* – shared ways of making meaning. For Strauss, each social world has at least one primary activity, particular sites, and a technology for carrying out its projects. People typically participate in multiple social worlds simultaneously. Becker asserted that *entrepreneurs*, deeply committed and active individuals, cluster around the core of the world and mobilize those around them. Shibutani viewed social worlds as identity and meaning-making segments in mass society.

Complex social worlds characteristically have *segments* or subworlds that shift as commitments realign, Bucher noted. Two or more worlds may intersect to form a new world, or one may segment into two or more. Larger *arenas* are constituted of multiple social worlds focused on a particular issue and prepared to act in some way, usually in struggles for power and legitimacy. In arenas, Strauss argued, various issues are debated, negotiated, fought out, and manipulated by representatives of participating worlds and subworlds.

Methodologically, to understand a particular social world, one must understand all the arenas in which that world participates and the other worlds in those arenas and their related discourses. All are mutually influential – co-constitutive of the focal world. Social worlds and arenas become the units of analysis in studies of collective action and discourse. The *boundaries* of social worlds may cross-cut or be more or less contiguous with those of formal organizations. Society as a whole, then, can be conceptualized as consisting of layered mosaics of social worlds, arenas, and their discourses.

Social worlds/arenas theory is a conflict theory. There typically exist intra-world differences as well as more expected inter-world differences of perspective and commitment. For Strauss, *negotiations* – persuasion, coercion, bartering, educating, discursively and otherwise repositioning, etc. – are routine strategies to address conflicts. Clarke (2005) asserts that there can also be *implicated actors* in a social world, actors silenced or only discursively present, constructed by others for their own purposes. Star and Griesemer developed the concept of *boundary objects* for things that exist at junctures where varied social worlds meet in an arena of mutual concern (e.g., treaties among countries, software programs used in different settings, courses that are part of different majors). The boundary object is "translated" to address the specific needs or demands of the different worlds involved.

The social worlds/arenas framework is the conceptual infrastructure of a new mode of grounded theory for qualitative research–situational analysis (Clarke 2005). Making maps of social worlds and their arenas is part of the data analysis, providing portraits of collective action at the meso level. The key analytic power of social worlds/arenas theory is the elasticity of the various concepts to analyze at multiple levels of complexity.

SEE ALSO: Mesostructure; Networks; Reference Groups; Symbolic Interaction

REFERENCE

Clarke, A. E. (2005) *Situational Analysis: Grounded Theory After the Postmodern Turn*. Sage, Thousand Oaks, CA.

SUGGESTED READING

Strauss, A. L. (1993) *Continual Permutation of Action*. Aldine de Gruyter, New York.

ADELE E. CLARKE

socialism

Socialism refers to those practices and doctrines based on, and emphasizing the benefits of, collective property, social equality, human cooperation and communal forms of economic and political association. Yet, beyond these shared features, socialism as both practice and doctrine is characterized by tremendous diversity. This is evident in the historical development of socialism.

First used in English in the 1820s and French and German in the 1830s, the term "socialism" had been preceded by movements whose aims and practices resonated with what we now recognize as socialist values. These included early Christian-inspired movement such as the Levelers and the Diggers in seventeenth-century England, and the Anabaptists in sixteenth- and seventeenth-century Central Europe. It was not until after the French and Industrial Revolutions, however, that socialist doctrines began to be more systematically elaborated. Comte de Saint-Simon (1760–1825), Francios-Charles Fourier (1772–1837), and Robert Owen (1771–1858), for example, all penned treatises that expressed an antipathy towards individualism and, conversely, a celebratory attitude towards community, cooperation and social solidarity.

Such ideas gained a broader hearing in Europe in the 1830s and 1840s, largely in response to accelerated industrialization and urbanization, and the problems that they brought in their wake. It was out of this milieu of social and political ferment that the ideas of Karl Marx and his collaborator Frederick Engels began to develop. While not beginning their intellectual careers as socialists, their early radical democratic sensibilities had given way to a more explicitly socialist position by the mid-1840s. This so-called "scientific socialism" was underpinned by a distinctive view of history and of capitalism, and would be elaborated and refined over the coming three decades. In this view, history involves the progressive unfolding of distinctive stages, driven by class struggle, with each stage being defined by a dominant set of production relations. With the advent of capitalism, and its immanent drive to improve labor productivity through technological innovation and intensified exploitation of the modern proletariat, the material and political preconditions for socialism were laid.

Although Marx never outlined any blueprints for a socialist society, there are three key sources that illuminate his views on the socialist future and the transition from capitalism to socialism. First, *The Class Struggles in France, 1848–1850*, argue that the transition to socialism would require a new transitionary political form that he labelled as the "dictatorship of the proletariat." Second, the possible content of this new state form was discussed in Marx's responses to the Paris Commune of 1871. In particular, Marx was impressed by the way in which the Commune sought to overcome the capitalist division between economic and political life. This was principally manifested in the election of workers to local and national delegations of workers' deputies, which combined executive, legislative, and judicial functions, with worker representatives recallable at short notice. Finally, in his *Critique of the Gotha Programme*, Marx makes a distinction between a first and second stage of communism, which would later be recognized as one between socialism (first stage – where a state is still necessary) and communism (second state – where the state has withered away).

After Marx's death in 1883, a key debate within the European socialist movement revolved around the question of reform or revolution. In the revisionist controversy within German Social Democracy, Eduard Berstein claimed that much Marxist orthodoxy had been invalidated by contemporary developments within capitalism. These included the increased dispersal of ownership, improved conditions for workers, and the growing parliamentary influence of organized labor. Defenders of revolutionary orthodoxy responded that the instrument of workers' oppression, the capitalist state, could not be the instrument of their liberation, and that the basic structure of capitalist exploitation remained even if workers' conditions were ameliorated by social reform. Moreover, if capitalist private property and profit were truly threatened, the coercive nature of the capitalist state would reveal itself. Therefore, a revolutionary path to socialism was indispensable.

In the twentieth century, this same divide reappeared in several guises. The Bolshevik revolution in Russia in 1917 became a new revolutionary orthodoxy, and in the eyes of many, supporters and antagonists alike, became synonymous with socialism. This would severely discredit the very idea of socialism, especially once Stalinism had been consolidated in the Soviet Union. Democratic socialists in the west rejected this model, and instead advocated a reformist, market socialism, which was at least partly embodied in the development of the modern welfare state. The socialist credentials of such states were challenged, however. Socialist feminists, for example, pointed to the gendered assumptions on which many welfare policies were based, and to the very different implications of welfare state policies for working class and middle class women.

Since the collapse of "already existing socialism," socialists have been on the defensive. But it would be wrong to write off socialism as doctrine or practice. Many of the same problems that inspired socialist ideas in the first place remain with us, and these ideas continue to contribute to our understanding of the world as it is and as it could be.

SEE ALSO: Capitalism; Communism; Global Politics; Marx, Karl; Property, Private

SUGGESTED READINGS

Castro, F. (1972) *Revolutionary Struggle, 1947–1958*. MIT Press, Cambridge, MA.

Lenin, V. I. (1932) *State and Revolution*. International Press, New York.

Lipset, S. M. & Marks, G. (1999) *It Didn't Happen Here: Why Socialism Failed in the United States*. Norton, New York.

Marx, K. (1998) *The Communist Manifesto*. Verso, London and New York.

LLOYD COX

socialist feminism

Socialist feminism, which draws on aspects of both Marxist feminism and radical feminism, emerged in the 1970s as a possible solution to the limitations of existing feminist theory. Marxist feminism, drawing on the work of Marx and Engels, cites capitalism as the cause of women's oppression. The oppression of women is a byproduct of the economically determined oppression experienced by the working class. The liberation of women is dependent upon the abolition of capitalism and the liberation of the working classes. In contrast, radical feminism argues that women are oppressed through a system of patriarchy in which men systematically oppress women. Gender oppression precedes all other forms of oppression, for example class and economic oppression. Marxist feminism has been criticized for its inability to explain women's oppression outside of the logic of capitalism, and radical feminism for producing a universalistic, biologically based account of women's oppression, which pays insufficient attention to patterned differences between women. Socialist feminism attempts to overcome these problems through the production of historically situated accounts of women's oppression that focus on both capitalism and patriarchy. Attending to both the public and private areas of women's lives, Socialist Feminism makes links between the personal and the structural. There are different strands of Socialist Feminist thought.

In Mitchell's (1975) psychoanalytic model, capitalism – the economic system – is allocated to the material level; patriarchy – the rule of law – is allocated to the ideological level and assumed to operate at an unconscious level. While Eisenstein (1984) retains Mitchell's conceptualization of capitalism, she reassigns patriarchy to the conscious cultural level and dismisses any distinction between the two, leading to the term "capitalist patriarchy." In contrast, Hartmann (1979) produces a materialist understanding of patriarchy and capitalism as two distinct but interactive systems, which center on men's exploitation of women's labor. Challenging Eisenstein's single-system theory, Hartmann states that patriarchy predates capitalism and exists beyond its boundaries; thus, it is inappropriate to regard them in terms of a single system.

The allocation of patriarchy to either the material, cultural, or ideological level does not permit an analysis of the pervasive nature of patriarchal structures across all three levels. Simultaneously, it assumes that all social structures can be reduced to the workings of either capitalism or patriarchy, whilst assuming there is a symbiotic relationship between the two. A focus on paid work dismisses radical feminist concerns with sexuality and violence.

Walby's (1990) dual-systems approach attempts to overcome these problems through a historically and socially defined understanding of patriarchy as a system of six interrelated structures, which in contemporary society are in articulation with capitalism and racism. The six interrelated structures are paid work, household production, culture, sexuality, violence and the state. This model enables Walby to chart the dynamic nature of patriarchy over the last 150 years, including the move from a private to a public form of patriarchy.

SEE ALSO: Liberal Feminism; Patriarchy; Radical Feminism; Socialism

REFERENCES

Eisenstein, H. (1984) *Contemporary Feminist Thought.* Allen & Unwin, London.

Hartmann, H. I. (1979) Capitalism, patriarchy, and job segregation by sex. In: Eisenstein, Z. R. (ed.), *Capitalist Patriarchy*. Monthly Review Press, New York.

Mitchell, J. (1975) *Psychoanalysis and Feminism*. Penguin, Harmondsworth.

Walby, S. (1990) *Theorizing Patriarchy*. Blackwell, Oxford.

ANN CRONIN

socialist medicine

The term socialist medicine applies to a health care delivery system designed to provide preventive, diagnostic, clinical, rehabilitative, educational, and custodial services to a designated population free of charge at the time of the service. The prototype of socialist medicine is also known as Soviet socialized medicine.

At a time when health care is being recognized as a basic human right, Soviet socialist medicine has often been cited as a model for the universal provision of health care. The nature and structure of Soviet socialist medicine reflected the ideological and political orientation of the Soviet regime. There were two major ideas underlying the health care system of the former Soviet Union. One was that illness and premature mortality were primarily the product of a flawed system (capitalism) and its exploitation of the working class. This exploitation exposed workers to a series of pathogenic elements that affected their health and well-being: poor pay, child labor, long working hours, miserable housing conditions, inadequate nutrition, and a noxious social environment (Engels 1958: *The Condition of the Working Class in England*). Thus, capitalism was indicted as the major etiological factor in illness and early death. Only socialism (and eventually communism) would eliminate the sources of most socially caused ill health.

The second idea was that the provision of health care under capitalism meant that workers were, in most instances, deprived of access to such care because they could not afford it. The removal of that payment by the patient meant the elimination of the barrier to health care. Under socialist medicine, it was society (i.e., the polity) that would henceforth shoulder the responsibility for the provision of health services to the entire population. The Soviet Union was the first country in the world to promise universal and free health services as a constitutional right (Sigerist 1937: *Socialized Medicine in the Soviet Union*; 1947: *Medicine and Health in the Soviet Union*). This would also permit physicians to stop being engaged in a "commercial" transaction and enable them to treat patients without being fettered with questions of money. By the same token, hospital and other health institutions would also offer free services at the expense of the state. The promise of gratuitous and universal (though not necessarily equal) medical care to the entire nation was one of the few redeeming factors of an otherwise bleak totalitarian regime. It was often held as an example to emulate worldwide, and served as important propaganda for use at home and abroad.

SEE ALSO: Health Care Delivery Systems; Socialized Medicine

SUGGESTED READING

Field, M. G. (1967) *Soviet Socialized Medicine: An Introduction*. Free Press, New York.

MARK G. FIELD

socialization

Socialization is a concept embracing the ways people acquire the competencies required for participation in society. At the societal level, socialization helps explain how large numbers of people come to cooperate and adapt to the demands of social life. At the organizational level, it summarizes how newcomers to groups and organizations move from outsiders to participating members. At the personal level, it refers to the development of the mental, emotional, and behavioral abilities of individuals.

Sociology offers three broad orientations to socialization – functional, interactional, and critical. Functionalists view socialization as a process of role learning by which people adopt prescribed orientations to life which limit the ends to which they aspire and the means they use to achieve them. From this perspective, socialization is the imprinting of cultural patterns on personalities and a major means of integrating people into the patterns that constitute society's institutions. This is a deep process leading people to treat external values and norms as definitive of their identity.

Functionalism has been criticized for portraying people as passive recipients of social influence. The interactionist perspective leans in the opposite direction by emphasizing the individual's active role in socialization. For interactionists, the crux of socialization is the formation of self-concepts in the context of social relationships. Selves emerge and develop as people mutually construct versions of reality through communicative processes based on shared symbols. By learning how to communicate with symbols, individuals come to incorporate the responses of others into their actions and selves.

Interactionism and functionalism have been criticized for discounting power and inequality in social life. The various critical orientations to socialization, such as Marxism and Feminist Theory, are unified by deep concerns with power in society and the reproduction of inequalities. Proponents of critical perspectives agree that socialization is a primary mechanism of social control. Pierre Bourdieu's critical view of socialization has gained prominence in contemporary sociology. For Bourdieu, socialization is the acquisition of "habitus," which points to processes by which people who share similar positions in society inculcate in each other deeply ingrained patterns of subjective adjustments to external social conditions.

Sociological research on socialization is organized around substantive domains. Much of this research frames socialization as a mediating process between self, social organization, and broader social conditions. Examples of these domains include the family, schools, and the media.

Families are often framed as principal agents of socialization. Family socialization has often been conceptualized as children learning their parents' beliefs, values, worldviews, and behaviors. Some researchers argue that families are seedbeds of a child's basic orientations to society, and that parental attitudes serve as predictors of children's attitudes throughout life. Researchers suggest that children learn to conceptualize themselves in gendered, religious, political, racial and class terms in and through routine interactions within family life.

Studies of socialization in schools tend to highlight how socialization extends beyond the official academic curriculum. Schools provide students with early life encounters with institutional evaluations of their competencies as people, sometimes with significant effects on their self-conceptions. A prominent theme here is that teachers' expectations of students exert powerful influences on the actual gains they make. Schools also use categories that affect the way teachers treat students and how students treat each other. Such labels not only inform the self-concepts of children, they also help students draw distinctions between themselves along various lines, including race, class and gender.

People acquire quite a bit of knowledge of the social world from mass media. Some theorists argue that the information disseminated by media mutes distinctions between fact and fiction in daily life. People's relationship to "reality" is found to be altered by the mediating images of television, cinema, Internet, and print media. A prominent theme suggests that consumption of television, magazines, and music reinforce unrealistic, negative, or stereotypical images of gender, sexuality, race and ethnicity.

Two debates about the implications of societal change for socialization beg for more attention from sociologists. First, sociologists recognize how emerging technologies are reshaping many aspects of how people relate to each other, but more research is needed on the effects of new media and computer technologies on child socialization. Second, although sociologists pay considerable attention to societal changes in family formations, they have conducted comparatively few studies of the long-range implications of social changes in families for personal development.

SEE ALSO: Socialization, Agents of; Socialization, Adult; Socialization, Primary

SUGGESTED READINGS

Gecas, V. (1992) *Contexts of Socialization.* In: Rosenberg, M. and Turner, R. (eds.), *Social Psychology: Sociological Perspectives.* Transaction Publishers, New Brunswick

Wentworth, W. (1980) *Context and Understanding: An Inquiry into Socialization Theory.* Elsevier, Oxford

SAL ZERILLI

socialization, adult

Socialization refers to the process by which people learn and internalize the attitudes, values, beliefs, and norms of our culture and develop a sense of self. The concept of socialization is among the most important in sociology, because it attempts to illustrate and explain the tremendous impact living in society has on shaping the individual. The individual becomes a human being through socialization, and what it means to be an individual evolves over the life course.

Early sociological and psychological theories of socialization, largely reflecting cultural beliefs about development in the early twentieth century, focused on self and moral development up to what we today know as adolescence. Mead's (1934) theory of the self, for example, posited three stages: infancy, play, and game stages. The final game stage occurs during adolescence when the individual is able to learn and respond to the community's norms and standards and act accordingly in everyday life. Mead assumed that the socialized self acquired through adolescence generally remains stable throughout the remaining life span.

Symbolic interactionist thinkers following Mead have attempted to refine his theory to account for the apparent changes in the adult self-concept present in modern society. Shibutani (1961) adapted Merton and Kitt's (1950) structural notion of *reference group* to interactionist thinking to illustrate how adults can be expected to be members of various groups which in turn serve as audiences to the self. In effect, the adult learns to be different selves to accommodate the multiple complex situations that mark modern life.

ADULT SOCIALIZATION IN EVERYDAY LIFE

Sociologists of everyday life contend that the process of becoming an adult in our society is rich, ongoing, and worthy of detailed ethnographic analysis. Studies of adult socialization are no longer limited to traditional elderly settings. Kotarba (2006), for example, explores the many ways baby boomers continue to use rock 'n' roll music and culture as resources for refining their sense of self as they occupy the role of parents, lovers, and others. They shape and modify the musical values they acquired during adolescence to fit the needs of later adulthood, so that they may continue to attend rock 'n' roll music concerts but may prefer comfortable seating in the shade near the stage as opposed to more adventurous lawn seating.

SEE ALSO: Socialization; Socialization, Agents of; Socialization, Gender

REFERENCES

Kotarba, J. A. (2011) *Baby Boomer Rock 'n' Roll Fans and the Becoming of Self.* Ashgate, Burlington, VT.

Mead, G. H. (1934) *Mind, Self and Society.* University of Chicago Press, Chicago, IL.

Merton, R. K. & Kitt, A. (1950) Contributions to the theory of reference group behavior. In: Merton, R. K. & Lazarsfeld, P. F. (eds.), *Studies in the Scope and Method of "The American Soldier."* Free Press, Glencoe, IL.

Shibutani, T. (ed.) (1961), *Society and Personality.* Prentice Hall, Englewood Cliffs, NJ.

JOSEPH A. KOTARBA

socialization, agents of

Socialization is the process of social interaction through which people acquire personality and learn the ways of their society. It is an essential link between the individual and society. To aid in this process, we have agents of socialization (significant individuals, groups, or institutions in which learning takes place). These include:

- *The family*: Family is by far the most significant agent of socialization. It is within the family that the first socializing occurs. Families teach the child the language of their group, acceptable gender roles, and important values.
- *Schools*: For children in modern industrial societies, school is an important, formal, agent of socialization. Besides teaching the basics, there is often a "hidden curriculum" as well, things like following rules, being punctual, and not being absent unless you have a legitimate excuse.
- *Peers*: these are friendship groups of roughly equivalent age and interests, who are social equals. They are particularly important for teens and young adults; peers can ease the transition to adulthood. They tend to be more egalitarian than some of the other agents and influence a person's attitudes and behavior.
- *Mass media and technology*: in modern societies, these are important agents of socialization. Most people believe that people's attitudes and values are affected by what they see and hear in the media. A positive influence is the fact that televisions and commercials can introduce young people to unfamiliar ideas, lifestyles, and cultures.
- *Public opinion*: what people think about controversial issues is important, but not everyone's views are equally influential. Better educated, wealthier, and well-connected people's views often carry more clout. This agent influences appropriate gender roles, notions of right and wrong, and beliefs about controversial topics such as abortion or gay marriages.
- *Religion*: religion is important and relevant for some people, but in the modern world, religion is losing some of its power and influence. For those that follow religious tenets, the norms influence people's values, the desired size of families, the likelihood of divorce, rates of delinquency, and behaviors considered appropriate (or not).
- *Workplace*: the workplace teaches us appropriate values, work ethic (or lack of it), and appropriate attire. In modern societies, full-time employment confirms adult status and awards us a personal identity. In a culture that has few rites of passage, that is important.
- *The state*: increasingly agencies like nursing homes, mental health clinics, and insurance companies have taken over functions previously filled by families. The state runs many of these institutions or licenses and regulates them. In a sense, the state has created new rites of passage, such as the age a person can legally drive, purchase and consume tobacco and alcohol, marry without parental consent, or officially retire.
- *Total institutions*: these are an important agent of resocialization for some; they are places where residents are confined for a set period of time and kept under the influence of a hierarchy of officials. Every aspect of life is controlled, from the time you get up until you go to bed. The goal of a total institution is to resocialize you, to totally change you and make you into something new (and presumably "better").

SEE ALSO: Mass Media and Socialization; Socialization; Socialization, Gender; Socialization, Primary; Total Institutions

SUGGESTED READING

Giddens, A. & Duneier, M. (2000) *Introduction to Sociology*, 3rd edn. W. W. Norton, New York, pp. 76–84, 186–91, 370–2.

DELORES F. WUNDER

socialization, gender

As children grow up they develop a sense of who they are, how they should relate to others, and the role they play in a larger society. The lessons children learn and the processes through which cultural norms are passed from one generation to the next is known as socialization. The focus on gender socialization highlights that there are roles, or cultural expectations and norms, which are associated with each sex category ("male" or "female"). Sociologists make distinctions between sex and gender. While sex is based on biological categories, gender is the result of cultural processes that construct different social roles for men and women. Gender socialization, then, is the process through which boys and girls learn sex appropriate behavior, dress, personality characteristics, and demeanor.

While gender socialization is lifelong, many sociological theories focus on early childhood socialization. Four such perspectives are the psychoanalytical, cognitive development, social learning, and social interaction perspectives.

The most famous psychoanalytical explanation of gender socialization is Sigmund Freud's identification theory. Freud argued that children pass through a series of stages in their personality development. During the first two stages (the oral and anal stages), boys and girls have similar behavior and experiences. Around age four, however, boys and girls become aware of their own genitals and that members of the opposite sex have different genitalia. It is during this phallic stage that children begin to identify and model their behavior after their same-sex parent, thus learning gender appropriate behavior, although this process differs for boys and girls.

While Freud's theory has been largely discredited, sociologists have drawn on it to extend psychoanalytical explanations of gender socialization. Nancy Chodorow (1978) drew on Marxist theory and psychoanalytic object-relations theory to argue that gender socialization processes are key for the reproduction of the capitalist economy. She argued that identification is more difficult for boys than for girls because boys need to psychologically separate themselves from their mothers and model their fathers, who are largely absent from the home as a result of the breadwinner-homemaker division of labor. This results in boys being much more emotionally detached than girls, who do not experience this psychological separation.

The second perspective points to cognitive development as a way to explain gender socialization, arguing that socialization occurs as children try to find patterns in the social and physical world. From this perspective, children's earliest developmental task is to make sense of a seemingly chaotic world. As they observe and interact with their environment, they develop schema, or organizing categories. Because children rely on simple cues to understand the world and because there are clear differences in how women and men look and act, biological sex provides a useful schema.

The social learning perspective posits that gender socialization is learned. This theory draws on the psychological concept of behaviorism to argue that children learn gender by being rewarded for gender appropriate behavior and punished for gender inappropriate behavior.

The social interaction perspective offers a fourth approach to gender socialization. This perspective has deep sociological roots. In 1902, sociologist Charles Cooley argued that individuals develop a sense of self by imagining how they appear to others, interpreting others' reactions to their actions, and developing a self-concept based on these interpretations. Thus, a person's sense of self, which he called "the looking-glass self," is an ongoing process embedded in social interaction. From this perspective, interaction forms the basis of gender socialization.

Social institutions are crucial to gender socialization. Parent–child interactions do not occur in isolation, but are embedded in the social institution of the family. Other social institutions important to gender socialization in childhood are school, sports, and mass media.

In sum, sociologists offered a variety of theories to explain gender socialization. The most fruitful to date has been the social interaction perspective because it recognizes that gender is an ongoing process and that gender roles are produced and reproduced in social institutions. A great deal of theoretical and empirical work remains to be done, however. Much of the scholarship on gender socialization has examined middle-class, white heterosexuals. Thus, sociologists need to examine how their theories and data apply across class, race, ethnic, and sexual boundaries.

SEE ALSO: Gender Ideology and Gender Role Ideology; Sex and Gender; Socialization, Primary

REFERENCE

Chodorow, N. (1978) *The Reproduction of Mothering.* University of California Press, Berkeley, CA.

SUGGESTED READINGS

Thorne, B. (1993) *Gender Play: Girls and Boys in School.* Rutgers University Press, New Brunswick, NJ.
West, C. & Zimmerman, D. (1987) Doing gender. *Gender & Society* 1: 121–51.

DEANA A. ROHLINGER

socialization, primary

Socialization is the process by which humans learn the ways of being and doing considered to be appropriate and expected in their social environments. Primary socialization occurs when the individual is a newly born member of society experiencing this process for the first time. Primary socialization has the social psychological characteristic of primacy, meaning that its position as first in the acquisition of social knowledge renders it a filter and a foundation for the subsequent information internalized by the fledgling social being. Primacy also makes early socialization remarkably resilient, in that it is much more difficult to change primary habits and beliefs than those learned later in the life course.

Primary socialization is an initial set of significant symbols by which the individual interprets the perceived social world, formulates a conception of personal identity or identities, and through which he or she communicates understanding and desire with others. Through the symbolic structure of language, coupled with nonverbal communication and other cultural cues, the individual negotiates an understanding of the agreed-upon realities of social settings with significant others in their environment.

An early social philosophy of childhood portrayed the newborn social participant as a *tabula rasa*, or a blank slate upon which society then inscribed an identity. Later theorists, however, questioned the passivity of this model of child socialization. George Herbert Mead (1934) drew upon the "looking-glass self" model formulated by Charles Horton Cooley (1902). Unlike Cooley, however, Mead located the self as more than a passive reflection of social observation and response. Mead's novice social being was an active participant and negotiator in the socialization process, and his conceptualization of this agency has influenced subsequent theorizing on the subject.

There may be biological preconditions for primary socialization to be effective. Although any stage theory should be treated with caution, Piaget's (1954: *The Language of Thought and Child*) schema indicates that a child may not be capable of socialization beyond a certain point if physical development is inadequate. However, children also require sociability in order to thrive emotionally, mentally, and physically. Kingsley Davis (1947: "Final note on a case of extreme isolation") and others who studied children raised in isolation provide evidence of the essentiality of interaction with human others for the full development and ongoing physical wellbeing of the child.

Complex learning processes that may occur during primary socialization include operant conditioning to environmental or social contingencies, observational learning (imitation), and internalization of social norms and values. The content of primary socialization is likely to include language and other forms of communication, identities and role-taking, negotiation and meaning construction, and cultural routines.

Society exists before the individual arrives, and primary socialization allows new members to be integrated into existing social arrangements. This process also enables the perpetuation of culture via intergenerational transmission. In primary socialization, the earliest agents of socialization are crucial to the fundamental construction of new social beings. Changes in the composition of families in contemporary society, however, such as single parent households, grandparents parenting, and day care for working families, may create changes in the sources and character of primary socialization.

SEE ALSO: Looking-Glass Self; Socialization, Adult; Socialization, Agents of

REFERENCES

Cooley, C. H. (1902) *Human Nature and the Social Order*. Scribner, New York.

Mead, G. H. (1934). *Mind, Self, and Society*. University of Chicago Press, Chicago, IL.

LESLIE WASSON

socialized medicine

Socialized medicine is a system of health care delivery in which care is provided as a state-supported service. The term was introduced in 1954 by an American academic – Almont Lindsay – on a study visit to the United Kingdom. On his return to the USA, he published a book called *Socialized Medicine in England and Wales* (Lindsay 1962), describing the history, organization, and structure of the National Health Service (NHS). However, the term "socialized medicine" is one that tends to be used by "observers" (particularly North American observers) of the UK health service and it is less commonly heard within the UK itself (Webster 2002: 1). This may be because the British NHS is considered by many analysts to be a unique example of socialized medicine. Indeed, it is often described as "a socialist island in a capitalist sea." In this respect it forms part of a welfare system which rests on collective provision, social justice, social equality, and democracy in order to mitigate the adverse effects of capitalism. The fundamental principles of the NHS are therefore: that it should be publicly funded (predominantly by taxation); health care should be universal and be provided on the basis of health "need" rather than the ability to pay; and services should be comprehensive in that they should include preventive health services as well as treatment for those who are ill.

SEE ALSO: Health Care Delivery Systems; Health and Medicine; Socialist Medicine

REFERENCE

Webster, C. (2002) *The National Health Service: A Political History*. Oxford University Press, Oxford.

SARAH NETTLETON

society

The idea of society as a generalized term for social relations appeared, like sociology, during the transition to modernity. Implicit concepts of the social can be identified much earlier, for example in Platonic and Aristotelian philosophy, but premodern philosophies did not generally differentiate "society" from the political organization of the state. The use of the adjective "social" as "pertaining to society as a natural condition of human life" derives from Locke (1695). With the decline of feudalism the idea of the state as the property of the sovereign gave way to the principle of impersonal governance bound by juridical rules, while the state differentiated into administrative, judicial, and representative functions. By the eighteenth century theorists such as Adam Ferguson depicted a "civil society" associated with the new commercial social order, the rise of public opinion, representative government, civic freedoms, plurality, and "civility." In these terms, society came to depict a realm of contractual and voluntary relationships independent of the state, which in turn became merely one area of social activity among others. Society was increasingly conceptualized as a realm of diffuse voluntary associations, in which individual self-interested actions result in an equilibrium of unintended consequences.

However, this liberal Enlightenment emphasis on free association and individualism conflicted with Catholic conservative reactions to the 1789 French Revolution and its aftermath. For conservatives such as de Bonald and de Maistre, enlightened individualism and the Revolution had destroyed the organic bases of society that lay in sacred moral authority and the institutions of church, monarchy, and patriarchal family. Although not sociologists, their emphasis on questions of the foundations of organic social solidarity set the scene for the organic functionalist theories of society of Comte and Durkheim, and in the twentieth century, Parsons and Luhmann. For Durkheim, society is an internally differentiated yet functionally integrated system whose operations could be understood only from the point of view of the whole. This complex system is an entity *sui generis*, that is, a discrete reality that cannot be reduced to or explained with reference to another ontological level such as biology or psychology. For systems theory, core problems of society are those of achieving sufficient internal integration to persist over time and boundary maintenance, that is, preserving borders between internal and external systems. This concept underpins systemic functionalist analysis, although mechanisms of integration are viewed differently in different theorists – moral integration in Durkheim; a more complex process of adaptation, goal attainment, integration, and latency in Parsons; and complexity reduction in Luhmann.

This approach has been criticized from at least two perspectives. First, Marxist and other critical theories have emphasized the centrality of power, exploitation, and conflict as central organizing principles in society such that "society" is a field of contestation around class, gendered, and racialized structures. In these terms, "society" has only an illusory unity which critical analysis deconstructs to reveal patterns of hegemonic domination and resistances.

Secondly, individualistic theories drawing on liberal pragmatism appear in writers such as Simmel, Mead, Becker, and Goffman. They approach "society" as at best a metaphor for an aggregation of human interactions rather than an entity *sui generis*. Indeed, Simmel held the view that we should not speak of "society" in abstraction from the forms of association that connect individuals in interaction.

This central issue has been core to many debates in sociological theory – that is, how to comprehend society both as social action and as a system of interrelated practices with unintended consequences. One can say that "society" refers to all forms of mutual and intersubjective communication in which the perceptions and behavior of actors are oriented to those of others. These may be specific others – such as family members, colleagues, friends, rivals, enemies, and authority figures – or they may be generalized others in the form of internalized expectations derived from cultural, moral, practical, and communicative practices. These intersubjective networks can exist across a continuum between informal and voluntarily entered relationships (such as friendship), through formal institutional interactions (e.g., in workplaces and with officials), to highly coercive ones such as prisons. Social relationships at each of these levels can be constituted by expressive (affective) orientations or by instrumental ones. Relationships can be highly personal and influenced by the particular characteristics of others or highly impersonal and formalized encounters, such as a money exchange or phoning a call center. "Society" thus refers to the complex patterns of social relationships that will be sustained through time and space, although encounters may be anything from fleeting to lifelong and proximate to distant. Any social interaction though will summon up or, as Giddens (1979) puts it, "instantiate" vast amounts of tacitly held, taken-for-granted background cultural knowledge about how to perform and attribute meaning to social interaction. This means that as well as situated interactions and communications, "society" also refers to the latent structures of linguistic, affective, cultural, and normative rules that are deployed piecemeal in any actual interaction. Systems of power and domination also inhere within these structures, although they can be accessed and subject to critical reflection and practice through intersubjective communication.

Although core to sociological analysis, the concept has recently been questioned for example by Urry (2000) and Beck (2000) for whom globalization renders obsolete the idea of discrete societies bound by national borders. However, understood in the way outlined here there are not grounds to jettison the concept of "society" because some communicative networks are now organized globally. Indeed we need to understand how global processes are sustained through socially situated interactions of "the social" (Ray 2007: 60–6).

SEE ALSO: Civil Society; Functionalism/Neofunctionalism; Globalization; Social Worlds; Society and Biology; Sociology

REFERENCES

Beck, U. (2000) *What Is Globalization?* Polity Press, Cambridge.

Giddens, A. (1979) *Central Problems in Social Theory*. Macmillan, London.

Locke, J. (1695) *Essay Concerning Human Understanding*, 2nd edn.

Ray, L. J (2007) *Globalization and Everyday Life*. Routledge, London.

Urry, J. (2000) Mobile Sociology. *British Journal of Sociology* 51 (1): 85–203.

SUGGESTED READING

Ray, L. J. (1999) *Theorizing Classical Sociology*. Open University Press, Buckingham.

LARRY RAY

society and biology

Biology and society is one of the new transdisciplinary fields for sociology that emerged in the 1990s. Owing to its strong links with genetic research, medicine, health, agriculture, environment, science, and technology it has developed a number of important research centres.

In the 1990s it became clear, from work in the sociology of health, the sociology of the body and science and technology studies, that it was no longer possible to conceive of a sociological domain that was separable from the biological. Critically, social phenomena operate in material and biotic contexts in which important transfers of materials, information, prehensions, and inscriptions take place.

Sarah Franklin (2007) argues that we can identify three shifts in the way life itself has been considered in modernity.

First, in the nineteenth century nature was *biologized*. According to this view, *life* originates in narratives of evolution and natural selection. It became possible to think of human difference in biological terms (such as race). Equally, individuals could be explained in conception stories of eggs and sperm, and of genetic blueprints. These were "the facts of life."

Second, biology itself become geneticized in the latter half of the twentieth century and now social issues surrounding human behavior, pathology and risk were geneticized: social planning and management now involved *genetic* assessment. Social life orientated itself to genetic genealogy and referenced "genetic parents," "genetic relatedness," "genetic risk," "genetic identity," and "genetic variation." Concern over genetic-inheritance gave way to socially significant technologies of control such as genetic screening, the human genome project and human gene therapy.

Third, geneticization became inseparable from its instrumentalization or the uses that could be made of it. In addition to being able to make new life and change existing life at will (theoretically) geneticization made possible completely new forms of property and power. More can be *done* with genes, such as the captitalization of life itself. The commodification of genomics drove international scientific competition to claim biotechnical market share but also expertise in the management and surveillance of genetic risk. Patents were now possible for new life. In turn, such altered understandings contextualize the ways in which life itself can be owned, capitalized and patented.

But it is not just life that changes but *being*. Creatures such as Dolly the Sheep and "Oncomouse" weren't born but *made*; they were not beings but "done-tos." More social life will focus on accumulation strategy deals between corporate wealth generation and molecular biology. And as this happens sociologists are beginning to ask whether society itself will become recombinant?

Newton (2003a) argues that genetic technologies and future technologies to tackle hitherto uncontrolled natural forces such as weather and volcanic activity will dissolve the distinction between biology and society: "What remains of interest is how far human techno-linguistic skill will enable us to increasingly plasticize biological and physical processes and "short-circuit" seemingly millennial natural stabilities. Are we moving toward plastic bodies (with "clonable" parts) and a pliable world where we will be able to play with *all* the times of nature?" (pp. 27–8).

The study of society and biology will not only monitor social change emerging from new technologies and their implications, but also its *contested* nature in the realm of *biopolitcs*. Rose (2001) argues that: "[T]he biological existence of human beings has become political in novel ways" (1). He traces the history of biopolitics beginning with the nineteenth to mid-twentieth century when those in power sought to discipline individuals, through health and hygiene regimes and breeding programmes, "in the name of the population." Further into the twentieth century the massive political apparatus of health would not have been possible without the increasing health aspirations of the people themselves. This alliance between state and people shifted in the second half of the twentieth century from an emphasis on avoiding sickness to an emphasis on attaining well-being (an optimization of health, but also beauty, fitness, happiness, sexuality, and more). As he says: "ethical practices increasingly take the body as a key site for work on the self" (Rose 2001: 18).

SEE ALSO: Biodemography; Biosociological Theories; Biosociology

REFERENCES

Rose, N. (2001) The politics of life itself. *Theory, Culture and Society* 18 (6): 1–30.

Newton, T. (2003a) Truly embodied sociology: marrying the social and the biological. *Sociological Review* 51 (1): 20–42.

SUGGESTED READINGS

Franklin, A. (2002) *Nature and Social Theory*. Sage, London.

Franklin, S. (2000) *Life Itself: Global Nature and the Genetic Imaginary*: www.comp.lancs.ac.uk/sociology/soc048sf.html.

Franklin, S. (2001) *Are We Post-Genomic?*: www.comp.lancs.ac.uk/sociology/soc047sf.html.

Newton, T. (2003b) Crossing the great divide: time, nature and the social. *Sociology* 37 (3): 433–57.

ADRIAN FRANKLIN

sociocultural relativism

INTELLECTUAL AND SOCIAL CONTEXT

While the word "culture" was first used in 1877 by Edward Tylor to describe the totality of humans' behavioral, material, intellectual, and spiritual products, it was Franz Boas who gave the term one of its most distinctive elaborations. Unlike some other anthropologists (e.g., Malinowski), Boas refused to devalue cultures regardless of how primitive they might appear to outsiders. For Boas, the principal task was to describe accurately and understand completely the cultures of the world, not to rank them from good to bad. Students of Boas, especially Benedict and Herskovits, carried on his legacy, especially his commitment to cultural relativity. They adopted cultural relativity as a principal way to generate respect and tolerance for human diversity, while defending indigenous peoples from threats to their collective and individual well-being.

Sociocultural relativism is a postulate, a method, and a perspective. One implication of the postulate of relativity is that actions and attributes vary from time to time, place to place, and situation to situation. If anything "real" or "objective" exists in the social world, it is the intrinsically situational nature of both rules and reactions and the dynamic, negotiated nature of social order. A second implication of the postulate of relativity is that collective *definitions* of actions and attributes are elastic and also vary from time to time, place to place, and situation to situation. Things that are mightily upsetting to one generation may be trivial to the next (or vice versa), and a particular trait of an individual can be admired by friends but despised by enemies (Goode 2001: 37). The concept of relativism is based on the fact that at certain times and places, acts and attributes that an outsider might find distressing or wrong are not defined as such by individuals living in those times or places. Sociocultural relativism is a method, too. It demands an actor-relevant approach in which social scientists take the role of their subjects and understand the world through the subjects' eyes. While this does not guarantee freedom from ethnocentrism, it does make this bias less likely. In Goffman's (1961: 130) words, "the awesomeness, distastefulness, and barbarity of a foreign culture can decrease to the degree that the student becomes familiar with the point of view to life that is taken by his [her] subjects." Sociocultural relativism requires that you put yourself in the shoes of another, maybe even an adversary's, in order to understand why someone might wear those shoes at all.

Sociocultural relativism is also a perspective, as it is possible to find relativism or nonrelativism in human experience depending on how an observer's eye is slanted. If you are looking for vacillation, drift, and indeterminacy, they are easy to find in this constantly changing, multiplex world of ours; if, however, you are looking for stability and constancy, you can find them, too. Not all sociologists consider themselves relativists, but *all* sociologists must wrestle with the ethical, philosophical, logical, theoretical, and empirical issues that surround a discussion of sociocultural relativism.

Respect for diversity must be tempered with the knowledge that some conditions can neither be easily overlooked nor dismissed as an example of the equivalency of human cultures. We have neither a convincing moral code that can be applied to all places and times nor any theory that makes it possible to understand human experience separate from its social context. Nonetheless, situations will be found in which it is impossible to maintain an attitude of indifference. Sociocultural relativists do not have to believe in the absolute equivalency of values, norms, or customs and blindly accept whatever they find. Romanticizing diversity blunts our ability to recognize the genuine tragedy, pathos, and harm that deviant social practices can produce.

A relativizing motif is a driving force of sociological consciousness, and sociologists call into question what most other people take for granted. One of sociology's strengths is that it can make sense of groups and relationships in a world in which values have been radically relativized. Sociologists uncover and critically evaluate the pretensions and propaganda individuals use to hide, distort, or legitimize what they are doing. They shift from one perspective to another, ranging from the impersonal and remote transformations of the wider society to the inner experiences of individuals in order to understand the interconnections between the two. Sociologists participate mentally in the experiences of individuals differently situated from themselves no matter where or when they are found. Sociocultural relativism can help us to understand the experiences of people in groups and subcultures *within* the boundaries of any one society, as well as the experiences of people drawn from different societies and cultures.

SEE ALSO: Cultural Relativism; Moral Panics

REFERENCES

Goffman, E. (1961) *Asylums*. Doubleday/Anchor, Garden City, NY.

Goode, E. (2001) *Deviant Behavior*, 6th edn. Prentice Hall, Upper Saddle River, NJ.

SUGGESTED READING

Hatch, E. (1997) The good side of relativism. *Journal of Anthropological Research* 53: 371–81.

JOHN CURRA

socioeconomic status, health, and mortality

Socioeconomic status (SES) – a marker of an individual's or a group's position in the societal structure – exerts a profound influence on all dimensions of health and mortality. Health is a measure of the quality of life, whereas mortality defines the risk of death and can be used to measure length of life. High mortality captures the extreme consequences of socioeconomic disadvantage and in some cases reflects the ultimate state of poor health. The examination of health and mortality outcomes is a useful way to understand the negative effects of socioeconomic disadvantage.

SES is measured in a variety of ways, depending on data availability and the specific research questions posed. Typically, SES includes measures of education, income, and occupation. Education is often regarded as the most important dimension of SES because it usually occurs prior to employment, may be a prerequisite for occupational advancement, engenders a broader world perspective, contributes to a sense of personal control, and provides the requisite knowledge and skills to obtain and apply health information. Education has a graded effect on health and mortality, with higher educational levels contributing to better health and survival prospects.

Overwhelming evidence supports the strong and persistent effects of income on health. Low income increases the likelihood of poor health and contributes to higher risks of death. Methods of measuring income include per capita income, poverty rates, income-to-needs ratios, and various consumption thresholds. Income can also be measured through relative comparisons. Whereas incomes can directly affect health through access to health care and opportunities for healthy lifestyles, income inequality can indirectly affect health outcomes and mortality through underinvestment in social spending, erosion of social cohesion, and stress.

Occupational research shows that mortality and morbidity decrease with increases in employment, occupational status, and occupational prestige. Compared to individuals who are not in the labor force, employed individuals are generally healthier, in part because they have access to income, workplace camaraderie, workplace health factors such as gyms and exercise programs, and health insurance. Occupations can be further classified by occupational status and occupational prestige using measures such as the Nam-Powers Occupational SES Scores (OSS), Duncan's Socioeconomic Index (SEI), and innovative measurements of job desirability and physical and mental demands.

Occupational status and prestige can affect health through differential experiences with workplace hazards, physical risks, and demands, toxic exposures, or through detrimental stress related behaviors.

SES is associated with health behaviors and structural conditions that have lasting impacts on health throughout the life course. For instance, researchers have made a persuasive case that higher levels of SES include access to resources that translate into behaviors that minimize the risks associated with morbidity and mortality. Compared to individuals with lower SES, individuals with higher SES are more likely to live in areas characterized by health promoting resources and low crime and they are more likely to engage in healthy behaviors – exercise, abstention from smoking, more nutritious diets, avoidance of drug use or excessive alcohol consumption – which translate into lower risks of death from such causes as cardiovascular disease, many forms of cancer, diabetes, accidents, and homicide.

SES is usually conceptualized to include multiple dimensions (knowledge, employment, and economic status) and is often indexed by educational and occupational attainment and income. Individuals who are situated in elevated positions in the social hierarchy tend to experience superior levels of health and survival. Individuals who are employed, with higher levels of education, and with greater incomes tend to enjoy better health and lower mortality than socioeconomically disadvantaged individuals.

SEE ALSO: Health and Culture; Mortality: Transitions and Measures

SUGGESTED READINGS

Link, B. G. & Phelan, J. (1995) Social conditions as fundamental causes of disease. *Journal of Health and Social Behavior* (extra issue): 80–94.

Mirowsky, J. & Ross, C. E. (2003) *Education, Social Status, and Health.* Aldine de Gruyter, New York.

Rogers, R. G., Hummer, R. A., & Nam, C. B. (2000) *Living and Dying in the USA: Behavioral, Health, and Social Differentials of Adult Mortality.* Academic Press, New York.

JARRON M. SAINT ONGE AND RICHARD G. ROGERS

sociolinguistics

Sociolinguistics is the systematic study of the social uses of language. It proceeds by observing the way people use language in different social settings. People adjust their vocabulary, sounds, and syntax depending upon who they are speaking to and the circumstances of the conversation. Such adjustments are often linguistically subtle and socially meticulous and largely subconscious. They are not taught or consciously learned, but are part of the innate linguistic competence of all normal people.

Philosophers have always recognized that socialization is the primary function of language. Yet linguistic research into its social significance is relatively recent, having emerged as an international movement only in the second half of the twentieth century. Sociolinguistics extends social science methods to the venerable study of language, which since Plato has been conceived as the abstract study of the combinatorial possibilities of parts of speech (syntax) and speech sounds (phonology).

Around 1960, linguists began tracking social variables in speech acts, such as the age, sex, and social class of the participants, and correlating them with dependent linguistic variables.

Variation in language is socially motivated and linguistically insignificant. To take a simple example, it is possible in English to say either *John doesn't need any help* or *John doesn't need no help*. Those two sentences convey the same linguistic meaning and both are readily understood by anyone who speaks the language. Linguistically, they are perfect paraphrases. Socially, however, they are not equivalent at all, with the former deemed to be correct, educated, standard usage, and the latter, though it differs by only one small word, deemed to be incorrect, uneducated, or rustic.

Social factors largely determine the linguistic realization of speech acts. Janitors speak differently to lawyers in the office block than they do among themselves, and vice versa. Young mothers meeting by chance at the local doctor's office chat to one another more familiarly than they do to elderly neighbors in the same situation. Men and women in sex-exclusive domains such as locker rooms tend to slant both the topics of their conversation and their speech styles in different ways.

In modern industrial societies the speech of the educated middle class in capital cities tends to gain acceptance as the national norm and get codified (in somewhat idealized form) in dictionaries, grammar books, and usage guides. Working-class varieties typically differ from the standard dialect both grammatically and phonologically, and the differences are socially stratified, so that they become greater down the social hierarchy, with lower working class more different from the standard than middle working class, and so on. Within social classes, women tend to use fewer stigmatized and nonstandard features than men, a robust difference that apparently holds in all complex societies. The age groups at the social extremes also tend to differ most from the standard, with the oldest groups preserving some features that have become archaic or old-fashioned in the dialect, and adolescents accelerating changes and adopting innovations at a greater rate than their elders.

Adjustments in style are usually explicable in terms of self-monitoring. As social settings become more casual, participants become less self-conscious about their behavior. Linguistically, they use more vernacular variants. This explanation presupposes that the vernacular is more natural than standard speech, more relaxed, and presumably more deeply embedded in the language faculty. Under special circumstances, stylistic adjustments are highly self-conscious, as when a white adolescent adopts African American features with his peers (called "crossing," Rampton 1995), or an adult with social airs adopts features of the higher social class (called "aspirers," Chambers 2003: 101–5). Self-conscious adjustments like these attract attention and are sometimes subject to criticism, whereas style-shifting toward the vernacular in casual settings generally goes unnoticed.

Sociolinguistics has discovered nuances such as social subcategories and age-graded changes in coming to grips with the manifold ways in which interacting variables of class, sex, age, ethnicity, and style affect the way people speak. For the first time, a branch of linguistics studies grammar and phonology as they are enacted in the service of communication. Sociolinguistics is necessarily variant, continuous, and quantitative, and in all those respects it differs from older branches of linguistics. For centuries, thinking people have recognized, at least tacitly, that our speech expresses who we are and how we relate to the social setting, as well as what is on our minds. The social uses of language are so deeply engrained in our human nature that they were thought to be beyond human comprehension, as were consciousness and genetic coding. Like them, when sociolinguistics came into being in the second half of the twentieth century, its very existence represented an assault on the presumed limits of knowledge. Also like them it made rapid progress, a consequence undoubtedly of the fact that there was everything to learn. It is now firmly established as a core area in the study of language.

SEE ALSO: Language; *Langue* and *Parole*

REFERENCES

Chambers, J. K. (2003) *Sociolinguistic Theory: Linguistic Variation and Its Social Significance*, 2nd edn. Blackwell, Oxford.

Rampton, B. (1995) *Crossing: Language and Ethnicitiy among Adolescents*. Longman, New York.

J. K. CHAMBERS

sociological imagination

The term "sociological imagination" comes from a book with that title by American sociologist C. Wright Mills (2000 [1959]) and describes an understanding of one's own position and experiences as reflective of broader social and historical forces. According to Mills, the sociological imagination is more than just a theoretical concept or heuristic device: it is a "promise."

In general, the promise of the sociological imagination is to allow individuals to understand their place in the broader social and historical context. As Mills says in the first sentence of *The Sociological Imagination*, people today increasingly feel that their private lives are a series of "traps" (p. 3). The promise of the sociological imagination is to understand the nature of these traps and to determine if they are in fact private in nature, or if, as Mills suggests, their actual origin lies with broader social and historical forces.

More specifically, the "promise" of the sociological imagination involves the linking of "personal troubles" to "public issues" (p. 8). Described by Mills as a form of "self-consciousness," the sociological imagination directs attention to the linkages between "the personal troubles of milieu" and "the public issues of social structure" (pp. 7–8). "Troubles" reflect one's personal problems and are "private matter[s]" undeserving of sociological attention, whereas "issues" reflect problems that transcend the private sphere of the individual, and are therefore "public matter[s]" (p. 8).

One example offered by Mills concerns unemployment. When one person is unemployed, he notes, it is a personal matter. However, when a significant number of people are unemployed, it becomes a public issue concerning a lack of economic opportunity. Thus, broad social and historical trends, such as deindustrialization, produce outcomes felt and experienced by individuals as private or "personal troubles," masking their structural origins. The key, therefore, is in linking personal experiences such as unemployment to broader social and historical trends (e.g., deindustrialization). When many people experience similar personal troubles or find themselves in a similar set of "traps," it suggests structural rather than personal origins.

In this respect, the sociological imagination is reflective of a broader sociological preoccupation with the micro–macro linkages of society. For Mills, many of the individual, or micro-level, problems that people face in fact reflect broader structural, or macro-level, phenomena. Thus, by focusing on these macro-level or structural arrangements, one can grasp a better sense of one's own life experiences or "biography." Rather than individuals blaming themselves for their own problems, Mills offers the sociological imagination to the American public as a way of linking personal troubles and the "traps" of daily life to larger social and historical trends. As Mills suggests, many of the pressing problems in our daily lives are problems of social structure; the key is in linking individual outcomes or "biographies" to broader social structures and structural trends.

SEE ALSO: Micro-Macro Links; Mills, C. Wright

REFERENCE

Mills, C. W. (2000) [1959] *The Sociological Imagination*. Oxford University Press, New York.

CHRISTOPHER ANDREWS

sociology

Sociology is a form of social inquiry that takes wide-ranging forms. As is the case with many disciplines, it is contested and there is no generally accepted definition of what constitutes sociology. But we should not draw the conclusion that the contested and diverse nature of sociology amounts to the absence of any sense of self-understanding and that the discipline has lapsed into irreversible fragmentation. Sociology can be partly defined by citing examples of what sociologists actually do, but it can also be defined by referring to some of the major intellectual statements of the discipline, such as classic works or theoretical and methodological approaches that are characteristically sociological. To begin, it is helpful to look at sociology in terms of its subject matter, its approach, and some of the classical works that have shaped the discipline.

Many disciplines have a clearly defined subject matter, although very often this is due to the absence of methodological scrutiny and uncritical consensus, as in the general view that "the past" is the subject domain of historians while political scientists study "politics." Sociologists generally have a tougher time in defending their territory than other disciplines, even though they unhesitatingly take over on the territory of others. Sociology's subject domain can arguably be said to be the totality of social relations or simply "society," which Durkheim said was a reality *sui generis*. As a reality in itself the social world is more than the sum of its parts. There has been little agreement on exactly what these parts are, with some positions arguing that the parts are social structures and others claiming that society is simply made up of social actors and thus the subject matter of sociology is social action. The emphasis on the whole being greater than the sum of the parts has led some sociologists to the view that sociology is defined by the study of the relations between the different parts of society. This insight has tended to be reflected in a view of society as a movement or process. It would not be inaccurate to say that sociology is the social science devoted to the study of modern society.

In terms of theory and methodology, sociology is highly diverse. The paradigms that Thomas Kuhn believed to be characteristic of the history of science are more absent from sociology than from other social sciences. Arguably, anthropology and economics have more tightly defined methodological approaches than sociology. As a social science, sociology can be described as evidence-based social inquiry into the social world and informed by conceptual frameworks and established methodological approaches. But what constitutes evidence varies depending on whether quantitative or qualitative approaches are adopted, although such approaches are not distinctively sociological. There is also considerable debate as to the scientific status of sociology, which was founded to be a social science distinct from the natural sciences and distinct from the human sciences. The diversity of positions on sociology today is undoubtedly a matter of where sociology is deemed to stand in relation to the experimental and human sciences. While it is generally accepted that sociology is a third science, there is less consensus on exactly where the limits of this space should be drawn. This is also a question of the relation of sociology to its subject matter: is it part of its object, as in the hermeneutical tradition; is it separate from its object, as in the positivist tradition; or is it a mode of knowledge connected to its object by political practice, as in the radical tradition?

A discipline is often shaped by its founding figures and a canon of classical works. It is generally accepted today that the work of Marx, Weber, and Durkheim has given to sociology a classical framework. However, whether this canon can direct sociological research today is highly questionable and mostly it has been relegated to the history of sociology, although there are attempts to make classics relevant to current social research. Such attempts, however, misunderstand the relation between the history of a discipline and the actual practice of it. Classic works are not of timeless relevance, but offer points of reference for the interpretation of the present and milestones in the history of a discipline. For this reason the canon is not stable and should also not be confused with social theory: it was Parsons in the 1930s who canonized Weber and Durkheim as founding fathers; in the 1970s Marx was added to the list – due not least to the efforts of Giddens – and Spencer has more or less disappeared; in the 1980s Simmel was added and in the present day there is the rise of contemporary classics, such as Bourdieu, Bauman, Luhmann, Habermas, and Foucault, and there are recovered classics, such as Elias. It is apparent from a cursory look at the classics that many figures were only later invented as classical sociologists to suit whatever project was being announced. The word "invented" is not too strong here: Marx did not see himself as a sociologist, Weber was an economic historian and rarely referred to sociology as such, and Foucault was a lapsed psychiatrist; all of them operated outside disciplinary boundaries.

The impact of Foucault on sociology today is a reminder that sociology continues to change, absorbing influences from outside the traditional discipline. The range of methodological and theoretical approaches has not led to a great deal of synthesis or consensus on what actually defines sociology. Since the so-called cultural turn in the social sciences, much of sociology takes place outside the discipline itself, in cultural studies, criminology, women's studies, development studies, demography, human geography, and planning, as well as in the other social and human sciences. This is increasingly the case with the rise of interdisciplinarity and more so with post-disciplinarity, wherein disciplines do not merely relate to each other but disappear altogether. Few social science disciplines have made such an impact on the wider social and human science as sociology, a situation that has led to widespread concern that sociology may be disappearing into those disciplines that it had in part helped to create.

Sociology is the only science specifically devoted to the study of society in the broad sense of the term, meaning the social world and the open field of the social. Like many of the social and human sciences it does not have a clearly defined subject matter. This situation often leads to the assumption of a crisis. Sociology today is often faced with three broad choices. One is the classical vision of a field that is based on the interpretation of the results of other sciences from the perspective of a general science of society guaranteed by a canonized sociological heritage.

Second, those who reject the first as too generalist, parasitic, and lacking a clearly marked out specialized field argue that sociology must confine itself to a narrow territory based on a tightly defined conception of sociological research and disciplinary specialization. Third, those who reject the highly specialized understanding of sociology and resist the generalist understanding of sociology tend to look to post-disciplinarity, whereby sociology is not confined to the traditional discipline and occurs largely outside sociology.

These are false dilemmas, despite the fact that there are major challenges to be faced. Interdisciplinarity is unavoidable today for all the sciences, but it does not have to mean the disappearance of sociology any more than any other discipline. It is also difficult to draw the conclusion that sociology exists only in a post-disciplinary context. However, it is evident that sociology cannot retreat into the classical mold of a general science. Sociology is a versatile and resilient discipline that takes many forms. One of its enduring characteristics is that it brings to bear on the study of the social world a general perspective born of the recognition that the sum is greater than the parts.

SEE ALSO: American Sociological Association; Body and Cultural Sociology; British Sociological Association; Economy (Sociological Approach); Environment, Sociology of the; Institutional Review Boards and Sociological Research; Knowledge, Sociology of; Marxism and Sociology; Political Sociology; Scientific Knowledge, Sociology of; Society; Sociological Imagination

SUGGESTED READINGS

Berger, P. (1966) *Invitation to Sociology: A Humanistic Approach*. Penguin, London.

Bourdieu, P. & Wacquant, L. (1992) *An Invitation to Reflexive Sociology*. University of Chicago Press, Chicago, IL.

Calhoun, C., Rojek, C., & Turner, B. (eds.) (2005) *Handbook of Sociology*. Sage, London.

Clawson, D. (ed.) (1998) *Required Reading: Sociology's Most Influential Books*. University of Massachusetts Press, Amherst, MA.

GERARD DELANTY

sociology in medicine

Sociology in medicine, in its most extreme form, encompasses work aimed at the provision of technical skills and problem solving for the medical community while neglecting contributions to the parent discipline. Medical sociology experienced dual roles early in its institutionalization. Sociology in medicine and sociology of medicine were the names designated for applied and pure work, respectively, by Robert Straus in 1957. Sociology in medicine represents the thrust toward reform, advocacy, and application. During the 1950s and 1960s, the primary aim of medical sociology was to serve medicine, with a large majority of medical sociologists employed by health science, and only 30 percent holding appointments in traditional sociology departments. This ascendancy was short lived as the effects of the cold war, which equated sociology with socialism, decreased the influence of sociology on public health issues and policy. Through increasing opportunities during the 1980s, sociology in medicine again became an exciting career choice for medical sociologists.

The work of sociologists in medicine is directly applicable to health issues, focusing on disease processes or factors influencing patients' responses to illness, with goals of improving diagnosis and treatment. It may examine doctor–patient relationships, various therapeutic situations, or social factors that affect and are affected by specific health disorders. The sociologist in medicine may also have responsibilities of educating health science students in sociology of health and illness. The major contributions of sociology in medicine have been to medical education, social epidemiology, and knowledge of utilization and compliance. Sociologists in medicine seek to answer questions of interest to their sponsors and institutions rather than to the discipline of sociology.

Sociology in medicine, then, treats sociology as a supporting discipline to medicine, which involves achieving the goals of medicine. For this reason, sociology in medicine has been severely criticized since its inception. Sociologists in medicine are less compelled to defend the significance of their work to the academic community than are conventional sociologists. The demands placed upon the sociologist in medicine are for practical applications rather than sociological significance. Therefore, sociology in medicine has consistently battled with the question of whether or not it is real sociology. Aside from criticisms of its parent discipline, sociology in medicine has historically faced problems within its working environment as well. Communication, status, and relationship issues have surrounded it since the first tenure-track position was created for a sociologist in a medical school in 1953.

When the distinction was made between pure and applied work of medical sociologists, the predominant opinion of sociologists was that the two were incompatible. Academic sociologists believed sociologists in medicine showed loyalty to the medical institution and did not contribute to the discipline. Those working in medicine considered themselves to be quite practical sociologists, as their work was directly applicable to human health. The opinion of incompatibility has changed dramatically and will continue to change. Straus, who named the distinction in 1957, wrote in 1999 that it is possible for the medical sociologist to do both pure and applied work. Many current medical sociologists consider the structural position of the scholar to be irrelevant today, and have called for a re-naming of the work of medical sociologists. Rather than distinguishing between sociology in medicine and sociology of medicine, work of medical sociologists may be aptly called sociology *with* medicine.

SEE ALSO: Medical Sociology; Medicine, Sociology of

REFERENCES

Straus, R. (1957) The nature and status of medical sociology. *American Sociological Review* 22: 200–4.

Straus, R. (1999) Medical sociology: a personal fifty year perspective. *Journal of Health and Social Behavior* 40: 103–10.

SUGGESTED READING

Cockerham, W. C. (2007) *Medical Sociology*, 10th edn. Prentice Hall, Englewood Cliffs, NJ.

CAREY L. USHER

sociometry

The word "sociometry" was coined by Jacob Levi Moreno (1889–1974), in studying emotional structures in small groups. Moreno also founded a journal, *Sociometry* (now the *Social Psychology Quarterly*), published by the American Sociological Association.

In sociometric surveys respondents are asked to name their friends, or to rate other group members on some dimension. These "choices" can be displayed as a sociogram, a diagram in which points represent individuals and arrows represent choices.

Research in natural settings and laboratories shows that sociometric choices result from: (1) propinquity (proximity) – attraction forms between individuals who encounter each other in daily life; (2) reciprocity – attraction is mutual; (3) perceived similarity – individuals choose others they think are like them; and (4) status – individuals choose others with high prestige. Since interaction occurs between persons who have positive bonds, such persons tend to influence each other.

Cognitive balance theory is useful to sociometry. Heider proposed that people seek agreement with others they view positively and disagreement with those viewed negatively; such *balanced states* are stable while imbalanced states change. This explains reciprocity and similarity and predicts that relationships among three or more persons become transitive.

SEE ALSO: Interpersonal Relationships; Networks; Social Influence; Social Psychology

SUGGESTED READINGS

Heider, F. (1958) *The Psychology of Interpersonal Relations.* Wiley, New York.

Moreno, J. L. (1934) *Who Shall Survive? A New Approach to the Problem of Human Interrelations.* Beacon House, Boston, MA.

BARBARA F. MEEKER

solidarity

Solidarity, defined as the perceived or realized organization of individuals for group survival, interests, or purposes, may result from either external threats or internal needs. Solidarity, reflecting various dimensions and forms of organizing, may best be described in Durkheimian terms as ranging from organic to the inorganic. That is to say, we may describe solidarity that derives from some intrinsic characteristic of the participants or from extrinsic characteristics. When we speak of intrinsic characteristics, related to organic solidarity, we typically include such types as family, racial/ethnic groups, national and to some extent religious affiliation. Alternatively, inorganic solidarity, related to the more voluntary, associational characteristics of such organization, suggests greater volition on the part of its members. When we speak of inorganic solidarity we typically make reference to neighborhood associations, clubs, political organizations, and the like. Given the more transient nature of today's populations, religion and national identity may also fall into this latter category for obvious reasons associated with mobility and personal choice. Depending upon type, solidarity comes into being for multiple reasons. Social and political movements, community organizing, and social activism rely upon the ability of respective leaders to organize and solidify significant groups for the purposes of social action. The capacity of groups to solidify is directly associated with their capacity to organize about significant issues, events, visions, and/or threats. Thus the capacity to solidify is evidence of the capacity to survive, thrive, persist, and promote group interests, viability, and/or vitality.

Differing forms of solidarity (to include dimensions, levels, and types of solidarity) may be associated with different types of groups, institutions, or organizational components. Hence, along the organic continuum and within the family, issues of kinship and major life events such as marriage, births, deaths, reunions, holidays, celebrations, and so on form the basis of specific events that may evoke episodes of solidarity. These events, repeated over time, and depending upon frequency, intensity, and level of interaction, produce a sense of family solidarity. Thus we can talk about solidarity in the family as being a process experienced over these various and collective life events.

Alternatively, within religious or other cultural institutions, we can likewise talk about events which serve to enhance, inspire, or evoke episodes of solidarity. Such events typically revolve around the ceremonial, but may also include the commemorative, induction of new members, proselytizational, and other significant life events of members which have been serialized within the cultural institution (e.g., typically marriage, birth, coming of age, and so on find expression within religious and other cultural institutions and also serve as solidifying events). Religious and other cultural institutions also provide, encourage, and to a great extent require vision and visionary leaders that serve to express institutional-wide ideas, values, and purpose which not only transcend the everyday events and issues of its members, but also give members a sense of collective identity, thus encouraging solidarity. These visions and visionaries, occurring periodically through the institutional memories of members, serve to produce and sustain group cohesion.

Collectively, then, within religious and cultural institutions, the ceremonial, those life events that are commemorated, and visions and visionary leaders provide the organizational glue that accounts for solidifying events. These events over time are what we refer to when we speak of solidarity within religious and cultural institutions.

Often solidarity is held out to various groups (e.g., racialized, gendered, political) as if it were some actuality that can be achieved. As such, and given the reality that it is often presumed to be associated with specified dominant groups, it only manifests itself oppositionally. Solidarity, for heterogeneously large groups, presumes a level, form, and/or quality of unity which is prevented by the very nature of heterogeneously large groups. What solidarity does come into being tends to be experienced not universally but partially by specific sections of groups whose interests, goals, and/or opportunities are perceived to be challenged, effected, or affected. More generally and typically, members of groups seek to organize or mobilize as a consequence of perceived organization or mobilization by external groups, forces, and/or threats. Consequentially, solidarity is not an event but a process that is never quite complete and is dependent upon such things as perceived threat, advantage, and disadvantage to which and by which organizational resources are expended. The nature of these organizational resources is defined by the resource base(s) of the group, the historical progression or context to which the group owes its existence, and the ability of group members to effectively acquire, access, and mobilize resources and members for the purposes of obtaining levels of solidarity.

SEE ALSO: Class Consciousness; Diversity; Ethnic Enclaves; Social Movements; Solidarity, Mechanical and Organic

SUGGESTED READINGS

Amit-Talai, V. & Knoles, C. (ed.) (1996) *Re-Situating Identities: The Politics of Race, Ethnicity, and Culture.* Broadview, Peterborough, Ontario.

Scott, J. C. (1985) *Weapons of the Weak: Everyday Forms of Peasant Resistance.* Yale University Press, New Haven, CT.

Scott, J. C. (1990) *Domination and the Arts of Resistance: Hidden Transcripts.* Yale University Press, New Haven, CT.

RODNEY COATES

solidarity, mechanical and organic

French sociologist Émile Durkheim (1858–1917) coined the terms mechanical and organic solidarity to describe types of social organization, that is, ways in which individuals are connected to each other and identify with the groups and societies in which they live. For Durkheim, social solidarity is a state of unity or cohesion that exists when people are integrated by strong social ties and shared beliefs, and also are regulated by well-developed guidelines for action (i.e., values and norms that suggest worthy goals and how people should attain them).

The central question Durkheim poses in his first book, *The Division of Labor in Society* (1893), is what is the basis of social solidarity in modern societies, where there is a great diversity of people living in vastly different settings? How do the parts of modern society (individuals, groups, institutions) become more interdependent while at the same time becoming more distinct from each other? Durkheim argues that social solidarity takes different forms in different historical periods, and varies in strength among groups in the same society. However, reflecting the popularity of social evolutionary thought in the late nineteenth century, Durkheim summarizes all historical forms of solidarity into a traditional-modern dichotomy. Mechanical solidarity is a simple, pre-industrial form of social cohesion, and organic solidarity is a more complex form of cohesion that evolves in modern societies (by which he means the western capitalist democracies).

Specifically, mechanical solidarity occurs in small, simple societies such as settlements of small kinship groups scattered across territories. Each kinship group is organized similarly. Within each group, members perform all functions needed to survive (e.g., familial, economic, political, and religious); there is no specialization or differentiation of function across groups living in the same area. Each member feels connected to group life in a manner similar to other members because everyone has an experience of the world that comes from a religiously-based common culture, which reproduces in each person the same ways of thinking, feeling, and acting. By mechanical, Durkheim does not mean machine-like or artificial. He means that the conditions of life are the same for everyone so there is little diversity in people's experiences and ideas. Individuals do not have a sense of identity separate from being a member of a family, clan, or a warrior caste. Consequently, "the ideas and tendencies common to all the members of the society are greater in number and intensity than those which pertain personally to each member" (Durkheim 1964 [1893]: 129).

Over time these simpler societies disappear, urban areas emerge, and complex divisions of functions appear within cities, among institutions, and within nation-states. Organic solidarity is found in societies where there is a complex division of labor and diversity of ways of thinking, feeling, and acting. No one household, neighborhood, town, or economy can produce everything its members need to survive. Economies depend not only on the family but on educational institutions to produce dependable workers with a range of needed skills. There is a great diversity of occupations, racial and ethnic backgrounds, religious beliefs, and political views. Such diversity of people, groups, and institutions is organized into distinct yet interdependent roles and functions.

Durkheim's argument about the distinction between mechanical and organic solidarity identifies two key variables that continue to be important in sociology today. "Social life comes from a double source, the likeness of consciences and the division of labor" (Durkheim 1964 [1893]: 226):

- *Extent (degree of complexity) of the division of labor*, which refers to level of differentiation of an activity into distinct functions or roles. For example, the one-room schoolhouse developed into a complex system of kindergartens, elementary schools, middle schools, and high schools.
- *Extent of the collective consciousness*, which refers to the number of values, beliefs, norms, emotions, and ways of acting that are shared within a group or society, and the intensity with which members share/experience these practices.

With mechanical solidarity, the division of labor is absent or weak, while the collective consciousness is strong because a large number of beliefs, values, and traditional practices are shared intensely by members. Durkheim argues that when the division of labor becomes more complex, the collective conscience changes. With organic solidarity, there is a complex division of labor yet a weakened collective consciousness because practices and beliefs shared by everyone are far fewer and are more abstract and ambiguous (thus less constraining). Thus, in modern societies, people are more interdependent due to the division of labor, yet are more distinct. Durkheim observes that perhaps the only value widely shared and strongly-held in modern western societies is the abstract notion of individualism – the inherent dignity, worth, and freedom of the individual.

SEE ALSO: Collective Conscience; Division of Labor; Durkheim, Émile; Norms

REFERENCE

Durkheim, E. (1964) [1893] *The Division of Labor in Society*, trans. G. Simpson. Free Press, New York.

SUGGESTED READINGS

Alexander, J. & Smith. P. (eds.) (2005) *The Cambridge Companion to Durkheim*. Cambridge University Press, Cambridge.

Bellah, R. N. (ed.) (1983) *Emile Durkheim on Morality and Society*. University of Chicago Press, Chicago, IL.

Lukes, S. (1973) *Émile Durkheim: His Life and Work*. Penguin, Harmondsworth.

ANNE M. HORNSBY

space

Space has many faces: the situated space defined for social interactions, the bubble of individual space, the private spaces we maintain for our personal lives, the public spaces of wider social activity, and space as a scarce distributed resource in the organization of human social life. Although some theorists use the terms space and place interchangeably, they are in fact not the same concept.

Hall's (1966) groundbreaking book *The Hidden Dimension* treats space as a sociological category of experience. For Hall, as well as LeFebve (1991), space is ordered by human custom and definition. The reverse is also observed: the design of a space can affect the sort of activities and meanings that occur within it.

Spaces can be flexible to different definitions of the situation and accompanying interactions. A small space beneath a kitchen table may be room for feet and legs, a cave or a castle to a young person, or the land of bountiful opportunity to the family dog.

Individuals carry an invisible bubble of space around them in order to feel comfortable interacting with others. The size of this cushion of space varies from one individual to another and across cultures. For example, a person in one of the Arabic cultures needs to get very close, about one foot away, in order to communicate effectively. In other cultures, about four feet is the acceptable communication distance. Most Americans need about 30 inches (Sommer 1983). The implication for diplomatic missions and everyday conversation is that others may be perceived as either too pushy or too cold and distant for reasons that have nothing to do with the content of their communications, and much to do with the amount of intervening space.

Oldenburg (1999) demonstrates the importance of everyday spaces to the construction of social relationships and meanings. His examination of the "third spaces" that people spend time in, after home and work, highlights the importance of semi-private and public spaces in providing meaning and continuity to human life. Historians and political scientists have examined the roles of taverns and coffeehouses as community facilitators and sites for political discourse and organization. Milligan (1998) looks at what happens to the definition of a place when it is moved into a new space. Community bonds forged in the crucible of one intense social space lose their integrity when those facilities and their limitations are no longer extant. Du Bois (2001) provides examples of special designs that encourage social interaction in nursing homes, bars, and other public spaces.

SEE ALSO: Place; Time–Space; Urban Space

REFERE
Du Bois … n behavior: the sociol… , W. & Wright, R. D. … *g a Better World.* Allyn … .
LeFebve… *of Space*, trans. D. Ni… shing, Oxford.
Milligan … nd potential: the social … ment, *Symbolic Intera…*
Oldenbu… *ace: Cafes, Coffee Shops, … d Other Hangouts at th…* edn. Marlowe, Emer…
Somme… *ng Buildings with People in Mind.* Prentice Hall, Englewood Cliffs, NJ.

LESLIE WASSON

species-being

Species-being (*Gattungswesen*), a controversial Feuerbachian-inspired term refashioned in Marx's critique of Hegel's idealist philosophy, is central to Marx's conception of alienation and true communism. Hegel had argued the form and substance of knowledge developed historically. The conscious mind (*Geist*) initially experiences reality as external and separate; it does not know that alien world. From its first sensory encounter, the mind becomes conscious of itself and through a complex, dialectical subject/object interaction process develops an increasingly comprehensive intellectual grasp of reality, culminating in an absolute spirit (*Geist*). Overcoming the original perception of separation – alienation – mind's full potential is actualized in the totality of absolute being.

Hegel's philosophy buttressed nineteenth-century Prussia's intolerant, protestant state. Ludwig Feuerbach's *Essence of Christianity* – a democratically inspired critique of God's existence – challenged the state's religious foundation. In religion, Feuerbach argued, the powers of humankind are alienated from it, extrapolated, made infinite, and then impose themselves on humanity as an absolute God. Feuerbach's anthropologically based critique of theology undermined religion and idealism by emphasizing humankind's material being as a species (*Gattungswesen*) – the real, existent, identifiable, characteristics of humankind that religion hypostatized.

Species-being in Marx emanates from his critiques of Hegel and Feuerbach. Following Feuerbach, Marx began with real, active humans, but "inverting" Hegel's idealism produced a dramatically different conception of species-being. For Marx, humankind was a materially active, social being, compelled to produce (labor) in order to exist. Production (labor) – the ontological basis to praxis – changes and develops humankind's knowledge, conditions of being, and social arrangements. Labor, the material mediation of subject and object, is the ontological basis for humankind's mental, creative, social, and material development. This is a central component of humankind's species-Essence. Species-being is not a set of fixed natural characteristics – our species' being is materially active, interactive, and creative, producing our material life, thereby changing our circumstances.

At the same time, as Marx (1975: 62) emphasized in correspondence with Feuerbach, humankind is social: "The unity of man with man, which is based on real differences between men, the concept of human species [*Menschengattung*] brought down from the heaven of abstraction to the actual earth, what is this other than the concept of *society*." After this letter, while continuing work on the 1844 manuscripts, Marx began using "social" to replace the more abstract term "species-being."

Under conditions of private property, the true social character of humankind's creative laboring activity is torn asunder by social – i.e. class – division. Rather than developing workers and their social interrelationships, the externalization process creates products, a process, and a system that confronts and stultifies workers' physical, emotional, and political development while creating and supporting social division. Only by overturning private property can humankind's socio-material potential fully flourish in freedom.

SEE ALSO: Alienation; Feuerbach, Ludwig; Hegel, G. W. F.; Labor; Praxis

REFERENCE

Marx, K. & Engels, F. (1975) *Marx-Engels Gesamtausgabe* (*Marx–Engels Complete Works*), part 3, vol. 1. Dietz Verlag, Berlin.

SUGGESTED READINGS

Gould, C. (1978) *Marx's Social Ontology*. MIT Press, Cambridge, MA.
Hegel, G. W. F. (1977) [1804] *Phenomenology of Spirit*, trans. A. Miller. Clarendon Press, Oxford.

ROB BEAMISH

sport

Like play and games, sport is ancient, ubiquitous, and diverse. Given the multitude of sport forms and the variety of specific sports, and granted the magnitude and complexity of sport in modern society, a full description of sport requires treating the social phenomenon at different levels of analysis, including sport as a unique game occurrence, sport as a particular type of ludic activity, sport as an institutionalized game, sport as a social institution, and sport as a form of social involvement. But for purposes of concise consideration herein, sport is highlighted as an embodied, structured, goal-oriented, competitive, contest based, ludic, physical activity.

SPORT IS EMBODIED

The degree of physicality varies by sport, but the body constitutes both the symbol and the core of all sport participation. Embodiment in sport is clearly revealed in the many kinds and degrees of physicality associated with sporting activities, including physical activity, physical aggression, physical combat, physical exercise, physical prowess, and physical training. Embodiment in sport is a mirror of social relations in society, as for example, elitism (class vs. mass bodies), sexism (male vs. female bodies), racism (black vs. white bodies), ageism (young vs. old bodies), ableism (able vs. disabled bodies), and homophobia (straight vs. gay bodies). In short, sporting bodies represent a range of desiring bodies, disciplined bodies, displaying bodies, and dominating bodies.

SPORT IS STRUCTURED

Sport is highly structured in at least four ways. First, all sports (whether informal or formal) are *rule governed* by either written or unwritten rules of play. Second, most sports are *spatially circumscribed* by the sites of their venues, whether they be arenas, courts, fields, pools, rings, rinks, stadiums or tracks. Third, nearly all sports are *temporally circumscribed* as illustrated by designated time periods such as innings, halves and quarters; or number and time of bouts and rounds; or allocated attempts within a specific time period. Indeed to prevent indefinitely long sporting encounters sports have instituted tie-breakers, "sudden death" playoffs, and shorter versions of selected sports (e.g., one-day cricket matches). Fourth, modern sports are typically *formally administered*, whether by local clubs, schools, universities, professional teams and/or sport federations.

SPORT IS GOAL ORIENTED

Individuals, teams and corporate organizations are explicitly goal directed in sport situations, especially in terms of the perennial overriding goal of winning. Athletes and coaches alike continually attempt to achieve various standards of excellence. And numerous forms of self-testing take place in all sporting encounters. Most predominantly, the sporting media constantly stresses the theme of being Number One in terms of number of games won, total points earned, number of medals earned, top rank on the money list, most career victories, or number of Grand Slam titles.

SPORT IS COMPETITIVE

Perhaps the key feature of all forms of sport is competition demanding the demonstration of physical prowess. Such competition may be between individuals or teams, and may involve either an animate object of nature (e.g., a bull in a bullfight), or an inanimate object of nature (e.g., surmounting the highest mountain in the world). A spectator typically perceives three basic forms of competition (McPherson et al. 1989): *Direct competition* where two opponents, either individuals or teams, directly confront one another, as for example, in boxing or football. *Parallel competition* wherein participants compete against one another indirectly by taking turns as in bowling or golf; or contesting in separate spaces, as for example, swimming or running in assigned lanes in the case of aquatic and track competitions. *Competition against a standard*, as for example, trying to make the "minimal standard" of a qualifying time for an Olympic running event, or trying to achieve an "ideal standard" of a world record in an Olympic event.

SPORT IS CONTEST BASED

Many, if not most, sporting encounters are contests, i.e., competitive activities characterized by two or more sides, agreed upon rules, and criteria for determining a winner, with a non-reciprocal outcome (i.e., they are zero-sum contests wherein the victor takes all). Two basic categories of sporting contests are *sporting matches* and *agonal games.* Sporting matches involve demonstrations of physical superiority in terms of speed, strength, stamina, accuracy, and coordination. Agonal games are games whose outcome is largely determined by the demonstration of superior physical prowess in combination with superior strategy and tactics. A chief characteristic of sporting contests are uncertain outcomes which lend excitement to the contests for players and spectators alike. Efforts to insure "a level playing field" represent attempts to guarantee an uncertain outcome by matching opponents by age, weight, skill level, or some type of handicap system as seen in bowling, golf and horse racing.

SPORT IS LUDIC

Even the most highly professionalized sports possess some ludic or play-like elements. Two major ludic elements in all sports are *artificial obstacles* and *realized resources*. Individuals and groups are confronted in daily life by obstacles that they must attempt to overcome. However, individuals and groups often do have the requisite resources to adequately cope with the specific obstacles that they confront. Uniquely, in the ideal play world of sport and unlike real-life situations, athletes and sport teams are typically provided with the needed resources (e.g., coaching, equipment, training, etc.) to cope with their artificially created obstacles. The history of sport shows that there is always controversy as to what constitutes "legitimate" realized resources in a given sport. For example, many drugs and steroids are illegal, and there are constant rule changes as to what constitutes legal sporting equipment, be it the size of a tennis racquet, the horse power of a racing car, the type of grooves on a golf club, or the design of prosthetics for disabled athletes. In sum, the ludic element of sport is the core of the tension balances associated with the expressive and instrumental aspects of sport since time immortal.

SEE ALSO: Globalization, Sport and; Sexuality and Sport; Social Theory and Sport; Sport and Capitalism; Sport and Culture

REFERENCE

McPherson, B. D., Curtis, J. E., & Loy, J.W. (1989) *The Social Significance of Sport: An Introduction to the Sociology of Sport*. Human Kinetics, Champaign, IL.

SUGGESTED READINGS

Hargreaves, J. (1986) *Sport, Power and Culture*. Polity Press, Cambridge.

Loy, J. W. (1968) The nature of sport: a definitional effort. *Quest* 10: 1–15.

Loy, J. W. & Coakley, J. (2007) Sport. In: Ritzer, G. (ed.), *The Blackwell Encyclopedia of Sociology*. Blackwell Publishing, Oxford, pp. 4643–53.

Weiss, P. (1969). *Sport: A Philosophic Inquiry*. Southern Illinois University Press, Carbondale, IL.

JOHN LOY AND JAY COAKLEY

sport and capitalism

As an "ideal type," "capitalism" is a social formation where people's needs and wants are predominantly met through enterprises employing individuals who are free, and compelled by lack of other legal ways to adequately meet their needs, to sell their labor power. The capitalist ethos involves a predictable legal system and rational accounting so enterprises can pursue their primary objective – asset accumulation. Enterprises strive to extend their sphere of influence as far and as advantageously as possible, using all available, legal means. Instrumental reason pervades capitalism as people, objects and events are assessed in means/ends terms (see Weber 1927: 352–68).

"Sport" is an abstraction denoting various embodied, competitive, agonistic cultural practices that occur and develop within a socioeconomic formation. "Sport" as concrete practice is shaped by capitalism and its ethos.

Under capitalism, sport becomes a market opportunity for owners or promoters to purchase athletes' skills and produce a spectacle they sell to spectators, sponsors, and various media. Just as the education system develops future workers, youth sport prepares and sorts those who will become athlete-workers. To mitigate the unconstrained application of instrumental reason in profit oriented spectacles centered on maximizing human physical performance in zero-sum competitions, sport leagues, governing bodies, and governments must regulate some aspects of sport.

Early promoters and owners competed with each other to produce the most commercially appealing spectacles. To prevent their self-destruction, owners in many sports formed leagues which acted like cartels, controlling costs, regulating player movement, reducing economic competition internally, and setting prices. Professional baseball enjoys immunity from American anti-trust laws and other leagues act as though they are also.

Drastically underpaid, toiling under conditions set completely by owners and tied in perpetuity to teams through "the reserve clause," players sought basic employees' rights in bitter struggles with owners. Following failed, drawn out court challenges, athletes turned to unionization to change the balance of power. Despite internal player division and owner opposition, basketball (1954), hockey (1967), football (1968–87; 1993), and baseball (1968) formed certified bargaining units that negotiated improved working conditions and compensation.

Opposed to the rampant materialism of nineteenth-century capitalism, Pierre de Coubertin launched the modern Olympic Games to reestablish Europe's traditional values. However, from 1896 to the present, commercial interests and nationalist political objectives – seen especially in the 1936 Nazi Games, the cold war confrontations between 1952 and 1989 and more recently Beijing 2008 – the Games have become as commercialized and profit driven as any professional sport in modern times. Requiring a full-time commitment by the 1970s, the International Olympic Committee removed amateurism from its eligibility code in 1974, opening the Games to the world's best (professional) athletes – enriching athletes and the IOC.

Dominated by instrumental rationality, the Games have had to face difficult questions about child labor, athletes' rights, athlete abuse, performance-enhancing substances and financial and ethical corruption. Initiated as the antithesis of the capitalist spirit, the Olympic Games are now deeply entrenched in the drive for profit, accumulation and personal financial gain through the widespread use of instrumental reason and a purely utilitarian approach to human athletic performance.

Oppositional forms like "extreme sports" and other alternative sport forms have sprung up to resist the logic of capital but they have been quickly incorporated into the marketplace and begun to display the same ethos as mainstream, commercial and high-performance sport.

SEE ALSO: Capitalism; Sport;

REFERENCE

Weber, M. (1927) [1923] *General Economic History*, trans. F. Knight. Free Press, Glencoe, IL.

SUGGESTED READINGS

Beamish, R. & Ritchie, I. (2006) *Fastest, Highest, Strongest*. Routledge, London.

Gruneau, R. (1999) *Class, Sports and Social Development*. Human Kinetics, Champaign, IL.

ROB BEAMISH

sport and culture

For sociologists subscribing to a hierarchical model of culture, sports may be regarded as its antithesis: a bodily practice, of little cultural consequence, gazed on by passive spectators for the enrichment of the leisure and media industries. However, taking sports seriously as culture does not necessitate the abandonment of formative sociological questions of structure, agency, and power, but helps to "rehabilitate" and extend them into hitherto neglected areas. Sport's raw popularity as spectacle alone marks it out as a pivotal element of contemporary society and culture. For example, the estimated cumulative audience for the 2002 Korea/Japan World Cup of association football was 28.8 billion viewers; 9 out of 10 people in the world with access to television watched some part of the Sydney 2000 Olympic Games; and the worldwide audience estimate for the Opening Ceremony of the 2008 Beijing Olympics alone was 1.2 billion viewers. Such "mega-media" sports events are profoundly instructive about cultural change in (post) modernity.

The major dimensions of the sports–culture relationship concern the impacts of the industrial development of sport, the social ideologies that circulate within the "media sports cultural complex" (Rowe 2004: 4), and the positioning and influence of sports within the wider sociocultural sphere. Sport is a key instance of the penetration of the logic of capital into everyday culture and of the industrialization of leisure time and practice, inducing since the nineteenth century spectators to pay to enter the controlled space of the sports stadium in order to watch paid athletes perform. Although these spatialized aspects of sports culture remain important – major stadia, for example, are invested with the quasi-spiritual qualities that support the proposition that sports is a secular religion – the most important force in the development of sports has been its increasingly intense relationship with the media, without which sports would be hampered by the restrictions of time and space. Because of its intimate involvement with, and omnipresence through, the media, sports is a highly effective bearer of social ideologies disguised as natural, self-evident truths, including those concerning innate competitiveness, corporeal meritocracy, national and racial superiority, and an inevitably unequal gender order.

Sports discourse and language increasingly frame the wider society in its own image – the "sportification" of society. Sports metaphors, such as those involving "level playing fields," regulatory "hurdles," and "races" for company acquisitions and profit goals, routinely insinuate themselves into news bulletins. Similarly, the language of sports suffuses political discourse in liberal democracies, with electoral contests, parliamentary debates and policy disagreements framed in the manner of sports encounters. Advertisers also "pitch" products and services in sporting terms, with companies and consumers represented as "teams" and "oppositions," and the visual imagery of sports used to depict producers and consumers. Such representations of diverse organizations, relations, and practices as analogous to sports phenomena require skeptical sociological examination given their cultural-symbolic reduction of complex social, economic, and political processes to simple, imagined sports contests and outcomes.

The sociological analysis of sports and culture must deal adequately with the size, complexity, scope, and volatility of its immediate subject, and encompass its deep intrication with the sociocultural world as a whole. The power that can be wielded within sports culture is highly variable and clearly related to other resources of power (including economic, military, and geopolitical). The form that sports culture takes in different national and transnational contexts is both highly diverse and globally connected, and demands a rejuvenated, theoretically rigorous, historically informed, and culturally attuned sociology of sports and culture.

SEE ALSO: Body and Cultural Sociology; Sport and Culture

REFERENCE

Rowe, D. (2004) *Sport, Culture and the Media: The Unruly Trinity*, 2nd edn. Open University Press, Maidenhead.

SUGGESTED READING

Miller, T., Lawrence, G., McKay, J., & Rowe, D. (2001) *Globalization and Sport: Playing the World.* Sage, London.

DAVID ROWE

standardization

Standardization is a procedure used in science to increase validity and reliability. It assumes that objective scientific findings ought to be non-contradictory and replicable and that the best way to achieve this is to ensure that research instruments and methods remain uniform within a particular study and from one study to the next. The concept standardization is used in two distinct but related senses in science. In a purely descriptive sense, standardization establishes a lingua franca, facilitating confidence among researchers that they and others are gathering new knowledge about the same empirical phenomena. In the second sense, standardization ensures excellence. In this sense, standards not only keep research uniform but keep it "good." In survey research, considerable efforts are made to both promote the standardization of question formats and other kinds of measurement instruments across studies and to ensure uniformity of procedure amongst interviewers working on the same study. Critics of standardization sometimes argue that procedures that ensure findings can be replicated do not ensure those findings are valid. Other critics suggest that standardization inevitably entails coercion as proponents of different standardized procedures wrangle with one another for supremacy. Still others suggest that standardized methods can impose artificial frameworks on research that might distort rather than improve understanding. These critics suggest that a more naturalistic and spontaneous approach can sometimes facilitate a more nuanced sensitivity to the nature of phenomena under investigation. More recently, sociologists of science have shown that the use of standardized procedures must inevitably require discretionary assessments as to whether those procedures have been implemented properly. Because these discretionary assessments themselves can never be fully reduced to standardized protocols, we must remain cognizant of the fact that standardization can never completely eliminate the idiosyncratic influence of specific individuals and specific social contexts on the conduct of scientific research.

SEE ALSO: Reliability; Validity, Quantitative

SUGGESTED READINGS

Maynard, D. W., Houtkoop-Steenstra, H., Schaeffer, N. C., & van der Zouwen, J. (eds.) (2001) *Standardization and Tacit Knowledge: Interaction and Practice in the Survey Interview.* Wiley Interscience, New York.

Timmermans, S. & Berg, M. (2003) *The Gold Standard: The Challenge of Evidence-Based Medicine and Standardization in Health Care.* Temple University Press, Philadelphia.

DARIN WEINBERG

state

Few concepts are as central to social analysis and political practice as the state. Many assume that the state is synonymous with the elected government. All the non-elected state administrators, coercive apparatuses, and sociocultural institutions that constitute modern states are often ignored. Despite the crucial nature of state power, major political and methodological disputes remain over the nature and role of the state and how to acquire and maintain state power. Some argue that state institutions are interwoven with social and economic relations in society. Others view the state as distinct from non-state institutions because they perform coercive, taxing, judicial, and other administrative roles that private institutions cannot perform. Despite the privatization of various state industries and services, there is little prospect that the state (and millions of state employees) will be abolished and that all its current roles will be performed by private businesses. Sociologically and politically, Marxists argue that class and power relations in society hold the key to understanding state institutions and the way states maintain ruling-class power, ideology, and cultural practices. Conversely, liberals, conservatives and Weberians either reject the existence of a ruling class or see the state as independent of class divisions in society. Many radicals, liberals, and conservatives simplistically reduce complex state institutions to mere instruments, or to a homogenous actor or subject, like Machiavelli's Prince, capable of moral, immoral or amoral behavior and having a "collective mind" or political will. Others stress the historical uniqueness of each state and ignore those numerous aspects shared by contemporary states.

Without a notion of state institutions it is difficult to explain how stateless societies (such as indigenous communities) differ from societies with elaborate forms of military, fiscal, and administrative state power. Revolutions, imperialism, world wars, welfare states, and numerous other developments would be unintelligible if the vital roles played by state institutions were ignored. State theory has always been intimately related to particular historical and political developments. Political philosophers from Aristotle to Machiavelli analyzed political power in city-states and empires. Between the fifteenth and eighteenth centuries, religious conflict and secular opposition to religious authority led to a redefinition of church–state relations. Absolutism gave rise to liberal ideas about state sovereignty and property rights, constitutional checks on tyranny, and the belief in a "social contract" between rulers and citizens. Hobbes, Locke, Rousseau, and Hegel produced differing conceptions of the relationship between civil society and state institutions. States were either conceived as embodying the highest spiritual, legal, and political values, or as a constant threat to the freedom and privileges of citizens. The eighteenth- and nineteenth-century political economists – from Adam Smith to Karl Marx and J. S. Mill – helped lay the foundations of contemporary liberal and Marxist analyses of the role of states in developing capitalist societies.

The 1920s Italian Communist leader Antonio Gramsci analyzed the complex relationship between capitalist states and civil society. Capitalist hegemony required both coercion and consent via an elaborate set of cultural and educational practices, values, and socioeconomic relations. The visible state in the industrial capitalist west, Gramsci argued, could not be captured by revolutionaries (as Lenin had done in the largely agrarian Russia of 1917) if the less obvious "earth-works" (shoring up the state) of cultural and social hegemony remained largely intact. Fifty years later, neo-Marxist state theorists used Gramsci's work to reconceptualize contemporary state–civil society relations.

State coercion and consent were also central in the work of Weber. He differentiated between traditional forms of spiritual and princely authority or legitimacy and the development of an impersonal legal-rational authority that underpinned modern organizations – especially bureaucracies of the modern state. Weber defined the modern state as an organization that has "a monopoly of the legitimate use of physical force." Although state authorities do not like sharing armed power with other groups in nation-states, Weber's definition is limited in that many state officials tolerate both non-state criminal organizations and illegitimate coercion and corruption within state armed forces and police. Various state administrations and secret police have practiced state terrorism and illegal torture without the knowledge of citizens or other branches of government, thus mocking the notion of a monopoly of "legitimate violence."

Between the 1930s and 1960s liberals became increasingly divided over theories of democracy and the modern state. Conservative liberals continued to favor a laissez faire, "minimal state" that primarily defended private property rights against demands for social equality. The Great Depression of the 1930s, followed by the defeat of fascism in 1945, led various Keynesian liberals and "social market" liberals to champion new interventionist welfare states and international steering bodies such as the International Monetary Fund or supra-states like the European Union. Nevertheless, most liberals believe parties or individuals in government might pursue sectional interests, but view the state as neutral, serving all citizens impartially. Marxists, however, argued that it was impossible for the state to be a neutral umpire in a class-divided society. The 1970s neo-Marxist renaissance in state theory also stimulated interest in *the state* by feminists who focused on the *patriarchal state* which reproduced male dominance and worked against the interests of women in all spheres of social policy and power relations (Chappell 2003). Environmentalists also analyzed the absence of a *green state* or an *ecological state* (Eckersley 2004).

Despite their differences, Marxists, feminists and greens agreed that without state institutions private market forces would be unable to manage society, sustain profitability, or, equally importantly, defend capitalism against working-class and other social movement opposition.

SEE ALSO: Anarchism; Civil Society; Liberalism; Marxism and Sociology; Nation-State; Neo-liberalism; State and Economy; Welfare State

REFERENCES

Chappell, L. (2003) *Gendering Government*. UCB, Vancouver.

Eckersley, R. (2004) *The Green State: Rethinking Democracy and Sovereignty*. MIT Press, Cambridge, MA.

Jessop, B. (2002) *The Future of the Capitalist State*. Polity, Cambridge.

SUGGESTED READING

Frankel, B. (1983) *Beyond the State?* Macmillan, London.

BORIS FRANKEL

state and economy

HOW DOES CAPITALISM AFFECT DEMOCRATIC STATES?

Pluralists argue that a wide variety of economic actors, including representatives from business, labor, consumers, and others, struggle to influence the policy making process. Policymakers tend to respond most favorably to those groups who have the most resources, organizational skills, and access to policymakers.

Other scholars maintain that the business community has a significant advantage in this political competition. It has more resources than other groups in society and so is generally able to capture, dominate, or otherwise influence the policy making process to its advantage. Furthermore, policymakers have little choice but to promote continued business investment and economic growth or else they will be voted out of office, tax revenues will dry up, and the state will suffer political and fiscal crises.

Still other researchers suggest that states enjoy far more autonomy over economic policy making than these other perspectives acknowledge because politicians and state bureaucrats have interests of their own that they use the state to pursue. Some go so far as to suggest that states are predatory in the sense that their rulers are driven to maximize the revenue their states extract from the economy in order to increase their own power.

HOW DO DEMOCRATIC STATES AFFECT CAPITALISM?

The state always influences the economy. First, governments provide and allocate *resources* to business through direct subsidies, infrastructure investment, and procurement, which create incentives for firms to engage in many kinds of behavior. Second, states establish and enforce *property rights* and regulate firms in ways that affect their behavior and organization. Antitrust law, for instance, influences whether firms merge or not. Third, the *structure* of the state affects business. For example, decentralized states provide different opportunities for firms to relocate their operations within national borders than do centralized states. Finally, nation-states engage other nation-states in *geopolitics*. Such international activity often impacts national economies. Notably, when war breaks out, economies can be devastated or revitalized, as occurred in Western Europe and the United States, respectively, during World War II.

HOW ARE STATE-ECONOMY RELATIONS ORGANIZED?

Scholars often recognize three types of state-economy relationships in capitalist countries. First is the *liberal* model (e.g., USA, Britain) where the state tends to maintain an arms length relationship from the economy, grants much freedom to markets, pursues relatively vigorous antitrust policy, and relies heavily on broad macro-economic and monetary policies to smooth out business cycles, and tries not to interfere directly in the activities of individual firms. Second is the *statist* model (e.g., France, Japan) where the state is much more involved in the economy and exercises much greater influence over individual firms, such as by providing finance and credit directly to them. Third is the *corporatist* model (e.g., Germany) where the state promotes bargaining and negotiation among well organized social partners, notably business associations and labor unions, in order to promulgate economic and social policies that benefit all groups in society.

In sum, government can be an arm's-length regulator, a strong economic player, or a facilitator of bargained agreements. But the state and economy are *always* connected in important ways in capitalist democracies. And this has always been true – even in the most laissez faire examples of the nineteenth century when states prevented capitalist self-interest from getting out of hand to the point where it hurt workers, consumers, and the environment so much that it would have undermined capitalism itself (Polanyi 1944).

SEE ALSO: Capitalism; Polanyi, Karl; State; Welfare State

REFERENCE

Polanyi, K. (1944) *The Great Transformation*. Beacon Press, Boston, MA.

SUGGESTED READINGS

Katzenstein, P. J. (ed.) (1978) *Between Power and Plenty*. University of Wisconsin Press, Madison, WI.

Lindberg, L. N. & Campbell, J. L. (1991) The state and the organization of economic activity. In: Campbell, J. L., Hollingsworth, J. R., & Lindberg, L. N. (eds.), *Governance of the American Economy*. Cambridge University Press, New York, pp. 356–95.

JOHN L. CAMPBELL

statistical significance testing

One of the central goals of quantitative social science research is to establish relationships or associations between variables of interest as a means of providing empirical support for a theoretical proposition. Due to logistical constraints, researchers are usually unable to examine every single case in the population of interest and have to rely on a representative sample which is used to draw inferences about the population of interest. The adequacy of statistical inferences depends to a large extent on the representativeness of the sample.

Due to the necessity to work with samples rather than populations, tests of statistical significance, otherwise termed hypothesis testing or inferential statistics, are extremely important for dealing with the possibility that relationships derived from a sample data are based on chance. The goal of statistical inference is to be able to infer something about the truth of a hypothesis without collecting data from the entire population.

In hypothesis testing, the statistical hypothesis identifies an *assumed* value or relationship about a population – null hypothesis – which is assumed true until the sample data provide contradictory evidence. The null is rejected if an event can be shown to be *highly unlikely* to occur if the hypothesis is assumed true and the alternative hypothesis is affirmed. That is, if the sample result is contrary to what is expected when the hypothesis is assumed true, then the null hypothesis is rejected as a possibility.

The alternative hypothesis can be stated as a one-tailed or two-tailed test. If the researcher is unsure about the direction of the difference between and sample statistic and population parameter, then a 2-tailed test is specified. In this case, the researcher is most interested in whether there is difference between the sample and population but not the direction of the difference. In a 1-tailed test, on the other hand, the researcher can explicitly state whether the sample statistic is expected to be greater or smaller than the population parameter.

The decision to reject the null hypothesis in favor of an alternative hypothesis depends on the *alpha* level which is chosen prior to data analysis. For example, if the difference between the sample statistic and the hypothesized parameter is due to random chance, fewer than 5 times in 100 (i.e., $\alpha < 0.05$, or a 5 percent level of significance), then the results are deemed statistically significant. As decisions based on probabilities will not be correct 100 percent of the time, it is always possible that an error has been made in the statistical inference resulting from the decision on whether to reject null hypothesis.

SEE ALSO: Descriptive Statistics; Quantitative Methods; Statistics; Validity, Quantitative

SUGGESTED READINGS

Healey, J. F. & Prus, S. (2009). *Statistics: A Tool for Social Research*, 1st Canadian edn. Nelson, Toronto.

Levin, J. & Fox, J. A. (2007). *Elementary Statistics in Social Research*, 10th edn. Allyn & Bacon, Needham Heights, MA.

STEPHEN OBENG GYIMAH

statistics

In an early text on statistical reasoning in sociology, Mueller et al. defined the concept of statistics in two related manners: "(1) the factual data themselves, such as vital statistics, statistics on trade, production, and the like; and (2) the methods, theories, and techniques by means of which the collected descriptions are summarized and interpreted" (1970: 2). Moreover, Blalock (1972) identified five steps that all statistical tests have in common. First, assumptions concerning the population and the ability of the generalizations from the sample must be made. The assumptions also influence the formal stating of hypotheses (e.g., the null hypothesis is a statement of no association, and the research hypothesis is the alternative to the null). Then, the theoretical sampling distribution must be obtained or the probability distribution of the statistic must be rendered. Next, an appropriate significance level and critical region for the statistic must be selected. Fourth, the test statistic must be calculated. Lastly, based on the magnitude of the test statistic and its associated significance, a decision about the acceptance or rejection of hypotheses must be made.

The field of social statistics, in practice, is probably more concerned with the levels of measurement and the various types of statistical tests rather than the laws and rules that make such analysis possible in the first place. Indeed, the level at which social phenomena are measured dictates the type of statistical test that can be calculated. Concepts are measured at four levels: nominal, ordinal, interval, and ratio. Once a characteristic is measured, and the characteristic shows variation, then it is called a variable. Ratio measurement is the most precise because the distance between values is both equal and known, and variables measured at the ratio level may contain a true zero, which signifies the total absence of the attribute. As with variables expressed at the ratio level, interval-level variables are continuous, and the distance between values is also both known and constant. However, for variables measured at the interval level, no true zero point exists; the zero in interval-level data is arbitrary. Variables measured at the nominal and ordinal levels are categorical. With ordinal-level data, the response categories are both mutually exclusive and rank-ordered. The categories of a variable measured at the nominal level have no relationship with one another; they simply signify the presence or absence of a particular quality.

Statistical tests are generally univariate, bivariate, or multivariate in nature. Univariate statistics involve the description of one variable. If the variable was measured at a nominal level, then it is possible to report the mode (i.e., the most commonly occurring value), proportions, percentages, and ratios. When the variable is measured at the ordinal level, it becomes possible to calculate medians, quartiles, deciles, and quartile deviations. Then, at the interval and ratio levels of measurement, univariate procedures include means (i.e., the arithmetic average), medians (i.e., the midpoint), variances, and standard deviations. Measures of central tendency include the mode, median, and mean; measures of dispersion or the spread of the values for a given variable are typically reported as a quartile, percentile, variance, or standard deviation.

Bivariate statistics involve tests of association between two variables. Again, the level of measurement determines the appropriate bivariate statistic. For example, when both the dependent variable (i.e., the effect or the characteristic that is being affected by another variable) and the independent variable (i.e., the cause or the characteristic affecting the outcome) are measured at a nominal level, then the chi-square statistic is most commonly used. Unfortunately, the chi-square test only reveals if two variables are related; in order to determine the strength of a bivariate relationship involving two nominal variables, other statistics such as lambda or phi are used. When the dependent variable is measured at an interval or ratio level, and the independent variable is categorical (i.e., nominal or ordinal), then it becomes necessary to compare means across the categories of the independent variable. When the independent variable is dichotomous, the t-test statistic is used, and when the independent variable contains more than two categories, an analysis of variance (ANOVA) must be used. When both variables are measured at an interval or ratio level, then statistical tests based on the equation for a line, such as Pearson's correlation and least-squares regression, become appropriate procedures. Multivariate statistics often test for the relationship between two variables while holding constant a number of other variables; this introduces the principle of statistical control.

SEE ALSO: ANOVA (Analysis of Variance); Measures of Centrality; Multivariate Analysis; Random Sample; Regression and Regression Analysis; Statistical Significance Testing

SUGGESTED READINGS

Blalock, H. M. (1972) *Social Statistics*, 2nd edn. McGraw-Hill, New York.

Blalock, H. M. (ed.) (1974) *Measurement in the Social Sciences: Theories and Strategies.* Aldine, Chicago, IL.

Mueller, J. H., Schuessler, K. F., & Costner, H. L. (1970) *Statistical Reasoning in Sociology*, 2nd edn. Houghton Mifflin, Boston, MA.

WAYNE GILLESPIE

status

Status originates from Latin and means in the social sciences standing in society; status commonly denotes the state of affairs and legal position of a person. In sociology, the notion of status or social status designates location and position of collectivities – communities, groups or strata – in the social hierarchy of honor and prestige. Positions are distinguished from one another in terms of differentiated duties and rights, immunities and privileges gained in professions or other significant areas of social life, and are usually associated with a common lifestyle and consumption pattern. In turn, these distinguishing traits are attributed a hierarchical value that generally represents the scale of social worth in society.

Ralph Linton, an anthropologist, defines status as a position in a "particular pattern" (1936: 113). The status of an individual is the "sum total" of the positions he has acquired in society. Status is moreover gained mainly by achievement or ascription. It is achieved through personal efforts and it is ascribed on the basis of traits individuals have, for instance, their gender or ethnicity. Linton's approach departs from an earlier definition of status as the legal position of a person and accentuates that social standing is defined according to the degree of attributed prestige, esteem, and respect rather than possession of wealth and power.

Max Weber argues that status denotes "a quality of honor or a lack of it" (1974: 405), which is differentially attributed, constituting a system of social stratification based on custom and communal values. Status groups enjoy the same level of honour and are characterized by a common consumption pattern and a lifestyle. These groups strive to enhance the position of their members by claiming rights and privileges, while resisting status loss. In Weber's view, status groups differ from classes, however, in the long run both become "knitted" and interlinked: a highly valued status group will acquire wealth and power, and a wealthy class will acquire a high status (Weber 1974: 180–94.

Scientific preoccupation with status in western societies has been significant in exploring the constitution of social order and the relation of individuals to this order. Contemporary studies in status could be categorized in three broad areas: status and occupational stratification, status and "expectation states theory," and "status conversion" or "inconsistency." The first area of research comprises the paradigm best known as occupational stratification. This paradigm attempts to measure the standing of occupations in order to determine the structure of social stratification and (upward) social mobility. It also attempts to define the significance of occupation in determining the location of individuals in the social hierarchy. Research is mainly quantitative and some of the main criteria or "variables" employed are education, type of occupation, and income, best known as the socioeconomic index. Terms such as social or occupational status and occupational prestige are used interchangeably.

Expectation states theory, the second major research area in status, generally involves an attempt to uncover processes of evaluation among members of a well-defined group. Experimental findings indicate that individuals who are viewed as having a higher status are also considered by fellow group members to perform better even if this is not the case. Status clues, status characteristics and status symbols are concepts to describe how individuals exchange information in a tacit manner about their social status.

A third broad area of research and theorizing refers to phenomena of "status conversion" and "status inconsistency." Benoit drawing on Weber discusses status equilibration and status conversion mechanisms. The terms denote that different "types" of status tend to reach a common level; that is, an individual's high status in the economic hierarchy will match the achieved status in the "political hierarchy" and this in turn will be equivalent to the status in the "hierarchy of prestige" (Benoit 1966: 80). Hughes on the other hand examines status inconsistencies. The term means that a person occupies simultaneously different statuses, as for example women employed in highly esteemed economic or political positions. In practice, these persons are made invisible to clients or are directed to tasks that presumably fit better their "natural" social roles (1971). Hughes's approach touches upon the interrelational aspect of status: it is enjoyed when, if, and as long as it is granted by others. This aspect forms the crux of the matter in issues of inequality and social exclusion. The concept of status is thus still relevant today in studying social processes and outcomes related to unequal access to and use of social goods and services.

SEE ALSO: Class; Status Attainment; Status Construction Theory

REFERENCES

Benoit, E. (1966) [1944] Status, status types, and status interrelations. In: Biddle, B. J. & Thomas, E. J. (eds.), *Role Theory: Concepts and Research*. J. Wiley, New York, pp. 77–80.

Hughes, E. C. (1971) *The Sociological Eye: Selected Papers*. Aldine-Atherton, Chicago, IL.

Linton, R. (1936) *The Study of Man*. Appleton-Century, New York.

Weber, M. (1974) [1948] *From Max Weber: Essays in Sociology*, trans. & ed. H. H. Gerth & C. Wright Mills. Routledge & Kegan Paul, London.

VASILIKI KANTZARA

status attainment

Status attainment research begun by sociologists in the USA in the 1970s laid the foundation for the study of the transmission of socioeconomic advantage from one generation to the next (also called intergenerational social mobility). Status attainment research seeks to understand how characteristics of an individual's family background (also called socioeconomic origins) relate to his or her educational attainment and occupational status in society. It developed a methodology – usually path analysis and multiple regression techniques with large survey data sets – to investigate the intergenerational transmission of status.

In the classic study, *The American Occupational Structure* (1967), Peter Blau and Otis Dudley Duncan used national-level data obtained from the 1962 Current Population Survey from the US Census Bureau and presented a basic model of the stratification process in which father's education and occupational status explain son's educational attainment, and all three variables, in turn, explain son's first job and subsequent occupational attainment. They found that the effect of son's education on son's occupational attainment was much larger than the effect of father's occupation on son's occupational attainment; thus they concluded that in the USA in the mid-twentieth century, achievement was more important than ascription in determining occupational status.

International studies of social mobility have contributed greatly to our understanding of how family socioeconomic status shapes educational and occupational outcomes. The influence of the Blau–Duncan model is clearly evident in this international research; most studies conceptualize socioeconomic status as either father's education and occupation or a composite measure of these and other family background factors. Some researchers have had to alter this approach due to data limitations or considerations of the local context, but still, the systematic approach to the measurement of family background is striking. As a result of these efforts, status attainment models now exist for many nations in all regions of the world.

Status attainment research constitutes one of the largest bodies of empirical research in the study of social stratification. It reshaped the study of social mobility by focusing attention on how aspects of individuals' socioeconomic origins relate to their educational attainment and occupational status in society. Nonetheless, critics have noted several limitations with this line of research. First, status attainment research does a better job of explaining the social mobility for white males than females or minorities. Second, this line of research has limited explanatory power because, even for white males, status attainment models can explain only about half of the variance in occupational attainment. This indicates that even the most complex status attainment models still do not get very close to approximating the even more complex reality of the attainment process. Third, in its focus on individual characteristics, status attainment research has tended to neglect the role of structural factors in determining individual educational and occupational outcomes. Changes in the economy or changes in the opportunity structure of occupations caused by large-scale policy changes (e.g., equal employment opportunity policies) are just two examples of factors that create societal shifts that can impact status attainment processes at the individual level. Since the 1990s, more research has expanded status attainment research to account for such social structural or organizational factors that may play a role in individual mobility.

SEE ALSO: Horizonal and Vertical; Status

SUGGESTED READINGS

Campbell, R. (1983) Status attainment research: end of the beginning or beginning of the end? *Sociology of Education* 56: 47–62.

Sewell, W. H., Haller, A. O., & Portes, A. (1969) The educational and early occupational attainment process. *American Sociological Review* 34: 82–92.

CLAUDIA BUCHMANN

status construction theory

Status construction theory is a theory of how widely shared status beliefs form about apparently nominal social differences among people, such as sex or ethnicity. Status beliefs associate greater respect and competence with people in one category of a social difference (e.g., men, whites) than with those in another category of that difference (women, people of color). When widely shared in a population, status beliefs have consequences for inequality among individuals and groups.

The theory focuses on the aggregate effects that emerge from interpersonal encounters between socially different actors when these encounters have been framed and constrained by macro structural conditions. In interdependent encounters between categorically different people, interpersonal status hierarchies form just as they do in virtually all cooperative, goal-oriented encounters. Since the actual origins of such influence hierarchies are typically obscure to participants while the categorical difference between them is salient, the theory argues that there is some chance that the participants will associate their apparent difference in esteem and competence in the situation with their categorical difference. If the same association is repeated for them in subsequent intercategory encounters without being challenged by those present, the theory argues that participants will eventually form generalized status beliefs about the categorical difference.

Once people form such status beliefs, they carry them to their next encounters with those from the other group and act on them there. By treating categorically different others according to the status belief, belief holders "teach" some of the others to take on the belief as well. This creates a diffusion process that has the potential to spread the new status belief widely in the population.

Whether the new status belief does in fact spread widely and which categorical group it casts as higher status each depends on the structural conditions that shape the terms on which people from each group encounter one another. Of central interest is whether structural conditions create an unequal distribution between the groups of some factor such as material resources or technology that is helpful in gaining influence in intercategory encounters. The unequal distribution of such a "biasing factor" means that people from the group with more of the factor are systematically more likely to emerge as the influential actors in intercategory encounters than are people from the group with less of the factor. Thus, the "biasing factor" shapes intercategory encounters in such a way that these encounters continually produce more status beliefs favoring the structurally advantaged group than the other categorical group. Eventually, opposing status beliefs are overwhelmed as status beliefs favoring the structurally advantaged group spread to become widely shared in the population.

The theory's arguments about how encounters between socially different people create and spread status beliefs have been tested and supported in a series of laboratory experiments. Computer simulations of the diffusion process also support the theory's arguments about how structural conditions shape the aggregate consequences of encounters and cause widely shared status beliefs to emerge. The theory has been applied to explain the persistence of established status beliefs, such as those about gender, as well as to the emergence of new status beliefs.

SEE ALSO: Class, Status, and Power; Expectation States Theory; Status

SUGGESTED READINGS

Ridgeway, C. L. (1991) The social construction of status value: gender and other nominal characteristics. *Social Forces* 70: 367–86.

Ridgeway, C. L. (2006) Status construction theory. In: Burke, P. (ed.), *Contemporary Social Psychological Theories*. Stanford University Press, Stanford, CA, pp. 301–23.

Ridgeway, C. L. & Erickson, K. G. (2000) Creating and spreading status beliefs. *American Journal of Sociology* 106: 579–615.

CECILIA L. RIDGEWAY

stereotyping and stereotypes

Stereotyping is a way of representing and evaluating other people in fixed, unyielding terms. The stereotypes which result from this process homogenize traits held to be characteristic of particular categories of people, make them appear natural, necessary and unchangeable, reduce people to them without qualification and reproduce notions of others as radically different from those among whom the stereotypes circulate. The force of a stereotype is strongest when it is commonly held to be irrevocable. This is especially the case when stereotypes are connected to alleged biological determinants of, say, gender or ethnicity, for in such cases they can exert a tremendous pull, drawing description and assessment back towards their essentialist measures of difference.

Essentialism involves seeing others through the singular characteristic that is supposed to be definitive of who they are and what they do. It is the opposite of individualism, which conceives of each individual as personally unique regardless of their formation in particular cultural worlds. Against this exaggerated version of selfhood, stereotypes essentialize by refusing the distinction between individuality and group membership. Stereotypes make categories seem categorical, and so are a form of individualism in reverse.

Stereotyping is a sign of power, or a bid for that sign. The forms of representation it deals with provide support for existing structures of power, relations of domination and oppression, and inequalities of resource and opportunity. Yet those with relatively little power or privilege also engage in stereotyping, at times as a way of salvaging status and esteem from conditions which damage or destroy them. Their stereotypes of others may serve as scapegoats for feelings of frustration, disaffection, or anger, again because of social power and inequality. Travelers, foreign workers, and refugees (or so-called asylum-seekers) are examples of people who have suffered from this displaced aggression, not least when it is exploited by populist media with a main eye for circulation and sales. Stereotypes implicitly affirm those who stereotype in their own sense of superiority, and may also extend beyond this in validating a social order or culturally sanctioned hierarchy. The symbolic boundaries which stereotypes construct and reproduce strategically exclude those who are targeted, stating that "you do not belong here" or "you are not one of us." Stereotyping always operates via strict demarcations between "us" and "them," even when power issues are not immediately involved, as for example when it involves the selective idealization of others (e.g. the elevation of certain limited notions of feminine beauty or behavior, or the heroic status accorded by certain whites to black jazz, blues, or rap artists). Stereotypes may then appear to deal in positive images and affirmative identifications, but these are still one-sided projections and may have negative consequences for the other, as for example in confining them to a set role or ability.

Stereotyping may not be confined to the modern period, but it has certainly increased enormously during this time and become characteristic of modern societies or societies becoming modern, one that follows from their increased rate and pace of social change, movements of people and encounters with cultural difference. The need for informational short cuts and readymade devices of discourse and representation that help us process the otherwise overwhelming data of daily social realities creates fertile ground for stereotypes. Once established, they obstruct critical enquiry or fuller forms of portrayal because of their facile convenience and fixed manner of representation. Stereotyping may also be encouraged when the speed of social change results in a drive to order, reassertion of proprieties and norms, and antagonism towards fluidity and ambivalence. When these attain a resolute presence in media which are accredited as sources of authority or truth, the rhetorical force of stereotypes is increased, whether this involves young people reading teen magazines or adults watching the news on television.

Stereotyping is not just a psychological problem, attendant on the question of how to regard others as we strive to make sense of the world around us. It is also a sociological problem, attendant on the question of how others are conceived and represented. Contesting stereotypes involves untying their tight knots of symbolic figuration in the name of self-determination, and we should take heart from those who have done so, for they show that it is possible to challenge the closure of stereotypical representations and achieve greater inclusiveness within society, greater opportunities and scope, and a more positive social identity.

SEE ALSO: Essentialism and Constructionism; Social Control

SUGGESTED READING

Pickering, M. (2001) *Stereotyping: The Politics of Representation*, Palgrave Macmillan, New York.

MICHAEL PICKERING

stigma

The term stigma refers to a social or individual attribute that is devalued and discredited in a particular social context. As Goffman (1963) noted, however, this definition requires an important qualification, one that defines stigma in terms of "a language of relationship" that can link attributes to particular stereotypes, rather than a priori objectified attributes. The language of relationship between attributes and stereotypes is extremely important because an attribute, in and of itself, does not carry an inherent quality that makes it credible or discredible outside the nature of the stereotype that corresponds to it.

Link and Phelan (2001) defined stigma in terms of the presence and convergence of four interrelated components. First, people distinguish and label human differences. Second, members of the dominant cultural group link labeled persons with certain undesirable attributes. Third, negatively labeled groups or individuals are placed in distinct and separate categories from the non-stigmatized. Fourth, as a result of the first three components, labeled individuals experience status loss. Finally, the process of stigma placement, and therefore management, is dependent on the degree of one's access to social, economic, and political power.

Regardless of how stigma is defined, however, in order for an attribute to be designated as a mark of stigma, two conditions must be present. First, the designation of stigma must be informed by a collectively shared understanding by all participants of which attributes are stigmatizing in the available pool of socially meaningful categories in a particular social context. This statement is important because an attribute that is stigmatizing in one social context may not be stigmatizing in another. The second condition relates to the degree to which a mark of stigma is visible. The degree of visibility determines the stigmatized person's feelings about themselves and their interactions and relationship with non-stigmatized groups and individuals, particularly in situations perceived as potentially stigmatizing encounters.

There are two general categories of stigma attributes. The first category refers to attributes that are immediately or potentially visible upon social encounters. Three types of stigma attributes can be outlined within this category. The first relates to outward and clear physical deformations. The second relates to what Goffman described as "the tribal stigma of race, nation, and religion." The latter is transmitted through lineage, and affects all members of the stigmatized group.

This type of stigma can be characterized as collective or group stigma, while the first, physical deformities, affects only individuals, and can therefore be referred to as individual stigma.

The second broad category relates to stigma attributes that are not clearly and outwardly visible, but may or may not become visible upon social interaction and where the stigmatized person believes that their stigma is not known to those with whom they interact. The distinction between whether or not a particular stigma attribute is visible is important because it determines the nature of social interaction between those who are perceived as stigmatized and the normals. More importantly, it situates the nature of the reactions and information management by stigmatized individuals that appear to reveal their stigma attributes. In the case where the stigma attribute is readily and clearly visible, the process of information management involves attempts to minimize tensions generated during social interactions.

If the stigma attribute is visible, the process of information management shifts from mere tension management to information management about one's feelings of having a spoiled identity. The concern of the stigmatized in this case becomes one of whether or not to display discrediting information, and ultimately leads to what Goffman described as information management techniques.

There are a number of information management techniques employed by stigmatized individuals. One common technique is "covering." Covering refers to attempts by stigmatized individuals to conceal signs commonly considered stigma symbols. Another strategy is "distancing," where stigmatized individuals or groups disassociate themselves from those roles, associations, and institutions that may be considered as stigmatizing. Still another strategy is "compartmentalization," where individuals divide their worlds into two social worlds: a small and intimate one to which the stigmatized reveals their identity, and a larger group from which the stigmatized individual conceals their identity. Finally, individuals may engage in "embracement" through the expressive confirmation of the social roles and statuses associated with stigma (Snow & Anderson 1987).

SEE ALSO: Deviance; Facework; Goffman, Erving

REFERENCES

Goffman, E. (1963) *Stigma: Notes on the Management of Spoiled Identities*. Prentice Hall, Englewood Cliffs, NJ.

Link, B. & Phelan, J. (2001) Conceptualizing stigma. *Annual Review of Sociology* 27 (3): 363–85.

Snow, D. & Anderson, L. (1987) Identity work among the homeless: the verbal construction and avowal of personal identities. *American Journal of Sociology* 92: 1334–71.

SUGGESTED READING

Kusow, A. M. (2004) Contesting stigma: on Goffman's assumption of normative order. *Symbolic Interaction* 27 (2): 179–97.

ABDI M. KUSOW

stranger, the

In Simmel's essay, "The Stranger" (1971 [1908]) the notion of distance is important where the stranger is both remote and close; a part of the group as well as outside of it. His unusual social position leads others to assume that he possesses a unique objectivity. Therefore, group members are more inclined to divulge private information that they often keep hidden from intimates. This objectivity provides the stranger with more freedom because his atypical social position allows him to assess more accurately situations, even close ones, from a distance, with minimal personal bias.

Simmel writes that group members tend to highlight the general abstract traits that they share with the stranger. Therefore, the stranger is close to others based upon general similarities like nationality, social position, or occupation, but these same universal attributes make him remote because they also pertain to many others.

Because there is an emphasis on these general qualities, they also tend to stress the individual characteristics that they do not share with the stranger, which results in tension. Simmel also claims that there is a level of strangeness in even the most intimate associations. When entering into romantic relationships people tend to concentrate on what is unique and distinctive, but as time passes, each participant will come to question their relationship when they realize that it is not particularly exceptional. All close relationships must endure this assessment because they are never especially unique. This awareness results in an overall level of strangeness within the relationship.

Simmel argues that although varying degrees of remoteness and nearness are present in all relationships, there is a "special proportion and reciprocal tension" between farness and nearness that produce the unique social type of the stranger (Simmel 1971 [1908]: 149). But, Simmel warns, we cannot define or quantify this special proportion with great certainty.

SEE ALSO: Simmel, Georg; Social Distance

REFERENCE

Simmel, G. (1971) [1908] The Stranger. In: Levine, D. N. (ed.), *George Simmel: On Individuality and Social Forms.* University of Chicago Press, Chicago, IL, pp. 143–9.

TERRI LEMOYNE

strategic essentialism

Strategic essentialism is an approach developed by Gayatri Chakravorty Spivak, which describes the political use of what is considered to be an "essence" with a critique and recognition of the essentialist nature of the essence itself. This concept operates in relationship to the concept of the *subaltern*. The *subaltern* is a term often used to represent the oppressed or "Other" in society and Spivak recognizes that what constitutes the *subaltern* is defined by the elites.

Strategic essentialism seeks to identify the use of labels out of political interest while acknowledging the complexities of the core meaning (or essence). For example, a group of disabled veterans may be fighting for benefits owed to them by the government; the elites. At the same time they are recognizing the complexities of what it means to be a "disabled veteran" as defined by the elites. The literal categorization of the term "disabled veteran" may not mesh with the current cultural understanding both inside and outside of the group itself. The group identity serves as a basis of struggle and yet within the group, there is also debate related to what "disabled veteran" actually means.

There are a number of critiques of strategic essentialism, including Spivak who sees the concept evolving into a means for promoting essentialism rather than as a means of analysis. Some question the concept's accountability for the intricacies of identities, due to the focus on specific issues within a certain political, geographic, historical context. The concept has morphed into a theory rather than remaining a technique or strategy for understanding the complexity and fluidity of subject/object positions, of identity and power.

SEE ALSO: Deconstruction; Essentialism and Constructionism

SUGGESTED READING

Spivak, G. C. (1996) *The Spivak Reader*, ed. Landry, D. & MacLean, G. Routledge, London.

KRISTINA B. WOLFF

stratification: functional and conflict theories

The classic, functionalist statement on social stratification is by Kingsley Davis and Wilbert Moore (1945). "Starting from the proposition that no society is 'classless,' or unstratified," they sought "to explain, in functional terms, the universal necessity that calls forth stratification in any social system" (p. 242). The main functional requisites that stratification fulfills are the need to distribute people in the social structure, motivate them to strive to fill important, demanding positions and then to perform. Because not all positions are equally pleasant, demanding in skills or important "to societal survival," the differential rewards of social stratification induce people to fill significant, demanding positions. Thus social inequality is "an unconsciously evolved device by which societies insure that the most important positions are conscientiously filled by the most qualified persons" (p. 243). The positions offering the most rewards – financial, respect, status, and lifestyle comforts – are the most important and require the greatest talent and training. Any position that is easily filled, no matter its importance, does not require significant reward. "[I]f the skills required are scarce by reason of the rarity of talent, or the costliness of training, the position, if functionally important, must have an attractive power that will draw the necessary skills in competition with other positions" (p. 244).

After presenting their main premises and argument, Davis and Moore discussed how stratification operated functionally in the spheres of religion, government, technical knowledge, and wealth, property and labor.

Davis and Moore's article stimulated considerable debate. Conflict theorists posed several fundamental criticisms. Critical of functionalists' highly abstract conception of society as a natural, boundary-maintaining system with specific functional requisites, conflict theorists argued that social formations (and the stratification systems found throughout history) are constituted through specific, contested struggles between groups with differing aims. Social groups (particularly classes), power, history, historical location and social context which are central to understanding stratification are absent from the functionalist position.

More specifically, while functionalist theory might help account for the emergence of stratification as social groups begin to experience increasing social differentiation, over the long term there are specific actions that groups take to either retain their positions of social advantage and power or to challenge emerging social inequalities. Thus, even if stratification arose because some positions were genuinely important and required hard-to-find or costly-to-develop skills, once individuals or groups occupy those positions they then have the power and resources to consolidate their positions of privilege, close or narrow access to those positions and create an ideology of legitimacy that serves their particular interests. As a skilled group, sharing specific abilities and desires, those individuals can mobilize resources and organize themselves more effectively than larger, disparate groups pushing for greater access or more equity in the allocation of social rewards. Moreover, in the short-run, restrictions to equality of opportunity and existing inequalities of condition mean that the alleged functionality of stratification is limited – even precluded – by the power wielded by those at the top of the hierarchy.

Finally, critics noted that Davis and Moore's premises presupposed a key relationship that they needed to demonstrate – that increased social differentiation must result in stratification.

SEE ALSO: Conflict Theory; Functionalism/Neofunctionalism; Stratification: Gender and; Stratification and Inequality, Theories of;

REFERENCE

Davis, K. & Moore, W. (1945) Some principles of stratification. *American Sociological Review* (10): 242–9.

SUGGESTED READINGS

Horton, J. (1966) Order and conflict theories of social problems as competing ideologies. *American Journal of Sociology* 71: 701–13.

Wrong, D. (1959) The functional theory of stratification: some neglected considerations. *American Sociological Review* (24): 772–82.

ROB BEAMISH

stratification, gender and

Although social stratification lies at the heart of macro-sociology, the study of gender and stratification is comparatively recent, and developed from feminist scholarship. The traditional sociological view is that the oppression of women is adequately covered by class analysis. Feminist theory insists that the class structure, and the oppression of women within patriarchal systems, are separate but interacting social processes.

Conventional class analysis treats all members of a household as having the same social class as the main breadwinner, who is usually a man. Feminists debated whether wives should be allocated to classes on the basis of their husband's occupation or the wife's current (or last) occupation. It is now agreed that women's position in society, and in the labor force, should be studied separately from class analysis. Empirical research has shown that the sex segregation of occupations, and the pay gap between men and women, cut across social classes in ways that vary from one society to another, and vary across time. Occupational segregation and the pay gap develop and change independently within labor markets due to variations in female employment, anti-discrimination policies and other social policies – including family-friendly policies that have been counter-productive in their effects. Similarly, women's position in the family is studied independently of their position in the class structure, and depends on their education (relative to that of their spouse) as much as their earning power and occupational status.

The feminist assumption that dual-earner and dual-career families would become universal after equal opportunities policies took effect has been proven wrong, even for ex-socialist countries. Instead, couples choose between three family models, corresponding to women's three lifestyle preferences: a minority of work-centered women who adopt the male profile of continuous full-time employment and are financially self-supporting; a minority of home-centered women who are dependent on their spouses after marriage; and a majority of adaptive women who are secondary earners within their households rather than careerists, and have varied employment patterns. This heterogeneity of women's lifestyle preferences, and thus employment profiles, cuts across social classes, education levels, and income levels. This diversity of female lifestyle choices produces a polarization of female employment profiles over the lifecycle, and is a major cause of rising income inequality between households in modern societies – as illustrated by income differences between dual-career childless couples and one-earner couples with several children to support.

Currently, female social stratification differs from male social stratification, because women have two avenues for achieving higher social status and class position – through the labor market or the marriage market. Both are actively used by women, even today. Men rarely use the marriage market for advancement because the vast majority of women resist the idea of role reversal in marriage, with the woman as the main income-earner.

Overall, stratification and inequality among women tends to be larger than among men. For example, in Britain at the start of the twenty-first century, there were more female than male millionaires, because some women achieved success and wealth through their own gainful work, and some achieved wealth as rich men's ex-wives or widows.

The picture in developing societies depends a lot on whether women have independent access to the labor market/market economy, have access primarily through male members of their family (father or spouse), or are expected to refrain from market activities and devote themselves exclusively to homemaking and childrearing activities. In agricultural societies, technology is also an important factor in women's social and economic position – as illustrated by large differences in women's position in economies depending on the hoe or on the plough.

SEE ALSO: Gender, Work, and Family; Inequality/Stratification, Gender; International Gender Division of Labor; Stratification and Inequality, Theories of

SUGGESTED READINGS

Crompton, R. & Mann, M. (eds.) (1986) *Gender and Stratification*. Polity Press, Cambridge.

Hakim, C. (2000) *Work–Lifestyle Choices in the 21st Century: Preference Theory*. Oxford University Press, Oxford.

Hakim, C. (2004) *Key Issues in Women's Work: Female Diversity and the Polarisation of Women's Employment*. Glasshouse Press, London.

CATHERINE HAKIM

stratification, race/ethnicity and

An important research field in the stratification literature is concerned with inequalities along the ascribed characteristics of race and ethnicity. The term race connotes biological differences among people (skin color, facial features) that are transmitted from generation to generation. As such, these biological differences are seen as permanent characteristics of people. However, the notion of race does not make much sense as a biological concept, because the physical characteristics that make people distinctive are trivial. Even though biological differences are superficial, they are important sociologically. For if people believe that others are biologically distinctive, they tend to respond to them as being different. Furthermore, skin color is transmitted from generation to generation by assortative marriage, a prime sociological phenomenon.

Race is considered a social construct and in that sense incorporated in the more general notion of ethnicity. An ethnic group is a subpopulation of individuals who are labeled by the majority and by the members of a group itself as being of a particular ethnicity. The term ethnicity refers to the (perceived) historical experiences of a group as well as its unique organizational, behavioral, and/or cultural characteristics. Thus, ethnic groups can be distinguished by their country of origin, religion, family practices, language, beliefs, and values. The more visible the characteristics marking ethnicity, the more likely it is that those in an ethnic category will be treated differently.

Ethnic inequality is documented in different ways. Important aspects of inequality include education (school dropout, educational attainment), the labor market (unemployment, occupational status, income), wealth, housing quality, and health. These issues are examined at the national level, telling us something about the distribution within a population, and at the individual level, informing us about mobility. Questions on mobility include examinations of the life course of people (i.e., intragenerational) and studies comparing parents and their children (i.e., intergenerational).

The literature on ethnic stratification is divided into three different research lines. The first is concerned with the position of *indigenous populations* that were annexed through military operations and colonization, such as the American Indians in North and South America, Aboriginals in Australia, and Maori in New Zealand. The second focuses on ethnic groups that are the offspring of *slaves* or *involuntary migrants*, such as African Americans in America. The third is concerned with the economic position of *voluntary migrants* and their offspring, such as the Italians who moved to the US at the turn of the twentieth century.

Many researchers use notions of discrimination to explain group differences in ethnic stratification. Two different types of ethnic discrimination (i.e., the unequal treatment of minority groups) are outlined: attitudinal and institutional. Attitudinal discrimination refers to discriminatory practices influenced by prejudice. Research shows that prejudice, and, in turn, discrimination, tends to increase when ethnic groups are perceived as threatening to the majority population in terms of cultural, economic, or political resources. Ethnic groups that are numerically large and that are distinct culturally are especially vulnerable to discrimination. This led to theories about ethnic competition and split labor markets.

Another important theory is that of statistical discrimination.

Institutional discrimination refers to rules, policies, practices, and laws that discriminate against ethnic groups. This type of discrimination is used to explain the economic difficulties that African slaves and their offspring experienced in the USA. For instance, through the first half of the twentieth century, they were formally excluded from acquiring or inheriting property, marrying whites, voting, testifying against whites in court, and attending higher-quality schools.

Various research designs have been used to study ethnic stratification. The classical design is the case study, in which a single ethnic group in a single receiving context is examined. Because this design provides little information on contextual effects, comparative macro designs have also been developed. One such popular framework is the "comparative origin" method, which compares multiple ethnic groups in a single location, yielding important insights into ethnic group differences. Similarly, researchers have paid attention to the role of the receiving context by comparing a single ethnic group across multiple destinations, such as cities or nations ("comparative destination" design). More recently, these macro approaches have been combined into a "double comparative" design, which studies multiple-origin groups in multiple destinations simultaneously. This design provides a better understanding of ethnic origin, the receiving context, and the specific interaction between origin and destination ("ethnic community").

Researchers nowadays agree that ethnicity plays a role in people's life chances, that ethnic groups gradually improve their economic standing across generations, and that the process of assimilation can be interpreted in terms of human capital accumulation. At the same time, it is found that assimilation rates of ethnic groups vary. Initially, researchers have relied on theories of biological traits and cultural dispositions to explain such group differences, but they have been largely replaced by extensions of the human capital theory, ideas on discrimination, the concept of ethnic capital, and spatial differences in economic opportunities. In recent work, researchers have combined the theories explaining group differences with micro-level approaches explaining individual assimilation.

SEE ALSO: Assimilation; Ethnic Enclaves; Ethnicity; Race; Stratification and Inequality, Theories of

SUGGESTED READINGS

Aguirre, A. & Turner, J. H. (2004) *American Ethnicity: The Dynamics and Consequences of Discrimination.* McGraw-Hill, New York.

Alba, R. & Nee, V. (2003) *Remaking the American Mainstream: Assimilation and Contemporary Immigration.* Harvard University Press, Cambridge, MA.

Gordon, M. M. (1964) *Assimilation in American Life.* Oxford University Press, New York.

FRANK VAN TUBERGEN

stratification and inequality, theories of

The term stratification system refers to the complex of institutions that generate inequalities in income, political power, social honor, and other valued goods. The main components of such systems are: (1) the social processes that define certain types of goods as valuable and desirable, (2) the rules of allocation that distribute these goods across various roles or occupations in the division of labor (e.g., houseworker, doctor, prime minister), and (3) the mobility mechanisms that link individuals to these roles or occupations and thereby generate unequal control over valued goods. It follows that inequality is produced by two types of matching processes: The social roles in society are first matched to "reward packages" of unequal value, and individual members of society are then allocated to the roles so defined and rewarded.

There is a growing consensus among academics, policymakers, and even politicians that poverty and inequality should no longer be treated as soft "social issues" that can safely be subordinated to more fundamental interests in maximizing total economic output. This growing concern with poverty and inequality may be attributed to such factors as: (1) a spectacular increase in income inequality in many late-industrial countries that was entirely unpredicted and contradicted the reigning paradigm that late industrialism would bring increasingly diffused affluence; (2) the persistence of various noneconomic forms of inequality (e.g., racially segregated neighborhoods, gender pay gap) despite decades of quite aggressive egalitarian reform; (3) the mounting evidence that extreme income inequality, far from increasing a country's economic output, may be counterproductive and in fact reduce total output; (4) an emerging concern that poverty and inequality may also have negative macro-level effects on terrorism, ethnic unrest, and other collective outcomes; (5) a growing awareness of the negative individual-level effects of poverty on health, political participation, and a host of other life conditions; (6) the rise of a "global village" in which spatial disparities in the standard of living have become more widely visible; (7) an idiosyncratic constellation of recent news events that have exposed troubling inequalities (e.g., Katrina, executive compensation scandals); and (8) a growing commitment to a broader conception of human entitlements that encompasses "rights" to basic social amenities (e.g., housing) as well as rights to basic forms of social participation, such as employment.

The first task in understanding inequality and poverty is to specify the types of assets that are unequally distributed. It is increasingly fashionable to recognize that inequality is "multidimensional," that income inequality is accordingly only one of many forms of inequality, and that income redistribution in and of itself would not eliminate inequality. When a multidimensionalist approach is taken, one might usefully distinguish between the eight types of assets listed in the left column of Table 1, each understood as valuable in its own right rather than a mere investment item. It is now fashionable, for example, to examine the structure of inequality with respect to such outcomes as computer literacy, mortality and health, risk of imprisonment, and lifestyles.

Arguably, the most dramatic social scientific finding of our time is that income inequality has increased markedly since the 1970s, reversing a longstanding decline stretching from the eve of the Great Depression to the early 1970s. We have since witnessed one of the most massive research efforts in the history of social science as scholars sought to identify the "smoking gun" that accounted for this dramatic increase in inequality. Initially, the dominant hypothesis was that deindustrialization (i.e., the relocation of manufacturing jobs to offshore labor markets) brought about a decline in demand for less-educated manufacturing workers, a decline that generated increases in inequality by hollowing out the middle class and sending manufacturing workers into unemployment or the ranks of poorly paid service work. This line of argumentation still has its advocates but cannot be reconciled with evidence suggesting that the computerization of the workplace

Table 1 Types of valued goods and examples of advantaged and disadvantaged groups

Assets		*Examples*	
Asset group	*Examples of types*	*Advantaged*	*Disadvantaged*
1 Economic	Wealth	Billionaire	Bankrupt worker
	Income	Professional	Laborer
	Ownership	Capitalist	Worker (i.e., employed)
2 Power	Political power	Prime minister	Disenfranchised person
	Workplace authority	Manager	Subordinate worker
	Household authority	"Head of household"	Child
3 Cultural	Knowledge	Intelligentsia	Uneducated
	Popular culture	Movie star	High-culture "elitist"
	"Good" manners	Aristocracy	Commoner
4 Social	Social clubs	Country club member	Non-member
	Workplace associations	Union member	Non-member
	Informal networks	Washington "A list"	Social unknown
5 Honorific	Occupational	Judge	Garbage collector
	Religious	Saint	Excommunicate
	Merit-based	Nobel Prize winner	Non-winner
6 Civil	Right to work	Citizen	Illegal immigrant
	Due process	Citizen	Suspected terrorist
	Franchise	Citizen	Felon
7 Human	On-the-job	Experienced worker	Inexperienced worker
	General schooling	College graduate	High school dropout
	Vocational training	Law school graduate	Unskilled worker
8 Physical (i.e., health)	Mortality	Person with long life	A "premature" death
	Physical disease	Healthy person	Person with AIDS, asthma
	Mental health	Healthy person	Depressed, alienated

and related technological change has been a driving force behind a heightened demand for highly educated workers. Because of this result, the deindustrialization story has now been largely supplanted by the converse hypothesis that "skill-biased technological change" has increased the demand for high-skill workers beyond the increase in supply, thus inducing a short-term disequilibrium and a correspondingly increased payoff for high-skill labor. At the same time, most scholars acknowledge that this story is also an incomplete one and that other accounts, especially narrowly political ones, must additionally be entertained. Most notably, some of the rise in income inequality in the USA is clearly attributable to the declining minimum wage, a decline that in turn has to be understood as the outcome of political contests that increasingly favor pro-inequality forces.

Although inequality scholars have long sought to understand how different "reward packages" are attached to different social positions, an equally important task within the field is that of understanding the rules by which individuals are allocated to these positions. The language of stratification theory makes a sharp distinction between the distribution of social rewards (e.g., the income distribution) and the distribution of opportunities for securing these rewards. It follows that social scientists have become interested in the study of opportunity and how it is unequally distributed. This interest leads to analyses of the net effects of gender, race, and class background on labor market rewards. The size of such net effects may be uncovered statistically by examining between-group differences in income (and other rewards) in the context of models that control all merit-based sources of remuneration. Additionally, experimental approaches to measuring discrimination have recently become popular, most notably "audit studies" that proceed by: (1) sending employers resumes that are identical save for the applicant's gender, race, or class, and (2) then examining whether call-back rates (for interviews) are nonetheless different across such groups.

SEE ALSO: Income Inequality and Income Mobility; Mobility, Horizontal and Vertical; Poverty; Status Attainment

SUGGESTED READING

Grusky, D. B., Ku, M. C., & Szelényi, S. (2008) *Social Stratification: Class, Race, and Gender in Sociological Perspective*, 3rd edn. Westview Press, Boulder, CO.

DAVID B. GRUSKY

structural functional theory

Structural functional theory holds that society is best understood as a complex system with various interdependent parts that work together to increase stability. For most of the twentieth century the structural functional perspective (also called functionalism) was the dominant sociological approach in the USA and western Europe. Although the label structural functional theory has subsumed multiple perspectives, there are a few basic elements that generally hold for all functionalist approaches in sociology: social systems are composed of interconnected parts; the parts of a system can be understood in terms of how each contributes to meeting the needs of the whole; and social systems tend to remain in equilibrium, with change in one part of the system leading to (generally adverse) changes in other parts of the system.

HISTORICAL DEVELOPMENT

Talcott Parsons was perhaps most instrumental in promulgating structural functional theory in the twentieth century (Parsons 1937). He constructed a theory of social action which argued that individual action is rooted in the norms of society and constrained by its values. In this way, individuals carry out actions that benefit the whole of society. Drawing on Spencer's work, Parsons also asserted that all societies must meet certain needs in order to survive. His AGIL scheme (Parsons 1951) proposed that all societies must fulfill an adaptive function, a goal-attainment function, an integrative function, and latent pattern maintenance (latency).

Following Parsons, Robert K. Merton laid out a working strategy for how to "do" structural functional theory in distinguishing between manifest (or intended) functions and latent (or unintended) functions, noting that the same acts can be both functional and dysfunctional for the social whole. Merton (1968) proposed that sociologists can examine the functional and dysfunctional elements of any structure, determine the "net balance" between the two, and conclude whether or not the structure is functional for society as a whole.

CENTRAL ELEMENTS

Although structural functional theory has taken various forms, there are a few basic elements that are central to the perspective. First, the theory leads to a focus on the functions of various structures. By "functions," theorists in the perspective generally mean consequences that benefit society as a whole, contribute to its operation, or increase its stability. "Structure," in its broadest sense, can mean anything that exists independent of individual actors. Social arrangements such as stratification systems therefore are social structures, as are social institutions such as marriage. Structural functional theorists tend to examine social structures in terms of the functions they serve for society. Davis and Moore (1945), for example, developed a functional theory of stratification in which they argued that a stratification system is a functional necessity, with positions in society that are more functionally important garnering higher rewards.

A second basic element of structural functional theory is rooted in the organic analogies of Comte and Spencer. The theory treats society as an integrated whole with a series of interconnected parts. Further, the theory holds that the various parts contribute to the functioning of the whole. Durkheim, for example, proposed that when all of the parts of the social whole are fulfilling their necessary functions, then society is in a "normal" state. When individual parts are not fulfilling their functions, Durkheim argued, society is in a "pathological" state.

Third, structural functional theorists assume that society rests on the consensus of its members, and that there is widespread agreement on what is good and just for society. Davis and Moore's theory of stratification, for instance, rests on an assumption that members of society generally agree on which social positions are most important for society.

CRITICISMS

In the middle of the twentieth century, structural functional theory became the dominant sociological perspective in the USA and western Europe. In the 1960s, however, criticisms of the theory began to mount. These criticisms took a variety of forms, but two were perhaps most common: the theory deemphasizes social conflict and it does not adequately address social change.

According to critics, structural functional theory overemphasizes social cohesion while ignoring social conflict. By treating society as an interconnected whole, structural functional theory emphasizes integration among the various parts of society. With this approach, critics hold that the theory disregards social conflict. Moreover, because of its focus on social consensus and integration, any attention the theory does pay to conflict tends to treat it as disruptive.

Critics also contend that structural functional theory is ill-equipped to deal with social change. Another consequence of viewing society as a system of interconnected parts is that any changes are seen as having the consequence of disrupting the entire system. To early thinkers in the functionalist perspective, change was a major threat. Herbert Spencer, for example, held that any change made with the objective of benefiting society will have unforeseen negative impacts. While more contemporary theorists in the structural functional paradigm have not been as hostile to social change as was Spencer, the theory still has difficulty in dealing with change. This has led to a criticism of the perspective as being conservative in nature.

CONTEMPORARY FUNCTIONALISM

Perhaps the best-known contemporary variant of structural functionalism is the neofunctionalism of Alexander and colleagues (Alexander 1998; Alexander & Colomy 1990). Neofunctionalism is largely a reconstruction of Parsons's body of work, avoiding many of the pitfalls of earlier structural functional theorists. It accomplishes this in part by not taking social integration as a given, by giving greater weight to social action, and by specifying the role that the perspective should play in the production of knowledge.

SEE ALSO: Functionalism/Neofunctionalism; Merton, Robert K.; Parsons, Talcott

REFERENCES

Alexander, J. C. (1998) *Neofunctionalism and After.* Blackwell, Oxford.

Davis, K. & Moore, W. (1945) Some principles of stratification. *American Sociological Review* 10: 242–9.

Merton, R. K. (1968) *Social Theory and Social Structure.* Free Press, New York.

Parsons, T. (1937) *The Structure of Social Action.* McGraw-Hill, New York.

Parsons, T. (1951) *The Social System.* Free Press, Glencoe, IL.

JEFFREY W. LUCAS

structuralism

Structuralism is a catchall term for a set of explanatory approaches in the social sciences that emphasize the causal force of the relations among elements in a system rather than the character of the elements individually. Various structural approaches have at times been popular in linguistics, psychology, anthropology, and sociology. In the latter two fields, distinct forms developed that can both be traced back to Émile Durkheim, while sociology has also produced strains of structuralism influenced by Georg Simmel. Arising from Durkheim and Simmel as well has been the programmatic contention that only structural approaches provide a basis for distinguishing sociological-anthropological explanations from psychological or economic ones.

Anthropological structuralism achieved celebrity through the writings of Claude Lévi-Strauss. He offered novel and intriguing structural explanations of marriage systems, of totemism, and of primitive systems of myth, but his work soon came under attack. It was seen as too systematic and scientistic by some scholars in the humanities, whose critiques were instrumental in launching poststructuralism and postmodernism as intellectual currents. At the same time, some anthropologists and sociologists (e.g. Harris 1968) criticized it as a form of self-validating idealism. It never propagated as a method.

In sociology, structuralism has had a longer, more varied, and less meteoric career. One strand of structural analysis follows Durkheim in viewing elements of culture as determined by social structure. Another carries forward Simmel's view of social structure as having formal properties that condition behaviors well beyond the domain of culture. They join in viewing social structure as the source of what Durkheim called *social facts*, that is, causal currents that generally operate outside the awareness of social actors.

As an example of the Durkheimian strand, sociologist Guy Swanson argued in *The Birth of the Gods* that the structure of relations among organized groups in society determined how the spiritual world was conceptualized. Swanson showed, for instance, that the concept of a "high god" directing lesser spiritual agents occurred more frequently in societies with a significant number of hierarchically organized "sovereign groups," each having jurisdiction over an array of human affairs. Societies with lesser numbers of such groups believed either in unorganized spiritual forces or in multiple, competing divinities. Thus the structure of sociopolitical organization was shown to determine relative monotheism within the cultural domain.

While the Durkheimian strand of structuralism has largely explained variation in culture, the Simmelian strand has taken a more systematic approach to defining and mapping social structure, and used the result to explain a wider range of social behavior. Its main objective is to show how well-defined properties of social structures (or occupancy of particular positions within them) constrain behavior. The structures range from small-scale friendship or work groups, mapped sociometrically, to entire societies, viewed in terms of specific structural properties.

Network theories, for instance, use features of social structure such as the comparative intimacy of social relationships, the proportion of weak to strong ties among individuals, and the relative frequency of bridging ties among groups, to explain an array of social phenomena ranging from the capacity of communities to mobilize politically to the comparative catholicity of cultural tastes. An interesting feature of network theories has been their suggestion that occupants of positions that are connected to other positions in similar ways should behave similarly, as Ronald Burt argues in *Toward a Structural Theory of Action*. The explanatory power of the principle of structural equivalence is only now being explored.

A somewhat different approach was taken by Peter Blau in *Inequality and Heterogeneity*, which views the skeleton of social structure as composed of the different dimensions along which people are differentiated from one another. Among these might be wealth, education, gender, religious confession, political party, and so on. Societies vary in the number of dimensions involved in drawing distinctions (their heterogeneity) and the tendency of dimensions to be ranked (their inequality). They also vary in the degree to which positions allow for interaction with diverse others (the relative intersection of dimensions) and the degree to which ranking on one dimension predicts ranking on others (relative consolidation of dimensions). Blau explored many features of social life that are dependent upon these variables: for instance, greater intersection of dimensions seems to decrease the likelihood of intergroup conflict.

Programmatic structuralism advances the claims of Durkheim and Simmel that the integrity of sociology as a scientific discipline depends upon establishing a realm of causation distinct from those explored by psychology or economics. This position has been most forcefully argued and illustrated by Donald Black (1976; 2000). Neither Durkheim nor Simmel, he argues, had the strength of their convictions, since both consistently relied on individual psychologistic explanations. All classical and most modern sociology, suggests Black, focuses more on understanding people than on understanding social life, with the consequence that it is more psychological than sociological. To finally become sociological, sociologists must replace their interest in people with an interest in social life and how it can be explained structurally. Black exemplifies this by explaining the behavior of law as a result of structural variation in social life.

Structuralism has been handicapped by a lack of consensus over how to define social structure. Were consensus reached, though, problems of measurement would still plague it, since many of its propositions will be hard to test unless and until metrics are established that allow comparisons across the important dimensions of social structure. Until this methodological problem can be solved, structuralist theorizing is apt to remain suggestive rather than successfully separating sociology from psychology and economics.

SEE ALSO: Postmodern Social Theory; Poststructuralism; Social Structure

REFERENCES

Black, D. (1976) *The Behavior of Law*. Academic Press, New York.
Black, D. (2000) Dreams of pure sociology. *Sociological Theory* 18: 343–67.
Harris, M. (1968) *The Rise of Anthropological Theory: A History of Theories of Culture*. Crowell, New York.

MARK A. SCHNEIDER

structuration theory

In its early form structuration theory was developed by the British sociologist Anthony Giddens in a series of publications in the 1970s and early 1980s as he attempted to define a distinctive approach to the study of social relations. Structuration has since been further refined, strengthened and reinvigorated in the course of debate, critique, counter-critique, and through the lessons of diverse empirical applications.

Giddens wanted the term "structuration" to signal an approach that subverted more static notions of social "structure" and gave due weight to the dynamic qualities of agency. He presented social life in terms of parallel and intersecting sequences in which agents – who are both constrained and enabled by their particular social conditions (structures) containing varying contents and combinations of power relations, norms and meanings – draw on their structural context in producing actions that collectively combine to produce the shape of subsequent structures, and so on. Agents *draw on* this context through, for example, their understanding of it, through the skills and dispositions they have derived from it, and through the power resources it provides. Social life is thus said to be characterized by a "duality of structure" whereby agents draw on structures (as the *medium* of action) to produce actions that then change or maintain structures (the *outcome* of action). The attention given to the temporal sequencing of such "situated action" is coupled with an equal concern with spatial conditions and dynamics. The inclusion of both structures and agency within structuration meant that Giddens was able to fashion a path between the deterministic tendencies of Marxism and Positivism, on the one hand, and the overly voluntaristic, free-floating approaches of interpretive sociologies such as ethnomethodology and symbolic interactionism, on the other. Many have noted the similarities between Giddens's approach here and that of the French theorist Pierre Bourdieu.

Structuration's emphasis on process and agency means that the very concept of "structure" must be re-conceptualized in terms of the situated praxis of agents acting in conditions of power, norms and meanings. The very existence of social structures relies on their continuing to be "put to work" by the agents within them; a living institutional structure such as a library only continues to exist in a meaningful form as long as people continue to run it and use it as a library. This, in turn, requires that these people must share an internalized, phenomenological, understanding of what a library is and of how to "do" things such as cataloging, searching, lending, borrowing, reserving, and so on. These understandings are stored within stocks of mutual knowledge embodied within agents, and existing as part of wider sets of beliefs and views of the world containing all sorts of formative cultural, social, and religious influences. Methodologically structuration insists that it is necessary to hermeneutically interpret and understand these actors' worldviews or "frames of meaning" in order to be truly able to grasp what they do and why they do it.

Giddens's invaluable formulations were ultimately limited by their preoccupation with more abstract and generalizing philosophical issues (ontology-in-general) at the expense of concerns with forging links between this level and more in-situ, empirical, issues (ontology-in-situ). Subsequent contributors to the tradition, such as Nicos Mouzelis, Margaret Archer and Ira J. Cohen, have taken on this difficult terrain with tangible effect. Rob Stones has synthesized recent advances under the label of Strong Structuration Theory, elaborating a fourfold cycle in which one can now distinguish between: (1) structures external to a given actor, which act as her conditions of action, both constraining and enabling in various ways; (2) the actor's internalized, phenomenologically inflected sense of the external structures. These "internal structures," in turn, can be divided into the perception of external structures in the immediate context (*conjuncturally-specific internal structures*), and those enduring and transposable dispositions, capacities and discourses that have been acquired from past contexts (borrowing from Bourdieu these can be seen as *internal structures as habitus*); (3) active agency, including such things as degrees of critical reflection, creativity and improvisation employed when actors draw upon internal structures in producing practical action; and (4) the consequences of action on outcomes. There have been corresponding empirically sensitive refinements in working through the epistemological and methodological implications of structuration's basic concepts, and in elaborating on the nature of the relational meso-level terrain within which agents-in-focus act and interact.

SEE ALSO: Bourdieu, Pierre; Ethnomethodology; Phenomenology; Structure and Agency

SUGGESTED READINGS

Cohen, I. J. (1989) *Structuration Theory: Anthony Giddens and the Constitution of Social Life*. Macmillan, London.

Giddens, A. (1984) *The Constitution of Society*. Polity Press, Cambridge.

Stones, R. (2005) *Structuration Theory*. Palgrave Macmillan, London.

ROB STONES

structure and agency

The concepts of structure and agency are central to sociological theory. Structures are typically seen as the more fixed and enduring aspects of the social landscape. As used by Durkheim and others working within a similar tradition, *structure* is a metaphor that denotes qualities of society that are akin to the skeleton of a body in the field of anatomy, or to the frame of a building in architecture. Durkheim insisted that there are structured ways of acting, thinking, and feeling that are general throughout particular societies; that act as external pressures and constraints; and that are not reducible to biology or psychology. This was also to emphasize the role of society in the process of causation as opposed to individual or group agency. Some writers taking issue with this position went to the other extreme. Weber, for example, emphasized the role of individuals and rejected the idea that terms such as "society" or "group" could refer to any reality other than that of individuals and their actions. Others, seeking to embrace *both* structure and agency in their analytic frameworks, which is by now the dominant conception in contemporary social theory, maintained the Durkheimian emphasis on structures but conceived agency as the more processual, active, dimension of society – analogous to the physiology of an organism. Agency here is the dynamic ability of individuals or groups, such as class movements, governments, or economic corporate bodies, to "make things happen".

Although mutually entwined, structure and agency can still be conceptualized independently. Lopez and Scott (2000) argued that there are two primary ways of conceptualizing structure, both deriving from Durkheim, and a third mode that can be found in more contemporary theorizing. The first is the *relational* notion of structure, referring to networks of social relations that tie people together into groups and social systems. These networks of interdependencies, characterized by mutual reliance within divisions of labor, are typically clustered into specialized sectors of social relations such as kinship, religion, the economy, the state, and so on. Durkheim referred to these as *collective relationships*. Georg Simmel similarly saw society as a dynamic complex of social forms and interactions that structure agents' behaviour, just as Norbert Elias's *figurational sociology* emphasized the webs and networks of relationships within which individual agents act.

The second notion of structure, the *institutional*, refers to the beliefs, values, symbols, ideas, and expectations that make up the mutual knowledge of members of a society and that allow them to communicate with each other. Durkheim (1984) referred to this dimension of structure as society's *collective representations*. The structural-functionalist tradition associated with the work of Talcott Parsons, Robert Merton, and others, captured this aspect of structure under the rubric of "social institutions." Other writers characterized it in terms of cultural patterns. Parsons' focus was on the rules and normative expectations into which agents were socialized as children, and on their adaptation to the various roles and positions they occupied as adults. This emphasis on rules and norms held in individual minds within institutions merges into Lopez and Scott's third notion of structure, that of *embodied* structure, and the combination of both can be seen in diverse strands of current writing, including new institutionalism, Jeffrey Alexander's cultural sociology, and in the theories of Pierre Bourdieu (habitus) and Anthony Giddens (practical consciousness).

Agency theorists argue that structural approaches fail to recognize the central role played by agency in the production of structured patterns or of social change. Two overlapping traditions have dominated here. One includes Weber, Schütz, Berger and Luckmann, Garfinkel, and, more recently, Luc Boltanski and Laurent Thevenot, in the neo-Kantian and phenomenological traditions. The emphasis here is on types of action and on the storehouse of preconceptions, typifications, of objects and practices – the latter as "recipe knowledge" – that we draw upon in appropriate circumstances, and also on the array of competencies, skills, and moral commitments that are intrinsic to agents' routine accomplishments. There is also an emphasis on the shifting role played by the agent's situational "horizon of relevance" in affecting how she draws upon stocks of knowledge. The other tradition – that of pragmatism and symbolic interactionism – includes Mead and Blumer, and has more recently influenced Hans Joas, Alexander and Nicos Mouzelis, who emphasize the reflection, reflexivity, and creativity inherent in the very process of interaction itself, and in the making of selves. Critical realist Margaret Archer has also made valuable contributions to this strand through her discussions of the relationship of reflexivity to "internal conversations," whilst Andrew Sayer has launched a critique of the neglect of values and emotions – "what people care about" – within theoretical understandings of agency.

Major contemporary theorists such as Bourdieu, Giddens, and Jürgen Habermas, along with many of the other more recent theorists mentioned above, have attempted to synthesize and combine the three notions of structure and the two traditions of agency outlined. Other current trends focus on explicit links between such syntheses and the empirical, *in-situ* level.

SEE ALSO: Agency (and Intention); Bourdieu, Pierre; Phenomenology; Schutz, Alfred; Structuralism; Structuration Theory

REFERENCES

Durkheim, E. (1984) [1893] *The Division of Labour in Society*. Macmillan, London.

Lopez, J. & Scott, J. (2000) *Social Structure*. Open University Press, Philadelphia.

SUGGESTED READINGS

Emirbayer, M. & Mische, A. (1998) What is Agency? *American Journal of Sociology* 104: 962–1023.

Stones, R. (2009) Theories of social action. In: Turner, B. (ed.), *The New Blackwell Companion to Social Theory*. Blackwell, Oxford.

ROB STONES

student movements

Student movements have emerged in many modern and modernizing societies. Increasing student numbers provide the necessary critical mass for movements, but political conditions provide the most general reasons for their development.

In the 1960s student movements spread in opposition to the Vietnam War and, in France in May 1968, threatened revolution. They inspired women's, personal liberation and environmental movements, developed "movement entrepreneurs," and contributed to the legitimation of protest and the "participatory revolution" in liberal democracies.

The 1960s student movements arose out of an extraordinary conjunction of demography and social change, sustained rises in living standards, expansion of higher education in response to changes in technology and occupational structures, and an effective vacuum of political opposition. Universities had expanded, but graduate unemployment was negligible and students' complaints were not primarily self-interested.

Are student movements likely to reappear? The status of "student" has become less determinate as students are increasingly integrated into the social and economic mainstream, and distinctively student politics more closely resemble the politics of other sectional interests.

Student movements have continued to play important roles in authoritarian states, keeping alive democratic aspirations and contributing to the collapse of regimes. From Spain to Thailand to Taiwan, they provoked political crises that expanded civil liberties and democratic rights. Student protests against more systematically repressive regimes have been aggressively suppressed, as in Beijing's Tiananmen Square in 1989.

It was generally students who first challenged oppressive regimes in the name of universalist principles of liberty, morality and democracy. The critical conditions for the emergence and development of student movements are a moralistic political grievance and absence within the polity of effective opposition from more powerful actors.

SEE ALSO: Anti-War and Peace Movements; Global Justice as a Social Movement; Social Movements; Social Movements, Networks and

SUGGESTED READINGS

Burg, D. E. (1998) *Encyclopedia of Student and Youth Movements*. Facts on File, New York.

Rootes, C. (1980) Student radicalism: politics of moral protest and legitimation problems of the modern capitalist state. *Theory and Society* 9 (3): 473–502.

CHRISTOPHER ROOTES

subculture

Subculture came into vogue in US sociology in the mid to late 1950s stemming from the Chicago School's ethnographic emphases and empirical studies of youths informed by Robert Merton's strain theory. Drawing from US sociology, subculture gained ascendance in the United Kingdom during the 1970s through studies of working class youth, soccer hooligans and the critical ethnographies at the Centre for Contemporary Cultural Studies.

Subculture stems from culture – one of English's most complex words (Williams 1958). From its origin in tending nature, by analogy culture soon included training the mind and then an overall state of mind; expanding to represent a society's general intellectual achievements, culture stood for the arts and finally denoted a whole way of life – spiritual, intellectual and material.

Subculture arose in response to culture as an all encompassing idea and reference. By focusing on the socio-material creation of habits of mind, outlooks, innovative artistic expression, presentation and "performance," subcultural studies indicated how youths, delinquents, rebels, even athletes, gamers and conformists produced separate, shared activities, knowledge, referents and lifeworlds that distinguished them from the "mainstream."

With current postmodernist emphases on social fragmentation, subculture has lost much of its former, analytic popularity.

SEE ALSO: Deviance; Chicago School; Cultural Studies; Culture; Subcultures, Deviant

REFERENCE

Williams, R. (1958) *Culture and Society*. Chatto & Windus, London.

SUGGESTED READING

Gelder, K. & Thornton, S. (eds.) (1997) *The Subcultures Reader*. Routledge, London.

ROB BEAMISH

subcultures, deviant

The term "*sub*culture," like "culture," refers to a shared collection of traits, such as beliefs, values, interests, language, behaviors, and collective identity. The terms "subculture" and "culture" can alternately refer to a *group* or *population* of persons characterized by distinctive cultural traits. Distinctive cultural groups become "sub" cultures by contrast to the conventional or mainstream traits of a larger cultural group, often enjoying greater status and power. Because members of a subculture differ from members of a larger, dominant or mass culture, their differences are often evaluated as *deviant* – they violate conventional standards or fall short of conventional expectations. Deviant subcultures appear in a diversity of forms, associated with gangs, prison inmates, drug addicts, religious cults, hippie communes, and punk rock.

The study of deviant subcultures has traditionally been associated with the study of juvenile delinquency, deviance and crime, but has expanded well beyond its traditional concerns and disciplinary boundaries. While early treatments employed the concept of deviant subculture to explain the delinquency of a specific type of group, typically comprising urban, working class, male youths, subsequent studies have explored deviant subcultures among people of different ages, genders, class positions, and locales. Whereas early theories were often concerned to understand the social causes of delinquency, and treated subcultures as largely dysfunctional cultural adaptations, current literature has expanded well beyond criminological concerns to encompass a wider variety of deviance, by a wider variety of perspectives. The study of deviant subcultures is today a very diverse interdisciplinary study drawing, for example, from cultural studies and neo-Marxist social criticism as well as from traditional positivist criminology.

SEE ALSO: Counterculture; Deviance; Subculture

SUGGESTED READING

Gelder, K. & Thornton, S. (eds.) (1997). *The Subcultures Reader*. Routledge, New York.

T. J. BERARD

subjectivity

Subjectivity is a concept that opposes the methodological possibility of a disembodied objective perspective and works to explicate the emergence of the reflexive actor in society. The extent to which sociology can or should detach itself from the actor's subjective experience, and even whether subjectivity is itself illusory, is highly contested and essential to sociology's self-identity.

Subjectivity rejects the possibility of a position independent outlook of the world and stipulates that all knowledge is knowledge from particular points of view. There are four main avenues through which subjective value judgements could permeate sociology: (1) the selection of problems (2) the determination of the contents of conclusions (3) the identification of fact and (4) the assessment of evidence (Nagel's 1961 essay: "The value-oriented bias of social inquiry"). Charles Taylor (1971) argued in the seminal essay "Interpretation and the sciences of man" that subjectivity is absolutely unavoidable for sociology, although social relations rest on intersubjective rules and the sharing of a common world. He suggested we are bound by a hermeneutic circle when engaging in sociology (or any other social science) because it is impossible to appeal to verification through "brute data," as in the natural sciences, to verify claims. Instead, one must rely on value-based intuitions.

Relatedly, subjectivity has come to be understood as undermining the traditional view of a consistent, stable and autonomous self as sole author of interactions with other selves and a description of the external forces that come to construct the subject. The supposed philosophical illusion of an integrated self was challenged, in particular, by four separate, but sometimes interdependent, movements of thought: Marxism, Psychoanalysis, Structuralism, and Feminism. Marxists outlined how the modes of production produced false consciousness; Psychoanalysts revealed a fragmentary unconscious of irrational impulses; Structuralists, like Levi-Strauss, Lacan and Althusser developed the linguistic analysis of de Saussure to reveal how underlying anthropological, psychological and state structures were formative influences on the subject; Feminism illustrated how the subject was engendered in a society dominated by patriarchal norms.

These efforts themselves came to be criticized for implicitly attempting to liberate a "real self" behind a veil of socio-structural influences. Foucault's intention, arguably, was to show this subject as a discursive fiction constructed in a power nexus. As such, the subject is, in fact, another remnant of the Enlightenment tradition, which allows normative appeal for a unified, autonomous, rational self. Thus, without the foundations of tradition or reason, the subject dissolves into an overwhelmed post-modern spectator of a hyper-real social environment, a playfully pastiche consumer of late capitalism.

Anti-subjective arguments have been heavily criticized for their methodological, empirical and normative shortcomings. Taking stock of the dramatic technological and cultural changes of recent decades, there has been a re-evaluation of what processes of subjectivity are still relevant to our understanding of the reflexive subject. Structural inequality has emerged as a particular focal point. Accordingly, feminist standpoint theory, whereby each subject is a situated knower in a system of particular social relations, is providing invaluable theoretical and methodological resources. Drawing upon these, for instance, a realist theory of identity has been developed, as represented in Alcoff and Mohanty (2006) *Identity Politics Reconsidered*, which rejects the thesis that the subject is a mere fiction but positions subjectivity against essentialism in recognition of anti-subjective concerns.

SEE ALSO: Epistemology; Feminist Standpoint Theory; Foucault, Michel; Hermeneutics; Identity Theory; Objectivity; Postmodern Social Theory

REFERENCE

Taylor, C. (1971) Interpretation and the sciences of man. In: Martin, M. & MacIntyre, L. C. (eds.) (1994) *Readings in the Philosophy of Social Science*. MIT Press, Boston, MA.

SUGGESTED READINGS

Foucault, M. (1984) *The Foucault Reader*, ed. P. Rabinow. Penguin: London.

Harding, S. (2003) *The Feminist Standpoint Theory Reader: Intellectual and Political Controversies*. Routledge: New York.

Martin, M. & MacIntyre, L. C. (1994) *Readings in the Philosophy of Social Science*. MIT Press, Boston, MA.

JOSEPH PATRICK BURKE

suburbs

In the USA, a city's suburbs are the set of incorporated municipalities located outside the city's political boundaries, but adjacent to the city or to its other suburbs. Suburbs form a band around the city that has lower population density overall than the city, but predominately urban land uses. "Suburb" refers to this band of suburbs and also to a particular municipality within this band. "Suburban" can refer to a way of life identified with suburbs.

The definition of suburb and characteristics of suburbs differ around the world, in part because of differences in local government. US municipalities, including suburbs, have substantial political and fiscal autonomy; the property tax is their major source of revenue. Thus a municipality with a shopping mall or industrial park can fund services, including schools, more easily than a residential suburb.

Early US cities absorbed people and activities by using land more intensively and by expanding on the edge. Cities routinely annexed newly-urban land. Annexation became less common as state laws made annexation difficult while facilitating the incorporation of a new municipality. Incorporated places soon ringed many older cities, blocking city expansion and providing inexpensive land near the city. This process accelerated after World

War II, when diverse federal and state policies subsidized new schools, sewer lines, and other infrastructure. Some cities, especially in the west, continued to annex, creating substantial differences among US cities and their suburban bands.

The suburbs of any US city tend to be different from each other, yet internally homogeneous. Age produces some differences; the extent land use is residential produces others. Differences that affect the municipality's ability to fund services are the most consequential. A suburb with both wealthy residents and substantial non-residential development can provide services more easily than a primarily residential community with low-income residents. Over time, these differences can produce substantial "stratification of place" among a city's suburbs.

SEE ALSO: City; Segregation; Urban Ecology; Urbanization; Urban Policy

SUGGESTED READING

United States Bureau of the Census (2009) www.census.gov.

JUDITH J. FRIEDMAN

suicide

Suicide is among the top ten leading causes of death. Over 30,000 Americans take their own lives each year, or about 85 each day. While Americans fear being murdered more than dying by their own hand, the suicide rate is currently double the murder rate.

Sociological analysis of suicide has stressed Durkheim's (*Suicide*, 1897/1966) concept of social integration. Bonds or the subordination of the individual to society is thought to provide meaning and prevent selfishness or "egoism." Groups lacking in ties to society are expected to be at higher than average risk of suicide.

FAMILY INTEGRATION

Marriage and parenting provide a set of responsibilities to spouse (e.g., giving and receiving emotional support) and children. Both act as protections against excessive self-involvement. A review of 132 studies found strong support for this thesis in 77.9 percent of the findings. For example, in Austria, the suicide rate of divorced persons is 4.22 times higher than the suicide rate among married persons. Also, divorce rates are the best predictor of suicide rates in the 50 states in the United States for all census years.

RELIGION AND SUICIDE

Religious beliefs and practices tend to be associated with lower suicide risk. A belief in a blissful afterlife can give persons encountering stressful life events (e.g., divorce, unemployment, death of a loved one) the strength and courage to persevere. Further, friends from church (coreligionists) may provide emotional and material support for suicidal individuals. A review of 162 studies found that 87 percent contained evidence that religion protects against suicidality.

ECONOMIC STRAIN AND SUICIDE

Most research has found that lower status persons have higher, not lower, suicide rates. For example, data for the USA indicate that laborers have a suicide rate of 94.4 suicides per 100,000, 8 times the national suicide rate. The high suicide rate of lower class persons is partly a consequence of associated high rates of mental troubles, alcoholism, and family disruption.

Unemployment can influence suicide by affecting suicide risk factors such as lowering household income, self esteem, work-centered social networks, and increasing depression levels. For example, in Austria the suicide rate for the unemployed was nearly 4 times that for the general population.

MEDIA AND SUICIDE

The last major research focus concerns media effects. From news and other coverage of suicide, depressed people may learn that there are troubled individuals who commit suicide in response to life's problems. Imitation effects have been documented in many studies. For example, during the year of publication of *Final Exit*, a guide recommending suicide through asphyxiation for the terminally ill, there was an increase of 313 percent in suicide by this method in New York City. A copy of *Final Exit* was found at the scene of 27 percent of these suicides.

Widely publicized suicides are most likely to trigger copycat suicide if the model is a celebrity, someone with whom many people identify. Studies of the suicides of entertainment or political celebrities are 14 times more likely to find a copycat effect than studies of ordinary suicides. When famous movie stars commit suicide, there are, on average, 217 additional suicides during the month of news coverage of their suicide.

SEE ALSO: Divorce; Durkheim, Émile; Mental Disorder; Unemployment

SUGGESTED READING

Stack, S. (2003) Media as a risk factor in suicide. *Journal of Epidemiology and Community Health* 57: 238–40.

STEVEN STACK

surplus value

Determining the source of social surplus was the most important scientific and political question classical political economists addressed. The Physiocrats claimed that nature was the source of all social surplus (all other products simply circulated in the economy as an exchange of equivalents). Adam Smith maintained that the division of labor in manufacturing was the source of social surplus, suggesting that any tariffs or impediments to industry would restrict the wealth of nations. Karl Marx developed a theory of "surplus value" – *Mehrwert* (literally more-value) – by focusing on capitalist production.

Marx accepted British political economists' argument that a product's "value" is based on the number of hours of labor required for its production. Whether it is agricultural work, raw material extraction, or the fabrication of manufactured goods, a given product contains a theoretically calculable amount of socially necessary, simple, abstract labor time. This calculation includes the value of the raw materials and labor power congealed within it and a portion of the value of the machinery, facility and power costs, and other inputs transferred piecemeal into the product during manufacture.

Marx's theory has four key premises. First, on the whole, all commodities exchange as equivalents of value. Surplus does not arise through unfair or unequal exchange. Second, while workers do not have direct access to the means of production or the requisites needed to live, they are free to sell their ability to do work (or labor power) in order to survive. Third, like every commodity, labor power has a particular value; its value is equivalent to that of the value of the goods needed to produce and maintain labor power (the socially determined requisites needed to function as a worker). Finally, workers and employers exchange equivalents – workers agree to work a specified period of time in return for their labor power's full value. Employers do not create surplus value by paying below workers' value.

Working under conditions their employers determine, at some point in the workday workers will have congealed, in the products they produce, a specific number of hours of socially necessary, simple, abstract labor equivalent to the value of their labor power. But workers do not stop production at that point; they were hired to work a full workday. During this next phase of the workday, as they produce additional products, workers are still congealing value – hours of socially necessary, simple, abstract labor – into products producing "more value" (i.e., "surplus value") for which the capitalist does not have to compensate the workers since they had already agreed to a wage equivalent to the value of their labor-power – additional compensation would remunerate workers above the value of their labor-power. Employers may increase that surplus value by extending the working day's length (increasing absolute surplus value) or intensifying production to reduce the time required to cover the value of labor power (increasing relative surplus value).

The key to surplus value is the unique ability of labor power, in a system of equivalent exchange, to produce, over the course of a workday, more value than the value exchanged with the worker (the bearer of labor power). According to Marx, labor power is the sole source of surplus value and thus workers and their labor power are the source of social surplus in capitalist societies.

SEE ALSO: Exchange-Value; Labor/Labor Power; Marx, Karl; Value

SUGGESTED READINGS

Marx, K. (1976) [1890] *Capital*, 4th edn., vol. 1, trans. B. Fowkes. Penguin, Harmondsworth.

Marx, K. (1935) *Wage-Labor and Capital*, trans. J. L. Joynes. Charles H. Kerr & Co., Cooperative, Chicago.

ROB BEAMISH

surveillance

Surveillance, from the French verb, *surveiller*, means "watching over." It involves the observation of behaviors, actions and activities to collect data and personal information on the part of governments, law enforcement agencies, and others such as credit and banking institutions, corporations, and research companies.

Surveillance functions as social control. Michel Foucault's concept of the Panopticon is a metaphor for surveillance society and accompanying disciplinary apparatuses. State power is no longer exercised through torture; rather, it is hidden in the everyday corpus of technologies to make populations self-police their own behavior. For example, why drive within the speed limit? Because someone (or some camera) may be watching.

Today, new information technologies have multiplied ways of conducting surveillance: monitoring Internet usage and connections on social networking sites, phones and text messaging, traffic and street cameras, fingerprinting, medical and educational records, credit card records, satellite imagery, GPS tracking and RFID chips, government issued ID cards and census-taking, and so on.

Reasons for increased surveillance have also multiplied: direct advertising, employee productivity, insurance premiums, credit history, intelligence to combat the "war on terror" (Lyon 2003), voting districts and welfare policies, among many others. In this way, surveillance underscores the characteristics of modernity: rationality, record keeping, bureaucracy, systemization, and efficiency.

The increase of new surveillance technologies prompts the term "surveillance society" and the expansion to large-scale populations brings about the term "mass surveillance." Such heightening of surveillance raises concerns about whether these new technologies keep people safe or whether they are intrusive and violate personal privacy.

Everyone who pays with a credit card and who uses a cell phone participates in the processes that make possible widespread surveillance. It is not a top down process: from neighborhood watch programs to looking out for suspicious persons at the airport, surveillance is part of the social fabric pushed forward by new technologies, routines, conveniences, and concerns for safety.

SEE ALSO: Foucault, Michel; Panopticon

REFERENCE

Lyon, D. (2003) *Surveillance after September 11.* Polity Press, Cambridge.

SUGGESTED READING

Foucault, M. (1995) [1978] *Discipline and Punish: The Birth of the Prison*, trans. A. Sheridan. Vintage Books, New York.

HEATHER MARSH

survey research

Survey research refers to systematic investigations designed to gather information from populations or samples for the purposes of describing, comparing, or explaining phenomena. Survey research involving samples often is distinguished from census surveys, which involve the study of populations.

Several types of research approaches are described in the survey methodology literature. *Descriptive or status* survey research focuses on accurately characterizing information about defined units of analysis, such as individuals, social groups, geographic areas, or organizations. In descriptive research applications, surveys are used to quantify phenomena such as unemployment rates in a state, the health status of citizens of the USA, or the number of certified teachers in a school district. Public opinion surveys or polls (e.g., Gallup Poll or Harris Survey) are a type of status survey designed to quantify information from defined samples about their subjective preferences, beliefs, or attitudes. *Correlational* survey research is directed toward examining interrelationships among variables. An example of correlational survey research might involve using surveys to examine familial and community factors associated with juvenile delinquency. *Explanatory* survey research typically involves hypotheses testing to explicate relationships between attribute or predictor variables and criterion variables of interest.

Commonly employed survey research designs include cross-sectional and longitudinal designs. In cross-sectional designs, information is collected at a single point in time from a sample of respondents. Three common types of longitudinal designs include panel, trend, and cohort. Panel designs involve data collected at different points in time from the same sample. In trend designs, different samples from the same general population are used at each measurement occasion. Cohort designs involve identifying a specific population who share a common attribute, such as infants born in the USA in 2005 or those who graduated from high school in Texas in 2004. The same specific population is involved in the cohort study over time, but a new sample from this population is selected each time survey data are gathered.

Sampling decisions are important in survey research, particularly when the intent is to evaluate the precision of sample estimates in relation to population characteristics. Three interrelated processes are associated with sampling decisions: defining the sample frame, determining sample size, and choosing a sampling method. The sample frame is the list of people or objects that comprise the accessible population. Survey samples are selected from the frame by specifying sample size and determining whether probability or nonprobability sampling methods will be used to select units. Probability sampling permits use of statistical tools to estimate the amount of sampling error. Random sampling error occurs due to chance variations in different samples drawn from the same population. Systematic sampling error occurs when inadequate sampling procedures are used. Coverage error is a form of systematic sampling error. An example of coverage error would be surveying only individuals with access to computers when the variables of interest are related to having or not having computer access. Errors in sampling also can arise from poor definitions of the sampling frame and the use of small sample sizes.

Modes of survey administration involve face-to-face, telephone, mail, and web-based formats. Use of computers in survey research is becoming commonplace, including laptops and personal data assistant (PDA) devices. Each mode has its strengths and limitations. Decisions related to the mode of administration to be used typically involve considerations of the characteristics of the sample to be surveyed, the types of questions to be asked, the response rate desired, and time and cost considerations.

SEE ALSO: Convenience Sample; Interviewing, Structured, Unstructured, and Postmodern; Random Sample

SUGGESTED READINGS

Alreck, P. L. & Settle, R. B. (1994) *The Survey Research Handbook*, 2nd edn. McGraw Hill, New York.

Fowler, F. J. (1993) *Survey Research Methods*, 2nd edn. Sage, Newbury Park, CA.

PATRICIA SNYDER

sweatshops

Sweatshops, in short, are now found not only globally but in every pore of production. When "sweated labor" first won attention in the 1840s, it was thought to be an archaic phenomenon that would yield to modern industry. But actually sweated labor is ancillary to industry, not an outdated survival. Sweatshops encircle the globe because the factory system is global.

The "sweating system" was originally a form of labor subcontracting in which factory workers enlisted outside helpers. T. J. Dunning of the Bookbinders Union gave a concise explanation in 1860. The factory owner pays a piece wage to the regular employee, the "sweater," "who takes out work to do, at the usual rate of wages, and who gets it done by others at a lower price; the *difference,* which is his profit, being 'sweated' out of those who execute the work." Sweated labor was thus an adjunct to industry. The sweater worked in a factory with motor-driven machines, but the products often needed finishing touches applied by hand. This led to subcontracting, since semi-finished items could be taken to outworkers for finishing. The sweater needed only material (furnished by the capitalist) and willing hands. The expropriation of the peasantry ensured that willing hands were available in abundance. And the sweated sub-workers, paid a fraction of the standard piece wage, were not merely exploited but ultra-exploited.

Initially, sweated labor was mainly handwork. Women, children and others crowded into dank cellars and cottages, where they toiled long hours at menial tasks. "Sweatshop" was not yet a standard term. The sweated workers, many of whom were small children, often called their worksites schools: "mistresses' schools," "lace schools." But in the 1860s the sewing machine drove the smallest children out of the sweatshop; this increasingly led sweated workers to concentrate in factory-like sites, often in tenements. Immigration, in the 1880s and after, provided fresh sources of labor. Increasingly, factory owners organized the subcontracts personally, to cut costs but also to undercut unions (by giving work to outworkers, especially Jews and Italians). An anti-sweatshop movement arose fueled by humanitarian and proletarian concerns. Several strikes, by Jewish and Italian seamstresses and male cloak workers, led to breakthrough labor agreements and solidified the garment unions.

Weakened by agitation and legislation, sweatshops faded into obscurity. But after World War II new technology, from computerization to containerization, gave capital enhanced mobility. Globalized subcontracting in many forms, from "outsourcing" to "offshoring," became familiar. "Feeder plants" funneled into industry in the 1940s. Now the dynamic is to expand indefinitely in every direction. Every production process pulses along a vast supply chain – and most supply chains terminate in sweatshops, especially among new waves of immigrants and in export processing zones. And with the ascent of Walmart and other oligopoly retailers, the global retail sector has emerged as a unifying realm, merging supply chains of all kinds.

This is the present situation, in which sweatshops now serve (in Marx's phrase) as the factory's "external departments" on a worldwide scale. This is plainest in the apparel industry, where the nimble fingers of ill-paid young women apply finishing touches to apparel and accessories in sweatshops all over the world. Globalization includes, and presupposes, the globalization of sweated labor.

Politically, the notion of the "sweatshop" presupposes the legitimacy of the factory. Only when factories appear "normal" do sweatshops appear pathological by contrast. Today, the unity of these systems is even more obvious, since the "sweater" is usually a subsidiary or client of the firm that owns the factories. So, directly or indirectly, factory and sweatshop workers tend to have the same employers. Yet the global chain of links has grown so long that workers have a tough time seeing beyond their own workplace. The evils of sweatshops are easily seen, but the ties that bind sweatshops in Manila to investors in London are less readily visible.

SEE ALSO: International Gender Division of Labor; Labor/Labor Power; Marx, Karl

SUGGESTED READINGS

Dunning, T. J. (1860) *Trades Unions and Strikes*. Self-published, London.

Esbenshade, J. (2004) *Monitoring Sweatshops*. Temple University, Philadelphia.

Marx, K. (1867) [1976] *Capital*, vol. 1. Penguin, Harmondsworth.

DAVID NORMAN SMITH

symbolic classification

Symbolic classification – literally, complex arrangements of symbols into wholes – refers to the process of classifying and ordering by means of which individuals are able to make sense of the natural and social world. They do so by means of models of categorization that are culturally and socially determined as well as the outcome of a complex interplay between personal experience, socio-cultural context and linguistic forms. Such categories are cast in concrete images that we may call symbols, which are, by definition, polysemic and relativistic.

Durkheim and Mauss were among the first social scientists to reflect on the ways human beings conceive of time, space, causality, unity, plurality, and so on. Their ideas are elaborated in an article published in *L'Année sociologique* (1903) and later translated in English as *Primitive Classification* (1963). The importance of this publication lies in the fact that some of the issues illustrated here were eventually discussed in structuralist social theories several decades later; moreover, it may be regarded as an early contribution to the sociology of knowledge and to sociological epistemology. The central argument of their essay is that there exists a connection between the classification of natural phenomena and the social order. The act of classifying does not occur through the effect of a "spontaneous" attitude of the mind, based for example upon the principles of contiguity, similarity, and opposition among objects or among living beings, but originates within the organization of social life. They oppose both the idea that categories exist before experience (built-in or *a priori* categories) and that categories are the product of experience (empiricism) and assert that ideas and worldviews are constructed on a model that reproduces the society from which they have emerged. Durkheim would later take this up in *Les Formes élémentaires de la vie religieuse: le système totémique en Australie* (1912).

The work of Levi-Strauss and Mary Douglas is also grounded in the Durkheim and Mauss paradigm. Lévi-Strauss analyzes symbolic classification at a much deeper, i.e., unconscious, level. Native categories of thought are the output of universal mental processes (e.g., binary or dual oppositions), which manifest themselves in different ways. Both the cosmologies of "primitive" societies and the scientific thought of industrial societies are founded upon the same bases – the unconscious but structured regularities of human thought. The British anthropologist Mary Douglas departs from the epistemology of Durkheim and Mauss' notion of symbolic classification and refines their sociology of knowledge. She avoids their evolutionary typology, i.e., the distinction between primitive and modern symbolic schemata, and insists on the importance of classificatory impurities. To understand the environment, individuals introduce order out of the chaos by means of classification. Yet in this process individuals discover that a few objects, living beings, actions, or ideas appear to be anomalous – matter out of place – which may pollute the entire classificatory system. What does not fit must be dealt with ideologically to keep the anomaly under control, both in the natural and in the social world. Recent undertakings in symbolic anthropology have moved away from structural problems and focused rather toward issues of practice. This is evident, for example, in recent studies on social justice dealing with how welfare policy systems classify potential recipients (Thévenot 2007); or on ethnicity which deconstruct the ethnic anomalies stressed by a hegemonic system of classification in multi-ethnic societies.

SEE ALSO: Durkheim, Émile; Knowledge, Sociology of; Semiotics; Signs; Symbolic Exchange; Structuralism

REFERENCE

Thevenot, L. (2007) The plurality of cognitive formats and engagements: moving between the familiar and the public. *European Journal of Social Theory* 10 (3): 409–23.

SUGGESTED READINGS

Douglas, M. (1966) *Purity and Danger: An Analysis of the Concepts of Pollution and Taboo.* Penguin, Harmondsworth.

Lévi-Strauss, C. (1966) [1962] *The Savage Mind.* University of Chicago Press, Chicago, IL.

SIMONE GHEZZI

symbolic exchange

Symbolic exchange is the organizing principle, the cellular structure, of the earliest forms of society. The exchanges that take place within and between clans, within and between tribes and between chiefs and other members of the tribe are more than economic exchanges as we know them in modern societies, and their circulation integrates the members of these societies. Marcel Mauss conceptualizes these exchanges as a form of gift giving, and the gift is a "total social phenomenon." They are multi-dimensional: economic, moral, religious, mythological, juridical, political, aesthetic and historical.

Mauss created his concept from the work of nineteenth- and early twentieth-century anthropologists in Melanesia, Polynesia, and northwest America. Like Durkheim, he also wanted to demonstrate the social basis for exchanges as a refutation of the utilitarian notion that individual interests were the foundation for the creation of market relations. There was no "natural" economy that had preceded political economy. Further, while the tribes of the Americas, Africa and Asia seemed so different, so "other," to Europeans, Mauss wanted to demonstrate through comparative analysis the underlying similarities as well. The complex structure of the gift made it more difficult for Europeans to see these groups as inferior primitives whose annihilation or assimilation would be of no loss to humanity.

Gift giving was obviously an economic phenomenon, although it did not involve the exchange of equivalent values as it does in market economies. In the Kwakiutl tribe the *potlatch* ritual exchanges were competitive and required a reciprocal exchange at a later moment that was of more value than the original gift. This was how the chief, the clan, or the tribe maintained prestige and power; the chief would distribute the gifts later received to the members of his clan or tribe. The chief was the member of the tribe who shared the most. The goods exchanged were often destroyed in festivals which made the accumulation of wealth difficult. Gift giving also involved a relation with nature and created a balanced reciprocal relation between society and nature. The domination of nature is a modern phenomenon; these tribes lived in nature.

Gift giving also included an ethic of reciprocity. The members of tribes were obligated to give gifts as well as receive gifts. Failure to do either would mean a loss of status, perhaps enslavement or possibly war if it occurred between two tribes. The norm of reciprocity bound clan to clan, men to women and tribe to tribe, and the circulation of gifts reproduced these tribes as tribes.

Thorstein Veblen brought the analysis of symbolic exchange to the consumer practices of wealthy Americans. Veblen developed his concepts of vicarious consumption and conspicuous consumption from the same sources as Mauss, from tribal cultures and agrarian societies. The leisure class originally derived its prestige from avoiding ignoble work and devoting its time to pursuits that had little practical significance: sports, indolence, war, religious activities and government. They also derived prestige through the idleness and vicarious consumption of their wives, families and servants. Further, as the members of the middle class took up practical positions as professionals and managers, they derived their prestige from conspicuous consumption.

Jean Baudrillard developed his analysis from a critical reading of Mauss, John K. Galbraith and Thorstein Veblen. Symbolic exchange for Baudrillard was a way to escape the consumer society and the political economy of the sign. He demonstrated in his early writings how the code of consumption and the system of needs had completed the system of production. The use value of the commodity provided an "alibi" to exchange value. Consumers were even more alienated in their private lives than they were at work. They were unconscious of the process of semiosis that led through their acts of consumption of commodities with their coded differences to the reproduction of the capitalist mode of production. The only way out of this system was a return to symbolic exchange where the accumulation of wealth and power was impossible and where exchanges were reciprocal and reversible.

SEE ALSO: Baudrillard, Jean; Exchange-Value

SUGGESTED READINGS

Baudrillard, J. (1988) *Symbolic Exchange and Death.* In: Kellner, D. (ed.), *Jean Baudrillard*, Stanford University Press, Stanford, CA.

Kellner, D. (1994) *Baudrillard.* Blackwell Publishers, Oxford.

Mauss, Marcel, (1967) *The Gift.* W. W. Norton, New York.

Veblen, T. (1953) *Theory of the Leisure Class.* Mentor, New York.

MICHAEL T. RYAN

symbolic interaction

Symbolic interaction, grounded in Pragmatism and the writings of George H. Mead, postulates use of language to create common meanings for thinking and interacting. Herbert Blumer (1969: *Symbolic Interactionism: Perspective and Method*) coined the term and elaborated its premise that humans act on the meanings which objects have for them. Early Chicago sociologists W. I. Thomas, Robert Park, and Everett Hughes contributed a parallel view but gave social forces more emphasis than Blumer. Howard Becker (1982: *Art Worlds*) and Anselm Strauss (1993: *Continual Permutations of Action*) fused the two lines as Interactionism.

KEY ASSUMPTIONS AND CORE CONCEPTS

G. H. Mead noted two distinctive human qualities: handedness and language. The hand allows sensing and modifying the environment. Together they facilitate thinking and communication for coordinated action. As humans develop, they are socialized into society; learn meanings and uses of objects. They develop a reflexive self. From this foundation there are five assumptions: process, emergence, agency, conditionality, and dialectics.

Social objects are always in process even when maintaining stability. Structures exist as processes.

- Emergence means combinations that create qualitatively different manifestations. A group is more than the sum of individuals. Handedness and language produce social organization and culture. Emergence also means unpredictability and contingency. Agency is the capacity to exert some control over self, others, and circumstances. Social action is not predetermined but constructed and capable of alteration.
- Constructed conditionality embeds two processes. Humans construct societies and then live with the consequences which condition but do not determine subsequent activity. Interactionists reject dualistic thinking in favor of dialectical thinking. The self is composed of a social (me) and a personal (I), which dialogue with each other. Self-society and structure-agency are processually implicated in each other.

A set of core concepts draws upon these assumptions. The dyad or joint action is the basic social unit. From this form and process are built greater complexity. Dyads with relative stability have general agreements subject to modification. Joint action occurs because each actor builds upon and completes the actions of the other. Actors often recognize routine situations and produce the appropriate actions. In problematic situations, interaction is required for definition and concomitant behavior. Collective action, joint action by multiple actors, whether small or large, requires coordination. Collectivities are networks which connect multiple others, but vary in the degree of coordination, duration, and spatial location.

Interactionists question the state of conventional organizational forms. The term social organization is preferable to social structure because it suggests greater fluidity. Constraints and inequality are recognized but there are also contingencies that provide dynamic possibilities. Bureaucracies are "negotiated orders" conditioned by position and resources.

SCHOOLS OF THOUGHT

Interactionism lacks a consensual, integrated body of ideas. Major faultlines surround Blumer's interpretation of Mead. Some believe Blumer minimized obduracy, rejected a positivist approach, and emphasized symbolic aspects more than social organization.There are two orientations that stand in some contrast to conventional symbolic interaction. The Iowa School, developed in the 1950s under the leadership of Manford Kuhn pursued a scientific, structural study of the self. In the 1970s, Carl Couch and colleagues developed the "new" Iowa School systematically studying coordinating behavior in different relationships. Couch used these studies to explore the evolution of complex forms of social coordination across space and time. The second form, Dramaturgy (Goffman 1959: *The Presentation of Self in Everyday Life*),.uses a theatrical metaphor to focus on actor-audience interactions and emphasizes expressive behavior, staging, and nonverbal elements. Many have used dramaturgy to expand the scope of Interactionism.

METHODOLOGY

Interactionists use a variety of methods and techniques. Many conduct fieldwork and depth interviews to access actors' perspectives, biographies, and experiences. Others, focusing on action and process, conduct systematic observations of behavior. A third approach utilizes questionnaires and statistics to explore connections between self, roles, and social structures. A final category involves content analyses of documents and media to elicit thematic elements. Clarke (2005: *Situational Analysis: Grounded Theory after the Postmoden Turn*), integrated discourses and structural contexts with grounded theory, resulting in a more comprehensive qualitative methodology. Because the researcher's self is the instrument of data gathering and writing, recent focus emphasizes its effects on the research and presentation. One consequence has been the adoption of a narrative style that is self-consciously explicit about rhetorical structure and dramatic appeal.

Interactionists commonly use multiple methods in their research in order to examine problems with different information.

RECENT CONTRIBUTIONS

The renascence of pragmatism has led to new topics such as temporality, physical objects, and science. Scholars have also examined power, institutions, and large-scale social processes (Hall 1997: "Meta-power, social organization, and the shaping of social action"). New attention has been devoted to inequality processes. Significant ventures have transformed collective behavior and social movements, eliminating irrational actors and group minds, adding cultural/symbolic analysis, and expanding the temporal and spatial dimensions. Interactionists were among the first to study emotions focusing on the interplay between cognition, norms, and feeling. They are now attentive to recent neurocognitive research and its relationship to mind, self, emotions, and actions.

SEE ALSO: Blumer, Herbert George; Goffman, Erving; Mead, George Herbert; Pragmatism; Role; Self; Social Psychology

SUGGESTED READING

Reynolds, L. & Herman-Kinney, N. (eds.) (2003) *Handbook of Symbolic Interaction*. Altamira Press, Lanham, MD.

PETER M. HALL

system theories

Within sociology there have been several system theories, differing from one another in the extent to which, for example, human agency, creativity, and entrepreneurship are assumed to play a role in system functioning, formation and reformation; conflict and struggle are recognized; power and stratification are part and parcel of the theorizing; structural change and transformation – and more generally historically developments – are taken into account and explained.

There are at least three general social system approaches: functionalist and neo-functionalist theories (identified particularly with Parsons); the historical, Marxian approach; and actor-oriented, dynamic system theories.

FUNCTIONALIST SYSTEMS THEORIES

The theorists in this tradition explain the emergence and/or maintenance of parts, structures, institutions, norms or cultural patterns of a social system in terms of their consequences, that is, the particular functions each realizes or satisfies. This includes, for instance, their contribution to the maintenance and reproduction over time of the larger system. The major functionalist in sociology is arguably Talcott Parsons. Society in a Parsonian perspective is not just an aggregate of social structures but a functioning or operating system, with a relatively high degree of coherence, integration, and effectiveness.

Of particular importance is Parsons's theory of universal functions or *requisites*. He identified four universal functions (AGIL) with which any society must deal in order to be sustainable: *Goal attainment (G)*; *Adaptation or economic efficiency (A)*; *Latency (L)*; *Integration (I)*. The performance and effectiveness of AGIL institutions in accomplishing relevant functions may be treated as variables, thus suggesting varying degrees of societal effectiveness and sustainability of any given system. Another important development related to Parsonian systems theory is Niklas Luhmann's autopoietic systems theory.

HISTORICAL, POLITICAL ECONOMIC SYSTEMS THEORY

The Marxian approach to system theorizing clearly points to sociologically important phenomena: the material conditions of social life, stratification and social class, conflict, the reproduction as well as transformation of capitalist systems, the conditions that affect group mobilization and political power, and the ways ideas functions as ideologies. Marx's historical approach conceives of all societies as evolving in a series of stages. Each stage is characterized by a particular structure, a certain mode of production, the "superstructure" of politics, and a culture derived from and dependent on the substructure of production. Human beings generate these structures through their own actions, but not always under the conditions of their own choosing or in the ways they intend. Marx and Marxists focused their theoretical and empirical research on the emergence and transformation of capitalist systems. Because of systemic contradictions – between, for instance, the "forces of production" (such as new knowledge, techniques, and scientific developments that contribute to generating such forces) and the "relations of production" (such as the private ownership of the means of production) – the capitalist system undergoes crises, leading eventually to its transformation. Among other related major developments, world systems theory should be mentioned. Inspired by Marxist theories, it emphasized global exchange and trade relations, focusing on dependency among nations and imperialism and putting the evolution of capitalist systems in a global and comparative perspective.

ACTOR-ORIENTED, DYNAMIC SYSTEMS THEORIES

This family of theories – inspired to a great extent by Walter Buckley and developed by Margaret Archer and Tom R. Burns and Helena Flam, among others – is non-functionalist. Complex, dynamic social systems are analyzed in terms of stabilizing and destabilizing mechanisms, with human agents playing strategic roles in these processes. Institutions and cultural formations of society are carried by, transmitted, and reformed through individual and collective actions and interactions. On the one hand, such structures – temporally prior and relatively autonomous with respect to social action – exhibit causal force. They constrain and enable people's social actions and interactions. On the other hand, individual and collective agents through their interactions generate the reproduction, elaboration, and transformation of those very same structures. Such an approach entails systematic theorizing of individual as well as collective agents, institutions and cultural formations and their part in processes of social reproduction and transformation and, in general, the endogenous and exogenous drivers of system stability and change. One identifies and explains the real and variegated structures which have emerged historically and are elaborated and developed in ongoing interaction processes.

System theories have contributed generally to the development of conceptual and methodological tools to investigate system interdependencies and their dynamics and interaction-structure loops explaining, for instance, institutional reproduction and transformation.

SEE ALSO: Dependency and World-Systems Theories; Functionalism/Neo-functionalism; Parsons, Talcott

SUGGESTED READINGS

Archer, M. S. (1995) *Realist Social Theory: The Morphogenetic Approach*. Cambridge University Press, Cambridge.

Buckley, W. (1967) *Sociology and Modern Systems Theory*. Prentice Hall, Englewood Cliffs, NJ.

Burns, T. R. & Flam, H. (1987) *The Shaping of Social Organization: Social Rule System Theory with Applications*. Sage, London.

Luhmann, N. (1995) *Social Systems*, trans. J. Bednarz, with D. Baecker. Stanford University Press, Stanford, CA.

Wallerstein, I. (2004) *World-Systems Analysis: An Introduction*. Duke University Press, Durham, NC.

TOM R. BURNS

T

taxes: progressive, proportional, and regressive

Progressive taxes are taxes that require those who earn more money to pay higher taxes. Personal income taxes in the US are progressive. Proponents of progressive taxes argue that wealthy individuals have a moral obligation to society to pay higher taxes. Opponents argue that progressive income taxation has a negative effect on capital formation and economic growth.

Proportional taxes refer to taxes that equally burden all income groups in a society. Proportional taxes are sometimes referred to as a flat tax. For example, if a society had a proportional income tax of 15 percent, a family with an annual income of $100,000 would pay $15,000 a year in income taxes, while a family with an annual income of $10,000 would pay $1,500 a year in income taxes.

Regressive taxes burden lower-income groups more than higher-income groups. Less affluent individuals spend a higher proportion of their income on regressive taxes, such as sales taxes and excise taxes, than do more affluent individuals. Sales tax is tax that is placed on all items that are sold: food, clothing, furniture, etc. Excise taxes are placed on certain items such as alcohol, tobacco, and gasoline.

The generation of government revenue and the redistribution of income among the population are two central reasons for taxation. When all forms of taxation are considered, some countries, such as the US, actually have more income inequality after taxation than before. Therefore, while taxation does much to generate revenue for the government, it may do little to redistribute resources.

SEE ALSO: Class; Economic Development; Income Inequality and Income Mobility

SUGGESTED READINGS

Davies, D. (1986) *United States Taxes and Tax Policy*. Cambridge University Press, New York.

Fullerton, D. & Rogers, D. L. (1993) *Who Bears the Lifetime Tax Burden?* Brookings Institution, Washington, DC.

CHRISTINE A. WERNET

Taylorism

The emergence and spread of Taylorism occurred in the 1880s, which was the same decade that New Jersey and other states passed laws that made it easier for industrial firms to use the joint-stock holding company. Although capitalists developed other means to organize and control the labor process in the increasingly large corporation, their strategies resulted in labor unrest that was manifested as absenteeism, labor turnover, and strikes. In response to these conditions, Taylor (1911) claimed that there was a need for "greater national efficiency" and that efficiency is best achieved through systematic management of people. He argued that his system would improve efficiency and appeal to workers' economic self interest by increasing profits, which would permit capitalists to increase wages thereby eliminating workers' desire to join unions. By the 1920s, Taylorism and others forms of scientific management were adopted in the USA and other industrial societies.

The technical dimensions of Taylorism focused on the "one best way" to perform work. Taylor maintained that workers retained knowledge over the production process, and incorporated rest breaks into the production process (i.e., soldiering) that were so sophisticated that capitalists and their foremen could not detect them. To increase control over the labor process, Taylor collected information from workers and centralized it in a planning department where engineers used it to create rules governing how to complete each task and the amount of required time to do it.

Drawing from the Marxian-Hegelian conception of alienation, Braverman (1974) maintained that the separation of conception from execution in Taylorism dehumanizes the worker because it limits the opportunities for individuals to use their creative capacities. This separation occurs when engineers transform craft knowledge into work rules (i.e., bureaucratic controls) and machines (i.e., technical controls). Although the application of scientific management eventually subordinated operating managers to centralized control, they retained a substantial degree of control over the labor process throughout the middle decades of the twentieth century.

There are important long-term effects of Taylorism. First, after management gained control over the labor process, Taylorism encouraged managers and engineers to disregard workers' knowledge, which created conflict and obstacles to improving efficiency. Second, the reimbursement system initiated by Taylor contributed to inequality by establishing a system of pay differentials between managers and workers, which reached a historical high point in the late twentieth and early twenty-first centuries.

SEE ALSO: Alienation; Capitalism; Fordism/Post-Fordism; McDonaldization

REFERENCES

Braverman, H. (1974) *Labor and Monopoly Capital*. Monthly Review Press, New York.

Taylor, F. W. (1967) [1911] *The Principles of Scientific Management*. W. W. Norton, New York.

HARLAND PRECHEL

technology, science, and culture

Science and technology were once commonly seen as free from cultural influences. This view was championed in the 1920s by scientists and philosophers known as the "Vienna Circle" (Rudolf Carnap, Karl Hempel, Moritz Schlick, and others), who maintained that science produces objective, supra-cultural knowledge via direct observation and logic. The heyday of this notion was brief. By the 1930s, scholars like Boris Hessen, Ludwig Fleck, and Robert Merton argued that cultural, social, political, and economic factors affect science, influencing even the content of scientific theories. Thomas Kuhn asserted in his 1962 *Structure of Scientific Revolutions* that science experiences sudden changes in fashion – sometimes following broader cultural changes – after which theories and data acquire new meaning. This view was debated by a generation of historians, sociologists and anthropologists of science, spawning what became known as the "social constructivist" view of science, which held that what is taken to be true among scientists reflects social consensus, and not bedrock facts about nature. Scholars advocating the "Social Construction of Technology" (SCOT) have similarly described how technologies do not evolve through an inevitable logic of their own, but are constituted through ongoing negotiations between engineers, consumers, users, marketers, etc., reflecting a mosaic of social and cultural assumptions. As such, science and technology bear the imprint of the cultural circumstances in which they arise, while at the same time, our culture bears the imprint of science and technology that play an increasingly central role in almost every aspect of our lives.

Expanding on the pioneering work of Bruno Latour, many scholars today picture social and cultural artifacts, human actors, and natural objects as linked in a single "network." The identity of each element of the network is constituted, in varying degrees, by all other elements in the network. In Latour's system, it makes little sense to track social and cultural "influences" on science or technology or the "social construction" of scientific knowledge or technological artifacts, because these formulations overlook the fact that society, artifacts and nature are mutually constituted. This model, though not without problems, captures nicely the inextricability of science, technology, and culture.

SEE ALSO: Science; Science and Culture; Science, Social Construction of

SUGGESTED READINGS

Knorr Cetina, K. (1999) *Epistemic Cultures: How the Sciences Make Knowledge*. Harvard University Press, Cambridge, MA.

Latour, B. (1993) *We Have Never Been Modern*. Harvard University Press, Cambridge, MA.

NOAH EFRON

technopolitics

Technopolitics is increasingly entering the complex political terrain of the 21st century as an agonistic intersection of politics and technology, or as a conscious "strategic practice of designing or using technology to constitute, embody, or enact political goals" (Hecht 1998: 15).

Since the Enlightenment, promoting democracy and developing new technologies have been intimately associated with global ideas about humanity, progress and modernity. New media technologies, from the printing press to the Internet, have always been identified as contested terrains of ideological struggle and accompanied with great hope for their radical potential to provide the wider public with information, or to improve critical political debate.

For Marx, worker control of the means of production could result in the radical transformation of the modern society as a whole. Dewey also called for broad citizen responsibility and participation in communities of inquiry. From the same analytic point of view, Walter Benjamin, in the spirit of

Brecht, hoped for the "refunctionalization" of new technologies in the direction of societal and human betterment.

By the middle of the twentieth century, the complex relationship between technology and democracy had been systematically problematized in largely varying ways. This was mainly associated with an increasing concern about the potential threat to democratic politics posed by the rapid growth in the size and complexity of technological systems, rendering them beyond rational political control and deliberation. Such a theme was emphatically taken up by the Frankfurt School (e.g. Marcuse, Adorno, and Horkheimer) and is still visible in contemporary work by Langdon Winner, and Andrew Feenberg.

One response to this "growth" has been to encompass the technical dimension of our everyday lives through a wide variety of political interventions (e.g. protests and boycotts), active collaboration with experts, and experiments with public participation in technoscientific decision making. Another type of response is to be found in recent works by Bruno Latour, Andrew Barry, Annemarie Mol, and Noortje Marres who have called for a return to the democratic "politics of objects" (first raised by Dewey). The latter view emphasizes the democratizing impact of technology's complexity and uncertainty on political processes.

Of course, the idea of technopolitics directly opposes technological determinism, according to which technical means and systems are wholly autonomous entities (with "purposes" of their own), which always and inevitably become "ends in themselves". Technopolitics strongly encourages a creative and active working with media and culture, regarded as progressive "tools" able to provide democratic alternatives previously excluded from the established order, rather than pessimistically viewing them as promoting social reproduction and passivity.

In addition, technopolitics appears to genuinely further a reflexive line of inquiry which moves us beyond the reductivistic extremes of virulent technophobia – that is, the hypercritical conception of domination from technological development (Ellul, Virilio) – and the naïve technophilic celebration of the coming "computopia". That means, it allows the philosopher/sociologist of technology to critically grasp "the full range, effects and possibilities of the high-tech adventure that we are currently undergoing" (Kellner 1999: 123). In recent years, continuing technopolitical struggles, which tend to coordinate with really existing politics, increasingly advance local issues, raise hot bioethical debates and point to alternative (less promethean) technologies from scientists and technical experts in fields such as biology, genetics, medicine and environmental protection.

In the context of contemporary infosociety and cyberculture, "technopolitics," as a technologically mediated form of political engagement and action, is a radical tool potentially available to oppositional, oppressed or excluded, social groups and communities. It is thus an important means of consciousness-raising and empowerment (*globalization from below*), which optimistically signifies the critical use of technology (digital media of communication and other cultural forms) to enact small (everyday) revolutions in the here-and-now, to increase the sense of community, and to serve the vital need for global peace, equality, and justice. This perspective possibly amounts to a subversive shift from passive online consumers to *active technocitizens*.

SEE ALSO: Information Society; Information Technology; Technological Determinism

REFERENCES

Hecht, G. (1998) *The Radiance of France: Nuclear Power and National Identity after World War II*. MIT Press, Cambridge, MA.

Kellner, D. (1999) Virilio, war and technology: some critical reflections. *Theory, Culture & Society* (16) (5–6): 103–25.

SUGGESTED READING

Armitage, J. (ed.) (1999) Special issue on machinic modulations: new cultural theory and technopolitics. *Angelaki: Journal of the Theoretical Humanities* 4 (2).

CHARALAMBOS TSEKERIS

terrorism

The term terrorism derives from the Latin verb *terrere*, "to cause to tremble or quiver." It began to be used during the French Revolution, and especially after the fall of Robespierre and the "Reign of. Terror," or simply "the Terror," in which enemies of the Revolution were subjected to imprisonment, torture, and beheading, the first of many modern examples of state terrorism.

Over the past two centuries, terrorism has been a highly contested and volatile category. Those accused of terrorism are vilified as enemies of the state and social order, but many labeled "terrorists" insist that they are "freedom fighters," strugglers for national liberation, or *mujaheddin* (holy warrior) or *fedayeen* ("prepared for martyrdom"), ready to die for righteous causes. Many decry terrorists' indiscriminate violence against civilians, while other critics like Chomsky (1988) and Herman (1982) document state use of violence and terror against its perceived enemies.

Sociologically, terrorist groups often recruit disaffected and alienated individuals, often motivated by strong ideologies like nationalism or religion to commit terrorist acts against innocent civilians. These in turn generate societal fear and exacerbate conflicts and hatred within the social fabric.

The term has also been associated in the twentieth century with indiscriminate or excessive use of state violence and has been leveled against actions of Nazi Germany, the Soviet Union, the United States, Israel, and other countries. For instance, Chomsky (1988) and Herman (1982) document a wide range of US state terrorist actions in Southeast Asia, Africa, South America, and elsewhere, with Chomsky pointing out that the USA is the only country that has ever been convicted of an international act of terrorism by the World Court, which condemned US acts against Nicaragua during the 1980s.

From the 1970s to the present, terrorists have constructed spectacles of terror to promote their causes, attack their adversaries, and gain worldwide publicity and attention. Terror spectacle has become an increasingly significant part of contemporary terrorism and various groups systematically use spectacles of terror to promote their agenda.

On September 11, 2001, terror attacks against the World Trade Center in New York and the Pentagon in Washington, DC became a global media spectacle. The September 11 terror spectacle was the most extravagant strike on US targets in its history and the first foreign attack on its territory since the war of 1812. The 9/11 attacks inaugurated a "war on terror" by the Bush administration and was the prelude to highly publicized terrorist bombings in London, Pakistan, Bali, and elsewhere, and Bush administration military interventions in Afghanistan and Iraq as "preemptive" actions in the "war on terror." Many critics accused the Bush administration of state terrorism in its invasion and occupation of Iraq.

Terrorism and terror war have thus become defining features of the twenty-first century. Governments throughout the world have attempted to more precisely define and criminalize terrorism, while terrorist activities multiply. As weapons of destruction become more deadly and widespread, social divisions between haves and have-nots multiply, and conflict rages throughout the world, terrorism will likely continue to be a major issue and problem of the present era.

SEE ALSO: Violence; War; World Conflict

REFERENCES

Chomsky, N. (1988) *The Culture of Terrorism*. South End Press, Boston, MA.

Herman, E. (1982) *The Real Terror Network*. South End Press, Boston, MA.

SUGGESTED READING

Kellner, D. (2003) *From September 11 to Terror War: The Dangers of the Bush Legacy*. Rowman & Littlefield, Lanham, MD.

DOUGLAS KELLNER

theology

The modern conception of theology as both a faithful and rational or scientific way of talking about God dates from the Christian Middle Ages. Theology as a term is rooted in Greek philosophy, which consisted of three parts: the mythology of the gods, theology as a form of philosophy of nature, and political theology as a public cult. Christendom only reluctantly accepted the term. It is only from the twelfth century onwards that the term theology is commonly used for this science of Christian faith in contrast to the term philosophy. The late Middle Ages finds the term entirely accepted and it is even taken over by Martin Luther. In modern times it is especially used to distinguish between religious philosophy and religious studies on the one hand and Christian doctrine on the other.

Christian theology finds its roots in the biblical tradition. In its first phase since the second century, theology was dominated by the apologetical defense of faith from external attack as well as inner gnostic debate. Clement of Alexandria and Origen developed the first conceptions of systematic knowledge and of an understanding of faith. From the thirteenth century a new prototype of theology as science of faith was established. The west and east developed differently, with western theology concerned with inner processes of systematization and rationalization, while the east was more liturgically and spiritually oriented. Furthermore, philosophy and theology in the west were separated, and challenged faith and science to bring forth their inner connection. Thomas Aquinas thought of God from the rational as well as the revelational points of view. The plurality of theologies was already apparent in the Middle Ages. Thus, scholastic theology with its tendencies to rationalize and intellectualize faith went hand in hand with forms of theology with ties to Augustinian-Neoplatonic thinking or those which were more biblically or affectively oriented, such as the *devotio moderna*.

Nominalism in the late Middle Ages came under the pressure of the medieval synthesis of faith and reason until it fell apart during the Reformation.

Modern western theology is marked by schism and conflict with modern society and culture. Reformation, due to the negation of scholastic theology, fell back on the Bible and on patristic theology, as well as trends of mysticism. For Luther, the object of theology was no longer the unity of faith and reason, but "the culpable and forlorn individual and the justificatory or saving God" (WA: 327). Modern trends in Protestant theology are marked either by the search for a connection with modern culture (e.g., the theology of the Enlightenment and liberal theology) or a stress on separation (e.g., Pietism and dialectical theology).

Theology conceives of its modern form in processes of inner differentiation which follow the general development of society and science. When it began in the twelfth and thirteenth centuries it was still homogeneous in its interpretation of the Bible, reflection on faith, and introduction to religious practices. The beginnings of the separation of biblical and systematic theology reach back as far as the Middle Ages. In its function of thinking about faith, theology consists of three basic structures: historical, systematic, and practical science. Historical theology gained its modern form through the development of the historical-critical method, which leads to tensions with systematic theology. Pastoral theology reacts to the modern differentiation of religion and society and helps establish practical theological disciplines which specialize in the practical role of the church in society. It is a specific part of modern theology that it reflects and copies the plurality of scientific approaches and disciplines. Today, theology signifies the connection between historical disciplines (contemporary history and exegesis of the Old and New Testament, church history), systematic disciplines (philosophy, fundamental theology, dogmatics, moral theology, social ethics), and practical disciplines (pastoral theology, liturgics, canon law, missionary science, religious education). The unity within the plurality of theologies is nowadays mainly expressed in the challenges it faces: the overcoming of confessional separation, the dialogue between religions, the variety of cultures, and the separation of the world into the poor and the rich. Theology is challenged to demonstrate the unity of the Christian promise of salvation and the culturality of Christian faith. It proves to be most fruitful where it succeeds in interpreting faith as part of a sociopolitical and cultural sphere with a view to its capability for experience and action. This is all the more clear in outlines of contextual theology developed across confessional boundaries, the best known of which are feminist theology, the theology of liberation, the theology of enculturation, and the theology of religions. In the sciences, theology nowadays appears to be an indispensable science of the cultural memory and a challenge to overcome the limitations of the modern understanding of science as a system of hypothetical-deductive propositions within interdisciplinary dialogue.

SEE ALSO: Hermeneutics; Orthodoxy; Secularization

REFERENCE

Luther, M. (2002) *Werke. Kritische Gesamtausgabe* [= WA] Bd. 40, II. Böhlau, Weimar.

SUGGESTED READING

McGrath, A. E. (1994) *Christian Theology: An Introduction*. Blackwell, Oxford.

KARL GABRIEL

theoretical research programs

A theoretical research program includes a set of interrelated theories, working strategies, and empirical models regarding social processes to be studied.

The interrelation among theories in a program arises from a *core set* of key ideas used in different ways throughout the program. Each way represents a distinct pattern of theoretical growth. Core ideas may be *elaborated* to provide a more specific account of the phenomenon under study. They may be combined with new ideas to *proliferate* a theory that explains phenomena in a new domain. Two *variant* theories may propose slightly different versions of the core ideas to account for a process they both explain. *Competing* theories use very different core ideas to address the same phenomenon. Finally, ideas in one theory may be *integrated* with ideas from another theory to provide a deeper or more complete account of phenomena.

Working strategies help determine, for example, what the core ideas in a program should be and how to construct and test theories with them. Working strategies may only emerge gradually as theories in a program develop, broaden, and deepen understanding of the ideas under investigation. Additionally, models help specify ways the core ideas in a program may be employed to deal with the complexity of an application situation.

A focus on theoretical research programs reveals *multiple* kinds and sources of knowledge growth.

Knowledge grows through the construction of new theories within programs, through articulation and refinement of working strategies, and through assessments of the empirical adequacy and instrumental utility of models.

SEE ALSO: Theory; Theory Construction; Theory and Methods

SUGGESTED READING

Berger, J. & Zelditch, M., Jr. (1993) *Theoretical Research Programs: Studies in the Growth of Theory*. Stanford University Press, Stanford, CA.

DAVID G. WAGNER

theory

HISTORY

The "sociological canon" includes Karl Marx, Max Weber, and Émile Durkheim – authors whose seminal books, most published before 1800, are assigned in practically all sociological theory courses. Along with several of their contemporaries and near-contemporaries, their masterworks comprise sociology's body of classical theory. Although this body of work was prone to grandiose rhetoric and minimal empirical validation, today these demerits are usually forgiven in view of the trailblazing nature of the work.

Between the classical period and the 1980s or so, contemporary theorizing resided in what is sometimes called the modern era. Sociology experienced a great upsurge of activity and visibility between around 1920 to 1970. Some of this activity was due to the rise of critical theory led by Theodor Adorno, Max Horkheimer, and others. An ascension of American sociology also occurred during this period, owing to the Chicago School (W. I. Thomas, Florian Znaniecki, Robert Park, Charles Horton Cooley, and Herbert Blumer), Harvard University (including Pitirim Sorokin, Talcott Parsons, and Georg Homans), and Columbia University (including Robert K. Merton, Paul Lazarsfeld, Daniel Bell, C. Wright Mills, and William J. Goode). Every school of theorizing spawned multiple offspring: feminist, postmodernist, agency-structure, and modernity approaches, to cite just a few.

SCHOOLS

Theories may be distinguished by major traditions or "schools." These tend to be general, thematic approaches, relatively open to varying interpretations, and difficult to test in direct and rigorous ways. Sociology encompasses dozens of schools, but several are foundational.

- Functionalism (also called structural functionalism) once dominated sociology. It treated social systems as having differentiated, interdependent substructures with corresponding functions that operate in a coordinated fashion to maintain the integrity of the system as a whole. Early proponents included Auguste Comte, Herbert Spencer, and Durkheim, and later Merton and Parsons. The core ideas have continued to evolve through lines of work such as human ecology, organizational ecology, neofunctionalism, evolutionary approaches, and others.
- Conflict approaches focused on destabilizing factors such as social inequalities and social change. Marx helped to usher in these ideas, and other early versions were articulated by Weber and Georg Simmel, with later refinements by Ralf Dahrendorf, Lewis Coser, Jonathan Turner, Randall Collins, and others. Neo-Marxist theories, resource mobilization theory, theories of social revolutions, and breakdown theories of social movements all have roots in the conflict perspective.
- Symbolic Interactionism gives primacy to the individual in social contexts. Cooley focused on the emergence of self-concepts out of social interaction, and in the 1930s George Herbert Mead became a leading figure, making theoretical connections between institutions, the social self, and the minds of human actors. Other key figures have included Blumer, Park, Jacob Moreno, Edmund Husserl, Alfred Schütz, Manford Kuhn, and the field has helped spawn newer lines including phenomenology, ethnomethodology, role theories, identity theories, emotion theories, sociolinguistics, dramaturgical analysis, and conversation analysis.
- Structuralism is concerned with the social consequences of patterns among social objects ranging from individual cognitions to nations. It first emerged from certain strands within Marxist, Durkheimian, and Simmelian theorizing, and later was influenced by Claude Lévi-Strauss' cognitive-linguistic approach; Alfred Radcliffe-Brown's ideas on the effects of social structures; and around the mid-twentieth century by such work as Moreno's sociometry, Alex Bavelas's communication network studies, Fritz Heider's balance theory, and Peter Blau's macrostructural theory. More recent approaches emerging from structuralist traditions

include social network analysis, Pierre Bourdieu's cultural conflict theory, Anthony Giddens's structuration theory, and many others.

- Others: many other schools achieved at least some level of prominence at various times, including critical theory, ethnomethodology, feminist theories, postmodernism, systems theories, neofunctionalism, exchange theories, neo-Marxism, evolutionary theory. On the positive side, our theoretical traditions provide us with a superb "database" of ideas from which to draw solutions to intellectual and social problems. On the negative side, these schools have waxed and waned mainly due to factors other than explanatory power and empirical testing. Sociology would do well to improve systematically on its most promising ideas and relegate the rest to the historical record.

THEORETICAL METHODS

Theories may be distinguished according to methods employed in their construction. Sociology is widely considered to be a social science. A central tenet of science is that research is oriented toward developing and evaluating clear, testable theories. A scientific theory is a set of general, parsimonious, logically related statements containing clearly defined terms, formulated to explain accurately and precisely the broadest possible range of phenomena in the natural world. Only a relatively few modern and contemporary sociological theories manifest such properties, and sociologists generally do not teach or learn methods for developing such theories.

Much theoretical work in sociology entails the analysis of other theoretical writings. Whereas the value of such activities may be questioned from a scientific standpoint, they may offer previously unrealized nuances and insights. At the same time, a writer's status, personal charisma, or rhetorical skill may receive undue consideration in the evaluation of such work. Other work aims to produce atheoretical descriptions of complex empirical phenomena. These may range from discursive "thick descriptions" to statistical relationships in a causal model, either of which may serve as a platform for inducing general theory. Finally, even the blatant promotion of ideological or philosophical positions has been called theorizing in some corners of the field.

Between the highly rigorous and the nonscientific is a range of theoretical styles. Computer simulations may embody the terms and arguments of a theory. Grounded *theorizing* is method used to develop a relatively abstract theory to fit a concrete set of observations. *Typology construction* produces categorization schemes that assist in conceptual development. *Propositional inventories* are listings of general statements intended to encapsulate some body of theoretical knowledge.

SEE ALSO: Conflict Theory; Grounded Theory; Knowledge, Sociology of; Metatheory; Postmodern Social Theory; Theory and Methods

SUGGESTED READINGS

Calhoun, C., Gerteis, J., Moody, J., Pfaff, S., & Virk, I. (eds.) (2003) *Contemporary Sociological Theory*. Blackwell, Malden, MA.

Cohen, B. P. (1989) *Developing Sociological Knowledge*. 2nd edn. Nelson-Hall, Chicago.

Münch, R. (1994) *Sociological Theory*, vol. 1: *From the 1850s to the 1920s*; vol. 2: *From the 1920s to the 1960s*. Nelson-Hall, Chicago.

Turner, J. H. (2003) *The Structure of Sociological Theory*, 7th edn. Wadsworth-Thomson Learning, Belmont, CA.

BARRY MARKOVSKY

theory and methods

Theories reside in a realm of ideas, establishing meanings and organizing our beliefs about reality. Theories are expressed through sets of abstract, general, logically related statements. In contrast, *methods* pertain to concrete objects in the natural world which, in sociology, usually implies one of two things: (1) *research methods* – procedures enacted in the natural world in service of recording observations; (2) *data analysis methods* – manipulations of recorded observations for the purpose of summarizing empirical observations or making inferences about them. Data analysis methods include a large palette of qualitative and quantitative techniques. When formulated without the benefit of strong ties to the natural world, theories should be regarded with much skepticism and deserve only highly provisional support. By the same token, when applied without the benefit of a clear theoretical purpose, methods are no more useful to us than unlabeled snapshots of unfamiliar scenes.

Although it receives relatively little attention in the general sociological literature, the theory-method interface is critical. That is because we want our theories to be relevant to the natural world in order to increase our understanding and our ability to intervene in desired ways. Although theories and methods are intimately connected, sociological writing at times obscures important distinctions between theoretical statements and observation statements. These are separate spheres of operation, each with its own rules and standards.

The interface of theory and methods – where elements in the theoretical realm connect to elements of the natural world – becomes most apparent when theories are written simply and clearly, and their connections to objects in the natural world are unequivocal. There are three essential components to the theory-methods connection: (1) statements in the theory, (2) statements that link terms in the theory with observations, and (3) statements about particular observations. Each is described next.

1 Theories employ conditional statements, often called propositions or assumptions, to make general claims that can be subjected to analysis. For example, "*If* a group has a role structure, *then* that group has a system of rewards and punishments." The general form of this proposition is that of a conditional statement: If the first part is true, then it is claimed that the second part will be true as well.
2 Terms in propositions must be connected to actual empirical phenomena. The terms themselves are relatively simple abstract constructs. It is this abstractness that permits theories to be general, i.e., applicable to a wide range of empirical cases. So a highly specific observation statement such as "The Chess Club now active at Fairview High School has three elected positions" may serve as an instance (often called an "operationalization") of the "group with role structure" part of the proposition. "The Chess Club now active at Fairview High School has trophies for outstanding performance, and rescinds the membership of any member caught cheating" could be an instance of having a "system of rewards and punishments."

Definitions of theoretical terms, such as "role structure," "reward," and "punishment" in the example above, guide this process. Unless terms are clearly defined, researchers cannot be certain whether the theory has been applied correctly. At the same time, definitions must be broad enough so that the theory applies in a wide range of cases. Good theories strike a useful balance between specificity and generality.

3 Now that we have connected theoretical terms and observable phenomena, we can derive testable *hypotheses*. In our example: "If the Chess Club at Fairview High School has multiple elected and appointed positions, then it will have trophies for outstanding performance and rescind the membership of any member caught cheating." Ideally, this would be just one of many hypotheses for a variety of empirical settings that could be derived from the theory and tested.

With the theory having guided the choice of empirical indicators, research methods now can be used to gather data such as using experiments, surveys, participant observation, text analysis, or other means. The choice of research methods, in conjunction with the specific questions the researcher would like to answer, together determine the most appropriate data analysis methods.

SEE ALSO: Experimental Methods; Social Indicators; Theoretical Research Programs; Theory; Theory Construction

SUGGESTED READINGS

Cohen, B. P. (1989) *Developing Sociological Knowledge: Theory and Method*, 2nd edn. Nelson Hall, Chicago.
Kerlinger, F. N. & Lee, H. B. (2000) *Foundations of Behavioral Research*, 4th edn. Wadsworth, Belmont, CA.
Schutt, R. K. (2004) *Investigating the Social World*, 4th edn. Pine Forge Press, Thousand Oaks, CA.

BARRY MARKOVSKY

theory construction

The ideal *theory* is a set of explicit, abstract, general, logically related statements formulated to explain phenomena in the natural world. *Theory construction* is the process of either formulating and assembling components of theories into coherent wholes, or revising and expanding theories in light of logical, semantic, or empirical analyses.

At their core, theories are *arguments*. As such, they are sets of statements (called axioms, propositions, assumptions, etc.) that provide logical support for one or more other statements (conclusions, theorems, derivations). Every statement in a theory consists of *terms*, and the meaning of every term should be clear to intended readers. Some terms are part of the logical system (e.g., "If ... then ..."; "{ ... + ... }/ ... = ..."). The meanings of all other terms must already be shared by readers, or else must be defined explicitly. Finally, *scope conditions* state conditions under which a theorist considers the theory to be applicable.

Good theories promote clear communication, rigorous testing, accurate measurement, and broad applicability. To achieve these qualities, theorists must take care to eliminate any contradictions, ambiguities and ambivalences from their terms and arguments. Further, good theories are constructed using abstract language so that they may be applied in many kinds of empirical settings. Another kind of specialized statement, sometimes called operationalization, instantiation, or interpretation, connects the abstract theoretical terms to observable terms.

Once expressed, good theories are *deductive* in the sense of having clearly stated propositions from which conclusions follow logically. As well, most theories also are *inductive* in the sense that their propositions, and modifications to their propositions, typically originated as conjectures and intuitive leaps.

SEE ALSO: Theory; Theory and Methods; Theoretical Research Programs

SUGGESTED READING

Cohen, B. P. (1989) *Developing Sociological Knowledge*. Nelson-Hall, Chicago, IL.

BARRY MARKOVSKY

third world and postcolonial feminisms/subaltern

Third World feminism has taken important liberal and nationalist forms in both politics and the academy. Liberal feminist movements of the 1970s and 1980s drew on social science literature that linked women's economic disadvantage to occupational and educational discrimination. Public policy responses included Women in Development (WID), promoting women's participation in international development planning; and later, Gender and Development (GAD), emphasizing the relationship of development programs and processes to changes in gender relations.

Nationalist feminisms stress the transmission and interpretation of third world women's voices and their engagement in civic and non-governmental organizations. Nationalist academic writing of the late 1980s and the 1990s drew heavily on the work of Fanon (1961), Memmi (1965) and others to explore the shared and enduring subjective experiences of colonial oppression and marginalization. It engaged as well post-structural and postmodern critical and interpretive methods to interrogate, deconstruct, and reinterpret representation in literature, art and other cultural forms. Resulting feminist postcolonial theories have explicated gendered representations produced in colonial and postcolonial settings.

"Subaltern" is a term used historically by the British military to identify officers of lesser rank. It is now used more broadly to characterize socially subordinate groups. Antonio Gramsci described the subaltern both as incipient challengers to traditional dominant classes and relatively powerless groups subject to constraining ideological power. The term's meaning has expanded again, however, as postmodern and postcolonial feminists have argued that the conceptual and discursive meanings of Marxist and neo-Marxist thought, including Gramsci's theorization of the subaltern, reproduce binary and essentialist thinking that has limited Third World women's political options. Feminist sociologists more generally echoed these concerns in their theoretical and methodological recognition of the situated and subjugated knowledges of women and other socially marginalized groups.

Academic and policy makers' current discussions of globalization and the internationalization of investment and trade have to an extent supplanted the debates of the 1980s and 1990s about the ideological and subjective meanings of colonialism, postcolonialism, and nationalism. Methodological and epistemological challenges to structuralist categorizations of history and culture continue to engage feminists and other critical theorists and activists. However, recent recognition of the breadth and depth of global interdependence has reinvigorated the scholarly quest to understand the dynamics of global capitalism and the transformative political spaces therein. The third world feminist challenge is ever more complex as the interstices of international domination and national self-interest multiply and become less distinct, changing the terms of meaningful collective action.

SEE ALSO: Colonialism (Neocolonialism); Liberal Feminism; Socialist Feminism

SUGGESTED READINGS

Gramsci, A. (1991) *Prison Notebooks*. Columbia University Press, New York.

Fanon, F. (1961) *The Wretched of the Earth*. Grove, New York.

Memmi, A. (1965) *The Colonizer and the Colonized*. Orion Books, New York.

Spivak, G. C. (1988) Can the subaltern speak? Speculations on widow sacrifice. In: Nelson, G. and Grossberg, L. *Marxism and the Interpretation of Culture*. University of Illinois Press, Urbana, IL, pp. 271–313.

MARIETTA MORRISSEY

Thomas, William I. (1863–1947)

William I. Thomas was born in 1863 in Virginia and raised there in a rural Protestant milieu. In 1884 he received his bachelor's degree from the

University of Tennessee. He then studied for two years in Germany followed by teaching English and sociology at Oberlin College. In 1893 he entered the sociology program at the University of Chicago Thomas as part of its first group of graduate students (he worked under Albion Small), receiving his doctorate in 1895. That same year he joined the newly formed faculty of sociology at the University of Chicago. He died in 1947, an independent researcher in Berkeley, California.

Thomas is well known for his collaboration with Florian Znaniecki in *The Polish Peasant in Europe and America*. Other celebrated works include *The Unadjusted Girl* and, with Robert Park and Herbert Miller, *Old World Traits Transplanted*. His reputation has lived on in sociology largely in the legacy he left symbolic interactionism in the theoretic sections of the *Polish Peasant*. Today Thomas is widely recognized as one of the founders of this field.

Thomas had an enduring interest in the pragmatic tradition in sociology, one center of which at the time was the University of Chicago. For him sociology concentrated on human activities, wherein people demonstrated conscious control in developing art, religion, language, forms of government, and the like. More precisely, sociology looks at *attention*, the attitude that takes note of the outside world and then manipulates it. From this stance he wrote a great deal about attitudes and attention, later preferring to conceptualize both as *definition of the situation*.

A dictum from a work co-authored with his wife, Dorothy Swain Thomas, "if people define situations as real, they are real in their consequences," (Thomas & Thomas 1928: 571–2) is still frequently quoted.

SEE ALSO: Chicago School; Social Psychology

REFERENCE

Thomas, W. I. & Thomas, D. S. (1928) *The Child in America*. Alfred A. Knopf, New York.

SUGGESTED READING

Thomas, W. I. & Znaniecki, F. (1918–20) *The Polish Peasant in Europe and America*. Richard G. Badger, Boston, MA.

ROBERT STEBBINS

time–space

All social life is ordered over time and through space. However, when sociologists attend to the "situated" character of social life, they do not treat time–space as simply the temporal and spatial environment of the phenomena they study. They see social life as not just being "in" time–space, they see time–space as central to all social interaction. The "situatedness" of social life involves time–space as a constitutive feature in the construction and reconstruction of what people do and in the way they do things together. The ordering of social life comes about because social practices are routinely made to come together across time–space as shared experiences. This binding of time–space is expressed in the ways in which societies, institutions, and individuals organize time–space.

Anthony Giddens draws attention to three features that need to be addressed by sociologists when seeking to understand the way in which social life is ordered across time–space. The first involves the construction and reconstruction of regularized social interaction across time–space through informed practices. Take, for example, the actions and interactions relating to the lending and borrowing of a library book. These are knowledgeable activities involving the understanding of a range of time–space relations by both lenders and borrowers. A borrowed book has to be returned before the elapse of a specific time period. The library staff gather and process information on the whereabouts of the books they have lent out.

The second feature involves the association of social interaction with purposefully designed spatial and temporal environments. Taking once again the example of a library book, such transactions are embedded in purposefully designed spatial and temporal settings for the storage, distribution, and collection of books. The design features of a library building are integral to the spatial and temporal coordination of library transactions and are integral to what a library is.

The third feature involves the organizational mechanisms which are used to regulate the timing and spacing of social interaction. The lending and borrowing of a library book are organized by means of various time–space organizing devices. A library will have specific opening hours. The annual cycle of opening hours may include holiday closures. Other time–space schedules, such as a library's borrowing and cataloging system, regulate the location of books, and the length of the borrowing period.

The development and use of information, communication, and transportation technology impact on all three of the features set out above. David Harvey's term "time–space compression" describes the reduction of distance experienced through the decrease in the time taken, either to cross space physically by means of transportation, or symbolically by means of communication. People can, for example, increasingly download reading material digitally and so cancel out the need for physical transportation altogether. The use of the Internet also impacts on libraries as purposefully designed spatial and temporal settings. For example, library users may browse through books on a computer screen rather than in the open book stacks in a library building. Finally, Internet use impacts on the organizational mechanisms which are used to regulate the timing and spacing of library transactions. People can, for example, consult a library's cataloging system even outside a library's opening hours.

Time–space compression allows for the stretching of social life across time–space, a phenomenon that lies at the heart of globalization. Tomlinson (1999) writes of "the 'proximity' that comes from the networking of social relations across large tracts of time–space, causing distant events and powers to penetrate our local experience." However, as he makes clear, the compression of time–space is not just about physical distance. It is also about social-cultural distance.

SEE ALSO: Distanciation and Disembedding; Space

REFERENCE

Tomlinson, J. (1999) *Globalization and Culture*. Polity Press, Cambridge.

SUGGESTED READINGS

Giddens, A. (1984) *The Constitution of Society*. Polity Press, Cambridge.

Heidegger, M. (1962) *Being and Time*. Blackwell, Oxford.

Thrift, N. (1996) *Spatial Formations*. Sage, London.

JAMES SLEVIN

Tocqueville, Alexis de (1805–59)

Born into a French aristocratic family in 1805, Alexis de Tocqueville was a French political theorist, sociologist, and cultural and historical commentator whose contributions are equally claimed by the disciplines of sociology, political science, American studies, and American history. In 1831, together with his colleague Gustave de Beaumont, Tocqueville embarked on a tour of the nascent American democracy in an effort to understand the inner workings of the democratic spirit in the everyday lives and social institutions of the American people. On returning to France he wrote his famous two-volume investigation, *Democracy in America* (1835). Tocqueville uncovered within American society a tension between democracy's conflicting imperatives: the egalitarian character of democratic societies, while successfully eliminating forms of despotism identified with feudalism, did not provide sufficient integration of the individual into the social fabric. Hence, democratization, if extended unchecked and in irresponsible ways, could produce excessive individualism (a term Tocqueville coined for this purpose), and ultimately new forms of despotism. In a comparison of the American and French experiences with democracy, Tocqueville pointed to the dangers posed by the French case, in which a sudden leveling of social hierarchies following the French Revolution eliminated the intermediary institutions that maintained the integration of individuals within the larger social fabric, leading to revolutionary despotism, a theme developed more completely in his other major work, *The Old Regime and the Revolution* (1856).

The American case, on the other hand, fostered voluntary democratic institutions which ensured local involvement and instructed in the methods and techniques of self-rule. The American case, however, was possessed of the equally ominous threat of the "tyranny of the majority," or leveling and homogenizing of public opinion by the belief in the ultimate sovereignty of the views held by the greatest number.

Tocqueville's legacy is still very much in dispute, particularly in debates around the welfare state, civic engagement, and democratic citizenship. On the political right, Tocqueville is cited as a critic of the tyranny of the welfare state and of public assistance as a means of redressing inequality. On the left he is taken up as an advocate of an active role for the state in offsetting the atomization of society through policies that enable associative engagement of individuals in democratic and community participation. Tocqueville's imprint is also visible in contemporary sociological concerns with declining social capital and the erosion of civic engagement in urban, mediated, and postmodern societies.

SEE ALSO: Citizenship; Civil Society; Democracy; Individualism; Welfare State

SUGGESTED READINGS

Goldberg, C. A. (2001) Social citizenship and a reconstructed Tocqueville. *American Sociological Review* 66 (2): 289–315.

Putnam, R. (2000) *Bowling Alone: The Collapse and Revival of American Community*. Simon & Schuster, New York.

SAM BINKLEY

tolerance

The history of tolerance as guiding principle for states, governments, and the life of their citizens is linked to the Enlightenment and political liberalism. The philosophers of the Enlightenment proclaimed toleration as the notion that all human beings are essentially the same, independent of their religious beliefs. Political liberalism transformed these ideas into its own paradigm of individual rights and autonomy, value pluralism and private beliefs, and linked it to its ideals of justice and freedom.

Tolerance is a principle invoked in a world of deep pluralism, and in the face of religious and political conflict. In Europe, tolerance emerged as a mechanism of social order as early as in the Middle Ages when cities like Toledo, Granada, and Sarajevo thrived on tolerance between Muslim, Christian, and Jewish citizens in countries under Islamic governments. The Confederation of Warsaw (1573) is the earliest document of religious tolerance guaranteed by the state, followed in 1598 by the Edict of Nantes in France. The USA was the first to guarantee it in its constitution (1787).

Tolerance is best defined as a *minimalist concept* and in a *negative* way. Tolerance embodies a sense of *disapproval*, and is the deliberate choice *not to interfere* with beliefs, life styles and behaviors, which one disapproves of; as such it is a mechanism of "regulating aversion" (Brown 2006). Tolerant attitudes and behaviors are situated between a *positive and negative extreme*; at its positive extreme, tolerance includes respect for others, acceptance and embracement of social diversity and individual difference. At its negative extreme, tolerance is characterized by total neglect, disregard, ignorance and avoidance of those individuals and groups who are different.

Tolerance owes its prominent role in the formation of modern societies to its essential character as *non-interference*. It is decisive in the cultural change from "passions to interests" (Hirschmann 1997 [1977]), in the transition from *Gemeinschaft* to *Gesellschaft* (Tönnies), and the formation of weak ties (Granovetter 1973). Tolerance creates links *between* different social groups, and facilitates the everyday interactions of their members. Tolerance is seen as an indispensable "underpinning of democracy" and cornerstone of civic culture (Sullivan and Transue 1999).

In particular its roots in liberalism have given rise to critical re-evaluations of tolerance and its role in polity and society. In his essay "Repressive tolerance" Marcuse (1969 [1965]) was one of the first to point out the asymmetrical nature of tolerance. The majority decides when and how tolerance is appropriate, and grants it to minorities, thereby retaining the right (and power) to define the realm of what and who will be tolerated. In responding to the political, social and cultural challenges to tolerance in contemporary societies, political theory and philosophy have re-configured the concept of tolerance in terms of identity and difference, and redefined its links with liberalism. Traditional notions of political and religious tolerance need to be critically evaluated and broadened in order to account for all aspects of new forms of diversity in contemporary societies, and to relate them to the institutional frameworks of democracy, justice, and human rights.

SEE ALSO: Affirmative Action; Citizenship; Civil Society; Democracy; Discrimination; Prejudice

REFERENCES

Brown, W. (2006) *Regulating Aversion: Tolerance in the Age of Identity and Empire*. Princeton University Press, Princeton, NJ.

Granovetter, M. (1973) The strength of weak ties. *American Journal of Sociology* 78: 360–80.

Hirschmann, A. O. (1997) [1977] *The Passions and the Interests: Political Arguments for Capitalism before its Triumph*. Princeton University Press, Princeton, NJ.

Marcuse, H. (1969) [1965] Repressive tolerance. In: Wolff, R. P., Moore, B. Jr., & Marcuse, H. (eds.), *A Critique of Pure Tolerance*. Beacon Press, Boston, pp. 95–137.

Sullivan, J. L. & Transue, J. E. (1999) The psychological underpinnings of democracy: a selective review of research on political tolerance, interpersonal trust and social capital. *Annual Review of Psychology* 50: 625–50.

SUGGESTED READING

Horton, J. & Mendus, S. (eds.) (1999): *Toleration, Identity and Difference*. Macmillan, London.

SUSANNE KARSTEDT

Tönnies, Ferdinand (1855–1936)

Ferdinand Tönnies was born near Oldenswort, Germany, in the northern province of Schleswig-Holstein. He came from a well-to-do farming family and grew up at a time when Germany was expanding as a colonial empire and undergoing profound changes such as population growth, urbanization, and industrialization. Tönnies's oldest brother was involved in mercantile endeavors and thus he experienced the world of the peasant farmer as well as the town merchant. He received his doctorate in philosophy from the University of Tübingen in 1877, then returned to his native province, and later taught for over a half century as a private lecturer and professor at the University of Kiel.

Tönnies was interested in social philosophy and social science. His best-known work was his first, *Gemeinschaft und Gesellschaft*, published in 1887. Translated into English as *Community and Society* (1957), this book on social change and modernization had a pioneering influence in the new discipline of sociology. Its later editions served to enhance Tönnies's reputation as an important social theorist. *Gemeinschaft* referred not so much to a geographic place as to a "community feeling," intimate and holistic relationships, and a common meeting of minds characteristic of people living in a village or small town. By contrast, Tönnies used *Gesellschaft* to describe the impersonal, limited, and contractual relationships people have in an urban-industrial world, an "associational society." The two terms were meant to call attention to the dramatic shift occurring in the late nineteenth century in social groupings and interpersonal relations.

Tönnies believed all social relationships were governed by human will, the need to belong to groups or associate with others. He spoke of "natural will," the motivation for action derived from the temperament, character, or intellect of the individual. This will is typified by *Gemeinschaft* and is found in kinship groups, neighborhoods, and friendship circles. People are bound together by blood, locality, or common interest and naturally work together or help each other as an end in and for itself. Tönnies believed "rational will" is characteristic of *Gesellschaft*. People associate with one another as a means to an end, for economic or political gain in capitalist society, to rationally choose their associations for practical results rather than personal motives. Tönnies developed his concepts to be ideal-types of historical relationships found in medieval or rural, as opposed to modern or urban, societies.

SEE ALSO: Community; Society; Solidarity, Mechanical and Organic

REFERENCE

Tönnies, F. (1957) *Community and Society*, trans. C. P. Loomis. Michigan State University Press, East Lansing, MI.

RAYMOND M. WEINSTEIN

total institutions

The concept of total institution (TI) appeared with the publication of Goffman's essays, "Asylums" (1961). The essential features of the total institution are the rigid regimens, tight supervision and complex rules that routinize the daily movements of large groups of cohorts, socialize them to the culture of that institution, and yet somehow seek to return them to society at large. They seek to exclusively frame the experience of those so processed. Concrete examples range from the benign to the violently coercive, from schools to prisons. While these organizations present a range of variation in underlying functions, contradictions, and modes of entry and exit, the essence of total institutions is that they are bounded, sealed off physically and interactionally from civil society. The total institution controls the time and interests of the inmates: they sleep, work and play in one place. While the concept is implicit in the wide range of materials Goffman cites, including his field notes – from St Elizabeth's Hospital in Washington, DC, a large publicly funded mental institution – his aim is to assemble an analytic framework illuminating such organizations.

Goffman defines institutions as places where a particular activity regularly goes on (1961: 3) and total institution (TI in Goffman 1961: p. xiii) as "a place of residence and work where large numbers of like-situated individuals, cut off from the wider society for an appreciable period of time, together lead an enclosed, formally administered round of life." He asserts that in such institutions a split, both formal and informal, develops between "staff" and "inmates." This produces parallel social worlds. Description of the inmate and staff worlds and their contacts through ceremonies occupies the bulk of the essay.

The work of the place is ritualized: managing human needs takes place by bureaucratic rules and procedures applied to blocks of people – "whether effective in achieving the goals of the institution or not" (p. 6). The lived round of life – always under close surveillance – dramatizes the boundaries between the staff and inmate worlds. Because there is no paid work in the usual sense, and no family life, whatever is done for intimacy and reward is arbitrarily structured within the TI. The supervised public round of life reduces complexity to simplicity and thus the connection between "expression" and the self, the sense of personhood, is truncated. Sameness is sought and reinforced by responses by others, primarily staff, that are standardized and circumscribed radically. Unlike civil society in which diverse careers are produced and respected, the total institution shapes a single moral career for all. This is done by stripping and assaulting the self and then reducing the sense of self and self-determination to nil (p. 44). An institutionalized and all encompassing self emerges.

The organization varies in the rationalizations that it provides for these humiliating processes (pp. 45–6). The primary question is the "fit" between the institution and the person, not the fit between the person and their idiosyncrasies, feelings, failures and choices. (p. 47). The house rules and the privilege system combine to form an arbitrary system of rewards and punishments that embeds the person in the institution and creates an artificial connection between work and reward; time effort and output. This scheme is an artifice for control, but not for the accomplishment of any stipulated goal. Inmates create modes of adaptation which form an oppositional culture (not Goffman's term), "playing it cool," avoiding alliances with the staff, but also creating a distance for the survival of the self. The inmate culture has as a dominant theme a sense of self-concern (why am I here?) and an abiding sense that time has been wasted "inside." The irony of this degradation process is that the inmate adapts in ways that are not useful in civil society.

The staff world contrasts with the inmate world. It assumes that "people are material to work on" (p. 76): complex bundles of status, roles, feelings, selves and internalized drives are constructed as inanimate. The inmates are "ends" as well as means and the movement between these objectifications creates social chaos. Since formal organizations always fail to reach their stated goals (p. 83), staff must rationalize their failures in what might be called institutional accounts based on a "theory of human nature" (p. 87) that is nurtured in the organization. The two worlds, staff and inmate, are unified in division; that is ceremonies both recognize the two worlds and aim to blur them by finding compatible social space within which both can reside (p. 110).

SEE ALSO: Bureaucratic Personality; Goffman, Erving; Institution; Organization

REFERENCE

Goffman, E. (1961) *Asylums: Essays on the Social Situation of Patients and Other Inmates*. Doubleday Anchor, Garden City, NY.

SUGGESTED READING

Lemert, E. (1951) *Social Pathology*. McGraw-Hill, New York.

PETER MANNING

tracking

Tracking is the process of grouping students for instructional purposes based on actual or assumed differences in academic development or interests. In theory, such practices can maximize learning by allowing instruction to be tailored to the needs of each classroom of students. In practice, the quality of instruction often varies dramatically based on the course level such that low track students receive few learning opportunities while high track students are exposed to a rich and rigorous curriculum. When group placements are related to ascribed characteristics such as social class or ethnicity, tracking contributes to social stratification by perpetuating social inequality in not only individuals' current learning opportunities but also future educational and occupational attainment.

The terms *tracking*, *ability grouping*, and *streaming* are frequently used as synonyms for students' position in the academic status hierarchy within a classroom or school. When distinctions are made, ability grouping usually refers to sorting of elementary school students in a given grade level into groups that progress through a common curriculum at different speeds. These groups are usually given labels such as *low*, *average*, and *high* or *remedial*, *basic*, *regular* and *advanced* to reflect expected differences in students' ability to handle more or less challenging instructional material. In contrast, tracking usually refers to differences in high school students' academic programs, which consist of courses that differ in topics covered or level of difficulty. Traditionally tracks were given labels such as *vocational*, *general/academic*, *college preparatory*, and *elite college preparatory* to reflect whether students were expected to enter the workforce or attend college after graduating. Regardless of the terms used, tracks identify students who share similar educational experiences.

Tracking is a feature of modern school systems, although the process and extent of stratification and segregation varies dramatically. Placement procedures that utilized performance on standardized assessments are described as *contest mobility systems*, in which individuals earn the right of entry into the elite. In contrast, more subjective criteria are used for making placement decisions in *sponsored mobility systems*, in which individuals with unusual qualities are singled out for special assistance. In the USA during the late 1980s, many schools officially eliminated tracking (i.e., *detracked*) in response to political pressure. However, *de facto* tracking continues as a result of schools' sorting of students into courses or academic programs within the constraints of the master course schedule. While most schools' assignment policies appear basically meritocratic, minority and poor students have historically been less likely to be in higher tracks than equally talented white students or children of college educated parents.

Tracking clearly differentiates students' learning opportunities where some are given mentally challenging experiences that promote learning while others are relegated to classes with curricula so diluted that they are caricatures of regular courses. Critical theorists argue that these differences in curriculum reflect students' social origins and are one of the major mechanisms through which social stratification is perpetuated across generations. Lower track courses basically prepare working class children for menial jobs while college track courses prepare the social elite's children for professional or managerial careers.

Finally, whether through direct intervention of parents or a more criterion-based system, students' social backgrounds influence their sorting into courses such that they tend to take classes with others similar to themselves. This social class segregation within schools may allow formation of micro-communities with distinct norms and values relating to academic performance. Thus, regardless of their own backgrounds, students are likely to benefit academically from attending classes with others from more advantaged social backgrounds, which perpetuates social stratification in both economic and health benefits related to higher levels of educational attainment.

SEE ALSO: Conflict Theory; Educational Inequality; Meritocracy;

SUGGESTED READINGS

Hallinan, M. T. (1994) Tracking: from theory to practice. *Sociology of Education* 67: 79–84.

Oakes, J. (1985) *Keeping Track: How Schools Structure Inequality*. Yale University Press, New Haven, CT.

KATHRYN S. SCHILLER

tradition

"Tradition" is generally understood as a body of values, beliefs, rules, and behavior patterns that is transmitted generationally by practice and word of mouth and is integral to socialization processes. Connoting fixity, stability, and continuity, it guides daily behavior and justifies shared beliefs and practices. In small-scale societies, where tradition offers the dominant blueprint for acceptable behavior, its status is that of sacred lore. Where orally transmitted, however, tradition is always open to variation, contestation and change, and becomes a model of past practices rather than a passively and unreflectively inherited legacy.

Heuristically, tradition can be usefully conceptualized as a resource, employed (or not) strategically by individuals and groups. Tradition is subject to a range of moral evaluations by its carriers over time; it is understood by all as a symbol but no one can agree on its meaning, since understandings are embedded within rival groups and become part of competing political ideologies. Tradition can be invoked just as effectively to manifest ethnocentrism and disunity, by emphasizing local differences and reinforcing boundaries, as it can when functioning as a political symbol of unity (in which case it is deliberately left vague and internally undifferentiated, so as to minimize its potentially divisive aspect).

Since the 1990s, the historical turn in anthropological theory has led scholars to contextualize the emergence of particular constructions of tradition within colonization, missionization and post-war "development" and in articulation with the global political economy. Since it burgeoned in the 1980s, the topic of tradition has proved remarkably durable, engendering a multilayered body of knowledge about constructions of the past in contemporary societies. Social actors' received notions of tradition as the solid foundation that underpins customary behavior have been deemphasized in scholarly analyses in favor of conceptions of it as constantly subject to reinterpretation and rereading by each new generation of carriers, who construe their past in terms both of present perceptions and understandings and future hopes and needs.

SEE ALSO: Authority and Legitimacy; Belief; Socialization, Agents of

SUGGESTED READINGS

Hobsbawm, E. & Ranger, T. (eds.) (1983) *The Invention of Tradition*. Cambridge University Press, Cambridge.

Tonkinson, R. (1993) Understanding "tradition" – ten years on. In Lindstrom, L. & White, G. M. (eds.), Custom today. *Anthropological Forum* (special issue) 6 (4): 597–606.

ROBERT TONKINSON

transgender, transvestism, and transsexualism

The term transgender, although not accepted universally, has been used since the 1980s to refer to a range of practices and identities that cross between or lie outside the traditional western dichotomy of male and female, man and woman.

The term transvestite was coined by Hirschfeld in 1910 to refer to those men and women who, to varying degrees and for varying lengths of time, dressed as, behaved as and sometimes wished to *be*, members of the other sex, and he argued that this did not necessarily involve homosexuality as others assumed. In the early 1950s the endocrinologist Benjamin began to use the term transsexual to refer to those people who sought to "change sex" by means of newly developing hormonal and surgical procedures.

With transsexualism linked to "sex reassignment," transvestism came to be limited to forms of cross-dressing. Despite Benjamin's advocacy of "sex reassignment," it remained outside mainstream medicine until the 1960s when it began to be carried out on an experimental basis in some medical centers. This provided opportunities for some sociologists to encounter patients seeking such procedures. Other opportunities for sociological research opened up during the 1960s as subcultural groups and organizations began to develop. This enabled empirical studies of transvestites and transsexuals and their social worlds.

The late 1960s also saw the (re)emergence of the women's movement and the interest in gender. The new sociologists of deviance were generally "on the side" of those who were questioning conventional norms at that time. Those who were questioning the gender norms, however, were feminists and, on the face of it, transvestites and transsexuals appeared to be embracing what feminism was questioning. The critique of transgender phenomena that developed in some feminist circles culminated in Raymond's *The Transsexual Empire* (1980).

By the late 1980s some transvestites and transsexuals were beginning to use the term transgender in an inclusive, "umbrella" sense to encompass both identities. In time some authors included other "gender variant" people (e.g., drag queens and kings and intersexed people) within the term (sometimes controversially). By the early 1990s it became common to find references to the "transgender community," although, again, this concept has not been without controversy.

Since the early 1990s there has been a surge of anthropological interest in transgender, principally in Southeast Asia and in South America. Some of this literature has focused on conceptions that have developed without the influence of western medicine, such as the idea of an institutionalized "third" gender or liminal gender space. Nevertheless, it is also evident that western discourses of transgender have been exported to many parts of the world. The attention of social scientists has also begun to focus on those people with intersexed conditions. This has been partly stimulated by the development of a more visible and vociferous intersex community.

Transpeople who were originally assigned as female were not much in evidence in either the medical literature or the transgender community before the early 1990s but since then they have become much more visible and in fact have come to play key roles within that community and within transgender politics and theory.

The rise in popularity of the term transgender has paralleled the rise of queer theory, within which crossing the gender border is seen as subversive and transgressive. Stone's (1991) article which can be seen to provide the starting point for this approach has been particularly influential with some transactivists and academics, and raises radical questions about the binary and fixed nature of gender categories themselves.

Despite this late-modern/postmodern approach with its emphasis on diversity, fluidity, and moving beyond the rigidities of the binary gender divide and its celebration of new combinations of masculinity and femininity, for most in the professional and transgender communities, as in society at large, the binary view of gender prevails.

SEE ALSO: Drag Queens and Drag Kings; Female Masculinity; Intersexuality; Queer Theory; Sex and Gender; Sexual Citizenship

REFERENCE

Stone, S. (1991) The empire strikes back: a posttranssexual manifesto. In: Straub, K. & Epstein, J. (eds.), *Body Guards: The Cultural Politics of Gender Ambiguity*. Routledge, New York.

SUGGESTED READINGS

Califia, P. (1997) *Sex Changes: The Politics of Transgenderism*. Cleis Press, San Francisco, CA.

Ekins, R. & King, D. (2006) *The Transgender Phenomenon*. Sage, London.

Stryker, S. & Whittle, S. (eds.) (2006), *The Transgender Studies Reader*. Routledge, London.

DAVE KING AND RICHARD EKINS

transition economies

The term *transition economies* apply mainly to post-socialist countries in central and eastern Europe, and also in East Asia, despite its wider use in the economic or sociological literature. The term *transition* is used to describe the process through which a society or economy introduces the institutional facets associated with advanced capitalist economies, such as the legal system, ownership structures, institutions of financial and labor markets, the party system and the institutions of the independent and democratic state. Whilst the term *transition* is often restricted to a small time span of an economic change in which new economic institutions are formed and established, or relates only to an economic view of post socialist societies, or describes the fixed result of the changes as "the" western type of a market economy or capitalism, the term *transformation* has been more widely used in the sociological literature, especially in Europe. The latter term covers a social process of fundamental political, economic, technological, and cultural change, both managed and evolutionary, or self organized, in structures and values, including all areas and levels of the society, organizations, and the individual and collective actors. At the societal level, *institution transfers vs. institution building*, or re-institutionalization of social processes has been at the center of interest, including conflicts between inherent values of the transferred institutions and the local national value systems. Different transition strategies can be observed, ranging from early shock therapy to an incremental change finally leading to a distinctive mixture between public and private enterprise, and with the strong influence of social networks and groups with particular interests that have underpinned economic activities and institutions. The emergent, or newly embedded, institutions are therefore the result of a "recombination" of properties or "bricolage" based on the culture of the past and transformation experiences with the transferred institutions. At the level of individual and collective actors, the emergence and shape of *new social groups of actors*, especially entrepreneurs or managers and their influence on the development of new organizational forms, values, and the (re-)construction of new institutions can be stated based on an elite reproduction instead of a radical change within the economic elite.

SEE ALSO: Capitalism; Economy (Sociological Approach); Socialism

SUGGESTED READINGS

Fligstein, N. (1996) The economic sociology of the transition from socialism. *American Journal of Sociology* 101 (4): 1074–81.

Nee, V. & Matthew, R. (1996) Market transition and societal transformation in reforming state socialism. *Annual Review of Sociology* 22: 401–35.

RAINHART LANG

transnationalism

The concept of *transnationalism*, described as an integral part of the globalization process, is becoming increasingly popular in social and political sciences. Originally coined in international economics to describe flows of capital and labor across national borders in the second half of the twentieth century, this concept was later applied to the study of international migration and ethnic diasporas. The transnational perspective became increasingly useful for exploring such issues as immigrant economic integration, identity, citizenship and cultural retention. Transnationalism embraces a variety of multi-faceted social relations that are both embedded in and transcend two or more nation-states, cross-cutting sociopolitical, territorial and cultural borders. The ever-increasing flows of people, goods, ideas and images between various parts of the world enhances the blending of cultures and lifestyles and leads to the formation of "hyphenated" social and personal identities (Chinese–American, Greek–Australian, etc.).

Some authors argue that transnationalism may actually be a new name for an old phenomenon, in the sense that most big immigration waves of the past were typified by ethno-cultural retention and contacts with the homeland. Indeed, historic studies of ethnic diasporas show that immigrants never fully severed their links with the country they left behind. Yet, due to technical and financial limitations of the time, for most migrants these links remained mainly in the sentimental and cultural realm, and were seldom expressed in active shuttle movement or communication across borders. Economic ties with countries of origin were typically limited to monetary remittances to family members. Although up to one-quarter of transatlantic migrants of the late nineteenth and early twentieth centuries eventually returned to their homelands, the decision to repatriate was in fact another critical and irreversible choice to be made. Hence, for the majority of historic migrants, resettlement was an irreversible process always involving a dichotomy: stay or emigrate, or else stay or return.

In the late twentieth century efficient and relatively cheap means of communication and transportation (time- and space-compressing technologies) made this old dichotomy largely irrelevant. As Castells (1996) has pointed out in his book *The Rise of the Network Society*, new technologies have virtually created new patterns of social relations, or at lest strongly reinforced pre-existing tendencies. They allowed numerous diasporic immigrants to live in two or more countries at a time, via maintaining close physical and social links with their places of origin. Transnational activities and lifestyles became widely spread, embracing large numbers of people and playing a significant role in economy, politics and social life of both sending and receiving countries. Guarnizo and Smith (1998) have introduced a useful distinction between *the two types of transnationalism* – "*from above*" and "*from below*." The former refers to institutionalized economic and political activities of multinational corporations and organizations such as *UN*, *Amnesty International* or *Greenpeace*, which set in motion large-scale global exchange of financial and human capital. On the other hand, the increasing role in these networks belongs to ordinary migrants – grassroots agents of transnationalism who run small businesses in their home countries, organize exchange of material (e.g., ethnic food) and cultural (e.g., tours of folk artists) goods within the diaspora, pay regular visits to their birthplace and receive co-ethnic guests. This is called a *transnational lifestyle*.

Most transnational networks in business, politics, communications and culture organize along ethnic lines, i.e. include members of the same ethnic community spread between different locales on the map. Common language and cultural heritage are the key cementing factors for the *transnational diasporas*. In most cases, transnationals become bi-lingual and bi-cultural, but different communities may exhibit various extent of cultural separatism versus acculturation in the host society.

Migration experience in the context of global society, where constant exchange of people, products and ideas is reinforced by global media networks, has attained a whole new quality. The full-time loyalty to one country and one culture is no longer self-evident: people may actually divide their physical pastime, effort and identity between several societies. Citizenship and political participation are also becoming bi-focal or even multi-focal, since some sending countries allow their expatriates to remain citizens, vote in national elections and establish political movements. In this context, international migrants are becoming *transmigrants*, developing economic activities, enjoying cultural life and keeping dense informal networks not only with their home country, but also with other national branches of their diaspora. The split of economic, social and political loyalties among migrants, and gradual attenuation of loyalty to the nation-state as such, is seen as problematic by some receiving countries. Yet, some recent studies show that dual citizenship may in fact promote immigrants' legal and socio-political attachments to both their home and host country rather than reinforce the so-called post-nationalism.

SEE ALSO: Globalization; Immigration Policy; Network Society; Transnationals

REFERENCE

Guarnizo, L. E. & Smith, M. P. (1998) The locations of transnationalism. In: Smith, M. P. & Guarnizo, L. E. (eds.), *Transnationalism from Below*. Comparative Urban and Community Research series, vol. 6. Transaction, New Brunswick and London, pp. 3–34.

SUGGESTED READINGS

Portes, A., Guarnizo, L. E., & Landolt, P. (1999) The study of transnationalism: pitfalls and promise of an emergent research field. Introduction to special issue on Transnational Communities. *Ethnic and Racial Studies* 22 (2): 217–37.

Van Hear, N. (1998) *New Diasporas: The Mass Exodus, Dispersal and Regrouping of Migrant Communities*. University College of London Press, London.

LARISSA REMENNICK

transnationals

The term transnational corporation (TNC) is often used interchangeably with that of multinational corporation (MNC) or multinational enterprise (MNE) to mean a firm that owns or controls income-generating assets in more than one country. Other transnational organizations include intergovernmental bodies such as the UNO, regulatory agencies and NGOs. The focus here will be on corporations.

Trading organizations spanning territorial frontiers predate the modern nation-state. Today they still serve to integrate world markets and, more controversially, may affect a convergence in lifestyles. In the 1980s the level of foreign direct investment (FDI) between countries overtook that of exports/imports. There was also a shift from previously dominant patterns of trade and investment. This took the form of i) a search for new, often cheaper, sources of labor ii) a search for new local product markets. In pursuing these opportunities TNCs have dispersed stages in the design, production and distribution of goods to form chains of interdependent activities undertaken in different countries. The emergence of information technology, as well as new transportation systems, has facilitated a "reduction of time and space" between dispersed activities.

The effect on the sovereignty of host states is often seen as erosive. Governments can become increasingly dependent on FDI to provide both jobs and taxes. A global contest between national governments for the location of plants increases the risk of later withdrawal, thus shaping future policy. The local "outsourcing" of services actually multiplies this dependency. Most governments seek to regulate these domestic activities. The more educationally "developed" is the host economy, the more likely the exchange to be an equitable one.

The indirect effects of FDI can also be considerable. The pricing of the transfer of goods and services between plants is controlled within the MNC in a way that can significantly shape the trade balance of the host country. The effect of workplace organization on the self-identity of local communities can be significant. New employment disciplines may be unfairly exploitative – the so-called "race to the bottom." But in rural regions TNC employment regimes can also provide a "modern" life-style and, with it, new collective aspirations. At the other end of the TNC hierarchy evidence of increased recruitment of senior executives across borders, together with professionals associated with other transnational agencies, suggest the emergence of a new global elite.

SEE ALSO: International Gender Division of Labor; Transnational Movements

SUGGESTED READINGS

Bartlett, C. A. & Ghoshal, S. (1989) *Managing Across Borders: The Transnational Solution*. Harvard Business School Press, Boston, MA.

Dicken P. (2006) *Global Shift*. Sage, London.

RAY LOVERIDGE

trust

Trust has become a significant topic of study in the social sciences over the past decade. Trust can be defined in relational terms as the belief that the trustor will take the trustee's interests to heart. In the encapsulated interest view of trust articulated by Hardin (2002) one party A trusts party B with respect to x (a specific domain of activity) when A believes that her interests are included in B's "utility function" such that B values what A desires *because* B wants to maintain good relations with A or wants to maintain a reputation for being trustworthy in the network of relations in which the A–B relation is embedded. The shadow of the future casts a protective veil over the relationship. Others define trust as the belief that the trustee will not take advantage of the vulnerability of the trustor. Often theorists do not make a clear distinction between trust and trustworthiness. Perceived trustworthiness lowers the likelihood of monitoring in many situations. In this way trust reduces the cost of monitoring and in some contexts it may also reduce transaction costs since investment in contracts or credible commitments are not required to secure the transaction.

The Nobel-prize winning economist Kenneth Arrow (1974: 23) recognized much earlier the pragmatic value of trust. Arrow (like the sociologist Luhman) viewed trust as an important lubricant of a social system: "It is extremely efficient; it saves a lot of trouble to have a fair degree of reliance on other people's word." In Arrow's view trust not only saves on transaction costs, but it also increases the efficiency of a system enabling the production of more goods (or more of what a group values) with less cost. But it cannot be bought and sold on the open market and it is highly unlikely that it can be simply produced on demand. A lack of mutual trust is one of the properties of many of the societies that are less developed economically, Arrow argues, reflecting a theme that was picked up two decades later by Francis Fukuyama.

The lack of mutual trust makes collective undertakings difficult, if not impossible, since individuals cannot know if they engage in an action to benefit another that the action will be reciprocated. It is not only the problem of not knowing whom to trust, it is also the problem of having others not know they can trust you. The difficulty that arises is how to coordinate the interests of individuals in society to produce more of what they need as a collectivity. This problem is at the heart of the work on social dilemmas in the social sciences and it has attracted much attention in the past few decades. As Arrow notes, the lack of mutual trust represents a distinct loss economically as well as a loss in the smooth running of the political system which requires the success of collective undertakings.

Shapiro (1984) argues that financial transactions do not occur easily without trust because contracts are incomplete. Trust thus provides the social foundations for relations of exchange and production. Monitoring is ineffective. Sanctioning can be costly. Transaction costs may be high. To the extent that actors are trustworthy with respect to their commitments such costs can be reduced within organizations and in the economy more broadly. But without the institutional backing of contract law and other forms of legal protection few societies rely strictly on the vagaries of personal relations. In economies under transition from one major form of economic organization to another, as in the transitions that occurred in post-communist societies, reliance on personal networks and trust relations is often an important step in the evolution to systems of trade that require interactions with strangers in the context of market economies. New linkages between economics, psychology, political science and sociology are being developed, as topics such as trust take on broader social significance, especially in uncertain times.

SEE ALSO: Exchange Network Theory; Game Theory; Intimacy; Social Exchange Theory

REFERENCES

Arrow, K. J. (1974) *The Limits of Organization*. W. W. Norton, New York.

Shapiro, S. (1984) *Wayward Capitalists*. Yale University Press, New Haven, CT.

SUGGESTED READINGS

Cook, K. S. (ed.) (2001) *Trust in Society*. Russell Sage, New York.

Hardin, R. (2002) *Trust and Trustworthiness*. Russell Sage, New York.

KAREN S. COOK

U

unemployment as a social problem

All industrialized or post-industrial societies consider themselves to be working societies. Work – or more precisely, *gainful* work – defines an individual's worth and status. It is for most people the main means of earning a living and frequently the prerequisite to be eligible for social security coverage. Unemployment endangers the livelihood of the unemployed individual and, possibly, also that of his or her family. It is the most important cause of poverty and is also frequently associated with problems such as crime, right-wing extremism, suicide, and illness. Therefore, unemployment is a principal social and political challenge.

Usually, the unemployment of individuals with low education is markedly higher – generally by a factor of 2 to 4 – than that of highly qualified workers. Often, the unemployment of younger and older workers is also above average. Marked gender differences can be perceived in continental European countries, where women's unemployment is often significantly higher than men's, while there are hardly any gender differences in Anglo-Saxon countries with their liberal labor markets or in the Scandinavian countries with their greater emphasis on gender equality. In most cases, ethnic and racial minorities suffer significantly higher unemployment rates than the native-born majority.

Persistent unemployment on the societal level is frequently associated with the concepts of underclass and exclusion. The term underclass was coined by Gunnar Myrdal and describes a social group that is even below the "working class" and thus cut off from mainstream society; in American inner-city ghettos this tendency is exacerbated by spatial segregation (Wilson 1987). The term underclass was also used to ascribe to people certain traits such as the inability to work due to a lack of skills or the unwillingness to work due to certain values and attitudes; its use in sociology is therefore controversial. The term exclusion plays a bigger role in Europe. Here, unemployment by definition damages the "social contract". In critical perspective, the term is used to indicate that contemporary capitalism offers fewer and fewer opportunities to participate socially, especially for the "less productive."

Unemployment is frequently explained by the transition of capitalist societies to post-industrial and post-Fordist economies. Technological changes lead to a continual rise in productivity so that one frequently talks about "jobless growth." In a global world capital becomes more mobile; as some jobs are "exported," new jobs are created. Firms increasingly act as multinational or transnational enterprises and work is distributed over many countries and linked by computer networks. The outcomes of these developments for national labor markets may vary considerably between countries. Yet it is obvious that the European economies, based largely on medium- and high-skilled jobs, have to increase their investments in human capital substantially if they do not want to lose ground and if they want to maintain their higher levels of equality. Also, inclusion of women in the labor market is still lagging considerably behind many Western European countries. At the same time, it may be increasingly necessary to loosen the hitherto tight connection between paid work and entitlements to welfare benefits, as job insecurity most likely will continue to grow and episodes of unemployment will be part of the life course of many individuals for the coming decades.

SEE ALSO: Labor Markets; Social Exclusion; Unemployment; Welfare State

REFERENCE

Wilson, W. J. (1987) *The Truly Disadvantaged: The Inner City, the Underclass, and Public Policy*. University of Chicago Press, Chicago, IL.

SUGGESTED READINGS

Andersen, J. G., Clasen, J., van Oorschot, W., & Halvorsen, K. (eds.) (2002) *Europe's New State of Welfare: Unemployment, Employment Policies and Citizenship*. Policy Press, Bristol.

Gallie, D. & Paugam, S. (eds.) (2000) *Welfare Regimes and the Experience of Unemployment in Europe*. Oxford University Press, Oxford.

JUTTA ALLMENDINGER AND
WOLFGANG LUDWIG-MAYERHOFER

unions

Unions are collections of workers that join together to defend their common interests as employees. In unionized workplaces, employers' authority over the workplace is qualified by collective bargaining agreements (or contracts) which codify the terms and conditions of the labor process. Agreements specify workers' wages, hours, benefits, seniority and grievance systems, their right to strike, and managerial prerogatives (whether or not management has the sole right to hire, fire, discipline, plan production, change production, etc.) for a specified period. Contracts also normally allow for union representatives (called stewards or committeepersons) within the workplace, who instruct workers regarding their rights and represent them in their grievances against employers. Most contemporary contracts prohibit strikes during the term of the agreement, but unions are free to call strikes when contracts expire. Alternatively, workers sometimes take matters into their own hands by conducting "wildcat" strikes, which occur without union authorization.

US unions include two basic types: craft (vertical) unions, which organize skilled workers by crafts, and industrial (horizontal) unions, which organize all workers within particular workplaces by industries (e.g. auto, rubber, steel), but many unions have a mix of both types. National unions (like the United Farm Workers) normally belong to federations such as the American Federation of Labor-Congress of Industrial Organizations (AFL–CIO) and also have subordinate bodies at the regional and local levels. Although the mainstream US labor movement considers "dual unionism" (two unions, usually from different federations, simultaneously organizing workers within a single industry or trade) to be harmful, some scholars contend that it may enhance innovation in organizing and/or union growth.

Unionization rates vary over time, place, and industry. The proportion of workers organized in unions varies from very low in the USA and France to very high in the Scandinavian countries. Periods of increase in USA union density tend to coincide with the initiation of new and successful labor organizations, and the periods of decline have been more gradual. US union density hit its peak during the 1950s, and has declined steadily until very recently, when it stabilized.

Union organizing and collective bargaining has been associated with conflict as well as a good deal of violence, especially in the USA. Prior to the 1930s, US employers had considerable leeway in protecting their property and sometimes summoned the aid of state and federal troops. Taft and Ross (1969) indicate that troops intervened in over 160 disputes. Overall they estimate that 700 died and several thousand suffered serious injuries in US labor disputes.

Some union organizing is conducted in alliance with political parties. In Europe, unions tend to organize along industrial lines and to be affiliated with left-of-center political parties (some European countries also have (or have had) rival Christian, socialist, and/or communist unions). US unions have participated in, but seldom form formal ties with, political parties but have both reacted to and influenced legislative change. The severely anti-union legal environment of the early period was altered by pro-union legislation in the 1930s, but post-war legislation has mainly moved in an anti-union direction. Likewise, in Great Britain the Combination Acts restricted and the Trade Union Act of 1871 liberalized labor laws.

The level of internal union democracy has been an issue of heightened public concern, especially during specific periods. The main charge has been that unions are oligarchies that are unresponsive to workers' needs, or that they are corrupt. Internal democracy movements have appeared in several non-democratic unions to work towards union responsiveness, and the Landrum–Griffin Act, passed in 1959, requires a baseline level of democracy and that unions report on their internal affairs to government agencies. But studies show that while some unions lack the fundamentals of democracy, others are highly democratic, and provide workers with important voice in the workplace.

SEE ALSO: Class Consciousness; Deindustrialization; Fordism/Post-Fordism; Work, Sociology of

REFERENCES

Taft, P. & Ross, P. (1969) American labor violence: its causes, character, and outcome. In: Graham, H. & Gurr, T. (eds.), *Violence in America: Historical and Comparative Perspectives*. New American Library, New York, pp. 270–376.

SUGGESTED READINGS

Freeman, R. & Medoff, J. (1984) *What Do Unions Do?* Basic Books, New York.

Stepan-Norris, J. & Zeitlin, M. (2003) *Left Out: Reds and America's Industrial Unions*. Cambridge University Press, Cambridge.

JUDITH STEPAN-NORRIS

urban

Derived from the Latin word *urbanus* (meaning characteristic of, or pertaining to, the city), *urban* essentially holds that same connotation to most people. Yet varying criteria exist among the 195 countries in defining *urban*. These criteria include *administrative function* (national or regional capital), *economic characteristics* (most residents in non-agricultural occupations), *functional nature* (a developed infrastructure), and *population size* or *density*. Administrative function is used solely in 89 countries and in combination with other criteria in another 20. Economic is one of several criteria in 27 countries, as is functional in 19 countries; functional is also used solely in 5 countries. Population size or density is the sole criterion in 46 countries and in combination in another 42. No definition exists in 24 countries, while Guadeloupe, Hong Kong, Kuwait, Monaco, Nauru, and Singapore designate their entire populations as urban.

Such differences make cross-national comparisons difficult. For example, the lower-range population limit for an urban area ranges from 200 in Iceland to 10,000 in Greece. A universal standard, perhaps the midpoint of 5,000 inhabitants, would be inappropriate in populous countries such as China or India, where rural settlements with no urban attributes at all could easily contain such large numbers. Using each country's own criteria, the United Nations Population Division (2008) identified 47 percent of the world's population as urban. Significant variations existed: Africa, 36 percent urban; Asia, 37 percent; Europe, 71 percent; Latin America and the Caribbean, 75 percent; North America, 79 percent. The lowest (10 percent) was in Burundi, while the highest (100 percent) were in the six countries previously identified.

German sociologist Ferdinand Tönnies (1887) described the contrasting elements of urban and rural life from a cultural perspective. His concept of *gemeinschaft* (community) characterized the small village and surrounding area where people united by close ties of family and neighborhood shared traditional values and worked together for the common good. In contrast to this "we-ness," *gesellschaft* (association or society) denoted the "me-ness" of the city of a future-oriented heterogeneous population, leading Tönnies to pessimistically view the city as characterized by disunity, rampant individualism, and selfishness, even hostility. This typology of *gemeinschaft* and *gesellschaft* had a lasting influence on other urban sociologists.

Émile Durkheim (1962) also had an enduring effect. His emphasis on contrasting social bonds offered another perspective on urban and rural distinctiveness. He suggested that urban social order rested on an *organic solidarity* in which individual differences, greater freedom, and choice thrive in a complex division of labor where inhabitants are interdependent. Rural life, on the other hand, is organized around *mechanical solidarity*, with social bonds constructed on likeness (common beliefs, customs, rituals, and symbols), where inhabitants are relatively self-sufficient and not dependent on other groups to meet all of life's needs.

These twofold typologies dominated for much of the twentieth century with most studies, based on a spatial emphasis on the central city, examining different variables in comparison to non-urban areas. In recent decades, however, changing settlement patterns and the evolution of a global economy reduced the analytical value of this simplistic urban–rural dichotomy.

The post-World War II suburban boom in developed countries initiated an exodus from cities and a growing preference for that lifestyle. At first, suburbs were mostly bedroom communities on the cities' outskirts, where inhabitants typically lived in one-family houses, but worked, shopped, and enjoyed leisure activities in the city. By ringing the central cities, the suburbs reinforced the original conception of *urban* in a spatial context, and were essentially viewed as residential appendages to the cities. That changed with the development of suburban office and industrial parks, shopping malls, megastores, hospitals, and places of worship. As the suburbs became more self-sufficient, the definition of *suburban* changed into that of a third entity, an alternative to *urban* and *rural*.

Even so, larger cities still extended their sphere of influence beyond their boundaries, particularly in such areas as culture, fashion, media, professional sports, sightseeing, and tourism. The term *metropolitan* denotes that reality throughout the world, as does the US Census Bureau term *metropolitan statistical area* (MSA). The official US urban population thus includes not just those living in cities, but also in *urbanized areas* with populations of 2,500 or more, as well as in *urbanized zones* (unincorporated communities of less than 2,500, but on the fringes of metropolitan areas).

Sometimes metropolitan areas overlap each other in their spheres of influence, creating what Jean Gottman (1961) conceptualized as a *megalopolis*, citing the region extending from Boston to Washington. The Census Bureau identifies 18 such regions in the US and calls them *consolidated metropolitan statistical areas* (or CMSAs).

Disparities in urban definitions and the blurring of urban and non-urban elements led social scientists into new theoretical approaches. *Convergence theory* argues that technology will lead cities and communities everywhere to develop similar organizational forms. In contrast, *divergence theory* posits that increasingly dissimilar organizational forms will emerge because of differences in (1) cultural values and histories; (2) timing and pace of urbanization; (3) form of government and planning approaches; and (4) hierarchy of countries in the global economy. Another perspective, *postmodern theory*, rests on the premise that cities develop in ways that are no longer rational or manageable. Instead, global capitalism serves as the underlying rationale for actions by increasingly fragmented urban power structures. The economic welfare of cities now results from causes existing beyond their boundaries. This interplay of global, national, regional, and local forces is an additional complicating factor in explaining what we mean by *urban*.

Urban still remains subject to varying interpretations, with or without a spatial premise; with a local, regional, national, or global perspective; and with either a positive or negative emphasis. Regardless of theoretical or conceptual approach, the term nonetheless remains mostly suggestive of its Latin origins: that of particular qualities associated with people and patterns indeed found in cities.

SEE ALSO: Metropolis; New Urbanism; Urban Policy; Urban Political Economy; Urban Space; Urbanization

REFERENCES

Gottman, J. (1961) *Megalopolis*. Twentieth Century Fund, New York.

Tönnies, F. (1963) [1887] *Community and Society*. Harper & Row, New York.

United Nations Population Division (2008) *World Urbanization Prospects: 2007 Revision*. United Nations, New York.

SUGGESTED READINGS

Durkheim, É. (1962) [1893] *The Division of Labor in Society*. Free Press, New York.

Parrillo, V. & Macionis, J. (2009) *Cities and Urban Life*, 5th edn. Prentice Hall, Upper Saddle River, NJ.

VINCENT N. PARRILLO

urban ecology

Urban ecology is the study of community structure and organization as manifest in cities and other relatively dense human settlements. Of particular concern is the dynamic evolution of cities and contrast in urban structure across time periods, societies, and urban scale. The notion of community is central to urban ecology; a premise of the ecological approach is that the aggregation of persons into communities has important implications for their life chances, for the behavior of groups, and for aggregate outcomes. Urban ecology is interdisciplinary, touching on sociology, demography, geography, economics, and anthropology. Early ecological thinking drew a parallel for human behavior with the topic of ecology in biology, and hence the name.

Contemporary urban ecology maintains this orientation, but has been spurred further by new data forms and methodological developments. The concern for social exclusion and the increasing ethnic diversification of high-income societies provides increasing impetus for the ecological approach and encourages revisiting Robert Park's notion that spatial distance reflects social distance. Contemporary treatments emphasize dynamic changes in residential environments, extending classical concerns for the process of residential sorting and succession. In a related thread ecology investigates the restructuring of urban areas in light of significant transportation, communication, and industrial transformations. Scholars have used this framework to understand new urban forms and how systems of interurban hierarchy emerge.

Urban ecology readily lends itself to the exploitation of multi-level or contextual data and associated statistical approaches. In multi-level data, individual information (microdata) is merged with characteristics of neighborhoods or a wider geographic area. Individual outcomes are predicted not only from individual traits, but also from characteristics of the wider community. The "neighborhood effects" literature, both substantively and methodologically, can be seen as a major intellectual development consonant with the approach of urban ecology. Similarly, the broad interest in the sociology of the macro–micro link overlaps significantly with ecologists' interest in community, in multiple levels of aggregation, and in dynamic interchange. The multi-level ecological approach can be engaged at varying geographic scales, from tracing household mobility to neighborhood composition through examining how individual health and socioeconomic outcomes are influenced by structural conditions measured at the regional level.

The predisposition of urban ecological analysis to spatial phenomena has made urban ecology readily receptive to the use of geographic information systems (GIS). More than merely mapping, GIS technology applied to urban ecology allows the analyst to redefine communities and networks, and to link micro to macro. Whereas social scientists were once bound by the community aggregation defined by others (such as a census agency's tract or ward boundaries), the increasing availability of point data allows a more refined analysis of the relationship between human organization, sustenance activity, community and territory. Such technological developments have stimulated a re-connection with biological ecology. Urban ecological analysis provides a framework for examining integrated human-natural systems. Here again human activity is seen as dynamic and community-based, both influencing and influenced by its surrounding environment.

While urban ecology may be identified most clearly with American urban sociology and the Chicago school particularly, its adherents and manifestations are much broader. It has been applied in analyses of urbanization in socialist countries as well as in the developing world. Still, the level of knowledge about urban ecology for settings outside of high-income societies is less clearly codified. It is far from certain that the models once applied to North America and Europe (and selected other locations) will apply so readily to other portions of world geography, especially to urban settings in low-income countries. Yet, themes of internal urban structure, geographical disparities in well-being, and community change are relevant to all of these settings.

SEE ALSO: Compositional Theory of Urbanism; New Urbanism; Park, Robert E. and Ernest W. Burgess; Urban; Urban Space

SUGGESTED READINGS

Micklin, M. & Poston, D. L. (eds) (1998) *Continuities in the Study of Human Ecology*. Plenum Press, New York.

Hawley, A. (1950) *Human Ecology: A Theory of Community Structure*. Ronald Press, New York.

Saunders, P. (2001) Urban ecology. In: Paddison, R. (ed), *Handbook of Urban Studies*. Sage, London, pp. 36–51.

MICHAEL J. WHITE & ANN H. KIM

urban policy

Urban policy is best understood as the cluster of policies that are aimed at influencing the development of cities and the lives of those living in cities, although this can only be the starting point in exploring its meaning. It is not possible to generate any clear cut or simple definition that makes it easy to determine what makes urban policy "urban" or even the nature of the "urban" on which it is targeted. Much social and public policy (for example in education, housing or policing) affects urban areas directly, but is only sometimes given the label "urban." And the "urban" areas on which it is targeted have also varied widely (from neighbourhoods to localities; from inner cities to suburbs; from communities to city regions).

The nature of the urban problem on which any explicit urban policy is focused has also changed dramatically at different times and in different places: from slums and poverty to poor infrastructure and crowding; from failing housing markets to gentrification; from dysfunctional to sustainable communities; from economic decline to criminality and threat; from failing schools to broken windows; from racial tensions to property development. In recent years British urban policy has oscillated between regeneration and renaissance; neighbourhood renewal and sustainable communities. In the USA the urban agenda has come to be associated with the demands and needs of black urban populations.

Meanwhile, a global urban policy has emerged which emphasizes the economic importance of cities and their residents as drivers of economic growth, and sometimes even creativity. Within this framework, instead of being problems, entrepreneurial and competitive cities become the basis on which prosperity and well-being may be constructed. From this perspective, the global slums and those who live in them are seen as sources of enterprise, not pools of failure.

It is these ambiguities and inconsistencies that give urban policy its importance. As well as reflecting contemporary understandings of the role of cities in economic and social development, it also helps to create those understandings in practice.

SEE ALSO: New Urbanism; Urban Ecology; Urban Poverty

SUGGESTED READING

Cochrane, A. (2006) *Understanding Urban Policy: A Critical Approach*. Blackwell, Oxford.

ALLAN COCHRANE

urban political economy

One of sociology's foundational questions has been: How does the city shape social life? The answer provided by urban political economy is: As a mechanism in the accumulation of wealth, with all the power and inequality that result. An interdisciplinary paradigm, urban political economy localizes and spatializes the concerns of "political economy," the broader field investigating how material processes of production and exchange shape and are shaped by institutional decisions and activities. Characteristically, urban political economy emphasizes *production within cities* (urban labor relations, local business costs, and infrastructure) and *of cities* (which literally builds the settings for community and everyday life).

Starting in the 1960s, urban political economists analyzed urban form and growth as expressions of *historical relations of industrial production*. In this Marxian view, the twentieth-century flight of manufacturing to the urban periphery and the growth of residential suburbs serve industrialists' interests in, respectively, avoiding the business costs of aging and inflexible urban infrastructure and dispersing urban hotbeds of labor unrest. Next, urban political economy joined the neo-Marxian scholarship on *capital accumulation* by emphasizing financial investment in land and the built environment, which offers capital a crucial alternate site for investment when industrial economies soured. This theoretical turn also drew attention to landlords, developers, and other capitalists who generate rents (land-based profits) as a specifically urban "ruling class." Subsequently, urban political economists turned to neo-Weberian questions of how growth and rents organize the collaboration and political dominance of urban elites. Here, a particularly robust theory involves the *growth machine*, a territorially defined coalition of elites from public, private and civic sectors that promotes growth in order to advance common interests in intensifying land-based exchange values: higher rents for developers and landlords, increasing tax revenues for local governments, new readers for local newspapers, more rate-payers for utilities, more jobs for local trade unions, and so on.

Since the 1980s, urban political economy has furthered scholars' understanding of capitalism's "flexible" mode of accumulation by identifying how space, markets, and networks assume a coordinating role formerly contained within corporate bureaucracy. This is evident in *flexible industrial districts* where sectors of skilled labor, entrepreneurial companies, and specialized support systems cluster: finance (New York, London, Tokyo), high technology (Silicon Valley), film (Hollywood), fashion (Paris), even neighborhoods producing bohemian art and lifestyle. Often lauded for their prosperity, these cities and regions reveal the polarization of the *dual city*. While well-paid workers revitalize once-staid urban economies, gentrify declining neighborhoods, and stimulate the growth of high-end consumer services, the loss of manufacturing and other activities that support decent-paying jobs leave working classes less secure, and new immigrants leapfrog over older ethnic and racial groups to manage and fill low-wage service, sweatshop, and informal economy jobs.

As the dynamics of growth and decline increasingly extend beyond the scale of any one city, region, or even nation, urban political economists continually reevaluate what constitutes the "political." Does the customary emphasis on capitalists' pressure politics and growth machine hegemony still have explanatory value? If so, how, and at what scale?

SEE ALSO: Global/World Cities; Political Economy; Urban Renewal and Redevelopment

SUGGESTED READINGS

Harvey, D. (1982) *The Limits to Capital*. University of Chicago Press, Chicago, IL.

Logan, J. & Molotch, H. (1987) *Urban Fortunes*. University of California Press, Berkeley, CA.

Mollenkopf, J. & Castells, M. (eds.) (1991) *Dual City*. Russel Sage Foundation, New York.

LEONARD NEVAREZ

urban poverty

The study of urban poverty attempts to understand the roots of urban dilemmas such as crime and delinquency, single motherhood, unemployment, and low education. The causes and consequences of spatially concentrated poverty and the intergenerational transmission of poverty are core questions.

The sociological study of urban poverty dates back to W. E. B. Du Bois's *The Philadelphia Negro* (1899). Two decades later, Chicago School sociologists viewed urban poverty as a temporary stage in the incorporation of migrants from rural areas and abroad, as immigrant groups moved from poor, central city neighborhoods to better-off areas. The Great Migration, which brought Southern blacks to Northern and Western cities in the early to mid-twentieth century, challenged the Chicago School model, as blacks were blocked from economic advancement experienced by white ethnics. Focus shifted to the intergenerational transmission of poverty. Some scholars emphasized lack of opportunity while others argued for a "culture of poverty" characterized by intergenerational norms disparaging education and two-parent families and encouraging crime.

The demographics of poverty shifted dramatically during the twentieth century. Improvements in government income supports reduced poverty among the elderly, while the increase in single-parent families increased poverty among unmarried mothers and their children, the "feminization of poverty."

With *The Truly Disadvantaged* (1986), W. J. Wilson refocused attention on the neighborhood context of urban poverty. He argued that the black urban poor were disadvantaged by both family and neighborhood poverty. As middle-class blacks left inner-city neighborhoods in the 1970s, the decline of the manufacturing economy led to joblessness among working-class males, especially blacks. An "underclass" emerged, a concentrated population characterized by single motherhood, joblessness, school dropout, and participation in the underground economy, socially, culturally, and economically isolated from mainstream society. Massey and Denton (1993) charged Wilson with ignoring racial segregation's magnification of the consequences of economic segregation.

One current strand of research investigates the consequences of neighborhood disadvantage for individuals, which include exposure to negative peer influences, collective socialization by neighborhood adults, and formal institutions, which distribute material resources and effect contact with non-neighborhood adults. A second strand seeks to understand out-of-wedlock and teenage childbearing among the urban poor. The male marriageable pool hypothesis holds that a shortage of economically attractive mates leads poor women to eschew marriage. Edin and Kefalas (2006) argue that poor urban women hold marriage and childbearing in such high regard that they delay marriage when success is uncertain but have children lest they miss out on motherhood. The peer culture explanation for teenage childbearing holds that early sexual activity and childbearing are sources of status among peers (Anderson 1999).

As research continues, the study of urban poverty faces methodological and theoretical challenges. First, today's urban poor are heterogeneous. Latinos and other immigrants have become an important understudied segment of the poor. Second, how the urban poor are socially isolated or socially connected to others is poorly understood. Third, studying the dynamics and consequences of high-poverty neighborhoods requires new data and methods for measuring neighborhood social and cultural characteristics.

SEE ALSO: Chicago School; Ethnic Enclaves; Urban Policy

REFERENCES

Anderson, E. (1999) *Code of the Street.* Norton, New York.

Edin, K. & Kefalas, M. (2006) *Promises I Can Keep.* University of California Press, Berkeley, CA.

Massey, D. & Denton, N. (1993) *American Apartheid: Segregation and the Making of an Underclass.* Harvard University Press, Cambridge, MA.

SUGGESTED READING

Jencks, C. & Mayer, S. E. (1990) The social consequences of growing up in a poor neighborhood. In: Lynn, L. E., Jr. & McGreary, M. G. H. (eds.), *Inner-City Poverty in the United States.* National Academy Press, Washington, DC, pp. 111–86.

DAVID J. HARDING

urban renewal and redevelopment

The built environment deteriorates with the passage of time and the stresses of use and neglect. Unemployment, poverty, shortages of affordable housing, health epidemics, and transportation problems often accompany physical decay in modern cities. Attempts to relieve these social problems through the maintenance, rehabilitation, and rebuilding of the physical environment are known as urban redevelopment.

European governments implemented the first large-scale urban redevelopment projects in the nineteenth century. Louis Napoleon Bonaparte of France led the way with his massive renovation of Paris that began in 1853. Thousands of residents were displaced by the creation of a system of wide boulevards that "pierced" diagonally through dense, older neighborhoods of the city. Another wave of urban redevelopment began after World War II. In Europe, government acquisition and demolition of properties played a major role in the rebuilding of cities destroyed by war. Cities in North America meanwhile embarked on their first major effort at demolition and rehabilitation of the built environment. Title II of the 1949 Federal Housing Act, known as "urban renewal," responded to a very different problem: the long-term trend of suburbanization that threatened the stability of the central city.

Understood as a process, redevelopment involves the mobilization of substantial resources controlled by state as well as non-governmental actors. Community development corporations, tax increment financing (TIF), eminent domain, tax exempt bonds, human capital, and social trust are some of the many resources commonly involved in attempts to improve distressed neighborhoods. Valued resources may be controlled by real estate owners, financial institutions, developers, neighborhood residents, historic preservationists, or environmental groups. Sociological studies of redevelopment tend to revolve around questions relating to how the composition and dynamics of urban governing coalitions influence strategies of redevelopment.

In the last section of his classic book *Urban Villagers* (1962), Herbert Gans described how destruction of the built environment caused by urban renewal disrupted relationships among neighbors and extended families in Boston's Italian West End. Gans introduced the important distinction, overlooked by local planners, between a slum and a low-rent district. The West End definitely fell into the latter category, according to Gans, which benefited greatly the working-class families residing there. Gans's work influenced a generation of urban planners to be skeptical towards the view that older neighborhoods must be demolished in order to be saved.

By the 1970s a growing body of research validated earlier criticisms of urban renewal. Most of this work was done by scholars versed in neo-Marxist and political economy literature. They used case methods to develop theories of how class interests – especially those of corporate business and real estate – influence government intervention in the physical redevelopment of cities. But the sacrifices of some would repay in the prosperity of the city as a whole.

Over the past century the physical decline of cities has corresponded more and more with patterns of socioeconomic distress. In the name of relieving distress, officials have facilitated redevelopment of the built environment. At times, government action has contributed to greater decline and distress, such as occurred with federal urban renewal. More often, redevelopment projects have mixed results. Understanding the institutions and coalition forms most conducive to more sustainable growth that meets the needs of all urban residents remains a high-priority agenda for future research.

SEE ALSO: Built Environment; Gentrification; New Urbanism; Urban Political Economy; Urban Poverty; Urbanization

SUGGESTED READINGS

Gotham, K. F. (ed.) (2001) *Critical Perspectives on Urban Redevelopment, Research in Urban Sociology*, vol. 6. Jai Press, New York.

Molotch, H. L. (1976) The city as a growth machine. *American Journal of Sociology* 82 (2): 309–30.

Peterson, P. (1981) *City Limits*. University of Chicago Press, Chicago, IL.

GREGORY J. CROWLEY

urban revolution

The urban revolution refers to the emergence of urban life and the concomitant transformation of human settlements from simple agrarian-based systems to complex and hierarchical systems of manufacturing and trade. The term also refers to the present era of metropolitan or megalopolis growth, the development of exurbs, and the explosion of primate or mega-cities. Archeologist V. Gordon Childe coined the term *urban revolution* to explain the series of stages in the development of cities that preceded the Industrial Revolution of the nineteenth century. For Childe, the first revolution – the "Agricultural Revolution" – occurred when hunting and gathering societies mastered the skill of food production and began to live in stable and sedentary groups. The second revolution – the "Urban Revolution" – began during the fourth and third millennia BCE in the civilizations of Mesopotamia and the Near East. The urban revolution ushered in a new era of population growth, complex urban development, and the development of such institutions as the bureaucratic state, warfare, architecture, and writing. For Henri Lefebvre (2003), the urban revolution not only signifies a long historical shift from an agricultural to an industrial to an urban world, but also refers to a shift in the internal organization of the city, from the political city of pre-medieval times to the mercantile, then industrial, city to the present phase, where the "urban" becomes a global trend. Today, many scholars use the term urban revolution to connote profound changes in the social organization of societies, but they disagree over the conceptualization, causes, and trajectory of the change.

One major point of debate focuses on issues of conceptualization and addresses questions about when, where, and why the first cities arose. In his oft-cited essay "The urban revolution," Childe (1950) described the features of early communities in Mesopotamia that marked the beginning of urban settlements. A key feature of the first cities was their immense population size, up to 20,000 residents; their dense geographic concentration; production of an agricultural surplus; and a specialized labor force and system of governance. Today, scholars argue that there is not one urban revolution but several. A "Second Urban Revolution," for example, began about 1750 as the Industrial Revolution generated rapid urban growth in Europe. The economy, physical form, and culture of cities changed dramatically as feudal power broke down and trade and travel increased. Increasing size, density, and diversity of cities combined with the growth of commerce to make urban life more rational, anonymous, and depersonalized. Since about 1950, a "Third Urban Revolution" has been occurring in less developed countries, where most of the world's largest cities are located. The increasing number of primate or mega-cities of more than 8 million inhabitants illustrates profound demographic and population trends of the past century. In 1950, only two cities, London and New York, were that size. In 1975, there were 11 mega-cities, including 6 in the industrialized countries. In 1995, there were 23 in total, with 17 in the developing countries. In 2015, the projected number of mega-cities is 36, with 30 of them in the developing world and most in Asia. In short, the urban revolution is a global trend that is taking place at different speeds on different continents.

SEE ALSO: Global/World Cities; Metropolis; Urban; Urbanization

REFERENCES

Childe, V. G. (1950) The urban revolution. *Town Planning Review* 21 (April): 3–17.
Lefebvre, H. (2003) [1970] *The Urban Revolution*, trans. Robert Bononno. University of Minnesota Press, Minneapolis, MN.

KEVIN FOX GOTHAM

urban space

Defining urban space would appear to be a fairly straightforward task. In a certain sense, urban space might simply be understood as the material space that is commonly seen as constitutive of the "city." And yet ascribing a precise definition to urban space remains difficult. In part, this difficulty arises from the nature of the term itself. In order to define urban space it is necessary to ask what is meant by "urban" and what is meant by "space." Certainly, the process of urbanization in which individuals migrate from the countryside to the city has been an important feature of industrial society and continues to rapidly transform parts of the world industrializing for the first time. From a structural perspective, understanding urban space requires that attention be paid to the economic arrangements and institutional relations that characterize processes of urbanization, rather than simply the space in which urbanization occurs.

While significant scholarship has focused on the increasing populations of cities and the emptying of the countryside, other scholars have taken a more conceptual approach to understanding the "urban." Indeed, critical geographers and sociologists such as David Harvey and Manuel Castells have theorized urban space with an emphasis on certain structural features of capitalism and the economic processes through which the capitalist mode of production reproduces itself. For Harvey, the "urban" is characterized by capital's need for a "spatial fix" to the problems of over-accumulation. The creation and destruction of the built environment therefore provides opportunities for productive reinvestment of capital. From this perspective, urban space may not only be defined by the boundaries of the "city" conceived of by authorities and urban planners but, rather, as a process rooted in the very nature of accumulation under capitalism. Here, the existence of suburbs and even exurbs might also be viewed as constitutive of the urban, for they too are representative of the economic arrangements through which these processes become materialized. Other conceptions of urban space are even less concerned with its material dimensions. Manuel Castells suggests that urban space is increasingly a "space of flows"; centers for the tangible and intangible transmissions of information that serve to organize the global economy.

If the "urban" can be defined by certain economic processes and institutional arrangements that create new patterns of work, commerce, and production, space is generally conceived of as the dimension in which social encounter takes place. Indeed, from the perspective of social relations, one may conceive of urban space as the collection of a large number of individuals with diverse lifestyles living in close proximity. The changing ecology of human settlement over time has led to a shift in social relations. Rather than the informal ties (*Gemeinschaft*) that may characterize smaller communities, social order among a large diverse population requires the creation of more formal roles and relations (*Gesellschaft*). From a historical-institutional perspective, in order for such a large number of persons to co-exist, a centralization of social life becomes necessary for providing services to the population.

As urban space developed during industrial society, diversity in lifestyles and work increasingly lent itself to the hierarchical organization of space. Social class has generally characterized the organization of urban space, even while the nature of this spatial hierarchy continues to change with shifting values and lifestyles. Though for much of the twentieth century the upper classes sought to escape the urban core, contemporary processes of gentrification have reconfigured space in many urban centers. The gradual "upscaling" of formerly working class neighborhoods has led many to question who has the right to occupy urban space. In some cases, city redevelopment efforts have implicitly framed certain spaces as intended for white-collar users, rather than for the working class, poor or homeless. What all of these processes highlight is the definitively social aspect of urban space and its connection to changing relations as well as broader structural forces. For this reason, urban space is a continually contested dimension that provides unique opportunities to examine both human encounter and institutional structure.

SEE ALSO: New Urbanism; Space; Urban Policy; Urban Renewal and Redevelopment

SUGGESTED READINGS

Castells, M. (1989) *The Informational City: Information Technology, Economic Restructuring, and the Urban Regional Process*. Blackwell, Cambridge, MA.

Harvey, D. (1989) *The Urban Experience*. Johns Hopkins University Press, Baltimore, MD.

Mitchell, K. (2000) The culture of urban space. *Urban Geography* 21: 443–9.

JACOB LEDERMAN

urban tourism

Urban tourism refers to a variety of social practices and institutional forms that involve the production, representation, and consumption of urban culture, history, and environment. In conventional accounts, tourism is a set of discrete economic activities, a mode of consumption, or a spatially bounded locality or "destination" that is subject to external forces producing impacts. Other research, in contrast, conceptualizes tourism as a highly complex set of institutions and social relations that involve capitalist markets, state policy, and flows of commodities, technology, cultural forms, and people. One can find conceptualizations of tourism as a search for authenticity; an expression of leisure and performative identity; a malevolent form of colonialism; a form of pilgrimage to culturally significant places; a type of ethnic relation; a force for historical and cultural commodication; and a process of mobility and demographic migration. In John Urry's famous concept of the "tourist gaze," tourists view or gaze upon particular sites and sights because "there is an anticipation, especially through day-dreaming and fantasy, of intense pleasures, either on a different scale or involving different sense from those customarily encountered" (1990: 132).

One major debate in tourism studies concerns whether tourism is a global process of simulation that reflects and reinforces people's alienation from society and social relations. Early, Dean MacCannell (1973) developed the concept of "staged authenticity" to refer to the manufacturing of local culture to create an impression of authenticity for a tourist audience. MacCannell conceived of culture as primordial and viewed tourists as alienated consumers who strive to experience an authentic experience and encounter with authentic sites, objects, or events. In contrast, Ritzer and Liska (1997) maintain that rather than seeking authenticity as MacCannell suggests, people prefer inauthentic and simulated tourist attractions and experiences because these can be made to be highly predictable and efficient vehicles for delivering fun and entertainment. Other scholars have used the concept of Disneyfication to examine the spread of Disney theme-park characteristics to cities and urban culture. This city-as-theme-park explanation suggests that urban cultural spaces are being refashioned to attract visitors and enhance entertainment experiences through the production of fake histories and phony cultures that masquerade as "authentic."

In contrast, more recent research eschews a conception of tourism as eroding urban culture and examines the ways in which tourism practices invigorate local culture and relations. Gotham (2007) has elaborated on the concept of touristic culture to examine the actions of local elites in using tourism practices, images, symbols and other representations to build a New Orleans community identity during the first half of the twentieth century. As he points out, powerful groups and organized interests often deploy symbols and imagery in an attempt to unite local citizens and build a supportive constituency for tourism development. Tourism practices can support and invigorate existing modes of authenticity, help reconstruct old forms of authenticity, and promote the creation of new meanings of authenticity and local culture. Rather than viewing authenticity as immutable and primordial, Gotham examines the process of authentication, focusing on how and under what conditions people make claims for authenticity and the interests that such claims serve. Findings suggest that tourism discourses, practices, modes of staging and visualization can shape and constrain the availability of symbols and themes people use to construct meanings and definitions of authenticity. The implication is that tourism discourses, practices, and framings can mobilize people to create new authenticities, reinvent culture, and foster new conceptions of place identity.

SEE ALSO: Grobalization; Sex Tourism; Urban; Urban Space

REFERENCES
Gotham, K. F. (2007) *Authentic New Orleans: Race, Culture, and Tourism in the Big Easy*. New York University (NYU) Press.
MacCannell, D. (1973) Staged authenticity: arrangements of social space in tourist settings. *American Journal of Sociology* 79 (3): 589–603.
Ritzer, G. & Liska, A. (1997) "McDisneyization" and "post-tourism": contemporary perspectives on contemporary tourism. In *Touring Cultures: Transformations in Travel and Leisure*. London: Routledge.
Urry, J. (1990) *The Tourist Gaze*. Sage, Thousand Oaks, CA.

KEVIN FOX GOTHAM

urbanism, subcultural theory of

Claude Fischer's (1975; 1995) urban theory is designed to explain how and why social relationships vary by size of population in settlements. According to the theory, urban life is bifurcated into public and private domains. In the public domain social relationships are typically superficial because people are usually interacting with others whom they do not know personally and may not see again. Such interactions are based mainly on the obvious roles people are playing at the time, such as bus rider, store clerk or customer, and pedestrian. Thus, the public domain, which varies directly with the size of the population, is characterized by anonymity, impersonality, tolerance, and lack of social bonding with others.

However, urbanites, even those in settlements with very large populations, have private lives characterized by interpersonal networks of friends, associates, and family, just as do people in smaller settlements. In addition, urbanites are more likely to be involved in other private networks with people who share interests that are somewhat uncommon and often unconventional. Through interaction concerning those peculiar interests, people within such networks develop distinct norms, a particular set of meanings and legitimations, status systems, and other social characteristics that distinguish them as *subcultures*. Thus, in their private worlds, urbanites are no less socially bonded interpersonally than people in other places and, in addition, they are more likely to be involved in subcultural networks.

Cities promote subcultural formation because their large populations make it more likely that a number of people will share a given interest even though it may be statistically rare or unconventional. Moreover, the freedom implied by an anonymous, impersonal, tolerant public domain permits urbanites with peculiar interests to locate each other and interact sufficiently to produce subcultures. Fischer uses the term *critical mass* to refer to a situation where there are enough people with similar but unusual interests to form a subculture. The larger the city, the greater the number of critical masses and the larger the likelihood of subcultures of many types.

Because so many and so many different kinds of subcultures blossom and grow in cities, urban dwellers become more tolerant of the peculiar behaviors or interests that various subcultural affiliates embrace. In addition, subcultural affiliation provides supportive networks, distinct normative expectations, and social controls to encourage those who participate in them to embrace the behaviors around which the subcultures are oriented.

SEE ALSO: Subcultures, Deviant; Urbanism/Urban Culture

REFERENCES
Fischer, C. S. (1975) Toward a subcultural theory of urbanism. *American Journal of Sociology* 80: 1319–41.
Fischer, C. S. (1995) The subcultural theory of urbanism: a twentieth-year assessment. *American Journal of Sociology* 101: 543–77.

CHARLES R. TITTLE

urbanization

Urbanization refers to the process whereby ever larger numbers of people migrate to and establish residence in relatively dense areas of population. It is a phenomenon that has existed throughout the ages, from ancient times to the present. Large numbers of people have gathered and created urban sites in places like ancient Rome and Cairo as well as in ancient Peking in China. Yet, in recent times, the process of urbanization has gained increasing momentum and with it greater attention as well. Today, more than half of the world's population live in what are considered urban places, and demographers project that by the year 2050 much of the world's population will reside in them.

If urbanization were simply about large numbers of people living in dense residential settlements, it would hold little interest for sociologists. In fact, it is about considerably more. One of the questions posed about urbanization has to do with the reasons why people move into urban areas. What, in particular, draws people into urban areas and, once there, why do they remain? Even more importantly, what happens to people and to their lives as human beings once they move into the compact spaces of urban areas? These are questions that have prompted some of the most interesting and perceptive of sociological writings.

Urbanization is something that holds great interest for sociologists and the theories they develop about the way the world works. The first of the major sociological theorists to write about urbanization and its connections to social life was the German social theorist, Georg Simmel. He saw in the nature of urbanization and the growth of the modern metropolis elements that were characteristic not merely of cities, but of the broader development and change unfolding in the modern world. Simmel insisted that the modern city compelled people to treat one another in an indifferent and cool manner. People did not relate to one another as intimates, for example, but rather in an instrumental and calculating fashion: what can you do for me, in effect, rather than let us get to know one another better.

The next major perspective on urbanization and urban areas came from a scholar who helped to create the Chicago School of sociology, Louis Wirth. Wirth, in effect, synthesized many of the key insights of Simmel in a work that would become perhaps the most famous essay about the urban condition in the twentieth century, "Urbanism as a way of life." Wirth insisted that the pace of life in the city forced people to deal with one another in an impersonal fashion. People tended to become anonymous in the city; as a result, this influenced their own sense of comfort and security. The city, because of its size and the pace of its life, could become a place that helped to produce various forms of social disorganization, including divorce and crime. Urbanization also placed people into new relationships with one another, the effect being to undermine or to deemphasize the intimacy they had found in smaller places. Moreover, the city also gave birth to new and singular social developments, among them a range of new organizations, such as voluntary associations, not to say also new business groups. In effect, Wirth formalized and extended the basic insights of Simmel, creating both a sociological and a social psychological portrait of the city – a portrait that would remain in place for many decades and provide both an inspiration and a foil for subsequent sociological research.

Other writers and researchers from the Chicago School, among them Park and Burgess, helped to embellish and to flesh out this vision of what urbanization and cities were all about. The Chicago School, in effect, became that branch of sociology that would be devoted to understanding, interpreting, and even seeking remedies for the urban condition created in the modern world.

In recent years scholars have begun to rethink the way they conceive both of cities and of the broader process of urbanization. Lefebvre urged students of urbanization to turn their attention to urban areas as spaces, and to investigate the way such spaces were created. In particular, he insisted that the broader social forces of modern capitalism have much to do with the configuration and arrangement of spaces in the city. Thus, for example, the nature of work and the way that people must travel to work helps to account not only for the development of transportation routes and modes of transportation, but also for the nature of social life and the sites of residential settlements in urban areas.

SEE ALSO: Chicago School; City; Global/World Cities; Urbanism/Urban Culture

SUGGESTED READINGS

Lefebvre, H. (1991) *The Production of Space*, trans. D. Nicholson-Smith. Blackwell, Oxford.

Orum, A. M. & Chen, X. (2003) *The World of Cities: Places in Comparative and Historical Perspective*. Blackwell, Oxford.

Park, R. E., Burgess, E. W., & McKenzie, R. D. (1925–6) *The City*. University of Chicago Press, Chicago, IL.

ANTHONY M. ORUM

use-value

There are many things in the world; each is a concrete object with physical properties determined in the natural order. Some things have no apparent use while others are useful. Although "use" and "use-value" seem the same conceptually, they are not. Use-value applies to commodities and differentiates them from non-commodity things.

A commodity is a particular thing; it is secured or produced to enter a social relation of exchange. It is a qualitatively distinct, concrete object with a particular use; this is its form. That form simultaneously constitutes the material embodiment of the abstract, socially necessary labor – the value – entailed in its procurement or production. Thus, a commodity is and has use-value. The use-value's form is concrete and centers on use; its substance is social and abstract and centers on its value. Commerce must attend to the concrete use and abstract value of a commodity to secure profit.

The capacity to do work, in general, is not a commodity (or use-value) although it has ontological significance for humankind and is used in one's private activities. As a qualitatively unique, concrete capacity, engaged in social labor that is congealed in a product that will enter the social relations of exchange, the capacity to labor is a commodity. It has a concrete, human form and potentially calculable, abstract, social substance (the value required to restore labor-power after a period of expenditure). Labor-power is a unique use-value because, under given conditions of social production, it can produce more value than needed to replace it. Marx argued this was the unique source of surplus-value – hence profit.

SEE ALSO: Exchange-Value; Labor/Labor Power; Marx, Karl; Value

SUGGESTED READING

Marx, K. (1976) [1890] *Capital*, 4th edn., vol. 1, trans. B. Fowkes. Penguin, Harmondsworth.

ROB BEAMISH

V

validity, qualitative

Validity regards how scientific knowledge is made credible. As a social construction, the very calculus of credibility has shifted across time, place, and various fields. Discourse practices of validity in contemporary qualitative research exemplify a proliferation of available framings. The traditional foundations of knowledge are challenged by an epistemological indeterminacy that weakens any "one best way approach" to validity.

A post-epistemic focus situates validity as the power to determine the demarcation between science and not-science, for example, recent moves by the federal government to warrant experimental design as the "gold standard" for good science. In contrast, qualitative researchers argue that the "problem" of validity is about deep theoretical issues that technical solutions cannot begin to address. Across the earlier naturalistic and constructivist paradigms of Lincoln and Guba to discourse theory, ethnographic authority, critical, feminist, and race-based paradigms and more recent poststructuralisms, validity in qualitative research ranges from correspondence models of truth and assumptions of transparent narration to practices that take into account the crisis of representation. And some call for new imaginaries altogether, where validity is as much about the play of difference as the repetition of sameness.

Rather than exhausting the problem, post-epistemic, socially grounded practices displace normative criteria of quality and exemplify how any criteria are situated, relational, temporal/historical. Unlike standardized regulatory criteria, such criteria move toward contextually relevant practices that both disrupt referential logic and shift orientation from the object to the relations of its perception.

SEE ALSO: Validity, Quantitative; Qualitative Methods

SUGGESTED READINGS

Kvale, S. (1995) The social construction of validity. *Qualitative Inquiry* 1 (1): 19–40.

Lather, P. (1993) Fertile obsession: validity after poststructuralism. *Sociological Quarterly* 34 (4): 673–93.

Lincoln, Y. & Guba, E. (1985) *Naturalistic Inquiry*. Sage, Newbury Park, CA.

Patton, M. (1990) [1980] *Qualitative Evaluation and Research Methods*. Sage, Newbury Park, CA.

PATTI LATHER

validity, quantitative

In quantitative research, validity is considered when a researcher is designing a survey or conducting an experiment for collecting data about some phenomena. Validity, in terms of quantitiave research, relates to accuracy, or, in other words, it relates to how accurately or precisely a given concept is being measured by the researcher. A valid measure is one which actually or validly measures the concept it is supposed to be measuring. Researchers use four criteria for designing their measures: face validity, content validity, predictive validity and construct validity: (1) Face validity is when "at face" a measure appears logical. For example, when a person is measuring height, they would not ask "How heavy are you?" (2) Content validity is when a measure covers the range of meanings of a concept. For example, to measure the concept "generosity," just asking the question "how much money have you donated in the last month?" will not do. Rather, the researcher needs to ensure that a set of questions (or a single question) address all possible concepts of generosity. (3) Predictive validity examines whether a measure can predict the potential behavior or outcome that it is supposed to predict. For example, "GRE scores have a high degree of success in predicting success in graduate schools" therefore GRE scores are considered to have good predictive validity. (4) Construct validity seeks agreement between a theoretical concept and a measure. For example, in criminology, strain theory suggests that a variety of different societal pressures cause an individual to experience strain and therefore commit crime. Contrarily, a researcher finds in his research that strain leads to success in life. In this case, his measure is not in agreement with the dominant strain theory and he needs to question his construct validity.

SEE ALSO: Reliability; Validity, Qualitative;

SUGGESTED READING

Creswell, J. (2009) *Research Design: Qualitative, Quantitative, and Mixed Methods Approaches*, 3rd edn. Sage, Thousand Oaks, CA.

SHEETAL RANJAN

value

Karl Marx's labor theory of value and Georg Simmel's cultural theory represent the extremes of sociological positions on value.

Under capitalist production, Marx argued, concrete human labor congeals materials into a qualitatively distinct form which determines a commodity's use. Simultaneously, that concrete labor creates an abstract substance of socially necessary, simple, abstract labor. The quantity of this abstract substance constitutes the commodity's value. Fundamental change under capitalism must address the actual, social, and material process through which value is produced and distributed.

Simmel's conception of value stemmed from his interest in various heuristic concepts sociologists could use to understand social relationships. Individuals, Simmel argued, assess and attach value or values to objects to overcome the separation between them and the objects of their interest.

In exchange, people assess their relationship to an object and others' expectations to form a particular, subjective value of the object – expressed as money. As a measure of money, value becomes a "cultural objectivation" created by a subjective understanding and assessment that stems from and further develops a specific worldview.

Marx's and Simmel's analyses of value met in a concern over alienated existence in commodity-based societies and served as the departure point for more comprehensive analyses. Nevertheless, a material, production based theory of value versus a cultural objectivation theory fundamentally separates sociologists over how fundamental social change occurs.

SEE ALSO: Exchange-Value; Labor/Labor Power; Surplus Value; Use-Value

SUGGESTED READINGS

Marx, K. (1976) [1890] *Capital*, 4th edn., vol. 1, trans. B. Fowkes. Penguin, Harmondsworth.

Simmel, G. (1978) [1907] *The Philosophy of Money*, trans. T. Bottomore & D. Frisby. Routledge & Kegan Paul, London.

ROB BEAMISH

values

Values represent beliefs and ideals which form the basis for choices and preferences, both at an individual and collective level; generally speaking, a value is defined as that which is "good" and which is desired and is able to make one happy. Long-lasting and immaterial ideas regard both current conduct and one's ultimate objective in life: they are different from simple interests which are not particularly characterized by duration and also from moral laws which indicate what is the "right thing to do"; values propose a certain lifestyle and "how to be" rather than purely concrete rules of behavior.

The utilization of the concept in the sociological ambit has been, in the last decades, the object of lively debate, owing to the difficulty of clearly defining what is meant by "values". Sociologists often put in evidence how difficult it is to provide a definition that is usable in empirical research and, on the other hand, they underline the relativity and subjectivity of the definition itself. All the researchers in any case unanimously highlight the connection between the values, the social structure and the actual behavior of the social subjects. Hechter (1993) identifies some difficulties in the study of values: first, they are not visible; second, there are no theories capable of satisfactorily explaining the connection between the values and the behaviors both at individual and at collective levels: besides we lack theories explaining how values are formed and, lastly, they are not easily measurable.

Values are not to be confused with attitudes, norms, needs and with the peculiarities of personal traits. Values are centred on ideals, hence they have an abstract role in building self identity, while attitudes are directly referred to the actual behavior of the individuals. Compared to norms, then, values are perceived by the individuals not as imposed from outside, but rather as outcomes of free personal choice. Besides, while needs refer to the biological sphere, values highlight the various cultural responses that can be given to such needs. The need for food or sex meets different responses according to the values of the different cultures where such needs are felt. Finally values differ from traits because, while these refer to the actual fixed aspects of personality, the former are abstract judgement criteria constantly inclined towards self transcendentalism.

Although the search is highly personal, the values of the individual are part of his/her social and cultural context. From a sociocultural point of view, values constitute a specific element of every culture: they are closely linked to the symbols, laws and rituals which regulate the various dimensions of collective life. Thus it is clear that values have the function of uniting individual and social praxis and it is this unity which coherently guarantees the link between the individual and society. From a sociological point of view, it is the complex mechanism of the transfer of values from one generation to another which constitutes the socialization process: via this there is the interaction between society and the individual and thus various aspects of culture become important for the individual.

Values, seen from the perspective of social sciences, do not regard the dimension of absoluteness and the transcendent of the philosophical context but are linked to precise historical, geographical and social contexts which are related to various economic, political and religious structures.

SEE ALSO: Culture; Fundamentalism; Identity Theory; Social Change

REFERENCE

Hechter, M., Nadel, L., & Michod, R. E. (eds.) (1993) *The Origin of Values*, de Gruyter, New York.

SUGGESTED READING

Hitlin, S. & Piliavin, J. A. (2004) Values: reviving a dormant concept. *Annual Review of Sociology* 30: 359–93.

GIUSEPPE GIORDAN

variables

A variable (indicator, item) is a superordinated attribute, characteristic, or finding that exists in at least two distinct subordinated categories (classes, groups, units of measurement, values). Cases (individuals) can differ on the variable concerning the category they belong to. All cases of a sample or population can be allocated to variables. All cases assigned to the same category count as "the same" (concerning this variable). If two cases are allotted to different categories, they are regarded as being dissimilar. Categories should be mutually exclusive, meaning that any individual can only be allocated to one category. They should also be exhaustive (i.e., each individual should be assignable to one category). If for some reason one does not know what category a case belongs to, this is called missing data or missing value.

In surveys, each question in a questionnaire (usually) can be considered as one variable, each possible answer to a question as a category (value). Using a coding system, the answers given have to be coded (i.e., they have to be transformed into figures in order to make them processible by statistics). Here, the problem of measurement arises (i.e., the verbal responses have to be correctly transferred into numbers without distorting their meaning). Defining a concept in a way that it can be measured is called operationalization.

There are multiple ways of classifying types of variables. First, variables can be classified by the number and discernibility of their categories (see Table 1). Secondly, variables can differ concerning the level of analysis (level of aggregation) of the cases concerned. Researchers can study individuals: (1) variables can describe these individuals' genuine characteristics; (2) relational variables describe a case's interrelationship to other cases; (3) contextual variables capture a case's embeddedness in a collective. Researchers can also examine collectives (aggregates, higher levels of analysis). These collectives can be regarded as individual cases themselves, but they also consist of individuals of lower analysis levels. Global (integral) variables are variables describing characteristics genuine to the aggregate. Analytical (aggregative) variables have to be calculated from variables measuring characteristics of lower-level cases. Structural variables are calculated from information on the relation

Table 1 Classification of variables by characteristics of categories

		Example	
Type of variable	*Characteristics of categories*	*Variable*	*Categories/values*
Binary variable (= Dummy variable)	Two categories with clear boundaries that should be coded with "1" and "0"	Gender	Male, female
Discrete and polytomous	More than two (but finite number of) categories with clear boundaries	Continent	Africa, America, Asia, Europe, Australia
Continuous	Large (often infinite) number of categories that make the boundaries between categories hard to distinguish	Income in US $	Any value from 0 to an infinite number

Table 2 Classification of variables by level of measurement

Measurement level	*Variable type*	*Characteristics of categories*	*Example*	
			Variable	*Categories/values*
Low	Categorial variable (= Index, Nominal variable, Qualitative variable)	Categories are just different, but there is no rank between categories.	Gender	Male, Female
↑	Ordinal variable (= Dimension, Scale in the narrow sense)	Additionally, categories can be ranked.	Attitude toward tax cuts	Completely agree, Partly agree, Partly disagree, Completely disagree
↓	Metric variable (Variable of interval scale)	Additionally, the distance between any two adjactent categories is the same	IQ	Any value from about 80 to about 180
High	Variable of ratio scale	Additionally, a true point of zero exists	Number of children	Any value from 0 to about 20

between lower-level cases. Thirdly, variables differ in level of measurement (scale in the broader sense); that is, on the question how categories can be arranged (see Table 2). The higher the scale type, the more severe are the measurement rules, but the more statistical methods are allowed as well. Fourthly, variables differ on how they can be operationalized. Manifest variables can be observed and measured directly, while latent variables cannot be directly observed but have to be reconstructed using special methods, such as factor analysis. Fifthly, for some variables, individual values can be interpreted directly, without knowing other cases' values. For other variables, one needs to know the whole range of values to assess the meaning of a single case's value.

SEE ALSO: Computer-Aided/Mediated Analysis; Quantitative Methods; Statistics; Variables, Control; Variables, Dependent; Variables, Independent

SUGGESTED READING

Bartholomew, D. J. (ed.) (2006) *Measurement*, 4 vols. Sage, Thousand Oaks, CA.

NINA BAUR

variables, control

Control variables are variables included in multivariate analyses to identify spurious associations. In assessing whether X causes Y, it is important to examine whether the covariation between them persists after the effects of other variables on this association are removed. A variable is controlled when its influence on the other variables in the model is held constant.

In laboratory experiments, Z can be controlled by setting a fixed value for it and observing the relationships between X and Y for that fixed value. The experiment can then be repeated at other fixed values of Z and see whether the same results occur. However, in most social research, values of variables such as education, age, and income cannot be manipulated before obtaining the data. Therefore, the part of association between X and Y that is caused by variation in Z can be removed by comparing only cases with equal or similar values of Z at a time. Spurious relationship exists if both X and Y are dependent on Z, so that the association disappears when Z is controlled.

Social research establishes causal claims by demonstrating temporally ordered covariation among variables and by discrediting alternative explanations. It is not always evident which variables should be controlled in causal analysis using multivariate techniques. Researchers should thus develop a thorough knowledge of the theory and past research relating to their empirical inquiry so that plausible spurious relationships can be quickly detected and potential confounding variables appropriately controlled for.

SEE ALSO: Dependent Variables; Independent Variables; Multivariate Analysis

SUGGESTED READING

McClendon, M. J. (2002) *Multiple Regression and Causal Analysis*. Waveland Press, Long Grove, IL.

HUNG-EN SUNG

variables, dependent

Dependent variables are presumed outcomes that can be influenced or predicted by other, *independent variables*. For example, providing scholarships to permit low income students to attend college (independent variable) might affect their occupations and income (dependent variables).

Dependent variables differ in the type of *measurement* (i.e., rules used to assign numerical values) they represent. Stevens (1946) identified four *scales of measurement*. In *nominal* scales, categories (e.g., teacher, lawyer) are arbitrarily assigned numerical values that convey no information other than category membership. *Ordinal* scales indicate the relative quality or amount of the variable of interest via rank ordering (e.g., drop out = 1; high school diploma = 2, associate's degree = 3, bachelor's degree = 4), but differences between ordinal scores are not meaningful (above, $2 - 1 \neq 4 - 3$). In *interval* scales (e.g., Fahrenheit temperatures), differences between numbers are invariant across the measurement scale (e.g., $42° - 37° = 84° - 79°$). However, 84° Fahrenheit is not twice as hot as 42° Fahrenheit. Such statements can only be made for *ratio* scales, which have an absolute zero signifying absence of the thing being measured (e.g., Calvin temperatures, income in dollars). Thus, the level of measurement constrains the type of statistical analyses that are appropriate.

In interpreting the information provided by measurement of dependent variables, it is also essential to consider their reliability and validity. *Reliability* refers to the accuracy or precision of measurement. *Validity*, on the other hand, refers to the appropriateness and utility of the data for a given interpretation or use. Although data must be reliable in order to permit valid interpretations, misguided or erroneous interpretations of reliable data are possible. Thus, reliability is necessary but not sufficient for validity. Several approaches are used to gauge both reliability (e.g., internal consistency, test-retest) and validity (e.g., content, criterion-related).

SEE ALSO: Experimental Design; Hypotheses; Measures of Centrality; Reliability; Variables, Independent

SUGGESTED READING

Stevens, S. S. (1946) On the theory of scales of measurement. *Science* 103: 677–80.

ERNEST GOETZ

variables, independent

Independent variables are the presumed causes whose effects are measured via changes in the values of *dependent variables*. For example, winning a state lottery (independent variable) might increase expenditures on luxury items (dependent variables). According to Cohen, Cohen, West, and Aiken (2003), there are four requirements for concluding that an independent variable (X) causes or influences a dependent variable (Y):

1. X precedes Y in time (temporal precedence).
2. Some mechanism whereby this causal effect operates can be posited (causal mechanism).
3. A change in the value of X is accompanied by a change in the value of Y on the average (association).
4. The effects of X on Y can be isolated from the effects of other potential variables on Y (nonspuriousness or lack of confounders). (p. 64)

It is important to note that (3) above represents a probabilistic view of causality that is particularly important in the social sciences. A change in an independent variable is likely to be associated with a change in the dependent variable, but the occurrence, size, and direction of the change may differ from one individual or occasion to the next. In social science research, multiple observations are used to address this problem.

Experimental research has long been considered the "gold standard" in providing evidence of causality. In experiments, causal relationships are tested by manipulating the independent variable (or variables) of interest while keeping other factors constant.

Although such control is not possible in social science research, researchers can attempt to control or account for other potentially confounding variables. Thus, one might study the effect of mode of presentation of a political story (newspaper vs. television) in a study in which potentially confounding variables (e.g., sex and age of audience members) are controlled by random assignment to conditions, matching, or statistical procedures.

SEE ALSO: Experimental Design; Hypotheses; Reliability; Variables, Dependent

SUGGESTED READING

Cohen, J., Cohen, P., West, S. G., & Aiken, L. S. (2003) *Applied Regression/Correlation Behavior Analysis for the Behavioral Sciences*, 3rd edn. Lawrence Erlbaum Associates, Mahwah, NJ.

ERNEST GOETZ

variance

Variability is one of the key characteristics of a set of scores. Measures of variability are used to provide an indication of the extent to which characteristics of people (e.g., income, occupation), events (e.g., attendance at concerts), or things (e.g., capacity of concert venues) differ from one another. Although there are other measures of variability (e.g., *range*), *variance* and *standard deviation* are used most frequently.

Variance and standard deviation depict variability of a set of scores in terms of their distances from the mean, or *deviation scores* (i.e., score – mean); therefore, they can only be computed for *interval* or *ratio* scales, in which differences between scores are meaningful and consistent. However, the sum of the deviation scores is zero for all sets of scores, so the average deviation score is of no value as a measure of variability. This difficulty is overcome by squaring the deviation scores.

Computation differs depending on whether you have all data of interest or want to use a sample drawn from a larger population to draw inferences about that population. Statistical notation differs in these two cases as well (mean: μ for population, M for sample; standard deviation: μ for population, M for sample). If you have data for the entire population of interest, variance is found by summing the squared deviation scores and dividing by the number of scores (N):

$$\frac{\sum (X - \mu)^2}{N}$$

Application of this equation to estimate population variance from a sample, however, systematically underestimates the true value. To correct for this bias, squared deviation scores are divided by the number of scores (n) minus 1:

$$\frac{\sum (X - M)^2}{n - 1}$$

Variance is at the core of statistical analysis (e.g., *analysis of variance*, *correlation* and *regression, hierarchical linear modeling, structural equation modeling*), but calculation of the variance yields a metric in which the unit of measurement is squared; therefore, variability is most often reported in terms of the standard deviation, which is the square root of the variance.

SEE ALSO: ANOVA (Analysis of Variance); Confidence Intervals; Statistics

SUGGESTED READING

Keith, T. Z. (2006) *Multiple Regression and Beyond.* Pearson, Boston, MA.

ERNEST GOETZ

verstehen

Usually translated as "understanding," the concept of *verstehen* has become part of a critique of positivist approaches to the social sciences. Rather than explain behaviour with reference to impersonal "causes" *verstehen* places understanding of social meanings as central to a sociological approach. Whereas natural science (and positivistic methods in social science) constitutes a world of objects to be explained, *verstehen* regards human actors as subjects with whom the researcher enters into dialogue. Wilhelm Dilthey (1833–1911) was crucial in the development of hermeneutic philosophy into a sociological method arguing that since sociologists were part of the world that they studied sociology can develop deeper and more intimate knowledge of its subject matter than is possible in natural sciences. As members of society we learn to decode symbols and develop the capacity for empathy – reconstructing and "reexperiencing" emotions, intentions, social situations etc. By drawing on shared experiences we have the ability to project ourselves into a text or form of life and understand its meaning. As cultural scientists we are surrounded by cultural objects, "Roman ruins, cathedrals, and summer castles," fragments of the history of mind that can be understood only by interpretive techniques grounded in the life process of individuals (Dilthey 1986). This approach was resolutely universalistic in its assumption that whatever humans had created can be understood through reconstruction of their meanings and in intentions.

Max Weber (1864–1920) used the method of *verstehen* most famously in *The Protestant Ethic and the Spirit of Capitalism* where he supplemented structural and economic accounts of the origin of capitalism in Europe with reconstruction of the worldview of seventeenth-century Protestants. His claim that the Calvinist belief in predestination provoked "an unprecedented inner loneliness" and consequent search for signs of salvation in the worldly but ascetic pursuit of capital accumulation, placed the understanding of meaningful action at the center of his explanation of the rise of capitalism. *Verstehen* has subsequently been central to the methods of interpretive sociology, notably symbolic interactionism.

However, the use of *verstehen* is open to criticism. First, critics have argued that this is not a distinct method, but an elaboration of what all social actors do routinely in everyday life. Second, there is no way of validating *verstehende* interpretations since they cannot be tested against replicable evidence. Third, it is claimed that interpretation of meanings adds no new knowledge and by definition recycles what is already known about society. Fourth, *verstehen* is at best a source of hypotheses that then require testing against evidence. Fifth, it is accused of over-emphasizing meaning at the expense of material structures and unintended consequences of actions. Finally the emphasis on understanding might have a conservative orientation that gives too little attention to power relations. To some extent these criticisms focus on *verstehen* as a form of introspection or imaginative reconstruction of meanings rather than as a systematic dialogue with a range of social materials – texts, archives, conversations, worldviews, and cultural artifacts – in which suggested interpretations can be "tested" with reference to the extent that they open up new layers of understanding.

SEE ALSO: Hermeneutics; Positivism; Weber, Max

SUGGESTED READINGS

Dilthey, W. (1986) Awareness, reality: time. In: Mueller-Vollmer, K. (ed.), *The Hermeneutics Reader*. Blackwell, Oxford, pp. 149–64.

Ray, L. J. (1999) *Theorizing Classical Sociology*. Open University Press, Buckingham.

Weber, M. (1984) *The Protestant Ethic and the Spirit of Capitalism*. Allen & Unwin, London.

LARRY RAY

victimization

Victimization is the action of victimizing, or fact of being victimized. Until a variety of factors converged during the 1960s, individual victims were not always given much attention by the criminal justice system. During this time, the women's movement began to address the victim-blaming often seen with sexually violent crimes. Child abuse as a societal problem was also coming to the attention of local and state leaders. Finally, rapidly growing crime rates between 1960 and 1980 brought greater scrutiny to the criminal justice system, in part through President Johnson's 1967 Commission report. Victimization was one focus of this report. The culmination of these factors began the discussion about the victim's role in the criminal justice process, what services should be provided to victims, and data gathering about victimization in the USA.

Certain demographic factors are associated with greater risks of victimization. The risk of victimization decreases with age after peaking in the 16–24 age group. The elderly (ages 65 and older) have much lower victimization rates than younger individuals. Men in general are more likely to experience a violent crime than are women. Women are more likely to experience rape or sexual assault than are men, as well as simple assault with minor injury. Blacks are more likely to experience crimes of violence than other minorities and whites but are slightly less likely than whites to experience simple assault (Bureau of Justice Statistics 2003).

However, demographics alone cannot fully explain victimization and criminal behavior. Theories of victimization began in the 1940s with Hans von Hentig and his theory of victim–perpetrator interaction. Von Hentig observed that victims often contributed to their victimization by somehow provoking the offender or by putting themselves in situations that would make them prone to criminal acts. Ezzat Fattah stressed the link between victimization and offending and argued that the criminal act as a whole needs to be examined because of the interaction of the victim and offender. Victims can be offenders and vice versa.

Hindelang, Gottfredson, and Garofalo developed the lifestyle theory of crime in 1978. Changing gender roles (women working outside the home) and work schedules means that people live different lifestyles, spend varying amounts of time in public, and interact with different kinds of people. This theory is based on several propositions, including that increased time spent with non-family members and in public places increases the chances for victimization.

SEE ALSO: Crime; Hate Crimes; Race and Crime; Violent Crime

REFERENCE

Bureau of Justice Statistics (2003) *Criminal Victimization in the United States, 2002 Statistical Tables*. US Department of Justice, Office of Justice Programs, Washington, DC.

SUGGESTED READING

Doerner, W. G. & Lab, S. P. (1995) *Victimology*. Anderson Publishing, Cincinnati, OH.

TANCY J. VANDECAR-BURDIN

violence

Violence is a form of power. It is really power in action, "action-power," as Popitz (1999: 43) says, a way of action based on the power physically and materially to hurt other creatures or to be harmed. Violence means to kill, to harm, to destroy, to rob, and to expel. These are the five basic forms of violence. All varieties of violence are variants and hybrids of these forms.

Among the basic forms of violence, killing stands out especially. It represents the extreme limit of violence. With killing there is *absolute* violence, an extreme limit of all social conflict, the end of dominance, power, and sociation. As power over life and death, absolute violence is the experiential area for the idea of complete power, the source of absolute impotence – and the source of absolute freedom. Deadly action-power constitutes the antinomy of absolute power and the fact that all power of human beings over one another is imperfect. Both can become the trigger for fundamental legitimations: for the god-like superiority of the killer and for unconditional opposition.

Like all power, violence needs legitimation, which comes up again in the debate about the concept of violence. The idea of what violence *is* is historically, interculturally, and intraculturally highly variable. The concept is loaded with value judgments and normative expectations and routinely becomes part of symbolic struggles. In the controversies about the concept of violence one discovers the fundamental ambivalence of violence and power as the guarantors and gravediggers of freedom and order.

SEE ALSO: Crime; Domestic Violence

REFERENCE

Popitz, H. (1999) *Phänomene der Macht*. Mohr, Tübingen.

SUGGESTED READING

Collins, R. (2008) *Violence: A Micro-Sociological Theory*. Princeton University Press, Princeton, NJ.

TRUTZ VON TROTHA

violent crime

Violent crime is the illegal, intentional, and malicious physical injury of one person by another. Social scientists seeking to document and explain violent crime typically rely on official statistics from police, court, and public health agencies, and on victimization and self-report surveys. While each of these sources has limitations and biases, they can be used to estimate the prevalence of and trends in violent crime, and the characteristics of the people involved in it.

Violent crime rates vary greatly over time. In Europe and North America, for example, serious interpersonal violence decreased dramatically after the sixteenth century, probably as a result of the expansion of state powers, the Protestant Reformation, and the rise of modern individualism. Violent crime rates also vary greatly among societies, even relatively similar ones. In countries with extreme inequalities in income and wealth, weak collective institutions of social protection, and few restrictions on firearms, violent crime rates are higher.

Young, economically disadvantaged males predominate among both victims and perpetrators of violence. Females are more likely to be victims than perpetrators and most female victims are attacked by males they are related to or intimately involved with. Violent crime is much more likely to occur between relatives or persons well known to each other than between strangers. Sociological explanations of violent crime focus on the individual, situational, and/or structural-cultural levels of analysis. Individual-level analyses look for characteristics that predispose people to or fail to discourage them from violence. Situational approaches attend to the context and processes immediately surrounding violent events, such as the presence of weapons or bystanders. Structural-cultural approaches look at broader social forces, processes, and value systems shaping violent motivations and opportunities. With recent changes in global politics and governance, sociologists are currently evaluating accepted knowledge about violent crime by studying such violent behaviors as terrorist acts and war crimes.

SEE ALSO: Hate Crimes; Violence

SUGGESTED READINGS

Eisner, M. (2003) Long-term historical trends in violent crime. In: Tonry, M. (ed.), *Crime and Justice: A Review of Research*, Vol. 30. University of Chicago Press, Chicago, IL, pp. 83–142.

Jackman, M. (2002) Violence in social life. *Annual Review of Sociology* 28: 387–415.

ROSEMARY GARTNER

virtual communities

Following the dramatic loss or decline of real human communities, the highly contentious sociological conception of "virtual communities" signifies a decisive historic break with material human geography and the subsequent emergence of Net-based "social aggregations" (Rheingold 1993), complex electronically grounded networks of interactive social relations. In particular, the advent and rapid growth of Internet bulletin boards, electronic mailing lists, chat rooms, MUDs, MUSHes, MOOs, IRCs, forums and blogs since the mid-1990s has triggered radically new and diverse modes of social bonding, subjectivity, experience, identity formation and political intervention (e.g. cyborg politics).

Virtual communities, originally anticipated by J. C. R. Licklider and R. W. Taylor as early as 1968, increasingly move towards the overwhelming creation of a global (or local/global) virtual society which optimistically promises unlimited democratic freedom of speech and self-expression, as well as the general revision and revival of the public sphere: "The vision of a citizen-designed, citizen-controlled worldwide communications network is a version of technological utopianism that could be called the vision of 'the electronic agora' " (Rheingold 1993: 14). In that sense, a virtual community, as an essentially anonymous online community of common interests, tasks, goals and orientations, is much "more than just an array of computer-mediated communication messages; it is a sociological phenomenon" (Matusitz 2007: 24).

This ultimately requires new automated data extraction techniques, quantitative methods of rigorous analysis and robust empirical findings about the organization, governance and performance of the large Internet-connected communities, where the real/corporeal (or physical) as we have known it is dynamically reconfigured. However, serious epistemological doubts have been repeatedly raised about the extent to which the public and urban places of social and cultural life, rich human experience and real face-to-face interaction could be actually telemediated, or reconstructed within imagined, unaccountable, solipsistically self-referential or "hyper-realistic" electronic regimes.

In principle, there is nothing more social than virtual communities; they are genuine collective discursive products. Everyone is freely communicating and socializing with everyone (who is not physically present!) and through the computer humanity (as a whole) is reflexively communicating with itself. Yet, the most social of the social worlds is at the same time the loneliest of the lonely worlds. Like in Husserl's transcendental monadology, the world is our subjective representation (an ideal world or a mindscape) and, in the absence of the *embodied other*, we can thus never be sure that we are not alone in the world and that virtual communities are not only a dream (or a nightmare)!

Nevertheless, virtual communities still provide *real* alternative humanistic choices and opportunities for self-realization, self-awareness, political conscious-raising, empowerment (letting dissenting voices speak out) and critical discussion of public issues (with adequate human feelings) that may otherwise not be discussed on such an open macro-scale, albeit with continuing serious problems of access and discrimination that need to reflexively and meaningfully be addressed by *both* participants *and* policy makers.

SEE ALSO: Cyberculture; Online Social Networking; Web 2.0

REFERENCES

Matusitz, J. (2007) The implications of the Internet for human communication. *Journal of Information Technology Impact* 7 (1): 21–34.

Rheingold, H. (1993) *The Virtual Community: Homesteading on the Electronic Frontier.* Addison-Wesley, Reading, MA.

CHARALAMBOS TSEKERIS

W

war

War – oftentimes defined as longlasting conflict between political groups (especially states or nation-states) and carried out by armed forces – has never been at the center of sociological theorizing. This has something to do with the historical origins of sociology which regarded itself as the science of capitalist and industrial society, a type of society in which processes of capital accumulation and technological innovation might create enormous conflicts, but usually only those *within* a society, not *between* societies. Thus, war as an intersocietal process or a phenomenon between states was pushed at the margins of sociological reasoning.

Although in the works of the sociological classics like Max Weber, Émile Durkheim, or Georg Herbert Mead one will always find scattered though certainly interesting hints at the consequences of warfare for societal development, it was not until the rise of historical sociology in the late 1970s that war, and especially *the consequences of war*, really began to be theorized in a systematic and theoretically meaningful way beyond the very specialized field of military sociology. Starting with Theda Skocpol's *States and Social Revolutions* (1979), the debate focused very much on how European modernity was shaped by the impact of wars. Whereas Skocpol had argued that especially the French and the Russian Revolutions and their outcomes can only be understood by focusing on international contexts, and particularly on the crises of state administrations weakened by longlasting or lost wars, others emphasized how the modern state and its monopoly of violence were the result of violent interstate conflicts: it was only by constant warfare that large state bureaucracies were built in Europe, bureaucracies for the purpose of extracting resources out of civil society in order to finance large standing armies. Even the rise of democracy and welfare states historically seemed to be closely connected with war since suffering populations could organize and successfully demand suffrage and social rights. And, last but not least, war was also linked to internal repression since the militarization of societies as a consequence of war sometimes led to ethnic cleansing or even genocide.

As historical-sociological research also made clear: War is not a homogeneous variable so that different kinds of war have very different effects. Even within the context of the nineteenth and twentieth centuries at least four types of war are to be distinguished: (1) interstate wars between neighboring or competing nations; (2) colonial wars in which mostly European expeditionary forces usually defeated indigenous groups and populations in various parts of the world; (3) civil wars between established state apparatuses and rebels; and (4) wars of national liberation against mostly European colonial powers, a type of war that only came into being after 1945.

The common feature of all these types of war is that a more or less powerful state is at least on one side of the conflict. The phenomenon of state-failure and state breakdown in some world regions, however, structured macro-violence in a surprising way so that since the late 1980s some analysts have begun to talk about so-called "new wars" (Kaldor 1999). These supposedly new conflicts usually take place in spaces where the state monopoly of violence has vanished so that various types of combatants – armed bandits, ethnic groups, parts of former state elites, etc. – are fighting for resources. These conflicts – so the argument goes – are not shaped by clearly defined ideological or political goals any longer as, for example, the wars of liberation in the period of decolonization especially after 1945.

SEE ALSO: Anti-War and Peace Movements; Democracy; Ethnic Groups; Genocide; Liberalism; Military Sociology; Modernity; Nation-State; World Conflict

REFERENCE

Kaldor, M. (1999) *New & Old Wars. Organized Violence in a Global Era*. Stanford University Press, Stanford, CA.

SUGGESTED READINGS

Joas, H. & Knöbl, W. (2008) *Kriegsverdrängung. Ein Problem in der Geschichte der Sozialtheorie*. Suhrkamp, Frankfurt/M.

Skocpol, T. (1979) *States and Social Revolutions: A Comparative Analysis of France, Russia, and China*. Cambridge University Press, Cambridge.
Wittrock, B. (2001) History, war and the transcendence of modernity. *European Journal of Social Theory* 4 (1): 53–72.

WOLFGANG KNÖBL

weak ties (strength of)

Weak ties are relationships between individuals marked by relatively low intensity and emotional closeness; strong ties are defined as having the converse characteristics. The importance of weak ties to a variety of sociological phenomena has been most influentially articulated by Mark Granovetter (1973) in one of the best cited articles in sociology, "The strength of weak ties" (SWT).

In SWT Granovetter introduces the concept of a bridge: a line in a network which provides the only path between two points. He also distinguishes between the former, and "local bridges," the latter being a line in a graph that provides the only local path between two points.

According to Granovetter, because of the principles of Balance Theory, weak ties are not automatically bridges, but *all bridges are weak ties*. Granovetter asserts that in large networks it is unlikely that a specific tie provides the only path between two points, but local bridges may be functionally important. The significance of weak ties is that those which are local bridges create more and shorter paths. Consequently, whatever is to be disseminated can reach a larger number of people, and cross greater social distance when it is diffused through weak ties rather than through strong ones.

Also based on principles of Balance Theory, Granovetter reasons that strong ties should tend to be people who not only know one another, but also have few contacts not tied to ego as well. An ego's weak ties in general, by contrast, will not be tied to one another, but will tend to be tied to individuals not tied to ego. Thus weak ties are of importance because they are the conduits through which ideas, influences, or information socially distant from alters may reach her. In a later article, Granovetter clarified his argument by emphasizing that it is only bridging weak ties that are of particular importance, and reiterated that weak ties are far more likely to be bridges than are strong ties.

In his SWT article, and a related book, Granovetter goes on to describe the results of a study he undertook examining the role contacts play in helping one to get a job amongst recent professional, technical, and managerial job changers in a suburb of Boston. In his study the majority of jobs were obtained through weak ties. Granovetter's SWT insights have spawned substantial work on the relationship between the tie strength between egos and contacts and job search outcomes.

Granovetter's SWT insights also have implications for understanding collective action. Granovetter has argued that at the level of whole networks, weak ties are important because they are more likely (than strong ties) to serve as bridges between otherwise isolated cliques in a community.

Marsden and Campbell (1984) have provided a thorough conceptual and empirical review of the notion of tie strength. Based on an analysis of empirical data they concluded that closeness (the measure of the emotional intensity of a tie) is the best indicator of tie strength.

The SWT argument is implicitly connected to a number of substantive and theoretical problems in sociology; some of these include small world studies, network sampling, estimating personal network size, techniques for assessing and improving the accuracy of responses, and understanding the creation of weak ties.

SEE ALSO: Network Society; Social Network Theory

REFERENCES

Granovetter, M. (1973) The strength of weak ties. *American Journal of Sociology* 78: 1360–80.
Marsden, P. V. & Campbell, K. E. (1984) Measuring tie strength. *Social Forces* 63: 482–501.

DAVID B. TINDALL

wealth

Wealth is defined as assets held by an individual or household. These assets may include financial wealth such as savings accounts, stocks, or bonds as well as property such as the family home, farm or business. Some estimates of household wealth also include consumer durables such as vehicles and refrigerators.

Wealth is an important dimension of stratification because property can be passed down from generation to generation. Families use accumulated assets or savings to bridge interruptions in income, preventing downward social mobility. In spite of its importance, sociologists tend to leave wealth out of their measures of socioeconomic status, because of the difficulties in obtaining valid and reliable data on household assets. This is particularly true when engaged in cross-cultural research, because economic assets vary tremendously and are defined differently for different countries. Using the data that are available, sociologists and economists have determined that in general, the distribution of wealth varies a lot, but is far more unequal than the distribution of income. The USA exhibits the highest levels of wealth inequality in the developed world.

For economists, wealth represents income that is saved rather than being spent on daily necessities or consumer desires. Of course not all individuals are equally able to save. The accumulation of assets is extremely difficult for the poor and working poor because nearly all of their income goes to fulfill daily needs. In most "third world" countries (and some in the "second world") household needs are not subsidized by their employer through medical or childcare benefits.

Recent economic indicators suggest that more and more American families are having trouble saving a portion of their incomes. Net household liabilities have exceeded net asset accumulation in the USA since 1999, which means that Americans are not only failing to accumulate wealth, they are accumulating personal debt at unprecedented rates. Decreasing home values and stock prices means that even wealthy Americans, as are individuals in other countries, are experiencing a decrease in net worth. Some research indicates that US households in the bottom quintile have no wealth at all, and a large portion of these have negative wealth (i.e. debt). These experiences are being reproduced in other "first world" countries.

Throughout history, various government initiatives have sought to encourage the acquisition of wealth for some households. These programs have enabled many families to secure home ownership and save for retirement. Unfortunately, many of these government subsidies have benefited the wealthy class far more than other groups, resulting in a large wealth gap typically patterned by race and ethnicity. For example, on average, African American households possess only eight cents in wealth for every dollar possessed by white families. This disparity persists, even though the income gap between African American and white households has shrunk. African American households are also more likely to possess wealth in the form of residential property than in a more liquid form such as stocks or bonds. These disparities exist in countries around the world, although some are based on economic (or political) status rather than race/ethnicity.

SEE ALSO: Bankruptcy; Consumption; Income Inequality and Income Mobility

SUGGESTED READINGS

Collins, C. & Yeskel, F. (2000) *Economic Apartheid in America: A Primer on Economic Inequality and Insecurity*. New Press, New York.

Keister, L. (2000) *Wealth in America: Trends in Wealth Inequality*. Cambridge University Press, New York.

JUANITA M. FIRESTONE AND CLAUDIA W. SCHOLZ

Web 2.0

The term Web 2.0 first entered the public sphere in 2004 following conferences and events organized by O'Reilly Media. Initially the term was little more than an ill-defined buzzword. However, in a much-cited discussion, O'Reilly (2005) gave the concept greater analytic content. He argued that it was possible to identify a shift toward user-generated web content of various sorts. The early signs of this growth came with the emergence of blogs, but these were very quickly followed by a range of other forms of contributory practice such as "tagging," "feeds," "commenting," "noting," "reviewing," "rating," "mashing up," "making friends," and so on.

A very crude set of distinctions might be drawn between Web 1.0 (1993–2003) and Web 2.0 (2004 onwards). If Web 1.0 was primarily about "reading" or "browsing" web pages, Web 2.0 is still about this, but with the added ability that people can now "write" and "contribute" as well. If the primary unit of content of Web 1.0 was the "page," within Web 2.0 it has shifted toward the "post" or the "record." If the primary state of Web 1.0 was "static," the primary state of Web 2.0 is "dynamic": Not only do more things move about on the screen, but actual content changes as more and more people contribute, post, respond, edit, amend, link, and so on. If Web 1.0 was primarily viewed through a computer screen using a web browser of some sort, Web 2.0 can be viewed through an increasingly wide range of devices – PCs certainly, but now also myriad mobile devices. If content within Web 1.0 was generally created by web coders and designers, within Web 2.0 content is created by all users, albeit within the context of templates provided by coders and designers. If the social and cultural base of Web 1.0 was primarily that of web designers and "geeks," Web 2.0 is viewed as a "cooler" domain offering up the possibility of a new culture of public research. Finally, if Web 1.0 was still generally "consumed" by users, Web 2.0 represents an ontological blurring of the distinction between "consumption" and "production" as more and more users "work" without financial reward in order to produce web content.

Although the unity of Web 2.0 derives from this large-scale shift toward user-generated web content, the *form* that this takes is highly varied.

- Blogging has quickly become part of the cultural mainstream. A blog – a compression of "web log" – is a website where an individual offers commentary, reflections, and/or descriptions of phenomena.
- Wikis can be understood as user-generated resources constructed and edited by anyone who wishes to contribute. The most well known is the online encyclopedia Wikipedia.
- Folksonomies involve the locating and marking or classifying of a web page with a metadata label. Tags act as metadata operating behind web pages enabling them to be organized into classified networks. Two of the most widely used are Flickr and YouTube.
- Mashups are "hybrid applications, where two or more technologies or services are conflated into a completely new, novel, service" (Maness 2006: 9). The point of mashups is that they present existing information in new ways. Mashups utilizing maps are, for example, a form of web-based "do-it-yourself" geographic information system.
- Social network sites (SNS) are perhaps the most socially significant of the Web 2.0 applications, particularly as the number of users continues to escalate. SNS users build profiles about themselves, posting photos, videos, information about their backgrounds, views, work, consumption preferences, and so on, and make "friends" with other users. Examples include Facebook and Myspace.

The sociology of Web 2.0 is in its infancy but the phenomenon demands that we radically rethink many of the binaries we have traditionally worked with: consumption/production; expert/amateur; public/private; virtual/real; and many others.

SEE ALSO: Consumption and the Internet; Internet

SUGGESTED READINGS

Beer, D. & Burrows, R. (2007) Sociology and, of and in Web 2.0: some initial considerations. *Sociological Research Online* (12) 5: www.socresonline.org.uk/12/5/17.html.

Maness, J. M. (2006) Library 2.0 theory: Web 2.0 and its implications for libraries. *Webology* (3) (2): www.webology.ir/2006/v3n2/a25.html.

O'Reilly, T. (2005) *What Is Web 2.0: Design Patterns and Business Models for the Next Generation of Software*: oreillynet.com/1pt/a/6228, accessed December 7, 2006.

ROGER BURROWS

Weber, Max (1864–1920)

German sociologist Max Weber was born in Erfurt, Thuringia, April 21, 1864. He studied history, economics, and philosophy at the University of Heidelberg in preparation for a career in law. However, after receiving his doctorate and briefly practicing law he decided to take up an academic career.

Early in his marriage to Marianne Schnitger, a distant cousin, he took an academic appointment in economics at Freiburg, soon to be followed by his appointment to the professorial chair in political economy at Heidelberg in 1896. In the following year he suffered a psychological breakdown and was unable to resume scholarly work until 1902. Beginning in 1903 he authored several "methodological" essays. The most important of these was his 1904 "'Objectivity' in Social Science and Social Policy," in which he presented his notion of "ideal-type" concepts, conceived as instruments for representing the most relevant aspects of a given object (e.g., "city" or "capitalism") for purposes of social-scientific inquiry. Ideal-type concepts are central to Weber's methodological perspective, which has been variously characterized as methodological individualism, atomism, constructivism, or nominalism.

In addition to the "objectivity" essay, written to inaugurate his editorship of the social science journal, *Archiv für Sozialwissenschaft und Sozialpolitik* (*Archives for Social Science and Social Policy*), Weber published in the same journal in 1904–5 "The Protestant ethic and the 'spirit' of capitalism," eventually to become his best known work. Over the next few years he wrote further on religious sects in North America, conducted research on the psychophysics of industrial work, and wrote about agrarian conditions in ancient Roman society.

Beginning around 1910 Weber began to identify his academic work and interests with the emerging discipline of sociology while retaining his interests in the historical dimensions of social and cultural phenomena, including the legal, political, economic, and religious spheres. He took an academic appointment at Munich in 1919–20, lecturing on economic history and sociology. He had completed revisions to his "The Protestant Ethic and the 'Spirit' of Capitalism" when he contracted pneumonia and died in Munich on June 14, 1920.

In addition to being claimed as a leading founder of sociology and a major contributor to modern political science, public administration, and political theory, Weber has been recognized for significant contributions to the fields of economic history, historical jurisprudence, the study of ancient civilizations, and the field of the comparative study of religions.

Weber was a historian who became a sociologist, a sociologist who remained an economist, a serious student of ancient society who contributed significantly to the understanding of modern western culture. He was equally captivated by the study of economics and religion, of material and ideal factors, of social structure and individual action. In sociology his contributions are recognized especially in the areas of law, religion, and the economy; in the study of social stratification, political, urban, and rural sociology, and the sociology of culture. In terms of the method and general conception of sociology, Weber insisted that social action is the conceptual foundation of our understanding of societal structures. Insofar as action carries meaning it is intelligible through the use of *Verstehen* (understanding) in the context of interaction and of sociological observation. As important as action is, Weber gave even more attention to what he called order and to what sociologists later came to view as social structure. Action and structure, for Weber, interact in complex loops, with structure emanating either directly or indirectly as a result of action, yet with subsequent action both enabled and constrained by existing structure. Weber is rightly regarded as the founder of structural sociology (stratification, institutions) as well as the sociology of action.

Weber's sociology was largely historical and comparative, conceived as a complement to the historical study of economics, politics, and religion. His greatest substantive contributions to sociology came through two great macro-sociological projects of the last decade of his life.

ECONOMY AND SOCIETY IN WORLD-HISTORICAL PERSPECTIVE

Weber's first major project became known as *Economy and Society*. Published posthumously, this comprehensive reference work, called by Guenther Roth a kind of "sociologist's world history," represents an achievement of encyclopedic scholarship with a global reach. There he presented a vision of "interpretive" sociology based on both the understanding and the causal explanation of intelligible human conduct. Weber regarded "social action," which is subjectively meaningful to the acting individual and oriented toward other people, as the core of human social life. Any social action has subjective meaning and objective conditions, both important in sociological explanation. Weber's dualistic conception of social action can be understood as a synthesis of two scholarly traditions: hermeneutics, emphasizing the understanding of meaning, and positivism, focusing on the causal explanation of empirically observable conditions.

Economy and Society includes many abstract typologies, ranging from types of social action and social relationships to organizations, institutional structures, and social stratification. The best known is the threefold typology of political authority or legitimate domination (*Herrschaft*). *Rational-legal authority* rests on a belief in the legality of a framework of enacted rules by which rulers are selected and by which they govern. *Traditional authority* rests on a belief in the time-honored sanctity of traditions. Finally, *charismatic authority* rests on a belief in the special qualities (*charisma* or "gift of grace") of a person to rule.

Also in *Economy and Society* Weber elaborated his well-known concept of *bureaucracy*. He was interested primarily in the role of bureaucracy in modern western societies where he found it to be particularly consonant with the rational-legal type of political domination. All the designated properties of bureaucracy, especially its governance of action by impersonal standards and systematic procedures, its organization of work activities in the name of efficiency, and its codification of rules and records, were consistent with rational-legal domination as opposed to traditional or charismatic rule.

In Weber's view the development of bureaucratic forms of organization in the modern west was part of a marked trend toward *bureaucratization* across a broad range of institutions, and as part of a historical process of *rationalization*, viewed as the extension of various types of rationality. Bureaucracy represents *formal*, as opposed to *substantive*, *rationality*, given the character of bureaucracy as merely an instrument or tool that can serve virtually any set of ends or purposes.

THE COMPARATIVE STUDIES OF CIVILIZATIONS: *THE ECONOMIC ETHIC OF THE WORLD RELIGIONS*

Weber's second major project was conceived under the rubric of *The Economic Ethic of the World Religions*. This study focused on each of several "world religions" including Confucianism, Taoism, Buddhism, Hinduism, ancient Judaism, Islam, and Christianity. These were comparative civilizational studies, showing how religion is implicated in all the major spheres of society and culture. The starting point of this comparative-historical project can be traced to his renowned study of the relation of the Protestant ethic to the "spirit" of modern capitalism, dating from 1904–5.

In *The Protestant Ethic and the Spirit of Capitalism* Weber sought to find the contribution made by Protestant religious beliefs and practices to the development of modern ("rational") capitalism as found in Western Europe and the USA. Marking this modern form of capitalism as new were especially the emphasis on the systematic organization of work done by laborers hired on a formally free market, and enterprises devoted to the pursuit of increasing profit without the constraints of traditionalism.

Weber found the historical origins of capitalism's ascetic, yet secular, modern spirit, an ethos prescribing the acquisition of money from one's occupational activity while abjuring consumption and luxury as waste of time or money, to lie in early Protestantism, especially Calvinism. The central Calvinistic doctrine was the belief in the "predestination" of one's soul to ultimate salvation or damnation, a fate that the individual believer could neither know nor change. Individuals were admonished to avoid self-doubt regarding their status as members of "the elect," for such doubts could be the devil's work. The best way to sustain self-assurance of one's salvation was to work tirelessly in one's chosen economic vocation.

In Weber's interpretation the significant result of following such religious counsel was the production of a *this-worldly rational asceticism* – *this-worldly* in being visible in the mundane world of work; *rational* in that the individual took control over one's actions and life course; *ascetic* in that self-discipline and avoidance of temptations (idleness, pleasure, materialism) through complete devotion to labor came to dominate one's everyday life.

According to Weber, this Protestant asceticism nourished the secular spirit of capitalism exemplified by Benjamin Franklin in the late eighteenth century. With this new spirit employers and workers were more likely to dedicate themselves to the program of capitalistic enterprise free of the distractions of the world outside the factory, the workshop, or the firm. To the extent that Calvinism actually had these effects, they were, paradoxically, unintended consequences of the religious doctrines. By the twentieth century, Weber noted, the motivation to work had devolved into a mere compulsion in order to support an ever more prosperous and materialistic lifestyle, a compulsion likened by Weber to a "steel-hard casing."

SEE ALSO: Authority and Legitimacy; Bureaucracy; Capitalism; Ideal Type; Political Sociology; Rational Legal Authority; Religion, Sociology of; Verstehen

SUGGESTED READINGS

Kalberg, S. (1994) *Max Weber's Historical-Comparative Sociology*. University of Chicago Press, Chicago, IL.

Weber, M. (1988) *Max Weber: A Biography*, trans. and ed. H. Zohn. Transaction Books, New Brunswick, NJ.

Weber, M. (1946) *From Max Weber: Essays in Sociology*, trans. and ed. H. H. Gerth and C. W. Mills. Oxford University Press, New York.

Weber, M. (1968) *Economy and Society: An Outline of Interpretive Sociology*, 3 vols., ed. G. Roth & C. Wittich, trans. E. Fischoff, H. H. Gerth, et al. Bedminster Press, New York.

Weber, M. (2009) *The Protestant Ethic and the Spirit of Capitalism with Other Writings on the Rise of the West*, 4th edn., trans. and intro. S. Kalberg. Oxford University Press, New York.

JOHN DRYSDALE

welfare dependency and welfare underuse

Welfare dependency refers to the use that people make of publicly provided cash benefits/transfers or human services. Welfare underuse is the term applied when people entitled to publicly provided benefits and services fail to do so.

Welfare dependency is a feature of advanced industrial societies with developed welfare states, whose citizens enjoy specific "social" rights, for example, to social security, healthcare, social support and education. The premise on which the advocates of state welfare provision promoted it was that, as societies become more complex, the "states of dependency" that arise at various points in the human life-course may be "recognised as collective responsibilities" (Titmuss 1955: 64). The policy makers who fashioned the modern welfare states of the post-World War II era favoured guaranteed basic minimum state provision, but they also, to varying degrees, expected people to depend so far as possible on income from paid employment and on support from their families.

Since the 1970s preoccupations with the nature and extent of welfare dependency have increased as support for state welfare provision has declined (e.g. Esping-Andersen 1996). Neoliberals urged that current levels of state welfare spending were unaffordable, while neo-conservatives blamed an alleged moral decline in western society upon welfare dependency. Critics of the latter thesis draw on evidence which suggests that people who depend on state welfare exhibit no signs of a "culture" of dependency but subscribe to the same values as everybody else. Additionally, longitudinal social data enable us to see that for unemployed people and lone parents, for example, welfare dependency is generally a relatively short-lived, not an enduring experience.

Welfare underuse can in part be attributed to the stigma potentially associated with welfare dependency. It is important to distinguish between the underuse of cash benefits, transfers or their equivalent in kind (e.g. food stamps or food cards), as opposed to the underuse of public or social services. The underuse of cash benefits is often referred to as a failure of "take up." This can result from the stigma attaching to certain kinds of benefit (especially conditional or means-tested benefits), to ignorance on the part of potential claimants, and/or to the administrative complexity of the schemes.

The underuse of public services may similarly result from the structural and administrative features of those services. Of particular concern is the differential use of services by different social classes or minority groups. Healthcare and education, may be more extensively used and provide greater benefits to middle-class families than to the poorest families who need them the most. Benefits from advances in medical science and health technologies tend to be unequally distributed, not only globally, but even within rich countries. In this way, inequalities in income may be translated into inequalities in life chances and of power.

The majority of the population in capitalist welfare states will during particular stages of their lifecourse make use of publicly provided or state financed health, education and welfare services. Policy-makers and sociologists may be concerned about whether, by whom and why dependency upon such provision becomes excessive; or conversely about whether, by whom and why such provision may be underused.

SEE ALSO: Citizenship; Social Services; Stigma; Welfare State

REFERENCE

Titmuss, R. (1955) A lecture republished in Alcock, P. et al. (eds) (2001) *Welfare and Wellbeing: Richard Titmuss's Contribution to Social Policy*. Policy Press, Bristol.

SUGGESTED READINGS

Dean, H. and Taylor-Gooby, P. (1992) *Dependency Culture: The Explosion of a Myth*. Harvester Wheatsheaf, Hemel Hempstead.

Esping-Andersen, G. (ed.) (1996) *Welfare States in Transition*. Polity, Cambridge.

HARTLEY DEAN

welfare state

The essence of the modern welfare state lies in the institutional commitment to reconcile equity issues with the efficient operation of markets in industrial and post-industrial capitalist societies. Since capitalism institutionally relies on the free competition of autonomous agents in markets to achieve economic efficiency, the unfettered operation of competitive forces is unlikely to result in an egalitarian distribution of economic well-being in society given an unequal distribution of wealth and resources, economies of scale in production, significant transaction costs and imperfect information regarding prices and preferences among economic agents. As an institutional antidote, modern welfare states have developed various policy instruments to realign distributional and efficiency concerns, and to institutionally organize social solidarity in complex and heterogeneous societies.

Historically, the foundations of the modern welfare state emerged in late nineteenth century Europe when governments responded to social upheaval generated by the transition to full-fledged industrial economies. From the introduction of public health and pension insurance in Bismarckian Germany in the 1880s onwards, governments began to recognize the need for institutional mechanisms that ensured mass participation in economic growth generated by technological progress and an intensified transition to the capitalist mode of production. From their roots in the social integration of the working class, modern welfare states have considerably expanded their scope and objectives, and nowadays consist of a broad array of policies and programs – ranging from traditional public assistance to social insurance through pension, health care and unemployment insurance, to service provision to the elderly, families or the unemployed, and a tax system raising the financial means necessary to fund these various instruments of government intervention – that aim to secure adequate standards of living, broadly defined, for an encompassing majority of the population.

However, while similar programs exist in most of today's most advanced economies, different power constellations and historical trajectories have led to variation in the structure and generosity of welfare state institutions in the western world. Due to strong labor movements and a long history of social-democratic governance, Scandinavian countries feature particularly extensive welfare states that combine universalist transfer systems with encompassing public service systems and a large public sector to provide these. In contrast, Catholic social policy and predominantly conservative governments have created Continental European welfare states that are typically more bent towards regulation, prefer social insurance to universal transfer systems and are weaker on public service provision than their Scandinavian counterparts. In comparison, the interventionist role of welfare programs is traditionally more limited in the USA, and, after significant rollbacks during the 1980s, Britain, Australia, and New Zealand, but also in most post-communist countries of Eastern Europe.

The welfare state constitutes a veritable intervention into private agents' economic decision-making, and significantly affects the structure of economic incentives and constraints in society. Transfers that compensate for social risk alter the nexus between market income and household standards of living, government subsidies and service provision deliberately alter price structures in the education, health and care sector, as well as households' market power by providing information, legal services and regulation. There is widespread consensus about the fact that welfare state institutions generate a considerable amount of economic redistribution vertically (from the wealthy to the poor), horizontally (between different groups in society, e.g. from households without children to families with dependent children) and intertemporally (across individual life courses). Besides, important equity effects also result from the redistribution of educational opportunity through public education, stipends and public job training programs. On the other hand, unless properly designed, the availability of benefits as well as the progressive income taxes required to fund welfare state programs could create economic disincentives that reduce economic activity, undermine economic growth and hence question the long-term viability of the welfare state. Finally, the public provision or subsidization of education, health care and social services has created demand for these services, thus providing employment opportunities for women and integrating traditionally female occupations into the formal labor market.

SEE ALSO: Family Poverty; Taxes: Progressive, Proportional, and Regressive; Welfare Dependency and Welfare Underuse; Welfare State

SUGGESTED READINGS

Barr, N. (1998) *The Economics of the Welfare State*, 3rd edn. Oxford University Press, Oxford.

Esping-Andersen, G. (1990) *The Three Worlds of Welfare Capitalism*. Polity Press, Cambridge.

Goodin, R. E., Headey, B., Muffels, R. & Dirven, H.-J. (1999) *The Real Worlds of Welfare Capitalism*. Cambridge University Press, Cambridge.

MARKUS GANGL

whiteness

Despite numerous claims of universality, racelessness, and "colorblindness" (Bonilla-Silva 2006), whiteness is not only still present but remains racially particular in its own right. "White" is a racial category, and "whites" something of a racial group, of course partaking of huge variation across space and time.

Whiteness has been largely invisible in the "modern world-system" of European creation, especially in the nations of the global North and West. This invisibility is somewhat unique among the racial categories. Contrary to many common sense notions, the uniqueness of whiteness does not consist of its "normalization": the idea that whiteness is the "default" racial status, that whites are "just people" who "don't have a race." Nor does this uniqueness consist in the "transparency" of whiteness: the way in which whiteness is taken for granted in the world's powerful countries and thus not seen. In many places, especially where one racially-defined group predominates, that group's raciality is also relatively invisible. Rather, the uniqueness of whiteness's invisibility lies in the contradictions therein: while whiteness partakes of normality and transparency it is also dominant. And it is also beleaguered, nervous, and defensive. These qualities in turn belie claims for the "normality" and "transparency" of whiteness, the default status of the concept.

Whiteness can hardly be hidden in a social system based on racial domination, one in which races are necessarily relational matters. White supremacy has never gone unresisted, for one thing, so whites (colonists, settlers, planters, etc.) have always had to "circle the wagons": they had to theorize whiteness, defend its "purity," and justify their rule. They had to take up their "White Man's Burden" (note the gender element), carry out their "Mission Civilizatrice," fulfill their "Manifest Destiny."

Thus the chief distinction between the racial category of whiteness and other racial designations is not some supposedly all-encompassing negativity of white identity; indeed the claim that whiteness is merely the "absence of color" is quite ridiculous. Rather the concept's problematic nature stems from its continuing (if often flexible and today often disavowed) involvement with domination.

SEE ALSO: Race; Race, Definitions of

REFERENCE

Bonilla-Silva, E. (2006) *Racism without Racists: Color-Blind Racism and the Persistence of Racial Inequality in the United States*, 2nd edn. Rowman and Littlefield, Lanham, MD.

SUGGESTED READING

Jacobson, M. F. (1968) *Whiteness of a Different Color: European Immigrants and the Alchemy of Race.* Harvard University Press, Cambridge, MA.

HOWARD WINANT

womanism

In 1983, Alice Walker contrasted Afrocentrism, black feminism, and white feminism using the term *womanist* to render a critique of possibilities for women and men who felt ostracized by the mainstream women's movement in the United States. Walker's much cited phrase, "Womanist is to feminist as purple is to lavender," reflects this comparison. In her classic essay "In search of our mothers' gardens," Walker describes womanism as being rooted in black women's particular history of racial and gender oppression in the United States. Yet, womanists are "traditionally universalists." Womanism is a gender-progressive worldview that emerges from black women's unique history, is accessible primarily to black women yet also extends beyond women of African descent. Womanism is a pluralist vision of black empowerment that requires women and men to be aware of gendered inequalities and seek social change. In the late 1980s, womanist theologians such as Cannon and Kirk-Duggan sought to clarify women-centered aspects of biblical studies, church history, systematic theology, and social ethics. Hudson-Weems (1993) argued that the feminist–womanist tie should be separated by locating womanism in the words of Sojourner Truth and Afrocentric cultural values (i.e., Africana womanism). Hudson-Weems identified the characteristics of Africana womanism. Some include self-defining, family-centeredness, struggling alongside men, adaptability, black sisterhood, authenticity, strength, mothering, and spirituality. It should be noted that although Africana womanists see sexism as an important problem, some do not see sexism as an objective more important than fighting racism. This perspective reflects the nationalist roots of womanism and is a critique of womanism.

SEE ALSO: Black Feminist Thought; Feminism; Women's Movements

REFERENCES

Hudson-Weems, C. (1993) *Africana Womanism: Reclaiming Ourselves*. Bedford, Troy, MI.

Walker, A. (1983) *In Search of Our Mothers' Gardens: Womanist Prose*. Harcourt, Brace Jovanovich, New York.

APRIL L. FEW-DEMO

women and sexuality

The framing of women's sexuality as passive, responsive and inferior to men's sexuality can be traced back to the works of early Greek philosophers such as Plato and Aristotle, as well as Galen, a second century physician. Galen's thesis that women's sexuality was *similar, although inferior*, to men's sexuality remained popular well into the eighteenth century. In this "one-sex" model (Lacquer 1990) female sexuality was not clearly distinguished from men's and both sexes were framed as potentially sexually desiring/active. The shift to a "two-sex" model in the late eighteenth century was the result of social, political and economic changes in which sexual differences were articulated in order to support shifting gender arrangements. Although women were no longer seen as inverted replicas of men, the association of women's bodies and sexuality with reproduction and nurturance, as opposed to sexually desiring/active, was reinforced.

The nineteenth century sexologists, Richard von Krafft-Ebing and Havelock Ellis, drew on biological and evolutionary understandings of sexuality which continued to endorse the inevitability of male domination and female submission. Women were seen as being weakened by their reproductive biology and women's sexual activity was primarily for reproductive purposes. While nineteenth-century sexologists and medical practitioners reproduced discourses of women's sexuality as passive and inferior, sex researchers in the mid-twentieth century, such as Kinsey and Masters and Johnson, focused on *similarities* in men's and women's sexual response. Their work was seen as emancipatory because it acknowledged the importance of women's sexual pleasure/orgasmic satisfaction. However, for Masters and Johnson women's sexuality was still positioned as *responsive* (with orgasm resulting from penile–vaginal penetration), while for Kinsey sex was framed as a straightforward biological function and a purely physical phenomenon.

Much feminist theorizing in the 1980s and 1990s draws on the work of Michel Foucault, and post-structuralism more broadly, to explore the ways in which sexuality is constructed in discourse. This work challenges essentialist understandings about gender and sexuality, including critiques of radical feminist framings of women's sexual pleasure as "eroticized submission."

Queer theory has also influenced contemporary understandings of sexuality. Queer disrupts the assumed links between sex-gender-sexuality and draws on the notion of "performativity" as a way of understanding the ways in which sexuality and gender are "done" (Butler 1990). Poststructuralist feminism and queer theory have facilitated a shift to exploring the diversity and fluidity of sexual identities, preferences, practices, and meanings.

In contemporary critical theorizing and research on women and sexuality a central debate revolves around the degree to which there has been a "democratization" (Giddens 1992) or equalization of heterosexual relations, that is, the extent to which dominant, oppressive norms and practices of heterosexuality have been undermined with changes in heterosexual relations. While there has been an apparent erosion of the sexual double standard and an increasing emphasis on women's right to sexual pleasure and freedom of sexual expression, sexual asymmetries between women and men still persist. Much contemporary research explores how women are both active, desiring sexual agents *and* how their agency is potentially compromised by the normative construction of heterosexuality.

SEE ALSO: Foucault, Michel; Lesbian Feminism; Queer Theory; Sex and Gender; Sexual Politics

REFERENCES

Butler, J. (1990) *Gender Trouble: Feminism and the Subversion of Identity*. Routledge, New York.

Giddens, A. (1992) *The Transformation of Intimacy*. Polity, Cambridge.

Laqueur, T. (1990) *Making Sex: Body and Gender from the Greeks to Freud*. Harvard University Press, Cambridge, MA.

TIINA VARES

women's health

Women's health encompasses physical, emotional, and social health associated with female reproductive and sexual development over the lifecycle, or any medical condition more common among women. The sociology of women's health includes the study of gendered politics within medicine, medical training, doctor–patient interactions, self-care, illness behavior, and health care utilization. Women's health can be more broadly construed to include the relationships between gender inequality and health, even among men.

In most countries women on average live longer than men, but appear to experience more sickness and ill-health than men. This gender paradox in health where "women are sicker, but men die quicker" is an overly simplistic generalization, because while women tend toward more physical illness, disability days, and health care utilization, men experience more life-threatening ailments such as heart disease, respiratory disease, and cancer. Biomedical explanations argue that physiological sex differences contribute to different sex-specific disease rates. Sociomedical explanations consider social constructionism and gender role theories: gender differences in material circumstances, social roles, social support, and lifestyle explain the gender patterning of health and mortality.

Perhaps the predominant sociological focus on women's health has been the medicalization of women's lives. As women are more often patients than men, women's lives may be more easily subject to medicalization. Examples of medicalization research in women's health include: Barbara Katz Rothman's analysis of the expanding definition of "high-risk" pregnancy; Anne Figert's study of the politics that define PMS as a medical and psychological disorder; Margaret Lock's research on the divergent medicalization of menopause in the USA and Japan; and Emily Martin's study of how biomedical textbooks unnecessarily use gendered language to describe gamete production, conception, menstruation, and menopause.

Feminism enhanced women's entry into medical fields. Now about a quarter of physicians in the US are women, but nursing remains a nearly exclusively female occupation. Gender stratification operates at all levels within these fields, with women doctors more likely to specialize in pediatrics, family practice, and obstetrics/gynecology than men. The predominant dyads within medicine (doctor–patient and doctor–nurse) are gendered and hierarchical. Thus, medical settings have contributed to studies of dominance, authority, and gender.

Inclusion of women as physicians has contributed attention to the differential treatment of women as second-class patients relative to men and to the exceptional treatment of women as patients who receive excessive intervention. Such treatment may not result from overt discrimination, as the gender system is strongly related to ideas about illness, etiology, and treatment. McKinlay (1996) identified patient, provider, health system, and technologic influences on the gendered detection of heart disease.

The modern women's health movement succeeded in the 1970s by demanding informed consent for sterilization surgery and drug package inserts for the Pill, buoying larger movements in self-help and consumerist health care. Following public pressure to change the way biomedicine was conducted and organized in the USA, in 1990 the National Institutes of Health founded an Office of Research on Women to oversee the systematic inclusion of women in clinical studies.

SEE ALSO: Gender, the Body and; Health and Culture

REFERENCE

McKinlay, J. B. (1996) Some contributions from the social system to gender inequalities in heart disease. *Journal of Health and Social Behavior* 37: 1–26.

SUGGESTED READINGS

Figert, A. E. (1996) *Women and the Ownership of PMS: The Structuring of a Psychiatric Disorder*. Aldine de Gruyter, Hawthorne, NY.

Fisher, S. (1988) *In the Patient's Best Interest: Women and the Politics of Medical Decisions*. Rutgers University Press, New Brunswick, NJ.

Lock, M. (1993) *Encounters with Aging: Mythologies of Menopause in Japan and North America*. University of California Press, Berkeley. CA.

Martin, E. (1987) *The Woman in the Body: A Cultural Analysis of Reproduction*. Beacon Press, Boston, MA.

Rothman, B. K. (2000) *Recreating Motherhood*, 2nd edn. Rutgers University Press, New Brunswick, NJ.

DIANE S. SHINBERG

women's movements

Movements on behalf of women arise from the gendered social constructions that have accompanied the biological differences between male and female that pervade social life. The political processes by which rules are made and valued objects and services are distributed have institutionalized gender differences since the beginning of human history. Traditional systems of religious and political thought have relegated women to a secondary status. Thus, the potential beneficiaries of "women's movements" conceivably encompass more than half of humanity. Yet women are also divided by all of the social distinctions and sources of subordination to which the human experience gives rise. These differences present both obstacles to mobilization and a multiplicity of competing claims characterized in terms of identity struggles.

To speak of "women's" movements requires attention to the distinction between movements made up of women as a constituency or organizational strategy and those movements in which the empowerment of women is both a goal and source of theoretical and ideological negotiation and contestation, that is, "feminist" movements (Ferree & Mueller 2004). Although feminist mobilizations are always concerned with the subordination or self-actualization of women, the elasticity of that definition has led to enormous variety in movements. According to Karen Offen (2000), the term itself is a product of intellectual discourse in late nineteenth-century France. Among feminists the most consistent division globally and historically has been that between liberal and socialist feminisms. Since 1848 an intense rivalry developed in Europe that was echoed in most parts of the world. The pervasive socialist/liberal difference is still found in Raka Ray's (1999) comparison of feminist organizing in Bombay and Calcutta; in European and North American feminists' responses to neo-liberal political and social restructuring; and in Latin American women's responses to authoritarian governments.

As one of the major social movements developing in the modern period, feminist movements have, to some extent, shared the same repertoire of collective action as labor, environment, male suffrage, and other "rights" movements. They have embraced a familiar repertoire of mass meetings, petitions, demonstrations, and electoral campaigns. At the same time, nineteenth-century feminists challenged cultural norms and values through a more symbolic and discursive repertoire associated today with "new social movements."

By the time European powers dominated the world in the nineteenth century, many of the ideas associated with feminism had become embedded in the larger cultural package of "modernity." Indigenous leaders in the European colonies sometimes entertained these ideas along with other modern systems of thought as a way of coming to terms with the imperial powers. With the overthrow of colonial powers in the twentieth century, feminist ideas have been attacked for their association with western imperialism and other discredited "modern" ideas. Similarly, when the Soviet system collapsed late in the twentieth century, ideas about women's equal participation in politics and the paid labor force were discredited in many countries of Eastern Europe because of their association with an imposed Soviet-style socialism.

Like most long-running international movements, feminists have gone through periods of highly public mobilizations followed by "abeyance" periods (Rupp & Taylor 1987), but the transformative moments redefining the relationship of women to men and to society have historically been quickly suppressed by counter-movements that reestablished women's traditional subordination. This was true until the suffrage movements of the late nineteenth and early twentieth centuries offered a foundation in the polity for resisting counter-movements and offered the potential for global mobilization through new international governmental and non-governmental organizations.

SEE ALSO: Cultural Feminism; Feminism, First, Second, and Third Waves; Liberal Feminism; Socialist Feminism

REFERENCES

Ferree, M. M. & Mueller, C. (2004) Feminism and women's movements. In: Snow, D. A., Soule, S. A., & Kriesi, H. (Eds.), *The Blackwell Companion to Social Movements*. Blackwell, Oxford, pp. 576–607.

Offen, K. (2000) *European Feminism: 1700–1950*. Stanford University Press, Stanford, CA.

Ray, R. (1999) *Fields of Protest*. University of Minnesota Press, Minneapolis, MN.

Rupp, L. & Taylor, V. (1987) *Survival in the Doldrums*. Ohio State University Press, Columbus, OH.

CAROL MUELLER

work, sociology of

The sociology of work takes one into the heart of sociological analysis. Humankind's mediated relationship to the natural world is inescapably ontological to human life and interrelationships. From the artifacts of *Homo sapiens*' early existence, through records found within all social formations including the texts of world religions, classical and contemporary thought and scientific and technological undertakings, one sees how work has occupied human thinking and created some of humanity's most complex and significant questions and issues.

During structural-functionalism predominance in North America during the 1950s and 1960s, sociologists tended to study the "sociology of occupations" but as Marxian and other continental perspectives entered mainstream sociology, the terminology and concerns shifted. The terms labor and work rose to prominence opening discussions of the labor process, labor history, paid and unpaid labor, segmented and dual labor markets, for example, while issues like alienation, collective action, power and resistance, class conflict, docile bodies, and power/knowledge pushed discussions of the occupational structure, hierarchies, status, mobility, career paths, and modernization theory from center stage.

The sociology of work centers on and expands outward from the employer/worker relationship. In the contemporary period, employers (private or public) hire workers to produce goods or services which others purchase for direct consumption or further processing. Through paid work, workers earn money to meet individual and/or domestic needs and wants. The struggle over wages is among the most obvious features of the employer/worker relationship – but it involves far more. The employer/worker relationship occurs within and impacts upon numerous aspects of the social whole; three of the most important are the production, ownership, distribution, and control of social wealth; socio-historically created patterns and perceptions of consumption; the legitimation of existing social relations.

Employers hire workers for their abilities and capacities to perform work for a specified time-frame but employers cannot separate workers' bodies from their labor capacities – the whole person is hired, creating important complexities. Living within society, workers are shaped by, and also perceived through, various socially constructed conditions and perceptual frameworks – e.g. class, gender, ethnicity, racialization, educational background, aspirations, and understandings of the world, in general, and work, in particular. These influence interactions among workers, employers, and supervisors and those interactions feed back into the larger society.

Employers possessing capital and resources and specific corporate, positional, and personal motives and interests offer workers money, certain intrinsic satisfactions, levels of (in)security, status and some form of employment record or career. Workers possess particular resources of skill, knowledge, physical ability, and capacity for learning along with specific motives and interests. In exchange for wages, workers surrender a significant measure of personal autonomy, give forth effort and suffer, in the process, various measures of impairment and fatigue. Issues concerning wages, the basis, size, history and trajectory of the wage gap existing between men and women, racialized and non-racialized groups, or normative and non-normatively constructed workers; part-time versus full-time work; career disruptions; and paid versus unpaid labor stem from this aspect of the employer/worker relationship.

The numerous tensions within the employer/worker relationship are usually managed within fairly specific parameters but the dynamic is a continuous source of pressure that can lead to small- or large-scale change.

Employers use encouragement, incentives, the wage-contract and possibly some (moderately) coercive practices and other forms of sanction to get work done. The ease or difficulty involved in putting workers' labor capacities to work depends on the tasks to be performed (pleasant, intrinsically rewarding ones are easier than dull, routine, physically demanding, and/or dangerous work), workers' social and economic situation, as well as their aspirations, motives, experiences, interests and subjective willingness to work. As a result, the quantity and quality of work is also subject to an ongoing, dynamic tension. Through work, products are released into the market linking work to consumption and all of the complex issues related to consumer society, immaterial production and consumption, globalized markets, and the "McDonaldization" of society.

The tension between employers and workers is not usually overt but remains covertly present as an ongoing conflict of interests. Workers and employers strive to improve their position by drawing upon a wide array of personal and systemic resources. In that process a balance is established but it will be challenged and fluctuate over time.

Employers control the formal rules of the workplace and manage production demands but they do so within the context of a broader, increasingly globalized, market which pressures them to minimize costs and increase productivity through management strategies and technological innovation. Questions of scientific management, human relations strategies, Fordist mass production, lean production, technological innovation, surveillance, deskilling, docile and disciplined bodies, and work games all stem from this aspect of the employer/worker relationship.

Workers are pressured to maximize their wages by the market, dominant cultural practices, various media images, personal ambitions, and conditions within their domestic household to care for dependents and educate children within a changing fiscal environment. As employers seek increased productivity, workers want better pay, greater control over and fulfillment through work, reductions in the physical costs and impairment of labor, and safe working conditions. These objectives tend to pressure workers towards collective action leading into questions about local, regional and national labor history; labor's political affiliations and formal political involvement; the strategic and democratic differences among dialogical, consensual, or bureaucratic decision making processes within a collective bargaining unit; determining common interests among diverse, unionized workers with heterogeneous wants; and the willingness and ability to mobilize and sustain collective action all come into focus.

The two opposing tendencies – increased control by the employer versus that of workers – create a system of perpetual tension and change which extends beyond the immediate employer/worker relationship into broader social processes as a whole.

SEE ALSO: Alienation; Fordism/Post-Fordism; Gender, Work and Family; Labor/Labor Power; Labor Process; McDonaldization; Taylorism; Unions

SUGGESTED READINGS

Krader, L. (1979) *Treatise on Social Labor.* Van Gorcum, Assen.

Offe, C. (1985) *Disorganized Capitalism: Contemporary Transformations of Work and Politics.* Polity Press, Cambridge.

Watson, T. (2003). *Sociology, Work, and Industry.* Routledge, London.

ROB BEAMISH

World Bank

The World Bank is a multilateral development bank that provides low-interest loans and interest-free credits to developing countries. The Bank's twin goals are to reduce poverty and increase economic growth. It originated in the 1944 Bretton Woods conference with its sister organization, the International Monetary Fund. The Bank raises funds through the sale of bonds on the international market and through donations from member states. Voting is weighted by the size of its member nations' economies and the United States has the most influence. Since the debt crisis of the 1970s, the Bank has required structural adjustment policy reforms as a condition of its loans. Critics charge that World Bank policies have hurt the most vulnerable and increased poverty.

The World Bank has two components, the International Bank for Reconstruction and Development (IBRD) and the International Development Association (IDA). The IBRD loans funds to creditworthy developing countries that are members of the Bank. This "hard loan window" has more favorable terms than commercial loans, with a typical loan term of fifteen to twenty years and an initial grace period of three to five years. Its capital comes from sales of its AAA-rated bonds on the world capital market to financial institutions, pension funds, and central banks. The IDA was added in 1960 to accommodate the poorest member nations. The IDA's "soft-loan window" provides interest-free loans with a term of 35 to 40 years and a 10-year grace period. It is funded through donations by member nations in replenishment rounds every 3 years.

The World Bank is governed by two boards. The Board of Governors meets once a year with jurisdiction over major policy decisions and admissions to the Bank. Every member nation has a high-level representative on the Board of Governors. The Board of Executive Directors is based at Bank headquarters in Washington, DC, and meets twice weekly as the operational authority. It is headed by the president of the World Bank and has twenty-four members. Voting shares in the Bank are weighted by the size of member nations' economies. The United States has 16.4 percent of votes and Japan has 7.9 percent. Germany has 4.5 percent of votes while France and the U.K. have 4.3 percent. China, Russia, and Saudi Arabia each have 2.8 percent of votes. By custom, the largest shareholder nominates the president of the Bank who has always been a United States national.

For the first few decades, the World Bank loaned funds primarily for infrastructure improvements such as transportation, dams, and communications. Under Bank president Robert McNamara (1968–1980), loans focused directly on poverty reduction and basic needs such as food, housing, water, and sanitation, especially in rural areas. When developing countries could not repay their loans during the 1970s debt crisis, the Bank instituted policy reform as a condition of new loans. The structural adjustment packages required borrowers to liberalize trade policies and decrease expenditures on social programs such as housing, health and education. By the 1990s, the Bank's evaluation units found that structural adjustment policies had resulted in increased inequality, less foreign investment, and particular hardships for the rural landless poor. Under James Wolfensohn (1995–2005), the Bank renewed its focus on reducing poverty with programs such as the Heavily-Indebted Poor Country (HIPC) initiative in 1996. Critics charge that even with these changes, the Bank has not reduced worldwide poverty and that developing nations pay more to wealthy nations in debt payments than they receive in aid.

SEE ALSO: Development: Political Economy, Global Economy, Income Inequality: Global, Neoliberalism, World Trade Organization; International Monetary Fund

SUGGESTED READINGS

Woods, N. (2006) *The Globalizers: The IMF, the World Bank, and Their Borrowers.* Cornell University Press, Ithaca, NY.

World Bank (2007) *A Guide to the World Bank*, 2nd edn. World Bank, Washington, DC.

SUSAN HAGOOD LEE

world conflict

"World conflicts" are not limited to the violence of all-out war. "Terrorism" currently refers to non-state violence directed at civilians and combatants in contests of will, power, and systems. Terrorism also includes any kind of organized violence against civilians. Hence, nations killing their own or other civilians qualify as "state terrorists" as distinct from "extra-state terrorists" all the way from ad hoc suicide bombers to organized guerrilla movements.

Globalization is another form of world conflict, which is sometimes physical (war) and sometimes structural (domination, exploitation, humiliation). Whatever its multiple meanings, globalization includes major clashes between employers and workers, from those in developed countries who are fired or forced to accept wage and benefits cuts to those working for low wages under degrading conditions in less developed countries. Increasingly, nations' economies compete with each other in brutal ways and devastate ecologies and national self-sufficiency, frequently causing vast involuntary population movements and straining natural resources to their breaking points.

World conflicts also include wars between ethnicities (Hutus and Tutsis in East Africa), religions (Catholics and Protestants in Northern Ireland), and fusions of religions and ethnicities (Sinhalese and Tamils in Sri Lanka, Jews and Palestinians in Israel/Palestine). As with wars between nation states, these conflicts blend anger over differences in wealth and territorial control with belief in one's own group's legitimacy and the illegitimacy of the opponent.

In addition to political, economic, ethnic, and religious dimensions of world conflicts, perhaps the least attended crucial aspect is social psychological: anger. Like all emotions, anger originates in an innate predisposition joined with real experiences that trigger it. Enraged people commonly are so consumed with anger that it frightens them to the point where they cannot figure out where to direct it.

Societies routinely lift anger away from its usual mundane contexts of family, work, politics, citizen–government relationships, and countless miscellaneous instances wherein people get frustrated with and hurt by each other. The anger of countless citizens is then diverted to structures where it is released against entire other groups who rarely if ever deserve it.

War is the largest-scale way of deflecting anger away from its original settings. Others include all forms of domination which are, social psychologically, forms of reciprocal anger of dominators and dominated, with one side ordinarily having the upper power hand over the other.

There are ways to engage in conflict besides violence which are slowly entering into public consciousness. These include countless forms of non-violent conflict resolution. In the recent period, its exponents and practitioners trace a line from Thoreau through Gandhi, Martin Luther King, Jr., the Dalai Lama, Thich Nhat Hanh, and Aung Sang Suu Kii, among others.

Peace visions in this era include addressing the needs of all people on the globe for cooperative associations increasingly replacing competitive ones, environmental health and safety, adequate health care, decent housing and nutrition, vibrant and viable communities and societies, and productive, fulfilling lives in relationship with selves, others, and the planet.

Organizations and movements that promote and practice peace number in the thousands throughout the world. They are less developed, known, and experienced than organizations and movements promoting and practicing war and other forms of physical and structural conflict, but they are clearly in motion. If they gain the momentum they need to banish war to the history books, we will still face a slew of grave conflicts that will require inventiveness, patience, and determination to solve satisfactorily. Once violent conflict is ended, the resolution of conflicts will move from death and devastation to creative forms of engagement, recognition, and compromise. There is no greater challenge facing our planet than this.

SEE ALSO: Anti-War and Peace Movements; Globalization; Global Justice as a Social Movement; Terrorism; War

SUGGESTED READINGS

Berman, P. (2003) *Terror and Liberalism.* Norton, New York.

Fellman, G. (1998) *Rambo and the Dalai Lama: The Compulsion to Win and Its Threat to Human Survival.* SUNY Press, Albany, NY.

GORDON FELLMAN

world trade organization

The World Trade Organization (WTO) is a multilateral body that regulates world trade and provides a forum for negotiations to reduce trade barriers. It began in 1995 as the successor to the General Agreement on Tariffs and Trade (GATT) and includes over 150 member states. Unlike the GATT, the WTO has a mechanism for settling trade disputes between member states and authorizing sanctions. Negotiations are guided by a set of principles and take place in rounds of talks, with agricultural subsidies the most contentious issue. The WTO has been the focus of anti-globalization protests highlighting negative consequences of trade liberalization.

The WTO operates under several broad principles, including the bedrock commitment to free trade. The member states agree to extend their best tariff rates to all other member states, a principle known as most-favored nation treatment. They commit to national treatment for foreign goods and services, treating them equally once in the domestic market. States agree to set ceiling rates on tariffs, avoid trade-distorting subsidies, and refrain from dumping products below cost. They also recognize that the least developed countries (LDCs) deserve special protection.

Each negotiating round has a set of items for discussion in a package arrangement. No items are concluded until all have been discussed and an agreement reached on each one. The rationale behind this package approach is that compromises essential in negotiations can be unpalatable back in the home countries. Each state wants some victories to offset the inevitable concessions. It is typically difficult to reach agreement on every item and so rounds take years to conclude.

Three main agreements serve as the framework for WTO regulations and negotiations. The first is the General Agreement on Tariffs and Trade (GATT), the original agreement covering trade in manufactured goods and agricultural products. The second is the General Agreement on Trade in Services (GATS) such as shipping, tourism, and financial services. The third is the Agreement on Trade-Related Aspects of Intellectual Property Rights (TRIPS), establishing minimum levels of protection for the intellectual property of member states. To resolve trade disputes, the WTO's Dispute Settlement Body appoints panels to investigate complaints brought by member states. If a member state is found out of compliance with rules specified in the agreements, it must revise its policies or face retaliation.

In 2001, the agenda for a new round of negotiations was set in Doha, Qatar. Trade ministers designed the negotiations as a development round, focused on issues important to the poorest countries. By far the most contentious issue has concerned agricultural subsidies that encourage overproduction and drive down prices. Developed countries compensate farmers for market downturns but developing countries do not have sufficient resources for subsidies. When developed countries' subsidies depress prices, farmers in poor countries are hurt the most, deepening their poverty. The reluctance of developed countries to reduce farm subsidies has undercut the credibility of the WTO and disillusioned developing countries, who feel the Doha Development Round has not lived up to its promise.

The WTO has been the object of wide-ranging anti-globalization protests such as the "Battle in Seattle" in 1999. Opponents decry the negative impact of liberalization on poor farmers, the lack of transparency in negotiations, damage to the environment by multinational corporations, and high unemployment brought about by unfair competition.

SEE ALSO: Global Economy; Globalization

SUGGESTED READINGS

Stiglitz, J. E. & Charlton, A. (2005) *Fair Trade for All: How Trade Can Promote Development*. Oxford University Press, Oxford.

World Trade Organization (2007) *Understanding the World Trade Organization*. World Trade Organization, Geneva.

SUSAN HAGOOD LEE

Y

youth/adolescence

"Youth" and "adolescence" represent contrasting approaches for sociologists. "Youth" is conceptualized as a socially constructed life phase between childhood and adulthood: a collective experience shaped by culturally and historically specific social structures, age-specific institutions, and societal expectations. In contrast, "adolescence" – associated with developmental psychology and clinical medicine – emphasizes processes of individual social and/or physiological and psychological development. Often equated with puberty, adolescence is represented as a time of experimentation and emotional storm and stress.

Early sociological conceptualizations of youth were influenced by *functionalism*, which regarded the period of youth as a means of facilitating smooth transitions from particularistic values within the family to the normative values of broader society, whilst Mannheim's *generational theory* emphasized how young people's attitudes and actions are shaped by their shared "generation location." *Youth cultural studies* originated in the *Chicago School* and was developed by the UK's *Centre for Contemporary Cultural Studies* into a class-based critique of young people as consumers and producers of mass and ghetto cultures, although many cultural studies scholars now use the language of "post-subculture" to argue that class is no longer relevant to understanding youth cultures. The *youth transitions approach*, particularly influential in Northern Europe and Australasia, has highlighted the emergence of *fractured* and *extended transitions* to adulthood, emphasizing the impact of structural factors on young people's lives. Beck's *individualization thesis* has also been utilized by researchers seeking to understand the experience of youth in "late modernity." While the proliferation of individualized biographies might suggest that class, ethnicity, and gender no longer determine young people's life chances, critics argue that the old indicators remain firmly in place.

SEE ALSO: Childhood; Birmingham School; Life Course; Mannheim, Karl

SUGGESTED READING

France, A. (2007) *Understanding Youth in Late Modernity*. Open University Press, Buckingham

Henderson, S., Holland, J., McGrellis, S., Sharpe, S. & Thomson, R. (2006) *Inventing Adulthoods*. Sage, London.

SUE HEATH

Z

Zimbardo prison experiment

In 1971, social psychologist Phillip Zimbardo (born 1933) conducted his widely known "Stanford prison experiment." Originally planned for two weeks, the study investigated the impact of anonymity and loss of identity on prisoners and guards in a simulated penal institution.

From a pool of volunteers, Zimbardo selected well-adjusted young men who were randomly assigned to the role of prisoner or guard. Zimbardo himself assumed the role of "superintendent." The guards were dressed in anonymizing uniforms, equipped with night-sticks and told to run the prison in whatever way they wished, except through physical violence. Prisoners were arrested by real police officers, blindfolded, and brought to a mock prison in the basement of a Stanford University building. To increase the sense of anonymity and humiliation, prisoners only received rubber sandals and a "Muslim smock" showing their prisoner number as clothing.

The study quickly devolved into a situation of great hostility, in which prisoners and guards absorbed their respective roles. Following a crushed prisoner revolt, the guards' regime became increasingly sadistic and abusive, relying on public humiliation, solitary confinement, sleep deprivation and starvation. The result was depression and extreme emotional disturbance among the prisoners, five of whom had to be released prior to the termination of the experiment. Zimbardo, immersed in his own role in running the prison hierarchy, failed to stop most of the human rights abuses. The experiment was ended after only six days after a social psychologist unrelated to the study objected to its horrifying conditions.

According to Zimbardo, the results of this experiment illustrate that the fulfillment of social roles within a closed social system can overwhelm any individual moral standards – including his own. The prison study is also known as an ethical fiasco because researchers failed to protect the human rights of their research participants.

SEE ALSO: Authority and Conformity; Experimental Methods; Role theory

SUGGESTED READING

Zimbardo, P. G. (2007) *The Lucifer Effect: Understanding How Good People Turn Evil.* Random House, New York.

MARKUS KEMMELMEIER

Index